KING GEORGE VI

King George VI, 1937

KING GEORGE VI

His Life and Reign

BY

JOHN W. WHEELER-BENNETT

ST MARTIN'S PRESS

New York

AUTHOR'S NOTE

T HE following Note is offered to the reader in explanation of the scope and organization of this book.

The official biography of King George V was a dichotomized work; the *private* life was entrusted to Mr. John Gore, who published his admirable and important book, *King George V, a Personal Memoir*, in 1941, and the *public* life to Sir Harold Nicolson, whose *King George V, his Life and Reign*, published in 1952, is one of the outstanding biographical and historical studies of our time. This procedure was not followed in the case of King George VI, and when, in November 1952, I was invited to undertake this task I was informed that I was to deal with both the personal and the public life of His Majesty.

I have therefore conceived of my task as being to depict the King both as a Sovereign and as a man, and also to give some account of the great events which occurred during his reign and which formed the background for his own thoughts and actions. With some of these events King George was not directly identified, and yet I found it impossible to make clear to myself, and consequently to others, his reactions to national and international problems without providing a broad outline of what these problems were. In so doing it has been my earnest endeavour to keep 'the Life' in proportion to 'the Times'.

By gracious permission of Her Majesty the Queen I was most kindly enabled to work in Buckingham Palace and was accorded unrestricted access to the Royal Archives both there and at Windsor. In addition I have received much kindness and invaluable assistance from Her Majesty Queen Elizabeth the Queen Mother.

The Royal Archives, which I have consulted, included:

1. The diaries of King George V and of Queen Mary; letters from them to the King as Prince Albert and as Duke of York; reports from Mr. Hansell and from those who held authority over the young Prince at Osborne, Dartmouth, as a Cadet in the training cruiser *Cumberland*, and as a junior naval officer.

2. Letters from the King to his parents and to and from other members of the Royal Family.

3. The King's own diaries: King George VI was by no means as regular a diarist as his father but during the periods in which he did write a journal his records were kept meticulously. There were four such periods:

   (i) A sporadic record for the year 1912 in a quarto commercial diary, presented to him by Queen Mary.

   (ii) From the beginning of his cadet cruise in *Cumberland* on January 18, 1913, until May 5, 1915. This diary was kept in a green leather volume, with a brass lock and the initial A on the cover. The record appears to have come to an arbitrary conclusion coincidental with the end of the volume;

   (iii) a record written in a brown leather loose-leaf notebook in pencil during the East African tour of the Duke and Duchess of York, December 1924–April 1925; and

   (iv) a daily diary, written in a series of blue leather notebooks from the outbreak of the Second World War until the eve of his departure for the South African tour, *i.e.* September 1, 1939–January 31, 1947.

4. The main files containing the King's official correspondence, his notes and memoranda and also the letters and memoranda addressed to Ministers by the King's Private Secretaries.

5. The King's diary of engagements from 1920 to 1951.

6. Cabinet Minutes, documents and memoranda.

I have read through all this material and have supplemented it in three respects. First, I have consulted the works listed in the Bibliography at the end of this book; secondly, I have talked with all sorts and conditions of men and women — over 150 of them —who knew the King at some stage or other of his life, and in so doing I have made numerous visits in England and Scotland and also in the United States of America, Canada, Norway, the Netherlands, France, Switzerland, Malta and Eire; and, thirdly, I have been greatly assisted by those who have made available to me their diaries and also originals of letters written to them by His Majesty. I would like to express my sincere gratitude to all those who have aided me by giving thus generously of their recollections and their records.

The note references in the book are of two sorts. The numerical references indicate sources, a full list of which is to be found on pp. 835-58. The alphabetical references indicate substantive notes at the foot of the page.

I must acknowledge most warmly the invaluable help
afforded me by the three sons of Mr. Lionel Logue who, after
their father's death, placed his papers at my disposal; by
Dr. Herman Kahn and the staff of the Franklin D. Roosevelt
Library at Hyde Park, N.Y., to whose hospitality and co-
operation I owe much; by Mr. J. C. Smuts, as Literary
Executor of his father, and the Trustees of the Smuts Archives
in supplying me with the letters to Field-Marshal Smuts printed
on p. 650 and p. 692; by Susan, Lady Tweedsmuir in allowing me to use the letter from Lord Tweedsmuir to a friend on
p. 380; by Lady Stair in sending me the King's 'rhododendron
letter' on pp. 260-61; by Lady Greig in giving me such free
use of her husband's papers; and by the Trustees of the British
Museum.

In an enterprise of this magnitude one's gratitude is infinite
to all those who have by word or deed given aid and succour
in greater or lesser degree; one's regret is also profound that,
because of dictates of space, it is impossible to thank each
individually. Certain of my benefactors, however, I must
name. To Sir Alan Lascelles, Private Secretary and Keeper
of the Archives to King George VI and Queen Elizabeth II,
my indebtedness is unbounded. No critic could be more wise,
more trenchant or more constructive; to his friendly guidance and never failing encouragement I owe, perhaps, more
than anything else. I am also greatly obliged to his predecessor, Lord Hardinge of Penshurst, and to his successor, Sir
Michael Adeane, who has on every occasion afforded me the
most friendly co-operation. Sir Owen Morshead, The Queen's
Librarian at Windsor, and Sir Norman Brook, the Secretary
to the Cabinet, have been my kindly arbiters and I am greatly
beholden to them for the wisdom of their counsel; while in
Sir Harold Nicolson I have had a sage and generous mentor,
whose kindness is proverbial.

I must acknowledge my gratitude to Admiral of the Fleet
Earl Mountbatten of Burma for applying his expert scrutiny
to the Genealogical Table.

To Miss Helen Gardiner and her staff at Buckingham
Palace my debt is great for their invaluable co-operation and
help, and also to Miss Leta Smith of the Windsor Archives.
My niece, Juliet Fiennes, was my secretary throughout the

period of research and the greater part of the composition of the book, and for her loyal, wholehearted and unflagging zeal I can never be too grateful. I am also greatly indebted to her successor, Miss Frances Coulson, for her faithful and efficient service. I must tender my sincere thanks to Mr. Rex Allen for his meticulous and painstaking work in proof-reading and indexing, and, finally, my keen appreciation of the great care and trouble which my publishers and the printers have taken in the final production of the book.

JOHN W. WHEELER-BENNETT

Garsington Manor,
Oxon.
November 1952–May 1958

ACKNOWLEDGEMENTS

THE author wishes to acknowledge the Gracious Permission of Her Majesty Queen Elizabeth the Queen Mother for the use of the Sargent and Laszlo portraits of King George VI when Duke of York, and the painting of Queen Alexandra at Sandringham by Frederick Morgan and T. Blinks. The Laszlo portrait of Her Majesty Queen Elizabeth the Queen Mother when Duchess of York is reproduced by kind permission of the Hon. David Bowes-Lyon.

The author also wishes to make the following acknowledgement in respect of copyright material, for the use of which permission has kindly been granted: For the verses from THE SCHOLARS by Rudyard Kipling. Copyright 1919 by Rudyard Kipling. Reprinted by permission of Doubleday & Co. Inc.

CONTENTS

APPENDICES

ILLUSTRATIONS

PART I

PRINCE ALBERT
1895–1920

PRINCE EDWARD AND PRINCE ALBERT, YORK COTTAGE, 1898

PRINCE EDWARD AND PRINCE ALBERT WITH M. HUA, 1903

CHAPTER I

THE NURSERY AND THE SCHOOLROOM
1895–1908

(i)

ON Saturday, December 14, 1895, a second son was born to the Duke and Duchess of York at York Cottage, Sandringham.[a] The Duchess's confinement had been an easy one; she was not taken ill until eleven o'clock the previous evening, and the child was born about four hours later.[b]

For days the Home Secretary, Sir Matthew Ridley, had been a worried man, keeping in constant touch with Sandringham and expressing anxiety lest he 'should not arrive in time'.[c] Sir Dighton Probyn[d] had advised him on December 7 that the

[a] The children of the Duke and Duchess of York, later King George V and Queen Mary, were six in number: *Prince Edward* (born 1894, subsequently Prince of Wales and King Edward VIII and now Duke of Windsor: married, 1937, Mrs. Wallis Warfield Simpson); *Prince Albert* (born 1895, subsequently Duke of York and King George VI: married, 1923, Lady Elizabeth Bowes-Lyon); *Princess Mary* (born 1897, now Princess Royal: married, 1922, Viscount Lascelles, later Earl of Harewood); *Prince Henry* (born 1900, now Duke of Gloucester: married, 1935, Lady Alice Montagu-Douglas-Scott); *Prince George* (born 1902, subsequently Duke of Kent: married, 1934, Princess Marina, daughter of Prince Nicholas of Greece: killed on active service 1942); *Prince John* (born 1905, died 1919).

[b] There appears to be some uncertainty as to the exact time of the baby's birth. The *London Gazette* gave the round hour of 3 o'clock, the Duke of York recorded the time as 3.40 a.m. (Sandringham Time) in his diary and the Duchess as 3.10 in hers. In his telegram to Queen Victoria the Duke stated the time as 3.30.

[c] Rt. Hon. Sir Matthew White Ridley (1842–1904) was Home Secretary in Lord Salisbury's Cabinet from 1895 to 1900, when he became the first Viscount Ridley. The custom necessitating the attendance of the Home Secretary at royal births had no constitutional basis and did not, as is commonly believed, even date from the 'Warming-Pan Incident' of 1688, when the Whigs alleged that the baby born to James II's Queen, Mary of Modena, had died shortly after birth and that a substitute had been smuggled into the palace in a warming-pan, to become eventually the Old Pretender, or, to the Jacobites, King James III. There is, in fact, no clue to the origin of the custom, which was abandoned on the occasion of the birth of Prince Charles, Duke of Cornwall, on November 14, 1948.

[d] General the Rt. Hon. Sir Dighton Macnaghten Probyn, V.C., G.C.S.I., G.C.B., G.C.V.O. (1833–1924), an Indian Mutiny veteran and successively equerry, Comptroller and Treasurer, and Keeper of the Privy Purse to King Edward VII from 1872 to 1910, and Comptroller to Queen Alexandra from 1910 to 1924.

Duke of York saw no reason for his arrival until the event was 'taking place'; that this was expected by the thirteenth of the month but that it might occur 'any day between this and Christmas'. A card of trains to Wolferton, the nearest railway station to Sandringham, was sent to the Home Secretary for his greater peace of mind but, alas, he detected a mistake in the list and this occasioned renewed anxiety and further correspondence with Sir Dighton.

On December 10 a new complication intervened. Sir Matthew was invited to dine with the Queen at Windsor; what should he do in the event of a telegram summoning him to Sandringham? The Master of the Household, Lord Edward Pelham-Clinton,[a] admonished him to reply to Sandringham that he had been commanded to Windsor, but later reversed his judgment, and all was relayed by the Home Secretary by telegraph to Sir Dighton Probyn.[1] In the end, however, Sir Matthew arrived at York Cottage 'shortly after' the birth of the Prince, a fact which was duly noted in the special supplement of the *London Gazette*[2] and in the daily press.[b]

Unlike his elder brother, Prince Edward, whose birth eighteen months before, in the middle of Ascot week, had been toasted by his grandfather, the Prince of Wales, amid general rejoicings, at a great ball in the Fishing Temple at Virginia Water,[3] the new little Prince entered the world on a note of apology. It was not a tactful day which the future King George VI had chosen for his birthday, for his advent had coincided with that *dies irae* in the life of Queen Victoria, the anniversary of the deaths of the Prince Consort in 1861 and of Princess Alice in 1878. It was still an occasion of great sorrow and mourning in the family and it was clear that the Duke of York viewed this unhappy concatenation of events with apprehension. He had hoped for a girl as his second child and had

---

[a] Lord Edward William Pelham-Clinton, G.C.V.O., K.C.B. (1836–1907), second son of the fifth Duke of Newcastle, Master of Queen Victoria's Household, 1894–1901.

[b] 'Amid the chorus of congratulations there will be a note of condolence with Sir Matthew White Ridley, the Home Secretary, who was not present at the great event on Saturday morning', commented one editor on December 16, 1895. 'A few days ago, when at Sandringham, he excused himself from attending a public meeting on the grounds that his presence there was necessary. Yet on the fateful day the Home Secretary is discovered to be in London! Does this remissness involve a penalty, and, if so, what?'

expressed this wish within his family,*a* but, putting aside his disappointment on this score, he wrote in his diary :

A little boy was born, weighing nearly eight lbs. at 3.40 a.m. S.T.*b* Everything most satisfactory, both doing well. Sent a number of telegrams, had something to eat. Went to bed at 6.45, very tired.⁶

One of these telegrams was to his redoubtable grandmother, Queen Victoria, then at Windsor mourning her dead on this 'terrible anniversary':

Darling May was safely confined of a son at 3.30 this morning both doing well. GEORGIE⁷

was the message sent to the Queen, and much depended upon her reception of the news. The Duke had cut out and pasted into his diary a cutting from the *Globe* of December 14 that struck a note which he clearly hoped would have a respondent echo in the heart of the aged Queen :

Under any circumstances [ran the editorial] the birth of a second son to H.R.H. the Duke of York would be of significance as insuring to all appearances for many years to come the devolution of the Crown in the male line, but the auspicious news has additional interest when we remember that December 14 has been a black day in the annals of our Royal House, marking as it does the anniversary of the death of the Prince Consort and also that of Princess Alice. Henceforth it is permissible to hope that the august lady, in whose joys and sorrows the nation claims a right to share, may find in the felicitous event of December 14, 1895, a solace for the mournful memories of December 14, 1861, and December 14, 1878.

This note was re-echoed by the *Standard* two days later in a ponderous editorial. After reciting the threnody of tragic memories which the anniversary held for the Royal Family the editor continued :

But, surely, the Fourteenth of December may, henceforth, bear its white mark. Not that the Past can ever be forgotten, not that

a 'We were all so delighted that it was another boy', wrote the Princess of Wales to her son, 'though I hear you wished very much for a girl, but better luck next time!!!'⁴ And her brother, King George of Greece, wrote equally consolingly: 'I am sure you would have preferred a girl — she may come after — much later. Two boys following the one upon the other with one year between them is so much better.'⁵

b The initials S.T. do not stand for 'Summer Time' but for 'Sandringham Time'. The clocks at Sandringham were always kept half an hour fast. King Edward VIII on his accession abolished this practice.

even the sound of the joy-bells of the present hour can ever deaden
our ears to the recollections of a sadder and graver note. It is the
distinguishing characteristic of the higher natures, and equally of
the more serious communities, never to part wholly with their
reminiscences, even though these should give to existence a certain
air of sombreness. But the 'Too much sorrow', on which Shakespeare comments with disapproval, is incompatible with the healthy
activities either of individual or of national life; and all of us,
from our beloved Sovereign downward, will, we are quite sure, hail
with eagerness the new cause given us by the Duchess of York
for looking on the Fourteenth of December as not by any means
one of the days devoted exclusively to mourning and regret.[a]

The Queen's children were also anxious that she should not
permit the cumulative sorrows of bereavement to prejudice her
against the latest addition to the Royal Family.

I cannot say how much I rejoice! [the Dowager Empress
Frederick wrote from Berlin to her mother on December 17]. On
the one hand I thought it rather to be regretted that the dear little
Baby was born on a day of such inexpressibly sad memories to us,
— but on the other — it is a gift from Heaven and a very precious
one, — and there is something very touching in the thought — that
on this *darkest* day of your Life a ray of sunshine is sent in after
years! and I like to look at it in this light![8]

But the first reaction from Windsor must have been far
from reassuring to the anxious father at Sandringham.

Grandmama was rather distressed that this happy event should
have taken place on a darkly sad anniversary for us [wrote the
Prince of Wales to his son on December 14], but I think — as well
as most of us in the family here — that it will 'break the spell'
of this unlucky date.[9]

Two days later, however, things were looking a little
brighter, though all danger of the royal displeasure was not
entirely past. A second letter from his father urged the Duke

[a] In the midst of all this guarded and almost apologetic rejoicing at the advent
of the little Prince, it is refreshing to find that *Punch* celebrated his birth with a
cartoon (January 4, 1896) and that the *Morning Advertiser* seemed positively —
and prophetically — glad to greet him: 'The little Prince belongs to the nation
as well as to his parents. He may never be called upon, as his father was, to step
into the place on the steps of the throne, vacated under such sorrowful circumstances by an elder brother. But his birth is a second guarantee of the direct
succession to the British Crown — that greatest of all inheritances, as Mr. Gladstone once finely called it.' (December 16.) In addition slackness of business on
a Saturday provided an opportunity for a display of loyalty on the Stock Exchange,
and 'For two hours' after closing time excited members celebrated the event after
their own fashion' (*Financial Times*, December 16, 1895).

of York to suggest to the Queen that she should become the baby's godmother and that he should be named Albert.

Grandmama is not the least annoyed with you about anything [the Prince continued], but she only regretted that the little boy was born on the 14th though we have all told her that it will dispel the gloom of that sad anniversary. She is ageing rapidly — & has always been very kind & affecte. to you that I really think it would gratify her if you yourself proposed the name of *Albert* to her.[10]

The Duke adopted this propitiatory proposal with alacrity :

I am afraid, dear Grandmama [he wrote to the Queen, who had now repaired to Osborne], you were rather distressed that he was born on the 14th, that doubly sad day to you & all our family, but we hope that his having been born on that day may be the means of making it a little less sad to you. Dear Grandmama, we propose with your permission to call him *Albert* after dear Grandpapa & we also hope that you will be his Godmother.[11]

Amid this welter of apprehension and apology, which is illustrative of the awe and veneration in which her family held Queen Victoria to the last moment of her life, the one person who remained stably unconcerned was the Queen herself. With her unfailing and outstanding good sense, she set the matter in a proper perspective. She appreciated the fact that her son and grandson were regretful that what should have been for her a happy event would inevitably be clouded by the untowardness of its timing, but she was far too sensible to allow her sorrow to prejudice her against the small offender who had thus trespassed unwittingly upon her grief.

Found telegrams from Georgie and Sir J. Williams [a] saying that dear May had been safely delivered of a son at three this morning [the Queen wrote in her diary], Georgie's first feeling was regret that this dear child should be born on such a sad day. I have a feeling it may be a blessing for the dear little boy and may be looked upon as a gift from God![12]

Moreover, she was clearly delighted at the request of the parents for her personal blessing. Not only did she consent to be a godmother but she conferred upon her godson-to-be the infinite proof of her approval in the shape of a bust of the late Prince Consort as a christening present.

[a] Sir John Williams, Bart., G.C.V.O. (1840–1926), a leading authority on obstetrics who had attended the delivery of the Prince.

I cannot tell you how much pleased & gratified I have been by your dear letter [she wrote to her 'Darling Georgie']. But before I answer it let me express my joy at dear May's doing so well & recovering so quickly. Thank God! she is, *unberufen*, very strong. She gets through these affairs like nothing. It is a great satisfaction to us all that it should be a second boy & I need not say how *delighted* I am that my great wish — viz. that the little one born on that sad anniversary shd. have the dear name of *Albert* — is to be realised. Most gladly do I accept being God-mother & this dear little Boy born the day when his beloved great grandfather entered on a new greater life will be especially dear to me. — I thank you lovingly for your very kind letter & will write again soon, but I must end to save the Post.

Ever   Your devoted Grandmama

V.R.I.[13]

The Queen's feelings towards her granddaughter-in-law were no less warm :

I am all impatience to see the *new* one [she wrote to the Duchess of York], born on such a sad day but rather the more dear to me, especially as he will be called by that dear name which is the byeword for all that is great & good.[14]

The great-grandmother was, in fact, all agog to receive the details of the baby's other names and who the other god-parents were to be. She would have liked the christening to be at Osborne so that she could be present at it, but conceded the stronger claims of Sandringham.

The dire consequences feared from the inopportune date of the baby Prince's advent were therefore averted, and, thus regally sponsored, he was duly christened at the Church of St. Mary, Sandringham, on February 17, 1896, by the Bishop of Norwich, assisted by the Rev. Edgar Sheppard, sub-dean of the Chapels Royal, Canon J. N. Dalton, the Duke of York's old tutor, and the Rectors of Sandringham, Wolferton and Dersingham. In addition to the Queen, the other god-parents were the Empress Frederick,[a] the Grand Duchess of Mecklen-burg-Strelitz,[b] the Grand Duke of Mecklenburg-Strelitz, the Crown Prince of Denmark,[c] the Duke of Connaught[d] and

[a] Former Princess Royal of England and mother of Kaiser Wilhelm II.

[b] Sister of the Duchess of Teck and aunt of the Duchess of York.

[c] Subsequently King Christian X of Denmark and brother of the Princess of Wales.

[d] Brother of the Prince of Wales.

Prince Adolphus of Teck.[a]   The infant Prince, attired in the lace robe which was worn by all the children and grandchildren of the Prince and Princess of Wales,[15] received the names Albert Frederick Arthur George,[b] but to his family he was always known as 'Bertie'.

The ceremony did not go off entirely unmarred.   Prince Edward, who had evinced considerable surprise at being confronted with a new baby brother,[16] had subsequently become much interested in this most recent recruit to the family, and it was with evident pleasure that he accompanied his parents to the christening.   He remained absorbed and silent until the solemn moment of actual baptism when his brother, lying in the arms of the Bishop of Norwich, let forth so sturdy a yell that the elder Prince was moved to follow suit.   He howled in sympathy, and to such purpose that he had to be removed to the vestry.[17]

Of course he is very young to come to church [his father commented in the account he sent that night to Queen Victoria], but we thought that in years to come it would give him pleasure to know that he had been present at his brother's christening.[18]

(ii)

The era into which Prince Albert was born in December 1895 was at the zenith of its ample comfort and its peaceful calm. No signs were apparent of the two cataclysms which were to convulse the world before his death.   It was an age of colonial empires and of good living, of 'localized' wars and an effective Concert of Europe.   Politically the world in 1895 had changed little — apart from the emergence of the German Empire — since the statesmen of Europe had delineated its boundaries at Vienna eighty years before.   Europe was still the centre of influence and culture; the United States had not yet emerged as a world power and was not destined to do so for nearly a quarter of a century; Asia was still virtually unawakened. East of the Franco-German border stretched the possessions of

[a] Brother of the Duchess of York, and subsequently created first Marquess of Cambridge in 1917.

[b] *Albert* for his grandfather and great-grandfather, *Frederick* for his great-uncle by marriage, the second German Emperor, *Arthur* for his great-uncle the Duke of Connaught, and *George* for his father.

the Hohenzollerns, the Habsburgs and the Romanovs ; and a host of Russian grand dukes, Austrian archdukes and German princelings enlivened all the capitals of Europe.   Moreover, the Turkish Empire at this time still occupied a substantial portion of the Balkan Peninsula, though these European *san-jaks* were eyed with acquisitive envy by the Christian princes in Athens, Belgrade, Bucharest, Cetinje and Sofia.

But it was to England that the world looked with respect and fear, albeit in certain cases with envy and jealousy.   The Great Queen, who was grandmother to half the ruling houses of Europe, had become, by virtue of her very age, both a national and an international institution.   It was difficult to conceive of either Britain or Europe without the Queen of England, and though Britain's policy of 'Splendid Isolation' and her maddening *Superbia Britannorum* might enrage the governments and peoples of the Continent, their dislike of Britain was held in check by their involuntary veneration of that country's tremendous sovereign.

In 1895, moreover, the power of Britain and the might of her Empire had gone unchallenged since the Crimean War. That pinnacle of imperial grandeur, the Diamond Jubilee, was still two years ahead, and two more years separated England from the day when a handful of armed farmers in South Africa should tax the full resources of the Empire before their overthrow was encompassed.   It was still an England of gracious living and a certain smug complacency, of primitive plumbing and Chantrey Bequest pictures, of an income tax at 8d. in the pound and mild taxation generally, though the Harcourt death-duties had been introduced in 1894.   An agricultural labourer, though his wages might be only 15s. per week, could get a pint of beer or an ounce of tobacco for 2½d. and was not too fiercely resentful of the discrepancy between his earnings and the incomes of the wealthier classes.

In the fifty-six years of the life of King George VI the world, and with it Britain, underwent the most shattering changes in tempo and character.   The age of the clipper ships and dashing equipages, of oil lamps and the stereopticon, had given place to an era of atomic energy and radar, of psychiatry and television and the radio, of relativity and three-dimensional moving pictures, with the Comet aircraft consuming the distance from London to Johannesburg in twenty-two hours.

At the King's birth there were twenty reigning monarchs in continental Europe. At his death there were but seven. The German, Russian, Austro-Hungarian and Turkish Empires had disappeared from the map. The British Empire of Dominions beyond the Seas had become a Commonwealth of self-governing nations and the Indian Empire had dissolved itself into two parts, one a Dominion and the other a Republic. Even the political structure of the United Kingdom itself had changed, for the Republic of Ireland had contracted out of both the Kingdom and the Commonwealth.

Within the King's youth there came into usage electric light, the motor-car and the gramophone, and he was an adult before he first heard a radio broadcast. He was eight years old when the Wright Brothers made their historic flight at Kitty Hawk in 1903, and he was the first King of England to wear an airman's wings. As a young man he witnessed the social revolutions which were wrought in England during his father's reign by the Liberals before the First World War and by both Labour and Conservative Governments after it, and as Sovereign he presided over the destinies of his country through the era of far more sweeping changes under the Labour Government after the Second World War. In both great conflicts he served his country with courage and fidelity, in the first as a junior naval officer, being the first British Sovereign to have seen action in battle since William IV — who as a young man took part in the Battle of Cape St. Vincent — and in the second as the ruler of his peoples.

King George VI watched the transition of his times from the relaxed complacency, the assured security and the established society of the late Victorian era to the strain and stress and tension, the international uncertainty and the shifting fluidity of our own day. It is against this changing background that the story of his life must be read and understood.

(iii)

The structure of the Royal Family at the birth of Prince Albert was that of a pyramid. At the apex was the aged and legendary figure of Queen Victoria ('Gangan'), nearing her seventy-seventh year, infirm of body but undimmed in activity of mind, moving within a circuit of Windsor and Osborne and Balmoral, with rare visits to Buckingham Palace. To her great-grand-children she seemed a personage of another world, removed from them not only by years but by periods and epochs; a benign matriarch not wholly dissociated from the Deity; the focal point around which the whole family constellation revolved.

Slightly nearer, though yet considerably apart, were the Prince and Princess of Wales ('Grandpapa' and 'Grannie'), whose devoted benevolence was a constant source of immense pleasure to the younger generation and whose presence at Marlborough House and Sandringham was the occasion for wonderful visits from the grandchildren, moments of unalloyed happiness and riotous enjoyment.

The prevailing factor in the lives of Prince Edward and Prince Albert was, however, the parental influence of the Duke and Duchess of York. The future King George V was now in his thirty-first year and in the closing stages of his career as an active naval officer. He had risen by merit and hard work to the rank of Captain, and is so described in the Parish register of St. Mary's, Sandringham, on the occasion of the christening of his second son. Until recently he had been but third in succession to the throne, and his whole life and happiness had been centred in the naval career which he had made, most successfully, his own.

But with the death on January 14, 1892, of the Duke of Clarence, the elder son of the Prince of Wales, the destiny of the Duke of York underwent a material change. He was now his father's direct heir and his active naval life had accordingly to be abandoned.[a] Deprived at one stroke of a beloved brother and of a much loved career, the Duke turned sadly from the sea to the affairs of State, setting himself to master the problems of internal politics and international relations.

On July 6, 1893, he married Princess Mary of Teck,[b] who

---

[a] The Duke of York's last active command was in H.M.S. *Crescent* during an eight weeks' target practice in the Irish Channel in May and June of 1898.

[b] Princess Mary (1867–1953) was the daughter of Francis, Duke of Teck, the son of Duke Alexander of Württemberg by a morganatic marriage with the Hungarian Countess Rhédy, and Mary Adelaide, daughter of Adolphus, Duke of Cambridge, son of George III.

had previously been betrothed to the Duke of Clarence, and together they settled down at York Cottage, a small and depressing residence in the grounds of his parents' estate at Sandringham.

Though he was now to assume the rôle of a country gentleman — and let it be said that with the passing of the years his affection for Sandringham waxed almost as great as his love for the sea — the Duke of York ever retained the temperament of the naval officer, with its rigidity of outlook, its categorical sense of duty, its expectation of immediate obedience, impeccable conduct and extreme orderliness, and, in addition, its cheery gusto. He accepted unquestioningly his position of 'second-in-command' to his father — whom he loved and revered — and with it the self-effacement and dependence which this status inevitably entailed.

It may be doubted whether the Duchess of York shared, at any rate at the outset, the self-abnegation of her husband. As one of the biographers of King George V has tactfully written : [19]

The Duchess had married into a family which for years had been self-sufficient, a family which the Princess's genius for affection had turned into something that was certainly a closely guarded clique and was not far short of a mutual-admiration society. It was a family little given to intellectual pursuits, without much in the way of artistic tastes or taste, a family not easily to be converted to any other manner of life than that which they had found all-sufficing in an age wherein privilege vigorously survived.

The Duchess was intellectually on a higher plane ; she was already well educated and constantly seeking to increase her store of knowledge in many fields beyond the range of the Princess of Wales and Princess Victoria. She was full of initiative, of intellectual curiosity, of energy, which needed outlets and wider horizons. Their recreations were not hers. Their manner of life could not satisfy her notions of the ideal in the intellectual life of those days. And she was living in a small house on an estate which drew its inspiration wholly from the Prince and Princess, whereon every smallest happening or alteration was ordered and taken note of by the Prince. The very arrangement of her rooms, the planting of her small garden, were matters which required reference to Sandringham House, and the smallest innovation would be regarded with distrust. There was so much that she might usefully have done on the estate. Her ideas might have influenced a score of local institutions and increased the well-being of the neighbourhood. But such matters were the prerogative of the Princess, whose charm and kindliness often made up for her lack of system and order.

Sometimes the Duchess's intellectual life there may have been starved and her energies atrophied in those early years. For she came of a younger, more liberal generation, with far more serious notions of woman's sphere of usefulness, and very strong ideas of the responsibilities demanded of the first ladies in the realm. For many women, then as now, the daily call to follow the shooters, to watch the killing, however faultless, to take always a cheerful, appreciative part in man-made, man-valued amusements, must have been answered at the sacrifice of many cherished, many constructive and liberal ambitions. It is fair to assume that the self-effacement which conditions at Sandringham in those years demanded of a fine and energetic character must have fallen hardly on the Duchess, and fair also to suggest that the Prince and Princess might have done more to encourage her initiative and to fill her days, and with a more understanding sympathy to have alleviated the shyness with which she entered upon her ceremonial duties.

Nor can the immediate surroundings of her married life have enchanted the Duchess of York. It was to York Cottage, Sandringham, a small annexe standing a few hundred yards from the 'Big House', that she was taken as a bride to spend her honeymoon, and York Cottage has to be seen to be believed.

'It was, and remains, a glum little villa', Sir Harold Nicolson has written in terms of restraint rather than of exaggeration,

encompassed by thickets of laurel and rhododendron, shadowed by huge Wellingtonias and separated by an abrupt rim of lawn from a pond, at the edge of which a leaden pelican gazes in dejection upon the water lilies and bamboos. The local brown stone in which the house was constructed is concealed by rough-cast which in its turn is enlivened by very imitation Tudor beams. The rooms inside, with their fumed oak surrounds, their white overmantels framing oval mirrors, their Doulton tiles and stained glass fanlights, are indistinguishable from those of any Surbiton or Upper Norwood home. The Duke's own sitting-room, its north window blocked by heavy shrubberies, was rendered even darker by the red cloth covering which saddened the walls. Against this dismal monochrome (which was composed of the cloth used in those days for the trousers of the French army)[a] hung excellent reproductions

[a] The Duke of Windsor in his memoirs (p. 27) records his belief that this scarlet covering had been destroyed by moths. This is, in fact, not so. The room still retains the full glory of its remarkable decoration.

of some of the more popular pictures acquired by the Chantrey Bequest.[20]

Nor was this all. The plumbing equipment in 'this most undesirable residence' was of the most primitive and the bedroom accommodation of the most cubicular. The bed- and dressing-rooms of the Duke and Duchess were of a normal size, but those allotted to the children and to members of the Household were dark and charmless. The little cell reserved for the lady-in-waiting was situated immediately above the pantry and separated from it by the thinnest of flooring, through which every sound penetrated. On one occasion the occupant of this chamber sent down word that, if the footmen cleaning the silver beneath her did not object to her overhearing their conversation, she, for her part, had no objection to overhearing it. As for the servants, the Duke himself once remarked vaguely that he supposed they must sleep in the trees.

It was at York Cottage, however, that he lived in complete happiness for thirty-three years, from the date of his marriage until he took possession of Sandringham House in January 1926 after the death of Queen Alexandra. Here five of his six children were born, and here he cherished so dearly that Sandringham way of life, the love of which was inherited by his second son. 'Dear old Sandringham', he called it, 'the place I love better than anywhere else in the world.'

It was also to be 'home' to his family. For though as children they would follow the family migrations to Osborne, to Frogmore, to Abergeldie, and later to Marlborough House and Buckingham Palace, it was Sandringham, with its garden and seashore attractions and its 200-acre park, that formed the abiding basis of their mixed memories of childhood.

This childhood, like that of so many brought up in the late Victorian and Edwardian eras, was essentially one of separation. The modern theory of parents being 'companions' to their children had not yet been evolved, and contact with their elders was unusual rather than usual in young lives. Children were brought to their parents at stated and regular times and were otherwise in the hands — and sometimes at the mercy — of nurses, footmen and other servants. The relationship of both parties had, as a result, a certain unnaturalness about it. To the children these regular meetings with their parents, the occasions on which they were brought to the dressing-room or drawing-room, were awesome, though exciting and often rewarding ; to the parents they were pleasant occasions, but often exacting and sometimes bewildering. It was a system which might evoke affection but which could rarely promote intimate understanding.

It was not unnatural that this condition of affairs, so widely prevalent at the time, should also obtain in the family *ménage* at York Cottage. The Duke of York, like many another Victorian father, was devoted to children and, as he said, 'got on with them like a house on fire'. This, however, as so often happened, tended to mean 'other people's children', and it was true — as many of the younger members of the Royal Family, his nephews and nieces and young cousins, as well as the schoolchildren at Sandringham and Balmoral, could testify. Yet with his own children, though he was a model family man and a loving and devoted father, bathing them in turn, weighing them, playing with them on occasion, instructing them in the use of gun and rod and in the saddle, he remained a distant figure inspiring reverence, reserved affection and sometimes genuine fear. Lacking the tolerance and easy *bonhomie* of his father, he was impetuous by nature and gave vent to his feelings instantly and without reserve. 'His manner of chaffing them or interrogating them added to the shyness and tied the tongues of those by nature the most diffident, and the same qualities which gained him the devotion of his Staff and servants and the admiration of his wider family as their ideal head, sometimes created a barrier which separated him from his own sons', though it is important to note that no misunderstandings or lack of sympathy continued beyond the dates of their respective marriages.[21]

The same constricting *mores* of the period affected the relations of the Duchess of York with her children. She was deeply devoted to them, and they to her, with a sincere and warm affection. Yet it was difficult for her to stand between them and the sudden gusts of their father's wrath and equally difficult for them to make a confidante of her. The qualified misunderstanding between the parents and their children was probably neither more nor less than that existing in many other families at that time, but, for all that, it was none the less sad.

(iv)

The Royal nursery at York Cottage did not escape the vicissitudes and upheavals which affected other similar British establishments of the period. The first head nurse was discharged
for being insolent to the Duchess of Teck, the Duchess of
York's mother, and her successor appears to have been both
sadistic and incompetent. She showed a marked preference
for the elder of her charges ; indeed, her devotion was so
fanatical that, in order to demonstrate the superiority of her
power over him to that of his parents, she would twist and
pinch the unfortunate Prince Edward's arm before bringing
him into the drawing-room. As a result a sobbing, bawling
infant was speedily returned to his nurse, who miraculously
quietened him, having, by these perverse methods, established
her own moral ascendancy.[22]

Prince Albert the nurse frankly ignored to a degree which
amounted virtually to neglect. So completely did she disregard his wants and comforts that he was frequently given his
afternoon bottle while driving in a C-sprung victoria, a process
not dissimilar from a rough Channel crossing — and with corresponding results. It is not surprising that the baby developed
chronic stomach trouble, which may well have laid the foundation for the gastric complaint from which he was later to suffer
so acutely.

Eventually, however, it was discovered that all was not well
in the nursery, and this Freudian character was dismissed, to
be succeeded by Mrs. Bill — the beloved 'Lalla' — who had
been under-nurse to both her predecessors. She soon established an efficient and humane régime, based on a sage amalgam
of love and discipline, under which her three charges — for
Princess Mary had been born on April 25, 1897 — throve and
flourished.

Of the six children of the Duke and Duchess of York, the
first three constituted a group by themselves. Less than three
years separated the eldest from the youngest, and Prince
Albert was eighteen months younger than his brother and
sixteen months older than his sister. This position as the
second of the three was not advantageous to his development. By nature a shy, nervous and affectionate child, easily

frightened and somewhat prone to tears, he compared un-
favourably with the gaiety of his more forthcoming elder
brother and the inevitable charms of his baby sister. As a
result he was apt to drop into the background and even to be
ignored altogether. For example, Queen Victoria in her diary
records a visit from them as follows: 'The dear little York
children came, looking very well. David is a delightful child,
so intelligent, nice and friendly. The baby is a sweet pretty
little thing.' [23] There is no recorded impression of little Bertie.

They were, however, a very happy and united trio. Prince
Albert was devoted to his sister and entertained an almost
extravagant admiration for his brother, whose lead he followed
into all kinds of mischief. But somehow or other the blame
for these pranks usually seems to have been attached to him
rather than to the others. He early gained a reputation for
childish disobedience, and parental chidings were not even
omitted from birthday greetings. 'Now that you are five
years old', his father wrote to him, 'I hope you will always try
& be obedient & do at once what you are told, as you will
find it will come much easier to you the sooner you begin. I
always tried to do this when I was your age & found it made
me much happier.' [24]

The first break in this family pattern came very shortly
thereafter, at the beginning of Prince Albert's sixth year. In
most quarters the Boer War was believed — though erroneously
— to be drawing to its close, and on the Sandringham front the
four [a] children of the Duke and Duchess of York were quarantined against German measles, which Prince Edward had
developed just after Christmas. Their parents had gone to
London on January 17, 1901, to attend a great reception and
dinner in honour of the returned hero, Lord Roberts, who, as
Commander-in-Chief, had brought victory out of defeat for
the British forces in South Africa. That night, at the Marlborough Club, the Duke of York was informed by his father
that Queen Victoria, then at Osborne, had suffered a slight
stroke that afternoon. Two days later the reports of her health
were more reassuring and the Duke and Duchess returned to
Sandringham. They did not see their children for fear of infection and on Monday, January 21, they left hurriedly again

[a] Prince Henry was born on March 31, 1900.

PRINCE HENRY, PRINCE EDWARD, PRINCE ALBERT, PRINCE GEORGE, PRINCE JOHN

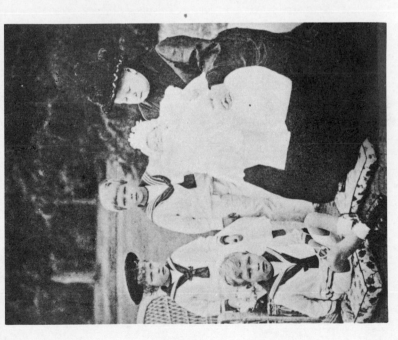

'The last portrait taken of Her late lamented Majesty Queen Victoria with the children of the Duke and Duchess of York' (contemporary postcard)

for London. Word reached the nursery that 'Gangan' — the mythical, legendary, ancestral 'Gangan', whom they, her great-grandchildren, had regarded with a mixed reverence, awe and apprehension [a]— was sinking, and the following day she died.

Despite his precautions the Duke of York did not escape the infection. On arrival at Osborne with his father and his cousin, the German Emperor, he was feeling far from well and, although he forced himself to attend the new King to London for the Accession Council at St. James's Palace, and to take the Oath in the House of Lords, on his return to Osborne on January 24 he fell seriously ill with German measles. He was confined to his room, nursed devotedly by his wife, until February 10.

It so happened, therefore, that the heir to the throne was unable to accompany the Great Queen on her last silent journey from Osborne, through London, to Windsor, but his three elder children were released from Sandringham for the event. At the special request of the Duchess, Queen Alexandra arranged for them to see the funeral service in St. George's Chapel and to be present two days later at the final interment beside the Prince Consort in the private mausoleum at Frogmore.[25]

Thus, on that bitterly cold afternoon of February 2, 1901, the five-year-old Prince Albert stood amongst the kings,[b] the scores of princes and the multitude of dignitaries, who sorrowfully — and almost disbelievingly — watched the burial

[a] There is ample evidence to the effect that both Prince Edward and Prince Albert were frankly terrified in the presence of Queen Victoria, though it is difficult to discover whether their terror was caused by the ancient lady herself or by the somewhat fearsome Indian orderly officers who frequently attended her. Whatever the cause, both boys would frequently burst into tears, and this both saddened and annoyed the Queen, who would ask, with the petulance of old age, what she had done wrong now. It also mortified the children's parents.

[b] Four kings followed Queen Victoria's coffin on horseback: King Edward VII; the German Emperor, Kaiser Wilhelm II; King George I of the Hellenes; and King Carlos of Portugal; a fifth, the aged King Leopold II of the Belgians, drove in a carriage. There were also present the German Crown Prince and the Crown Princes of Rumania, Greece, Denmark, Norway and Sweden, and Siam. The Emperor of Austria was represented by the Archduke Franz Ferdinand, the Tsar by the Grand Duke Michael Alexandrovitch, and the King of Italy by the Duke of Aosta. In addition, there was a host of German minor Royalties, including the Grand Dukes of Baden and Hesse, and the Dukes of Saxe-Coburg-Gotha, Saxony and Württemberg. Of those mentioned above, two Kings (Greece and Portugal) and both the Austrian and Russian representatives were destined to die by assassination.

of Queen Victoria. It was the first of three such occasions which he would attend in St. George's Chapel, and, half a century later, kings and princes would attend his own funeral there.

Less than two months after the death of Queen Victoria there occurred the first prolonged dislocation of the family circle at York Cottage. On March 16 the Duke and Duchess of Cornwall and York[a] sailed in S.S. *Ophir* for Australia, to open, on behalf of the new Sovereign, the first session of the Commonwealth Parliament, and they were away nearly eight months. The Duke left strict instructions that his two elder sons were to write regularly to their parents and, in addition to his own replies, long and instructive letters to the Princes were written from the various ports of call by Mr. Walter Jones, the village schoolmaster of Sandringham, an old friend of the Duke's youth, whom he had attached to his suite.

Prince Albert took this injunction very seriously and even wrote his first letter four days before his parents sailed, so that it might reach them at Gibraltar :

MY DARLING MAMA AND PAPA
We hope you are quite well and not seasick. Did you have a big wave when you went through the Bay of Biscay ? We send you love and a lot of kisses,

From your loving

BERTIE [26]

Like most children of their age, those left behind at York Cottage soon became reconciled to the absence of their elders. In the first place, they were released from a somewhat strict parental supervision, remaining under the benevolent despotism of 'Lalla' Bill, supplemented by the conscientious but ineffective educational efforts of their governess, Mlle Hélène Bricka, an Alsatian lady who had taught their mother as a girl; and in the second, they were grossly and enthusiastically spoiled by their grandparents. King Edward and Queen Alexandra adored their grandchildren and liked nothing more than to have them with them. Thus, for nearly eight months,

[a] On the accession of King Edward VII the Duke of York, as heir to the throne, succeeded him as Duke of Cornwall, and thereafter was known as the Duke of Cornwall and York. It was not until November 9, 1901, after his return from Australia, that the King conferred on his son the title of Prince of Wales.

the three Princes and Princess Mary, together with their nursery entourage, followed the peregrinations of the Court from Marlborough House to Sandringham and from Osborne to Balmoral. The bonds of discipline were definitely relaxed. King Edward, with his jovial *bonhomie* and enjoyment of life, and with formidable recollections of his own early instruction, discouraged lessons as constituting an unnecessary inhibition to fun. Both he and the Queen encouraged the children in their boisterous expression of animal spirits and delighted to show them off before distinguished visitors at luncheon at Buckingham Palace and Sandringham, when they were allowed to romp openly in the dining-room.[a]

This freedom was the more enjoyed and the more exploited because of the earlier and stricter parental régime. For the same reason, it took hold upon the children the more firmly. They became really unruly, and it is not altogether surprising that, when their father returned to England in the autumn of 1901, he swiftly decided that a corrective was not only necessary but long overdue, and that his elder sons had reached an age when they could no longer be controlled by feminine supervision.

(v)

The year 1902 was momentous in the lives of Prince Albert and his elder brother, for it marked their removal from the benign suzerainty of 'Lalla' Bill to masculine discipline, and also their transition from the nursery to the schoolroom. The first change came with the New Year when the two boys were told that thenceforth they would be in the charge of Frederick Finch,

---

[a] The happy relationship between King Edward and his grandchildren was a very real one and Prince Albert appears to have been a favourite. There are in the Royal Archives at Windsor a number of little notes from his grandfather, dashed off from such varied addresses as Buckingham Palace, Ajaccio and the Jockey Club, of which the following is an example :

MY DEAREST LITTLE BERTIE
 You have written me a very nice little letter. How fortunate that Bland caught Papa's parrot that had flown away or else he might have been shot! I shall hope to see you again next week — & find you all well. Now that the weather is fine again you might have to play golf!
Ever your devoted Grandpapa,
EDWARD R.

hitherto the nursery footman.[a]   Finch was then thirty years old and his charges seven-and-a-half and six respectively.   He was handsome, stalwart and muscular, 'naturally respectful but without a trace of servility'.[27]   For the next eight years he was to be, at first, the nursemaid, and, later, the arbiter, trusted confidant and loyal champion to the two Princes.   It was Finch who attended to their clothes and saw that they themselves were personally clean.   It was Finch who heard their prayers morning and evening, and who tucked them up in bed, and it was Finch also who, when occasion demanded, administered condign chastisement upon their small persons. They were devoted to him and he to them.

The second change was more vital.

The education of Princes has long been among the more perplexing of the personal problems with which Sovereigns are confronted.   The choice of mentor, the curriculum of study selected, have more than once changed the course of history and have certainly moulded the minds of young heirs to the throne in formulating their views towards the enigmas which they have later encountered.   The Prince Consort's precise and tidy mind had summed up the problem apophthegmatically in 1849 : 'Upon the good education of Princes, and especially of those who are destined to govern, the welfare of the world in these days greatly depends'.[28]

Acting upon this precept, the Prince, while his eldest son was still in his cradle, devised, with the aid of the inimitable Baron Stockmar, that severe and heavily documented discipline under which the future King Edward VII groaned throughout his boyhood [b] and of which his biographer wrote : 'The system, however well intentioned, was obviously vitiated

---

[a] Frederick Finch (1871–1953), the son of a young footman in the service of the first Duke of Wellington, was born at Stratfield Saye and entered the service of the Duke of York in November 1899, at the age of twenty-seven.   He transferred to the household of Prince Edward, when Prince of Wales, in 1910, and served him first as valet and later as Steward until 1935, when he retired on pension to live in Berkshire.

[b] Of the succession of young tutors whose duty it was to implement the Stockmar system, one, Frederick Waymouth Gibbs, who held the onerous position from 1851 to 1860, has left a discreet but not unrevealing diary of which some excerpts were published under the title of 'The Education of a Prince' in the spring issue of the *Cornhill Magazine* for 1951.   Mr. Gibbs shrewdly observed that many of the shortcomings of his somewhat difficult and unruly pupil arose 'from want of contact with boys of his own age . . . and from himself forming the centre around which everything seems to move. . . .'

by its scorn of the idiosyncrasies of a normal boy whatever his station in life'.[29]

Mindful of his own unhappiness, King Edward, when his turn came to select a preceptor for his sons, chose with care and anxiety the Reverend John Neale Dalton, of whom so penetrating a study is presented by Sir Harold Nicolson in his biography of King George V.[30] Mr. Dalton succeeded in winning the affection and admiration of his pupil, whose intimate friend and counsellor he remained until his death as Canon of Windsor in 1931, when over ninety years of age.

Whereas King Edward's recollections of his childhood and education had been unhappy ones, King George's were quite the reverse, and whereas King Edward had sought to provide for his sons the opposite of his own experiences, King George endeavoured to re-create the happy relationship which had existed between his brother and himself and Mr. Dalton. For this purpose he selected Mr. Henry Peter Hansell, to whom he handed over his sons in the spring of 1902.

Mr. Hansell at this time was thirty-nine years of age. The son of a country gentleman of Wroxham in Norfolk, he had been educated at Malvern College, where he had gained distinction in English and History and as a member of the School XIs in cricket and football, and at Magdalen College, Oxford, where he took Second Class Honours in History. He then became a schoolmaster, first at Rossall and then at Ludgrove, and had been chosen by the Duke of Connaught to be private tutor to his son, Prince Arthur,[a] whom he had recently shepherded into Eton. He was tall and good-looking, in appearance not unlike the late Mr. Ramsay MacDonald, a bachelor without much sense of humour, and a keen golfer. But what commended him particularly to the Prince of Wales, apart from the fact that he was a Norfolk man, born and bred on the Broads, was that he was also a keen yachtsman. His was not a warm personality and he was prone to fall into long

---

[a] Prince Arthur of Connaught (1883–1938), only son of the Duke of Connaught, married in 1913 the Lady Alexandra Victoria Alberta Edwina Louise, daughter of the first Duke of Fife and the Princess Royal, eldest daughter of King Edward VII, who, on the death of her father, became Duchess of Fife in her own right. Prince Arthur served as Governor-General of the Union of South Africa from 1920 to 1923. He predeceased his father, and his only son, the second and last Duke of Connaught, died in Ottawa at the age of twenty-eight in 1943.

periods of abstraction, when, pipe in mouth, he would gaze vacantly into space; but he succeeded in capturing the strong and abiding affection of his young charges,[a] who called him 'Mider' — a childish corruption of 'Mister' — and corresponded devotedly with him long after they had passed from his authority.[b]

It must be admitted, however, that Mr. Hansell was not a born teacher, nor an ideal preceptor. On the other hand, in fairness to him, it must be added that he was fully conscious of his own shortcomings and was from the first apprehensive of the success of the experiment. To his credit he realized that much had changed since the 1870's when Mr. Dalton had directed the studies of Prince Eddy and Prince George, and he appreciated the truth, which Mr. Gibbs had discovered half a century before, that many of the youthful deficiencies of princes are derived from lack of contact with boys of their own age. He was personally convinced, and more than once he expressed this conviction to the Prince of Wales, who vetoed it out of hand, that Prince Edward and Prince Albert would be far better off at a good preparatory school where they would experience competitive games and work, learn to take the rough with the smooth and, in short, lead a normal school life.[c]

In his own strange way Mr. Hansell endeavoured to create at York Cottage as much of this school atmosphere as possible. He fitted up a classroom with two standard desks, a blackboard, bookshelves, etc., in a corner room on the first floor; here from 7.30 till 8.15 the boys would do their preparation before breakfast; and from 9 till 1 and between tea and supper they did their lessons. On some occasions, with the

---

[a] Their devotion to Mr. Hansell did not, however, prevent the Princes from indulging in numerous practical jokes at his expense — usually when their parents were absent from York Cottage. There are still those at Sandringham who remember seeing the front door burst open and the boys rush out and rapidly climb into a tree, to be shortly followed by their tutor who would call and look for them in evident bewilderment at their sudden and complete disappearance.

[b] Mr. Hansell continued as mentor to Prince Edward, when, as Prince of Wales, he was an undergraduate at Magdalen College, Oxford, and later during his residence in France as the guest of the Marquis de Breteuil. He served with gallantry and distinction in the First World War and died in 1935 at the age of seventy-two.

[c] At a later period the idea of sending young princes to a preparatory school was accepted, and both King George's younger sons, Prince Henry and Prince George, attended St. Peter's Court at Broadstairs.

co-operation of Mr. Jones, Mr. Hansell would organize immature football matches in pick-up sides in which the Princes joined with boys of the village school, but it is doubtful whether these games gave very much enjoyment to anyone.

Mr. Hansell's principal defect, however, was one of excessive virtue, and the virtue of his period and background. He might, in fact, have stepped straight out of the pages of one of Dean Farrar's great school romances. His was the muscular Christianity of *St. Winifred's*, and this might not have occasioned too great a difficulty had he not expected his pupils to be equally imbued with the characteristics of *Eric, or Little by Little*. This they most certainly were not. They were quite ordinary little boys with no more of original sin about them than any others of their age and weight, but equally with no more outstanding virtues than their contemporaries. They were high-spirited and intelligent and to ignite within them the spark of ambition to learn must have constituted a challenge to any tutor. Mr. Hansell's efforts to ignite this spark appear to have resulted in something of a damp squib.

There exist in the Royal Archives at Windsor a series of leather-bound note-books containing the weekly, and sometimes daily, reports of Mr. Hansell to the Prince of Wales on the progress and conduct of his sons. In them, even making allowances for that inevitable exasperation which, most understandably, afflicts periodically those who teach the young, the tutor seems rarely to rise above the petulant and at times to achieve the querulous. 'Both boys must give a *readier* obedience. I often describe them to myself as obedient boys at the second time of asking' (September 20, 1902) is a typical entry, as is also: 'The work in simple division sums is most disheartening. I really thought we had mastered division by 3 but division by 2 seems to be quite beyond him [Prince Albert] now' (July 25, 1903) ; and again: 'I am very sorry to say that Prince Albert has caused two painful scenes in his bedroom this week. On the second occasion I understand that he narrowly escaped giving his brother a very severe kick, it being absolutely unprovoked & Finch being engaged in helping Prince Edward at the time.' (January 16, 1904.) Mr. Hansell was not one to play down the youthful peccadilloes of his charges.

Mr. Hansell did not labour single-handed. In the course of time he assembled quite a varied teaching staff. In addition to Mr. Jones, he was assisted by two heavily bearded European colleagues, M. Hua, who had taught French to the Prince of Wales, then Prince George, in *Britannia*, and subsequently became a master at Eton,[a] and Professor Oswald, a German scholar ; [b] and there was also Mr. Martin David, a mathematics master at Tonbridge School. Of these Mr. Hansell regarded himself as a Headmaster and the Report Book is indicative of his methods :

On this, the last page of the second volume of the Report Book [he wrote on May 20, 1905], it will not be out of place if I put down a few observations on the important subject of how the Princes are to be kept up to the mark in their work and in their conduct. A careful survey of the Report Book for each day will show that reports of bad work have been noted and dealt with by me. The strong lever of a report book, to be handed in to His Royal Highness after each lesson will be used by Dr. Oswald, Mr. David and Monsieur Hua. With regard to my own work & the responsibility of surveillance, I propose only to make a direct report for special misbehaviour or idleness, such report only to be made after due consideration and with full conviction.

It may be imagined what effect reports of this nature would have had on the temperament of the Prince of Wales, with his background of naval discipline and his rigid Victorian upbringing. Their receipt was not infrequently followed by that summons of his sons to their father's Library which betokened a terrifying 'dressing down' for the culprit. All the children, even Princess Mary who for a brief period came under Mr. Hansell's authority,[c] were subjected to these

---

[a] The Prince of Wales entertained a similar sentimental attachment for M. Hua as he had for Canon Dalton, which even persisted after his death in 1909. The Prince paid periodic visits to his grave at Kensal Green cemetery.[31]

[b] Dr. Oswald was clearly not a strict disciplinarian. On one occasion he complained to the Prince of Wales of Prince Albert's inattention, and, when pressed for details, explained in embarrassment, 'Your Royal Highness, it isn't only that Prince Albert is inattentive, but when I scold him he just pulls my beard'.[32]

[c] Princess Mary's passage through the York Cottage schoolroom appears to have been a disruptive one. 'I must keep Princess Mary apart from the others as much as possible, whenever it is a matter of work', reported Mr. Hansell. 'Her disposition is mercurial ; one can enforce discipline and order of a sort but the fact remains that, so long as she is in the room, her brothers cannot concentrate their attention on any serious work.' (May 9, 1903.) Shortly thereafter the Princess was withdrawn to the stricter supervision of Mlle José Dussau.

rodomontades, but they were dreaded by Prince Albert most of all, partly because he was the most sensitive of the elder children and partly because he was already suffering from that impediment in his speech which was to afflict him throughout his life and against which he fought so gallant, and ultimately so victorious, a battle.

The origins and causes of Prince Albert's stammer are difficult to discover. He was undoubtedly a highly strung, easily excitable and nervous child, and his early nursery experiences were not calculated to have ameliorated this condition. He was sensitive, easily rebuffed and prone to take his weaknesses and mistakes too seriously. This would find expression either in acute depression or in outbreaks of anger, as much at himself as at others. But he did not stammer when he first began to talk, and it appears to have developed during his seventh and eighth years. It has been attributed to his being naturally left-handed and being compelled to write with his right hand. This would create a condition known in psychology as a 'misplaced sinister' and may well have affected the speech. Whatever the cause, however, the affliction of speech impediment had descended upon him.

Only those who have themselves suffered the tragedies of the stammerer can appreciate to the full their depth and poignancy — the infuriating inhibitions and frustrations, the bitter humiliation and anguish of the spirit; the orgies of self-pity; and the utter exhaustion, mental and physical; perhaps, above all, the sense of being *different* from others and the shrinking from help prompted by pity. Only by the exercise of the greatest tact and sympathy and understanding can the lot of the sufferer be mitigated, and these factors were not predominant in the climate of ideas at York Cottage.

Small wonder then that Mr. Hansell reported Prince Albert as being backward in oral work and disinclined to take part in French and German conversation exercises with M. Hua and Dr. Oswald — the boy had difficulty enough in expressing himself in his own tongue, let alone in a foreign language — and small wonder that, when hauled up before his irate father, he stood tongue-tied, unable to defend himself.

His stammer cut him off in some respects not only from his parents but from his brothers and sister too. Although more at his ease with them and therefore less inhibited in speech, he was precluded from taking an active part in the badinage and repartee which are a part of family life, and bitterly resented the imitation of his affliction to which, with the unthinking and unintentional cruelty of the young, he was subjected. Driven in upon himself, he alternated between periods of dreamy abstraction, during which it seemed impossible to command his concentration, and outbursts of emotional excitement, sometimes of high spirits and exuberance, sometimes of passionate weeping and depression. '*Le tempérament excitable du Prince Albert, sa disposition hâtive, la facilité avec laquelle il se rebute devant le moindre raisonnement sont les obstacles contre lesquels il y a à lutter et qu'il faut vaincre . . .*' wrote M. Hua, with only partial comprehension (July 14, 1908).

Nor was this the only tribulation which the Prince had to bear at this time. Like their father, all the Prince of Wales's sons, with the exception of the eldest, suffered from knock-knees, and to correct this failing Sir Francis Laking [a] had devised a system of splints in which Prince Albert had to pass certain hours of the day and in which, for a time, he had to sleep at night. They were painful and wearisome to the wearer, but he persevered with them. 'This is an experiment!' he wrote to his mother at Marlborough House. 'I am sitting in an armchair with my legs in the new splints and on a chair. I have got an invalid table, which is splendid for reading but rather awkward for writing at present. I expect I shall get used to it.' [33]

The splints also occasioned Mr. Hansell some mental anguish. '*Prince Albert*'s early morning work is rendered almost useless by the *splints*, which, I must say, appear to suit him much better and to be doing good already', he reported. 'Under the conditions however small results can only be obtained by very great and sustained efforts on the part of the teacher' (May 21, 1904), and again: 'Practically all *Prince Albert*'s work with me has been combined with the splints. It is now quite certain that *such a combination is impossible*.' (July 2, 1904.) Later, however, Mr. Hansell was appeased by the fact that Sir Francis Laking ordained that the offending appliances need only be worn at night, leaving the day free

[a] Sir Francis Henry Laking, Bt., G.C.V.O., K.C.B., M.D. (1847–1914), Physician-in-Ordinary and Surgeon-Apothecary to the Prince of Wales.

for mental improvement.[a] The treatment, one is glad to know, proved entirely successful.

It must not, however, be thought that Prince Albert's childhood was lived in the atmosphere of Florence Montgomery's *Misunderstood*. Stormy it may have been, chequered it certainly was, but there were many and long periods of halcyon sunshine. There was much happiness in the family circle at York Cottage and at Marlborough House. In the evenings the Princess of Wales would preside at the piano over juvenile sing-songs and there were other, country, diversions. The boys learned to ride and were initiated by Mr. Hansell into the early mysteries of the game of golf. In London their tutor took them to the usual sights, including the Zoo, and the White City, and to watch cricket at Lord's.

In the preparations for the Coronation of their grandfather on June 26, 1902, the two Princes received their first taste of royal pageantry and of their own historic heritage. With Mr. Hansell they went to the Tower of London to be shown the Crown Jewels that their grandparents would later wear, and to Westminster Abbey to see the Coronation Chair in which their ancestors for the past six hundred years had been crowned Sovereigns of England.[b] They experienced, with Britain and the Empire, the sickening shock of disappointment and, to some extent, the anxiety, occasioned by the King's sudden illness and the postponement of his crowning. But when the great day arrived at last on August 9 they were present in the Abbey — two small boys, both of whom were to be Kings but only one of them to be crowned — in the Royal box reserved for the Princesses, wearing the 'Balmoral costume' and under

[a] On one occasion Prince Albert pleaded so hard not to have the splints put on at night and wept so bitterly that Finch, whose duty it was to see that they were properly adjusted, relented and allowed him to sleep without them. On this being reported to the Prince of Wales by Sir Francis Laking, Finch was sent for to the Library where, having heard his explanation, the Prince stood up and, drawing his trousers tight against his legs, displayed his own knock-knees and said in a loud voice: 'Look at me. If that boy grows up to look like this, it will be your fault.'

[b] The Coronation Chair has been used at every Coronation of a British Sovereign since Edward I, with the solitary exception of Queen Mary I, whose Coronation was unusual in that the two Primates and the Bishop of London were held in the Tower as traitors and heretics, and the ceremony was performed in a somewhat perfunctory manner by the Bishop of Winchester and the Dean of Westminster. Even Oliver Cromwell used the Chair at his installation as Lord Protector.

the joint guardianship of Mr. Hansell and Finch. An eye-witness recalls that they fidgeted and whispered incessantly but watched with awe their father do homage to the newly crowned King. The catastrophe, however, which overtook one of their great-aunts who, in a tense moment in the ceremony, dropped her heavily embossed Order of the Service over the edge of the box into a large gold vessel below with a deafening clatter, was altogether too much for their sense of decorum and caused them such mirth that they had to be sternly repressed by the Princess of Wales.[34]

Of all the changes of residence through which they followed their parents, it was to the annual summer visit to Scotland that the children most looked forward. There, at Abergeldie, a fascinating and romantic castle of the fourteenth century, a few miles from Balmoral, they cast off all restraint. For weeks before the date of departure from London they counted the days. Then there was the excitement of the night journey in the Royal train, the early awakening and the peeping through the curtained windows for a first glimpse of Scotland in the dawn; the drive from Ballater station, and then, at last, dear, wonderful, enchanting Abergeldie. There the Princes and their sister ran wild together. They explored the rugged scenery of Deeside, and in due course they were taught the skill and technique of salmon fishing, grouse shooting and deer-stalking. They were thrilled with the most agreeable terror at the thought that the castle tower was alleged to be haunted by the ghost of an unfortunate female who had been burned as a witch, and they delighted in the excitement afforded on windy days by the swaying of the foot suspension bridge across the Dee. Above all joys, however, were the breakneck bicycle rides in which, going full pelt and crouched over the handle-bars, they recklessly risked their necks, while Finch toiled in the rear, shouting hoarse and unregarded warnings. Gradually the long days shortened and there loomed the approaching sadness of the last week before their return to London, the farewell visits to their favourite haunts, the penultimate sorrow of the dispatch of the bicycles by train to Sandringham, and the final desolation of leaving Scotland for another whole year.

These annual visits in his childhood imbued Prince Albert

with that love for Balmoral which was to rival his affection for Sandringham in his later life and to make him the first Sovereign who inherited the full and deep attachment of Queen Victoria to this Scottish home.

It was shortly after their return from the Scottish holiday of 1905 that the Prince and Princess of Wales were again separated from their children. From the middle of October until the beginning of the following May, they were absent from England on a State Visit to India. The Princes and their sister were once again left under the supreme protection of their grandparents and the immediate authority of Mr. Hansell and Mlle Dussau. The conditions were somewhat different from those of four years before. King Edward was more deeply concerned with affairs of State than he had been in 1901 when he was last *in loco parentis*. The rifts within the Conservative Party had caused Mr. Arthur Balfour to resign in December 1905, and the immense majority with which Sir Henry Campbell-Bannerman and the Liberal Party returned from the General Election of January 1906 carried with it the first mutterings of those fierce constitutional storms which were to darken the latter days of King Edward's reign and the opening of his successor's.

For this and other reasons the King and Queen were less at Sandringham than formerly, but when they did come the wonderful relationship between them and their grandchildren was re-established, and the fabulous visits from York Cottage to the Big House began once more. The bonds of discipline were again relaxed — 'It was quite impossible for me to hold an examination as they returned so late from Sandringham', wrote Mr. Hansell — and the attractions of their grandparents' company caused the young Princes to neglect, or, at any rate, to become confused in, their filial duties of correspondence. This lapse brought its inevitable reproof from Delhi. 'You & David seem to have misunderstood that we wanted you both to write to Mama & I every alternate week, as Mary does', the Prince of Wales admonished his second son. 'David ought to have written last week instead of this week to me, & you ought to have written to me this week. I don't know how the confusion has come.' [35] And to Mr. Hansell: 'The two boys ought to write to the Princess & I each week alternately so that they both write each week'.[36]

Discipline tightened up again with the return of the parents but it was clear that all was not well in the York Cottage schoolroom.   Prince Edward was getting too old for such confined educational instruction and Prince Albert was beginning to resent his elder brother's superiority.   'It is extraordinary how the presence of one acts as a sort of "red rag" to the other', Mr. Hansell reported (January 18, 1907).   The immediate problem was solved by the departure in the spring of Prince Edward as a Cadet to the Royal Naval College, Osborne.   He was succeeded in the schoolroom by Prince Henry.   'Last Monday we started seriously on a summer term for our new Schoolroom', wrote Mr. Hansell on May 11. 'Prince Albert is now the head-boy and *Prince Henry* has taken the second boy's place.   I am very glad to say that Prince Albert gives promise of taking a serious and sensible view of his responsibilities.'

But the success of this somewhat unusual arrangement of a private school with a 'captain' and one other boy continued to elude Mr. Hansell.   By the end of the year he was sorrowfully reporting to the Prince of Wales, 'I should say that Prince Albert has failed to appreciate his position as "captain"' (December 20, 1907).

The truth was that the Prince was woefully weak in Mathematics, a subject in which an elementary proficiency was necessary for the entrance examination to Osborne which he was to take in a year's time.   He seemed unable to master its fundamentals, and its intricacies evaded his comprehension altogether.   Moreover, he loathed the subject, yet was keenly conscious and somewhat ashamed of his weakness in it.   Despair would seize hold of him as problem after problem resisted his efforts to solve them and he would ultimately dissolve into angry tears.   'You must really give up losing your temper when you make a mistake in a sum', his father wrote to him. 'We all make mistakes sometimes, remember now you are nearly 12 years old & ought no longer to behave like a little child of 6',[37] and he followed this up with an injunction to Mr. Hansell: 'You must be very strict & make him stick to it & do many papers'.[38]

Thanks to the Trojan efforts of Mr. Martin David and not a little to a newly developing pertinacity in the Prince himself, the offending subject was mastered, at any rate sufficiently for him to face his examiners. He appeared before the Board [a] for his oral interview on November 5, 1908, and, although it was generally agreed that he was the most shy and nervous candidate to come before them, he displayed that capacity of rising to an emergency which was to characterize him throughout life. He began by stammering badly, but as his confidence grew he mastered his nervousness and answered the questions put to him 'brightly and well'. The Board had no doubts about its decision. As one member put it later : 'If he had been a costermonger's son there would not have been the slightest hesitation in passing him'.[39]

A month later he took the written examination and was adjudged to have done 'extremely well' in English, History and French, his oral French being almost perfect. In company with most of the candidates, he found the Geography paper rather beyond his range, but on his result in the fateful Mathematics paper the comment was 'very fair indeed, except that in Geometry he seems to have been below the average'. He had passed his ordeal 'most creditably'.[40]

Not for the last time in his life had Prince Albert shown a salient characteristic. He may be described, perhaps, as a 'bad starter', a prey to anticipatory nervousness, sceptical as to his own ability — and, in his early years, admittedly prone to indolence — yet once the race was on, once he was faced with the reality, he never failed to measure up to the emergency. He was one of those who need the spur of actual challenge to evoke their finest effort.

And so, at the end of his twelfth year, Prince Albert completed the second stage of his life. The first — the nursery — had been dominated by 'Lalla' Bill; the second, the schoolroom, by Finch and Mr. Hansell. Over both there had been the all-permeating authority of his parents. It was a very cloistered life that he had led. He had never been 'on his own', never had contact with the world outside the routine of the royal peregrinations, never mixed with boys of his own

[a] The Examining Board consisted of Admiral Sir Wilmot Fawkes (Chairman) ; Mr. Charles Lowry, Headmaster of Tonbridge School; Colonel Brittan, Assistant Adjutant-General of the Royal Marines ; Lord O'Hagan ; Commander Ellerton, Flag-Commander, Devonport ; and Mr. Wedgwood Benn, M.P. (later Viscount Stansgate).

age, save in those decorous football games with the schoolboys
of Sandringham, in which, as Prince Edward wrote later: 'No
doubt, Mr. Jones's whistle served to restrain the natural exuberance of the other boys'.[41] The lacerated shins, black eyes
and bloody noses which most boys have encountered before
the conclusion of their twelfth year had not been his, nor had
he really been taught the art of learning. He was now to be
precipitated, tender and unprepared, into the hard world of
competitive life, where standards of achievement were more
than a little likely to be set by physical prowess, and where the
fact that he was the son of the Prince of Wales would prove
neither asset nor protection. Like his elder brother, he was
not to find it a wholly agreeable experience.

    . . . I can state as a fact that he has reached a good standard
all round [runs Mr. Hansell's final report to the Prince of Wales]
but we must remember that he is at present a 'scatter-brain' and
it is perfectly impossible to say how he will fare . . . at Osborne
under the influence of all the excitement attendant on the new
life. . . . Like his brother he cannot get on without 'a bit of a
shove' and, after our experience of Prince Edward's first two terms,
I do hope that he will not be left too much to himself.[a] At present
they *must* have a certain amount of individual help and encouragement, especially encouragement, a too literal interpretation of the
direction that they are to be treated exactly the same as other boys,
who have had three or four years at a private school, must lead to
disaster. However, I think that the experience has been bought
and that Prince Albert will profit by it. . . . At the same time he
requires a firm hand, but in that respect the excellent discipline of
Osborne will be just what he requires. I have always found him a
very straight and honourable boy, very kind hearted and generous ;
he is sure to be popular with other boys.

    [a] The Duke of Windsor has recorded his experiences at Osborne in chapter iv
of his memoirs, 'The Navy will teach David'.

On Leaving Dartmouth

CHAPTER II

OSBORNE, DARTMOUTH AND 'CUMBERLAND'
1908–1912

(i)

IN the year 1844 Queen Victoria and her husband, then a young married couple and twenty-four years old, were in search of some country property which, while not too far distant from London and the seat of government, might yet provide them with the means of escape for a time from the oppressive splendour and state of Court life into the comparatively retired and simple ways of the rest of mankind. What they wanted in fact was a house of their own and, in the words of the Prince Consort's biographer, Sir Theodore Martin: 'The simple domestic tastes of the Queen and Prince, no less than their profound delight in natural beauty, gave, in their case, intensity to this natural desire for some quiet loop-hole of retreat'.[1]

In the course of their 'house-hunting' their attention was drawn by Sir Robert Peel to the property of Osborne House, on the north shore of the Isle of Wight, then owned by Lady Isabella Blatchford. Their first inspection of it in October 1844 resulted in their enchantment with its repose and privacy; its noble sea-view of Portsmouth with the great roadstead of Spithead, and its splendid stretch of seashore, ideal for bathing. Negotiations for purchase were begun at once and soon concluded, and early in the New Year the Queen and Prince had achieved their ambition of acquiring their own home, bought and paid for from the Queen's private funds, and theirs to create and develop without let or hindrance. 'It sounds so snug & nice', wrote Queen Victoria in announcing the purchase to her uncle, King Leopold of the Belgians,[a] 'to

---

[a] The text of the letter from Queen Victoria to her uncle here given is taken from the original in the Royal Archives at Windsor. It is not without humour

have a place of *one's own* — quiet & retired — & free from all
Woods and Forests & other charming departments, which really
are the plague of one's life.'[2]

Neither the original house nor the original property was
sufficient for the needs of the Royal Family and their Household. The neighbouring estate of Barton Manor was soon
acquired and this, together with other smaller additions,
swelled the holding to some 2080 acres. Under the personal
direction of the Prince Consort, Mr. Thomas Cubitt designed
a new and larger and more impressive residence in a strangely
Italianate style, which essayed, and to some extent successfully,
to recapture in the green and pleasant countryside of the Isle
of Wight the exotic charms of the Italian Riviera.

The estate [wrote Sir Theodore Martin] afforded scope for the
exercise of the Prince's skill in laying out grounds, in planting, in
agricultural improvement. . . . His labours were amply repaid by
the results. His plantations, rich in an unusual variety of conifers
and flowering shrubs, gladdened his eyes by the vigorous luxuriance
of their growth, and in them the nightingale 'trilled her thick-
warbled note the summer long'. Of all the songs of birds he
loved these the most, listening for them 'in the happy peaceful walks
he used to take with the Queen in the woods, and whistling to them
in their own long, peculiar note, which they invariably answered',
or standing out at night on the balcony, to hear their song.[3]

With these idyllic memories of happiness it was not surprising that Queen Victoria, after the death of the Prince
Consort, made Osborne her favourite home, second only to
Balmoral, which again she and he had bought and planned
and built together. It was to Osborne that the Court for
many years came annually from July 18 to August 23, and
again from December 18 to February 23. Here the ancient
Queen gathered about her her children and grandchildren
and great-grandchildren each year at Christmas-time. Among
the great-grandchildren who had played decorously in the
mosaic-floored corridors or on the shaven lawns or in the
sunny sitting-room, where the legendary 'Gangan' sat surrounded by photographs of her family, were Prince Edward
and Prince Albert, and during their last summer visit there

to find that Sir Theodore Martin in quoting the letter (on p. 248 of his first volume)
has seen fit to edit the Queen's English, replacing 'snug & nice', which he apparently
regarded as unqueenly, by 'pleasant'.

had been taken that famous photograph, the last of Queen Victoria in her lifetime, with an infant prince in her arms.[a] Here the Queen died on January 22, 1901.

It had long been the ardent desire of Queen Victoria that her eldest son should retain Osborne as an official residence, but few of her children, save Princess Beatrice, shared her affection for the place — one of them indeed had described it as a 'family necropolis'[4]— and one of King Edward VII's early acts was to dispose of it. After consultation with his advisers and with the concurrence of the Prince of Wales, he gave the whole of the Osborne Estate to the nation, the State Apartments and the grounds to be open to the public and the remaining portion of the house, except those rooms which had been in the personal occupation of Queen Victoria and which were to be kept closed,[b] to be utilized as a Convalescent Home for Officers of the Fighting Forces.[c]

This, however, was not all. As a part of the Goschen-Selborne-Fisher reforms in the naval educational system the decision had been taken to build a Royal Naval College at Dartmouth to replace that ancient and time-honoured nursery of naval officers, *Britannia*, the training-ship in which Prince Eddy and Prince George had received their early instruction in the 'seventies. King Edward VII laid the foundation-stone of the new college in March 1902, but, because the entry age of cadets had been lowered under the famous Selborne Scheme from between fourteen-and-a-half and fifteen-and-a-half years of age to between twelve and thirteen years, it was necessary to find additional accommodation to house and teach them, and this was not apparently easily forthcoming.

[a] So frail was the Queen on this occasion and so fearful lest she might drop the baby, that Mrs. Bill, concealed behind her chair, stayed up her arm until the prolonged ordeal of a Victorian 'snap' was over.

[b] These apartments, maintained in exactly the same condition as when Queen Victoria died, save for certain minor alterations in her own bedroom, remained closed to all but members of the Royal Family and certain privileged visitors until 1954, when, on the instructions of Her Majesty Queen Elizabeth II, they were thrown open to the public.

[c] To give effect to King Edward's wishes the Osborne Estate Act of 1902 (2 Edward VII, c. 37) was passed by Parliament. By this Act certain small portions of the estate were reserved for the use of members of the Royal Family, Osborne House and the surrounding grounds being placed under the management of the First Commissioner of Works, while the remainder was allotted to the charge of the Commissioner of Crown Lands (formerly H.M. Department of Woods and Forests!).

The Admiralty's difficulty was solved by that erratic naval genius, Admiral Sir John Fisher, then Second Sea Lord and in charge of personnel, who suggested to King Edward that use might be made of the remaining portions of the Osborne Estate for a junior Royal Naval College. The coach-house and stables, he proposed, could be converted into class-rooms and the level portions of the park made into playing fields. Other accommodation for dormitories, gun-rooms and officers' quarters could be built and, in addition, a great hall, 'Nelson', which would serve as a quarter-deck and place of general assembly. The King was most favourably disposed to the idea and so rapid was the progress of construction and conversion that, although work on the foundations did not begin until March 1903, the buildings were sufficiently completed to be opened formally by the King, accompanied by the Prince of Wales, on August 4 of the same year.[a] Both were delighted with what they saw. 'Papa and I went to see the new College for cadets at Osborne, which is quite charming', the Prince wrote to the Princess of Wales from the *Victoria and Albert*, '. . . I should like to be a cadet again to go and live there'.[5]

This desire of the Prince of Wales was vicariously fulfilled, as we have seen, in his sons. Prince Edward entered the Royal Naval College, under the personal escort of his father, in February 1907, as a member of the Exmouth Term. Two years later (January 15, 1909) Prince Albert followed him to Osborne.

(ii)

'Cadet H.R.H. Prince Albert of Wales'— as he was entered on the books of the College — had, therefore, a certain connection of background with the old world of Osborne, but in the new world, of which he had suddenly become a denizen, he was very much a stranger. He found himself a member of the Grenville Term on a parity of footing with some seventy-odd other thirteen-year-olds, the large majority of whom had

[a] The speed with which the work was carried out and the fact that the buildings were but temporary erections of usolite — the intention being to reconstruct them in brick later, a time which never came — accounted for their fragile and jerry-built nature, and many a cadet received punishment for accidentally — or possibly intentionally — poking his hand or foot through a wall ! These temporary buildings had not been replaced when the College was finally closed in 1921. All trace of it has now been virtually obliterated.

had the material advantages — advantages physical, mental and psychological — of three, and in most cases four, years at a private school.   It was all very well for the Prince of Wales to give orders that his son was to be treated in all respects exactly as any other cadet.[a]   This instruction was intended to prevent any favouritism being shown him as the son of the heir to the throne, but it could not create for him an equality which clearly did not exist.   He was in fact at a considerable disadvantage *vis-à-vis* his contemporaries.   For, besides being shy and nervous and abnormally homesick, he had never played a serious game of cricket or football, had never sat in a class of more than three, and had never really had the spark of learning kindled within him.   Moreover, his stammer incited the natural brutality inherent in small boys and there were not wanting among his fellow cadets those who could not resist the temptation to boast that they had once kicked a Prince of the Blood Royal.

In addition to these personal handicaps the sudden transition to the life of a Naval College, with its rigid routine and its strenuous life spent mostly at the double,[b] which was difficult enough for an ordinary schoolboy to assimilate, seemed the more strange and bewildering to one who had been brought up in the bosom of a family, however strict may have been the parental authority.   Prince Albert, therefore, had much to learn, much leeway to make up, and, despite the brave mendacity of his first letter home to his mother : 'I have quite settled down here now',[8] and the various assurances of Prince Edward that 'Bertie is getting on well',[9] it was some long time before he could get his bearings.   The Prince of Wales displayed considerable understanding of his son's difficulties, and

[a] Messrs. Gieves, the famous naval tailors, received instructions from the Prince of Wales that Prince Albert's outfit should be exactly the same as that of any other cadet entering Osborne.   These were rigidly observed except in the case of the rough blue woollen rug, which, embroidered with the owner's initials in scarlet, lay folded at the foot of each cadet's bed.   In the case of Prince Albert, the late Mr. Gieve took it upon himself to depart from the strict letter of the Prince of Wales's orders and insisted on supplying a rug of fine soft quality cashmere ! [6]

[b] 'There can be little doubt that in the early days of Osborne (and Dartmouth) cadets were hustled too much', wrote a former Dartmouth master.   'The limited time allowed them for saying their prayers and brushing their teeth (almost by numbers) made for neither godliness nor cleanliness, and everything was done at the double, whether there was need for haste or not.' [7]

wrote accordingly to Mr. Hansell, who was in direct communication with the College authorities: 'No doubt it will
take a term or two for Bertie to really settle down'.[10]

In their dichotomy of authority the Royal Naval Colleges
at Osborne and at Dartmouth resembled nothing so much as
'lordly Lacedaemon, the city of two kings'. There was a
Commanding Officer responsible for administration, discipline
and naval instruction, and a Headmaster, who presided over
the broader aspects of education, and this divided control was
reflected in the life of the individual cadet. Each boy had a
tutor, a master who kept a record of his positions and reports
throughout his course, but his local deity was, in reality, his
Term Officer, an executive lieutenant of about twenty-six or
twenty-seven, chosen for his character and his technical or
athletic abilities. It was the Term Officer who set the tone
and moulded the characters of the cadets in his charge, awarding praise and blame where required; and it was he who
organized games and dealt out punishments. The relationship was a highly important one, for, whereas at a public
school, however much a house-master may be liked and
respected by his boys, few of them form their style on him,
cadets modelled themselves, both consciously and instinctively,
on their Term Officers. There were, after all, only six such
demi-gods and they were picked from the wardrooms of the
whole Navy. It was not surprising, therefore, that four hundred
potential hero-worshippers fresh from school should find in
them admirable qualities. 'Their example and teaching', wrote
one naval officer, 'were the moulds into which, year by year,
the molten metal of the Navy's officer-personnel was poured,
thence to be scattered about the seven seas, tempered by winds
and stress, and, in God's good time, tested to the uttermost.'[11]

Prince Albert was singularly fortunate in his superiors at
Osborne. The Captain of the College, Captain Christian,[a]
and the Headmaster, Mr. Godfrey,[b] were men of first-class

---

[a] Admiral Arthur Henry Christian, C.B., M.V.O. (1863–1926), Captain of the
Royal Naval College, Osborne, 1908–1910, Rear-Admiral Eastern Mediterranean,
1915–1917; commanded the naval forces at the landing at Suvla Bay and in the
subsequent evacuation operations.

[b] Charles Godfrey, M.V.O. (1873–1924), succeeded Mr. Cyril Ashford as
the Headmaster of R.N.C., Osborne, in 1905, having been Senior Mathematics
Master at Winchester. He remained at Osborne until the College closed in 1921,
when he became Professor of Mathematics at the R.N.C., Greenwich.

ability in their respective fields, who took as direct an interest
in his development and welfare as was possible from their
Olympian heights, and his tutor, Mr. James Watt, the Second
Master and head of the Science Department, had a stimulating
mind. But the compelling influence of his life at Osborne was
undoubtedly the Term Officer of the Grenvilles, Lieutenant
William Phipps, whose character and temperament made him
a natural and ideal pattern on which those in his charge
might model themselves. A splendid athlete and a strict
disciplinarian, Lieut. Phipps had also that intelligent comprehension of human frailty which made him a just and
appreciative preceptor; above all, one who could distinguish
between the accomplished idler and the genuinely bewildered.
To the first he was ruthless, to the second a friend in need.
Prince Albert keenly admired his Term Officer and remembered him in after years.[a]

The 'settling down' period took Prince Albert well into
the summer term, but by that time he had begun to make an
impression. His personality — a friendly, gay, easy-going
personality — began to be appreciated by all, and his efforts
at games earned him warm commendation. He was not a
natural player of either rugger or cricket but he tried hard
and in athletics gave early indication of that fleetness of foot
and physical endurance in races which stood him in good
stead at both Osborne and Dartmouth. 'He shows the grit
and "never say I'm beaten" spirit which is strong in him —
it's a grand trait in anybody's character', was the enthusiastic
opinion of Captain Christian.[12]

Now, too, he began to make those early friendships among
his fellow cadets which were to remain fast throughout his naval
career, and these he never forgot in after-life. Popular though
he was, he did not make friends easily. A natural shyness
made him reserved in human relationships throughout his life,
but once he made a friend he was a friend for always. The
little circle of intimates at Osborne included 'Jimmie' James,
Colin Buist, George Cavendish, 'Bill' Slayter and Miles Reid,
with all of whom he continued to keep in touch long after he

[a] Captain William Duncan Phipps, C.V.O., R.N., retd. (b. 1882), was
appointed a Gentleman-Usher-in-Ordinary to King George VI in 1937, and to
H.M. the Queen in 1952.

had left the Navy. What appealed to them in him was his sense of fun and mischief, his complete lack of 'side', his integrity and courage, and his general capacity for 'good-fellowship'. He was, they agreed, a fellow who would never let you down.

With them he was completely at his ease and uninhibited, and his stammer virtually disappeared. This was not so in class, where he found it a severe handicap, and his refusal to expose his defect puzzled and annoyed his masters, who attributed his silences either to stupidity or to undue shyness.[a] Here, again, his father showed a deeper understanding. 'Watt thinks Bertie shy in class', the Prince wrote to Mr. Hansell. 'I expect it is his dislike of showing his hesitating speech that prevents him from answering, but he will I hope grow out of it.' [13]

The end of the summer term of 1909 was enlivened by news of the preparations for the State Visit of the Tsar, who was to arrive at Spithead in the Imperial Yacht *Standart* on August 2. The Empress, the young Grand-Duchesses and the little Tsarevitch were also aboard, and for these younger members of the Imperial party Prince Edward, Prince Albert and Princess Mary were to be companions. While staying with his parents at Barton Manor shortly before the visit Prince Albert had been suffering from a severe cold and cough, which, he said, had been prevalent among the cadets at the end of the term, but on the eve of the Tsar's arrival it became abundantly clear that the boy had whooping-cough. He was quickly quarantined at Barton Manor and there held *incommunicado* until after the Imperial party had departed. There was no little anxiety lest the Tsarevitch should contract the infection, in which case a ruptured blood-vessel from excessive coughing might have had a disastrous effect upon his haemophilic condition. No such unfortunate result occurred, however, and the Tsar's children played unscathed upon the beach at Osborne, bought picture postcards and were shown over the College by Prince Edward.[14]

This illness of Prince Albert, though childish and unimportant in itself, was yet eventful in that it brought into his

---

[a] Like many another stammering schoolboy, however, Prince Albert was not above using his affliction as a cover for an unprepared lesson!

life a man who, in later years, was to exercise considerable and beneficial influence upon him. The assistant medical officer at the College was a young Scotsman, a Surgeon-Lieutenant, one Louis Greig, then twenty-nine years old, a graduate of Glasgow University and a hero to the cadets, not so much perhaps for his medical skill as that he had played International Rugby football for Scotland and coached the College teams with a wealth, ferocity and lucidity of language which left no illusion as to his meaning. Prince Albert took a strong liking to this tough, debonair young man, whose gaiety cheered him in the tedium of his sickness. He gave to Lieutenant Greig his confidence, his affection and his admiration, and a friendship was engendered between them which was to play a highly important part in the development of his personality and character.[a]

The infectious period over, Prince Albert emerged run-down and debilitated. It was arranged that he should recuperate at Alt-na-Guithasach, an estate some ten miles from Balmoral, situated just above Loch Muick, with Mr. Watt to minister to his mind and the faithful Finch in attendance.[b] Here in the pure and bracing Highland air he regained health and strength. He caught many trout, and his tutor, himself a fine fisherman, taught his pupil many of those delicate touches which distinguish the accomplished fly-fisher from the ordinary water-flogger, and together they tramped the moors and made up for lost time in work. Though his convalescence occupied the better part of September, he showed no sign of boredom, supporting the comparative seclusion with an equanimity remarkable in a boy of his years cut off from companionship of his own age.[16] Eventually, after a week's extra leave, he returned to Osborne at the end of September.

Nearly a year passed by, and, in the first week of May 1910, Prince Edward and Prince Albert were at Frogmore, preparing to return to Dartmouth and Osborne respectively at

---

[a] Group Captain Sir Louis Greig, K.B.E., C.V.O. (1880–1953), served with the Prince in *Malaya* in 1917, accompanied him as equerry when he transferred to the Royal Air Force and at Cambridge University, and was his Comptroller as Duke of York from 1920 till 1923.

[b] 'I am awfully impressed with Finch's care of him', wrote Watt to Hansell. 'There is really only one word for it and that is devotion. I have never seen anyone who was so thoughtful and considerate.'[15]

the conclusion of their Easter leave. Word came suddenly
that King Edward VII, who had returned from Biarritz to
London on April 27 in indifferent health, was less well, and on
May 5 the Prince of Wales telegraphed to the Captains of the
Royal Naval Colleges that he wished his sons to remain in
London as the King was very ill indeed.[17] He died a few
minutes before midnight on the following day. The news was
not broken to the two Princes, but the next morning (May 7),
on looking out of their old schoolroom window at Marlborough
House, Prince Albert saw the Royal Standard flying at half-
mast over Buckingham Palace. He drew his brother's attention
to it and in silent sorrow they realized that their beloved
'Grand-papa', whom they had adored so deeply and who had
so gladly indulged their affection, had been taken from them.

Two days later, at 9 a.m., the Accession of King George V
was proclaimed from the balcony of Friary Court, St. James's
Palace. Prince Edward and Prince Albert, in the uniforms of
naval cadets, witnessed the ceremony from the garden wall of
Marlborough House. They stood at the salute. The King
and Queen had also, from behind a curtain in the schoolroom,
looked down on Friary Court, and the King wrote in his
diary that night:

May and I watched from the window of the boys' room. Most
touching when the crowd sang the National Anthem.[18]

Once again the Dead March from 'Saul' and the Chopin
Funeral March soughed through the streets of London ; once
again the Kings gathered to attend the last journey of a
British Sovereign.[a] Whereas Queen Victoria had been borne
to her grave in the bitter cold of February, King Edward's
funeral day on May 20 was blazing and sultry ; men and
women fainted in the silent crowds. In one of the State
coaches the two Princes, in naval uniform, rode with their

---

[a] Apart from King George V and the German Emperor, King Edward's
funeral was attended by seven other sovereigns, the Kings of Denmark, Portugal,
Norway, Spain, Belgium, Greece and Bulgaria. The Dowager Empress of Russia,
the Queen Dowager of the Netherlands, the Crown Princes of Rumania, Montenegro, Servia and Greece, the Archduke Franz Ferdinand of Austria, the Grand
Duke Michael of Russia and the Duke of Aosta, representing the King of Italy,
were also present. The United States of America were represented by ex-President
Theodore Roosevelt as special envoy, and France by her Foreign Minister,
M. Stephen Pichon.

sister and the new Queen, their mother. At Windsor they joined the procession on foot and marched behind their grandfather's coffin from the station to St. George's Chapel.

On his return to Osborne, 'Cadet Prince Albert' (no longer 'of Wales') was confronted with the serious question of whether or not he could make the grade for Dartmouth, whither he was supposed to go in six months' time. It cannot be claimed that at any time during his career at Osborne or Dartmouth he was a natural student. As his College reports, now preserved in the Royal Archives at Windsor, show, he had resolutely stuck within the last half-dozen places in his Term and more often than not occupied one or other of the last two. This had disconcerted his masters and enraged his father but had apparently left Prince Albert himself not deeply concerned.

'He is always very penitent with me, assures me that he is doing his best & so on', wrote Captain Christian. 'I am sure the boy has determination & grit in him but he finds it difficult to apply it to work, tho' with games it comes out strongly.'[19] But his tutor's comments were more bewildered. 'With Prince Albert's mercurial temperament all things are possible . . .' and again: 'I don't think he regards a rebuke any more seriously than his work'.[20] There had, moreover, been more than one stern parental rebuke:

MY DEAREST BERTIE [the Prince of Wales had written]
. . . I am sorry to have to say that the last reports from Mr. Watt with regard to your work, are not at all satisfactory, he says you don't seem to take your work at all seriously, nor do you appear to be very keen about it. My dear boy this will not do, if you go on like this you will be at the bottom of your Term, you are now 71st & you won't pass your examination & very probably will be *warned*[a] this term if you don't take care. You know it is Mama's & my great wish that you should go into the Navy & I believe you are anxious to do so, but unless you now put your shoulder to the wheel & really try & do your best to work hard, you will have no chance of passing any of your examinations. It will be a great bore, but if I find that you have not worked well at the end of this term, I shall have to get a master for you to work with all the holidays & you will have no fun at all. Now remember,

[a] If a cadet's work was consistently unsatisfactory or he failed to pass his examinations, he was officially 'warned' that he would not be able to return to the College.

everything rests with you, & you are quite intelligent & can do very well if you like. I trust that you will take to heart what I have written & that the next report will be a good one & the others to come until the end of the term. Our weather here is fine but not as warm as it might & as it ought to be for Ascot. . . .[21]

In the months which followed, Prince Albert seems to have avoided successfully both the humiliation of a 'warning' and the inconvenience of a holiday tutor. But the margin of escape had been a slender one, and, though there had been moments of pronounced improvement,[a] he was still perilously near the bottom in his terminal position. There was, however, apparent to those who taught him, a definite improvement in his powers of concentration and his willingness to use them. His temperament, though still volatile, was less liable to those violent fluctuations which had marred his earlier years. In his two years at Osborne, if he had not distinguished himself scholastically, he had assimilated many other things which would be of even more lasting value to him. For one thing, he had learned to live a normal boy's life, to hold his own with his contemporaries and to adopt a philosophical attitude to the minor tragedies of life which are apt to loom so large at the age of fourteen.

As the final examinations approached in December 1910, there was considerable perturbation at Osborne, not only as to how Prince Albert would do in them but what the effect would be, if he did badly, upon the King his father. No uncertain starter on the eve of a great race was watched with greater care and anxiety than that lavished by Mr. Watt on his unpredictable pupil, on whose 'form' he sent regular and frequent reports to Mr. Hansell.

The results, however, were calamitous. Though he had been working well up to the eve of the examinations, Prince Albert, like many another of his age, was overcome by the excitement of going home for the Christmas holidays and, despite his tutor's report: 'I am still of opinion that His Royal Highness has done better and more consistent work than he

---

[a] 'The enclosed Report on Prince Albert's work is much more satisfactory', wrote Captain Christian to Mr. Hansell on one occasion. 'I would, however, suggest that you should not tell the Prince of Wales as it may be only a flash in the pan !' [22]

has done in any previous term',[23] the fact remained that his final position in the Term was 68th out of 68.

'I am afraid there is no disguising to you the fact that P. A. has gone a mucker', wrote the despairing Mr. Watt to Mr. Hansell. 'He has been quite off his head, with the excitement of getting home, for the last few days, and unfortunately as these were the days of the examinations he has come quite to grief. . . . I am afraid Their Majesties will be very disappointed, and I can well understand it. But after all the boy must be at the least stable part of his mental development, and I expect another year will produce a great change in him.'

There is no record of Prince Albert's reception on his return to Sandringham for Christmas.

(iii)

There was a world of difference between Osborne and Dartmouth. Though founded within two years of one another, Dartmouth achieved that sense of permanency which Osborne always lacked, and it had, furthermore, an inherited tradition. The new buildings of the College, set on the side of a steep hill and commanding a magnificent view of the lowest reach of the river to where it flows between its twin castles to join the open sea, are but the young heirs to those two sea-veterans, *Britannia* and *Hindoustan*, which, moored a little up-river just below Philips's shipyard, had nurtured generations of naval cadets on the broad bosom of the River Dart.[a]

Here, in the fine natural harbour, protected by the hills on either side and by the sudden bend of the river, cadets could get their first practical lessons in seamanship; they learned to sail and pull small boats in sheltered waters and later their training took them out to sea. Those who were romantically and historically minded derived interest from the fact that it

---

[a] The *Britannia* was established as a training ship at Dartmouth in 1863 and was joined by *Hindoustan* a year later. In 1869 the original *Britannia* was superseded by a bigger ship, *Prince of Wales*, which, to maintain the tradition, was re-christened *Britannia*. Even after the opening of the College these vessels were retained for technical instruction until, in July 1916 when the demands and losses of war had rendered Britain's supplies of metal dangerously low, they were towed out of harbour to be broken up for the sake of their copper. The whole College mustered on the embankment to witness their passing.[24]

was from Dartmouth Harbour that Richard I had sailed on crusade to the Holy Land, ten of his vessels being Dartmouth-built. Hence Humphrey Gilbert and John Davis had gone forth on that voyage which was to result in the discovery of Newfoundland; and to Dartmouth, in recognition of its quota of ships contributed to the English fleet, Drake sent the first prize taken from the defeated Armada. The romance of history means more to the boy of fourteen than he is prepared to admit — even to himself — and the same is true of the beauty of his surroundings. Here, again, the College is singularly well favoured. The sparkling river, winding between deep woods which run down to the water's edge, makes Dartmouth one of the most beautiful spots in England and its charms were not altogether lost upon the young barbarians who, in the hot stillness of a summer half-holiday, picnicked in the reaches of Mill Creek or made the long pull up to Dittisham, with the reward of strawberries and Devonshire cream at the end of it, before the lazy drift home on the seaward current.

These pleasures were, however, as yet unknown to Prince Albert when, as a small and rather frightened new-comer, he reached the railway terminal at Kingswear in the closing greyness of a January afternoon in 1911. Here, with Prince Edward, now Prince of Wales,[a] who was in his last year at Dartmouth, he said good-bye to Mr. Hansell who had escorted them from London and, crossing the river by steam launch to the College jetty, entered the new world.

The transition for the cadet from Osborne to Dartmouth was a considerable one. A greater manliness [b] and sense of responsibility were now expected from those who, in less than three years, would become midshipmen in His Majesty's Navy. At the same time there were greater freedoms and greater opportunities — both for pleasure and for mischief. The formal structure remained the same and Prince Albert was again fortunate in his Captain[c] and in his Headmaster,

[a] King George V created his eldest son Prince of Wales on his sixteenth birthday, June 23, 1910.

[b] Symbolic of this was the fact that Dartmouth cadets were issued with the regulation full-length naval overcoat, as distinct from the short reefer jackets worn at Osborne.

[c] The Captain of Dartmouth during Prince Albert's period as a cadet was the subsequent Admiral Sir Hugh Evan-Thomas, G.C.B., K.C.M.G., M.V.O. (1862–1928), who commanded the Fifth Battle Squadron at Jutland in 1916.

Mr. Ashford, who, having launched the College at Osborne, had been translated to Dartmouth.[a] He came under two excellent Officers in the Term, Lieutenant Henry Spencer-Cooper (known to the Greynviles,[b] with the affectionate disrespect of youth, as 'Scoops') and in Engineer-Lieutenant Sydney P. Start.

Perhaps somewhat more urbane in personality than Lieutenant Phipps, Lieutenant Spencer-Cooper carried on the work of developing the character of Prince Albert which had been so admirably begun at Osborne. Realizing that the boy was still very young for his age and lacked confidence in his own abilities, he set himself to win his confidence and thus to bring out in him the sterling qualities which lay so close below the surface. He fostered the Prince's love of riding, and went out with him, recognizing in the boy's plucky and even reckless horsemanship a release from inhibitions in other aspects of his life. He encouraged Prince Albert to follow the beagles and to go in for cross-country running where, with his long loping stride and capacity for endurance, he could acquit himself very creditably and excel among his fellows. The same was true of tennis, of which Prince Albert was very fond and in which he became an excellent left-handed player. In the field of organized games he was never more than a competent performer, but, under instruction, he soon became a useful member of a 'black cutter's' crew and could handle a 'blue boat' with credit and ability.

Lieutenant Start, to whom Prince Albert was quickly assigned for extra tuition in deference to his weakness in Mathematics and Engineering, was also a character to command the respect and admiration of cadets — not least, again, because he was a 'Rugger' International and had played for the Navy against the Army. He succeeded in instilling a certain grip of the two offending subjects into Prince Albert

[a] Sir Cyril Ashford, K.B.E., C.B., M.V.O. (1867–1951), had taught as an assistant master at Clifton and at Harrow before being appointed Headmaster at Osborne at the founding of the College in 1903. On the opening of R.N.C., Dartmouth, he became the first Headmaster and remained there until his retirement in 1927.

[b] There would appear to be no adequate explanation for the different spellings of the name 'Grenville' at Osborne and Dartmouth. No Admiralty ruling exists on this point and it is believed that the decision in favour of the spelling 'Greynvile' at Dartmouth was due to the personal preference of a Captain of the College.

and, as a reward for his pupil's perseverance and industry, presented him on one occasion, shortly before the beginning of the holidays, with a set of teaspoons made of an amalgam of metals (alloy of bismuth, cadmium, tin and lead), which, when burnished, were indistinguishable from silver, but which would melt at 160°. The satisfying use of these implements lay in the joy of substituting them for the real articles and then watching the consternation of those who saw the spoon disintegrate in the cup as they stirred their tea. The Prince reported on his return to the College that he had tried the trick at Sandringham with excellent results but that it had not been greatly appreciated by his father.

The actual circumstances of Prince Albert's entry into Dartmouth could, however, scarcely have been less auspicious. Barely a month after the term had begun, a great epidemic of measles, which swept through England generally, assailed the College and crippled its activities. It was a particularly virulent and persistent form of the disease, in which the sufferers recovered and then re-contracted infection as often as three times, and there was the added complication of mumps. At one moment more than two-thirds of the cadets were in the sick-bay simultaneously, of whom two died in the course of the epidemic.

The Prince of Wales and Prince Albert were both among the victims and suffered from both diseases quite severely — sufficiently so for bulletins to be issued to the Press; [a] but by the beginning of March they were discharged from medical attention and were granted sick-leave to recuperate at Newquay. There, at the Headlands Hotel, under the supervision of Mr. Hansell — their beloved 'Mider' — they played golf and visited the historical monuments and beauty spots of Cornwall, to which Duchy the Prince of Wales, now its Duke, was paying his first visit. They returned to Dartmouth two days before the end of term.

Prince Albert's initial sojourn at Dartmouth had there-

[a] The *Lancet* also made reassuring reference to their health : 'The Princes are at the age of least danger, and the important measure of confinement to bed, to the lack of which so many complications and *sequelae* are frequently due, is being enforced. It is to the complications and *sequelae* of the disease, rather than to the disease itself, that the danger principally attaches, and these are very largely to be avoided by a proper appreciation of the risks.' [25]

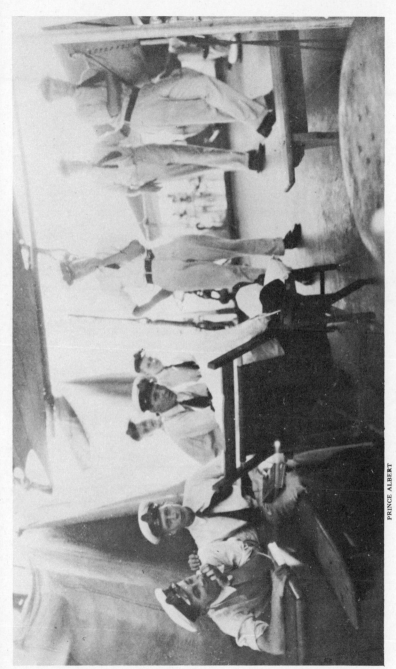

PRINCE ALBERT

H.M.S. *CUMBERLAND*; TRAINING CRUISE, 1913

fore lasted a bare four weeks, scarcely time to settle down ;
and, though this process was completed in the summer, the
second term was also interrupted by the great occasion of the
Coronation of King George V, for which he was given leave of
absence. He arrived in London on June 20, two days before
the ceremony, and on the great day itself he drove in cadet's
uniform to the Abbey, in the Prince of Wales's Procession.
With him in the carriage were the Prince of Wales, in coronet
and Garter robes,ᵃ the Princes Henry and George in Highland
costume, and Princess Mary in a robe of State. On reaching
the Abbey the Prince of Wales was conducted to his chair,
and after he was seated his three brothers and his sister saluted
him solemnly as they passed to their appointed places. Princess
Mary curtsied deeply and the Prince rose and gravely bowed
to her.

The age-old ceremony moved on with the splendour of its
majestic ritual and the King's younger children watched with
awe the Coronation of their father, the homage of their elder
brother and the crowning of their mother. Then there followed the long drive back to Buckingham Palace through the
ecstatic crowds and the appearance of the King and Queen
with their family on the balcony in response to the cheering
multitudes in the Mall. On the following day Prince Albert,
with his brothers and sister, accompanied King George and
Queen Mary on the State Drive through London, and on
June 24 he embarked with his parents, together with the
Prince of Wales and Princess Mary, in *Victoria and Albert*, to
view the mighty gathering of warships at Spithead. That
night he was allowed to go with the King to the Semaphore
Tower of Portsmouth Dockyard to watch the fireworks and the
illumination of the Grand Fleet.

It can readily be understood that after these exhilarating
experiences the return to the more monotonous régime of the
Royal Naval College, Dartmouth, was something of an anti-

ᵃ The appointment by King George of his eldest son to the Order of the
Garter was accelerated in order to regularize his position at the Coronation. As
Prince of Wales he took precedence over the peers of the realm and should
normally have worn a peer's robes, but as he was not of age and was therefore too
young to take his seat in the House of Lords, this was impossible. To obviate
this very real difficulty the King decided to invest him as a Knight of the Garter
shortly before the Coronation, and this ceremony was performed on June 10,
1911.[26]

climax. Prince Albert's imagination and innate ebullience had been thoroughly roused, and, though he was in no way *entêté* by what he had seen and done, it was in his nature that it should take some time for the excitement to subside. It is not, therefore, surprising that his instructors found him wanting in concentration. 'He can concentrate', wrote his tutor [a] in his end of term report, 'but at present he will not force himself to do so for more than a minute or two; it is a spasmodic effort to satisfy us, not the deliberate choice of his own mind.' [27] The net result was that he was placed 67th out of 68, and this time the parental threat of a holiday tutor was brought into effect. Mr. Watt appeared at Balmoral and for at least two hours a day that summer they were engaged in the study of Physics and Mathematics. The results were, on the whole, satisfactory, [b] and despite the incursion of lessons Prince Albert thoroughly enjoyed his leave. He shot his first stag on August 18, and at the Gillies' Ball at Balmoral his charm and vivacity of manner were generally remarked.

But King George had a serious talk with his second son before his return to Dartmouth, and followed it up with a letter of stern admonition.

I trust you will take to heart all I told you before you left & remember yr. position & that it is for you to set an example to the others & you must really work hard & try your best & soon I hope go up several places, as it does look so bad that you are practically last in your term & everyone says that you can do much better if you like. [29]

Prince Albert would appear to have marked well his father's censure, for by the end of the year he was 63rd in his term (a rise of four places) and his tutors' reports were accordingly commendatory, but it was not considered advisable to

[a] Prince Albert's tutor at Dartmouth was the Rev. Ernest Henry Arkwright, M.V.O. (1868–1950), who, having served on the teaching staff and as Chaplain at Osborne from 1903 to 1905, was transferred in the same capacities to Dartmouth, where he remained until 1919. He then left to become Chaplain at Harrow School and subsequently followed a parochial career.

[b] 'His main failings', wrote Watt to Hansell, 'are inaccuracy in detail, and, what is more serious, a tendency to give in when he meets with a difficulty rather than to endeavour to overcome it by himself. My efforts, in consequence, have been directed towards encouraging in him a certain amount of initiative, and to getting him to see that if only he were to display a little more determination, and self-reliance, many of the difficulties which he is inclined to regard as insuperable, would prove to be well within his powers.' [28]

cause a further interruption in his studies by allowing him to go on leave to attend the State Welcome accorded to King George and Queen Mary in February on their return from the Durbar Tour in India.   There is plenty of evidence, however, that he was maturing and developing along other lines and he was certainly learning to enjoy himself.   His capacity for mischief — always a sure barometer of good spirits — was also on the increase, as the entries against his name in the Punishment Book at Dartmouth bear witness:

'Skylarking' in the Gallery outside the Quarter Deck (with eight others)	1 day's No. 1A punishment
Talking before Grace	1 day's No. 3 punishment
Talking outside Study	1 day's No. 3 punishment [a]

And there was a celebrated incident when, with sixteen other malefactors, he received 'six of the best' for letting off illicit fireworks on Guy Fawkes' Night.   Even after he became King, Prince Albert always maintained that a modicum of injustice attached to this punishment in that, since the cane broke at the fourth stroke, he should not have received the remaining two.   This view of the case was not shared by his Term Lieutenant.

There was a good deal of 'skylarking' at Dartmouth at that time and on one occasion a bold spirit in the Greynviles succeeded in putting out all the lights on the Quarter Deck during a Saturday-night dance and introducing a flock of sheep, supplemented by a quantity of cocks and hens, during

---

[a] Punishment No. 1A entailed an hour's strenuous physical drill with a loaded wand held above the head under the eye of a petty officer. Exercises were carried out partly at the walk but mostly at the double. Punishment No. 3 was the same as the above, with the additional penalty of being confined to College grounds and the loss of other privileges.

The most severe punishment inflicted on a cadet was an official caning, which was rendered as formal and serious an affair as possible. Sentence was passed on the Monday but was not put into effect until the Thursday, so that the offender had a good seventy-two hours to ruminate upon his sins and anticipate their retribution. On the day itself he was formally examined by the Chief Surgeon, who had to pronounce him fit for punishment. He was then paraded in the gymnasium, where, in the presence of the Captain of the College, the Commander, the Surgeon, his Term Officer and the members of his term, he was strapped to a vaulting horse and received up to 12 cuts with the cane administered by a petty officer. The punishment was also reported to the Admiralty.

the ensuing darkness. The pandemonium which resulted may be conjectured rather than imagined, and, though he had had no part in the initial crime, Prince Albert joined with enormous gusto and immense enjoyment in the riot which accompanied the efforts of all present to recapture the errant livestock.

And then there was the affair of 'The Statue'.

Two statues, one of King George and the other of Queen Mary, had been presented to Dartmouth College and installed in the Long Gallery on either side of the entrance to the Quarter Deck. A visit of inspection to the College by Their Majesties had been arranged for March 1912, and all efforts of 'spit and polish' were bent towards this great event. It was a moment, however, at which the youth of England was seized with a fit of disrespect for public monuments as a whole. A statue was whitewashed at Cambridge, and at Oxford some enterprising character saw fit to decorate the pinnacle of the Martyrs' Memorial with an article of domestic but usually unheralded utility which had to be displaced by gunfire. These events, which received a moderate degree of Press publicity, constituted a challenge to that part of the youth of England who were embryo naval officers, and certain unruly spirits in the senior Term — which, it should be made quite clear, was not the Greynviles — let it be known that they intended on some suitable occasion to decorate the King's statue with red paint. It is doubtful whether this enterprise ever got — or was intended to get — beyond the 'talking stage', but psychological warfare, as we were later to learn, is comprised more of *suggestio falsi* than *suppressio veri*, and the impression made upon the minds of Captain Evan-Thomas and his Commander, when the rumour reached them, was that some dastardly outrage was undoubtedly contemplated.

With a Royal visit in the offing this prospect was fraught with additional horrors, and the Captain ordered a twenty-four hour watch to be mounted on the statue. This entailed enlisting the assistance of civilian servants in the College in addition to the naval ratings, petty officers and Red and Blue Marines. But the civilian element resented being thus drafted for service 'over and above the call of duty'; some of them threatened to go on strike, and some of the potential strikers were dismissed.

At this point Prince Albert saw fit to acquaint his parents with these happenings :

Papa's statue has been placed at the end of the quarterdeck to-day with Grandpapa's picture on the right of it [he wrote to his mother]. It looks very well indeed. Have you seen that small paragraph in to-days Daily Graphic on page 9. It is headed 'The Statue and the Strike'.ᵃ It is supposed that some cadets were going to paint it, so the cadets' servants were told to watch it at night, to prevent anybody from doing so. The weather here is much finer now and warmer. Mr. Dixon Wright talked to me last night about my confirmation. . . .

Best love to all

Your devoted son

BERTIE.[31]

The result of the receipt of this letter at Buckingham Palace may be easily imagined. The conjunction of the idea of the use of 'red' paint on his statue, combined with the fact that the country was in the grip of a coal strike, moved King George deeply. He at once wrote for an explanation to Captain Evan-Thomas, from whom he presumably received a satisfactory reply.ᵇ To Prince Albert he wrote: 'I saw that idiotic paragraph in [the] Daily Graphic. I suppose one of the servants who was sent away invented it.'[32] 'I am glad you saw that paragraph in the Daily Graphic about the statue', replied his son. 'It shows how very idiotic people can be.'[33]

The situation was eased somewhat by the fact that, after all, the King and Queen were prevented from visiting Dartmouth by the serious conditions arising from the great coal strike of the spring of 1912, which lasted for five weeks and cost the country the loss of thirty million working days.[34] In

---

ᵃ The small paragraph in question, which Prince Albert thoughtfully enclosed in his letter for his parents' perusal, read as follows :

A statue of King George placed recently in the Royal Naval College, Dartmouth, quickly attracted the attention of some of the cadets, and it was rumoured that they intended decorating it after their own ideas.

The College authorities thereupon gave orders to the cadets' servants to keep an hourly watch over the statue at night. The men objected to the extra duty, and a strike is regarded as probable.[30]

ᵇ On the back of the envelope of Prince Albert's letter to Queen Mary there appears a brief memorandum in King George's hand : 'I have just sent my letter off to Thomas to ask him what the paragraph meant. No matter. I would like to hear his explanation. G.' Unfortunately neither a copy of the King's letter nor Captain Evan-Thomas's reply is to be found in the Royal Archives at Windsor.

the midst of the general disappointment the incident of 'The Statue' was decently buried and forgotten,[a] but Prince Albert was unable to persuade his father to fall in with the request that he voiced on behalf of 'most of the cadets', that they should be granted an additional week in their summer leave to make up for the cancelled Royal visit.[35]

It was at this time that there occurred Prince Albert's first spiritual awakening. His confirmation was approaching and he was being prepared for it by one of the College Chaplains, the Rev. Henry Dixon-Wright. He took the matter seriously but without the morbidness which not infrequently accompanies these early religious stirrings. He began to drop into the College Chapel for brief periods of prayer and meditation and would discuss religious questions, not only with the Chaplain but also with his Term Lieutenant, with a complete lack of embarrassment and with considerable fluency of thought and expression.

The ceremony of his confirmation took place on April 18, 1912, in the parish church at Sandringham, where Prince Albert had been baptized, and was performed by Bishop Boyd-Carpenter, the Clerk of the Closet,[b] assisted by Canon Edgar Sheppard.[c] 'A beautiful day', Queen Mary recorded, 'Bertie was confirmed at 12 — by Bishop Boyd-Carpenter, who gave a charming address.'[36]

The Bishop, who was an eloquent preacher, took as his text the words of Christ in St. Luke's Gospel, 'Do this in remembrance of Me'.[37] Unfortunately, as his address was extemporaneous, no record of it remains, but what he said

---

[a] King George's statue was later moved to the far end of the Quarter Deck, where it still stands, having, though slightly damaged, triumphantly withstood the bombing of the College by German aircraft in September 1942. The statue of Queen Mary was subsequently sent to India.

[b] Rt. Rev. William Boyd-Carpenter, K.C.V.O. (1841–1918), who had been Hon. Chaplain to Queen Victoria, 1879–1883, was Clerk of the Closet to King Edward VII and King George V from 1903, and sub-Dean and Canon of Westminster from 1911, until his death. He was Bishop of Ripon from 1884 to 1911.

[c] Canon Edgar Sheppard, K.C.V.O. (1845–1921), who had been Chaplain-in-Ordinary to Queen Victoria and King Edward VII and was Domestic Chaplain to King George V, became sub-Dean of the Chapels Royal in 1884 and Canon and Precentor of St. George's Chapel, Windsor, in 1907, both of which positions he held until his death. His son, Very Rev. Hugh Richard Sheppard, C.H. (1880–1937), is remembered as the famous 'Dick Sheppard' of St. Martin-in-the-Fields, who ultimately became Dean of Canterbury from 1929 to 1931.

evidently made a deep impression on Prince Albert, for two years later he wrote to him from H.M.S. *Collingwood*:[a] 'It is just two years ago tomorrow that you confirmed me in the small church at Sandringham. I have always remembered that day as one on which I took a great step in life. I took the Holy Sacrament on Easter Day alone with my father and mother, my eldest brother and my sister. It was so very nice having a small service quite alone like that, only the family.'[38][b]

To his intense delight Prince Albert was allowed, before his return to Dartmouth for the summer term, to accompany the King on his review of the Fleet off Weymouth from May 7 to 11, 1912. It was a thrilling and wonderful experience for a boy who had dedicated himself to the career of a naval officer, and at its close Prince Albert wrote a clear and factual account, which is preserved in the Royal Archives at Windsor. Fog interfered with much of the programme and on two days it was so thick that the gunnery display had to be abandoned as the ships could not see their targets. But there was much of interest to be seen and enjoyed. With his father he inspected the newest and mightiest of Britain's naval strength and the high point of adventure was a visit to the submarine D.4. Here the King and his son not only went over the whole ship under the escort of her commanding officer, Lieutenant Martin Dunbar-Nasmith,[c] but put to sea in her and submerged. 'We steamed out past the breakwater', wrote the Prince. 'There we dived and went about three miles under water which took about 20 minutes. When we came up again there was a thick fog, but it cleared off very quickly and we returned to the Yacht.' In those days, when the submarine was as yet a new and virtually untried branch of the Service, this was nearly as revolutionary an experience for the Sovereign and his son as to go up in an aeroplane.

[a] The extract from this letter is published by the courtesy of the Trustees of the British Museum. The volume in the Boyd-Carpenter collection, of which it forms a part, is still reserved from public use.

[b] Prince Albert recorded in his diary that he made his first Communion on April 21, 1912.

[c] This officer, afterwards Admiral Sir Martin Dunbar-Nasmith, V.C., K.C.B. (b. 1883), became one of the submarine heroes of the First World War, and while in command of the famous E.11 distinguished himself by destroying ninety-six Turkish vessels in the Sea of Marmora, an exploit for which he was decorated with the Victoria Cross. In the Second World War he was Commander-in-Chief at Plymouth and the Western Approaches, and Flag-Officer in Charge, London.

But there was one other incident during those four days, the importance of which was certainly not apparent at the time. The First Lord of the Admiralty, Mr. Winston Churchill, came on board *Victoria and Albert* to greet the King, and this was the first occasion on which Prince Albert met the man with whom he was to work in later years in such close accord for the salvation of their country.[a]

His last six months at Dartmouth disclosed that Prince Albert had to a great extent justified Mr. Watt's prophecy in his final report from Osborne. Dartmouth had wrought a considerable change in him. He was still very young for his age, and certainly no intellectual giant, but his pastors and masters had ceased to wonder whether he was either incorrigibly lazy or merely grossly stupid, and there was a new note of general approval running through their reports.[40] His final position, that of 61st out of 67, was — on the hypothesis that all things are relative — a considerable improvement, and the final judgment of his Captain was, 'I think he will do'.

There was also a development in the broader and more human issues. Prince Albert had achieved a general popularity with his masters and officers and fellow cadets, and also with the College servants, to whom he was unfailingly courteous and considerate. This was not the easy admiration acquired by the outstanding school athlete or by a brilliant and 'flashy' personality, for he was neither of these; it was a respect acquired in deference to his general conduct and character. He never shirked, never malingered,[b] never gave up in a game or race or sport. He was generous and loyal, with an abundance of fun and mischief, and one of his most pleasing traits was that he never talked 'up' or 'down'. 'Quite unspoiled and a nice honest, clean-minded and excellent mannered boy' was the opinion of one of his preceptors.

[a] Their second meeting occurred a few months later when the First Lord came to Dartmouth to inspect the College. On this occasion Prince Albert, with several other cadets, dined with him on the Admiralty yacht, and played 'Coon-Can' with Mrs. Churchill.[39]

[b] Indeed the reverse was true, for it was found later that the gastric symptoms, which subsequently caused Prince Albert so much trouble, had made their first appearance at Dartmouth, and the Prince, dismissing them as 'bilious attacks', had temporarily disposed of them by the self-imposition of a *jour maigre* and had never reported sick.

In addition, being sensitive himself, Prince Albert had learned to be considerate of others. Lieutenant Spencer-Cooper, who kept a small shoot, one day invited a group of cadets to look at the young pheasants. One of the boys was town-bred and of modest background, and his ignorant comments provoked a general laugh. It came as an evident surprise to Prince Albert that anyone should be so completely lacking in knowledge of preserving and shooting, but it was he who on the return journey explained the technique of these subjects to his companion. Already there was emerging that 'common touch' which was to be his lodestar through life.

(iv)

The goal to which every naval cadet looked forward almost from the first day of his appointment was the final training cruise in foreign waters, at the close of which he would qualify for the dirk and patches of a midshipman. Prince Albert shared this ambition no less than any other cadet and it was with a sense of mingled excitement, trepidation and adventure that he joined the 9800-ton cruiser *Cumberland* at Devonport on January 17, 1913.

The object of the cruise was to provide a further stage in the progressive preliminary training of a naval officer. At Osborne and Dartmouth the cadet had received a good grounding in physics and mathematics, he had familiarized himself with the various types of engines and other mechanical contrivances with which ships of war were provided, and had generally acquired something more than a rudimentary knowledge of the subjects essential to the culture of a naval officer. The cruise provided the translation from the realm of theory to the field of practice. The cadet moved from the classroom and the workshop to the quarter-deck and engine-room platform of a modern man-o'-war, where theory and practice were blended in an effective amalgam. He learned in a wider sphere than heretofore the lessons of obedience and responsibility in addition to a practical knowledge of the tasks of those whom one day he would have to command. Thus, for example, cadets coaled ship like everyone else on board and stood their watches under the supervision of their officers, while at the same time pursuing their technical and intellectual studies in classes. Added to this instruction were the inestimable advantages of what was for many of them their first contact with the great world outside. Hitherto their general horizon had been bounded by the playing-fields of the Royal Naval College. Now for the first time they visited foreign climes, met strange peoples and derived some idea of the vastness of that far-flung Empire which in due course they would be called upon to serve and defend.

For Prince Albert there was an additional and important factor. Hitherto he had suffered at Osborne and at Dartmouth from a constant, if unavoidable, comparison with his elder brother. Prince Edward's scintillating charm, his facility of manner, his good looks and ready nimble mind had provided an inevitable criterion against which the shy, retiring, persistent, more introspective and inhibited personality of Prince Albert was always measured. 'It was like comparing an ugly duckling with a cock-pheasant', said one of his contemporaries in later years. 'One could wish that he had more of Prince Edward's keenness and application', Mr. Watt had written from Osborne,[41] and the same note had been evident in the reports from Dartmouth. Now, however, Prince Albert was on his own in a world where this comparison could no longer be made, for, much to his disappointment, the Prince of Wales had had to forgo the training course at the end of his time at Dartmouth by reason of having to play his important rôle at the Coronation of his father.[42] This continual contrasting by their elders had caused no breach or ill-feeling between the brothers, who were probably ignorant of its existence. They remained wholly devoted to one another, and, throughout the cruise, each wrote to the other by every mail.[43]

Captain Aubrey Smith[a] commanded *Cumberland*, but Prince Albert was in the special charge of Lieutenant-Commander Spencer-Cooper, and, in addition, the ship's surgeon was his old friend of Osborne days, Lieutenant Louis Greig. They sailed

[a] Admiral Sir Aubrey Clare Hugh Smith, K.C.V.O., K.B.E., C.B. (1872–1957), had been Naval Attaché in Russia, Sweden and Norway, before assuming command of *Cumberland*. He was head of the British Naval Mission to Greece, 1921–1923, and British Naval Representative with the League of Nations from 1923 to 1927, when he retired.

from Devonport at noon on January 18 [a] and it soon became evident that the Prince, like Lord Nelson, was a poor sailor, and remained so throughout his naval career. But he was not alone on this occasion, for, as the chops of the Channel gave place to the steady roll of the Bay of Biscay, most of the cadets, and indeed some of the officers, were incapacitated by sea-sickness. Before they arrived at the Canaries on the 24th, however, all was again normal and they were greeted with the traditional Spanish hospitality.

It was at Teneriffe that the first of a series of slight deviations was made from the strict instructions which the King had given that, as at Osborne and at Dartmouth, Prince Albert was to be treated like any other cadet. The town was *en fête* for the son of the King of England, and Captain Smith decided that some gesture must be made in response. He arranged therefore for a drive through the streets; a decision which was wholly unwelcome to the Prince. 'In the afternoon I drove round the town with Captain Smith and Major Golding [the British Consul], as the people wanted to see me', he wrote to his mother. 'They followed the carriage all the time and made a great noise. They decorated all the streets very well.' [44]

The enthusiasm of the King's British subjects in the West Indian Islands was still greater. At Trinidad, Barbados, and Jamaica, and also Bermuda, the demonstrations and enthusiasm were immense — much to the embarrassment of Prince Albert. He had a great aversion even to semi-public appearances and his stammer made him the more shy and retiring. The climax was reached at Jamaica, where he was called upon to open the new wing of the Kingston Yacht Club, of which the main building had been opened by his father in 1901. He had prepared his speech with great care and had rehearsed it assiduously until it seemed that he was word-perfect. But as he stood up to speak he found himself encompassed about both below and behind by clusters of young Jamaican ladies whose one ambition in life was to touch even the trousers of the White Prince. As he spoke they prodded his ankles and thighs in an excess of loyal admiration and one was overheard

[a] *Cumberland*'s cruise was from January 18 to July 8, 1913. Her itinerary was Teneriffe — St. Lucia — Trinidad — Barbados — Martinique — San Domingo — Puerto Rico — Jamaica — Havana — Bermuda — Halifax — Quebec — Gaspé — St. John's, Newfoundland — Plymouth.

to whisper to another : 'Say, have you touched the Prince ?', to which her friend replied ecstatically, 'Yes, three times.'[45] Such an ordeal might well have thrown a more practised speaker off his balance and it is no wonder that Prince Albert stammered badly, but he kept on doggedly to the end of his prepared text.

After this experience the Prince decided to take his own measures for protection. Amongst his friends in the Greynviles was a cadet whose likeness to him was so great that once at Dartmouth the other's father had mistaken the Prince for his own son. These two entered into a pact of secrecy, the outcome of which was that on certain occasions during the rest of the cruise when Prince Albert was due to make an appearance (but not to speak) at some minor public function and had something better to do, such as playing lawn-tennis, his friend would take his place as a 'stand-in' and smile charmingly at the crowds. This substitution was carried out more than once and always without detection. No word of it, at least, reached Captain Aubrey Smith, but Lieutenant-Commander Spencer-Cooper may have had his suspicions.

On another occasion later in the cruise, when representatives of the Canadian press swarmed on board *Cumberland* and demanded an interview with Prince Albert, he persuaded another of his friends to be a substitute for him. This youth was a boy of imagination and Puckish humour. Speaking as the Prince, he assured the pressmen that he was treated exactly as every other cadet on board, ate the same food, slept in the same hammocks, had the same duties ; the only difference was that he wore a bowler hat on Sundays.

But Prince Albert did not spend all his time avoiding publicity. There was much fun to be had during the cruise and one of the most agreeable incidents was a gymkhana in Barbados in which he won the Distance Handicap of four furlongs open to polo ponies, and was placed in the Polo Scurry of two furlongs. He also won the Farmyard Race, in which the mounted competitors had not only to cover the course but also to imitate some bird or animal of the farmyard at the finish. Prince Albert was allotted a donkey for imitation, and his braying was awarded the prize on the grounds of both resonance and verisimilitude.[46]

When *Cumberland* reached Puerto Rico on March 19, she received news of the assassination of Prince Albert's great-uncle, the King of Greece,[a] and the colours were promptly lowered to half-mast. King George, who was greatly distressed, wrote to his son from Windsor :

We were all terribly shocked & grieved last Tuesday, the 18th inst, to receive the sad news that dear Uncle Willy the King of Greece had been assassinated at Salonica, by a Greek. It is too horrible he was out for a walk as usual in the street, when this brute came up behind him & shot him through the heart.[47]

How deeply affected Prince Albert was by the loss of his beloved grandmother's brother it is difficult to say, for there is no mention of it in his diary nor in his letters to his parents, but he had expressed vehement views on political assassination on the occasion of the unsuccessful attempt on the life of King Victor Emmanuel III in the previous year.[b] 'I saw in the papers the other day that one of those beastly anarchists tried to kill the King of Italy', he wrote to his father at that time. 'What a good thing it was he was killed by the crowd.' [48]

Slowly the cruise ran its course and *Cumberland* passed from the tropical charms of the Caribbean to the more rugged and virile scenery of Canadian waters, reaching Halifax on May 15. Here began for Prince Albert a new and wonderful experience. Like most Englishmen, he had no idea of the magnitude and magnificence of the Dominion of Canada, over which his father ruled. The size of the Canadian lakes and the immense distance which it is possible to cover by water in penetrating into the heart of the country came as a revelation

[a] Prince William George of Schleswig-Holstein-Sonderburg-Glücksburg (1845–1913) was the second son of King Christian IX of Denmark and younger brother of Queen Alexandra. In 1863, after the expulsion of King Otto, a prince of the house of Wittelsbach, from the Greek throne, the British Government nominated Prince William, then a naval cadet of eighteen, for the vacant crown, and the Greek National Assembly made a formal offer to him, which he accepted, taking the title of King George I. Under his rule Greece acquired in the course of the Balkan Wars the better part of Macedonia and the port of Salonica. It was during his first visit to this newly liberated city that King George was assassinated by a Greek named Schinas. He married Princess Olga, daughter of the Grand Duke Constantine of Russia and granddaughter of Tsar Nicholas I, and their youngest son, Prince Andrew of Greece, became the father of Prince Philip, Duke of Edinburgh.

[b] This was the attempt on March 14, 1912, by the Roman bricklayer, Antonio Dalba, who fired twice point-blank at the King as he drove along the Corso to the annual commemorative Service held for his father, King Umberto.

to him. From that moment he loved Canada and looked forward to a return visit. But he had to wait for a quarter of a century before he could make it.

A fascinating day of tourist interest was one which began at Toronto at seven in the morning and ended at Quebec twelve hours later, during which the cadets visited Niagara Falls, sailed through the lovely scenery of the Thousand Isles and shot the rapids at Long Sault. The only unpleasant element was the persistent attention of the press and public, which disturbed Prince Albert a good deal.

I was hunted all the time by photographers and also by the Americans who had no manners at all and tried to take photographs all the time [he wrote in his diary as he recorded the events of the day]. We arrived at Lewiston at 10.30 and then got into a special tramcar on the Belt Line on the American side of the Niagara River. We took photographs of the rapids and the famous Whirlpool on the way to the falls. At Niagara Falls New York, the town we got out and then saw the American Falls from Goat Island. Some of us went under the falls which was a curious experience. We took off all our clothes and then put on flannels and oilskins. We then went down an elevator and walked along a path till we got to the bridge which goes under the falls. The spray is tremendous and soaks you absolutely. When we were actually under the falls we could neither see nor breathe, because the water and spray hits you full in the face and you can only gasp for breath. . . . Afterwards I went with a few cadets under the Horseshoe Falls on the Canadian side. They have built a tunnel which goes 150 feet out under the falls. Then we went to see the Ontario Power station which can transmit electricity for about 500 miles. The voltage is 60,000 volts they can generate with thirteen water turbines. . . . We shot the rapids to Montreal. We struck a rock while shooting the Long Sault Rapids but no harm was done. The Lachine Rapids were the most exciting.[49]

It was a wonderful day and one which Prince Albert enjoyed a good deal more than the social functions which followed at Quebec. He was still profoundly shy in the company of those whom he did not know and at the various balls which were given for the cadets nothing would tempt him on to the dance floor. He preferred to get away into a corner from which he resisted all efforts to dislodge him. Again and again pretty Canadian girls were introduced and, though he was never boorish, it was observed that the conversation soon

flagged.   On one occasion, however, his reserve melted.   Lieutenant-Commander Spencer-Cooper, gripping his trousers with
both hands, confided to him that the ultimate catastrophe had
happened — the two back braces buttons had come off.   The
Prince was delighted.   All his shyness left him, and partner
after partner was informed, with a giggle, of the predicament
which afflicted the Lieutenant-Commander.   He was quite sorry
when that ball ended.

But what delighted him still more was the salmon-fishing
on the Gaspé peninsula and in Newfoundland.   Here he was
really in his element and enjoyed himself hugely.   It was noticeable, too, that with his fishing hosts he was completely at his
ease, comporting himself with a complete lack of shyness or
stammer.

Nor was the Canadian part of the cruise without its own
excitements.   At one moment off the Canadian coast *Cumberland* ran into a considerable storm and a large wave coming
aboard caught Prince Albert and one or two others and sucked
them to the side of the ship.   When the wave subsided he
emerged, soaked to the skin and in high good humour, but, as
one who was present observed, 'He was as near as a toucher
washed overboard'.

Cumberland returned to her home port of Plymouth on July
8, 1913, and the cadets were granted a week's leave before
completing the remainder of the training period on manœuvres
off the Nore.   King George and Queen Mary were staying
with Lord Derby at Knowsley in the course of a Royal tour
of the Duchy of Lancaster, and it was there that Prince Albert
rejoined his parents after an absence of six months.   The King
was gratified by his son's appearance.   Before the beginning
of the cruise he had been uncertain as to how he would make
out, but he now perceived a great change in him.   The boy
was no longer callow.   He had grown up very much and had
achieved a certain amount of *savoir-faire* and self-confidence,[50]
and he was no longer so tongue-tied in his father's presence.
When, a few weeks later, at the conclusion of the naval
manœuvres, the King joined his fleet at Cowes, he visited
Cumberland and complimented all concerned.   To Prince Albert's
Term Officer he said simply, 'Thank you.   I am pleased with
my boy.'

CHAPTER III

NAVAL CAREER

1913–1917

(i)

PRINCE ALBERT received his appointment as a Midshipman on September 15, 1913, and thus made his official entry upon the career of a naval officer, which, like his father before him, he thought would be his major work in life.[a] He had become a serious devotee of his calling, keen and alert, and his ultimate ambition at this stage of his life was to have his own independent command and to rise, as his father had done, to the rank of Captain on the active list.

There was, however, a major difference between the attitudes of King George V and his son towards their chosen vocation; King George loved both the Navy and the sea; Prince Albert loved the Navy, but, as an indifferent sailor, it is doubtful whether he inherited his father's maritime passion and he certainly did not share his delight in yachting. Much of the Prince's service was a continual battle against sea-sickness, and it says much for both his moral and physical courage that he persisted.

His first appointment was to the 19,250-ton battleship *Collingwood* (Captain James Ley),[b] at that time flying the flag of Vice-Admiral Sir Stanley Colville, commanding the First

---

[a] Prince Albert held the following ranks in the Royal Navy:

Naval Cadet	.	. 1909–1913
Midshipman	.	. September 15, 1913
Acting Sub-Lieutenant	.	September 15, 1915
Sub-Lieutenant	.	. May 15, 1916
Lieutenant	.	. June 15, 1916
Commander	.	. December 31, 1920
Captain	.	. June 30, 1925
Rear-Admiral	.	. June 3, 1932
Vice-Admiral	.	. January 1, 1936
Admiral	.	. January 21, 1936
Admiral of the Fleet	.	December 11, 1936

[b] Admiral James Clement Ley, C.B., C.V.O. (1869–1946).

Battle Squadron of the Home Fleet. Admiral Colville was an old friend and former shipmate of King George,[a] but this made no difference to the status of the newly joined Midshipman Prince Albert.

The Midshipman has now disappeared from the sea-going Navy [b] but in his time he was regarded as 'the lowest form of marine life' and treated with scant courtesy. He was subject to a very rigid discipline at the hands of his superiors, at whose beck and call he was, rather in the manner of a 'fag' at a public school. When off duty his world was the Gunroom, and his local deity was the junior Sub-Lieutenant, who exercised his autocratic powers according to his own character, sometimes as a benevolent despot and sometimes as a bloody tyrant.[c] Moreover, the Midshipman enjoyed no sense of privacy. On the flat outside the Gunroom, which he shared with a dozen others or more, his clothes and personal belongings were stored in his sea-chest and above this he slung his hammock at night and stowed it away in the morning. There was nowhere he could be alone — a considerable privation when one is seventeen.

Prince Albert lived the normal daily life of the 'snotty', without the slightest deviation or privilege, standing watch, taking his picket-boat from ship to shore, labouring in the pitch-black hold of a dirty collier in the gruelling work of coaling ship, and finishing up with the traditional meal of bread and cheese, onions and beer before turning in. For practical purposes he was known as 'Mr. Johnson', a sobriquet used by both his superiors and his contemporaries.

To be an integral part, however insignificant, of so great a living entity as a ship's company, with its delicately adjusted

[a] Admiral the Hon. Sir Stanley Cecil James Colville, G.C.B., G.C.M.G., G.C.V.O. (1861–1939), had served with King George V in the corvette *Canada* in 1883 and in 1888 in the battleship *Alexandra*, the flagship of the Duke of Edinburgh, Commander-in-Chief, Mediterranean. During the First World War he commanded the Orkneys and Shetlands and later became Commander-in-Chief, Portsmouth. At his death in the spring of 1939 he was Vice-Admiral of the United Kingdom and Lieutenant of the Admiralty.

[b] Under the Admiralty education reforms of 1954 the age entry into the R.N.C., Dartmouth, was raised to eighteen years, the term Naval Cadet was abolished and those who entered the College did so as Midshipmen.

[c] It is believed that Mr. Charles Morgan's much debated novel, *The Gunroom*, published in 1919, is a not exaggerated picture of the life of a Midshipman under certain conditions, before the First World War.

balance of obedience and responsibility, was an experience which played a vital part in the development of Prince Albert's character. To be compelled to subject himself without question to the commands of his superiors and yet to be ready to take responsible command of a picket-boat with a subordinate petty-officer old enough to be his father ; to bring aboard a boat-load of drunken 'liberty-men' without accident ; and to cox his own cutter crew in a squadron regatta, was an inestimable training which he never forgot and which matured within him not only his own moral qualities but also that human understanding and the common touch which in later life he displayed to such admirable effect.

The First Battle Squadron sailed from Devonport on October 28, 1913, to join in manœuvres in the Mediterranean, and later to cruise in Egyptian and Aegean waters.[a] It was Prince Albert's first contact with continental Europe, and moreover, as part of a fleet-in-being, he gained his first practical experience of British naval sea-power and an acquaintance with those strategic points, Gibraltar, Malta and the Egyptian ports, which formed the first links in the long line of communication with the Indian Empire.

The manœuvres were highly successful and at their conclusion the Fleet sailed for Alexandria. The Commander-in-Chief, Admiral Sir Berkeley Milne, and Sir Stanley Colville were invited to stay with Lord Kitchener at the Agency in Cairo, taking with them Prince Albert and a fellow midshipman. The great soldier was not one to miss a trick in the endless game of oriental diplomacy in which he was engaged with the wily Khedive of Egypt. He saw to it that Prince Albert was present at the Agency when the Khedive returned the Commander-in-Chief's call, and Abbas II was suitably impressed at being presented to the son of the British Sovereign.[b]

[a] The First Battle Squadron took the following course : left Devonport, October 28 — Gibraltar, November 3 — Majorca, November 7 — Malta, November 11 — Alexandria, November 21 — Salamis Bay and Athens, November 28 — Malta, December 3 — Naples, December 8 — Toulon, December 13 — Barcelona, December 17 — Gibraltar, December 22 — Devonport, December 29.

[b] Abbas Hilmi Pasha (1874–1944), a great-great-grandson of Mohammed Ali, succeeded his father Tewfik Pasha as Khedive of Egypt in 1892. He was no cordial friend of Britain, and, when a British protectorate was proclaimed over Egypt on December 18, 1914, he was deposed on the following day in favour of his cousin, Hussein Khamil, who became the first Sultan of Egypt, and he was excluded from the succession when Egypt became a Kingdom in 1922.

The Field-Marshal assigned one of his staff to show the sights to the two midshipmen, and at the top of the Great Pyramid their guide pointed out to Prince Albert the initials A E scratched roughly in the stone; they were those of his grand-father, King Edward VII, who had carved them there fifty years before at the age of twenty.

There was entertainment on a considerable scale for the naval visitors, and over a thousand guests inaugurated the new ballroom at the Agency. 'We all went on to the ball given by Lord Kitchener at the Agency to the Fleet', Prince Albert recorded. 'I went to bed at 3.0 a.m. having danced nearly every dance.'[1] And this was the boy whom, not six months before, wild horses could not drag on to a ballroom floor in Quebec!

Prince Albert I think enjoyed it very much [wrote Admiral Colville to King George]. He was taken about by Major Blair & shewn most things; was introduced to the Khedive when he made his return call at the Agency & was present at Ld. Kitchener's Ball — but I would not let him dine at the Agency official dinner, in spite of Kitchener wanting him to do so; I knew it was not Your Majesty's wishes and I felt if the rule was once broken, it would be so difficult to refuse at other places.[2]

From Alexandria the Fleet proceeded to Greece and anchored in the Bay of Salamis for inspection by the Greek King and Queen. Prince Albert had been looking forward to spending a week-end leave with his Greek cousins in Athens, and great was his disappointment when a severe cold necessitated a curtailment of this pleasure. When King Constantine[a] and Queen Sophie visited *Collingwood* the Prince had to receive them in Admiral Colville's spare cabin.

[a] This was that unhappy King Constantine of Greece (1868–1923) who, having succeeded to the throne on the assassination of his father a few months before, was forced to vacate it on two occasions; the first in 1917, at the behest of the British and French Governments; and the second in 1922, as a result of the disastrous defeat of the Greek forces in Asia Minor by Mustapha Kemal Pasha. After the first Abdication King Constantine was succeeded by his second son, Prince Alexander, who died in 1920 as the result of the bite of a monkey. After his second Abdication King Constantine was succeeded by his eldest son Prince George, who became King George II (1890–1947), and was himself twice forced to vacate his throne — once in 1923 on account of a revolutionary movement, and once again, after the restoration of 1935, because of German aggression in 1941. The monarchy was restored by plebiscite in 1946. King Constantine married Princess Sophie Dorothea of Prussia (1870–1932), sister of the late Kaiser Wilhelm II.

I unfortunately had rather a cold so was obliged to remain in bed. Uncle Tino and Aunt Sophie came down from Athens in the morning and went round the fleet which was dressed in the 'Hussar' [he wrote to his father]. They had lunch with Sir Berkeley Milne in the 'Inflexible', and then they came on board to see me. I was very sorry at not being able to go and stay with them for the two days, but I am going up there on Monday morning, the 1st of December, to spend the day with them.[3]

Fortunately he was fully recovered for his day of sightseeing :

I got up at 7.0 and left here [Salamis Bay] at 9.0 a.m. and arrived at Athens at 10.0. I saw Uncle Tino, Aunt Sophie and the cousins and then I went with George and Alexander to see the Acropolis and museums. After lunch I looked at some photographs of the war. After tea I motored down to the Piraeus with Aunt Sophie and returned to the ship in the barge. I changed and then helped with the main derrick. After supper we left Salamis Bay for Malta. I turned in at 9.30.[4]

The Fleet returned to Gibraltar by way of Naples, Malta and Toulon, and Prince Albert was confronted with his first birthday and his first Christmas away from home, and was naturally regretful. But he was really enjoying life very much, and his anniversary marked a particular step along the path to manhood. 'My 18th birthday and I am allowed to smoke', he recorded in his diary ;[5] and the recognition of this new emancipation had been anticipated in Queen Mary's birthday present. He wrote to thank her from Toulon :

DARLING MAMA,

Thank you very much for your letter, and for the lovely cigarette case you gave me for my birthday. Sir Stanley Colville gave it me this morning. It is a great pity that I shall not be at home for Christmas, and I shall think of all of you together. I am looking forward to coming home very much.

We arrived here on Saturday the 13th. The French Vice-Admiral Marin-Darbel, the senior officer here, came on board to see Sir Stanley Colville in the morning and I was introduced to him. Sir Francis Bertie [a] is staying on board here now. The French fleet are giving us a very good time here, and have arranged all kinds of dances and theatres for us. Last night I went to a ball

---

[a] Rt. Hon. Francis Leveson, first Viscount Bertie of Thame, G.C.B., G.C.M.G., G.C.V.O. (1844–1919), a distinguished diplomatist who served as Ambassador in Paris from 1905 to 1918. His diaries, published in 1924, provide a valuable contribution to the diplomatic history of the First World War.

given by the Municipality, which was a very funny affair. There were 6000 guests, and it was in a theatre. There was no room to dance and you could not move at all. All the guests were the ordinary people in the town and most of them got drunk at supper. I went away very early.

I am so glad that you enjoyed your visit to Chatsworth, and that you made some expeditions, and that you found the house interesting with some old things.

Best love to all

Your devoted son

BERTIE.[6]

Christmas Day in a battleship was no period of idle and nebulous celebration. It was filled with a progress of events which followed one another according to well-established ritual. After church on deck there was the formal exchange of visits between the Wardroom and the Gunroom, and these were followed, according to the immemorial custom of the Service, by a tour of the garland-hung mess-decks by the officers, who halted at each mess to exchange the compliments of the season and to sample the traditional 'figgy-duff' (plum cake). 'Properly observed,' a naval officer has written, 'this ritual would put the normal stomach out of action for the remainder of the day.' But there are different methods of sampling, and the caps of the officers became the surreptitious repositories for lumps of cake, cigarettes, walnuts and other gifts.

In fine warm weather *Collingwood* rode at anchor in Gibraltar harbour on Christmas Day, 1913, and although Prince Albert's thoughts may have strayed to the family party gathered at York Cottage, his time was certainly too well filled for any prolonged nostalgic reflection. He was a responsible personage in the ship that day, for he was in charge of the Christmas mail and his routine began additionally early for that reason.

I got up at 5.30 and went in the cutter to land the postman [he wrote in his diary that evening]. After breakfast I went to divisions and church on the upper deck. After that I went into the wardroom with all the members of the gunroom and then they came into the gunroom to return the visit. At 11.30 we all went the rounds of the mess deck. All the messes were beautifully decorated, and we were offered pieces of cake etc. After our own lunch I wrote letters. At 8.45 the Admiral gave all the Wardroom Gunroom and Warrant Officers dinner in his cabin. After that we had a concert in the wardroom.

A few days later the First Battle Squadron returned to its home port and Prince Albert rejoined his family at Sandringham on New Year's Eve. It was a happy home-coming, for again the King could discern in his son further signs of that late maturing, the tardiness of which had so worried him in the past. For the Prince it had indeed been an eventful year. He had journeyed over 13,000 miles and had seen more of the world in a twelvemonth than many men see in a lifetime. In his diary on New Year's Eve he listed, without comment, the formidable array of places which he had visited and the total distance travelled.

There followed six months of normal service with his ship, interspersed with brief spells of leave spent at Buckingham Palace and Windsor and in occasional visits to his elder brother at Oxford. Once, for ten days in April 1914, the Prince of Wales was the guest of Captain Ley in *Collingwood* during a tour of duty up the west coast of Scotland, an event which gave both brothers much pleasure.

In England, during the last months of the old order, popular interest was divided between the new manifestations of modern scientific progress and the anxiety as to the repercussions of the Government's determination to give Home Rule to Ireland, and both were reflected in the letters of King George to his son :

Hamel ᵃ gave us a splendid exhibition in flying on Monday & looped the loop 14 times, he is a very nice young fellow & our best aviator now.[7]

But it was Ireland that was uppermost in the King's mind. In opening Parliament on February 10 he laid great stress in

---

ᵃ Gustav Hamel (1889–1914) was an intrepid young aviator who caught the imagination of the British public. The son of a Surbiton doctor, of Danish origin, Hamel took his pilot's certificate in 1911 and that year carried the first aerial mail, between Hendon and Windsor. In 1912 he was second, and in 1913 first, in the Aerial Derby, and he perfected the technique of 'looping the loop', which feat he was twice commanded to demonstrate before the King and Queen at Windsor. On May 23, 1914, while flying a Morane monoplane with an 80-h.p. Gnome engine, he disappeared over the English Channel and was presumed drowned. The King and Queen sent a message of condolence to his parents.

the Speech from the Throne on the paragraph about Home Rule, in which he appealed for a peaceful settlement. 'I read my speech in the House of Lords as usual which was very full', he wrote to Prince Albert. 'This will be a momentous session as the Irish question has got to be settled & I trust civil war in Ulster prevented.' [8] The King's hopes seemed doomed to destruction, for, on opening his newspaper on the morning of Saturday, March 21, he read of the Curragh Incident, in. which certain officers of the Cavalry Brigade stationed in Ireland resigned their commissions when asked if they would fight against Ulster.[9] King George was deeply distressed at this deplorable episode, not only because of its impact on the immediate situation but also because of its more far-reaching effects on the Army as a whole. 'I fear already the Army has greatly suffered,' he wrote to his son, '& it will be years before they get over it.'[10]

To the Midshipman in *Collingwood*, however, these grave considerations were of less immediate moment than the minor problems arising out of his everyday life.

On Friday night after I was turned in, I fell out of my hammock, with the help of someone else, and hit my left eye on my chest [he wrote to his father]. It swelled up very much and yesterday it was bandaged up. I did not cut it, or actually hurt the eye-ball but it was very sore all round. It is much better to-day, but I expect I shall have a black eye for a few days.[11]

This was the kind of incident which the King, with his memories of his own days as a 'skylarking snotty', could well appreciate and he replied sympathetically:

Sorry that with the help of someone else you fell out of yr. hammock & hit your eye on yr. chest, it must have hurt a good deal, but glad it didn't damage yr. eye permanently. I should do the same to the other fellow if I got a chance.[12]

Collingwood, as a unit of the First Battle Squadron, was at Portland when the news reached England of the assassination on June 28 of the Archduke Franz Ferdinand, who had been King George's guest at Windsor six months before. It made as little impression on Prince Albert as it did on the majority of Englishmen. The weather was fine and hot, and the possibility that this untoward event in the Balkans would have

far-reaching repercussions seemed infinitely remote. What
was of more immediate importance was that for the next few
days the ship lay off Brighton where: 'After lunch at 2.30 50
girls arrived from the Rodine [sic] School. We showed them
over the ship and danced before tea.'[13]

But in Whitehall the shots fired at Sarajevo had sounded a
warning note which cut through the clamour of 'the haggard,
squalid, tragic Irish quarrel which threatened to divide the
British nation into two hostile camps'. By good fortune the
British Cabinet, on the initiative of Mr. Churchill, had decided,
as early as the previous autumn, to hold a Test Mobilization
instead of the routine summer manœuvres, and this process
actually began on July 15, 1914. The Naval Reserve, though
not legally liable, had been invited to join their ships, and
upwards of 20,000 reservists reported to their depots. There
was a general concentration of warships at Spithead, where on
July 17 and 18 King George held a grand review of his Navy,
inspecting ships of every class.[14] Prince Albert accompanied
his father in *Victoria and Albert*, and on the night of the 18th
sat down to dinner with sixteen Admirals. On the morning
of Sunday July 19 the great armada, with *Collingwood* amongst
its ships, put to sea for exercises of various kinds. It took more
than six hours for the Fleet to pass before the King. 'We
cheered ship when we passed Papa in the Royal Yacht', the
Prince recorded.[15]

The exigencies of the Service had prevented a farewell
between Prince Albert and his family and he wrote to his
father regretting this but expressing hope that he would get
leave shortly.[16] The King replied from Buckingham Palace
on July 28:

DEAREST BERTIE
Many thanks for your letter of 26th. I was also sorry not to
have said goodbye to you last Sunday before leaving the 'Collingwood'.[a] I quite understand you were in your turret. I also missed
you on bd. the Yacht, as we were late in getting into harbour & it
was raining so hard. I have just heard from yr. Captain that for
the moment all leave is stopped on account of the European situation & he has asked for my instructions concerning your coming on

---

[a] The King referred to Sunday July 19, not to Sunday July 26, the Sunday
immediately preceding the date of his letter.

Queen Alexandra at Sandringham, with Prince Edward, Prince Albert and Princess Mary, by Frederick Morgan and T. Blinks

leave on Friday as arranged. I have answered that of course you
could not have leave until the situation became normal again. I
am sure you would be the last to wish to be treated differently to
anybody else. But I do hope that things are going to come right
& that there will be no war & that you may be able to come on
Friday or very soon after. The Irish question is a very serious &
critical one especially after what took place on Sunday in Dublin.[a]
I have had to give up my visit to Goodwood where I was to have
gone yesterday & up till now, on account of the political situation,
I have made no arrangements yet for going to Cowes on Saturday.
I shall indeed be disappointed if we are unable to go. I hoped to
have raced in the 'Britannia' at least 4 times next week. Harry
who has had a chill comes home tomorrow & George on Thursday.
Our weather has been quite cold & blowing hard each day, a great
change to all the nice warm weather we had before.

I shall be most disappointed if you are unable to come on
Friday, but hope we shall meet very soon.

 With love from Mama

   Ever my dear boy   Yr devoted Papa

                  G.R.I.[17]

Alas for hopes of leave and dreams of Cowes; father and
son were not to meet again for many weeks. The shadows
were closing in over Europe in all their sombre reality. Even
as the King wrote (July 28) Austria was declaring war on
Serbia; on the same day the percipient mind of Mr. Churchill
descried the necessity for the Fleet to go to its War Station
and the order went forth for the Battle Squadrons to leave
Portland and concentrate with all speed and secrecy at Scapa
Flow. 'We may picture this great Fleet', Mr. Churchill has
written, 'with its flotillas and cruisers, steaming slowly out of
Portland Harbour, squadron by squadron, scores of gigantic
castles of steel wending their way across the misty, shining
sea, like giants bowed in anxious thought. We may picture
them again as darkness fell, eighteen miles of warships running
at high speed and in absolute darkness through the Narrow
Straits, bearing with them into the broad waters of the North
the safeguard of considerable affairs.'[18]

Prince Albert's diary entry for July 29 presents a more

 [a] This was the unhappy incident of Bachelor's Walk, on July 26, 1914, when
a company of the King's Own Scottish Borderers, returning to Dublin after an
encounter on the Howth road with a body of Nationalist Volunteers who had just
taken delivery of a ship-load of German Mauser rifles, were jeered at by the crowd
and fired into it, killing three persons and injuring some forty others.

prosaic account of this great naval migration as seen through the eyes of a midshipman :

We left Portland at 7.0 and steered west, and then turned east. We went to General Quarters during the forenoon to try all the navyphones. The Captain gave us our war stations before lunch. We started war routine at 1.0 p.m. We were all in 3 watches. The watchkeepers, control officers, searchlight officers etc. I kept the afternoon watch alone, as I was one of the 3 midshipmen of the watch. After tea everything was rigged for night defence, and all boats were placed on the deck, and cables and wire hawsers were lashed and stowed below. After dinner I kept the 1st watch, and we went [to] night defence stations. The 4" guns were all ready for a destroyer attack. We passed the Straits of Dover at 12.0. I then turned in.

On Mr. Churchill's initiative the Fleet was not dispersed when the allotted time for the reservists had expired. Instead, it was placed on a permanent mobilization footing on August 1 in response to the German declaration of war on Russia. Five days later the make-believe was over and the old world had crumbled.

I got up at 11.45 and kept the middle watch till 4.0 [Prince Albert wrote]. War was declared between us and Germany at 2.0 a.m.[a] I turned in again at 4.0 till 7.15. Sir John Jellicoe took over the command from Sir George Callaghan. After divisions we went to control. I kept the afternoon watch till 4.0 p.m. Two German trawlers were captured by destroyers. Papa sent a most interesting telegram to the fleet. I put it down in words.

'At this grave moment in our National History I send to you and through you [i.e. Sir John Jellicoe] to the officers and men of the fleets of which you have assumed command, the assurance of my confidence that under your direction they will revive and renew the old glories of the Royal Navy, and prove once again the sure shield of Britain and of her Empire in the hour of trial.' [19]

Back in London, after the cheering crowds, which had demonstrated in front of Buckingham Palace, had dispersed, King George had also written in his diary: 'Please God it may soon be over & that he will protect dear Bertie's life'.[20]

---

[a] The British ultimatum to Germany actually expired at 11 p.m. on the night of August 4, 1914.

(ii)

In the unremitting watch and ward which the Royal Navy had now assumed over the coasts of Britain, *Collingwood* played her part, and in Turret 'A' Prince Albert performed his routine duties. The officer of his turret, Lieutenant Campbell Tait, had become a personal friend both of the Prince and of the Prince of Wales during the latter's visit to the ship in April, and though this entailed no favouritism nor remission of duties for Prince Albert, it did make for a felicitous comradeship which he remembered in after-life.[a] He now experienced the monotonies and strain of long periods at sea interspersed with brief snatches of shore leave at Rosyth where the facilities for recreation were limited.

He had, however, the satisfaction of knowing that a sense of warm relationship and understanding was developing between himself and his father. 'Little did I think when I saw you last in the fore turret of the "Collingwood" only three weeks ago, that we should now be at war with Germany', wrote the King. 'It has all come so suddenly. . . . Always do your duty. May God bless & protect you my dear boy is the earnest prayer of your very devoted Papa',[21] and again, a few days later, 'You can be sure that you are constantly in my thoughts'.[22]

The anxiety which both the King and Queen entertained for the health of their son was justified all too soon. Scarcely had he settled into the routine of the Navy at war when Prince Albert sustained the first of a series of gastric illnesses which were to hamper his war service and cause him acute suffering, in body and in mind.

> After lunch I kept the afternoon watch [he wrote in his diary on August 23], I then went to the sick bay with a violent pain in the stomach and I could hardly breathe. They put hot fomentations on it, which eased it. . . . Morphia was injected into my arm. I was put to bed in the Commander's cabin at 8.0 and I slept the whole night.

Two days later the inescapable verdict was that of appendi-

---

[a] Admiral Sir William Eric Campbell Tait, K.C.B., M.V.O. (1886–1946), finished his naval career as Commander-in-Chief of the South Atlantic Station from 1942 to 1944. On his retirement King George VI appointed him Governor of Southern Rhodesia in 1945, in which post he died in the following July.

citis, but he was not too ill to be moved from *Collingwood* to the hospital ship *Rohilla* at Wick.　Here he was visited by Sir James Reid,[a] an eminent Scottish physician in attendance on the Royal Family for many years, who had been instructed by the King to take charge of the case.　Sir James confirmed the diagnosis of the Fleet Surgeon and agreed that the patient should be transferred to shore as soon as possible. He did not feel, however, that the Prince was yet ready to be moved.

Here a difficulty arose.　British Intelligence reports indicated that the German High Seas Fleet, or, at any rate, a part of it, was meditating a foray into the North Sea, which was, of course, what the Grand Fleet had been waiting for ever since the declaration of war, and every preparation for action was made in the strictest secrecy.　This entailed the transfer to shore of any serious cases who might be in the sick-bays of their respective ships and who could not be taken into action, and Sir James Reid was informed that *Rohilla* had been recalled to the Fleet at Scapa Flow for that purpose.　He at once decided to remain with his patient until the boy could be landed at Aberdeen.

In dense fog and moving through mined waters — in which two local trawlers had been blown up just before — *Rohilla* sailed from Wick under a destroyer escort on the afternoon of Wednesday, August 26.　An enemy submarine had been reported in the vicinity and there were some anxious hours before the hospital ship rejoined the Fleet in safety that evening. The Commander-in-Chief and Sir James Reid held a conference the next morning when, on learning that Prince Albert would be fit to be landed by Saturday, Sir John Jellicoe agreed to send *Rohilla* direct to Aberdeen the following evening (Friday, August 28) provided that she was not required for the transfer of wounded as a result of 'certain operations' which might be imminent.　Security forbade his saying more, but that afternoon those on the hospital ship watched a part of the Grand Fleet, with Sir John Jellicoe in *Iron Duke*, steam

---

[a] Sir James Reid, first Baronet, G.C.V.O., K.C.B. (1849–1923), a graduate of Aberdeen University, who had been Resident Physician to Queen Victoria from 1881 to 1901 and had married one of her Maids of Honour, the Hon. Susan Baring.　He was subsequently Physician-in-Ordinary to King Edward VII and King George V.

off into the mists. They encountered the enemy, and, in the Battle of the Heligoland Bight, achieved the first formal naval victory of the war, sinking three German cruisers and two destroyers.

The Commander-in-Chief kept his word. *Rohilla* received her orders to proceed to Aberdeen forthwith and by noon on Saturday, August 29, Prince Albert was comfortably installed in the Northern Nursing Home.[23] Here he recuperated from the immediate attack until he was sufficiently recovered for the operation. This was performed on September 9 by Professor John Marnoch of Aberdeen University,[a] in the presence of Sir James Reid and Sir Alexander Ogston.[b] 'The Prince behaved admirably, and showed no sign of fear or nervousness', Sir James wrote to the King that evening, in announcing the success of the operation. Prince Albert evidently concealed his emotions for he subsequently confessed to his father : 'He [Professor Marnoch] is really a very nice man. One gets to know the surgeon so much better after the operation. I was afraid of him at first, but that soon wore off.' [24]

Though naturally greatly disappointed at missing the excitement of the first Fleet action of the war, the Prince proved himself an excellent patient, appreciative of all that was done for him and considerate of those in attendance. He was anxious also to assuage the anxiety of his parents :

I am afraid you must have been rather frightened when you heard I was ill [he wrote, in pencil, to his father]. I am much better now and feel quite happy. Sir James Reid arrived yesterday and he examined me. The pain has practically gone away now although it hurt a good deal last Sunday. [Everyone] has been very kind to me in every way and everything is most comfortable here. You must be very sorry at not being able to go up to Scotland this year as usual. You must be very tired after all this very trying time with so much work to do, and so many people to see, and never getting a rest. . . .

Best love to you dearest Papa, Mama and Mary, and my thoughts are always of you all

Your most devoted son
BERTIE.[25]

[a] Sir John Marnoch, K.C.V.O. (1867–1936), was at this time Regius Professor of Surgery at the University of Aberdeen, and Hon. Surgeon in His Majesty's Household for Scotland.

[b] Sir Alexander Ogston, K.C.V.O. (1844–1929), was Extra Surgeon to the King in Scotland and Professor of Surgery at Aberdeen University.

The inevitable loneliness of his sojourn in the Nursing Home was alleviated on two occasions by visits from the Prince of Wales and Mr. Hansell: 'David and Mider arrived here at 11.0 to see me. They both thought me looking well';[26] and from Princess Mary and Mlle Dussau. But he was delighted to leave Aberdeen on October 4 and rejoin his parents in London, and his convalescence was passed uneventfully between Buckingham Palace and York Cottage. He longed to be back with his friends in *Collingwood*, to whom he wrote wistfully, and had confidently expected that, after a spell of sick-leave, he would be able to rejoin his ship. A relapse and recurrence of pain in November, however, banished these hopes and he was condemned to a further period of inactivity.

Prince Albert was deeply despondent at this time. Deprived of companionship of his own age and of his immediate friends in the Navy, he suffered also, with the acute sensitivity of a young man in war-time, from the feeling that he was not 'doing his bit'. It was the period of heavy casualties. The flower of England was being decimated on the fields of France and Flanders, at Ypres and La Bassée, including many of his friends — and he could only attend their memorial services in London; Louis Greig, serving with the Royal Naval Division, had been taken prisoner at Antwerp, and the Prince of Wales had left for B.E.F. Headquarters, where he was to be aide-de-camp to Sir John French, the Commander-in-Chief. His younger brothers were away at school. The King was engulfed by the manifold duties of a monarch in war-time, and the Queen's time was much occupied. The Prince himself was condemned to alternate between Sandringham and London with his sister as companion, occupying his time with books and riding and shooting, and such minor and most welcome crises as might arise.

The big stag in the Park had become very dangerous, so Bland wanted me to shoot it, which I did yesterday morning [he wrote to King George with evident satisfaction from York Cottage]. He had attacked Bland the same morning as he went for Mary and me while we were riding, Bland thought it better to get rid of him. I went with Gamble and Mr. Jones. He weighed 21 st. 8 lbs. 11 points. He smelt extraordinarily nasty owing to the time of year.[27]

Moreover, it seemed that the powers that be were against him. Sir Frederick Treves,[a] the King's Surgeon, whose private opinion it was that the Prince ought never to go to sea again, had been adamant in prolonging his convalescence. At length, however, in deference to Prince Albert's persistent pleas, Sir Frederick did reluctantly agree to his eventually rejoining his ship, but only after a spell of service ashore. This was better than nothing, and it was with enthusiasm and relief that, towards the end of November, the Prince received word from his father, on the eve of the King's departure for the Front, that arrangements had been made for him to join the War Staff at the Admiralty, an appointment in which he could wear uniform.[28] 'I am very pleased with your arrangement about me going to work on the War Staff at the Admiralty', Prince Albert wrote in reply, 'it will be very interesting, and now people cannot say that I am not doing anything.'[29] The enforced inactivity had lain heavily upon his conscience, for in a letter to the Queen three days later (November 29) he used the same words : 'It is a good thing as now nobody will be able to say that I am doing nothing'.

So to the Admiralty he reported on December 2, where he was received by Mr. Churchill and later inducted into the secret mysteries of the War Room, being given the task of keeping up to date the great charts on which the position and movements of every British warship — and, as far as possible, those of the enemy also — were daily plotted. In this work he was well occupied and happy and it gave him particular pleasure to pass on to the King — sometimes in advance of the 'usual channels', and enjoining upon him the necessity for strict secrecy — items of information concerning naval actions. This was the case in the Battle of the Falkland Islands.[b]

---

[a] Sir Frederick Treves, first Baronet, G.C.V.O., C.B. (1853–1923), Surgeon-Extraordinary to Queen Victoria and Serjeant-Surgeon to King Edward VII and King George V.
[b] On November 1, 1914, a British Squadron commanded by Rear-Admiral Sir Christopher Craddock had been defeated at the Battle of Coronel off the coast of Chile by a German Squadron of superior strength under Admiral Graf Spee, with heavy losses, including *Good Hope* and *Monmouth*. Five weeks later, on December 8, Admiral Spee's force was destroyed off the Falkland Islands by a cruiser squadron under Admiral Sir F. Doveton Sturdee. An admirable account of the action was written by Commander Spencer-Cooper, who took part in it : *The Battle of the Falkland Islands; Before and After* (London, 1919).

I have just returned from the Admiralty and have heard that the 'Nürnberg' has been sunk by the 'Kent', one of the 'Cumberland' class [he wrote on the night of December 10 to King George, then at Sandringham]. There are very few people who know this, so please don't tell anybody as I don't know whether it will be in tomorrow's papers or not. I thought you would like to know, and I am so glad to be the first person to tell you.

On this occasion he had not succeeded in getting in first, as his father somewhat crushingly informed him.[30]

Soon, however, the monotony of office routine began to irk him and he yearned for the day when he should rejoin his ship. He was nineteen years old and felt that this was no age to be 'on the beach'. The fact that the second Fleet action of the war, the Battle of the Dogger Bank,[a] took place while he was still ashore added to his dejection. 'Life here is very dull', he wrote to his old Term Officer, Commander Spencer-Cooper, 'and I am longing to get back to the "Collingwood" ', and the entries 'Nothing to do as usual' and 'It seems such a waste of time to go there every day and do nothing' appear frequently in his diary. At length, on February 4, 1915, after an interview with the Second Sea Lord, in which he was successful in obtaining permission to return to sea, there comes the joyous entry, 'I went to the Admiralty for the last time', and a week later (February 12) he rejoined his ship at Portsmouth.

Like many a young man returning from sick-leave in wartime, Prince Albert was torn between relief at being able again to do a man's work in the service of his country and regret at leaving his parents and his home. 'I was really very sorry to leave last Friday and I felt quite homesick the first night, not being used to a hammock', he wrote to his father. 'But of course I knew that it was quite right for me to go back, now that I have quite recovered from my appendicitis.'[31] 'I miss you still very much especially at breakfast', the King replied a few days later.[32]

The life to which he returned was very different from that which he had left six months before. Units of the Fleet now

---

[a] Sir David Beatty's battle cruiser force encountered and defeated a part of the High Seas Fleet at the Battle of the Dogger Bank on January 24, 1915, sinking the battle cruiser *Blücher* and severely damaging a number of other German warships.

only went out into the North Sea for three days at a time and
remained in harbour at Scapa Flow for ten, and this new
routine entailed corresponding changes in the duties of midshipmen.   Prince Albert was now a senior Midshipman and
therefore no longer kept watch at sea, but alternated between
being in control of searchlights by night and in charge of submarine look-outs by day.   In harbour he worked as an assistant
to the Gunnery and Torpedo Lieutenants and ran the steam
pinnaces and picket-boats under the supervision of the Commander.   For recreation there were gymnastics and boat-
pulling exercises and hockey and football ashore, but in none
of these was Prince Albert allowed to take part.   He was
permitted to play golf, however, and there was occasional week-
end leave for fishing.

The monotony of the three days' patrol at sea was occasionally relieved by moments of vivid excitement :

Yesterday afternoon we heard that several submarines were
somewhere near us [Prince Albert reported to his father].   A very
careful look out was kept for them.   We discovered one on the
horizon and reported it to the Flagship.   At about 1.0 p.m. we
heard that the 'Neptune', who was just astern of us, and last of
the line, had been fired at by a submarine.   The torpedo passed
astern.   At 1.15 the 'Dreadnought' made a signal to say she had
rammed and sunk a submarine.   The officer of the watch saw the
periscope, and then felt a bump.   A few minutes later they saw
the submarine's bow come out of [the] water, and they saw U29
in relief on it, the number having been painted out.   The C in C
is not going to have it published yet, as he wants to see whether
the Germans will admit it.[33]

The letters exchanged between the King and Prince Albert
during this period were very much the same as those passing
between any other father and son at the time, and indicate a
deepening of common understanding and mutual sympathy.
They reflect a shocked sadness at the heavy increase of casualties
on the Western Front, where the Battle of Neuve-Chapelle and
the Second Battle of Ypres [a] had taken a terrible toll of British
manhood, and the death of the son of Lord Stamfordham, the
King's Private Secretary, caused them deep personal sorrow.

[a] At Neuve-Chapelle, March 10–13, 1915, the British casualties were approximately 13,000.   During the Second Battle of Ypres, April 22–May 24, 1915, the
British Army lost 60,000 men.

'Poor John Bigge's death came as a great shock to me', wrote
Prince Albert. 'He was such a very nice man. Lord Stamfordham must be heartbroken about it.'[34]   In addition, there
was the anxiety caused by the acute shortage of shells — 'We
must have more ammunition before we can try another
advance', wrote the King. 'We can't turn it out fast enough,
drink I am afraid has something to do with it, so I have set
the example by giving it up during the war'[35] — and a mounting tide of horror and anger at the unbridled use by Germany
of the U-boat weapon. 'We heard to-day that the "Lusitania"
had been sunk off the south-west coast of Ireland', Prince
Albert wrote. 'A terrible catastrophe with so much loss of
life.[a] It makes one so angry to think that after a thing like the
"Lusitania" going down we cannot do anything in revenge.
Here we are absolutely ready the whole time and still we have
to wait.'[36] 'The sinking of the "Lusitania" was a dastardly
outrage & a great crime against civilisation',[37] replied the King.

For the first three months after his return to *Collingwood* the
Prince appeared to be in excellent health and to have recovered from his gastric troubles, but with the approach of
summer the danger signals reappeared.[b] 'I have been very
fit on the whole since I returned to here but just lately the
infernal indigestion has come on again', he wrote to Mr. Hansell
on May 15. 'I thought I had got rid of it but it has returned
in various forms.' Thereafter the attacks became more frequent
and he was unable to ignore them as he had at Dartmouth.
Much against his will he was forced to report to the sick-bay
more and more often. The uncertainty — for he never knew
when an attack might not seize him while on duty — and the
generally debilitating effect of the complaint itself, began to
prey upon his physical and nervous condition. He lost both
weight and confidence, and by the beginning of July matters
had become sufficiently serious for the Fleet Surgeon to seek
consultation with the distinguished surgeon Sir Watson Cheyne,
then serving as a temporary consultant to the Fleet.[c]   The

---

[a] The *Lusitania* was torpedoed on May 7, 1915, off the Old Head of Kinsale,
with the loss of 1198 lives.
[b] Unfortunately Prince Albert ceased to keep a diary after May 5, 1915.
[c] Sir William Watson Cheyne, first Baronet, K.C.M.G. (1852–1932), Professor
of Clinical Surgery at King's College, London, served as a consultant to the
Fleet with the rank of Surgeon-Rear-Admiral from 1914 to 1917.   He was

outcome was a recommendation that Prince Albert should be transferred to a hospital ship for a period of observation, and this decision was approved by King George during his three days' visit to the Grand Fleet from July 7 to 9, 1915. This fortunately did not coincide with one of Prince Albert's periods of incapacitation, so that father and son were able to enjoy each other's company after a separation of nearly six months.

Thus, for the second time in his naval career, Prince Albert was compelled to forsake *Collingwood* for a hospital ship — the *Drina* — but with the understanding that he would be visited daily by someone from his ship and would be able to continue his preparation for the examinations which were due later in the summer, for promotion to the rank of acting Sub-Lieutenant. He had also received a further and very important assurance from his father, from his captain and from Sir Watson Cheyne, that if the Fleet put to sea for action he should return to *Collingwood*.

When he was established in *Drina* on July 12, under the personal care and attention of Dr. Willan,[a] it was confidently anticipated that he would soon respond to treatment and be able to rejoin his ship in a comparatively short space of time. His complaint had been diagnosed as caused by the weakening of the muscular wall of the stomach and a consequent catarrhal condition. The treatment consisted of a quiet, regular life, careful dieting and the artificial evacuation of the residuum from the stomach at night.[b] He was again a good patient, and indeed grateful for the rest and relief from nausea, pain and anxiety. His friends from *Collingwood* visited him every afternoon and he took gentle exercise ashore with the chaplain. Moreover, he was buoyed up by the assurance he had received that, should *Collingwood* put to sea for Fleet action, he would be in her.

At the end of a month, however, it was clear that, though

President of the Royal College of Surgeons from 1914 to 1917 and a Member of Parliament for the Universities of Edinburgh and St. Andrews in 1917, and for the Scottish Universities from 1918 to 1922.

[a] Dr. Robert Joseph Willan, C.B.E., M.V.O. (1878–1955), a graduate of Durham University, at which he subsequently became Professor of Surgery, served as a temporary surgeon in the Navy during the First World War and as Surgeon-Rear-Admiral and Consultant in Surgery for Scotland in the Second.

[b] In a letter to Queen Mary of July 21, 1915, Prince Albert enters into a detailed description of his treatment, in which he was intensely interested.

he was making good progress and was putting on weight, Prince Albert's recovery was not going to be as rapid as had been hoped and expected. His anxiety to get well and his faith in his treatment were apparent and favourable factors, but his progress was retarded by disconcerting relapses, and both his surgeons and his Captain became increasingly anxious as to the honouring of the pledges which had been given him.

With some diffidence Captain Ley placed his quandary before the King on August 10.

I am, Sir, in some difficulty with regard to my undertaking which I made to Your Majesty and to Prince Albert, namely that I would certainly get him back to 'Collingwood' in the event of the Fleet putting to Sea.

Ten days ago Dr. Sutton [a] told me that it would be most unadvisable, even dangerous to his health, to do so. Since then he has been improving steadily but to-day he has again informed me that taking everything into consideration, he does not consider that the Prince's condition would allow of his being embarked at the present time.

I have every confidence in Dr. Sutton and Dr. Willan and feel bound to accept their decision in the matter. I have told Dr. Sutton so, while repeating to him how important it is that the Prince should not miss Active Service. At the same time I feel strongly that should I, acting on their decided opinion, go to sea without him, I should be breaking my word to Your Majesty and to Prince Albert. Nevertheless, I consider that this would be my right course.

I greatly hope that he will be on board when the time comes, but the Doctors cannot say just yet how soon they think his condition will permit him to return.[38]

There was no doubt in King George's mind as to the answer which he would send to this letter. He knew what his own reaction would be if, in his son's place, he were compelled to choose between risking his life or health and missing the opportunity of taking part in a Fleet action. He rightly believed that his son's choice would be the same. If Prince Albert was to remain on the Active List of the Navy he must be spared, at whatever cost and danger, the mortification and the disappointment of seeing his ship proceed to sea in the face of the enemy without him. The father, fully cognizant of the risks involved and the possible bereavement to himself,

[a] Surgeon-Rear-Admiral Edward Sutton, C.M.G. (1870–1940).

also understood fully what lasting effect such an event would have upon his son's mind. He therefore replied, by the hand of his Private Secretary, in Roman sentiments :

DEAR CAPTAIN LEY,

The King desires me to answer your letter of the 10th inst., to which H.M. has given careful consideration. He attaches the utmost importance to keeping faith with Prince Albert with regard to the promise given H.R.H. that in the event of the Fleet putting to sea, he should return to 'Collingwood'.

Dr. Rolleston *a* recognised that this arrangement was a compromise, but one which ought to be carried out loyally : for no doubt the idea of the Prince's not being allowed to proceed into action with his ship would prey upon his mind and undo all the good effects of his treatment. Therefore H.M. cannot agree to Dr. Sutton's suggestion.

There is in the King's opinion only one alternative and that is to declare that the Prince is medically unfit for service ; to send him on sick leave and place him in a nursing home under special treatment. This course His Majesty would however strongly deprecate.

From what you report, H.R.H. has evidently improved considerably ; there is no reason to expect any early naval engagement, but even were the unexpected to happen and the Fleet were ordered to sea the day after you receive this letter, the King would prefer to run the risk of Prince Albert's health suffering than that he should endure the bitter and lasting disappointment of not being in his ship in the battle line.

In these circumstances please say nothing to Prince Albert and let us hope that he will continue to progress every day & be able to return to duty before 'the day' comes.

Yours very truly

STAMFORDHAM.

The King further feels that, Dr. Sutton having left, Dr. Willan may have different views of the case. H.M. also remembers that you think that the Prince's illness gets somewhat on his nerves which seems to be another reason for refraining from any action likely to upset H.R.H.

S.³⁹

Though there is no doubt that the opinions expressed in King George's reply represented not only his own views but

---

a Sir Humphry Davy Rolleston, first Baronet, G.C.V.O., K.C.B. (1862–1944), served as Consultant Physician to the Navy throughout the First World War, with the temporary rank of Surgeon-Rear-Admiral. He subsequently became Regius Professor of Physic at Cambridge University, 1925–1932; President of the Royal Society of Medicine, 1918–1920, and of the Royal College of Physicians, 1922–1926: and Physician-in-Ordinary to King George V, 1923–1932.

those of Prince Albert, it soon became clear that, admirable though these might be, a strict adherence to them was not possible. The Prince, who had been transferred to the hospital ship *China* in the meanwhile, though consistently reported as making 'satisfactory progress', was equally consistently considered as being 'not yet fit for sea duty'. At the end of two months' semi-invalid existence — greatly cheered by a week's visit by the Prince of Wales at the end of August — he was becoming bored and depressed, wearied by the severity of his treatment and increasingly apprehensive at the approach of his Sub-Lieutenant's examinations. King George counselled patience — 'You can't expect to get well in a minute, anything to do with the stomach must take a little time to get right'[40] — but at length the King himself became impatient and sought the assistance of his old friend Sir Stanley Colville in finding a solution.

The upshot of a conference between Admiral Colville and the doctors was that what Prince Albert required, after having been confined in a hospital ship for over eight weeks, was a complete change of scene and air to complete his cure, and Sir Stanley suggested to the King that he should recuperate at Abergeldie, under the supervision of Dr. Willan. 'As regards the Fleet going to sea', he added, 'well, I am positive that it is best for Prince Albert not to go at present but get absolutely well, it will be real bad luck if "The Day" came off whilst he is away, but if it does "Kismet". I have discussed the whole thing with Prince Albert, as Your Majesty wished me, and he quite agrees to everything.'[41]

So to Abergeldie Prince Albert and Dr. Willan went in mid-September, where they were joined by Mr. Hansell, and there they remained for a month. Amid the happy memories of his childhood and in the keen air of the Highlands the Prince made good progress, but his complaint was obstinate, and, on his return to Sandringham in October, he was still unfit for duty. He was shocked and alarmed at the news of King George's accident in France at the end of the month,[a] and this emotional

---

[a] On October 28, 1915, while inspecting men of the 1st Wing of the Royal Flying Corps at Hesdigneul, King George met with a serious accident. His horse took fright at the cheers, and, rearing, fell backwards, pinning the King under her. His Majesty received severe injuries.

excitement caused a further set-back. By the end of the year it was all too apparent that his recovery was still incomplete and the Naval Medical Board, having refused to sanction his rejoining his ship, granted him three months' sick-leave, during which time he was attached to the Admiralty for 'light duty'.

A happy interlude in this period was a four-days' visit to the Prince of Wales at the Headquarters of the Guards' Division at La Gorgue at the end of January 1916. This had been proposed by the Prince, and King George's initial hesitancy in agreeing had been overcome by Queen Mary. It was an unqualified success. Under the guidance of his brother Prince Albert saw as much of war conditions as was compatible with security. He watched a bombardment of the enemy position by British artillery and later the German retaliation. 'I saw several houses shelled by the Boches and the women and children running out by the back door', he wrote to a friend in *Collingwood*. 'That makes one think of the horrors of war and those people are shelled every day.' He visited the scenes of the fighting in the previous September and names such as Loos, Hulluch and La Bassée, of which heretofore he had only read in the newspaper, took on a new significance for him. Above all, the visit gave him a fresh interest in life. After dreary weeks of invalid existence, he felt that he was once more in the world of action — though only, alas, as an onlooker. Nevertheless he returned to London with renewed confidence in himself, and with fresh courage to pursue the dishearteningly slow progress towards that happy day when he himself could return to active service.

It was considered expedient at this time to allow Prince Albert to begin his official career as a member of the Royal Family and to relieve the King of some of his many minor duties. His first public function was in the Palace of Westminster where a new rifle range had been installed for the use of members of both Houses of Parliament. This Prince Albert opened on March 17 with the following words:

It is a great pleasure to me to open this range in the Palace of Westminster. I am very grateful to the many distinguished members of both Houses of Parliament for coming to support me. I trust that this excellent range may be a source of both instruction and

recreation. Our congratulations are due to those who originated
and carried it out, whilst we thank the kind friends and sympathisers
who subscribed the necessary funds. I shall declare the range open
by firing the first shot and I will try my very best to obtain a bull's-
eye.[a]

A few weeks later he was deputed by the King on April 1
to welcome the Crown Prince of Serbia [b] on his arrival at
Charing Cross for a visit to England in the interests of his
country which had suffered so cruelly at the hands of the
enemy. This was an opportunity for Prince Albert to display
his linguistic ability, for the conversation had to be conducted
in French, and he acquitted himself manfully. 'I am still
leading the quiet life with a Serbian Prince thrown in last
week', he wrote to Louis Greig.[c] 'Pretty stiff time with him, as
he can't talk English.'

But his heart was not in public functions, and every letter
he wrote at this time was pregnant with his desire to get back
to *Collingwood*. The welcome news that he had passed his
examinations as an acting Sub-Lieutenant was followed in mid-
April by his appointment to substantive rank; at the end of
the month the doctors relented and countenanced his return
to sea duty. He rejoined his ship on May 5.

(iii)

By the spring of 1916 there were significant indications in
Germany that the High Seas Fleet was preparing to abandon
the policy of quiescence which had been faithfully pursued
since the Battle of the Dogger Bank and that 'The Day' to
which the British Navy had looked forward with such high
hopes for nearly two years might be at hand. The changes in
the Naval High Command in March, in the course of which

[a] The shot was an inner, just above the bull.

[b] Prince Alexander Karageorgević (1889–1934), second son (the eldest,
Prince George, was insane) of King Peter I of Serbia, was Commander-in-Chief
of the Serbian Army at this time. He became Prince Regent in 1918 and succeeded his father as King Alexander I of Yugoslavia in 1921. On October 9,
1934, he was assassinated at Marseilles, during a State visit to France, together
with M. Louis Barthou, the French Foreign Minister.

[c] Dr. Louis Greig, who had been taken prisoner at Antwerp in 1914, had been
later exchanged and was now serving with the Fleet as a Staff-Surgeon.

von Capelle *ᵃ* succeeded Grand Admiral von Tirpitz as Minister of Marine, and von Scheer *ᵇ* took over the command of the High Seas Fleet, was followed by successive manifestations of a more active strategy. Offensive action against the British at sea was imperative if the German Navy was to justify its existence in the eyes of the German people. A nation in gradual process of disillusionment as to ultimate victory and groaning under the increasing severity of the British blockade was calling ominously for retaliation by the Fleet, for the creation of which they had borne such heavy burdens of taxation in peace-time. Moreover, the adverse fortunes of German arms on land had to be offset at sea. The appalling sacrifices which had been made in the desperate effort to win the Verdun salient had so far been made in vain.*ᶜ* For the first time since the outbreak of war the spirit of the German people was sick. Their *Vernichtungswille* (the will to destroy) was waning, and the Fleet alone was their present hope of a restorative.

All circumstances, therefore, were confederate to the advancement of Admiral von Scheer's own predilection for a policy of boldness, and in the month of May he developed a plan for a bombardment of Sunderland by his battle-cruisers under von Hipper,*ᵈ* which should tempt Sir David Beatty to sally forth from his base at Rosyth to destruction by the concentration of U-boats which would be lying in wait for him. By pure coincidence Sir John Jellicoe had simultaneously perfected his own plan, of which the objective was to force von Scheer to make just this move.[42]

In point of fact the inclemency of the weather prevented either plan from being put into effect. Von Scheer was

---

ᵃ Admiral Edward von Capelle (1855–1931) was German Minister of Marine from 1916 to 1918. He was an opponent of von Tirpitz's advocacy of unrestricted U-boat warfare.

ᵇ Admiral Reinhold von Scheer (1863–1928) commanded the German High Seas Fleet from 1916 to 1918, when, for a short time, he became Chief of the Admiralty Staff. After the war he published *Germany's High Sea Fleet in the Great War* (Eng. trans., London, 1920).

ᶜ In the course of the Battle for Verdun, which lasted from February 21 to December 20, 1915, the German losses were 336,831.

ᵈ Admiral Franz von Hipper (1863–1932) commanded the German battle-cruiser force throughout the First World War. In November 1918 he suffered the mortification of seeing mutiny break out in the squadron which he had trained and led into action.

dependent on aerial reconnaissance by Zeppelins for protection against the danger of being caught unawares by one of Admiral Jellicoe's periodic sweeps down the North Sea, and day after day the weather conditions were such that it proved impossible for the dirigibles to go up. The U-boats had already gone forth to their rendezvous, and the time was drawing near when they would have to return to base. May 30 was the last day to which von Scheer could possibly postpone his operations, and when, on that day, he found that the weather was still against him, he ordered von Hipper to proceed to the Skagerrak, ensuring that his presence off the Norwegian coast became known to the British Admiralty, while he himself would follow secretly with the battle fleet. Von Hipper's movements were duly reported to London and on the night of May 30 the British Battle Fleet from Scapa and Cromarty under Sir John Jellicoe, and the fast scouting squadrons from Rosyth under Sir David Beatty, proceeded to sea. The scene was set for the greatest naval battle of the war.

Here we must leave the general for the particular, for it is neither the duty nor the purpose of the biographer of King George VI to describe in detail — however great the temptation — that great Battle of the Mists, which the British call Jutland and the Germans Skagerrak, much less to enter into the disputes and conflicts which later ensued as to the conduct of that battle. His concern is with the rôle played in the engagement by *Collingwood* and the share of Prince Albert in that rôle, his actions and reactions. These are perhaps best told in the Prince's own words and in those of his immediate superior during the battle, Lieutenant Campbell Tait, his turret commander.[a]

Although he had been in excellent health during the three weeks since he had rejoined his ship, Prince Albert was unfortunately in the sick-bay and feeling very sorry for himself when *Collingwood*, with the First Battle Squadron, put to sea on the night of Tuesday, May 30. This indisposition was not,

---

[a] Prince Albert's account of the battle as he saw it is to be found in a report written for King George, supplemented by a memorandum entitled 'Incidents of the Naval Action of May 31, 1916', and in letters to the King (June 3), to the Queen (June 6) and to the Prince of Wales (June 3, 10 and 25). Lieutenant Tait's comments were in letters to the Prince of Wales (June 5) and to Captain Spencer-Cooper (April 8, 1937).

however, so much caused by a recurrence of his old gastric
trouble as by the effects of a surfeit of 'soused mackerel'
partaken of in the course of a hearty supper with a fellow
lieutenant in *Invincible* on the previous Sunday night. He
remained on the sick-list and in a state of acute depression until,
in the early afternoon of Wednesday, he suddenly received a
tonic which worked a wondrous cure — the call to action.

'Suddenly at about 2 p.m. a signal was received that the
German High Seas Fleet was out and engaging our battle
cruisers only forty miles away and that the battle was coming
in our direction', wrote Lieutenant Tait to the Prince of Wales.
'Huge excitement. Out at last. Full speed ahead. Sound of
"Action" — you can imagine the scene! Out of his bunk
leaps "Johnson".[a] Ill? Never felt better! Strong enough to
go to his turret and fight a prolonged action? Of course he
was, why ever not?'[43]

And to his turret he went, to remain there until the guns
were firmly secured next day.[b] Though *Collingwood* was under
heavy attack from torpedo craft, those aboard her saw little
more of the main German battle fleet than the distant orange
flashes of their guns; but they saw other evidence of the
carnage of battle. They passed the wreck of *Invincible*, the
flagship of the Second Battle Cruiser Squadron (in which
Prince Albert had supped so incautiously but three nights
before); they watched the tragedy which overwhelmed Sir
Robert Arbuthnot's cruiser squadron when, caught between
the two fleets, enveloped in a shifting cloud of smoke, spray
and bursting shells, they seemed to fall to pieces as if bashed
by a gigantic hammer. Unable to do anything but watch —
for the enemy was still hidden — they saw first *Defence* and then
Black Prince disappear beneath a pall of spray and smoke.
Their own turn came when *Derfflinger* suddenly loomed up in
the mist, leading a division of the enemy and deploying into
line, and into this enormous target they fired three salvoes at
8000 yards' range with great effect. But though through their

---

[a] Prince Albert's *nom de guerre* (see above, p. 67).

[b] 'Prince Albert', reported Captain Ley to King George, 'was in bed on sick
list when we prepared for action, but got up and went to his turret, where he
remained till we finally secured guns next day. Though his food that evening and
night was of an unusual description, I am glad to tell Your Majesty that he has
been quite well since and *looks* quite well again.'[44]

glasses they could see huge holes torn in the enemy's side, exposing the main deck which glowed like a furnace, with flames leaping up through a rent in her quarter-deck, they could not administer the final *coup de grâce*, and their quarry turned away to be hidden again in the rolling mists. It was nine o'clock by now and nearly dark, so, as Prince Albert wrote to his brother, 'We packed up for the night and manned the 4″ guns for repelling destroyer attacks, which never came'.[45]

Prince Albert's own account of *Collingwood*'s share in the battle is clear and factual, reflecting a good sense of balanced *rapportage* : [46]

The Grand Fleet went to sea on Tuesday evening the 30th and steamed in an easterly direction towards the Skagerrak. During the forenoon on Wednesday reports came in that the Battle Cruisers were in action with the German battle cruisers. A bit later the 5th Battle Squadron was also reported to be in action. The 5 Queen Elizabeths made up this squadron, and are usually known as the Fast Battle Squadron. The 1st, 2nd and 4th Battle Squadrons were together in 6 divisions with the destroyers and light cruisers deployed all round them.

We went to 'Action Stations' at 4.30 p.m. and saw the Battle Cruisers in action ahead of us on the starboard bow. Some of the other cruisers were firing on the port bow. As we came up the 'Lion', leading our Battle Cruisers, appeared to be on fire the port side of the forecastle, but it was not serious. They turned up to starboard so as not to cut across the bows of the Fleet. As far as one could see only 2 German Battle Squadrons and all their Battle Cruisers were out. The 'Colossus' leading the 6th division with the 'Collingwood' her next astern were nearest the enemy. The whole Fleet deployed at 5.0 and opened out. We opened fire at 5.37 p.m. on some German light cruisers. The 'Collingwood's' second salvo hit one of them which set her on fire, and sank after two more salvoes were fired into her. We then shifted on to another light cruiser and helped to sink her as well. Our next target was a battle cruiser, we think the 'Derrflinger' [*sic*] or 'Lützow', and one of the 'Collingwood's' salvoes hit her abaft the after turret, which burst into a fierce flame. After this she turned away from us and disappeared into the mist. By this time it was too dark to fire and we went to Night Defence stations. The 4″ guns were manned to repel destroyer attacks. Our 12″ firing was very good, though rather slow, as we could only fire at the flashes of the German guns. The range at the commencement was 10000 yds and ceased at 8000 yds. The Germans fired some of their torpedoes but only one of them took effect in the 'Marlborough', the flagship of the 1st Battle Squadron. One of her boiler rooms, one of her hydraulic rooms, and one of her dynamo rooms were flooded, and her speed was reduced to 14 knots. She succeeded in getting into the Humber. One torpedo passed ahead of the 'Collingwood' and another astern. We had no casualties and no damage done to us, though we were 'straddled' several times. That is some of the shots in a salvo falling short of the ship and others over.

The 'Colossus' was hit once in the superstructure which wounded 9 men, and put the main derrick out of action. The 'Barham' and 'Malaya' and 'Warspite' in the 5th Battle Squadron were hit. The latter had to go to Rosyth at once. The 2 former had a good many killed and wounded. The 'Barham' 28 killed, 41 wounded, and the 'Malaya' 38 killed, 53 wounded. The dead were buried at sea. The cruiser 'Defence' was concentrated on by the German battle cruisers, and was hit by several salvoes at once. She blew up in a huge sheet of flame and smoke, and when this sank down, she had utterly disappeared.

The 'Warrior' was totally disabled and had to be abandoned. Several of our destroyers were sunk and some were taken in tow by others. Whether they have all got in is not yet known.

The German Fleet all turned away from us after dark, followed by our light cruisers and destroyers who attacked them during the night. The result is not yet known as to whether they accounted for any more of the enemy. We were not attacked at all during the night and everything was very quiet.

The Fleet steamed south 40 miles off the Danish coast all night. The Action was fought about 40 miles south of the Skaggerak and 40 miles off the Danish coast. We went to action stations at 2.0 a.m. on Thursday June 1st but there was no sign of the enemy to be seen. We saw a Shütze-Lanz airship at 4.0 a.m. who came out to make a report as to where we were. She was fired at by several ships. Her range was about 12000 yds. She made off as soon as we fired at her. We remained at action stations all day till 5.30 p.m. We returned to Scapa Flow at noon on Friday June 2nd, and coaled and ammunitioned at once.

———

I was in A turret and watched most of the action through one of the trainer's telescopes as we were firing by Director, when the turret is trained in the working chamber and not in the gun house. At the commencement I was sitting on the top of A turret and had a very good view of the proceedings. I was up there during a lull, when a German ship started firing at us, and one salvo 'straddled' us. We at once returned the fire. I was distinctly startled and jumped down the hole in the top of the turret like a shot rabbit!!

I didn't try the experience again. The ship was in a fine state on the main deck. Inches of water sluicing about to prevent fires from getting a hold on the deck. Most of the cabins were also flooded.

The hands behaved splendidly and all of them in the best of spirits as their heart's desire had at last been granted, which was to be in action with the Germans. Some of the turret's crew actually took on bets with one another that we should not fire a shot. A good deal of money must have changed hands I should think by now.

My impressions were very different to what I expected. I saw visions of the masts going over the side and funnels hurtling through the air etc. In reality none of these things happened and we are still quite sound as before. No one would know to look at the ship that we had been in action. It was certainly a great experience to have been through and it shows that we are at war and that the Germans can fight if they like.

The episode on the roof of 'A' Turret may be elaborated in one degree. When the salvo came out of the mist and passed over Prince Albert's head, causing him to jump 'down the hole in the top of the turret like a shot rabbit', he omits to state that, in making a similar dive for safety, a petty officer of ample girth became wedged in the hole, resisting all efforts of the Prince and a midshipman to push him down. They succeeded in doing so only as the second salvo came over, so close that the turret officer, who remained outside, could see the colour of the shells.

The psychological effect of the battle upon Prince Albert was very great, and fully justified the belief which King George had always held that his son must, if at all possible, bear his share in a fleet action. In all his letters written after the battle, the burden of the Prince's thoughts is 'thank God I was back in time'. It had brought him new experience and new trials. He had felt the excitement of battle, though he declared it to have been a dull engagement and greatly deplored the fact that *Collingwood* carried no scar from the fighting.[a] He had known the pride of sharing with others in victory and the sorrow that this victory had been robbed of its ultimate fulfilment. 'Oh, if only they would come out again

---

[a] 'Bertie is very proud at having been in action but is sorry that his ship was not hit (although she was straddled by several salvoes) as she has nothing to show she has been in the fight', wrote King George V to the Duke of Connaught.[47]

and we could meet them, but this time in the early morning, we should have better light and more daylight to deal with them', he wrote to the Prince of Wales. 'In a war on such a scale as this of course we must have casualties and lose ships & men, but there is no need for everyone at home to bemoan their loss when they are proud to die for their country. They don't know what war is, several generations have come and gone since the last great battles.'[48] Above all, he had seen death and dealt it out, and had learned the strange absence of fear in action. 'When I was on top of the turret I never felt any fear of shells or anything else', he wrote again to the Prince of Wales. 'It seems curious but all sense of danger and everything else goes except the one longing of dealing death in every possible way to the enemy.'[49] In a single summer afternoon he had passed into the full dignity of manhood and when, a few days after the battle, King George paid his surprise visit to the Grand Fleet, he could again say: 'I am pleased with my son'.[a]

The pride of victory was, however, tempered by the tragedy of a national loss. The Grand Fleet, after waiting in vain for the Germans to reappear and continue the battle off Jutland, returned to Scapa and three days later Lord Kitchener embarked upon his fateful mission to Russia. In the long summer twilight of June 5 the cruiser *Hampshire* passed through the ships of the Fleet, *Collingwood* amongst them, and the men cheered and cheered again as the tall grey figure on the bridge in field uniform, his greatcoat buttoned around him, stood at the salute. A heavy sea was running, so heavy that the *Hampshire*'s destroyer escort was compelled to turn back almost immediately. A few hours later, within sight of the Orkneys, the cruiser struck a mine, and in fifteen minutes had disappeared, taking with her the ship's company of 800 officers and men, and the Field-Marshal and his staff.

The writer of today, looking down the corridors of time illuminated by the little lamp of history, may be tempted to qualify Lord Kitchener's death with *Felix opportunitate mortis*. There had undoubtedly been errors of judgment and Lord Kitchener's prestige had become dimmed, but this was only

---

[a] Prince Albert was among those officers commended for their services by Admiral Sir John Jellicoe in his dispatch made public on September 16, 1916.

appreciated by a comparatively small circle, and to the great majority of Englishmen the term 'K' still retained that magic quality which had raised the First Hundred Thousand. The news of his death was received as a national calamity throughout the Empire from the Sovereign to the men of 'Kitchener's Armies' in France and Flanders, who were about to make their great onslaught of the Battle of the Somme.[a]

The sinking of the 'Hampshire' with Ld. Kitchener on bd. was a terrible blow to me [wrote the King in deep distress to his son]. His loss to the Nation is so very great & we could ill spare him now, but this will make us redouble our efforts to win this war. . . . He was a great friend of mine, I had known him for 30 years & he always told me everything. He has left a terrible blank.[50]

The summer passed in the monotony of the resumed watch on the German Fleet, which, however, showed no further desire to try conclusions at sea. For Prince Albert it was enhanced by a growing hope and belief that at last his illness and weakness were behind him. 'I really think now that I have got over all my inside troubles', he wrote to his father in July. 'I have not had any recurrence of pains or sickness.'[51]

As if the Fates mocked him he was struck down not six weeks later. On the evening of August 26 he went sick with acute pain. The Fleet Medical Officers believed an immediate operation to be necessary, but the arrival of Sir William Macewen[b] and Sir James Reid on board resulted in his being transferred to the Naval Hospital at South Queensferry, and soon thereafter to Windsor, where Queen Mary thought him looking 'rather thin' and in need of rest.[52] Had he but known it he had left *Collingwood* for ever,[c] for a further conference of doctors, this time Sir Frederick Treves, Sir Bertrand Dawson[d]

---

[a] The Battle of the Somme opened on July 1, 1916.

[b] Sir William Macewen, C.B. (1848–1924), Professor of Surgery at Glasgow University, was Hon. Surgeon to His Majesty in Scotland and Surgeon-General for the Royal Navy in Scotland.

[c] From the point of view of his career as a naval officer Prince Albert was not sorry to leave *Collingwood*, in which he had served for the better part of three years. Most of his friends had left for service in torpedo craft and submarines and he himself was hoping for a new appointment.

[d] Rt. Hon. Bertrand, first Baron Dawson of Penn, G.C.V.O., K.C.B., K.C.M.G. (1864–1945), Physician-in-Ordinary to King Edward VII, King George V, King Edward VIII and King George VI.

and Dr. Hewett,[a] agreed that his complaint was now without doubt a duodenal ulcer, and that a prolonged period of rest was necessary.

In this moment of bitter disappointment Prince Albert had two sources of consolation. The resumption of a balanced diet and a regular life banished the gnawing pain which had begun to distract him, and the definite diagnosis of its cause relieved his acute depression, since it destroyed the illusion that he was suffering from some undefinable, or, worse still perhaps, some malignant disease. A duodenal ulcer could, after all, be cured or, at worst, be removed surgically. It needed only additional patience to await the day of his deliverance. So with a new philosophy he submitted to rest and treatment until the beginning of November, when, after a fortnight's leave at the Imperial Hotel, Torquay, accompanied by Lieutenant Campbell Tait, he reported to Portsmouth, for service on the staff of the Commander-in-Chief, Sir Stanley Colville.

The routine of an office desk never appealed to the Prince. It was something better than quiescence at home but not to be compared with service at sea. Though he conscientiously applied himself to his duties, he kept up a concentrated barrage of attack on his father, on Admiral Colville and on the Admiralty for a new appointment afloat. It was nearly six months before he succeeded in gaining his objective.

In the meantime, life was not entirely without incident. King George's old friend and equerry, Sir Charles Cust,[b] paid a visit to the Commander-in-Chief, who for his interest and that of Prince Albert, arranged a visit to the new submarine K3. 'We went out into the Solent and dived', the Prince later wrote to the King. 'It was rather an unfortunate dive as we stuck her nose in the mud for a $\frac{1}{4}$ of an hour. Her crew were quite new, and they had forgotten to flood one of the forward tanks when they flooded the remainder. So when

[a] Sir Stanley Hewett, K.C.B., K.C.V.O., K.B.E. (1880–1954), a graduate of Cambridge University, served as Surgeon-Apothecary to King George V and King George VI.

[b] Captain Sir Charles Leopold Cust, third Baronet, G.C.V.O., C.B., C.M.G., C.I.E. (1864–1931), was the lifelong friend of King George V, with whom he had been a naval cadet and midshipman, and whom he served as personal equerry from 1892 until his death.

they did flood it, her bows went down very fast into the mud. It was not serious and they soon blew the water out again. It was most interesting and a great experience.'[53]

Prince Albert was now approaching his twenty-first birthday and man's estate (December 14, 1916). He was granted leave of absence to spend it at Buckingham Palace, and to his intense pride and pleasure was invested by his father with the Order of the Garter. Whether King George had any particular motive in bestowing this honour upon his second son it is impossible to say, since the event passes without record in his diary and only secures a bare mention in that of Queen Mary. He had made the Prince of Wales a Knight of the Garter under exceptional circumstances at the age of seventeen,[a] but, since he also appointed his two younger sons to the Order on their twenty-first birthdays,[b] it is probable that he regarded this as no more than a proper recognition of the attainment of their majority. Prince Albert, however, chose to look on it as an exemplification of the King's confidence and esteem, and was deeply touched thereby. 'I cannot thank you enough for having made me a Knight of the Garter', he wrote. 'I feel very proud to have it, and will always try to live up to it'; [54] and to Queen Mary, 'You don't know how proud I felt when Papa gave me the Garter'.[55] 'I am glad you say you will try & live up to the Garter', replied the King. 'Remember it is the oldest Order of Chivalry in the world.'[56]

On May 8, 1917 — a year and three days after he had rejoined *Collingwood* before Jutland — Prince Albert reported again for sea duty, this time to the 27,500-ton battleship *Malaya* (Captain the Hon. Algernon Boyle),[c] with the rank of acting Lieutenant, and here to his great delight he was shortly joined by Dr. Louis Greig, who was appointed in June as the ship's second surgeon. 'It is so nice having a real friend as a messmate and he is very cheery', he wrote to the Queen,[57] and from this time they remained virtually unseparated for the next six years.

It was a welcome discovery also to find Commander

---

[a] See above, p. 51.

[b] Prince Henry was appointed a Knight of the Garter on March 31, 1921, and Prince George on December 20, 1923.

[c] Admiral the Hon. Sir Algernon Boyle, K.C.B., C.M.G., M.V.O. (1871–1949).

Campbell Tait, with common memories of *Collingwood*'s forward turret at Jutland,[a] and there were others among the Prince's shipmates who in later years were to become 'Rulers of the Queen's Navee'; two young lieutenants named Brind and McGrigor were marked by destiny, and, in addition to Tait, there were six others among *Malaya*'s younger officers who subsequently achieved executive flag rank.[b] In after years that vintage of *Malaya*'s officers would pride themselves on having had four embryonic Commanders-in-Chief and two Admirals of the Fleet simultaneously as members of the Wardroom.

Father and son met briefly during the King's visit to the Grand Fleet in the third week of June. Less than a fortnight later Prince Albert had tragic news to report. On the night of July 9, the battleship *Vanguard*, moored in Scapa Flow, was destroyed by an internal explosion. Her war-time complement was nearly 1000 men, of whom by good fortune more than half were ashore at the time of the explosion, but of those left on board only one officer and two ratings survived, and a week later one of these had died. It is one thing to see a ship sunk by enemy gunfire in the heat of battle, and quite another to witness the sudden and complete disintegration of a great vessel in the peaceful calm of home waters. The horror of the shock is still remembered by those who were present in neighbouring ships. Prince Albert wrote of the disaster to his father:

She blew up at 11.15 p.m. last Monday. The explosion was not very loud as a certain amount of people didn't hear it. I was asleep at the time having gone to bed early. Most ships sent boats away to the scene of the accident at once, to pick up bodies, etc.

[a] Lieutenant-Commander Tait was appointed acting Equerry to Prince Albert as from July 1, 1917.

[b] Admiral Sir Patrick Brind, G.B.E., K.C.B. (b. 1892), after having been Commander-in-Chief of the Far Eastern Station from 1948 to 1951, was, on the organization of the N.A.T.O. High Command, appointed Commander-in-Chief, Allied Forces, Northern Europe, a position which he held from 1951 to 1953.

Admiral of the Fleet Sir Rhoderick McGrigor, G.C.B., D.S.O. (b. 1893), was Commander-in-Chief of the Home Fleet, 1948–1950, Commander-in-Chief Plymouth, 1950–1951, and First Sea Lord and Chief of the Naval Staff from 1951 to 1955.

The six future admirals were: Vice-Admiral Geoffrey Burghard, D.S.O.; Vice-Admiral Clifford Caslon, C.B., C.B.E.; Rear-Admiral Clement Ellis, C.B.; Rear-Admiral Charles Norris, C.B., D.S.O.; Vice-Admiral Frederick Parham, C.B., C.B.E., D.S.O.; and Vice-Admiral Sir Charles Woodhouse, K.C.B., who was Commander-in-Chief, East India Station, from 1948 to 1950.

The sea all around was covered in wreckage and oil fuel. The next morning nothing was to be seen of the ship at all above the water. The northern shore of Flotta was covered with wreckage which had been washed ashore, and several bodies amongst it. Working parties ashore were hard at work clearing it all away for 2 days. The 'Vanguard' was lying in the billet which we had left only two days before. We had gone to a buoy next to the 'Queen Elizabeth' for our regatta.

It gave us a great shock at the time; but now things have settled down again normally.[58]

Until a Court of Inquiry had established the cause of the disaster the possibility that a U-boat had penetrated the anti-submarine defences of Scapa and torpedoed the battleship could not be excluded from consideration, and on July 16 the Fleet moved south to Rosyth. There were, however, supplementary reasons not unconnected with morale : 'Scapa Flow is now in an awful state, it appears, as all the bodies from the "Vanguard" have been coming to the surface. I expect that is the reason why we are here now', wrote the Prince to his father. 'This isn't official, but I met somebody who had heard from one of the ships left up there.'[59]

But Prince Albert's naval career was drawing to its close. When his great-uncle, the Duke of Connaught, visited the Fleet on July 26, he found the Prince laid up with a recurrence of his gastric trouble, and ten days later he was transferred to South Queensferry Hospital from *Malaya*, with Louis Greig in attendance. He was in a poor condition physically, and the ship's chaplain [a] who visited him in hospital found him looking very thin and ill. He was deeply depressed, and though King George, in great distress, exhorted him to have patience and courage,[60] he himself now knew that the great disappointment which had overhung his life for the last three years could no longer be evaded. He had to face up to the issue, and characteristically he faced it squarely. He dearly loved the Navy, but he realized that the strain of sea-duty made greater demands upon his constitution than that over-taxed organism could support, and with this decision his doctors agreed. 'Personally I feel that I am not fit for service at sea, even when I recover

---

[a] *Malaya*'s chaplain at this time was the Rev. Hubert John Matthews, now the Ven. the Archdeacon of Hampstead.

from this little attack', he wrote to his father.[61]   It was the
final and honourable surrender in the face of superior forces.

Accompanied by Louis Greig and Campbell Tait, he
returned to Windsor on August 13, and after a month's rest
and quiet went to recuperate with Sir Harry and Lady Joan
Verney in North Wales. But it was evident that, even when
leading the quietest of lives and eating the simplest of food,
his complaint would not yield to treatment, and with the
medical support of Louis Greig, he wrote imploring his parents
to agree to an operation which would remove the cause of all
his trouble. 'I don't think I can get any better without an
operation and I should like to get it over and done with', he
wrote to the King in great depression from Llangurig.[62]

The King's medical advisers were divided on the wisdom
of an immediate operation, and for nearly two months the
Prince awaited the issue of their debate with deepening dejection. In the meantime it had been decided that he should be
transferred from the Navy that Floats to the Navy that Flies,
and his appointment to the Royal Naval Air Service Station
at Cranwell was gazetted on November 13. This plan had
originated with the Prince himself, and rather to his surprise
it received immediate parental approval — 'My own suggestion
for once came off and Papa jumped at the idea', he wrote to
Mr. Hansell. 'Greig is going there as well . . . he is a perfect
topper.'[63]

Alas, however, for these plans. Shortly after his appointment
had been announced the Prince was prostrated by a further
attack. This at least had the effect of causing his doctors to
make up their minds, and Queen Mary noted in her diary:

November 28, 1917.
It is decided that poor Bertie is to have an operation to-morrow
as he does not seem at all well & has constant pain. He is most
cheerful about it. . . .

November 29, 1917.
Dr. Rigby [a] performed the operation at 10, which was most
successful. Sir Fred. Treves, Sir Bertrand Dawson, Dr. Hewett &
Dr. Greig were present & came to report to us later. The operation
was very successful & they found the cause of all the trouble he has
been having since 1915.

[a] Sir Hugh Rigby, first Baronet, K.C.V.O. (1870–1944), was Serjeant-Surgeon
to King George V from 1928 to 1932.

One cannot but believe, in view of this discovery, that had the Prince's complaint been correctly diagnosed two years before, and had the decision to operate been taken earlier, he would have been spared much mental and physical anguish and the Navy would not have lost a promising young officer. For, although if measured in terms of time the period actually spent by Prince Albert as an active naval officer was not great,[a] it was yet sufficient for him to impress his superiors with the sterling qualities of his character. His commanding officers thought highly of him. They have left it on record that his work was above the average, that he was zealous and hard-working, possessed of good common sense and upright character, and could handle men well. There was no doubt in their minds that had it been possible for him to continue in the Service he would have proved himself as valuable and efficient a senior officer as his father.

His contemporaries found the Prince an agreeable shipmate, shy and self-effacing and reliable, gay, good-humoured and considerate of others, save when he was swept by those squalls of temper which, though of brief duration, left him exhausted in both mind and body. His suffering and disappointments during this period had not, however, been in vain. They had taught him many things: patience and endurance in the face of prolonged pain and frustration, and above all a sense of grateful appreciation for those who ministered to him; and these lessons he never forgot. Years later, in the full flower of renewed health and vigour, he was to say on a public occasion: 'I myself know what it is to need the services of a sick nurse and what a wonderful comfort it is to have that need well supplied and so my admiration and gratitude towards the nursing profession for their never failing help and watchful care is very real and very great'.[b] This note of gratitude born of adversity was to recur again and again in his public speeches.

[a] In the three years and eleven months (Sept. 1913 to Aug. 1917) during which Prince Albert was a serving naval officer, he was actually at sea for twenty-two months: in *Collingwood*, September 1913–August 1914, February–July 1915, and May–August, 1916; in *Malaya*, May–August 1917.
[b] The occasion was the laying of the foundation stone of the Nurses' Home at the Liverpool Infirmary, July 25, 1923.

CHAPTER IV

CRANWELL AND CAMBRIDGE
1918–1920

(i)

THE expansion of modern aviation from the lambent dream of dedicated pioneers to a recognized factor of everyday life was encompassed entirely within the lifetime of King George VI. He was just eight years old when the Wright Brothers took off in the teeth of a 27-mile-an-hour gale [a] at Kitty Hawk, North Carolina, on December 17, 1903, and established the fact that the age of the flying machine had come at last; he was a naval cadet when Louis Blériot, on July 25, 1909, shattered the illusion of British insular isolation by flying the Channel in forty minutes; and he was a Midshipman when Hamel was looping the loop at Windsor in 1914. Within the span of his war service he saw Britain's air strength grow from the 150 machines available in August 1914 to the 14,000 in service at the date of the Armistice; and in later years he was to see this great science develop magically — both for destructive and constructive purposes. Warsaw and Belgrade and the great centres of Germany and Japan were to be laid waste by its agency. London and other British cities were to suffer cruelly and his own home of Buckingham Palace was not to go unscathed. But, on the other hand, civil aviation was to make great strides; and his last public appearance was to be at London Airport, waving farewell to his daughter and her husband on their flight to East Africa — a long step from that half-mile flight over the sand-dunes of North Carolina.

[a] The term 'gale' was used by Mr. Orville Wright in the narrative of the flight which he wrote for the Aeronautical Society of Great Britain; and indeed, to as primitive an aircraft as the 'Flyer', a wind of 27 m.p.h. must have seemed almost a hurricane. In fact, however, according to the Beaufort Scale, adopted by the British Admiralty in 1838 and by the International Meteorological Committee in 1874, a 'strong wind' does not become a 'gale' until it has achieved a velocity of 38 m.p.h.

It was not inappropriate, therefore, that he should have been identified with the Royal Air Force from its inception, nor that he should have been the first British Monarch to hold a pilot's licence.

The circumstances attendant upon the nativity of new celestial bodies are not infrequently chaotic. Nietzsche, indeed, has written: 'There must be chaos that out of chaos may come forth new stars', and this is not inapplicable to the conditions preceding the birth of the Royal Air Force. When in 1911 a sub-committee of the Committee of Imperial Defence recommended 'the creation of a British Aeronautical Service, to be regarded as one, and to be designated "The Royal Flying Corps"', it added the further recommendation that the Corps should consist of a Naval Wing, a Military Wing and a Central Flying School for the training of pilots, and these proposals were authorized by Royal Warrant in the following year. But the soldiers and the sailors naturally approached the subject of aviation from the angle of their own professions and, moreover, there was the difference in service language which complicated the matter of the common training of pilots. It was not long before the Navy had declared its virtual independence, in command, in training and in supply; the Naval Wing became known as the Royal Naval Air Service and established its own training depots. As a result of this step the Royal Flying Corps became part of the Army.[1]

With the advent of war and the growth of aerial warfare in volume and importance, the defects of this dual system of control became increasingly apparent. Various attempts were made to gather together the threads of aeronautical command and to place them under one central authority, but these were obstinately resisted by both sides until, in the autumn of 1917, the severity of the German raids on London stimulated the Government into making a further effort, this time with success. The Air Force (Constitution) Bill was presented to Parliament early in November 1917, and received the Royal Assent on November 29. Under its provisions a unified air service, to be known later as the Royal Air Force,[a] was to

---

[a] King George V approved the title of 'Royal Air Force' on February 19, 1918, and the Royal Proclamation announcing this fact was published on March 7, 1918.

THE DUCHESS OF YORK, BY PHILIP LASZLO, 1925

come into existence on April 1, 1918. Lord Rothermere [a] was
appointed first Secretary of State for Air, and Major-General
Sir Hugh Trenchard,[b] the 'Father of the Royal Air Force',
first Chief of the Air Staff.

King George had been very favourably disposed towards
the idea that one of his sons should be identified with the new
Service; and, since Prince George had now entered the Navy
as a cadet [c] and it was the evident desire of Prince Albert
to transfer, he deemed it expedient that his second son should
join the Royal Naval Air Service pending its amalgamation in
the Royal Air Force. As an added precaution for Prince
Albert's health it was arranged with the Admiralty that Staff-
Surgeon Louis Greig should also be seconded to the same
branch of the Service. Prince Albert received his appointment
to H.M.S. *Daedalus* on January 1, 1918, and reported there a
month later.

Named after that intrepid aeronaut of mythology, of whom
Maurice Baring wrote:

> Bright gifts and festal crowns to him they bore;
> The brave, the wise, the mighty and the fair
> Acclaimed him lord of the unconquered air,

Daedalus was in fact a barren stretch of land at Cranwell on the
wind-swept plateau of Lincolnshire, some twelve miles to the
north-east of Grantham, which had become a great training
station both for pilots and aerial gun-layers in aeroplanes and

---

[a] Rt. Hon. Harold Sidney Harmsworth, first Viscount Rothermere (1868–
1940), a younger brother of Lord Northcliffe, was Secretary of State for Air from
1917 to 1918.
[b] Marshal of the Royal Air Force Hugh Montague, first Viscount Trenchard,
G.C.B., O.M., G.C.V.O., D.S.O. (1873–1956), was an early pioneer of military
aviation, having been Assistant Commandant of the Central Flying School from
1913 to 1914. He commanded the Royal Flying Corps in the field from 1915 to
1917, and held the appointment of Chief of the Air Staff from January to April
1918 and again from 1919 to 1929. In the interim he was Commander-in-Chief
of the Independent Air Force, and later of the Inter-Allied Independent Air
Force, under the supreme authority of Marshal Foch. It was during his second
term as Chief of Staff that the R.A.F. took on its permanent form and established
its tradition as a Service. He was Commissioner of the Metropolitan Police of
London, 1931–1935.
[c] Prince George left Dartmouth in May 1920 to join the cruiser *Téméraire*
for the training cruise. 'He has kept up the best traditions of my family by passing
out of Dartmouth 1 from bottom, the same place as I did!!!!' Prince Albert
wrote to a friend.

dirigibles. 'She' was commanded by Rear-Admiral Luce, the hero of *Glasgow*,[a] and was governed by strict naval discipline and terminology, which rendered it neither unusual nor humorous for the command to be given to cut the grass on the quarter-deck. Nor for the officer of the watch to pace solemnly, telescope under arm, the narrow gallery which surrounded the clock-tower about the drill-hall of the camp.

There was nothing about *Daedalus* in January 1918 to suggest the dignity and magnificence of the Royal Air Force Cadet College which was destined to replace it in later years.[b] It was composed of a collection of hangars for aircraft and of temporary hutments — some of which still remain in the starkness of what may be called the 'corrugated-iron perpendicular period' — in which were housed 86 officers and some thousands of men and boys for the purposes of training. Of these the boys, drawn from both the R.F.C. and the R.N.A.S. and numbering at first 500, later 1500, and eventually 2500, became Prince Albert's special charge, as O.C. No. 4 Squadron, Boy Wing. It was in a sense his first real command, and he wrote proudly of it to the King:

I am going to run them as an entirely separate unit to the remainder of the men, and I am known as the Officer Commanding Boys. I shall have to punish them myself and grant their requests for leave etc. At present I have not got a proper office but hope to get one shortly. The work is entirely new to me and I find it rather difficult to begin with, but I shall get used to it. They live in small huts, 20 boys in each, and these give me the most trouble as they won't keep them clean without my constantly telling them off to clean them out of working hours.[2]

The Prince proved himself something of a strict disciplinarian, a quality not entirely appreciated by all of those under his command. In addition to this work, he acted as what was known, in those early days before the official nomen-

---

[a] Admiral John Luce, C.B. (1870–1932), had commanded *Glasgow* in the disastrous action off Coronel, in which she was the sole survivor of the British Squadron. He had the satisfaction of commanding her also in the Battle of the Falkland Islands (see above, p. 81, f.n. b).

[b] The Royal Air Force Cadet College was inaugurated at Cranwell on February 5, 1920, and was originally housed in the huts of the war-time establishment. The foundation-stone of the present College was laid in April 1929, and the new buildings were officially opened on October 11, 1934, by the Prince of Wales.

clature of the new Service was settled, as 'Assistant Adjutant' of the East Camp, where the Boy Wing was housed.[a]

Not only the work but the whole life of Cranwell was new to him. It was very different from that of a battleship. On the whole he found his fellow officers 'very nice, though a curious mixture of people, in every walk of life',[3] and his practised eye of a naval officer found much to be desired in the type of petty officer to be found in the R.N.A.S. 'One finds a tremendous difference between them and the proper Naval P.O.', he wrote to his father. 'But with a little persuasion I hope to make them understand what I want.' He proved himself a 'good mixer', however, becoming known to his seniors as 'P.A.', and entered upon his new duties with pleasure and enthusiasm, displaying a conscientious competence.

The life suited him; the strong air of Lincolnshire, together with the hard day's work, sent him to bed a tired but healthy man. In his spare time he rode a horse, played a lot of tennis and also learned to drive a car, developing into something of a 'demon driver'. In due course he had his first flight in an aeroplane which, like many another, he experienced with mixed emotions. The day on which the flight had been arranged proved to be one of storm and rain. Cranwell had had a number of fatal flying accidents and the officer in charge of training urged a postponement. Prince Albert demurred. He was not in the least anxious to go up, he said, but he would be no more anxious tomorrow or the next day. The thing had been arranged, and, since he had to do it some time, he preferred characteristically to get it over and done with. He went up and the flight was successful. 'It was a curious sensation', he wrote later to Queen Mary, 'and one which takes a lot of getting used to. I did enjoy it on the whole, but I don't think I should like flying as a pastime. I would much sooner be on the ground!! It feels safer!!'[4]

Moreover he was happy. Dr. Greig and his wife had taken

[a] A memorial plaque commemorating this fact was placed on the wall of the room which Prince Albert occupied on one of the few brick buildings then existing at Cranwell, now known as York House. When King George VI visited the College in 1945 he protested against the use of the word 'Adjutant' which, he said, was a purely Army office and which he had never held, never having been a soldier. He asked the then A.O.C. Cranwell to have the wording on the tablet changed; this officer, however, died suddenly a few days later and the alteration was never made.

a small cottage at South Rauceby, some four miles from Cranwell, the supreme ugliness of whose Victorian Gothic exterior was belied by the charm within of the three-hundred-year-old oak beams and winding staircases. Here Prince Albert joined them, and here for the first time he experienced home life on a small scale and it delighted him. It was very pleasant and restful after his day's work to come back to the cottage and the happy companionship of the Greigs; to work in the garden and build a chicken-run and to do the dozen or so odd jobs demanded by domestic life in war-time. Interest in his work, pleasure in his surroundings and the incomparable joy of his renewed health were making a new man of him. 'I never trouble my head about myself now, as I feel a different person', he wrote enthusiastically to his mother.[5]

King George and Queen Mary made a visit of inspection to Cranwell on April 11, 1918, a few days after the Royal Air Force had officially come into existence, and it was with immense satisfaction that Flight-Lieutenant Prince Albert,[a] Officer Commanding Boys, watched his charges, now increased in number to 2500, whom he had groomed and drilled with zealous care, do him credit as they paraded before their Sovereign. 'We motored to Cranwell which has now become the largest aerodrome in the world', King George recorded in his diary of this visit. 'Inspected the boys whom Bertie is in charge of, visited the sheds & saw all the different kinds of machines, also the classes at instruction & we saw the airships in their hangars, unfortunately it was misty & foggy so we could not see any flying.'

Never had the motto of the Royal Air Force — *Per Ardua ad Astra* — seemed more appropriate than during the weeks immediately following its official birth. No sooner had the new Service come into existence on April 1, 1918, than differences in temperament and outlook resulted in a monumental disagreement between the new Secretary of State, Lord

[a] Prince Albert held the following ranks in the Royal Air Force:

Flight-Lieutenant	. . .	April 1, 1918
Squadron Leader	. .	August 1, 1919
Wing Commander	. .	June 1, 1920
Group Captain	. .	June 30, 1921
Air Chief Marshal	. .	January 21, 1936
Marshal of the Royal Air Force	.	December 11, 1936

Rothermere, and the new Chief of the Air Staff, Major-
General Trenchard, as a result of which the latter's resignation
was accepted on April 13.[a] Almost immediately afterwards
the Vice-President of the Air Council, Lieut.-General Sir David
Henderson,[b] also resigned on the ground that he could not
work with the new Chief of the Air Staff, Major-General Sykes,[c]
and on April 25 it was announced that the Secretary of State
had followed suit, on grounds of health, to be succeeded by
Sir William Weir.[d][6]

This unfortunate congeries of events, which was rendered
the more serious by virtue of the fact that it coincided with the
great German offensive on the Western Front and the defeat
of the British Fifth Army, had a most disheartening effect
upon the officers of the new Service, many of whom had
served under General Trenchard's dashing leadership of the
R.F.C., and to whom he had become a figure of popular
acclaim and admiration; and the consternation caused by his
departure was reflected in the letters exchanged between Prince
Albert and King George. 'Everything here as you may

[a] Sir Hugh Trenchard actually tendered his resignation to the Secretary of
State on March 19, before the new Service came into being. Because of the
unfortunate effect which such an announcement might have had on the formation
of the Royal Air Force, Lord Rothermere delayed placing the matter before the
Cabinet until April 10. It was accepted on April 13 — exactly six years to the
day after the creation of the Royal Flying Corps. For the superstitious it may be
of interest to note how this so-called 'unlucky' day is associated with the Air
Service. The R.F.C. was formed on May 13, 1912; the German air-r aid on
London which stimulated the establishment of the R.A.F. was on June 13, 1917;
and the first Chief of the Air Staff tendered his resignation on March 13, 1918.

[b] Lieut.-General Sir David Henderson, K.C.B., K.C.V.O. (1862–1921), was
also a pioneer of military aviation, having been, before his appointment to the
Air Council, Director of Military Aeronautics from 1913 to 1914, and in command
of the R.F.C. in France from 1914 to 1915. He returned to the War Office as
Director-General of Aeronautics in August 1915, a post which he held until a
few months before the formation of the R.A.F.

[c] Major-General the Rt. Hon. Sir Frederick Sykes, G.C.S.I., G.C.I.E.,
G.B.E., K.C.B., C.M.G. (1877–1954), had served in the Royal Flying Corps from
its inception. He commanded the Military Wing until 1914, and, for a brief
period, took over the command of the R.F.C. in France. He later transferred
to the R.N.A.S., which he commanded in the Eastern Mediterranean from 1915
to 1916. Having served as Chief of the Air Staff from 1918 to 1919, he entered
Parliament, where he sat as a Conservative member from 1922 to 1928, and
again from 1940 to 1945. He was Governor of Bombay from 1928 to 1933.

[d] Rt. Hon. William Douglas, first Viscount Weir, G.C.B. (b. 1877), was
Controller of Aeronautical Supplies and a member of the Air Council from
1917 to 1918. He remained as Secretary of State for Air from April to December
1918.

imagine is in a very unsettled state, owing to the changes in the Air Board,' wrote the Prince, 'and nothing is settled yet as to what routine we are working under. We are now having a mixture of naval and military routine, which is not a great success.' [7]

I am sorry that Genl. Trenchard's resignation has produced an unsettled state of affairs in the Air Force, which is only to be expected [the King replied]. But I hope nobody will lose their heads, but will try & work loyally under the new Air Board. I know Genl. Sykes is not popular in the Force, but that can't be helped, everyone ought to try & do their best at such a serious moment as the present.[8]

And again a week later :

I feel sure now that Ld. Rothermere and Sir Henry Norman have left the Air Brd. & that Sir W. Weir has become the new Minister of the R.A.F. that everything will go right. I had a long talk with him on Saturday, he is a first rate man & very popular with everyone & he is going to give Genl. Trenchard an important position in the R.A.F.[a] so I hope everything will work well now & that all the officers will rally round him.[10]

It was inevitable, however, that, with the best will in the world, conflicts between military and naval customs and traditions would produce friction in the early days of the R.A.F. Cranwell was no exception. Officers and instructors came and went with bewildering rapidity and the already established system of training boys, which had been Prince Albert's special care and interest, was completely disrupted. Having been in charge of all the boys he was, not unnaturally, annoyed at finding his command cut to a mere fraction, with newly appointed and inexperienced officers placed over him. 'I am rather depressed about the whole affair as you may imagine, as I was very keen on this job, and was doing my best to make it a success', he wrote in a long letter to his father in the middle of May, protesting against the removal of his old

---

[a] This was the suggestion put forward by the Air Council to the War Cabinet on May 13, 1918, that the time had come to constitute an Independent Force for large-scale bombing operations over Germany. It was proposed that General Trenchard should have this independent command. This proposal was given effect in June and was the forerunner of the Inter-Allied Independent Air Force, which came into existence in the following October, and of which General Trenchard became Commander-in-Chief.[9]

instructor. 'Now I am afraid I have rather lost interest until I know exactly what is going to happen. I am telling you all this as I am certain you would want to know what sort of things do go on, and this is quite a serious question and I am involved in it personally.'[11]

A month later the position had not improved. 'The whole of my show is upside down,' the Prince wrote to a friend, 'and no one knows what is likely to happen. I am pretty fed up and don't feel like staying here for good.' He was not fated to do so. By the middle of July it had been decided that, to broaden his experience of Air Force training, he should be attached to a cadet unit at St. Leonard's-on-Sea; and thither the Prince and Louis Greig were transferred on August 1.

The summer of 1918 was one of victory. The spring had proved the darkest moment in the Allied military fortunes. The German offensive — that final gambler's throw which Ludendorff had made on March 21 — had carried the enemy almost to the gates of Paris and to the Channel ports. Defeat, and the consequent necessity for a negotiated peace, had been narrowly averted, partly by the military genius of Marshal Foch, partly because the German armies lacked the final ounce of strength required to break the Allied line, partly owing to the indomitable spirit of the British and French infantry. On July 15 Ludendorff began his ultimate offensive in Champagne, that *Kaiserschlacht* launched under the imperial eye of the All-highest War Lord in person; in two days it had been brought to a standstill and on July 18 Marshal Foch dealt the enemy the first of those hammer blows which were to breach the German line on August 8 — that 'black day' of the German army [a]— and were not to abate until the final surrender in the railway-carriage at Réthondes.

A major reason for the daring and success of Marshal Foch's operations was the existence of some two million fresh American troops in reserve. Although United States divisions had been in France since June of 1917 and had seen hard fighting, it was this immense reserve of manpower which had finally turned the scale of battle in the Allies' favour. Many of the young Americans never saw action, some indeed never

[a] '*Der 8. August ist der schwarze Tag des deutschen Heeres in der Geschichte dieses Krieges*', Ludendorff was to write later in his *Erinnerungen* (p. 547).

crossed to France, but the might of his reserves gave the Marshal that assuredness of superiority which he needed for final victory.

London therefore was full of Americans at this time, and Independence Day (July 4) was selected for special demonstrations of Anglo-American unity. At a great meeting in Westminster Hall, Mr. Winston Churchill proclaimed that the new Declaration of Independence was 'No peace till victory; no pact with unrepentant wrong', but the general manifestation was the baseball game between the United States Army and Navy, which was staged at the Chelsea Football Ground, Stamford Bridge, that afternoon.

The King and Queen attended, with Prince Albert on special leave, and others of the Royal Family, and in stifling heat and amid scenes of indescribable enthusiasm, were introduced to the amazing exhibition of excitement and self-expression which is an integral part of an American baseball game. The British are apt to take their sports — according, at least, to foreigners — seriously and sadly. Not so the Americans; they are serious too, but deliriously ebullient; and the presence of the 'cheer-leader' and the 'rooter' is as essential to the proper conduct of games as that of the teams themselves — though this is perhaps truer of football than baseball. On this occasion, however, the friendly rivalry of the American armed services was in frenzied evidence and the British spectators were as fascinated and entertained by the encouragement and insults offered to the players — and, above all, to the umpire — by the American onlookers as by the game itself. 'It was a revelation of America at play,' was the comment of *The Times*, 'and the afternoon was as strenuous as a pillow-fight in a boys' dormitory.'

The Royal Party were delighted. The King, who found the whole affair 'quite exciting',[a] autographed a ball at the request of the Anglo-American Baseball League and this was sent as a souvenir to President Woodrow Wilson. It was an experience which Prince Albert never forgot.

There was another and more serious reason, however, for

---

[a] 'We all went to see a baseball match between the American Army & Navy, played at Stamford Bridge', the King wrote in his diary. 'Large crowds, the Navy won by 2 runs to 1. Quite exciting; only got home at 6.0.'

his presence in London at this time. King George and Queen Mary celebrated their Silver Wedding on Saturday, July 6, with a studied avoidance of display but with all the solemn dignity which the occasion demanded. The Prince of Wales was absent in France, but Prince Albert, Prince Henry, Prince George and Princess Mary accompanied their parents to the special service of Thanksgiving at St. Paul's, and later to a gathering at the Guildhall, where King George paid tribute to the gallantry of his forces and the fortitude of his peoples.

These celebrations over, Prince Albert reported to R.A.F. Headquarters at St. Leonard's, and here he came under the command of Brigadier-General Critchley,[a] whose dynamic personality was infusing a spirit of health and enthusiasm into the young men of the Air Force. Appointed to No. 5 R.A.F. Cadet Wing, Prince Albert first passed through the Cadet School for a fortnight's course and then took command of a squadron. The keen interest in the physical and technical training of young men which had been born in him at Cranwell — and somewhat rebuffed — was now quickened under the stimulus of General Critchley's ardour, and he took an enthusiastic pride in the cadets under his charge.

Once again King George inspected his son's base of operations, on August 30, and once again he was moved to warm commendation :

I was quite delighted with my visit to you last Friday [he wrote] and I must say Genl. Critchley is a wonderful man, the very man for the job. Tell him from me that I never saw such keen boys as his cadets & I thought his system of training quite first rate & that I consider his by far the best training establishment that I have seen & I have seen a great many in the last 4 years. I congratulate him on the splendid spirit he is putting into the boys which I am sure they will never lose when they become pilots. I thought your squadron did wonderfully well considering they had only been at drill for a week. The flag was very good on the hill. You say you think the General was rather nervous. He said to

[a] Brigadier-General Alfred Cecil Critchley, C.M.G., C.B.E., D.S.O. (b. 1890), was a Canadian by birth and, although educated in England, began his military service in the Canadian Army; from this he was seconded to the Royal Flying Corps in February 1918 and thence to the Royal Air Force. In the Second World War he organized and commanded the Initial Training of all air crews for the R.A.F. until 1943. A keen sportsman, he introduced greyhound racing into Great Britain in 1926.

me during the march past, 'now the 5th squadron is coming, your son has been as nervous as a cat since yesterday'. I thought you did it very well & he certainly makes you march a good pace. I certainly think you are in a better place than at Cranwell, the whole spirit is different.[12]

Prince Albert was delighted with his father's praise of his commanding officer and of himself. His work with the cadets fired his imagination, and in fact it was at Cranwell and at St. Leonard's, and later at Folkestone, where he spent a few weeks with another cadet unit, that he became first imbued with those early ideals of sport and fitness which in later life he made a slogan in his public speeches and which found expression in his work with the Industrial Welfare Society, the National Playing Fields Fund and, above all, in his own Duke of York's Camp.

In the West the war was drawing to a close. The German armies were falling back stubbornly but steadily before the Allied waves of attack and in the skies General Trenchard's Independent Air Force, together with the R.A.F., had established a definite superiority. Prince Albert longed to get to France before the final collapse of the enemy and it was with the keenest satisfaction that he found himself posted to General Trenchard's staff. With Louis Greig he flew the Channel on October 23 and reported to the Headquarters of the R.A.F. at Autigny.

General Trenchard's command covered the wide Nancy area of the Western Front, and Prince Albert was enabled to witness operations for both day and night bombing, not only by British but also by American, French and Italian squadrons. This was his first contact with aerial warfare in the offensive — he had experienced anti-aircraft operations in England — and it mightily impressed him. 'The officers all seem in very good spirits and never look upon a raid as more than an ordinary flight, which of course is only right', he wrote to Queen Mary.[13] But it was to the Commander-in-Chief of the Independent Air Force that he gave his highest admiration. 'General Trenchard won't allow anybody to talk about peace here', he wrote to King George early in November, when the first hint of armistice negotiations was in the air. 'I have never seen a man more engrossed in his command. He knows a great deal more about what a Squadron should have than the Squadron Commander. He fairly keeps everybody up to their work.' [14]

The rumours of peace then circulating about the I.A.F. Headquarters were true, nevertheless, and the end came very swiftly. At eleven o'clock on the morning of November 11 the guns along the Western Front were stilled and the slaughter which had endured for four years suddenly ceased. 'The great day has come & we have won the war', wrote King George to his son. 'It has been a long time coming, but I was sure if we stuck to it, we should win & it is a great victory over one of the most perfect military machines ever created.' [15]

Like many another young officer, Prince Albert found himself without immediate employment. The Independent Air Force was disbanded immediately after the Armistice and General Trenchard returned to England. The Prince had been transferred to the staff of Major-General John Salmond,[a] commanding the Royal Air Force in the West with headquarters at Cambrai, but he did not know whether it was his father's wish that he should stay in this appointment, and before taking up his new duties he stayed with Lord Derby, the British Ambassador in Paris, awaiting the King's pleasure.

His new orders were not long in coming and they were of a particularly interesting nature. Through Prince Arthur of Connaught the King of the Belgians had asked King George to send a personal representative, a member of the British Royal Family, to accompany him in his official entry into Brussels on November 22. The first suggestion was that the Prince of Wales should go, but this King George considered undesirable as the Prince had duties with the Canadian Corps to whose headquarters staff he was then attached. The second choice put forward was that of the Duke of Connaught, who had recently been in France; but he had returned to England and was unwilling to go out again. So it was to his second son

[a] Marshal of the Royal Air Force Sir John Salmond, G.C.B., C.M.G., C.V.O., D.S.O. (b. 1881), had been seconded to the Royal Flying Corps in 1912 as an instructor at the Central Flying School. He was appointed Director-General of Aeronautics and a member of the Army Council in October 1917 and took over the command of the R.F.C. in the field from General Trenchard in January 1918, becoming the Commanding Officer of the R.A.F. on the Western Front from 1918 to 1919. After holding important R.A.F. commands after the First World War, he succeeded Sir Hugh Trenchard as Chief of the Air Staff, a position which he held from 1930 to 1933.

that King George entrusted this historic mission, the first on which he represented his father on a matter of State.[a]

It was a moving and unforgettable experience. For four years the lovely city of Brussels had kept her head high and her pride intact, despite every artifice and ruthless attempt by the occupying Power to compel her to humility. For four years King Albert and Queen Elisabeth, clinging to that last segment of Belgian soil which remained free, had carried on the fight against the oppressor. The capital of Belgium and her Sovereign had each looked forward with hope and confidence — now flickering, now quickening — to the day when they should be reunited in freedom; and now the day had come, a golden day of brilliant autumn, of dazzling sunshine and blue skies.

King Albert and his family had slept the night of Thursday, November 21, in the Château of Laeken, and the following morning they drove to the Port de Flandre, where they were met by Prince Albert, wearing the khaki uniform of the R.A.F. There the whole party mounted: the King in field uniform and a battered trench helmet; the Queen in a faded and worn habit of dove grey; Prince Leopold, Duke of Brabant; Prince Charles, Count of Flanders; and Princess Marie-José. Through the streets of the city they rode, and the cheers of the loyal Bruxellois, now and again choked with tears of joy, swelled mightily to greet the Sovereign, who symbolized the return of liberty and the prospect of early peace. Arrived at the Place de la Nation, they were received by Burgomaster Max, the hero of Brussels, and by Cardinal Mercier, the spiritual flame of Belgian resistance. Contingents of Allied troops passed before them and then they entered the Chamber of Deputies, where awaiting them were General Léman, the defender of Liège, and General Sir Herbert Plumer. Prince Albert sat with Prince Leopold beside the rostrum and listened while, for ten minutes, King Albert, nervously gripping his old tin helmet, retold the story of Belgium's fortitude and sacrifices during the long war years, and affirmed, to an audience which was not

---

[a] A curious confusion of identity arose at the time, resulting in the belief of many that it was in fact the Prince of Wales and not Prince Albert who accompanied the Belgian Royal Family into Brussels. This error has persisted till the present day and is repeated by Mr. Sidney Cunliffe-Owen in his recent biography of Queen Elisabeth of the Belgians (p. 94).

ashamed to weep openly, Belgium's everlasting gratitude; then out into the sunlight where cheers and tears again mingled.

That night, after the excitements and emotions of this memorable day were over, Prince Albert sat down in the Palace of Brussels to write to his father :

The entry into Brussels went off very well to-day. I met the King and Queen outside the town this morning and rode in with them. The King told me how delighted he was that you had sent me to represent you. I rode on his right side. It was a very impressive sight and he received a wonderful welcome from his people. A Belgian Division marched past, and also detachments representing the British, French & American Armies. . . .[16]

There followed the visit of King George V to France (November 27–December 11) in the course of which he was received with fervour by the crowds that packed the Champs-Élysées, in what he described as 'a great demonstration of gratitude to England for what she has done for France'. Thereafter he toured the battlefields, the war cemeteries and the devastated areas, and throughout he was accompanied by his two eldest sons. The Prince of Wales and Prince Albert thoroughly enjoyed the festivities in Paris, and, during the later pilgrimage, exerted themselves to prevent their father from becoming over-tired. They were in constant attendance on him, save once when they slipped away for a day by themselves in Mons and Charleroi. At the latter place they saw a film of the Royal entry into Brussels, with Prince Albert in evidence. 'It was a very bad film', one of her sons wrote to Queen Mary.

The question now arose as to how the King's sons should be employed in the intermediate stage between Armistice and Peace. The return of the British armies and their demobilization was one of the thorniest of the problems which beset Mr. Lloyd George's post-war Government, and King George, with his deep sense of correct conduct, was determined that no finger should be pointed at members of his family on account of their premature return to civilian life. There had already been unworthy whispers during the winter of 1917 as to Prince Albert's prolonged absence from active service and the King decided that both Princes should remain in France at any rate until the spring. In this decision both willingly concurred.

'Bertie can be of far more use in this way than sitting in England where he has spent most of the war not that this was his fault!!' the Prince of Wales wrote to Queen Mary. 'But by remaining with the armies till peace is signed he will entirely erase any of the very unfair questions some nasty people asked last year as to what he was doing you will remember.' [17]

Thus Prince Albert found himself at Christmas-time once more attached to General Salmond's staff, now at Spa, that Belgian watering-place which had but a few short weeks before housed the imperial entourage of Wilhelm II and the High Command of the German Army. This was not the only reminder which he was to have of the former Imperial German régime. At the close of the year he went to visit General Currie, the commander of the Canadian Corps, who was quartered in the Schaumberg Palace at Bonn, the residence of Princess Viktoria of Prussia,[a] the sister of the ex-Kaiser, whom the Prince now met for the first time. He was to receive his first experience of that mass mobilization of sympathy in which the entire German nation engaged during the years immediately following the First World War, and which constituted so valuable a foundation of propaganda for Hitler and the future Nazi régime.

Princess Viktoria professed the most supreme ignorance of all German atrocities during the war, and to be completely unable to understand the deep sense of resentment entertained by the Allies. 'She seemed to have very little idea of what our feelings are towards Germany', Prince Albert wrote to his parents. 'All the atrocities and the treatment of prisoners seemed to be a revelation to her, as everything like that had always been kept secret from them. . . . Greig told her some of his experiences as a prisoner which I think gave her an idea of how things were then. She asked after you and the family, and hoped that we should be friends again shortly. I told her politely I did not think it was possible for a great many

[a] Princess Frederika Wilhelmina Amelia Viktoria of Prussia (1866–1929) was the second daughter of the Emperor Frederick III and Princess Victoria of Great Britain. Her early infatuation for the romantic ruler of Bulgaria, Prince Alexander of Battenberg, having been blighted by Bismarck, she married firstly, in 1890, Prince Adolphus of Schaumberg-Lippe who died in 1916, and secondly, and more eccentrically, in 1927, Alexander Zubkov (d. 1936).

The Schaumberg Palace at Bonn is now the official residence of the Chancellor of the German Federal Republic.

years ! ! ! ! She told everybody there that her brother did not want the war or any Zeppelin raids or U boats, but that of course was only a ruse to become friendly with us. . . .' [18]

Your answer to Cousin Vicky (who of course I have known all my life) was quite correct [replied the King]. The sooner she knows the real feeling of bitterness which exists here against her country the better. [19]

It was shortly after his return to Spa that Prince Albert received the news of the death, on January 18, 1919, of his youngest brother, Prince John, at the age of thirteen. This handsome and lovable, but unfortunately quite abnormal, boy had lived in complete seclusion at Sandringham in the charge of Mrs. Bill and a male attendant, and his sudden and peaceful death could only be regarded as a release from further suffering and misery. The Prince did not return to England for the funeral but wrote in affectionate sympathy to both his parents.

It was characteristic of Prince Albert's thoroughness that he now determined to learn to fly. He was not enamoured of flying and though, since his arrival in France, he had flown frequently as a passenger, he had not overcome that fundamental dislike of aerial transport which had been born of his first flight at Cranwell. Nevertheless, if he was to continue in the Air Force it must not be as a 'Quirk',[a] he must achieve his wings. Subduing his natural disinclination, therefore, he applied to Sir John Salmond for permission to learn to fly, which was granted; and two Avro machines and an instructor were sent over from England for this purpose. After the Prince had received a certain amount of instruction, he and General Salmond, reflecting that the whole thing was entirely un-authorized by the Air Ministry, felt that the matter should be placed before the King. Prince Albert also wished to return to England permanently and hoped that the two issues might be combined. He felt that his usefulness with the Air Force in France had been exhausted and that he should extend his knowledge of the Service by working in the Home Establishment while at the same time learning to fly. An additional reason for his wishing to return to London was his anxiety to take remedial measures for his stammer, which, although

[a] A 'Quirk' was an R.N.A.S. term for an officer who had not taken his flying tests.

improved, together with the general state of his health, was still a source of worry and embarrassment to him. A new specialist in speech defects had been discovered and the Prince wished very much to take instruction from him.

All these points he placed before his father by letter at the end of January, and the King replied with understanding :

You propose that you should soon come home as you would like to get your wings, in other words learn to fly & become a pilot & to do that the best instructors & machines are at home, which of course is quite true. I thought you told me that you had no wish to fly, therefore I questioned yr. remaining in [the] R.A.F. I suppose now you have changed your mind & you can certainly do so if you wish.[20]

The transfer arrangements were soon completed and by the end of February Prince Albert was ensconced in the Air Ministry in London, where, as he was later to tell his fellow Civil Servants, 'I found myself being moved from one branch to another rather like a human "buff slip" marked "Passed to you for action, please" '. Nevertheless his contact with the Civil Service brought him a wider vision and a greater wisdom. Like many before and after him, who have learned by practical experience something of the inner workings of that great organism, which Lord Rosebery once described as 'the springs and wheels of the Juggernaut Car of State', he acquired a profound admiration for the devotion and efficiency of its members. 'They never spare themselves,' he once said, 'but continue to serve their country until at last the sad day comes when they, like their files, must be stamped with the fatal letters P.A. ['Put Away'] and disappear.'[a]

Prince Albert's flying instruction took place at the beginning of March at Waddon Lane Aerodrome, Croydon, a site which was later absorbed into Croydon airport. With considerable courage and devotion, Louis Greig, then a man of nearly forty years of age, took the course with him and also qualified. Their instructor was Lieutenant W. A. Coryton,[b] and the

---

[a] Speech at a Civil Service Dinner, on February 10, 1928.

[b] Air Chief Marshal Sir William Alec Coryton, K.C.B., K.B.E., M.V.O., D.F.C. (b. 1895), was seconded from the Rifle Brigade to the Royal Flying Corps in 1917. In the Second World War he was A.O.C. of a Bomber Group from 1942 to 1943, Assistant Chief of the Air Staff from 1943 to 1944, and commanded the Third Tactical Air Force from 1944 to 1945.

FRANCE, 1918

machines they used were two Mono Avros of the Air Council Communication Squadron.[a]

Lieutenant Coryton found Prince Albert possessed of one priceless attribute in a flyer ; he had an instinctive co-ordination of eye and hand and brain, born perhaps of his proficiency as a horseman and a tennis player. He was a conscientious and intelligent pupil and within a few months had mastered the intricacies of cross-country flying, landing on a mark, and such acrobatics as looping, stalling and Immelmann turns. But the medical examiners, basing their judgment on his general physical and psychological condition, advised that he should not fly solo, and he was expressly forbidden to do so by Sir Hugh Trenchard.

When the time came, therefore, for his final tests, he was accompanied by Lieutenant Coryton, who, however, sat in the front seat with his hands on the bottom of the struts and without once touching the controls. Prince Albert, having passed his Modified Test at Croydon on July 28, and his Air and Ground tests three days later, received his wings as a certified pilot on July 31, 1919, his certificate being signed by the Brigadier-General commanding the South-East Area of the R.A.F. His permanent commission as a Squadron Leader was gazetted on the following day.

Prince Albert had therefore attained his ambition. He was a fully qualified pilot, the only member of the Royal Family, and, later, the only British Sovereign to achieve this distinction.[b] He had not greatly enjoyed the experience and he never overcame his fundamental distaste for flying, but his determination to accomplish what he had set out to do had carried him through to ultimate success — and with it the relief attendant on such accomplishment.

(ii)

The England to which Prince Albert's generation returned as men in 1919 was very different from that from which they had

---

[a] The control-stick of the aircraft in which he actually qualified was presented to King George VI by Sir Alec Coryton in 1950.

[b] The Prince of Wales also learned to fly in 1929 under the instruction of Squadron Leader Don, and later purchased a Gypsy Moth for his personal use. Prince Henry and Prince George were also taught by Air Commodore Sir Edward Fielden, now Captain of the Queen's Flight. None of them, however, received an official pilot's certificate as did Prince Albert.

gone forth as boys four and a half years before. That which in 1914 had been designated the Governing Class had suffered appalling losses, and a crippling taxation precluded any possibility of a return to the standards of a pre-war way of life, even had that been considered desirable. Moreover, the authority of this class to govern was now for the first time being seriously challenged. Though Mr. Lloyd George's Coalition Government had been returned at the General Election of December 1918 with 526 out of 707 seats, a majority of 345, the official Opposition had passed into the hands of Labour, whose 59 members constituted the alternative Government. The Liberal Party, with its majestic past, which had formed the King's Government at the outbreak of the war with a membership in the House of Commons of 272, had suffered annihilation and had returned with a mere handful of 33 seats, their leader Mr. Asquith being himself defeated.[a]

The term 'Ideology' had come into use in the course of the war, its origins lying in the 'Wilsonism' of Washington and the 'Leninism' of Moscow, and its repercussions resounded throughout the post-war world. The Optimists truly believed that they had fought a 'war to end war' and 'to make the world safe for Democracy'. They spoke of a League of Nations, and of conserving for purposes of peace at home that spirit of common effort and sacrifice which had been engendered in war-time. The Realists aimed at the obviation of Germany's resurgence as an aggressive power. The Pessimists spoke gloomily of 'the next war' and the dangers of Bolshevism, and John Maynard Keynes cheerlessly foretold the economic consequences of the Peace.[b]

[a] Mr. Asquith's defeat at East Fife caused great distress to King George, who had always retained for his first Prime Minister feelings of particular esteem. 'I regret very much that Mr. Asquith has been defeated', he wrote to Prince Albert on December 31, 1918. 'It is very ungrateful after all he has done for his country.'

The other significant result of the 1918 Election was the virtual disappearance of the historic Irish Party of Redmond and Parnell, which was reduced from 84 to 7 seats, and the sweeping victory of Sinn Fein with 73 members, all of whom, however, refused to take their seats in the House of Commons.

[b] John Maynard, first Baron Keynes (1883–1946), resigned from the British Delegation to the Paris Peace Conference, on which he was the principal representative of the Treasury, in protest against its reparation policy. The publication of his book, *The Economic Consequences of the Peace*, in 1919, caused considerable dissension, but the prophecies contained therein were in great measure fulfilled before the Lausanne Conference of 1932 brought about a 'final' settlement of the reparation problem.

At home the Government's incautious policy of demobilizing the armies — a policy based on the principle of releasing first of all the 'key men' required by industry, who had been in effect the last to be called up — provoked grave resentment and disorders. There were riots in Glasgow and Belfast, and at Luton the town hall was burned down by an angry mob. The situation was only saved from becoming really serious by the courage and energy of Mr. Churchill at the War Office in producing a more equitable system of release, based on length of service and number of wounds.

There were other causes of discontent, apart from de-mobilization. The shortage of housing, the rise in the cost of living, the increase of unemployment; the dissatisfaction among munition workers, who had earned large wages during the war, at finding themselves dependent on the dole; and the resentment of the returning ex-soldiers against the munition workers who had stayed at home and made good money, all combined to render the early days of reconstruction a restless and hazardous era, in which the portents of greater danger were all too apparent.

For the ideology of Moscow was as potent in its attractions as that of Washington. Mr. Wilson's gospel of 'self-determination' aroused the nationalistic aspirations for independence amongst small peoples, but Lenin's wholesale use of the Marxist slogan, 'Workers of the World, Unite!' fell with a no-less-dulcet and alluring note on the ears of workers who had only now realized their strength and power. Moreover, the toppling of thrones in Central and Eastern Europe had not been without its impact further west, and, though the Belgian monarchy had been if anything strengthened by the stresses and adversities of war, in the Netherlands it required courage and resource on the part of Queen Wilhelmina and her ministers to counteract the activities of Troelstra and his republican movement.[a]

Against this background of unrest Prince Albert resumed civilian life. His generation had grown to manhood during

[a] Pieter Jelles Troelstra (1860–1930), a leader of the Dutch Social-Democratic Workmen's Party, was influenced by the German Revolution of November 1918 to arouse a revolution of the proletariat in the Netherlands. Though there was little genuine public support for his movement, there were moments of danger at which a less firm stand than that taken by the Queen and her Government might have turned the tide in his favour.

the war and had known death and danger at an age when normally their highest ambition might well have been to make a century at Lord's or to graduate with honours from the University. They came back now to resume the disrupted tenor of their lives.

In the case of Prince Albert the King decided that the time had come when he should begin to assume his part in public life. The Prince of Wales had many calls upon him, and, in any case, was about to embark upon his series of Empire tours, and his place in this country would have to be taken by his brother. At the same time King George was persuaded that there was much to be gained by Prince Albert and Prince Henry rounding off their formal education by reading for a few terms at Cambridge as members of Trinity College. Prince Albert was not unwilling to abandon his office routine in the Air Ministry, and to take up a new life which would prepare him for his future tasks. 'I am giving up a Service career now, and go to Cambridge in October for a year, to learn everything that will be useful for the time to come', he wrote to his old Dartmouth Term Officer in July 1919. 'My brother is so overwhelmed with work that I am going to help him with it now. It is really the best thing to do, now that there is so much going on in every way.'

The tradition that the sons of the Sovereign should attend a British university had been established by the Prince Consort as a part of that monumental scheme for the education of princes which he had devised for his eldest son. Between the years 1859 and 1862 King Edward VII as Prince of Wales attended — with the now defunct status of a 'nobleman' — no fewer than three Universities — Edinburgh, Oxford and Cambridge — under what one of the Prince Consort's biographers has described as 'a meticulous curriculum appropriate for one who aimed at spending his life in the amply billowing gown of a don, but quite unsuited for one destined by the gods to wear a crown rather than a mortar-board. Tutors, professors, scientists, historians, mathematicians and preachers — marionettes dancing to the manipulation of the Prince Consort — tortured the boy's intelligence like the morbid spectres in a nightmare provoked by a surfeit of plum-pudding.'[21]

While at Cambridge King Edward was a member of Trinity College, residing outside the College at Madingley Hall, and, despite the apparently indigestible intellectual pabulum which he himself had absorbed there, his eldest son the Duke of Clarence was admitted to the same College as a 'Pensioner' in the summer of 1883. King George V, under the influence of Mr. Hansell, himself a Magdalen man, sent the Prince of Wales to Magdalen College, Oxford. Now, however, Prince Albert resumed the family tradition at Trinity, Cambridge.

There were many other young naval officers up at the same time, for the Admiralty had sent some hundreds of them, whose education had been interrupted by the war, to various colleges at Cambridge. This experiment aroused considerable interest, and some scepticism, and Mr. Rudyard Kipling was moved to commemorate it :

Oh, show me how a rose can shut and be a bud again!
Nay, watch my Lords of the Admiralty, for they have the work in
        train.
They have taken the men that were careless lads at Dartmouth in
        'Fourteen
And entered them at the landward schools as though no war had
        been.
They have piped the children off all the seas from the Falklands to
        the Bight,
And quartered them on the Colleges to learn to read and write !

Their books were rain and sleet and fog — the dry gale and the
        snow,
Their teachers were the hornéd mines and the hump-backed
        Death below.
Their schools were walled by the walking mist and roofed by the
        waiting skies,
When they conned their task in a new-sown field with the Moon-
        light Sacrifice.
They were not rated too young to teach, nor reckoned unfit to guide
When they formed their class on Helles' beach at the bows of the
        'River Clyde'.

.   .   .   .

They know the price to be paid for a fault — for a gauge-clock
        wrongly read,
Or a picket-boat to the gangway brought bows-on and full-ahead.
Or the drowsy second's lack of thought that costs a dozen dead.

They have touched a knowledge outreaching speech — as when
  the cutters were sent
To harvest the dreadful mile of beach after the *Vanguard* went.
They have learnt great faith and little fear and a high heart in
  distress,
And how to suffer each sodden year of heaped-up weariness.

.   .   .   .   .

Soft — blow soft on them, little East Wind! Be smooth for them,
  mighty stream!
Though the cams they use are not of your kind, and they bump,
  for choice, by steam.
Lightly dance with them, Newnham maid — but none too lightly
  believe.
They are hot from the fifty-month blockade, and they carry their
  hearts on their sleeve.
Tenderly, Proctor, let them down, if they do not walk as they
  should,
For, by God, if they owe you half-a-crown, you owe 'em your four
  years' food!

Hallowed River, most gracious Trees, Chapel beyond compare,
Here be gentlemen tired of the seas — take them into your care.
Far have they come, much have they braved. Give them their hour
  of play,
While the hidden things their hands have saved work for them day
  by day:
Till the grateful Past their youth redeemed return them their
  youth once more,
And the Soul of the Child at last lets fall the unjust load that it
  bore![22]

The two Princes, together with Wing Commander Louis
Greig, now officially attached to Prince Albert as equerry, and
Mrs. Greig, came up to Cambridge in mid-October. The
King had leased 'Southacre' for them, a small and exceedingly
ugly but comfortable house with a pleasant garden, off the
Trumpington Road, about a mile from Trinity, and they made
the journey to and from the College on bicycles. Their official
mentor was Mr. R. V. Laurence, the Senior Tutor of the
College,[a] with whose pungent humour and remarkable personality they were deeply impressed, assisted by two of the
younger dons, Mr. J. R. M. Butler, son of the great Master of

[a] Reginald Vere Laurence, C.V.O., M.A. (1876–1934), Fellow and Senior
Tutor of Trinity College, and University Lecturer in History.

Trinity,[a] and Mr. D. H. Robertson,[b] both men of great charm
and ability.

Whereas Mr. Gladstone had remarked of King Edward
VII that he knew everything except what was in books; and
Sir Herbert Warren, President of Magdalen, Oxford, had pronounced a similar judgment on the Prince of Wales : 'Bookish
he will never be',[23] Prince Albert and Prince Henry soon
impressed those who taught them with their anxiety to get
the greatest advantage possible out of their university studies.
They displayed shrewdness as well as keenness, and, though
the methods of teaching were unfamiliar to them, they started
at once to apply their wits in the way suggested to them, with
encouraging results. Their freshness and willingness to learn
made for a very pleasant relationship between tutor and pupil,
and all who came into contact with them, old or young, were
delighted with their naturalness and friendliness.

There were two points, however, on which those charged
with their instruction were concerned — the briefness of their
intended period of study at Cambridge and the fact that they
were missing something of the fullness of University life by not
living in College. 'It will be a great pity, from the point of
view of their education, if their time here is cut any shorter
than is absolutely necessary, though of course I realize what
important other demands there must be on their future',
Mr. Butler wrote to Lord Stamfordham. 'One year, and still
more a fraction of a year, seems a very short time to get the
full advantage of the place.' The King was prepared to let
Prince Henry remain at Cambridge until the summer of 1920,
but in the case of his second son he was reluctant to agree,
moie particularly without discussing the matter with him;
but in the end he too spent the full year at the University.

In the matter of residence, however, the King was adamant.
Both Mr. Butler and Mr. Robertson were of the opinion that :

The Princes would gain educationally if it were possible for
them to live in College. They would certainly see more of men of

---

[a] Sir James Ramsay Montagu Butler, M.V.O., O.B.E., M.A. (b. 1889), Vice-
Master of Trinity College and Chief Historian of the Official Military Histories
of the Second World War, was Regius Professor of Modern History at Cambridge
from 1947 to 1954.

[b] Sir Dennis Holme Robertson, C.M.G., M.A., F.B.A. (b. 1890), a Fellow of
Trinity College and Professor of Political Economy in the University of Cambridge
from 1944 until 1957.

their own age and so would get more of that mixing with other minds with similar interests which is a very important part of the university system of education . . . as a matter of fact, there are a large number of undergraduates who have held commissions *a* — some quite senior commissions — so that Prince Albert's case, and still less Prince Henry's, would not be at all exceptional.[24]

This matter had already been under discussion and, as Lord Stamfordham had told Mr. Butler, King George somewhat unexpectedly desired his sons to have a greater degree of freedom than was, as he thought, permitted to those who resided in College. He therefore remained as impervious to Mr. Butler's reasoning as, for quite different considerations, he had been obdurate in the face of Mr. Hansell's arguments in favour of sending Prince Edward and Prince Albert to a preparatory school instead of educating them at home.[b]

Though the King realizes the obvious advantages to be gained by residence in College [wrote Lord Stamfordham to Mr. Butler on November 27] he feels that both Princes, having already passed through the disciplinary period *in statu pupillari*, it would be hardly fair to ask them again to give up just that little extra freedom which is enjoyed by living outside walls and gates! At the same time His Majesty hopes that both Princes will take every possible opportunity of making friends and mixing with the other Undergraduates and profiting by those advantages which you so rightly claim to residence in College.

Whether the Princes did in fact enjoy greater freedom by living out of College may be questioned; it can hardly be doubted that, in spite of the hospitality always shown at 'Southacre', they would have seen more of their contemporaries, and made friends more easily, if they had 'kept' in College rooms. It is significant of this that few, if any, of Prince Albert's friendships in after-life dated from his days at Cambridge.

There were, however, other advantages to be gained from residence at 'Southacre', for it was at this period of his life, more, perhaps, than at any other in their happy relationship, that Prince Albert derived the greatest benefit from his association with Wing Commander Louis Greig. Maturing late in life, the Prince at twenty-four had carried into manhood

---

a Among these was Prince Albert's cousin, Lieutenant Lord Louis Mountbatten, who was in residence at Christ's College.

b See above, p. 24.

certain of those traits which more often disappear at an earlier age. He was still prone to depression in the face of minor difficulties, though he had learned to confront major problems, as, for instance, those of his health and speech, with a fine courage. In the sports in which he was proficient, such as golf and tennis, he was easily discouraged by defeat or by his own poor performance on an 'off day', even to the extent of abandoning the match; and he had difficulty in controlling his temper. With infinite patience and sometimes brutal frankness, yet in the true spirit of friendship, Louis Greig set himself to help Prince Albert to overcome these weaknesses, to take a beating without lowering the standard of his sportsmanship and generally to learn the lesson of Rudyard Kipling's hackneyed but nevertheless essential verity, that in meeting triumph and disaster one must 'treat those two impostors just the same'.

'My principal contribution was to put steel into him', Louis Greig once said of Prince Albert at this period of his life. It was a contribution of inestimable and lasting value, and it evoked a warm response. For, though in later years there were circumstances in which the iron might have entered into his soul, the steel was always there to meet it, and his own great inner courage overcame the threatening spectres of despair.

Prince Albert's studies at Cambridge embraced history, economics and civics, but what particularly interested him was the development of the Constitution. This he learned from Dicey's solid and uncompromising *Law of the Constitution*, relieved by the brilliant and scintillating pages of Walter Bagehot. The instruction was not all unilateral, moreover. The Prince offered a variety of new impressions about our Constitutional history, and his description of an interview between Queen Victoria and Sir William Harcourt is still remembered vividly by one of his supervisors.

Though unfortunately he did not leave on record, as his father had done,[a] the fruit of his reading in Bagehot's fascinating work, *The English Constitution*, many of the author's

---

[a] Sir Harold Nicolson, in his biography of King George V (p. 62), quotes the text of a memorandum written by the King in 1894, when Duke of York, after his study of Bagehot's *Constitution* with Mr. Tanner.

apophthegms must have remained in Prince Albert's mind and recurred to him in later years. 'Royalty is a government in which the attention of the nation is concentrated on one person doing interesting actions', wrote Bagehot, 'Royalty will be strong because it appeals to diffused feeling',[25] but he adds, of monarchy: 'Its mystery is its life. We must not bring in the daylight upon magic.'[26] On the domestic side of monarchy he was also illuminating. 'A *family* on the throne is an interesting idea also. It brings down the pride of sovereignty to the level of petty life. . . . A princely marriage is the brilliant edition of a universal fact, and as such it rivets mankind . . . a Royal Family sweetens politics by the seasonable addition of nice and pretty events. It introduces irrelevant facts into the business of government but they are facts which speak to "men's bosoms" and employ their thoughts.'[27]

Mr. Bagehot was also admonitory. 'We have come to regard the Crown as the head of our *morality*', he wrote. 'We have come to believe that it is natural to have a virtuous sovereign, and that domestic virtues are as likely to be found on thrones as they are eminent when there.'[28]

To all Bagehot's principles of Monarchy — its necessary dignity, its social value and its essential morality — Prince Albert dedicated himself with a solemn rectitude and an upright probity. He believed, as did his father, that the Crown must of necessity represent all that was most straightforward in the national character, that the Sovereign must set an example to his people of devotion to duty and service to the State, and that, in relation to his Ministers, he must closely adhere to — and never abandon — the three inalienable rights of the King in a constitutional monarchy : the right to be consulted, the right to encourage and the right to warn.

In their lighter moments Prince Albert and his brother enjoyed to the full the various pleasures of Cambridge life. They tore about the country on motor-bicycles; they punted on the Backs; they took their morning draught at the Hawks Club; they entertained generously at 'Southacre', where once again, as at the cottage at Rauceby in his Cranwell days, Prince Albert delighted in the happy domestic life with the Greigs and their children. He was duly 'progged' and relieved of the sum of 6s. 8d. for smoking in academic dress —

'I was made to regard the cigarette which I was then smoking as one of the most expensive I have ever sampled', he later told the Union *a* — and found generally 'in the atmosphere of Cambridge and in the particular environment of Trinity a steadying and mellowing influence'.*b* When he went down in 1920 at the end of the Easter Term it was with genuine regret. 'I am very sorry at leaving after the splendid time I have had', he wrote to Mr. Butler. His first loyalty may well still have been to the River Dart, but a part at least of his affections remained on the banks of the Cam. He revisited the University, both as Duke of York and as King, and never failed to proclaim his pride at being a Cambridge man.

Prince Albert's period of residence as an undergraduate was not one uninterrupted round of academic work and pleasure. The claims of his public duty often impinged upon his University life, summoning him to London and elsewhere as his father's representative, and of the disadvantages of this he was well aware. Scarcely had the Michaelmas Term of 1919 begun — the Prince's first term at Cambridge — when he was called to London on October 24 to become a member of the Worshipful Company of Drapers and to receive, four days later, the Freedom of the City of London. On October 30 he went to Dover, as the King's representative, to greet the Shah of Persia, Sultan Ahmed, the last of the Kajar dynasty,*c* whom he accompanied in the royal train to Victoria station, where they were welcomed by the King in person. Prince Albert was the constant companion of the imperial visitor throughout the greater part of his State visit, taking him round the City of London, acting as his guide in a tour of Windsor Castle, sitting next to him at the Covent Garden Ballet and at the Guildhall Banquet, and even accompanying him to receive a deputation of Parsees at the Persian Embassy. He

a This was on the occasion of the Centenary of the Cambridge Union on November 15, 1921, when he returned as Duke of York to take part in the Society's celebrations. 'Prince Albert did not speak easily in those days, at any rate in public', wrote Professor Butler years later, 'and the courage with which he persisted in finishing his speech on what he called the most frightening occasion of his life was notable.'[29]

b This statement was made on June 3, 1947, when King George VI and Queen Elizabeth attended the celebrations of the fourth centenary of Trinity College, and the King proposed its health.

c The Kajar dynasty ruled Persia from 1794 to 1925, when Sultan Ahmed was deposed by the founder of the present Pahlevi dynasty, General Reza Khan.

was, moreover, the agonized witness — agonized by reason of barely restrained mirth — of the Padishah, a man of considerable rotundity, first tripping and then rolling down the great staircase of Lord Curzon's house in Carlton House Terrace during a party given by the Foreign Secretary for His Imperial Majesty.[30] Throughout this somewhat exacting programme Prince Albert kept up a fluent conversation with the young Shah in French, and on more than one occasion was observed to have won a smile and a laugh from that usually enigmatic monarch. Scarcely had he returned to Cambridge when he had to go through the same routine again, this time greeting the President of the French Republic and Madame Poincaré on their arrival from France on November 11.

Now, too, his speaking engagements began to multiply. In the course of his time as an undergraduate he attended a score or more of public functions in various parts of the country, each of which entailed making a speech. This was always an ordeal, for his stammer still troubled him. The specialist under whom he had worked on his return from France had produced only disappointing results, but another had been found, an Italian professor, who seemed to be more successful.

Prince Albert persevered doggedly both with his treatment and with his speeches. He had early discovered that he could talk more easily impromptu than from a written text, and, while this was rarely possible, he did so whenever he could. It was particularly successful when he was called upon during his first term at Cambridge to speak at the official luncheon to the recipients of honorary degrees from the University. This was a difficult task for any young man to perform, for, in addition to the fact that those honoured were among the great commanders of the war, under some of whom the Prince had served as a very junior officer,[a] there was also present that accomplished and silver-tongued orator, Mr. Arthur Balfour, who had that morning been installed as the new Chancellor of the University. The Prince chose to speak extemporarily, and with excellent effect. 'I don't know if Greig told you that at

---

[a] Those honoured with degrees at Cambridge on November 27, 1919, were : Admiral of the Fleet Sir Henry Jackson, Admiral Sir Charles Madden, Rear-Admiral Sir Roger Keyes, General Sir William Robertson, General Lord Byng of Vimy, Air Marshal Sir Hugh Trenchard and Air Vice-Marshal Sir John Salmond.

the luncheon to the "recipients of honorary degrees" on Thursday Prince Albert for the first time discarded the written draft of his speech and spoke in his own words', Mr. Butler reported to Lord Stamfordham. 'I was not at the luncheon, but the speech seems to have pleased people very much.'[31] Nor was this the only commendatory report that the King received. 'Trenchard told me what a good speech you made at the R.A.F. dinner the other night', he wrote to his son, '& that you only hesitated once, which shows that yr. Italian friend is doing you good which is a great thing, if you could only stick to it & persevere now, he will very likely cure you entirely. . . .'[32]

But his public appearances were occasions of pain and grief to Prince Albert. He dreaded them as one dreads a visit to the dentist, and their approach filled him with foreboding. 'I am longing to get the Academy Dinner over and that dreadful speech', he wrote to Queen Mary from 'Southacre'. 'I hope it will go off all right, though it is something of an ordeal to go through.'[33]

King George had watched with close attention the development of his second son. He was pleased with what he had seen. He was satisfied that Prince Albert had made the most of his months of study at Cambridge. He believed that he was making an effort to overcome his speech defect and that, in spite of his difficulties, he was taking his place as a King's son in the public life of the country. He was beginning to appreciate the fact that the Prince's character needed the stimulus of encouragement and understanding to call forth the best that lay within. The Birthday Honours List of June 3, 1920, included the following announcement:

The KING has been pleased to direct Letters Patent to be passed under the Great Seal of the United Kingdom of Great Britain and Ireland, to bear this day's date, granting unto His Majesty's Son, His Royal Highness Prince Albert Frederick Arthur George, K.G., and the heirs male of his body lawfully begotten, the dignities of Baron Killarney, Earl of Inverness and Duke of York.[34]

PART II

DUKE OF YORK
1920–1936

THE DUKE OF YORK, BY JOHN SARGENT, APRIL 1923

CHAPTER I

ENGAGEMENT AND MARRIAGE
1920–1923

(i)

WHEN in 1890 the Prince of Wales desired that the title of Duke of York should be conferred upon his eldest son, Prince Eddy, Queen Victoria demurred in no uncertain manner. To the Queen this title, ancient and traditional though it was in the Royal Family of Britain, was too recently associated with her Hanoverian uncles to commend its revival. She expressed a preference for the titles of Duke of Rothesay or Earl of Chester as dignities for her grandson, but agreed to compromise on his being created Duke of Clarence.[1]

Two years later, however — the tragic death of Prince Eddy having occurred on January 12, 1892 — the issue was reopened in the case of Prince George, and again the Prince of Wales desired the title of Duke of York for his heir. This time the Royal Matriarch assented, albeit with a rather bad grace, and in the Birthday Honours of May 24, 1892, Prince George became the first Duke of York since that grand old holder of the title 'who had ten thousand men'.[a] He also received the dignities of Earl of Inverness and Baron Killarney. 'I am glad you like the title of Duke of York', the Queen wrote to her grandson, 'I am afraid I do not and wish you had remained as you are. A Prince *no one* else can be, whereas a Duke any nobleman can be, and many are! I am not very

---

[a] Frederick, Duke of York (1763–1827), the second son of George III, followed a military career with varying success. His operations against the French in the early years of the Revolutionary Wars were largely unsuccessful owing in great measure to disheartening and impossible conditions. He was Commander-in-Chief of the British Army from 1798 until his death in 1827, with the exception of a brief interval from 1809 to 1811, and though no military genius, he was, in the opinion of the historian of the Army, Sir John Fortescue, from the point of view of administration the best Commander-in-Chief the British Army has ever had.

fond of that of York which has not very agreeable associations.'²

Twenty-eight years later King George V, with no such hesitation, conferred these titles upon his second son. 'I made Bertie Duke of York, Earl of Inverness and Baron Killarney to-day, the same titles that I had', he wrote in his diary on June 5, 1920. 'A pleasure to us all', Queen Mary recorded on the same evening.

Prince Albert received the news at Cambridge and was deeply touched by this additional mark of the King's approbation. 'I must write and thank you again ever so very much for having made me Duke of York. I am very proud to bear the name that you did for many years, and I hope I shall live up to it in every way', he wrote to his father,³ and the King's reply must have warmed his son's heart.

DEAREST BERTIE,
I was delighted to get your letter this morning, & to know that you appreciate that I have given you that fine old title of Duke of York which I bore for more than 9 years & is the oldest Dukedom in this country. I know that you have behaved very well, in a difficult situation for a young man & that you have done what I asked you to do. I feel that this splendid old title will be safe in your hands & that you will never do anything which could in any way tarnish it. I hope you will always look upon me as yr. best friend & always tell me everything & you will find me ever ready to help you & give you good advice.
Looking forward to seeing you to-morrow
Ever my dear boy
                                                Yr. very devoted Papa
                                                          G. R. I.⁴

It was never easy for King George to express the genuine affection which he felt for his children, nor for his children to appreciate its depth and sincerity. A martinet by nature, and one who held tenaciously to the standards and conventions of his upbringing, the King found it difficult — well-nigh impossible — to adjust himself to that new world, with its strangely altered criteria, which had emerged from the First World War. To a very great degree, the younger generation to which his children belonged remained to the end an insoluble enigma to him, but he discerned in Prince Albert those basic qualities of character which he himself possessed in such full measure and which struck the chords of his recognition and respect.

The new Duke of York also derived much pleasure and gratification from the obvious satisfaction with which his new honour was received in all quarters. 'I want mine to be one of the first letters of congratulation that you receive', wrote the Prime Minister's Secretary, Mr. Philip Kerr,[a] from 10 Downing Street on the eve of the publication of the Honours List. 'This new honour which you are to receive will give pleasure to *all* your friends & nothing has ever been more richly deserved. . . . I hope your life will run on easy lines & that you will have all the happiness & success that the world can offer.' And Campbell Tait, his old friend and turret-commander in *Collingwood*, now appointed to *Victoria and Albert*, wrote : 'I am sending you a white rose, your new emblem, just for luck! We've got a house over in Alverstoke now, quite out in the country, and the flower came out of the garden. I brought it on board this morning for my cabin, but it just struck me that it would be nice to send it to you with my best wishes and congratulations. I remember that more than once you talked to me and wondered whether you would be York or Clarence or Gloucester or one of the others. Well, at any rate York is the most distinguished to judge by the encyclo-paedia I have consulted — whole paragraphs more than any of the others — and it is now up to you to add appreciably to those paragraphs ! I know you can do it.'

The Duke took his seat in the House of Lords on June 23, his supporters being the Duke of Connaught, who had per-formed the same office for King George more than a quarter of a century before, and the Duke of Northumberland. He was very nervous, and, as he advanced to the Woolsack to be received by the Lord Chancellor, he was almost tottering. But Lord Birkenhead saved the situation. As he bent forward to take the new peer's hands between his own, he whispered,

---

[a] Rt. Hon. Philip Henry Kerr, eleventh Marquess of Lothian, K.T., C.H. (1882–1940), having been one of Lord Milner's 'Kindergarten' in South Africa, returned to London to become the first editor of the *Round Table*. He served Mr. Lloyd George as Private Secretary from 1916 to 1921, and joined Mr. Ramsay MacDonald's National Government first as Chancellor of the Duchy of Lancaster and later as Parliamentary Under-Secretary for India. He was Secretary of the Rhodes Trust from 1925 to 1939. Shortly before the outbreak of the Second World War he was somewhat unexpectedly appointed British Ambassador in Washington, where he died suddenly in December 1940, at the height of a spectacularly brilliant diplomatic career.

'Been playing much tennis lately, Sir?' and the Duke's composure was completely restored.

Tennis was indeed very much in the Duke's mind at that moment, for, with Louis Greig, he had entered the R.A.F. Doubles Competition and, somewhat to their surprise, they found themselves first in the semi-final and then, on July 8, in the final; this, to their enormous satisfaction, they won after a hard-fought match. In addition, they met in the semi-finals of the Singles, which the Duke lost to Dr. Greig. King George, who with the Queen was on a visit to Edinburgh, telegraphed his congratulations and the Duke of York replied on July 9:

MY DEAREST PAPA,

Very many thanks for your telegram which I received last night. We are both very pleased at having won the Air Force Cup for the Doubles. Our hardest match was the semi-final as we lost the 1st set and after winning the 2nd set easily we only just won the 3rd, after our opponents were 4-1 in games.

I was very surprised to get through the 3 rounds of the Singles into the Semi-Finals. The 1st round was a walk over as my opponent scratched.

The 2nd & 3rd rounds were all very long matches, & I lost the 1st set in each, but won the last 2 sets.

Greig defeated me easily in the semi-final, which I knew he was sure to do. Greig scratched in the final of the singles as he had played 4 matches in the day and was very tired. As it was, in the doubles we both nearly collapsed from fatigue. I don't think I have ever played so well in my life, and I did not lose my head at the critical moment which was very lucky.

I am afraid the weather has somewhat spoilt your visit to Edinburgh, but I see that you have not had to upset any of your arrangements. I hope you have heard from David about his railway accident, which might have been serious, but he seems to be quite all right and none the worse for it.[a]

Best love to you, Mama and Mary

I remain   Ever

Your very devoted son

BERTIE.

---

[a] The Prince of Wales was at this time touring Western Australia, and his train was derailed on a sharp curve where the track had been weakened by heavy rains. The Prince's coach and one other toppled over the embankment and arrived upside down at the bottom. As the Prince and his Chief of Staff, Admiral Sir Lionel Halsey, extricated themselves unhurt from the wreckage, they heard

Perhaps the most satisfactory aspect of the whole episode was that it gave to the general public the clinching evidence that the Duke had not only recovered his health but was in a state of fitness which enabled him to undergo a gruelling physical ordeal.

He had need of all his physical stamina for, in addition to his own heavy programme of visits and speeches in the country, King George was delegating to him more and more official duties. On July 20, 1920, for the first time he held an investiture at Buckingham Palace in place of his father, who was attending the funeral of the Empress Eugénie; and thereafter there were similar occasions, giving the Duke increasing experience and confidence. In the following February the King sent him to Brussels to present the Distinguished Flying Cross to King Albert, and to confer decorations on Burgomaster Max and other Belgian subjects in recognition of their war services to Britain. It was his first experience of a State visit, and he acquitted himself very creditably. 'I cannot conclude this long letter', wrote the British Ambassador to Lord Stamfordham, 'without telling you how well the Duke of York played his part here. He talked in the most pleasant way to the Belgians whom I had the honour of introducing to him, and many of them told me afterwards how pleased they had been to have had the opportunity of meeting His Royal Highness.'[5]

The year 1922 brought the Duke into direct contact with Balkan Royalty and Balkan politics. Queen Marie of Rumania had invited King George to be the chief sponsor, or 'Koom', at the wedding of her daughter to the King of the Serbs, Croats and Slovenes, and to send one of his sons to represent him at the ceremony in Belgrade. The invitation must have awakened many sad and difficult memories. It had been traditional in the past for this office to be held at the marriages of the Kings of Serbia by the Tsar of Russia; but now there was no longer a Tsar, and King George's affection for his ill-

cries of protest and alarm coming from one who had been apparently trapped in the up-ended toilet, and recognized the voice of a member of the local State Legislature at whose hands they had suffered many things in the past few days. The Prince records that on this occasion Admiral Halsey growled: 'If I had planned to square accounts with the old blighter, I could not have done it better myself' (Duke of Windsor, *A King's Story*, p. 160).

fated cousin Nicholas was well known. Indeed the last occasion
on which Nicholas II had been 'Koom' to a King of Serbia
had been followed by a tragedy second in horror only to his
own murder.

It had been in the summer of 1900 at the marriage of
King Alexander Obrenović, the last of that tragic dynasty,
to his mistress Draga Mashin. Three years later, on the
night of June 11, 1903, the King and his consort were butchered
and defenestrated by military assassins in the royal palace of
Belgrade, under particularly brutal circumstances; while in
the city the Prime Minister, General Tsinsar-Marković, and
his Minister of War, and also the Queen's two brothers, were
murdered by members of the same conspiracy.[a]

A spasm of horror convulsed a world as yet uncalloused
by the wholesale atrocities of the Bolshevik and Nazi régimes.
As 'Freedom shrieked when Kosciusko fell', so Europe recoiled,
shocked and revolted, from the picture of those naked and
mutilated corpses lying deserted in the rain at the breaking
of a summer day, on the lawn of the royal palace. In press
and pulpit and parliament a storm of protest broke, and King
Edward VII expressed his own indignation by taking the
initiative in withdrawing his Minister from Belgrade, an
example which was followed by virtually every other European
court and government.

Nor was King Edward's anger easily appeased. Though
it was clearly established that the new ruler of Serbia, King
Peter, a member of the rival dynasty of Karageorgević, whom
the conspirators had summoned from his exile in Geneva to
fill the vacant throne, was completely innocent of any com-
plicity in the crime, he did not — or could not — at once free
himself from associations with those who were, by their affinities
or actions, thus implicated;[b] and King Edward made this
factor the touchstone of his attitude. When in 1905 the Tsar
and the King of Italy [c] joined in urging the resumption of

[a] Miss Rebecca West has written a vivid and terrible account of these events
in the first volume of her book, *Black Lamb and Grey Falcon* (i, pp. 575-582).

[b] One of King Peter's earliest acts on ascending the throne, however, was to
remove the ban on foreign newspapers so that the full tide of the world's condemnation swept into Belgrade. 'Serbia', he said, 'shall henceforth know what
other countries think of it' (West, *op. cit.* i, p. 589).

[c] King Victor Emmanuel III of Italy and King Peter I of Serbia had both
married daughters of King Nicholas of Montenegro.

diplomatic relations with Serbia, King Edward informed their ambassadors that neither he nor his Government could consider such a step until the last of the regicides had been banished from King Peter's entourage.[6] 'And, besides this reason,' he added, 'I have another, and so to say, a personal reason. *Mon métier à moi est d'être Roi.* King Alexander was also by his métier "un Roi". As you see, we belonged to the same guild, as labourers or professional men. I cannot be indifferent to the assassination of a member of my profession, or, if you like, a member of my guild. We should be obliged to shut up our businesses if we, the Kings, were to consider the assassinations of kings as of no consequence at all. I regret, but you see that I cannot do what you wish me to do.'[7]

The ambassadors retired rebuffed, and the King remained adamant. It was not until June 1906, three years after the murder, when the last of the regicides had been placed on the retired list, that a British Minister again presented his credentials at Belgrade.

Much had happened between 1906 and 1922. The guild of the Kings had suffered sorely under the impact of war and revolution. Its international significance was no longer as great as it had been in King Edward's day, but the need for solidarity was no less great. The House of Karageorgević had given good government to its country, and Serbia had proved herself a steadfast and loyal ally of Britain in the First World War. And thus it came about, by the ironies of time and history, that the son of King Peter — another Alexander, himself fated to die by the assassin's bullet — was betrothed to a great-niece of King Edward,[a] and that King Edward's son was to stand as 'Koom'.

For King George, after consultation with the Foreign Office, accepted the invitation of Queen Marie of Rumania, and sent the Duke of York to deputize for him at the marriage, on June 9, 1922. As representative of the 'Koom', the principal figure in the ceremony after the bridal couple, he was received in great state and rode in the procession immediately before the bridegroom's carriage. The Serbian royal stables had

[a] Princess Marie of Rumania, who married King Alexander, was the daughter of Queen Marie, the eldest daughter of Queen Victoria's second son, Prince Alfred, Duke of Edinburgh, and the Grand Duchess Marie Alexandrovna of Russia.

recently been replenished with a number of fine Irish horses, all well trained with the exception of that assigned to the Duke. That animal was excessively restive and the onlookers were impressed and delighted with the Duke's excellent horsemanship, which not only permitted him to keep his mount under restraint but also to acknowledge with apparent gaiety the enthusiastic cheers of the crowds who thronged the route. His next most popular act was to scatter handfuls of silver coins amid the throngs of children in answer to the traditional cry: 'O Koom, your purse is burning'. During the complicated and exhausting marriage ritual of the Orthodox Church the Duke of York bore his part with dignity, and left behind him in Belgrade a reputation which could scarcely have been enhanced.

He did his part beautifully & his presence was most popular in Serbia [wrote Queen Marie of Rumania to King George]. Everyone much appreciated that you sent one of your sons and were awfully pleased. . . . Somehow your boy in some ways reminded me so much of you, though he has exactly May's smile, but his movements were yours and his hands. . . .[8]

Four months later he was back in the Balkans, this time as King George's representative at the coronation of King Ferdinand and Queen Marie of Rumania at Alba Julia on October 16.[a] Here, again, he created a wholly admirable impression, and reports of his prowess were forwarded to London. 'The Duke's soldier-like appearance, his bearing, his good looks, and horsemanship during the procession through the entire town [of Bucharest], as well as in the parade at Alba Julia, were all the subject of many flattering observations', wrote the British Minister to Lord Stamfordham. 'Among the officials too, both of the Court and of Government, I have had personal occasion to hear nothing but the most sympathetic comment. . . . M. Duca [Foreign Minister] was especially

---

[a] King Ferdinand had succeeded his uncle, King Carol I, on the Rumanian throne in 1915. In the following year Rumania entered the war on the side of the Allies, but was defeated by the German armies. As a result, however, of the Peace Settlement of 1919, she received large tracts of former Austro-Hungarian territory, including Transylvania, the Banat and Bukovina, and, by a special agreement between the Powers, the Russian province of Bessarabia. It was in celebration of this Greater Rumania, much of which was subsequently lost to Hungary and Russia, that the coronation ceremonies of 1922 were held.

At Balmoral, 1927

(Photograph taken by King Boris of Bulgaria)

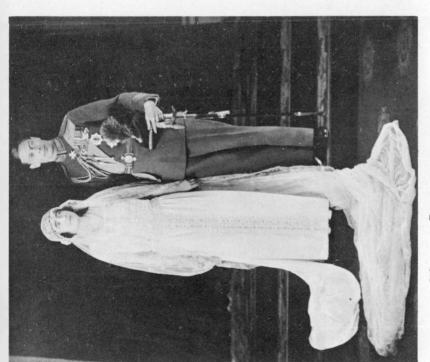

Wedding Photograph of the
Duke and Duchess of York, April 1923

impressed, and said that the Duke was by far the most popular of the Royal Representatives who had come on this occasion. . . . I hope you will be good enough to tell His Majesty that in my long experience of such ceremonies I have never experienced greater pride in recognizing the suitability, and complete popularity, of my country's Special Representative.' [9]

Whether King George dismissed this praise as unduly fulsome or whether he merely failed to recognize his son's capabilities in undertaking these missions abroad, is not entirely clear ; but it is evident that he was not wholly appreciative of the Duke's achievement, even in face of the corroborative evidence of Colonel Ronald Waterhouse [a] and Admiral Sir Henry Campbell, [b] who had accompanied him. This fact was clearly recognized by Lord Stamfordham who, in a letter to Queen Mary, took occasion to redress the balance of injustice :

I venture to trouble Your Majesty with this letter [he wrote] in case you may not quite realise what an unqualified success the Duke of York was in Rumania.

I happened to be in the King's room when His Majesty was talking on this subject to Your Majesty. *I* had been talking to Colonel Waterhouse — by no means a 'gusher' — and I felt that His Majesty's praise was quite inadequate. For Colonel Waterhouse said he could not exaggerate how admirably in every way His Royal Highness had done — and that when once he got away 'on his own' he was a different being and never failing to 'rise to the occasion', and proved himself to be far away the most important of the foreign visitors at the Coronation. [10]

It was not always easy for the sons of King George V to please their father.

(ii)

On coming down from the University the Duke of York found himself a very busy young man. Besides the normal routine duties of a member of the Royal Family, and his State visits

[a] Lieut.-Colonel Sir Ronald Waterhouse, K.C.B., C.M.G., C.V.O. (1878–1942), a soldier and civil servant of wide experience, was Private Secretary and Equerry to the Duke of York in 1921, but left his service a year later to become Principal Private Secretary to the Prime Minister, a position which he held until 1928, serving successively Mr. Bonar Law, Mr. Stanley Baldwin and Mr. Ramsay MacDonald.

[b] Admiral Sir Henry Hervey Campbell, K.C.V.O., C.B. (1865–1933), had been the first Governor to the Prince of Wales whilst serving in H.M.S. *Hindoustan* in 1911.

abroad, he was engaged with the work of the Industrial Welfare Society, which took him on tours and visits throughout the country; and later he had the absorbing interest of his Duke of York's Camp. In his spare time he hunted with the Pytchley and a number of other packs, proving himself an admirable rider to hounds and, indeed, the best horseman in his family. At Sandringham and Balmoral he gave evidence of becoming an outstandingly good shot with gun and rifle. In addition, he was a frequent figure at the small private dances which were given in London during the early post-war years.

It was a full and useful existence that the Duke was leading; but in the midst of it all he had a sense of loneliness, of a lack of understanding and appreciation, of affection never returned in full measure. Buckingham Palace was still 'home' to him, and all that that implied, but the parental supervision was still irksome and his comings and goings were often the subject of comment and inquiry.

Moreover he was in love; and what the Victorian lady-novelists would have called 'the object of his affections' was the Lady Elizabeth Bowes-Lyon. They had first met in 1905 at a children's party at Montague House, when, it is said, she gave him the crystallized cherries off her sugar cake; but they did not meet again until the summer of 1920 at a small dance given by Lord Farquhar. The Duke paid a visit to Glamis Castle from Balmoral that autumn, but it was not until a year later, when he stayed there a second time, that he gave any indication of his affections. Then: 'It is delightful here & Elizabeth is very kind to me', he wrote to Queen Mary. 'The more I see of her the more I like her.' Thereafter there was frequent mention of her in his letters to the Queen.

Lady Elizabeth Bowes-Lyon was the youngest but one of the ten children of the fourteenth Earl of Strathmore,[a] who

[a] The children of Lord and Lady Strathmore were as follows: (1) Violet Hyacinth, 1882–1893; (2) Mary Frances, b. 1883, married sixteenth Baron Elphinstone; (3) Patrick, fifteenth Earl, 1884–1949, married Lady Dorothy Godolphin Osborne; (4) John Herbert, 1886–1930, married Fenella Hepburn-Stuart-Forbes-Trefusis; (5) Alexander Francis, 1887–1911; (6) Fergus, 1889–1915, married Lady Christian Norah Dawson-Damer, killed in action; (7) Rose Constance, b. 1890, married fourth Earl of Granville; (8) Michael Claude Hamilton, 1893–1954, married Elizabeth Margaret Cator; (9) Elizabeth Angela Marguerite, b. 1900, married the Duke of York; (10) David, b. 1902, married Rachel Pauline Spender-Clay.

had married Miss Nina Cecilia Cavendish-Bentinck, a first cousin of the sixth Duke of Portland. She was born on August 4, 1900, at St. Paul's Walden Bury in Hertfordshire. So wide a gap divided her and her younger brother David from the rest of the family, that Lady Strathmore used to call them her 'two Benjamins', and would say that they would be mistaken for her grandchildren.

But though widely separated in age, the Bowes-Lyon children were a very united and loving family, deriving much from the affection of their parents and particularly from the talents and qualities of their mother. For Lady Strathmore was one of those fortunate and gifted persons who excel in whatever field of activity they adopt, and not only did she herself give to her two youngest children the rudimentary foundations of their formal education, but also their early instruction in drawing, painting, music and dancing. It was from her that her daughter inherited much of her capacity for human understanding, as well as her vitality of spirit and variety of interest, and in addition the exquisite complexion of the Cavendish-Bentincks. It was also to her mother that Lady Elizabeth owed that serenity of soul which in later life was to prove so great a source of comfort both to herself and to her husband.

Lady Elizabeth's early childhood was divided between the thousand-year-old castle of Glamis, with its historic memories and its tales of ghosts stretching from Macbeth and Malcolm II to Prince Charles Edward and Claverhouse, and the Queen Anne beauty and elegance of St. Paul's Walden Bury, with the peace of its garden, its pleached alleys and its long green vistas between clipped beech hedges. Both places were redolent of the happiness of home and family, and if the two youngest children were too small to join in the sports and games of their elders, they were never allowed to feel left out of the circle.

Because of the war years, during which Glamis became a convalescent hospital and Lady Elizabeth was engaged in doing her young best to assist her mother and sisters in entertaining the patients, she did not come south until the first mad post-war seasons, but when she did come she took London by storm. Not only was she quickly voted the best dancer in any London ballroom, but her charm and grace, her beauty both of face and spirit, brought her a host of admirers. She became a close friend of Princess Mary, and when King George's daughter was married to Lord Lascelles in 1922 Lady Elizabeth Bowes-Lyon was one of her bridesmaids.

The Duke of York's enjoyment of his visits to Glamis and St. Paul's Walden Bury can be readily understood. The relations of Lord and Lady Strathmore with their children and the happy badinage and affection of a large and closely knit family were a revelation to him, providing a climate of ideas to which he instantly responded, and in which his own personality throve and blossomed. He was deeply in love and was delighted to find that both the King and Queen warmly favoured his idea of marriage with Lady Elizabeth. 'You'll be a lucky fellow if she accepts you', said King George.

But Lady Elizabeth entertained a very natural reluctance to abandon the unfettered liberty of a great noble's family for the restricted freedom of membership of the Royal circle, where every action was public property, every step must be watched, every word guarded. There were uncertainties and delays and, although the Duke pressed his suit with dogged pertinacity, he had to be a patient suitor for over two years. Finally, however, his persistence triumphed, and on January 13, 1923, a telegram from St. Paul's Walden Bury to Sandringham carried the prearranged signal, 'All right. Bertie', which told Queen Mary that he had been accepted.

Two days later he himself announced his engagement to his parents.[a] 'Bertie with Greig arrived after tea and informed us that he was engaged to Elizabeth Bowes-Lyon, to which we gladly gave our consent. I trust they will be very happy', King George wrote in his diary on January 15; and Queen Mary also recorded, 'We are delighted and he looks beaming'. 'You & Papa were both so charming to me yesterday about my engagement', the Duke wrote to Queen Mary from London next day, '& I can never really thank you properly for giving

[a] The betrothal of the Duke of York to Lady Elizabeth Bowes-Lyon, 'to which the King has gladly given his consent', was formally announced in the Court Circular on January 16, 1923. The formalities, however, were not completed until February 12, when, at a special meeting of the Privy Council, the King signed the document signifying his consent in pursuance of the Royal Marriages Act of 1772.

your consent to it. I am very very happy & I can only hope
that Elizabeth feels the same as I do. I know I am very
lucky to have won her over at last.' [11]

On January 20 Lord and Lady Strathmore with their
daughter spent the week-end at Sandringham to meet the
King and Queen and Queen Alexandra. It was an ordeal
not to be underestimated, but Lady Elizabeth came through
it with flying colours. 'Elizabeth is charming, so pretty &
engaging & natural. Bertie is supremely happy', Queen Mary
wrote that night, and the King's comment was no less enthusiastic : 'She is a pretty and charming girl & Bertie is a
very lucky fellow'.

Indeed, from the first moment, King George took Lady
Elizabeth into his heart. He admired her fearlessness, her
beauty and her wit, and even his stern insistence on punctuality
was not proof against her charm. To no one else would he
have said — as he did, when his son and daughter-in-law
arrived two minutes late for dinner and she apologized —
'You are not late, my dear, I think we must have sat down
two minutes too early'. 'The better I know & the more I see
of your dear little wife', he was to write to his son from Balmoral
shortly after the marriage, 'the more charming I think she is
& everyone fell in love with her here.' [12]

The marriage of the Duke of York and Lady Elizabeth
Bowes-Lyon was solemnized in Westminster Abbey on April
26, 1923, amid great splendour. Not for five hundred and
thirty years, when the young King Richard II married Princess
Anne of Bohemia in 1383, had a prince of the Royal House
been wed in the Abbey, and the whole Empire was stirred by
the event. A proposal by the British Broadcasting Corporation
to broadcast the service, though it won the approval of the Dean
of Westminster, was vetoed by the Chapter, for whom so
revolutionary an idea was altogether too startling.[13] No sound
record of the ceremony exists, therefore ; but the press and
moving-picture industry of the world bore testimony to the
deep feeling of approval, loyalty and affection which moved
the whole nation.

'A princely marriage is the brilliant edition of a universal
fact, and as such it rivets mankind', the Duke of York had
read as an undergraduate at Cambridge in Walter Bagehot's

sparkling work.[a] The imagination of the British public, whose inherent love of pageantry had been starved during the austerity of the war years, and but whetted by the two previous royal weddings since the war,[b] was fired by the romance and glamour of the occasion, and certainly no royal function since the Coronation in 1911 had been so universally acclaimed in popularity. There was, as *The Times* pointed out editorially, 'but one wedding to which the people look forward with still deeper interest — the wedding which will give a wife to the Heir to the Throne and, in the course of nature, a future Queen to England and the British peoples'. And another writer added: 'Whilst the Princes of Wales have almost invariably been compelled to accept the brides that State policy selected, the Dukes of York have nearly always obeyed the dictates of their hearts'.[15]

There was something immensely and warmly appealing about this bridal couple. They were so young and fresh and happy; they were so good-looking, the Duke with the clean-cut litheness of good health, his Duchess with that wistful beauty which has been caught so vividly in Laszlo's portrait. The fact that she was a Scotswoman also delighted the nation, and the genealogists derived much pleasure from demonstrating the fact that both she and the Duke were descended from King Robert I of Scotland.[c] The people of Scotland derived particular satisfaction from the fact that King George conferred the Order of the Thistle upon his son on his wedding day.

Many now realized for the first time the sympathy and respect which the Duke of York had justly earned by his struggle against ill-health during the war. 'Young as he is and great as is his station', wrote one, the Duke has 'known enough of frustration to make all admirers of pluck and

---

[a] Mr. Bagehot also added, in a burst of cynical realism: 'We smile at the Court Circular; but remember how many people read the Court Circular! Its use is not in what it says, but in those to whom it speaks.'[14]

[b] There had been two Royal weddings in Westminster Abbey since the end of the war, that of Princess Patricia of Connaught to Captain Alexander Ramsay, on February 27, 1919, and of Princess Mary to Lord Lascelles on February 28, 1922.

[c] King Robert I, the Bruce (1306–1329), was a direct ancestor of Mary Queen of Scots, and therefore by descent of the present Royal Family of Britain. King Robert II (1371–1390), a grandson of Robert the Bruce, gave his daughter, Lady Jean Stewart, in marriage to Sir John Lyon, Thane of Glamis and Chamberlain of Scotland, the ancestor of the Earls of Strathmore, in 1379.

perseverance the more anxious to wish him happiness and success in the venture.'[16]

Now also came tributes of popularity and affection to his self-effacing work on behalf of industrial welfare and in his annual Camp. Amongst those in the great crowds who cheered the Duke of York on his progress to and from the Abbey were many who had found him suddenly standing beside them at the loom or the lathe or the assembly-line, always with a cheery word of personal interest and understanding. There were boys, too, who had swum with him and played push-ball in shirt and shorts at his Camp at Romney. All these joined in sincere and heartfelt wishes of good-will.

The wedding day itself was one of typical April weather, with quick showers of rain and sudden sunshine, but, as King George recorded, 'It stopped raining at about 9.30 & the sun actually came out as the Bride entered the Abbey'. She was attended by six bridesmaids,[a] the bridegroom by the Prince of Wales and Prince Henry. The Archbishop of Canterbury read the service and the Archbishop of York gave an address, described by King George as 'beautiful', and by Queen Mary as 'charming'. In the course of it he told the bride and bride-groom : 'You have received from Him at this Altar a new life wherein your separate lives are now, till death, made one. With all our hearts we wish that it may be a happy one. But you cannot resolve that it shall be happy. You can and will resolve that it shall be noble. The warm and generous heart of this people takes you today into itself. Will you not, in response, take that heart, with all its joys and sorrows, into your own ?'

The Archbishop made special reference to the Duke's activities in connection with industry : 'You, sir, have already given many proofs of your care for the welfare of our working people. You have made yourself at home in the mines and ship-yards and factories. You have brought the boys of the workshop and the public school together in free and frank companionship. You have done much to increase the public sense of the honour and dignity of labour.'

[a] The Duchess of York's bridesmaids were : Lady May Cambridge, Lady Mary Cambridge, Lady Katherine Hamilton, Lady Mary Thynne, Miss Diamond Hardinge and Miss Betty Cator. Her two nieces, Miss Elizabeth Elphinstone and Miss Cecilia Bowes-Lyon, were also in attendance.

In the late afternoon they left to spend the first part of their honeymoon at Polesden Lacey, near Dorking, the home of Mrs. Ronald Greville. Later they went to Glamis, where the Duchess contracted whooping-cough — 'So unromantic to catch whooping-cough on your honeymoon', wrote the Duke to Queen Mary [17] — and to Frogmore, where the Duke recalled his childhood memories. 'So funny being here again', he wrote to Mr. Hansell. 'Nothing has changed at all except that it has been lent to us!! Old memories come rushing back all the time & our old schoolroom is just the same, even to the ink-stains on the writing table. The Mary Moser room at the end of the colonnade still seems to contain old Hua & his famous mark book with V.M., M., F. & Mod. It makes one feel so much older.'

The Duke may well have speculated on the feelings of those in the home which he had now left behind him. His mother, he thought, would miss him. 'I do hope you will not miss me very much', he wrote to her, 'though I believe you will as I have stayed with you so much longer really than the brothers.' [18] But what of his father? The answer came in a letter from King George, illustrative at once of his somewhat unpredictable reactions, his basic, if sometimes somewhat clandestine, affection for his children, and the fact that, whatever strictures he may have passed upon them while they remained under the parental roof-tree, were forgiven and forgotten once they had married and gone forth on their own.

DEAREST BERTIE [wrote the King]
    . . . You are indeed a lucky man to have such a charming & delightful wife as Elizabeth & I am sure you will both be very happy together & I trust you both will have many many years of happiness before you & that you will be as happy as Mama & I are after you have been married for 30 years, I can't wish you more. . . . It must have been with a pang that you left your home after 27 years. I miss you very much & regret your having left us, but now you will have your own home which I hope will be as happy as the one you have left. You have always been so sensible & easy to work with & you have always been ready to listen to any advice & to agree with my opinions about people & things, that I feel that we have always got on very well together (very different to dear David). I trust that this state of affairs will always remain the same between us & that you will come to me for advice whenever

you want it. . . . By your quiet useful work you have endeared
yrself to the people, as shown on Thursday by the splendid reception
they gave you.   I am quite certain that Elizabeth will be a splendid
partner in your work & share with you & help you in all you have
to do.

Wishing you & Elizabeth every good luck & a very happy
honeymoon.

Ever my dear boy

Yr. most devoted Papa

G. R. I.[19]

(iii)

The Duke of York's marriage was the first great climacteric
of his life.   Not only did it entail emancipation from a home
environment which, despite the sentiments of his father's letter,
had not been entirely congenial to him, but it brought him
much for which he had long craved in deprivation — love,
understanding, sympathy, support.   All these things were now
his in generous abundance, and his whole conspectus of life
changed accordingly.   Hitherto he had been painstaking in his
duties and had taken his pleasures equally seriously;   but
there had been a tendency to morbidness and introspection and
self-pity.   Now, under the influence of married happiness and
companionship, the flower of his natural gaiety blossomed
forth and a new spontaneous zest was evident in his whole
personality.   The world took on a fresh and magical hue for
him, and, as the years passed and he became established in his
own home with his wife and daughters, his family life came to
be his salient joy and comfort.

'I am quite certain', King George had written to his son,
'that Elizabeth will be a splendid partner in your work &
share with you & help you in all you have to do.'   No prophecy
could have been more completely fulfilled, no expression of confidence more entirely justified.   The Duchess was not only to
be the partner of his happiness but his inspiration of encouragement in the face of adversity, his enduring source of strength
in joy and sadness.   Hers was the ability to sustain or reward
him by a single smile or gesture in the public battles which he
waged with his stammer;   hers the capacity to calm with a
word that passionate temper which ever and anon would

burst its bounds. Their marriage was not only an auspicious union of complementary personalities and attributes, but also a fusion of soul and spirit in dedication to the joys of family life and the service of the State.

For the essential significance of this marriage lay in the fact that the Duke and Duchess of York embarked immediately upon a way of life which was to exemplify to the full the truth of Bagehot's requisite of monarchy, namely the fulfilment of the public expectation that 'domestic virtues are as likely to be found on thrones as they are eminent when there'. At this time the British public still hoped for a Princess of Wales who should in due course be her husband's consort upon the throne; but, as the years passed and the Prince remained a bachelor, there came an ever-increasing acceptance of the fact that, in the nature of things, the Duke and Duchess of York would one day become King and Queen. Their happiness in themselves and in their children, and their untiring devotion to, and apparent enjoyment of, their public duties, became a source of public delight and admiration. This found expression years later in the cry which rang out above the cheers greeting their appearance as they drove out of Buckingham Palace on the occasion of King George V's Jubilee : 'There goes the hope of England'.

CHAPTER II

INDUSTRIAL RELATIONS

(i)

PRIOR to his accession to the throne, the great contribution of King George VI to the national life of Britain was in the interests of industrial welfare, in which field he was a virtual pioneer. The world of industry and commerce, where the great forces of Capital and Labour combined in the production of those commodities which were the very life-blood of national existence, was a veritable *terra incognita* to the Royal Family and, in the four years preceding the outbreak of the First World War, not more than twenty factories had been visited by King George and his sons.

The impact of the war years was perhaps more extensive in the industrial sphere of the national life than in any other. New ideas of freedom had shaken the old order, new demands for leisure were being made by the forces of Labour, which had felt power and influence for the first time. The good relations of employers with their workmen became vital to the post-war recovery and reconstruction of Britain, and the maintenance of industrial peace ranked parallel in importance with that of international amity.

It was essential that some personal link should be established between the Royal Family and the world of manufacture, and it was this liaison rôle which the Duke of York performed with such remarkable and outstanding success. Fully to appreciate the importance of the Duke's contribution, however, it is necessary to understand the circumstances of its birth and development.

(ii)

The collapse of Imperial Russia in March 1917 sent a seismic shock throughout the world; and, in the reactions of many, alarm and expectation, apprehension and hope, were inextricably mingled.   Those who had long hoped for the establishment of a constitutional government in Russia and the consequent disappearance of the *malaise* which had beset her war effort, felt their hopes rise with the birth of Prince Lvov's Provisional Government, while those who feared the growth of revolution saw in the downfall of the Tsarist régime the first wave of a cataclysm which might engulf the whole monarchical system.   To the world proletariat the Russian Revolution betokened the dawn of a new era of power and opportunity; and even in Britain, where Republicanism was believed to be dead and buried since 1872, there arose a call for an English Revolution on Russian lines.

On March 31, 1917, a mass meeting, over which Mr. George Lansbury presided, was held in the Albert Hall, to celebrate the fall of Tsardom, and on April 21 Mr. H. G. Wells wrote a letter to *The Times* asserting that the moment had come for the British people to rid themselves of 'the ancient trappings of throne and sceptre' and advocating the immediate formation of Republican Societies.

Much of this academic revolutionary enthusiasm waned with the advent to power of the Bolsheviks in November 1917 and the subsequent brutal and horrifying massacre of the Imperial Russian family in July of the following year, but there was no denying that the events of Petrograd and Ekaterinburg had had their far-reaching repercussions in every state in Europe.   Monarchy seemed to be at a discount.

In England there was undoubted discontent and disillusionment.   The shortage of food and its high price and the alleged inequality of distribution of existing food stocks, the industrial unrest due in great measure to general war-weariness, personal hardships and afflictions, and the ever-increasing conflict between Capital and Labour, combined to create a far from felicitous climate of ideas, and one which was not palliated by Mr. Lloyd George's promises of a post-war millennium.

At this difficult time the example set by the Royal Family was outstanding.   Though the Russian Revolution and the murder of the Tsar and his family had shaken King George's confidence in the innate decency of mankind,[1] yet he never failed in his duty or his courage or his determination.   His early gesture of banishing alcohol from his table for the duration of the war had caught the public imagination — though his example was not universally followed — and the King's visits to the Front, and his untiring and enheartening tours of the camps and hospitals and munitions plants at home, endeared him to the British public, impressing them with the genuine and simple sincerity of his character. Indeed, in assessing the different factors which enabled Britain to weather the stormy period of 1917 and 1918, 'a very high place', as Mr. Lloyd George has testified, 'must be given to the affection inspired by the King and the unremitting diligence with which he set himself in these dark days to discharge the functions of high office.' [2]

Yet, as Lord Cromer wrote in August 1918 :

In spite of the unceasing labours and devotion to public duties of the King and Queen during the last three years, the fact remains that the position of the Monarchy is not so stable now, in 1918, as it was at the beginning of the War. It seems therefore imperative that in the critical times with which the Country is now faced no stone should be left unturned in the endeavour to consolidate the position of the Crown. The Crown is the link of Empire and its fate is inseparable from that of all British Possessions.' [3]

And there were more shocks ahead. The conclusion of the war brought about a further weakening of the monarchical principle and tradition. The overthrow of the Imperial dynasties of Germany and Austro-Hungary, and the emergence of the President of the United States, Woodrow Wilson, as the new saviour of mankind, combined to make Republicanism an attractive panacea for those ills with which the world found itself beset in its struggle to readjust its standards to the new post-war order. Could the British Monarchy withstand the wave of revolution which had swept Romanovs, Habsburgs and Hohenzollerns from their thrones? Was the monarchical principle sufficiently deeply rooted in Britain to enable it to confront and surmount the problems presented by demobilization, unemployment, industrial unrest and the great social changes which the war had brought about?

We stand at the parting of the ways [wrote Lord Esher to Lord Stamfordham at this juncture (November 4, 1918)]. Some risks will have to be run. The Monarchy and its cost will have to be justified in the future in the eyes of a war-worn and hungry proletariat, endowed with a huge preponderance of voting power.

I see a great future for the King in connection with the consolidation of 'Imperial' control of our public affairs; but imagination and boldness will be required, necessitating the abandonment of many old theories of Constitutional Kingship.

The King and Queen will have to take risks. The strength of Republicanism lies in the *personality* of Wilson! and the use he has made of his position. It is a lesson. He has made the 'fashion' of a Republic. We can 'go one better' if we try.[4]

The essential and imminent truth of these words was borne out only ten days later.

On November 14, the Thursday of Armistice Week, the announcement of a General Election was made in the House of Commons. The Labour Party at once withdrew from the Coalition Government and that same evening launched their election campaign at a meeting at the Albert Hall. There, amid tumultuous scenes, Mr. Bob Williams, Secretary of the Transport Workers' Union, announced, 'I hope to see the Red Flag flying over Buckingham Palace', and warned that unless the workers' grievances were redressed by constitutional process, organized labour would resort to 'other means'. Willie Gallacher, who proudly described himself as 'a Bolshevik from Glasgow' — and subsequently sat in the House of Commons as a Communist — admitted frankly that he was out for revolution. More moderate speakers, such as Mr. J. R. Clynes, were howled down; and, before dispersing, the meeting sang 'The Red Flag' and gave hearty cheers for 'The Bolsheviks', 'Lenin and Trotsky', and, amid much laughter, 'The Bloody Revolution'.[5]

On November 23, King George rode with the Prince of Wales and the Duke of Connaught, and, accompanied by Queen Mary, Queen Alexandra and Princess Victoria, in an open carriage, to review some 35,000 Silver Badge ex-Servicemen in Hyde Park. He was given an enthusiastic reception, and in riding down the lines (as he recorded in his diary) 'they broke through & came round me to shake hands & I was nearly pulled off my horse'. But there was also another spirit abroad. The men were genuine enough in their loyalty but they were not to be baulked of the opportunity of laying their grievances concerning the inadequacy of their pensions and their lack of houses and work before the King in person. As if by a pre-arranged signal, hitherto concealed banners with slogans were defiantly unfurled among the milling humanity which pressed about the King. In so tense an atmosphere there were possibilities of serious trouble, but fortunately the police were able to extricate the King without incident. With his eldest son he rode silently back to Buckingham Palace. There, having dismounted, he said to the Prince of Wales, 'Those men were in a funny temper' — and shaking his head, as if to rid himself of an unpleasant memory, he strode indoors.[a]

But the unpleasant memory persisted; it would not be exorcized, and to it were added tidings of further disturbance and disgruntlement at home, and of the weakening of the ties of Commonwealth. How could the position of the Crown be consolidated? How could the Crown become identified with the peoples of Britain and of the British Dominions beyond the Seas?

The answer to the second of these questions, in so far as the Dominions were concerned, was provided by the fertile brain of Mr. Lloyd George. It was he who suggested that the Prince of Wales should embark upon a series of Empire tours to thank the peoples of the Commonwealth, in the King's name and as his representative, for their contribution to the war. King George was quick to grasp the import of this project. Not only would these tours serve to carry his gratitude to the Empire but they would also permit the Prince to gain a comprehensive idea of the extent and variety of his dominions and the conditions in which his peoples lived, while at the same time affording his subjects an opportunity of seeing their future monarch. The Prince departed on the first of his great imperial journeys on August 5, 1919.[6]

There remained the home country, and here the solution came from an unexpected quarter, having its origins in the

[a] King George in his diary makes no mention of this adverse demonstration, but the Duke of Windsor in his memoirs (pp. 128-129) gives a vivid description of it. The Duke's account, however, is in error on two points of detail. He states that Prince Albert was present on this occasion, which is impossible, as he only returned from France on the following day, November 24. The Duke also recalls that the demonstrators referred to Mr. Lloyd George's election pledge of 'a land fit for heroes to live in'. The speech in which the Prime Minister made this promise was also not delivered until the day after the parade, November 24.

early days of the war. In the course of a tramp across the Epsom Downs one Sunday afternoon in November 1915, Mr. Seebohm Rowntree [a] revealed to Mr. Lloyd George, then Minister of Munitions, the primitive conditions under which many of those engaged in the manufacture of munitions had to live and work. There was no tradition of care for the health and comfort of the workers beyond the minimum already compulsory under the Factory Acts. Many temporary factories and extensions to existing buildings had no equipment for the very necessities of life. There were neither lavatories, cloakrooms, first-aid centres, mess-rooms, nor canteens. There was, moreover, much immorality.

Mr. Lloyd George decided then and there to create a Welfare Department of the Ministry of Munitions, and invited Mr. Rowntree to become the head of it. He accepted, and at first concentrated on welfare work among the women munition workers. It soon became evident, however, that a parallel problem existed among the thousands of lads employed in the munitions industry, and to meet this situation Mr. Rowntree, on the advice of Dr. Christopher Addison,[b] enlisted in April 1916 the assistance of an East End clergyman, the Rev. Robert Hyde,[c] Vicar of St. Mary's, Hoxton, and Head of the Maurice Hostel Settlement, who had specialized in work amongst boys.[7]

Mr. Hyde, on joining the Welfare Department of the Ministry, discovered that he had both a flair and a vocation for such work; so much so that he became determined that it should be a permanent and living force in British industrial life and that he would devote the rest of his own life to it. But he found difficulties in officialdom. The Government were un-

[a] B. Seebohm Rowntree, C.H. (1871–1954), sociologist and philanthropist. Chairman of Rowntree & Co. Ltd., 1925–1941.

[b] Rt. Hon. Christopher, first Viscount Addison, K.G., M.D. (1869–1951), Minister of Munitions in succession to Mr. Lloyd George, 1916–1917, and subsequently Minister in charge of Reconstruction, President of the Local Government Board, Minister of Health, Minister of Agriculture, Secretary of State for Commonwealth Relations, Paymaster-General and Lord Privy Seal. He sat as Liberal M.P. for Hoxton Division of Shoreditch, 1910–1922; as Labour M.P. for Swindon, 1929–1931 and 1934–1935. He was raised to the Peerage in 1937 and created a Knight of the Garter in 1946.

[c] Sir Robert Robertson Hyde, K.B.E., M.V.O. (b. 1878), Vicar of St. Mary's, Hoxton, 1912–1916; served in Welfare Department of the Ministry of Munitions, 1916–1918. Founder, and for many years Director, of the Industrial Welfare Society, Sir Robert Hyde relinquished holy orders on being awarded a K.B.E. in 1949.

willing to continue their welfare work except under legislation and through Civil Servants. They wished to combine it with the activities of the Home Office Factory Department or the Ministry of Labour. Mr. Hyde, however, was convinced that success did not lie through these means, but rather that welfare work must depend for its direction and control not upon a State Department but upon the good-will, the experience and the co-operation of employers and the representatives of labour.

Forthwith he resigned from the Ministry of Munitions in July 1918 and founded the Boys' Welfare Association, thereby providing an organization through which industry itself might be responsible for the development of the growing movement for the betterment of working conditions, the setting up of works' committees, the provision of health centres and canteens in factories, and of proper facilities for the maximum of enjoyment in the workers' free time. It was not an easy task that he had set himself. At the outset there was considerable opposition from the unenlightened among both the employers and the workers. Industrial management, in certain cases, denounced welfare work as a species of Bolshevism, while some Trade Unionists were equally opposed to it for the dual reason that it might steal some of their influence with the workers and that it was not entirely to their advantage to have too great a degree of harmony between Capital and Labour in industry.

Mr. Hyde, however, persevered; and with the backing of certain prominent industrialists, such as Sir William Beardmore,[a] and certain Labour leaders, such as Mr. J. H. Thomas, Mr. Arthur Henderson and Mr. John Hodge, he contrived in the space of half a year to make the Boys' Welfare Association something which could command the interest, respect and commendation of over a hundred firms.

It was at this moment that Mr. Hyde had the happy idea of Royal patronage. This had been accorded to sport, to charities and to the fighting Services, but never to industry. Why should not one of the King's sons become interested in Industrial Welfare? And, since the Boys' Welfare Association

[a] Sir William Beardmore, Bt., first Baron Invernairn (1856–1936), head of the shipbuilding firm of Beardmore & Co. It was said of him by David Kirkwood, the I.L.P. leader, to Mr. Lloyd George in December 1915, 'I am as much a slave of Sir William Beardmore as if I had the letter "B" branded on my brow'.[8]

had neither party nor political attachment, and occupied a neutral position as between the so-called 'sides' in industry, why should not this become the channel of interest?

The means of approach lay ready to Mr. Hyde's hand. He was a member of the Archbishop of Canterbury's Commission on Christianity and Industrial Problems; [a] so was the Archbishop's Chaplain, Dr. George Bell.[b] They became close friends, and to him Mr. Hyde broached his plan. What did the Archbishop's Chaplain think of the idea of one of the King's sons becoming President of the Boys' Welfare Association? If he thought favourably of it, would he and the Archbishop take the matter up with Lord Stamfordham? [9]

The proposal went forward and the King approved it. It would, he thought, be an admirable thing for Prince Albert to become identified with some activity which would take him out into the industrial towns of Britain at the same time that his elder brother was touring the Dominions. It would be good experience for the Prince and beneficial to the Monarchy.

Prince Albert's reaction was also favourable. Back from France and about to go up to Cambridge, he saw in Mr. Hyde's suggestion an opportunity for something wider, something more absorbing and constructive, in addition to the routine formal functions which would fall inevitably to his lot as a member of the Royal Family — the laying of corner-stones, the commemoration tree plantings, the opening of new highways, and so forth. His habitual shyness and the consciousness of his stammer made him shrink from ceremonial affairs with set speeches and rigid formality, and in agreeing to serve he made one condition. 'I'll do it,' he said, 'provided that there's no damned red carpet about it.' Apart from this, he expressed himself as 'more than willing' to accept.[10]

Prince Albert threw himself into the new field of activity

[a] The Commission on Christianity and Industrial Problems was appointed by Archbishop Davidson in connection with the National Mission of Repentance and Hope during the First World War. Its chairman was the Rt. Rev. Edward Talbot, then Bishop of Winchester, and its membership included, among many others, A. L. Smith, Master of Balliol College, Oxford; W. L. Hichens; R. H. Tawney; George Lansbury; and Bishop Gore.

[b] Rt. Rev. Dr. George Kennedy Allen Bell (b. 1883), Chaplain to the Archbishop of Canterbury, 1914-1924 (whose biography he wrote, *Randall Davidson, Archbishop of Canterbury*, 1935), Dean of Canterbury, 1924-1929, and Bishop of Chichester, 1929-1958.

with all his characteristic energy and devotion. He was determined that the job should be no sinecure. He attended meetings of the Association's Council and embarked at once on the great series of visits to industrial centres which in time was to give him so deep an insight into the industrial life of the nation. True to his initial condition of acceptance, he insisted that on these occasions he should see the factories and their workers under normal conditions, free from all ceremony and all preparations of the kind that had been regarded as an essential part of a Royal visit in the past. Once his wish became known and understood it was loyally respected.

The effect and influence of Prince Albert's interest was immediately apparent. The men, women and boys whose work he inspected were first surprised and then delighted to find the King's son moving among them unselfconsciously and with the minimum of fuss, clearly and genuinely interested in them and in their work. 'I feel sure you will be gratified to learn that already his [Prince Albert's] action has been of the highest service', wrote Mr. Hyde enthusiastically to Archbishop Davidson:

I feel more than ever certain that if those tendencies which we all deplore are to be checked and guided aright it can only be accomplished if the goodwill which exists in every section of the community is enabled to unite and find expression. The Prince's contribution in this direction is of no small importance. [11]

Prince Albert's activities in this new sphere were closely and carefully noted in Buckingham Palace. King George was pleased with his son's serious application to his new interest and within a year Queen Mary had made the suggestion that the range of the Association's operations, which had so far been restricted to work among men and boys, should be extended so that the benefits of industrial welfare should be enjoyed by all workers.

The Queen's suggestion was warmly welcomed; and at a general meeting of the Association on May 22, 1919, at the opening of which Prince Albert presided, it was formally adopted. The organization was renamed the Industrial Welfare Society (I.W.S.) and its objects were declared to be the formulation and development of the many activities, industrial, educational and recreational, indicated in the word 'Welfare' for the benefit of all those engaged in industry.

Prince Albert continued in the office of President and reaffirmed his interest and confidence in the work in a letter to the new Society: 'I realise from my visits to various Works and from my attendance at your Council meetings, what an important scheme we are undertaking, and I feel confident, if we all pull together, that it will turn out a very real benefit to the Industrial Workers of our Country'.[12]

This extension of the scope of the Society's activities brought with it inevitably an increase in Prince Albert's own share in them and a widening of his horizon. He acquired a technical knowledge of industry which enabled him to ask questions surprising in their perspicacity both to workers and to managers alike in the factories which he visited, and proving that he was no superficial inquirer. He went down coal mines, clambered up scaffolding, drove locomotives as well as petrol runabouts, and once a tramcar through the crowded streets of Glasgow — to the consternation of those who were responsible for his safety, poured molten metal from crucibles, blasted by pressing a button many thousands of tons of rock — and all in a desire to learn at first hand how things were done and how the working days of the nation were spent. As the manager of a large business put it after one of Prince Albert's visits: 'Of all the many visitors we had here, I never met one who asked more sensible questions or showed greater understanding of our fundamental problems. He does like getting to the bottom of things.' [13]

Nor was the Prince perturbed — on the contrary, he was greatly entertained — by occasional but inevitable failures of the equipment which he inspected. As he himself once confessed: 'It seems that I place an evil spell on the machines in which I show a special interest and they sometimes break down and stop. Once, to my surprise and dismay, I was dropped in a lift. Another time a fool-proof stamping machine threw out forty unstamped letters for my benefit. The threads of looms seem to break whenever I approach those machines. And yet I find that industrialists are ready to welcome me in their midst.'

He never shirked the seamier side of what he regarded as his job. Once when he was visiting a soap works he learned that, associated with the plant, there was a glue department, at best a somewhat noisome place. On asking to see it he was told that the process was very unpleasant and the smell almost unbearable. He replied that if the place was good enough for the people who worked there, it was good enough for him to see — and in he went. His well deserved title of 'the Industrial Prince' was earned the hard way.

With the experience gained from these personal contacts there came also a deepening of Prince Albert's understanding of the basic issues involved. He quickly sensed from his early industrial visits that there was a great deal of unrest and unhappiness in the country. Those were the days when the hopes based on Mr. Lloyd George's 1918 election pledge to make Britain 'a land fit for heroes to live in' were wearing very thin, and there were many who shared the view of the contemporary political satirist that, under the mismanagement of the post-war Coalition Government, Britain had become a land in which only heroes could live. Prince Albert was deeply concerned by what he saw and heard. To mitigate these conditions he was tireless in his efforts to secure improvements in industrial life, and he also developed a keen desire to give a personal lead in the promotion of good human relationships. This thesis he elaborated before a general meeting of the Industrial Welfare Society in 1920 :

To me the importance of the welfare question lies in the fact that it helps the worker to free himself from the grip of the machine and enables him to make fuller use of his leisure.

There is a new industrial philosophy abroad with which we must identify ourselves and of which we must be pioneers.

The saving and brightening of the worker's life should be, and must eventually be, an industrial issue, and when the community realizes that the country is richest which nourishes the greatest number of happy people, a big step will have been taken towards the contentment and prosperity of the nation.

The happiness of the worker and the dignity of labour became recurring theses in Prince Albert's industrial philosophy, and from it he drew the moral that a happy worker did his work better than one working under restraint and dissatisfaction. This theme he would illustrate by the story of a workman engaged in redecorating the interior of a church, who was keeping time with great sweeps of his paint-brush while crooning to himself the tune of 'Horsie, keep your tail up'. Shortly thereafter the Rector entered and was aghast at this secular accompaniment to labour. 'If you must sing at your work, at least sing a hymn', he admonished. Therewith he left and, returning some time later, found that the workman had adjusted his rhythm to the dreary and languorous tempo of 'Abide with me'.

When Duke of York, and settled as a married man in his own home, he carried his system of contacts still further. Captains of industry and Trade Union leaders became regular callers at 145 Piccadilly, and the Duke's influence made itself felt throughout the industrial life of Britain. The King was delighted, and on one occasion when the Prime Minister of the day brought up in audience some question of industrial relations, His Majesty replied, 'Oh, that's my second son's department', and chuckled; and the Duke's brothers referred to him as 'the Foreman'.

Nor was public recognition lacking:

It may not have been the case that industry was actually despised, but that members of the Royal House had not found a way to intimacy of touch with it [wrote the editor of the *Yorkshire Post*]. Even an appearance of neglect could hardly fail to have a bad effect upon the mentality of the worker. At heart he was a little ashamed of manual toil, which to him appeared to be lacking in dignity. Advancement in social status was associated in his mind with black-coated tasks.

The wisest influences in the ranks of industry are nowadays turned to the cultivation of pride in work well done rather than to shame of an overall and grimy hands. And the Duke is taking his part in this task. Throughout the country he is fast becoming a leader in something more than name in the ranks of industry. He has thrown upon it the glamour and prestige of his position. Without show, formality, fuss or bother, he has deliberately and consistently made personal contact with men of all classes connected with productive enterprise.[14]

There was also a lighter side to the Duke's work, as witness the famous golf match in the Rhondda Valley.

In January 1923, in the course of an I.W.S. dinner, Mr.

Frank Hodges,[a] the Miners' Trade Union leader, invited the Duke of York to play a game of golf on a miners' course in South Wales. The Duke at once responded to the challenge and it was hoped that the match would follow shortly afterwards. Owing to a number of circumstances it was impossible to arrange the game until the spring of the following year, but on May 17, 1924, a two-ball, nine-hole game was arranged on the Ton Pentre Welfare Scheme Golf Course in the Rhondda Valley between the Duke and his Comptroller, Captain Basil Brooke, with Mr. Frank Hodges — by that time Civil Lord of the Admiralty in Mr. Ramsay MacDonald's first Labour Government — and Mr. Evan Williams,[b] President of the Mining Association of Great Britain, both of whom had been spirited antagonists in many a coal-mining dispute.

The course had originally been laid out by a small band of golfing enthusiasts among the local miners, who acquired an acre or two of rough ground, cut holes in the pitch with no tools but ex-Service jack-knives, and played golf on the course without tees, without greens, without everything but live enthusiasm. In 1922 a golf club was founded, with the help and co-operation of two mining companies, and the two-acre patch was extended to a course of fifty acres. This was laid out by the miners themselves, giving voluntary labour after working hours, and the result by the time of the Duke's visit was at least a playable golf course.

Great excitement had been aroused by this match and even before the train had reached its destination the loyal Welsh people all along the line had put out their flags and cheered the Duke as he passed. A good deal of washing was hanging out also, and occasionally this included a red petticoat, on the appearance of which the Duke would say : 'Hodges, another member of your party !'

The Duke was entertained to lunch by the Ocean Recreation Union, the Chairman of which was Colonel David Davies,[c]

---

[a] Frank Hodges, M.P., J.P. (1887–1947), General Secretary Miners' Federation of Great Britain, 1918–1924 ; Civil Lord of the Admiralty, 1924 ; Secretary of International Miners' Federation, 1925–1927 ; M.P. for Lichfield, 1923–1924.

[b] Sir Evan Williams, Bt. (b. 1871), President of the Mining Association of Great Britain, 1919–1944 ; President of National Board for Coal Mining Industry, 1921–1925.

[c] David Davies (1880–1944), created Baron 1932 ; landed proprietor and industrialist ; Liberal M.P. for Montgomeryshire, 1906–1929 ; Parliamentary

who spoke of the work of the I.W.S. in providing a common
ground where persons of all shades of opinion and thought
might meet together and find mutual interests. 'Today is
symbolical of that work. Not always, Sir, have your opponents,
Mr. Evan Williams and Mr. Frank Hodges, played together. I
have known them, doughty warriors both of them, in other
fields, fighting hard, stern battles — you have created this
partnership.'

The Duke and Captain Brooke were defeated by their
opponents and the day, which had had many hilarious moments
— not the least of which was the appearance on the last green
of a small dog, who, obviously a souvenir collector, ran away
with the Duke's ball, which was never recovered — concluded
with an unrehearsed and unauthorized incident at the Ystrad
railway station when a Boy Scout, who had managed to 'gate-
crash' the platform, suddenly sounded the Last Post as the
Duke's train drew away.

It was with the greatest satisfaction that the Duke watched
the gradual but progressive acceptance and extension of ideas
which he himself had early assimilated and developed. It had
not always been easy to secure the co-operation and the confidence of Capital and Labour for his welfare schemes, and
these voluntary organizations were apt to be regarded by some
government officials as the 'opposition show'. Indeed there
had been those who had feared lest his association with the
I.W.S. might not end by setting the King's son against the
King's Government. But these apprehensions soon evaporated
in the indisputable evidence of the success of the work, and the
Duke could write triumphantly to Mr. Hyde in 1934 :

Leaders throughout the world are now generally recognizing
that the greater the mechanization of industry, the greater is the
need for acknowledging that indefinable element we have always
described as the human factor. The I.W.S. proclaimed this
message many years ago, when ears were not always attuned to
hear, & it must [be] as gratifying to you as it is to me to know
that its truth is now being so widely accepted.[15]

From the fruits of his experience the Duke evolved for

Private Secretary to Mr. Lloyd George, 1916–1919. He was closely associated
with the work of the League of Nations Union, and was Founder and Chairman
of the New Commonwealth Society.

R. A. LISTER & CO., 1931   IN CAMP, 1936

'UNDER THE SPREADING CHESTNUT TREE', SOUTHWOLD, 1937

himself a new philosophy of relations between Capital and
Labour based on the welfare of the worker, and this he made
public at the general meeting of the I.W.S. on November 20,
1935. Had he known, it was the last such gathering that he
was able to attend, for he was within a year of those great and
tragic events which were to lay upon his shoulders that burden
of the affairs of State which he was never to lay down save with
his life. Looking back over the sixteen years of his presidency,
he said :

I feel there is a change of spirit abroad, recalling many of the
best features of working life in the Middle Ages, a spirit which, to
a large extent, was lost in the development of the factory system.
We must prove that throughout history there has always been an
impulse to make a society in which men are able to work together
in harmony.

In days gone by, the master craftsman lodged his apprentices.
To-day the employer has to provide houses for his work-people.
The master was responsible for feeding his hands. To-day he
instals a canteen. The ambition of the apprentice was to obtain
his independence as a master craftsman. This is not always possible
now, but by introducing promotion schemes and pension funds a
firm is able to offer security in later life. The master watched over
the health of his work-people. To-day the employer develops
medical services and sickness funds. In those far-off days the
master was responsible for the discipline of his young people during
their leisure. To-day, that responsibility exists no longer, but the
wise employer provides, where there is need, facilities for recreation.
I may even suggest that the modern works council is in direct
following of the close domestic tie which existed between the master
and the apprentice which, if the story-books are to be believed,
often led to a happy marriage with the employer's daughter.

Through the advent of large industrial groups, many of these
old human associations disappeared, and with them nearly all
sense of partnership. Since our work began, however, we have
shown that partnership promotes the well-being of the workers and
adds to the efficiency of the enterprise. Much that was best in the
relations that existed in the age of the Craft and the Guild is being
re-established to-day.

This was the essence of the great work to which, as a young
man, he had set his hand and in which he laboured until the
eve of being called to greater things. With his characteristic
thoroughness he spared himself nothing. In the years 1919–
1935 he made numerous tours of British industrial areas and

visited between 120 and 150 works and factories. His interest
in the thousands of men, women and boys with whom he came
into contact was never that of a shallow observer and they knew
it. Whether he went to the light manufacturing plants or to the
heavy industries — the forges and the foundries, or to the ship-
yards and construction sites; whether he crouched beside
miners underground at the coal face, or appeared suddenly in
the offices and shops where women worked, the effect was the
same, one of simple understanding and sincerity of interest.
With these men and women he lost his shyness and forgot his
stammer. His human interest transcended all and by his
words and actions he set a standard for human relations at
work that made Britain a better place to work in.

Indeed, he did more. He brought to the country a new
concept of Royalty, of Royalty closely identified with the
people, genuinely interested in their affairs. It was a steadfast
belief which was to remain with him all his life and which was
later to constitute one of his cardinal principles of Kingship.

CHAPTER III

'MY CAMP'

ALTHOUGH on his accession to the throne King George was known to many thousands of men and women in industry through his work with the Industrial Welfare Society, it was with the Duke of York's Camp that his name was more peculiarly and prominently associated in the public mind. This annual affair had become a national institution by 1936, and its founder could be justly proud of an achievement which, in inspiration and conception, owed virtually everything to his initiative and support.

From his earliest connections with the Industrial Welfare Society the Duke had sought for a means by which he himself might make some personal contribution to the promotion of good human relations in society. He was not content with the example which was set by his interest in the extension of welfare work in industry; he wanted to give some practical lead in drawing attention to the simple truth that friendship and common interest transcend in importance the superficialities of class distinctions and class prejudices. The common goodness and kindness of heart which, behind the barriers of class and reserve, is innate in the British people, frequently requires a cataclysm to bring about its revelation. It became abundantly apparent in the suffering of the Second World War, in the air-raid shelters, in life-boats and in the sacrifices demanded by everyday hardships and privations. It was not so apparent in the 'twenties, when bitterness and dissension were perhaps more acute than at any time subsequently.[a] The Duke's ideas came as a surprise to a

[a] It will be remembered that it was to meet the prevalent industrial unrest that Parliament passed in 1920 the Emergency Powers Act, by which, after a proclamation of a state of emergency by the Sovereign, the Government of the day was enabled to exercise special and far-reaching powers for the safeguarding of the well-being of the community. In the ensuing quarter of a century these powers have been called into operation on five occasions: by King George V, at the request of Mr. Lloyd George in 1921, and again at that of Mr. Baldwin in the

country riven by industrial disputes and which had never experienced the social benefits of national military service in times of peace.

For more than a year the Duke had kept his ideas to himself, and the opportunity for their realization came quite unexpectedly. In March 1921 the welfare officer of the Briton Ferry Steel Company in South Wales, an associate of the Industrial Welfare Society, wrote asking that some football fixtures might be made for a team of boys in the works who had saved up their money for a visit to London. Three games were arranged for the visitors; the first with the personnel of the Ordnance College, Woolwich, the second with the Boys' Club of the McVitie & Price Biscuit Works, and the third with Westminster School. At this last game, played on March 10 on the Vincent Square ground, the Duke of York was present, and with him were Sir Alexander Grant,[a] Sir Charles Wakefield [b] and Mr. Hyde of the I.W.S. The game was played with great keenness and good sportsmanship and the result was a draw, neither side having scored.

This was the first occasion on which industrial boys and public school boys had met on equal terms, and all present were impressed by the success of the experiment as exemplified by the demeanour and spirit of the players. To Sir Alexander Grant there came the vision of the projection of this experiment on broader lines. The short period of a game did not offer sufficient time for the players to hobnob; the opportunity must be found to achieve this same association on a bigger scale. As they left Vincent Square he spoke to the Duke of

General Strike of 1926, twice by King George VI, on the advice of Mr. Attlee, to meet the crises of the Dock Strikes of 1948 and 1949, and by Queen Elizabeth II, on the advice of Sir Anthony Eden, in the emergency of the railway strike of 1955.

[a] Sir Alexander Grant, first Bt. (1864-1937), Chairman and Managing Director of McVitie & Price Biscuits Ltd., was a close friend of Mr. Ramsay MacDonald and a generous benefactor to many causes. In 1923 on behalf of the Scottish nation he gave £100,000 towards the reconstruction of the Advocate's Library of Edinburgh, to be known in future as the National Library of Scotland.

[b] Charles Cheers, first Viscount Wakefield, G.C.V.O., C.B.E. (1859-1941), was Governing Director of the oil manufacturing firm of C. C. Wakefield & Co., Ltd. An alderman of the City of London, he had been distinguished for his recruiting activities during the First World War and for his public benefactions, among which was the purchase and endowment of Talbot House, Poperinghe, the birthplace of the Toc H Movement. Like Sir Alexander Grant, he had been an early supporter of the Industrial Welfare Society.

York of what was in his mind, urging that much good would result if some plan could be devised whereby boys from industry and from public schools could be brought together on terms of equality.

The Duke had come to know and respect this tough, visionary Scotsman, who had raised himself to a position of leadership in the world of industry and commerce. It was to the Willesden factory of McVitie & Price that he had paid his first visit under the auspices of the Industrial Welfare Society, in April 1919; and, as he was later to testify, it was as a result of this visit that he had conceived the ambition of making a personal contribution towards a better understanding between the workers and the so-called 'leisured class'. 'The idea which started the first time I came to your works at Willesden, became a living thing in the Camp,' the Duke of York wrote to Sir Alexander years later, '& through your great generosity you enabled me to make a great experiment in the lives of a great many boys, whose lives, ideas and upbringing were totally different.' [1] Up to this moment this ambition had lacked a means of expression but now his imagination was fired by Sir Alexander Grant's vision.

The Duke lost no time. A few days later he invited Mr. Hyde to Buckingham Palace to discuss Sir Alexander's idea, and with him came Commander B. T. Coote, who, a pioneer of physical training in the Navy and later associated with Sir Robert Baden-Powell in the early days of the Boy Scout movement, had been recruited to the staff of the Industrial Welfare Society. A number of proposals were discussed at this meeting but none commended themselves to the Duke. His own ideas were taking shape. If people were to get to know one another they must live together, he argued; why should not a group of boys from the public schools and from industry spend a week together somewhere, somehow, as his guests? Then suddenly the final idea struck him. 'Let's have a camp,' he said.

Thus the great idea was born, and again the Duke allowed no grass to grow under his feet. Within a very short space of time preparations for the first Camp, to be held in August of the same year, were actually under way. Mr. Hyde and the I.W.S. undertook to sound out the various industrial firms;

Dr. David of Rugby,[a] at that time Chairman of the Public Schools Headmasters' Conference, was consulted and expressed the warmest approval of the scheme; Sir Alexander Grant assumed the financial responsibility of the first Camp; and Commander Coote was given a free hand to organize the enterprise.[b] A suitable Camp site was found in a disused aerodrome at New Romney on the Kentish coast, near Hythe, where well-built, roomy huts with modern sanitation, electric light, adequate kitchen equipment and a vast dining-hall offered ideal accommodation, together with a hundred acres of playing fields; all within a short distance of the sea, where safe bathing could be indulged in at all hours of the day. The Duke was enthusiastically interested in all details.

There was nothing, of course, intrinsically novel about the idea of a holiday camp. School missions and university settlements had organized them for boys from the East End of London and elsewhere for many years. The Scout Movement, the Boys' Brigade, Cadet Corps and Boys' Clubs had done likewise. These, however, had meant handling disciplined units of a homogeneous character in which all members were more or less known to one another. The Duke's scheme had none of these features. In effect it meant that one hundred public schools and one hundred industrial firms were each invited to send two boys between the ages of seventeen and nineteen to meet and mix as the Duke's guests for a week's holiday, working, playing and sleeping together on terms of complete equality. The system of inviting them in couples was adopted because it was felt that individuals of both groups might feel unduly shy and diffident in the presence of complete strangers. Apart from this provision the boys were unknown to one another, and all were strangers to the Camp staff.

So great an experiment in social integration was not without

---

[a] Rt. Rev. Albert Augustus David, D.D. (1867–1950), Headmaster of Clifton from 1905 to 1909, and of Rugby from 1909 to 1921, was consecrated Bishop of St. Edmundsbury and Ipswich in 1921. He was translated to the See of Liverpool in 1923, where he remained until his retirement in 1944.

[b] Commander Coote served as Camp Chief from 1921 to 1926, when he was succeeded by Captain J. G. Paterson, who had been identified with the scheme from the first as a Section Leader and continued as Camp Chief until the last Camp in 1939. A long and unpublished memorandum by Captain Paterson on the history of the Duke of York's Camp has been of great assistance in the writing of this chapter.

its difficulties and obstacles, but most of these were overcome by the patronage and personality of the Duke of York, whose avid interest in the scheme removed much of the suspicion and scepticism which were manifested on both sides. 'If anybody but a member of the Royal Family had started the Camp', Sir Robert Hyde has written, 'I have no doubt that the average parent of the public schoolboy would have been a little timorous about the advisability of allowing Claude to associate with Bill, lest he should "catch" something detrimental to his health, or, far worse, to his manners. On the other hand, the Camp would certainly have been regarded as a trap to tame young Bolshevists.' [2]

As it was, there was not in fact much competition to go to the first Camp. The novelty of the idea carried with it the grounds of apprehension. Among the schools and the firms who originally had been approached there were some who were unco-operative and who produced rather naïve excuses for declining the Duke's invitation. Among the boys themselves who did attend there was at the outset a vague idea that they were taking part in some new and peculiar social experiment. They were quite uncertain as to what it was all about or what was expected of them. Consequently some of them arrived at the appointed meeting-place, the Riding School in the Royal Mews of Buckingham Palace, on the opening day of the first Camp, Saturday July 30, 1921, with bowler hats and umbrellas, while others appeared in 'gents' natty suitings' direct from 'the peg'.

The boys were welcomed informally by the Duke of York as soon as all had assembled in the Riding School and then the four hundred strangers sat down to luncheon. There was no magical breaking of barriers, no sudden melting of reserve. The normal processes of boy-psychology took their course, and it was natural, therefore, that some time was spent in sizing one another up, and that the boys' expressions registered interest or displeasure, according to the person at whom they happened to be looking. 'Let it be confessed that there was an almost ominous quiet about the atmosphere when they all sat down to lunch', Captain Paterson recalls. 'It required complete confidence in the ultimate success of the experiment to preserve the morale of the staff at that stage of the proceedings and I think that many of the boys themselves would have "deserted" if they could have summoned up the courage to do so.' Clearly the initial success or failure of the Duke of York's great experiment was hanging in the balance and for purely natural causes — the normal inimicality of boy for boy.

A special train provided by the Southern Railway — no mean gesture of co-operation in the midst of August Bank Holiday week-end traffic — carried the Duke's guests from Cannon Street to Dymchurch whence, after a three-mile walk, they reached the Camp site at New Romney. The walk did something to break the ice but, even so, segregation was still apparent, and it was noticeable that like walked with like.

It is to the eternal credit of the Camp Chief, Commander Coote, and his Section Leaders, some of whom were members of the I.W.S. staff, some public schoolmasters, club leaders, welfare workers and young employers, that the Duke of York's enterprise did not founder in those first few hours. By superhuman efforts, and inspired by a sense of loyalty to the Duke, they kept the ship afloat until an even keel had been achieved. In the common reaction to strange conditions, and in the common donning of the regular Camp garb of shorts and shirt, the boys lost their diffidence and self-consciousness. The Etonian and the Harrovian, the Welsh miner and the Lancashire cotton hand came to discover that in the very incongruity of their backgrounds lay the great secret of the whole scheme — a great scheme devised by their host, the Duke of York, to promote a sense of equality and comradeship between the upper and lower classes of England.

The Camp staff staked everything upon the double chance of the section system and competitive games. The whole four hundred were divided up, and thoroughly commingled, into twenty groups of twenty each, and all games were between sections. Each boy participated in the Camp games not for himself but for his section, and on the last day of the Camp the score in points of each group was read out and the two leading ones were presented with medals; the groups were so equally matched that difference in scores between the first and the last was usually extremely small.

The games and competitions had to be carefully planned so that all should have an equal opportunity to excel. Thus orthodox cricket and football were ruled out as giving the public schoolboys too great an advantage ; and as one participant, later to become a distinguished member of the diplomatic service, wrote in his local paper on returning home, the games played were 'perfectly novel and unorthodox and had probably never been seen, much less played, by anyone before. . . . It was a work of genius to have devised games which were so fair for all, and these games struck the key-note of the Camp — an equal chance for all, with the individual, whether schoolboy or factory hand, working for his side and not for himself.' [3]

The Duke of York visited his guests on August 3. He crossed in the Royal Yacht from Cowes to Dover and completed the journey to New Romney by car. He may well have been apprehensive as to what he might find. After all, there was no precedent for what he had done. No member of the Royal Family had ever before taken so active and personal a part in such an enterprise. For better or for worse, he had given the prestige and the great influence of his name to a project which was to be carried out by people he hardly knew, and, although he was deeply and sincerely convinced of the need and justification of his experiment, the general mood of the times was scarcely confederate to its success. In the early 'twenties there was an atmosphere of suspicion and truculence abroad with which he had come into contact in his industrial visits, and even the best of motives were open to mistrust and misconstruction. The Trade Unions had been disturbed by the idea, and open scepticism had been expressed by many on the 'other side'. Inquisitive eyes were on him and, through no fault of his own, the scheme had had an unsympathetic press. To continue in the face of these difficulties had required both patience and fortitude — qualities, however, in which the Duke of York was never lacking — but, as he made the journey from the Isle of Wight to Kent, it would not have been surprising if he wondered whether the great ideals underlying his experiment would ever come to fruition or whether he had achieved anything more than providing four hundred fortunate young men with a unique holiday.

Any such misgivings which may have disturbed him must have been very quickly dispelled on his arrival at the Camp.

The spirit of happy comradeship was evident on all sides, as were the warmth of his reception and the regret at his departure. During the few hours of his visit he received genuine and spontaneous expressions of appreciation and good-will made in the most informal and charming manner, which banished all suspicion of insincerity or mere politeness, and when he left that evening it was with the certitude that his initial effort had been completely justified by the result. 'He was no longer vulnerable. He could now go on with confidence', writes Captain Paterson. 'He had four hundred staunch supporters. He had found the perfect means of exposing some of the nonsense that was talked about class relationships and placed the seal of his influence and leadership on a venture destined to go from strength to strength during the difficult years between the wars, and there can be no doubt of its contribution to strengthening the ties between the Crown and the people.'

After the success of the first Camp there was no question in the minds of any concerned as to the desirability of a second or a third. Experience had taught much to the organizers, and their task was made the more easy by the offers of help and support which were forthcoming. Though Sir Alexander Grant continued to bear the greater part of the financial burden, others were ready to assist in service and in kind. Sir Charles Wakefield, whose house was near by, contributed all manner of seasonal delicacies. The catering was taken over by the managing director of a great chain of hotels, and the head of a large London electrical company became Camp Bursar. From first to last the indefatigable Mr. Hyde doubled the rôles of Padre and Camp Jester with inimitable success.

There was keen competition, too, to serve as Section Leaders and, as the years went by, those who had attended earlier Camps as boys returned in this capacity. All were inspired by the spirit of the Duke of York's ideal that 'the Camp is playing a part in oiling the wheels of industry with good fellowship and understanding',[4] and the leaven of the Duke's inspiration was working throughout the country.

The four hundred boys who had been the Duke's original guests carried away from that first Camp an experience which they never forgot and which they were anxious for others to share. 'In this short week', wrote one of them, 'a great end was achieved — the public schoolboy came to know his brother, the factory hand (and vice versa) — came to know him as a keen sportsman and a staunch comrade; in fact this camp came at a time when it was much needed, when men are striving after a false shadow of democracy which tends towards Bolshevism, when the two classes are at loggerheads.'

The 'first four hundred' were closely questioned on their return to their schools and industries, but their answers were the same: 'Come and try it'. Never again was there a lack of response to the Duke of York's invitation — indeed a rule had to be imposed that no boy could attend Camp twice — and never again was there that sickening silence at the outset when the boys first foregathered in the Riding School of Buckingham Palace. There was still a natural shyness, but, as one boy wrote later in his school magazine: 'Few of us can have held the slightest expectation that a camaraderie so spontaneous, natural and far-reaching would exist in so short a time between boys drawn from spheres so diverse'. Sons of industrialists occupied adjacent palliasses to their fathers' employees and struck up warm friendships, and on one occasion a prominent colliery owner who was a Section Leader found himself sleeping in the same hut with two of his pit-boys who were at that time out on strike, a circumstance which embarrassed none of them, nor disturbed their comradely relationship.

As the years passed, the Duke of York's interest and enjoyment in the success of the enterprise quickened, a fact which was manifested in the nature of his visits. At first his natural shyness and diffidence had been as great as anyone's and his first visit did not extend beyond a few hours, during which he wore a bowler hat and a lounge suit. This soon changed, and 'the Duke's Day' became the climax of the week. It had been suggested to him that he might spend the whole period in camp but this he vetoed with his usual common sense, saying: 'If I stay you will only be saying every morning: "What the devil shall we do with him next?" and your own work would be neglected'.[5] On the other hand, his own idea that he should drive down at midnight, dress in Camp kit in the morning and wander about unrecognized and free, was reluctantly abandoned as liable to attract too great a degree of publicity.

His custom became, therefore, to arrive in the morning before lunch, join in the meals and games and bathing and to leave after the evening entertainment.

Whilst in Camp the Duke, although dignified with the title of 'Great Chief', was just one more boy on holiday, taking an enthusiastic part in all activities. On one occasion a push-ball game had been arranged and he was asked if he would referee. 'Referee be damned,' said he, 'I'm going to play.' Shortly thereafter a lusty young Harlequin, burrowing his shoulder into the ribs of the man in front of him with the exhortation to 'push like Hell !', received the Duke's immediate answer, 'Damn it, I *am* pushing like Hell !'

When 'Under the Spreading Chestnut Tree' became the Camp song the Duke joined in vociferously, with all the accompanying manual gestures, and it may well be that this song, sung by the six thousand young men who attended the Camps held between 1921 and 1939, may have had as beneficial an influence for the Monarchy as 'Lillibullero' had a deleterious effect on James II, when it 'sang him out of three kingdoms'.

It was perhaps in the evening entertainments that the Duke showed himself in his happiest vein. A salient feature of the Camp, and one in which he took a particular interest, was the visits of distinguished public men, who might be Cabinet Ministers, labour leaders, great industrialists or eminent publicists.[a] Each was invited to make a three-minute address and was warned that at the end of this period a time signal would be given. What he was not told was that the signal was the discharge of a blank cartridge from a revolver. The Duke took a particular and impish delight in the efforts of great orators, accustomed to developing their views at length, to confine themselves to the three-minute limit and their chagrin at being cut short in mid-peroration. The speakers were listened to with interest and attention by the boys, but were also regarded as fair game. When a man could be observed making a desperate effort to keep within the time-limit, the audience, often egged on by the Duke, would cheer him to the echo, thus causing him either to proceed under difficulties or, by

[a] Among those who visited the Camp in this capacity were Lord Reith, Lord Macmillan, Lord Citrine, Colonel David Davies and the Rt. Hon. John Hodge, then Minister of Labour.

pausing, to lose some precious portion of his allotted span. On one occasion a speaker asked for an additional minute to complete his point and the Duke whispered, 'Give him four', meaning four minutes in all. Whether this was accompanied by a wink is unknown, but the time-keeper, misinterpreting the instruction, cut the appalled speaker short with four deafening discharges from the revolver.

That the Duke thoroughly enjoyed his day with his guests in Camp was clear to all. Of all the eighteen Camps held he only missed one, in 1934, when blood-poisoning of the hand from the prick of a rose thorn made it impossible for him to do more than greet the boys at the Riding School. Apart from everything else his day in Camp gave him an excuse for slipping away from the Cowes Regatta, which he never enjoyed ; but it also gave him the opportunity to take a personal part in the great project, which of his own initiative he had set on foot, and the sense of achievement as well as the complete absence of formality made him relaxed and happy.

Moreover he never forgot a boy whom he had met in Camp. Over and over again in his great industrial tours of Britain he would stop at a bench or an assembly-line beside a young man with : 'Hullo, you were in my Camp in such and such a year. How are you getting on ?' to the amazement of those about him. It was the same with the public schoolboys. An ambassador who came to kiss hands on his appointment to a capital behind the Iron Curtain was surprised to find that King George VI did not discuss with him the conditions of the country to which he had been accredited, but exchanged recollections of their common experiences at Camp. A few years later the same ambassador again had audience of his Sovereign, this time to receive the accolade of knighthood, and once again the King, having completed the ceremony, reverted to the topic of 'my Camp'.

Of the boys' reactions it is only necessary to offer two instances from the many hundreds available to indicate the success which the Duke's great project achieved. The first is one of a public schoolboy who wrote : 'Perhaps we were inclined to enter Camp, like the animals in Noah's menagerie, two by two, but we went out of it in clusters, and nothing really separated these clusters save the partitions in the carriages of the train. We felt it quite a wrench to say good-bye to so many good fellows, of only a week's acquaintance, but the best of friends all the same.'

The second instance is one of a young Glaswegian who also expressed his appreciation of the Duke's hospitality, but in his own way. He was known by his employers to be of 'Red' proclivities, but this neither hampered their selection of him to attend Camp nor his complete acceptance of and by his fellows when he got there. He returned a confirmed admirer of the Duke of York and years later, in his native Glasgow, broke up the meeting of a Communist agitator who had spoken disparagingly of the Monarchy.

The course of the Duke of York's Camp was not, however, without its ups and downs, and, because the Duke had assumed the ultimate responsibility, it was to him that the major problems were referred for decision. The site at New Romney, which in 1921 had been secluded and ideal, became a centre of tourist attraction. In addition, a number of holiday visitors had infiltrated into the immediate surroundings and their encroachment upon the privacy of the Camp presented too many embarrassments and diversions for the site to be suitable any longer.

Because the whole basis of the Camp was on an *ad hoc* footing and the decision to hold it from year to year was the Duke's alone, the problem was put before him, and, after consideration, he determined that it would be better to discontinue the Camp temporarily rather than hold it in unsatisfactory surroundings.

In communicating this decision to Sir Alexander Grant, he wrote :

As you know, I have decided, owing to the unsuitability of the site & the accommodation at New Romney, not to hold another Camp there again. The place is already over-crowded, & I dare not run risks of any kind with the boys who come to Camp as my guests. The Camp, I have always felt, is my own private enterprise & I do not want people to look upon it as a yearly institution, in the same way as they look upon others of a similar character.

For this reason, & for others with which I will not burden you, I have decided not to hold a Camp at all this year. I am very sorry that this decision has had to be made, but I hope that by next year a suitable site will have been found, & that the Camp will continue to play as valuable a part in the National life as it has done in the past.[6]

So there was no Camp in 1930, and the break in continuity was not unbeneficial. It emphasized the fact, as the Duke had written, that it was 'his own private enterprise' and not a permanent institution, and it also made imperative the finding of a new site. The Duke's hope that such a site would be forthcoming in the intervening year was realized through the public-spirited generosity of the people of the Suffolk seaside resort of Southwold, who, through their Mayor and Corporation, offered the amenities of Southwold Common to the Duke of York as a permanent site for his Camp if he should so desire it. The offer was cordially accepted for 1931, and for the next eight years the Camp was held there, its privacy being scrupulously respected by both townspeople and visitors.

Though the Duke always regarded the Camp as his own private enterprise — as indeed it was — he confined his participation to an ever-increasing interest and to a readiness to help in any emergency. He was always prepared to discuss any detail of organization, however small, but he never interfered. His complete confidence in those who ordered the direction of affairs and his never-failing gratitude were a source of constant pleasure and encouragement.

Although I am very bad at expressing myself [he once wrote to Captain Paterson] I cannot tell you how much I appreciate the way you run the Camp while it is in progress, but also for the immense trouble you take in getting employers to send the right type of boy.

I know how much work it entails both before and after and I thank you very much indeed for your great help to me in this work. I hope you will be able to be my Camp Chief for many years.[7]

Never until the closing ceremonies of the last Camp, held under unique circumstances in 1939,[a] did the Duke's interest flag, and the success and influence of his experimental project were so great that, as the result of a conversation in 1927 during his Australian tour with Lord Somers,[b] then Governor

[a] See below, Part III, pp. 397-9.
[b] Arthur Herbert Tennyson, sixth Baron Somers, K.C.M.G., D.S.O., M.C. (1887-1944), was Governor of Victoria from 1926 to 1931. He served as Deputy Chief Scout for Great Britain from 1936 to 1941, and as Chief Scout of the United Kingdom and British Commonwealth from 1941 until his death in 1944.

of Victoria, an Australian camp on similar lines to his own was established in the following year.

In assessing the contribution made by the Duke of York's Camp, it is difficult to over-emphasize the importance both to the Duke himself and to the social life of the country. To the Duke it offered an opportunity for personal service and activity, which he both desired and needed, and a unique means of expression for that practical idealism which was so essential a part of his character. It was an early manifestation also of that theory of monarchy which he was later to put into practice so successfully, the theory of a Sovereign who was in touch with his people, interested in their welfare and promoting it in so far as it lay within his power to do so.

To do something difficult and 'on his own' always gave the Duke immense pleasure, and the problems presented by the initiation and subsequent development of his Camp were of no mean dimensions. In view of the industrial situation in Britain in 1921 it is surprising that he was able to realize his ideal at all, and it is the more surprising to consider that in 1926 the Camp was able to continue after the bitterness engendered by the General Strike, and in the midst of the great Coal Strike which persisted long after the General Strike had collapsed.

Though the success of the Duke's enterprise was clearly apparent, the secret of that success is more difficult to define. Perhaps the most adept endeavour to do so was made by a visitor to the Camp of 1923, a Cabinet Minister, who broadcast for the B.B.C. an account of his experiences and impressions. On the material side, he said, he did not think that it differed very perceptibly from other camps. 'What did distinguish it was the real vital and spiritual force which animated alike the organizers and the Camp — the vital and spiritual force of help, of co-operation — in one word, of Love.'[a]

[a] This broadcast was made on August 16, 1923, by the Rt. Hon. Sir Anderson Montague-Barlow, K.B.E., when Minister of Labour. As a young man he had been Secretary of the Cambridge House Settlement in South London.

CHAPTER IV

WIDENING EXPERIENCE
1923–1926

(i)

THE Duke and Duchess of York returned from their honey-moon at the beginning of June 1923 to the residence which King George had granted them for their home — White Lodge in Richmond Park.

Standing between Sheen Gate and Robin Hood Gate, with a fine view over the Deer Park to Richmond, the Lodge had been built between 1727 and 1729 by George II as 'a place of refreshment after the chase'. In its original design it was a pleasant and simple house, called at first 'Stone Lodge', but very soon it came to be known as 'New Lodge' to distinguish it from 'Old Lodge', another residence in Richmond Park which the historian Lysons records as having been built on the site of 'a manor in the parish of Kingston, known as Hart-lington' and held in 1624 'in possession from the King *in capite*, by the 40th part of a knight's fee'.[1] It has long since disappeared.

Though originally intended by George II as a rural retreat from hunting, the New Lodge soon became the favourite resort of Queen Caroline, who loved to stroll in the long elm-lined avenue of close-shaven turf, now known as the Queen's Walk, and it was here that Sir Walter Scott, in *The Heart of Midlothian*, laid the scene of the famous interview between the Queen, the Duke of Argyle and Jeanie Deans, when the Scots girl pleaded so effectively for the pardon of her sister Effie, then under sentence of death for child murder.[2]

Princess Amelia, daughter of King George II, lived in New Lodge as Ranger of Richmond Park. She greatly en-larged the house, building on two wings in brick and changing the name to White Lodge. She was followed by Lord Bute and he by Henry Addington, first Viscount Sidmouth, during whose long occupancy of some fifty years, from 1792 to 1844, White Lodge was visited by many distinguished figures. Here, on the morning of September 10, 1805, Lord Nelson, driving over from Merton to visit his old friend before leaving for Portsmouth to embark in *Victory*, outlined the plan of attack which he intended to pursue should he be so fortunate as to bring the combined Spanish and French fleets to action. 'Rodney', he said, 'broke the enemy's line in one place, I will break it in two', and, with a finger dipped in wine, he drew upon 'a little round study table' the general character of the assault — which he subsequently carried out at Trafalgar — to be made in two lines led by himself and Collingwood.[3]

In Queen Victoria's reign White Lodge became in 1858 the first independent establishment of the Prince of Wales, though perhaps 'independent' is too extreme a term, since the future King Edward VII was housed in one wing in a state of monastic seclusion, with two tutors and three equerries operating under a rigorous code of disciplinary rules for the furthering of their charge's military and intellectual studies and also his manners and deportment.[4]

After the death of her mother in 1861 the Queen and the Prince Consort spent a part of their last summer together at White Lodge reading over the Duchess of Kent's diaries and correspondence, and a few years later, in 1869, it was bestowed upon the Duke and Duchess of Teck.

For Queen Mary, therefore, the house had a special significance. This was the home of her childhood; the house from which she had left to be married, and to which she returned for the birth of her first-born son. Here, too, both her parents died.[a] It was with Queen Mary that the idea had originated that the young Duke and Duchess of York should make their first home there — 'to keep it in the family' — and it was she who had superintended the greater part of the organization and decoration of the house against their return.

Like most young married couples the Duke and Duchess

---

[a] The Duchess of Teck died at White Lodge in 1897, the Duke in 1899.

were engaged at the outset with the myriad problems entailed
in getting into a new house, the engagement of staff, the
arrangement of furniture and the fitting in of their own personal
belongings, both new and old. At last all was complete, and in
some trepidation they invited King George and Queen Mary
to luncheon on the Thursday of Ascot week, June 28. 'I had
better warn you', the Duke wrote to his mother, 'that our cook
is not very good, but she can do the plain dishes well, & I
know you like that sort.' 5 The visit, however, was a great
success. The King and Queen not only enjoyed the 'plain'
luncheon but also toured the whole house and were delighted
with what they saw. 'May & I paid a visit to Bertie and
Elizabeth at White Lodge & had luncheon with them,' the
King recorded that evening. 'They have made the house so
nice with all their presents', and Queen Mary also thought
that they had made their home 'very nice'.6

But almost from the first the Duke and Duchess found
White Lodge an incubus and a liability. It was too big and
too expensive to maintain, and, moreover, it was very inconvenient. Whereas two hundred years before George II and
his Queen had found it a pleasantly secluded and rural retreat,
this was no longer true. Richmond Park, from being practically
in the country, had now become very easily accessible from
London, and on week-ends and holidays hordes of sightseers
arrived in cars and charabancs. They pressed around White
Lodge and its approaches so closely that the Duke and Duchess
scarcely dared to put their noses out of doors, and all sense of
privacy departed. Yet this propinquity to London was in a
sense only 'one way'. Richmond was really too far out for
those attending functions in the city, and an extra half-hour
for the journey had to be added to the time-table of any
engagement. Moreover in winter it was very foggy, and on
more than one occasion the chauffeur lost his way and spent
a dispiriting hour or more wandering around Richmond
Park.

By 1924 the Duke was pressing for a change of residence,
and urging the necessity for a home in London. This, however,
was not so easy to arrange. In the first place, suitable London
houses were hard to find and, in the second, the regulations
governing the Royal residences in the parks of Richmond and

Windsor made it difficult to find a fitting incumbent for White Lodge. Three years passed in prolonged negotiations before the difficulty could be resolved, and it was not until after their return from Australia and New Zealand that the Duke and Duchess were able to settle in 145 Piccadilly, which was to be their home for the next ten years.[a]

Nor was the housing problem the only personal issue with which the Duke was confronted in the early days of his marriage; there was also the question of his Household. Hitherto he had had an equerry in attendance, first Lieutenant-Commander Campbell Tait and later Wing Commander Louis Greig, but on his creation as Duke of York in 1920 Greig had become the Comptroller of his Household, with Captain the Hon. James Stuart [b] as equerry, and, for the space of one year, Colonel Waterhouse served as Private Secretary prior to his appointment to the Prime Minister's office. It was Louis Greig, however, to whom he had given his early affection at Osborne, who had been the constant friend, companion and mentor of his bachelor life, and the relationship, a wholly felicitous one, had been of the utmost benefit to him. He knew that he owed much to Louis Greig and he was both appreciative and grateful. With the Duke's marriage, however, and the setting up of an independent *ménage*, it was natural that a change should come, and both realized the necessity for this. Wing Commander Greig retired from the Duke's Household at the beginning of 1924, though he retained for the remainder of their lives the personal friendship and confidence of both King George V and his son.

The new Comptroller of the Household was Captain Basil Brooke, [c] a naval officer only recently retired, and as his equerry the Duke appointed Lieutenant Colin Buist, an old

---

[a] In 1927 White Lodge was leased to Lord Lee of Fareham, the donor of Chequers to the nation. It remained in private occupancy for a number of years, and was used by the Government as a residence for Marshal Tito and his retinue, when the President of Yugoslavia made a State visit in 1953. In 1955 it was granted as a permanent school for the Royal Ballet.

[b] Rt. Hon. James Stuart, C.H., M.V.O., M.C., M.P. (b. 1897), the third son of the seventeenth Earl of Moray, served as Secretary of State for Scotland from 1951 to 1957.

[c] Rear-Admiral Sir Basil Vernon Brooke, G.C.V.O. (1876–1945), remained as Comptroller of the Duke of York's Household until 1937, when he became Groom-in-Waiting and Extra Equerry to King George VI and Treasurer to the Queen.

friend and fellow term-mate in the Grenvilles at Osborne and at Dartmouth.*

(ii)

Both the Duke and Duchess of York desired to travel and see something of the British Commonwealth before settling down to the regular routine of married life.   In the course of the Imperial Conference in the summer of 1923 the Duke hinted to one of the Dominion Premiers that they might be invited to visit his country, and the Prime Minister undertook to sound the King on the subject.   King George was not averse to the principle of this, but felt that it could not take place at once 'because the young people had just been married and must settle down' — a view exactly contrary to that of the 'young people' concerned — and there the matter ended for the time.

In the autumn, however, an opportunity for foreign travel did present itself, though not of the nature which they had originally desired.   A double event of some significance was to take place in Belgrade on October 21 and 22, 1923.   The infant son of King Alexander of Yugoslavia was to be christened, and King Alexander's cousin, Prince Paul, was to wed Princess

---

* The appointments to the Household of the Duke of York may be summarized as follows :

Private Secretary

1921–1922	Lieut.-Colonel R. Waterhouse
1927–1934	Mr. Patrick Hodgson
1934–1936	Commander Harold Campbell, R.N.
1936–1937	Sir Eric Miéville

Comptroller

| 1920–1923 | Wing Commander Louis Greig |
| 1923–1937 | Captain Basil Brooke, R.N. |

Equerries

1917–1918	Lieut.-Commander Campbell Tait, R.N.
1918–1920	Wing Commander Louis Greig
1921–1922	Captain the Hon. James Stuart
1922–1923	Wing Commander Louis Greig
1924–1928	Lieut. Colin Buist, R.N.
1928–1936	Major Terence Nugent
1930–1934	Commander Harold Campbell, R.N.
1934–1937	Viscount Coke

Olga of Greece.[a] At the first of these ceremonies the Duke and
Duchess of York were invited to stand as god-parents ('Koom'
and 'Koomitsa') to the infant Prince Peter, and it was suggested that at the second the Duke might be the official representative of King George.

The prospect of a third visit to the Balkans was not one
which commended itself to the Duke of York, who was planning
a holiday at Holwick Hall, a property of the Strathmore family
in County Durham. Neither the King nor the Foreign
Secretary, Lord Curzon, had put pressure upon him to accept
the Yugoslav invitations, and, having virtually dismissed the
idea, he was already installed at Holwick when the Foreign
Office changed its mind. For various reasons of State it was
now considered highly expedient that the Duke should be
present at these two ceremonies in Belgrade and Lord Curzon
urged this upon the King so strongly that His Majesty telegraphed somewhat apologetically from Balmoral on September
23, asking his son to leave almost at once.

The Duke was not best pleased. As a bachelor he might
not have found so sudden a change of plan inconvenient, but
it was not so easy for the Duchess to depart at a moment's
notice. In any case, this precipitate disarrangement of their
holiday plans was far from his liking. 'Curzon should be
drowned for giving me such short notice', he wrote in exasperation to Louis Greig on September 24, '. . . he must know
things are different now.' But despite the inconvenience and
the brief period afforded for preparations, the Duke and
Duchess left London on October 18 for Belgrade.

Once again the splendour of Balkan royal pageantry was
spread forth. The importance of the occasion lay in the fact
that it was intended, erroneously enough, to celebrate the
assured succession of the House of Karageorgević upon the
throne of the new Triune Kingdom of the Serbs, Croats and
Slovenes (soon to be simplified into 'Yugoslavia'), and, at the

———

[a] Prince Paul was the son of Prince Arsène Karageorgević, brother of King
Peter I of Serbia, and Aurora Demidoff, a member of a wealthy aristocratic
Russian family. Born in 1893, he was left without a home a few years later, on
the separation of his parents, and was brought up by King Peter with his own
sons. Princess Olga was the eldest daughter of Prince Nicholas of Greece, third
son of King George I, and the Grand Duchess Helen Vladimirovna of Russia.
Her youngest sister, Princess Marina, married Prince George, Duke of Kent, in
1934.

same time, to strengthen further the dynastic ties which bound the Balkan Royal Families together. No effort was spared by the indefatigable Queen Marie of Rumania to emphasize the family connection with Britain, and also the solidarity of the Balkan monarchies, whom she had sought to unite by a web of family alliances.[a] All the relations were there. 'We were quite a large family party & how we all lived in the Palace is a mystery', the Duke wrote to his father. 'We were not too comfortable & there was no hot water ! !'[7]

The gift of futurity of vision is perhaps never one to be desired, but had it been available to any of the participants in these twin ceremonies, the effect might well have been one of gloom. For of the two principal figures, the infant prince was to be driven by the forces of Nazi aggression from the throne which he had ascended at the tender age of eleven, while the bridegroom was to take such action in the moment of his country's peril as to call down upon himself the obloquy of the world.

No such foreboding, however, marred the two ceremonies. At the first, on October 21, the Duke had a prominent, and slightly embarrassing, part to play. Having received a suit of hand-embroidered underwear from the parents of the child, in exchange for the traditional 'Koom's' gift of a gold coin, the Duke had entire charge of the baby, which he carried on a cushion, for the greater part of the service. It was indeed due to his quick thinking that a calamity was avoided. The moment arrived when the Patriarch of the Serbian Orthodox Church, a man of great dignity and many years, had to receive the baby from the 'Koom' for total immersion, and the infirm old gentleman, losing his grip on the Crown Prince, allowed him to slip completely into the font. With a quick movement the Duke scooped up the baby and returned him to the shaking hands of the Patriarch. Thereafter the Duke bore his charge, screaming with resentment at such treatment, three times around the altar, preceded by a deacon with a thurible emitting clouds of incense.

You can imagine what I felt like carrying the baby on a cushion [the Duke wrote later to King George]. It screamed most of the

---

[a] Of Queen Marie's children, one daughter became Queen of Greece and the other Queen of Yugoslavia. Her son, King Carol II, married Princess Helen of Greece. Both the Greek marriages ended in divorce.

time which drowned the singing & the service altogether. It was made as short as possible, which was lucky & the chapel was of course over-heated as they were frightened of the baby catching cold. Poor Mignon[a] was in bed all the time as she had some complication which started after she was up. I expect she got up too soon.[8]

According to Serbian tradition the duties of 'Koom' by no means end with the formalities of the christening. He is responsible for the supervision of the child's education and later, when the question of marriage arises, he must be consulted on the choice of a bride. The Duke of York never assumed any obligation lightly, and in the years to come he was to discharge his responsibilities to his godson in no mere superficial manner.

On the following day the marriage of Prince Paul and Princess Olga was solemnized by the Patriarch of Serbia, and after the ceremony the Royal relations, with the Duke and Duchess of York, watched the bride carry out the traditional Serbian wedding customs of stepping over a strip of cloth, symbolizing the moat of her husband's house, of scattering corn and kissing a boy-baby — in this case the newly christened Crown Prince Peter.[9] Of the wedding the Duke wrote :

Cousin Missy[b] as usual was in great form. Aunt Sophie[c] was there too. She has aged a great deal, poor lady, after all she has been through. She sent you & Mama many messages & is longing to come back to England. . . .[10]

This was the Duchess of York's first encounter with the continental relations of that great family network into which she had married. With the exception of the bride and bridegroom, she had met none of the galaxy of Balkan royalty, regnant and exiled, with which she was now confronted. She survived the ordeal with complete success, and her charm carried all before it. The Duke wrote proudly to his father :

They were all enchanted with Elizabeth especially Cousin Missy. She was wonderful with all of them & they were all strangers except two Paul & Olga.

[a] Queen Marie of Yugoslavia.
[b] Queen Marie of Rumania.
[c] The exiled Queen of Greece.

On the Duke's return to England there were questions both large and small to claim his attention. The Conservative Government, in which Mr. Stanley Baldwin had succeeded Mr. Bonar Law as Prime Minister in May 1923, had encountered substantial difficulties at home and abroad. The Ruhr Crisis[a] and the Corfu Incident[b] had exacerbated Britain's relations with France and Italy respectively, and the domestic economic situation seemed to Mr. Baldwin to demand revolutionary fiscal measures — namely, Protection — for its amelioration. On November 12, therefore, two weeks after the Duke's return to London, the Prime Minister asked King George for a dissolution of Parliament in order that he might seek a mandate from the country for the introduction of tariff reform. The King used every means at his command to dissuade Mr. Baldwin from such a decision — but in vain — and took the gloomiest view of the Conservative prospects in an election.

His forebodings were justified. The country rejected the doctrine of Protection by a large majority. Mr. Baldwin was heavily defeated at the polls on December 8. The Conservatives lost 88 seats, their membership in the House of Commons being reduced from 346 to 258. Labour returned with a representation of 191, and the Liberals, momentarily reunited under the banner of Free Trade, increased from 117 to 158. A situation without precedent had arisen.

The Duke of York shared his father's anxiety and, like many others in England, looked with apprehension upon the future. 'The result of the General Election must be very

[a] On January 11, 1923, French and Belgian troops occupied the Ruhr Basin in the enforcement of sanctions for the failure of Germany to maintain her reparation payments. The British Government (Mr. Bonar Law) had refused to participate in this adventure, whose only effect was to inflame German nationalism and destroy the value of the Mark, which by the end of the year stood at the fantastic figure of RM. 22,300.000,000 to the pound sterling. The French regarded British non-participation as a betrayal of the Entente.

[b] The Italian Fleet, on the order of Signor Mussolini, bombarded Corfu on August 31, 1923, as a punitive measure for the murder by bandits a few days before of General Tellini, the Italian representative on the Greco-Albanian Frontier Commission. A number of fatal casualties resulted from the bombardment and the Greek Government referred the matter to the League of Nations, of which both the Council and the Assembly were then in session at Geneva. The British representative on the Council, Lord Robert Cecil, thundered against Italian aggression, but the Great Powers, fearful of the Duce's reactions, obtained the transfer of the dispute to the Conference of Ambassadors in Paris, who fined the *Greek* Government half a million pounds! Despite this gesture of appeasement, Signor Mussolini never forgot or forgave what had been said at Geneva.

worrying to Papa now. I wonder what is going to happen', he wrote to Queen Mary on December 10.

King George was in no uncertainty as to what was going to happen. He insisted that Mr. Baldwin must meet the House of Commons and only resign after being defeated. When this occurred, on a combined Labour and Liberal vote, he sent for Mr. Ramsay MacDonald on January 22, 1924, and confided to him the task of forming Britain's first Socialist Government.[11] In the meantime, he adjured his son:

You ought to go to the House of Commons when you can, there will be some very interesting debates which will become historical.[12]

Acting on this advice the Duke did attend several debates in the House at this time, being present on the occasion of Mr. Baldwin's defeat, and gained thereby a first-hand knowledge of parliamentary procedure and personalities.

For the winter of 1923-1924 the Duke and Duchess took 'The Old House' at Guilsborough in Northamptonshire, which was convenient for both the Pytchley and the Whaddon Chase, and here the Duke hunted as often as his engagements allowed. Often he would attend a meet in the morning, motor back to London later in the day to be present at, for example, the Church Lads' Parade at the People's Palace, and return to Guilsborough to hunt again on the following day. His life was strenuous at this time, but he never allowed his pleasures to interfere with his public engagements.

With the spring, however, they returned to the problems of White Lodge and the exasperating delays of building contractors. 'The Office of Works actually finished the boiler by Wednesday', the Duke wrote to Queen Mary, '& marvel of marvels they worked on Sunday!!'[13] But it was clear that, with the numerous engagements of a busy social season ahead, the continuation of White Lodge as a base of operations was impossible, and it was with relief that they accepted the offer of the loan of Chesterfield House, the London home of Viscount Lascelles and Princess Mary.

It was indeed a brilliant and crowded season. Londonderry House, Wimborne House, Forbes House, Derby House and Crewe House were still great centres of private hospitality at that time and, in addition to the public engagements in and out of London which always thronged his calendar, there was the gay social life of their own which the Duke and Duchess led among their friends. During this summer also there were two State Visits, in both of which, although the Prince of Wales was also there to share the burden, the Duke had to play a leading part. On May 12 the King and Queen of Rumania arrived, to be followed on May 26 by the King and Queen of Italy; while on July 7 the Duke was charged with the task of meeting the heir to the throne of Ethiopia, Ras Taffari,[a] on his arrival in London, and of conducting him on the following day to Buckingham Palace for an audience of the King.

Scarcely had the Lion of Judah departed when the Duke and Duchess of York on July 19 began an official visit to Northern Ireland. In the space of a crowded week the Duke unveiled a War Memorial to the members of the Queen's University, Belfast; received the Freedoms of Belfast and Londonderry and an honorary degree from the Queen's University; laid several foundation stones, and visited local industries. This was the first occasion since the momentous opening of the first session of its Parliament by King George V three years before[b] that a member of the Royal Family had visited Northern Ireland, and all the deep loyalty and attachment of the Ulsterman to the British Crown were made abundantly manifest in honour of the Duke and his Duchess. Both were deeply touched by their reception, and from Baron's Court, Newtownstewart, the residence of the Duke of Abercorn, where they stayed for two nights before returning to England,

[a] Ras Taffari (b. 1891) was the son of Ras Makonnen and the cousin of the Emperor Menelek of Ethiopia. After the revolution of 1916 which led to the enthronement of the Empress Zauditu, he was proclaimed Regent and heir to the throne, to which he succeeded in 1930 as the Emperor Haile Selassie. Driven from his country by Italian aggression in 1936, he took refuge in England, whence in 1940 he flew to Khartoum and took a prominent part in the reconquest of his country. He re-entered Addis Ababa at the head of the liberating forces in 1941.

[b] Under the Government of Ireland Act of 1920, a separate parliament and executive government were established for the six counties of Northern Ireland (Antrim, Armagh, Down, Fermanagh, Londonderry and Tyrone), and the parliamentary boroughs of Belfast and Londonderry. The first session of the Northern Irish Parliament was opened in person by King George V on June 22, 1921, amid scenes of wild enthusiasm.[14]

the Duke wrote a letter to his father which showed not only the impression which these demonstrations had made upon him, but also his keen appreciation of the part played by the Duchess :

Our reception has been quite astounding. There is no other word to describe the wonderful enthusiasm of the people of Belfast. They turned out in the streets at any time of the day & night, & the noise they made cheering was quite deafening. One could feel all the time that they were really genuine about it, & that they were pleased to see us. . . . We were received in the same wonderful way wherever we went even in the poorest parts, which shows how very loyal they all are to you. . . . Elizabeth has been marvellous as usual & the people simply love her already. I am very lucky indeed to have her to help me as she knows exactly what to do & say to all the people we meet. . . .[15]

(iii)

In the winter of 1924 the long cherished desire of the Duke of York to see something of the British Empire at first hand was at last gratified. Both he and the Duchess were badly in need of a holiday from the gruelling round of their official duties, and King George gave his consent for a visit to East Africa and the Sudan, which was to combine certain official duties with a good deal of big game hunting. The Duke was overjoyed, and, with a small suite,[a] they left England on December 1 to travel, via Paris, to Marseilles where they were to board the P. & O. liner *Mulbera*.

I don't think I really thanked you properly for allowing Elizabeth & me to go [the Duke wrote in farewell to King George just before leaving]. I am sure we shall enjoy the trip thoroughly in every way & besides being very interesting we shall gain a great deal of experience through what we shall see and do.[16]

The *Mulbera* sailed from Marseilles on December 5 in calm and sunny weather, but the Mediterranean soon justified its reputation for versatility and it was with thankfulness that the party arrived at Port Said five days later after a very cold and stormy passage. Here they found British warships stationed

---

[a] The Duke and Duchess of York were attended on this tour by Captain Basil Brooke, Lieut.-Commander Colin Buist and Lady Annaly.

on account of the tense situation created by the recent murder of the Sirdar, Sir Lee Stack,[a] but the Duke was delighted to find among them his old ship *Malaya*, in which he dined. An afternoon spent at Aden on the 16th was the occasion for a visit to the famous Tanks which supply water to the town, and are locally attributed to the far-sighted construction of King Solomon. Between Aden and Mombasa the *Mulbera* 'crossed the Line', and with the time-honoured tributes and indignities the Duke and some fifty other neophytes were made free of King Neptune's domains. On December 22 they landed at Mombasa.

Here they received their first introduction to that strange amalgam of ritual and rhythm which is so great a part of the mystery of Africa. A great native dance festival, or *ngoma*, had been organized in their honour, to which they went after a garden party given at Government House by Sir Robert Coryndon.[b] It was held in a great open space and presented a most imposing sight. Five thousand native men and women were assembled, in every kind of dress and colour, representing every tribe, and each in turn performed their own special tribal dance. They had already been dancing for three days and were drunk with rhythm, with the weird haunting strains of strange instruments and the never-ceasing throb of the tomtoms.

Representatives of all the different tribes had been collected [the Duke wrote to King George] & they danced their own particular dances, some of which were very weird. The music was also very odd & it consisted of numerous tom toms & a special kind of horn which they' blew through & the noise at times was quite deafening. It was most interesting to have seen.[17]

The Duke was anxious to gain as much insight as possible

[a] Major-General Sir Lee Stack, G.B.E., C.M.G. (1868–1924), Governor-General of the Sudan and Sirdar of the Egyptian Army, was mortally wounded in Cairo on November 19, 1924, by Wafdist gunmen. He died on the following day. As a result the British Government insisted that all Egyptian troops should be withdrawn from the Anglo-Egyptian Sudan, the garrisoning of which was henceforth to be undertaken entirely by British troops.

[b] Sir Robert Coryndon, K.C.M.G. (1870–1925), was Cape Colony born, and had been private secretary to Cecil Rhodes from 1896 to 1897, and during the parliamentary inquiry into the Jameson Raid. He was Governor of Uganda from 1917 to 1922, when he was appointed Governor of Kenya and High Commissioner of Zanzibar. His sudden death on February 10, 1925, caused a complication in the programme of the Duke of York's tour.

during his travels into the working of colonial government and before leaving Mombasa that night he had a long talk with the Governor, asking the kind of questions which indicated that he had briefed himself fully before leaving England. He reported to his father :

Sir Robert Coryndon seems to be a very nice man & very alive to his responsibilities out here. I had a talk with him last night & he told me what a wonderful future this Colony has before it. Both during & after the War things were not too bright here but now things have settled down & the place is growing steadily. There is a very good type of settler out here & most of them are gentlemen in the true sense of the word.[18]

The Christmas which the Duke and Duchess of York spent at Government House, Nairobi, could scarcely have been in greater contrast to those passed previously at Sandringham, at St. Paul's Walden Bury or at Glamis. The journey which they had made from Mombasa in the Governor's train had taken them through a wonderland of jungle and mountain and plain, and at almost every moment their interest and curiosity were held by some new sight, some fresh experience. Snow-capped Kilimanjaro towered sixty miles away, as the train bore them to the famous Athi Plains, and, when they reached the Game Reserve, they moved to a seat in front of the engine the better to see the wonders of the country.

The train journey was most interesting [wrote the Duke]. A distance of 325 miles through absolutely wild country ; untouched as yet by man through lack of surface water, though it will be in time, where we saw different animals including zebra, hartebeeste, ostrich, baboons, & wildebeeste quite near the line. The country is very fairly open all the way with grass & stunted trees. Nearer Nairobi you reach the Athi Plains which are quite flat & the animals roam about just outside the town. We had a wonderful reception at the station & on our way to this house. The people have been too kind to us in every way & I am sure we are going to have a real holiday.[19]

There followed some six weeks of safari, with game hunting which could not have been better calculated to delight the heart of a keen sportsman and an excellent shot such as the Duke, though, like every new-comer, he did not show himself at his true form for the first day or two. The brilliant light and the clear atmosphere affect everyone when first shooting on safari, and, though this had been explained to the Duke, it worried him somewhat.

I found it difficult to gauge the distance of the shots in the morning as the light was very odd [he confided to his diary [a]]. This does happen to people when they start shooting out here & it is very disconcerting.   Also everything is so new now.[20]

But this difficulty was quickly overcome, and the Duke was soon shooting as well as ever.   So also was the Duchess, who showed her proficiency with a 0·275 Rigby rifle to excellent effect.[b]

Even on holiday, however, the Duke could not escape the attention of the press.   News reports were issued weekly from the camp for the pressmen in Nairobi, and these were decked out in glowing and spurious exaggeration.   An alarming report appeared in the English press of the Duke's being charged by a rhinoceros, and fears were expressed for his safety lest he should be taking unnecessary risks.   The incident had been magnified out of all proportion, as the Duke's own diary account shows :

We found one Oryx alone shortly afterwards & we got up to him within 200 yds by keeping a tree between us & him.   I took a rest off the tree & fired & hit him.   He was facing me.   He went off & we followed & I hit him 3 more times when he lay down.   I was going to finish him off when we saw a Rhino on the edge of a thick patch of bush.   We forgot about the Oryx & went after the Rhino.   We followed him into the bush & suddenly came upon not one but 2 Rhinos lying down in the thickest part of the bush 8 yds away.   One got up towards us & Anderson fired & killed it. I did not fire as I could not see him properly.   It was most exciting. The other one ran away.   After this we went back & finished off the Oryx.   It was very hot by now at 11.30 & we were glad of the mules to ride home on.   Elizabeth came out with us in the afternoon after tea to look at the Rhino.

This is the Rhino the papers said had charged me.[21]

To his parents he wrote reassuringly : 'I am so sorry about

[a] The Duke of York kept a full and careful diary in pencil of his tour from his arrival at Mombasa on December 22, 1924, to his departure from Port Sudan on April 10, 1925.   It is preserved in the Royal Archives at Windsor.

[b] The Duchess of York obtained a specimen of the following animals : rhinoceros, buffalo, waterbuck, oryx, Grant gazelle, dik-dik, Kenya hartebeeste, steinbuck, water-hog and jackal.

the Rhino incident. It was quite untrue that she charged us properly. She was lying down only 8 yds from us & she got up towards us, that was all. . . . We are not out to take unnecessary risks but there is always a chance of them happening.' [22]

It was indeed a happy and exciting time, not unmixed with the hardships inevitable when on safari, but with new and fascinating adventures at every turn. The long hot days of hunting; the journey back with the game to the base camp by car or on mule-back; the cool velvety nights spent under canvas, when the silence might suddenly be broken by the galloping hoofs of zebras pursued by lions and hyenas, or the whole camp devastated by sudden fierce storms of wind and rain, with the tents of all collapsing around them and their belongings scattered in the sodden darkness; all these were experiences to be savoured to the full and cherished as memories. The Duke and Duchess fell in love with Kenya, its romance and its possibilities. In writing home about it, however, it is perhaps significant that it was to his mother rather than to his father that the Duke chose to express his enthusiasms and his criticisms, and, in the light of subsequent events, his views have an added interest:

We are both so impressed with this wonderful country [he wrote to Queen Mary] & it has certainly come up to & passed our expectations. I am certain people at home have no idea what its possibilities are & what its future one day is going to be. Everything is so new & utterly different to other parts of the Empire, & being so young it should be made gradually by the best people we can produce from home. By this I don't mean the settlers who are a very nice lot & for the most part real gentlemen, but the official side of the life of Kenya. I have had several talks with the Governor Sir Robert Coryndon & he is sorry to have to say that things are not quite as they should be owing to lack of first hand & personal knowledge of the officials at home. Ormsby-Gore,[a] who has just returned from a lengthy visit here, I understand has gone home with very different ideas to those with which he came out. I know you won't mind me telling you all this but I feel it is an important thing for this vast country to be better understood. [23]

[a] Rt. Hon. William George Arthur Ormsby-Gore, fourth Baron Harlech, K.G., G.C.M.G. (b. 1885), as Under-Secretary for the Colonies was chairman of the Parliamentary Committee which visited East Africa in 1924. He subsequently served, amongst other Government positions, as Secretary of State for the Colonies from 1936 to 1938, and U.K. High Commissioner in South Africa from 1941 to 1944.

Unfortunately Queen Mary's reply to this letter is not to be found, but it must have been a sympathetic one, for on March 21 the Duke wrote again :

Thank you so very much for your letter of the 8th Feb, in which you say you received mine safely. I was sure what I wrote would interest you as you are always so keen on getting first-hand knowledge. I was so struck at the time at the funny ways things were done at home, & the awful results that will ensue unless somebody is told before it is too late, & Kenya is much too valuable to mishandle.

The conquest was mutual, for Kenya reciprocated to the full the enthusiasm and the interest which the Duke and Duchess displayed so warmly. Greatly to his surprise — and no little to his embarrassment — the Colony expressed the wish to present the Duke with a farm, the offer coming through Sir Robert Coryndon. He was deeply touched by this mark of affection, and referred the matter to his father. It was not, however, considered expedient for him to accept the gift.

Of course it was kind of the Governor to have offered you a gift of a farm on behalf of the Colony [wrote King George]. I at once consulted the Colonial Office & I entirely agree with them that it would *not* be possible to accept it, (as I have telegraphed to you) it would create a precedent, which would mean that other members of the family might be offered farms in other colonies when they visited them. What would you do if the farm didn't pay ? The only way would be to buy a farm yrself (& you have no ready money) like David did in Canada & I thought that was a mistake.[24]

The Duke's holiday in Kenya was brought to a sudden and tragic conclusion on February 10, when word came to him of the death of Sir Robert Coryndon, after an emergency operation for pancreatitis. The Duke and his party were at that moment staying with Lord and Lady Francis Scott [a] at Rongai, two hundred and fifty miles from Nairobi, but he at once cancelled all engagements, and, with Captain Brooke and Lieutenant-Commander Buist, sped back to the Colony's capital to be present at the funeral of one who had endeared himself to

[a] Lieut.-Colonel Lord Francis George Montagu-Douglas-Scott, K.C.M.G., D.S.O. (1879–1952), sixth son of the sixth Duke of Buccleuch, settled in Kenya after the First World War and became a leader of the European inhabitants of the Colony, serving as a member of both the Executive and Legislative Councils. He married Lady Eileen Elliot, daughter of the fourth Earl of Minto.

Kenya as a fine soldier, a renowned big game hunter and a great administrator.

The Governor was buried with military honours [the Duke recorded in his diary]. All the inhabitants, whether European, Indian or Native turned out to watch the procession. It was a fine sight & showed how high a reputation Sir Robert Coryndon had in the Colony. He will be a great loss at this time as he did understand what was wanted & was all out for getting it. He will be a difficult man to replace.[25]

Nor was this the Duke's only anxiety. News reached him of the serious illness of King George, who on February 15 had developed an acute attack of bronchitis. Cables from London, however, were reassuring, telling him that his father was recovering but that the doctors had insisted upon a cruise in southern waters. 'I was so sorry to hear you had been ill but was greatly relieved by your cable', wrote the Duke. 'So you are going for a cruise in the Yacht to the Mediterranean which I hope will make you quite fit again.'[26]

Out of respect for the mourning for the Colony's dead Governor, the Duke cancelled the remainder of his Kenya tour, including, to his great regret, a lion hunt by spearmen in the Nandi country, and proceeded at once to Uganda, leaving Kisumu on February 15 and concluding his visit on March 5 at Nimule on the borders of the Sudan. His own account of these eighteen days' travel, with its variety of incidents, is contained in a letter to King George:

We left Kisumu by steamer & crossed the Victoria Nyanza & after seeing the Ripon Falls which is the source of the White Nile at Jinja we reached Entebbe the next day. Mr. Jarvis the acting governor met us & the following 2 days we were in Kampala where we visited the Kabaka of Buganda when I invested him with the K.C.M.G. He was very pleased about it. On the Sunday we went to church in the Cathedral & visited the Catholic Missions who are all doing good work among the natives. For the last week we have been on safari in the Semiliki Valley where we had good sport, as there was plenty of game & they were not too difficult to get up to. The Valley runs parallel to the Ruwenzori range which is in the Belgian Congo. The country is so different to Kenya & much more tropical & much hotter. Uganda is not so attractive as Kenya in any way. This is not a good time of year to see it as it is the dry season, & the natives burn all the elephant grass which

grows to a great height, & the smoke from the fires cause a great
cloud which shuts out the sun & the ashes are blown everywhere
& settle on everything.   We did see the snow tops of Ruwenzori
one evening from the valley.   We reached Lake Albert 2 days ago
& after calling at Butiaba on the lake we went on to our next camp
for elephant.   When we got there we discovered that they had
gone inland again so we went on in the steamer the 'Samuel Baker'
down the White Nile to another place after 3 hours steaming.   We
landed at Katengeri & made our camp & in the afternoon I went
off with Salmon the game ranger & in the evening I shot a very
good elephant whose tusks weighed 90 lbs each.   It was very lucky
as there are not very many big ones left.   I got a smaller one 2 days
later, Brooke got a 70 pounder & a 45 pounder & Buist also got an
elephant the last day.   So we did well in the home of the elephant.
The next day March 3rd we reached Rhino Camp & I went out
& shot a White Rhino with a horn 33" long which is quite good.
Out here they are considered a very fine trophy & so they are,
but they are quite easy to shoot & do not charge people like the
Kenya ones do.   We saw at least 30 of them but they were all small.

We finished our Uganda visit yesterday morning having arrived
at Nimule the night before.   The rudder post of the 'Samuel
Baker' got bent the night before so we had to stop to make it good
which took all night.

We are now on board the 'Nasir' a river steamer where we
arrived yesterday after motoring from Nimule to Rejaf a distance
of 90 miles on a very bad road.   I am sure it will be an interesting
trip down the Nile & we should see plenty of game of all sorts.[27]

The Duke's expectations were not disappointed.   Their
journey down the Nile was full of pleasure.   The weather was
very hot and because of the scarcity of water, herds of white-
eared Kob and other game would come down to the river-
bank to drink.   Sometimes expeditions were organized from
the river-boat and on other occasions they would tie up for a
day or two and go inland to shoot.   At Tonga they arrived in
time for the annual native tribal gathering at Talodi, at
which some 12,000 Nubian tribesmen marched past and
afterwards gave an exhibition of the particular form of wrestling
for which they were famous.

One of the features of these games is the Nuba wrestling [he
wrote to the King].   They are enormous men, & wrestle all dressed
up; that is, what they call dressing.   They have a belt covered
in bells round the middle from which hang monkey's tails & all
sorts of things they can get hold of.   They seem to understand

sportsmanship as they never argue over a decision & there is no fouling of any sort.[28]

At length they reached Khartoum,

> Where the Blue Nile into the White Nile slips
> And the long betrothed at last take hands,

and stayed at the great palace that Kitchener had built on the site of that simpler residence where Gordon had met his lonely, tragic death, and which the Mahdi had destroyed. Here they were entertained by the new Governor-General, Sir Geoffrey Archer,[a] and taken to the battlefield of Omdurman, where the Dervish hordes had been scattered, the power of the Emirs broken for ever, and the murder of Gordon finally avenged.[b]

On April 9 the Duke and Duchess embarked in the P. & O. liner *Maloja* at Port Sudan and ten days later they arrived back in London, in time to greet King George and Queen Mary on April 25 on the return from their Mediterranean cruise. It was not a complete family reunion, for the Prince of Wales had departed a month before on his tour of South Africa. The King had quite recovered his health, and in his son and daughter-in-law he saw two young people whose eyes had been opened and whose horizons had been broadened by their weeks of travel, and who had proved themselves calm in emergency and cheerful in hardship.

(iv)

Fresh from the experiences of his East African tour and fired with the new enthusiasm which his travels had kindled, it may be imagined with what zest and energy the Duke of York threw himself, on his return to London, into his duties as the President of the British Empire Exhibition. Little more than

---

[a] Sir Geoffrey Archer, K.C.M.G. (b. 1882), a Colonial civil servant, was appointed Governor-General of the Sudan in December 1924 after the murder of Sir Lee Stack. He remained in this post until 1926.

[b] On December 2, 1898, Sir Herbert Kitchener, with a force of some twenty-three thousand British and Egyptian troops, attacked and conclusively defeated the army of the Khalifa, fifty thousand strong, at Omdurman, thus freeing the Sudan from the corrupt government of the Emirs. It was at this battle that there occurred the famous charge of the 21st Lancers in which Mr. Winston Churchill took part and of which he gives so vivid a description in *The River War*.

a year before, the thousands who had packed Wembley Stadium
had watched the slim golden-haired figure of the Prince of
Wales, as he formally requested the King his father to open
this great gathering of imperial effort which had been brought
together in his honour and in honour of the British Empire.
In response King George had spoken briefly, and for the first
time many hundreds in Britain had heard their Sovereign's
voice, for this was the first occasion on which he broadcast.[29]
'Everything went off most successfully', the King had noted in
his diary.[30]

Now the Duke of York had succeeded his elder brother as
President of the Exhibition, and the date chosen for the second
opening was May 10, 1925, the fifteenth anniversary of the
accession of King George V. Keenly anxious to stimulate
public interest in this great display of Empire, the Duke
adopted the course of appealing directly to the public. He
arrived back from Africa on Sunday, April 19, and on the
following Tuesday a message appeared in *The Times* over his
signature.

> The British Empire Exhibition aims to complete in 1925 the
> educational work for Empire unity and Empire trade so well begun
> in 1924. The task of showing fresh aspects of our great heritage
> has been taken up with vigour and enthusiasm, and the new picture
> of the Empire will be even more vivid than the old. I ask for it the
> fullest measure of public support.
>
> ALBERT, President.

But the Duke was desperately apprehensive about his own
part in the forthcoming ceremony. His stammer was still a
grievous burden to him, and he also suffered the normally shy
man's dread of the microphone. His speech was a brief one
and he rehearsed it feverishly, both at home and at Wembley,
and it was on this latter occasion that his distrust of the microphone received an additional fillip. Standing in the vast empty
expanse of the Stadium he began to speak so that the engineers
might test the amplifiers. After a few sentences he realized
that no sound was coming through and turned to draw the
attention of the officials to this fact. He succeeded beyond
his expectations, for his remark : 'The damned things aren't
working' was carried in a mighty roar throughout the Stadium
— the switch had been thrown at that particular moment.

As the day of the opening approached, the Duke's anxiety mounted. Not only had he to speak to this great expectant multitude and the even greater 'cloud of witnesses' of the radio listeners, but it was the first occasion on which he had spoken before his father, and his heart quailed within him. 'I do hope I shall do it well', he wrote to the King. 'But I shall be very frightened as you have never heard me speak & the loud speakers are apt to put one off as well. So I hope you will understand that I am bound to be more nervous than I usually am.' [31]

When the day actually arrived he passed through the ordeal better than he had hoped. There were moments when he failed to articulate, but he refused to be stampeded into defeat, and kept on resolutely to the end. 'Bertie got through his speech all right, but there were some rather long pauses', the King wrote to Prince George on the following day.[32]

It was becoming increasingly clear, however, both to the Duke himself and to those around him, that courage and resolution were not sufficient. If he were to take his full part in the life of the country — and he longed to do so with the yearning of one who saw how much there was to be done — some better means must be found of curing his speech defect. But eighteen months or more were to elapse before this means was to be found, and in the interim he continued to suffer and to persevere.

In the winter of 1925 the Duke suffered a major bereavement. While he and the Prince of Wales were out hunting in Leicestershire on November 19, the news reached them that their beloved grandmother, Queen Alexandra, who, sixty-two years before, had been welcomed to England as 'the Sea-King's daughter from over the sea', had had a severe heart attack at Sandringham; and when they arrived at Wolferton Station the next afternoon they were told that she had died. They reached the house in time to join their parents for prayers around the bedside, mourning the passing of one who represented the last link with those happy interludes of their childhood.[33]

But a great happiness was approaching. At 2.40 in the morning of April 21, 1926, the Duchess of York gave birth to her first child, a daughter, who was third in succession to the throne. The baby was born at 17 Bruton Street, the home of the Duchess's parents, and the news was at once reported to Windsor. The King and Queen motored to London that afternoon to view their first granddaughter.[a]

We were awakened at 4.0 a.m. by Reggie Seymour [Queen Mary wrote in her diary] who informed us that darling Elizabeth had got a daughter at 2.40. Such a relief and joy . . . at 2.30 we went to London to 17 Bruton Street to congratulate Bertie & we found Celia Strathmore there, saw the baby who is a little darling with a lovely complexion & pretty fair hair.

The Duke was overjoyed both at the arrival of his daughter and at the evident satisfaction of his parents. There may have been some uncertainty as to an assured welcome for a girl, but there is no doubt as to the felicity which her advent had conferred upon her mother and father. 'You don't know what a tremendous joy it is to Elizabeth and me to have our little girl', the Duke wrote to Queen Mary. 'We always wanted a child to make our happiness complete, & now that it has at last happened, it seems so wonderful & strange. I am so proud of Elizabeth at this moment after all that she has gone through during the last few days, and I am so thankful that everything has happened as it should and so successfully. I do hope that you & Papa are as delighted as we are, to have a grand-daughter, or would you have sooner had another grandson. I know Elizabeth wanted a daughter. May I say I hope you won't spoil her when she gets a bit older.'[34]

There followed almost immediately the national emergency occasioned by the General Strike of May 4-12. Because of his considerable understanding of industrial conditions and his deep concern for the fundamental issues involved, the Duke, putting aside his new-found pride in parenthood, took a lively interest in the course of the crisis. He attended daily in the House of Commons, listening attentively to the debates and to the cold logic with which Sir John Simon pronounced the Strike to be unconstitutional, and he bore away his impressions for future contemplation.

In the meantime, however, a vitally important domestic question had been exercising the minds of the Duke and

[a] The first grandchild of King George and Queen Mary was the elder son of Princess Mary and Lord Lascelles who had been born on February 7, 1923.

Duchess of York — the naming of their daughter. The Duke
wrote to ask his father's consent to their choice:

Elizabeth and I have been thinking over names for our little
girl & we should like to call her

Elizabeth Alexandra Mary

I hope you will approve of these names, & I am sure there will be
no muddle over two Elizabeths in the family. We are so anxious
for her first name to be Elizabeth as it is such a nice name & there
has been no one of that name in your family for a long time.

Elizabeth of York sounds so nice too.[35]

King George readily approved. 'I like it & think it is a
pretty name', he replied; [a][36] and with the King and Queen,
Princess Mary, the Duke of Connaught, Lady Elphinstone
and Lord Strathmore as her god-parents, the infant princess
was christened by the Archbishop of York on May 29 in the
private chapel at Buckingham Palace. 'Of course poor baby
cried', wrote Queen Mary in her diary.

[a] 'I have heard from Bertie about the names,' the King wrote to Queen
Mary, 'he mentions Elizabeth, Alexandra, Mary. I quite approve & will tell
him so, he says nothing about Victoria. I hardly think that necessary.[37]

THE CHRISTENING OF PRINCESS ELIZABETH, MAY 29, 1926

CHAPTER V

THE WORLD TOUR AND AFTER
1927–1929

(i)

ON July 9 in the year 1900 the Commonwealth of Australia (Constitution) Act, having passed through both Houses of Parliament, received the Royal Assent. By virtue of this legislation New South Wales, Victoria, Queensland, South Australia, Western Australia and Tasmania ceased to be Colonies and became 'States', federated for special purposes under one Dominion Government. The Act came into operation on January 1, 1901, and was the last imperial measure of the Victorian era, which had seen the beginnings of the transition of the British Dominions into independent statehood.[a] Three weeks later the Great Queen was dead.

King Edward VII, after some initial reluctance at being parted from his son so soon after his accession to the throne,[1] signified his recognition of the importance of the infant dominion by sending the Duke of Cornwall and York to open on his behalf the first session of the Commonwealth Parliament on May 9, 1901, and this precedent was about to be revived.

Originally both the Commonwealth Government and that of the State of Victoria were housed in Melbourne, but in 1911 the Australian Government had acquired from the State of New South Wales an area of some 900 square miles, on which it was intended to create the Capital of the Commonwealth in federal territory. The planning for the site of the new city of Canberra had been interrupted by the First World War, but building operations were begun in 1923 and it was intended that the seat of government should be formally transferred to

[a] New Zealand had achieved self-government in 1852, though the designation of 'Dominion of New Zealand' was not assumed until 1907. The Dominion of Canada came into existence in 1867, and other possessions to obtain Dominion status before the accession of King George VI were the Union of South Africa in 1909, Newfoundland in 1917 and the Irish Free State in 1921.

the federal capital in 1927, when Parliament would meet for the first time in the new legislative buildings. To mark this milestone in Australian history the Commonwealth Premier, Mr. Stanley Bruce,[a] had in June 1926 requested King George that one of his elder sons might follow in his footsteps and perform the opening ceremony.

The Prince of Wales had already toured Australia in 1920 amid scenes of delirious enthusiasm,[2] and the King decided after consideration that it was now opportune for his second son to undertake a mission of first-rate imperial importance. He had, however, a certain hesitancy in making this decision. Despite the testimony of all those concerned with the Duke of York on his missions abroad as to the admirable, dignified and felicitous manner in which he had always comported himself, the King still retained a certain lack of confidence in his son's capacity to meet the responsibilities of a Royal Tour such as was now envisaged; and, in addition, there was the problem of his stammer. This was indeed a major factor. Mr. Bruce, who had heard the Duke speak on several occasions during the period of the Imperial Conference of 1926, was appalled at the prospect of the King's representative being so gravely inhibited; and the Duke himself, than whom there was none more acutely conscious of the difficulty, half-doubted his ability to carry out the heavy programme of speeches which formed an inevitable part of a Royal Tour. He was now thirty years old and, notwithstanding the courage with which he had stubbornly faced his ordeals of public speaking, and in spite of the understanding, the encouragement and the compassion which he received so unstintingly from the Duchess, the disillusionment caused by the failures of previous specialists to effect a cure had begun to breed within him the inconsolable despair of the chronic stammerer and the secret dread that the hidden root of the affliction lay in the mind rather than in the body.

But the hour of deliverance was at hand. October 19, 1926, was to be a momentous day in the life of the Duke of York, for on that day he had his first interview with Mr. Lionel

[a] Rt. Hon. Stanley Melbourne, first Viscount Bruce of Melbourne, C.H., M.C. (b. 1883), was Prime Minister of Australia from 1923 to 1929, and Australian High Commissioner in the United Kingdom from 1933 to 1945.

Logue, who has left his own record of the meeting: 'He entered my consulting room at three o'clock in the afternoon, a slim, quiet man, with tired eyes and all the outward symptoms of the man upon whom habitual speech defect had begun to set the sign. When he left at five o'clock, you could see that there was hope once more in his heart.'

Mr. Logue's career had been in many ways phenomenal. Born in South Australia in 1880, his education and training had been towards the calling of an engineer. He was in no way a qualified medical man and his gift of healing speech defect was revealed to him in dramatic and almost miraculous circumstances during the First World War. Later he specialized and became highly proficient in the art, and in 1924 he came to practise in London. His fame soon spread, and in the late summer of 1926 he was brought into touch with the Duke's Private Secretary, Mr. Patrick Hodgson.

The Duke was at first ill-disposed towards the idea of seeing Mr. Logue. He had had his fill of specialists who claimed to be able to cure stammering and he was thoroughly discouraged by a series of failures. It was the Duchess who persuaded him to make 'just one more try', and as a result a new aspect of life opened before him.

Mr. Logue's approach was both physical and psychological. His presence and personality inspired confidence, but by the very simplicity and sincerity of his nature rather than by any cultivated 'bedside manner'. Those who sought his professional advice felt immediately that not only did he believe in his own power of healing but he was able to inspire them with a similar belief both in him and in themselves. With a complete understanding of his own subject, he knew that the stammerer's first fear was of seeming 'different' from others. His first objective, therefore, was to convince his patient that stammerers were entirely normal people with a perfectly curable complaint. His treatment consisted of teaching the stammerer to breathe correctly, if necessary developing his lungs by physical exercises, and to control his diaphragmatical rhythm. The fundamental secret of his success was that, whereas from the first contact he caused the patient to believe in the certainty of a cure, he also made it absolutely clear that this certainty depended as much upon the patient as upon himself, and even more. 'There is only one person who can cure you and that is yourself' was a favourite dictum. 'I can tell you what to do but only you can do it.' The patient, having acquired initial confidence, was thereby brought into active partnership in his own treatment and was made to see that the ultimate goal of a successful cure was his for the gaining.

It was this element of challenge which appealed to the Duke of York. Deeply impressed by Mr. Logue's confidence and sincerity, he placed himself unreservedly in his hands. For the next two and a half months the Duke visited his consulting-room almost daily and religiously adhered to the system of exercises prescribed. The Duchess of York was also keenly interested. She too was a frequent visitor to Harley Street, acquainting herself with the details of the treatment in order to be of help to the Duke in the great odyssey on which they were both about to embark.

The progress in the Duke's speech was almost immediately manifest. After only a month's treatment he was writing with renewed hope to King George:

I have been seeing Logue every day, & I have noticed a great improvement in my talking, & also in making speeches which I did this week. I am sure I am going to get quite all right in time, but 24 years of talking in the wrong way cannot be cured in a month.

I wish I could have found him before, as now that I know the right way to breathe my fear of talking will vanish.[3]

Although in effect he never did lose his dislike of public speaking, and especially of broadcasting, the horrors of it were vastly mitigated for the Duke by Mr. Logue's treatment, and in the years ahead this was to become more and more apparent as greater demands were made upon him. For the moment the chief benefit was the removal of his immediate fears as to his capacity to carry out the Royal Tour, and, on the eve of his departure, he wrote to Mr. Logue in gratitude:

I must send you a line to tell you how grateful I am to you for all that you have done in helping me with my speech defect. I really do think you have given me a real good start in the way of getting over it & I am sure if I carry on your exercises and instructions that I shall not go back. I am full of confidence for this trip now.[4]

As will be seen, the Duke's confidence in himself was not misplaced. His speeches in Australia and New Zealand were, in the main, highly successful, though his stammer had a tendency to return if he became over-tired. This achievement developed the new-born faith in himself, and a greater sense of security in his relationship with his father. No longer was he tongue-tied in King George's presence. He was able now to speak fluently and forcefully. Later in the year, after his return from Australia, he wrote to Mr. Logue from Balmoral :

Up here I have been talking a lot with the King, & I have had no trouble at all. Also I can make him listen & I don't have to repeat everything over again.[5]

And King George was equally appreciative of his son's prowess in speech.

Delighted to have Bertie with me [he wrote to Queen Mary], he came yesterday evening, have had several talks with him & find him very sensible, very different to D.[6]

(ii)

The Duke and Duchess of York sailed from Portsmouth in the battle-cruiser *Renown* (Captain N. A. Sulivan) on January 6, 1927.[a] The King and Queen had bidden them farewell at Victoria, and the moment of their parting was a sad one, for it meant a separation from their baby daughter, Princess Elizabeth, then not quite a year old. 'I felt very much leaving on Thursday, and the baby was so sweet playing with the buttons on Bertie's uniform that it quite broke me up', the Duchess later wrote to Queen Mary. Twenty-six years before, the King and Queen had themselves made the same sacrifice at the call of Empire, leaving their young family behind them, and it was now their turn to be indulgent grandparents. They sent frequent bulletins on Princess Elizabeth's progress and

[a] On February 17, 1927, the Duke of York's tour was the subject of an attack in the House of Commons by certain members of the Labour Party on the grounds that a 'pleasure trip of this kind' should not be undertaken at a moment of industrial depression. In reporting this debate to King George the Prime Minister, Mr. Baldwin, sought to make light of the incident. This view, however, was not accepted by His Majesty, who not only expressed himself forcefully on the sentiments expressed by the Labour members, in a letter from Lord Stamfordham, but also rebuked Mr. Baldwin for his light-hearted treatment of the affair.[7]

behaviour, and themselves received the usual parental admonitions against spoiling. 'I am glad to be able to give you the most excellent accounts of your sweet little daughter, who is growing daily', wrote the King. 'She has 4 teeth now, which is quite good at 11 months old, she is very happy & drives in a carriage every afternoon, which amuses her.'[8]

I am so glad little Elizabeth is behaving herself so well with you [replied her father]. I do hope you will not spoil her too much, as I have always been told grandfathers are apt to.[9]

But separation from his daughter was not the only care weighing on the Duke of York's mind at the moment of his departure. He had a keen sense of the responsibilities ahead and was deeply appreciative of the imperial task which the King had assigned to him. 'This is the first time you have sent me on a mission concerning the Empire, & I can assure you that I will do my very best to make it the success we all hope for', he wrote to his father as *Renown* ploughed her way westwards,[10] and as an earnest of this he held frequent conferences with his Chief of Staff, General Lord Cavan,[a] and his Political Secretary, Mr. Harry Batterbee,[b] who had been attached to his suite.[c]

The route which *Renown* was to follow had not been decided upon without certain imperial searchings of heart. The invitation to visit Australia had been quickly followed by one from the Government of New Zealand, and this too had been accepted. The Australian Government, however, maintained that, as the opening of the Commonwealth Parliament at Canberra on May 9 was the *fons et origo* of the Royal Tour, the Duke and Duchess should proceed to Australia first and that New Zealand should be visited afterwards. These reasonings

---

[a] Field-Marshal Frederic Rudolph Lambart, tenth Earl of Cavan, K.P., G.C.B., G.C.M.G., G.C.V.O., G.B.E. (1865–1946), having commanded the Guards Brigade, and subsequently Guards Division, in the First World War, served as Chief of the Imperial General Staff from 1922 to 1926.

[b] Sir Harry Batterbee, G.C.M.G., K.C.V.O. (b. 1880), was at this time an Assistant Secretary in the Dominions Office. He subsequently served as United Kingdom High Commissioner in New Zealand from 1939 to 1945.

[c] Apart from the above, the suite of T.R.H. consisted of: Lieut.-Commander Colin Buist, R.N., and Major Terence Nugent, as Equerries; Mr. P. K. Hodgson, Private Secretary; Surgeon-Commander H. E. Y. White, R.N., Medical Adviser; and the Countess of Cavan and the Hon. Mrs. J. Little-Gilmour, Ladies-in-Waiting.

of prestige gave little reck, however, to considerations of climate and to the demands which would be made on the powers of endurance of the Duchess of York, and, in deference to these, it was decided that Their Royal Highnesses should go out by way of the Pacific, visit New Zealand first and conclude their tour with the great moment at Canberra. This decision was not well received in Australia: 'The question of the Duke and Duchess of York's visit to New Zealand and its place in Their Royal Highnesses' itinerary has upset the equanimity of the Commonwealth Government', wrote Lord Stamfordham to Sir Charles Fergusson,[a] the Governor-General of New Zealand [11]— but the decision was adhered to nevertheless.[b]

At Las Palmas and Jamaica, where they were received with enthusiasm, the Duke revived old memories of the *Cumberland* cruise of fifteen years before, but once the West Indies had been left behind and *Renown* had turned her bows towards the Panama Canal, all was new and unknown. They entered the Pacific Ocean on January 28 and four days later 'crossed the Line' with the traditional ceremony of initiation on entering into King Neptune's dominions. The Duke was hailed with the lines:

> Now is the winter of our discontent
> Made glorious summer by this sun of York,

and though he had himself been initiated during the voyage from Aden to Mombasa at the outset of his East African tour,[c] both he and Captain Sulivan offered themselves as the first victims for Neptune's marauding 'Bears'.

At early dawn on February 22 *Renown* passed the narrow

[a] General Sir Charles Fergusson, seventh Bt., G.C.B., G.C.M.G., D.S.O., M.V.O. (1865–1951), commanded the 5th Division, and subsequently the 2nd and 17th Corps, in the First World War, and was Military Governor of the British Zone of Occupied Germany from 1918 to 1919. He served as Governor-General and Commander-in-Chief of the Dominion of New Zealand from 1924 to 1930.

[b] The itinerary of the Royal Tour was as follows: Sail from Portsmouth, January 6, 1927 — Las Palmas — Jamaica — Colón — Panama — the Marquesas Islands — Fiji — arrive New Zealand (Auckland), February 22 — leave New Zealand (Kingston), March 22 — arrive Australia (Sydney), March 26 — leave Australia (Perth), May 23 — Mauritius — Port Said — Malta — Gibraltar — return Portsmouth, June 27. Accounts of the tour were later published by two accompanying journalists, Ian F. M. Lucas, *The Royal Embassy* (London, 1927), and Taylor Darbyshire, *The Royal Tour* (London, 1927).

[c] See above, p. 199.

straits into the bay of Waitemata, the port of Auckland, and a few hours later the Royal visit to New Zealand had officially begun — in sheets of rain. Two days before, the Duke had received a telegram from King George and Queen Mary:

You are about to land in New Zealand and start on the first stage of your mission; and we shall more than ever follow your doings with affectionate interest. There is a strenuous time before you but we know that you both will do everything to secure the success which has already attended your efforts.

G.R.I. & M.[12]

Just how strenuous the programme of welcome was may be judged from the letter which the Duke, tired but triumphant, wrote to Queen Mary five days later from Rotorua. 'I had to make 3 speeches the first morning. The last one in the Town Hall quite a long one, & I can tell you that I was really pleased with the way I made it, as I had perfect confidence in myself & I did not hesitate at all. Logue's teaching is still working well, but of course if I get tired it still worries me.' [13]

This was but the beginning. The Duke and Duchess now embarked upon an almost terrifying schedule of dinners, receptions, garden-parties, balls and other official duties — relieved by brief fishing excursions — which might well have daunted the courage and endurance of a less determined couple. Everywhere they were received with demonstrations of the most genuine enthusiasm and loyalty — for the New Zealanders are if anything *plus royalistes que le roi* — and everywhere the impression left by their visit was of something which had surpassed all expectations. This impression was no mere fleeting *feu follet*; it had its more vital and more lasting effects.

It is quite unnecessary to say that they both made themselves adored by everyone [the Governor-General wrote to the King]. This I know sounds like a newspaper expression but it is no more than the truth.

I want to tell Your Majesty of an incident. On the second day of the visit, Mr. Coates[a] met by chance a man who is a noted Communist agitator in Auckland. He said to Mr. Coates, 'I've done with this —— Communism.' Mr. Coates asked why this sudden conversion had taken place. The man said: 'Why, they're human! Yesterday I was in the crowd with the wife, and one of

[a] Rt. Hon. Joseph Gordon Coates, M.C. (1878–1943), was Prime Minister of New Zealand from 1925 to 1928.

the children waved his hand, and I'm blessed if the Duchess didn't wave back and smile right into my face, not two yards away. I'll never say a word against them again. I've done with it for good and all.'[14]

Indeed the vivid charm of the Duchess of York was a very real factor in the success of the tour. A more responsive personality than the Duke, she was able to complement his greater shyness by a radiance which carried all before it. 'She shines and warms like sunlight', a young Scotsman wrote of her at this time. 'I never used to believe the stories one reads about people swearing themselves "ready to die" for Mary, Queen of Scots, or Maria Theresa. But if they were anything like the Duchess of York I can easily understand it.'

The Duke made his own impression. He was most dignified, but it was noted that he had an unerring instinct for unbending just at the right moment to the right people on the right occasion. Moreover, his ever-genuine desire to acquaint himself with the interests of the people whom he met in city and country, and his unsparing efforts to understand their point of view, produced the same warm response that it had in Britain. His speeches were felicitous and sincere, and the emphasis which he frequently laid on child welfare was particularly appealing. It was now that he coined the slogan which was to be repeated by him and others throughout the Empire: 'Take care of the children and the country will take care of itself.'[a] Also, in a country of keen sportsmen, the fact that he showed himself a more than competent horseman, fisherman and tennis-player was an additional reason for the affection with which he came to be regarded by all New Zealanders.

Misfortune, however, was on the way. Their Royal Highnesses had completed their tour of the North Island and had reached Christchurch in the South Island when, on March 12, the Duchess succumbed to the strain of the Tour with an attack of tonsillitis and, on the orders of her medical advisers, was compelled to return to Wellington, there to rest and convalesce at Government House.

For the Duke this was a major tragedy. In addition to his natural anxiety, to be deprived of his wife's encouragement

[a] In a speech at a Government Luncheon at Wellington, on March 8, 1927.

and support at this moment was a blow which seemed at first to take the heart out of him.   In his innate shyness and modesty, he believed that it was the Duchess whom the crowds were really cheering and that it was she whom they really wanted to see. His first thought was to cancel the latter part of the tour of the South Island and to return to Wellington with her, but this very natural instinct was overcome by his sense of duty, and with a saddened heart he determined to complete the programme.

Nor was his spirit lightened to receive a letter from his father which indicated that King George was indeed following his son's tour with keen and critical interest.   The photographs of the Duke's arrival at Las Palmas had arrived in London late in January and the King had written: 'I send you a picture of you inspecting Gd. of Honour (I don't think much of their dressing) with yr. Equerry walking on yr. right next to the Gd. & you ignoring the Officer entirely. Yr. Equerry should be outside & behind, it certainly doesn't look well.' [15]

Wearily the Duke replied :

. . . I have your letter of the 25th Jan. to thank you for. I noticed the same thing about the photograph you sent me, & I can explain it easily. I had finished inspecting the guard of honour & was walking back to join Elizabeth. Buist was taking a message from me. It was an unfortunate moment for the photograph to be taken. . . .[16]

In a sense, however, the illness of the Duchess was not an unmixed evil, for it provided that element of challenge to which the Duke was ever responsive. The fact that he had to go on alone called out all his reserve powers and induced him to make a special effort — and with remarkable success. In Christchurch and Dunedin, in Ashburton, Timaru, Waitaki and Oamaru, and in the country districts which he visited, the people thronged about him with a gladness and a sympathetic loyalty that was the warmer for their appreciation of his coming to them at the cost of a certain self-sacrifice. He finished the tour with a new confidence in himself born of the welcome which he had received.

The Duke and Duchess were reunited in *Renown* on March 22 in perilous circumstances. If the weather on their arrival in New Zealand had been inclement, at the moment of their departure it was positively vicious. *Renown* had arrived at Invercargill in the Foveaux Strait at the southern tip of South Island to take the Duke aboard. A gale was blowing and a heavy sea running, and the battle-cruiser proceeded to Bluff, where it was hoped that an easier embarkation might be effected. Even so the Duke and his party were compelled to make use of a harbour tug in place of the New Zealand cruiser *Diomede* for the transit from shore to ship, and so rough was the passage that on reaching *Renown* the Duke had literally to be dragged on board by two seamen. The Duchess watched anxiously from the deck. 'I was glad to be on board', she wrote later to Lady Alice Fergusson, 'when I saw my husband being thrown (literally) from the bridge of the tug on to our quarter-deck at Bluff. It looked most unpleasant, but he did not seem to mind much.'

Thus ended the first lap of the Royal Embassage. 'I won't go on telling Your Majesty that the tour was a success, as that can be more properly estimated by others', wrote Sir Charles Fergusson to King George. 'But from New Zealand's point of view it could not possibly have given greater pleasure. . . . May I just say, Sir, how everybody appreciated to the full the way in which His Royal Highness threw himself heart and soul into the work of the tour. He never spared himself and went out of his way to give the utmost pleasure to everyone.' [17]

It was a fitting and well deserved encomium.

(iii)

The distance between Australia and New Zealand is considerably greater than the twelve hundred miles of the Tasman Sea which separates them geographically. In temperament, culture and general way of life New Zealand belongs to the Old World, and the fact that she has experienced a succession of Labour governments does not alter the fact that she is basically conservative, with a fine veneration for established institutions, especially the Monarchy, and a close attachment to the Crown Imperial.[a]

[a] New Zealand did not ratify the Statute of Westminster of 1931 until 1947, being the last Dominion to do so.

The spirit of the Island Continent is very different. If New Zealand belongs to the Old World, Australia belongs to both the Old and the New. She is a country in the full splendour of youth, already grown to statehood, with a concomitant vitality and independence, yet retaining many of the traditions of, and a great affection for, the Old Country. If New Zealand feels that her fundamental allegiance is to the Crown Imperial in London, Australia is equally definite in holding to the Crown in Australia. Both are staunchly monarchical, but with that variety of interpretation which makes the British Commonwealth a practical, viable and workable conception — and at the same time quite incomprehensible to the foreigner. Above all, Australians are respecters of persons for what they are rather than for what they represent, and it was in this spirit that they gave their unstinting welcome to the Duke and Duchess of York.

The conflict of prestige as to whether Their Royal Highnesses should first visit New Zealand or Australia, which had complicated the planning of their itinerary, had been repeated ın microcosm in the preparations for their landing at Sydney, involving a delicate point of relationship in federal government. Because they would first set foot on Australian soil in the capital of New South Wales, the authorities of that State claimed the honour of extending the initial welcome. The Commonwealth Government, however, argued that the Royal visit was to Australia as a whole and not to any particular State, and that the privilege of first welcoming the Duke and Duchess was clearly their prerogative. As neither party would abandon their contention, recourse was had to the way of compromise — ever a possible solution in British imperial affairs. A pontoon was built out from the shore, and this was recognized as Federal Territory on which the Commonwealth Ministers would make their act of greeting, while the New South Wales dignitaries waited to make theirs on the mainland.

No hint of discord, however, marred the harmony of welcome on the morning of March 26 as, in perfect weather, the great battle-cruiser with her escort of destroyers from the Royal Australian Navy passed The Heads, and entered the stirring beauty of one of the greatest harbours in the world.

You can imagine the arrival of the Renown in Sydney Harbour on a perfect autumn morning — brilliant sunshine & just enough breeze to blow the flags out [wrote the Governor-General, Lord Stonehaven,[a] to Lord Stamfordham]. She dropped her anchor under the windows of Admiralty House in Neutral Bay to the minute. (This was a good start which was favourably contrasted with the arrival of the American Fleet which took 35 minutes to pick up its moorings & bungled a good deal at that.) The harbour was filled with craft of all sorts, which however entirely respected the request not to hoot or whistle or make a noise until the anchor was down. This silence added immensely to the impressiveness of the arrival. Once the Renown was at anchor the air was made hideous for several minutes by all manner of welcoming shrieks & noises — that was of course inevitable.[18]

The enthusiasm of the welcome at Sydney struck the note for the whole Australian tour. In the ensuing two months the Duke and Duchess of York passed from State to State of the Commonwealth in a blaze of eager ecstasy, which evoked an equally eager response. 'To say that they instantly made the best possible impression seems almost an impertinence', reported Lord Stonehaven, 'and it only faintly expressed the real pride & joy to which their presence gave rise. . . . I don't believe such a scene could have been reproduced anywhere outside the empire and I am certain that nothing could have given rise to it except a Royal Visit.'

The Duke was completely at home with the lack of formality which he encountered. He was not afraid to dissent in discussion and would express his own views freely yet discreetly. He soon earned the reputation of being, as one Australian put it, 'a really genuine young man with decided opinions of his own and that is what we like'.[19] Both he and the Duchess were deeply moved at the personal warmth of their reception and the spirit of devotion to the Crown with which they met on every side. 'The people here have got a most wonderful spirit of loyalty to you & the Empire', the Duke wrote to his father from Brisbane. 'No one can understand it until they have

[a] Rt. Hon. John Lawrence Baird, first Viscount Stonehaven, G.C.M.G., D.S.O. (1874–1941), having served in the Diplomatic Service, entered Parliament in 1910 and became Minister of Transport and First Commissioner of Works in the brief Conservative Ministry of 1922–1923. He was appointed Governor-General of Australia in 1925, and on the completion of his term of office in 1930 he returned to England to become Chairman of the Conservative Party Organization from 1931 to 1936.

been out here. It is such a wonderful thing & we are so glad to be able to stimulate it by coming here for you.' [20]

As parents also they were both touched and surprised at the general interest displayed in their daughter, Princess Elizabeth. 'It is extraordinary how her arrival is so popular out here', the Duke wrote to the Queen. 'Wherever we go cheers are given for her as well & the children write to us about her.' [21] Their post-bag was indeed most amply filled, and the capacity of the staff was taxed to the full in answering its contents. 'The letters of good wishes and welcome have been almost overwhelming', wrote the Duke's Private Secretary to Queen Mary. 'Some of them were very amusing. A large number were written by children, one of whom began with the words, "I am four and a half months old and I should like a photograph of Princess Betty". This, needless to say, was an attempt of a parent to secure a photograph for herself. Another correspondent evinced a passionate desire to exhibit her varicose veins to Their Royal Highnesses.' [22]

Of the many moving episodes which the Duke experienced in Australia, perhaps the most dramatic were the ceremonies of Anzac Day at Melbourne on April 25. To Australians and New Zealanders this day, with its poignant echoes of Gallipoli, of France and Flanders, and of Palestine, is one of solemn remembrance, guarded and cherished with fitting sentiment. On this occasion it was the more significant since the salute of those parading was to be taken by the son of the Sovereign for whom they had gone forth to make the sacrifice which they remembered on this day. Citizens from the whole State of Victoria poured into Melbourne and lined the route in thousands, and ex-Servicemen from every part of the Commonwealth and from New Zealand assembled for the march past.

Having laid a wreath on the Cenotaph before the Parliament House, the Duke joined the Governor-General and the Governor of Victoria at the saluting base and the parade began. First *Renown*'s Marine Band, then Sir John Monash [a] and his staff, and then eight abreast, rank on rank, came some

[a] General Sir John Monash, G.C.M.G., K.C.B. (1865-1931), commanded the Third Australian Division and later the Australian Army Corps during the First World War.

twenty-five thousand ex-Servicemen, among them twenty-nine recipients of the Victoria Cross, each wearing his coveted decoration. Though it was then nine years since the war, the men marched with a proud carriage and rigid military precision. The Duke found their appearance 'most impressive'.

The parade was followed by a special veterans' service in the Exhibition Building, which was attended by at least twenty thousand. There, after the singing of the 'Old Hundredth', 'Nearer, my God, to Thee' and Kipling's Recessional Hymn, Sir John Monash made an appeal to the Australian people to 'keep Anzac Day sacred'. The Duke of York, in one of the most emotional speeches of his whole tour, spoke in support of the same theme. He said:

It is a very great privilege to take part in to-day's ceremony to celebrate the landing in Gallipoli twelve years ago of the Australian and New Zealand Army Corps, which has made for ever famous the name of Anzac.

That great feat of arms and the heroic deeds of all who shared in it will be remembered so long as the Empire lasts. They gave their all for the King and Empire, and their sacrifice will remain for ever a shining example of what human will and endurance can accomplish.

A memorial to those whom we commemorate to-day has been raised in Gallipoli — soil for ever sacred to British hearts. But the best and worthiest memorial we can offer them is to seek inspiration from their example, to endeavour to learn the lesson they teach of courage, patience and self-sacrifice, and to consecrate ourselves afresh to those great purposes for which they gave their lives.

Therefore I would beg you to regard this day, not so much as one of mourning for the dead as one of earnest resolve on the part of us, the living, to emulate their example. Let us try to live more worthily of those who made the great sacrifice for us, and to do the utmost that lies in our power to maintain and hand down to the children who come after us those traditions of loyalty, fortitude and devotion to duty which animated those gallant men, and on the preservation of which the whole welfare and security of the Empire depend.

To the veterans of Anzac this was the crowning moment of their day, and it was evident from their demeanour as the Duke passed among them after the service, shaking hands and conversing with many, that his words had entered into their hearts.

The great day of the opening of Parliament was approaching, and the eyes of the Commonwealth were turning to Canberra. In choosing the site of the federal capital those concerned could hardly have selected a place more untouched by the hand of man. On a gently undulating plain, cattle and sheep had grazed quietly in the folds of the low hills and beside a river flowing between willow-fringed banks, the blue mountains forming a grand background to a peaceful panorama. Here a tiny township had grown up in the 'forties, all unaware that three-quarters of a century later it would become the capital of a great country. Yet perhaps the spirit of prophecy had been abroad in the old Canberra, for on a tombstone in the burial-ground of the Church of St. John the Baptist someone had graven, in 1845: 'For here we have no continuing city, but seek one to come'.

The boundless faith of Australians in their own destiny has been exemplified in the vision of the choice of their capital and in the imagination of its development. The first sod had been turned in 1918, and when the Prince of Wales visited Canberra in 1920 he described it as 'a city of hope and foundation stones'. Yet the hopes flourished and the foundation stones justified their promise of great buildings.

May the 9th was warm and cloudless : a day historic in itself and also full of memories, for just twenty-seven years ago another Duke of York had performed the same function for the Commonwealth that his son was about to undertake. Because of the immense crowd which had come to attend the ceremony, the Duke had proposed a change in the original programme, suggesting that the actual moment of the opening of the great doors of the new Parliament House should be the occasion for him to make a brief speech to those assembled outside, in addition to the formal ceremonial address within the Chamber. Some opposition was incurred but the Duke carried his point, at some inconvenience to himself, for the ordeal of an additional speech was never welcome to him. His deep sense of the association of the Monarchy with the people convinced him that so vitally historic an event as this should have a special popular appeal, not only to the thousands gathered in the immediate vicinity but to the people of Australia as a whole.

THE DUKE OF YORK AND PRINCESS ELIZABETH

He was himself strongly affected by the whole occasion. His sensitive spirit was acutely aware of its momentous character, of what it meant to the pride of a young people and to the ancient Crown and Monarchy whose representative he was. He was desperately anxious to give of his best in doing justice to the responsible rôle which was his. He slept ill the night before and awoke with his nerves in a jangle of apprehension. No sign of this was apparent, however, when a few hours later he stood at the entrance to the Parliament House and faced a crowd of twenty thousand.

The power of tradition and the dignity of monarchy were perhaps never better exemplified than on this occasion. There seemed nothing incongruous in the procession of State carriages, with their attendant scarlet-clad postilions and outriders in perukes and cockaded hats, driving over a wide Australian plain bright with autumn sunshine, for this was the fitting ritual inherent in the ceremonial opening of Parliament under the British Crown in whatever land or clime, whether in Westminster, Ottawa or Delhi. In the same way the new bright Parliament House had assumed the stately attributes inseparable from the age-long tradition of legislature. The King's majesty carries its own grandeur wherever it is called upon to play a part.

The Duke of York's speech, after he had unlocked the doors of the Parliament House with a golden key, was, in the opinion of many, the most moving and successful of the long series which he delivered during his tour. 'The speech outside on the steps after unlocking the door was a tremendous success & entirely H.R.H.'s own idea', Lord Cavan wrote next day to King George.[23] It was not only heard by the thousands present but was relayed by radio throughout Australia :

We are gathered here this morning to open this first meeting of the Parliament of the Commonwealth of Australia in a new Capital City, and I should like, if I may, to try to give expression to some of the thoughts that come to me at this historic moment.

It is impossible not to be moved by the significance of to-day's events as a great landmark in the story of Australia. I say this not only because this day sees the opening of a new Parliament House and marks the inauguration of a new Capital City — but more because one feels the stirrings of a new birth, of quickened national activity, of a fuller consciousness of your destiny as one of the great self-governing units of the British Empire.

To-day marks the end of an epoch and the beginning of another, and one's thoughts turn instinctively to what the future may have in store. One's own life would hardly be worth living without its dreams of better things, and the life of a nation without such dreams of a better and larger future would be poor indeed.

Standing on this spot, and looking out over the beautiful site that has been chosen for the Federal Capital, I think of those great men who worked for a Federated Australia and whose aim was realised when my Father opened the first Federal Parliament in 1901. We are now building on the foundations which they laid.

I think we should all have in our hearts one other vision. On Anzac Day we commemorated those gallant men and women who laid down their lives in the War. Though they have passed into the Great Beyond, they are still speaking to those who choose to listen. And if Australia listens to the Voices of the Noble Army of the Dead, and if the Great Army of those Living and those yet Unborn is determined to march in step with them towards the ideals for which they died, then the glorious destiny of this Country will be assured for all time.

The scene within the building was ceremonially impressive, but the conditions of discomfort were acute. The Senate Chamber is a small one and in it a special lighting system had been installed for the benefit of camera-men from the press and cinema. 'So terrific was the light', wrote Lord Cavan, 'that it raised the temperature of the Senate from 65 to 80 degrees in twenty minutes, in spite of the fact that by special request, one-third of it was turned off.' Nevertheless the Duke's great speech, which he made from the throne after his Commission to open Parliament in the King's name had been read, 'was perfectly admirable in delivery', and the closing passages were marked by his audience with evident and particular satisfaction :

The British Empire has advanced to a new conception of autonomy and freedom, to the idea of a system of British nations, each freely ordering its own individual life, but bound together in unity by allegiance to one Crown and co-operating with one another in all that concerns the common weal.

It is the King's earnest prayer, in which I fervently join, that under Divine Providence the future years may see the same advance in the development and prosperity of the Empire and all its parts, the same spirit of mutual understanding and sympathy, and the same determination to support one another to the uttermost, should need come.

It is, perhaps, particularly fitting that we should celebrate the birth of this new Capital City just after the close of an Imperial Conference, which represents the beginning of another chapter in our Empire story.ᵃ   May this day's ceremony mark the rededication of this Commonwealth to those great ideals of liberty, fair dealing, justice and devotion to the cause of peace, for which the Empire and all its members stand.

A fanfare of trumpets, a Royal Salute of twenty-one guns, as the clocks of Canberra struck noon, and the Parliament of the Commonwealth was open.

The day ended with a Review of troops representing the Australian Army, Navy and Air Force, during which, however, a note of tragedy was struck by one of the aeroplanes taking part in the Review crashing to the ground, the pilot dying some two hours later.   This was the second serious air accident of the Australian tour.   In the course of the drive of Their Royal Highnesses to the Parliament House at Melbourne on April 21 two of their air escort collided and crashed, the crews of both aircraft being killed.   By good fortune the wreckage fell clear of the enormous crowds in the streets.   'The R.A.A.F. is a most smart & efficient body of men, but being young & keen they try & do too much in the way of formation flying, & their machines unfortunately are not of the very best', was the Duke's comment on these accidents in a letter to his father.

The Duke had accomplished his great mission in the King's name most creditably and successfully, and it was with supreme relief and with justifiable pride that he wrote :

The ceremony of opening the door of Parliament House was made a separate one, so that the public could see & hear the proceedings.   Stands were erected to accommodate the visitors from

ᵃ The Imperial Conference of 1926 had adopted a Report which contained, as the fruit of Lord Balfour's wisdom, the following definition of the status and relationship of the Dominions and the Mother Country :

They are autonomous communities within the British Empire, equal in status, in no way subordinate one to another in any respect of their domestic or internal affairs, though united by a common allegiance to the Crown, and freely associated as members of the British Commonwealth of Nations.

It was to this definition that the Statute of Westminster gave final and legal form in 1931.

overseas & foreign countries, & also for people from the various states. All together I should think there were 20000 people.

The reading of your message & commission was done in the Senate Chamber. The members of both Houses were the only ones present at that ceremony. It was a very small room & not a very easy one in which to speak. I was not very nervous when I made the Speech, because the one I made outside went off without a hitch, & I did not hesitate once. I was so relieved as making speeches still rather frightens me, though Logue's teaching has really done wonders for me as I now know how to prevent & get over any difficulty. I have so much more confidence in myself now, which I am sure comes from being able to speak properly at last.

It is a great relief to me that the object of our mission is now over, & more especially when I played my part successfully, at least I think & hope so.'[24]

Less than a fortnight later, on May 23, *Renown* set out from Fremantle on her long journey home. The Duke and Duchess said farewell to Australia with reluctance, for they had greatly appreciated the spontaneous and unquestioned warmth of their reception there, and there could be no doubt as to the impression they had left behind them. 'His Royal Highness has touched people profoundly by his youth, his simplicity and natural bearing', Sir Tom Bridges, the Governor of South Australia,[a] wrote to King George, 'while the Duchess has had a tremendous ovation and leaves us with the responsibility of having a continent in love with her. The visit has done untold good and has certainly put back the clock of disunion and disloyalty 25 years as far as this State is concerned.'[25]

The voyage home across the Indian Ocean was not without incident. Thursday, May 26, broke fine and warm and clear after several days of storm. Through a substantial swell, *Renown* pursued her course toward Mauritius, where she was due in four days' time. It was Queen Mary's birthday and in accordance with the traditions of the Service a Royal Salute was fired at noon. Some two hours later, in the shimmering heat of a stifling afternoon, word was brought to the Duke that a serious fire had broken out in one of the boiler-rooms, caused by the overflow of oil fuel running down from one tank to

[a] Lieut.-General Sir Tom Bridges, K.C.B., K.C.M.G., D.S.O. (1871–1939), had commanded Australian forces in the South African War. He was Governor of South Australia from 1922 to 1927.

another. The place soon became an inferno and the boiler-room staff, having done what they could to meet the emergency, were forced to withdraw, four of them having been gassed and burned.

Renown was in wireless contact with H.M.A.S. *Sydney*, but she was now 800 miles, or a minimum of three days, distant. The immediate danger was that the whole main oil supply might catch fire, in which case there would have been little chance of the ship's escaping complete destruction. A working party stood by to flood the ammunition chamber, and all plans were made ready to abandon ship, though by reason of the heavy seas through which she had recently passed a number of *Renown*'s boats were out of action. Thanks to the strenuous efforts of the fire-fighting party, these precautions were happily unnecessary; by half-past ten that evening the fire was out, and all danger had passed; but before this was achieved the blazing fuel had come within a few feet of the main oil tanks.

Throughout this period of alarm the Duke and Duchess remained quite imperturbable, though, as the Duke commented to the King with masterly understatement: 'Oil is a dangerous substance for a fire & it might have been serious'.[26] He had remained as near the scene of action as safety would permit throughout the afternoon, and on the following morning inspected the gutted boiler-room and visited the injured in the sick-bay.

The remainder of the journey home, with its visits to Mauritius, Malta and Gibraltar, was uneventful, save for one minor incident of unconscious humour. As *Renown* left Gibraltar harbour, she was played out to a musical programme by the massed bands of the garrison. To the Duke's intense amusement the final strains which floated across from shore to ship were those of 'Now thank we all our God'.

On the morning of Monday, June 27, the Duke and Duchess set foot again in England. They were greeted at Portsmouth by the Duke's three brothers, and on the platform at Victoria the King and Queen were waiting to receive them. King George had issued minute instructions as to the uniforms to be worn by the Duke and his staff on this occasion ('Frock-coat & epaulettes, without medals & riband, only stars') and had added a last injunction to his son : 'We will not embrace at the station before so many people. When you kiss Mama take yr. hat off.' [27]

In the six months of his journey around the world the Duke of York had travelled thirty thousand miles by sea and several thousand miles by land. He had witnessed the abiding loyalty of all classes in Australia and New Zealand to the Crown and the Empire, and their affection for the Mother Country. With his quick perception he had seen deeper than the cheering crowds and waving flags, and had realized that this loyalty was not only to the person and family of the King, but also in a wider sense to all those things of which the Crown and the Empire were symbols — justice, liberty, fair play and love of peace. His impressions had left him buoyant and enthusiastic for the future of the British Commonwealth of Nations, and it was in this spirit that he addressed an audience at Guildhall in a celebration of welcome on July 15 :

I return a thorough optimist. When one has travelled over the vast extent of the Empire; when one has witnessed what our fathers have accomplished ; when one has seen how the grit and creative purpose of our kinsmen have triumphed over the most tremendous difficulties, it is impossible to despair of the future of the British race. The same qualities which carried us successfully through the war will, I am convinced, so long as we remain united as members of one family, enable us to surmount all difficulties that may beset us, however formidable or however perplexing. If we hold together we shall win through. . . .

(iv)

The Duke returned from his tour not only with a new vision of Empire but with renewed confidence in himself. He had accomplished a difficult mission with outstanding success and, above all, he had established an ascendancy over the impediment in his speech. Throughout the tour he had kept up Mr. Logue's exercises in so far as his strenuous programme had permitted and had kept touch with him by letter,[a] and

---

[a] A telegram had been dispatched to Mr. Logue by the Duke's Private Secretary from Canberra on the night of May 9, 1927, telling him how well the two speeches had been delivered that day at the opening of the Commonwealth Parliament.

within four days of his return to London he had resumed the regular visits to Harley Street.   It was therefore with a lightened heart that he faced again the many demands made upon him which entailed public speaking.

With this new-born confidence there came a desire for a closer knowledge of the rudiments of statecraft.   Now that he was assuming a definite and more prominent part in the life of the country, a part which brought him into contact with leaders of public affairs, in the opinion of the Duke's House-hold, and indeed of the King's advisers also, it was highly desirable that he should acquaint himself with certain of the inner workings of international and Commonwealth affairs as disclosed in the reports of British representatives in foreign countries and in the Dominions.   Here, however, the opposi-tion of King George was encountered.   His Majesty was averse to such a procedure, holding that it was no part of the duties of his elder sons to have access to such confidential informa-tion, yet ignoring the fact that they were expected, in some indefinable manner, to appear conversant with world affairs and to give the impression of being informed and knowledge-able.   Not even in the case of his heir, the Prince of Wales, did the King permit his presence at audiences granted to Ministers nor to peruse the contents of those ever-present dispatch boxes containing the submissions of the Prime Minister and the heads of Government departments, and he discouraged his association with political leaders.[28]   The only privilege which he would concede to the Prince and the Duke of York was permission to see a very limited selection of Foreign Office and Dominion Office telegrams — and this only with the greatest misgivings and after considerable resistance.

But the time was approaching when the Duke of York was to be called upon to play an important part in the functions of the Crown.   On October 19, 1928, he represented his father at the funeral in Denmark of the Dowager Empress of Russia,[a] and on his return attended the King at the opening of Parliament

[a] Princess Marie Dagmar of Denmark (1847–1928), daughter of King Christian IX and sister of Queen Alexandra and of King George I of Greece, married Tsar Alexander III in 1866 and became the mother of Tsar Nicholas II. After the Revolution of 1917 she escaped from the Crimea in a British cruiser and passed the remainder of her life in Denmark.

on November 6 and at the Armistice Day ceremonies at the Cenotaph. Here King George contracted a severe chill, which he neglected, and ten days later he was in the grip of serious illness. A blood test taken at midnight on November 21 indicated acute septicaemia, the centre of infection being identified as at the base of the right lung. His condition became steadily more grave, and the Prince of Wales, then on tour in East Africa, was warned that there 'was cause for anxiety'; he at once decided to return to England but could not arrive before December 11. A bulletin from Buckingham Palace on December 1 referred to 'a decline in the strength of the heart'.

The Duke of York, who had been hunting at Naseby, returned to 145 Piccadilly immediately at the first news of his father's illness, and remained in London in great anxiety. On December 2 it was obvious that the King would be incapacitated for a long time and that Counsellors of State must be appointed to transact public business during his illness.[a] Six Counsellors were nominated: The Queen, the Prince of Wales, the Duke of York, the Archbishop of Canterbury (Dr. Lang [b]), the Lord Chancellor (Lord Hailsham [c]) and the Prime Minister (Mr. Baldwin) — and a meeting of the Privy Council was summoned for December 4 for the Sovereign to give his assent to the transfer of power into their hands.[29]

The Duke was one of the Privy Counsellors who formed the quorum on this occasion.[d] The King was very weak and the effort required made a heavy demand upon him. Standing with Mr. Baldwin and Lord Stamfordham in the doorway which separated the Audience Chamber from the King's bedroom, the Duke watched Sir William Joynson-Hicks enter alone and, approaching to within a few yards of the King's bed, read the Order; heard the King's voice, husky with

[a] For a note on the appointment, powers and functions of Counsellors of State, see Appendix A, p. 809.

[b] Dr. Lang had only been appointed Archbishop of Canterbury a few days previously (November 12), on the resignation of Archbishop Davidson. He had not done homage, and was unable to do so until March 27, 1929, when the King was recuperating at Bognor.

[c] Rt. Hon. Douglas McGarel Hogg, first Viscount Hailsham (1872-1950).

[d] The Privy Council quorum comprised the Home Secretary (Sir William Joynson-Hicks), acting as Lord President; the Duke of York; the Prime Minister; and the King's Private Secretary. The Duke of York had been introduced into the Privy Council on June 25, 1925.

illness yet quite clear, answer 'Approved'; and saw Lord Dawson of Penn hold the paper which the King signed.

Two days later the Duke wrote two letters to his elder brother, then speeding home by the swiftest means possible, which the Duke of Windsor has included in his memoirs. They gave him the first details of the King's illness, and the second letter contained an item, the inclusion of which indicates that, despite the gravity of the situation, the King's sons had not lost their sense of humour :

There is a lovely story going about which emanated from the East End [wrote the Duke], that the reason of your rushing home is that in the event of anything happening to Papa I am going to bag the Throne in your absence ! ! ! ! Just like the Middle Ages. . . .

The first crisis in the King's illness was reached on December 11, the very day on which the Prince of Wales reached London, and Lord Dawson faced the necessity of an operation. That evening the Duke of York met his brother at Victoria and during the three-minute drive to Buckingham Palace conveyed to him the deep sense of foreboding which hung like a pall over Britain.

He prepared me for the shock that my father's appearance would bring [the Prince wrote later]. 'You will find him greatly changed', he said, 'and now Dawson says an operation will be necessary in a day or two.' Then he spoke admiringly of my mother. 'Through all the anxiety she has never once revealed her feelings to any of us.' This seemed to trouble him, for he quickly added, 'She is really far too reserved ; she keeps too much locked up inside of her. I fear a breakdown if anything awful happens. She has been wonderful.'[30]

The operation was duly performed and throughout Britain and the Empire men and women waited and listened, with that reverent sense of loyalty and affection for the Crown which is especially evoked in moments of great crisis, for news of the King's struggle for life. Churches were kept open night and day for prayers of intercession, and day after day, night after night, in the bitter cold, silent crowds waited outside the Palace for tidings of their stricken Sovereign, as though the sick man had been of their closest kin.

Christmas came and went, a saddened season ; but by the close of the year the King had won the battle and it was possible to announce that 'Convalescence is now in sight'. Early in February he was moved by ambulance to Bognor, whence he returned to Windsor in May. It was not, however, until the middle of June that he was pronounced sufficiently recovered to bear the strain of a public ceremony. On Sunday, July 7, 1929, accompanied by the Queen and attended by his children, he drove in state to Westminster Abbey for a Service of Thanksgiving, which was broadcast to every corner of the world.[a]

The King's illness had aroused a passion of loyal concern which was without parallel. 'Science may discover some formula for the miracles which may be wrought, even in the physical sphere, by the concentrated will of great masses of men', wrote one of his biographers. 'Our ancestors, more piously and perhaps more wisely, would have attributed his recovery to the prayers of his people.'[b][32]

(v)

The illness of his father, with its weeks of tense anxiety, had cast fresh burdens and duties upon the Duke of York; he bore the one with calmness and discharged the other with efficiency. The stress was considerable but it did not disturb his equilibrium, and he was able to write with satisfaction to Mr. Logue: 'Through all this nervous strain my speech has *not* been affected one atom'.[33] He was master of himself.

[a] Few of those who were present in the Abbey, or who lined the streets on that great day of rejoicing, were aware that the King's wound was still unhealed. His own comment to Lord Dawson after his return to the Palace, was characteristic: 'Fancy a thanksgiving service with an open wound in your back'.[31]

[b] The popular upwelling of gratitude for the King's recovery found practical expression in contributions to the National Radium Fund and King Edward's Hospital Fund, which were merged in a National Thanksgiving Fund. This was inaugurated by the gift of 100,000 guineas from a gentleman who for some time withheld his name but whose identity was subsequently disclosed to be that of Sir George Roberts. King George himself gave a donation of £1000 to the Fund.

CHAPTER VI

LORD HIGH COMMISSIONER TO THE GENERAL ASSEMBLY OF THE CHURCH OF SCOTLAND, 1929

(i)

THE close affinity of the Royal Family for Scotland is derived not so much from their descent from the tragic and ill-fated Stuarts, nor even from the romantic *agape* of 1822, when the Hanoverian King George IV first startled and then delighted the Scots by appearing in Edinburgh wearing a kilt of the Stuart tartan. Rather does it stem from that discovery of the Highlands by Queen Victoria and Prince Albert in 1842, that early glimpse which resulted in love at first sight, and implanted the desire for a home, a private retreat, among these delightful and comparatively inaccessible surroundings.

The desire grew powerfully. The relative advantages and attractions of various properties were canvassed and the first choice of the Queen and her husband was Ardverikie, on Loch Laggan, a house belonging to Lord Abercorn. This had particularly appealed to them because, as they drove along the Kingussie road, the surrounding country 'reminded us much of Thuringen'. The prospects of Ardverikie, however, were literally washed out by rain when the Queen paid a visit there in 1847 during a period of execrable weather. Thereafter the search for a house in a more clement climate was pursued farther to the eastward, and was eventually crowned with success a year later when the sudden death of Sir Robert Gordon made the Deeside estate of Balmoral available; the lease was taken over from the Earl of Mar.

Residence was actually established in September 1848, and the Queen wrote happily to the King of the Belgians:

This house is small but pretty, and though the hills seen from the windows are not *so* fine, the scenery all around is the finest almost I have seen anywhere. It is very wild and solitry, aand yet cheerful and *beautifully* wooded, with the river Dee running between two sides of the hills, Loch Nagar is the highest hill in the immediate vicinity, and belongs to us.

Then the soil is the driest and best known almost anywhere, and all the hills are as sound and hard as the road. The climate is also dry, and in general not very cold, though we had one or two very cold days.[1]

An added attraction was that here again the scenery recalled to the nostalgic Prince Albert the wild and wooded landscape of his native Thuringia ; but the Queen's affection was for the country itself. 'I love my peaceful wild Highlands,' she again wrote to her Uncle Leopold, 'the glorious scenery, the dear good people, who are so much attached to us, and who feel their *Einsamkeit* sadly, very much.'[2]

As at Osborne, however, what the Queen and the Prince really wanted was 'a home of their own' and, in addition, the 'small but pretty' house was in fact too small. When, therefore, the lease acquired in 1847 expired five years later, Prince Albert bought the Balmoral estate from the trustees of the Earl of Fife for £31,500. The existing house was pulled down and on a neighbouring site the present Castle was erected, designed by Prince Albert himself in the Scottish baronial style. The new house was first occupied on September 7, 1855,[a] and a year later the Queen wrote in her diary : 'Every year my heart becomes more fixed in this dear Paradise, and so much more so now that *all* has become my dear Albert's *own* creation, own work, own building, own laying out, as at Osborne ; and his great taste, and the impress of his dear hand, have been stamped everywhere'.[3]

Various accretions of property were made from time to time : Birkhall, with its 6000 acres and charming Georgian house, the lovely and ancient keep of Abergeldie [b] and the

---

[a] In September 1955, in commemoration of the centenary, there was published Mr. Ivor Brown's delightful and informative work, *Balmoral*.

[b] Birkhall was originally bought from the Gordon family for the Prince of Wales (King Edward VII) during his father's lifetime. It ultimately proved too small for him and he was given Abergeldie Castle as his residence. The Queen and the Prince Consort endeavoured to buy Abergeldie also from the Gordons but were unable to succeed ; and, though successive Sovereigns have repeated the attempt to purchase, the property is still held on lease.

picturesque bothie of Alt-na-Guithasach, which the Queen acquired for her own greater privacy. All these combined with Balmoral to give the Royal Family a Scottish retreat where they could rest and recuperate far from the madding Court and enjoy themselves in country pursuits as uninterrupted as was possible by the inevitable demands of public business.

For the Queen and the Prince went to Balmoral primarily for health and enjoyment. 'To them it was the nineteenth-century equivalent of hydro, clinic, sea voyage and watering-place rolled into one.'[4] Not only did they enjoy themselves but they made their enjoyment obvious, not standing aloof from the traditional pleasures of the Scots; and, though the appearance of the Prince Consort in the Royal Stuart tartan perhaps never completely escaped the bizarre, they avoided the mistake of trying to play the part of a Scottish laird *manqué*.

But though Queen Victoria loved and enjoyed to the full her Highland home in the happy flood-tide of her married life, and found solace there during her long and lonely widow-hood in revisiting, and commemorating with stone cairns, the scenes which she and Prince Albert had gazed upon so adoringly together, it remained for her great-grandson to inherit her affection for Balmoral. King Edward VII was no countryman, and preferred the attractions of continental watering-places to those of Deeside; while King George V, though he was certainly the Squire of Sandringham, was never the Laird of Balmoral. King George VI, however, combined the attributes of both, and it would be difficult to assess a priority of his affections in respect of his two country estates, with both of which he identified himself so closely.

Certain it is that Balmoral, and all that it implied, lay close to the heart of King George. At Abergeldie he had spent some of the happiest moments of his childhood, and his tutor had commented on the contented and cheerful manner in which he had supported a long convalescence at Alt-na-Guithasach.[a] As Duke of York he passed many happy autumns at Birkhall, and as King he looked forward with increasing impatience to his annual residence at Balmoral. Here he found peace and relaxation; here, although he could not wholly escape the cares of State, he could at least be free from the

[a] See above, p. 43.

routine of life in London ; here in bodily exertion he recaptured
tranquillity of spirit. Gun in hand, dog at heel, he would climb
the hills and tramp the moors, sometimes in company, sometimes attended by a single gillie. It pleased him to exercise
his consummate skill with gun and rifle ; it pleased him also
to worship simply and humbly in the village church of Crathie.

(ii)

The strong ties — personal, marital and hereditary — which
bound the Duke of York so tenaciously to Scotland were
materially strengthened when, in 1929, he was appointed by
King George V to be Lord High Commissioner to the General
Assembly of the Church of Scotland. This was the first time
that a member of the Royal Family had held this office since
1679, when another Duke of York, later King James II, had
been sent as High Commissioner by the King his brother.

The year 1929 was a momentous one in Scottish Church
history, for it was the Year of Reunion. Eighty-six years before,
the Presbyterian faith in Scotland had suffered a grievous
schism, which had its origins in the fundamental problems of
the relations between Church and State, and the immediate
issue of local patronage in the appointment of ministers.[a] Successive Cabinets in London, notably those of Lord Melbourne
and Sir Robert Peel, considered the claims of the Church to
'exclusive jurisdiction' in spiritual affairs with apathy and
lack of understanding, and seemed fatally prejudiced against
the Scottish case by its points of resemblance to the Oxford
Tractarian Movement, then also making a bold bid for religious

---

[a] The issue of local patronage may be defined as one of whether the 'call'—
the signed document addressed by a congregation to a minister-elect inviting
him to accept the pastoral charge over them — or the will of the patron should
be the dominant factor in the appointment of ministers. The Patronage Act of
1712 had given the right to patrons to present ministers, and in many cases the
'call' had become merely the ratification of the patron's choice. In such cases
where the 'call' had been refused, some patrons had insisted upon the appointment
of their nominees, and the principle of the Veto Act of 1825, which was passed by
the Assembly but rejected by the Courts in London, sought to establish it as a
fundamental law of the Church that 'no pastor shall be intruded on any congregation contrary to the will of the people'. Authorities who may be consulted
on the origins and causes of the dispute are : T. Brown, *Annals of the Disruption*
(1892) ; R. Buchanan, *Ten Years' Conflict* (1849) ; and Hugh Watt, *Thomas
Chalmers and the Disruption* (1943).

independence within the Church of England. Finally, at the end of ten years of bitter conflict, there came the Great Disruption of 1843, when, on May 18, in the session of the General Assembly held in St. Andrew's Church, Edinburgh, the Moderator, Dr. David Welsh, read a solemn protest against the refusal of the British Government to consider the 'Claim of Right', and then left the Assembly, followed by two hundred other 'Protesters' and 'Non-Intrusionists'. On that day the Free Church of Scotland was born, and to it adhered over four hundred ministers, who for conscience' sake abandoned the churches they loved and the positions they had prized.

So great an act of dissent was vastly impressive, occurring as it did in the midst of the 'hungry 'forties', for it represented a deep and flaming spiritual conviction on the part of its adherents, as well as a considerable self-sacrifice in matters material. It has been described as 'the most honourable fact for Scotland that its whole history supplies', and Lord Jeffrey expressed a widespread opinion when he declared : 'I'm proud of my country. There is not another country on earth where such a deed could have been done.'

Thenceforward there had been two great Churches in Scotland, though only one, the Church of Scotland, was officially recognized in London.[a] Much bitterness had been engendered by the Disruption, but with the lapse of time these passions cooled and the efforts of wise and enlightened men in both Churches were ardently bent towards reunion.

The task was not an easy one ; but the manifestation of greater understanding in London of the problems involved, the redressing of certain outstanding grievances, the gradual subsidence of partisan feeling and the general sense of greater national unity brought about by the First World War, were all influences towards a healing of the breach and the dawn of the great day when the Church of Scotland would be reunited in 'the One, Holy, Catholic and Apostolic Church'.[b]

[a] In 1900 there was brought about a successful merging of the Free Church with the United Presbyterians, the new body becoming the United Free Church of Scotland.

[b] The chief artificers of reunion were, on the Church of Scotland side : Dr. Archibald Scott ; Lord Balfour of Burleigh ; Dr. Wallace Williamson of St. Giles, Edinburgh ; Dr. John White of the Barony, Glasgow ; and Lord Sands. On the United Free Church side they were : Dr. Archibald Henderson of Crieff ; Principal Martin of New College, Edinburgh ; and Dr. R. J. Drummond.

By the summer of 1928 the Moderators of the two Churches were able to inform the Prime Minister that reunion would be accomplished within a twelvemonth, and suggested that some Royal recognition of this momentous event would be appropriate. Mr. Baldwin therefore approached Lord Stamfordham with the idea that the Duke of York should be appointed High Commissioner to the first General Assembly of the reunited Church in the following May, and that the King himself might attend one of the sessions.[5] King George at once concurred with the proposal of the appointment of his son but felt that, in so far as his own attendance at the Assembly was concerned, this would only be possible if the session were held in the autumn when he could come to Edinburgh on his way back to London from Balmoral. It was therefore agreed that the last meetings of the two independent assemblies should take place at the usual season in May with the Duke as High Commissioner, and that the first session of the United Assembly should be postponed until October in order that His Majesty might be present.[6]

These arrangements had, of course, been made prior to the King's illness and, as the spring of 1929 approached and the announcement of the Duke's appointment became imminent, he grew increasingly apprehensive and uncertain as to whether it was still the King's wish that he act as his representative in Scotland. A visit to his father at Bognor on March 7, in order to say good-bye before leaving to attend the wedding of the Crown Prince of Norway,[a] presented an opportunity for raising the matter ; but the Duke did not take it, and on his return to London sought the intervention of Lord Stamfordham :

I went down to Bognor to-day & found a really wonderful change in the King. He is so much stronger now & can walk about his room alone, & he talked quite a lot without getting tired. I mentioned to the Queen about the question of the King being told that the Prime Minister had approached me, & that I have consented to act as Lord High Commissioner this year in Edinburgh. But I should like you to inform the King as to this

[a] The Crown Prince Olav, only son of King Haakon VII of Norway and Princess Maud, daughter of King Edward VII, was married to Princess Martha of Sweden on March 29, 1929. The Duke of York, with the Duchess, attended the wedding as King George's representative.

before it is announced. I understand that the P.M. had already talked over the matter with the King last November, but of course he will not have remembered it, & if he sees the appointment in the papers he might ask why he had not been consulted. I hear you are going to see the King on Saturday, so perhaps you would take that opportunity of mentioning it. The Queen thinks it would be advisable.[7]

Lord Stamfordham undertook this embassage and in due course sent a reassuring reply.[8] The announcement of the Duke's appointment was duly made on March 28.

The office of Lord High Commissioner to the General Assembly of the Church of Scotland is both ancient and venerated,[a] and represents the relationship of the chief court of the Church to the ruling powers of the State. After the Reformation there was some doubt as to the legality of the proceedings of the Assembly of the new Church without the sanction of the Sovereign, and, although John Knox declaimed, 'Take from us the freedom of assemblies and take from us the Evangel', the Assembly voted in 1561 to request Queen Mary to appoint a representative who should keep her informed of their transactions. The practice dates from that time. One King of Scotland, James VI, himself sat in the Assembly and actually voted in the election of a Moderator, but, with the exception of his grandson, no other member of the Royal Family had held the office until the son of King George V.[b]

During the time for which his commission runs, which is the duration of the General Assembly, the Lord High Commissioner is, as the King's representative, the first subject in the realm, taking precedence even of the King's eldest son. He does not preside over the Assembly, for that is the function of the Moderator, but from the Throne, which is deemed to be 'outside the House', he opens the session in the King's name, attends daily, and, in the same name, closes the session in due course, appointing another Assembly to meet in the following

[a] The title in its present form dates only from the early decades of the nineteenth century. In earlier days he was referred to as His Majesty's Commissioner, the Royal Commissioner, the Great Commissioner and sometimes simply as the Commissioner.

[b] Subsequently, however, both King George V's younger sons held the office of Lord High Commissioner, the Duke of Kent in 1935, and the Duke of Gloucester in 1949.

year.[a] In order, however, to assert the right of the Church to meet without a Royal Commissioner at all, the Moderator also performs the act of opening and closing the Assembly, in each case immediately before the Commissioner. The Lord High Commissioner bears the title of 'His Grace', resides in royal state in the Palace of Holyroodhouse, and his suite includes a purse-bearer and a chaplain, while the Solicitor-General is *ex officio* his legal adviser. When he goes to or from the Assembly a silver mace is borne before him and he is entitled to a mounted escort, a guard of honour and a salute of twenty-one guns.

In the case of the Duke of York certain changes of privilege and title were introduced. He was addressed as 'Your Royal Highness' instead of 'Your Grace', and received a Royal Prince's escort of a subaltern and twenty-eight, as distinct from twenty, troopers. These were drawn from the Scots Greys and their appearance, in full scarlet and bearskins, reminded at least one of those who saw them of the ironic historical coincidence that, just two hundred and fifty years before, another Duke of York had ridden through Edinburgh as the King's Commissioner, with the avowed intent of suppressing Presbyterianism in Scotland, and that the chief instrument in this suppression had been the regiment of dragoons now known as the Scots Greys.[b] [9]

Perhaps the person who derived the most pleasure from the brave showing of the Royal Escort was King George V — then recovering at Windsor from his relapse of May 20 — when he saw the pictures in the illustrated papers. The fact that they appeared in full dress uniform filled the King 'with feelings of delight which I can hardly describe', Lord Stamfordham wrote to General Sir William Peyton.[c] 'His Majesty

[a] In 1910 the Earl of Stair, having been elected to the Assembly before being appointed Lord High Commissioner, chose to discharge the functions of both offices. Having delivered the King's message, he appeared on at least one occasion on the floor of the House.

[b] James, Duke of York, came to Edinburgh as Lord High Commissioner in 1679, in which same year three troops of dragoons were raised for the standing army in Scotland. Three more were added in 1681, and the six were then combined as the 2nd Regiment of Dragoons, later known as the Scots Greys.

[c] General Sir William Eliot Peyton, K.C.B., K.C.V.O., D.S.O. (1866–1931), served with distinction in the Sudan campaign, in the Boer War and in the First World War, when he commanded the 40th Division. He was G.O.C. Scottish Command from 1926 to 1930.

hardly dares ask how this has been accomplished.'[10] The
explanation of the miracle — for miracle it was in those days of
national economy and austerity [a]— was that the Commanding
Officer of the Scots Greys had in his possession, left over from
pre-war equipment, a sufficient number of the uniforms prescribed for Royal Escorts by the King's Regulations. He
sought permission from the G.O.C. Scottish Command to dress
the escort accordingly, and General Peyton, having ascertained
that no cancellation of the Regulations had been issued, gave
the necessary authority. But, as he wrote to Lord Stamfordham : 'So as to avoid any misunderstanding I did not refer
the matter to the War Office'.[11]

The Duke, as Lord High Commissioner, took up residence
in Holyroodhouse on May 20, and that evening at a State
dinner the traditional ceremony of the Presentation of the
City Keys was performed by the Lord Provost of Edinburgh.[b]
On the following morning, after a levee, he drove with his
escort in an open landau with outriders — an innovation
made in deference to his Royal rank — to perform his function
at the opening of the General Assembly, with its curious
mingling of ecclesiastical and State ceremonial. The appointment of the King's son to this high office, and the presence
with him of his Scottish wife, had greatly pleased Scotland,
and the popular acclaim which they received on their drive
from Holyroodhouse to St. Giles' Cathedral, and later by way
of the Lawnmarket to the historic Tolbooth Church, wherein
the Assembly met, was both vociferous and heartfelt. The
citizens of Edinburgh — ever romantic where the Monarchy
is concerned — were delighted with this display of Royal
pageantry and made no secret of their gratification. At the
outset of the State drive a white *haar* had drifted in from the
North Sea, softening the sharp outlines of the Castle Rock and
making the crowds assembled in the streets seem endless; but

---

[a] The situation was also somewhat complicated by the fact that the sessions
of the Assemblies coincided with the strenuous political campaign of the General
Election of May 31, 1929, at which the Labour Party was returned as the largest
single party with 287 seats, the Conservatives and Liberals gaining 261 and 59
seats respectively. As a result, Mr. Ramsay MacDonald became Prime Minister
on June 5 for the second time.

[b] The City Keys are customarily presented to the Sovereign on arrival at the
railway station in Edinburgh, but to the High Commissioner on the first evening
of his official residence at Holyrood.

this had vanished by the time the Duke and Duchess of York emerged from the Cathedral and it was in sunshine as well as amid cheers that they drove to the Tolbooth.

Within the church the Assembly waited for the King's message of commendation on their efforts for reunion, and the Duke gave it with clear resonance :

The scheme for the Union of the Church of Scotland and the United Free Church of Scotland, prepared with long and anxious care, has now been completed, and has secured in both Churches that general assent of the local Church courts which is one of the historical features of your system of Church Government. It still awaits the approval of the two General Assemblies. But I rejoice to know that the final Act by the Assemblies which meet to-day, of this great act of union, is universally expected.

His Majesty the King was desirous of marking his personal sympathy and interest in this important Assembly by appointing me to the honourable office of High Commissioner.

The Duke and Duchess were received with tumultuous applause by the assembled commissioners, and these scenes were repeated a few days later when they visited the Free Church General Assembly, where the Duke conveyed a similar message. The fact that the sessions of the two Assemblies coincided with the celebration of the six-hundredth anniversary of the presentation to the city of Edinburgh of its Charter by their common ancestor, King Robert the Bruce, imposed upon the Duke and Duchess a heavier burden of engagements than was normally the lot of a High Commissioner and his wife ; but they performed their exacting duties with unfailing dignity and good humour, and even found time to make an addition of their own to the programme in the shape of a novel kind of garden party at Holyroodhouse, where they invited children to meet them. Their general demeanour of kindness, interest and grace was acknowledged on all sides, and of the Duchess the *Scotsman* lyrically proclaimed that 'it may well be that the frail ghost of Mary Queen of Scots revisiting the Castle felt the stirrings of jealousy'.[12]

For the Duke and Duchess of York themselves there was but one cause for sorrow — the absence of their daughter.

The only thing I regret, is that we have not got Lillibet here [the Duchess wrote to Queen Mary]. I fear that it has been a very great disappointment to the people. Not that they would have seen her, but they would have liked to feel that she was here. In the solemn old Assembly, the Moderator mentioned in his welcoming address 'our dear Princess Elizabeth', which is, I believe, almost unique. It almost frightens me that the people should love her so much. I suppose that it is a good thing, and I hope that she will be worthy of it, poor little darling.[13]

When the Duke of York laid down his office as Lord High Commissioner on May 29, the Act of Reunion of the Churches in Scotland was an accomplished fact; and there was still a widespread hope, amounting almost to expectation, that King George would come in person to the first Union Assembly in the following October. This, however, was not to be. On May 20, the day on which the Duke had begun his official residence in the Palace of Holyroodhouse, the King had suffered a relapse, which was sufficiently severe to necessitate his receiving his new Ministers at Windsor instead of at Buckingham Palace. He had genuinely desired to be present at the momentous session of the Assembly, and postponed his final decision in the matter as long as possible on the urgent appeal of the Duke of York, who realized the keen disappointment which would be caused in Scotland by his father's absence. However, Lord Stamfordham was regretfully compelled to inform the Moderators that the King's doctors had finally advised against it,[14] and, as it turned out, though His Majesty's health had just, but only just, sufficiently improved to allow him to attend the Service of Thanksgiving at the Abbey on July 7, he was not well enough to visit Scotland at all that year.

Thus it was that on the great day of Union, October 2, the Duke of York was again his father's representative. This time there was no pomp — no landau, and no escort — but the solemnity of the occasion provided its own magnificent and moving dignity. After a wild night of wind and rain the day dawned in storm, but with some fair weather and gleams of sunshine later. The two Assemblies met separately for the last time, in the Tolbooth Church and the Assembly Hall, and then moved in two processions, the one down the Lawnmarket, the other up the Mound and Bank Street, to meet on the Royal Mile where St. Giles' stands in full view. There the two Moderators ^a clasped hands and, with their followers mingling behind them, strode with full hearts through John Knox's parish to John Knox's church.

After the service in the Cathedral the High Commissioner and the congregation proceeded to a vast garage which had been transformed into an Assembly Hall, the only building capable of housing so great a gathering.

The actual Union Ceremony was very impressive [the Duke wrote to his father], even though the Hall was really a garage. There were quite 10,000 people present. It was just as well that we had no carriages or escort as there was a fearful gale blowing & it was raining. . . .[15]

The scene within the Hall was indeed impressive. The great officers of Scotland's Church and State were assembled there, together with prominent members of all the professions, soldiers and sailors of high rank, the Archbishop of Canterbury and his predecessor, Lord Davidson of Lambeth, both of whom later addressed the Assembly, and representatives of other Protestant Churches in Europe, America, South Africa and the Antipodes. As one who was present recorded: 'It was incomparably the largest, the most cosmopolitan and the most representative assemblage of Christian men and women ever brought together for such a purpose'.[16] From the thousands gathered in the hall there arose, in the majestic beauty of the metrical psalms, a glorious volume of praise and thanksgiving that two Christian Churches 'each in fidelity to its own great heritage, are now become One Church in Christ Jesus, under the designation of the Church of Scotland'.

Sitting above this great assemblage, and indescribably moved by what he saw, the Duke of York listened while the King's Letter was read, and heard the words which touched not only his heart but the hearts of all those present:

We have thought it fitting that our most dear son, Albert, Duke of York, whom we appointed to represent us at the last Assembly of the Church prior to the Union, should again act as our representative at the first Assembly of the United Church. We trust that our choice will commend itself to you, the more so as his

^a The Moderators were the Rt. Rev. Dr. Joseph Mitchell of the Church of Scotland and the Rt. Rev. Dr. Alexander Martin of the United Free Church. Dr. John White was elected first Moderator of the United General Assembly.

reception at your former meetings gave happy evidence of the
loyalty to the Throne which has always heartened us by its constancy and fervour.

When the warm applause which greeted him had subsided,
the Duke made his own address, in the course of which he spoke
of his personal rejoicing at the consummation of reunion, and
of the King's sorrow at having to cause disappointment by his
absence. 'His Majesty also is most keenly disappointed, and
he has asked me to inform you that he had, before his illness,
been eagerly contemplating the prospect of a visit to an
Assembly which marks such a significant event in the history
of his beloved Scottish people.'

By the following evening the ceremonies of reunion were
completed, and, the ritual of closure having been performed
by the Lord High Commissioner and the Moderator, the
Assembly sang its Psalm of Demission, 'Pray that Jerusalem
may have peace and felicity', and dispersed. All who had
been present at these sessions and had heard the memorable
addresses delivered by divines and laymen, Episcopalian as
well as Presbyterian, were sensible of having participated in
a great and searching spiritual experience. 'We came back to
the world', wrote one, 'with a new conscience of our shortcomings in the past, and of the tasks awaiting our faith in the
days to come.' [17]

No part of this great experience was unshared by the Duke
of York, on whom the events of these two days had made a
deep impression. He, too, had felt the presence of the Spirit
of God in the Assembly, and had been profoundly moved at
the message of the Church of England, conveyed by its Primate,
to the Reunited Church : 'May the celebration of your unity
quicken our faltering steps in the quest of the city of our
dreams — the One, Holy, Catholic Church'. He carried
away from Edinburgh a host of memories and much food for
thought, and in the peace of the moors around Balmoral he
pondered on what he had seen and heard.

There was much cause also for his personal satisfaction.
His two periods as Lord High Commissioner had enabled him
— as in England, as in Australia and New Zealand — to
identify himself with the people of Scotland even more closely
than before ; to understand the inner depths of their national

character, to learn more of their special interests.   In addition, there came from Sandringham the brief expression of his father's approbation.   'I congratulate you on yr. speeches connected with the Union of the Scottish Churches', wrote King George.[18]

CHAPTER VII

SIX QUIET YEARS
1930–1935

(i)

WITH the opening of the third decade of the twentieth century there became faintly apparent those premonitory symptoms of the disaster which was to mark its close. The high hopes for the safeguarding of world peace which had been born of the Locarno Agreement of 1925, and had reached their ephemeral apogee with the signature of the Kellogg-Briand Pact for the Renunciation of War in August 1928, had begun to totter under the impact of the world-wide economic depression, the decline of democratic government in Germany and the steady upsurge of imperialist expansion in Japan. An era in which, theoretically, war had been renounced by the nations of the world as an instrument of national policy, was destined to witness more naked and unbridled aggression than any other period of modern history, and to close with the outbreak of the most savage conflict which mankind had ever known. In this same period, moreover, the British Monarchy experienced a crisis the repercussions of which were to shake it to its foundations.

For the Duke of York, however, the first six years of this decade were to be a period of quiet and domestic life. It was almost the last span of untroubled peace that he was to know, and one in which a felicitous balance seemed to have been struck between his arduous duties as a servant of the State and his happy existence as a husband and father.

In the second week of January 1930 the Duke went to Rome as King George's representative at the wedding of the Crown Prince of Italy and Princess Marie-José of Belgium.[a]

---

[a] Umberto, Prince of Piedmont (b. 1904), only son of King Victor Emmanuel III of Italy and Queen Elena, married on January 9, 1930, Princess Marie-José, only daughter of King Albert and Queen Elisabeth of the Belgians. Prince

The ceremony, performed in the Pauline Chapel of the Palace of the Quirinal on January 9, was of special significance since it marked the first-fruits of that reconciliation of the House of Savoy and of the Italian State with the Vatican which had been brought about during the previous year by Signor Mussolini and Pope Pius XI in the Treaty of the Lateran.[a] Apart from this, it was distinguished by a monumental chaos of disorganization, due largely to the fact that the Grand Marshal of the Italian Court, a venerable member of the Roman nobility, was approaching his hundredth birthday and refused to delegate his powers. The result was confusion, in the midst of which the Grand Master himself was overheard to make a general appeal: 'Can anyone tell me who is the bridegroom?' and the ex-King of Afghanistan was accorded precedence over all other royalties.[1]

The Duke, who was suffering from the dual disability of a heavy cold and the fact that the Duchess, who had had an attack of bronchitis, was unable to accompany him to Rome, was greatly displeased at the complete breakdown of the arrangements and did not hesitate to express himself forcefully to the British Ambassador, Sir Ronald Graham. It was not the happiest of royal gatherings.

In the summer of the same year a second daughter was born to the Duke and Duchess of York. They were at Glamis, and by some oversight and miscalculation the doctors had informed the Home Secretary, Mr. J. R. Clynes,[b] that his presence would be required early in August. Instead of awaiting a more definite summons, he arrived in an excess of zeal on August 5, to find himself decidedly premature; he was

---

Umberto became Lieutenant-General (*i.e.* Regent) of the Kingdom on June 5, 1944, and following the abdication of King Victor Emmanuel III on May 9, 1946, he became King, but his reign only lasted until June 13 when, as the result of a referendum, Italy declared herself to be a Republic.

[a] The Treaty and Concordat of the Lateran between the Kingdom of Italy and the Holy See were signed on February 11, 1929, and ratified on June 7, 1929, thereby establishing the Vatican City State, restoring to the Pope his liberty as a temporal Sovereign, and ending the fifty-eight-year-old quarrel between the Vatican and the House of Savoy.

[b] Rt. Hon. John Robert Clynes (1869–1949), President of the National Union of General and Municipal Workers, entered Parliament in 1906. He was Food Controller during the latter years of the First World War, and on the advent of the Labour Party to office in 1924 became Lord Privy Seal. He was Home Secretary in Mr. MacDonald's second Government of 1929–1931.

taken in by the Dowager Lady Airlie at Cortachy and settled
down for a long spell of waiting. Five days later the Duke
was writing to Queen Mary: 'I feel so sorry for Mr. Clynes
having to be here for so long. I always wanted him to come
up when he was sent for, which would have been so much
simpler.'[2] On August 13 Mr. Clynes was still waiting, and
the Duke wrote somewhat apologetically to the King on the
continued presence of the Home Secretary.[3] The baby finally
arrived on the evening of August 21, and Mr. Clynes was
released from his long vigil. 'Got the news that Elizabeth
had a little girl last night at 9.30 at Glamis, both doing well',
the King recorded in his diary.[4] The King and Queen left
Sandringham for Balmoral on the 22nd, and on August 30
they visited their latest granddaughter at Glamis. They found,
Queen Mary wrote, 'E. looking very well and the baby a
darling'.[5]

The naming of the new Princess was a matter for grave
consideration.

I am very anxious to call her Ann Margaret [the Duchess wrote
to Queen Mary] as I think that Ann of York sounds pretty, &
Elizabeth and Ann go so well together. I wonder what you think?
Lots of people have suggested Margaret, but it has no family links
really on either side.[6]

King George, however, was averse to the name of Ann;
and, though disappointed, the parents bowed to his wishes in
the matter. The Duchess wrote resignedly but with determination to Queen Mary:

Bertie & I have decided now to call our little daughter 'Margaret
Rose', instead of M. Ann, as Papa does not like Ann — I hope
that you like it. I think that it is very pretty together.[7]

Apparently the King raised no objection to this decision,
for on October 30 the Princess was christened Margaret Rose
by the Archbishop of Canterbury at Buckingham Palace.

Some months later the question arose of the appointment
of a successor to Lord Willingdon,[a] whose retirement as
Governor-General of Canada was imminent; and the outcome provides an interesting sidelight on the attitude of

[a] Rt. Hon. Freeman Freeman-Thomas, first Marquess of Willingdon, G.C.S.I.,
G.C.M.G., G.C.I.E., G.B.E. (1866–1941), was Governor-General of Canada
from 1926 to 1931, and Viceroy of India from 1931 to 1936.

254   DUKE OF YORK   1931

Mr. MacDonald's Labour Government to the connection between the Royal Family and the Commonwealth. In the discussion of likely candidates between the British Government and Mr. R. B. Bennett,[a] the Conservative Prime Minister of Canada, the name of the Duke of York was considered among others. But, according to a memorandum from Sir Clive Wigram to Lord Stamfordham, Mr. J. H. Thomas,[b] then Secretary of State for the Dominions, 'was not very keen about the Duke of York and I asked him for the reason; he said that they did not want a Royalty in Canada as it was too close to the U.S.A. and the Canadians pride themselves on being as democratic as the Americans. I cannot believe that this is true — however there it is!'[8]   This view was violently contested by Lord Stamfordham. 'I *do not believe* it', he minuted to King George on January 3. 'The Americans are the greatest worshippers of Royalty — people of title etc. . . . When Thomas was at Balmoral he was *insistent* that the Princes should go to the Dominions as G.G.s or even as Governors of the Australian States!'[9]

Mr. Thomas, however, stuck to his opinions, and the King, in duty bound, followed the counsel of his constitutional advisers of the day. The Duke of York's name was dropped from consideration, and in the end Lord Bessborough [c] was agreed upon and appointed.

Whether the Duke of York would have willingly accepted the office of Governor-General of Canada is uncertain. There had been a time when he was anxious to see as much of the Commonwealth and Empire as possible, and his experiences in Australia and New Zealand had been of the happiest and most successful. But he was now a family man with a desire to settle in his own home. Had the desirability of his appointment to Ottawa been put to him as a matter of duty he would unquestionably have gone there, for with him public service

[a] Rt. Hon. Richard Bedford, first Viscount Bennett (1870–1947), Leader of the Conservative Party in Canada from 1927 to 1938, and Prime Minister and Minister of External Affairs from 1930 to 1935.

[b] Rt. Hon. James Henry Thomas (1874–1949), General Secretary of the National Union of Railwaymen, was Secretary of State for the Colonies in both Mr. MacDonald's Labour Governments, and for the Dominions from 1930 to 1935.

[c] Rt. Hon. Vere Brabazon Ponsonby, ninth Earl of Bessborough, G.C.M.G. (1880–1956), served as Governor-General of Canada from 1931 to 1935.

ever transcended personal inclination, but it is to be believed
that he was not too disappointed, and that he now turned his
attention with satisfaction to the making of a home.

(ii)

In September 1931 King George offered the Royal Lodge in
Windsor Great Park to the Duke and Duchess of York as their
country home.   Originally known as 'Lower Lodge', a humble
appendage of 'the Great Lodge', it had been granted by
William Augustus, Duke of Cumberland ('The Butcher'), to
Thomas Sandby,[a] who as Private Secretary had served with
him at the battles of Dettingen and Culloden and whom, when
the Duke became Ranger of the Great Park in 1746 and took
up residence in the larger house, which he renamed Cumberland Lodge, he appointed as his Deputy Ranger.   Sandby
lived there until his death in 1798.

When George, Prince of Wales, became Prince Regent in
1811 he had need of a country-house within easy reach of
London and Windsor.   It was impossible for him to live at
the Castle, since it was at once the asylum of George III
and the home of Queen Charlotte and her daughters.   He
therefore fixed upon Cumberland Lodge ; but until this could
be reconditioned he took up temporary residence in the Lower
Lodge, which he decreed should be thatched in accordance
with the prevailing fashion of a *cottage orné*.   Gradually,
however, the Prince became more and more attached to the
smaller house, now known as 'the Royal Lodge', which he
used exclusively as his own residence, keeping Cumberland
Lodge to house his guests.   He continued this custom even
after he became King in 1820, living there during the extensive
alterations which were being carried out in Windsor Castle.

As the King's unpopularity with his subjects increased, he
sought to shield himself from the public within the privacy
of Royal Lodge.   He sensed his estrangement from the dis-
contented working classes, who, in the opening days of his
reign, had espoused the cause of Queen Caroline largely out of
dislike for her husband.   Unlike his jovial successor upon the

[a] Thomas Sandby and his brother Paul were both Foundation Members of
the Royal Academy.

throne, who met the gathering storm of radical feeling with a bourgeois familiarity towards all and sundry, George IV retired into seclusion at Royal Lodge. He withdrew because he was unpopular; he was unpopular because he withdrew. It was a vicious circle that was never broken.

As ever, George IV could not keep from making additions, alterations and general ornamentation. He decreed the construction of 'a stately pleasure dome', first at the hand of John Nash and latterly at that of Sir Jeffry Wyatville.[a] The cost was immense and became the subject of unfavourable comment in the House of Commons, but the King remained undeterred; there was no finality to his building schemes, and indeed he was still adding to Royal Lodge when he died in 1830, leaving unfinished a great banqueting saloon designed by Wyatville.

The tide of 'Peace, Retrenchment and Reform', which characterized the reign of King William IV, literally swept away the strange house whose construction had so entertained his predecessor for eighteen years. When the house-breakers had completed their task of demolition, nothing remained save the Chapel and Wyatville's great saloon, which was still unroofed. Here the King and Queen Adelaide used frequently to picnic; and the Queen subsequently caused a charming octagonal room to be built on to the end of it, hung inside with chintz in the manner of a marquee. Later, she reconstructed from the fragments which remained of the house a tea pavilion in the Home Park, known as Adelaide Cottage, which remains there to this day.

During the century which supervened between the destruction of George IV's dream house and the occupancy of Royal Lodge by the Duke and Duchess of York, the truncated remnant

---

[a] Sir Jeffry Wyatville (1766–1840), was the nephew of James Wyatt, who as Surveyor-General of Works had carried out extensive alterations to Windsor Castle for George III. He himself renovated the Castle for George IV, and on the occasion of the laying of the new foundation-stone in 1824, petitioned the King to be allowed to assume the suffix -ville in order to differentiate himself from his kinsfolk who were architects, builders and contractors. To this request the King is said to have returned the somewhat disconcerting reply: 'Ville or mutton, call yourself what you like; it's all one to me'. Contemporary opinion is reflected in the epigram which appeared in a daily paper next morning:

> Let George, whose restlessness leaves nothing quiet,
> Change, if he must, the good old name of Wyatt;
> But let us hope that their united skill
> Will not make Windsor Castle 'Wyat-ville'.

accommodated, as a grace-and-favour residence, a variety of members of the Royal Family and friends and retainers of the Sovereign. To meet their successive needs a number of alterations and additions were made from time to time, most of them ineptly. Wyatville's lofty saloon had been roofed and partitioned into three rooms, and to reach the front door the incomer had to traverse a long glass greenhouse. Inconvenience and dilapidation were the keynotes of the house when the Duke and Duchess first visited it in September 1931, and it is a tribute both to their perspicacity and their courage that they saw the possibilities of the place, and, having done so, were not daunted by the difficulties of realizing them. 'It is too kind of you to have offered us Royal Lodge', the Duke wrote to King George after their first inspection, '& now having seen it I think it will suit us admirably.' [10] 'I am so pleased to hear that both you & Elizabeth liked *the* Royal Lodge & would like to live there', the King replied from Balmoral. '. . . I hope you will always call it *the* Royal Lodge, by which name it has been known ever since George IV built it.' [11]

It was by no means an ideal time for home-making. The New York Stock Market crash of October 1929 had heralded a new and grave phase of the post-war economic depression throughout the world. In 1930 a wave of political and economic unrest spread over Latin America, causing governments and dictatorships to rise and fall with bewildering rapidity, and bringing with it a material decrease in the volume of trade. Economic distress and financial embarrassment became vividly apparent in Australia, and the collapse of the Kreditanstalt Bank in Vienna in May 1931 began a period of unparalleled economic eruptions throughout Europe. The tide of crisis reached Britain in the month of July, and Mr. Ramsay MacDonald's Labour administration proved quite incapable of meeting the financial emergency, with the result that, after an historic Cabinet meeting, they were compelled to resign on August 24. At this juncture King George gave an outstanding instance of constitutional wisdom. He invited Mr. MacDonald to form a National Government composed of all parties, with a mandate to take the necessary measures for the salvation of the national economy. When taken, these included a drastic

Economy Bill and the ultimate abandonment of the Gold Standard on September 21.[a]

The crisis had its repercussions throughout the economic life of the country, and strict curtailment of expenditure, both public and private, became the order of the day. In this the Royal Family set an outstanding example. One of the King's first acts after the appointment of the National Government was to inform the Prime Minister of his decision that, while the emergency lasted, his Civil List should be reduced by £50,000. 'I am going to give up the shooting in Windsor Park', he wrote to the Duke of York, 'as I can't afford it, I am sorry as the birds fly so well there, perhaps David might like to take it on.' [12]   But the Prince of Wales was also taking his share in the movement for the reduction of expenditure, and he at once contributed £50,000 to the National Exchequer.

The Duke of York was faced with similar financial restrictions, not the least of which was the sacrifice of his hunting and his stable. 'I shall be unable to hunt with the Pytchley this year', he wrote to the Master, Mr. Ronald Tree. 'It has come as a great shock to me that with the economy cuts I have had to make my hunting should have been one of the things I must do without. And I must sell my horses too. This is the worst part of it all, and the parting with them will be terrible.' [13]   It was indeed a severe wrench to part with his stable, which he had built up with care and discrimination, and which had given him so many happy hours. 'I am only doing this after careful consideration of facts (damned hard facts)', he wrote to his equerry, Commander Colin Buist, who had undertaken to superintend the sale, 'The horses are looking so well, too'.[b] [14]

Slowly the pressure of the economic cyclone eased; the nations of the world emerged from their storm-shelters and

---

[a] The majority of the Labour Party refused to follow Mr. MacDonald's lead in support of the National Government. At the General Election of October 27 they paid the price for this decision, losing 200 seats. The National Government was returned with a majority of 502 (471 Conservatives, 35 Liberal Nationals, 33 'Pure' Liberals, 13 National Labour, 2 'National'). The Opposition consisted of 52 Labour members and 4 Lloyd George Liberals. A brilliant account of the crisis of 1931 is to be found in chap. xxvii of Sir Harold Nicolson's biography of King George V.

[b] The Duke's six horses were sold in his presence at the Leicester Repository on Saturday, November 7, 1931. The total fetched was nine hundred and sixty-five guineas (*The Times*, November 9, 1931).

began to take stock of their immediate situation. Emergency measures gave place to more considered legislation; the stringency of personal restrictions abated. As the crisis passed and the Duke and Duchess found themselves again at liberty to attend to the demands of the Royal Lodge, they concentrated all their efforts upon making this their real home — to which they could retire and relax from the eternal programme of official and semi-official engagements, the home that they could make for themselves, of which the keynote was to be gaiety and love and laughter; above all, a home where their children might grow up with the boon and the blessing of a family life replete with affection and understanding, such as the Duchess had enjoyed and the Duke had never known.

Little by little, as circumstances permitted, improvements were planned and carried out, until a considerable mansion had once more arisen on the site of King George IV's original 'Cottage'. Wyatville's great saloon, now disencumbered of its party-walls and restored to its magnificent proportions, became the central feature, forming a large and delightful living-room, with new wings added on either flank, and the whole exterior pink-washed in a colour of warm rose. No two people — not even Queen Victoria and Prince Albert — could have been happier in their home-making than were the Duke and Duchess of York.

The development of the gardens was also a great delight, and here the Duke found opportunity for the expression of one of his chief interests. He had a genius for landscape gardening which soon gained him an acknowledged position as an authority in this field, for he combined considerable horticultural lore with a gift for design and display, and the priceless possession of a 'green finger'. He was no fair-weather gardener, who merely liked to stroll among his lawns and flower-beds on a pleasant day; he knew indeed of what he spoke, and, with the assistance of Mr. Eric Savill,[a] the Deputy

---

[a] Sir Eric Savill, K.C.V.O., C.B.E., M.C. (b. 1895), was appointed Deputy Surveyor of Windsor Parks and Woods in 1931, and to this King George VI added the appointment of Deputy Ranger of Windsor Great Park in 1937. To him is largely due the credit for the many great improvements carried out at Windsor in recent years, not the least of which is the creation of the bog-garden, a place of great beauty in early summer, which the King named the Savill Garden.

Surveyor of Windsor Parks and Woods, he created at Royal Lodge one of the most beautiful smaller gardens in the country, distinguished alike for its display of colour and its perfection of arrangement.

The Duke's speciality was shrubs, and within this category his particular interest lay in rhododendrons. In this world he was a recognized connoisseur — in the words of one of the experts employed by the Commissioner of Crown Lands, on the subject of rhododendrons 'Nobody could stump him' [15]— and he entered with enthusiasm into the collector's passion for the exchange of information and species with other masters in the same field. So great did his interest become, and so wide his knowledge, that he once wrote to the Countess of Stair after a visit to Lochinch Castle, in the 'language of rhododendrons'.

DEAR LADY STAIR,

I must write & thank you both so very much for asking me to come to Lochinch. I did so enjoy my visit & you gave me such an Agapetum (delightful) time.

It was a great disappointment to me that my wife was unable to come too, & she is miserable at having missed the two Formosum (beautiful) days we had there. I am glad to tell you that she is much better, though I found her looking Microleucrum (small and white).

It was nice of you to say that I deputised well for her on Saturday but I feel that she could have done everything much better, as she has the Agastum (charming) way of Charidotes (giving joy). As we had arranged our visit for her, she Pothinum (much desired) to be there, & it was very sad for her to have missed it. However it is Sperabile (to be hoped for) Timeteum (to be honoured) with a future invitation.

As to my visit, I am overjoyed Eclecteum (to be chosen out) and Aberrans (wandering) Cyclium (round) so many Erastum (lovely) and Arizelum (notable) gardens in so short a time, has left me Charitostreptum (gracefully bent) with a Recurvum (bent back), & somewhat Lasiopodum (woolly footed). I must say I am filled Coeloneurum (with impressed nerves) at all the Agetum (wondrous) & Aperantum (limitless) beauties of the gardens cyclium (round) Lochinch.

But despite being Asperulum (slightly roughened) & having had time to examine my feet, Denudatum (naked) and Detersile (clean) I am glad to find that they are neither Hypoglaucum (blue beneath) Hypolepidotum (scaly) nor Hypophaeum (grey) but merely Russatum (reddened). This Rufuscens (becoming reddish) will have Comisteum (to be taken care of) otherwise they will not be Eudoxom (of good report) for Clivicola (living on hillsides) in August. As a diversion I much enjoyed our chase after those Tephropeplum (ashy grey colour) Dumicola (dwellers in thickets) which we were lucky enough to find Telopeum (conspicuous) Lochmium (from a coppice). Knowing you to be an Ombrochares (lover of rain) I hope you will soon get some to revive the Species of Rhododendron; which as we are told by one Wallace: 'Of course it is over', and to make the snipe bogs Paludosum (marshy). It is too kind of you to have given me so many Axium (worthy) & Eucallum (beautiful) plants which will be Eritimum (highly prized) by me & are most Apodectum (acceptable).

After this I feel I cannot write English any more. It was really too kind of you to have had me to stay & I did so enjoy every moment of it. Thanking you both again so very much.

Yours very sincerely

ALBERT.[16]

To this letter Lady Stair replied in kind, with equal wit and ingenuity:

SIR,

Your Royal Highness's letter has much charopoeum (causing joy) us. It was a assumistum (very pleasing) letter & I feel timetum (to be honoured) at receiving it. I feel a desire to attempt a reply in the same asteium (elegant) strain but I fear my effort may not be axium (worthy). Your Basilicum (Royal) Highness' standard is protistum (first of the first).

I am anxious to report to you that at the Garden party we received much chrysodoron (golden gift), argenteum (silver) & acrugenosum (verdigris coloured) for our hospital. All together the grand sum of £1982 was taken. This was praeclarum (very remarkable) & inopinum (unexpected) owing to the population of this county being minus (smaller) than most. I think it will be jucundum (pleasant) for you to know that though deeply dis-appointed at not having the pleasure of seeing your horaeum (beautiful) Duchess, I heard on all sides that people were delighted with the eximium (excellent) way in which you took her place.

The pulchrum (beautiful) weather continues & is very jucundum (pleasant) but many rhododendrons are pendulum (hanging). We have been removing seed heads & watering as long as the midges would let us.

We have again visited the garden at Logan. The hemi-trichotum (half hairy) elder brother, Kenneth McDouall was peramoenum (very pleasing) at having shown his garden to our

Diaprepes (distinguished) guest & expressed delight at your insigne (remarkable) knowledge of rhododendrons. The barbatum (bearded) brother said nothing, this was characteristic. We have not been to the garden of the calvescens (becoming bald) gentleman at Lochryan again, because his rhododendrons are all 'Erastum (lovely) but past'.

I would like to go to the show at the Horticultural Hall on Tuesday to see if there are any good late flowering rhododendrons or azaleas but I shall have to go to Eton instead for the 4th of June.

I hope the plants we propose sending you will flourish.

I have the honour to be Sir

Yr. obedient servant

VIOLET STAIR.[17]

(iii)

The mid-thirties of the twentieth century were a period of great stability for the British Monarchy. On the Continent of Europe the advent to power of Adolf Hitler and the Nazi régime in Germany, and the disquieting disunity of France were sources of anxiety to many, and the great experiment of President Roosevelt's New Deal across the Atlantic was the cause of wonderment to not a few; while the unchecked aggression of Japan in China and of Italy in Ethiopia shattered the hopes of the disciples of Collective Security, and gave rise to new and growing apprehension. At home, however, the National Government had weathered the economic crisis and when, in the autumn of 1935, Mr. Baldwin replaced Mr. MacDonald as Prime Minister and was returned to power after a General Election with a handsome majority [a] it appeared that domestic stability was assured. The marriages of the King's two younger sons, the Duke of Kent and the Duke of Gloucester,[b] had given great public satisfaction, and the tremendous upwelling of popular affection and devotion on the occasion of the King's Silver Jubilee on May 6, 1935 — though it appears to have surprised King George himself, whose

[a] At the General Election of November 14, 1935, Mr. Baldwin and the National Government were returned with a majority of 245, showing a loss of 79 seats. They were confronted with an Opposition of 180, Labour having increased its representation from 95 seats to 154.

[b] The Duke of Kent on November 29, 1934, married Princess Marina, daughter of Prince Nicholas of Greece and sister of Princess Paul of Yugoslavia. Almost exactly a year later, on November 6, 1935, the Duke of Gloucester married the Lady Alice Montagu-Douglas-Scott, daughter of the seventh Duke of Buccleuch.

comment on returning from his drive through the East End of London was, 'I'd no idea they felt like that about me. I am beginning to think they must like me for myself' [18] — came to the vast majority of his subjects as confirmation of that deep-seated affection and loyalty which had for twenty-five years existed as much towards the personality of the Sovereign as to the Crown.

It seemed to the Duke of York that the pattern of his life was now firmly established, and that his lines were laid in very pleasant places. He was supremely happy in his family and his home. The upbringing of his daughters was a source of never-failing interest and care to him, and because of his memories of his own clouded childhood he was determined that, come what might, Princess Elizabeth and Princess Margaret should look back upon their early years as a golden age. The love, the understanding and the companionship of the Duchess were part of his living entity. Indeed, so essential were they, that it is impossible to imagine him deprived of these vital parts of his spiritual organism.

The Duke was fully appreciative of his status as his father's second heir to the throne. Admittedly the King's health was failing; admittedly, also, the Prince of Wales remained un-married. But even in the event of the death of his father and the accession to the throne of his brother, it seemed most unlikely to the Duke of York that he would occupy the throne, or not at least for an appreciable period of time, since, actuarially speaking, they came of a long-lived family and only eighteen months separated him in age from his elder brother. Never at any time did he appear to consider it within the bounds of probability that he would become King. He continued to pursue the full round of his official engagements, with an un-diminished devotion to duty, and at the same time he enjoyed to the full the supreme felicity of his domestic life. Beyond this he gave no thought, save in the realm of ultimate pos-sibility, to his own succession.

The days of this peaceful existence were, however, numbered. The life of King George V was drawing to its close and the events which followed were to lay upon the Duke of York's shoulders burdens of responsibility unasked, unlooked-for and unwelcome.

(iv)

For some time the King's health had been causing anxiety. There had been a disquieting renewal of his bronchial trouble in February 1935, which had necessitated a period of recuperation at Eastbourne. He had survived the exacting ceremonies of his Silver Jubilee with surprising resilience, however, and his appearance, when he went down to review the Fleet at Spithead in July, had given rise to the hope that he was fully recovered. The nation's relief from anxiety was voiced in the prayer of the Poet Laureate:

> O God, vouchsafe him many years
> With all the world as England's friend,
> And England bright among her peers
> With wisdom that can never end.[a]

But the prayer was not to be granted. On his return from Balmoral in the autumn, those closest to the King noticed a serious deterioration. The death of his sister, Princess Victoria, early on the morning of December 3, dealt him a shattering blow. For what was perhaps the first and last time in his life his tremendous sense of public duty faltered, and, at short notice, he cancelled the State Opening of Parliament scheduled for that day, feeling that under the burden of his bereavement he could not face the ordeal of a public appearance. He went to Sandringham for his usual Christmas festivities and made his last broadcast to the Empire, from which many of his listening public deduced a marked decline in his state of health.

On January 15 a small house-party had gathered at Sandringham. The King went for a short ride on his white pony, with the Queen walking beside him. Next morning he complained of a cold and remained in his room all day. 'Most worrying', Queen Mary recorded in her diary. 'I sent for Bertie to help me with the party.'[19]

The Duke of York had had his own anxieties, for the Duchess had recently suffered an attack of influenza from which pneumonia had developed. She was lying ill at Royal Lodge, but both agreed that the Duke must make an

---

[a] 'A Prayer for the King's Majesty', by John Masefield.

immediate response to his mother's appeal, and he left at once for Sandringham, arriving late in the afternoon of January 16.

On the following day the King was very ill. 'I feel rotten', he wrote in the last recorded entry in his diary. He remained drowsy all day and the Queen sent for the Prince of Wales, who was shooting at Windsor, and for Lord Dawson of Penn, both of whom arrived the same evening, the Prince by air.[20] The two following days were filled with increasing gloom. Sir Maurice Cassidy [a] arrived and pronounced the King's heart to be failing; all hopes for his recovery faded. The Prince of Wales returned with the Duke of York to London on January 19, and informed the Prime Minister that his father was not expected to live more than two or three days.[21]

On the morning of January 20 a Privy Council was held for the purpose of appointing Counsellors of State,[b] and the events of the day are told with poignant simplicity in Queen Mary's diary. Weak and dying, the King sat propped up in a chair, just visible to the Privy Counsellors through the open door of his sitting-room.

Ld. Dawson managed to get G. to say 'Approved' & he was able to sign 2 little crosses, as he was unable to sign his name which distressed him. . . . David & Bertie returned at 2.30 in D.'s airplane. . . . G. became weaker during the evening and we realized the end was approaching. We family dined alone & then went to G.'s room at intervals & at 5 to 12 my darling husband passed peacefully away — my children were angelic.[22]

On an extra page of her diary the sorrowing Queen added this passage:

Words commemorating King George V's death: 'The sunset of his death tinged the whole world's sky'.

[a] Sir Maurice Alan Cassidy, G.C.V.O., C.B. (1880–1949), was Physician Extraordinary to King George V, King Edward VIII and King George VI.

[b] The Privy Counsellors present on this occasion were: the Lord President, Mr. Ramsay MacDonald; the Archbishop of Canterbury, Dr. Lang; the Lord Chancellor, Lord Hailsham; the Home Secretary, Sir John Simon; Lord Dawson and Lord Wigram, with Sir Maurice Hankey as Clerk to the Council. The Counsellors of State thus appointed, who functioned only until the proclamation of King Edward VIII the next day, consisted of the Queen, the Prince of Wales and the Dukes of York, Gloucester and Kent.

CHAPTER VIII

THE REIGN OF KING EDWARD VIII : JANUARY–DECEMBER 1936

(i)

A NEW reign and a new era, brief but significant in the annals of our history, began on January 20, 1936. It opened in a blaze of glowing and effulgent hope — to close on a note of major tragedy. No British Sovereign ascended the throne with a greater measure of good-will from his peoples, or with higher expectations, than did King Edward VIII. In Britain and around the Commonwealth and Empire he had endeared himself as Prince of Wales, by reason of his radiant comeliness, his gaiety, his lack of formality, his courage and, above all, his ability to talk as man to man with 'duke's son, cook's son, son of a millionaire'. Prince Charming he had been justly termed ; to the men and women of his generation he typified all that was best in the twentieth century, and they looked forward to the promise of a modern monarch, cognizant of the problems of his peoples and closely identified with their interests and aspirations.

No man is more willing to make friends, and none has a greater regard for the obligations of friendship [*The Times* wrote of the new King]. At the same time he values humanity in the widest sense of the old aphorism. Men, not books, are his library, as they were for the last King Edward, and he has the same power to learn from them. He is gifted with a genuine interest, which more 'democrats' profess than feel, in all sorts and conditions of people, and he is rich in a study that is admirable and endearing in any man and inestimable in a Sovereign — the study of mankind.[1]

The tone and tempo of the new reign were apparent from the outset. It was not for nothing that the King's first act was to abolish 'Sandringham time',[a] nor that his first journey as

---

[a] See above, p. 5 and fn. *b*.

Sovereign was by air.ᵃ He came of a generation to whom
speed was the essence of life, whose thinking was 'stream-
lined', and who sought to cast off what they regarded as the
outworn shibboleths of the Victorian era. How closely King
Edward sympathized with and shared these views may be
gathered from his own words :

I was, after all, the first King of the twentieth century who had
not spent at least half his life under the strict authority of Queen
Victoria. My father was already halfway through his life-span
when his grandmother died ; and by the gravity of his temperament it was to her, rather than to the livelier example of his own
father, that he looked for a model of the Sovereign's deportment.
His Court retained a Victorian flavour to the end ; and I had come
to look upon it as at least sexagenarian in composition and outlook.²

The personal regimen of the late King George had been set
in the framework of strict and regular adherence to certain
individual precepts and certain established features of the social
calendar. His son was of a less rigid nature. King George
went to church every Sunday. King Edward attended Divine
Service when he felt like it. Unless some State emergency or
serious illness interfered, the old King never missed the Derby
or the Two Thousand Guineas or Cowes Regatta. He would
be on the grouse moors every August 12. On the rare occasions
when he dined out it was in the private houses of the restricted
circle of his personal friends.

But this new young Monarch was different [as he wrote of
himself]. While he worked overtime in so far as his duties were
concerned, August would probably find him playing golf at Biarritz
or swimming off Eden Roc, or stooking wheat on his ranch in
Canada. He had abandoned hunting for the less virile pursuit of
gardening. He preferred golf to yacht racing, and in place of the
stereotyped shooting parties still in vogue for those who could afford
them, he would be off stalking chamois in the Tyrol, or shooting par-
tridges as a guest of Regent Horthy of Hungary. His free evenings
were more likely to be spent *en petit comité* with a few intimates or
at the Embassy Club than in the great houses or salons of London.³

Such, then, was the *leitmotiv* of the new reign and the new
Monarch. He was ready and willing to assume the responsi-

ᵃ It was King Edward VIII who created 'The King's Flight' under the direction of his personal pilot, now Air Commodore Sir Edward Fielden. Originally
composed of the King's own aeroplane, it was later expanded to include a number
of aircraft.

bilities of kingship, but on his own terms. He did not intend, for example, to withdraw into that tight possessive world of officialdom from which, as Prince of Wales, he had already begun to escape. Though, as he himself has suggested in his memoirs, it may well have been possible that, had the choice been left to him, he might not have consciously chosen the throne as the most desirable goal of all his aspirations,[4] now that he *was* King, he wanted to be a successful King, though a King in a modern way.[a] He was determined that, within the constitutional limits of his position, he would be his own master. It was his intention that his era should be one of hard work and modernity; an era in which formality and 'red tape' were to be reduced to a minimum; an era in which the King might enjoy his hard-earned leisure where he wished and how he wished, and with whom he wished, unrestricted by the rigidity of Court etiquette. 'He was', writes the Duchess of Windsor, 'excited and challenged by what he took to be his mission to modernize the monarchy within its traditional glory and strength.'[5] There were those who welcomed his departure from tradition, but there were also those who wondered how it might end.

(ii)

For the Duke of York the new reign brought new burdens of responsibility. He was now his brother's immediate heir, separated from the throne by but one life, and there was no present prospect of the King's marriage. Yet, despite this new imminence, he steadfastly refused to contemplate the prospect of his own succession, either then or in the months that followed.

At this moment, indeed, there was much to occupy him in mind and body. His immediate anxiety for the Duchess was allayed by her rapid recovery from pneumonia, and he felt free to play his part in helping the new Sovereign in the

[a] In an interview given to the American magazine *Parade* on June 16, 1957, twenty years after his marriage, the Duke of Windsor made the following statement: 'There has been criticism in some quarters through the years that I did not want to be King, that I put my personal feelings above the throne and above my duty, that I left because of a craving for private happiness. This is a lie. I say it now and for all time : all my life I trained for the job and for twenty-four years as Prince of Wales I served my country and the Commonwealth devotedly. For a year as King I worked as hard and selflessly as I knew how. Of course I wished to be King. More, I wished to *remain* King.'

many tasks which beset him.   On the morrow of King George's death, King Edward and the Duke flew to London for the Accession meeting of the Privy Council at St. James's Palace, and then returned to Sandringham to supervise the arrangements for the funeral.

It had been the special desire of Queen Mary that the late King should not remain unburied more than a week,[6] and, in accordance with this wish, the body was brought from Sandringham to London on January 23.   From King's Cross the coffin on its gun-carriage, wrapped in the Royal Standard with the Imperial Crown atop, escorted by a bearer-party of the Grenadier Guards and followed by the King and his brothers, passed through the silent mourning crowds to the Great Hall of the Palace of Westminster.[a]   There, set on a catafalque beneath a splendid pall, it lay in state for five days, while there filed before it an endless stream of men and women and children, many of them weeping, in a final act of homage to one whom they had always revered and loved.

At each corner of the catafalque stood the motionless figure of an officer of the Brigade of Guards, his head bowed, his hands clasped on the hilt of his drawn sword ; but on the last night of the vigil, on the initiative of King Edward, their places were taken for a while by the four sons of the dead King, who, in the uniforms of their respective Services, kept the last watch about their father's bier.

On the grey and wintry day of January 28, King George V was borne through the streets of London and of Windsor to his grave in St. George's Chapel.   Behind him walked his four sons, and five foreign rulers bore him company.[b]   There

[a] It was in the course of this progress through London that the Maltese Cross on the Imperial Crown, a jewel set with a great sapphire, eight medium-sized diamonds and one hundred and ninety-two lesser diamonds, fell from the gun-carriage into the gutter.   It was swiftly retrieved by the Company-Sergeant-Major of the Grenadier Guards bringing up the rear of the bearer-party.   Quick as his action had been, the incident had not passed unnoticed, and to the superstitious it seemed an ill augury for the opening of the new reign.

[b] The five rulers were : King Christian of Denmark, King Haakon of Norway, King Carol of Rumania, Tsar Boris of Bulgaria, King Leopold III of the Belgians, and the President of the French Republic, M. Albert Lebrun.   Of these, King Christian became a virtual prisoner of the Nazis, and King Haakon was forced to fly from his country as a result of German aggression.   Tsar Boris died under mysterious circumstances, King Carol and King Leopold were compelled to abdicate, and President Lebrun was displaced from office by Marshal Pétain.

followed a great concourse of foreign statesmen and warriors, some of whom made strange companions : Marshal Pétain, the hero of Verdun and the man of Vichy ; Maxim Litvinov, then in fleeting popularity as the entrepreneur of a short-lived honeymoon of amity between the Soviet Union and the West, Marshal Tukachevsky, destined to be executed as a traitor a year later, and the Grand Duke Dmitri, a cousin of the murdered Tsar ; Freiherr von Neurath, the German Foreign Minister, who ten years later was to be condemned at Nuremberg as a major War Criminal, Field-Marshal von Blomberg, a future victim of the Führer's caprice, and the aged and arthritic Duke of Saxe-Coburg-Gotha. From Austria came the dashing Prince von Starhemberg, who endeavoured unsuccessfully to enjoy the protection of both Hitler and Mussolini — and suffered accordingly ; and from Finland the veteran Field-Marshal Baron von Mannerheim, that romantic figure who was to resist so gallantly the assault of the Red Army upon his country. All these followed King George V to Windsor, and with them went the mourners of England and the Empire, the greatest and the humblest in the land, to take their sorrowful leave of one whose passing marked the end of the Victorian era.

> When Time has sifted motives, passions, deeds,
>   Now complex to results and made appear
> The unexpected fruits of scattered seeds,
>   And scattered dust in the expected ear,
> Then watchers of the life of man will know
>   How spirits quickened in this ended reign
> Till what was centuries stagnant 'gan to flow ;
>   And what was centuries fettered moved again ;
> How with this Ruler entered into rest
>   The country's very self from slumber stirred,
> Took charity as guide and hope as guest,
>   And ventured to a nobler marching word.[a]

(iii)

The salient features of King Edward's reign were his desire for economy and for the institution of changes which he

[a] 'Ode on the passing of King George V', by John Masefield.

regarded as having been too long delayed, changes which should bring his life and environment as a Sovereign into greater compatibility with the demands of the age in which he lived. He considered that a twentieth-century monarch must lead a twentieth - century existence, attuned to the standards of the twentieth century and not to those of the nineteenth. To the King it seemed that his father's whole life had been a stubborn rearguard action against the acceptance of the march of his own times, and this he was determined should not continue.

It was perhaps natural that his first assault should be upon Sandringham, which he regarded as the epitome of this 'Sleepy Hollow' mentality, and where, in his own words, King George's 'private war with the twentieth century had ended in the almost complete repulse of the latter'. He himself had lost his early love for this home of his childhood. Fort Belvedere had become his spiritual home, and the Sandringham estate figured in his mind only as a voracious 'white elephant', the upkeep of which could only be maintained at its traditional standard by a consistent and, to his view, prodigal dipping into the Privy Purse.

The King was determined that substantial reforms must and should be effected at Sandringham, and it was with this purpose that, in the first month of his reign, he asked the Duke of York to conduct an enquiry into the whole question of how the running expenses could be most effectively reduced. The Duke took with him a mutual friend, Lord Radnor,[a] an experienced landowner, and the two of them devoted a fort-night to surveying the estate.[7]

This report, which was written in large measure by the Duke himself, was a remarkable example of clarity and common sense, which would have done credit to his great-grandfather, the Prince Consort. Approaching the problem with realistic objectivity, it set forth a clear and considered programme of retrenchment. The Duke's own deep affection for Sandringham was clearly indicated, but it was not permitted to obscure his judgment in recommending decisions which, though they may

[a] William Pleydell-Bouverie, seventh Earl of Radnor, K.C.V.O. (b. 1895), was appointed Lord Warden of the Stannaries in 1933, and Chairman of the Forestry Commission in 1952.

have cost him something to put forward, he nevertheless considered to be essential, and the majority of them were subsequently put into effect during his own reign.

Indeed this report epitomized much of the Duke of York's attitude towards the new state of affairs created by his father's death. He, too, had chafed beneath the parental yoke, but not to the same degree or for the same reasons as his elder brother. He was, moreover, fundamentally his father's son in a way which King Edward never had been and never could be. The conflicts and vagaries of his relationship with the late King were of minor significance if set against the many tastes and characteristics which they shared in common. This circumstance was recognized as a fact by both the father and the brother. 'You have always been so sensible & easy to work with & you have always been ready to listen to any advice & to agree with my opinions about people & things, that I feel that we have always got on very well together (very different to dear David)',ª King George had written to the Duke of York at the time of his marriage, and King Edward has admitted that, in the midst of the difficulties with which he speedily found himself beset, he took comfort from the fact that his brother, his heir and successor:

. . . was in outlook and temperament very much like my father. The patterns of their lives were much the same, with the steady swing of habit taking them both year after year to the same places at the same time and with the same associates.[8]

Yet, though the Duke of York had much in common with his father, he was also possessed of a highly twentieth-century outlook — quite as strong as, though different in slant and face from, that of his elder brother. He was not unaware or unappreciative of the necessity for change and progress, but he realized that in order to bring this about, it was not essential to be at war with the memories of the past. For if, as King Edward has stated, King George V had fought a private war against the twentieth century, King Edward himself had been throughout his life an avowed rebel against the Victorian age.

His brother, both as Duke of York and as King, waged no

ª See above, p. 154.

vain battle with the present nor fought in phantom conflict
with the past. He too sought changes, but in order to bring
about that transmutation essential to progress with as little
dislocation or destruction of existing conditions as possible.
He was a progressive, not a revolutionary nor an iconoclast,
and, though impatient in his own temperament, he realized
and counselled the value of patience in public and in domestic
affairs, favouring the gradual rather than the precipitate course
of action.

Changes of personnel and establishment were also effected
by King Edward at Balmoral, during a brief visit to Deeside.
In this case, however, the decisions were taken by His Majesty
in consultation with the Crown authorities alone, and without
reference to his brother, although the latter was in residence at
Birkhall.

The Duke of York was pained at being thus ignored. He
was also disturbed at the nature of King Edward's decisions
regarding his Scottish home and its retainers. To the Duke
the Deeside country and its people meant home and happiness.
His love for them was heartfelt and sincere, and what touched
their well-being stirred his interest also. 'I know so much
about this place & I feel I am part of it. I like the people &
I believe they like me', he wrote to Lord Wigram [a] at this
time, and his heaviness of heart was revealed in a letter to
his mother, written from Glamis :

David only told me what he had done after it was over, which
I might say made me rather sad. He arranged it all with the
official people up there. I never saw him alone for an instant. . . .[9]

He entertained the hope that he might prevail upon the
King to stay longer at Balmoral in the following year, and to
become more intimately associated with the properties of which
he was laird and landlord. But when the King came again
to Scotland it was not King Edward VIII.

[a] Rt. Hon. Clive, first Baron Wigram, G.C.B., G.C.V.O., Royal Victorian
Chain (b. 1873), entered the Indian Army and served as A.D.C. to two Viceroys,
Lord Elgin and Lord Curzon, and on the staff of the Prince of Wales (King
George V) during his Indian tour of 1905–1906. In 1910 he was appointed
Assistant Private Secretary to King George V, becoming Private Secretary in
1931 and, in addition, Keeper of the Privy Purse, on the death of Lord Sysonby
in 1935 ; both of these offices he held until the death of King George V. He
served King George VI as Permanent Lord-in-Waiting throughout his reign.

(iv)

Slowly the fateful year of King Edward's reign drew to its tragic climax, though to the people of his realm there was as yet no breath or hint of tragedy. Preparations went forward for the Coronation in the following summer, and there was rising excitement at the prospect of this great spectacle. With the termination in July of the six months of official mourning, the King fulfilled a number of public engagements. He reviewed numerous units of the Navy, the Air Force and the Household Troops, and it was on his return to Buckingham Palace from presenting new colours to certain battalions of the Brigade of Guards in Hyde Park, on July 16, that there occurred that curious incident when a demented character with a grievance, one George Andrew McMahon — whose real name was Jerome Bannigan — sought to draw attention to himself by making a public disturbance. He had armed himself with a revolver, though there is little doubt that his object was self-advertisement rather than an attack on the King's person, and raised his arm in a menacing manner as the King, with the Duke of York on his left, rode slowly down Constitution Hill. As the King passed him McMahon stepped forward and threw his revolver, which was loaded in four of its five chambers, in the direction of His Majesty, striking the near hind leg of the King's horse. The affair was of negligible importance, and it was remarked that, apart from a muttered remark from the King and an answering grin from the Duke, neither checked his horse nor showed any sign of concern.[a]

The King's last public engagements of the season were the unveiling of the Canadian War Memorial on Vimy Ridge, and his attendance at the garden-party given at Buckingham Palace for the pilgrims from Canada who had crossed the Atlantic to be present at this great occasion of remembrance. These duties discharged, the King departed with a party of friends on a cruise in Balkan waters in the yacht *Nahlin*, which he had chartered from Lady Yule.

[a] It is not without interest that just ninety-six years before, on July 10, 1840, the lunatic Edward Oxford was condemned to be confined during Her Majesty's pleasure for his attempt upon the lives of Queen Victoria and Prince Albert on June 10, at almost exactly the same spot on Constitution Hill.

The Duke and Duchess of York repaired to Birkhall with
their daughters, there to contemplate the infelicitous prospect
before them.

Throughout the gaiety of the summer season, throughout
the preparations for the Coronation, there had been for the
King's family and for many of his most loyal and devoted
retainers an overshadowing cloud : the fact that the King
was in love with a lady who already had two husbands still
living and to one of whom she was still married.   Moreover, it
was becoming more than a suspicion that the King wished to
marry her himself.

It had been in the winter of 1930 that the Prince of Wales
had met Mrs. Simpson at Melton Mowbray.[a]   She had been
born Wallis Warfield, and her parents came of old and established aristocratic families in Maryland and Virginia.   In 1916
she had married Lieutenant Winfield Spencer, of the United
States Navy, from whom in 1927 she obtained a divorce on
a charge of desertion.   Six months later she was married
in London, at the Chelsea register office, to an Englishman,
Mr. Ernest Simpson.

The acquaintance between the Prince and Mrs. Simpson
had grown into friendship, and friendship into love.   The
matter had not escaped the notice of King George V and
had clouded the last years of his life.   No public association
of Mr. and Mrs. Simpson with the Prince occurred, however,
until after his accession to the throne, when their names
appeared in the Court Circular on two occasions, as having
dined with the King at York House, in company with the
Prime Minister and Mrs. Baldwin, Mr. and Mrs. Winston
Churchill, and Colonel and Mrs. Charles Lindbergh and
others.   In the King's own words : 'Secrecy and concealment
were not of my nature.   We saw each other when we could.' [10]
Mrs. Simpson became a frequent week-end visitor at Fort
Belvedere, with other of the King's friends, and she was among
his guests on the cruise in *Nahlin* in the summer, and later, in
the autumn, at Balmoral.

At this time the name of Mrs. Simpson was virtually

---

[a] The Duke of Windsor in *A King's Story* (p. 254) gives the date of their first
meeting as 1931, but the Duchess in her memoirs specifically denies this and places
the meeting a year earlier (p. 165).

unknown in England. It was, however, widely known in the great world outside, as was her friendship with the Sovereign. During the summer the uninhibited newspapers and magazines of the United States discussed more and more openly the possibilities of a 'Royal Romance', and when in October it became known that Mrs. Simpson had filed an undefended petition for divorce against her husband, the Hearst Press stated openly that as soon as these proceedings had been completed she would marry the King.

These rumours inevitably made their way to London and to the Dominions. As the summer waned, an ever-increasing volume of letters of the most critical kind, written mainly by British residents in the United States, began to reach Buckingham Palace, Marlborough House, Downing Street, Lambeth Palace and Printing House Square, where they occasioned grave dismay. No word, however, appeared in the British Press, and the country as a whole was still in complete ignorance of the rapidly darkening situation.

But if there was dismay in official circles in London, how much greater was the sorrow and alarm among the members of the King's own family. Queen Mary, perhaps the greatest palladium of the essential virtues and obligations of the Monarchy, was deeply distressed at her eldest son's intractability, while for the Duke of York the prospect was one of unrelieved gloom.

For him the impending crisis held a twofold sadness. He loved the King warmly and sincerely, and had admired in him all those qualities in which he felt himself to be deficient. As young men they had been friends and comrades, and, after the Duke's marriage, the gaiety and companionship of the Duchess had been an added link in their friendship. Now he felt shut off from his brother, neglected, ignored, unwanted. The situation at Balmoral, during the King's brief visit, had been like a nightmare, not only because of the decisions reached without his knowledge, but because of the hopelessly complicated personal element. He felt that he had lost a friend and was rapidly losing a brother.

But this was not the only aspect of the nightmare. That which the Duke had steadfastly refused to contemplate, that which he prayed might never be his destiny, was becoming ever more imminent. If these rumours were true, if the King persisted in taking a wife who had already divorced one husband and was preparing to divorce a second, it was manifest to all — save to the person most intimately concerned — that he could no longer remain Sovereign, and then the formidable burden of kingship would descend upon his brother's shoulders.

The Duke, however, would not abandon hope, would not bring himself to believe that, if faced with the choice of the Crown or this marriage, the King of England would opt unhesitatingly for Mrs. Simpson. He persisted in this belief until, very shortly after his return to London from Scotland, he received a visit from the King's Private Secretary, Major Alexander Hardinge.[a] The purport of his message was that, on October 20, the Prime Minister had, after deep consideration and much searching of heart, sought an audience of the King, and, having shown him samples of the letters which had been received from many sources deprecating His Majesty's association with Mrs. Simpson, had begged him to persuade her to have the divorce proceedings withdrawn. But the King had been adamant. He had not the right, he said, to interfere with the affairs of an individual. The case must go forward.

The possibility of abdication could no longer be ignored, yet the Duke recoiled from it with consternation and incredulity. In his mind he sought to free himself from the nightmare web that was slowly enmeshing him, but in his heart he began to realize the inevitability of his destiny.

On Tuesday, October 27, Mrs. Simpson received her decree *nisi* at Ipswich.

(v)

By mid-November London and the university cities had become fully apprised of the situation, and gossip was rife. The British Press, however, with most commendable and almost superhuman restraint, had remained silent. This was the result

[a] Rt. Hon. Alexander Henry Louis, second Baron Hardinge of Penshurst, G.C.B., G.C.V.O., M.C. (b. 1894), the eldest son of that distinguished diplomat and friend of King Edward VII, who was Viceroy of India and twice Permanent Under-Secretary of State in the Foreign Office, was appointed Assistant Private Secretary to King George V in 1920 and Assistant Keeper of the Privy Purse in 1935. King Edward VIII appointed him his Private Secretary in 1936, and he continued to serve King George VI in this same capacity until 1943.

neither of collusion among the newspaper proprietors themselves nor of pressure brought to bear on them from high quarters. It sprang from a healthy respect for the libel laws of England (considerably more strict than those across the Atlantic) and also from a very proper consideration for the private life of the Sovereign — so long as it remained private.

There had, it is true, been an agreement between the London and provincial Press not to make sensational exploitation of Mrs. Simpson's divorce suit. This had resulted from a consultation which the King had had with Lord Beaverbrook on October 16, and a meeting which Lord Beaverbrook and Mr. Esmond Harmsworth had called of their Press colleagues on the same day at Warwick House.ᵃ But at this point neither the proprietor of the *Daily Express* nor the proprietor of the *Daily Mail* had any suspicion that the King had already decided to marry Mrs. Simpson whenever she should be free. They simply told their colleagues of the King's anxiety to protect the lady from unpleasant publicity, and it was agreed that, when the suit came up, it should be reported purely factually with no hint that it possessed any more interest than the hundreds of other undefended petitions heard each year in the Courts.[11] This 'Gentlemen's Agreement' was scrupulously kept — a fact for which the King bore witness of his gratitude [12] — but it extended no further than the reporting of the divorce suit.

Thus, while the French Press reported the Simpson divorce case under such headlines as '*L'Amour du Roi va bien*', and the Press of America lashed itself into a libidinous lather on the subject of the King's intended marriage, the British Press maintained a voluntary silence; but it was clear that this could not continue indefinitely, and that it needed only a spark of indiscretion to ignite the whole powder-barrel of publicity.

Meantime, Mrs. Simpson, chaperoned by her aunt, continued to be a frequent week-end visitor at Fort Belvedere, a fact which caused increasing anxiety to His Majesty's Ministers, since it indicated that her relationship with the King was quite unchanged. When her decree of divorce became absolute she would be free to marry him. If the King married her,

---

ᵃ *The Times*, the *Morning Post* and the *Daily Telegraph* were not invited to this meeting as their discretion was not in question.

she would be Queen; once Queen, then both she and the King would be crowned by the Archbishop of Canterbury in Westminster Abbey in a solemn service of Holy Communion and with the rites of a Church of which the King was the Head and which holds that Christian marriage is for all time. These were the facts with which the Prime Minister was now faced. It was imperative that the position should be clarified, that the King should be made aware of the deep concern with which his constitutional advisers viewed his apparent intentions, and of the grave implications which were inherent in their concern.

It was at this moment that the King's Private Secretary, Major Hardinge, undertook, with the approval of the Prime Minister, the painful and delicate task of enlightening his master. His right and duty to do so were unquestioned, since it is the responsibility of the Private Secretary to acquaint the Sovereign of any impending crisis, but it was an obligation which he would willingly have evaded had it been possible.

The King had opened his first, and last, Parliament on November 3, and had attended the traditional ceremony at the Cenotaph on Armistice Day. Thereafter he had spent three days with the Home Fleet at Portland, a visit which had proved a long series of personal triumphs. It was an unexcelled example of his great talents for inspiring enthusiasm and managing large bodies of men. 'He seemed to know personally every officer and seaman in the Fleet', wrote his Minister-in-Attendance.[a] '. . . Here, indeed, was the Prince Charming, who could win the hearts of all sorts and conditions of men and women and send a thrill through great crowds.' [13]

Flushed with this personal success and warmed by the evidence of his popularity with the public, the King returned to London on November 13, and went straight to Fort Belvedere. There he found awaiting him the following letter from Major Hardinge: [b]

---

[a] King Edward was attended on this occasion by the First Lord of the Admiralty, Sir Samuel Hoare, later Viscount Templewood, whose memoirs of the period are of great value.

[b] Lord Templewood (p. 219) states that the King received Major Hardinge's letter at Buckingham Palace, but in his own memoirs (p. 326) the King says definitely that he found awaiting him on his arrival at the Fort a red dispatch box marked 'Urgent and Confidential', which contained the letter.

BUCKINGHAM PALACE
SIR,   13 November 1936
        With my humble duty.

As Your Majesty's Private Secretary I feel it my duty to bring to your notice the following facts which have come to my knowledge, and which I *know* to be accurate.

(1) The silence of the British Press on the subject of Your Majesty's friendship with Mrs. Simpson is *not* going to be maintained. It is probably only a matter of days before the outburst begins. Judging by the letters from British subjects living in foreign countries where the Press has been outspoken, the effect will be calamitous.

(2) The Prime Minister and senior members of the Government are meeting to-day to discuss what action should be taken to deal with the serious situation which is developing. As Your Majesty no doubt knows, the resignation of the Government — an eventuality which can by no means be excluded — would result in Your Majesty having to find someone else capable of forming a Government which would receive the support of the present House of Commons. I have reason to know that, in view of the feeling prevalent among members of the House of Commons of all parties, this is hardly within the bounds of possibility. The only alternative remaining is a dissolution and a general election in which Your Majesty's personal affairs would be the chief issue, and I cannot help feeling that even those who would sympathize with Your Majesty as an individual would deeply resent the damage which would inevitably be done to the Crown — the corner-stone on which the whole Empire rests.

If Your Majesty will permit me to say so, there is only one step which holds out any prospect of avoiding this dangerous situation, and that is for Mrs. Simpson to go abroad *without further delay* — and I would *beg* Your Majesty to give this proposal your earnest consideration before the position has become irretrievable. Owing to the changing attitude of the Press the matter has become one of great urgency.

I have the honour . . .

ALEXANDER HARDINGE

P.S. I am by way of going after dinner to-night to High Wycombe to shoot there to-morrow — but the Post Office will have my telephone number, and I am of course entirely at Your Majesty's disposal if there is anything at all that you want.

The effect of Major Hardinge's letter upon the King was to render His Majesty both 'shocked and angry', but it undoubtedly had the more far-reaching effect of influencing him

to take the decision to make his position finally and unequivocally clear to the Prime Minister.[a]

He summoned Mr. Baldwin to Buckingham Palace at 6.30
on the evening of November 16 and told him categorically
that he intended to marry Mrs. Simpson as soon as she was
free to marry.   If he could do this as King, so much the better ;
but if the Government were irrevocably opposed to his wishes,
he was prepared to abdicate.

The Prime Minister was shocked and dismayed.   Whatever else he had expected, he had not foreseen this obduracy.
His reply, as he later told the House of Commons, was : 'Sir,·
this is most grievous news, and it is impossible for me to make
any comment on it today'.   So shaken was he, indeed, that
having, on his return to Downing Street, informed his senior
Cabinet colleagues as to what had occurred at his audience
with the Sovereign, he found himself temporarily at the end of
his tether. 'David,' he said to his Chief Whip, Captain David
Margesson,[b] 'I have heard such things from my King to-night
as I never thought to hear.   I am going to bed.'   And to bed
he went, feeling unequal even to seeing the King's Assistant
Private Secretary, Mr. Alan Lascelles,[c] who had waited patiently
for his report.

The King, however, was in no way thus affected.   He had
taken a long step along the road towards his heart's desire, and
the prospect of married happiness was now opening before him.

[a] The Duke of Windsor only printed extracts from Major Hardinge's letter
in his memoirs (pp. 326-327).   The full text was not made public until November
29, 1955, when its author included it in an article in *The Times* entitled 'Before
the Abdication ; Private Secretary's Letter to King Edward VIII'.

It is to be noted that King Edward returned no reply to Major Hardinge's
letter, and thereafter held no further converse with his Private Secretary.   At
his request, Mr. Walter Monckton, who had been his Attorney-General as Duke
of Cornwall from 1932 to 1936, acted as his liaison officer with Downing Street
for the brief remainder of his reign.

[b] Captain the Rt. Hon. Henry David Reginald, first Viscount Margesson,
M.C. (b. 1890), was Parliamentary Secretary to the Treasury and Government
Chief Whip from 1931 to 1940, and Secretary of State for War from 1940 to 1942.

[c] Rt. Hon. Sir Alan Frederick Lascelles, G.C.B., G.C.V.O., C.M.G., M.C.
(b. 1887), had served as Assistant Private Secretary to the Prince of Wales from
1920 to 1929, and as Secretary to Lord Bessborough, when Governor-General
of Canada, from 1931 to 1935, in which year he was appointed Assistant Private
Secretary to King George V.   In this office he also served King Edward VIII
and King George VI until, in 1943, he succeeded Sir Alexander Hardinge as
Private Secretary, a position which he continued to hold under Queen Elizabeth II
until his retirement in 1953.

In a painful interview that same evening the King told
Queen Mary of his unalterable resolve, and on the following
day he similarly informed first the Duke of York, and later
his two younger brothers.

(vi)

The story of the later stages of the Abdication Crisis has been
told in detail by the two principal protagonists, the King and
the Prime Minister, each from his own point of view.[a] The
circumstances surrounding the failure of the suggestion, propounded by Lord Rothermere, for a morganatic marriage
between the King and Mrs. Simpson; the passionate and
romantic plea by Mr. Churchill for time and patience; the
departure of Mrs. Simpson from England; and the King's
final decision to abdicate in view of the advice proffered to
him unanimously by his Governments at home and overseas,
are known to all. The one aspect of this unhappy matter
which has never been revealed is the feelings of the King's
heir, the man who, in an agony of apprehension, watched the
gradual but unrelenting approach of that dreaded moment
when he would have to take up the burdens and responsibilities
of kingship which his brother was preparing to lay down.

There is preserved in the Royal Archives at Windsor a
contemporary narrative of these tragic days in the history of
the British Monarchy, written in the Duke of York's own hand,
a simple and poignant chronicle depicting vividly his thoughts
and sufferings.

Ever since the moment on his return to London from
Scotland in October when the possibility of the King's abdication had been revealed to him, the Duke, appalled at the
prospect, had sought on many occasions to reason with his
elder brother — but in vain.

I have been meaning to come & see you but I wanted to see
David first [he wrote to Queen Mary in the first week of November].
He is very difficult to see & when one does he wants to talk about
other matters.

    [a] See *A King's Story*, pp. 337-415, and Mr. Stanley Baldwin's statement to the
House of Commons on December 10, 1936; also Mr. G. M. Young's *Stanley
Baldwin*, pp. 232-244, and the Duchess of Windsor's memoirs, *The Heart has its
Reasons* (*passim*).

It is all so worrying & I feel we all live a life of conjecture; never knowing what will happen to-morrow, & then the unexpected comes. . . .[14]

At this moment of trial and testing, it was to Queen Mary, still in the early sorrow of her widowhood, that the Royal Family turned as their oriflamme and guidon. 'Thank God we have all got you as a central point, because without that point it [the Family] might easily disintegrate', one of them had written to her. It was their fervent hope that she, with her great sense of the dignity of the Crown and her deep understanding of the obligations of Monarchy, might prevail upon her first-born son to subordinate his longing to pursue his love to his duty as a Sovereign.

After the momentous interviews of November 16 and 17, however, even this hope receded. The King's determination to marry Mrs. Simpson was beyond all deterrent, and his consequent abdication became the more inescapable. On the 25th the Duke of York was writing to Sir Godfrey Thomas,[a] with some degree of resignation: 'If the worst happens & I have to take over, you can be assured that I will do my best to clear up the inevitable mess, if the whole fabric does not crumble under the shock and strain of it all'.

On the night of November 29 the Duke and Duchess of York travelled to Edinburgh where the Duke was to be installed as Grand Master Mason of Scotland in succession to the Prince of Wales. He left London with great reluctance and with the sense of his impending fate heavy upon him. 'I hate going to Scotland to do what I have to do as I am so worried over this whole matter', he wrote to Sir Eric Miéville[b] on the night of his departure. 'I feel like the proverbial "sheep

[a] Rt. Hon. Sir Godfrey John Vignoles Thomas, tenth Baronet, G.C.V.O., K.C.B., C.S.I. (b. 1889), having first served in the Diplomatic Service, became Private Secretary to the Prince of Wales in 1919 and so continued until the Prince's Accession in 1936 when he was appointed an Assistant Private Secretary to the King. In 1937 he became Private Secretary to the Duke of Gloucester and so continued until his retirement in 1958.

[b] Sir Eric Charles Miéville, G.C.I.E., K.C.V.O., C.S.I., C.M.G. (b. 1896), entered the Far Eastern Consular Service in 1919 and served as Private Secretary to successive Ministers in Peking, 1920–1927; to the Governor-General of Canada, 1927–1931; and to the Viceroy of India, 1931–1936. He was Secretary to the Executive Council of the Governor-General of India from 1935 to 1936, in which year he was appointed Private Secretary to the Duke of York. He continued to serve King George VI as Assistant Private Secretary from 1937 to 1945.

being led to the slaughter", which is not a comfortable feeling.'
As the Duke and Duchess drove about the city, their reception
was tumultuous and the cheers seemed to have a specially
significant fervour. But their own hearts were heavy, as day-
by-day developments were reported to them from London.
For behind them, in England, the storm had broken.

On Tuesday, December 1, the Bishop of Bradford, Dr.
Walter Blunt, in addressing his Diocesan Conference, commended the King to God's Grace, of which all Christian
people stood in need — 'for the King is a man like ourselves'.
The Bishop then added: 'We hope that he is aware of his
need. Some of us wish that he gave more positive signs of his
awareness.' The words of Bishop Blunt, directed entirely
towards the King's irregularity in attending Divine Service
on Sunday, were the key which unlocked the door of silence.[a]
Next day the provincial Press reported his remarks with comments, and the London Press quoted the provincial. By Thursday all reserve had been jettisoned and the news of the King's
desire to marry Mrs. Simpson was made public for the first time
— proclaimed in glaring print from the newspaper placards.

Such was the position when the Duke of York returned to
London on Thursday, December 3, and it is here that his own
chronicle begins :

I returned to London from Edinburgh on the morning of
Thursday Dec 3rd. At Euston I was both surprised & horrified to
see that the posters of the Daily Press had the following as their
headlines in block letters 'The King's Marriage'.

Knowing what had already been told me by my brother on
Tuesday Nov 17th that it was his intention to marry Mrs. —— &
that he had told Queen Mary & the Prime Minister the night
before, I went to see Queen Mary on Wed Nov 18th, to the Prime
Minister on Thursday Nov 19th, & again to Queen Mary later
that day. I saw Queen Mary again on the evening of Nov 23rd,
& my brother on the evening of Tuesday 24th.

I then went to Edinburgh on Sunday evening Nov 29th. to be
installed as Grand Master Mason of Scotland on Monday Nov

---

[a] It has been stated that, although Bishop Blunt had not heard of Mrs.
Simpson's association with the King when he originally wrote his speech, he was
aware of it when he delivered the speech some six weeks later. He is quoted as
saying that he had considered not giving it at all 'but took the risk because of
the danger that silence was doing to the Crown and to the Empire'. The Bishop
died on June 4, 1957.

30th. in the place of my brother. I was kept fully informed of what was going on. On my return I hastened to see Queen Mary & to tell her how surprised I was that the whole matter had been published. I saw my brother, (together with Walter Monkton[a]) who was in a great state of excitement, who said he would leave the country as King after making a broadcast to his subjects & leave it to them to decide what should be done.[b] The Prime Minister went to see him at 9.0 pm that evening & later (in Mary's & my presence) David said to Queen Mary that he could not live alone as King & must marry Mrs. ——. When David left after making this dreadful announcement to his mother he told me to come & see him at the Fort the next morning [Friday Dec. 4th].[c] I rang him up but he would not see me & put me off till Saturday. I told him I would be at Royal Lodge on Saturday by 12.30 p.m. I rang him up Saturday. 'Come & see me on Sunday' was his answer. 'I will see you & tell you my decision when I have made up my mind.' Sunday evening I rang up. 'The King has a conference & will speak to you later' was the answer. But he did not ring up. Monday morning [December 7] came. I rang up at 1.0 p.m. & my brother told me he might be able to see me that evening. I told him ' I must go to London but would come to the Fort when he wanted me'. I did not go to London but waited. I sent a telephone message to the Fort to say that if I was wanted I would be at Royal Lodge. My brother rang me up at 10 minutes to 7.0 pm to say 'Come & see me after dinner'. I said 'No, I will come & see you at once'. I was with him at 7.0 pm. The awful & ghastly suspense of waiting was over. I found him pacing up & down the room, & he told me his decision that he would go. I went back to Royal Lodge for dinner & returned to the Fort later. I felt having once got there I was not going to leave. As he is my eldest brother I had to be there to try & help him in his hour of need. I went back to London that night with my wife.

[a] The spelling of Sir Walter Monckton's name is inaccurate throughout the paper. The Rt. Hon. Walter Turner, first Viscount Monckton of Brenchley, K.C.M.G., K.C.V.O., M.C., Q.C., (b.1891) served as Attorney-General to the Prince of Wales from 1932 to 1936 and as Attorney-General to the Duchy of Cornwall from 1936 to 1947 and 1948 to 1951. During the Second World War he was Director-General of the Press and Censorship Bureau, 1939–1940; of the Ministry of Information, 1940–1941 ; and of the British Propaganda and Information Services at Cairo, 1941–1942. He was appointed Solicitor-General in the Caretaker Cabinet of 1945 and also served as United Kingdom representative on the Allied Reparation Commission at Moscow. In the Cabinets of Sir. Winston Churchill and Sir Anthony Eden he was Minister of Labour, 1951–1955, Minister of Defence, 1955–1956, and Paymaster-General from 1956 until his retirement and elevation to the Peerage in 1957. He then became Chairman of the Midland Bank.
[b] This suggestion was made by the King to the Prime Minister on December 4 and rejected at a special Cabinet Meeting held on the following day.
[c] The dates and names in square brackets have been inserted.

I saw Queen Mary on Tuesday morning. [December 8.]

I saw Walter Monkton that afternoon (who was not allowed to see me before) & he told me all the facts. From this knowledge I went to Queen Mary & told her, & went to Royal Lodge where I met my brother Harry & told him what was going on. While telling Harry I was summoned urgently to the Fort by Monkton to meet my brother & the Prime Minister. We dined together. A dinner I am never likely to forget. While the rest of us (8 in all) D. P.M. D. of K. E.R.P. W.M. A.G.A. U.A. D. of Y.ᵃ were very sad (we knew the final & irrevocable decision he had made) my brother was the life & soul of the party, telling the P.M. things I am sure he had never heard before about unemployed centres etc (referring to his visit in S. Wales). I whispered to W.M. '& this is the man we are going to lose'. One couldn't, nobody could, believe it.

Later I returned to London.

I saw Queen Mary Wednesday morning [December 9] to arrange for her to see my brother at Royal Lodge.

Later that morning I saw Peacock & Monkton, then the P.M. & later Bircham my lawyer. I met my brother at Royal Lodge & he & his mother were together for some time. After this I went to the Fort where D. & I, Bircham & Allen (A.G.A.) had a talk. I had to stop it as it involved too much (& had a word with W.M. who had just returned from No. 10.). I then had a long talk with D but I could see that nothing I said would alter his decision. His mind was made up. I motored up to London with W.M. (much to our mutual surprise) as D. had been very suspicious previous to my talk with him, & we were then able to discuss what we liked in confidence. I went to see Queen Mary & when I told her what had happened I broke down & sobbed like a child.ᵇ A few minutes later I was told from No 10 that I was wanted to witness together with my 2 younger brothers D's instrument of abdication at 10.0 a.m. on Thursday Dec 10th. I saw Wigram at R.L. [Royal Lodge] first & was present at the fateful moment which made me D's successor to the Throne. Perfectly calm D signed 5 or 6 copies of the instrument & then 5 copies of his message to

---

ᵃ D. (David); P.M. (Prime Minister); D. of K. (Duke of Kent); E.R.P. (Sir Edward Peacock, Receiver-General of the Duchy of Cornwall); W.M. (Mr. Walter Monckton); A.G.A. (Mr. George Allen, private solicitor to the King); U.A. (Sir Ulick Alexander, Keeper of the Privy Purse); D. of Y. (Duke of York); Major Thomas Dugdale, the Prime Minister's Parliamentary Private Secretary, was also present (*A King's Story*, p. 402).

ᵇ 'Bertie arrived very late from Fort Belvedere, and Mr. Walter Monckton brought him and me the paper drawn up for David's abdication of the Throne of this Empire because he wants to marry Mrs. Simpson ! ! ! ! !' Queen Mary wrote in her diary of this interview. 'The whole affair has lasted since 16 November and is very painful. It is a terrible blow to us all and particularly to poor Bertie.'[15]

Parliament, one for each Dominion Parliament.   It was a dreadful moment & one never to be forgotten by those present.   One or two curious incidents happened later re. the servants.   I was there all the morning & afternoon.   I went to R.L. for a rest as the tension was getting unbearable at the Fort.   But I could not rest alone^a & returned to the Fort at 5.45.   Wigram was present at a terrible lawyer interview which terminated quietly & harmoniously. E. R. P. was a very great help.   Wigram & E. R. P. dined with me at R.L.   I later went to London where I found a large crowd outside my house cheering madly.   I was overwhelmed.

I went to see Queen Mary.

Friday [December 11] that dreadful day I was busy arranging details of my own Accession Council & Proclamation & seeing Crown Lawyers about D's title etc.

I went to the Fort as King with Harry arriving at 7.0 pm. All D's servants called me His Majesty.   Sir J. R. [John Reith] wished to announce D as Mr. E. Windsor for his broadcast.   I put that right.^b   One other matter I settled too.

Dinner at R.L.   Mama, David, Mary, Harry, George, Aunt Alice [Princess Alice, Countess of Athlone], Uncle Algy [Earl of Athlone], & self.^c

When D & I said good-bye we kissed, parted as freemasons & he bowed to me as his King.^d

And so there passed from the throne of Britain a Sovereign who had taken what he confidently believed to be for him the right decision.   As he drove to Portsmouth that stormy December night he had regret only for the circumstances, not for the decision itself;^e but 'there was an overwhelming

---

^a An additional anxiety for the Duke of York was that the Duchess had contracted influenza and was lying ill at 145 Piccadilly.   He was therefore deprived of her comforting presence and was compelled to suffer his ordeal alone.

^b See below, p. 295.

^c Of this dinner-party the Duke of Windsor writes : 'Dinner passed pleasantly enough under the circumstances.   I hope I was a good guest but I rather doubt it' (*A King's Story*, p. 412).   It was from this dinner that the Prince, now no longer King, went to Windsor Castle to make his farewell broadcast.   He returned to Royal Lodge for his final farewells.

^d At the particular request of King Edward, Mr. Baldwin had included in his speech to the House of Commons on the previous afternoon the text of a pencilled note which he had received from His Majesty.   It read :

Duke of York.   He and the King have always been on the best of terms as brothers, and the King is confident that the Duke deserves and will receive the support of the whole Empire.

^e In an article written for the *Daily Express* on June 3, 1957, the Duke of Windsor stated : 'But make no mistake, it is the circumstances, not the decision itself, that I regret.   If twenty years were to be erased and I were to be presented with the same choice again under the same circumstances, I would act precisely as I did then.'

sadness in my heart at leaving Great Britain and its people'.[a]

At two o'clock on the morning of Saturday, December 12, His Royal Highness Prince Edward of Windsor left Portsmouth in the destroyer *Fury* for Boulogne,[b] and at eleven o'clock King George VI attended his Accession Council at St. James's Palace. The minds of many present went back involuntarily to that day not quite a year before when they had witnessed the Accession of the King who had just sailed away. He had been debonair, self-possessed, full of youthful charm and buoyancy. The Sovereign who now presented himself to his Privy Counsellors was very different. He was shy and hesitant, one who had ever shunned the limelight. Upon his face were the traces of the ordeal through which he had so lately passed. Truly are 'acceptable men tried in the furnace of adversity'.[16]

Pale and haggard, yet with an innate dignity and integrity which compelled the respect and reverence, as well as the protective instinct, of his hearers, the King addressed them in a low, clear voice, but with many hesitations :

Your Royal Highnesses, My Lords and Gentlemen,
I meet you to-day in circumstances which are without parallel in the history of our Country. Now that the duties of Sovereignty have fallen upon Me I declare to you My adherence to the strict principles of constitutional government and My resolve to work before all else for the welfare of the British Commonwealth of Nations.
With My wife and helpmeet by My side, I take up the heavy task which lies before Me. In it I look for the support of all My peoples.
Furthermore, My first act on succeeding My brother will be to confer on him a Dukedom and he will henceforth be known as His Royal Highness the Duke of Windsor.

The King's first act was thus one of grace and, as will be seen, of wisdom also.

In the afternoon he was proclaimed King with all the pageantry of traditional ceremonial;[c] and on the following

---

[a] See interview in *Parade*, June 16, 1957.

[b] Just two hundred and forty-seven years before, King James II, the last King of England to vacate the throne, had stolen silently across the Thames from Mill-bank in the early hours of December 11, 1689, and, pausing only to drop the Great Seal into the river, had departed on his road to exile.

[c] 'Have had good crossing', telegraphed the Duke of Windsor through the

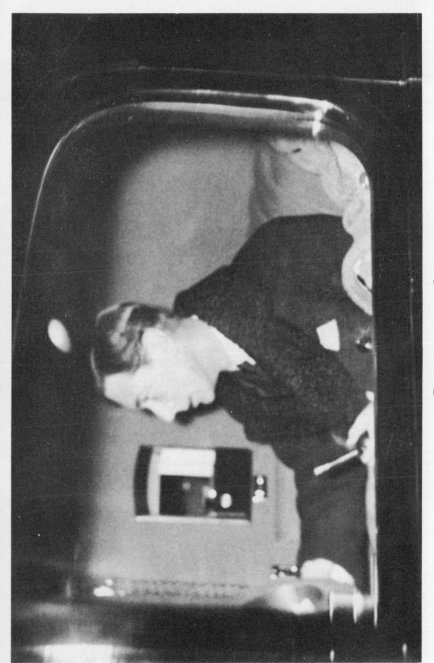

December 11, 1936

day, Sunday, prayers were offered for him in every place of
worship throughout the Empire. In the great metropolitan
cathedrals and the little grey country churches there arose
the invocation to Almighty God : A prayer for the King's
Majesty, our most gracious Sovereign Lord King George . . .
so replenish him . . . endue him . . . grant him . . .
strengthen him . . . bring him . . . A prayer for the Royal
Family . . . our gracious Queen Elizabeth . . . the Princess
Elizabeth . . . endue them . . . enrich them . . . prosper
them. . . .

As one worshipper later reflected : 'It was almost as if one
were hearing these prayers for the first time, so deep their
significance'.[17]

Admiralty on the same day. 'Glad to hear this morning's ceremony went off so
well. Hope Elizabeth better. Best love and best of luck to you both. David.'

PART III

KING GEORGE VI
1936–1952

CHAPTER I

THE FIRST YEAR

1936–1937

(i)

KING GEORGE VI was *Roi malgré lui*, and perhaps no monarch has succeeded to the Throne more reluctantly. From every aspect his new dignity was unwelcome to him; the sudden and tragic circumstances of its coming, his personal dislike of publicity and limelight, and his practical unpreparedness, all tended at first to overwhelm him.

Now was displayed the fallacy of King George V's policy of refusing to allow his second son to be initiated even into the ordinary everyday working of government. The new King stood appalled at the volume and the nature of the business which emerged day by day from those leather-clad dispatch boxes which inexorably dog the life of every British Sovereign. He was, moreover, more than ever conscious now of his own physical disability and of what he believed to be his inferiority in comparison with his brother.

All this sense of deficiency found utterance in a passionate outpouring of spirit to his cousin, Lord Louis Mountbatten,[a] on the first night of his reign. The two were at Fort Belvedere, watching Prince Edward of Windsor making his last preparations for departure. 'Dickie, this is absolutely terrible,' the new King said in great distress. 'I never wanted this to

---

[a] Admiral of the Fleet the Rt. Hon. Louis Francis Albert Victor Nicholas, first Earl Mountbatten of Burma, K.G., G.C.B., G.C.S.I., G.C.I.E., G.C.V.O., D.S.O. (b. 1900), is the second son of Admiral of the Fleet Prince Louis of Battenberg, subsequently first Marquess of Milford Haven, and of Princess Victoria of Hesse. Entering the Navy in 1913 he served in the First World War, and in the Second achieved early distinction as a Captain of Destroyers. He became Chief of Combined Operations in 1942 and in the following year was appointed Supreme Allied Commander in South East Asia (SEAC), in which post he remained until 1946. He was the last Viceroy of India, March–August 1947, and the first Governor-General of the Dominion of India, 1947–1948. He then resumed his naval career, becoming Commander-in-Chief, Mediterranean, in 1952, and First Sea Lord in 1955.

happen ; I'm quite unprepared for it. David has been trained
for this all his life. I've never even seen a State Paper. I'm
only a Naval Officer, it's the only thing I know about.' And
Lord Louis was able to give him consolation. 'This is a very
curious coincidence,' he replied. 'My father once told me
that, when the Duke of Clarence died, your father came to
him and said almost the same things that you have said to
me now, and my father answered : "George, you're wrong.
There is no more fitting preparation for a King than to have
been trained in the Navy ".'

The truth of this remark was to be made immediately
evident in a hundred ways. The fact that the King had lived
and worked as a member of a ship's company gave him an
understanding of humanity and of human nature upon
which he was to draw again and again with profit ; while his
predisposition, as a naval officer, to the use of pragmatic
common sense often enabled him to arrive at a practical
point of view, or even the solution of a problem, which had
eluded his advisers.

Never was this more clearly demonstrated than in the
first major decision which the King was called upon to make
at the outset of his reign. The authorities were divided as to
the name and title by which King Edward VIII was to be
known after his abdication. There was no historical precedent
to which reference might be had, since James II, the last British
monarch to be thus displaced, had never formally abdicated,
but was declared by Parliament to have vacated the Throne.
He remained 'the King over the Water' until his death, and
as such afforded no small embarrassment to his successor.

The pundits were confounded, and in their dilemma they
sought the counsel of King George on this extremely delicate
subject. In a memorandum annexed to his record of the
Abdication Crisis, the King gives an account of an interview
with the Lord Chancellor's representative on the morning of
Friday December 11, and of his solution of the problem :

Lord Wigram & Sir Claud Schuster [a] (as representative of the
Lord Chancellor) came to see me in the forenoon, as Schuster

---

[a] Claud, first Baron Schuster, G.C.B., C.V.O. (1869-1956), was Clerk of
the Crown and Permanent Secretary to the Lord Chancellor from 1915 to 1944.

wanted to ask me what my brother King Edward VIII was going to be known as after his abdication. The question was an urgent one, as Sir John Reith (Director of the B.B.C.) was going to introduce him to the air that night as Mr. Edward Windsor. I replied :— That is quite wrong. Before going any further I would ask what has he given up on his abdication? S. said I am not sure. I said, It would be quite a good thing to find out before coming to me. Now as to his name. I suggest HRH D of W[indsor]. He cannot be Mr. E. W. as he was born the son of a Duke. That makes him Ld. E. W. anyhow. If he ever comes back to this country, he can stand & be elected to the H. of C. Would you like that? S replied No.

As D of W he can sit & vote in the H of L. Would you like that? S replied No. Well if he becomes a Royal Duke he cannot speak or vote in the H of L & he is not being deprived of his rank in the Navy, Army or R. Air Force. This gave Schuster a new lease of life & he went off quite happy.

The immediate problem of how the former Monarch should be described over the radio that night was also decided by King George personally. It was on his specific instruction that Sir John Reith introduced him as 'His Royal Highness Prince Edward', and, as we have seen, the King announced at his Accession Council on the following morning his intention to create his brother Duke of Windsor.[a]

It was not, however, until after the Coronation that the style and title of the Duke of Windsor was given legal form. In the *London Gazette* of May 28, it was announced that by Letters Patent issued under the Great Seal of the Realm — that is to say on the advice of Ministers — the Duke was accorded the title of 'Royal Highness' for himself alone, the Duchess being precluded from using it.[b] The statement was as follows :

The King has been pleased by Letters Patent under the Great Seal of the Realm bearing date the 27th day of May, 1937, to declare that the Duke of Windsor shall, notwithstanding his Instrument of Abdication executed on the 10th day of December, 1936, and His Majesty's Declaration of Abdication Act, 1936, whereby

[a] See above, pp. 287-8. This decision commended itself to the older members of the Royal Family also. 'I am so pleased that you created him *Duke* of *Windsor*', the old Duke of Connaught wrote from Bath to his great-nephew. 'I so thoroughly approve of the title & I am sure that all at Windsor will be proud to have him as *their Duke*.' [1]

[b] The Duke of Windsor and Mrs. Simpson were married at the Château de Landé, Monts, France, on June 3, 1937.

effect was given to the said Instrument, be entitled to hold and
enjoy for himself only the title style or attribute of Royal Highness
so however that his wife and descendants if any shall not hold the
said title style or attribute.[a]

(ii)

Common sense and human understanding, great personal
integrity, combined with a deep humility, a keen sense of
public service, moral and physical courage above the ordinary,
and a sincere recognition of dependence upon the grace and
guidance of Almighty God, were the outstanding qualities
which King George VI brought to his high office. And it was
these qualities which accomplished his quick recovery from
the initial impact of shock. At first he had been emotionally
disturbed ; then a merciful numbness had supervened, to be
followed, however, by a gradual reawakening to the realities
of life, which demanded all his courage. As always, it was to
his wife that he turned for comfort and support, and, as always,
these were abundantly forthcoming. Together they faced the
future with a natural awe but without fear. 'I can hardly now
believe that we have been called to this tremendous task and
(I am writing to you quite intimately) the curious thing is that
we are not afraid. I feel that God has enabled us to face the
situation calmly', Queen Elizabeth wrote to the Archbishop of
Canterbury.[2]

It was characteristic of King George that, three days
after his accession, he should signalize his forty-first birthday
(December 14), his first as King, by bestowing the Order of
the Garter upon the Queen, as his father had done before
him. 'He had discovered that Papa gave it to you on his,
Papa's, birthday, June 3rd,' the Queen wrote to Queen Mary,
'and the coincidence was so charming that he has now followed
suit, & given it to me on his own birthday.'[3] There was more,
however, than mere family coincidence in the King's act.
His appointment of his Queen to the most ancient Order of
Chivalry at this first opportunity was also a public declaration
of gratitude and affection to one who had shared with him so

[a] It is a matter of interest that the Great Seal used on this occasion was that
of King George V. A new Seal is prepared after the Coronation of each new
Sovereign and there had been no time for that of King George VI to be made.

bravely the burdens of the past, and was to bear with him so nobly the trials of the future.

Emotionally and physically exhausted, the King and Queen looked forward with relief to their Christmas holiday at Sandringham. There with their children they could find a brief respite from all but the more pressing affairs of State. There life flowed on in an accepted pattern, both restful and relaxing. In the peace of Sandringham, beloved of his father and himself, the King could take stock of the stupendous events which had occurred during the twelve months since his father's death. A year earlier the peoples of the British Commonwealth had listened to King George V's last Christmas broadcast, and many had judged from it of the Sovereign's impaired state of health. This Christmas there was to be no Royal broadcast. The new Monarch was not yet ready to assume that part of his father's great heritage. The happenings had been too momentous, too overwhelming, for him to address his peoples thus familiarly.[a]

Since that Christmas a year before, one King had died and another had abdicated. The structure of the British Monarchy had sustained a very severe shock, and had survived it. But there was much to be done, hard and patient work, in shoring up and repairing that structure, and the King knew that this was his first and most important task. He faced it with characteristic determination and in a spirit of dedication ; the same spirit which had inspired the concluding words of his first message to Parliament a few days previously : ' It will be my constant endeavour, with God's help, and supported as I shall be by my dear wife, to uphold the Honour of the Realm and promote the Happiness of my peoples'. Now, on the last day of the old year, he sat down to write to his Prime Minister :

I am new to the job [he wrote simply] but I hope that time will be allowed to me to make amends for what has happened.[4]

[a] The King did, however, broadcast a New Year's message of self-dedication to the peoples of the Empire and Commonwealth. After a touching reference to the past, he said :

I realize to the full the responsibilities of my noble heritage. I shoulder them with all the more confidence in the knowledge that the Queen and my mother Queen Mary are at my side. . . . To repeat the words used by my dear father at the time of his Silver Jubilee, my wife and I dedicate ourselves for all time to your service, and we pray that God may give us guidance and strength to follow the path that lies before us.

And Mr. Baldwin replied in words which must have heartened his King:

> Sir, if I may say so, you need have no fear for the future, so far as you are concerned. The whole country is behind you with a deep and understanding sympathy.[5]

(iii)

At the date of the King's accession it was impossible to assess the extent to which the Abdication Crisis had affected the fabric of the Monarchy. All that could be said with certainty was that it had been shaken to the foundations, but that it still stood firmly. But how firmly? The structure had not been destroyed, but how gravely had it been undermined, how deep were the fissures?

The nation had passed through an agony of suspense which, though it had lasted but a week, had been the more severe by reason of the suddenness with which the crisis had broken. The newspaper headlines which had so shocked the Duke of York on his arrival at Euston on the morning of December 3 were also the first tidings which the average Englishman had received of the constitutional convulsion in which King Edward and his Ministers were involved. The general reaction was one of dismay and bewilderment, and, at first, of incredulity. There was deep sympathy for the King, but this had waned when it became clear that he preferred abdication as a means of escaping from his dilemma. Though, since the Norman Conquest, several English monarchs had died otherwise than in possession of their regal functions, there was no case on record of an English sovereign who had renounced the throne when not only were there other courses open to him, but these were actually being urged upon him by his Ministers.

Thus, while crowds gathered around Buckingham Palace shouting 'Down with Baldwin, we want the King', there were also many of King Edward's subjects whose deep moral feelings were gravely disturbed, and among whom there arose a sense of resentment in that it seemed to them that he was not sticking to his job. Their disillusionment was keen and, in some cases, bitter.

This disillusionment, moreover, went further than the individual; it reflected upon the whole position of the Monarchy. It is idle to believe that, because the Abdication Crisis was of short duration and because it was skilfully handled, there are no grounds for the assumption that it was not of the utmost gravity, and that in slightly different circumstances the stability of the Monarchy might not have been imperilled. For example, the late Sir Arnold Wilson, a staunch Conservative Member of Parliament,[a] gave it as his opinion that if a straight vote of the House of Commons had been taken not less than a hundred votes would have been cast in favour of the establishment of a republic.[6] Whatever the truth of this statement, the Commons certainly heard Mr. Maxton,[b] speaking in the Abdication debate on behalf of the Independent Labour Party, declare: 'We are doing a wrong and a foolish thing if, as a House, we do not seize the opportunity with which circumstances have presented us of establishing in our land a completely democratic form of government which does away with old monarchical institutions and the hereditary principle.'[7] They also heard him move the following amendment to the Abdication Bill:

This House declines to give a second reading to a Bill which has been necessitated by circumstances which show clearly the danger to this country and to the British Commonwealth of Nations inherent in an hereditary monarchy, at a time when the peace and prosperity of the people require a more stable and dignified form of government of a republican kind, in close contact with, and more responsive to, the will of the mass of the people, and which fails to give effect to the principle of popular election.

Though Mr. Maxton's amendment was defeated by the overwhelming vote of 403 to 5, the fact that it could be moved

[a] Lieut.-Colonel Sir Arnold Talbot Wilson, K.C.I.E., C.S.I., D.S.O. (1884–1940), after a successful career in the Indian Political Department, entered the House of Commons in 1933 as a National Conservative Member for the Hitchin Division of Hertfordshire, and held the seat until his death. He was also editor of the *XIX Century Review* from 1934 to 1938. He was an ardent supporter of Mr. Chamberlain's policies of appeasement, but eventually reacted so violently from them that, although well over age, he volunteered for the R.A.F. at the outbreak of war, and died in action over London as an air-gunner on May 31, 1940.

[b] James Maxton (1885–1946), a Member of Parliament from 1922 to 1946 and Chairman of the Independent Labour Party from 1926 to 1931, and again from 1934 to 1939. Although a violent radical and a would-be revolutionary, Jimmy Maxton was one of the most beloved members of the House of Commons.

at all is not without its significance. That grave and bitter political consequences did not arise from the Abdication Crisis, that so little rancour and recrimination were in fact engendered, is due to two things : the dignity and willingness with which King Edward VIII accepted the constitutional position, and the personal qualities of his successor.

That the new King appreciated to the full the gravity and the potential danger of the situation has already been shown. To Sir Godfrey Thomas he had gloomily envisaged the possibility that the whole fabric of the Monarchy might 'crumble under the shock and strain' of the Abdication,[a] and in writing to Mr. Baldwin after his accession he had expressed the hope 'that time will be allowed to me to make amends for what has happened'.[b] Though not fearful of the tasks which lay ahead of him in this respect, he was certainly oppressed by their magnitude; but he set himself steadfastly to fulfil them, and it was not long before he impressed those about him by a new development of strength and confidence.[8]

The basic theme of conscious policy was that of a return in great measure to the criteria and traditions of the reign of King George V; a reign in which the family life of the Sovereign had been in considerable evidence. Indications of this reversion are to be found in the King's immediate choice of 'George VI' as his style and title, and of his recall of his father's old friend and adviser, Lord Wigram, who had retired from his post of Private Secretary in 1935, but who was now appointed Permanent Lord-in-Waiting.[c] More closely personal still was the fact that the King's handwriting and his initial of 'G.R.I.' were virtually indistinguishable from those of his father.

But King George's great and outstanding achievement in these early days of his reign — perhaps a greater achievement than is often realized — was to show simply and quietly that

---

[a] See above, p. 283.

[b] See above, p. 297.

[c] Exhausted by the strain of the Abdication Crisis, Major Alexander Hardinge, having been knighted by the King, was granted three months' sick leave which he spent in India. During his absence, the Private Secretary's office, though in the hands of his assistants, Mr. Alan Lascelles and Sir Eric Miéville, was under the general supervision of Lord Wigram.

a true sense of duty could touch as deeply the imagination and sympathy of his peoples as could more glamorous appeals. Within a few weeks of his accession it was clear to all that there could be no 'King's Party' to oppose a King who sought nothing for himself and all for his realm. As one observer wrote on New Year's Day of 1937: 'Thus twice in the same year the state trumpeters blew for an accession; but for so healing a blast as their second, history would have to go back many years'.[9]

(iv)

With the passing of winter the gloomy memories of the Abdication Crisis were crowded from the public mind by the approach of spring, and with it the glories of the Coronation Day, which, as had already been announced, was to be on May 12, 1937.

Under normal conditions the interval of time between a Sovereign's accession and his Coronation is some eighteen months. This period, while primarily caused by the six months' full mourning and the year of half-mourning for his predecessor, is also designed to give the new monarch an opportunity to prepare for the Coronation ceremonies, and for the ceremonies themselves to be arranged and organized. In addition it is usually during the latter part of this period that there occur such time-absorbing matters as the presentation of addresses to the Sovereign by Privileged Bodies.

The circumstances of the accession of King George VI, however, were far from normal, and, since it was thought inexpedient even to consider the idea of postponing the date for the Coronation which had been set by King Edward, much of the preliminary ceremonial had to be compressed into six months. The inevitable strain was very considerable, but both the King and the Queen had emerged from their initial ordeal with seemingly boundless energy, and they flinched from nothing in the heavy calendar of preparatory engagements with which they were confronted. It was, however, necessary for the King to take a major decision early in the New Year which caused grave disappointment to himself and to millions of his Indian subjects.

King Edward had agreed that an Accession Durbar should take place at Delhi during the cold-weather season of 1937–1938. If the King should be prevented from being present in person, then the Viceroy should hold the Durbar on his behalf. His Majesty had approved in principle the idea of a personal visit to India but, in view of the gravity of the international situation, it had been considered unwise to make any explicit public pronouncement. A guarded reference to the King's hope to revisit his Indian Empire after his Coronation had been included in the Speech from the Throne at the opening of Parliament on November 3. After the accession of King George a further and slightly more definite announcement was made (on January 2) reiterating Their Majesties' hope to visit India in the winter of 1937–1938 for the holding of a Durbar.

There then occurred a conflict of advice. The King's intimate advisers urged a postponement of the Indian visit on the grounds that His Majesty required time to settle down and learn how the machinery of government functioned at home, more especially as it was almost certain that, as soon as the Coronation was over, he would be working with a new Prime Minister. Moreover, it was argued, to launch the King and Queen into the exhausting programme of a Durbar immediately after the strain of the Coronation, with its restricted and crowded period of preliminary ceremonies and functions, would be to weary them beyond endurance; and with this view their chief medical adviser, Lord Dawson of Penn, concurred. It was also considered unwise for the King to leave the United Kingdom and to appoint Counsellors of State so soon after the shock of the Abdication Crisis; and a final argument for postponement was advanced that a visit by the King-Emperor to India should be timed to coincide with the announcement of some progressive step in regard to self-government — as had been the case with King George V in 1911 — and, though the new Government of India Act, establishing an All-Indian Federation but not conceding full self-government, had reached the Statute Book in 1935, it was still in its preliminary stages of operation and the time was not considered yet ripe for the granting of dominion status.[10]

As against these arguments it was urged by the Secretary

of State for India, Lord Zetland,[a] and the Viceroy, Lord Linlithgow,[b] that a postponement of the King's visit would cause grave disappointment to the masses of India, who had displayed great loyalty on the occasion of King George V's Silver Jubilee and at the time of his death, and would be interpreted as an indication that the Imperial Government feared the Indian Congress Party, which had recently passed a resolution that it would take no part in a Durbar. By the winter of 1938–1939 the Congress Party might be in an even stronger position and still more hostile towards a Royal visit; and by that time also, pressure might well have been brought to bear on His Majesty to visit some others of his Dominions, and should he do this before being crowned King-Emperor, it would, it was believed, have a disastrous effect upon India.[11]

Faced with these divergent counsels, King George weighed the arguments of both sides with careful consideration. He was personally anxious to go to India, partly because it was a part of his dominions of which he had no previous experience; partly because he was anxious to follow in his father's footsteps and be crowned in full solemnity as King-Emperor in Delhi; and also partly because he realized the difficulties adduced by the Government of India and wished to become personally acquainted with the complexities of the situation. On the other hand, he was acutely conscious of his own inexperience in the practice of statecraft and the urgent necessity that this be remedied. It was this factor which materially influenced him in making up his mind in favour of postponement, a decision which he conveyed to Lord Zetland in a personal letter:

Much as I should like to meet the wishes of yourself and the Viceroy, I do feel that from a personal point of view it would be better to postpone the visit until the winter of 1938–1939. As the Viceroy himself said in his recent telegram (which you quoted in your letter of January 18) 'I do need time to settle in'. I have

[a] Rt. Hon. Lawrence John Lumley Dundas, second Marquess of Zetland, K.G., G.C.S.I., G.C.I.E. (b. 1876), having been Governor of Bengal from 1917 to 1922, served as Secretary of State for India from 1935 to 1940. In 1928 he published the authorized biography of the Marquess Curzon of Kedleston.

[b] Rt. Hon. Victor Alexander John Hope, second Marquess of Linlithgow, K.G., K.T., G.C.S.I., G.C.I.E., O.B.E. (1887–1952), was Chairman of the Joint Select Committee on Indian Constitutional Reform from 1933 to 1935, and served as Viceroy and Governor-General of India from 1936 to 1943.

not had the advantage of my predecessors of serving a long
apprenticeship as Prince of Wales and becoming, to some extent
at any rate, acquainted with the duties and responsibilities of the
Sovereign.

It must also be remembered that, when I open Parliament
next November, I shall have a new Prime Minister, and I believe
that it would not be advisable and helpful for me to be absent
from this country within a year of my accession to the Throne.

I feel sure that you and the Viceroy will appreciate the reasons
which I have put forward, and assist me to carry out what I cannot
but think to be the right course.[12]

The postponement of the Durbar was a source of no little
disappointment to King George, and was in fact to mean that
he would never see his Indian Empire,[a] but its wisdom was
undoubted under the given circumstances.   This decision
— clear and incisive — was a further example of that pragmatic common sense, that ability to take first things first,
which was so invaluable an asset to the King throughout his
life, and more particularly in making up his mind in these
early days when he was feeling his way, steering by faith
through strange waters.

Meantime the preparations for the Coronation were in
full progress, and here King George reaped the benefit of
that wise precaution which had impelled King Edward to
have his brother present at all his preliminary conversations
with the Earl Marshal and the Archbishop of Canterbury.

In the frequent discussions which Dr. Lang[b] held with
King George and with the Queen, all were at one in their
belief that the ceremony in Westminster Abbey should be

---

[a] The King's visit to India was again postponed, this time indefinitely, in
January 1938, partly on account of the burden which a State visit would throw
upon the Indian taxpayer, and partly because of the difficulties encountered in
implementing the Government of India Act of 1935.   There were, indeed, those
among His Majesty's advisers who deprecated the idea of his visiting India until
she had achieved full self-government, and could receive him on a basis of equality
with his other Dominions.   He himself was impatient of this counsel.   'The
King hopes that his visit will not have to wait until Dominion Status has been
attained', Sir Alexander Hardinge wrote to Lord Zetland on March 3, 1938,
'for he feels that this would mean relegating it at least to his old age!'

[b] Most Rev. and Rt. Hon. Cosmo Gordon, 1st Baron Lang of Lambeth,
G.C.V.O., Royal Victorian Chain (1864–1945), was ordained in 1890 and consecrated Bishop of Stepney in 1901.   He was Archbishop of York from 1908 to
1928 and of Canterbury from 1928 to 1942.   The Archbishop was Lord High
Almoner to King George V, King Edward VIII and King George VI.

made the occasion for bringing home to the peoples of the British Commonwealth the real and spiritual significance of the Coronation, to associate them with it in a way never before attempted, and to establish the position of the Sovereign, in Bagehot's phrase, as the 'head of our morality'. It was their endeavour to emphasize that the Church of England still embodied the religious aspect of the nation, and never more notably than in the solemn service of the Coronation in which the King represents the State and the Archbishop the Church. No service, indeed, could be designed to bring out more magnificently the true meaning of a Christian State, with these two figures dominating the scene of pageantry and splendour. As the late Archbishop of York, Dr. Cyril Garbett,[a] has written:

It is the Archbishop who presents the King to the people for their acclamation; it is he who anoints the King, who hands the Sword to him, who delivers the Orb with the cross shining upon it, who places in his hand the Sceptre and receiving the Crown from the Altar sets it on the King's head. All through the service the Archbishop blessing and exhorting the King is also hallowing the State. And throughout the rite the King is seeking the help of God for his great office, now kneeling previous to the anointing while the Holy Spirit is invoked, afterwards for the Archbishop's blessing, later to make his oblation, and finally to receive Holy Communion.[13]

This was precisely King George's own concept of his Coronation, and it was one in which he wished his peoples to share to the greatest extent possible. To this end he supported the views of the Archbishop of Canterbury [b] against those who were opposed to the broadcasting of the service from inside the Abbey, realizing that by this agency it would be brought to many millions not only within his dominions but in the world at large. This opposition was not easily overcome, but at length all obstacles were removed, and the British Broadcasting Corporation was given full facilities; though,

[a] Most Rev. and Rt. Hon. Cyril Forster Garbett, G.C.V.O. (1875–1955), was ordained in 1900 and consecrated Bishop of Southwark in 1919, being translated to Winchester in 1932. He was Archbishop of York from 1942 until his death.

[b] Dr. Lang had originally been among the most reluctant converts to the uses of the wireless, and his biographer states that his conversion was 'undoubtedly reinforced by the discovery that he was himself the possessor of a perfect broadcasting voice' (Lockhart, p. 409).[14]

at the request of the Earl Marshal, the suggestion for tele-
vising the ceremony was not pressed.[a][15] It was, however,
filmed.

With the King's approval four major changes were made
by the Archbishop in the Order of the Service from that used
at the Coronation of King George V. The first was to
remove the Litany from its place within the Service and to
have it chanted by the Westminster Canons as they moved
down from the Altar before the Service, after their procession
up to it bearing the Regalia. The second was to omit the
Sermon; and the third was to restore the old order of the
Anointing, rising from the hands to the head, instead of
descending from the head to the hands.

The fourth and most important change concerned the
Oath, both as to its place in the Rite and in its form. In 1911
the Oath had been taken by King George V after the beginning of the Communion Service, but this ceremony was now
restored to its ancient place immediately after the Recognition
and before the office of Holy Communion. The major change,
however, was constitutional, not liturgical, and was imposed
by the wholly new position of the King's self-governing
Dominions as created by the Statute of Westminster.

This altered status affected not only the Oath but the
form of Recognition. Since the Coronation of William III
and Mary, all Sovereigns had been presented for Recognition
in the simple form of 'The undoubted King of *this Realm*',
but this formula did not now suffice. The King was no
longer 'King of Great Britain and Ireland and Ruler of the
British Dominions beyond the Seas'. He was as much King
of Canada, Australia, New Zealand, South Africa and Eire [b]
as of Great Britain, and each Dominion wished *their* King to
be crowned and consecrated at the same time and with the
same ancient usage. The difficulty presented was to satisfy
this wish by arriving at some form of Recognition and Oath

[a] The circumstances of the broadcasting of King George's Coronation mark
a milestone in progress between the complete interdiction placed upon the B.B.C.
with regard to his wedding as Duke of York (see above, p. 151) and the dignified
and impressive rendering of the full rites of Queen Elizabeth II's Coronation on
television.

[b] For the altered status of Ireland in the Commonwealth as a result of the
Abdication Crisis, see below, pp. 324-7.

acceptable to the sensibilities of Ottawa, Canberra, Wellington, Pretoria and Dublin.

This proved to be a question, as the Archbishop of Canterbury recorded, 'of the utmost intricacy and difficulty',
with the result that 'for weeks the air was thick with messages'
between the Dominions Office in London and the Governments of the Dominions. The main complications were
raised by South Africa and Eire and it required all the great
patience and tact of the Secretary of State for the Dominions,
Mr. Malcolm MacDonald,[a] before general consent was
obtained. An agreed formula was, however, at last found.
For the Recognition it consisted in the simple solution of
omitting the words '*of this Realm*' and presenting the Sovereign
as 'King George, your undoubted King'. As to the Oath,
the King was required to answer affirmatively to the question:

> Do you solemnly promise and swear to govern the peoples of
> Great Britain, Ireland, Canada, Australia, New Zealand, and the
> Union of South Africa, of your possessions, and the other territories
> to them belonging or pertaining and of your Empire of India, accord-
> ing to their respective laws and customs? [b]

No sooner, however, had this difficulty been overcome
than another emerged. The Oath is followed in the Coronation Rite by a solemn promise on the part of the Sovereign
to maintain the Protestant Faith. This had always applied
to the Church of England in England, but with the broadening
of the Oath it clearly had other implications. Mr. de Valera,
for Ireland, Mr. Mackenzie King on behalf of the French
Canadians, and the Roman Catholic Prime Minister of
Australia, Mr. Lyons, demanded that some new formula be
found which confined the King's promise to his rôle as King
of Great Britain and not as Sovereign of their respective
Kingdoms.

[a] Rt. Hon. Malcolm MacDonald (b. 1901) was the second son of Mr.
Ramsay MacDonald, and sat in the House of Commons from 1929 to 1945, first
as a Labour Member and later as National Labour. He was Secretary of State
for the Dominions from 1935 to 1938, and for the Colonies from 1938 to 1940,
when he became Minister of Health. He served as U.K. High Commissioner
in Canada, 1941–1946; Governor-General of Malaya, 1946–1948; and Com-
missioner-General of the U.K. in South-East Asia, 1948–1955, in which year he
was appointed U.K. High Commissioner in India.

[b] The new form of Oath, although agreed by the Commonwealth Governments, was not embodied in any legislative enactment. Its legality has been
questioned on this ground.

Again the machinery of consultation between Whitehall and the Dominions Governments groaned beneath the weight of the communications entailed by this knotty point, and again the conciliatory powers of Mr. MacDonald were taxed to the utmost. But forbearance and consideration triumphed once more, and a compromise agreeable to all was achieved. The King was required to maintain 'the true profession of the Gospel' ('There was no objection to *that*', commented the Archbishop), and to maintain the Protestant Reformed Religion only as it is by law established *in the United Kingdom*; and this constitutional requirement was separated from the promise to maintain the rights and liberties of the Church of England.[a] [17]

(v)

As the Coronation approached, there occurred a certain unpleasant manifestation of that popular failing to be ready to believe evil of public characters, which, though unimportant and contemptible in itself, yet had some significance. Coming from none knew where, passed from mouth to mouth, in some cases unheedingly, in others with malignant intent, there

[a] King George VI was only the third monarch (his father was the first) to use the new form of the Declaration on the Protestant Faith which, under the Bill of Rights of 1689, is exacted by the Lord Chancellor from each acceding Sovereign before making the Speech from the Throne at the first State Opening of Parliament. In its original form the Declaration required from the King the repudiation of the doctrine of transubstantiation, and the assertion that 'the invocation or adoration of the Virgin Mary or any other Saint and the Sacrifice of the Mass as they are now used in the Church of Rome are superstitious and idolatrous'. King Edward VII protested against this gratuitous insult to his Roman Catholic subjects and, although he read the compulsory words, did so in a low voice. He urged successive Prime Ministers to amend the intolerant wording of the declaration, but although legislation was introduced to this effect, it was never enacted in the King's lifetime. In full support of his father's views, King George V absolutely refused to open Parliament until a more tolerant and less offensive form of words had been substituted, and, as a result of his obduracy, a new formula was, after some difficulties, passed through both Houses of Parliament and received the Royal Assent on August 3, 1910. It ran as follows:

I do solemnly and sincerely in the presence of God profess, testify and declare that I am a faithful Protestant, and that I will, according to the true intent of the enactments to serve the Protestant succession to the Throne of my Realm, uphold and maintain such enactments to the best of my power.[18]

This was the Declaration which King George V read from the Throne when he opened his first Parliament on February 6, 1911, and Sir Sidney Lee's statement (II. 25) that 'King Edward's successor took the oath in its old form' is therefore erroneous.

swept through London a wave of idle and malicious gossip which embraced not only the general health of the King and the Royal Family but also his ability to discharge his functions as a Sovereign. The announcement that the Durbar was to be postponed was seized upon as the basis of a whispering campaign that the King was in such frail health that he might not be able to support the fatigue and strain of the Coronation ceremony itself. The order of service, it was said, was being cut to the barest minimum, and indeed there might be no Coronation at all. And there was the crowning calumny that, even if he succeeded in getting through the ordeal of the Coronation, the King would never be able to undertake all the arduous duties which would fall to him, that he would never be able to speak in public, and that he would be a recluse or, at best, a 'rubber stamp'.

The newspapers were at pains to deny and condemn this spiteful bruit,[19] but it remained for the Reverend Robert Hyde, the King's comrade and colleague in his Camp and Industrial Welfare work, to make a public riposte. Speaking on May 6, 1937, at a luncheon of the Industrial Co-Partnership Association, Mr. Hyde referred in no uncertain terms to the current rumours, and then recalled his long association with the King as Duke of York and the diverse circumstances which they had shared together. Many of these had made arduous demands upon the King's physical stamina and mental equipment, and had disclosed the forcefulness of his character. 'Never have I found any evidence of those shortcomings, of physical and mental weaknesses, which notorious gossip has attached to him. Those of us who have watched him for the past twenty years conquering that hesitation in his speech which filled him with real anguish have only been filled with admiration. . . . Those of you who hear this gossip, do not heed it; it is unkind, unworthy and untrue.' [a] [20]

King George was in fact in excellent health. But he was admittedly nervous about his stammer, and apprehensive regarding the Coronation broadcast which he would make to

[a] Mr. Hyde's speech was well reported and warmly approved. 'There will be full public endorsement of the condemnation by the Director of the Industrial Welfare Society of malicious, cruel and unfounded gossip regarding the health of the King' was the comment of the *Sunday Chronicle* on May 9, 1937.

his peoples. Mr. Lionel Logue was in frequent consultation, and together they rehearsed the text not only of the broadcast but also of the speech which the King was to make at the unveiling of the King George V memorial in St. George's Chapel, Windsor, his first public utterance since his accession.

Mr. Logue had been incensed by the public attention which had been drawn to the King's speech defect by the Archbishop of Canterbury in his famous Abdication broadcast on December 13, 1936. Dr. Lang had said on this occasion: 'In manner and speech he [King George VI] is more quiet and reserved than his brother. (And here I may add a parenthesis which may not be unhelpful. When his people listen to him they will note an occasional and momentary hesitation in his speech. But he has brought it into full control, and to those who hear it need cause no sort of embarrassment, for it causes none to him who speaks.)' [21]

Though the Archbishop had spoken with the best possible intention, it was felt that his remarks had increased the King's nervousness and had led the listening public to anticipate something altogether worse in the way of a hesitation than that which actually existed. Both these conclusions were in fact correct, but, to the happy relief of all concerned, the speech in St. George's Chapel on April 23 was highly successful, though it was evident that the King spoke under the stress of strong personal emotion. Standing in the crowd, Mr. Logue had the supreme satisfaction of hearing a man say to his wife: 'Didn't the Archbishop say this man had a speech defect, my dear?' and her reply: 'You shouldn't believe all you hear, dear, not even from an Archbishop.' [22]

(vi)

On Wednesday, May 12, 1937, King George VI and Queen Elizabeth were crowned in Westminster Abbey with all the pageantry and grandeur of a thousand-year-old tradition. They had spent the week-end quietly at Royal Lodge, returning on the Sunday evening to London to meet the Archbishop of Canterbury at Buckingham Palace. This final act of spiritual preparation had been timed to coincide with the evening services then being held all over the country at which prayers would be offered for Their Majesties. 'After some talk on the spiritual aspects of the Coronation', the Archbishop recorded, 'and of its spiritual meaning for themselves, they knelt with me; I prayed for them and for their realm and Empire, and I gave them my personal blessing. I was much moved, and so were they. Indeed, there were tears in their eyes when we rose from our knees. From that moment I knew what would be in their minds and hearts when they came to their anointing and crowning.'[23]

It was thus refreshed and sustained that the King and Queen went to their Coronation, with humility and steadfastness, with dedication and devotion. They had been called to the highest office in the State and they made of the rite of their formal installation a genuine act of worship and self-offering, an avowal of their dependence upon Almighty God for the spirit, strength and power needed for so heavy and exacting a charge.

Nor was this hidden from those about them; it was apparent to all. 'I am quite sure', wrote Bishop Furse of St. Albans [a] to the Queen, 'that those whose privilege it was to be near Your Majesties must have felt — as I did — that this sense of reality was mainly due to the lovely way — in spite of all the elaborate ritual & ceremonial — in which Your Majesties, together, made us all realize that Your Coronation meant for You both, first & foremost, the Offering of Yourselves and all You had to give in life-long service to God & Your fellow men, in simple faith that He would give You the power equal to the task.'[24]

The King, like his father, was a religious man, a man of simple faith. To him the outstanding aspect of this great pageant was the sacred fact that here, before the High Altar of the Abbey, he was being consecrated to the service of his peoples to whom he had sworn a grave oath. He had been imbued with this spirit of service from the very beginning of his public life, and now, on the threshold of his reign, it was hallowed and enhanced. There was, too, a great sense of thankfulness to his subjects. He had been deeply moved by

[a] Rt. Rev. Michael Bolton Furse, K.C.M.G. (1870–1955), was Bishop of Pretoria from 1909 to 1920, and Bishop of St. Albans from 1920 to 1944. As 'Mike' Furse to all, he was greatly beloved.

the evident affection as well as the loyalty of the enthusiasm with which he had been received on all sides since his accession, and he acknowledged this in his Coronation broadcast: 'If, in the coming years, I can show my gratitude in service to you, that is the way above all others that I would choose . . . for the highest of distinctions is the service of others, and to the Ministry of Kingship I have in your hearing dedicated myself, with the Queen at my side, in words of the deepest solemnity. We will, God helping us, faithfully discharge our trust.'

The King's own record of his Coronation, written as a memorandum that same evening, is a very human document, not without its gaiety; combining a Sovereign's recognition of the gravity of the event with a naval officer's meticulous perception of untoward lapses in ceremonial:

We were woken up very early, about 3.0 a.m., by the testing of the 'loud speakers' which had been placed in Constitution Hill; one of them might have been in our room. Bands & marching troops for lining the streets arrived at 5.0 a.m. so sleep was impossible. I could eat no breakfast & had a sinking feeling inside. I knew that I was to spend a most trying day, & to go through the most important ceremony in my life. The hours of waiting before leaving for Westminster Abbey were the most nerve racking. At last the time came & we drove in the State Coach to the Abbey in our Robes.

On our arrival our pages & train bearers met us to carry our robes to our retiring rooms.

Elizabeth's procession started first but a halt was soon called, as it was discovered that one of the Presbyterian chaplains had fainted & there was no place to which he could be taken. He was removed however after some delay & the procession proceeded & arrived in position.

I was kept waiting, it seemed for hours due to this accident, but at last all was ready for my progress into the Abbey. This went off well & my pages & I negotiated the flight of steps going up to the Sacrarium. I bowed to Mama & the Family in the gallery & took my seat. After the Introduction I removed my Parliamentary Robes & Cap of Maintenance & moved to the Coronation Chair. Here various vestments were placed upon me, the white Colobium Sindonis, a surplice which the Dean of Westminster insisted I should put on inside out, had not my Groom of the Robes come to the rescue. Before this I knelt at the Altar to take the Coronation Oath. I had two Bishops, Durham, & Bath & Wells, one on either side to support me & to hold the form of Service for me to follow. When this great moment came neither Bishop could find the words, so the Archbishop held his book down for me to read, but horror of horrors his thumb covered the words of the Oath.

My Lord Great Chamberlain was supposed to dress me but I found his hands fumbled & shook so I had to fix the belt of the sword myself. As it was he nearly put the hilt of the sword under my chin trying to attach it to the belt. At last all the various vestments were put on & the Archbishop had given me the two sceptres. The supreme moment came when the Archbishop placed the St. Edward's Crown on my head. I had taken every precaution as I thought to see that the Crown was put on the right way round, but the Dean & the Archbishop had been juggling with it so much that I never did know whether it was right or not. The St. Edward's Crown, the Crown of England, weighs 7 lbs, & it had to fit.[a] Then I rose to my feet & walked to the throne in the centre of the amphitheatre. As I turned after leaving the Coronation Chair I was brought up all standing, owing to one of the Bishops treading on my robe. I had to tell him to get off it pretty sharply as I nearly fell down. The Homage of the Bishops & Peers went off successfully. My two Brothers Gloucester & Kent did their Homage after the Archbishop of Canterbury, & were followed by the senior Duke (Norfolk), the senior Marquess (Winchester), the senior Earl (Shrewsbury), the senior Viscount (Hereford) & the senior Baron (De Ros).[b]

There swept over England a wave of gay celebration and joyous thanksgiving; wherever they went the King and Queen were acclaimed with expressions of personal regard and affection. There was often no formality about the greetings, but only reverence and love and admiration.

> The King and Queen of England, what fair names
> That for a thousand years have lit the flames
> Within their people's hearts; what trumpets sound
> Through timeless vistas as They both are crowned!
> The tapestries where, falcon chained to wrist,
> The giants of the past ride through the mist

[a] The Archbishop's explanation of this incident is as follows: 'The King was very anxious that the Crown should be placed on his head with the right side to the front. Accordingly it was arranged that a small thin line of red cotton should be inserted under one of the principal jewels on the front. It was there when I saw the Crown in the Annexe before the ceremony. But when the Dean brought the Crown to me on its cushion from the Altar and I looked for my little red line, it was not there. So I had to turn the Crown round to see if it was on the other side; but it was not. Some officious person must have removed it.' (Lockhart, p. 420.)

[b] There are two inaccuracies in King George's account of the Homage of Peers. The Marquessate was represented, not by the senior Marquess, Lord Winchester, but by Lord Huntly, and the Barons by Lord Mowbray, in place of Lady De Ros, who held the senior Barony.

> Of History, are stirred, as bugles blow
> From Agincourt and Mons and Waterloo
> To wake the Lion and the Unicorn
> From deep heraldic sleep to new life born ;
> What whispering of trees in country lane
> 'Again, an English King is crowned, again,
> Another George, a new Elizabeth,
> To add fresh laurels to the English wreath !'
> In cities, multitudinous voices swell
> 'We have a King who loves His subjects well,
> We have a Queen, and never was more fair ;
> Long may They reign and ever grow more dear !' [a]

On the day after the Coronation the King and Queen drove through the streets of London in an open carriage and were received tumultuously. There followed the Naval Review at Spithead on May 20, and on May 24, Empire Day, a service of public Thanksgiving at St. Paul's. After a great review of ex-Servicemen in Hyde Park on June 27, short State visits were paid to Scotland (July 5–11), in the course of which the King invested the Queen with the Order of the Thistle in St. Giles' Cathedral, and to Northern Ireland (July 27–29).

The King did not allow his crowded programme to prevent him from making his annual visit to what was still called the Duke of York's Camp. He flew up to Southwold on August 3 and spent a happy day of complete relaxation among his youthful guests, returning to London the same night.

Two months of hard-earned and much-needed rest followed at Balmoral, but at their close the strenuous round began again. The King spent three days among the industries of Yorkshire in October, and on October 26 he opened Parliament in State. This occasion of his first Speech from the Throne caused him much anxiety. By reason of the fact that it is delivered sitting, the Sovereign's Speech presents, in any case, an additional difficulty, since it is always easier to speak standing ; but for a stammerer a sitting position is particularly inhibiting for reasons of rhythm and breathing, and the King feared that he might be defeated. 'My father always did this

---

[a] 'Ode for the Coronation of Their Majesties, May 12, 1937', by Sir Osbert Sitwell. A copy of this poem was found among King George VI's private papers after his death, and is preserved among the Royal Archives.

sort of thing so well', he said to Mr. Logue, and was only partly consoled by the reply that it had taken King George V years of experience and practice before he attained his admittedly high standard. Sitting in his study at Buckingham Palace, with the Crown upon his head, King George VI practised indefatigably, first with the text of his father's last Speech from the Throne in 1935 and then with the draft of his own. His efforts were rewarded with a success which, if tempered by some hesitation, was considerably greater than he had ever expected.[25]

The routine was unrelenting. On November 16 King Leopold III of the Belgians arrived on a State visit to London, and in the first week of December the King and Queen toured Cornwall to receive the feudal dues from the tenants of the Duchy.

It was a wearied but gratified and happy Monarch who arrived at Sandringham for the celebration of Christmas, a season to be spent untrammelled by the shadows and anxieties of the previous year. This year King George spoke to his peoples on Christmas Day. It was not his intention at this time to continue the tradition of his father, and he so informed his listeners : 'But as this is the first Christmas since our Coronation, the Queen and I feel that we want to send to you all a further word of gratitude for the love and loyalty you gave us from every quarter of the Empire during this unforgettable year now drawing to its end. We have promised to try and be worthy of your trust, and this is a pledge that we shall always keep.'

So ended the first year of the reign of King George VI ; how momentous it had been, how great the changes. Twelve months before, he had been still bowed under the great destiny which had so unexpectedly befallen him. Today, as he looked back across the brilliant months of his Coronation and its attendant festivities, he could no longer feel any hesitation and uncertainty. His head and heart were high, his feet set firmly and confidently upon the path of service, and he had been made aware in a thousand ways of the affection, the admiration and the fealty of those whom he was pledged to serve.

In the months which had passed, the King had successfully followed in the old ways of his father, yet with a new and

youthful vigour. Into everything that he had had to do he
had thrown himself with an energy, and an ever-ready cheer-
fulness and amenity. Now alone, now with the Queen, he
had been constantly in the public eye, and the 'man in the
street', with his unerring judgment, had little difficulty in
discerning that the passage of time was proving within his
King all the discretion, the patience and the firmness of
principle which are numbered among the foundations of
wisdom.

It falls to me as much I suppose as to any public man to meet
all sorts and conditions of people, from Cabinet Ministers to 'the
man in the street', and to learn what is in their minds [the Archbishop of Canterbury wrote to him at this time]. I find everywhere
the same testimony to the impression which Your Majesty and the
Queen have made upon Your people during the first year of Your
reign.

At first, the feeling was one of sympathy and hope. It has
now become a feeling of admiration and confidence. . . . I *know*
this to be true.

I have noticed, all who have in any way come into contact
with Your Majesty have noticed, how remarkably and steadily, if I
may presume to say so, You have *grown into* Your high office. Thus
the courage with which a year ago You accepted the burden of a
great responsibility suddenly thrust upon You, has been amply
vindicated.[26]

CHAPTER II

THE KING'S HERITAGE

(i)

ON May 27, 1937, fifteen days after the Coronation, Mr. Ramsay MacDonald resigned as Lord President of the Council and on the following day Mr. Stanley Baldwin retired from the office of Prime Minister. Thus ended that remarkable association of personalities which, either severally or together, had governed Britain since the resignation of Mr. Bonar Law in 1923. As leaders of their respective parties they had been political opponents until the Economic Crisis of 1931 had called both to the common duty of saving their country, and since that time they had alternated as Prime Minister and President of the Council in the National Government. Their joint administration had seen the restoration of Britain's national economy and the revival of Imperial Preference in the Ottawa Agreements. It had also witnessed the beginning of the decay in international confidence which was to end in war. Their departure from the political stage marked the end of an epoch, for the three years' term of office of their immediate successor, which preceded the beginning of the Churchillian era, was a period distinct in itself.

It had been Mr. Baldwin's desire that a peerage should be conferred on his colleague, and he had so advised King George, who whole-heartedly approved. Mr. MacDonald was sounded, and was somewhat tempted by the offer. 'It would be a grand thing to be Earl of Lossie,'[a] he said wistfully to Harold Nicolson at this time, but on consideration he thought better of it 'on personal grounds', and when the King repeated the offer at his final audience, he begged leave to decline.[1] Mr. Baldwin, however, on the recommendation of his successor, was created an earl and a Knight of the Garter.[b]

---

[a] Mr. MacDonald had been born at Lossiemouth, in Morayshire, in 1866.

[b] At the same time Mrs. Baldwin was created a Dame Grand Cross of the Order of the British Empire.

Though it had been an accepted fact that Mr. Baldwin would retire as soon as the Coronation was over, it was with genuine regret that King George parted with his first Prime Minister, who had served his father long and loyally and whose wise counsel had sustained the King himself in the first difficult months of his reign. He wrote to this effect on May 29 :

I would like you to know with what real sadness I accepted your resignation yesterday morning. I do, however, appreciate to the full your wisdom in laying down your burden while your health is good, without waiting for any possible impairment from exhaustion or overwork to injure either yourself or the Government of which you have been the head.

During the years when you have held the onerous office of Prime Minister, you have had to face crises of a gravity unprecedented in time of peace. By your handling of them — as well as by the high standard which you have always set in public life — you have won for yourself the admiration and confidence, and, if I may say so, the affection of the vast majority of your countrymen. You take with you into retirement the abundant goodwill of our people — and, heavy as their loss will surely be, I regard it in one sense as my gain — for in my inexperience I shall look to you for guidance and advice in the difficulties with which I know that I must from time to time be faced — and I hope, and believe, that I shall not ask in vain.[a]

The Queen and I send our best wishes to you and Mrs. Baldwin, and we look forward to seeing you frequently in the future.

With deep gratitude for your great services to my Father and myself. . . .

GEORGE R.I.[2]

The new Prime Minister, Mr. Neville Chamberlain, long designated as Mr. Baldwin's successor and leader of the Conservative Party, brought to his office gifts and qualities very different from those of his predecessor. Son of the 'Great Joe', and half-brother to Sir Austen Chamberlain, one of the artificers of the Locarno Agreement, he shared perhaps more of the characteristics of his father. His approach to public affairs was rather that of the head of a great corporation — he had been a successful Lord Mayor of Birmingham — than of a politician. As his biographer has written:

[a] Lord Baldwin continued to render considerable assistance to King George, and not least by means of small dinner-parties given in his London home at which the King was enabled to meet leaders and members of all political parties unofficially and informally.

THE DUKE OF YORK, BY PHILIP LASZLO, 1931

Masterful, confident, ruled by an instinct for order, he would give a lead, and perhaps impart an edge, on every question. His approach was ordinarily careful but his mind, once made up, hard to change ; he would make relevance a fundamental and have the future mapped out and under control, thus asking his departmental ministers to envisage two-year programmes.[3]

He had, moreover, the reputation in every office he had held of consistently knowing his own bills better than the men who drafted them.

Colder and more austere in thought than Mr. Baldwin, Mr. Chamberlain had little of his predecessor's amiable long-suffering with what he might regard as 'erring and straying men'. His combative intelligence could not pretend to a sentiment which he did not share, nor conceal a dislike which he felt, and when he thought men to be wrong he hit them hard. A man of great integrity and high principle, and of considerable courage, both moral and physical, his failings were those prompted by a certain self-sufficient obstinacy which caused in him a tendency, particularly in the conduct of foreign affairs, to refuse to believe what he did not wish to believe.

The relations of the Prime Minister with his Sovereign were always those of the most cordial nature. Indeed King George's feelings for him were very much the same as those of his father for Mr. Asquith ; he was keenly appreciative of the fact that Mr. Chamberlain kept him fully apprised of every aspect of affairs of State, and his sympathy was evident for the efforts that his Prime Minister was to make in dealing with the sombre prospect with which both were confronted.

It was indeed a barren heritage in world affairs to which King George VI and Mr. Chamberlain had succeeded. The authority of the League of Nations, already weakened by the withdrawals of Japan in 1931 and of Germany in 1933, had virtually disappeared with the failure of the policy of sanctions against Italy in 1935 ; and a year later the collapse of the Locarno Treaty System, in the face of Hitler's remilitarization of the Rhineland, without let or hindrance, had dealt the final blow to the hopes of those who had placed their confidence in the principle of collective security. Though France and Britain might reiterate their mutual promises of guarantee and assistance, the fact remained that Belgium had withdrawn from the Western Security system and had resumed that fantastic belief in the international guarantee of her neutrality which had failed to protect her from attack in the First World War and was to prove equally ineffective in the Second. The northern flank against Germany was therefore left undefended, and in the south Italy stood in sullen hostility, while Spain was convulsed in a civil war which, by its international repercussions, menaced the peace of Europe. A rapidly rearming Germany had allied herself with an already fully armed Japan in the Anti-Comintern Pact of 1936, and with Italy in the Rome-Berlin Axis agreements of the same year. The Central European states — though knit together and to the Great Powers by a network of pacts and alliances — stood, in reality, defenceless against Nazi penetration and attack, and in the Far East Japan's aggression against China had strained to the acutest tension her relations with Great Britain, the United States and Russia.

Thus it was that in May of 1937, when King George was crowned and Mr. Chamberlain took office, the international prospect was lowering and overcast. The German menace stood upon the Rhine, naked and unashamed, and Adolf Hitler had given full warning to all who wished to be warned of the measure of his ambitions, not only in respect of the destruction of the Treaty of Versailles and all that that implied, but also for the establishment of his Thousand Year Reich, with frontiers stretching from the Baltic to the Brenner, and from the Strasburger Kirche to the Riga Dom. The problem which confronted King George's Prime Minister was this: was war already inevitable sooner or later — or could the structure of the existing European system be shored up and peace be preserved? With commendable courage Mr. Chamberlain refused to accept the fatalistic course, and determined to make a new attempt for the salvation of peace. That he did so is unquestionably to his credit, irrespective of the fact that, in the view of many, he chose the wrong means of achieving his end.

The choice of two methods lay to Mr. Chamberlain's hand: he could either take the lead in forming an alliance of anti-Axis Powers outside the League of Nations, or he could appease the Axis Powers themselves. To choose the first would have entailed for Britain explicit obligations *vis-à-vis* France, in whom the Prime Minister placed little confidence, and also drawing more closely to the Soviet Union, of whom he was frankly suspicious. It would, moreover, have involved Britain to some degree in the undertakings which France had given to her protégés in Central, Eastern and South-Eastern Europe.

To many it seemed that only by an association of this sort could Western Europe hope to contend successfully against the formally allied Dictators' Bloc, but to Mr. Chamberlain it became an article of faith that Europe must be preserved at all costs from division into two armed camps. As an alternative policy he preferred and pursued the Way of Appeasement.

It is unfair to saddle Mr. Chamberlain with the responsibility for the choice of the term Appeasement. It had in fact been used by Mr. Anthony Eden,[a] who, in pronouncing the funeral oration over the corpse of the Locarno System on March 26, 1936, had assured the House of Commons that 'it is the appeasement of Europe as a whole that we have constantly before us'.[4] Mr. Chamberlain's policy was in effect only a projection of Mr. Eden's, but with a significant shift of emphasis. Whereas Mr. Eden had advocated the appeasement of Europe as a whole, Mr. Chamberlain now embarked upon a policy of appeasing the dictators of Germany and Italy and Japan at the expense of the democracies.

Mr. Chamberlain was induced to adopt this policy from three motives : first, like all right-thinking men, he had a detestation of war, with all its attendant horrors; secondly, he was genuinely convinced that much might be accomplished by personal diplomacy in conference, that there 'must be something in common' between different peoples since 'we

---

[a] Rt. Hon. Sir Anthony Eden, K.G., M.C. (b. 1897), sat in the House of Commons from 1923 to 1957 with the following offices: Under-Secretary of State for Foreign Affairs, 1931–1933; Lord Privy Seal, 1934–1935; Minister without Portfolio for League of Nations Affairs, 1935; Secretary of State for Foreign Affairs, 1935–1938 and 1940–1945; Secretary of State for Dominion Affairs, 1939–1940, and for War, 1940. With the return to power of the Conservative Party in 1951 Mr. Eden was once again at the Foreign Office, where he remained until he succeeded Sir Winston Churchill as Prime Minister in 1955. He resigned on grounds of ill-health in January 1957. He was created a Knight of the Garter in 1954.

are all members of the human race' and, as a corollary to this,
that the dictators must have their human side.[5] He shared the
view held by many of his contemporaries that discussion can
change the nature of facts and the course of events.

The Prime Minister's third motive was a practical one.
He knew, and none better, the lamentable state of Britain's
armaments and defences. The first tentative steps in rearmament had been taken by Mr. Baldwin's government in
1935, with the disclosure of the existence of the Luftwaffe in
strength; and during what Mr. Churchill has felicitously
called the 'loaded pause', which followed the Nazi reoccupa-
tion of the Rhineland, Britain began to rearm more vigorously,
though still without great conviction. Mr. Chamberlain, as
Chancellor of the Exchequer, had warmly advocated an
acceleration of the tempo of rearmament, and had favoured
fighting the General Election of 1935, first and foremost, on
Defence. He had subsequently urged an increase in the pitch
of the rearmament programme, and had obtained some satisfaction in this respect in the programmes put forward in the
Defence White Papers of 1936 and 1937. Mr. Chamberlain
had thus done his best to put the nation's defences in order, a
fact to which Mr. Churchill was among the first at the time to
bear witness,[a] but he knew well how pathetically little he had
been able to achieve, and how cavernous was the gap between
the blue-print of a White Paper and the finished product of a
nation in arms.[b] But, though the achievement of the Government for attaining the latter state was still small in comparison
with the efforts of their antagonists across the Rhine, the Prime
Minister had at least done something, and in the teeth of

[a] On May 31, 1937, speaking to a Conservative Party meeting, Mr. Churchill
said : 'When the late Government were at length convinced of the urgent need
to rearm . . . no one was more active than Mr. Chamberlain'.

[b] Mr. Chamberlain's biographer has written of British armament at this time
that it was 'low in the extreme'. 'Tied till the end of 1936 by the London Treaty,
we had 15 capital ships (3 only of post-war construction) as against 69 in 1914,
and 50 cruisers as against 108. The Army was 20,000 below establishment, the
Territorial Force 40,000, while the Air Force was lagging dangerously behind a
German front-line strength which high authority put at 1500.' To repair these
gaps the White Paper of 1936 offered wide remedial measures. 'A rebuilding of
the battle fleet, an increase of cruisers up to 70, replacement of destroyer strength ;
an increase in front-line numbers of the Home Air Force, from the 1500 planned
in 1935 to 1750, exclusive of the Fleet Air Arm; modernization of the Army
and recruitment of four new battalions.' (Feiling, p. 313.)

bitter opposition from the Labour Party, who, while criticizing the Government for pusillanimity in foreign affairs, were steadfastly and vehemently opposed to any major measure of rearmament.

What was less certain, and what perplexed members on both sides of the House of Commons, was what Mr. Chamberlain proposed to do next. Was the ultimate objective of his policy to cry a halt to the Nazi demolition of the structure of the Peace Settlement of Paris, or was he prepared to recognize a state of 'co-existence' (though this term had not then been coined) with the dictatorships, and, having placed Britain's defences in a condition when she would be free from menace, tacitly condone the steps taken by Hitler and Mussolini to make good by peaceful means their territorial ambitions? In other words, were the Dictators to be given a free hand in Central and Eastern Europe and in the Balkans?

The answer to this question we now know. Mr. Chamberlain began by following the second of these policies and was compelled by force of circumstances to abandon it for the first. But before he abandoned the Way of Appeasement he had indicated the very great lengths to which he would go to gain a general settlement, even though at the first he was sceptical of success: 'I don't believe myself that we could purchase peace and a lasting settlement by handing over Tanganyika to the Germans, but if I did, I would not hesitate for a moment', he once told the House of Commons,[6] but in the end the sacrifices made in the cause of peace amounted to a good deal more than this.

An essential consideration in assessing Mr. Chamberlain's policies is that, from first to last, they received the wholehearted support of a considerable majority of his fellow-countrymen and also — which was of equal importance — of the King's Governments in the British Commonwealth. The Imperial Conference of 1937, which closed on June 15, formally endorsed the views of the British Prime Minister in the following terms:

The members of the Conference, while themselves firmly attached to the principles of democracy and to parliamentary forms of government, decided to register their view that differences of political creed should be no obstacle to friendly relations between governments and countries and that nothing would be more damaging to the hopes of international appeasement than the division, real or apparent, of the world into opposing groups.[7]

The Conference also recorded its belief that a healthy growth of international trade, accompanied by an improvement in the general standard of living, was 'an essential step to political appeasement',[8] and it was thus made evident that faith in conciliation and appeasement was the guiding principle of Commonwealth foreign policies.[9]

Despite, therefore, the thunderous admonitions of Mr. Churchill and his small band of adherents, despite also the paler fulminations of the Labour opposition, Mr. Chamberlain could feel confident that he had the majority of the Conservative Party behind him, the general approbation of the people of England and the approval of his colleagues in the Dominion Governments. Within his own Government, as he had reconstructed it on taking office,[a] though there might be some waverers, he was assured of the support of a staunch and powerful team in Lord Halifax, Sir John Simon, Sir Samuel Hoare and Sir Thomas Inskip.

(ii)

It was in the field of Commonwealth relations that Mr. Chamberlain's Government essayed one of its earliest experiments in appeasement.

In December 1936 the Government of Mr. de Valera had seized upon the opportunity presented by the ratification of the Act of Abdication of King Edward VIII to re-define the status of Ireland *vis-à-vis* the British Crown and the British Commonwealth. Simultaneously with the Abdication Act, another measure, the External Relations Act, was passed through the Dail, by which Eire acknowledged the King's position in external affairs in regard to such formal matters as diplomatic representation in foreign countries where Irish Ministers would be accredited in the King's name and by instruments signed by the King, though these documents were henceforth written exclusively in Erse. At the same time

[a] For the various changes of Governments and in Cabinet appointments which took place during the reign of King George VI see Appendix C.

notice was given that the people of Eire would be presented with a new Constitution to replace the fundamental law pursuant to the Treaty of 1921, by which the Irish Free State became a member of the Commonwealth.

This new Constitution, which defined Ireland as a Republic, was approved by the Dail on June 14, 1937.[a] By its provisions the King was eliminated in respect of internal affairs, in which formal action was to be taken by an elected President of the Republic. Mr. de Valera had thus at last achieved the realization of that formula of the 'external association' of Ireland with the British Crown, to which he so tenaciously adhered, in fair weather and in foul, and in the face of all possible difficulties, ever since he had first propounded it to Mr. Lloyd George in the initial Anglo-Irish negotiations of July 1921.

The Imperial Conference of 1937, with perhaps more wisdom than logic, had agreed to accept the complex situation created by these two pieces of Irish legislation as constituting no fundamental change in Eire's relationship to the Commonwealth,[10] and this attitude was formally enunciated as the policy of His Majesty's Government in the United Kingdom on December 30, 1937.[11]

With the New Year, therefore, the British Government opened negotiations with a view to resolving the various points left outstanding by the Anglo-Irish Treaty of 1921, which had been emphasized by the new situation. The discussions[b] were very nearly wrecked at the outset by the insistence of Mr. de Valera that the reunion of Ireland was an essential prerequisite to any full and lasting Anglo-Irish friendship and that, since the Partition of Ireland was something for which the Government of the United Kingdom was responsible, it was for them to undo it. To this Mr. Chamberlain and his colleagues could not agree, but they did go so far as to offer to make a statement which in effect indicated that, although any change in the existing relations between Eire

[a] It was adopted by a plebiscite on July 1, and came into force on December 6.

[b] The United Kingdom was represented in the discussions by Mr. Chamberlain, Sir John Simon, Sir Samuel Hoare and Mr. Malcolm MacDonald, and Eire by Mr. de Valera, Mr. Séan Lemass, Mr. Séan MacEntee and Dr. James Ryan; while Lord Craigavon and Mr. John Andrews held a watching brief for the Government of Northern Ireland.

and Northern Ireland would require the consent of the Belfast Government, the United Kingdom would not oppose but would indeed welcome any modification of the existing position to which Northern Ireland would agree. This proposal, though accepted in principle by Mr. de Valera, was rejected by Lord Craigavon and Mr. Andrews, and the statement was never made.

A certain degree of success was, however, achieved in other spheres. With regard to finance and economics, it was agreed that in order to terminate the financial dispute which had existed since 1921, the Government of Eire would pay a lump sum of £10 million as a final settlement of much larger British claims. In return, the United Kingdom agreed to abolish the special duties on imports from Ireland which had been imposed in 1932, and there was a similar repeal by Eire of the retaliating duties imposed on British goods.

The most striking feature of the Anglo-Irish Agreement of 1938, however, was the decision of the United Kingdom Government to return the Irish Treaty Ports to the control of the Eire Government, and to surrender the rights regarding them which Britain had enjoyed since 1921.[a] This proved to be a measure of considerable controversy. There were those who considered it a grave strategic disaster thus to weaken the defensive system of the United Kingdom at a moment when the international situation was in a state of progressive deterioration, and Mr. Churchill later stigmatized it as 'a major injury to British national life and safety', and 'an improvident example of appeasement'. His judgment was : 'a more feckless act can hardly be imagined — and at such a time'.[12] But Mr. Chamberlain thought otherwise. To him it seemed absurd that, when the policy of Britain and of the Commonwealth was directed towards pacification and con-

[a] Article 7 of the Anglo-Irish Treaty of 1921 provided that :

The Government of the Irish Free State shall afford to His Majesty's Imperial Forces :

(a) In time of peace such harbours and other facilities as are indicated in the Annex hereto, or such other facilities as may from time to time be agreed between the British Government and the Government of the Irish Free State ; and

(b) In time of war, or of strained relations with a foreign Power, such harbours and other facilities as the British Government may require for the purpose of such defence as aforesaid.

ciliation in Europe, the opportunity should not be seized upon to ease a state of tension nearer home, which had grown dangerously acute in recent years and the termination of which might have a far-reaching effect within the Commonwealth as a whole. He had established a very friendly personal relationship with Mr. de Valera and he hoped, moreover, that this display of British trust would be rewarded, for example, in the event of war, by the possibility of setting up munition works in Ireland, remote from danger of enemy air attack.[13] In this he was disappointed.

King George was concerned for the success of these Anglo-Irish negotiations and was kept informed of their fluctuating progress, with its tale of crises, deadlocks and concessions, through a series of lengthy letters from Mr. Malcolm MacDonald, the indefatigable Secretary of State for Dominion Affairs. These reports the King read 'with great interest and occasional bewilderment',[14] and it was with evident relief that he learned from the Prime Minister that the final text of the Agreement had been signed in the Cabinet Room at No. 10 Downing Street at 3 o'clock on April 25. The Prime Minister added that at the end of the ceremony he had handed to Mr. de Valera the field-glasses which he had surrendered to a Captain Hintzen on the occasion of his arrest almost exactly twenty-two years before, on April 30, 1916, during the Easter Rebellion in Dublin.[15]

The King was gratified that an agreement had been reached after so many set-backs and apparent *impasses* had been encountered, and he signified his approval in a letter to Mr. Chamberlain:

I heartily congratulate you and your colleagues on this happy ending to the negotiations of recent months, and I share your confidence that, as a result, the relations between the two countries will now enter upon an era of increasing friendliness.[16]

Some hope was entertained at this time of the possibility of Mr. de Valera's being received in audience by the King, who welcomed the chance of meeting this former rebel against the Crown; but in the end it was judged to be inopportune, and despite the fact that Mr. de Valera continued to direct the destinies of Eire until 1948, a sufficiently propitious moment for his reception by King George VI never occurred.

(iii)

In respect of international affairs, therefore, the lot of the King's heritage had not fallen to him in a fair ground. Menacing clouds darkened the horizon, lions beset the way, and the cause of peace seemed to be in increasing jeopardy. To counter these threats, to dispel the dangers involved, the King's Prime Minister had elected to follow the Way of Appeasement, and it may therefore be asked what the attitude of His Majesty was towards this policy.

King George was very deeply a man of peace. The prospect of the peoples of his Commonwealth and Empire being plunged into war shocked and appalled him. To him the counsels of patience and reason were ever more welcome than those of precipitance, and, whereas he viewed with horror the more bestial aspects of the dictatorships, he was at one with his Prime Minister in believing that no reasonable effort must be spared to prevent the dictators from involving the world in a general conflagration. Moreover, he had boundless confidence in Mr. Chamberlain, whose personality he found agreeable and assuring, and he was convinced of the wisdom of a policy which, if it was not finally successful in preserving peace, would at least make abundantly clear to the world with whom lay the responsibility for war.

CHAPTER III

THE TWILIGHT OF PEACE
NOVEMBER 1937–MARCH 1939

(i)

IT was not long before Mr. Chamberlain's adherence to the policy of appeasement produced a rift within His Majesty's Government which ultimately caused first the Secretary of State for Foreign Affairs and later the First Lord of the Admiralty to part company with the Prime Minister. In pursuit of his policy Mr. Chamberlain's major objective was to effect a general settlement in Europe by means of mutual concessions on the part of all, and the conclusion of a Four-Power Agreement between Great Britain, France, Germany and Italy, which should guarantee the execution of such a settlement. In order to gain the ultimate goal, however, it was first necessary to weaken the Axis, if possible by detaching Italy by means of a bilateral agreement which, among other concessions, would accord British recognition — hitherto withheld — of Italy's East African conquest and of King Victor Emmanuel's claim to the style and title of Emperor of Ethiopia. At the same time a similar bilateral agreement was envisaged with Germany for the settlement of all questions outstanding between herself and Britain.

It was in the pursuance of this latter aim that the Prime Minister and his colleagues took advantage of the opportunity presented by the invitation received by the Lord President of the Council, Lord Halifax,[a] in his capacity as Master of the

---

[a] Rt. Hon. Edward Frederick Lindley Wood, first Earl of Halifax, K.G., O.M., G.C.S.I., G.C.I.E. (b. 1881), sat in the House of Commons from 1910 to 1925 and was successively Parliamentary Under-Secretary for the Colonies, 1921–1922; President of the Board of Education, 1922–1924; and Minister of Agriculture, 1924–1925. Created Baron Irwin, he was appointed Viceroy of India in 1926, and so continued until 1931, when he returned to serve in the National Government as President of the Board of Education, 1932–1935; Secretary of State for War, 1935; Lord Privy Seal, 1935–1937; Lord President of the Council, 1937–1938; and Secretary of State for Foreign Affairs, 1938–1940. He

Middleton Foxhounds, to attend an international hunting exhibition organized by Goering in Berlin. To Lord Halifax as a sportsman the invitation presented little enticement, more especially as a *battue* of foxes was proposed as one of the main attractions. His first reaction was to consign it to the waste-paper basket, but before doing so he mentioned it to his colleagues in Cabinet, with the result that both Mr. Chamberlain and Mr. Eden were in agreement that it offered a favour-able occasion for establishing unofficial contact with the Nazi leaders and for exploring their minds. Lord Halifax therefore went to Germany, where, avoiding the slaughter of foxes by gunfire, he had talks with Goering in Berlin, and, on November 19, with Adolf Hitler at Berchtesgaden.

In the opinion of Lord Templewood,[a] the most able of the defenders of the policy of appeasement, 'the visit failed to produce any good result. There was nothing in common between Halifax and Hitler. The fact that Hitler completely underrated Halifax's qualities exposed the narrow limits of the Führer's outlook. If anything emerged from the talks, it was the bleak sight of the wide gulf that had to be bridged if peace was to be ensured.'[1] But this was certainly not the opinion of Mr. Chamberlain. 'The German visit was from my point of view a great success', he recorded in his diary on November 26, 'because it achieved its object, that of creating an atmosphere in which it is possible to discuss with Germany the practical questions involved in a European settlement. . . . I don't see why we shouldn't say to Germany, "Give us satis-factory assurances that you won't use force to deal with the Austrians and Czechoslovakians, and we will give you similar assurances that we won't use force to prevent the changes you want, if you can get them by peaceful means."'[2]

succeeded his father as Viscount Halifax in 1934. In 1941, on the death of the Marquess of Lothian, Lord Halifax became Ambassador in Washington, where he remained until 1946.

[a] Rt. Hon. Samuel John Gurney Hoare, first Viscount Templewood, G.C.S.I., G.B.E., C.M.G. (b. 1880), was a Member of Parliament from 1910 to 1944. He served as Secretary of State for Air from 1922 to 1929; for India, 1931–1935; and for Foreign Affairs in 1935. He resigned as a result of the criticism aroused by the Hoare-Laval Pact, but returned to the Cabinet in 1936 as First Lord of the Admiralty. He was Home Secretary from 1937 to 1939, Lord Privy Seal, 1939–1940, and for a brief period again Secretary of State for Air in 1940. He was then appointed Ambassador to Madrid and remained there until 1944.

Force, however, whether physical or psychological, was not a weapon with which the Führer was prepared to dispense, and in all fairness to Mr. Chamberlain it must be stated that neither he nor any of his colleagues could have known that on November 5, just two weeks before the Hitler-Halifax conversation, the Führer had outlined to his highest subordinates, in secret conclave, 'the fundamental principles' of his plans for aggression in Central and Eastern Europe, which he regarded as so vital that they must be considered, in the event of his death, as his last Will and Testament.³ The Führer's intentions were no whit altered by the visit of Lord Halifax, and he proceeded upon his evil way.

Probably the most important outcome of the German visit was that Lord Halifax carried back with him to London a very fair and accurate appraisal of Hitler's mentality, but the generally negative results of the visit only increased in the mind of Mr. Eden his already existent doubts as to the efficacy of the policy of appeasement.

The Foreign Secretary was the more disturbed when, on his return from a brief holiday in the South of France during the Christmas recess of Parliament, he found that in his absence the Prime Minister, without consulting any of his Cabinet colleagues, had, on January 12, rejected a proposal of considerable importance from President Roosevelt. The President had suggested that the United States should take the initiative in suggesting that certain Governments should join together in drawing up tentative proposals for subsequent submission to all nations as a basis for universal agreement.⁴ Doubtful of the effectiveness of such a plan — and indeed of the competence of the President to carry it through — Mr. Chamberlain saw in it a threat to his basic principle of avoiding the division of Europe into two armed camps, and regarded it as cutting across the lines which he had now established with Germany and with Italy. He had replied accordingly. The result was twofold : the President agreed to postpone his projected appeal, and the wedge between the Prime Minister and the Foreign Secretary was driven a little deeper. 'For while Chamberlain feared the dictators would pay no heed, or else use this "line-up of the democracies" as a pretext for a break', — writes his biographer — 'it was found on Eden's return that he would rather risk that calamity than the loss of American good will.' [5]   Whilst the incident did not lead to an immediate rupture, it was, in Lord Templewood's view, 'the underlying reason for Eden's resignation a month later'.[6]

For the tempo of events was rapidly increasing.   On February 12 Hitler summoned the Austrian Chancellor, Dr. Schuschnigg, to Berchtesgaden, and there subjected him to an ordeal of psychological intimidation which, when the details of it became known, shocked the world.   In Mr. Eden's mind it was the final argument against any further appeasement of the dictators, one of whom at any rate had now shown himself at last in his true colours.   But Mr. Chamberlain thought otherwise.   He too had been disturbed by Hitler's treatment of Schuschnigg, whom he regarded, according to his diary, as having been 'outrageously bullied',[7] but for him this did not constitute a reason for abandoning the fundamental principle upon which his whole foreign policy and that of the Commonwealth was based.   Indeed he was in high hopes of coming to an over-all agreement with the Italian Government, and thereby achieving his long-term aim of dividing the Axis.

Through his sister-in-law, Sir Austen Chamberlain's widow, the Prime Minister had received a message from the Duce indicating that an early agreement would be welcome in Rome, and that it would include provision for the withdrawal, by all parties concerned, of volunteers on both sides in the Spanish Civil War, a measure which had long been the objective of British diplomacy.   Preliminary conversations were in fact in process between Mr. Eden and Count Dino Grandi, the Italian Ambassador, at the time of Schuschnigg's summons to Berchtesgaden.   They had not progressed very far at that time, and thereafter Mr. Eden was less enthusiastic about them than ever.   Both Mr. Chamberlain and Count Ciano, the Italian Foreign Minister, were becoming impatient at what they regarded as unwarrantable delays, and the issue between the Prime Minister and his Foreign Secretary reached a crisis during the week-end of February 18–20, 1938.

On Friday, the 18th, a conversation took place at No. 10 Downing Street between Mr. Chamberlain, Mr. Eden and Count Grandi during which the various questions at issue

— Austria, Ethiopia and Spain — were canvassed. According to the Italian Ambassador's report to his Minister,[8] the conflict of views between the two British statesmen was evident during the discussion and, whether this be true or not, it is a fact that when they reviewed the conversation together after the departure of Count Grandi, it was apparent that there was great variance between them. The Prime Minister favoured the immediate opening of formal negotiations with the Italian Government as a means of preserving Austria's independence, which all agreed was now imperilled, and of accepting Mussolini's word, without further guarantees, about withdrawing his volunteers from Spain. The Foreign Secretary held completely opposite views. He was convinced that Hitler was acting towards Austria on the certainty of Mussolini's secret assurances that Italy would offer no opposition to annexation, and that hence the opening of Anglo-Italian negotiations would prove no deterrent.[a] As to withdrawals from Spain, the Italian record of previous broken promises was so bad in this respect that Mr. Eden wished to see the volunteers actually begin their return to Italy as an earnest of good faith before negotiations began. He was opposed to any form of compromise.

The cleavage of opinion was carried to the Cabinet, which met almost continuously throughout the 19th and 20th. By Saturday night the *impasse* was complete; the differences vital and unbridgeable. The Prime Minister could entertain no other course of action than that which he had previously advocated, namely that of opening negotiations with Italy; the Foreign Secretary could not square it with his conscience to defend before the House of Commons a policy in which he did not believe. In these circumstances he felt that he should resign, and intimated his intention of doing so. The Cabinet were unanimous in their support of Mr. Chamberlain.[b]

[a] On this point Mr. Eden's instinct was entirely correct, but he was slightly ahead of events. Hitler's personal emissary to the Duce, Prince Philip of Hesse, had been pressing Mussolini for some time to give just this assurance, but he did not succeed in getting it unequivocally until the night of March 11, the very eve of the German annexation of Austria. It was this news which provoked from Hitler the paroxysm of hysterical gratitude: 'Tell Mussolini I will never forget him for this, never, never, never'.

[b] The issues raised by Mr. Eden's resignation have been sharpened by the publication after the war of Count Ciano's diplomatic papers, amongst which was Count Grandi's famous report of February 19, 1938.[9]

After further discussion and attempts to dissuade him on the part of some of his colleagues, Mr. Eden formally resigned on Sunday night at 7.30, and with him went the Under-Secretary of State, Lord Cranborne.[a] They were succeeded in office by Lord Halifax and Mr. R. A. Butler.[b] 'I have won through', wrote Mr. Chamberlain to his friend Lord Rushcliffe,[c] 'but it has only been with blood and tears'.[10]

King George was at Royal Lodge during this momentous week-end. He had been informed by Sir Alexander Hardinge of the unusual event of the Cabinet being summoned on a Saturday, and was aware of the difference of opinion which existed between his Prime Minister and his Foreign Secretary, but neither Sir Alexander in London nor King George at Windsor was prepared in any way for the headlines with which the Beaverbrook and Harmsworth press announced on Sunday morning the imminent probability of Mr. Eden's resignation.

The King at once telephoned to his Private Secretary for confirmation of these reports, but because the Minutes of the Cabinet meeting of the previous evening were still being dictated, Sir Alexander failed to get adequate information from No. 10 Downing Street, and was compelled to seek for it elsewhere. It was not until after luncheon on Sunday that he was able to give His Majesty details of the acutely serious situation which had developed. He recorded:

It must be noted that no intimation of any kind was given to

---

[a] Rt. Hon. Robert Arthur James Gascoyne-Cecil, K.G., fifth Marquess of Salisbury (b. 1893), served, as Lord Cranborne, as Under-Secretary of State for Foreign Affairs, 1935–1938; Paymaster-General, 1940; and Secretary of State for the Dominions, 1940–1942. Called to the House of Lords as Lord Cecil of Essendon in 1941, he held office as Secretary of State for the Colonies, 1942; Lord Privy Seal, 1942–1943; and Secretary of State for the Dominions, 1943–1945. Succeeding his father in 1947, he again became Lord Privy Seal in 1951, Secretary of State for Commonwealth Relations, 1952, and Lord President of the Council in 1952. He resigned from Mr. Macmillan's Government in March 1957.

[b] Rt. Hon. Richard Austen Butler, C.H., M.P. (b. 1902), entered the House of Commons in 1929, and served as Under-Secretary of State at the India Office, 1932–1937, Parliamentary Secretary, Ministry of Labour, 1937–1938, Under-Secretary of State at the Foreign Office, 1938–1941, and Minister of Education, 1941–1945. He was Minister of Labour in Mr. Churchill's 'Caretaker Government' in 1945, and when the Conservatives returned to power in 1951 he became Chancellor of the Exchequer until 1955, when he was appointed Lord Privy Seal, in which capacity, combined with the office of Home Secretary, he continued to serve in Mr. Macmillan's government.

[c] Rt. Hon. Henry Bucknall Betterton, first Baron Rushcliffe, G.B.E. (1872–1949), Minister of Labour, 1931–1934.

The King regarding the crisis which had arisen at the Cabinet Meeting on Saturday 19th. The Minutes could not reach The King before the morning of the 21st, as Hankey [a] was still dictating them at mid-day on Sunday, and if it had not been for the accurate information supplied by Lords Beaverbrook and Rothermere there was no reason why The King should have known anything about it until Eden, and possibly other members of the Cabinet, had already resigned.[11]

King George was royally displeased at the seeming neglect with which he had been treated. He instructed his Private Secretary to convey the expression of his displeasure to the Cabinet Secretariat and to demand that some better machinery be devised for keeping him informed of such sudden events in the future.

His Majesty feels, with, in my humble opinion, much justification [wrote Sir Alexander Hardinge to Sir Maurice Hankey], that he should not have been left to learn from an unreliable Press of the difficult situation in which his Government was placed as the result of the Cabinet Meeting on Saturday night. I feel sure that you will agree that some arrangement should be devised to enable The King to receive immediate intimation of any serious developments of this nature, and I would welcome the opportunity of discussing the matter with you.[12]

In point of fact, the immediate circumstances of Mr. Eden's resignation had been so unusual that it would have been very difficult to say at what point the position had become sufficiently critical to report to His Majesty. Despite the reports in the Sunday press, neither the Prime Minister nor Sir Maurice Hankey had thought that the Foreign Secretary really intended to resign until the meeting of a small group of Ministers at which he actually announced his decision to do so. It was then 7.30 on Sunday evening, and although the Prime Minister's Secretariat should have telephoned to Buckingham Palace, in the excitement and preoccupation of the moment they forgot to do so. As a result of consultation between Sir Alexander Hardinge and Sir Maurice Hankey, it was agreed

[a] Rt. Hon. Maurice Pascal Alers, first Baron Hankey, G.C.B., G.C.M.G., G.C.V.O. (b. 1877), was Secretary of the Committee of Imperial Defence, 1912–1938; of the War Cabinet, 1916, the Imperial War Cabinet, 1917, and of the Cabinet, 1919–1938; Clerk of the Privy Council, 1923–1938; Minister without Portfolio, 1939–1940; Chancellor of the Duchy of Lancaster, 1940–1941; and Paymaster-General, 1941–1942.

that the Secretary to the Cabinet should make himself responsible for reminding the Prime Minister of his duty to inform
the King of any impending crisis and, in the event of his being
prevented from doing so immediately, the Secretary should
have discretion to get in touch with the King's Private Secretary. Later still, this method was further expedited when, at
His Majesty's own suggestion, it was arranged that in order
to enable him to keep abreast of rapid developments during
a serious situation, whether in internal or external affairs, a
draft copy of the conclusions of the Cabinet should be sent to
him at the same time as to the Prime Minister, instead of
waiting for the Cabinet Minutes in their final form.

The King's anxiety to be kept *au courant* with the movements and developments of events was prompted not only
by a keen interest in the happenings of the day but also by a
deep sense of duty in the proper discharge of the functions of
his high office. It is the accepted and inalienable threefold
right of the Sovereign to advise, to encourage and to warn in
moments of crisis, and to the practical and punctilious mind
of King George it was impossible for him to fulfil these responsibilities *vis-à-vis* his Ministers unless he was kept as well
informed as they. Thus zealously did he cherish and exercise
his prerogatives.

(ii)

Mr. Eden's resignation came as a surprise and a shock to the
people of England,[a] among whom he had long enjoyed the
deserved reputation of the *preux chevalier* of the League of
Nations.   Taken in conjunction with the third-degree
methods applied to Dr. Schuschnigg, news of which had just
preceded the Foreign Secretary's departure, and the Nazi
annexation of Austria which closely followed (March 12), it

[a] In commenting on Mr. Eden's resignation, Mr. Churchill wrote : 'On this
night of February 20, 1938, and on this occasion only, sleep deserted me. From
midnight till dawn I lay in my bed consumed by emotions of sorrow and fear.
There seemed one strong young figure standing up against long, dismal, drawling
tides of drift and surrender, of wrong measurements and feeble impulses. My
conduct of affairs would have been different from his in various ways ; but he
seemed to me at this moment to embody the life-hope of the British nation, the
grand old British race that had done so much for men, and had yet some more
to give. Now he was gone. I watched the daylight slowly creep in through the
windows, and saw before me in mental gaze the vision of Death.' [13]

constituted the first major blow to the general popular confidence which had been hitherto reposed in Mr. Chamberlain.
There were those who entertained the hope that Mr. Eden
would add his voice and the weight of his influence to the
efforts of Mr. Churchill in an effort to awaken Britain to a
sense of her danger. These, however, were disappointed.
Mr. Eden was a seceder, not a leader of a revolt nor even
an active rebel. With a superb loyalty to the Leader of his
Party he exercised great self-restraint.

It is to be believed that, though King George regretted
the departure of Mr. Eden from the Cabinet, he was more
greatly at ease with his new Foreign Secretary, Lord Halifax.
As the King was later to admit to one of his Dominion Prime
Ministers, he had not, at this time, been able to establish
close personal relations with Mr. Eden, whom he found it
difficult to persuade in conversation to depart from his brief.
It was not until later, and under the influence of Mr. Churchill,
that the King came to appreciate Mr. Eden's full worth. Lord
Halifax, on the other hand, with his ease of manner, his great
amiability, and his ripe experience of men and affairs, was
on very cordial terms with His Majesty, partly upon personal
grounds and partly by reason of the close identity of the new
Foreign Secretary's views with those of the Prime Minister.

The spring and summer of the year 1938 were pregnant
with anxiety. Scarcely had the first shock of the Nazi annexation of Austria begun to subside when it became apparent that
the assurances given by German statesmen to Czechoslovakia,
that the *Anschluss* was entirely 'a German family affair' and
that Czechoslovakia had nothing to fear from the Reich, were
patently false. On March 28, just two weeks after Hitler's
triumphant entry into Vienna, Konrad Henlein, the leader of
the Sudeten German Party in Czechoslovakia, was summoned
to Berlin to receive his orders for the preliminary work of
disrupting the Czechoslovak State, and on April 24 his
proclamation of the 'Karlsbad Programme' fired the first shot
in the battle which ended in Hitler's victorious entry into
Prague a year later.

Czechoslovakia sought confirmation from Paris that the
solemn mutual obligation for defence into which she had
entered with France would be honoured in the event of Nazi

aggression. The French Government returned no immediate reply to this enquiry but first sought assurances of support from the British Government.

Now was the beginning of Mr. Chamberlain's great ordeal, that tragic sequence in his life during which he was to rise to the peak of triumph with the Munich Agreement, and to crash in shocked and bitter disappointment six months later with the German occupation of Prague. The Prime Minister could not bring himself to believe that Germany would attack Czechoslovakia, nor that the maintenance of the territorial integrity of the Czechoslovak State, as created by the Peace Settlement of Paris, justified the outbreak of a second world war. With courage and determination, and in the face of fierce criticism, he held fast to his confident belief in the essential efficacy and the eventual success of the policy of appeasement.

In the meantime the Government had run into difficulties in the House of Commons on the question of rearmament and more especially in the matter of the expansion of the Royal Air Force. The Secretary of State for Air, Lord Swinton,[a] had succeeded in bringing together a remarkable team of public servants, both airmen and civilians, to whose combined genius was due the development in planning and invention of those types of machines and equipment to which Britain later owed her survival: the Hurricanes and Spitfires which won the Battle of Britain; the Blenheim and Wellington bombers, which later carried the war so devastatingly to the enemy's stronghold; the system of Radar and the 'shadow factories', all owed their inception to the inspiration and energy of Lord Swinton and his colleagues. Indeed, if Lord Trenchard be known as the Father of the Royal Air Force, Lord Swinton may very well be termed its Godfather.[b]

[a] Rt. Hon. Philip Cunliffe-Lister (né Lloyd-Greame), first Earl of Swinton, G.B.E., C.H., M.C. (b. 1884), served as President of the Board of Trade, 1922–1923, 1924–1929 and in 1931; Secretary of State for the Colonies, 1931–1935; Secretary of State for Air, 1935–1938; Minister Resident in West Africa, 1942–1944; Minister for Civil Aviation, 1944–1945; Chancellor of the Duchy of Lancaster and Minister of Materials, 1951–1952; Secretary of State for Commonwealth Relations, 1952–1955.

[b] In the opinion of one of his colleagues, Lord Winterton: 'Lord Swinton should be bracketed with Mr. Churchill and the late Lord Haldane as one of the three outstandingly successful Service Ministers of our time in preparing the Forces for which they were ministerially responsible before a great war for the task which they had to perform'.[14]

But, like all Service Department Chiefs in time of peace, the Air Minister had to contend with the Treasury's reluctance to finance the bill of costs entailed in translating a great production programme from the drawing-board to the finished article, and although the then Chancellor of the Exchequer, Sir John Simon,[a] had had the benefit of four years at the Foreign Office and of having met the Führer face to face, it would appear, in the words of one commentator, that he 'had evidently forgotten what he had learnt as Foreign Secretary from Hitler's own mouth'.[15]

By May of 1938 there was considerable parliamentary criticism of the Government's programme of aerial rearmament, centring chiefly on the delays in the production of new types of aircraft and in the setting-up of the 'shadow factories'. Mr. Churchill took the lead in this attack, though he was careful to differentiate in his strictures between the Government's policy and the personal contribution of Lord Swinton, and the Air Ministry were at a double disadvantage in replying. In the first place, they were unable, for reasons of security, to tell the House what progress had in fact been made, and, for reasons of propriety, to say that this progress would have been considerably greater had the money for the necessary expense been forthcoming. In the second place, their representation on the Front Bench was not of the ablest. When the Secretary of State for Air had assumed office in 1935 he had been Sir Philip Cunliffe-Lister, with a seat in the House of Commons, but he had accepted a peerage two years later and found it increasingly difficult to defend his Ministry's record from 'another place'. Meantime in the House of Commons, his deputy, Lord Winterton,[b] was unequal to the task of meeting the attacks of Mr. Churchill and his followers. 'I was too

[a] Rt. Hon. John Allsebrook, first Viscount Simon, G.C.S.I., G.C.V.O. (1873–1954), served as Solicitor-General, 1910–1913; Attorney-General, 1913–1915; Home Secretary, 1915–1916; Chairman of the Indian Statutory Commission, 1927–1930; Secretary of State for Foreign Affairs, 1931–1935; Home Secretary, 1935–1937; Chancellor of the Exchequer, 1937–1940; and Lord Chancellor, 1940–1945.
[b] Rt. Hon. Edward Turnour, sixth Earl Winterton (b. 1883), sat in the House of Commons as an Irish Peer for the Horsham Division of Sussex from 1904 to 1951. During this period he held the offices of Under-Secretary of State for India, 1922–1929; Chancellor of the Duchy of Lancaster, 1937–1939; Deputy Secretary of State for Air, March–May 1938; and Paymaster-General, January–November 1939.

"long-winded", too parenthetical, and too ready to reply to interruptions', he writes modestly of his own contribution.[16] The climax came after a particularly stormy debate on May 12.

Mr. Chamberlain was faced with the imperative necessity of strengthening the representation of the Air Ministry in the House of Commons. This he could do either by appointing a new and more adept deputy or by a new Secretary of State from the Lower House. He chose the second alternative, and dispensed with the valuable services of Lord Swinton on May 16, replacing him by Sir Kingsley Wood.[a] 'He [the Prime Minister] felt that he must have a Secretary of State in the House of Commons who could pacify the House', wrote the retiring Minister.[17]

The loss of Lord Swinton to the nation's counsels was felt acutely by those of his colleagues and opponents alike who knew the full tally of his achievement. This also was the feeling of King George, who was well acquainted with the facts and showed his appreciation of them.

I saw Swinton this evening [he wrote to Mr. Chamberlain] & I was very sorry to have had to say good-bye to him as Secretary of State for Air. He has done so well in the Air Ministry I feel & he will be a great loss to the country at this time.[18]

Nor was this impression erased with the passage of time. In the days to come, when the Battle of Britain had been fought and won, the King wrote in his diary: 'Men like Lord Swinton will be remembered' (October 4, 1940).

Spring gave place to summer and summer to autumn, and in Central Europe the storm-clouds of the Czech crisis brewed ever more dark and lowering.[b] The critical situation which had arisen during the week-end of May 20–22, when it appeared probable that Hitler meditated a descent in force upon Czechoslovakia, had been met by a display of determined

---

[a] Rt. Hon. Sir Kingsley Wood (1881–1943) served as Postmaster-General, 1931–1935; Minister of Health, 1935–1938; Secretary of State for Air, 1938–1940; and Lord Privy Seal from April to May 1940, when he became Chancellor of the Exchequer, which office he held until his death.

[b] The story of the Czech crisis from the point of view of Mr. Chamberlain has been told by his biographer (Feiling, pp. 347-382), but a much abler defence of the Prime Minister's policy is to be found in Lord Templewood's memoirs (pp. 285-326). For the views of Mr. Chamberlain's critics, see the trenchant accounts of Mr. Churchill (vol. i, pp. 250-288) and Mr. Duff Cooper (pp. 224-242).

opposition from Britain, France and Russia, but it was apparent to all that the danger had but passed for the moment and that some adequate solution of the claims of the Sudeten Germans for self-determination must be speedily achieved if war was to be averted.[a]

Acutely sensitive of this necessity, Mr. Chamberlain now conceived the idea of making a direct intervention in the hitherto abortive negotiations then in process between the Czech Government and the Sudeten German leaders by dispatching an unofficial British mission, with Lord Runciman[b] at its head, to assist and accelerate both parties in reaching an agreement. The Prime Minister had arrived at this 'original and hardy idea'[c] in the belief that the Czech Government were pursuing a deliberately dilatory policy in the hope that in the long run they would get a better bargain with the support of Britain and France. He also feared that, if the Sudeten German demands for complete political autonomy within the Czechoslovak State were not accommodated to some major degree, Hitler would seize the excuse of 'protecting' this German minority to settle the matter by force. Neither the Czech nor the French Government responded warmly to the original suggestion, and it was considered essential to gain the support of France. An opportunity of achieving this by direct contact was now presented.

On July 19 King George and Queen Elizabeth left England on a State Visit to the President of the French Republic. Their original date of departure had been set for June 28, but their

[a] In a speech before the Congress of the Nazi Party on September 12, 1938, Hitler admitted that on May 28 he had taken the momentous decision that the Sudeten Problem must be settled 'this year' — even if this involved a European war. It is also now known from the German documents presented in evidence at the trial of the Major War Criminals at Nuremberg in 1945–1946 that Hitler had on that same day issued the revised directive for 'Operation Green', recording his 'unalterable decision to smash (zerschlagen) Czechoslovakia by military action in the near future' and appointing October 1 as the dead-line for putting this Operation into effect. (International Military Tribunal Document, PS-388, item 11.)

[b] Rt. Hon. Walter, first Viscount Runciman of Doxford (1870–1949), had during his parliamentary career held the offices of President of the Board of Education, 1908–1911; President of the Board of Agriculture, 1911–1914; Commissioner of Woods and Forests, 1912–1914; and President of the Board of Trade, 1914–1916 and 1931–1937. He also served as Lord President of the Council from 1938 to 1939.

[c] It was in these words that Mr. J. L. Garvin hailed the appointment of the Runciman Mission in The Observer on July 31, 1938.

plans had been thrown into confusion by the sudden death at Glamis on June 23 of the Queen's mother, Lady Strathmore. A hasty postponement of the visit was inevitable and, on the suggestion of President Lebrun, the dates of July 19–22 were proposed and accepted.

At one moment it had been thought that the Queen might not be able to accompany His Majesty. Queen Elizabeth, however, though deeply saddened by this bereavement of one whose love and warm personality she had dearly cherished, would not allow her sorrow to deprive the King of her support nor to interfere with the obligations of public duty, more especially as the strengthening of the bonds of friendship between Britain and her chief ally in Europe were now of very pressing moment.

On the appointed day, therefore, the King, who had only just recovered from a somewhat severe attack of gastric influenza, and Queen crossed the Channel in H.M.S. *Enchantress*.[a] Twenty-four years before, on April 21, 1914, King George V and Queen Mary had made a similar visit to Paris, and the superstitious recalled that within four months Britain and France had been at war with Germany. The international situation in June 1938 was more openly threatening than on that occasion. Would the testing of Anglo-French solidarity come again so soon ?

This thought, however, was not permitted to dim the brilliance nor diminish the warmth of the welcome which France offered to the British Sovereign. Throughout the three days of their visit they were received with rapturous enthusiasm and an almost personal affection by the Parisian crowd. The Queen's charm and beauty carried all before them, and the simple splendour of her white *trousseau* evoked transports of admiration in the newspapers.[b]

[a] Their Majesties were attended by Lord Halifax, as Minister in Attendance ; the Duke of Beaufort, Master of the Horse ; Field-Marshal Lord Birdwood, Gold Stick in Waiting ; the Earl of Airlie, Lord Chamberlain to the Queen ; the Duchess of Northumberland, Mistress of the Robes ; Countess Spencer, Lady-in-Waiting ; Sir Alexander Hardinge and Sir Eric Miéville, Private Secretary and Assistant Private Secretary to the King ; Captain Charles Lambe, R.N., Equerry ; Captain Richard Streatfeild, Private Secretary to the Queen ; and Mr. Oliver Harvey, Private Secretary to the Secretary of State for Foreign Affairs.

[b] In deference to her mourning an all-white *trousseau* for the State Visit was devised for the Queen. It is notable that this was the first occasion on which she wore the crinoline dresses inspired by the Winterhalter portraits of the young Queen Victoria at Buckingham Palace.

The programme was a crowded one, and no opportunity was allowed to pass of stressing the solidarity of Anglo-French relations and of emphasizing the fundamental basis of that amity as one of peace. Their friendship was directed against no other Power, King George asserted at the Élysée banquet on the first evening : 'It is the ardent desire of our Governments to find, by means of international agreements, a solution of those political problems which threaten the peace of the world and of those economic difficulties which restrict human well-being. The action of our Governments is thus directed towards a common goal — that of assuring the happiness of the peoples of the world by means of true co-operation.'

Perhaps the last day of the visit (July 21) was the most memorable for the future. At a review of 50,000 troops at Versailles in the morning there passed before the King the outward and visible sign of the military might of France — so soon, alas, to be found lacking in inward and spiritual grace. The grim mechanical devices of modern armour, the dash and *élan* of the Moroccan cavalry recalling the warfare of a bygone age, mingled in a great pageant which inspired both awe and confidence.

The review was to have been accompanied by a fly-past by the French Air Force, but this was for some reason postponed somewhat infelicitously until the afternoon. As the King and Queen and their hosts were sitting with a great company at a concert in the chapel of the Château, wave after wave of aircraft passed over them, casting their fleeting shadows on the sunlit walls and intermittently drowning the music with the drone of their belligerent engines. There was something macabre in the experience which remained rooted in the memories of both the King and the Queen.

The visit ended that evening with a brilliant fête at the Quai d'Orsay, where the great *salons* and lantern-decked gardens of the Foreign Ministry presented a spectacle of fairy-like magnificence, and the ballet of the Opera danced with fantastic grace before Their Majesties. In the minds of few present could there have been the thought that within two years these same halls and gardens would be occupied by the forces of the invader.

On the following day the King went to Villers-Bretonneux,

there to unveil a memorial to thé eleven thousand members of
the Australian Imperial Forces who fell in France during the
First World War and have no known grave.

Their Majesties returned to London that night, secure in
the knowledge that their visit to France had been one of
unquestioned personal success. It had also been successful in
other ways, for in the intervals of the great festivities Lord
Halifax was enabled to exchange views with the French Prime
Minister, M. Édouard Daladier, and the Foreign Minister,
M. Georges Bonnet, and to gain their assent among other
matters, albeit somewhat grudgingly, to the dispatch of Lord
Runciman to Czechoslovakia.

The arrival of the Runciman Mission in Prague on August 3
produced a momentary easing of the tension of anxiety, and
the British public prepared to go off for their summer holidays
with a more tranquil mind. The King shared this lightening
of heart. At the end of July he visited the Royal Yacht
Squadron at Cowes in the *Victoria and Albert*, and then sailed
up the east coast to Aberdeen, *en route* for Balmoral. On the
way, he anchored off Southwold on August 1, and paid his
usual visits to his Camp, being borne ashore through the waves
from an open boat on the bare shoulders of his young guests.

King George had hoped to find some peace and relaxation
during his Scottish holiday, but scarcely had he arrived than
there began to beat in upon him the baleful tumult of the
gathering storm. For Hitler was now throwing off the mask.
He had not regarded Lord Runciman as a messenger of peace
and was beginning to clamour openly for the 'return' of the
Sudeten Germans to the Reich. The King sent a word of
sympathy to his harassed Prime Minister :

The German attitude to what you are trying to do to help the
Czechoslovakian situation, certainly gives cause for anxiety, &
their partial mobilisation on the Czech frontier under the guise of
large-scale manœuvres, might mean all sorts of things.[19]

The Prime Minister spent four days (August 31 – September 3) at Balmoral, but he could bring the King no
heartening tidings. Despite all efforts Lord Runciman and
his colleagues had failed to find a compromise formula acceptable to both the Czechs and the Sudeten Germans. The
danger of German intervention was growing, and it was now

accepted that if this occurred and the French acted in support of their Czechoslovakian allies, Britain could not long remain uninterested.

Mr. Chamberlain, however, had not abandoned hope. On his return to London he wrote with guarded optimism to the King on September 6 :

Developments seem very slow and I am afraid that we may have to wait another week or even more before we can speak with confidence about the issue. All the same I have a 'hunch', as J. P. Morgan says, that we shall get through this time without the use of force. Hitler cannot say that no progress is being made and the general opinion of the world would be more shocked than ever if Runciman's efforts were to be rudely interrupted before it could be established that they had failed. Even if things looked more threatening than they do at the moment I should not despair for I don't think we have fired the last shot in our locker.[20]

The developments in Prague had not been quite as dilatory as Mr. Chamberlain believed, for on September 4 President Beneš had summoned the leaders of the Sudeten German Party to the Hradschin Palace and, in what came to be known as 'Plan No. 4', had conceded to them virtually all the most extreme of their demands, including that which would establish for one section of the population a totalitarian system of government within the democratic Czechoslovakian Republic. Appalled at the fruits of their own victory, the party chieftains had fled to Nuremberg, there to confer with Hitler, who at once issued orders for a revolt of all Germans in Czechoslovakia. The first incident occurred on September 7 and this was held sufficient justification for the breaking-off of negotiations by the Sudeten German leaders. The Führer's time-table was approaching its dead-line.

All Europe, all the world, now waited in tense anxiety for September 12. On that day Hitler was to speak to his assembled legions at Nuremberg, and it was fully believed in Prague and elsewhere that the speech might well determine the issue of peace or war. The listening Czechs carried their gas-masks with them, for who could tell whether, within an hour of the beginning of the speech, the first German bombers would not be overhead ?

Hitler's speech did not bring war, however. It dripped

venom; it abounded in the grossest insults to President Beneš
and his countrymen — who that heard it can ever forget the
naked hatred in the Führer's voice as he articulated the words :
'*Ich spreche von der Tschechoslovakei*' ? But it did not bring war
and it did not even bring the demand for a plebiscite in the
Sudeten German areas. To the Sudeten German Party,
however, it brought the signal for revolt, and revolt they did
in real earnest, so that for two days there was hand-to-hand
fighting in the Sudetenland. Hitler had now created the
situation he desired.

On Wednesday September 14 to the King at Balmoral
there came a long letter from the Prime Minister, of which
the text must be given in full.[21]

10 DOWNING STREET
WHITEHALL
13th September, 1938

SIR,

With my humble duty, I write to inform Your Majesty that the
international situation has been engaging the constant and earnest
attention of Your Majesty's Ministers. The continued state of
tension in Europe which has caused such grave concern throughout
the world has in no way been relieved, and in some ways been
aggravated, by the speech delivered at Nuremberg last night by
Herr Hitler. Your Majesty's Ministers are examining the position
in the light of this speech, and with the firm desire to ensure, if
this is at all possible, that peace may be preserved.

On the one hand, reports are daily received in great numbers,
not only from official sources but from all manner of individuals
who claim to have special and unchallengeable sources of information. Many of these (and of such authority as to make it impossible
to dismiss them as unworthy of attention) declare positively that
Herr Hitler has made up his mind to attack Czecho-Slovakia and
then to proceed further East. He is convinced that the operation
can be effected so rapidly that it will be all over before France or
Great Britain could move and that they will not then venture to
try to upset a *fait accompli*.

On the other hand, Your Majesty's representative in Berlin [a]
has steadily maintained that Herr Hitler has not yet made up his
mind to violence. He means to have a solution soon — this month —
and if that solution, which must be satisfactory to himself, can be

[a] Rt. Hon. Sir Nevile Henderson, G.C.M.G (1882–1942), was British Ambassador in Berlin from 1937 until the outbreak of war in September 1939. His
book, *Failure of a Mission*, published in 1940, is an important source for the history
of these years.

obtained peacefully, well and good. If not, he is ready to march if he should so decide.

With these contradictory views before us, Your Majesty's Ministers have acted on the basis of the latter and more optimistic forecast. It has been obvious, however, that we must be prepared for the possibility of a sudden change for the worse and, if then we have any time at all for action, we must know beforehand what action we are going to take.

In these circumstances I have been considering the possibility of a sudden and dramatic step which might change the whole situation. The plan is that I should inform Herr Hitler that I propose at once to go over to Germany to see him. If he assents, and it would be difficult for him to refuse, I should hope to persuade him that he had an unequalled opportunity of raising his own prestige and fulfilling what he has so often declared to be his aim, namely the establishment of an Anglo-German understanding, preceded by a settlement of the Czecho-Slovakian question.

After sketching out the prospect of Germany and England as the two pillars of European peace and buttresses against communism, I should suggest that the essential preliminary was the peaceful solution of our present trouble. Since I assume that he will have declared that he cannot wait and that the solution must come at once, my proposal would be that he should agree that, after both sides had laid their case before Lord Runciman and thus demonstrated the points of difference, Lord Runciman should act as final arbitrator. Of course I should not be able to guarantee that Dr. Beneš would accept this solution, but I should undertake to put all possible pressure on him to do so. The Government of France have already said that they would accept any plan approved by Your Majesty's Government or by Lord Runciman.

The plan, which I have discussed with Your Majesty's Foreign Secretary and which I would also propose to reveal to the members of the Cabinet tomorrow, is a last resort, only to be embarked upon if the situation is thought to be otherwise desperate. I should hope that, if occasion should arise for me to adopt it, I should have Your Majesty's approval and permission to absent myself from the country at this time in a last attempt to save the peace of Europe.

I am, Sir, Your Majesty's humble, obedient Servant,

NEVILLE CHAMBERLAIN.

But events were now moving with hideous momentum, and scarcely had Mr. Chamberlain completed the writing of this letter when he was compelled to add a postscript:

Events on the Continent of Europe have moved so rapidly and the situation appears to have become so critical that I have

sent a personal message to Herr Hitler that I propose to travel to
Germany by air and I am ready to start tomorrow. I have asked
him to indicate the earliest time at which he could see me. I
trust that my action will have Your Majesty's approval.[22]

The King would in any case have returned to London in
such a moment of crisis but it so happened that he was travelling
south on the night of the 14th to attend the funeral of his
cousin, Prince Arthur of Connaught, who had died two days
previously. He therefore sent his approval of the Prime
Minister's proposed action by telephone on the afternoon of
the 14th, and Mr. Chamberlain departed by air for Berchtesgaden on the following morning.

On the King's arrival at Buckingham Palace on the
morning of the 15th, he at once conferred with those of the
Inner Cabinet who remained in London, Lord Halifax, Sir
John Simon, Sir Samuel Hoare, and Sir Thomas Inskip,[a]
and discussed the situation with them. To Lord Halifax he
put forward an idea of his own, which had matured during
his sojourn at Balmoral. He had prepared a draft of a personal
letter to Hitler on the basis of 'one ex-Serviceman to another',
urging him to spare the youth of Britain and Germany from
the horrors and the slaughter of a second world war. He did
not show the draft to Lord Halifax, but he asked him if he
thought that such an initiative on his (the King's) part might
be of some help towards strengthening the hands of the
Government in maintaining peace. The Foreign Secretary
replied guardedly that though he was doubtful of the efficacy
of the 'ex-Serviceman' aspect of such an appeal to the Führer,
the time might well come when a direct approach by His
Majesty might be of assistance, and he advised that the matter
should be referred to the Prime Minister on his return from
Germany.

King George shared to the full the nation's admiration for
the hardihood and courage of a man of nearly seventy setting

---

[a] Rt. Hon. Thomas Walker Hobart Inskip, first Viscount Caldecote, C.B.E.
(1876–1947), was a Member of Parliament, 1918–1929 and 1931–1939. He
served as Solicitor-General from 1922 to 1924, from 1924 to 1928 and from
1931 to 1932; and as Attorney-General from 1928 to 1929 and from 1932 to
1936. He became Minister for the Co-ordination of Defence in 1936, and Secretary of State for Dominion Affairs in 1939 and again in 1940. He was Lord
Chancellor from 1939 to 1940, and Lord Chief Justice from 1940 to 1946.

out on his first flight to challenge the dragon in his lair. The intrepid initiative of Mr. Chamberlain, which fired the imagination of all Englishmen and appealed to their sense of sportsmanship,[a] took hold upon him also, and he waited anxiously for the Prime Minister's return. A letter in the King's own hand awaited Mr. Chamberlain on his arrival at the airport on the evening of September 16.[b]

MY DEAR PRIME MINISTER,

I am sending this letter to meet you on your return, as I had no opportunity of telling you before you left how much I admired your courage & wisdom in going to see Hitler in person. You must have been pleased by the universal approval with which your action was received. I am naturally very anxious to hear the result of your talk, & to be assured that there is a prospect of a peaceful solution on terms which admit of general acceptance. I realize how fatigued you must be after these two very strenuous days, but if it is possible for you to come & see me either this evening or tomorrow morning, at any time convenient to yourself, I need hardly say that I shall greatly welcome the opportunity of hearing your news.

Believe me,

Yours very sincerely,

GEORGE R.I.[23]

By 9.30 the same evening the Prime Minister was at Buckingham Palace, having previously met with the Cabinet. He told the King of his first momentous interview with Hitler, of his conviction that the Führer was not bluffing but was fully determined to settle the matter of the Sudetenland by force and at once, and that only the intervention of his visit had held up the invasion of Czechoslovakia. He had won a breathing-space of a week during which the French Government must be persuaded to face the situation squarely and the Czechs induced to accept the principle of self-determination in the Sudetenland.

[a] Mr. Chamberlain's journey to Berchtesgaden inspired the Poet Laureate to write the following poem, which appeared in *The Times* on September 16 1938:

> As Priam to Achilles for his son,
> So you, into the night, divinely led,
> To ask that young men's bodies, not yet dead,
> Be given from the battle not begun.

[b] The file copy of this letter in the Royal Archives is endorsed as follows: 'Letter written in my own hand to the Prime Minister on his return from seeing Hitler in Germany. G.R.I.'

The King was both distressed and perplexed at this news. 'Everything is in a maze', he wrote to Mr. Lascelles at Balmoral, on September 17, 'The Cabinet is always sitting, so no news. The French arrive to-morrow & if they won't stand up to Hitler how can we & the World must be told it is their fault and not ours.'

MM. Daladier and Bonnet duly arrived and within that fateful week there was evolved the 'Anglo-French Plan', which the Czechoslovak Government accepted under pressure and protest. It was with this that Mr. Chamberlain returned to Germany on September 22 for his second meeting with the Führer at Godesberg.

The Prime Minister was back in London on September 25, and on the following day he lunched with the King at Buckingham Palace. This time he was visibly more depressed. After his first German visit he could at least report the tactical success of time saved, but the second visit could only offer the story of great disillusionment and further intransigence. The Prime Minister told his Sovereign of his initial meeting with Herr Hitler at the Hotel Dreesen, at which he had been shocked to find that the Führer had gone back on his agreement of a week before and was now demanding an immediate German occupation of the Sudetenland as an essential preliminary to a plebiscite. He spoke of his own outburst of righteous wrath at such double-dealing; of the long vigil at the Hotel Petersburg on the other side of the Rhine, while communications passed to and from Godesberg; of the suspense as to whether Hitler would break off negotiations there and then; and, finally, of the glimmer of hope which had emerged from their last talk late on the night of the 23rd, when Hitler had agreed to extend until October 1 the date by which the predominantly German areas must be evacuated by Czechoslovak forces.

Now it was 'up to the Czechs', to whom a hideous choice of alternatives had been presented: either they accepted Hitler's terms and surrendered peacefully large tracts of their territory; or they resisted and their resistance would be crushed by the united forces of Germany, Poland and Hungary, before adequate assistance could reach them from their Allies. The prospect of war seemed very near; for if the Czechs chose the path of resistance it was almost certain that France

CONVERSATION PIECE AT THE ROYAL LODGE, WINDSOR, 1950
BY JAMES GUNN

would be compelled to implement the pledges of her treaty of alliance, and once France was at war with Germany it would be but a matter of time before Britain became involved.

Emergency measures began to operate. The Air Raid Precautions system was put on a war footing on September 25, and deep cellars and basements were commandeered for shelters. On the following day came the evacuation of school children to the country, and the clearing of hospitals for casualties, of which, the gloomy whisper went, fifty thousand were expected during the first few days. The population of London was registered and fitted for gas-masks, which were to be distributed later, and, as a result of the official exhortation of 'keep calm and dig', there appeared in the parks and gardens of the capital that system of 'slit trenches' which was supposed to give shelter from aerial bombardment. On the Horse Guards Parade and on Westminster Bridge single anti-aircraft guns were mounted, and lonely Spitfires patrolled the skies above the city.

To King George the seemingly relentless approach of war was fraught with horror. He yearned to offer some personal contribution to the efforts which Mr. Chamberlain was still making to divert the oncoming disaster. When the Prime Minister was received in audience on Monday September 26, the King reverted to the idea, which he had already put forward to Lord Halifax, of a personal appeal to Hitler, and showed to Mr. Chamberlain the draft of a telegram which he considered might strengthen the hand of Sir Horace Wilson [a] who was then in Berlin, in a last attempt to warn the Führer of the ineluctable consequences of the use of force. The Prime Minister, however, was not convinced that the time was yet propitious for such a *démarche*, and once again King George was disappointed.

The gravity of the international situation inevitably kept

---

[a] Sir Horace John Wilson, G.C.B., G.C.M.G., C.B.E. (b. 1882), entered the Civil Service in 1900 and became Principal Assistant Secretary to the Ministry of Labour, 1919–1921, and Permanent Secretary, 1921–1930. He was appointed Chief Industrial Adviser to the Government in 1930, and was seconded to the Treasury for special service with the Prime Minister in 1935. A trusted confidant of Mr. Chamberlain, Sir Horace Wilson became his *fidus Achates* in foreign affairs and accompanied him on his three historic visits to Germany in September 1938. He served as Permanent Secretary of the Treasury and Head of the Civil Service from 1939 to 1942.

the King in London, and he was thus prevented from accompanying the Queen to Clydeside for the launching on September 27 of her namesake, the great liner *Queen Elizabeth*. He did, however, send through her a message of exhortation to his people which expressed his own faith in them. To the listening masses of England the Queen's voice came clear and confident :

I have a message for you from the King. He bids the people of this country to be of good cheer, in spite of the dark clouds hanging over them and, indeed, over the whole world. He knows well that, as ever before in critical times, they will keep cool heads and brave hearts; he knows, too, that they will place entire confidence in their leaders who, under God's providence, are striving their utmost to find a just and peaceful solution of the grave problems which confront them.

In ever-increasing anxiety the King followed each move in the desperate battle for peace as it was reported from No. 10 Downing Street.

The latest news is this : [he wrote to Queen Mary on the evening of the 27th]. The Prime Minister has just sent a telegram to Hitler & Beneš suggesting that they should get into touch with each other & to propose that Hitler should occupy Asch & Egerland on Oct. 1st. That an International Commn. should then arrange for the rest to be handed over peacefully by Oct. 10th.

Beneš has been told, as he well knows, that his country will be overwhelmed anyhow, & that it would be wise for him to take this course.

If Hitler refuses to do this then we shall know once & for all that he is a *madman*.

It is all so worrying this awful waiting for the worst to happen.[24]

This had been Mr. Chamberlain's last act before making his historic broadcast on the evening of September 27, and the King's first reaction to the news was to reiterate his offer to send a personal telegram to Hitler. But Mr. Chamberlain, who had by this time received Sir Horace Wilson's report of his acrimonious interview with the Führer that afternoon, feared that things had now gone too far, and that in his present mood Hitler might send and publish an insulting reply to the King which would merely add fuel to the flames. In the face of these arguments King George then finally abandoned his project.

It may be imagined with what emotions the King listened to the broadcast of the Prime Minister when, his world in ashes and deathly tired, Mr. Chamberlain told briefly of his journeys to Germany; his efforts for peace; his horror of war and his readiness to make yet a third visit to the Führer if he thought that by this means peace might be preserved; and finally, of the measures taken for the nation's defence. It was a speech of tragedy and weariness, but also of hope not quite abandoned, and it stirred the King's compassion. At its close he caused a message of warm sympathy and congratulation to be conveyed to the Prime Minister.

Later that night Mr. Chamberlain received from Hitler the letter which gave him the hope that all chance for the salvation of peace was not lost and which caused him to make his final appeal to Mussolini for the Duce's personal intervention with the Führer.

The effect of this approach was not known, however, when 'Black Wednesday', September 28, dawned over London and Paris. Men and women woke with the eerie feeling that this was 'the last day' and that by tomorrow night their homes might be in flames. In Paris they were fighting for seats on the trains, and the roads out of the city were choked with traffic; in London they were digging trenches.

The King held a Privy Council that morning to confirm by Royal Proclamation the preparations already begun — the mobilization of the Fleet, which Mr. Chamberlain had ordered on his own initiative, and the calling-up of the Auxiliary Air Force — and to declare a State of Emergency giving the Government the appropriate powers. His Majesty was informed of the latest steps taken and of the slender chance of peace which might result from the approaches being made that morning in Berlin; but for the moment there was nothing that he or his subjects could do but to wait impatiently for the final answer.

Relief from suspense did not come until the moment that afternoon when to the Prime Minister, in the midst of his narrative to the House of Commons of his efforts for peace, was handed a paper containing Herr Hitler's invitation to a Four-Power Conference at Munich on the following day.

That scene in the House and its sequel have become

historic. The relief from suspense, the gratitude for life preserved, the joy at the reprieve of peace — for none doubted that peace was now assured — found abundant utterance from the King's own heart. When on September 30 the Prime Minister returned in triumph from Munich to Heston and waved to the cheering crowds the text of the Agreement for Anglo-German Friendship, which he had signed with Hitler after the Pact of Munich, he found awaiting him a Royal welcome.

I am sending this letter by my Lord Chamberlain [a] [wrote the King], to ask you if you will come straight to Buckingham Palace, so that I can express to you personally my most heartfelt congratulations on the success of your visit to Munich.

In the meantime this letter brings the warmest of welcomes to one who by his patience and determination has earned the lasting gratitude of his fellow countrymen throughout the Empire.[25]

The Prime Minister obeyed the King's command and, with Their Majesties and Mrs. Chamberlain, appeared on the balcony of Buckingham Palace to receive the grateful plaudits of the men and women of London — and far wider afield — who believed with him that he had brought home 'Peace with Honour'.

Yesterday was a great day [the King wrote enthusiastically to Queen Mary]. The Prime Minister was delighted with the result of his mission, as we all are, & he had a great ovation when he came here.[26]

Like many of his subjects, the King viewed with delight the prospect of being able to resume his summer holiday which had been interrupted by the spectre of war. 'We may be returning to Balmoral tomorrow night', he wrote to his mother. 'I am hearing from the P.M. at lunch time today. He told us yesterday he could see no reason why we should not go. It will give us a fortnight there.' [27] And indeed, after

---

[a] Rt. Hon. George Herbert Hyde Villiers, sixth Earl of Clarendon, K.G., G.C.M.G., G.C.V.O., Royal Victorian Chain (1877–1955), served as Chief Conservative Whip in the House of Lords, 1922–1925, and as Chairman of the British Broadcasting Corporation, 1927–1930. In 1931 he was appointed Governor-General of the Union of South Africa, where he remained until 1937, and the following year became Lord Chamberlain of His Majesty's Household for the remainder of King George VI's reign.

the acute tension and nervous strain of the past two weeks, he was badly in need of rest.

But before he left on the night of Sunday, October 2, he issued to his peoples a message of sober thanksgiving and gratitude :

The time of anxiety is past, and we have been able to-day to offer our thanks to the Almighty for His Mercy in sparing us the horrors of war.

I would like now to thank the men and women of this country for their calm resolve during these critical days, and for the readiness with which they responded to the different calls made upon them.

After the magnificent efforts of the Prime Minister in the cause of peace, it is my fervent hope that a new era of friendship and prosperity may be dawning among the peoples of the world.

(iii)

Mr. Chamberlain would have been more than human if, in the first flush of his triumph, when every hour brought him fresh evidence of the gratitude and acclaim of his countrymen, and of the admiration of the world, he had not believed in the stability of what he had achieved at Munich. The supplication of the nations had been offered in his support; the thankfulness of the world was his in his success. 'The knowledge of all the heartfelt prayers that were going up for the success of my efforts has helped to sustain me in the terrible hours through which I have passed', he wrote to the Archbishop of Canterbury on October 2. 'I am sure that some day the Czechs will see that what we did was to save them for a happier future. And I sincerely hope that we have opened the way to that general appeasement which alone can save the world from chaos.' 28

It was almost immediately apparent, however, that, though the gratitude of Mr. Chamberlain's countrymen for their preservation from war was ·deeply sincere, there were many among them who were critical of the means by which this preservation had been achieved ; and more especially of the way in which the Czech Government had been compelled to make sacrifices for the salvation of the rest of Europe.

Mr. Duff Cooper[a] resigned from the Cabinet on October 2 and, in the debate in the House of Commons which opened on the following day, though the Prime Minister received the endorsement of the House,[b] his policy was caustically criticized not only by the Labour Opposition but by members of his own party.[c]

Though King George was staunch in his support of Mr. Chamberlain, he was ever fair and just in his judgment. Mr. Duff Cooper records that when he went to surrender his seals of office the King was 'frank and charming. He said he could not agree with me, but he respected those who had the courage of their convictions.'[29] As the debate proceeded, however, the King may be believed to have been in greater sympathy with the feelings of Queen Mary, who wrote:

> I am sure you feel as angry as I do at people croaking as they do at the P.M.'s action, for once I agree with Ly. Oxford who is said to have exclaimed as she left the H. of Commons yesterday, 'He brought home Peace, why can't they be grateful' — It is always so easy for people to criticise when they do not know the ins and outs of the question.[30]

By the time the King returned from Balmoral on October 18 much of the elation of three weeks before had subsided, and the Munich Agreement had begun to appear in clearer perspective. 'You have everything in your own hands now — for a time — and you can do anything you like. Use that time well, for it won't last,' had been the advice of Lord Baldwin to his successor in congratulating him on his return

---

[a] Rt. Hon. Alfred Duff Cooper, first Viscount Norwich, G.C.M.G., D.S.O. (1890–1954), served as Financial Secretary to the War Office, 1928–1929 and 1931–1934, and Financial Secretary to the Treasury, 1934–1935. He entered the Cabinet as Secretary of State for War in 1935 and became First Lord of the Admiralty in 1937. During the Second World War Mr. Duff Cooper became successively Minister of Information, 1940–1941; Chancellor of the Duchy of Lancaster, 1941–1943; Representative of H.M. Government with the French Committee of National Liberation, 1943–1944; and Ambassador in Paris, 1944–1947.

[b] The vote in support of Mr. Chamberlain's policy was 366 to 144.

[c] After the resignation of Mr. Eden the dissident Tories were divided into two groups: the followers of Mr. Churchill, consisting of Mr. Brendan Bracken and Mr. Robert Boothby; and the followers of Mr. Eden, comprising about twenty members, including Lord Cranborne, Sir Sidney Herbert, Mr. Harold Macmillan and Mr. Richard Law; Mr. Duncan Sandys acted as liaison officer between the two groups, attending the meetings of both. Both groups abstained from voting in the 'Munich division'.

from Munich,[31] and it is true that, in certain respects, Mr. Chamberlain took this advice to heart. He had received other advice as well. Driving back to London from Heston on that great and exalted afternoon of September 30, Lord Halifax had offered the Prime Minister two items of counsel : first, that, if pressed by the Conservative Central Office to exploit his present overwhelming popularity to have a 'snap' General Election, he should refuse ; and secondly, that he should now take the action he had intended to take should war have come, and reconstitute his Cabinet as a truly National Government by bringing into it such outstanding Conservative figures as Mr. Churchill, Mr. Eden and Lord Cranborne, thereby strengthening its character.

Mr. Chamberlain had accepted the first of these points of guidance at once, but had postponed decision on the other until he had had time for further thought. He had subsequently weighed it together with all the other concomitants of the new situation created by the Munich Agreement and had made up his mind as to how to proceed. When, therefore, he was received in audience on October 19 he was able to give the King the general outline of the policy which His Majesty's Government would pursue in the immediate future.

King George was deeply interested and, as was his wont when his interest was aroused, he made notes of the discussion in his own hand which were later put into memorandum form by his Private Secretary. On this occasion the record ran as follows : [32]

The P.M. agreed with The King that the future policy must be the cultivation of friendly relations combined with intensified rearmament. One must be strong in order to negotiate. At times the old diplomacy fails, and personal interviews with dictators are called for. It was essential that Cabinet should be united and back him up in this new foreign policy. He was determined to get more aeroplanes, better A.R.P., and some kind of National Register. With regard to the latter there are thousands of difficulties, e.g. if a man lives in Croydon and works in London, where can he do the best work ?

The U.S.A. must be left alone. They will never take a more active line if we preach at them. Cordell Hull's [a] policy is to bring

[a] Hon. Cordell Hull (1871–1955), Secretary of State in President Roosevelt's first three Administrations, 1933–1943.

U.S.A. into line with us, but the Trade Agreement is more than we can swallow as it stands. With regard to Russia, it was significant that neither France nor Russia ever asked each other any questions during the crisis. The P.M. considered that it was better to leave the Soviets alone.

As for the Anglo-Italian Agreement, the Cabinet were engaged in considering the matter now.

As regards reconstruction of the Cabinet on a broader basis, the Opposition might help in producing armaments, but would criticize the P.M.'s foreign policy as being a paradox to rearmament programme. Opposition would be kept fully informed, in confidence, of what policy the Government were pursuing.[a]

The formation of a Ministry of National Service or Supply was also discussed, but the Prime Minister thought that it was undesirable except in war-time, and would upset the manufacturers who were just settling down to production of armaments.[b] The manufacturers had a horror of government interference.

In the Balkans, the Cabinet had approved of the purchase of Roumanian wheat. One had to be careful in this matter to anticipate what effect a transaction with one country would be likely to have on another country. The King expressed the hope that something could be done for Greece.

The Prime Minister agreed that Runciman and Newton both deserved rewards in the New Year's Honours List.[c]

From this exposition it was evident to the King that his Government proposed to pursue the dual policy of intensified rearmament and renewed efforts at appeasement. The success of the second was recognized as being dependent upon the first, since both the Sovereign and his Prime Minister were agreed that, in order to gain the maximum from the new *détente* created by the Munich Agreement, Britain must be in a position to negotiate from strength and not from weakness. Satisfied with this prospect and fully in sympathy with his Ministers, King George turned again to the details of his own routine.

Almost at once, however, there was demonstrated the

[a] Mr. Chamberlain's only effort in the direction of broadening his Government was to invite Lord Samuel, the Liberal Leader, to join the Cabinet, on October 25, as Lord Privy Seal. The offer was declined.

[b] The decision to set up a Ministry of Supply was announced in the House of Commons on April 20, 1939. Mr. Leslie Burgin, a National Liberal, became the first Minister.

[c] Mr. Basil Newton, who had served as British Minister in Prague throughout the Czech Crisis, received a K.C.M.G.

difficulty, from the point of view of public opinion, of reconciling in one policy the claim of 'Peace in Our Time' with the necessity of further preparations for possible national emergency. On the morrow of Munich the British Government had decided to issue an appeal to the people of Britain for voluntary national service in time of need, and a booklet was prepared for circulation in the New Year to every home in the United Kingdom, giving details of the various forms this service might take. The King and the Prime Minister, after consultation with the various members of the Cabinet most closely concerned, agreed that this new effort to arouse fresh interest and initiative in national service would receive added importance if it were inaugurated by King George himself in a national broadcast. The full agreement of the Government and of the leaders of the Labour and Liberal Parties had been obtained by the end of October, the date of the broadcast had been set and the text of the King's speech prepared.

It was at this point that a hitch occurred. The Prime Minister had also consulted the Governor of the Bank of England, Sir Montagu Norman,[a] and the Chief Press Liaison Officer of the Government, Mr. George Steward,[b] both of whom had expressed alarm at the idea of the King's broadcast. It was feared that so momentous a statement by the Sovereign would be interpreted as meaning that war was imminent and the Governor of the Bank went so far as to say that it might well lead to a slump on the Stock Exchange. Neither Mr. Chamberlain nor his colleagues shared these views, but they felt that they could not take the responsibility of advising the King to ignore them. They therefore tendered the advice that a broadcast by the King should not be made and that the drive for voluntary national service should be launched instead by the Prime Minister.[c][33]

A State Visit on N vember 15–18 of King Carol of Rumania

[a] Montagu Collet, first Baron Norman, D.S.O. (1871–1950), was Governor of the Bank of England from 1920 to 1944.

[b] George Frederick Steward, C.V.O., C.B.E. (1884–1952), passed from journalism into Government service during the First World War. He served first with the Minister of Information and later with the News Department of the Foreign Office, being transferred to the Prime Minister's Secretariat in 1931. He was appointed Chief Press Liaison Officer of the Government in 1937, retiring in 1944.

[c] The Prime Minister made his broadcast on January 23, 1939.

and the Crown Prince Michael *a* gave King George the opportunity of learning at first hand the current situation of Balkan
politics and the repercussions in that area of the Czech Crisis,
which had resulted in the virtual dissolution of the Little
Entente, formed in the early 'twenties as an alliance between
Czechoslovakia, Yugoslavia and Rumania; and this information the King found of advantage in discussions with his
Ministers, who did not in all cases share King Carol's
apprehensions regarding Nazi designs upon South-Eastern
Europe.

Scarcely had the Rumanian monarch departed when King
George was saddened by the death of his aunt, the Queen of
Norway, *b* in a London nursing home on November 20. Queen
Maud had been a favourite daughter of King Edward VII,
who had bought for her, on her marriage, a house at Appleton,
hard by the main estate of Sandringham. Here she had
lived for much of her married life before the election of her
husband to the throne of Norway, and thereafter she continued to return on regular visits, for, though she had acquired
a great devotion to her adopted country, her love for England
remained very strong. King George sincerely mourned the
death of his aunt, for whom he had entertained a warm
affection. With King Haakon he followed the coffin from
Marlborough House to Victoria Station, on the first stage of

a Crown Prince Michael, the only son of King Carol II of Rumania (1893–
1953) and Queen Helen, was born in 1921. Before the death of King Ferdinand
in 1927 Prince Carol had been exiled from Rumania and had formally renounced
his rights of succession. Prince Michael therefore succeeded his grandfather, at
the age of six, under a Council of Regency. In 1930, however, Prince Carol took
advantage of the political complications in Rumania to make a dramatic return
by air to his country where, displacing his son, he was acknowledged as King.
In 1940 the Rumanian dictator, Marshal Antonescu, compelled King Carol to
abdicate and Prince Michael became King for the second time. Having dis-
lodged the pro-Nazi régime of Antonescu by a personally directed *coup d'état* in
August 1944, King Michael brought his country over from the Axis alliance to
the side of the Allies. Rumania was, however, oc pied by Soviet troops who
secured the establishment of a Communist régime in 946, and King Michael was
in his turn compelled to abdicate on December 30 1947. He married Princess
Anne of Bourbon-Parma in 1948.

b Queen Maud (1869–1938) was the third and youngest daughter of King
Edward VII and Queen Alexandra. She married in 1896 Prince Charles of
Denmark (1872–1957), who in 1905, after the dissolution of the union of Norway
and Sweden, was elected King of Norway and assumed the name of Haakon VII.
There was one child of the marriage, Crown Prince Olav (b. 1903), who in 1929
married Princess Marthe of Sweden (d. 1954), and succeeded his father as Olav V
in 1957.

its journey to Norway,ᵃ and sent the Duke of Kent to represent him at the funeral on December 8 at Oslo.

Christmas that year at Sandringham was a happy family affair. There was relief in the thought that war had been averted during the past year, and a merciful ignorance of the tragedy which was to overwhelm the world some nine months later. There was no Christmas broadcast. With his deep dislike of the microphone, the King had no intention of continuing his father's annual custom of addressing his peoples at this season, and was only persuaded to do so later under the compulsion of public duty.

The New Year opened with painstaking if fruitless efforts on the part of the British Government to extend and deepen the spirit of co-operation which, it was believed, had been engendered at Munich. The Spanish Civil War still presented a continuing danger, and the anti-Jewish pogroms, which took place in Germany in November in revenge for the murder by a half-witted refugee of a Secretary in the German Embassy in Paris, sent a shudder of horror throughout the civilized world. Moreover Italy had adopted an attitude of hostility towards France in countenancing the publicly expressed demand for the cession of Tunis, Corsica and Nice. On the other hand, France and Germany had signed, on December 8, a Declaration of Friendship, in counterpart to that which Mr. Chamberlain had signed at Munich, and the Prime Minister believed that nothing could be lost and perhaps something gained by establishing personal contact with the Duce.

Preliminary steps had already been taken. In the first week of November the British Government had announced that the Anglo-Italian Agreement concluded in April, after Mr. Eden's resignation, should come immediately into force, and to this Parliament had consented. Shortly thereafter King George, ever anxious to help in the cause of peace and a believer in direct communication between Heads of States, suggested that he should write a personal letter to King Victor Emmanuel expressing his satisfaction at the restoration of good relations between their two countries. This suggestion,

---

ᵃ Others who followed in the procession on November 23 were Crown Prince Olav, the King of the Hellenes, the Prince Regent of Yugoslavia and the Dukes of Gloucester and Kent.

though welcomed in principle by the King's advisers, was felt
to be somewhat premature and they considered that it would
be wiser to postpone carrying it out until the results of the
Agreement could be more clearly discerned. With this view
the King concurred,ª and welcomed the idea of a meeting of
his Prime Minister and his Foreign Secretary with Mussolini.[35]

So to Rome Mr. Chamberlain and Lord Halifax went on
January 11 for a four-day visit. They found Mussolini emphatic
in his assurances that he wanted peace and was prepared to
use his influence to maintain it, and the impression was
conveyed that in any Anglo-German dispute Italy hoped to
remain neutral. What particularly impressed the Prime
Minister were the crowds who thronged the streets and country
level-crossings to see him and who made no secret of their
desire for peace. This alone, he felt, had made the journey
worth while.

Though some of those with Mr. Chamberlain had found
the Duce curt and even discourteous at times, this was certainly
not the picture which the Prime Minister gave the King on
his return to London. 'Both Halifax and I were favourably
impressed with Mussolini', he reported. 'Talking with him
is a much pleasanter affair than with Hitler. You feel you
are dealing with a reasonable man, not a fanatic, and he
struck us both as straightforward and sincere in what he said.
Moreover he has a sense of humour which occasionally breaks
out in an attractive smile, whereas it would take a long surgical
operation to get a joke into Hitler's head.' [36]

I am glad that you found Mussolini was easier to talk to than
Hitler was in Munich. [The King replied from Sandringham.]
Your reception by the Italian people must have pleased you, apart
from the official side of the visit.
Although nothing concrete has come out of it, in the way of

_____

ª After the opening of the Norwegian campaign in April 1940, King George
again reverted to his suggestion of a personal approach to King Victor Emmanuel.
This time the proposal went further than before and the King actually wrote
and signed a letter dated April 22. Its dispatch, however, was left to the discretion
of the Prime Minister and the Cabinet. Their considered opinion was that the
effect of the letter in Rome might be to give the impression that there existed in
London anxiety as to Italian policy, and this, it was felt, would be unfortunate.
The King's letter, which had got as far as Paris for transmission in the diplomatic
bag to Rome, was therefore not sent and was returned to His Majesty, who said
that he 'quite understood'.[34]

pacts etc., I am sure that your visit has done good in the way of personal contact with Mussolini & Ciano.[37]

Alas, however, for the hopes of those who had trusted in the Way of Appeasement as a means for the preservation of peace. Hitler, cheated by the very liberality of the Munich terms of the fulfilment of his basic and primitive desire to destroy utterly the Czechs, had not ceased to plot and plan the disruption and ultimate disintegration of the rump of Czechoslovakia, which had been guaranteed by Britain and France under the Munich Agreement. His earliest moves toward this end had been taken in October 1938, and by March 1939 the seeds of propaganda and treason sown among the Czechs and Slovaks and Ruthenians were ready to bear fruit. In the first week of March the Ruthenian and Slovak autonomist leaders fled to the Reich to beseech the Führer to authorize their declarations of independence from the central government at Prague. The independence of both territories was proclaimed on March 14 and in the small hours of the morning of the 15th the miserable Czech President, Dr. Hácha, hastily summoned to Berlin, was submitted to an ordeal to which the agony that Schuschnigg had endured at Berchtesgaden was as nothing; he finally succumbed to the pressure of physical force and agreed to place the remnant of his country under German protection. By the evening of March 15 the Führer was in Prague and from the Hradschin Castle, the palace of the Kings of Bohemia, he issued to the German people the proclamation that 'Czechoslovakia has ceased to exist'.

In a matter of days, almost of hours, the Munich Agreement had been contemptuously torn up by the Führer and the doctrine of appeasement mocked and flouted. All that Mr. Chamberlain had sought to achieve, all that he had hoped to attain, was at one stroke rendered null and void. The mask was off; the deceit of the Führer was no longer covert. The promises that he had made of desiring none but Germans within the German Reich were now demonstrably false and perfidious. The full aim of his ambition was exposed in all its shamelessness.

To Mr. Chamberlain the shock was very great. On

March 10 he had announced publicly, 'the outlook in international affairs is tranquil'; a week later at Birmingham, on March 17, he was to denounce Hitler as a perjurer. The Prime Minister would not recant on Munich. He still believed, and rightly, that what he had done at that time had saved the world from war; he accepted none of the strictures of his critics. But the record of Hitler's broken pledges was now manifest to him and he did not hesitate to warn the Führer that while there was hardly anything that he would not sacrifice for peace, 'there is one thing that I must except, and that is the liberty that we have enjoyed for hundreds of years, and which we would never surrender'. Henceforth there must be resistance to aggression.

To King George, as he listened to the Prime Minister's speech on the wireless, there came a feeling of sympathy for the disappointment and indignation, the outraged righteous wrath, which was manifest in it. He knew how dearly Mr. Chamberlain had hoped to substantiate peace in Europe, and how great the obloquy which he had incurred in his efforts to do so. He shared to the full his Prime Minister's disillusionment, and he was moved next day to send him a message of condolence and of encouragement.

I feel I must send you one line to say how well I can appreciate your feelings about the recent behaviour of the German Government.

Although this blow to your courageous efforts on behalf of peace & understanding in Europe must, I am afraid, cause you deep distress, I am sure that your labours have been anything but wasted, for they can have left no doubt in the minds of ordinary people all over the world of our love of peace & of our readiness to discuss with any nation whatever grievances they think they have.[38]

Well might the Führer beware the danger of arousing 'the fury of a patient man'.[a]

    [a] 'Beware the fury of a patient man.'—John Dryden, *Absalom and Achitophel*.

CHAPTER IV

THE APPROACH OF WAR
MARCH–SEPTEMBER 1939

(i)

I N a period so crowded with great events as the reign of King George VI it is possible that the importance of the British Diplomatic Revolution of the spring of 1939 may not receive its just emphasis. It was, in point of fact, of immense significance, since it marked a reappraisal of that ancient principle of British foreign policy, namely that Britain would oppose with force the establishment of a hegemony of any one great Power upon the continent of Europe. In defence of this principle Britain had, through the centuries, fought the Spanish, Dutch, French and Germans ; and in pursuit of this principle Britain had become a guarantor of Belgian neutrality in 1839 and of the Western Locarno Pact in 1925. But beyond this principle she had refused to go, claiming for herself a strict right of its interpretation. By this means it was as possible for Lord Salisbury to reconcile 'splendid isolation' with the traditional fundamentals of British foreign policy as it was for Lord Lansdowne to square the *Entente Cordiale*. The chief difficulty confronting other European states was the uncertainty as to when the angel which every so often troubled the waters of the British conscience would pay his next visit to those deep and unplumbed pools, and there are many who hold that this failure to make clear in advance, and beyond peradventure, the attitude of Britain had been a material factor both in the outbreak of the First World War and in the achievement by Adolf Hitler of his 'peaceful victories'. Others have maintained that by not formally aligning herself Britain had contributed to the cause of peace, because no potential aggressor could be certain that he would *not* be confronted by an outraged British Commonwealth.

The recondite nature of her foreign policy had been of

particular salience in Britain's relations with France in the years between the wars. Ever since the failure of the still-born Anglo-American guarantee to France of 1920, Britain had made it clear to her chief European ally that, whereas she was prepared to give her full support in the event of unprovoked aggression by Germany against her or against Belgium, she was not prepared to join with France in guarantee-ing those military and political satellites in Central, Eastern and South-Eastern Europe with whom the French had entered into pacts and agreements of mutual assistance. It was on this rock that the several efforts of MM. Briand and Poincaré to achieve an Anglo-French alliance had foundered in 1922 ; it was the staunch adherence of Britain to this same tenet of policy which had nearly rendered abortive the negotiations for a pact of Western European Security in 1925 and had resulted in her incurring obligations to France, Belgium and Germany only and not to Poland and Czechoslovakia; and when in 1936, after the *débâcle* of the Locarno Treaty System, Britain renewed her pledges to France and to Belgium, it was on the same terms and in consonance with the same principle.

This steadfast devotion to the precept of strictly limited liabilities, and of keeping as close a control as possible over the decision as to when and why to go to war, was inherent not only in Britain's foreign policy but also in her relations with the other nations of the British Commonwealth. From the days of the Paris Peace Conference onwards the various govern-ments of the Dominions had evinced the greatest anxiety lest they should again be involved in war as a result of a decision in Westminster. At the time of the Chanak Incident in 1922,[a] when war seemed imminent, the Empire had been far from united, and certain of its component parts had made it abun-dantly clear that they did not feel themselves bound by obliga-

[a] In September 1922 the forces of the newly awakened Turkish Nationalist Movement under Kemal Pasha defeated the Greek Army decisively in Asia Minor, sacked and burned Smyrna and advanced upon Constantinople and Chanak. On September 16 the British Government informed the Governors-General of Canada, Australia, New Zealand and South Africa that, in agreement with the governments of France and Italy, the Commander-in-Chief of the Allied Army of the Black Sea had been instructed to resist aggression upon Europe by the Turks. The response of the Dominion Governments was alarmingly cool and it was fortunate that the courage and diplomacy of General Sir Charles Harington succeeded in bringing about the Armistice of Mudania on October 11.

tions incurred by the Government of the United Kingdom, nor compelled to take automatic action in the event of Britain becoming involved in war as a result of these obligations. This attitude had been implicitly reaffirmed three years later in relation to the Locarno Treaties, and His Majesty's Government in Westminster, therefore, became the more allergic to any extension, or indeed to any unnecessary clarification, of their existing liabilities.

In the months which had preceded the Munich Crisis Mr. Chamberlain — with the Commonwealth Governments in mind — had illustrated this point of view very vividly. On March 24, 1938 — less than a fortnight after the German annexation of Austria — in the course of a survey before the House of Commons of Britain's obligations abroad,[1] the Prime Minister said that it had been suggested that Britain should give forthwith an assurance that she would immediately come with all her power to the support of France in the event of the French being called upon, as a result of German aggression, to implement their pledges to Czechoslovakia; it had also been suggested that Britain should at once declare her own readiness to defend Czechoslovakia against unprovoked aggression, and should take the lead in inviting other nations to associate themselves with such a declaration. His Majesty's Government, said the Prime Minister, was not prepared to agree to either of these proposals, nor 'to any proposals which might result in Britain finding herself in a position where the decision to go to war should be automatically removed from the discretion of the Government'.

A more unequivocal restatement of the traditional British attitude could scarcely be desired, and although, as the Czech Crisis developed, it became increasingly apparent that, willy-nilly, the chances of Britain's remaining uninvolved in a war which developed out of the French honouring their treaty obligations to the Czechs were tenuous in the extreme, and although at Munich Britain had accepted participation in the guarantee of the truncated Czechoslovak State, this remained the basic principle of British foreign policy until the morrow of the day, a year later, on which German tanks rumbled into Prague.

The monumental and criminal folly of Adolf Hitler in

gratuitously tearing up the Munich Agreement had no greater historical result than the convincing of Mr. Chamberlain that German promises were not to be relied upon. The date of his conversion can be pin-pointed as March 16, 1939 — 'He [Hitler] finds it so easy to tear up treaties and throw overboard assurances, that no one can find any confidence in new ones', he wrote later [2] — and though, in his Birmingham speech of March 17, he explicitly omitted from British obligations any 'new unspecified commitments operating under conditions which cannot be foreseen', he was rapidly moving to a complete reversal of his previous policy.

For Hitler's malfeasance did not cease with the destruction of Czechoslovakia. On March 21 he made his first demands upon Poland for the retrocession of Danzig and the solution of the issue of the Polish Corridor, and, on the same day, compelled the Lithuanian Government to re-cede to Germany the territory of Memel. As if for good measure of proof of the general preference of the Axis Powers for a policy of aggression, Mussolini annexed Albania on April 7, Good Friday.

Mr. Chamberlain's reaction to this new outbreak of aggression was immediate and timely, for, as he later told the House of Commons, 'We did not know that Poland might not be invaded within a term which could be measured by hours and not by days'.[3] The occasion of a return State Visit to London by the President of the French Republic and Mme Lebrun on March 21–24 provided an opportunity for first-hand consultation with M. Georges Bonnet, who accompanied them as Minister in Attendance, and it was now that Mr. Chamberlain took his initial steps in the new policy for Great Britain.

The Prime Minister's first idea was for a four-Power declaration by Britain, France, the Soviet Union and Poland, as to their common attitude towards aggression. This was accepted by the French and Russian Governments but was rejected by Poland, who refused to be associated in any semblance of combination with Moscow. The Polish Government asked for an 'immediate' bilateral non-aggression treaty with Britain to supplement her already existing treaty with France, and it was in response to this request that Mr.

Chamberlain made his momentous statement in the House of Commons on March 31 :

In the event of any action which already threatened Polish independence, and which the Polish Government accordingly considered it vital to resist with national forces, His Majesty's Government would feel themselves bound at once to lend the Polish Government all support in their power. . . . I may add that the French Government have authorized me to make it plain that they stand in the same position as does His Majesty's Government.[4]

Never since the Diplomatic Revolution of 1756, by which Austria forsook her ancient alliance with Britain for that of her traditional enemy France, and Britain became the ally of Prussia, had there been so complete a reversal of British foreign policy. The decision to go to war — that independence of action which had been so jealously guarded by Britain for generations, and the limitation of which Mr. Chamberlain himself had refused to concede to France only a year before — had been placed unreservedly in the hands of a foreign power. For the first time in centuries Britain had given an unequivocal guarantee of automatic action. She had made her future in peace and war dependent upon the willingness of Poland to resist aggression. And not of Poland alone ; within a month the buckler of the Anglo-French unilateral guarantee had been extended on the same conditions first to Greece and Rumania (Ail 13), and then to Denmark, the Netherlands and Switzerland.[a] 'In a moment, in the twinkling of an eye', Britain had proclaimed that she stood four-square against the tempests of aggression.

Mr. Chamberlain's aim in offering thus liberally the Anglo-French Guarantee was not to trail his coat before the Axis Powers. 'I am no more a man of war today than I was in September', he told the House of Commons ; nor was it to present to the Dictators an intransigent front at every point — 'What we are concerned with', he wrote in his diary, 'is not

---

[a] The British unilateral guarantee to Poland was transformed into a reciprocal bilateral agreement on April 6, during the visit of Colonel Beck to London. Both Switzerland and the Netherlands, fearing that the Anglo-French offer of a guarantee would impair their traditional neutrality, declined it. Denmark accepted it, but in an effort to appease Hitler, signed a non-aggression pact with Germany on May 31. Greece and Rumania accepted unreservedly.

the boundaries of States, but attacks on their independence.'
The settlement of outstanding differences by means of peaceful
change was still his desire, but the interpretation of the term
'peaceful' must be one which did not include the connotations
of pressure, force and blackmail. It was the Prime Minister's
belief and hope that, as a result of the Anglo-French Guarantee,
two things would happen; first, that the Dictators might
abandon the tactics of aggression in the exercise of their
national policies, and secondly, that any smaller state which
entered into negotiations with Germany or Italy could do
so with a greater sense of security and assurance. The
keynote of the new British policy was not one of encircle-
ment but of self-defence against any threat to integrity and
independence.

That the attitude of Britain towards aggression might not
appear a gesture empty and without meaning, Mr. Chamberlain made a second revolutionary decision. On April 27 he
announced that, for the first time in the history of the country,
His Majesty's Government proposed to introduce compulsory
military service in time of peace. The House approved the
proposal by 376 votes to 145, but, owing mainly to the persistent opposition of the Labour Party, the Military Training
Bill did not pass its Third Reading before May 18.

Of prime importance in assessing this new initiative in
British foreign policy is the unifying effect which it had upon
the British public. At the time of Munich the country had
been divided. There would have been no united support for
war with Germany and grave opposition would have been
encountered from the Dominion Governments. This disunity
at home persisted until the German annexation of Czechoslovakia indicated clearly the impossibility of reliance upon
Hitler's pledged word. Thereafter the reactions of the great
majority of the supporters of Mr. Chamberlain's policy of
appeasement were those of the Prime Minister himself, namely
a conviction that a halt must be called to the Dictators' strategy
of aggression. This brought them into line — though not
always to reconciliation — with those critics of the Munich
policy who had held this view for some time longer. The
country, however, became united as it had not been for a
number of years, and its only anxiety was that the reality and

sincerity of the new departure in British policy should be understood and appreciated abroad, by friend and foe alike.

The riposte of the Dictators to the new British policy was not encouraging to Mr. Chamberlain's hopes for its success. On April 28 Hitler denounced simultaneously both the German-Polish Non-Aggression Treaty of 1934 and the Anglo-German Naval Agreement of 1935, and thereafter Germany and Italy entered into a military and political 'Pact of Steel' which identified their acts and policies very closely. Nevertheless Mr. Chamberlain continued to hope and to believe that the Führer now meditated no new and immediate move, and that some degree of deterrent might even have been provided. Thus persuaded, he took the responsibility of advising King George and Queen Elizabeth to carry out the plans which had been made for their journey to Canada and the United States in May.

(ii)

For the origins of the North American visit of the King and Queen, it is necessary to go back to the summer of 1937. Mr. Mackenzie King [a] arrived in London for the Coronation with the firm intention of gaining at least preliminary approval for a Royal visit to Canada. This ambition Mr. King had previously confided to his friend President Franklin D. Roosevelt, who instructed his special envoy, Mr. James Gerard,[b] to suggest to the King that if he went to Canada he should include a visit to Washington in his itinerary. Both proposals were cordially received; the idea of a Canadian tour was accepted in principle, and the King told Mr. Gerard that he would be delighted to accept President Roosevelt's invitation.[5]

---

[a] Rt. Hon. William Lyon Mackenzie King, O.M., C.M.G. (1874–1950), a veteran Canadian statesman, and grandson of that William Lyon Mackenzie who, in 1836, led an armed insurrection against the British authorities in Canada. Mr. King was leader of the Liberal Party from 1919 to 1948, and Prime Minister of the Dominion from 1921 to 1930 and from 1935 to 1948.

[b] Hon. James Watson Gerard, Hon. G.C.B. (1867–1951), was American Ambassador in Germany from 1913 until the entry of the United States into the First World War in 1917. His two books, *My Four Years in Germany* (1917) and *Face to Face with Kaiserism* (1918), had an important effect on the war-time thinking of the American people. Mr. Gerard represented the President of the United States at the Coronation of King George VI.

The visit to Canada was tentatively arranged for 1939, but its early planning was imperilled by the tension of the Czech Crisis in the previous summer, which caused both the King and his advisers to doubt the wisdom — or indeed the possibility — of proceeding with it. They sought the counsel of the Governor-General, Lord Tweedsmuir,[a] who added his pleading to that of Mr. King, urging that the idea of a visit by Their Majesties should not be abandoned unless the international situation were so threatening as to preclude all possibility. With some courage, therefore, the decision to proceed with the plans was taken, and when the Canadian Prime Minister met President Roosevelt at the dedication of the International Bridge at the Thousand Islands on August 18, 1938, it was with the news that the King and Queen would in all probability visit Canada in the following year.[6]

Mr. Roosevelt thereupon initiated the first personal correspondence to be exchanged between a President of the United States and a British Sovereign. His invitation was cordial and informal :

. . . I need not assure you that it would give my wife and me the greatest pleasure to see you, and, frankly, I think it would be an excellent thing for Anglo-American relations if you could visit the United States . . . if you bring either or both of the children with you they will also be very welcome, and I shall try to have one or two Roosevelts of approximately the same age to play with them![7]

The President's original plan was for a visit to the World Fair in New York and then 'three or four days of very simple country life' at his home at Hyde Park where the King and Queen would be free from formal entertainments and could enjoy a little rest and relaxation. He left to them the decision of whether they would wish to go to Washington in the height of the summer heat, where of necessity things would be more

[a] Rt. Hon. John Buchan, first Baron Tweedsmuir, G.C.M.G., G.C.V.O. (1875–1940), led a full and prolific public life which began as Private Secretary to Lord Milner in South Africa from 1901 to 1903, and closed with his appointment as Governor-General of Canada, an office which he held from 1935 until his death from an accident in 1940. He sat in the House of Commons as Member for the Scottish Universities from 1927 to 1935, and was Lord High Commissioner to the General Assembly of the Church of Scotland in 1933 and 1934. He will be long remembered with gratitude as a writer of romantic literature and as a biographer.

formal and the King would be under great pressure to be received by Congress if it were still in session.

You and I [the President wrote] are fully aware of the demands of the Protocol people, but, having had much experience with them, I am inclined to think that you and Her Majesty should do very much as you personally want to do — and I will see to it over here that your decision becomes the right decision.

King George received this letter at the height of the Munich Crisis — it arrived between the journeys of Mr. Chamberlain to Berchtesgaden and Godesberg — and, though he later described it as 'a pleasant relief at a time of great anxiety', he was unable to answer it until after the crisis had been brought to a peaceful conclusion and he had resumed his interrupted holiday at Balmoral. He then replied, with equal cordiality, on October 8, the date on which the announcement of his intention to visit Canada was made :

The Queen and I appreciate most sincerely your kind invitation to visit Mrs. Roosevelt and you in the United States in the event of our going to Canada next summer. I can assure you that the pleasure, which it would in any case give to us personally, would be greatly enhanced by the thought that it was contributing in any way to the cordiality of the relations between our two countries.

I hope that it will not be inconvenient if I delay my answer until the plans for a visit to Canada are further advanced, and I am in a position to judge how long it may be possible for me to be absent from this country. I will then communicate with you again.

Although the suggestions which you make for a visit sound very attractive, I am afraid that we shall not be taking the children with us if we go to Canada, as they are much too young for such a strenuous tour.

Before I end this letter, I feel that I must say how greatly I welcomed your interventions in the recent crisis. I have little doubt that they contributed largely to the preservation of peace.[a]

With all good wishes and many thanks for your kind invitation.

            Believe me
                  Yours very sincerely
                         GEORGE R.I.[8]

[a] President Roosevelt had intervened in the Czech Crisis on September 26 and 28, 1938, with appeals to both Hitler and President Beneš for a settlement of their differences by methods other than those of force. The first of these was supplemented by similar appeals by Mr. Cordell Hull to the Prime Ministers of Britain and France, and to the Governments of Poland and Hungary.

Undaunted by the uncertainty implied in the King's letter, Mr. Roosevelt replied on November 2 in some detail as regards possible plans, and this letter crossed one of November 3 from the King saying that he and the Queen would be delighted to include in their itinerary a four days' visit to the United States, which should embrace Washington, New York and Hyde Park.[a]

The decision that Their Majesties should enter the United States and make a State Visit to Washington raised a number of thorny problems, not the least difficult and delicate of which was the question of what Minister, if any, should accompany them in attendance. The King's original idea was that, though Mr. Mackenzie King, as his Prime Minister and Minister of External Affairs in Canada, would accompany him during his Canadian tour, Lord Halifax, as his Secretary of State for Foreign Affairs, should also accompany him to Washington, as had been the case in his visit to Paris in July 1938.

Here, however, complications arose. From a number of well-disposed American sources and also from Lord Tweedsmuir, who had a wide knowledge of American public opinion, there came the advice that, if Lord Halifax accompanied the King, the Royal Visit would be interpreted in some quarters in America as having political implications, and might savour of 'entangling alliances'. Lord Halifax himself, though he would have welcomed an opportunity for discussions with the President and with Mr. Hull, was doubtful of the wisdom of his inclusion in the Royal suite. At the same time other Dominion Governments contended that His Majesty should not be attended in a foreign country by a Canadian Minister only.

These reactions inclined King George to the opinion that he should not take any Minister in Attendance at all to Washington, and this view was communicated to the President. Mr. Roosevelt agreed in respect of Lord Halifax, saying that his presence would inevitably provoke talk of an alliance, but as regards Mr. Mackenzie King he felt that it would be con-

[a] The President wrote again on January 18, 1939, in even greater detail about the plans for the Royal visit, and to this letter King George replied on February 8. The originals of the King's letters are among the Roosevelt Archives at Hyde Park. Those of the President are in the Royal Archives at Windsor.

siderably easier. The Canadian Premier had often been in Washington before and the President could represent his presence as the visit of an old friend.

Mr. King, however, was under no illusions. He was quite determined to go to Washington. His right to be in attendance throughout the Dominion was, of course, never in question, since the Sovereign is as much King of Canada as of the United Kingdom, and his Canadian Ministers enjoy the same rights and privileges as do those in Britain. But Mr. King had no intention, as he said, that 'the King should cast him aside at the frontier like an old boot'. He moved all heaven and earth in his determination to attend His Majesty to Washington. He harangued the Governor-General; he wrote with deep feeling to the King's Private Secretary; he telegraphed at length to Mr. Chamberlain. No stone was left unturned, no avenue unexplored.

Finally, the King was advised that the matter of a Minister in Attendance was not considered to have any constitutional significance; it lay within his own Prerogative and was not one on which Ministerial advice would be tendered unless requested. He was also advised, however, that the absence of such a Minister precluded political conversations, just as his presence inevitably implied them.[a][9] His Majesty, therefore, decided not to take Lord Halifax with him to Washington, but he agreed to the presence of Mr. Mackenzie King, whose mind he set at rest with a personal letter at the end of March.[10]

The date for the departure of the King and Queen had been set for May 3, and the battle-cruiser *Repulse* assigned for their conveyance, but, as the date drew near, King George regarded with increasing reluctance the prospect of leaving

[a] It is to be remembered that King Edward VII was not infrequently accompanied on his travels abroad by Sir Charles Hardinge, the Permanent Under-Secretary at the Foreign Office, and not by a Minister in Attendance. The question also arose on the occasion of the Royal Visit to Italy in 1923 when King George V, being pressed by the King of Italy and by Mussolini to bring a Minister, asked the opinion of his Prime Minister, Mr. Bonar Law. The advice tendered was that it would be preferable for the King not to be so accompanied, as the moment was not considered opportune by His Majesty's Government for political discussions with Italy. Mr. Bonar Law's words were as follows: 'I would be very glad therefore if His Majesty would consider it from this point of view, as to whether there is less danger of the Visit proving less successful if it is made clear from the outset that no political result is to be expected from it'. This advice was taken by the King, and no Minister accompanied him.

Britain. Canada he longed to see, remembering the deep impression which his brief visit there as a Naval Cadet had made upon him, but the steady darkening of the international scene, which followed Hitler's wanton destruction of the Munich Agreement, evoked in him a desire to remain within the heart of the Commonwealth. His conversations with visitors from abroad, President Lebrun and M. Georges Bonnet, the enigmatic Colonel Beck and the observant M. Gafencu, gave him little cause for optimism; but his Ministers were agreed that the immediate moment of crisis was not yet and would probably not arise before the autumn, and on their advice he went forward with his preparations.

I feel that we must start for Canada on Saturday unless there is any really good reason as to why we should not [he wrote to Queen Mary].

I hate leaving here with the situation as it is, but one must carry on with one's plans as they are all settled, & Canada will be so disappointed.[11]

It was, however, a matter of concern to the King that he should be taking away *Repulse* at what might be a critical moment. It seemed to him that to withdraw one of his most powerful men-of-war at such a juncture would lend weight to the argument — then all too prevalent on the Continent and in the United States — that Britain did not 'mean business', whereas to cancel the arrangement and to leave *Repulse* with the Fleet might well help to dispel this wholly undesirable and quite unjustified impression. He put this question to the Admiralty,[12] who were at first disinclined to agree. But the wisdom of the King's reasoning prevailed and a week before his departure the decision was taken to withhold *Repulse*, which, however, accompanied the King half-way across the Atlantic as an escort.[a] The Admiralty chartered as a substitute the Canadian Pacific liner, *Empress of Australia*, which had previously carried both the Prince of Wales and the Duke of Gloucester to Canada. For the purposes of the voyage she

---

[a] Lord Halifax states in his memoirs that the British Naval Authorities considered it not impossible that the German battleship *Deutschland*, then cruising in Spanish waters, might be instructed to intercept the ship conveying the Royal Party for the purpose of holding the persons of the King and Queen. (*Fulness of Days*, pp. 203-4.)

was rated as a 'Royal Yacht', sailing under the White Ensign with the King himself in supreme command, and Vice-Admiral Sir Dudley North [a] commanding the whole Royal Squadron.

Thus it was with mixed emotions that the King and Queen sailed from Southampton in pale and watery sunshine on the afternoon of May 5. [b] Of the warmth of their reception on the other side of the Atlantic they were never for a moment in doubt, but it was an undeniable wrench to leave homeland and family under such uncertain conditions. [c] To those who cheered the great liner as she passed with her naval escort down Southampton Water there occurred the same sombre thoughts, and there were many who echoed in their hearts the spoken prayer of one of those watchers : 'For God's sake bring them safely back to us'.

The voyage itself was not without incident and was unexpectedly prolonged. [d] By ill luck it happened that for the first time in many years the ice-fields had come much further south than usual and this danger, in conjunction with that of dense fog, so delayed *Empress of Australia* that on the day on which she should have reached Quebec she was only just off Newfoundland.

For three & a half days we only moved a few miles [the Queen wrote to Queen Mary]. The fog was so thick, that it was like a

[a] Admiral Sir Dudley Burton Napier North, G.C.V.O., C.B., C.S.I., C.M.G. (b. 1881), was at this time Commander of H.M. Yachts. In the Second World War he commanded the North Atlantic Station from 1939 to 1940, and retired in 1942.

[b] Their Majesties' suite consisted of: Lady Nunburnholme and Lady Katherine Seymour, Ladies-in-Waiting; the Earl of Eldon, Lord-in-Waiting; the Earl of Airlie, Lord Chamberlain to the Queen; Mr. Alan Lascelles, Acting Private Secretary to the King; Captain Michael Adeane, Assistant Private Secretary; Lieut.-Col. the Hon. Piers Legh, and Commander E. M. C. Abel Smith, Equerries; Surgeon-Captain H. White, Medical Officer; and Mr. G. F. Steward, Chief Press Liaison Officer.

[c] On May 5 the King directed the issue of Letters Patent under the Great Seal of the Realm appointing five Counsellors of State to function in his absence. Although the Queen was to be absent from the United Kingdom she was named in accordance with the provision of the Regency Act of 1937. The other Counsellors were: the Duke of Gloucester, the Duke of Kent, the Princess Royal and Princess Arthur of Connaught.

[d] Several accounts of the Royal Tour have been written by journalists who accompanied Their Majesties. These include: *North America Sees our King and Queen*, by Keith V. Gordon (London, 1939); *Voyage of State*, by G. Gordon Young (London, 1939); *Merry America*, by H. R. Pratt Boorman (Maidstone, 1939); and *And the People Cheered*, by R. K. Carnegie (Ottawa, 1940).

white cloud round the ship, and the foghorn blew incessantly. Its melancholy blasts were echoed back by the icebergs like the twang of a piece of wire. Incredibly eery, and really very alarming, knowing that we were surrounded by ice, & unable to see a foot either way.

We very nearly hit a berg the day before yesterday, and the poor Captain was nearly demented because some kind cheerful people kept on reminding him that it was about here that the Titanic was struck, & *just* about the same date! . . . . ^a ¹³

The tension felt by all on board was somewhat relieved by the news of an unusual event — the purser's canary had laid an egg!

On May 17, however, *Empress of Australia* came safely to her berth at Quebec, and the King was able to write reassuringly to his mother:

I am afraid the Press will have made the most of our eventful voyage to Canada. It is quite true that we were held up by fog in the vicinity of icebergs for 3 days, & this occurrence has not been known for many years as the ice fields had come much further south than usual. Last Sunday when the fog cleared we spent the whole day in loose lumps of ice, & in the afternoon we had to push our way through a quarter of a mile of quite thick & solid ice. We saw several icebergs of varying sizes. The whole incident was a most interesting experience. It has delayed us two days, but it does not matter as we have rearranged our programme in Ottawa, so that we can catch up after those days.

As a matter of fact I have been able to have a good rest on the voyage, & the two extra days are all to the good for me, but I should not however have chosen an ice field surrounded by dense fog in which to have a holiday, but it does seem to be the only place for me to rest in nowadays!! [14]

The King had indeed been fortunate in obtaining a few days' extra rest, for, from the moment of his arrival in Canada to that of his departure a month later, he was to have little time for relaxation. Every hour of his days was filled with engagements, and many nights were spent in the Royal Train. The everyday duties of a Sovereign are sufficiently arduous, but the work of a Sovereign 'on tour' is exacting in the extreme.

^a At 2.30 a.m. on April 15, 1912, the White Star liner *Titanic*, then the largest ship in the world, and on her maiden voyage to America, sank after collision at full speed with an iceberg in the North Atlantic, with the loss of 1513 souls out of 2224 on board.

But the results were fantastic. The success of Their Majesties' visit had never been in doubt, but the magnitude of this success was wholly unexpected. Within a week of their arrival the King and Queen had completely won the heart of the whole North American continent. Those of their suite who were hardened veterans of many Royal tours stood amazed at the sincerity and the grandeur of the Canadian welcome and of its effect upon the proud nationalist spirit of Canada. There had been talk in the past of secession from the Commonwealth and of neutrality in time of war. If such sentiments had existed, they now disappeared 'like thin clouds before a Biscay gale'. As one Provincial Premier remarked to Mr. Alan Lascelles: 'You can go home and tell the Old Country that any talk they may hear about Canada being isolationist after to-day is just nonsense'.

In the height of their ardour some Canadians proclaimed, 'The King and Queen by what they are doing here have averted a European War', and, while this proved to be but a pious aspiration, there could have been no greater demonstration of the devotion and loyalty of the Canadian people had the Führer been but willing to mark and learn the lesson.

It was more even than this. The presence of the British Sovereign, for the first time in history, as King of Canada was a living symbol of the reality of the British Commonwealth, its essential vigour and effectiveness, despite its many superficial contradictions and seeming inconsistencies.[a] As the King was later to say in Guildhall on his return to London: 'In person I presided over the Canadian Parliament at Ottawa, and assented to legislation; in person I received the credentials of the new Minister of Canada's great and friendly neighbour, the United States; in person I signed the Trade Treaty between the two countries'.

[a] King George was himself fully aware of the bewildering anomaly which the British Commonwealth of Nations presented to outsiders, an anomaly which was enhanced by the fact that, in 1939, of his Prime Ministers, two (General Hertzog and Mr. De Valera) had been in arms against the Crown, and a third (Mr. Mackenzie King) was the grandson of one who had had a price set upon his head by the British Government. The reaction of the outsider, the King would say, must surely be that of the man who, on first seeing a giraffe, exclaimed: 'There ain't no such animal!'

It was these personal acts of the Sovereign, this personal attitude on the part of the King and Queen, which gave to their visit a far deeper significance than any other of its kind in history. And there was something else ; the fundamental fact that thousands of simple North American folk had met Their Majesties for the first time face to face and had found them to be so much nicer than they had ever imagined them. This above all, perhaps, succeeded in producing a result which far surpassed the expectations of even the most sanguine advocates of the tour.

When I induced Their Majesties to come out here last autumn I did not realize I was pulling the string of such a shower-bath ! [Lord Tweedsmuir wrote to a friend in Scotland, of the events in Ottawa.] The visit is going to have an enormous effect in Canada and in the United States, and, indeed, on the whole world, as a demonstration of our unity of spirit. . . .

Our Monarchs are most remarkable young people. I have always been deeply attached to the King, and I realize now more than ever what a wonderful mixture he is of shrewdness, kindliness and humour. As for the Queen, she has a perfect genius for the right kind of publicity. The unrehearsed episodes here were marvellous. For example, when she laid the foundation stone at the new Judicative Building I heard the masons talking and realized that some of them were Scots, and she made me take her and the King up to them, and they spent at least ten minutes in Scottish reminiscences, in full view of 70,000 people, who went mad ! Then at the unveiling of the War Memorial, where we had some 10,000 veterans, she asked me if it was not possible to get a little closer to them. I suggested that we went right down among them, if they were prepared to take the risk, which they gladly did. It was an amazing sight, for we were simply swallowed up. The faces of the Scotland Yard detectives were things I shall never forget ! But the veterans made a perfect bodyguard. It was wonderful to see old fellows weeping, and crying 'Ay, man, if Hitler could just see this '. The American correspondents were simply staggered. They said that no American President would ever have dared to do that. It was a wonderful example of what true democracy means, and a people's king.

Indeed the effect upon the American journalists was most striking, and those few among them who had come in a spirit of hostility to 'debunk' the British Royalty remained to praise and admire.

Nor were these scenes confined to the Dominion's capital. From Quebec, where French-speaking Canadians were talking to English-speaking Canadians for the first time of '*our* King and Queen' instead of '*your* King and Queen', through traditionalist Ontario, across the Prairie Provinces and the Rockies, and westwards to the Pacific Coast, the moving story of conquest was the same — the triumph of a true democracy and of a people's King.

(iii)

Shortly after ten o'clock on the night of June 9, 1939, a British reigning Sovereign entered the United States of America for the first time.[a]

The King and Queen had dined at the General Brock Hotel at Niagara Falls and had thereafter bidden a temporary farewell to the majority of the Canadian officials who had accompanied them to the West and back. They were particularly sorry to say good-bye to the orderlies of the Royal Canadian Mounted Police who had been their escort, and their regret was perhaps enhanced by the fact that it was known that members of the I.R.A. (Irish Republican Army) were reported to be active in Detroit and Buffalo, and in vengeful mood. The past three weeks had been a blaze of triumph ; but now they stood upon the threshold of a new experience, an experience which, in anticipation, was not without its uncertainties and hazards.

The British Royal Family were no strangers to the New World ; Americans recalled that both King George's grandfather and brother had visited the United States when Princes of Wales, and indeed that the future King Edward VII had with difficulty been restrained from allowing himself to be conveyed across Niagara Falls in a wheel-barrow by that celebrated tight-rope walker Charles Blondin.[15] What Americans probably did not remember — or, if they did, they were too tactful to draw attention to it — was that the first of the King's ancestors to set foot on American soil did so during the War of

---

[a] The occasion was rendered still further historic by the fact that, after the Royal Train had crossed the American border, the King knighted Mr. Alan Lascelles and invested him with the K.C.V.O. This was the first time a knighthood had been conferred by a British Sovereign on American soil.

Independence, when the son of George III, Prince William Henry, later Duke of Clarence and King William IV, was attached for a while to the Headquarters Staff of Admiral Digby on the Hudson River. The reception planned for the Prince by the insurgent colonists had been warm but courteous, for it had been arranged that he should be the object of a 'commando raid', and that both he and the Admiral should be conveyed, as prisoners but with all the honours of war, to the Continental Congress in Philadelphia. The scheme failed of success, but it had the blessing of George Washington,ᵃ and now, nearly a hundred and sixty years later, the great-great-grandnephew of Prince William Henry was about to pay a visit to General Washington's thirtieth successor in the office of President of the United States.

In his original conception of the visit of the King and Queen, President Roosevelt had had the international situation very prominently in mind, and with greater far-sightedness than many of his countrymen. Just as the presence of Their Majesties in Canada had presented to the world an irrefutable demonstration of Commonwealth solidarity, so, he hoped, would their visit to the United States offer a similar proof of Anglo-American friendship.

My husband invited them to Washington [wrote Mrs. Roosevelt] largely because, believing that we all might soon be engaged in a life and death struggle, in which Great Britain would be our first line of defence, he hoped that the visit would create a bond of friendship between the people of the two countries. He knew that, though there is always in this country a certain amount of criticism and superficial ill-feeling toward the British, in time of danger something deeper comes to the surface, and the British and we stand firmly together, with confidence in our common heritage and ideas. The visit of the king and queen, he hoped, would be a reminder of this deep bond. In many ways it proved even more successful than he had expected.[17]

ᵃ 'The spirit of enterprise so conspicuous in your plan for surprising in their quarters, and bringing off, Prince William-Henry and Admiral Digby, merits applause', General Washington wrote to Colonel Ogden of the 1st Jersey Regiment, on March 28, 1782, 'and you have my authority to make the attempt in any manner, and at such a time, as your judgement shall direct. I am fully persuaded that it is unnecessary to caution you against offering insult or indignity to the person of the Prince or the Admiral should you be so fortunate as to capture them. . . .'[16]

Certainly the reception given by the citizens of Washington to the first King and Queen that most of them had ever seen,[a] lacked nothing in warmth, cordiality or enthusiasm. In warmth their welcome matched the weather, for throughout the two crowded days of June 8 and 9,[b] the heat and humidity of the nation's capital was intense, and caused the King and Queen considerable discomfort. But their smiling fortitude under this additional trial won them an even greater measure of sympathy from the gay and happy thousands who thronged the streets to cheer them at every opportunity.[c] 'In the course of a long life I have seen many important events in Washington, but never have I seen a crowd such as lined the whole route between the Union Station and the White House', wrote Mrs. Roosevelt in her diary, and added, 'They have a way of making friends, these young people'.[18] Not for nothing did one newspaper print a headline : 'The British re-take Washington', and the more restrained and conservative *Washington Post* emphasized that the Capital's welcome was 'not the result of calculated Governmental dragooning to create the effect of popular enthusiasm but . . . wholly voluntary and sincere.'

Nor was this merely a crowd manifestation. Even the mordant pen of Harold Ickes recorded that 'The King and Queen made a very good impression. . . . They were gracious'[19] — high praise indeed from this acidulated chronicler.[d]

[a] King George VI was not the first reigning monarch to come to the United States; this had been the Emperor Pedro II of Brazil, who visited New York and Washington in 1876.

[b] The programme of the Washington visit included a State Dinner at the White House; a Garden Party at the British Embassy; a Congressional reception at the Capitol; visits to Mount Vernon, to the tomb of the Unknown Soldier at Arlington and to a C.C.C. Camp at Fort Hunt; a reception for British ex-Servicemen in the Embassy garden; and a farewell dinner-party at the Embassy.

[c] To protect herself from the blazing sunshine Queen Elizabeth held up a white silk parasol with a dark green lining, and parasols immediately became fashionable throughout the United States. The magazine *Life* was moved to comment: 'To makers of parasols and umbrellas the reign of George VI of England will be memorable not for the Munich Pact nor for the first North American trip of Their Britannic Majesties. To them the reign of George and Elizabeth will ever be the period when a Queen and a Prime Minister raised the parasol and umbrella to unprecedented pinnacles of international significance and chic.' (*Life* (U.S. Edition), July 24, 1939.)

[d] Harold L. Ickes (1874–1952), originally a Progressive Republican, who had followed Mr. Theodore Roosevelt at the Bull Moose Convention of 1912, served in President Franklin Roosevelt's Cabinet as Secretary of the Interior from 1933 to 1945, and so continued in President Truman's administration until 1946. His posthumously published diaries provide a valuable if unvarnished record of the

To persons reared in the belief that 'Royalty' was synonymous with 'stuffed-shirtedness', King George and Queen Elizabeth came not only as a welcome surprise but as a decided shock. It was the King's friendliness and humour, the Queen's grace and charm, and their evident and vivid interest in all they saw and heard, which captivated those who met them. From the Senator on Capitol Hill who, at the Congressional Reception, grasped the King's hand with the ecstatic exclamation : 'My, you're a great Queen-picker', to the boy in the Civilian Conservation Corps camp, who, looking incredulously at the hand the King had just shaken, remarked : 'Gee, I never even shook hands with a Congressman before ! I sure hope this gets me a job when I get out of the C.C.C.', the impression created was the same, one of essential 'humanness', yet withal of majesty.

One incident alone, which achieved considerable publicity, touched the hearts of Americans all over the country. The eight-year-old daughter of Mr. Harry Hopkins, President Roosevelt's close friend and collaborator,[a] had expressed disappointment that Their Majesties were not dressed like the kings and queens of her fairy stories, and at the Queen's suggestion she was in the hall of the White House as they left for the dinner-party at the British Embassy. There she saw pass close before her the King, wearing the insignia of the Order of the Garter, and the Queen radiant in her sweeping crinoline, her jewels and her diadem. Both stopped and spoke to her and, breathless and starry-eyed, she turned to her father : 'Daddy, oh Daddy, I have seen the Fairy Queen'.

Roosevelt era. Of the behaviour of his colleagues during the Royal Visit Mr. Ickes wrote trenchantly, more particularly of Vice-President Garner, who, being placed on the Queen's right hand at the State Dinner at the White House, is described as exercising 'no more self-restraint than he would have shown at a Church supper at Uvalde, Texas', and of Speaker Bankhead of the House of Representatives, who is said to have treated the King like 'a visiting Elk'.[20]

[a] Harry L. Hopkins (1890–1946) was associated in social welfare work with Mr. Roosevelt during his Governorship of the State of New York. He later served the President as head of the Federal Emergency Relief Administration and of the Works Progress Administration, and, from 1938 to 1940, as Secretary of Commerce. Throughout the period of the United States participation in the Second World War, Mr. Hopkins was Special Adviser and Personal Assistant to the President, on whose behalf he came to Britain on several occasions, and whom he accompanied on his war-time conferences abroad.

In many ways the most important effect of all was upon the President of the United States himself.   At the outset Mr. Roosevelt had been disposed to regard the King and Queen as 'two nice young people' who had a difficult position to fill and were doing it extremely efficiently and well.   He quickly discovered, however, almost from the moment of welcome at the Union Station and the first drive to the White House, that he had much in common with them, and that with the King he could discuss a diversity of interests as man to man.   As a result he looked forward with increasing pleasure to getting his guests away from the formality and protocol of Washington to the comparative peace and quiet of Hyde Park.

President Roosevelt's country home in Dutchess County, New York, was an important factor in his life.   Here on the steep bank of the Hudson River, beautiful in spring with dogwood, his family had lived for a hundred years.   Of patroon *a* ancestry, they came of that proud, solid Knickerbocker stock which even Ward McAllister,*b* New York's social arbiter of the 'eighties, had found 'unsnubbable', and which formed the backbone of that curious organism of New York society depicted in the novels of Henry James and Edith Wharton.   Here Mr. Roosevelt had been born; from here he had made his early forays into the field of New York State politics, and had begun his fruitless campaign for the Vice-Presidency.   Here, too, in the 'twenties, he came after his agonizing and gallant recovery from infantile paralysis; and hence he had gone forth in triumph as Governor of New York and as President of the United States.

The house itself was unpretentious but, with its Georgian silver and Duncan Phyfe sofas, its rosewood tables and Peale portraits, and even its Landseer engravings, it manifested an old-fashioned, spacious comfort, in sharp distinction to those monumental mansions of millionaires farther up the Hudson, whose baroque rooms and Roman atriums, imported tile by

a Under the Dutch system of administration in their North American possession, New Netherlands, during the seventeenth century, any member of the West Indian Chartered Company might establish a holding by purchasing land from the Indians and planting upon it a colony of fifty persons within four years of the beginning of the undertaking.   The founder of such a colony was styled a *patroon*.

b Samuel Ward McAllister (1827–1895), to whom is credited the invention of the term 'The Four Hundred', was also described as Mrs. Astor's 'Social Postilion'.

tile from Europe, exemplified a different and a later way of life.[a]

Deep love for his home went to the roots of Mr. Roosevelt's being. The plantations had been made under his personal supervision, and every tree was dear to him. The roads had been laid out to his design and, miraculously enough, despite his disability, he could drive his own car around winding turns and through thickly wooded sections. He had studied husbandry and forestry and even bee-culture, and turned them all to good profit. Here he was Squire, not President, and with his quick intuition he sensed that all this would appeal unfailingly to King George.

On the evening of Saturday June 10 the President and his wife, his mother and his family, sat in the library awaiting the arrival of the King and Queen from New York. They waited from six o'clock until nearly eight before their guests arrived, for the programme of the Royal Tour had got somewhat out of hand.

On the previous evening the Royal Train had left Washington for Red Bank, New Jersey, where next morning the King and Queen had embarked in the U.S. destroyer *Warrington*, with the Royal Standard at the fore, for a tour of New York Harbour. From the moment of their arrival their destinies had been in the hands of those vociferous showmen, the Mayor

[a] Hyde Park, New York, does not, as has sometimes been suggested, derive its name from the enthusiasm of a group of Anglophiles in nostalgic commemoration of Hyde Park, London. The name dates from the year 1705, when the then Royal Governor of New York, Edward Hyde, Viscount Cornbury, later third Earl of Clarendon, bestowed in the name of Queen Anne, upon three New York gentlemen, the princely gift of 3600 acres of Dutchess County on the left bank of the Hudson River. One of these fortunate recipients, Pierre Fauconnier, had been Lord Cornbury's Private Secretary, and had also served as Collector and Receiver-General of the Colony. Out of compliment and gratitude to his patron he named the estate, which he had made out of his share of the royal benefaction, Hyde Park. The property passed in time to the Bard family, and ultimately to the Vanderbilts, of whom one built upon it one of the mansions referred to. The local village community was first known as Stoutenberg, but by the last decade of the eighteenth century the dominant influence of the Hyde Park estate had caused it to be known by this name also. The village belonged to the township of Clinton, and when, in 1821, this was divided into two, the western portion was officially designated Hyde Park.

President Roosevelt's great-great-grandfather, Isaac Roosevelt, settled in Hyde Park in 1819 and built himself a house. This, however, is not the house in which the President was born; his birthplace, though built in 1827, was not purchased by his father until forty years later.

St. James's Church, Hyde Park, N.Y., June 11, 1939

The Queen   The King   President   James   Mrs. James   Mrs.   Mr.
                         Roosevelt   Roosevelt Delano   Franklin   Mackenzie
                                                           Roosevelt   King

of New York, Mr. Fiorello La Guardia, and Mr. Grover Whalen, President of the World's Fair. The result had been memorable, but detrimental to the punctual fulfilment of their schedule. A prolonged visit to the Exhibition, on Flushing Meadows, where the crowds had sung 'Rule, Britannia!' and 'Land of Hope and Glory', had been followed by a progress through New York City itself, where enormous crowds had greeted them, men and women cheering and stretching out their hands. It ended on Morningside Heights, where the King and Queen visited Columbia University, an institution which had been granted its original charter, as King's College, by George II in 1754.

The ninety-mile drive to Hyde Park was made along parkways lined with close-packed masses of people and cars. As the procession passed through the small townships, church bells rang, motor-cars hooted and flowers were strewn in the way. 'No American', said one who was present, 'ever received such an ovation from his countrymen.'

But the King and Queen were hours behind their time, and in the library at Hyde Park the Roosevelt family were waiting. At the King's command reports of their progress were telephoned to the President from various points along the route, and as they drew up at the door Mr. Roosevelt had a tray of cocktails waiting for them. 'My mother', he said, 'thinks you should have a cup of tea; she doesn't approve of cocktails.' 'Neither does my mother', the King replied, and gratefully took one.

The dinner-party which followed, and at which the President with felicitous impromptu proposed the health of Queen Mary, was not free from untoward incident. The President had brought up his coloured staff from the White House, with the result that his mother's English butler was so incensed at the thought of his King and Queen being waited upon by negroes that he took his holiday before their arrival rather than be a witness of this humiliation! And indeed it did seem as if some 'jinx' had settled on the house, for in the middle of the meal the side-table collapsed and a part of the dinner service crashed to the floor. The immediate silence was broken by one of the President's daughters-in-law anxiously exclaiming, 'I hope none of my dishes were among those broken', and a roar of laughter followed. Nor was this the only tragedy. After dinner the party adjourned to the library, which is on a lower level than the rest of the house; no sooner were they settled than there occurred a second appalling crash and a coloured butler, who had missed the step, shot into the room in a sitting posture, surrounded by decanters, bottles, jugs, glasses, and ice-cubes, which left a large lake upon the floor.[21]

Shortly thereafter the King, the President and Mr. Mackenzie King were left alone, and the talk turned to more serious subjects. There were few more charming personalities than Mr. Roosevelt, and few better conversationalists. The King was deeply impressed with his frankness of manner and easy friendliness. 'He is so easy to get to know,' he wrote subsequently, '& never makes one feel shy. As good a listener as a talker.'

They talked together of the thing which was uppermost in all their minds, the international situation and the seemingly inescapable drift towards war. Both the King and the President had laboured in the cause of peace, and would continue to do so, but neither could hide from himself or from each other the fact that their efforts seemed to have little chance of success. Both felt that, despite the surrounding peace of the Hudson River Valley in high summer, they were approaching the point at which one no longer said 'if' war should come, but 'when' war should come.

They spoke of the issue as it affected their two countries, and of the problems which confronted them as Heads of States. The President was deeply concerned for the safety of the Western Hemisphere. He had spent many fishing trips in the waters of the North Atlantic and the Caribbean, and as early as 1936 had conceived a plan of establishing bases in Newfoundland, Bermuda, Jamaica, St. Lucia, Antigua and Trinidad for the better protection of the American Continent, and to prevent their falling into the hands of a potential enemy.[22] The U.S. naval manœuvres of the winter of 1938–1939 had indeed been based on the idea of denying these waters to the warlike operations of belligerents, and especially to submarines and commerce raiders, and the idea of a Western Atlantic patrol had become firmly established. The President now spoke very frankly of this to King George, and also of what he hoped to be able to do, within his constitutional limitations, to help Britain in the event of war. The King spoke with equal frankness of the situation in Europe and the enigma of the Russian attitude.

The conversation held them all in deep interest until at 1.30 the President remembered his duty as a host and the strain to which his guest had been subjected all day. With fatherly concern he leaned forward and placed his hand upon the King's knee. 'Young man,' he said, 'it's time for you to go to bed.' [23]

The King went to his room, but not immediately to sleep, for he called in Mr. Mackenzie King from his adjoining room and kept him some little time to tell of how much he had appreciated all that this American visit had meant to him, how deeply he had been impressed by what the President had said, and how greatly he had enjoyed this frank exchange of views. 'Why don't my Ministers talk to me as the President did to-night?' he concluded. 'I feel exactly as though a father were giving me his most careful and wise advice.' [24]

Next morning all went to worship in the little parish church of St. James, where, as the Queen wrote to Queen Mary: 'The service is *exactly* the same as ours down to every word, & they even had the prayers for the King & the Royal Family. I could not help thinking how curious it sounded, & yet how natural.'[a] [25] There followed a brief interval, during which the Queen talked by transatlantic telephone to her daughters in London, finding them much amused that she was about to go to luncheon when Princess Margaret was about to go to bed.[26] Meantime the President drove the King over the estate. Now it was not the King of England talking to the President of the United States, but the Squire of Sandringham who was deeply interested in the developments and improvements which the Squire of Hyde Park had made on his property, and their friendship deepened on a new basis.

A picnic luncheon at the President's Cottage — at which, among other native American delicacies, the much publicized

[a] King George later presented a King James the First Bible to the Church of St. James, Hyde Park. Unfortunately, however, the danger of depredations by souvenir-hunters prevents its being used, and it has been placed in the Roosevelt Library and Museum.

'hot-dogs' were served — was followed by a swimming party.
Later King George and the President had a further long and
serious talk, from which Mr. Mackenzie King, who had gone
back to the house to rest, was, to his great chagrin, excluded ;
and, after a hilarious dinner, the King and Queen said good-
bye with genuine and deep regret. The Royal Train bore them
back to Canada.

For King George his twenty-four-hour visit to the President
at Hyde Park was an event of major importance, and he
regarded it as the apogee of his entire tour. Both he and the
Queen had found the Roosevelts most congenial : 'They are
such a charming & united family, and living so like English
people when they come to their country house', the Queen
wrote to Queen Mary — and between the King and the
President there had been engendered a genuine sense of
friendship and accord, based partly upon common interests
and mutual problems, but also prompted by that unspoken
bond which unites those who have triumphed over physical
disability. As the King confided more than once to Mr.
Mackenzie King (who repeated the confidence to the United
States Minister in Ottawa), 'he had never met a person with
whom he felt freer in talking and whom he enjoyed more',[27]
and again and again in their subsequent correspondence he
would refer to their conversations at Hyde Park.

These talks had impressed the King mightily — and
indeed with good reason — for, though they revealed Mr.
Roosevelt as being unduly optimistic as to how far he could,
or could not, persuade Congress to go along with him in the
event of war, they nevertheless contained the germ of the
future Bases-for-Destroyers deal, and also of the Lend-Lease
Agreement itself. With his usual methodical habit, the King
made a memorandum of their content the following morning
(June 12) before the Royal Train reached Sherbrooke, Ontario.
These notes are preserved in the Royal Archives :

I had two good conversations with the President, besides many
opportunities of informal talks on current matters in the car driving
with him. He was very frank & friendly, & seemed genuinely
glad that I had been able to pay him this visit. He gave me all
the information in these notes either in answer to my questions, or
he volunteered it.

Mr. Mackenzie King was present at the first conversation at Hyde Park. We talked of the firm & trusted friendship between Canada & the U.S.A. F. D. R. mentioned that he thought it was a waste of money to build a Canadian fleet as he had already laid his plans for the defence of the Pacific Coast of Canada, especially Vancouver Island. (Assembling plants for aeroplanes in Canada.) On mentioning the Neutrality Act the President gave us hopes that something could be done to make it less difficult for the U.S.A. to help us. Cordell Hull & others as well as himself were doing their best to lead public opinion on to the right tack. He gave us the following story to illustrate how he was tackling the subject in the Middle West & putting it in a way which they as farmers would understand.

'In the event of a war & say Germany & Italy were to win it, which means that the British Fleet & the French Army had been defeated, which at the moment are our first lines of defence, how would you like to lose one of your best customers the United Kingdom? Then again Hitler could say to our great neighbours to the south the Argentine & Brazil You cannot sell your wheat or your beef or your coffee in Europe except through me & Germany. I am the Master of Europe & in return I will send you the articles I *think* you will require in return at my price.'

I was alone with him for the 2nd conversation. We discussed Europe in a general way. He hoped France & Italy would try & get together.

He was doing his best to get New York to loan money to Roumania. I told him how difficult it was for us to help the Balkans as there was the Mediterranean to convoy things through, & they would want all they had got in a War. I explained to him Roumania's position as to frontiers having 4 to cope with. Because of the air we were only just becoming frontier-conscious ourselves. In the whole of N. America he has none. He was definitely anti-Russian. I told him so were we but if we could not have an understanding with her, Germany would probably make one.

He showed me his naval patrols in greater detail about which he is terribly keen. If he saw a U boat he would sink her at once & wait for the consequences.

If London was bombed U.S.A. would come in. Offensive air warfare was better than defensive & he hoped we should do the same on Berlin.

F. D. R.'s ideas in case of War

Trinidad Patrol. Base for his fleet at Trinidad to fuel & replenish stores. From this base he can patrol the Atlantic with ships & aeroplanes on a radius of approximately 1000 miles on a sector of

latitude of Haiti to latitude of Brazil. This patrol should locate
any enemy fleet which tried to get to S. Am. or the West Indies.

Bermuda Patrol. Base as above. To patrol N. Atlantic from
Cape Cod to Florida, with ships & aeroplanes to prevent submarines
from attacking convoys.

Brazil. Germans have an air base at Natal Cape St. Roque
also a landing ground on the island of Fernando Noronha 200 miles
from the coast. Brazil is pretty sure to kick out the Germans.
He would then use it himself.

Haiti, Cuba, & West Indies are potential friendly bases.

The idea is that U.S.A. should relieve us of these responsibilities,
but can it be done without a declaration of war?

Debts. Better not reopen the question. Congress wants repay-
ment in full, which is impossible, & a small bit is of no use, as they
will want more later.

Credits. U.S.A. will want Nickel from Canada. They will buy
our surplus rubber.

In return they can send steel sheets which can be cut for aeroplane wings.

Rough castings with bored cylinders to be machined at home.
Can be used for aeroplanes or motor boats.

On his return to London the King communicated the
essence of his talks with the President to the proper quarters,
and so greatly did he esteem their importance that he carried
the original manuscript of his notes about with him in his
dispatch case throughout the war.

Three days later, on June 15, Their Majesties sailed for
home from Halifax in the liner *Empress of Britain*. They bade
an affectionate farewell to their Canadian subjects, whose
hearts they had captured and whose tears were falling. As
the King said later: 'I nearly cried at the end of my last
speech in Canada, everyone round me was crying'.[28] The
tour had been of immense psychological importance to them
and they realized it as such. 'This has made us', they both
said on more than one occasion.

The North American tour was indeed a climacteric in the
King's life. It had taken him out of himself, had opened up
for him wider horizons and introduced to him new ideas. It
marked the end of his apprenticeship as a monarch, and gave
him self-confidence and assurance. No longer was he over-
awed by the magnitude of his responsibility, the greatness of
his office and the burden of its traditions. Now at last, he felt,

he could stand on his own feet and trust his own judgment. It had, moreover, provided him with a further means of implementing his old ideal of identifying the Royal Family with the people; that ideal which, twenty years before, he had demonstrated so eloquently in his activities with the Industrial Welfare Society and in his Camp. He had given to the Americans and Canadians — and indirectly to the world at large — a first glimpse of his new concept of kingship — the concept that the King must have a first-hand knowledge of his peoples and of their affairs, that he must have the common touch. 'There must be no more high-hat business,' he said to one of his advisers during the tour, 'the sort of thing that my father and those of his day regarded as essential as the correct attitude — the feeling that certain things could not be done.' Henceforth the King was determined to trust to his own judgment and to size up men for himself. With reluctance and uncertainty he had gone forth, to return in buoyant confidence.

Something of this new Monarch was disclosed in his speech at Guildhall, whither he went with the Queen in state on June 23, the day following their tumultuous welcome home to London. Speaking with great earnestness and some emotion, the King told his audience of what had impressed him most of all during his tour of the Dominion of Canada, showing thereby that he had been no superficial observer :

I saw everywhere not only the mere symbol of the British Crown; I saw also, flourishing strongly as they do here, the institutions which have developed, century after century, beneath the aegis of that Crown; institutions, British in origin, British in their slow and almost casual growth, which, because they are grounded root and branch on British faith in liberty and justice, mean more to us even than the splendour of our history or the glories of our English tongue. . . .

Even in the loyal enthusiasm shown to the Queen and myself by hundreds and thousands of my Canadian subjects, young and old, I thought I detected too the influence of those institutions. For it was not alone the actual presence of the King and Queen that made them open their hearts to us; their welcome, it seemed to me, was also an expression of their thankfulness for those rights of free citizenship which are the heritage of every member of our great Commonwealth of Nations.

It was the desire to serve the ideals of that Commonwealth which led me to undertake my journey to foster its sane and wholesome faith; to show, if I could, that its Headship, which I have been called upon to assume, exists to-day as a potent force for promoting peace and goodwill among mankind — these were the objects that I, and the Queen with me, set out to fulfil. It will be a source of thankfulness to us all our lives long if we have in some sort succeeded.

A Guildhall audience is perhaps more conditioned and hardened to oratory than most gatherings in this country, but even to this congeries of connoisseurs both the delivery and the content of the King's speech were a revelation, and the effect of its import was not lost upon the world outside. In Europe it was hailed as a declaration of beliefs and an indication that Britain was prepared to defend her democratic institutions; in America it struck a chord of response, warm and immediate; while from Canada Mr. Mackenzie King telegraphed to Sir Alan Lascelles: 'I am sure that no Sovereign has ever uttered words fraught with greater good for mankind'.

I have never heard the King — or indeed few other people — speak so effectively, or so movingly [wrote Sir Alan in reply]. One or two passages obviously stirred him so deeply that I feared he might break down. This spontaneous feeling heightened the force of the speech considerably. . . . The last few weeks, culminating in this final effort to-day, have definitely established him as a first class public speaker. It was very interesting to watch the effect of his words on such hardened experts as Winston Churchill, Baldwin & the Archbishop of Canterbury; it was patent that each of them & indeed everybody else in that historic place, was deeply moved.

The King's own reaction to his success as an orator was expressed, modestly and succinctly, in answer to a letter of congratulation from Sir Louis Greig. 'It was a change from the old days when speaking, I felt, was "hell" ', wrote His Majesty.[29]

(iv)

The European situation to which King George returned in June 1939 was one of ominous quiet. During the weeks which had elapsed since he left England, though the psychological condition had deteriorated, there had been no definite worsening of the international position, and there was no immediately perceptible threat of crisis. The alignment of Europe had been made somewhat clearer by the conclusion of the Pact of Steel between Germany and Italy on May 22, and both Britain and France had entered into preliminary discussions with Turkey for the provision of mutual aid in the Mediterranean in the event of war. Most important of all were the Anglo-French negotiations which had been opened in Moscow for a pact with the Soviet Union for mutual guarantee against aggression, though it was not, of course, known at the time that the Soviet Government was conducting parallel negotiations with Germany.

The King had been kept informed throughout his North American travels of the general position of affairs at home, but within a few days of his return to London he was placed in possession of all the latest first-hand information by his Prime Minister and Foreign Secretary.

The crux of the problem which confronted the King's Ministers, and also their French allies, was the essential necessity of making Hitler understand that never again could he count upon a repetition of the Munich Agreement and that, though Britain and France had no desire to provoke war and were anxious to settle all outstanding questions with Germany by free and peaceful negotiations, they were, nevertheless, no longer susceptible to blackmail and were prepared to meet force with force. The difficulty lay in conveying to the Führer the fact that, when, for example, Lord Halifax declared at a dinner of the Royal Institute of International Affairs on June 29: 'Our immediate task is . . . to resist aggression', he spoke for a country and a government that were in deadly earnest. If only, it was felt, Hitler could be convinced of this fact he might well be deterred from embarking upon further acts of depredation.

The King shared the anxiety of his Ministers to achieve this end, and sought for means by which he might aid them. After a review in Hyde Park on July 2 of 20,000 representatives of the Civil Defence forces, he issued a message, which was broadcast, telling them of the deep impression which had been made upon both him and the Queen of 'this demonstration of the spirit of service which is everywhere present in the nation to-day, and which shows itself in a determination to make the country ready to meet any emergency, whatever the sacrifices or inconveniences entailed. . . . You know that all our preparations are designed not to provoke war but to preserve peace.'

His Majesty, nevertheless, was ever anxious to make a personal contribution to assist the efforts of his Ministers, and had been ready to make a direct appeal to Hitler at the time of the Munich Crisis. Another possible initiative now suggested itself to him. His brother, the Duke of Kent, had been recently in Italy and had talked with his cousin, Prince Philip of Hesse,[a] the son-in-law of King Victor Emmanuel, who had served as the personal liaison officer between Hitler and Mussolini, and who was believed still to retain the Führer's confidence. Why, therefore, thought the King, should Prince Philip not be employed to good purpose ? 'Do you think it would be possible to get him over here', he wrote to Mr. Chamberlain, '& to use him as a messenger to convey to Hitler that we really are in earnest ?' He asked the Prime Minister to talk the idea over with Lord Halifax, and to communicate the result to him personally, 'as I am telling none of my secretariat'.[30] Neither Mr. Chamberlain nor Lord Halifax was greatly enamoured of the idea, however, and in deference to their views the King did not press it.

Summer — the last summer of peace for six years — was fast waning, and the King's thoughts, like those of his subjects, turned towards a summer holiday ; a holiday of which two events would ever remain with him as happy memories. The first of these was his return to Dartmouth College for the first time since leaving it as a cadet. On the afternoon of July 22 the Royal Yacht *Victoria and Albert* dropped anchor in the Dart and the King and Queen, the two Princesses, with Lord Louis Mountbatten and others, landed at the College steps — in sheets of pouring rain. A situation had arisen which must have stirred memories in the King's mind. A joint epidemic of mumps and chicken-pox had scourged the College, but this

---

[a] Prince Philip of Hesse (b. 1896) was the third son of Prince Frederick Charles, Landgrave of Hesse, and Princess Margaret of Prussia, sister of Kaiser Wilhelm II. He had thus the curious distinction of being, on his father's side, a great-great-great-grandson of George II of England, and also of George III on his mother's side. In 1925 he had married Princess Mafalda of Italy, who, having been arrested by Hitler and lodged in Buchenwald Concentration Camp, was killed during an Allied air raid in 1944.

could not dim the vociferous enthusiasm of the cadets' welcome. Those confined to dormitories leaned out of the windows as the Royal visitors passed by, and, to the King's great amusement, whereas the 'chicken-poxers' were able to raise a cheer, the 'mumpers' could only produce a throaty croak.

Memories of his own days as a cadet recurred incessantly as he went over the College and grounds, and he concluded his inspection by calling for the Punishment Book and reading aloud his own crime record, and those of his contemporaries, with appropriate comments, to the hilarious entertainment of all.

Because of the risk of infection the Princesses spent much of the time in the Captain's [a] house and garden, where, the sun having come out, they played croquet with various of the senior cadets. Here Princess Elizabeth met her cousin, Cadet Captain Prince Philip of Greece, Lord Louis Mountbatten's nephew. She had never seen him before, and this first meeting was to be of great moment in the history of Britain.

That evening the King and Queen entertained Prince Philip and his fellow cadet-captains to dinner in the Yacht, and the following afternoon, escorted as far as the harbour mouth by the hundred and ten boats belonging to the College, propelled by oars, sails, steam or petrol, *Victoria and Albert* steamed slowly out to sea.

The second memorable event of the King's holiday was his final Camp. This year, he had decided, it was to be on a much more personal basis. The number was to be halved, two hundred boys only, and it was to be held in the grounds of Abergeldie Castle, where he had spent so many happy days in childhood. The King himself was to be Camp Chief, and expeditions were to replace the usual competitions, the King taking a different party each day. The details of this new development had been set *en train* before the King's departure for Canada, and within three days of his return he had summoned Captain Paterson to Buckingham Palace to report.

The Camp, which opened on August 5, was, despite the weather, an outstanding success. But there was a difference;

---

[a] Admiral Sir Frederick Hew George Dalrymple-Hamilton, K.C.B. (b. 1890), was Captain of Dartmouth at this time.

half-realized, the threat of war was present, and though it was not permitted to spoil their enjoyment, the boys felt less inclined for ragging. Moreover, after a day's tramping — and they soon found that the King could out-walk any of them — they were in no mood for further physical exertion. It was more intimate, too. The fact that the boys were asked to tea in Balmoral Castle and that the Queen and the Princesses came to supper with them in camp, strengthened the personal aspect, and the reduced numbers made it easier to be quickly on familiar terms. The King's enjoyment of this new spirit was evident. He was always in his element at Balmoral and it was a delight to him to show its beauties and its fascinations to his guests. 'I saw much more of the boys as I went on their walks with them on the hill & was able to talk to them', he wrote to Queen Mary,[31] and never had he taken so active and personal a part in the actual running of the Camp.

This was another aspect of the new Monarch who had returned from the New World. Always informal in his Camp relations, he now showed a hitherto quite undisclosed ability for putting the boys at their ease, and it was remarkable how they responded to his mood.

They listened to him with rapt attention [writes Captain Paterson] while he described interesting features of the surrounding country, or pointed out activity going on all round them which their inexperienced eyes had failed to see. Herds of deer; birds of all kinds as they got up from the heather and bracken; the sparrow hawk hovering in the sky. These were all unfamiliar sights to the majority of them and they created a firm bond between the King and his young guests. They told him of their work and experience in the more crowded parts of his Kingdom and were not a little surprised by his own knowledge of their everyday world. It was a delightful experience and typified all that is grand and good in our democratic way of life and in the contemporary relationship between Throne and People.

On the last night of the Camp the great bonfire was lit in accordance with established tradition, this time by the King himself. The Balmoral pipers encircled it, playing stirring airs, and, finally, Auld Lang Syne and the National Anthem were sung with a fervour which would have surprised those who believe the British to be devoid of emotion. Then, led by the King, the boys trooped down the hill to the line of motor-coaches waiting to take them to Aberdeen and home. As he had greeted them, so now he sped them on their way, alone. Their last memory of him was of a figure caught in the headlights of the coaches, waving good-bye.

Within a few short weeks many of these young men would be members of the King's armed services or in the Civil Defence Force, fighting in defence of his kingdom and of their own rights and liberties. He would meet some of them again during his many tours of camps and air stations in Britain or during his visits to his armies in North Africa, Italy, Normandy and the Low Countries, or his inspections of the Fleet. Some he would never see again. They would always remember him as they saw him on the last evening of his last Camp — a figure, brightly lit, waving encouragement.

This was symbolic. It was the end. It was his own conception and with the willing help of others, his own achievement. It was fitting that these two hundred young men, representing the seven thousand who had enjoyed the unique privilege of meeting the King in such intimate circumstances, should take their leave of him from his own home, because what he had started as an experiment had become an integral part of His Majesty's personal interests.[a]

(v)

In Europe the sullen lull persisted; that moment of hot stillness before the cyclone breaks. In Britain summer had redeemed her reputation; the sun shone, the beaches and resorts were crowded, albeit some holiday-makers carried their gas-masks with their golf-clubs. The climate of ideas was full of contradictions, for whereas every day brought further evidence of national preparedness, there was as yet no feeling of hope abandoned and a widespread belief prevailed that, if the autumn passed without a crisis, a period of indefinite quiescence might be achieved.

The King shared these hopes. He had had to abandon his young guests at the Abergeldie Camp for one day, on

[a] Captain Paterson's Memorandum (see above, p. 398).

August 9, in order to inspect the Reserve Fleet at Weymouth, and had been greatly impressed by the spirit of the reservists. 'It is wonderful the way in which all the men have come back for duty at this time,' he wrote to Queen Mary on his return to Balmoral, '& I feel sure it will be a deterrent factor in Hitler's mind to start a war. If we can only get through these 2 months without a crisis all would be well." [32]

It was not to be. On August 22 the world shuddered at the announcement of the Soviet-German pact of non-aggression, and then groaned in anguished apprehension, for few doubted that this amazing event could but betoken war.

The King at Balmoral, on hearing the news, at once decided to return to London. He was apprised of the reaction of his Ministers in a letter from Mr. Chamberlain :

> 10 DOWNING STREET
> WHITEHALL
> 23rd August 1939

SIR,

　　Your Majesty will wish to receive at once from me some account of the events of the last twenty-four hours. These events moved so rapidly that it was, in the judgment of the Cabinet, essential to take immediately certain precautionary measures including the calling together of Parliament. I greatly regret that, owing to the pressure of the many weighty matters which had to be considered and acted upon with the least possible delay, I have had no earlier opportunity of submitting a report to you and that the intention to summon Parliament was announced publicly before a communication on the subject had been made to Your Majesty.

　　The Cabinet met at 3 p.m. yesterday afternoon and sat for about 3½ hours. I enclose the Minutes of the Meeting, which are the readiest means of acquainting you with all that has taken place.

　　Briefly, following the disclosure of the proposed Pact between Russia and Germany, it was decided that some immediate announcement must be made, indicating that what had happened in no way altered the policy of this country or our determination to fulfil our pledges. The Cabinet accordingly agreed to the issue of the statement which was made public last night, and to the despatch of a letter from myself to Herr Hitler. The terms of the letter were telegraphed in advance to Sir Nevile Henderson with instructions to seek an interview with Herr Hitler and communicate them to him. I enclose a copy of the statement and of the letter.[a]

When Parliament meets tomorrow it is our intention to ask for the passage into law during the day of the Emergency Powers (Defence) Bill. The Bill will not itself authorise action but will enable Regulations to be made, if the need arises, under which action necessary for the defence of the country can be taken. I propose, in submitting to the House the motion enabling all stages of the Bill to be taken in one day, to make a full statement on the international situation.

I have been glad to be informed of Your Majesty's immediate return to London, and shall welcome the opportunity of a full discussion of the position tomorrow.

I am, Sir,

Your Majesty's obedient humble subject

NEVILLE CHAMBERLAIN

His Majesty arrived at Buckingham Palace on the morning of August 24 to find a London still stunned by the news of the events in Moscow. He was greeted by a note from Queen Mary at Sandringham, a message of sympathy in his grave anxiety from one who recognized from the sad experience of the past the premonitory symptoms of conflict.[b] He plunged at once into a series of discussions with his principal Ministers, whom he left in no uncertainty that he approved the policy of determined opposition to Germany which they had adopted. He shared also the general dismay at the new and unnatural alignment which had resulted from the Nazi-Soviet Pact. He

[a] The statement by the Cabinet, which was broadcast by the B.B.C. on the evening of August 22, and appeared in the press on the following day, was as follows :

The Cabinet also took note of the report that a non-aggression pact between the German and Soviet Governments was about to be concluded. They had no hesitation in deciding that such an event would in no way affect their obligation to Poland, which they had repeatedly stated in public and which they are determined to fulfil.

The Prime Minister's letter to Hitler, the text of which is to be found in the *British Blue Book* on the events leading up to the outbreak of war (p. 96, No. 56), was handed to the Führer by Sir N. Henderson at Berchtesgaden shortly after one o'clock in the afternoon of August 23. In it Mr. Chamberlain recapitulated the steadfast attitude and intention of the British Government, and closed with the words : ' In view of the grave consequences to humanity which may follow from the action of their rulers, I trust that Your Excellency will weigh with the utmost deliberation the considerations which I have placed before you '.

[b] ' I feel deeply for you too,' Queen Mary also wrote to Queen Elizabeth, who had remained in Scotland, ' I having gone through all this in August 1914 when I was the wife of the Sovereign.' [33]

was alive, however, to the possibilities of extracting some advantage from it, more particularly from its repercussions on Japan, to whom it had come as almost as much of an unpleasant surprise as to the Western Powers, since it represented a complete jettisoning of the terms of the Anti-Comintern Pact of 1936, which had formed the basis of Japan's political association with Germany. Was not an opportunity presented here for the possible detaching of Japan from the Axis Powers?

The King has been closely watching the effect on Japan of the German-Soviet Pact [wrote Sir Alexander Hardinge to Sir Alexander Cadogan [a]], and will be disappointed if we do not succeed in deriving some benefit from it. His Majesty wonders, therefore, if it would help in any way if, at an opportune moment, he were to send a friendly message direct to the Emperor. His Majesty realizes perfectly that we must not do anything which looks as if we were throwing China overboard, and this aspect of the matter is, of course, one in which the King would rely for advice upon his Secretary of State.

His Majesty will be glad, therefore, if you will put the suggestion before Lord Halifax for his consideration, as he feels that, when dealing with Orientals, direct communication between Heads of States may be helpful.[34]

It was the considered view of the Foreign Office, however, that the behaviour of the Japanese at the time King George's suggestion was put forward was still too uncertain to eliminate all possibility of a rebuff, which must be avoided at all costs, and once again the desire of the King to serve personally the cause of peace was frustrated.

A further disappointment of the same nature awaited him. Warnings and appeals for a peaceful settlement of the German-Polish issue were flooding into Berlin and Warsaw from all quarters. They came, on August 23, from King Leopold III of the Belgians in the name of the smaller neutral states, Belgium, the Netherlands, Luxemburg, Denmark, Norway, Sweden and Finland; on August 24 from President Roosevelt and

---

[a] Rt. Hon. Sir Alexander George Montagu Cadogan, O.M., G.C.M.G., K.C.B. (b. 1884), having served as Minister and as Ambassador to China, 1933–1936, became Permanent Under-Secretary of State for Foreign Affairs in 1938 and so continued until 1946, when he was appointed Permanent British Representative to the United Nations until his retirement in 1950. He was later Chairman of the Governors of the British Broadcasting Corporation, and a Government Director of the Suez Canal Company.

from Pope Pius XII; and on August 26 from President
Roosevelt again and from Prime Minister Mackenzie King,
who also telegraphed to Mr. Chamberlain urging the advisability of a similar direct appeal by King George to Hitler.

The King was both anxious and willing to take an action
which he himself had suggested to the Prime Minister a year
previously at the time of the Czech Crisis, and he reverted to
the idea when he received Mr. Chamberlain in audience on
August 27. But once again Mr. Chamberlain was pro-
crastinatory. He admitted the possible desirability of such
an action by the King, but preferred to await a more suitable
moment. He would, he promised, keep the matter in mind.[35]

But the suitable moment never apparently arrived. The
sands of peace were fast running out and Adolf Hitler, undeterred by warnings or appeals, was shaping his course for
war. The final choice was now his and his alone. He had
been impressed by the British declaration of policy on August
23, and by the proof of its sincerity in the signing of the Anglo-
Polish Alliance two days later, and as a result he had made a
bid to separate Poland from her Western Allies. He rescinded
the order already issued to invade Poland on August 26, and
in his replies to Mr. Chamberlain [a] he asseverated his desire
for a friendly understanding with Britain, but that there must
first be a settlement of the differences between Germany and
Poland.

With all this the British Government had agreed, and
Lord Halifax had sought and obtained from the Polish Government an assurance of their willingness to negotiate in a con-
cessionary mood. This Mr. Chamberlain conveyed to the
Führer in a letter delivered on the evening of August 28, but
with the renewed assurance that Britain and France stood by
their pledges to Poland.

Hitler had therefore failed in his attempt to split the Anglo-
Franco-Polish Alliance. He knew now that an attack on
Poland would mean war with the Western Powers, whereas
the British reply gave him an opportunity of a settlement by
peaceful means. Faced with this alternative on August 29
he deliberately chose war, a choice which was to lead him
to the highest point of military conquest — but, finally, to

[a] *British Blue Book,* Nos. 60 and 68.

suicide and a nameless grave in the gardens of the Berlin Chancellery. The farce of offering terms to Poland for negotiation was gone through on August 30 and 31, and, at dawn on September 1, the Wehrmacht crossed the Polish frontier.

In London King George watched the progress of events during these last fateful days with deepening anguish. The idea of war, of the inevitable sacrifice and suffering of his peoples, was as abhorrent to him as to any other Englishman, yet he never faltered in his belief that the word of Britain was her bond. His days were fully occupied : meetings of the Privy Council, audiences to Ministers, visits to the War Office, the Admiralty, the Air Ministry and the Central War Room. The German invasion of Poland on September 1 was followed by a day of suspense, during which his Government strove to keep the French in line and finally dispatched an ultimatum to Berlin, bidding Hitler withdraw his troops behind his own frontiers as a preliminary to negotiations or accept the declaration of war by Britain and France. Many had believed that British and French action in support of Poland would be automatic and the delay in declaring war, coupled with the ambiguous reticence of the Prime Minister in the House of Commons, gave some to fear that a new Munich Agreement was imminent.[a]

But there was to be no turning back. The Anglo-French demands received no reply from Herr Hitler, and, the time limit having expired, Great Britain and France were at war with Germany from eleven o'clock on the morning of Sunday, September 3.

Under the stress of war King George decided to keep a diary.[b] For the next seven and a half years, until January 1947, he recorded faithfully and painstakingly — no matter how wearied he might be — the events of the day and fre-

---

[a] Mr. Chamberlain was unable on September 2 to take the House of Commons into his confidence in respect of the difficulties he was incurring with the French Government. His statement, consequently, made a deplorable impression ; the House was restive, resentful and suspicious, and the Labour Party particularly critical. It was in order to prevent a purely partisan speech from Mr. Arthur Greenwood, who rose to speak for the Opposition immediately after the Prime Minister, that Mr. Leopold Amery called across the House, 'Speak for England, Arthur'.

[b] 'I am keeping a War Diary now & have got it up to date', the King wrote to Queen Mary on September 24.

quently his own reactions to them. A more human and illuminating — and a less meteorological — chronicle than that of his father, it provides an invaluable record not only of the period but of the thoughts of a Sovereign.

Sunday September 3rd, 1939

As 11 o'clock struck that fateful morning I had a certain feeling of relief that those 10 anxious days of intensive negotiations with Germany over Poland, which at moments looked favourable, with Mussolini working for peace as well, were over. Hitler would not & could not draw back from the edge of the Abyss to which he had led us. Despite our protestations that the Polish Question could have been settled without force, Hitler had taken the plunge, with the knowledge that the whole might of the British Empire would be against him to help Poland, our ally.

France is our ally. Italy has declared herself neutral for the present.

At the outbreak of War at midnight of Aug. 4th–5th 1914, I was a midshipman, keeping the middle watch on the bridge of H.M.S. 'Collingwood' at sea, somewhere in the North Sea. I was 18 years of age.

In the Grand Fleet everyone was pleased that it had come at last. We had been trained in the belief that War between Germany & this country had to come one day, & when it did come we thought we were prepared for it. We were not prepared for what we found a modern war really was, & those of us who had been through the Great War never wanted another.

Today we are at War again, & I am no longer a midshipman in the Royal Navy.

For the last year ever since the Munich Agreement Germany or rather its leaders, have caused us incessant worry in crises of different magnitudes. Hitler marched into Czecho-Slovakia in March this year. Then Memel. We knew the Polish Question would be the next on the list of Hitler's bloodless victories. The whole country knew it, & had been preparing for it, by making arms, aeroplanes & all the engines of war in record time, to withstand the next real Crisis.

So today when the Crisis is over, & the result of the breakdown of negotiations is War, the country is calm, firm & united behind its leaders, resolved to fight until Liberty & Justice are once again safe in the World. . . .

The P.M. came to see me in the evening. He was very upset but very calm that all his work of the past months had been of no avail to keep the peace of the World. He knew that the Munich Agreement had prevented a European War last Year, & that he had been severely criticised after that for his foreign policy. He had at that time met Hitler face to face, & he hoped that he had made an impression on Hitler, that a repetition of his behaviour then would be the end of our patience.

I broadcasted a message to the Empire at 6.0 p.m.

King George's broadcast on that evening came at the close of a day of acute tension. The House of Commons had met for perhaps the first time in its history on a Sunday, and had heard the Prime Minister's final report of the last moments of peace. Thereafter Mr. Chamberlain had himself broadcast to the nation, and even as his words died away there came the first wail of the air-raid sirens that in the years ahead was to bring alarm into so many hearts. Though no attack had come, the incident had struck the note of war in a not unsalutary manner, alerting a people whom it is not easy to arouse.

The King's message was a declaration of simple faith in simple beliefs, and it is given here in full because there exists no better epitome of the fundamental principles for which Britain went to war. It was a message which gave encouragement, as perhaps nothing else could, to the British peoples in the face of the struggle which lay ahead, and united them in their determination to achieve victory.[a]

In this grave hour, perhaps the most fateful in our history, I send to every household of my peoples, both at home and overseas, this message, spoken with the same depth of feeling for each one of you as if I were able to cross your threshold and speak to you myself.

For the second time in the lives of most of us we are at war. Over and over again we have tried to find a peaceful way out of the differences between ourselves and those who are now our enemies. But it has been in vain. We have been forced into a conflict. For we are called, with our allies, to meet the challenge of a principle which, if it were to prevail, would be fatal to any civilized order in the world.

[a] It had originally been intended that copies of the King's message — one for every household — should be distributed throughout the British Isles, together with a facsimile of the King's signature. A public announcement to this effect had already been made, but circumstances immediately arose which made it impossible. There was an acute shortage of paper in the country and the estimated amount required for printing the broadcast was 250 tons. The Post Office was also seriously alarmed at the prospect of delivering an additional 15 million letters with their already depleted war-time staff. Finally it was found that the total cost of the enterprise would amount to some £35,000, and in the interests of war-time economy this was considered to be an unnecessary expenditure. On the King's initiative, therefore, the project was abandoned.

It is the principle which permits a State, in the selfish pursuit of power, to disregard its treaties and its solemn pledges; which sanctions the use of force, or threat of force, against the Sovereignty and independence of other States. Such a principle, stripped of all disguise, is surely the mere primitive doctrine that Might is Right. And if this principle were established throughout the world, the freedom of our own country and of the whole British Commonwealth of Nations would be in danger. But far more than this — the peoples of the world would be kept in the bondage of fear, and all hopes of settled peace and of the security of justice and liberty among nations would be ended.

This is the ultimate issue which confronts us. For the sake of all that we ourselves hold dear, and of the world's order and peace, it is unthinkable that we should refuse to meet the challenge.

It is to this high purpose that I now call my people at home and my peoples across the Seas, who will make our cause their own. I ask them to stand calm and firm and united in this time of trial. The task will be hard. There may be dark days ahead, and war can no longer be confined to the battlefield. But we can only do the right as we see the right, and reverently commit our cause to God. If one and all we keep resolutely faithful to it, ready for whatever service or sacrifice it may demand, then, with God's help, we shall prevail.

May He bless and keep us all.

CHAPTER V

THE WAR OF NERVES
SEPTEMBER 1939–MAY 1940

(i)

I T has been said with truth that, in September 1938 at the
time of the Munich Crisis, the chances of the various units
of the British Commonwealth entering in support of the
United Kingdom into a conflict with Germany, which had
arisen out of a French treaty commitment to Czechoslovakia,
were slender in the extreme. This thought had undoubtedly
been in the minds of both King George and his Prime Minister
in their assessment of the situation. If the majority of the
British public concurred — as it undoubtedly did — with
Mr. Chamberlain's view as expressed in his famous broadcast
of September 23, that it was fantastic to find themselves on
the brink of war 'because of a quarrel in a far-away country
between people of whom we know nothing', how much more
was this true of a French-Canadian *habitant*, a Queensland
sheep-drover or a dweller on the South African veldt?

The attitude of mind which had produced the refusal of
support in the Chanak Crisis and the specific reservations to
the Locarno Treaties, had become firm policy twelve years
later. Mr. Chamberlain's colleagues in Ottawa and Canberra
and Wellington and Pretoria had been wholly in favour of
his policy of appeasement as adumbrated at the Imperial
Conference of 1937, and had accepted it as their own, but
there would have been small chance of their approval if he
had asked them to abandon it little more than a year later,
whereas there was no question as to their whole-hearted
endorsement of the British Government's policy at Munich.[a]

---

[a] An example of the division which existed at this time is that of the Commonwealth of Australia, where, although the Government held that Australia
would be automatically at war when the King was at war in Britain, the Labour
Opposition held a completely contrary view. 'My doctrine is that so long as
the British Empire is constituted as it is to-day, it is not possible for Australia to

Such being the case, the decision of His Majesty's Government in the United Kingdom, in March 1939, to embark upon a complete reversal of this policy, and to enter into far-flung specific commitments on the continent of Europe, was the more remarkable and courageous. No Dominion was a party to the guarantees offered to Poland and to Greece and Rumania, nor to the Alliance with Turkey. The Governments of the Commonwealth were kept fully informed of all developments and, where time allowed, were consulted, but it was realized that neither information nor consultation was tantamount to commitment, even though it was recognized that the Dominions could not remain unaffected by the consequences of British policies in Europe. This, as Professor Mansergh has very rightly written, was 'a supremely important fact in 1939. On September 3 the United Kingdom declared war on Germany in fulfilment of the guarantee extended to Poland in the previous March, but for the rest the issue of peace and war had to be decided in the light of broader considerations.' [1]

Thus September 1939 was one of the great landmarks in the evolution of the British Commonwealth, and one which gave added point to King George's comment that an outsider might well believe that 'there ain't no such animal'. For, despite rifts and differences, and notwithstanding varieties of reasoning and approaches, the animal was disclosed as not only existing but very much alive.

The differences of agreement were indeed many and varied. [a] The Pacific Dominions held to their doctrine that neutrality on the part of the King in one part of the Commonwealth was logically incompatible with his being at war in another part. They therefore regarded themselves as being automatically belligerent, and their declarations of war upon

be neutral in a British war', the Attorney-General, Mr. Robert Menzies, had declared on behalf of the Government in September 1938; but the Leader of the Labour Party, Mr. Curtin, took 'the responsibility of going so far as to say that should war in Europe result . . . it will be a war that Australia would regret. But Australia . . . should not be involved in it.' In South Africa, however, both General Hertzog and General Smuts were agreed on a policy of non-belligerency should war have come in September 1938.

[a] An admirable study of the circumstances under which the various Dominions reached their respective decisions in September 1939, which has been of the greatest assistance in the writing of this section, is to be found in the chapter entitled 'In the Valley of Decision', of Professor Nicholas Mansergh's *Survey of British Commonwealth Affairs, Problems of External Policy, 1931–1939.*

Germany were made simultaneously with that of Great Britain on September 3. In the case of Australia, though Parliament was in session, it was not even summoned to endorse the action of the Cabinet, and the country rallied at once to the slogan: 'One King, one flag, one cause'. In New Zealand the motion approving and confirming the declaration of war was passed by the House of Representatives without a dissentient vote.

In Canada the *mores* were different, the result the same. Consistent with the view, which he had proclaimed for many years, that Canada would not go to war just because Britain, or indeed the rest of the Commonwealth, was at war until she had come freely and independently to the decision to do so, Mr. Mackenzie King did not summon Parliament until September 7, four days after the United Kingdom declaration of war. The debate which then followed indicated that three factors had occurred since 1938 which had helped to crystallize Canadian opinion: the barefaced manner in which Hitler had deliberately abandoned the basis of the Munich Agreement; his cynical pact with the Soviet Union; and the recent visit of Their Majesties. When the motion to declare war was moved on September 9, it was taken without a division, and Canada declared war as from the 10th.

In South Africa, however, the division was deep and bitter. The aged Prime Minister, General Hertzog,[a] had never departed from the view that behind Hitler and the Nazi régime stood the 'unholy Treaty of Versailles', on which, and on the victors who imposed it, rested the ultimate responsibility for the plight of Europe. For six years he had worked in close collaboration with General Smuts [b] to the end that the

[a] General the Hon. James Barry Munnik Hertzog (1866–1942) commanded the Boer forces of the South Western Division in the South African War and his rank of General derived from President Steyn of the Orange Free State. He became Minister of Justice under General Botha in the first Union Cabinet of 1910, and was leader of the Nationalist Party from 1924 to 1933, and of the United South African National Party from 1933 to 1939. He was Prime Minister of the Union from 1924 to 1939, and Minister for External Affairs from 1929 to 1938.

[b] Field-Marshal the Rt. Hon. Jan Christiaan Smuts, O.M., C.H. (1870–1950), served as State Attorney under President Kruger in the South African Republic in 1898 and during the South African War was in supreme command of the Boer forces in Cape Colony. He served as Minister of the Interior in the first Union Cabinet formed in 1910, and subsequently as Minister of Mines, Defence, Finance and Native Affairs, and was Prime Minister from 1919 to 1924. He was Minister of Justice in General Hertzog's coalition Cabinet from 1933 to 1939, and Prime Minister and Minister of Defence and External Affairs from 1939 to 1948. He

European peoples of South Africa might be reconciled and eventually fused into one nation, and up till the aftermath of Munich their views had wholly coincided in favour of a policy of non-belligerency for South Africa in the event of a European war.

Now in September 1939, however, there came the parting of the ways between these two great South Africans. General Hertzog remained consistent with his previous beliefs. His mind was rigid; that of General Smuts was still impressionable. In the year which separated the Czech and Polish Crises, General Smuts had moved steadily away from the views of the Prime Minister. He had studied, and had at length comprehended, the dark forces which were at work in Central Europe, and he was fully aware, moreover, of the danger which a victorious Germany would constitute to the Union of South Africa.

When, therefore, on September 2, 1939, General Hertzog informed his Cabinet that he was prepared to recommend a policy of neutrality to Parliament, General Smuts vehemently withstood him, and announced his intention of testing the issue on the floor of the House of Assembly. The Cabinet was divided five to seven against General Hertzog, but the Prime Minister would not yield. He believed that, with the support of Dr. Malan's Nationalist Party, he could command a majority in the House, and, although no longer the leader of a united Cabinet, he met Parliament on September 4. There he made an impassioned address in defence of neutrality, to which General Smuts replied with equal fervour in support of a declaration of war, with the reservation that South African forces should not be sent overseas. The historic debate which followed was protracted and bitter, bitter with the bitterness of the Afrikaner. Not till late in the evening of the second day was the vote taken, in an atmosphere of great tension. Sixty-seven members voted in favour of the Prime Minister's motion of neutrality, eighty for General Smuts' amendment for a declaration of war.

was a signatory of both the Peace of Vereeniging in 1902, and the Treaty of Versailles in 1919, and was elected Chancellor of Cambridge University in 1948. As a philosopher, he was an exponent of 'Holism' — 'the fundamental unity and continuity in nature'.

Even at this moment General Hertzog would not finally admit defeat. Believing that a general election would result in a majority in favour of his policy, he advised the Governor-General to dissolve Parliament; and only when this advice was rejected by Sir Patrick Duncan [a] did he tender his resignation. General Smuts at once formed a cabinet, and the South African declaration of war on Germany was announced on September 6.[b]

There remained Ireland. Here Mr. de Valera — that strange amalgam of dark mysticism, *Realpolitik* and statesmanship — had in a sense the easiest task of all. For just as the Antipodean Dominions regarded themselves as being automatically at war with the declaration by the United Kingdom, so, at the other end of the scale, the people of Eire regarded themselves as being 'automatically neutral'. This view was well-nigh universally accepted throughout the country, and all parties in the Dail were unanimous in support of it. Had Mr. de Valera himself felt otherwise and attempted to sway his countrymen towards war, he would have failed, even to the extent of having a civil war on his hands. For Ireland at this juncture, with characteristic paradox, would rather fight than go to war.[c]

But Mr. de Valera shared the views of his countrymen, though he had arrived at his conclusions as a result of wider considerations than most of them. Not only did he share their desire to remain neutral, recognizing the impossibility of bringing them to any other course had he wished to do so, but

[a] Rt. Hon. Sir Patrick Duncan, G.C.M.G. (1870–1943), was private secretary to Lord Milner in South Africa during the South African War, and was appointed Treasurer of the Transvaal in 1901, and Colonial Secretary from 1903 to 1906. He was Minister of the Interior and Education in General Smuts's Cabinet from 1921 to 1924, and Minister of Mines in General Hertzog's Cabinet from 1933 to 1936. He was appointed Governor-General of the Union of South Africa in 1937, and so continued until he died in 1943.

[b] On January 23, 1940, General Hertzog and Dr. Malan joined forces to challenge the Smuts Government on the issue 'that this House is of the opinion that the time has come for the war against Germany to be ended and for peace to be restored'. General Smuts, however, again carried Parliament with him. His policy of continued belligerency was confirmed by 81 votes to 59 in the House, and by 21 votes to 3 in the Senate.

[c] The threat of civil war in Eire at that time was no light one. The recrudescence of I.R.A. outrages in Northern Ireland, in Britain and in Eire itself, during 1938 and 1939, compelled Mr. de Valera to enact severe repressive measures, which he carried through with commendable resolution.

his own observations at Geneva, as President of the Assembly of the League of Nations in September 1932, had convinced him of the parlous condition of the world at large, of the barrenness of international polity, and of the primary necessity of keeping Ireland from being drawn into the inevitable maelstrom.

When, therefore, the Dail met on September 2, 1939, it was not to discuss *whether* Eire should remain neutral — this was assumed to be a matter already settled — but *how* her neutrality should be best secured, and the legislation then introduced, in the shape of an amendment to the Constitution of 1939 and of an Emergency Powers Act, was directed solely towards this end. Thus were the hopes of Mr. Chamberlain for the fruits of his earlier appeasement of Eire shattered and the worst forebodings of Mr. Churchill fulfilled. There were no naval bases in Eire for the British Fleet, but neither were there munition factories safe from aerial attack, and Mr. de Valera steadfastly rejected the several approaches made by the British Government to persuade him to abandon Ireland's neutrality,[a] a neutrality which, however, did not prevent thousands of Irishmen from volunteering for service in the armed forces and munitions factories of Britain.

The problem, therefore, which had so long vexed constitutional lawyers and interpreters of the Statute of Westminster, as to whether it was possible for the King to be at war through the action of certain of his Governments and neutral through the action of others, and whether a part of the Commonwealth so declaring itself neutral could remain within the fold, was accorded pragmatic recognition, and with certain curious constitutional results. Despite her neutrality, Eire was still considered to be a member of the Commonwealth in accordance with the decision of the Imperial Conference of 1937, and indeed the United Kingdom Government took a step, which many regarded as overdue, of putting their representation in Eire on a more formal basis. Hitherto a trade commissioner had sufficed for the handling of British interests,

[a] There were two such secret approaches made to Eire during the war: the first by Mr. Malcolm MacDonald in June of 1940, and the second by Lord Cranborne in December 1941, shortly after Pearl Harbour.

but in September 1939 Sir John Maffey[a] was appointed to Dublin as the first United Kingdom diplomatic representative.

On the other hand, the question of Irish representation abroad became an acute and immediate issue. When the post of Minister at the Eire Legation in Berlin became vacant, the credentials of a new Minister had, by virtue of the External Relations Act, to be signed by the King. But His Majesty could not accredit a diplomatic representative to a State with which he was at war, and, in consequence, Eire was compelled to be represented in the capital of the German Reich by a *chargé d'affaires*.

Thus did the King go forth to war in September 1939 at the head of an all but united Commonwealth, of which each component unit had reached its conclusion to participate in accordance with its own views and of its own free will. Nothing could have illustrated more definitely the sovereign status of the several Dominions, for the right of making war and peace has long been acknowledged as the acid test of sovereignty.[b] 'By 1939 the days of Dominion knight-errantry were over';[2] no longer was an appeal to traditional loyalties or to moral obligations sufficient to bring a united Commonwealth to war. Even the 'Ties of Common Funk', of which Rudyard Kipling had written, were loosened. The case for participation had to be argued in each case on the basis of national self-interest.

(ii)

The functions of a British Sovereign in war-time do not differ materially from those which he exercises in time of peace. He

[a] John Loader Maffey, first Baron Rugby, G.C.M.G., K.C.B., K.C.V.O., C.S.I., C.I.E. (b. 1877), entered the Indian Civil Service and became Private Secretary to the Viceroy from 1916 to 1920. He served as Governor-General of the Sudan from 1926 to 1933, and as Permanent Under-Secretary of State for the Colonies, 1933–1937. He was U.K. representative to Eire from 1939 to 1949.

[b] In sharp contradistinction was the position of the Indian Empire, which was declared by the Viceroy to be at war with Germany on September 3, by virtue of the authority vested in him by the Government of India Act of 1919, which still remained in force for purposes of central government because all attempts to implement the provisions of the Act of 1935 to create a government at the centre had failed.

does not, for example, automatically assume the command of his forces in the field, for he is already, as Sovereign, their Supreme Commander. His standard might fly in the flagship of any fleet or squadron he might be inspecting, but that would also be the case in peace-time. His constitutional position remains the same; he has neither more nor less power. But, if his functions do not change, war brings to a Sovereign, as to all others in authority, a vast increase in labour and responsibility and, to him alone, additional opportunities to utilize to the benefit of his Ministers his supra-party position as Head of the State.

In the First World War King George V had felt that his most useful function was 'not to inflict upon Ministers and Commanders his own view of policy or strategy, but, with constant vigilance, to advise, to encourage and to warn',[3] and on several occasions he offered his services to procure accommodation among party leaders and would comment 'with some severity upon the obstinacy of politicians who prolonged these recriminations in a time of national crisis'.[4] This, indeed, was the basic principle of conduct adopted by King George VI, but he was never satisfied that he had done enough. Though he toiled unremittingly at the tasks which fell to him — and they were many and arduous, filling almost every hour of his day — there appears in his diaries a recurrent note of disappointment that he could not do more. In his selfless service to his peoples he spared himself nothing, yet could not escape a feeling of frustration, even in his great weariness.

The first change with which the King was confronted at the outbreak of war was in the composition of his Government. Mr. Chamberlain's first act had been to reorganize his Cabinet, which he hoped could now be constituted on a national basis. In this, however, he was disappointed. Whereas the two leading dissidents among his own party, Mr. Churchill and Mr. Eden, accepted his invitation to serve — the one at the Admiralty, and the other at the Dominions Office, — his overtures to the Liberal and Labour leaders were declined with the same formula, that their parties could serve the national cause better from outside. His War Cabinet of nine members therefore consisted of his former 'Inner Cabinet', Lord Halifax, Sir John Simon and Sir Samuel Hoare, with the

addition of the three Service Ministers, Mr. Churchill, Sir
Kingsley Wood and Mr. Hore-Belisha, the Minister for the
Co-ordination of Defence, Lord Chatfield,[a] and Lord Hankey
as Minister without Portfolio.

The King was unprepared for both the size and the composition of the War Cabinet. He had expected a body of six
rather than nine, and, though he had known that Mr. Churchill
would be included, he seems to have been surprised that he
should be at the Admiralty.[5] He welcomed his new First
Lord warmly, however, and discussed with him the project
for American bases in the Atlantic, showing him the notes of
his conversations with President Roosevelt at Hyde Park.
When he received Mr. Eden, though, the King still found
him 'difficult to talk to'.[6]

The outbreak of war confronted the King with a personal
and delicate problem in the return to England of the Duke of
Windsor. Since his abdication, and his marriage in June
1937, the Duke had lived in Austria and France. There had
been strong differences of opinion over the Duchess's title, for
the Duke had been bitterly incensed at her exclusion by the
Letters Patent of May 28, 1937, from the use of the style of
'Royal Highness' and had not hesitated to make his views
known with some vehemence. An earlier suggestion for a visit
by the Duke and Duchess to England had not met with the
King's pleasure, but now the situation was different. England
was at war, and the Duke was anxious to serve his country,
in the armed forces of which he still held the rank of Field-
Marshal, Admiral of the Fleet and Marshal of the Royal Air
Force.

Though apprehensive of the difficulties which might arise
for all concerned from a prolonged residence of the Duke of
Windsor in England, the King was at first prepared to offer
his brother two alternative forms of war service. He could
either have a military appointment, with the temporary rank
of Major-General, on the staff of the British Mission in Paris,

---

[a] Admiral of the Fleet the Rt. Hon. Alfred Ernle Montacute, first Baron
Chatfield, G.C.B., O.M., K.C.M.G., C.V.O. (b. 1873), after a distinguished
naval career, during which he commanded the Atlantic Fleet (1929–1930) and
in the Mediterranean (1930–1932), and served as First Sea Lord from 1933 to 1938,
joined Mr. Chamberlain's Cabinet as Minister for Co-ordination of Defence from
1939 to 1940.

of which General Howard-Vyse *a* was the head, or serve as a civilian under the Regional Commissioner for Civil Defence for Wales, Lord Portal; *b* and with this choice the Duke was acquainted.

The brothers met on the afternoon of September 14. The King recorded in his diary:

I saw David on our return [from a tour of the London Docks]. I had not seen him since he left England on December 11, 1936. We talked for about an hour. There were no recriminations on either side. . . . I found him the same as I had always known him. He looked very well & had lost the deep lines under his eyes. . . .

And to the Prime Minister the King wrote: 'The whole tone of our meeting was a very friendly one. He seems very well, & not a bit worried as to the effects he left on people's minds as to his behaviour in 1936. He has forgotten all about it.' [7]

Of the alternative appointments offered him, it is to be believed that the Duke of Windsor would have preferred to serve on Lord Portal's staff in Wales.[8] The King, however, on considering the matter further, had decided otherwise. 'The conclusion reached by His Majesty', wrote Sir Alexander Hardinge on September 14 — the day of the meeting between the King and the Duke — to the Secretary of State for War, Mr. Hore-Belisha, 'is that His Royal Highness would be most suitably employed as a member of the Military Mission to France, of which General Howard-Vyse is the head.' [9] The Duke was informed of this decision next day by Mr. Hore-Belisha and received his appointment from the Chief of the Imperial General Staff, Sir Edmund Ironside, *c* as his personal

a Major-General Sir Richard Granville Howard-Vyse, K.C.M.G., D.S.O. (b. 1883), was Inspector of Cavalry from 1930 to 1934, and accompanied the Duke of Gloucester as Chief of Staff on his tour of Australia and New Zealand in 1935. He was head of the British Military Mission with the French High Command from the outbreak of war until the close of the Battle of France in June 1940.

b Rt. Hon. Wyndham Raymond, first Viscount Portal, G.C.M.G., D.S.O., M.V.O. (1885–1949), served as Regional Commissioner for Civil Defence for Wales, 1939–1940, as Parliamentary Secretary to the Ministry of Supply, 1940–1942, and as Minister of Works and Planning, 1942–1944.

c Field-Marshal William Edmund, first Baron Ironside, G.C.B., C.M.G., D.S.O. (b. 1880), commanded the Allied Expedition to Archangel in 1918–1919, and the Ismid Force and the North Persian Force, 1920–1921. He served as Quartermaster-General in India, 1933–1936; G.O.C.-in-C. Eastern Command, 1936–1938; Governor of Gibraltar, 1938–1939; Chief of the Imperial General Staff, 1939–1940; and Commander-in-Chief, Home Forces, 1940.

liaison officer with the French Army, acting under the administrative authority of General Howard-Vyse.

To Paris, therefore, the Duke went as a member of the British Military Mission, reverting temporarily to Major-General, but becoming junior in this rank to his younger brother, the Duke of Gloucester, then serving as Chief Liaison Officer with the British Expeditionary Force.[a] The Duke of Windsor remained in France until the *débâcle* of the summer of 1940 when, after an adventurous journey through Spain and Portugal, he was appointed Governor and Commander-in-Chief of the Bahama Islands, a post which he held until the end of the war.

The King, himself so convinced of the justice of the cause for which Britain fought, of the correctness of her conduct in fighting for it and of her ultimate victory, was disinclined to tolerate meekly the jeremiads and threnodies of those 'croakers' who could see nothing but darkness and despair at the end of the road. The spirit which had inspired Queen Victoria, during the South African War, to enunciate her famous dictum: 'There is no one depressed in *this* house; we are not interested in the possibilities of defeat; they do not exist',[b] was vibrant within her great-grandson, but King George gave it a different form of expression. On a scribbling pad on his desk he made the following memorandum: 'The schoolboy's definition of courage: That part of you which says "stick it" while the rest of you says "chuck it" '; and beneath this a verse from Isaiah: 'They helped every one his neighbour and every one said to his brother, Be of good courage'.[c]

[a] The Duke of Gloucester had been gazetted a Major-General on January 1, 1937.

[b] This incident took place at Windsor just after the 'Black Week' of December 1899, 'when all that was articulate in the country's public opinion had surrendered to one of those unreasoning fits of panic to which it is periodically liable'. Her Prime Minister, Lord Salisbury, being indisposed, the Queen sent for his nephew, Mr. Balfour, who 'began to speak to her with intent of consolatory reassurance, of the alarmist reports which filled the papers. But he was at once cut short with the characteristic, quick little bend of the head in which all regality seemed concentrated: "Please understand that there is no depression in *this* house; we are not interested in the possibilities of defeat; they do not exist." Mr. Balfour returned to his uncle enthusiastically appreciative. It had been splendid to pass from the clamorous croakers in Clubs and newspapers into the presence of this little old lady, alone among her women at Windsor, and hear her sweep away all their vaticinations into nothingness with a nod.' [10]

[c] Isaiah xli. 6.

When, therefore, the American Ambassador, Mr. Joseph Kennedy,[a] called upon him in the first week of the war, full of gloom for the future, King George took immediate steps to dispel his mood. Mr. Kennedy had been a fervent supporter of Mr. Chamberlain's policy of appeasement at the time of Munich, but in the ensuing year he had not progressed along the same road as the Prime Minister. He shared his abhorrence of war, but he carried it to the point of doubting whether war was ever worth while when, whatever the ultimate result, financial and material disaster seemed inevitable. He was unable to comprehend the deeper motives for which Britain had entered the struggle, seeing only that, since eastern Europe was of little use to her from a monetary standpoint, she might as well allow Hitler to occupy it. He had, moreover, been deeply shocked at the torpedoing of the liner *Athenia*,[b] with attendant loss of American lives.

These impressions Mr. Kennedy put before the King, and His Majesty reacted in no uncertain manner. He was distressed that the American Ambassador should hold such views personally, and was disturbed at the thought that they must certainly influence the reports which he made to Washington. He therefore wrote him the following letter, which he had first shown to his Prime Minister : [c]

September 12, 1939

DEAR MR. KENNEDY,

I was very glad that we had that talk yesterday.[d]

You certainly put the present international situation, as you see it, very clearly to me.

On thinking over what you said, I would like to make clear to you one or two matters which are in my mind. When referring to the fact that England would be broke at the end of this War, & that in this statement you also inferred that your country, the United States of America, would be likewise broke, is it not possible

---

[a] Hon. Joseph Patrick Kennedy (b. 1888) was United States Ambassador to London, 1937–1941.

[b] The S.S. *Athenia* was torpedoed by a U-boat off the north-west of Ireland on September 3, 1939, with a considerable loss of life.

[c] The copy of this letter in the Royal Archives is endorsed with the King's own hand : 'I showed this letter to the Prime Minister, the Rt. Hon. Neville Chamberlain, G.R.I.   12.9.39'.

[d] According to King George's diary, the interview took place on September 9, not on the 11th.

for you to put this fact before the American Press? As I see it, the U.S.A., France & the British Empire are the three really free peoples in the World, & two of these great democracies are now fighting against all that we three countries hate & detest, Hitler & his Nazi regime and all that it stands for. You were speaking about the loss of prestige of the British Empire under the changed conditions in which we live since the last war.

England, my country, owing to its geographical position in the World is part of Europe.

She has been expected to act, & has had to act, as the policeman, and has always been the upholder of the rights of smaller nations.

The British Empire has once again shown to the World a united front in this coming struggle.

Japan has been very rude to both our nations in the last few months, but with her preponderance of naval military & air armaments in that sphere even she has not dared to molest either of us, as she realises the prestige we both hold in the world.

I know that you appreciate things when they are plainly expressed, & that is why I do so now.

And I do it in a very friendly spirit as I have a tremendous admiration for your country, for your President & for yourself.

We stand on the threshold of we know not what. Misery & suffering of War we know. But what of the future? The British Empire's mind is made up. I leave it at that.

Believe me
Yours very sincerely
GEORGE R.I.

To this simple and courageous statement of the British case Mr. Kennedy replied, as the King recorded, 'very friendly like', and it is probable that its salutary effect was felt in Washington, where President Roosevelt was preparing to urge Congress to revise the neutrality legislation.[a]

King George's diplomatic ability was tested on more than one occasion during this period of the war, and, as will be seen, more frequently later. His capacity for honest and simple reasoning — as in the case of Mr. Kennedy — was an asset which came to be highly valued by his Ministers, who would turn to him in necessity for assistance, more especially in respect of his brother Sovereigns and heads of States.

[a] President Roosevelt delivered a message to a special session of Congress on September 21, urging the repeal of the existing Arms Embargo and the enactment of further neutrality legislation on the basis of 'Cash-and-Carry'. The Senate voted to repeal the Embargo on November 3, receiving the President's approval on the following day.

In this period of the war a diplomatic contest raged for the souls of those States which had proclaimed themselves neutral. The Nazi objective was to persuade as many States as possible to adhere to the Axis *bloc* in preparation for that New Order which the Führer proposed to create around the hard core of the German Reich. The diplomatic objective of Britain and France was to keep the neutrals neutral. During the comparative lull between the Battle of Poland and the German break-through in the West, the neutral States and their rulers watched anxiously for the next move on the military chess-board — and none more anxiously than in the Balkans. In Belgrade and Bucharest, in Athens and Sofia, a note of cold fear had been struck by the stark brutality of the second Nazi-Soviet treaty of alliance (September 29, 1939), which had not only partitioned Poland but had delivered to the U.S.S.R. large areas both in the Baltic lands and on the Rumanian borders. Hitler's *Realpolitik* and Stalin's avarice, either combined or severally, were capable apparently of any depredations, and the Balkan Sovereigns became increasingly uneasy in the face of alternate threats and blandishments.

Because of her key strategic position, considerable importance was attached to keeping Bulgaria within the neutral fold, and King George suggested to Lord Halifax that a semi-personal letter to King Boris,[a] on a 'Sovereign to Sovereign' basis, might have a beneficial effect upon his morale. The King had a genuine liking for the Bulgarian monarch, a man of considerable charm and ability, who with his Queen had been a visitor to Balmoral in the midst of the Czech crisis of the previous autumn. King Boris was an excellent shot, a fact which had further endeared him to King George, and together they had discussed the problems with which both were confronted in the international situation. The King had admired his guest's cool and quiet courage in the face of

[a] King Boris II of Bulgaria (1894–1943) succeeded his father, King Ferdinand (1861–1940), the 'Balkan Fox' of the First World War, on the latter's abdication in 1918. By nature a man of liberal beliefs, he was compelled by force of circumstances to take a more and more personal control of the affairs of his country, until by 1935 he had become a virtual dictator. He married in 1930 Princess Giovanna of Savoy, the youngest daughter of the King of Italy, by whom he had one son, Prince Simeon, who succeeded him briefly after his sudden and mysterious death on August 29, 1943. In addition to a passion for all outdoor sports, King Boris was an expert engine driver, and would frequently pilot his own royal train.

imminent political danger, and his admiration was enhanced when King Boris, while visiting Hitler a week before the Munich Conference, made a determined appeal that the influence of Germany should be cast into the scales in favour of peace, and was equally determined in his refusal to be drawn into the Nazi orbit.[a]

The King's idea of a personal message of encouragement to King Boris at this juncture commended itself to his Ministers, and, with their approval, he therefore addressed 'a personal note to you as a Brother Sovereign reigning over a brave people'. The letter recalled in terms of warm praise King Boris's efforts for peace in the previous year, and regretted their failure. It repeated in essence the reasons for Britain's going to war, and displayed an understanding of the difficulties with which Bulgaria was faced. At the same time the King urged the importance of maintaining Bulgaria's neutrality and of giving no grounds for suspicion to her neighbours:

. . . I know your country is placed in a particularly difficult and delicate position, and for this reason I and my Government have appreciated all the more the neutral attitude your nation has adopted in the present conflict. I sincerely hope that Bulgaria will, as I am sure she wishes to do, maintain that neutrality in all circumstances. You can, of course, rest assured that that neutrality will be respected in the fullest possible degree by my Empire so long as it is not violated by others. In that case I have no doubt that the Bulgarians will know how to give a good account of themselves.

I have always admired all that you have done for your country; and have welcomed the progress that Bulgaria has made under your enlightened leadership, until she now occupies a position in which she commands the respect of Europe as a whole.

I also know how strenuously you have laboured in the past to improve your country's relations with her neighbours, and I am sure I can count on you to continue your efforts in this direction. For this reason I am confident that nothing will be done, at Bulgarian instance, to increase those suspicions and fears between nations, which contribute so largely to the difficulties and dangers of the present time.[12]

[a] Hitler, also, was not unimpressed by King Boris. 'In my view, King Boris is a somebody', he is recorded as saying. 'There's nothing surprising about that, for he has been to a good school with his father, Tsar Ferdinand, the most intelligent monarch I've known . . . under the rod of the old fox, son Boris himself became a young fox.' [11]

The letter was handed to King Boris by the British Minister in Sofia on the evening of September 22. He was deeply moved, and more particularly by King George's references to his efforts for peace in 1938. 'How good of him to remember that', he repeated several times with tears in his eyes. Though his reply was somewhat, and perhaps necessarily, non-committal, the effect of King George's letter on his personal morale was excellent, and he was evidently greatly relieved to know that his brother Sovereign knew and understood 'the difficult and delicate position' in which Bulgaria found herself. The King's initiative undoubtedly proved a valuable factor in shaping King Boris's future attitude in persuading his Ministers to pursue Bulgarian neutrality, at any rate for the time being, although later he was unable to resist the demands and enticements of the Führer.[a]

More positively successful was King George's contribution to the conclusion of the Franco-British treaty of alliance with Turkey. This instrument was initialed on September 28, 1939, together with a military convention and a special agreement, which defined the various forms of financial and economic assistance to be given to Turkey, and contained a 'suspense clause' whereby the treaty would not come into force until the Western Allies had supplied Turkey with her immediate armaments requirements. A complication existed in the fact that the Turkish Foreign Minister had gone to Moscow for the purpose of negotiating a new pact of amity with the Soviet Union, and was there being placed under considerable pressure to modify the agreements already reached with Britain and France.

Such was the position when there arrived in London a Turkish military mission, headed by General Mehmet Orbay,[b] with a formidable 'shopping list' of armament requirements, in many of the items of which the British and French were

---

[a] See below, p. 491.

[b] General Mehmet Kazim Orbay (b. 1887), a veteran of the Italian, Balkan and First World Wars, and of the Turkish War of Independence in 1921, had accompanied President Inönü to the funeral of King George V in 1935. During the Second World War he became Chief of the General Staff in 1944 and was designated as Commander-in-Chief in the event of Turkey's becoming involved in hostilities. In 1946 he was appointed a Member of the Supreme Military Council and retired from the Army in 1950. He married a sister of Enver Pasha.

themselves sadly lacking. Despite the diplomatic explanations offered by the British and French negotiators, and the tactics adopted to do all possible for the General in the way of hospitality — 'in fact', as some one grimly remarked, 'to give him cutlets instead of cannon' — the conversations were going extremely badly, and the disgruntled General was displaying the premonitory symptoms of departure.

On October 11, however, General Orbay was received by King George. He had, as he later confessed, expected that this would be little more than a formality. In fact, the King received him in private audience alone and talked to him, simply and clearly, for some twenty minutes. 'It has been explained to Orbay that we need all our guns & aircraft here & in France, as the seat of war is now on the Western Front. I did my best to tell him this too,' the King modestly recorded.[13] The result was tremendous; and its effect was such that two days later, at a meeting at which the British and French put all their cards on the table, an almost unqualified success was achieved, and the Treaty was signed on October 19.

It has been quite impossible to let him [Orbay] have certain important items of which we ourselves are woefully deficient [General Ismay [a] wrote to Sir Alexander Hardinge]. Consequently, one cannot but think that he would have gone away a disappointed man, if it had not been for the tremendous impression created upon him by his private audience with the King.[14]

Patience as well as courage was a salient necessity in these early days of a conflict which had taken so bewildering a turn. In the East, the collapse of Poland before the combined might of Germany and Russia had brought immediate hostilities to a close. The seat of war, as the King had told General Orbay,

---

[a] General the Rt. Hon. Hastings Lionel, first Baron Ismay, K.G., G.C.B., C.H., D.S.O. (b. 1887), having served with distinction in the Indian Army, became Military Secretary to the Viceroy (Lord Willingdon) from 1931 to 1933, Deputy Secretary to the Committee of Imperial Defence in 1936, and Secretary to the Committee in 1938. During the Second World War he served as Chief of Staff to the Minister of Defence and Military Secretary to the Cabinet. During Lord Mountbatten's Viceroyalty, General Ismay was his Chief of Staff, and on the return to power of the Conservative Party in 1951 he was appointed Secretary of State for Commonwealth Relations. On the reorganization of the North Atlantic Treaty Organization in 1952, Lord Ismay became its first Secretary-General, and also Vice-Chairman of the North Atlantic Council. He retired from this post in 1957, when he was created a Knight of the Garter.

was now on the Western Front where the combined French
and British armies lay quiescent behind the Maginot Line.
The world anxiously awaited Hitler's next move, and the King
shared the general uncertainty. At Windsor he reviewed the
situation.

Sunday, September 24th

   After 3 weeks of War, many strange things have taken place. It
is all an amazing puzzle. Germany has overrun Poland, quicker
than was thought possible. The Poles have fought magnificently,
though their leaders were not prepared for the speed of the German
motorised divisions.   In fact the Germans were taken aback,
when the Red Army of Soviet Russia invaded Poland from the
East, earlier than was arranged in the German-Soviet Agreement
signed in August 1939, & advanced & took over the Galician oil-
fields. Soviet Russia has also occupied the Roumanian-Polish, &
the Roumanian-Hungarian frontiers to prevent Germany from
invading the Balkans. What will Germany do now ?
   Was Italy aware of the secret clause in the G-R Agreement ?
Russia's sudden swoop on the Balkan frontier cannot be to Italy's
liking or wish. She was surely keeping the Balkans for herself, &
would hate the Soviet in the Mediterranean & to have free access
from the Black Sea.
   Mussolini says he wants to stop the War, & we hear from
Ciano, his foreign minister, that Hitler will offer peace terms
when the Polish Question has been settled. But how is Stalin to
be reckoned with by the two Dictators, who have both stated that
Naziism and Fascism are anti-Bolshevism ?
   Our answer & that of the French will have to be 'Fight on'
& then what ?
   Germany has not interfered with our mobilisations in any way,
& has not raided us from the air. Why ? We must wait and see.

   The expected peace offer was not long in coming. It was
made by Hitler before the Reichstag on October 6 and was
rejected by the British and French Governments a week
later. Thereafter the fog of war closed down upon the Western
Front, and the conflict passed into that phase of sinister
inactivity which the Americans christened 'The Phoney War'
or, more satirically, the 'Sitzkrieg'. It was widely believed at
the time that Hitler, rather than risk a frontal attack upon the
legendary Maginot Line, was prepared to accept the strategy
of a war of attrition, and this was welcomed in the West, since

it was believed that Britain was well equipped to win such a war because of her superiority at sea. Hopes were raised for a struggle of endurance which might prove of comparatively little cost in loss of life. We now know that this reasoning was completely without foundation, and that Hitler had in fact intended to make his onslaught on the West at any propitious moment after the conclusion of the Polish campaign. His original date for attack was November 12. Only the inclemency of the weather prevented it from taking place, and continued to cause its postponement for a further six months.

A fleeting gleam from the dark-lantern gave evidence of the Führer's intentions. Tidings on November 6 from the Belgian legation in Berlin, where secret contact was maintained with anti-Nazi elements, sent King Leopold racing through the night from Brussels to The Hague by car to warn Queen Wilhelmina of the imminent danger of the invasion by Germany of their two countries, and of the necessity for concerted action for peace to forestall it. On the following day, November 7, a joint offer of their good offices as intermediaries was made by the two Sovereigns of the Low Countries to King George, President Lebrun and the Führer, and on November 12 the King replied on behalf of the British Government.

There had been no hesitation in the minds of King George or his Ministers as to what their answer should be. There was sympathy for the predicament in which the two Sovereigns found themselves, and appreciation for the sincerity of their offer, but there was no doubt as to how to reply to it. 'We cannot make peace with Hitler, as the old reason for our being at war with him still holds good', the King recorded in his diary.[15]

The King's reply, therefore, recapitulated the circumstances under which Britain had gone to war, her reasons for doing so, and the ultimate aim for which she must continue to fight. It concluded: 'Should Your Majesty be able to communicate to me any proposals from Germany of such a character as to afford real prospect of achieving the purpose I have described above, I can say at once that my Government would give them their most earnest consideration.'[16]

'I think that this reply puts our case very clearly', was the
King's comment.[17]

(iii)

In the first week of October the King had made his first war-
time visit to his Fleet, spending two days at Invergordon and
Scapa, where every mile of shore and stretch of water reminded
him of his service in the First World War. The flag officers
dined with him in *Nelson* — 'Not quite such a number as
there were in the Great War, when Papa came to visit the
Grand Fleet' — and were enthusiastic about the cheery spirit
of their men. 'I was very interested to see things as they are
at the beginning of a war', the King recorded. 'In rather a
muddle, but it is amazing how the Services put up with things,
& carry on under trying conditions.'[18]

Two months later he was with the British Expeditionary
Force [a] in France, from December 4 to 10. Here, in addition
to inspecting his own troops in their positions and conferring
with the Commander-in-Chief, Lord Gort,[b] he met President
Lebrun, M. Daladier, and General Gamelin ('A very reticent
man & speaks very little'), and was conducted over that
fantastic organism of fortification, the Maginot Line, which
he likened to 'an underground battleship'.

The King's visit was strenuous and crowded, and there
were present all the hard conditions of a field army on active
service in winter. He had to put up with a good deal of
discomfort, particularly with regard to ablution, for the
weather was bitterly cold and the comfort of a hot bath was a

[a] It had originally been intended to designate the British Army in France
the 'British Field Force', but the King had at once realized the importance of
maintaining the historical tradition of the British Expeditionary Force of the
First World War. He had accordingly made representations to the Chief of the
Imperial General Staff, General Sir Edmund Ironside, in the first week of the
war, to have the name changed.[19]

[b] Field-Marshal John Standish Surtees Prendergast Vereker, sixth Viscount
Gort, V.C., G.C.B., C.B.E., D.S.O., M.V.O., M.C. (1886–1946), served as
Chief of the Imperial General Staff from 1937 to 1939, and commanded the
British Expeditionary Force in France from the outbreak of war until the evacua-
tion from Dunkirk in June 1940. He was subsequently Inspector-General of
the Home Guard, 1940–1941; Governor and Commander-in-Chief of Gibraltar,
1941–1942, and of Malta, 1942–1944; and High Commissioner for Palestine and
Transjordan from 1944 to 1945.

rare luxury. The psychological importance of the visit was undoubted, since it came at a juncture when the Allied armies in the four months of war had seen very little action and there seemed no immediate prospect of a break in the stalemate. There had also been moments of difficulty between the British High Command in France and the Government in London, and the Anglo-French co-operation was in need of consolidation. In all respects, therefore, the King felt his visit to have been 'a timely one'.

It is of course obvious that the visit came at an opportune moment, and the very fact of the Sovereign being with his troops was an inspiration in itself [Sir Piers Legh [a] wrote to the Queen]. But the really salient feature to my mind was that the King showed a vital interest & understanding of the difficulties and problems which confront the highest and the lowest of all ranks of the B.E.F., and this fact was mentioned to me again & again during the visit.

It is impossible to imagine a greater success both from the British & French point of view, and I trust that His Majesty's natural modesty will not prevent him from realizing his achievement.[20]

The King was in fact conscious that he had been enabled to do valuable service during his visit, not only for the morale of his own troops but also in respect of the Anglo-French alliance. He returned home with a sense of satisfaction, which was strengthened by the welcome news of the elimination of the 'pocket battleship' *Graf Spee* by the Cruisers *Ajax*, *Achilles* and *Exeter* in the Battle of the River Plate.[b]

It had been agreed between King George and his advisers that the first Christmas of the war should be signalized by a

[a] Lieut.-Colonel the Hon. Sir Piers Legh, G.C.V.O., K.C.B., C.M.G., C.I.E., O.B.E. (1890–1955), had served as A.D.C. to the Duke of Connaught when Governor-General of Canada, from 1914 to 1915, and as Equerry to the Prince of Wales from 1919 to 1936. He was Equerry to King George VI from 1936 to 1946, and Master of the Household from 1941 to 1952.

[b] In the action of the River Plate off the coast of Uruguay on December 13, 1939, the British cruiser squadron so damaged the *Graf Spee* that she was compelled to put in to Montevideo. Here she was scuttled, by express order of the Führer, and her crew interned. Her commander, Captain Langsdorff, committed suicide three days later. On February 23, 1940, the ships' companies of *Ajax* and *Exeter* were inspected by the King on the Horse Guards Parade, and after a public investiture were subsequently entertained by the Lord Mayor of London in Guildhall. 'A most impressive ceremony,' the King recorded, '& watched by many thousands of the general public. It is the first time that such a ceremony has been staged. Before all investitures have been of a private nature.'

personal message to be broadcast by the Sovereign at the end
of the B.B.C.'s 'Round the Empire' programme on the afternoon of Christmas Day.   Since the beginning of his reign the
King had refused to continue his father's tradition in this
respect, and for two reasons.   In the first place, the Christmas
broadcasts of King George V had become almost legendary
throughout the Empire and Commonwealth, and his son was
doubtful of his ability to measure up to the standard thus
established ; and, secondly, there was his rooted personal
antipathy to the microphone.   The most urgent representations
and a full sense of the exigencies involved were necessary to
overcome his deep-seated repugnance.   'This is always an
ordeal for me & I don't begin to enjoy Christmas until after it
is over', he wrote in his diary.[21]

But the King need not have been concerned for his success.
His Christmas broadcast of 1939, the first of a series which
he made annually until his death, was memorable.   It was not
an easy moment to speak to his peoples.   The world was in a
mood of anti-climax, for the majority had expected that by
that time the full horror of war would have been loosed upon
London and upon Paris — but in effect nothing had happened.
There was danger of apathy and of complacency, and this
King George set himself to dissipate.   He spoke of the realities
of the situation, as he himself had seen them at first hand ; of
the Royal Navy and all its ancillary forces, 'upon which,
throughout the last four months, had burst the storm of
ruthless and unceasing war' ; of the Air Force, 'who were
daily adding laurels to those that their fathers had won' ; and
of the British Expeditionary Force in France : 'Their task is
hard.   They are waiting, and waiting is a trial of nerve and
discipline.'   Finally he warned his listeners of 'the dark times
ahead of us'.

A new year is at hand.   We cannot tell what it will bring.   If
it brings peace, how thankful we shall all be.   If it brings us continued struggle we shall remain undaunted.

In the meantime, I feel that we may all find a message of
encouragement in the lines which, in my closing words, I would
like to say to you :—'I said to the man who stood at the Gate of the
Year, "Give me a light that I may tread safely into the unknown ".
And he replied, "Go out into the darkness, and put your hand into

the Hand of God. That shall be to you better than light, and
safer than a known way." ' *a*
May that Almighty Hand guide and uphold us all.

(iv)

It is among the ironic tragedies of history that Mr. Neville
Chamberlain, 'a man of peace to the very depths of his soul',
should have been fated to be the head of a British Government
at the outbreak of a world war. His great humanitarian sense,
which had been deeply touched by the countless messages of
gratitude and relief which he had received after Munich, was
now as deeply afflicted by the horrors of war unleashed. His
soul shrank from the ruthlessness of conflict; his heart was
seared by every casualty. 'You will understand how hateful
I find my personal position', he wrote to the Archbishop of
Canterbury on September 5. 'I simply can't bear to think of
those gallant fellows who lost their lives last night in the
R.A.F. attack, and of their families who have first been called
upon to pay the price. *b* Indeed I must put such thoughts out
of my mind if I am not to be unnerved altogether.' [22] He
hated war too intensely to be a war Minister, and he knew it.
'I was never meant to be a war Minister,' he wrote again in
an agony of spirit, 'and the thought of all those homes wrecked
with the *Royal Oak* *c* makes me want to hand over my responsibilities to someone else.' [23]
     It was not surprising, therefore, that so great an aversion
to war should find its reflection in the Government's conduct
of the struggle. The 'Phoney War' was itself symptomatic of
this attitude of abhorrence and any suggestions put forward
for its more active prosecution were met with a spirit of nega-

----

     a The poem, 'The Gate of the Year', from which King George took this quota-
tion, had been sent to him shortly before the text of his broadcast was completed,
and he at once incorporated it. The poem, which was part of a collection of verse
entitled *The Desert*, published privately in 1908, was by Miss Marie Louise
Haskins, a lecturer at the London School of Economics, who served throughout
the First World War as a Supervisor of Women's Employment and Industrial
Welfare Work in a controlled factory. She died in 1957 at the age of 81.
     b On September 4, 1939, the R.A.F. attacked the German naval base at
Kiel and suffered casualties.
     c A German submarine penetrated the defences of Scapa Flow on October 14,
1939, and sank the battleship *Royal Oak*, with considerable loss of life.

tion. When Mr. Leopold Amery[a] proposed to the Air Minister that, in view of Germany's shortage of timber, some attempt should be made to set fire to the Black Forest, Sir Kingsley Wood replied that there was no question of the R.A.F. bombing even the munition works at Essen, 'which were private property'![24]

Criticism was rife among the Conservative back benchers, and even more so in the ranks of the Labour Party, where there was no confidence in Mr. Chamberlain and his immediate associates. The Opposition was frankly critical of the war measures taken by the Government which were not considered nearly rigorous enough,[25] and they did not hesitate to give public expression to their views.

King George was eager to give what support he could to his Prime Minister, and suggested that it might be advantageous if he were to have a talk with the Opposition and T.U.C. leaders, and to this idea Mr. Chamberlain assented.[26] The King received Mr. Attlee on the eve of a debate on the Government's policy in India, and there ensued an audience from which the Leader of the Opposition was reported by the Prime Minister to have emerged in 'a chastened mood'.[27]

More difficult and delicate were Mr. Chamberlain's relations with the Secretary of State for War, Mr. Leslie Hore-Belisha,[b] who had taken over the War Office in May 1937. In the years before the war he had introduced reforms which had modernized the pattern of the Army, reorganized its strategic distribution and increased the number of effective divisions for expeditionary service, and had, in addition, materially increased the comforts and heightened the morale of the private soldier. This feat had caused Mr. Chamberlain to record: 'He has done more for the Army than anyone since Haldane'.[28] Less popular with the Prime Minister was Mr. Hore-Belisha's vigorous advocacy of the introduction of

---

[a] Rt. Hon. Leopold Stennett Amery, C.H. (1873–1955), sat in the House of Commons as a Conservative member from 1911 to 1945. He served as First Lord of the Admiralty, 1922–1924; Secretary of State for the Colonies, 1924–1929, and for Dominion Affairs, 1925–1929; and as Secretary of State for India and Burma in Mr. Churchill's Coalition Government from 1940 to 1945.

[b] Rt. Hon. Leslie, first Baron Hore-Belisha (1893–1957), served as Minister of Transport from 1934 to 1937, and as Secretary of State for War from 1937 to 1940. He became Minister of National Insurance in Mr. Churchill's 'Caretaker Government' of 1945.

compulsory military service, and, as Mr. Churchill has written, to him 'belongs the credit of forcing this belated awakening. He certainly took his political life in his hands and several interviews with his chief were of a formidable character.' [29]

The Secretary of State for War had, moreover, his own ideas on strategy, and even before the war had been in favour of continuing the Maginot Line to the coast as the only means of stemming a German advance through northern France. With the outbreak of hostilities and the dispatch of the B.E.F., his anxiety regarding this gap between the northern end of the Maginot Line and the coast had increased immeasurably. He had argued the point with the British military commanders, and had raised it on several occasions in the War Cabinet, but General Gamelin and the Allied High Command were convinced that the Ardennes were impassable to large armies, and the British Cabinet and military leaders were hesitant of criticizing those whose armies were ten times as strong as their own. [30]

Mr. Hore-Belisha, however, would not be put off. He was eager and impatient and, to some extent, careless of other people's feelings. His vehement criticisms of the strategic conception caused considerable pressure to be placed on Mr. Chamberlain to replace him at the War Office, and — which was much worse — there developed between him and Lord Gort a lack of confidence which bred an almost perpetual friction.

Of this situation the King was fully cognizant. On several occasions the Prime Minister had confided his difficulties in audience, but always with the conclusion that, despite the difficulties of personality, he was anxious to keep the Secretary of State for War where he was. When the King visited the Expeditionary Force in France in December, he was given the views of the British High Command on the issue, and found that they bitterly resented Mr. Hore-Belisha's strictures, which they regarded as unwarranted, unsubstantiated and unjust. This His Majesty discussed with the Prime Minister on his return to London, and it was hoped that when Mr. Chamberlain himself went to the British Front later in the month he would be able to compose the differences between the Secretary of State and the Commander-in-Chief in the field. In this the Prime Minister was not entirely successful; however,

the King recorded : 'He [the P.M.] had had good talks with
Gort, but he is not thinking of removing Hore-Belisha from
the W.O.'.[31]   Thus the matter rested until after the Christmas
holiday, and on January 3 the King wrote to the Duke of
Gloucester : 'I don't think he [the P.M.] means to make a
change at the W.O.'.

Two days later an apparently static situation had become
fluid.   The Secretary of State for War had resigned, and the
press and public were demanding an explanation.   The King
was as much surprised as anyone.

When you receive my letter [he wrote from Sandringham to
the Duke of Gloucester], you will think I am mad in saying that I
did not think that Hore-Belisha would leave the War Office.   He
has now gone & Oliver Stanley [a] has taken his place.   I do not
know all the facts myself, as what has happened came about very
suddenly. . . .[32]

A full account of the circumstances of Mr. Hore-Belisha's
resignation was furnished to the King by his Prime Minister in
a letter dated January 8.   From this it emerged that, though
there existed no cleavage on policy between the two, Mr.
Chamberlain had reluctantly reached the conclusion that a
change at the War Office was desirable because of 'personal
relations'.   'I said that as I had told him repeatedly before
there existed a strong prejudice against him for which I could
not hold him altogether blameless', wrote the Prime Minister.
'I had hoped that after my recent visit to France it might be
possible for him to get things on a better footing but I have
since come to the conclusion that this will mean only a
temporary lull, and that a change would be necessary sooner
or later.   In these circumstances I felt the change had better
come when things were quiet than be forced later when perhaps
some crisis might have arisen.'   Anxious to retain the services
of his colleague in the Cabinet, Mr. Chamberlain had offered
him the office of President of the Board of Trade, but this

---

[a] Rt. Hon. Oliver Frederick George Stanley, M.P. (1896–1950), second son
of the seventeenth Earl of Derby, sat in the House of Commons from 1924 to
1950, and served successively as Minister of Transport, 1933–1934 ;   Minister of
Labour, 1934–1935 ;   President of the Board of Education, 1935–1937 ;   President
of the Board of Trade, 1937–1940 ;   Secretary of State for War, 1940 ;   Secretary
of State for the Colonies, 1942–1945.

Mr. Hore-Belisha had rejected, and had left the Government.[33]

When Mr. Hore-Belisha came to surrender his seals of office at Buckingham Palace on January 9, he was received at first with somewhat of reserve and was reproached for not having come to see His Majesty after his return from France in December, despite a summons to do so. This Mr. Hore-Belisha denied, saying that he never received such a summons and had, in fact, been greatly disappointed at not having done so, since he had been anxious to discuss with His Majesty his impressions of the British Expeditionary Force. The King was mollified, and they parted on warmer terms.

There is no mention of this incident in the King's diary, and his own somewhat laconic account of the audience is as follows :

I saw Hore-Belisha on my arrival at B.P. Luckily he was pleasant, and there was no need for me to open up the question of his resignation.[34]

The public was greatly mystified by the whole matter of Mr. Hore-Belisha's departure from the War Office, which in fact created a sensation. He was popularly regarded as one of the abler members of Mr. Chamberlain's administration, and his reorganization of the Army was commonly considered to be one of the outstanding achievements of the National Government. Since the Prime Minister's letter accepting his resignation stressed the point that there had never been any difference between them in policy, the suspicion became current that his efforts to democratize the Army had incurred the disapproval of the Higher Command, and fears were widely expressed that his work in this field was in danger of being undone. These rumours were denied by Mr. Chamberlain when Parliament met again on January 19 after the Christmas recess, but little further light was shed on the real reason for Mr. Hore-Belisha's dismissal. The House, however, being satisfied that the democratization of the Army would not be interfered with, did not pursue the matter further.[35]

Slowly the first bitter winter of the war gave place to the promise of spring, and with it the growing expectation of intensified warfare. In the peaceful seclusion of Royal Lodge, whither he had gone for the week-end, King George surveyed the situation as it appeared to him at the conclusion of the first six months of war, and set down his summation :

Sunday March 3rd

We have been at War for 6 months today.

Most people in this country, including the Govt., have been surprised that we have not suffered from air raids as was predicted. In the meantime, Govt. policy of the child evacuation scheme, so carefully worked out, has not been a great success owing to lack of danger, & many children have returned to their homes in cities & towns.

This time of comparative calm, has enabled us to get on with our armament programme, a prodigious one, without any outside hindrance. The question of supply of labour & raw materials is being carefully gone into, with the help & cooperation of the Trades Unions. But it is by no means an easy task with the Military Service Act in operation, affecting every man of the age of 20 yrs, unless they are in a 'reserved occupation'. Skilled labour is at a premium, & men in 'key' positions in industry, have had to be recalled from the B.E.F. in France. These men were in the Territorial Army. The Army, itself being so highly mechanised, needs all the skilled men it can get to look after it. Tanks, guns, motor vehicles etc. all need great attention.

The Royal Navy & Mercantile Marine have borne the brunt of the danger & discomfort of the War. Owing to the U-boats, the Convoy System for imports & exports has taken up the Navy's time with all available ships both large & small, all over the World. There has naturally been a good deal of dislocation of Trade, but remedies are being found to make it work under the new conditions. Most of the Neutrals have joined our Convoys as well. The U.S.A. & S. Am. have not been helpful, by introducing a 300 mile Territorial Zone round their coasts. We do not recognize it as we have Colonies within its boundaries. The R.A.F. has done good work, in cooperation with the Convoys with aircraft of the Coastal Command & with their many reconnaissance flights over Germany extending to Berlin & Vienna. Quite a number of fighters & bombers have been brought down over Gt. Britain, the North Sea & in France. The A.R.P. workers have had time to organise themselves. Their lot has been a trying time of waiting so far. The War in the first 6 months has been one of words and propaganda mainly from Germany. The Nazi regime is very good at it, & preaches by this means of its greatness. There have been several 'peace' moves, & 'scares' that Germany would invade Holland & Belgium, or else the Balkans.

Adjacent Neutrals in the N.W. & S.E. have had pressure put on them to induce them to send food & oil & raw materials into Germany, in return for armaments which seems to be her one export. Unfortunately every Neutral needs armaments & they cannot buy them from us. Germany sinks their merchant ships at sight for which there is no redress, & they have suffered more losses than the Allies in the way of tonnage. This 'War of Nerves' on Neutrals goes on relentlessly. Our own propaganda is getting better as time goes on.

The Germans maintain that we started the war to uphold our imperialist policy. Hitler is the imperialist in that *he* wants to conquer the world.

Germany cannot be altogether happy over our blockade. Reports show that they are suffering from lack of nutritious food, but then they have endured that hardship for years. I don't think the Army & the Nazi Party see eye to eye, & the Gestapo is a body to be feared by *all* Germans.

Yet, though unshaken in his belief of the rightness of his cause, and that ultimate victory was assured, the King was not at peace in his mind. The dashing and gallant episode of the 'cutting-out' of the prison ship *Altmark* [a] cheered him momentarily — 'I am delighted with this exploit', he wrote, 'I have been thinking of the "Altmark" for the last 2 days, & thank God we have rescued these men from a "living hell" ' [36] — but the visit of President Roosevelt's special envoy, Mr. Sumner Welles, [b] depressed him greatly, for it carried the conviction that the hopes which Mr. Roosevelt had expressed to him at Hyde Park for American aid to Britain had been over-optimistic. 'The fact is', he recorded after Mr. Welles's audience, 'the U.S. is not coming in to help us, & nothing yet will make them, but they are pro-British in the main.' [37]

Moreover, neither at home nor abroad did things seem to

[a] On February 15, 1940, the destroyer *Cossack* (Captain Philip Vian), having sighted the German merchantman *Altmark* in the Norwegian fjord of Josing, grappled her under cover of night and landed a boarding party, armed with cutlasses, which successfully liberated and brought off 300 British Merchant Navy officers and seamen who had been captured by the pocket battleship *Graf Spee* during her depredations in the first three months of the war, and were being taken to imprisonment in Germany.

[b] In February and March 1940, Mr. Sumner Welles, the U.S. Under-Secretary of State, visited Germany, Italy, France and Britain as the President's special envoy, for the purpose of discovering what the views of the four Governments might be as to the existing possibilities of concluding any just and permanent peace. Mr. Welles has given some account of this mission in his book, *The Time for Decision*.

be going as they should. The 'War of Nerves' was not only directed against the neutrals. It was showing its effects in Britain, where the general feeling of frustration found expression in an increasing discontent with the Government, and the failure of the Western Allies to send aid to Finland in her gallant struggle against Soviet aggression was now added grounds for criticism.[a]

I am very worried over the general situation [was the King's thought in the middle of March], as everything we do or try to do appears to be wrong, & gets us nowhere.[38]

Nor was his depression greatly lessened by the reshuffle in the Cabinet, occasioned by the death of the Minister of Shipping, Sir John Gilmour,[b] at the end of March. 'There is no new blood coming in', was his comment,[39] and, like the majority of his subjects, he longed for action. This, however, was not to be postponed for long. The reorganization in the Government had brought Mr. Churchill into greater prominence in the co-ordination of the Service Ministers and Chiefs of Staff [c] and the decision was at last taken to deprive Germany of Scandinavian resources by mining Norway's territorial waters. Unfortunately this decision was accompanied by Mr. Chamberlain's announcement that 'Hitler has missed the bus' (April 4), to be followed even more disastrously on April 9 by Germany's long-prepared invasion of Denmark and Norway.

(v)

The first popular reaction to the Norwegian campaign was one of relief that the stalemate of the past seven months had at last been broken. It was not doubted that in an operation with a strongly naval flavour the British would be more than a

[a] The Soviet Union had invaded Finland on November 30, 1939, and the Finnish Government, after a gallant resistance, appealed to Britain and France for assistance. When this did not materialize the Finns made their peace with Moscow on March 12, 1940.

[b] Lieut.-Colonel the Rt. Hon. Sir John Gilmour, Bart., G.C.V.O., D.S.O. (1876–1940), had served as Secretary of State for Scotland, 1924–1929; Minister of Agriculture, 1931–1932; and Home Secretary, 1932–1935. He had then retired, but was brought back into the Cabinet by Mr. Chamberlain in 1939 as Minister of Shipping.

[c] Lord Chatfield resigned as Minister for the Co-ordination of Defence on April 3, 1940.

match for the enemy, and expectations rose high. The King shared these hopes, for he too had chafed in inactivity. In the War Room of the Admiralty on the afternoon of April 9, he was shown the disposition of the British battle fleet off Norway, but received the gloomy news that the Germans were in possession of nearly all the Norwegian ports. Yet even now he felt the lack of that personal activity for which he longed. 'I have spent a bad day', he recorded that evening. 'Everybody working at fever heat except me.' [40]

The King was soon to have his ample share of work. Notwithstanding the confident utterances of Mr. Chamberlain and Mr. Churchill, it was unavoidably apparent by May 4 that, except for a precarious Allied foothold at Narvik, all Norway was in the hands of the enemy and that, despite the gallantry of their forces, Britain and France had suffered a heavy defeat.

The disastrous outcome of the Norwegian campaign released in Parliament, and in the country as a whole, the pent-up dissatisfaction with the Chamberlain Government which had so long been latent. In time of war a Government must be overwhelmingly strong to withstand failure, and after seven months of a war without movement Mr. Chamberlain's administration was too weak to survive disaster. The storm which it had just weathered after the failure to send aid to Finland was as nothing in comparison with the hurricane encountered when the Prime Minister and his colleagues faced the House of Commons on May 7 in the first day of the crucial debate on Norway.

Feeling ran high in the House during those two days, and the passion and drama of the debate were stronger even than at the time of Munich. The memories of older parliamentarians went back to the downfall of the Asquith Coalition in 1916 and the withdrawal of the Conservatives from the Lloyd George Coalition at the Carlton Club meeting of 1922 ; and historians sought precedent for so great a party convulsion in the Crimean War and the Roebuck motion.[a] For, in addition

---

[a] John Arthur Roebuck (1801–1879), a staunch supporter of the Government's policy in going to war against Russia but a virulent critic of their conduct of affairs in the Crimea, moved, on January 26, 1855, for a committee of enquiry. Lord John Russell resigned office as Lord President of the Council as soon as notice was given, and when the vote was taken, on January 29, the Roebuck Motion was carried by 305 to 148. The administration of Lord Aberdeen resigned next day.

to the attack of the gallant Member for Portsmouth North, Sir Roger Keyes,[a] resplendent in the uniform of an Admiral of the Fleet, and the dramatic appeal of Mr. Lloyd George to the Prime Minister to 'give an example of sacrifice because there is nothing which can contribute more to victory than that he should sacrifice the seals of office', it was of grim significance that five members of the Conservative Party spoke against the Government, and only six, apart from Ministers, spoke for them.   When Mr. Amery's impassioned peroration rang through the House, in the words of Cromwell to the Long Parliament — 'You have sat here too long for any good you have been doing. Depart, I say, and let us have done with you. In the name of God, go!' — it sounded the knell of Mr. Chamberlain's Government, despite the loyal effort of Mr. Churchill to redress the balance.

Mr. Chamberlain, however, did not at once accept the auguries of defeat. When he saw King George on the evening of the first day of the debate, May 7, he said smilingly that he had not come to offer his resignation and that he had not yet abandoned all hope of reconstructing his Government on the basis of a national coalition in which the Labour Party would join. 'I said to the P.M.', the King wrote, 'would it help him if I spoke to Attlee about the national standpoint of the Labour Party, & say that I hoped that they would realize that they must pull their weight & join the Natl. Govt.', but Mr. Chamberlain was of the opinion that such an appeal should be postponed until after the annual conference of the Labour Party, which would be held over the coming week-end at Bournemouth, as Mr. Attlee would then be more certain of the attitude of his followers.

The King was full of compassion for his Prime Minister in this hour of his ordeal. 'I told the P.M. that I did not like the way in which, with all the worries & responsibilities he had to

---

[a] Admiral of the Fleet Roger John Brownlow, first Baron Keyes, G.C.B., K.C.V.O., C.M.G., D.S.O. (1872–1945), had distinguished himself during the First World War both as Vice-Admiral commanding the Dover Patrol and in command of operations against Zeebrugge and Ostend on April 23, 1918.   On his retirement from the Navy he entered Parliament as a Conservative Member, representing Portsmouth North from 1934 to 1943.   In the Second World War he was appointed Mr. Churchill's special liaison officer with the King of the Belgians in 1940 and served as the first Director of Combined Operations, 1940–1941.

bear in the conduct of the war, he was always subject to a stab in the back from both the H. of C. and the Press.'[41] Thus encouraged, Mr. Chamberlain returned to the debate on the following day, and accepted the challenge of the Labour Party to press for a vote on a motion for adjournment. He was angered by the challenge and made it plain that he would make the vote one of confidence. He appealed to his friends in the House — 'and I have friends in the House' — to support him. This was a strategic error. Perhaps the Whips had misjudged the temper of the House and had misled him; perhaps he himself had overestimated the strength of party ties; but to be called upon to vote on party lines at that moment was not what the House desired, and when the division was taken members voted according to what they regarded as their patriotic duty and not to party loyalty.

This moment of testing was for many a searing struggle of conscience. One young officer in uniform, who had for long been a fervent admirer of Mr. Chamberlain, walked through the Opposition Lobby with tears streaming down his face,[42] and there were many who fought a similar battle with themselves.

So unexpectedly large was the number of Conservatives voting against the Government — we were forty-four in all — [wrote Mr. Amery] and so many remained ostentatiously in their seats determined not to vote, that, for a moment, we half thought we might have an actual majority. We streamed back into the House. But as the Whips marched up to the table, making their well-drilled three bows, the Government Whips were on the right. We strained our ears to hear David Margesson read out the figures : 281 to 200. A gasp, and shouts of 'resign, resign'. The drop from the normal majority of over 200 was enough to show that the confidence was no longer there, that the Government, as it stood, was doomed. Chamberlain stood up, erect, unyielding, sardonic, and walked out past the Speaker's Chair and over the feet of his colleagues, who then followed. The Government benches cheered, while the Socialists shouted : 'Go, in God's name, go !' [43]

The next two days were full of rumour, uncertainty and gossip. Mr. Chamberlain was at first unconvinced of the necessity for his resignation of the premiership. He was still flirting with the idea of heading a national coalition if he could persuade the Labour Party to co-operate. If this proved impossible, his preference for a successor fell on Lord Halifax. 'I would rather have Halifax succeed me than Winston', he had written.[44] Meantime the councils of the Conservatives were divided. The dissident Tories, though their choice of leader was certainly Mr. Churchill, agreed to support any Prime Minister who could form a truly National Government, that is to say, a Prime Minister under whom the Labour Party would consent to serve. The followers of Mr. Chamberlain were supporters of Lord Halifax, if a change in the premiership was absolutely necessary, for they could not easily forget the bitter criticisms which Mr. Churchill had heaped upon the leader of their party, nor forgive him for having proved so abundantly right.

The attitude of Labour was therefore the crux of the situation, and here also there was division. All were agreed that they could not and would not serve under Mr. Chamberlain, but bitter memories of Tonypandy [a] still rankled and precluded for many an immediate acceptance of Mr. Churchill. Indeed it would appear that the first choice of some of the Labour leaders, including Dr. Hugh Dalton, would have been Lord Halifax as Prime Minister, with Mr. Attlee [b] as Leader of the House of Commons and Mr. Churchill as Minister of Defence.[c]

[a] In the latter half of 1910 there was grave industrial unrest throughout England. There was rioting and looting at Tonypandy in Glamorganshire on November 8, and the Chief Constable of the county appealed for troops. Mr. Churchill, then Home Secretary, sent two hundred Metropolitan Police to the Rhondda Valley instead, but, when they were unable to keep order and were stoned by the mob, troops had to be sent after all. The Labour Party were long in forgiving Mr. Churchill for this incident.

[b] Rt. Hon. Clement Richard, first Earl Attlee, K.G., O.M., C.H. (b. 1883), was a Labour Member of Parliament from 1922 to 1955. He served as Under-Secretary of State for War, 1924, and as Chancellor of the Duchy of Lancaster, 1930–1931, and Postmaster-General, 1931. Elected as Leader of the Labour Party in 1935, he was successively, during the Second World War, Lord Privy Seal, 1940–1942; Secretary for Dominion Affairs, 1942–1943; Deputy Prime Minister, 1942–1945; and Lord President of the Council, 1943–1945. Mr. Attlee was Prime Minister and First Lord of the Treasury from 1945 to 1951 and Minister of Defence from 1945 to 1946. On his retirement from the leadership of the Labour Party in 1955 he was created an Earl and was appointed a Knight of the Garter in 1956.

[c] Dr. Dalton gives some account of the preferences prevalent at this time in his memoirs, *The Fateful Years, 1931–1945* (pp. 306-7). Mr. Amery, on the other hand, asserts in his memoirs (III, 370) that at one point during these two days, in the opinion of some of the Labour Front Bench, he himself was the Tory under whom they would sooner serve.

On the afternoon of May 9, Mr. Chamberlain held two important conferences at No. 10 Downing Street. The first was at 4.15 with Lord Halifax, Mr. Churchill and Captain Margesson, at which the question of a successor to the premiership — if such were necessary, for Mr. Chamberlain was still not wholly convinced of this — was discussed. A full description of it has been given by Mr. Churchill,[a][45] who did little talking and left it to Lord Halifax to urge the difficulty of a peer being at the head of a Government at such a time of crisis. Since Mr. Churchill would not express an opinion, the question was left unresolved, and at 6.15 the three Ministers met again to receive Mr. Attlee and Mr. Greenwood.[b] Much to the surprise of the Labour leaders, in view of the happenings of the past two days, Mr. Chamberlain renewed his invitation to them of the previous March to join a national coalition Government led by himself. They speedily undeceived him of even the remotest possibility of such a happening. Mr. Greenwood spoke in very forceful terms, and Mr. Attlee said that in any case the decision to serve in any coalition under any Prime Minister would be dependent on the approval of the Party Executive, who were at that moment with the Conference at Bournemouth. Mr. Chamberlain then asked them to put two questions to their colleagues:

1. Would they enter a Government under the present Prime Minister?
2. Would they come in under someone else?

Mr. Attlee promised to consult the Executive Committee next day and to telephone the result by two o'clock, but he left the Ministers under no great illusions as to what the answer to the first question would be.[46]

The following morning, May 10, brought the tremendous news that the full weight of the Wehrmacht had been hurled

---

[a] Mr. Churchill's description given in *The Gathering Storm* has the slight inaccuracy of placing the interview in the morning of May 10. The evidence that it took place on the afternoon of May 9 is, however, overwhelmingly conclusive.

[b] Rt. Hon. Arthur Greenwood, C.H. (1880–1954), Labour Member of Parliament, served as Minister of Health, 1929–1931. He was Minister without Portfolio, 1940–1942, in Mr. Churchill's Cabinet, and Lord Privy Seal, 1945–1947; and Paymaster-General, 1946–1947, in Mr. Attlee's. He was successively Deputy Leader, 1942; Treasurer, 1943; and Chairman of the Labour Party, 1952.

against the Low Countries and France, to which tidings
Mr. Chamberlain's first reaction was to abandon all thought
of resignation and to remain at his post. Even so devoted an
adherent as Sir Kingsley Wood, however, could not support
him in this view, and urged him to advise the King to send
for another Prime Minister. There followed shortly the news
from Bournemouth that the Labour Party Executive had
voted 'No' unanimously in answer to the first of Mr. Chamberlain's questions, and 'Yes' to the second.

Now there could be no question as to Mr. Chamberlain's
next action. He went to the Palace.

The King, meantime, was a prey to impatience and
anxiety. May 9 had been for him 'an unprofitable day',
spent in waiting for news of the conferences at No. 10 Downing
Street. His sympathy for his Prime Minister was enhanced
by the evidently increasing lack of confidence displayed in
him, and the result of the debate in the House had caused the
King displeasure: 'It is most unfair on Chamberlain to be
treated like this after all his good work. The Conservative
rebels like Duff Cooper ought to be ashamed of themselves for
deserting him at this moment.' [47]   His feelings towards the
treatment of Mr. Chamberlain were very much those of his
father at the time of the fall of Mr. Asquith in 1916.[48] Both
were loyal to Prime Ministers who had served them zealously
and with whom they had been on close personal terms.

The suspense was not relieved until the late afternoon of
the following day, and in the meantime the King gave thought
to the possibility of having to find a new Prime Minister. His
first and personal preference was, undoubtedly, Lord Halifax,
whose wisdom and urbanity had often dispelled the depression
of the past few months; and when Mr. Chamberlain came
for his final audience, the King advanced this view.

Friday May 10th

. . . I saw the Prime Minister after tea. He told me that
Attlee had been to see him & had told him that the Labour Party
would serve in the new administration of a new Prime Minister
but not one with himself as P.M. He then told me he wished to
resign so as to make it possible for a new Prime Minister to form a
Government. I accepted his resignation, & told him how grossly
unfairly I thought he had been treated, & that I was terribly sorry

that all this controversy had happened. We then had an informal talk over his successor. I, of course, suggested Halifax, but he told me that H. was not enthusiastic, as being in the Lords he could only act as a shadow or a ghost in the Commons, where all the real work took place. I was disappointed over this statement, as I thought H. was the obvious man, & that his peerage could be placed in abeyance for the time being.[a] Then I knew that there was only one person whom I could send for to form a Government who had the confidence of the country, & that was Winston. I asked Chamberlain his advice, & he told me Winston was the man to send for. I said good-bye to Chamberlain & thanked him for all his help to me, & repeated that I would greatly regret my loss at not having him as my P.M. I sent for Winston & asked him to form a Government. This he accepted & told me he had not thought this was the reason for my having sent for him. He had thought it possible of course, & gave me some of the names of people he would ask to join his government. He was full of fire & determination to carry out the duties of Prime Minister.[b]

In his conception of placing Lord Halifax's peerage 'temporarily in abeyance', the King was not using the term in the strictly technical sense in which it is known to peerage law. His practical mind had envisaged some simple and temporary arrangement whereby Lord Halifax, as Prime Minister, might be enabled to speak in the House of Commons. This would, of course, have required legislation.

Mr. Churchill completed the composition of his War Cabinet on the following day, May 11, including in it both Labour and Liberal leaders. The Prime Minister himself became Minister of Defence, with Mr. Chamberlain as Lord President of the Council; Mr. Attlee, Lord Privy Seal; Lord Halifax, Foreign Secretary; Mr. A. V. Alexander, First Lord of the Admiralty; Mr. Eden, Secretary of State for War; Sir Archibald Sinclair, Secretary of State for Air; and Mr. Arthur Greenwood, Minister without Portfolio. Other appointments

[a] It is not without interest that none of those who had previously expressed a preference for Lord Halifax as Prime Minister, including Mr. Chamberlain, saw any *constitutional* objection to a Prime Minister in the House of Lords and that Lord Halifax's own doubts on accepting the premiership did not include this.

[b] Mr. Churchill's own account is as follows: 'His Majesty received me most graciously and bade me sit down. He looked at me searchingly and quizzically for some moments, and then said: 'I suppose you don't know why I have sent for you?" Adopting his mood, I replied: "Sir, I simply couldn't imagine why". He laughed and said: "I want to ask you to form a Government". I said I would certainly do so.' [49]

to the Government within the next few days included Mr. Herbert Morrison as Minister of Supply, and Mr. Ernest Bevin as Minister of Labour and National Service.

(vi)

Thus did King George part from the second of his Prime Ministers and enter upon the splendid epoch of his third. It was not an easy transition. Both Mr. Baldwin and Mr. Chamberlain had been cast in the traditional mould of the Conservative politician, and as such they commended themselves to the King's liking. There was little of that mould about their successor. Mr. Churchill's political growth had been a free one, uninhibited by slavish loyalty to any one party, unencumbered by over-long devotion to outworn political shibboleths. Whether nominally a Liberal, Constitutionalist or Conservative, he had always been an independent at heart, unafraid of, and unresponsive to, the discipline of party ; cleaving resolutely to the line which at the time seemed to him best ; following an instinctive wisdom which, on occasion, carried him far above the statesmanship of his nominal leaders. Well and truly might he have said with the great Daniel Webster [a] that 'Inconsistencies of opinion arising from changes of circumstances are often justifiable. But there is one sort of inconsistence that is culpable ; it is the inconsistency between a man's conviction and his vote, between his conscience and his conduct. No man shall ever charge me with an inconsistency of that kind.' [b][50]

It was this independence of spirit which had placed Mr. Churchill in opposition to Mr. Baldwin at the time of the Abdication of King Edward VIII, and to Mr. Chamberlain in respect of the policy of appeasement, neither of which circumstances was a primary recommendation to King George.

[a] Daniel Webster (1782–1852), an outstanding American orator and patriot, represented the State of Massachusetts, first as Congressman and later as Senator, from 1823 until 1841. Throughout various political changes and vicissitudes he remained a staunch and consistent protagonist of the sanctity of the unity of the country as against secession. His classic utterance in this respect is known to every schoolboy in the United States : 'Liberty and Union, now and forever, one and inseparable'.

[b] Sir Winston Churchill said on one occasion : 'During my life I have often had to eat my own words and I have always found them a wholesome diet.'

At the time of the Coronation, however, the King had sent to Mr. Churchill a letter which the latter, in reprinting it in his memoirs, has described as 'a gesture of magnanimity' ; [51] but the condemnation of Mr. Chamberlain was less easily forgotten. It may have been also that His Majesty shared something of that uncertainty of mind which so many Englishmen at that time entertained with regard to Mr. Churchill, prompted by the kaleidoscopic nature of his past career. It may have been that he felt in fact somewhat overwhelmed by the very magnitude of Mr. Churchill's personality. It may have been his personal sorrow at parting with Mr. Chamberlain and his disappointment in regard to Lord Halifax. Whatever the reason, though the King accepted unquestioningly the advice of Mr. Chamberlain in inviting Mr. Churchill to form a Government, and gave him his full support, there was not immediately that personal degree of warmth between the Sovereign and his new Prime Minister that had animated his relations with the two predecessors.

I cannot yet think of Winston as P.M. [the King wrote in his diary on May 11]. . . . I met Halifax in the garden [a] & I told him I was sorry not to have him as P.M.[52]

This situation, however, was of but brief duration. The eminent good sense of the King and his keen appreciation of greatness ; the grandeur and the charm of Mr. Churchill ; the very gravity of the danger to nation and Commonwealth with which both were jointly confronted in the leadership of the State, were all conducive to a close relationship of collaboration, which waxed rapidly into a friendship of mutual affection and admiration. It was not long before the King was regarding the Prime Minister's audiences with pleasurable anticipation. He found them fruitful opportunities for a common unburdening of mind, and by September the formal audiences had been replaced by regular Tuesday luncheons at which the King and his Prime Minister, serving themselves from a side-table, would transact State business undisturbed save by an occasional air raid.[b] 'As a convinced upholder of

[a] Lord Halifax was at this time living in Eaton Square and had been accorded the privilege of walking through the gardens of Buckingham Palace on his way to the Foreign Office.

[b] This system of weekly luncheons began on Tuesday, September 10, 1940.

constitutional monarchy,' wrote Mr. Churchill, 'I valued as a signal honour the gracious intimacy with which I, as first Minister, was treated, for which I suppose there has been no precedent since the days of Queen Anne and Marlborough during his years of power.' [53]

By the New Year the relationship between Sovereign and Minister had passed the initial test. 'I could not have a better Prime Minister', the King wrote in his diary.[54]

CHAPTER VI

THE DECISIVE STRUGGLE
MAY 1940–JUNE 1941

(i)

BY pressure of circumstance and force of personality it so happened that, from the opening disasters of May 1940 till the final triumph of May 1945, Mr. Winston Churchill held the centre of the national stage in Britain, and later that, with President Roosevelt and Marshal Stalin, he dominated the international scene. In the type of war which was now loosed upon the world, the courage and the imagination and the steadfastness of one man were necessary for the survival of Britain, one man in whose leadership the British people could unwaveringly place their trust, whose inspiration could fire their own dogged resistance, and whose genius could interpret them to themselves. As Mr. Churchill himself modestly expressed it : 'It was the nation and the race dwelling all round the globe that had the lion's heart. I had the luck to be called upon to give the roar.' [a]   It was inevitable that he should fill this rôle. The Man and the Hour had met, and Mr. Churchill was 'the Lord of his Event'.

But behind the Prime Minister, supporting him with all the great weight of the strength and tradition of constitutional monarchy, stood the King, who, by the example of conduct set by himself and the Queen, afforded his people a standard of behaviour and a criterion of courage which none other than one in his high office could have proffered. Total war respects in its totality the monarch no more than the subject. To the people of Britain in their great ordeal the knowledge that their King and Queen shared their dangers and their privations, their losses and their sorrows, was a source of great comfort ; and the King's oft-repeated, and quite patently sincere and

---

[a] Sir Winston Churchill's speech in Westminster Hall on his eightieth birthday, November 30, 1954.

indomitable, belief in ultimate victory, even in the darkest hour, not only provided a factor of inestimable value in maintaining national morale but established throughout the land a deep and unshakable loyalty to the monarchy, bred of love and admiration.

The King's leadership, though less dramatic, less cosmic, less onerous than Mr. Churchill's, made, nevertheless, by its very simplicity and virtue, a vital contribution to victory, an example of personal self-sacrifice and unsparing devotion to duty which evoked on every hand a spirit of emulation.

No better crystallization of this leadership can be found than in the message broadcast by King George to his peoples on Empire Day, May 24, 1940, calling for a Day of National Prayer on the following Sunday. Realizing the momentous nature of the occasion, he was determined that the speech should be worthy of it. Days were spent in its careful preparation, hours in rehearsing its delivery with Mr. Logue, but so fluid was the military situation that up to the moment that he sat before the hated microphone he feared the possible necessity of a last-minute change in the text. 'I was fearful that something might happen to make me have to alter it', he wrote in his diary that evening. 'I was very pleased with the way I delivered it, & it was easily my best effort. How I hate broadcasting.'

The speech epitomized the King's own simple beliefs: recognition of the issue at stake, faith in the cause, confidence in ultimate victory, and, above all, a sublime trust in Almighty God.

The decisive struggle is now upon us. I am going to speak plainly to you, for in this hour of trial I know that you would not have me do otherwise. Let no one be mistaken; it is no mere territorial conquest that our enemies are seeking. It is the overthrow, complete and final, of this Empire and of everything for which it stands, and after that the conquest of the world. And if their will prevails they will bring to its accomplishment all the hatred and cruelty which they have already displayed. . . .

Against our honesty is set dishonour, against our faithfulness is set treachery, against our justice, brute force. There, in clear and unmistakeable opposition, lie the forces which now confront one another. The great uprising of the peoples throughout the Empire shows without doubt which will prevail. . . . In perfect unity of purpose they will defend their lives and all that makes life worth living.

Let no one think that my confidence is dimmed when I tell you how perilous is the ordeal which we are facing. On the contrary, it shines in my heart as brightly as it shines in yours. But confidence alone is not enough. It must be armed with courage and resolution, with endurance and self-sacrifice. . . .

At this fateful hour we turn, as our fathers before us have turned in all times of trial, to God Most High. . . . Let us with one heart and soul humbly but confidently commit our cause to God, and ask His aid that we may valiantly defend the right as it is given to us to see it. . . .

Keep your hearts proud and your resolve unshaken. Let us go forward to that task as one man, a smile on our lips, and our heads held high, and with God's help we shall not fail.

(ii)

From London, throughout those fateful days of a beautiful but fearful summer, King George watched the initial stages of the 'Decisive Struggle' unfold as the Wehrmacht swept across the Low Countries and northern France with relentless force. Nor was he a mere impassive observer. On May 13, for perhaps the first time in history, the long-distance telephone was used by one Sovereign to another in a cry for help.

I was woken by the police sergeant at 5.0 a.m. who told me Queen Wilhelmina of the Netherlands wished to speak to me [the King recorded]. I did not believe him, but went to the telephone & it was her. She begged me to send aircraft for the defence of Holland. I passed this message on to everyone concerned, & went back to bed. It is not often one is rung up at that hour, and especially by a Queen. But in these days anything may happen, & far worse things too.[1]

Later that morning there arrived from Holland Prince Bernhard and Princess Juliana with their two small daughters, the youngest, Princess Irene, only nine months old. From them the King learned at first hand of the parachute assaults upon the Netherlands by German troops, who were said to be descending by hundreds in all manner of disguises. Prince Bernhard, leaving his family in safety, returned to Holland, but scarcely had he left when Queen Wilhelmina was again on the telephone, this time, unexpectedly enough, from Harwich.

This intrepid royal lady,[a] having failed in her first attempt to obtain additional air support from Britain for her army, and being herself the object of German attempts to kidnap and hold her as a hostage to paralyse Dutch resistance, had left The Hague and embarked in the British destroyer *Hereward* at Rotterdam, with the purpose of joining that part of her forces which were still resisting the enemy in Zeeland. Prevented from landing at Breskens or Flushing because of German bombardment, and unable to make contact with the officer commanding her troops, the Queen had decided to go to England, there to make a further direct appeal to King George and the British Government for additional aid, and then to return to her own country. Her telephone conversation from Harwich at length convinced her, however, that, since her departure from The Hague that morning, the situation had so materially worsened that all thought of return to Holland was impossible. With deep reluctance she was persuaded to accept the inevitable and to proceed to London, where she received a warm and royal welcome. The King wrote in his diary :

I met her at Liverpool Street Station & brought her here [to Buckingham Palace]. I had not met her before. She told me that when she left the Hague she had no intention of leaving Holland, but force of circumstances had made her come here. She was naturally very upset, & had brought no clothes with her.[2]

The brave lady had indeed no more than what she stood up in, which included a tin hat given her by the commander of the destroyer. She was installed in the Palace with all consideration for her adversity, and her every want supplied.

Queen Wilhelmina was deeply touched by the sympathetic kindness of the King and Queen. Within the next few days she made two broadcasts, one to her own peoples and one to the peoples of the British Empire, and on both occasions King

[a] Queen Wilhelmina (b. 1880), the only daughter of King William III of the Netherlands and Princess Emma of Waldeck and Pyrmont, a sister of the Duchess of Albany, succeeded to the throne on the death of her father in 1890. She married in 1901 Prince Henry of Mecklenburg-Schwerin (1876–1934) and had one daughter, Princess Juliana Louise Emma Maria Wilhelmina (b. 1909) who, in 1937, married Prince Bernhard of Lippe-Biesterfeld (b. 1911). Queen Wilhelmina resigned the crown in favour of her daughter in 1948, and assumed the title of Princess of the Netherlands.

George insisted upon her speaking from the room which he himself used on similar occasions; while with compassionate understanding he received her news on May 15 that the Dutch Army had capitulated. Nor was this all. Queen Wilhelmina's younger grandchild, Princess Irene, was to have been christened with the due solemnity and pomp of the rites of the Dutch Reformed Church in the Cathedral of Amsterdam on May 31; now, at Queen Elizabeth's suggestion, the ceremony took place on the appointed date in the chapel of Buckingham Palace, where her own two daughters had been baptized. Both the admiration and the gratitude of Queen Wilhelmina were quickened by these acts of generous sympathy and spontaneous kindness on the part of the King and Queen at a moment of high tragedy in her life, and of stress and anxiety in theirs.

Tragic as were the circumstances of the Queen of the Netherlands, they were considerably less so than those of her brother Sovereign, King Leopold of the Belgians, who became the prisoner of his conscience.

The choice presented to all heads of States in the event of the total occupation of their countries is one of hideous complexity, and it inevitably arises when there is little time for calm consideration. To leave their homeland and follow their Governments into exile leaves them open to the charge of desertion by those who remain behind; yet to remain involves the risk of their being held hostage for the submissive conduct of their peoples held in the thraldom of a ruthless conqueror. This onerous alternative was forced upon Queen Wilhelmina, King Haakon of Norway, King Christian of Denmark and King Leopold. Two chose exile and the gallant continuation of the struggle from a foreign shore against a common enemy, with the justified hope of ultimate victory and liberation. Of the two who remained in their respective countries, King Christian, by his daily ride through the streets of his capital, became the symbol of resistance by the Danish people to a fate which they had been powerless to prevent but to which they were determined not to be resigned. But the decision of King Leopold to remain was one of the darkest personal tragedies of the war, and one in which King George took a great and sympathetic interest.

The King had a sincere liking for his young Belgian cousin, seven years his junior, whom he had first met on that historic day in November 1918 when together they had ridden with King Albert in triumph into Brussels, and whose subsequent life had been dogged by one calamity after another.[a] There was that in the character of King Leopold which aroused King George's sympathy, and, though he may have been critical of the international policies which the Belgian Sovereign had pursued, he was aware of the difficulties and complexities with which he was faced.   The feeling of friendship was reciprocated, and King Leopold had invited the King and Queen for a State Visit in October of 1939, which, to the disappointment of all, had had to be cancelled.

As the German attack swept through the Low Countries in May 1940, King George followed the fate of the Belgian Army with anxiety, for upon its sustained resistance much depended, including the covering of the left flank of the British Expeditionary Force.   It was the hope of all that, emulating the example of King Albert in 1914, King Leopold would maintain the Belgian Army as an active force, despite all initial reverses, and would continue to fight in support of the Allies.   This, however, was not to be.   Overwhelmed by the might of the Wehrmacht, Belgian military resistance was shattered, and by May 25 King Leopold, as Commander-in-Chief, became convinced that further opposition was hopeless. He therefore sued for terms of capitulation.   On this same day he wrote from his headquarters at Bruges a formal letter to King George explaining the necessity for his surrender and

[a] King Leopold III (b. 1901) was the great-grandson of Queen Victoria's 'Uncle Leopold', who became the first King of the Belgians in 1831.   He was educated at Eton and remains a loyal Old Etonian.   He succeeded to the throne on the sudden death, while mountaineering, of his father, King Albert, in 1934. In 1926 he married Princess Astrid of Sweden, who was killed in a motor accident in Switzerland, in which they were both involved, a year after his accession to the throne.   During his detention in Belgium by the Germans, King Leopold married in 1941 Mlle Marie Lilian Baels, daughter of a former Minister of the Crown, whom he created Princess de Réthy.   On the liberation of Belgium by the Allied Armies in September 1944, the constitutional position became somewhat involved.   King Leopold had not abdicated, but he was still in German hands, and the Belgian Parliament therefore elected his brother, Prince Charles, Count of Flanders, as Regent.   There followed a bitter political controversy.   When the Regency came to an end in July 1950, King Leopold delegated his powers to his eldest son by his first marriage, Prince Baudouin (b. 1930), in whose favour he formally abdicated on July 16, 1951.

also his reasons for his further fateful decision to remain with his people rather than accompany his Ministers to France, where they were still functioning as a Government.

King George was greatly disturbed at the news of the Belgian capitulation, which jeopardized in the extreme the movement of the British Army to the coast, whence its evacuation had already been ordered. 'This came as a great shock to me,' he wrote, 'as the evacuation of the B.E.F. will be almost impossible, with the Germans on three sides of us.' [3] At the same time he realized to the full the danger, not only to potential Belgian resistance but to the whole Allied war effort, involved in King Leopold's decision to remain in the hands of the enemy. Both the Belgian and British Governments had exhausted their efforts to persuade King Leopold to escape while yet he might, and both turned to King George with the request that he would make a personal appeal. On May 26, therefore, he telegraphed to his brother Sovereign in the following terms : [4]

I am very grateful for your letter.

I note that Your Majesty considers it to be your duty to your people and to your Allies to remain with your Army in Belgium. In taking this decision Your Majesty will not have overlooked the extreme importance of preserving a united Belgian Government with full authority outside the territory occupied by the enemy, and while paying tribute to Your Majesty's devotion I and my Government must express our grave concern at your decision.

While it would be presumptuous of me to advise you on your duty to your people, I can say that as regards the Allies and the fulfilment of their joint purpose in the war, I do not feel that Your Majesty is called upon to make the sacrifice which you contemplate.

Moreover I am bound to put to Your Majesty another point. If it were possible for you to remain in Belgium at liberty to mix with your people and to act and speak for them, there might be great value in the establishment of such a rallying point for the Belgian nation. But I can hardly hope that such would be the outcome of Your Majesty's decision to stay with the Army. It seems to me that Your Majesty must consider the possibility, even the probability, of your being taken prisoner, perhaps carried off to Germany, and almost certainly deprived of all communication with the outside world. Such a position would leave your people bereft of their natural leader without so far as I can see any compensating advantage.

But King Leopold would not be deterred from his chosen course of self-immolation. He had taken his decision and, rightly or wrongly, he would abide by it. He remained — and suffered accordingly.

King George, however, did not participate in the general storm of vilification, both public and private, vented upon the Belgian King. With his innate fairness of judgment he sought to examine all the available evidence before reaching his final conclusion on this terrible dilemma of divided loyalties. He questioned those British officers who had been in touch with the King: the Duke of Gloucester, Sir Roger Keyes, Lord Gort and Sir John Dill, who brought him a pathetic personal note of affection from King Leopold, and also the American Ambassador in Brussels, Mr. John Cudahy. The final verdict which he reached may be taken to be that which he expressed some six months later to Mr. Harry Hopkins as they sat, with the Queen, one afternoon in the air-raid shelter of Buckingham Palace, while above them raged the Blitz. 'He [the King] expressed a good deal of sympathy with the King of the Belgians', Mr. Hopkins wrote to President Roosevelt. 'It was perfectly clear that he felt that the King had had two responsibilities — one as Commander-in-Chief of the Belgian Army and the other his job as King, and that he had got the two jobs mixed up. He apparently had little or no criticism of him as Commander-in-Chief of the Army, but as King he thought he should have left the country and established his government elsewhere.'[5]

It was in accordance with this view that, when the question later arose of the deletion of the names of the Kings of Italy and of the Belgians from the roll of the Knights of the Garter, and the removal of their banners from St. George's Chapel at Windsor, His Majesty agreed in the case of King Victor Emmanuel, but was equally ready to concur with the view of his advisers that final judgment in the case of King Leopold should be held over until the end of the war. His banner was therefore permitted to remain, and still does so.[6]

In the Low Countries the fate of the British Expeditionary Force still hung in the balance. The capitulation on May 15 of the Dutch Army had jeopardized the British, Belgian and

French forces south of the Scheldt, and the B.E.F. could now
only be maintained through the northern ports of Nieuport
and Dunkirk. It was hoped, however, that the position would
be relieved by the large-scale counter-attack which General
Weygand was planning.

The reports which the King received both as regards the
strategic position and the general condition of the morale of
the French Government and High Command filled him with
the deepest anxiety, of which one of many entries in his diary
at this time is evidence.

Thursday, May 23rd

I wanted to see Newall [a] the C.A.S. not having seen him for
some time, & he came in the evening. He had just left a Chiefs of
Staff meeting with the Prime Minister & he told me that the
situation in France was critical. Gort had sent a message to say
that he was short of food & ammunition. Owing to the rapid
advance of the German tanks & motorised divisions, his lines of
communication had been cut through Amiens, & food had had to
be sent to France from here by air. German tanks had reached
Boulogne, & had captured a fort above the town & were shelling
the harbour. He feared the 2nd Irish Guards & 2nd Welsh Guards
had had many casualties as they were unable to stop the tanks with
anti-tank guns. The fort is to be bombed at once. Newall was
sorry to come with such a gloomy account & said that the French
command must have 'gone to seed' behind the Maginot Line.
They thought that the Meuse was impossible to cross at that one
point, & that the Ardennes Forest was an impossible place for an
army to deploy from. However the Germans have done it.
    . . . This news was so worrying that I sent a message to
Winston asking him to come & see me after dinner. I heard at
7.30 that the French had counter-attacked from the south, & that
they were reported to have entered Amiens, Albert, & Peronne.
This came from the W.O. The Prime Minister came at 10.30 p.m.
He told me that if the French plan made out by Weygand did not
come off, he would have to order the B.E.F. back to England.
This operation would mean the loss of all guns, tanks, ammunition,
& all stores in France. The question was whether we could get
the troops back from Calais & Dunkirk. The very thought of
having to order this movement is appalling, as the loss of life will
probably be immense.

[a] Marshal of the Royal Air Force Cyril Louis Norton, first Baron Newall,
G.C.B., O.M., G.C.M.G., C.B.E. (b. 1886), was Chief of the Air Staff from
1937 to 1940, and Governor-General of New Zealand from 1941 to 1946.

It was against this background of imminent disaster that the King made his Empire Day broadcast on the following day, and he had been fearful lest some further grievous news might necessitate the changing of his script at the last moment. Such news did in fact arrive twenty-four hours later in the capitulation of the Belgian Army which, taking effect at midnight on May 27/28, completely exposed the Allied left flank. Nothing now remained but to ensure the escape of the maximum number of troops of the B.E.F. from the Dunkirk–Nieuport perimeter, but two grave uncertainties existed : would German armour, pressing down the coast, reach the ports first and thus cut off the British from the means of evacuation ? Or, having reached the beaches, would the exhausted troops be bombed into annihilation by the Luftwaffe before they could be taken off ? In many minds there had arisen a third query : was evacuation possible at all ? But this had been answered in the emphatic affirmative by the determination of Mr. Churchill and the incredible capacity of the Royal Navy for improvisation.[a]

Of all these factors the King was cognizant. The fate of his army was hourly with him as, day by day, behind one of the most heroic rearguard actions in history, the miracle of Dunkirk — more prosaically named 'Operation Dynamo' — was performed as an unparalleled feat of co-operation between the three Services. 'I saw Anthony Eden after lunch who told me we had evacuated 30,000 men, mostly details, in the last 48 hours', the King wrote in his diary on May 29, and thereafter each evening he chronicled the day's record of salvation at the head of the daily entry.

Thursday May 30th
We have now evacuated 80,000 men of the B.E.F.

Friday May 31st
We have now evacuated 133,000 men of the B.E.F. and 11,000 Frenchmen.

Saturday June 1st
We have now evacuated 175,000 men of the B.E.F. and 34,000 Frenchmen.

[a] To carry out the evacuation of the British Expeditionary Force from the beaches, the Royal Navy assembled 887 vessels, 222 of which were naval craft, 91 passenger ships or merchant vessels, and the rest small craft of every kind, manned by yachtsmen and fishermen from all along the coast and up the rivers.

Sunday June 2nd

We have now evacuated 215,000 men of the B.E.F. and 60,000 Frenchmen.

At length the penultimate stage of the miracle was reached and the King could write with thankfulness and relief:

Monday June 3rd

We have now evacuated 224,000 men of the B.E.F. and 85,000 Frenchmen. The last of the B.E.F. have been evacuated.

Once again, as at Gallipoli in 1915, the impossible had been achieved. But the troops brought home barely more than their lives and what they could carry on their persons. Their artillery and armour were lost, their transport, stores and munitions abandoned [a] — but they themselves were safe, and for this the King and his people gave joyful thanks.

'Operation Dynamo' continued for two days longer in order to bring off those French elements of the rearguard who had survived. The King wrote:

Tuesday June 4th

We have now evacuated over 102,000 Frenchmen and the total is 327,000.

Wednesday June 5th

We have now evacuated over 111,000 Frenchmen and the total is 335,000.

On this last day, when the miracle had been accomplished, the King received some of those who had taken part in it, including the French Admiral Abriol, who had completed the demolition of Dunkirk, and the commanders of the Second and Third Corps of the B.E.F. 'They all told me the same story of heroism & devotion to duty of the Troops & of the difficulties which they had had to surmount', he wrote later that evening. 'Roads blocked with transport of all sorts, refugees by the thousand, a pitiable sight. They were tired but a long sleep had done them good.'

And indeed there was little time for rest, for the Battle of France was still being fought, albeit with a steadily decreasing resistance on the part of the French. On June 4 King George sent to President Lebrun, with the approval of his Ministers,

---

[a] Mr. Churchill has stated in his memoirs (II, p. 125) that the British losses in equipment were as follows: 7000 tons of ammunition; 90,000 rifles; 2300 guns; 82,000 vehicles; 8000 Bren guns; and 400 anti-tank rifles.

a telegram of sympathy and exhortation — 'We sympathize in the losses that France has sustained, but recognize in them the measure of French heroism and devotion' [7] — but it was soon apparent that the fighting spirit of France was exhausted. From Mr. Churchill the King learned of the rapidly deteriorating situation as the Prime Minister had seen it at his meetings with the French Ministers — the despairing gallantry of M. Reynaud, the bitter pessimism of General Weygand, the enigmatic defeatism of Marshal Pétain.[a] The end came quickly. On June 16 M. Reynaud abandoned the struggle and resigned; the Marshal formed a Government and late that same night sued for armistice terms. The soul of France was in eclipse.

British attention was now focused on saving the French Fleet from falling into German and Italian hands. For Italy had declared war on Britain and France on June 10. 'Mussolini gave no reason', the King wrote in his diary that evening. 'May he rue the day when he gave the order.' Again and again during these last fateful days Mr. Churchill had besought the French Government to dispose of the Fleet in almost any way they liked rather than allow it to be captured or impounded by the enemy, and had offered every kind of inducement, including the novel idea of a Franco-British Union. The French replies had been evasive. They would not send their ships to British ports, nor allow them to be interned in America; they proposed to send them to North Africa, there to be dismantled.

This, however, was far from satisfactory to the British Government, who enlisted the aid of King George in making a last appeal. Late on the night of June 22 — when, as it turned out, the Franco-German Armistice agreement had already been signed at Compiègne — the following telegram was despatched from His Majesty to President Lebrun : [8]

I learn with deep anxiety and dismay that Your Government under the cruel pressure of these tragic days contemplate sending the French Fleet to French North African ports where it would be dismantled. This must in effect leave the French Fleet where it would be in evident danger of falling into hostile hands.

[a] Vivid accounts of this tragic period are given by Mr. Churchill in chapters ix and x of the second volume of his war memoirs, and by Sir Edward Spears in Volume 2 of his *Assignment to Catastrophe*.

I need not remind you, Monsieur le Président, should this occur, how great would be the danger involved to our common cause and I rely on the solemn and explicit assurances already given to My Government that in no circumstances would Your Government assent to any conditions that involved this consequence.

Unfortunately the British Ambassador, Sir Ronald Campbell, to whom the telegram had been sent for transmission, did not receive it until the following morning when he had already left Bordeaux. Having no means of delivering it personally to the President, he forwarded it by telegraph from St-Jean-de-Luz. By the time it reached the distracted M. Lebrun the die had already been cast, and the tragic sequel was the action at Oran and Mers-el-Kebir on July 3, which was sadly to embitter Anglo-French relations.[a] To the King it was a source of regret that his appeal had arrived too late.[10]

(iii)

'Personally I feel happier now that we have no allies to be polite to & to pamper', the King wrote to Queen Mary after the fall of France,[11] and in these sentiments was at one with the vast majority of his subjects.[b]

The capacity of the British people for illogical virtue in politics is only equalled by their absolute refusal to recognize defeat and their ability to deck their disasters with the laurels of victory. The feeling of elation and pride which swept through England after the evacuation of Dunkirk was enhanced

[a] On July 3, 1940, Admiral Somerville proceeded to Oran and there presented to the Admiral commanding the French Fleet an ultimatum of four choices: (1) to join with the British Fleet and continue the war; (2) to place the ships under British control in a British port; (3) to send them for demilitarization to a French West Indian port (*e.g.* Martinique) or to entrust them to the United States until the end of the war; or (4) to sink the Fleet within six hours. Should all these solutions to the problem be rejected, Admiral Somerville was instructed 'to use whatever force may be necessary' to prevent the French ships from falling into enemy hands. After negotiations which lasted all day, the French Admiral remained adamant in rejecting the terms offered, and the British ships opened fire. The battleship *Bretagne* was blown up, *Dunquerque* ran aground and *Provence* was beached. *Strasbourg* escaped from the harbour and reached Toulon, where she was joined by cruisers from Algiers. Five days later *Richelieu* was immobilized by torpedo attacks at Dakar, and, later, after prolonged negotiations, the French Fleet at Alexandria was interned.[9]

[b] That this was no mere transitory feeling is evident from an entry in the King's diary on February 7, 1941 : 'I always feel that we have to be thankful France collapsed at once after Dunkirk, so that we were able to reorganize the Army at home, & gave us time to prepare the Air Force to repel the Blitzkrieg'.

rather than diminished by the knowledge that Britain now stood alone in the fight, stripped and girt for battle, and unimpeded by less determined friends.   A people which had lit the Armada beacons 'from Eddystone to Berwick-bounds, from Lynn to Milford Bay', and had watched undismayed the twinkling camp-fires of Napoleon's army at Boulogne, had now responded worthily to Mr. Churchill's grim promise of 'blood, sweat, toil and tears', and to the King's summons to the Decisive Struggle.   This spirit of pride and loyalty found expression in the greeting offered by an office-keeper in a Government department to a senior civil servant on the morrow of the fall of France :   'Well, we're in the final now, sir, and it's going to be played on our own ground'.   It also inspired verses which have subsequently become famous :

> Praise God, now, for an English war —
>   The grey tide and the sullen coast,
> The menace of the urgent hour,
> The single island, like a tower,
>   Ringed with an angry host.
>
> This is the war that England knows,
>   When all the world holds but one man —
> King Philip of the galleons,
> Louis, whose light outshone the sun's,
>   The conquering Corsican.
>
> When Europe, like a prison door,
>   Clangs ; and the swift, enfranchised sea
> Runs narrower than a village brook ;
> And men who love us not, yet look
>   To us for liberty ;
>
> When no allies are left, no help
>   To count upon from alien hands,
> No waverers remain to woo,
> No more advice to listen to,
>   And only England stands.
>
> .   .   .   .   .
>
> Send us, O God, the will and power
>   To do as we have done before ;
> The men who ride the sea and air
> Are the same men our fathers were
>   To fight the English war.[a]

[a] 'The English War', by Dorothy L. Sayers.

There was no bravado, no vainglory, no return to the old-time 'jingoism' of the 'nineties, which Rudyard Kipling had deplored in his 'Recessional', for in June 1940 both 'reeking tube and iron shard' were woefully lacking. The Army had come back from the Continent with added glory but with little else. The Home Guard were armed in many cases with pikes and pick-handles, and drilled with broomsticks. The spirit in which Britain 'stood alone' in 1940 was certainly one of pride, but of pride tempered with dedication to a defence, if need be to the death, of the decencies of life and common behaviour, set against a rule of dishonour, treachery and brute force; the pride of a people who, in the words of their King, had 'risen in just wrath against a thing which they detest and despise'.

Feverish preparations were set on foot to withstand the coming onslaught, for none then doubted that an invasion of Britain would be attempted, and none could say how soon. In point of fact Hitler did hesitate before carrying the war across the Channel, hoping that, in view of the adverse fortunes of war, the British Government might be persuaded to make peace. Though, on July 16, he gave to Keitel and Jodl the order to prepare plans for the attack, in his speech to the Reichstag three days later he made 'a final appeal to common sense' and urged upon Britain the futility of continuing the struggle. It was only when these approaches had been rejected with contempt and defiance that the Führer gave final orders to the Luftwaffe to prepare the way for the invasion of Britain which was given the code-name 'Operation Sea Lion'.

In the meantime Britain waited and looked to her defences,[a] an essential part of which was to ensure the safety of the Sovereign. There was much to be done. At the outbreak of war, despite the general impression that London would be bombed at once and terribly, there appears to have been no protection whatsoever provided for Their Majesties, or their household, at Buckingham Palace. Now a small room in the basement, a housemaids' sitting-room, was appropriated as a

---

[a] The official history of these stirring days is to be found in Mr. Basil Collier's *The Defence of the United Kingdom* and in Mr. T. H. O'Brien's *Civil Defence*. Mr. Peter Fleming, in his *Invasion 1940*, has also contributed a fascinating account of the period.

shelter, reinforced by balks of timber and divided into minute cubicles by partitions of beaver-board. It was not until 1941 that a full-scale concrete air-raid shelter was constructed adjoining the Palace, with the proper equipment of gas-proof chambers and ample bathing and kitchen accommodation.

An elaborate plan was drawn up for the speedy evacuation of the Royal Family from London in the event of invasion. For, although there was some discussion of the possibility of sending the Princesses to Canada in an emergency, there was never at any time the slightest idea that the King and Queen would leave the country. Nothing, in fact, was further from King George's mind. In those days when, in Mr. Churchill's words, 'we viewed with stern and tranquil gaze the idea of going down fighting amid the ruins of Whitehall', His Majesty had a shooting range laid down in the gardens of Buckingham Palace, and another at Windsor, at which he and other members of his family and his equerries practised regularly with rifles, pistols and tommy-guns.[12] As the King later told a visitor, it was his considered intention, in the event of a successful invasion of Britain by the Germans, and the establishment of a British resistance movement, to offer his services at once, in whatever capacity, to its leader.

The possibility of leaving London, however, had to be faced, and a number of houses were selected in various parts of the country to which Their Majesties might go. That most favoured was one in the West of England, which, some hundred and thirty years earlier, had been chosen for the same purpose when plans were being prepared for the safety of King George III and his family in the event of an invasion by Napoleon.[13]

Similar arrangements were made for other members of the Royal Family. Queen Mary, much against her will, left Marlborough House for Badminton, the home of the Duke of Beaufort — her nephew by marriage [a] — but the Duchess of Gloucester announced her intention to 'stay put' in Northamptonshire, trusting in God and the Barnwell Home Guard.

[a] Rt. Hon. Henry Hugh Arthur FitzRoy Somerset, tenth Duke of Beaufort, K.G., G.C.V.O., Royal Victorian Chain (b. 1900), was Master of the Horse to King George VI from 1936 to 1952, and subsequently to Queen Elizabeth II. He married in 1923 the Lady Mary Cambridge, elder daughter of Queen Mary's brother, first Marquess of Cambridge, formerly Adolphus, Duke of Teck.

The protection of Their Majesties was entrusted to a picked body of officers and men from the Brigade of Guards and the Household Cavalry, known as the Coates Mission, who, equipped with armoured cars, stood ready night and day to escort the King and Queen to a place of safety or to defend them against surprise attacks by German parachute troops.

This latter danger was considered to be a very real one, since the experience of both Queen Wilhelmina and King Haakon had shown that the purpose of the enemy was to seize, if at all possible, the person of the Sovereign of the country which they invaded.[a] Both the Dutch and Norwegian monarchs had been the subject of persistent attempts at capture and both impressed upon King George and Queen Elizabeth the dangers from such tactics.

King Haakon was particularly emphatic. Since his arrival with his son, Crown Prince Olav, from Norway on June 10, he had been lodged in Buckingham Palace, and on one occasion he asked King George what would happen if a parachute attack were threatened. The King explained the method of alerting the guard, and King Haakon, somewhat sceptically, asked to see it in operation. Obligingly King George pressed the alarm signal and, together with the Queen, they went into the garden to watch the result. There followed anti-climax ; nothing happened at all. An anxious equerry, dispatched to make inquiries, returned with the report that the officer of the guard had been informed by the police-sergeant on duty that no attack was impending 'as he had heard nothing of it'. Police co-operation having been obtained, a number of guardsmen entered the gardens at the double and, to the horror of King Haakon but the vast amusement of the King and Queen, proceeded to thrash the undergrowth in the manner of beaters at a shoot rather than of men engaged in the pursuit of a dangerous enemy. As a result of this incident precautions were revised and strengthened.

At this moment of dread quiet, the moment before the

---

[a] The Führer's intentions in the matter of the capture and treatment of the Sovereigns of those States which opposed him were expressed in an order to the Wehrmacht issued on April 2, 1940 — a week before the invasion of Denmark and Norway (see *Documents on German Foreign Policy, 1918–1945*, Series D, Vol. IX, pp. 67-68).

storm of fire and blast was to break over Britain, a final attempt was made to avert the tragedy. The aged King Gustav of Sweden,[a] doyen of the monarchs of Europe, secretly offered his good offices to King George and to Hitler to enable contact to be made between the two groups of belligerents in order to examine the possibilities of peace. King George received this secret letter on August 2, and promptly referred it to his Ministers for consideration and for consultation with the Dominions. His own reaction, as recorded in his diary, was very clear.

How can we talk peace with Germany now after they have overrun & demoralized the peoples of so many countries in Europe ? Until Germany is prepared to live peaceably with her neighbours in Europe, she will always be a menace. We have got to get rid of her aggressive spirit, her engines of war & the people who have been taught to use them.[14]

That this was also the unequivocal view of His Majesty's Governments in Britain and overseas was made forcefully clear in the reply which King George sent to the King of Sweden declining his offer. In view of the criminal record of the enemy, the King saw not the slightest cause to recede from the principles and resolves which he and his Ministers had already set forth.

. . . On the contrary the intention of My peoples to prosecute the war until their purposes have been achieved has been strengthened. They will not falter in their duty and they firmly believe that with the help of God they will not lack the means to discharge their task.[15]

The date of the King's reply is itself of significance. The letter was handed to the Swedish Minister on August 12, the day on which the preliminary phase of the Battle of Britain reached its close.[b]

[a] King Gustav V of Sweden (1858–1950) was the fourth in succession from Marshal Bernadotte, Prince of Ponte Corvo, who had been elected Crown Prince of Sweden in 1810. King Gustav, who had married Princess Victoria of Baden, came to the throne in 1907. He was succeeded on his death by his son, King Gustav VI, who married, firstly, Princess Margaret Victoria, daughter of the Duke of Connaught, and secondly, Lady Louise Mountbatten, daughter of Prince Louis of Battenberg, first Marquess of Milford Haven.

[b] 'The preliminary phase of the Battle of Britain lasted from 10th July until 12th August' (Collier, p. 170).

The Luftwaffe had carried out small-scale air raids before the armistice with France had been concluded ; since July 10 German aircraft had attacked various targets in force. The main battle, however, was not joined until August 13, when a full-scale attack began upon Channel shipping and the south coast ports. On August 26 the enemy switched his attacks to fighter airfields in the south and south-east. The assault on London began on September 7, by day and by night, and night raids on the capital continued with varying intensity throughout the winter. Heavy losses were inflicted on the enemy during these operations, but Britain's own loss in fighter pilots was also severe. In the battles over England that fateful autumn many a young Englishman made the discovery in sacrifice that 'Death opens unknown doors. It is most grand to die.' [a]

In the opening stages of the battle King George was indefatigable in his attention to the defences of Britain. Up and down the country he journeyed, inspecting the newly formed Home Guard, the R.A.F. fighter stations and the recently reorganized and re-equipped Army. Everywhere he brought encouragement and interest and — wherever possible — a note of humour. Nothing delighted him more than to be challenged by a nervous Home Guard sentry and to be asked for his identity card which, in common with all inhabitants of his beleaguered kingdom, he always carried with him. More particularly was he impressed by the men of the Royal Air Force, and by their rapid metamorphosis from civilian life. He talked freely with them, putting them at their ease. 'I was struck with their appearance', he once wrote in his diary. 'Just ordinary young men, who come from all trades & professions, are now flying & using the most intricate & modern inventions.' [16]

But it was when the brunt of the battle fell upon London that King George came into his own. Here, in grim and starkly practical form, was pragmatic proof of his own theory of monarchy — a Sovereign standing at the head of his people, sharing their dangers, deeply concerned for their suffering, encouraging them in their continued determination

[a] John Masefield, *The Tragedy of Pompey the Great*, 'Song of the Chief Centurions'.

SEPTEMBER 1940
THE KING AND QUEEN, WITH MR. CHURCHILL, INSPECTING BOMB
DAMAGE AT BUCKINGHAM PALACE

to resist the enemy. Again and again in those warm September days, when East and South London were staggering beneath the first shock of the enemy's bombardment, the King and Queen would appear suddenly and without formality among the rubble and the ruins. On one occasion, as the King paused in his inspection of a recently bombed area, a man cried out, 'Thank God for a good King', and there arose a ragged cheer. 'Thank God for a good people', was the King's instant response, and again there arose a cheer of defiance. A word of understanding here and there, and the Queen's smile, were sufficient proof of the sincerity of their sympathy. 'For him we had admiration, for her adoration', one said later ; and another eye-witness has a vivid recollection of a group of women standing before a bomb-shattered row of houses, their homes of yesterday, crowding about the Queen, calling to one another in unfeigned admiration, 'Oh, ain't she lovely ; ain't she just *bloody* lovely !'

If anything could have established the Monarchy even more firmly in the hearts of the people, it was this, and no one was more aware of the fact than Mr. Churchill : 'This war has drawn the Throne and the people more closely together than was ever before recorded,' the Prime Minister wrote to his Sovereign, 'and Your Majesties are more beloved by all classes and conditions than any of the princes of the past.'[a][17]

Shortly thereafter a further bond was forged between the King and his people. On September 9 the Luftwaffe shifted the force of its attack to the West End of London, and a bomb fell on the north side of Buckingham Palace, lodging itself under the stone steps outside the Regency Room. It did not explode and the King continued to use his study which was immediately above it. It went off, however, at 1.25 the next morning. No damage was done to the main structure, and there were no casualties as that part of the Palace had been evacuated for the night, but all the windows on all floors, including those of the Royal apartments, were shattered.

[a] On receiving the Freedom of the City of Edinburgh on October 12, 1942, Mr. Churchill took occasion to pay a public tribute to Their Majesties : 'The whole British Empire, and, most of all, the United Kingdom of Great Britain and Northern Ireland, owes an inestimable debt to our King and Queen. In these years of trial and storm they have shared to the full the perils, the labours, the sorrows, and the hopes of the British nation.'

The King and Queen, who now slept each night at Windsor and came up to London every morning, inspected the damage and, congratulating themselves on their escape, moved into quarters looking over the courtyard.[18]

Three days later the enemy struck again, and this time the escape was narrower.

We went to London & found an Air Raid in progress [the King wrote in his diary]. The day was very cloudy & it was raining hard. We were both upstairs with Alec Hardinge talking in my little sitting room overlooking the quadrangle; (I cannot use my ordinary one owing to the broken windows). All of a sudden we heard an aircraft making a zooming noise above us, saw 2 bombs falling past the opposite side of the Palace, & then heard 2 resounding crashes as the bombs fell in the quadrangle about 30 yds away. We looked at each other, & then we were out into the passage as fast as we could get there. The whole thing happened in a matter of seconds. We all wondered why we weren't dead. Two great craters had appeared in the courtyard. The one nearest the Palace had burst a fire hydrant & water was pouring through the broken windows in the passage. 6 bombs had been dropped. The aircraft was seen coming straight down the Mall below the clouds having dived through the clouds & had dropped 2 bombs in the forecourt, 2 in the quadrangle, 1 in the Chapel & the other in the garden. The Chapel is wrecked, & the bomb also wrecked the plumber's workshop below in which 4 men were working. 3 of them were injured & the fourth shocked. Looking at the wreckage how they escaped death is a wonder to me. E & I went all round the basement talking to the servants who were all safe, & quite calm through it all. None of the windows on our side of the Palace were broken. We were told that the bomb in the forecourt was a delay action (D.A.) bomb so we gave orders for all the east windows to be opened in case it exploded, & we remained in our shelter & had lunch there. There is no doubt that it was a direct attack on Buckingham Palace. Luckily the Palace is very narrow, & the bombs fell in the open spaces. The Chapel sticks out into the garden.[19]

'A magnificent piece of bombing, Ma'am, if you'll pardon my saying so', was the comment of one of the police constables, an old soldier, on duty at the Palace to the Queen, immediately after the raid.

The fact that the Palace had been bombed was, of course, known, but the imminence of the peril to the King and Queen was kept a close secret, and not even the Prime Minister was informed.[a] Moreover, the King had been badly shaken. 'It was a ghastly experience,' he wrote, '& I don't want it to be repeated. It certainly teaches one to "take cover" on all future occasions, but one must be careful not to become "dugout minded".' A week later he was still suffering from the effect of shock, and his symptoms will be recognized by many who recall the period. 'I quite disliked sitting in my room on Monday & Tuesday. I found myself unable to read, always in a hurry, & glancing out of the window.'[20]

The bombing of Buckingham Palace was a factor of considerable importance in unifying the Monarchy with the peoples of Britain and of the Commonwealth. Nor was its effect lost upon the United States. Though the narrow margin of escape of the King and Queen was unknown, the fact that their home had been attacked awakened a new feeling of loyalty and devotion and determination, born of common suffering. It was a major error in enemy psychological warfare. As Lord Louis Mountbatten wrote to the King: 'If Goering could have realized the depths of feeling which his bombing of Buckingham Palace has aroused throughout the Empire & America, he would have been well advised to instruct his assassins to keep off'.[b][21]

For the King and Queen also the psychological effect of the incident was very great. Even more than before they felt themselves at one with their people. 'I feel that our tours of bombed areas in London are helping the people who have lost their relations & homes,' the King recorded, '& we have both found a new bond with them as Buckingham Palace has been bombed as well as their homes, & nobody is immune

[a] The incident was not made public until after the war when Mr. Churchill was informed of it in the course of writing his memoirs. (Churchill, II, p. 334.) In all, Buckingham Palace was hit nine times during the war.

[b] On September 15, 1940, King George sent the following message to Mr. T. D. Williams, M.V.O., D.C.M., Superintendent of Buckingham Palace:

The Queen & I know only too well the strain to which the Staff of Buckingham Palace and others employed there, both men & women, have been subjected during the last week.

Under your able & tireless supervision the members of every department have cheerfully carried out their duties regardless of fatigue & with unfailing devotion to duty.

Please convey to everyone how greatly we appreciate the fine spirit which they have displayed.

GEORGE R.I.

from it.'[22]   And the Queen was equally emphatic : 'I'm glad
we've been bombed.   It makes me feel I can look the East
End in the face.'[23]

It was Queen Elizabeth's demeanour throughout this great
ordeal which inspired an American woman in Chicago to
write the following lines in her honour :

> Be it said to your renown
> That you wore your gayest gown,
> Your bravest smile, and stayed in Town
> When London Bridge was burning down,
>   My fair lady.

Few appreciated, however, the effort behind that 'bravest
smile', nor could know of the strain imposed upon Her Majesty
in these missions of consolation to the bombed areas.   'I feel
quite exhausted after seeing & hearing so much sadness, sorrow,
heroism and magnificent spirit', she wrote on one occasion to
Queen Mary.   'The destruction is so awful, & the people so
wonderful — they *deserve* a better world.'[24]

If at this moment King George could not guarantee to
his subjects a better future, he could at least formally recognize
their gallantry in the present, but he was exercised in his mind
as to what form this recognition should take.   There existed
many decorations and medals instituted by his predecessors
for the reward of gallantry and meritorious conduct, but
these, by their terms of reference, were restricted in the main
to members of the armed forces and only one of them, the
Victoria Cross, was open of award to all ranks.

In the days of Queen Victoria, and even in those of King
Edward VII, it had seemed incomprehensible that war in all
its fury should again directly afflict the British Isles, immune
from such a scourge for some two hundred years ; [a] and, moreover, the concept of total war, a war in which policemen
and firemen, and the ordinary men and women of the civilian
population, would be equally in the front line with the armed
forces of the Crown, and equally exposed to dangers of death
and wounds, was as alien to the imagination of King George
VI's predecessors as 'space travel' was to his own.   The

---

[a] The last battle to be fought on British soil was at Culloden in Inverness-
shire, where on April 16, 1746, the forces of King George II, commanded by the
Duke of Cumberland, defeated those of Prince Charles Edward.

British Isles were now under siege, their cities and ports subjected to the furious bombardment of the enemy. Every day, every night, there were performed prodigies of civilian valour, by the members of the police forces and the Fire Brigades,[a] by the men and women of the Civil Defence and A.R.P. Services, by the demolition squads who, at constant peril of their lives, rendered undetonated bombs harmless, and in rescue work carried out by ordinary members of the general public. For these there was no award or recognition.

It was to meet this evident need that the King created the George Cross and Medal.[b] It was the fruit of long deliberation and much careful study, both as to reference and design.

I have had it in mind for some time [the King wrote to Queen Mary], as I felt sure that a special medal would be needed to award civilians for work in air raids, & the cross for bravery & outstanding deeds in this sphere. The Services as well as civilians will be able to win the George Cross.[25]

The study of decorations was among King George's hobbies, and his collection of medals and ribbons at Windsor was among the most complete in the world. The planning of the George Cross and Medal was therefore of particular pleasure and interest to him, and the final design was almost entirely his own work, for he had sketched out an original device and

[a] At the outbreak of the war there were in Britain 1400 fire brigades, each independent of the other and each with its own local traditions and operational procedure. The organization of the country into Civil Defence Regions provided an early basis of co-operation, as a result of which many hundreds of pumps were moved over considerable distances; as, for example, from London to Manchester, Plymouth and Birmingham; Bristol to Birmingham; Birmingham to London, etc. The experience gained from these transfers of equipment proved conclusively that the wide diversity in procedure, training, ranks, rank-markings and general organization, as well as in apparatus, was too great to enable the brigades as then constituted to carry out efficiently the large-scale operations necessitated as a result of intensive enemy action. Unified command, with standard operational procedure throughout the United Kingdom, became an urgent need, and accordingly the National Fire Service was formed in August 1941. Designed as a temporary war measure, it was placed under the direct authority of the Home Secretary. By the Fire Services Act of 1947 the N.F.S. was transformed into separate Fire Brigades, controlled by County and County Borough Councils but retaining their common features of unified standardization.

[b] There did in fact exist for award to civilians two medals of the Order of the British Empire, instituted in 1922 in succession to the Silver Medal of that Order (1917). These were the Empire Gallantry Medal and the Medal for Meritorious Service, of which the first (the E.G.M.) was abolished in 1940 and its recipients became holders of the George Cross.

had studied and amended with meticulous care the subsequent drafts presented to him.

The decoration consists of a plain silver cross, with the Royal cipher 'G.VI' in the angle of each limb. In the centre is a circular medallion showing St. George and the Dragon, and surrounded by an inscription, 'For Gallantry'. The reverse is plain and bears the name of the recipient and the date of the award. The cross, which is worn before all other decorations except the Victoria Cross, is suspended from a dark blue ribbon threaded through a bar adorned with laurel leaves.

The terms of reference of the new decoration also bore the stamp of His Majesty's own hand. Intended primarily for civilians, it was to be awarded only for acts of the greatest heroism or of the most conspicuous courage in circumstances of extreme danger. Members of the fighting services were also eligible for the George Cross, but its award was to be confined to actions for which purely military honours would not normally be granted.

The King himself announced the creation of the George Cross in a broadcast to Britain and the Empire on September 23. He reminded them that they now stood in the front line, 'to champion those liberties and traditions that are our heritage'. The battle was now at their very doors, and the armies of invasion were massed across the Channel only 20 miles from their shores. 'To-night, indeed, we are a nation on guard and in the line.' He spoke a special word of gratitude to the men and women of the A.R.P. Services, saying that their devotion had won a new renown for the British name, and to those workers in the factories and on the railways who maintained all services of life and kept the fighting line supplied. 'Many and glorious are the deeds of gallantry done during these perilous but famous days. In order that they should be worthily and promptly recognized I have decided to create at once a new mark of honour for men and women in all walks of civilian life. I propose to give my name to this new distinction, which will consist of the George Cross, which will rank next to the Victoria Cross, and the George Medal for wider distribution.'

In conclusion the King paid a glowing tribute to London —

'that Mother City of the Commonwealth which is proving herself to be built as a city at unity with itself. It is not the walls that make the city, but the people who live within them. The walls of London may be battered, but the spirit of the Londoner stands resolute and undismayed.' He ended: 'Winter lies before us, cold and dark. . . . But after winter comes spring, and after our present trials will assuredly come victory and a release from these evil things. Let us then put our trust, as I do, in God, and in the unconquerable spirit of the British peoples.'

(iv)

The winter ahead was indeed grim, dark and cold, and it brought with it a personal sadness and loss for the King. Mr. Neville Chamberlain had remained as Lord President of the Council in Mr. Churchill's Cabinet, and had loyally supported the new régime. But he was a sick and failing man, and by the end of September he could no longer continue in office. In accepting his resignation the King wrote with sorrow and affection :

You were my Prime Minister in the earliest years of my reign, & I shall ever be grateful for your help & guidance during what was in many ways a very difficult period. For me too it will always be a pleasure to recall our many & intimate talks together. I have sympathised with you very much in seeing your hopes shattered by the lust & violence of a single man ; & yet, as I told you once before, your efforts to preserve peace were not in vain, for they established, in the eyes of the civilized world, our entire innocence of the crime which Hitler was determined to commit. For this alone, the country owes you a deep debt of gratitude.[26]

Having refused the award of the Order of the Garter,[27] Mr. Chamberlain retired to the vicinity of Basingstoke, whither the King and Queen drove to visit him in October. They found him a dying man. 'I am very sad about poor Mr. Chamberlain,' the King wrote to Queen Mary that same day after their return to Windsor, '& I know that I have lost a trusted friend. When he was P.M. he really did tell me what was in his mind, & what he hoped to do. I was able to confide in him, & even when he was Lord President of the Council we were able to have our talks.' [28]

The end was not far off. On November 11 the King noted
in his diary : 'Poor Neville Chamberlain died on Saturday
afternoon'.ᵃ The loss was severe and to be long mourned.
King George had never wavered in his loyalty to one in
whom he had had implicit faith and whom he regarded as
having been treated with ingratitude. In the retrospect of
the year which he drew up on December 31, he wrote of 'poor
Neville Chamberlain, whose resignation as P.M. was hard for
me to accept & whose untimely death has robbed me of an
adviser & friend'.

(v)

Britain remained beleaguered. Convinced at last that an
invasion of the islands was impracticable, and preoccupied
with the preliminary preparations for his surprise assault
upon Russia, Hitler had abandoned 'Operation Sea Lion', for
all but deception purposes, by the end of September 1940.
Nevertheless, he kept the island fortress closely invested, hoping
to starve the British people into surrender by severing their
supply lines upon the high seas or to batter them into submission by aerial bombardment.

Within the fortress King George continued to share the
dangers of his people, encouraging them by his presence and
himself encouraged and sustained by the many acts of heroism
which enriched this grim period. One such incident was the
epic of the *Jervis Bay*.

At the close of October the pocket battleship *Admiral
Scheer* and the 8-inch gun cruiser *Hipper* were at large in the
North Atlantic with orders to attack convoys *en route* from
Canada to Britain, from which battleship escorts had been
withdrawn to reinforce the Mediterranean. One such convoy
of thirty-eight vessels, 'strung like a procession of pilgrims
against the dawn', sailed from Halifax on October 27, under
the protection of the veteran 14,000-ton Australian freighter
Jervis Bay, a converted merchant cruiser, armed with seven
6-inch guns and commanded by a retired naval officer returned

ᵃ Mr. Chamberlain died on Saturday, November 9, and was buried in Westminster Abbey on November 14. The War Cabinet were his pall-bearers, and
King George sent the Duke of Gloucester as his personal representative.

to service, Captain Fogarty Fegen. Late in the afternoon of
November 5 the convoy, with its precious freight of vital
supplies, was intercepted by the *Admiral Scheer,* which opened
fire with her 11-inch guns. Captain Fegen at once reported
the situation by wireless to the Admiralty and then, fully conscious of the inevitable outcome of his action and undaunted
by the overwhelming odds against him, engaged the enemy
at full speed in order to gain time for the convoy to disperse
and escape. For an hour the unequal combat raged until,
her mission accomplished, the armed merchantman was abandoned, ablaze from stem to stern. She sank with the loss of
more than 200 men, including her gallant commander.

From the moment that the first reports of the action
reached him at Windsor on November 5, King George followed
it with the absorbed interest of a naval officer, stirred by the
epic of gallantry and self-sacrifice. Day by day he recorded
in his diary the fragmentary news of the engagement:

November 6 & 7 (Wednesday & Thursday)
   On Tuesday evening a report came in that a convoy in the
Atlantic was being shelled 'at leisure' by a German pocket-battle-
ship the 'Admiral Scheer'. The War Cabinet decided to send the
Fleet in various groups to its rescue in an attempt to catch the
'Scheer'. No news was heard from the convoy on either Wednesday
or Thursday.

November 8 (Friday)
   At last we have heard from one ship of the 'shelled' convoy,
which means that there are probably more safe.

November 9 & 10 (Saturday & Sunday)
   Fourteen ships of the convoy have now reached harbour.
There were 38 ships in it, but as they all disperse in an attack it is
difficult for them all to reform again at once.

November 11 (Monday)
   27 ships have now reported out of the 'shelled' convoy. The
AMC 'Jervis Bay' put up a gallant fight to give the convoy time
to disperse.

A week later the full story was available, and the King at
once took the initiative in bestowing upon the *Jervis Bay*'s
dead captain the highest award for valour. 'Survivors of the
"Jervis Bay" have been landed in Newfoundland', he wrote

in his diary on November 18. 'I have awarded Captain
Fegen the Victoria Cross posthumously. When he attacked
the "Admiral Scheer" he knew he was going to certain death
but he saved the convoy, 33 ships out of 38 being safe & have
reached port.' The incident had stirred the King deeply, as
indeed it touched the pride of all.[a] 'The story of the "Jervis
Bay" is an epic,' he wrote to Queen Mary, '& the award of
the Victoria Cross to her captain was my idea & I am glad it
has come out at once.'[29]

Before the close of this event, however, King George had
been brought face to face with calamitous destruction at home.
Early in November 1940 the German Air Force had conceived
a new plan for the strategic bombing of Britain, of which the
main operations were against the industrial centres other than
London. For these raids the Luftwaffe used their new naviga-
tional aid, the 'X' beam, by the assistance of which the
pathfinder aircraft of a special unit were able to find the
objective by radar, aim their incendiary bombs and so light
up the target that the main force of bombers could operate
by visual aids. The first application of this new method of
attack was against Coventry, on the night of November 14-15,
1940.

Late in the evening of November 14 a warning reached
Buckingham Palace from the Air Ministry that the 'X' beam
of the German Air Force had been detected as going straight
over Windsor Castle, though there was no means of telling
how far along the beam the raiders' objective for that night
lay. The Castle A.R.P. organization was alerted and later
that night the watchers on the battlements saw the enemy

---

[a] The epic of the *Jervis Bay* seized upon the imagination of many in the United
States and Mr. Gene Fowler was moved to write a long narrative poem, 'The
Jervis Bay Goes Down', which had considerable circulation in both Britain and
America. The final stanza may be quoted as an example :

The *Jervis Bay* goes down —
Goes down as a mere casualty of storm,
To rust out, fathoms deep, in common grave
With sisters unremembered by the years.
The *Jervis Bay* — of Australian registry
From somewhere south of Singapore —
Goes down in the history
Of an Isle that for a thousand years
Has prized the freedom
And the dignity of Man.

aircraft streaming overhead in full moonlight.   No bomb was dropped anywhere near Windsor, but soon there came news that the attack was on Coventry.

The moon was full, the sky clear, and the city with its high cathedral spire would have been an easy target even without the new devices of the enemy.   The people of Coventry, who had suffered previous raids, took their usual precautions. But this was no ordinary raid; it was on a scale hitherto unprecedented.   Five hundred German aircraft dropped 543 tons of high explosive bombs and incendiaries upon the stricken city.   Within an hour the whole of the centre of the town was a sea of flame ; 200 fires were started, many of which were not brought under control until the following morning. The greatest bombing concentration was in an area three-quarters of a mile by half a mile in the centre of the city. About a third of this area was completely devastated and another third required subsequent demolition.   During that night nearly six hundred people lost their lives.[a]

November 15 dawned upon a still burning Coventry, in which all public services had been disrupted, with dead and dying still buried beneath the ruins, and the living too stunned to do much else than thank God for their own survival.   A report of the destruction reached King George in the afternoon, and he at once decided to visit the place on the following day in an effort to cheer the grievously afflicted citizens.   With Sir Alexander Hardinge and Sir Piers Legh he motored from Windsor, to be met at the city limits by the Mayor and the Chief Constable, who guided them through mountains of rubble to what remained of the City Hall.   The streets were patrolled by troops for the prevention of looting ; at one point the cars were stopped, and only when the sergeant in charge had satisfied himself by personal inspection that the occupant of the second car was indeed the King, were they allowed to proceed.

In the ruins of the Mayor's Parlour, lit on that grey November day by candles stuck into beer bottles, the King was

---

[a] According to Home Office records the number of persons killed was approximately 568, and those seriously injured and detained in hospital some 865.   In the course of the raid, 2294 buildings were demolished and 45,704 buildings damaged.   In a period of 28 months all damaged houses were made habitable.

greeted by the Home Secretary, Mr. Morrison,[a] and the Regional Commissioner, Lord Dudley.[b] He received first-hand reports of the hideous effects of the raid, and thereafter went out himself to see the scenes of devastation.

I was horrified at the sight of the centre of the town [he wrote that evening in his diary]. The water, electricity & gas services had ceased to function. I talked to members of the emergency committee who were quite dazed by what they had been through. . . . I walked among the devastation. The cathedral, hotels, shops, everything was flat & had been gutted by fire. The people in the streets wondered where they were, nothing could be recognized. The regional services were working well & many had come in from 100 miles off. I talked to many of them & to many people. I think they liked my coming to see them in their adversity. . . . The morale of the people is excellent & is getting better each day. The shock to them was very great.[30]

The shock to the people of Coventry had indeed been very great, but the effect of the King's visit was immense and almost indescribable. His sudden appearance amid the smoking ruins and among the still bomb-shocked citizens gave a psychological fillip which was much needed, and could not perhaps have been provided in any other way. 'We suddenly felt that if the King was there everything was all right and the rest of England was behind us', said one of the survivors years later. 'We no longer felt that we were alone, we realized that what had happened to us, bad though it was, was but part of what was happening to all England and that England realized this.'

His visit has had a wonderful effect, & it fired the imagination & determination of the people to an unbelievable extent [Lord

---

[a] Rt. Hon. Herbert Stanley Morrison, C.H., M.P. (b. 1888), was first elected as a Labour Member of Parliament in 1923, and thereafter remained intermittently in the House of Commons. He was also Leader of the London County Council from 1934 to 1940. Mr. Morrison served as Minister of Transport from 1929 to 1931 in Mr. MacDonald's second Labour Cabinet, and joined Mr. Churchill's Cabinet in 1940 as Minister of Supply, and as Home Secretary and Minister of Home Security from 1940 to 1945. He served as Deputy Prime Minister to Mr. Attlee and Lord President of the Council from 1945 to 1951, and as Secretary of State for Foreign Affairs from March to October 1951. Mr. Morrison retired from the Executive Committee of the Labour Party on the election of Mr. Gaitskell to leadership of the Party in 1955.

[b] William Humble Eric Ward, third Earl of Dudley (b. 1894), served as Regional Commissioner for Civil Defence for the Midlands from 1939 to 1945.

Dudley wrote later to Sir Alexander Hardinge]. It was certainly very moving to see their faces light up as they recognized him & we are all more grateful to him than we can say for coming down there.[31]

For hours the King tramped among the rubble, and before he left he had satisfied himself that all possible aid would be forthcoming for the stricken city. 'Poor Coventry . . .', he wrote to Queen Mary on his return to Windsor, 'is in a very sorry state. The industrial part of the town was not badly hit, the old part & centre of the town looks just like Ypres after the last war. The people were all dazed from the shock of it, but the regional services were working well, & help is coming in from all parts.'[32]

Nor was this mission of compassion to Coventry an isolated event. Within the next few weeks Southampton, Birmingham and Bristol suffered the searing scourge of the Luftwaffe, and to each in turn, while the fires of their ordeal were yet burning, King George brought sympathy, encouragement and understanding. 'I feel that this kind of visit does do good at such a moment,' he wrote in his diary, '& it is one of my main jobs in life to help others when I can be useful to them.'[33]

That which he saw and heard during these visits to the afflicted provincial cities, and as he went about among his people of London, left upon King George a deep impression of the new spirit to which, with infinite pains and labour, Britain was giving birth. A fellowship of self-sacrifice and 'good-neighbourliness', a comradeship of adversity in which men and women gave of their noblest to one another, a brotherhood of man in which the artificial barriers of caste and class were broken down; this was the embodiment of the spirit which the King himself as Duke of York had striven to engender in his Camp and in his work for Industrial Welfare. He hailed it with a happy pride and even in the darkest hour of war sought for means to retain its benefits for the better days ahead. This was the message of his Christmas broadcast for 1940 :

Time and time again during these last few months I have seen for myself the battered towns and cities of England and I have seen the British people facing their ordeal. I can say to them that they may be justly proud of their race and nation. On every side

I have seen a new and splendid spirit of good fellowship springing up in adversity, a real desire to share burdens and resources alike.

Out of all this suffering there is growing a harmony which we must carry forward into the days to come when we have endured to the end and ours is the victory. Then when Christmas Days are happy again and good will has come back to the world we must hold fast to the spirit which binds us all together now. We shall need this spirit in each of our lives as men and women, and shall need it even more among the nations of the world. We must go on thinking less of ourselves and more for one another; for so, and so only, can we hope to make the world a better place and life a worthier thing.

'Life will not be easy after the war,' the King wrote in his diary that evening, ' & we shall all have to stick together to rebuild our towns & cities & make a new start in life.'

(vi)

During this period of the Decisive Struggle — when Britain stood alone — King George was not solely occupied with the internal affairs of his island fortress, pressing and pertinent though they were. The foreign relations of Britain were of vital importance at this time, for it was necessary to demonstrate to the world at large — and more particularly to that part of it which remained free — that, while Britain was both ready and competent to continue the immediate struggle against the Axis, she was not wholly thus preoccupied and was still fully capable of exercising her functions as a world power in diplomacy. Her efforts in this respect, which were directed towards France, Egypt, the Balkan countries and, above all, the United States of America, met with varying degrees of success; but in all of them King George, through his personal contacts with his fellow Sovereigns and heads of States, played a significant rôle.

The French situation which resulted from the Armistice of Compiègne remained confused and obscure. There were now two French 'Governments', the Vichy régime of Marshal Pétain, and the Free French Committee of General de Gaulle, both with a somewhat exiguous basis of legality and both contending for the adherence of the French overseas empire. The heartening gesture of General de Gaulle in providing a

rallying point in Britain for those Frenchmen who desired to
carry on the struggle for freedom had been received with
great enthusiasm, in which King George himself shared.[a]
But the fact soon emerged that the General, while a great
patriot, was not an easy partner, and, moreover, while his
appeals to the French colonial administrators to accept his
leadership as against that of the Marshal had met with a
certain success in Central Africa, in Asia and in the Pacific,
the rich and strategically vital North African possessions still
maintained a nominal loyalty to the Vichy régime.   German
and Italian Armistice Commissions were established in North
Africa, but enigmatic messages from General Weygand in
Algiers and General Noguès in Morocco indicated that,
while they accepted the supreme authority of Marshal Pétain,
neither desired an ultimate German victory.   It was essential,
therefore, to encourage even this negative form of French
resistance and, above all, it was essential to play for time.

In addition to these factors there was still cherished the
hope in London that, though Vichy France had ceased to be
an ally by virtue of the armistice, she would not become even
a tacit enemy and would resist to the utmost the blandishments
of Hitler to this end.

It was the delicate task of His Majesty's Government,
therefore, to give all possible assistance to the gallant
endeavours of General de Gaulle to weld anew the broken
sword of France and, at the same time, to encourage Marshal
Pétain to connive, in Mr. Churchill's phrase, at 'a kind of
collusive conspiracy'[35] for the maintenance of the maximum
of passive resistance to the enemy.   This latter purpose was
rendered the more difficult of achievement by the absence of
direct diplomatic representation between London and Vichy
and the necessity of conducting negotiations in a neutral
capital or, in the case of the French, by the employment of
unofficial envoys.

Despite these difficulties, however, a series of messages
were exchanged with the Marshal's Government during the
early autumn of 1940, the object of which was to obtain

---

[a] General de Gaulle writes in his memoirs: 'In England itself the Free
French were surrounded by esteem and sympathy.   The King, first of all, was
quick to give proof of these.'[34]

assurances from Vichy that they would not surrender what remained of the French Fleet to the Germans, nor allow Germany to obtain control of French overseas territory, nor would themselves attack the French colonies which had rallied to General de Gaulle. Should such assurances be forthcoming, the British Government, for its part, would be prepared to negotiate a *modus vivendi* whereby limited trade would be permitted to pass the British blockade between Metropolitan France and her North African territories.

These negotiations proved abortive, for the defeatism of the Marshal was proof against all such arguments. As the autumn drew on it became evident that the pressure exercised upon Vichy France to declare herself a 'collaborator' with Germany was increasing and, in consequence, the British Government made a final effort to counteract this constraining force. On October 21 Mr. Churchill made his famous broadcast to the French people [36] and, in addition, urged upon King George the wisdom of making a direct and personal appeal to the Marshal.

His Majesty willingly concurred with this suggestion, though his personal opinion, as expressed in his diary on October 12, had been : 'I feel that we should treat France as an enemy until she sees reason'. On October 25 he telegraphed the following message : [37]

M. LE MARÉCHAL,

At this serious juncture in the life of the British and French peoples, I send you a message of goodwill. The armistice which you were forced to make with the common enemy and his occupation of so many French ports and aerodromes for the attack on my country have been a very grievous addition to the burdens which my people have to bear. Nevertheless, these tragic events have not weakened in British hearts the sympathy and sense of comradeship which have grown up over many years of peace and war between the British and French nations. We are resolved to fight on to the end, and we are sure that the end will be a complete British victory over Hitler and his régime. We have solemnly declared that our victory will carry with it the restoration of the freedom and greatness of France.

Reports are reaching me of an attempt by the German Government to secure from you undertakings that would go far beyond the terms accepted by you at the time of the armistice. I recall that then you expressed your determination to accept no terms dishonouring to the name of France. I am confident that now also you will reject proposals that would bring dishonour to France and grave damage to a late Ally. The disaster that overwhelmed France deprived us of her assistance, but it would indeed be a sombre event in history if France were to range herself against us and afford direct assistance to our enemy. I do not doubt that, in refusing any such proposals that may have been made, you will carry with you the overwhelming assent of all those among both our peoples, and in other countries, who have put their faith in your honour as a soldier and who see in a British victory their hope of the salvation of France.[a]

The King's appeal reached the Marshal at a critical moment. On October 23 Hitler, at his interview with General Franco at Hendaye, had for the first time met his match in the wiles of diplomacy. On the following day there occurred the historic meeting with Pétain at Montoire, which, though later hailed by the Marshal's apologists as 'a diplomatic Verdun',[b] in effect resulted in the formal adoption by the Vichy Government of the principles of collaboration with Germany. It was on the morrow of his second capitulation to Hitler that Marshal Pétain received the King's message, and that it had little effect upon him may be judged by the fact that, on October 30, in a broadcast from Lyons to the French people, he announced that he had met with Hitler of his own accord. 'I have been under no *Diktat*, no pressure from him. Collaboration between our two countries was considered. I accepted the principles of it. The application will be determined later.'

[a] In October 1940 there arrived in London a certain M. Louis Rougier, who, acting on the personal instruction of Marshal Pétain, was received by Mr. Churchill and Lord Halifax. His object appears to have been to gauge the state of opinion in London and the prospects of the continued resistance of Britain to the enemy, but no agreement was concluded with the Vichy Government through him. M. Rougier later went to the United States with a plausible tale of his 'negotiations' in London, and in 1945 he published a book in Canada, entitled *Les Accords Pétain-Churchill*, which contained a number of misstatements regarding the relations between His Majesty's Government and the Vichy Government in the early days of that régime. In order to correct this misrepresentation of the facts, the Foreign Office issued a statement on July 17, 1945, followed on August 2 by a White Paper (Cmd. 6662), giving a complete dossier of the relevant documents. His Majesty the King gave permission for the text of his letter to Pétain and of the Marshal's reply to be included in this collection.

[b] Cp. Louis Dominique Girard, *Montoire, Verdun diplomatique* (Paris, 1948).

The Marshal's reply to the King was dispatched from Madrid on November 2. It was far from satisfactory. The King commented in his diary:

Pétain sent me a very unassuring reply to my message.[a] The gist is that he states that the French people felt deeply the aggressions which their country has suffered on several occasions at the hands of the Royal Navy, & also the support given by H.M.G. to Frenchmen who are rebels against their own country. He maintains that the Fr. Govt. have sought to avoid any action which could have aggravated the situation, that they will not make any unjustified attack, but will respect the essential interests of the French nation.[38]

It is probable that nothing could have deterred the Marshal at this time from his quasi-mystic belief that only by suffering and adversity could the soul of France be reborn, and that the form of such immolation which he considered best for her was collaboration with Germany rather than co-operation with Britain. The thought arises, however, that if the King's appeal was to have been effective at all, it should have been dispatched earlier. Had it reached the Marshal before his departure for Montoire, its efficacy might have been greater. As it was, it would appear that, as in the case of President Lebrun at the time of the French Armistice, the King's intervention had been sought too late for any prospect of success.

The ignoble entry of Italy into the war on June 10, 1940, at a moment when it seemed that the spoils of victory might be gratifyingly gained without the effusion of Italian blood — an act appropriately stigmatized by President Roosevelt on

[a] The text of Marshal Pétain's reply is as follows:

SIRE,

Le message de Votre Majesté a retenu toute mon attention.

Le peuple français, après avoir lutté aux côtés du peuple britannique, a ressenti profondément les agressions dont notre pays a été l'objet à plusieurs reprises de la part de la flotte britannique, ainsi qui le concours que le Gouvernement de Sa Majesté apporte à des Français rebelles à leur patrie. Sans se départir de son calme, le Gouvernement français a cherché à éviter tout ce qui aurait pu aggraver la situation. Il ne se livrera, pour sa part, à aucune attaque injustifiée ; mais, conscient de ses devoirs, il saura faire respecter dans l'honneur les intérêts essentiels de la nation française.

En raison des liens qui unissaient nos deux pays, c'est avec une grande douleur que je me vois obligé de parler à Votre Majesté avec cette franchise ; c'est en tout cas, à mon sens, le moyen le plus sûr d'appeler toute Sa haute attention sur un état de choses dont le Gouvernement français ne porte aucune responsabilité.

PÉTAIN.

that same day [a] — had its repercussions in Africa as well as in Europe; for from Libya Mussolini could launch his grandiose schemes for the rebuilding of the Roman Empire and the domination of the Mediterranean. The key to the success or failure of the Duce's dreams lay in Egypt, and to oppose him there stood General Wavell,[b] with 36,000 men, including one armoured division consisting of two partly equipped brigades.[c] This minute force was confronted by an army of 215,000 under Marshal Balbo, while in Italian East Africa lay a further army of 200,000 men under the Duke of Aosta. Small wonder was it, in the face of these overwhelming numbers, that General Wavell, whose melancholy fate it was to win battles but never to have sufficient resources at his disposal to effect a decisive victory, gave to his troops the standing order to 'make one man appear to be a dozen, make one tank look like a squadron, make a raid look like an advance'.[39]

An essential factor in the security of the British forces was that there should exist in Cairo an Egyptian Government well disposed toward Britain, and both willing and able to carry out the provisions of the Anglo-Egyptian Alliance; [d] and the Government of the then Prime Minister, Ali Maher Pasha, could not be described as such. In September 1939, Egypt had severed diplomatic relations with Germany, but, in agreement with the British Government, had not declared war. In June 1940, however, the Italian diplomatic mission remained undisturbed in Cairo after Italy's declaration of

[a] Speaking at the graduation ceremonies of the University of Virginia, President Roosevelt said à propos of the Italian declaration of war : 'On this tenth day of June 1940, the hand that held the dagger has struck it into the back of its neighbour. On this tenth day of June 1940 . . . we send forth our prayers and hopes to those beyond the seas who are maintaining, with magnificent valour, their battle for freedom.'

[b] Field-Marshal the Rt. Hon. Archibald Percival, first Earl Wavell, G.C.B., G.C.S.I., G.C.I.E., C.M.G., M.C. (1883–1950), was Commander-in-Chief in the Middle East from 1939 to 1941, Commander-in-Chief in India from 1941 to 1943, and Supreme Allied Commander in the South-West Pacific from January to March 1942. He was Viceroy of India from 1943 to 1947.

[c] General Wavell also had in his command some 47,000 men disposed in the Sudan, Kenya, British Somaliland, Palestine, Aden and Cyprus. He was later reinforced by Australian troops from Singapore.

[d] The Anglo-Egyptian Treaty of Alliance, signed on August 26, 1936, terminated the British military occupation of Egypt but recognized the special British interest in the defence of the Suez Canal Zone. The Treaty was abrogated by the Egyptian Government in 1951.

war on Britain, and Ali Maher persistently refused all British efforts to effect their expulsion.

The Prime Minister, the Court clique and many of the religious leaders were pro-Fascist and favoured appeasement. The situation was clearly impossible, and instructions were sent to the British Ambassador, Sir Miles Lampson,[a] to make forceful representations to King Farouk [b] that he must dispense with Ali Maher, and appoint as Prime Minister one who could form a robust and representative Government, which could also count on the support of the popular Wafdist Party, led by Nahas Pasha.

The audience which Sir Miles Lampson had of King Farouk at the Abdin Palace in Alexandria on the afternoon of June 17 was not a happy one. The King bitterly resented what he termed British 'interference' in the domestic affairs of Egypt and in the exercise of his own royal prerogatives, and he was particularly averse to the advice that he should consult Nahas Pasha, whom he had summarily dismissed from the premiership in 1937. The Ambassador, however, was insistent, and when he left for Cairo later that evening both he and the King knew that His Majesty had lost the battle.

King Farouk, however, did not surrender all at once. He was very angry, and for some time he considered the possibility of abdication. In the meanwhile he sent to London an irate and personal protest to King George, who received it from the hand of the Egyptian Ambassador on June 19.

Up to this time the relations between the two Sovereigns had been amicable. At the time of the German occupation

[a] Rt. Hon. Miles Wedderburn Lampson, first Baron Killearn, G.C.M.G., C.B., M.V.O. (b. 1880), had been British Minister to China from 1926 to 1933. In 1934 he was appointed High Commissioner to Egypt and took an active part in the successful negotiations of the Treaty of Alliance, becoming the first British Ambassador to Egypt in 1936. In 1947 he was Special Commissioner in South-East Asia, retiring in 1948.

[b] King Farouk (b. 1920) is a direct descendant of the Albanian satrap, Mehemet Ali, who in 1811 completed Napoleon's destruction of the Mameluke power in Egypt, becoming Khedive of Egypt and virtually independent of Turkey. Farouk succeeded to the Egyptian throne on the death of his father King Fuad (1868–1936) who, having become Sultan of Egypt in 1917, was proclaimed King in 1922 at the termination of the British protectorate. On July 23, 1952, as the result of a *coup d'état* carried out by a group of Army officers, headed by General Mohammed Neguib, King Farouk was compelled to abdicate in favour of his infant son, who, as Fuad II, was the nominal sovereign of Egypt, until June 13, 1953, when General Neguib proclaimed the republic.

of Czechoslovakia in March 1939, King Farouk had sent a personal message to King George assuring him that Egypt would stand loyally by her obligations under her treaty with Britain. A State visit of the Egyptian King and Queen to London had been arranged for the autumn of 1939, only to be cancelled at the outbreak of war, but King George had sent a message of friendship by Mr. Anthony Eden — when, as Secretary of State for the Dominions, he had visited Cairo in February 1940 — expressing his disappointment at the cancellation, and his appreciation of the facilities and assistance granted by Egypt to British forces. This had been well received.[40]

Now, however, King George was incensed by the criticism of the action of his representative in Cairo. 'I told the Egyptian Ambassador that I hoped Farouk would "play up" to the terms of our Treaty', he recorded. 'I sent Farouk a strong reply which I knew Lampson would act upon.' [41]

In his reply, which, after consultation with the Foreign Office, was handed to the Egyptian Ambassador on June 20, the King informed King Farouk that the British Ambassador's advice had been tendered at the express instructions of the British Government, who believed that the interests of the Egyptian people would be best served by the creation of a Government in Egypt 'as representative as possible, and determined to maintain a resolute attitude in the face of the Italian menace to Egyptian independence'. He further pointed out that reinforcements had been sent to Egypt at the request of the Egyptian Government. 'It is not the policy of my Government', the King continued, 'to urge that Egypt should declare war unless it is plainly proved by events that in the defence of her vital interests this step is inevitable.' [42]

King George's riposte contributed to the achievement of the desired result. The Italian Minister and his staff left Cairo on June 22, and when, fortified by the approval of his Sovereign and the support of the Government, Sir Miles Lampson, accompanied this time by General Wavell, had a further audience with King Farouk on June 23, they emerged triumphant. On the following day Ali Maher resigned, to be succeeded by the more amenable Hussein Sabry Pasha, who on June 28 formed a Coalition Government, endorsed but not joined by the Wafd Party, and pledged to the loyal execution of the Treaty.[a]

It was in eastern and south-eastern Europe that the effects of the collapse of France and the temporary establishment of a German paramountcy over continental Europe were felt most immediately. Hitler's designs upon the east European countries were economic, political and military rather than territorial. In his projected attack upon Russia, the earliest planning for which he initiated in July 1940, he had need of the economic resources of Hungary, Rumania, Bulgaria and Yugoslavia, their oil, grain and minerals, as well as their military and political support; and he cared not who suffered in the process of satisfying his needs. By threats and cajolery, by bribes and menaces, he succeeded very substantially in his ambitions, though he left a harvest of hatred behind him.

Rumania was his first victim, and the progressive constraint placed upon her King and Government is an admirable example of the Nazi technique of diplomatic pressure. On June 1, M. Gafencu, the friend of the Western democracies, was compelled to resign as Foreign Minister, and on June 30 King Carol, in an effort to appease the Führer and to enlist his sympathy in resisting the Bessarabian demands of Soviet Russia, formally renounced the Anglo-French guarantee given in April 1939. This had little effect, however, for Hitler was not minded at this moment to balk his Russian 'ally', and by the beginning of July Soviet troops had occupied all Bessarabia.

This was indeed a season for settling old scores. Incited by the success of Soviet depredations, encouraged by the tacit condonation of the Führer, the appetites of Rumania's other neighbours were whetted, and they hastened to make their demands for frontier adjustments. Caught between the assumed indifference of Hitler and the patent hostility of Stalin, Rumania could offer no resistance. One by one the fruits of former wars were stripped from her. On August 21 she ceded to Bulgaria that part of the territory of the Dobrudja acquired in 1913 after the Third Balkan War, and nine days

---

[a] On November 14, 1940, Hussein Sabry Pasha collapsed and died while reading the Speech from the Throne in the Chamber of Deputies. He was succeeded in the premiership by Hussein Sirry, whose Government led an uneasy existence until February 4, 1942, when, after a British military demonstration, King Farouk was at last forced to recall Nahas Pasha.

later by the Vienna Award of August 30 her representative was compelled by Ribbentrop and Ciano to surrender to Hungary the greater part of her Transylvanian spoils gained under the Treaty of Trianon.

In countries such as the Balkan States, where monarchy is closely identified with policy rather than raised above it, as in Britain, the penalty for failure is elimination, either figuratively, through abdication, or literally, by assassination. King Carol of Rumania, though prone to human frailties, had striven to keep his country out of Hitler's clutches. Though a Prince of the House of Hohenzollern, he had no love for the Germany of the Third Reich. It is not known whether or not the Führer aimed deliberately at getting rid of him, but if this were his object he could have employed no more effective technique than to heap cumulative humiliations upon Rumania. On September 6 the King abdicated in favour of his nineteen-year-old son, Prince Michael, whom he left, together with the fate of his country, in the hands of the pro-Nazi dictator, Marshal Antonescu. By the end of October there were eighteen German divisions in Rumania and the country was completely under German control. On November 23 Marshal Antonescu formally adhered to the Tripartite Pact in Berlin.

The weapon of Nazi pressure was now turned upon Bulgaria, where King Boris was successful in putting up a more prolonged resistance. Bulgarian neutrality was still a matter of great importance to Britain, both in itself and in respect of possible subsequent moves by the enemy against Greece and Yugoslavia. For this reason the British Government had not criticized the annexation of the Dobrudja and had been at pains to convey to the Government at Sofia the impression that, when Germany had been defeated, Bulgaria would be permitted to retain this territory. Hitler, however, was now dangling other glittering prizes before King Boris in the shape of the realization of Bulgaria's long-cherished ambition for an outlet to the Aegean, and this could only be attained at the expense of Greece, to whom Britain was bound by long-standing ties of friendship and, more materially, by the guarantee of April 1939.

A year earlier King George had made a major contribution

to the maintenance of Bulgarian neutrality by his personal appeal to King Boris,[a] and now, when the situation was considerably more adverse, he was urged by his Ministers to make a second attempt. It was considered in London that, in view of what had happened in Rumania, which was now virtually occupied by the German army, the pro-German tendency in Bulgarian policy was motivated more by fear than by hope of gain. A further message of encouragement from His Majesty to King Boris at this juncture might well serve to keep him on the right lines. King George, ever anxious to aid his Ministers, readily assented to their suggestion, and on October 12 he sent a telegraphic message, since by this time written communication with Sofia was both difficult and unreliable.

A little over a year has passed since I addressed a personal communication to Your Majesty, and I am anxious to let you know that since then your own welfare and the welfare of your country have often been in my mind.

As you are aware, my Government welcomed the recent settlement which Bulgaria reached with Roumania over the Southern Dobrudja ; for this settlement accorded with their general attitude towards efforts for territorial adjustment, as explained by my Secretary of State for Foreign Affairs in the House of Lords on September 5th. You may remember that the words he used were the following :—'His Majesty's Government have never supported a policy based on a rigid adherence to the *status quo*. On the contrary, the principle to which His Majesty's Government have lent their support is that they will be favourable to a modification of the *status quo* provided always such a modification is just and equitable in itself and is reached by means of free and peaceful negotiation and agreement between the interested parties and without aggression or compulsion.'

Further, I and my Foreign Secretary have been favourably impressed by the moderation shown by Your Majesty's Government in carrying into effect the settlement. We know very well that this has been largely due to the wise guidance of Your Majesty, whose efforts before the war to preserve peace are still fresh in our memories.

I and my Ministers trust that this guidance may continue, particularly in view of recent reports that Bulgaria is being pressed to throw in her lot with the Axis Powers. Bulgarians must be well aware that the object of those Powers is to use Bulgaria for their own purposes, and that any promises that may be made of a

---

[a] See above, p. 423.

reward for Bulgaria's cooperation will merely set the seal on her enforced subservience to Axis dictation and control. The recent history of Roumania is sufficient example of the future which awaits any small country which puts its faith in Germany: and clearly we have not yet seen the end of the chapter on that unhappy country. I and my Ministers sincerely trust, therefore, that Bulgaria will realise that her real interest lies in maintaining her present declared neutrality, and in refusing to be lured into a state of belligerency in the course of which she might well become the battlefield of the contending parties.

Meanwhile I send you my best wishes for the happiness and prosperity of Your Majesty and of Bulgaria during these troublous times.[43]

That King Boris was greatly touched by this message there is no doubt, and, though his reply indicated the increased pressure to which he was being subjected and his difficulty in resisting it, he may well have been sustained by the King's encouragement in the course of the ordeal which he shortly thereafter experienced when summoned to a personal meeting with the Führer at Berchtesgaden on November 17. He returned to Sofia without having committed Bulgaria to the Axis Pact, and was enabled to maintain his resistance until the following spring when, German pressure having become too great, Bulgaria adhered to the Pact on March 1, 1941.

There remained the critical factors of Yugoslavia and Greece. With the rulers of both of these States King George was allied by close ties of kin and friendship. For Prince Paul of Yugoslavia he felt a special sympathy in that the regency would shortly come to an end and the Prince was not unnaturally anxious not to hand over to his young nephew — King George's godson — a country plunged in war. Prince Paul was indeed a tragic figure, unsuited by temperament for the heavy burden of responsibility which fate had cast upon him, unskilled in statecraft and prone to despondency. The heavy defeats which the Allied cause had sustained in the summer of 1940 had thrown him into the deepest dejection, for his heart was with Britain and France, yet he found it increasingly difficult to withstand those of his advisers who bade him reach an accommodation with Germany.

At this time (July 1940) King George, at the advice of

the Foreign Office, had sent Prince Paul a long political letter containing information on Britain's war effort, and reiterating her determined intention to fight on until victory had been achieved. This appeared to have temporarily the desired effect of stiffening the attitude of the Regent, but by the close of October two events had occurred which again cast him into the Slough of Despond : the German occupation of Rumania, and the Italian assault upon Greece.

The unprovoked aggression of Italy against Greece on October 28 was recorded by the King in his diary with the following comment : 'Mussolini has told Greece that the reason for his ultimatum is that she has given G.B. [Great Britain] facilities for air bases etc. & tries to put all the onus on us. M. surpasses Goebbels in his lying propaganda'; and that night he authorized the broadcast over the Greek service of the B.B.C. of a message from himself to the Greek King and people. Thereafter he shared the general admiration of Britain for the courageous and successful resistance of the Greek forces to the invader, and hailed with satisfaction the bombing of the Italian Battle Fleet in the harbour of Taranto by the Fleet Air Arm on the night of November 11-12.[a]

The opening up of a new war front in the Balkans had its immediate effect upon Yugoslav policy. The unfortunate Prince Paul found himself under fire both from Berlin and from certain of his own advisers for his hesitancy in aligning himself with the Axis, and on November 1 he explained his difficulties at some length in a letter to King George, which displayed only too clearly his melancholy state of mind. Unfortunately the needs of Britain herself and the prior requirements of Egypt, Turkey and Greece precluded the offer of material to Yugoslavia, and rendered all the more complicated the task of saying to Prince Paul anything which could give him heart in his increasingly difficult situation. King George, however, after consultation, replied to the Regent on November 15, this time in a personal letter written in his own hand from Windsor Castle.

[a] On November 11 British fighters were also reported to have brought down 13 Italian and 12 German bombers in combat over Britain. 'The Italians fell very quickly out of the sky,' the King wrote in his diary. 'I try not to be vindictive, but this news has pleased me.'

My dear Paul,

We have been thinking so much of you and Olga since I last wrote to you in July. So much has happened everywhere, and the situation in your part of the world has become so much more critical in this time. Italy's attack on Greece has brought the war nearer to you than ever before.

I know and realise how difficult your position is, and that you may have to make concessions to the Axis on non-essential matters. At the same time I am sure you will never give way where the sovereignty of your country is concerned, and I do admire the skill and patience with which you are conducting this very difficult policy. I wonder whether you may think that now is a good moment from your somewhat lonely geographical position, to talk to your courageous neighbour Greece and also to Turkey on the subject of closer co-operation with these two countries.

I know that you are badly in need of armaments of different kinds and I only wish that it was possible for us to supply you with them at once. I am sure you realise that it is only a matter of time before we are in a position to do so. Of course owing to the tragic collapse of France we lost much of our material, but I am glad to say we are now making up fast our losses, and will soon be able to supply the needs of others besides our own.

I am sending you with this letter some notes I have had collected from the various Depts. as I know it will please you to see why we are so sure of ultimate victory.

I feel that whatever may lie ahead, the first and vitally important round of the Battle of Britain has ended in our favour. The Air Force is actually stronger now than it has ever been, and our aircraft industries are working on full time both by day and by night. And, in spite of the so-called 'total blockade', supplies of all sorts are pouring into this country from overseas and particularly from the U.S.A.

President Roosevelt's re-election was a great relief to us, as his Administration has been able to and will continue to supply to us many vital 'sinews of war' to augment the armaments we are ourselves producing.

I wish you could see the spirit of the people here, which, despite the violent and indiscriminate bombing of the last two months, is truly wonderful. You who I know are so fond of England will appreciate the truth in what I say.[44]

Two days after the dispatch of this letter to Prince Paul, the King received a long appeal from King George of Greece setting out very frankly the necessity for speed and quantity in the aid promised to Greece by Britain. The Greek King urged that, in view of the imminence of a German invasion of Greece in support of the defeated Italians, the Allies should forestall this event by assuming the offensive in Greece as soon as possible. He also proposed that the Balkan Front should be divorced as far as possible from the Egyptian Front, at any rate in so far as air activities were concerned.

What the King of Greece did not know was that General Wavell's offensive against the Italians in the Western Desert, which had already been delayed in order to send aid to Greece, was due to open on December 9, and that this naturally and inevitably curtailed the amount of support which could be spared for the Balkan Front. In view of this difficulty King George delayed his reply to the King of Greece until December 13, by which time the British had captured Sidi Barrani and were hustling Marshal Graziani's army across Libya towards Benghazi. After further consultation with his Ministers, he then took up in detail the points raised : [a]

I was very glad to get so frank an expression of your views as that contained in your letter of the 17th November, which reached me safely by the hand of Admiral Turle.

Before I attempt to answer the several points which you raise, I must tell you how overjoyed we have all been at the way in which your forces have dealt with the Italian aggression. It does your people the greatest credit, and it is also a remarkable tribute to your own unsparing efforts to build up a first-class fighting force. From the reports of my Military Attachés, I well know how much is due to your own personal attention to everything down to the smallest detail. The stand made by Greece and the example she has set have had a most encouraging and stimulating effect in this country and in every part of the world where people pray for the overthrow of Hitler and Mussolini. Certainly England will never forget what Greece has done this autumn and winter.

The points which you make in your letter are largely concerned with air assistance. First let me take the question of scale. The events of the last few days will have shown you why it was that we could not spare more machines for use in Greece. We were preparing our offensive against the Italian Army in Libya, which since the beginning of the war has been a constant threat to Egypt. The removal of this threat must be the first objective in our Mediterranean strategy. We can enjoy no liberty of manœuvre so long as Egypt is not made entirely safe, for I need hardly remind

[a] This letter was typewritten but begun and ended in the King's own hand.

you that its loss would entail the collapse of our position in the Middle East and bring in its train the collapse of Greece. We were therefore bound, in your interest as much as ours, to be prudent even at the risk of disappointing you, and to gauge the degree of assistance which we could afford to Greece by our estimate of what we should require for our offensive against the Italian Army in Libya. Great as was the damage inflicted at Taranto, it was not, and could not be, decisive, but the operations now being conducted against the Italians at Sidi Barrani will go far to relieve the whole situation in the Eastern Mediterranean. We may hope that they will also ease the pressure on your troops in Albania. This offensive, of which the results up to date are most encouraging, is evidence in itself of our determination to do everything we can to knock Italy out, and proof that we are not neglecting the opening which you have given us.

If as a result of our present operations we succeed in reducing the Italian air threat to Egypt I certainly hope that it may be possible to contemplate sending air reinforcements to Greece. Longer term reinforcements necessarily depend on the speed with which we can reinforce our air units in Egypt. As you will realise the limiting factors here are shipping and our own home requirements in the face of the German menace. As for the air assistance which has already reached you, you will appreciate that the reason why it seemed to you to be disappointingly slow in coming was the necessity of making ground preparations before the aircraft themselves arrived, and of providing adequate anti-aircraft protection for them. The speed with which any further reinforcements could reach you will depend to a considerable extent on the same factor, namely the rapidity with which your aerodromes and other facilities can be developed to meet your requirements. Here you could help us very much. Air Vice-Marshal D'Albiac and my Air Attaché have been told exactly what is needed, and we should be most grateful for anything you can do to make sure that their requests are quickly carried out by the authorities concerned.

Finally there is the question of the command of the British air units operating from Greece. I quite understand your desire for an independent command, but I fear that this might in fact have a result contrary to what you hope. The force based on your aerodromes is actually only a part of the air support which we are giving you, and it is intimately related to a much wider plan for striking at Italy, which must necessarily be controlled by one Headquarters; added to which our units in Greece depend for supply and maintenance on our organisation in Egypt. There is also the important point of the co-ordination of our Air Force operations with those of the Fleet Air Arm, and plans can only be approved by the two Commanders-in-Chief working in close collaboration. I think you will agree that these material considerations are overwhelming; but against this I can assure you that policy in regard to striking at Italy will be decided here and not in Egypt, and that our action will not be restricted by purely local considerations.

May I end as I began, by repeating once again the intense admiration we all have here for the exploits of the Greek army and the spirit of your people.[45]

The fortunes of war swung to and fro. On March 28, 1941, the Mediterranean Fleet defeated the Italians at the Battle of Cape Matapan, but three days later General Rommel, who had brought certain German reinforcements to North Africa, opened his counter-offensive, which compelled General Wavell to relinquish much of his hard-won gains.[a]

In the meantime the tempo of events in the Balkans had accelerated, and Prince Paul had become the victim of his fate. On February 14 Hitler, determined now to aid his Italian ally in Greece as well as in North Africa, summoned the Yugoslav Premier and Foreign Minister, MM. Cvetković and Cincar Marković, to Berchtesgaden, and demanded the adherence of their country to the Axis Pact for the purpose of securing passage for German troops to invade Greece. On March 1 Bulgaria joined the Axis and German troops appeared in Sofia and Varna. On March 4 Prince Paul himself went secretly to Berchtesgaden and gave a verbal assurance that Yugoslavia would follow the example of Bulgaria. The conflict of wills in Belgrade swung back and forth, until finally on March 20 a Cabinet crisis occurred, in which the Serbian Ministers resigned rather than accept the German terms.

At this juncture a joint plea was launched from Britain. Mr. Churchill addressed a warning to the Yugoslav Prime Minister,[46] while King George made a last appeal to the vacillating, harassed Prince Paul. A suggested form of words was put forward by the Foreign Office, but this the King rejected. 'I disliked the draft shown me & sent him a personal one of friendship', he wrote in his diary, adding a note of very human understanding: 'Paul must be terribly worried, especially as his regency comes to an end in 5 months'

---

[a] On June 30, 1941, General Wavell was succeeded as Commander-in-Chief in the Middle East by General Sir Claude Auchinleck.

time & he naturally does not want to hand over to Peter the country plunged into war.' [47]

The King's own message was as follows :

Reports are reaching me that you are being particularly hard pressed by the Germans to sign an agreement with them which, whatever the reservations, will certainly, if recent history is any guide, mark the first and fatal step in the loss of your country's independence and integrity.

Yugoslavia owes so much to your inspired example and steadfast leadership, our two countries share so many common ideals, and we have been close personal friends for so long, that I feel certain that we can rely upon you to take the right decision. I am absolutely convinced that both the true interests of your country and of your trusteeship demand that no agreement of any kind should be signed with the Germans whose word is never, and least of all now, to be trusted. We count on you.[48]

But neither the friendly counsel of King George nor the ringing exhortation of Mr. Churchill could restrain the leaders of Yugoslavia from their fatal course. Prince Paul and his two chief Ministers were now too far committed to draw back. With the approval of the Regent, MM. Cvetković and Marković again journeyed to the Reich. This time their destination was Vienna, whither they went with all secrecy lest the wrath of the Yugoslav people should be visited upon them. There, in the Belvedere Palace, on March 25 they signed the Axis Pact.

The sequel was swift and gallant. The news of the signature of the Pact came through the Belgrade radio to a stunned, and then an irate, people. The return of the Prime Minister and Foreign Minister next day was the signal for indignant and hostile demonstrations. The Prince Regent had left Belgrade for Zagreb. At dawn on March 27 a military revolution led by General Simović, head of the Air Force, proclaimed the Regency at an end and the assumption of power by King Peter. The movement received the support of the Church, the Army and the people. The streets of Belgrade rang with the cry, 'Better war than the pact with Germany', and the first act of the Simović Government was to repudiate the signatures of their predecessors.[a]

[a] A graphic eye-witness account of the events in Belgrade at this time is provided by King Peter himself in chapter vi of his memoirs. (*A King's Heritage*, pp. 57–76.)

Prince Paul, on arrival at Zagreb, was informed of the establishment of the new régime. He returned at once to Belgrade, only to leave that same night with his family for Greece.[a] 'Poor Paul, he has a lot to answer for I am afraid for the present position of the Balkans', King George wrote later in his diary.[49]

The reaction of Hitler to this turn of events in Belgrade was not long delayed. On April 6 there began the joint attack by German and Bulgarian troops upon Yugoslavia and Greece. The course of the operations bore a hideous resemblance to those of a year before in the Low Countries. In execution of the pledges of the British Guarantee of April 1939, British and New Zealand troops were at once dispatched to the support of Greece; but too little could be spared from General Wavell's hard-pressed army to stem the tide of the German advance. On April 17 the Yugoslav Field Army capitulated — though guerrilla resistance continued — and King Peter and his Ministers were evacuated by the R.A.F. from Kotor to Palestine.[b] On April 23 King George of Greece transferred the seat of his government to Crete and two days later the swastika banner waved above the Acropolis. By June 1 British and Greek troops had been driven from Crete, and the whole Balkan peninsula had passed under Nazi supremacy.

The King of Greece with his Ministers had escaped from Crete on May 25, and had found refuge in Cairo. There he received a touching message from King George:

The loss of Crete must be to Your Majesty and to all Greeks, as it is to us, a bitter blow. We share Your grief but we also share Your hopes. News reaches this country daily to prove that the tragedy of Greece has left unbroken the spirit of Your gallant people who have shown and continue to show a heroism and a disregard for odds unsurpassed in history. Your country has indeed been overwhelmed, but the spirit of the Greek people remains high and the fame of their resistance will outlast the transitory conquests of the enemy. Fortified by the Greek example

---

[a] After the evacuation of Greece Prince Paul and Princess Olga were transferred to South Africa, where they remained for the rest of the war.

[b] King Peter later came to England, arriving on June 21. 'I am his "Koom", a sort of permanent godfather in Serbia, & I held him at his christening. So I must look after him here. Perhaps it was destiny', King George wrote in his diary.[50]

we shall continue the struggle proud to have at our side those units of Your Fleet which survived the battle, the nucleus of a new Hellenic Air Force, and the cadres of a new Army. Meanwhile my Government learn that Hellenic communities overseas are expressing their determination to pursue the struggle for victory and asking how best they can help.

I greet through Your Majesty all who fought in the valiant Hellenic armies on the mainland, those who fought in Crete, and particularly the injured and bereaved; and I thank you one and all, each individually, for your cooperation; for the battles which you won, for the help you gave My soldiers; for the tremendous moral blow which you have struck for our common cause. To You and Your people we are for ever grateful and in our gratitude we do not forget that great soldier statesman John Metaxas who said to the Italians 'You shall not pass', nor his successor, Alexander Koryzis, who said 'No' to a yet more powerful foe.[51]

(vii)

Such was the year of the Decisive Struggle — when Britain stood alone. It was perhaps the most important twelve months in the life or times of King George VI. Though it both began and ended under the shadow of military defeat, with the evacuation of a British Army from the Continent of Europe, it also witnessed the determinative victory of the Battle of Britain, and the freeing of the island fortress, not from investment but from the menace of invasion. Over and above this, it had seen the people of Britain in 'their finest hour', when monarch and subject shared danger and suffering and the threat of death; when, in the words of the prophet Isaiah, which King George had taken for his own guidance,[a] 'They helped every one his neighbour; and every one said to his brother, Be of good courage.'

Historians of the future, looking back upon King George's reign, cannot but accord the tribute of greatness to Britain at this time, but they may also stand aghast at the narrowness of the margin of safety. Had Hitler but sacrificed his immediate dreams of invasion of Britain or Russia and, playing a game of politics with Stalin — who was only too anxious to continue playing it — concentrated his attack upon the Mediterranean and upon Britain's shipping and communications, how

[a] See above, p. 418.

different might have been the issue of the decisive struggle ! Had Rommel been sent to North Africa before rather than after General Wavell's defeat of Graziani; had Greece and Yugoslavia not made their gallant gesture of defiance, thereby causing Hitler to postpone the date of his attack on Russia, how disastrous might have been the result ! It is the 'Ifs' of History which change its course.

By the grace of God none of these things happened. On June 22, 1941, Britain no longer stood alone, for on that day German aggression brought her a powerful ally ;[a] and less than six months later, Japanese aggression was to bring her another. The Grand Alliance of Victory was based, in the first instance, on the errors of the enemy.

[a] At 4 a.m. on June 22, 1941, Germany invaded the U.S.S.R.

CHAPTER VII

ANGLO-AMERICAN RELATIONS
1939-1942

(i)

AMONG the many prominent events of the reign of King George VI, there is none of more vital importance than the substitution of the United States of America for France as Britain's chief ally. The events in Bordeaux and Vichy during the summer of 1940 marked not only the grave of the Third Republic but also that of the Anglo-French partnership which had been the keystone of British policy since the First World War. Though the *Entente Cordiale* might be revived, it was patent that France had forfeited, at least temporarily, the status of a Great Power which she had so long enjoyed, and that association with her would no longer constitute the chief consideration of British policy. Total war was to become global war, and 'global' was to remain the governing principle in the post-war world. Under such conditions Britain's outlook inevitably became reorientated. No longer did she look to the old world of Europe for her principal ally. Her new tenet of policy was to be that:

> And not by eastern windows only,
> When daylight comes, comes in the light;
> In front the sun climbs slow, how slowly,
> But westward, look, the land is bright.[a]

If the Anglo-French agreement, the *Entente Cordiale* of 1904, came as a surprising sequel to the relations between the two countries at the time of the Fashoda Incident and the Boer War, the circumstances precedent to the Anglo-American alliance were no less unpromising. During the early nineteen-twenties much damage had been done to British prestige in the United States by the allegedly 'impartial and dispassionate

---

[a] Arthur Hugh Clough, 'Say not the struggle naught availeth'.

approach' of certain historians to the subject of war-guilt, their
conclusions apparently being that Britain was only a degree
less culpable than Germany and that America had been be-
guiled into belligerency under false pretences. The anti-
British sentiments thus engendered in the United States were
exacerbated by the failure of the Coolidge Naval Disarmament
Conference and the Anglo-French Naval Compromise of 1928,
and were certainly not mitigated by the misunderstanding
arising from Mr. Stimson's 'Manchurian Gesture' of 1931
and the virtual repudiation of the British war debt a year
later. Anglo-American relations reached their nadir at the
time of the Munich Crisis, when American public opinion,
while firmly opposed to any action being taken by the United
States, was bitterly critical of a similar policy being pursued
by Great Britain. It may well have been forgotten that, in
the late 'twenties and early 'thirties of this century, unofficial
committees were formed in both Britain and the United States
for the study of possible means of mitigating the existing Anglo-
American hostility; while British statesmen were at pains to
emphasize that war between the two countries was 'unthinkable' — a sure sign that it had indeed been thought about.

The national characteristics of the two peoples, moreover,
were nearly as dissimilar as those of the British and French.
What was termed 'a common heritage of culture and language'
was, in fact, all too often the source of misunderstanding caused
by too great a familiarity and a consequent disregard of sensi-
tivities. The superficial similarities were themselves misleading
since they masked far more deep-seated differences of personality. Americans' hypersensitiveness, coupled with their not
infrequent habit of sharp criticism of others, were matched
by British bland indifference and by the maddening *superbia
Britannorum*. The warmth and *naïveté* of the American character encountered, too often disastrously, the more frigid
sophistication of the British, failing to penetrate behind the
façade; while the Englishman, schooled in the use of restraint
and under-statement, recoiled from the American addiction to
hyperbole and superlatives. Above all, there was a fundamental distrust by Americans of British diplomacy, in which,
it was held, hypocritical double-dealing was inherent.

It may therefore be thought surprising that from these

seemingly incompatible and divergent elements there should emerge an Anglo-American alliance, which, though susceptible to the stresses and strains inevitable between allies, nevertheless remained proof against 'the slings and arrows of outrageous fortune', and derives additional strength from the fact that it is unwritten.   The architects of this alliance were Mr. Churchill and President Roosevelt, its artificers Lord Lothian, Lord Halifax and Mr. Gilbert Winant; [a] but a substantial share of the credit must also be attributed to King George and Queen Elizabeth, who, in the course of their visit to the United States in the summer of 1939, disclosed to the American public the essential fact that 'Royalty' are 'people', and in three days did more to demolish anti-British feeling in America than could have been achieved in a quarter of a century of diplomatic manœuvring.   Theirs was the foundation upon which others builded; theirs the spark which others tended into flame.

The relationship between Mr. Churchill and the President was one of deep calling to deep; of two great war chieftains, imbued with the common desire of defeating a common enemy and forming an alliance of genius directed towards the preservation of a way of life and the ultimate triumph over tyranny and deceit; a union of great personalities brought together in a common cause.   The friendship between King George and Mr. Roosevelt was of a different nature, at once more simple and more personal.   It was based upon a community of interests altogether divorced from high policy, on correlative admiration devoid of any competitive element, and on a mutual understanding of the problems which confront the supreme leaders of great peoples and of the peaks of loneliness which are traversed by them alone.

The formulation of the Alliance was one of slow and delicate process.   Though at least 75 per cent of American public

[a] Hon. John Gilbert Winant, O.M. (1889–1947), a Republican by politics, having served in the State Legislature and Senate, was thrice elected Governor of New Hampshire, 1925–1927, 1931–1933, 1933–1935.   He was appointed Chairman of the Social Security Board by President Roosevelt in 1935, and became, first, Assistant Director, 1937–1938 and, later, Director, 1938–1941, of the International Labour Organization.   Appointed United States Ambassador at the Court of St. James in 1941 in succession to Mr. Joseph Kennedy, he remained in London until 1946 when he retired for reasons of ill-health.   He committed suicide at his home at Concord, New Hampshire, on November 3, 1947.

opinion favoured the allied cause in September 1939, at least 95 per cent were equally fervently opposed to America's becoming 'involved in Europe's wars' — with the exception of certain business men and lawyers who believed in doing business with the Nazis. The period of inactivity during the 'Phoney War' bewildered the Americans, who put to themselves and to the British and French officials in the United States the very understandable question: were the Allies serious in their fight against Hitler? The disasters of April, May and June 1940 caused even the most reasonable and level-headed to opine that Nazi Germany was invincible and that America would do well to bide her time and make the best arrangement possible later. The more intrepid and farsighted elements in the United States, however, realized the danger to their own country and to all civilization inherent in a Nazi victory. The movement to aid Britain 'by all means short of war' gained in weight and impetus as it became more clearly apparent that Britain could and would carry on the struggle, alone if need be. The valour displayed in the Battle of Britain and the Battle of the Atlantic; the unity of the British people in their determination to resist invasion and to withstand siege; the part played by the King and Queen in making that unity of spirit even greater, all had their favourable repercussions in the United States, but they did not obviate the very strong aversion of the American people to participating in a 'shooting war'.

The opinion may be safely ventured that, throughout the months which separated the Nazi invasion of Poland from the Japanese attack on Pearl Harbour, that is to say from September 1939 to December 1941, the attitude of the United States Congress was well behind the public sentiments of the American people, and the attitude of the President well ahead of it. From the earliest days of the Nazi régime, which had coincided almost exactly with his own assumption of office as President, Mr. Roosevelt had been fully aware of the dangers which it represented to the peace of the world. The economic interests of his own country, the intrinsic and traditional antagonism of the American people to 'entangling alliances', and the evident disinclination of the British and French Governments to oppose Nazi aggression by force of arms, precluded the President from following any course of action save that of exploring possibilities of a peaceful settlement of Europe's problems.

Nor were the American people any more responsive to the more proximate danger of Japanese aggression in Asia. President Roosevelt's attempt, in his reverberating 'Quarantine Speech' at Chicago on October 5, 1937, to use this danger to develop the thesis that if aggression were to be met at all it must be on a world-wide scale aroused the worst suspicions of the native isolationists and on the whole received little response from American public opinion.

At the outbreak of the war in Europe, therefore, American policy did not extend beyond the use of moral force, legal argument and economic measures — all so contrived as to avoid military and political commitments of any kind whatever. Yet American policy was not impartial in the strict sense of the word, and the 'Cash-and-Carry' legislation of the autumn of 1939 was illustrative of this. Once France had fallen, however, and the German army stood triumphant on Europe's Atlantic coast; once Britain stood in danger of defeat with the consequent control by Germany of the Eastern Atlantic, the United States Government, on the President's initiative, quickly abandoned at least a part of its policy of caution. Justifying its acts on the grounds of national defence, it now took steps to deprive Germany of certain of the economic and financial advantages of her conquests by 'freezing' the American assets of the occupied countries, and to give to Britain significant material aid and diplomatic support. 'The ultimate effect of thus identifying the British cause with the security of the Western Hemisphere', an American historian has written, 'was to bring the United States and Great Britain as close together as they could have been brought by a formal treaty of alliance. While localized differences continued to mar the singleness of Anglo-American endeavours, this tight and active association with the British Commonwealth remained the dominant theme.'[1]

(ii)

From the earliest days of the war King George had been preoccupied with the gigantic task of relief and reconstruction which would inevitably confront the victors at its close. In his view, immediate steps should be taken to set on foot the preparatory organization of what he termed 'an International Mission of help for after the war'.[2] He himself prepared a memorandum on the subject in the spring of 1940 which he discussed with Mr. Chamberlain and Lord Halifax, and the upshot was that the whole matter might most usefully be investigated by official committees in both Britain and the United States. It was further agreed, the King wrote in his diary, that 'I should write a personal letter to President Roosevelt, putting it to him that both our countries could help in this. . . . I feel so strongly that I must put this point to the President.'[3]

It was the suggestion of the Foreign Office that Mr. Sumner Welles, then on a 'fact-finding' mission of peace for the President,[a] should be asked to take the King's letter with him to Washington, but to this the canny American diplomat, conscious of the climate of ideas in his own country, demurred.

Sumner Welles was shown a copy of my letter to President Roosevelt [the King recorded on March 13], & his comment was that he could not take it as one passage mentioned the collaboration of the U.S.A. with us, & this would be taken to mean that we were asking the U.S.A. to help us in the War. I am very angry about it. It shows that the U.S. Administration & the U.S.A. are going to do nothing until after the Presidential election.

The letter, dated April 2, was, however, dispatched through the usual diplomatic channels, and was the first of a number exchanged between the King and the President in the course of the war. This correspondence, which formed a further and not unimportant strand in the bonds of Anglo-American friendship at this critical time, was, of course, unknown to the public of either country.

My dear President Roosevelt,
    In the midst of the preoccupations connected with the progress of the war, I have from time to time turned my mind to the question of what is likely to be the condition of affairs in Europe and perhaps elsewhere when the war comes to an end. This is a matter which no doubt is in your mind too.
    I think we must take it for granted that, at the moment.when

[a] See above, p. 436.

hostilities do cease, there will be in many parts of Europe and possibly elsewhere a serious dearth of the necessaries of life.

We cannot assume that, when that time comes, rapid initiative, followed by the requisite activity, will be forthcoming. On the contrary, I think it may be taken for granted that the responsible authorities will be very fully occupied. There is consequently a danger that, unless our preparations are made beforehand, there may be widespread distress and misery. I feel, therefore, that it would be wise to consider now whether some form of international organization should not be set up in the near future so that plans might be ready to be put into operation as soon as the right moment arrived. It seems to me that it is not too early even now to set on foot a preliminary study of potential stocks of the most vital articles of food and clothing, the sources of supply of these articles, and the possibilities of routing them to Europe and distributing them in the various countries which may stand most in need of them.

If you agree with me that a preliminary investigation of this kind would be of considerable value and importance, I should be very glad to have your views as to the best method of bringing it about.

Believe me

Yours very sincerely

GEORGE R.I.[4]

It is at once apparent how wise these long-term considerations of the King's were when one realizes that in 1940 he was foreseeing just the problems which actually arose some six or seven years later. The precipitate termination of Lend-Lease in 1945, the Marshall Plan and the establishment of the Organization for European Economic Co-operation in 1947, were exactly the type of eventuality which King George was prognosticating in this first letter to the President.

Mr. Roosevelt's reply on May 1 was friendly and co-operative.[5] He fully shared the King's views and was, he said, appointing a Government Committee to make an immediate study of the stocks of food and clothing then available in various parts of the world, as well as the manner through which production of those supplies which would be most vitally necessary might be effectively increased as an added reserve. He suggested that, if the British Government would establish a similar body in London, a useful and helpful exchange of information could be effected.

Before any such proposal could be acted upon, the whole

course of the war had been radically changed by the opening of
the German onslaught on May 10; and, with the Continent
largely dominated by Hitler, the consideration of post-war
problems assumed a more distant aspect. When King George
sent his reply on June 22, France had already fallen, but he
did not allow this fact to distract him from the ultimate and
eventual needs of the world. He wrote:

My dear President Roosevelt,

Your letter of May 1st dealing with the emergency conditions
which will exist at the end of the war, was very welcome to me.
Every day which passes goes to show that these conditions will
indeed be grave and the expert study which you suggest of available
stocks of food and clothing, and of the possibility of increasing
vitally necessary supplies should be of great value in making it
possible to direct effort in the best way when the time comes.

It has been decided to undertake, through a Governmental
Committee in this country, an enquiry on the lines indicated in
your letter, and I am hopeful that the interchange of information
through Governmental channels between the American and British
Committees may prove to be of real assistance in preparing to meet
this most serious problem.

I am very grateful for your ready cooperation in this work,
which will mean so much to the peoples of Europe.

     I am

       Yours very sincerely

          George R.I.[6]

Despite his preoccupation with the imminent danger of
invasion and the opening stages of the Battle of Britain, King
George did not abandon his interest in post-war problems.
An added importance was now provided in the necessity for
counteracting the 'New Order', by the proclamation of which,
it was anticipated, Hitler would attempt to consolidate Europe
under a Nazi paramountcy. To this the King gave his earnest
attention. At his command Sir Alexander Hardinge sent to
the Foreign Office a memorandum envisaging a joint declaration by Great Britain and the United States welcoming the
idea of a voluntary federation of European states after the
war, and promising their financial and economic support to
such an organization.[7]

The view of the King's advisers, however, was that though
the value of such a declaration would be undoubted, American

public opinion was still far from being sufficiently advanced for the United States Government to join in any such *démarche*, since it might be held to postulate their willingness to make themselves directly responsible for the formulation and maintenance of such a European federation. It was therefore suggested that the King's proposal should be held over until such time as America had become an active belligerent, when public opinion in the United States might then consider it of direct interest to the American people themselves to collaborate in the future rebuilding of Europe as an essential element in their own well-being. In accepting this advice, somewhat reluctantly, the King expressed the hope that the swing of the pendulum of American public opinion towards some participation in European affairs after the war might be accelerated by their realization that a Nazi-dominated Europe would constitute a menace to American security.[8]

The matter was therefore shelved for the time being, but the King's initiative was not entirely barren of results. A Ministerial Committee was set up to consider the possibility of creating some post-war European system on the basis of the federation. But the Committee had a second purpose, one which was always close to King George's heart. It was also charged with the task of the preliminary consideration of a scheme of social reform for the United Kingdom, designed to secure equality of opportunity and service among all classes of the community, thereby perpetuating the spirit of national unity achieved in the country during the war. It was from this preliminary investigation that there ultimately emerged the Beveridge Plans for social insurance and for full employment in a free society.

(iii)

On May 1, 1940, at the same time as he replied to King George's original proposals for post-war reconstruction, President Roosevelt wrote another and more informal letter to His Majesty. This second letter, arriving as it did in the midst of the downfall of the Chamberlain Government, must indeed have stirred memories of those happy, if crowded, hours which the King had spent at Hyde Park less than a year before.

For many weeks, and indeed months [wrote the President], I have been meaning to send you a personal line to tell you and the Queen how very much you have been in our thoughts.

Last June seems years distant. You will remember that the Saturday night at Hyde Park when I kept you up, after a strenuous day, I may have seemed pessimistic in my belief in the probability of war. More than a month after that I found the Congress assured that there could be no war, and for a few weeks I had to accept the charge of being a 'calamity-howler'.

I certainly do not rejoice in my prophecies but at least it has given me opportunity to bring home the seriousness of the world situation to the type of American who has hitherto believed, in much too large numbers, that no matter what happens there will be little effect on this country.

I hope much that the rather serious news of the past two weeks will have improved by the time you get this.

Always I want you and your family to know that you have very warm friends in my wife and myself over here, and you must not hesitate to call on me for any possible thing if I can help or lighten your load.

The other day I had a nice visit from Mackenzie King at my cottage at Warm Springs — and it is very good to know that Canada and the United States are on such a really intimate basis.

My very warm regards — and may I add that I really hope you are taking care of your own health because your continued fitness is of real moment to the world.⁹

At no moment could a reminder of Mr. Roosevelt's personal attitude have been more opportune, for it must have recalled to King George those momentous conversations at Hyde Park of which he had so careful a record. On his return to England in June 1939 he had passed on to the quarters best qualified to make use of them the views of the President concerning a Western Atlantic Patrol operating from British bases, and within a week (that is to say, three weeks after the talks at Hyde Park) President Roosevelt had made an oral, but very definite, approach on these same lines to the British Ambassador in Washington. The matter had hung fire until, on the outbreak of war, Mr. Churchill had returned to the Cabinet and to the Admiralty. The King discussed the President's views with the new First Lord, and Mr. Churchill's imagination was at once fired by the ideas presented. But again there was delay until, in the fateful summer of 1940 when Mr. Churchill had become Prime Minister, the issue was reopened in Washington by the British Ambassador, Lord Lothian.

President Roosevelt had already given ample proof of his anxiety and willingness to aid Britain at this moment of her extremity. On June 1, 1940, in answer to Mr. Churchill's appeal, he had authorized the sale of thirty-seven million dollars' worth of arms to help replace those lost in the evacuation from Dunkirk.[a] Mr. Churchill now appealed again for American aid, this time for destroyers, in which class of warship Britain's losses had been particularly heavy, and King George took occasion to back his petition.

Thank you so much for your personal letter of May 1st [he wrote to the President on June 26]. The Queen and I often think of the delightful days which we spent with you and Mrs. Roosevelt little more than a year ago. I remember very well our talk that night when you spoke of the probability of war. Your pessimism has proved to be only too well justified.

Since you wrote your letter, the British Empire has had to face a series of disasters for which it has been little to blame. But the spirit here is magnificent, and the people of these islands, strongly reinforced by the Dominion Contingents, are inspired by the thought that it is their own soil which they now have to defend against an invader. Their resolution and their confidence are supreme.

As you know, we are in urgent need of some of your older destroyers to tide us over the next few months. I well understand your difficulties, and I am certain that you will do your best to procure them for us before it is too late. Now that we have been deprived of the assistance of the French Fleet — to put the least unfavourable interpretation on the present position — the need is becoming greater every day if we are to carry on our solitary fight for freedom to a successful conclusion.[11]

The President's difficulties in complying with this request were considerable. Anxious as he was personally to acquiesce, he could not afford to ignore the domestic problems involved. To transfer fifty destroyers to the British was a distinctly un-neutral act, and there was the possibility to be considered that Hitler might regard it as a *casus belli* ; in addition, Congress had recently ruled that no American military property

---

[a] The American supplies thus purchased included half a million rifles stored from the First World War with 250 rounds of ammunition apiece, 900 field-guns with a million rounds, and 80,000 machine-guns.[10]

could be delivered to a foreign country unless it had been previously certified as surplus to the needs of the service involved. The President himself, moreover, desired a *quid pro quo*, and at first suggested that the destroyers should be delivered in return for a promise to send the British Navy to carry on the war from outlying parts of the Empire should Britain be herself successfully invaded. Mr. Churchill refused to make so explicit a public undertaking, since he did not wish to give the enemy the impression that Britain had even considered the possibility of a successful invasion. But he was ready to offer such a pledge personally and privately to Mr. Roosevelt, and he welcomed the President's subsequent suggestion that the transfer of destroyers should be linked with the grant to the United States of British bases in the Caribbean and North Atlantic. He wished, however, to keep the two transactions separate and unrelated, but this Mr. Roosevelt stubbornly resisted in his turn, since to him the reciprocal aspect of the agreement was essential to allay the extreme suspicions aroused in Congress and to justify his action before the domestic law and the domestic opinion of the United States, to the effect that he had obtained an asset for American security. Indeed Mr. Roosevelt's wisdom and courage on this issue can scarcely be overestimated. The risks which he took politically were considerably greater than were appreciated in Britain as a whole.

Though the difficulties were great they were overcome with remarkable celerity. On September 2 — less than fourteen weeks after Mr. Churchill's first appeal — an agreement was signed whereby fifty reconditioned U.S. destroyers of the First World War vintage were transferred to the Royal Navy,[a] in exchange for ninety-nine-year leases for the establishment of American air and sea bases in Newfoundland, Bermuda, the Bahamas, Jamaica, Antigua, St. Lucia, Trinidad and British Guiana.[b]

[a] The first eight destroyers were handed over to the British at Halifax on September 6.

[b] The Destroyer-Bases Agreement of September 2, 1940, was effected by means of an exchange of notes between the British Ambassador and the U.S. Secretary of State, and was published as a White Paper, Cmd. 6224. A full account of the negotiations is given by Mr. Churchill in his Memoirs (ii, pp. 353-368). See also the Memoirs of Mr. Cordell Hull, i, pp. 835-837; and Mr. Stimson's memoirs, *On Active Service*, p. 358.

Thus had come to fruition the dream which Mr. Roosevelt had unfolded to King George one summer evening at Hyde Park, and His Majesty wrote appreciatively to the President.

5th September 1940

MY DEAR PRESIDENT ROOSEVELT,

After what I said in my letter of June 26th, I feel that I must write to you again now that a solution of the destroyer question has been happily reached. I cannot tell you how much I have appreciated your efforts to help us, and admired the skill with which you have handled a very delicate situation. The friendly action of the United States in making these all-important ships available for us has evoked a warm feeling of gratitude throughout this country, and we hope that our offer of facilities in the Western Atlantic for the defence of North America will give equal satisfaction to your people. I remember so well the talk which we had on this particular subject at Hyde Park — but how far off all that seems now !

I have just seen your three Service Representatives, and I think you will find that the two who are returning will bring a reassuring account of conditions here. The outstanding and consistent success of the Royal Air Force in the recent battles has created a great feeling of confidence. The country's defences have now assumed a very formidable character ; enemy bombings have so far interfered but little with production, and the morale of the people is superb. No doubt we have a lot to suffer yet, but one is entitled to hope that the turn of the tide may not be so very far off.

Believe me

Yours very sincerely

GEORGE R.I.

P.S. The Queen joins with me in sending you & Mrs. Roosevelt our best wishes.

G.R.I.[12]

The course of the transfer of bases, however, did not run quite smoothly. Though the leasing of these areas had formed an integral part of the Agreement of September 2, 1940, the specific accord regarding them was not signed until March 21, 1941, and in the interval the United States authorities displayed less than the requisite amount of tact and discretion. In the West Indies particularly, where British traditions are deeply ingrained, the Americans exhibited an assertiveness which inevitably aroused resentment. In respect of the islands of Bermuda, St. Lucia and Trinidad, American demands went considerably beyond those originally mentioned, and entailed the stationing of substantial military forces which were considered to be in excess of those required for the establishment of Naval and Air Bases. In addition, a United States Economic Mission visited a number of the islands, and the assiduity of their enquiries awakened acute anxiety.

A marked fear developed among the inhabitants of the King's West Indian possessions that the establishment of United States bases on their territories would ultimately affect their status in the Empire, and would derogate from their cherished British sovereignty. In their anxiety they appealed to the King. The Bermuda House of Assembly in a memorial to His Majesty expressed themselves as 'deeply disturbed lest some new conception of American hemispheric defence may affect the status of this ancient colony as an integral part of the British Commonwealth', and the inhabitants of the Windward Islands voiced similar fears that the visits of recent United States missions were the thin end of the wedge of American penetration.

The seriousness of these events was not lost upon the Cabinet or the Sovereign. A Cabinet Paper was prepared by the Secretary of State for the Colonies, Lord Lloyd,[a] which caused the King deep concern.

I read a paper of Ld. Lloyd's on the West Indian Islands where the U.S. bases have been leased [he wrote in his diary]. I was much disturbed over it, as the U.S.A. is asking for more facilities than were originally agreed to, & wishes to fortify & have garrisons in Bermuda & Trinidad. I told Alec H. that there was no question of my giving my consent to hand over the sovereignty of these B.W.I. as I am the custodian of my subjects.[13]

The King's business with his Private Secretary was usually conducted verbally, but in this instance he committed his instructions to paper. 'The Americans have got to understand', he minuted to Sir Alexander Hardinge on December 30, 1940, 'that in leasing the bases the question of Sovereignty does not

[a] Rt. Hon. George Ambrose, first Baron Lloyd, G.C.S.I., G.C.I.E., D.S.O. (1879-1941), sat in the House of Commons as a Conservative from 1910 to 1918. He served as Governor of Bombay from 1918 to 1923, and returned to the House of Commons from 1924 till 1925, when he was appointed High Commissioner for Egypt and the Sudan, from which position he resigned in 1929. He was Secretary of State for the Colonies in Mr. Churchill's first Cabinet from 1940 until his death on February 4, 1941.

come in. These islands are part of the British Colonial Empire
& I am not going to see my West Indian subjects handed over to
the U.S. authorities.'[14]   He forthwith authorized Sir Alexander
Hardinge to convey these views to Lord Lloyd.

His Majesty quite realizes [wrote Sir Alexander on the following
day] that we cannot afford to supply the isolationists in America
with ammunition with which to attack the President, at a moment
which is so critical for our future. For this reason we may well
feel obliged to make concessions and submit to off-hand treatment,
such as we should not tolerate in ordinary times. Nevertheless, the
King, who, as the guardian of the Sovereignty of the people of the
West Indies, sets great store by their profession of loyalty and
devotion to the Crown, hopes that you will be able to emphasize to
them once more that their Sovereignty will not be in any way
affected by these concessions, and that everything possible will be
done to minimize interference with their conditions of life.[15]

Wiser counsels prevailed on both sides. The British West
Indians were persuaded to pocket their pride and contain
their apprehensions, while the Americans pursued a course of
conduct less likely to offend British susceptibilities. By the
time the final agreement was signed on March 21, 1941, most
of the greater difficulties had been overcome.

(iv)

Though the summer months of 1940 had seen the achievement
of Mr. Roosevelt's ambition for a Western Atlantic Patrol
based on British insular possessions, and had thus fulfilled the
most outstanding of the ideas which he and King George had
canvassed in the course of their conversations at Hyde Park,
there may well have been moments during that dolorous
autumn and winter when His Majesty recalled, with hope
deferred, the President's optimistic view that the bombing of
London would be followed by American intervention. The
gallantry and suffering of the British people did indeed evoke
the admiration and sympathy of the Americans. There was
popular endorsement for the aid which President Roosevelt
had given and there was every evidence that a policy of further
aid to Britain would receive public support, but it was also
abundantly clear that it must be 'all aid *short of war*'. There
was no large body of opinion in favour of belligerency. On

the contrary, the 'America First' Movement, in collaboration with Colonel Charles Lindbergh, provided a well-organized minority lobby, bitterly critical of the policies which the President had already pursued as being an approach to war. These factors inevitably weighed heavily with Mr. Roosevelt at a moment when he had committed himself to the unique experiment of running for a third term of presidential office.

The American electoral contest of 1940 was followed with deep interest and anxiety in London. The Republican candidate, Mr. Wendell Willkie,[a] was regarded as being personally favourable at least to continued aid to Britain, but his party were traditionally isolationist and it was feared that a change of administration in the United States at this juncture might well have a deleterious effect upon the Allied cause. The re-election of Mr. Roosevelt was hailed with satisfaction and relief, though there were many who, having indulged too greatly in wishful thinking, were disappointed at the immediately subsequent results. The mandate which the President had received was indeed for continued aid to Britain, but it was still to be 'all aid short of war', and, though Mr. Roosevelt went to the extreme limit of liberal interpretation of this precept, he could at no time have commanded a Congressional majority or, indeed, popular support, for active belligerency.

King George shared the general satisfaction at Mr. Roosevelt's re-election, and took the opportunity of sending a holograph letter of congratulation by the hand of his Ambassador.

November 11th 1940

MY DEAR PRESIDENT ROOSEVELT,

I feel I must take advantage of Lord Lothian's return to Washington, to send you a personal message saying how glad the Queen & I are to think that you are to be the President of the United States of America for a third term.

We all watched the election with deep interest, & are delighted & thankful at your victory.

In these grave & anxious days it is a great relief to feel that your wise & helpful policy will continue without interruption. It must have been a great sacrifice to you personally to have stood for re-election, & I hope that when you lay down your burden we

[a] Wendell Lewis Willkie (1892–1944), a brilliant lawyer and public utilities expert, was not a professional politician. His supporters stampeded the Republican Convention of 1940 at Philadelphia, and secured his nomination as presidential candidate in opposition to the party machine.

shall have achieved victory & peace, & that during your term of office our two countries will be more closely linked in both sympathy & fellowship.   We are keeping our end up here very well, & despite the constant & murderous bombing our people are full of courage & determination to win through.

The Queen & I send our best wishes to you & Mrs. Roosevelt.

        I am
                Your very sincere friend
                                        GEORGE R.I.[16]

To this letter President Roosevelt replied in terms of heartening friendship.   He wrote on November 22 from Hyde Park.

MY DEAR KING GEORGE

I have been intending to write to you for a month and more but, as you know, my time before the elections was of necessity taken up with a series of speeches and inspection trips.   Personally, I was much torn between the real duty to run for election again and a deep personal wish to retire.   Therefore, it was gratifying that the majority was so large, if there had to be any majority at all ! [a]

Also, I think and hope that there will be definite benefit to your Nation and to this by a continuity of existing policies.   There is absolutely no question that the appeasement element, the pro-Germans, the communists, and the total isolationists did their best for my defeat.

In regard to materials from here, I am, as you know, doing everything possible in the way of acceleration and in the way of additional release of literally everything that we can spare.

I think I realize a bit how splendidly all of your good people are standing up under these terrific air attacks — but I have what we call a 'hunch' — not necessarily based on cold figures, that you have turned the corner and that the break of the luck will be more and more with you.

May I also tell you that you, personally, and the Queen have deepened the respect and affectionate regard in which you are held in this country by the great majority of Americans.   All that is being done in Great Britain and the way it is being done make me feel very futile with respect to our own efforts.

At least the monthly production over here is speeding up and will continue to do so.

---

[a] The result of the Presidential Election of 1940 was as follows:

Franklin D. Roosevelt:	Popular Vote	27,243,466
	Electoral Vote	439
Wendell Willkie:	Popular Vote	22,304,755
	Electoral Vote	82

I am spending four days at home over Thanksgiving Day. Early in December I hope to get a bit of a holiday by going over to the Bahamas and several other prospective bases. That destroyer arrangement seems to have worked out perfectly. There is virtually no criticism in this country except from legalists who think it should have been submitted to the Congress first. If I had done that, the subject would still be in the tender care of the Committees of the Congress!

My wife joins me in sending our best wishes to you and to the Queen.

Yours very sincerely

FRANKLIN D. ROOSEVELT.[17]

In the midst of the elation at President Roosevelt's re-election Anglo-American relations suffered a most grievous loss in the sudden death, on December 12, of the British Ambassador at Washington, Lord Lothian. Few British representatives in America since the great Lord Bryce [a] have achieved so great an influence and so eminent a position as Philip Lothian. His appointment in July 1939 had not been received with universal approval, since he had been a supporter of Mr. Chamberlain's policy of appeasement, and had himself paid a visit to Hitler. The appointment, however, proved to be a stroke of genius. His earlier association with Lord Milner in South Africa, and with Mr. Lloyd George at the Paris Peace Conference, had given him a deep insight into imperial and international affairs, while his subsequent experience as Secretary of the Rhodes Trust had broadened his acquaintance with the Dominions and the United States, and had prepared him even further for the climax of his career.

A convinced believer in the 'manifest destiny' of the British Commonwealth and the United States to work together for the betterment of the world at large, Lord Lothian had the priceless advantage of an intimate knowledge of the American continent, an affection for and an appreciation of the American people and their way of life, and, withal, a clear understanding of the complexities and difficulties underlying Anglo-American relations, which he never underestimated. Taking up his appointment at Washington on the eve of war,

[a] Rt. Hon. James, first Viscount Bryce, O.M., G.C.V.O. (1838–1922), a distinguished historian and statesman, served as Ambassador at Washington from 1907 to 1913.

he revealed from the outset his persuasive powers, his states-
manlike qualities and his breadth of vision. In the difficult
months of his ambassadorship he played a leading rôle in the
intricate course of Anglo-American relations, often displaying
a courageous initiative which alarmed the more timorous of
his colleagues, but never misjudging the situation. From the
President, whose friendship he had enjoyed for over twenty
years, to the man in the street, he was known, trusted and
admired, and in his final address at Baltimore — read for
him, for he was on his death-bed — he gave a message which
bore fruit an hundredfold : 'If you back us you won't be backing a quitter. The issue now depends largely on what you
decide to do. Nobody can share that responsibility with you.'
He died the next day.

Ld. Lothian died to-day in Washington from food poisoning [a]
[King George wrote in his diary]. He will be a terrible loss to us,
as he was doing so well in the U.S.A. His place will be very
difficult to fill. He was a Christian Scientist & so would not call
in a doctor.[18]

That same day the King at Windsor received the following
telegram from President Roosevelt :

I am shocked beyond measure to hear of the sudden passing of
my old friend and your ambassador the Marquis of Lothian.
Through nearly a quarter of a century we had come to understand
and trust each other. I am very certain that if he had been allowed
by Providence to leave us a last message he would have told us
that the greatest of all efforts to retain democracy in the world
must and will succeed.

FRANKLIN D. ROOSEVELT.

The choice of a successor to Lord Lothian was indeed a
difficult one. Mr. Churchill's first thought was of Mr. Lloyd
George and, when this proved impracticable, he turned to
Lord Halifax. Here again the selection did not appear to be
inspired. To send to the United States at this juncture a
great aristocrat, noted as a Master of Foxhounds, who in his
political career had been closely identified with the policy of
Munich, and to whom the American continent was *terra
incognita*, did not at first glance seem to bristle with wisdom,

---

[a] His Majesty was misinformed. Lord Lothian died of uraemia.

more especially since he was to succeed the democratic, easy-going and informal Lord Lothian. Yet here again the critics were at fault. Lord Halifax adapted himself very successfully to the American scene, and established for himself a position of great authority and popularity.

But at the outset he was not happy at his appointment, being loath to leave England at a time when he believed that his judgment and experience could contribute a beneficial influence in the counsels of the War Cabinet. Some of his misgivings he placed before King George :

I saw Halifax who came down here to see me [wrote the King at Windsor on December 24]. He was very unhappy at the thought of leaving here now, & was perplexed at what might happen if anything happened to Winston. The team was not a strong one without a leader, & there were some hot heads among it. I told him he could always be recalled. By way of helping him I suggested that the post of my Ambassador in U.S.A. was more important at this moment than the post of Foreign Secy. here. But H. replied we would be very flattered if Cordell Hull came here as U.S. Ambassador but it would not make us change our policy. I said no, but Roosevelt has got to be helped by us to 'get over' his policy of Aid to Britain which is going well now, but should we suffer a disaster F. D. R.'s opponents would do their best to counter it. I think he understood this.

Lord Halifax's objections were overcome. With his great sense of public service and in deference to the wishes of his Sovereign, he bowed to the Prime Minister's wish that he should go to Washington, and all honour was done him in both countries. In addition to his position as Ambassador, he retained his membership of the War Cabinet,[a] and during his visits to Britain attended its meetings as of right. Moreover, when he arrived in Chesapeake Bay in the battleship *King George V* on January 24, he was to receive the distinction of being welcomed by the President in person.

King George was greatly touched by this honour accorded to his representative and to himself. 'It was indeed kind of you to have met my new Ambassador, Lord Halifax, when he landed from H.M.S. *King George V* at Annapolis', he wrote to Mr. Roosevelt on February 14, '— a gesture which I and

---

[a] Mr. Anthony Eden succeeded Lord Halifax as Foreign Secretary.

my countrymen deeply appreciated. I feel sure that the better you get to know him the more you will like him.' [19]

A fortnight later the King was at pains to repay the President's gesture in kind.

In the afternoon I met Mr. Winant, the new U.S. Ambassador, at Windsor Station [he recorded]. . . . I met him myself as a goodwill gesture between our two countries, & to return the compliment of F. D. R. having met Halifax personally on his arrival in America.[20]

'It was the first time in the history of Great Britain that a King had gone to meet an Ambassador', Mr. Winant wrote later. 'He was returning the courtesy which President Roosevelt had shown Lord Halifax and I didn't even have a battleship !' [21]

(v)

'Well, boys, Britain's broke, it's your money we want.' Such was the realistic message offered by Lord Lothian to the crowd of pressmen who had assembled to meet him at La Guardia airport on his last return from England in November 1940; and his words set off a chain of events in America which culminated some four months later in the enactment by Congress of the Lend-Lease legislation.

The Ambassador's remark was no exaggeration. By the end of 1940 Britain's dollar assets in America would be virtually exhausted, and she would therefore be unable to continue the policy of 'Cash-and-Carry'.[a] If America favoured 'all aid short of war' to Britain, it was becoming rapidly apparent that some other form of supplying the aid must be found than already existed, and that its safe delivery to Britain must be assured. It was also clear to many that United States policy

---

[a] Mr. Churchill in his memoirs (ii, p. 493) puts the position very clearly: 'Up to November 1940 we had paid for everything we had received. We had already sold 335 million dollars worth of American shares requisitioned for sterling from private owners in Britain. We had paid out over 4,500 million dollars in cash. We had only 2,000 million left, the greater part in investments, many of which were not readily marketable. It was plain that we could not go on any longer in this way. Even if we divested ourselves of all our gold and foreign assets, we could not pay for half we had ordered, and the extension of the war made it necessary for us to have ten times as much. We must keep something in hand to carry on our daily affairs.'

had moved a long way since September 1939. Even lip-service to the principle of neutrality had been by this time abandoned. The United States was now a non-belligerent, and the margin between non-belligerency and co-belligerency was visibly shrinking. The drift towards intervention was indubitable and was perceived by both the supporters and the opponents of the President. Yet none envisaged as yet a declaration of war.

King George was fully aware of the trend of events. In the 'Retrospect of 1940' written in his diary, he remarked that in re-electing Mr. Roosevelt as President of the United States the American people had responded to the theme of aiding Britain by the supply of armaments, adding, 'I hope that this theme will be put into practical effect very soon'.[22]

His hope was shortly to be realized in a very practical form. Before Lord Lothian's death negotiations had been set in train for a revolutionary change in the policy of American aid. On December 8 Mr. Churchill, in a long letter to President Roosevelt, had set out the sum-total of Britain's needs,[23] and a week later the President told a Press Conference that, in pursuing his policy of aid to Britain, 'I am trying to eliminate the dollar mark'. In the month of January Mr. Harry Hopkins arrived in London for consultation with the War Cabinet, and on January 10, 1941, the Bill, incorporating what Mr. Churchill has called 'the glorious conception of Lend-Lease', was introduced into the House of Representatives. Appropriately it was entitled, 'An Act to further promote the defence of the United States', and its number as a Bill was, significantly enough, 1776.

The object of the measure was to make arms and supplies from America more easily available to those Governments whose defence was deemed vital to the defence of the United States. For the value of these commodities an account would be kept but it would be left open for later settlement, the supplies being in the first instance 'leased' or 'lent'.[a]

The Bill was not accorded an entirely easy passage, and

---

[a] Some of the recipient countries, among them Britain, later concluded reciprocal aid agreements with the United States by which they undertook to provide assistance for the United States where this afforded the best means of achieving the common purpose, it being understood that such aid would be taken into consideration in the final settlement. For an account of this whole Allied transaction, see Edward R. Stettinius, *Lease-Lend, Weapon for Victory*.

the hearings on it before the Senate and House Committees afforded an opportunity for public debate of the President's war-time policies; however, it successfully weathered the rocks and shoals of controversy. It was passed by the House on February 8, and by the Senate a month later. The Act was signed by the President on March 11, and on the following day he sent to Congress the first appropriation for seven billion dollars. 'The American Lease & Lend Bill was signed today', King George noted in his diary.[24]

In the meantime the King had received Mr. Harry Hopkins.[a] 'He looked rather tired after his numerous visits & countless interviews with the powers that be', he recorded. 'He is much impressed by all he has seen of what we are doing to win the war & he is already cabling the President to send us more long distance bombers & flying boats. . . . Hopkins is anxious that I should write more informal letters to F. D. R. as he likes to receive my communications.'[25] For his part the King expressed the hope that a meeting would soon be possible between the President and Mr. Churchill.[26]

The opportunity for further correspondence with Mr. Roosevelt was not long delayed. The Battle of the Atlantic now presented the gravest threat to Britain's survival. An inexhaustible reservoir of supplies had been provided by the enactment of Lend-Lease, but the transport of these vital sinews of war in the teeth of German U-boat and surface raider activity was a most perilous and costly process. In April the United States Government instituted a patrol system whereby American warships and planes 'trailing' the merchant convoys could report the presence of enemy raiders to the British, and this, though lagging behind the measures which certain of the President's advisers wished him to take, was as far as he was prepared to go at the moment in 'un-neutrality'.[27]

The King was quick to express his appreciation.

The U.S. Ambassador, Mr. Winant, & Mrs. Winant came to lunch [he wrote on April 25]. I thanked him for what America is doing to help us. The new American patrols, which have just come into force, are going a long way to solve our difficulty of

---

[a] Mr. Wendell Willkie, the defeated Republican candidate in the Presidential election of 1940, also paid a visit to Britain at this time and was received by the King on February 4, 1941.

escorting convoys. Public opinion in U.S.A. is coming round to our way of thinking faster than before. The Winants are both very silent people.

But the patrol system was not enough. It became patently clear that if British freighters were to obtain safe passage across the Atlantic they must be escorted by warships, and, further, that the United States would have to bear a part in this operation. The brief but spectacular foray of the *Bismarck* into the North Atlantic aroused much anxiety in the United States,[a] and the President seized upon the opportunity presented to make a further advance in policy. On May 27 he announced that the present rate of Nazi sinkings of merchant vessels was more than three times the capacity to replace them and more than twice the combined British and American output. To meet this situation the President proclaimed an 'unlimited state of national emergency' and outlined the counter-measures he was prepared to take :

Our patrols are helping now to ensure the delivery of needed supplies to Britain [he announced]. All additional measures necessary for the delivery of goods will be taken. . . . The delivery of needed supplies to Britain is imperative. This can be done. It must be done. It will be done. . . . The only thing we have to fear is fear itself.

This declaration, for all intents and purposes, put the United States in a 'shooting war', for American escorting vessels now had orders to defend their convoys against attacks by the enemy. King George telegraphed his enthusiastic gratitude :

The Queen and I are deeply grateful for your magnificent speech.

It has given us great encouragement and will I know stimulate us all to still greater efforts till the victory for freedom is finally won.[28]

---

[a] On May 24, 1941, the *Bismarck* and *Prinz Eugen*, raiding in the North Atlantic, were brought to action, in the course of which the battle-cruiser *Hood* was sunk off Greenland. Pursued and shadowed by British warships throughout May 25 and 26, *Bismarck* was finally engaged on May 27 by *King George V* and *Rodney*, and was sunk by torpedoes from *Dorsetshire*.

A few days later he took occasion to send a long and informal letter to the President:

June 3rd 1941

MY DEAR PRESIDENT ROOSEVELT,

It is some time ago since I last wrote to you, & in doing so now, I would like to tell you how much your last speech of May 27th has encouraged everybody in this country to carry on, knowing that the immense potential industrial strength of your country is behind us.

I have read with great interest all that you have said & done during the past months, since you have been re-elected President, & I have been so struck by the way you have led public opinion by allowing it to get ahead of you.

I often think of those talks we had at Hyde Park, when you gave me your ideas of bases & patrols in the Atlantic, & I am very glad to know now, that those ideas have become real facts.

I have had some good talks with your Ambassador Mr. Winant, who with his charming wife have made first rate contacts here, & if I may [say] so everyone is delighted with your choice. I have also made the acquaintance of Mr. Harriman [a] and Mr. Biddle,[b] & others who have paid us a visit. All of them, I feel sure, understand the difficulties of our problems here.

After so many years of anxiety, when what we wanted to happen seemed so far from realisation, it is wonderful to feel that at last our two great countries are getting together for the future betterment of the world. I do thank God that it was possible for the Queen & me to come to America in those few months before war broke out in Europe, a visit which gave us the chance to meet you & so many Americans. I can assure you we both have a very real affection in our hearts for the people of the United States.

The fortunes of war are again going against us in the Mediterranean, but your gesture of sending, direct to Suez, much needed munitions of war, will shorten the all important time factor. The spirit of the people here under the strain of the terrible & indis-

---

[a] Hon. William Averell Harriman (b. 1891), a staunch supporter of President Roosevelt's New Deal programme in the early years of his administration, was appointed special representative of the President in Britain in March 1941, and in Russia in August 1941. He subsequently returned to both countries as U.S. Ambassador, in Moscow from 1943 to 1946 and in London from April to October 1946. He served as Secretary of Commerce in President Truman's Cabinet from 1946 to 1948 and as the President's Special Assistant from 1950 to 1951. In 1954 he was elected Governor of the State of New York.

[b] Hon. Anthony Drexel Biddle, jun. (b. 1896), served as U.S. Minister to Norway, 1935–1937, as Ambassador to Poland, 1937–1941, and to the exiled Governments in London, 1941–1944. He became Chief of Foreign Contacts division of SHAEF from 1944 to 1945, and returned to the same position in SHAPE from 1951 to 1953.

criminate bombing is truly remarkable. We have visited many a 'blitzed' city & town & we have found this same spirit everywhere.

My Prime Minister, Mr. Churchill, is indefatigable at his work, with his many & great responsibilities. He is a great man, & has at last come into his own as leader of his country in this fateful time in her history. I have every confidence in him. The sinking of the 'Bismarck' was a fine achievement, the effect of which will be felt all the world over, & shows that sea power still counts.

As I know you personally I would like to feel that I can write to you direct. So many communications between Heads of State have to go through 'official channels' & I hope that you will be able to write back to me in this personal way.

The Queen & I send you & Mrs. Roosevelt our kindest regards.
          Believe me
                    Yours very sincerely
                              GEORGE R.I.[29]

(vi)

The new phase into which the war passed with the German invasion of Russia on June 22, 1941, rendered a meeting between President Roosevelt and Mr. Churchill the more desirable. There were many aspects of the conflict and of Anglo-American co-operation which necessitated personal contact and a mutual knowledge of personalities. Both men had long desired a meeting, and King George himself had urged its expediency upon Mr. Hopkins six months before. The difficulty had been to decide upon the psychological moment and the most suitable rendezvous.

When, therefore, at the end of July Mr. Hopkins, on his second mission to Britain, brought to Mr. Churchill the President's invitation to a meeting in some northern bay early in August and the Prime Minister sought the King's permission to accept, it was granted with alacrity and satisfaction.

I am very glad [wrote His Majesty from Windsor on July 25] that you are at last to have the opportunity of making his [the President's] acquaintance and, as I told you before, I am sure that there is much to be gained by a meeting between you. I readily assent to your proposals, for I feel that circumstances are very different now from what they were when you first mentioned the idea to me at the end of February. In fact I do not think that one would be likely to find a better moment for you to be out of the country, though I confess that I shall breathe a sigh of relief when you are safely home again! As you rightly say, a flying boat could bring you back in a few hours from Newfoundland should any emergency arise.

Thus it was that on the morning of Saturday, August 9, the newest British battleship, *Prince of Wales*, sailed into Placentia Bay, Newfoundland, there to make rendezvous with the U.S.S. *Augusta*, and two 'former naval persons' [a] held their first historic meeting. Mr. Churchill's first act was to cable to the King the news of his safe arrival, and, on going aboard *Augusta*, he handed to the President a letter from King George.

MY DEAR PRESIDENT ROOSEVELT,

This is just a line to bring you my best wishes, and to say how glad I am that you have an opportunity at last of getting to know my Prime Minister. I am sure you will agree that he is a very remarkable man, and I have no doubt that your meeting will prove of great benefit to our two countries in pursuit of our common goal.

Believe me
Yours very sincerely
GEORGE R.I.[31]

The meeting of minds which occurred during the next three days had many beneficial results for the Allied war effort and for Anglo-American relations.[b] The President and the Prime Minister established a community of ideas from which evolved the first stages of that grand politico-military strategy which ultimately achieved a final victory. For many reasons also their thinking was directed even further afield, towards that day when victory should give them the opportunity and the responsibility for making peace. It was to this end that, before they separated, they agreed upon a joint declaration laying down certain broad principles which should give to the world a hope of better things to come.

[a] In the course of their political careers, Mr. Churchill had twice been First Lord of the Admiralty, and Mr. Roosevelt had served as Assistant Secretary of the Navy. At the outbreak of the war Mr. Chamberlain had arranged to keep the President informed on the war situation. He delegated this task to Mr. Churchill, and since these communications were, in a sense, unofficial, they were signed 'Naval Person'. When Mr. Churchill became Prime Minister the President addressed his replies to 'the former Naval Person' and, though after Pearl Harbour the exchange of messages was on a direct and official basis, this method of address continued to appear in informal messages.[30]

[b] For an account of the Atlantic Conference and of the formulation of the Atlantic Charter, see Mr. Churchill's memoirs, iii, pp. 380-400. See also H. V. Morton, *The Atlantic Meeting*, (London, 1943).

JOINT DECLARATION BY THE PRESIDENT
AND THE PRIME MINISTER
August 12th, 1941

The President of the United States of America and the Prime Minister, Mr. Churchill, representing His Majesty's Government in the United Kingdom, being met together, deem it right to make known certain common principles in the national policies of their respective countries on which they base their hopes for a better future for the world.

First, their countries seek no aggrandisement, territorial or other.

Second, they desire to see no territorial changes that do not accord with the freely expressed wishes of the peoples concerned.

Third, they respect the right of all peoples to choose the form of government under which they will live ; and they wish to see sovereign rights and self-government restored to those who have been forcibly deprived of them.

Fourth, they will endeavour, with due respect to their existing obligations, to further the enjoyment of all States, great or small, victor or vanquished, of access, on equal terms, to the trade and to the raw materials of the world which are needed for their economic prosperity.

Fifth, they desire to bring about the fullest collaboration between all nations in the economic field, with the object of securing for all improved labour standards, economic advancement, and social security.

Sixth, after the final destruction of the Nazi tyranny they hope to see established a peace which will afford to all nations the means of dwelling in safety within their own boundaries, and which will afford assurance that all the men in all the lands may live out their lives in freedom from fear and want.

Seventh, such a peace should enable all men to traverse the high seas and oceans without hindrances.

Eighth, they believe that all the nations of the world, for realistic as well as spiritual reasons, must come to the abandonment of the use of force. Since no future peace can be maintained if land, sea, or air armaments continue to be employed by nations which threaten, or may threaten, aggression outside of their frontiers, they believe, pending the establishment of a wider and more permanent system of general security, that the disarmament of such nations is essential. They will likewise aid and encourage all other practicable measures which will lighten for peace-loving peoples the crushing burden of armaments.

The effect of the Atlantic Charter upon the world at large was in the main salutary, but there were those who, while welcoming this profession of aspiration and intent, discerned with some apprehension a certain historical parallel with President Wilson's Fourteen Points.   Unless the United States became a belligerent and a full partner in the responsibility of rebuilding the post-war world, the whole onus of this task would fall upon Britain, imposing a staggering burden which she might not be able to carry alone.

These doubts and uncertainties were apparent among King George's first reactions to the Charter, as revealed in his record of conversation with his Ministers in London.   Its provisions would be very difficult to carry out, he told Capt. David Margesson, 'as we should have to do it ourselves.   The U.S.A. had deserted us after the Great War in Europe & might easily do so again if she does not come in and feel the effects' ; [32]   and to Mr. Mackenzie King he expressed the view that until the United States declared war upon Germany, 'the American people will never realize what the war means to *us* or to them in the long run'.[33]

The joint statement said all the right things [the King wrote to Queen Mary], but how are we going to carry them out ?   Most of the peoples of Europe will have forgotten that they ever had a Govt. of their own when the war is over.   America & ourselves will have to feed them in Europe for years & years.

I am so glad it was possible for those two men to meet at last, & to discuss all our problems together.   I knew Winston was longing for it, & this time was just the right moment for the meeting to take place.[34]

Some of His Majesty's misgivings were doubtless dispelled when on August 19 he received a report from Mr. Churchill on the whole course of the Atlantic Conference.

The Prime Minister came to lunch [he wrote in his diary].   He gave me a very full account of his meeting & talks with F. D. R., also those with the U.S.A. Service Chiefs.   F. D. R. told him that at the moment he would not declare war but that he would wage war with us, against Germany, as evidenced by taking over all convoy work to Iceland.   W. was greatly taken by him, & has come back feeling that he knows him.   He had several talks with him alone, when W. put our position to him very bluntly.   If by the Spring, Russia was down & out, & Germany was renewing her blitzkrieg here, all our hopes of victory & help from U.S.A. would be dashed if America had not by then sent us masses of planes etc,

or had not entered the war.   F. D. R. has got £3,000,000,000 to
spend on us here.   On the general situation W. told me the Atlantic
was much better, he thought Japan would remain quiet.

Mr. Churchill also brought to the King the following letter
from President Roosevelt, written in *Augusta* on the penultimate
day of the Conference.

MY DEAR KING GEORGE :
We are at anchor in this Newfoundland harbor close to H.M.S.
Prince of Wales and I have had three delightful and useful days
with Mr. Churchill and the heads of your three services.   It has
been a privilege to come to know Mr. Churchill in this way and I
am very confident that our minds travel together, and that our
talks are bearing practical fruit for both nations.
I wish that you could have been with us at Divine Service
yesterday on the quarterdeck of your latest battleship.   I shall
never forget it.   Your officers and men were mingled with about
three hundred of ours, spread over the turrets and superstructure —
I hope you will see the movie of it.
Will you be good enough to tell the Queen that her radio
address yesterday was really perfect in every way and that it will
do a great amount of good.
We think of you both often and wish we could be of more help
— But we are daily gaining in confidence in the outcome — We
know you will keep up the good work.
                    With my very warm regards,
                    Sincerely yours,
                                FRANKLIN D. ROOSEVELT.[35]

Throughout the autumn of 1941 the margin between
American co-belligerency and outright war dwindled perceptibly and public opinion in the United States rallied more
and more in support of the President — a remarkable feature
being that, since the Nazi invasion of Russia, the Communist
Party in America had become as wildly interventionist as it
had been previously uncompromisingly isolationist.   There
were now many who felt with Alice Duer Miller that

> In a world where England is finished and dead
> I do not wish to live.[a]

But there were also an appreciable number who perceived the
fact that in such a world the United States would have to

[a] *The White Cliffs.* King George had read this poem during a bout of
influenza and had noted certain passages from it in his diary.[36]

fight a grim battle alone for their independence and freedom. 'Public opinion is distinctly better than six months ago', President Roosevelt wrote to King George on October 15. 'In fact it is more strongly with us than is the Congress.'[37]

A month later, however, Congressional opinion had itself progressed in response to an appeal from the President, and the King could record with gratification the following entry in his diary :

Yesterday [November 14] [a] came the news that the House of Representatives in U.S.A. had passed by 18 votes the Bill to amend the Neutrality Act so as [to] allow U.S. merchantmen to sail to war zones. This is a very great help to us, though it appears the President had to send a special message to Congress to have it passed. America is not nearly ready for war. But she will wake up when the enemy sink armed U.S. merchantmen.[38]

It was, however, from the East and not from the West that there came the final impetus which drove America into war. The Sino-Japanese War had been maintained with desultory activity throughout the conflict in Europe, but the defeat of France and the collapse of her authority in Indo-China had presented fresh opportunities for Japanese intrusion upon that country and upon Siam. Shortly after the Atlantic Conference President Roosevelt had issued a solemn warning to the Japanese Government that further encroachment in the South-West Pacific would produce a situation in which the United States would be compelled to take such counter-measures as might be considered necessary to safeguard the rights, interests and security of the United States.[39]

The President had confided some of his anxieties to King George in his letter of October 15 : 'I am a bit worried over the Japanese situation at this moment', he had written. 'The Emperor is for peace, I think, but the Jingoes are trying to force his hand.' The United States Government spared no effort to sustain the endeavours of the moderates in Tokyo, with the apparently hopeful result that on November 15 there arrived in Washington a special emissary, Admiral Saburo Kurusu, who, with the Ambassador, Kichisaburo Nomura, was charged to explore the possibilities of a settlement.

[a] The Bill was passed by the House on November 13, 1941.

These, however, grew perceptibly fainter and the danger of an ultimate break became apparent in both London and in Washington. But the Japanese emissaries still continued their sterile talks with Mr. Cordell Hull, and on December 6 President Roosevelt, in an attempt to strengthen the Mikado's hand, addressed to him a personal plea for peace.[40] This final gesture was, however, fruitless. On the morning of December 7 the chicanery of Japanese policy was unmasked and treachery struck from a clear sky. The King received the news at Windsor :

Saturday, Sunday & Monday, Dec. 6th, 7th & 8th
A bomb shell arrived in the 9 o'clock News (B.B.C.) saying that the Japanese had bombed Pearl Harbour in Honolulu, the U.S. Fleet base, without any warning. The P.M. sent me word that Kelantan in Malaya had also been raided with troop landings, by the Japanese. On Monday the U.S.A. & ourselves declared ourselves at war with Japan as an answer to her unprovoked aggression on our respective territories. The Japanese negotiator Kurusu was talking to Mr. Hull when he received the news. The U.S.-Jap conversations were being prolonged on purpose so that the Japanese Fleet & Army could take up their strategic positions for a lightning attack on American islands in the Pacific without warning. The preparations must have taken weeks, probably months to prepare. F. D. R. sent a special message personally to the Japanese Emperor asking him to prevent war between their 2 countries.

The full tidings of the disaster were told to the King by Mr. Churchill at their weekly luncheon on the Tuesday (December 9).

The Prime Minister came to lunch. He gave me the latest news from America which was dreadful. In Pearl Harbour 3 U.S. Battleships were sunk & 3 seriously damaged. There are now only 2 effective U.S. ships in the Pacific, which means that U.S.A. has already lost command of the sea in the Pacific. A very serious situation for our ships the P of W & Repulse who are out there. The reaction on Americans will probably be an attack on F. D. R.'s Administration for not being prepared, not even the Fleet. Fancy the U.S. Fleet being in harbour when the authorities must have known that Japan was already on a war footing. W. told me he is anxious to go to Washington to arrange various matters with F. D. R.

Catastrophe, however, was not visited upon the Americans alone. Simultaneously with the Japanese attacks upon Hawaii and the Philippines came assaults upon Hong Kong and Malaya, each bringing with it a trail of calamity. The King had left London for a tour of South Wales industrial centres, and it was at Bargoed, on Wednesday December 10, that grievous news overtook him. He was about to leave when Sir Alan Lascelles was called to the telephone to be told that the great battleship *Prince of Wales*, which only a few months before had borne Mr. Churchill triumphantly to the Atlantic Conference, had been sunk by Japanese air attack, and that with her had gone the battle-cruiser *Repulse*.

This news, terrible in itself to any sailor, was doubly direful to one who knew the parlous condition of the Fleet; yet the King gave no sign to those about him of the shock which he had suffered. The tour continued as usual and His Majesty's demeanour was undisturbed. Only that evening did he write in his diary:

Just before leaving Bargoed I was told that both the 'P. of W.' & the 'Repulse' had been sunk by air attack off the Malayan coast. This came as a very real shock, knowing what their loss means to us in those waters We cannot spare any ships to replace them.

That same day in the Royal Train he wrote to the Prime Minister:

The news of the loss of the 'Prince of Wales' & 'Repulse' came as a great shock to the Queen & me when we were on our tour in S. Wales to-day. For all of us it is a national disaster, & I fear will create consternation in Australia. The lack of details makes the fact harder to bear, coming as it does on top of yesterday's bad news re the U.S. battleships. I thought I was getting immune to hearing bad news, but this has affected me deeply as I am sure it has you. There is something particularly 'alive' about a big ship, which gives one a sense of personal loss apart from consideration of loss of power.

In the comradeship of common loss His Majesty telegraphed to President Roosevelt:

My thoughts and prayers go out to you and to the great people of the United States at this solemn moment in your history when you have been treacherously attacked by Japan. We are proud indeed to be fighting at your side against the common enemy. We share your inflexible determination and your confidence that with God's help the powers of darkness will be overcome and the four freedoms established throughout a world purged of tyranny.[41]

And it was with the tragedies of Pearl Harbour and Malaya in his mind that he spoke to his peoples on Christmas Day: 'The range of the tremendous conflict is ever widening. It now extends to the Pacific Ocean. Truly it is a stern and solemn time. But as the war widens, so surely our conviction deepens of the greatness of our cause.'

CHAPTER VIII

THE TIDE OF VICTORY
1942–1943

(i)

W HEN Mr. Churchill returned to London in January 1942, after his first conference with President Roosevelt subsequent to America's entry into the war,[a] he told King George that 'he was now confident of ultimate victory, as the United States of America were longing to get to grips with the enemy and were starting on a full output of men and material; the U.K. and U.S.A. were now "married" after many months of "walking out".'[1] The Prime Minister was, in the long view, entirely justified in his optimism. The Japanese bombs which fell upon Pearl Harbour and Manila on December 7/8, 1941, achieved, at one stroke, what President Roosevelt, with all his genius of statesmanship, might never have accomplished; the virtual destruction of her Pacific Fleet brought a united America into the war. Nevertheless, the first seven months of 1942 were a record of almost unrelieved disaster for the Allied cause and it would have been a brave man who would have risked his reputation on the prophecy that by the end of that year the Tide of Victory would be running strongly.

To the initial catastrophes suffered by the American Fleet at Pearl Harbour and by the British squadron off the Malayan coast, there was added an additional naval mortification when the three German warships, *Scharnhorst*, *Gneisenau* and *Prinz*

[a] The sequence of events was as follows: Japan declared herself at war with the United States and the United Kingdom as from December 8, 1941. On the same day both these countries declared war on Japan. On December 11 Germany and Italy declared war on the United States and on the same day Congress responded with a formal declaration of war. Mr. Churchill left England for conferences in Washington and Ottawa on December 12, 1941, and returned on January 17, 1942.

Eugen, so long blockaded in Brest, so frequently the unattained target of aerial attack, effected their escape on the night of February 11/12 and fled unscathed up the Channel to the protection of northern minefields.   The incident, of minor importance in comparison with the reverses which had occurred and were to follow, nevertheless caused great indignation in Britain, where it was regarded as a serious blow to national and naval prestige.

This episode, however, paled into insignificance beside the news which followed four days later.   On February 15 the great island fortress of Singapore, with its garrison of some 60,000-70,000 men, surrendered to the Japanese after a siege of two weeks and despite Mr. Churchill's impassioned exhortation that 'Commanders and Senior officers should die with their troops.   The honour of the British Empire and of the British Army is at stake.'[2]

The reaction in Britain to what the Prime Minister himself described as 'the greatest disaster to British arms which our history records' was one of anger and dismay, and for the the first time since assuming office in May 1940, Mr. Churchill found his direction of the war the target of serious criticism from the press and public and in the House of Commons.   His leadership of the nation was not in question, but there was an increasing demand for the reconstruction of his administration, and for the greater delegation on his own part of some of the crushing burden of responsibility which hitherto he had carried alone.

To King George the ill-tidings of that black February week-end came as a severe shock and he was deeply despondent both for the fortunes of war and for the fortunes of his Prime Minister.   'I am very depressed over the loss of Singapore and the fact that we were not able to prevent the 3 German ships from getting through the Channel', he wrote to Queen Mary.   'We are going through a bad phase at the moment, and it will take all our energies to stop adverse comment and criticism from the Press and others.'[3]   It was the strictures upon his chief Minister that he greatly deplored.   That loyalty which he had shown to Mr. Chamberlain had now been transferred to Mr. Churchill and he resented the adverse comment in time of national crisis.   'I do wish people would get on with the job and not criticise all the time, but in a free country this has to be put up with ', he wrote at this time to his uncle, the Earl of Athlone, then Governor-General of Canada.

So distressed was His Majesty that he instructed his Private Secretary 'to find out what is in people's minds about all this', and in his diary, over the week-end of February 14/16, he recorded at Windsor the results of Sir Alexander Hardinge's inquiries. Those whom he had sounded were all

agreed & so is everyone else, that Winston is the right, & indeed the only person to lead the country through the war. But there is a growing feeling that owing to his innumerable preoccupations, there may well be aspects of Defence which do not get all the attention that they should. This feeling is developing into one of exasperation, as our reverses continue. These reverses will certainly continue for longer still, and it is therefore essential that a form of reorganization should take place now, otherwise the next storm may not be weathered, & the Government brought down with all its grave consequences.

There are 2 reasons for a reconstruction of the Government and a reorganization of the higher direction of the war.

(1) The persistent, if perhaps unavoidable, reverses to our arms are beginning to undermine the confidence of the people in the conduct of the war by their present leaders.

(2) The extension of the war to the Pacific is imposing too great a burden for any one individual to carry, who is both Minister of Defence and Prime Minister, and the impairment of Mr. Churchill's health would be in the nature of a national disaster.

I told Alec [was the King's comment] that probably he, Churchill, would make some alterations but that he would wish to remain Minister of Defence with all it entails.[4]

His Majesty's forecast could not have been more accurate. When the Prime Minister came to his weekly Tuesday luncheon on February 17 the King records that he was 'very angry about all this, and compares it to hunting the tiger with angry wasps about him'. He denied that he was directing the war as Minister of Defence but asserted that 'if he is to lead this country he must know everything'. He was determined to continue as Minister of Defence but was fully prepared to overhaul and reconstruct his Government. This in effect he did two days later.

Within the War Cabinet were retained Mr. Attlee, Mr. Eden, Sir John Anderson, Mr. Oliver Lyttelton and Mr. Ernest Bevin. Sir Kingsley Wood and Mr. Greenwood were dropped and the Prime Minister made the hardy experiment of adding Sir Stafford Cripps,[a] who had lately returned from Moscow, as Lord Privy Seal and Leader of the House of Commons. With this newly constituted team Mr. Churchill faced the House and won a vote of confidence on February 25.

The King heard of the changes with satisfaction. 'I am glad Winston has been prevailed upon to make them before and not after the debate', was his comment. 'The House of Commons wants Winston to lead them; but they don't like the way he treats them. He likes getting his own way with no interference from anybody and nobody will stand for that sort of treatment in this country.'[5]

Something even of Mr. Churchill's great confidence seems to have deserted him at this moment of Allied tribulation. At one of their weekly luncheons he told the King in a moment of despondency that 'Burma, Ceylon, Calcutta & Madras in India & part of Australia may fall into enemy hands', and his dejection was reflected in His Majesty's comment: 'Can we stick together in the face of all this adversity? We must somehow.'[6]

At the close of the fifth volume of his diary on February 28, 1942, he wrote: 'I cannot help feeling depressed at the future outlook. Anything can happen, & it will be wonderful if we can be lucky anywhere.'

There was no hint, however, of this depression in the letter which the King sent to President Roosevelt a few days later by the hand of his brother-in-law, Mr. David Bowes-Lyon, then proceeding to Washington on government business.

---

[a] Rt. Hon. Sir Stafford Cripps, C.H., K.C. (1889–1952), sat in the House of Commons from 1931 to 1950 as Labour member for East Bristol. He was Solicitor-General in Mr. MacDonald's second administration from 1930 to 1931, and thereafter his relation with the Labour Party became strained. In 1932 he formed the Socialist League and was later formally expelled from the Party. He was readmitted, however, in May 1940, and on the formation of Mr. Churchill's National Government he was appointed Ambassador to Moscow, 1940–1942. On his return to London he served successively as Lord Privy Seal, 1942, and as Minister of Aircraft Production, 1942–1945. With the return of Labour to power he became President of the Board of Trade, 1945–1947, Minister of Economic Affairs in 1947 and Chancellor of the Exchequer from 1947 till 1950, when he resigned for reasons of health.

March 11th, 1942

My dear President Roosevelt,

Since his return, my Prime Minister has told me of the many talks you & he had together at the White House, when you were able to settle so many matters vital to the war effort of our two countries. I am so glad that you & he have got to know each other, as I have always thought how important it would be for our complete cooperation. Much has happened since last December when Japan made those treacherous attacks on our territories to her advantage, but she has not counted the cost of the settlement we shall mete out to her with our combined strength when it comes into play. We have had to suffer reverses in the Pacific, but please God that the combined forces of our two countries will act together in redeeming them. Mr. Churchill has shown me your very encouraging reply to his long telegram in which you tell him how you can help us.[7] Shipping is our one great obstacle in retarding our immediate aims, but though it will take time & great effort on all our parts to prepare, the final issue i.e. Victory is without any doubt to be with us.[8]

A few weeks later King George was brought into personal contact with the representative of Britain's other major ally, the Soviet Union. Mr. Molotov arrived secretly in London on May 2, *en route* for Washington, with plans for the consolidation of those territorial advantages which Russia had obtained under her ill-fated pact with Hitler.

The U.S.S.R. was now demanding Britain's formal approval of her annexation of the Baltic States, of Eastern Poland and of Bessarabia, and the recognition of her new frontier with Finland. Such procedure was contrary to the views of Britain and the United States, who were anxious to postpone all discussion of territorial changes until after victory had been won and then to effect a general settlement in consonance with the principles of the Atlantic Charter, to which Stalin had adhered. As an alternative to the Soviet proposals Mr. Eden suggested an Anglo-Soviet Treaty of Alliance for twenty years, phrased in general terms and omitting all reference to frontiers, and to this Mr. Molotov eventually agreed with some reluctance. The Agreement was signed on May 26.

The King had received the Soviet Foreign Minister on May 22 and had gained the impression that 'he looks a small quiet man with a feeble voice, but is really a tyrant. He was quite polite.' He later wrote to Queen Mary:

. . . You will be surprised to hear that I saw Molotov the Soviet Foreign Minister before Whitsun, when he was here in conversations over the Treaty, which Eden & Stalin discussed in Moscow last December. He (M) was very difficult over the Frontier question of the Baltic States & Poland, & would not understand that we could not leave Poland in the lurch. The matter became a deadlock & Eden then gave Molotov a new Treaty to consider, which is a mutual assistance pact for now & after the war, & has nothing to do with frontiers. Winant helped us a lot over this when he impressed on Molotov that America did not like the Frontier Treaty as it went against the Atlantic Charter. The outcome of all this has been that Molotov came round & signed the new Treaty before going on to U.S.A. The secret has been well kept & it will not come out until M. returns to Russia. We now have some sort of hold over Russia & both sides seem happy about it. Molotov is a quiet man, but with a twinkle in his eye & a sense of humour. Maisky was interpreter. He was quite polite, & probably his visit here has made him understand the meaning of personal contacts. . . .[9]

But the tide of disaster persisted. On April 9 the surrender of General Wainwright at Corregidor brought to an end the last gallant resistance of the American and Philippine forces on the Bataan Peninsula. By the end of April the British and Netherlands possessions in the East Indies had been overrun by the enemy and Allied opposition to the Japanese in the South Pacific area had completely broken down. A month later British and Chinese forces had been driven from Burma and the Japanese armies stood upon the threshold of the Indian Empire. Almost it seemed that Mr. Churchill's recent prognostication would be fulfilled.

Now, too, there began at home that series of 'Baedeker Raids' by the Luftwaffe upon the historic cities of England in retaliation for British bombing of German industrial centres. Exeter, Bath, Norwich and York suffered heavily, with no material benefit to the enemy. The King was indignant. 'It is outrageous that the Germans should come & bomb our Cathedral cities & towns like Bath'; he wrote, 'which they know are undefended & contain no war industries, as "Reprisals" raids for what we are doing to their war industries.' [10]

Worse was to come. In Russia the German armies crossing the Don on a broad front reached Rostov; and in Africa Rommel's counter-offensive threatened the very gates of Cairo. Opening his attack on May 26, the 'Desert Fox' forced the evacuation by the French of Bir Hachim on June 11 and laid siege to Tobruk a week later. The unexpected surrender of this strongly garrisoned position took place on June 20 and Rommel swept eastwards out of Libya into Egypt, reaching El Alamein — 60 miles west of Alexandria — on July 1.

At this nadir in Allied fortunes it required a stout heart and staunch resolution to continue the struggle. Only the blind belief in the essential justice of the cause for which we fought and confidence that time was on our side could uphold the hope of ultimate victory, when all seemed dark. The faith of many was expressed in lines written by an Irish poet at this time :

> Through the dense fog of war
> I see nothing clearly ;
> Nothing at all, nothing at all.
> But one fixed star :
> England's star merely.
> By it I stand or fall,
> Loving her dearly.[a]

On the Westminster front the effect of this general depression and uncertainty found expression in open censure of the Prime Minister. Once again Mr. Churchill's critics nerved themselves to make a direct challenge to his leadership, and on June 23 Sir John Wardlaw-Milne [b] gave notice of a motion of censure on the Government for its direction of the war. Mr. Churchill was in Washington when the news reached him — he was in fact engaged in the early preparation for that operation in North Africa which was to change the undertow of defeat into the rip-tide of victory — but he immediately flew home and faced his critics in the House of Commons

---

[a] These lines by Conal O'Riordan appeared in *Punch* on July 1, 1942.

[b] Sir John Wardlaw-Milne, K.B.E. (b. 1878), had served on the Legislative Council of the Governor of Bombay and on the Council of the Governor-General of India. As Conservative Member for Kidderminster, he sat in the House of Commons from 1922 to 1945, being Chairman of the Select Committee on National Expenditure, 1939-1945, and Chairman of the Conservative Foreign Affairs Committee for the same period.

on July 1. There he listened to the proposal of Sir John Wardlaw-Milne that the office of Minister of Defence should be divorced from that of Prime Minister, and to his more reactionary suggestion — in that it harked back to the days of the Duke of Cambridge [a] — that the Duke of Gloucester should be appointed Commander-in-Chief of the British Army.

On this occasion, however, there was to be no repetition of those events which had brought down Mr. Asquith in 1916 or Mr. Chamberlain in 1940. Mr. Churchill, in winding up the debate with a reasoned and rational defence of his policies, had no difficulty in disposing of what he later described to King George as '"The weaker brethren" in the House of Commons'.[11] When the vote was taken the censure motion was defeated by 475 to 25, with about thirty abstentions, a result which the Prime Minister later described as 'proof to the world of the inflexible steadiness of Parliament and of its sense of proportion'.

The actual turning of the tide in the Second World War may be accurately determined as the first week of July 1942. After Rommel was repulsed at El Alamein on July 2 and turned away in deference to British resistance,[b] the Germans never again mounted a major offensive in North Africa; while in Russia the summer offensive of the Red Army marked the beginning of their ruthless and remorseless progress from the Don to the Elbe. In Asia and in the Pacific the Japanese advance had also been stayed, and the landing of American troops on the Solomon Islands on August 7 proved to be the first step on a bloody road to hard-won victory.[c] On all fronts the ascendancy passed from the enemy to the Allies and shortly thereafter there began that series of Conferences at which, parallel with the plans concerted for the ultimate

[a] Field-Marshal His Royal Highness Prince George William Frederick Charles, second Duke of Cambridge (1819–1904), a grandson of George III, was Commander-in-Chief of the British Army from 1856 to 1895.

[b] The British counter-attack before El Alamein on July 2 was directed in person by the Commander-in-Chief, Sir Claude Auchinleck, who had taken over the command of the 8th Army from General Ritchie. On August 18 General Auchinleck was succeeded as Commander-in-Chief Middle East by General Sir Harold Alexander, and Lieutenant-General Montgomery assumed the command of the 8th Army.

[c] The Japanese had already sustained naval defeats at the hands of the American Navy at the Battles of the Coral Sea (May 4) and of Midway Island (June 4).

defeat of Germany, Italy and Japan, policy was formulated for the exploitation of that victory when peace should be attained.

The position was adequately epitomized by President Roosevelt in a letter to King George :

Perhaps I can sum it up by saying that on the whole the situation of all of us is better in the Autumn of 1942 than it was last Spring, and that, while 1943 will not see a complete victory for us, things are on the up-grade, while things for the Axis have reached the peak of their effectiveness.[12]

(ii)

The constitutional path of King George VI's reign was smooth in comparison with that of his father. Though the changes in the political structure of the United Kingdom and of the British Commonwealth which occurred during his reign were of the most far-reaching, they were achieved in the main by consent and were not marked by the bitter controversy which clouded the latter years of King Edward VII and the beginning of King George V's tenure of the Throne. He was called upon to make no such vital constitutional decision as that involved in his father's pledge to Mr. Asquith to create a sufficiency of peers to secure the passage of legislation in the Upper House, nor were his choices in the matter of Prime Ministers accompanied by any major searchings of heart, save those of his own preference.

Nevertheless King George VI had the experience — surely unique among British Sovereigns — of having advice tendered to him on two occasions by his Prime Minister in respect of the succession to the premiership in the event of that office becoming vacant, not by political defeat or by death from natural causes, but by the death of the existing incumbent as a result of enemy action or of war-time contingencies.

The new totality of war — and the emphasis placed by Mr. Churchill on the importance of personal contact and discussion between himself and the political leaders of the United States and the Soviet Union — rendered him vulnerable in the course of his peregrinations to possible attack by enemy U-boats or aircraft or to the tragedy of fatal accident.

The possibility of this danger had occurred to some, if not to the Prime Minister himself, during Mr. Churchill's voyage to meet President Roosevelt off the coast of Newfoundland. On this occasion Mr. Attlee had expressed anxiety lest the German battleship *Tirpitz* should attempt to sink or capture the *Prince of Wales*, but to this Mr. Churchill had responded : 'I fear there will be no such luck'.[13]   However, when the King himself took cognizance of the hazards involved, the Prime Minister had to tender his advice.

At the Tuesday luncheon which preceded Mr. Churchill's departure for Washington in June 1942, the King asked the Prime Minister whom he would recommend as his successor in the untoward event of his death, and in a letter dated the same day (June 16) Mr. Churchill formally tendered advice that His Majesty should entrust the formation of a new government to Mr. Anthony Eden, 'who is in my mind the outstanding Minister in the largest political party in the House of Commons and in the National Government over which I have the honour to preside'.[14]

Thus the succession was secured, but, as the war proceeded, the duties of the Foreign Secretary took Mr. Eden himself more and more frequently on journeys abroad attended by the same dangers.   At length the time came — the occasion was the eve of the Yalta Conference of February 1945 — when both he and Mr. Churchill were to be absent simultaneously from the country.   King George again sought counsel of his Prime Minister and received from him the advice, unusual in itself, that, should both Mr. Eden and himself be killed on this forthcoming journey, the King should send for a person who was neither a professional politician nor a member of the Conservative Party.   Mr. Churchill gave his reasons for this choice clearly and in some detail :

10 DOWNING STREET
WHITEHALL

SIR,

The Prime Minister, with his humble duty, obeys Your Majesty's request to tender advice in respect of a successor to himself if both he and Mr. Eden, whose name has already been submitted, should be killed during this forthcoming journey.

The Prime Minister feels that this advice should be tendered by him in relation to the position which would be created if both he and Mr. Eden were killed at the same time during these next few months or even weeks when the war against Germany hangs in the balance and when a National Coalition Government is functioning. As Your Majesty is no doubt aware, Sir John Anderson [a] has not declared himself a Member of the Conservative Party, which has a very large majority over all other Parties in the House of Commons. He is returned as an Independent Member for the Scottish Universities. In ordinary circumstances Mr. Churchill would have advised Your Majesty to make sure that you send for a man whom the Conservative Party would choose as Leader, they having the Parliamentary majority. It may also be considered very probable that any Conservative for whom Your Majesty might send would immediately be chosen as Leader of the Conservative Party on account of the profound respect which that Party bears to the gestures of the Crown. However, till the end of the German war, it is necessary to consider the maintenance of the present harmonious Coalition whose services will, the Prime Minister is sure, never be forgotten by Your Majesty or by the people, having regard to the extraordinary perils through which we have safely passed. It would therefore seem very appropriate that during the continuance of the Coalition a Prime Minister should be chosen who would not necessarily be the Leader of the Conservative Party, though that might well follow, but would be adapted by character and outlook, and by the general regard attaching to him well qualified to sustain the existing all-Party Government.

In this case there can be no doubt that it is the Prime Minister's duty to advise Your Majesty to send for Sir John Anderson in the event of the Prime Minister and the Foreign Secretary being killed.

A new situation would possibly arise after a General Election had been fought. If a Conservative Party were returned with a majority perhaps as large as they have to-day, they might desire that Sir John Anderson should become a Member of their Party or they might choose a Leader of their own. It is very likely that there will be a substantial Conservative majority in the new Parliament; but it by no means follows that that majority would not accept Sir John Anderson as Prime Minister with or without his acceptance of the Leadership of the Conservative Party. The Prime Minister therefore feels that Your Majesty would be acting not only in harmony with Constitutional usage, but also with the practical needs of the time in sending for Sir John Anderson in the contingency referred to.

It would, of course, in Mr. Churchill's humble opinion, be

[a] Rt. Hon. John Anderson, first Viscount Waverley, G.C.B., O.M., G.C.S.I., G.C.I.E. (1882–1958), entered the Colonial Office in 1905; Governor of Bengal, 1932–1937; M.P. (Nat.) Scottish Universities, 1938–1950; Lord Privy Seal, 1938–1939; Home Secretary and Minister of Home Security, 1939–1940; Lord President of the Council, 1940–1943; Chancellor of the Exchequer, 1943–1945. He was awarded the Order of Merit on his sick-bed in December 1957, shortly before his death in the following month.

contrary to the spirit of the Constitution to send for anyone in any way obnoxious to the Party which holds predominance in the House of Commons at the actual moment.

With his humble duty Mr. Churchill remains

Your Majesty's faithful and devoted servant,

WINSTON S. CHURCHILL.[a]

This very remarkable document is of interest in a number of aspects. It is certainly unique that a living Prime Minister should have designated the succession of the premiership, as it were, 'to the third and the fourth generation', and it constitutes an important interpretation of the relative rôles of Sovereign and Minister. Mr. Churchill was undoubtedly within his rights in tendering his advice since the King had asked for it, but it is interesting to speculate on the reception which his recommendation would have been afforded in the event of the King's having had to adopt it. The proposal of a non-party man, of distinguished record, to lead a National Government is logical but without precedent and therefore daring, and one wonders whether the King, if he decided to pursue this course, would have consulted the various leaders of the parties composing the National Government before sending for Sir John Anderson. He would, of course, have been fully justified in so doing, since, as Sir Ivor Jennings has written: 'Except when the Government resigns after a defeat, he [the King] has a choice which he must exercise in such a way as to secure the strongest Government in the minimum time.' [15] To do this he must secure the best information available, whether from party leaders or elder statesmen. On the other hand, the King would have been equally correct in taking Mr. Churchill's precautionary counsel *au pied de la lettre* and in sending for Sir John Anderson without more ado.

Happily, however, the occasion for resolving these problems pragmatically did not arise.

(iii)

The summer of 1942 brought personal bereavement to King George. On August 25, his youngest brother, George, Duke of Kent, was killed in line of duty, in the fortieth year of his life.

---

[a] By an oversight Mr. Churchill omitted to put a date on the original of this letter which is among the Royal Archives. The archives of No. 10 Downing Street, however, establish the fact that the letter was written on January 28, 1945.

Animated, handsome and charming, the Duke of Kent had come into his own during the war. A happily married family man, at the outbreak of hostilities he was Governor-General designate of the Commonwealth of Australia, but he at once requested a more active part in the national war effort, his over-powering desire being to render useful service to his Sovereign and his country. The difficulties which attended the employ-ment of the King's brother in time of war were many, and not the least of them was the fact that his station carried with it the rank of Air Marshal. This difficulty the Duke himself solved at the outset. Waiving his pre-war rank, he accepted that of Air Commodore and for some time performed the normal routine duties which that rank entailed. This sphere of interest broadened, however, and the field that he made his own was that of the welfare and comfort of the Royal Air Force at home and abroad, his efforts yielding continuous and useful results. In the summer of 1941 he had made a wide tour of inspec-tion of the Empire training scheme in Canada, which had ended with a brief visit to the United States, where, in renewing memories of their first meeting in 1935, he had made a very favourable impression upon President Roosevelt. 'We had such a good time together at Hyde Park', the President wrote to King George, 'I had a great affection for him.'[16]

The affection was mutual, and when the younger son of the Duke and Duchess of Kent was born on July 4, 1942 — Independence Day — it was but natural that the President of the United States should be among his godfathers.

George & Marina's son was christened [the King wrote in his diary at Windsor on August 4]. Mama was here, also Uncle Charles [King of Norway], George of G[reece] & other members of the family. The baby was named Michael George Charles Franklin. F. D. R. is a godfather as he was born on July 4th.

Three weeks later the Duke was to leave on a further tour of R.A.F. establishments. On Tuesday August 25 he was airborne from Scotland *en route* for Iceland; shortly there-after he and all save one of his companions were dashed instantaneously to death.[a]

---

[a] Those of the Duke of Kent's party who were also killed with him were his secretary, Lieut. John Arthur Lowther, R.N.V.R., and Pilot Officer Michael Strutt, and the Duke's valet, Leading Aircraftsman John Walter Hales : of the crew of the aircraft only one survived, Flight-Sergeant Andrew Jack.

The King was at Balmoral with the Queen and the Duke and Duchess of Gloucester. The weather was vile; a low mist, rain and an east wind, — the worst flying weather — but the King and his party spent the day on the moors.

At dinner that night His Majesty was called from the table to take an urgent personal message from the Secretary of State for Air.

Archie Sinclair rang me up to say that George had been killed in an aeroplane accident on his way to Iceland. He had started from Invergordon in a Sunderland Flying Boat & after ½ hour flying had crashed into a mountain at Morven on the Langwell estate (Portland's). This news came as a great shock to me, & I had to break it to Elizabeth, & Harry & Alice who were staying with us. He was killed on Active Service.
We left Balmoral in the evening for London.[17]

The King was indeed greatly distressed, for he had been warmly attached to his youngest brother and had admired the sustained and the conscientious effort which he had made to play his part in the war. 'I shall miss him & his help terribly', he wrote to Louis Greig, and in his diary recorded with deep feeling of the funeral at St. George's Chapel, Windsor, on the 29th:

I was greatly moved by the Service, short & explicit. The R.A.F. detailed the Bearer Party, all N.C.O. Fighter Pilots, & Air Marshals & Air Vice Marshals acted as Pall Bearers.[a] I have attended very many family funerals in the Chapel, but none of which have moved me in the same way. . . . Everybody there I knew well but I did not dare to look at any of them for fear of breaking down. His death & the form it took has shocked everybody & I have had countless letters from friends extolling his merits. The war had brought him out in many ways. Always charming to people in every walk of life.[18]

The King returned to Balmoral on September 1 to resume the holiday which had been so tragically interrupted. But he could not rest until he had visited the scene of his brother's death and had thanked personally some of those who had assisted in recovering the bodies. This he did on Monday

---

[a] The six pall-bearers were:

Air Marshal H. Edwards.	Air Vice-Marshal A. C. Maund.
Air Marshal T. L. Leigh-Mallory.	Air Vice-Marshal R. Graham.
Air Vice-Marshal G. R. M. Reid.	Air Vice-Marshal F. H. McNamara, V.C.

September 14, accompanied by Sir Piers Legh.   He wrote in his diary :

I motored to Berriedale & walked from there to the site of the Sunderland crash where George was killed.   I met Dr. Kennedy, who found him, the farmer Morrison & his son who led search parties & Group Cpt. Pritchett of Wick R.A.F. Station.   The remains of the aircraft had been removed, but the ground for 200 yds long & 100 yds wide had been scored & scorched by its trail & by flame.   It hit one side of the slope, turned over in the air & slid down the other side on its back.   The impact must have been terrific as the aircraft as an aircraft was unrecognisable when found. I felt I had to do this pilgrimage.[19]

'The loss of this gallant and handsome Prince, in the prime of his life, has been a shock and a sorrow to the people of the British Empire, standing out lamentably even in these hard days of war ', Mr. Churchill said in the House of Commons. 'To His Majesty the King it is the loss of a dearly loved brother, and it has affected him most poignantly.' [a]

In his sorrow, King George's thought and consideration were for the widowed Duchess of Kent.   With characteristic kindness he at once arranged for her sister, Princess Olga (Princess Paul of Yugoslavia), to be flown back to England from South Africa in order that she might bear the Duchess company in her grief.

(iv)

When the King and Queen left Hyde Park, New York, in June 1939 they had been warmly sincere in urging the President and Mrs. Roosevelt to return their visit.   The events of history had postponed this possibility indefinitely, but on every occasion that Mr. Churchill had visited the White House he had spoken of the time when the visit should be paid — to celebrate victory.   But victory was still afar off and in the meantime the suggestion arose that Mrs. Roosevelt might usefully come to Britain with the dual purpose of learning at

---

[a] Speech in the House of Commons on September 8 on moving that a humble Address of Condolence be presented to His Majesty.   The House of Lords took similar action and the two Addresses were presented respectively by Lord Clarendon, the Lord Chamberlain, and Sir William Boulton, M.P., Vice-Chamberlain of the Household, on the moor at Balmoral on September 9.

first hand of the part which women had played in the British war effort and of the welfare conditions of the United States troops stationed in Britain.   Letters of sympathy and understanding had passed between the Queen and Mrs. Roosevelt since the outbreak of war and the idea of her coming was welcomed.

I wish much that I could accompany her, for there are a thousand things I want to tell you and talk with you about [the President wrote to King George].   I want you and the Queen to tell Eleanor everything in regard to problems of our troops in England which she might not get from the Government or military authorities.   You and I know that it is the little things which count but which are not always set forth in official reports.[20]

Mrs. Roosevelt's arrival had been planned for October 21, but she was held up by bad weather in Ireland, and on the 23rd the King recorded: 'We have been waiting two days now for Mrs. Roosevelt'.   The delay had not in fact been without advantage, for it had meant for the King a respite from audiences and other routine duties which he had cancelled in order to be at his guest's disposal.

She did in fact arrive that same afternoon and was met by the King and Queen at Paddington.   Thence they drove to Buckingham Palace with that apparent minimum of precaution with which British Sovereigns move and which contrasts so sharply with those all-enveloping security measures hedging the movements of the President of the United States. Her arrival in the battle-scarred palace gave her a very adequate idea of the living conditions of the King and Queen in war-time.   She was lodged in the Queen's own bedroom on the first floor but, because of the effects of bombing, its windows were without glass, and small casements of wood frames and isinglass had been installed.[21]   But what chiefly struck Mrs. Roosevelt was the size of her bedroom and its chill.   'Buckingham Palace is an enormous place, and without heat', she wrote in her diary.   'I do not see how they keep the dampness out.   The rooms were cold except for the smaller sitting-room with an open fire.   In every room there was a little electric heater.'   Her son Elliott, whom the King had invited to be present to welcome her, was so impressed with the vastness of her room that he told her that on her return to Washington she 'would have to take the long corridor in the White House as your bedroom because the one I have would never again seem adequate'.[22]

Mrs. Roosevelt was also impressed by the meals served at the Palace, which, as Lord Woolton, the Minister of Food, informed her, 'might have been served in any home in England and which would have shocked the King's grandfather'. A certain incongruity struck her in that the repast was served on gold and silver plates.[23]

The company at the dinner-party was notable, comprising, in addition to Lord Woolton, Mr. and Mrs. Churchill, General Smuts and his son, and Lord and Lady Mountbatten. The date also was a historic one, for on that day there had opened on the Egyptian frontier the great advance of General Montgomery from El Alamein which was ultimately to drive Rommel from Egypt, Cyrenaica and Tripolitania. Throughout the dinner and the subsequent showing of the film *In which We Serve*, the Prime Minister was observed to be distrait and withdrawn. Finally he could bear the suspense no longer, and, excusing himself, went to telephone to No. 10 Downing Street for news of the battle. That which he heard evidently pleased him, for he returned singing 'Roll out the barrel' with gusto.

The King and Queen provided every facility for their guest to see and hear everything, and personally conducted her on a tour of the bombed city of London — St. Paul's, the main City Control Centre at Moorgate and Guildhall, and a drive through the blitzed parts of the East End to the shelter at Stepney which held three thousand people. When she left them on October 25, the King sent the following message to the President.

. . . Mrs. Roosevelt left us this morning to continue her tour. I would like to tell you what real pleasure it gave us to have her to stay at Buckingham Palace. That she should have made the long journey in these dangerous war days has touched and delighted our people and they are very glad to welcome her here. We had some good talks and are looking forward to hearing her impressions of our women's war activities after she has completed the strenuous programme arranged for her.[a]

[a] Mrs. Roosevelt paid her farewell visit to the King and Queen at Windsor on November 13. 'She is much impressed with all she has seen and heard', the King wrote in his diary. Mrs. Roosevelt records that they both had bad colds.

Many thanks for your letter handed to me by Mrs. Roosevelt. I agree with what you say and only wish we could once again talk things over together. Let us hope this will be possible sooner than we think.

Best wishes from us both.

GEORGE R.I.[24]

The King and Queen had greatly enjoyed Mrs. Roosevelt's visit and had found her sympathetically understanding of the difficulties with which they and their people were faced and with the ideals which enabled them to go forward. Her own impressions Mrs. Roosevelt chronicled later :

The King and Queen treated me with the greatest kindness. The feeling I had had about them during their visit to the United States — that they were simply a young and charming couple, who would have to undergo some very difficult experiences — began to come back to me, intensified by the realization that they now had been through their experiences and were anxious to tell me about them. In all my contacts with them I have gained the greatest respect for both the King and Queen. I haven't always agreed with the ideas expressed to me by the King on international subjects, but the fact that both of them are doing an extraordinarily outstanding job for their people in the most trying times stands out when you are with them, and you admire their character and their devotion to duty.[25]

(v)

Much has happened since I started this volume 8 months ago [King George wrote on October 31, 1942]. Most of its contents are very depressing reading as very few of our military expeditions were successful. However, now with the battle in Egypt a week old to-day, I hope the next volume will contain some more exhilarating news of a success or two.

His Majesty had not long to wait for the fulfilment of his hopes. On the afternoon of November 4 he was rehearsing with Mr. Logue the speech from the Throne with which he was to open Parliament on the 11th. These periods of rehearsal were sacred from interruption save under the most urgent exigency and it was therefore with a quizzical look at his companion that the King greeted the ringing of the telephone. What he heard, however, evidently pleased him, for,

Mr. Logue records: 'He said excitedly: "Well, read it out, read it out", and I could hear coming across the wire the glorious news of the Libyan battle & Rommel's defeat. "The enemy is in full retreat." The King said: "Good news, thanks", and turned to me smiling.' [26]

That which was read to the King over the telephone was General Alexander's telegram to the Prime Minister:

After twelve days of heavy and violent fighting 8th Army has inflicted a severe defeat on the enemy's German and Italian forces under Rommel's command in Egypt. The enemy's front has broken and British armoured formations in strength have passed through and are operating in the enemy's rear areas. Such portion of the enemy's forces as can get away are in full retreat and are being harassed by our armoured and mobile forces and by our Air Forces. Other enemy divisions are still in position, endeavouring to stave off defeat, and these are likely to be surrounded and cut off.

The R.A.F. have throughout given superb support to the land battle, and are bombing the enemy's retreating columns incessantly.

Fighting continues.

'A victory at last, how good it is for the nerves', was the King's comment in his diary, and he pinned his copy of General Alexander's telegram to the entry page for that day.[27]

On the following day His Majesty wrote to felicitate the Prime Minister.

BUCKINGHAM PALACE
November 5th, 1942

MY DEAR WINSTON,

I must send you my warmest congratulations on the great Victory of the 8th Army in Egypt. I was overjoyed when I received the news & so was everybody else. In our many talks together over a long period I knew that the elimination of the Afrika Corps, the threat to Egypt, was your *one* aim, the most important of all the many other operations with which you have had to deal. When I look back & think of all the many arduous hours of work you have put in, & the many miles you have travelled, to bring this battle to such a successful conclusion you have every right to rejoice; while the rest of our people will one day be very thankful to you for what you have done. I cannot say more. At last the Army has come into its own, as it is their victory primarily, ably helped by the forces of the air, & of those that work under the surface of the sea.

I am so pleased that everybody is taking this victory in a quiet
& thankful way, though their rejoicing is very deep & sincere.
                    I remain
                         Yours very sincerely
                                        GEORGE R.I.

Less than a week later there was further great and good
news. '"Operation Torch" was lit early Sunday morning
as arranged', the King wrote in his diary on November 8,
and therein epitomized the fulfilment of five months of anxious
planning and preparation.

The Anglo-American landings in North Africa constituted
the first major full-scale operation of the war to be undertaken
on the initiative of the Allies themselves and not in response
to the ascendancy of the enemy. This success was of the
greatest psychological, political and strategic importance. It
proved to friend and foe alike that, despite the heavy reverses
in the Pacific and in South-East Asia, as well as the recent
defeat of British forces in the Western Desert, the combined
strength of the Anglo-American alliance was capable of mounting an operation of much greater magnitude than the Germans
had believed possible. It demonstrated, moreover, that the
Allies, through their command of the sea and their excellent
security and deception, could make a surprise assault of
decisive force in an unexpected quarter and at a great distance
from their own shores.

The sudden appearance of British and American Armies
in North Africa provided a rallying point on French soil for
French resistance to the enemy and placed finally beyond all
possibility the danger of an occupation of North Africa by the
Axis Powers. It offered a base for further military operations
against the 'soft under-belly of the Axis' and, more immediately,
it rang the knell of the German and Italian forces then reeling
back before the hammer blows of the 8th Army, for they were
now caught between two fires.

The subsequent success of 'Operation Torch' was, however, not without its problems and difficulties, and chief
amongst these was the mystery of Admiral Darlan. This
enigmatic figure had recently completed a tour of North
Africa and had returned to Vichy, but news of the serious
illness of his son had brought him back to Algiers on Novem-

ber 5, and he was therefore present at the moment of the
Allied landings. He was the man on the spot and he was the
master of all Vichy-French loyalties; it was with him, therefore, that General Mark Clark,^a the representative of the
Supreme Allied Commander, decided to deal.

Thus it came about that Admiral Darlan, who at the
outset had commanded resistance to the Allied landings,
ordered a 'cease-fire' on November 11, and assumed complete
authority throughout North Africa in association with the
Anglo-American forces. On the same day he telegraphed
orders to the French battle-fleet at Toulon to put to sea if in
danger of imminent capture by the Germans, whose immediate
reaction to the Allied landings in North Africa had been to
occupy the 'Unoccupied' zone of France.

There can be no doubt that the initial agreement between
Admiral Darlan and the emissaries of General Eisenhower ^b
was of essential value to the Allied cause, since it resulted in
the acceptance by the Vichy-French authorities in North and
West Africa of the situation created by the landing of the
Allied forces and saved thereby the loss of many British and

^a General Mark Wayne Clark (b. 1896) was appointed deputy Commander-
in-Chief of the Allied forces in 'Operation Torch', and, in preparation for the
Anglo-American landings, made the famous and perilous submarine expedition
to the North African coast on October 22–24, 1942. Allied Headquarters for
'Torch' were established at Gibraltar on November 6, and there General
Eisenhower remained until the 23rd. General Clark arrived at Algiers on
November 9 and, as General Eisenhower's deputy, took the decision to deal with
Darlan. He has given an entertaining account of his negotiations with the
Admiral and with Generals Mast, Giraud, Juin and Noguès in his book *Calculated
Risk*. General Clark later commanded the U.S. 5th Army and the 15th Army
Group in North Africa and Italy. He was Commander-in-Chief U.S. troops
in Austria from 1945 to 1947, and in 1952 he became Commander-in-Chief of
United Nations forces in Korea. On his retirement a year later he was appointed
President of the Citadel Military College at Charleston, South Carolina.
^b Hon. Dwight David Eisenhower (b. 1890) graduated from the Military
Academy at West Point in 1915 and thereafter, until the Second World
War, followed a normal military career. In 1941 he held the rank of Colonel,
and a year later was appointed Commander of U.S. Troops in the European
Theatre and Commander-in-Chief of the Allied Forces in North Africa. There-
after he became successively Supreme Commander Allied Expeditionary Forces
in Europe, 1944–1945, Commander of the U.S. Zone of Occupation in Germany,
1945, and Chief of the U.S. Army General Staff, 1945–1948. He was appointed
President of Columbia University, New York (1948–1950), but was recalled to
active service as Supreme Commander of the North Atlantic Treaty Forces in
Europe, 1950–1952. On his second retirement he was promoted to the rank of
General of the Army. Nominated as candidate of the Republican Party, he was
elected President of the United States in 1952, and re-elected in 1956.

American lives. 'Darlan was a political investment forced upon us by circumstances', General Mark Clark has written, 'but we made a sensational profit in lives and time through using him.'

Opinion in Britain, however, was deeply disturbed at the prospect of one whose record as an opportunist was well known being recognized as the head of the new French Administration in Africa, and the Prime Minister in particular came under criticism for an alleged submission to American influence. The scuttling of the French Fleet in the harbour of Toulon on November 27 removed some of the animosity against Darlan, since it was remembered that in 1940 he had promised that the Fleet should never fall into German hands, but it was not until December 10, in a secret session of the House of Commons, that Mr. Churchill was able to allay, in some respects at least, the suspicion of those who feared that, under the pressure of expediency, the Allies were in treaty with French Quislings.[a]

The King shared the general bewilderment and uncertainty. When the news of the scuttling of the French Fleet reached him, he recorded:

Darlan must have known that the Germans were only waiting a good opportunity to capture the Fleet & he appealed to them on Nov. 11 to come out. In 1940 when he was Minister of Marine in Pétain's government just after the collapse of France he promised us that the French Fleet would be scuttled before fighting with Germany; and it is. I wish I could understand this Darlan business. We must use him now but for how long? [28]

The answer to King George's question was not long in coming. On Christmas Eve the embarrassing problem of what to do with Admiral Darlan was solved by the bullet of a young Frenchman, named Bonnier de La Chapelle, who shot him down at the door of his office in the Palais d'Été at Algiers. Of this episode General Clark has written with a certain ruthless realism: 'Darlan's death was, to me, an act of providence. It is too bad he went that way, but, strategically speaking, his removal from the scene was like the lancing of a troublesome

---

[a] For a study of the Darlan episode see Mr. Winston Churchill's memoirs (iv, chapters 34 and 35). See also Admiral Docteur, *La Grande Énigme de la guerre: Darlan, Amiral de la Flotte*; and William Langer, *Our Vichy Gamble*.

boil. He had served his purpose, and his death solved what could have been the very difficult problem of what to do with him in the future.'

The situation in North Africa continued to deteriorate, however; three groups of Frenchmen now contended in Algiers for power and for Allied favours. There were the newly converted *epigonai*, who had acknowledged Vichy and the Marshal up to the moment of the Allied landings; there were the adherents of General Giraud, who, enjoying official Allied recognition, had been appointed Commander-in-Chief of French Forces; and there were the followers of General de Gaulle, who, because of his intransigence and his consequent conflicts with Mr. Churchill and President Roosevelt, found himself excluded from authority. The existence of these warring factions created no inconsiderable difficulties for the Supreme Commander and his political advisers.

And there were other Anglo-American problems. There was delay in the launching of the Allied assault on the Tunisian Front, of which Rommel did not fail to take advantage later, and it became evident that the Allied High Command in North Africa required co-ordinating. Moreover, the transport and supply of 'Operation Torch' had made heavy demands on shipping, and the Allied losses in the Atlantic at the hands of German raiders had been particularly heavy. Urgent appeals were flashed from Mr. Churchill to President Roosevelt for extra freighters to ensure the continued supply of food and materials to Britain.

Of all these circumstances the King was cognizant and, though elated by the magnitude of the success achieved in North Africa, he was fully aware of the difficulties which lay ahead. He was particularly dejected at the heavy losses in shipping. In his final diary entry for the year 1942 he wrote:

We shall be in a bad way here in mid-1943, & we shall have to reduce our war effort here, which will prolong the war & put more work on the U.S.A. to keep us all going. All this is not pleasant news to hear. Outwardly one has to be optimistic about the future in 1943, but inwardly I am depressed at the present prospect.[29]

Nor was the political and military course of the war the only cause of depression to King George in those days. The

loss of his brother, the Duke of Kent, and more particularly
its tragic suddenness, had shocked him deeply. In the New
Year he records that he took occasion to put his own affairs
in good order, because, 'ever since George's death, these matters
loom large in one's mind as one must be prepared for all
eventualities'.[30]

The need for further direct consultation between Mr.
Churchill and President Roosevelt on the direction of the
grand strategy of the war was becoming more and more
urgent, and the King hailed with relief and satisfaction the
news of their approaching conference at Casablanca in January.
He greatly favoured these meetings between the two men who
enjoyed his confidence and admiration, and indeed to some
extent his affection, but he always feared for Mr. Churchill's
safety during these long peregrinations. 'Ever since he became my Prime Minister', the King wrote to Queen Mary,
'I have studied the way in which his brain works. He tells
me, more than people imagine, of his future plans & ideas &
only airs them when the time is ripe to his colleagues & the
Chiefs of Staff. But I do hope & trust he will return home
at once.' [31]

The precautions for secrecy concerning the Casablanca
meeting were redoubled because, as King George recorded,
'F. D. R. is not supposed to leave U.S.A. while he is President
without the consent of Congress. But in a war like this people
have to meet to discuss matters in secret.'[32]

His Majesty sent to the President a personal letter, written
in his own hand, which was delivered by the Prime Minister.

MY DEAR PRESIDENT ROOSEVELT,
    I am so glad that you & Mr. Churchill are going to meet once
again. You will have many problems to discuss as to our future
strategy of the War in 1943.
    The efforts of our two countries, whether separate or combined,
have already shown to the World that we are determined to destroy
the enemies of civilization. Your deliberations on this occasion,
will, I feel sure, pave the way to a successful & victorious conclusion
of the War.
    My only regret is, that it is not possible for you to come here
for your conversations, when we could meet & renew the friendships
we made in the White House & at Hyde Park in 1939.
    The Queen & I were so delighted to entertain Mrs. Roosevelt

here last October, & we hope that she returned to you none the worse for her strenuous visit. I have asked Mr. Churchill to hand you this letter.

> With my very best wishes to you
>   Believe me
>   Yours very sincerely
>   GEORGE R.I.[33]

To this the President replied :

MY DEAR KING GEORGE,

I wish much that you could have been with us during the past ten days — a truly unique meeting in its thoroughness and in the true spirit of comradeship between each officer and his 'opposite number'.

As for Mr. Churchill and myself I need not tell you that we make a perfectly matched team in harness and out — and incidentally we had lots of fun together as we always do — Our studies and our various agreements must and will bear good fruit.

My wife was thrilled for all that she saw and learned in England — and I am most grateful to you and the Queen for all you did for her —

> My warmest regards to you both
>   Always sincerely yours
>   FRANKLIN D. ROOSEVELT.[34]

King George awaited the return of his Prime Minister to England with impatience and anxiety, and in the meantime he followed events in North Africa with the closest attention. In preparation for his talk with Mr. Churchill he received Mr. Mack,[a] the Foreign Office representative on General Eisenhower's staff, and put to him searching questions which resulted in the promise of a paper on the subject.[35]   This, however, only served to make the position the more obscure. 'The whole position in N. Africa is an enigma to me', the King recorded after reading Mr. Mack's memorandum.[36]

What His Majesty found difficult to understand, and his bewilderment was shared by many in Britain at that time, was the apparent lack of discrimination on the part of the American political and military authorities in North Africa in the selection of certain Frenchmen with pronounced Vichy

[a] Sir Henry Bradshaw Mack, G.B.E., K.C.M.G. (b. 1894), entered the Foreign Office in 1921. He served as Civil Liaison Officer to the Allied Commander-in-Chief, North Africa, 1942–1943, as U.K. Political Representative in Austria, 1944–1945, and as Minister to Austria, 1947–1948. He was appointed Ambassador to Iraq, 1948–1951, and to the Argentine Republic, 1951–1954.

records for posts of responsibility in the military command and civil administration. Both the President and the Prime Minister had become alienated by the hauteur and stubbornness of General de Gaulle, his unwillingness to co-operate with General Giraud and his refusal to accept any but complete authority. But the King understood full well — and perhaps better than the statesmen concerned — the feelings of those Frenchmen who in 1940 had risked all to maintain the honour and independence of France, and he certainly displayed a greater appreciation than either Mr. Roosevelt or Mr. Churchill of General de Gaulle's capacity for survival and his ability to get his own way.

The Prime Minister came to lunch [the King wrote on February 9]. He looked very well & cheerful & not tired after his long journey. He gave me a good account of the Conference, delighted with his Turkish visit[a] & was eulogistic over the smartness of the Eighth Army. He is furious with de Gaulle over his refusal to accept F.D.R.'s invitation to meet him & Giraud.[b] The latter made friends with F.D.R. & got on well. I warned W. not to be too hasty with de G. & the F. Fr. Nat. Comee. W. is seeing Massigli[c] to-day. I told W. I could well understand de G's attitude, & that of our own people here, who do not like the idea of making friends of those Frenchmen who have collaborated with the Germans.

Gen. Bergeret now an official in N. Africa signed the Armistice in 1940.[d] However Anglo-American relations are far more important than the wrangles between Frenchmen. Frenchmen can fight to redeem themselves now. I hope very much de G. & G. will come together.

[a] On January 30 Mr. Churchill had met and conferred with President Inönü at Adana in Southern Turkey.

[b] General de Gaulle had at first refused to accept President Roosevelt's invitation to come to Casablanca as he would not recognize the position of General Giraud. Under pressure from Mr. Churchill and on the advice of General Catroux, he at length relented, and arrived on January 22. There ensued a somewhat frigid meeting.

[c] René Massigli (b. 1888) was Political Director of the French Ministry of Foreign Affairs from 1937 to 1938 and Ambassador to Turkey from 1939 to 1940. He returned to Vichy France but escaped in 1943 to North Africa, where he became Commissioner for Foreign Affairs in General de Gaulle's Committee for National Liberation. He was Ambassador in London from 1944 till 1955, when he was appointed Secretary-General of the Ministry of Foreign Affairs. He retired in 1956.

[d] General Jean Marie Joseph Bergeret, Deputy-Chief of the Air Staff, was a member of the Commission appointed to negotiate the armistices with Germany and Italy on behalf of France. He did not, in fact, sign either of the agreements, which bear the signature of General Huntziger only, as Head of the delegation.

This hope, however, proved to be but a pious aspiration. The two French Generals, though nominally invested with joint authority, did not in any sense 'come together'. The political situation in North Africa continued to be chaotic. In addition, there was a serious deterioration in the military position, when, on February 12, Rommel, striking westwards in a well-directed counter-stroke, attacked the United States forces on the Tunisian front and drove them from Faid and Kasserene. On the 20th the German thrust broke through the Kasserene Pass. The American position was penetrated to the depth of 18 miles; their casualties were heavy and they lost some hundred tanks and a similar number of guns.

The King was deeply perturbed at this defeat and decided to discuss the position with the Prime Minister; but Mr. Churchill was in bed with influenza. His Majesty's concern was not only for the present reverse in Tunisia, which would certainly be redeemed — Allied forces did in fact reoccupy the positions on February 27/28 — but he feared for the political future. At Casablanca it had been agreed that the next move against the Axis was to be an assault on a grand scale against Sicily ('Operation Husky') and it was in His Majesty's mind that the political repercussions of the landings in North Africa might well be repeated on Italian soil: 'I feel we must have a cut & dried joint plan for this & that we must be firm & not deal with any of the Fascist régime or Mussolini's people, or any kind of quisling', was his comment.[37]

Deprived of the opportunity of discussing the situation with his Prime Minister, the King put pen to paper ('I wrote to him about the general political & military situation in North Africa. I am not happy about either'[38]); and there ensued that correspondence which Mr. Churchill has already printed in his memoirs.

BUCKINGHAM PALACE
February 22, 1943

MY DEAR WINSTON,
   I am very sorry to hear that you are ill, and I hope that you will soon be well again. But do please take this opportunity for a rest, and I trust you will not forget that you have earned one after your last tour, and you must get back your strength for the strenuous coming months. I missed being able to have a talk to you last Tuesday either, so I am writing to you instead.

I do not feel at all happy about the present political situation in North Africa. I know we had to leave the political side of 'Torch' to the Americans, while we were able to keep Spain and Portugal friendly during the time the operation was going on. I know we had to tread warily at the start, but is there nothing we can do now to strengthen Macmillan's and Alexander's hands in both the political and military sphere, to make the two French sides come together?

Now I hear that from the American point of view the date of 'Husky' will have to be postponed to the later one, whereas we can plan for the earlier one, which will be an aggravation of our difficulties in preparing the operation.

This fact will throw out all our careful calculations for convoys and escorts, and will upset our import programme again. I should not think of bothering you with these questions at this moment, but I do feel worried about them, and I would like an assurance from you that they are being carefully watched.

I cannot discuss these vital matters with anyone but yourself.

Believe me,

Yours very sincerely,

GEORGE R.I.

To this letter Mr. Churchill replied with a long and reasoned exposition of the situation, its wider political complications and its military aspects.[39] This to some extent allayed the King's anxiety.

I received a letter from the P.M. in which he assured me that the N. Afn. situation was going well [he wrote in his diary on February 23]. We had to use the French who were there. W. is still furious with de Gaulle & has refused him permission to go on a tour of N. Africa to Cairo etc. The Americans will learn through defeat, & the Germans will learn from the 8th Army when they meet in Tunisia.

The King's philosophy was justified. On February 4, 1943, General Alexander [a] had sent his famous telegram to the Prime Minister:

[a] Field-Marshal the Rt. Hon. Harold Rupert Leofric George, first Earl Alexander of Tunis, K.G., G.C.B., G.C.M.G., C.S.I., D.S.O., M.C. (b. 1891), at the outbreak of the Second World War commanded the 1st Division and later the 1st Corps of the B.E.F. and in this capacity completed the evacuation from Dunkirk. He was General Officer Commanding in Burma in 1942 and conducted the retreat before the Japanese invasion. Thereafter his commands were: Commander-in-Chief Middle East, 1942–1943; Commander-in-Chief 18th Army Group, North Africa, 1943: Commander-in-Chief Allied Armies in Italy,

SIR, The orders you gave me on August 15, 1942 *a* have been fulfilled. His Majesty's enemies, together with their impedimenta, have been completely eliminated from Egypt, Cyrenaica, Libya and Tripolitania. I now await your further instructions.

General Alexander's 'further instructions' were contained in the general reorganization of the Allied High Command in the Mediterranean area which had been envisaged at Casablanca. As a result of this he became General Eisenhower's immediate deputy — with control over all British, American and French Forces in North Africa. *b* The first-fruits of this reorganization were not entirely promising, since its announcement on February 11 was followed immediately by the defeat of the Americans at Kasserene. General Alexander, however, assumed active command on February 20 ('What a moment to do it', the King wrote in his diary) and speedily rectified the position. Thereafter he showed himself, in the King's words, 'a first-class strategist as well as a great commander in the field. He is also proving himself a diplomat with the Americans.' [40]

Closer Anglo-American liaison was also afforded in the political sphere by the appointment of Mr. Harold Macmillan *c* as Minister-Resident at Allied Headquarters.

1943–1944; and Supreme Allied Commander, Mediterranean Theatre, 1944–1945. In 1946 he was appointed Governor-General of Canada, returning to England in 1952 to become Minister of Defence in Mr. Churchill's Cabinet. He retired in 1954.

a The original of the hand-written instruction issued to General Alexander by the Prime Minister in Cairo (which was in fact dated August 10) was given by Mr. Churchill to the King, who placed it in the Archives at Windsor, keeping a copy in his diary. On the receipt of the Alexander telegram he copied it in pencil and pinned it with the other paper. The original of the telegram is now also at Windsor.

b On February 11, 1943, it was announced that, as a result of decisions taken at the Casablanca Conference, the Allied High Command in the Mediterranean Theatre of War would be reorganized as follows: General Eisenhower as Allied Commander-in-Chief, with General Alexander as his deputy; Admiral Sir Andrew Cunningham, Commander-in-Chief of all Naval Forces; and Air Chief Marshal Sir Arthur Tedder, Commander-in-Chief of all Air Forces. General Sir Henry Maitland Wilson became Commander-in-Chief Middle East.

c Rt. Hon. Harold Macmillan, M.P. (b. 1894), served in Mr. Churchill's National Government successively as Parliamentary Secretary, Ministry of Supply, 1940–1942: Parliamentary Under-Secretary of State for the Colonies, 1942; and Minister Resident at Allied Headquarters, North-West Africa and Italy, 1942–1945. He was Secretary of State for Air in the 'Caretaker Government' of 1945 and when the Conservatives returned to power in 1951 he was appointed Minister of Housing and Local Government, becoming Minister of Defence in

The destruction of the Axis Forces in Africa was now but a matter of time and hard fighting.   On March 20 the 8th Army opened its offensive against the Mareth line and began the conquest of Tunisia.   The final advance began on May 5; two days later British armour broke into Tunis and the Americans smashed their way into Bizerta.   Escape was now impossible and, huddled on the peninsula of Cap Bon, the last Axis forces surrendered on May 13.   'It is an overwhelming victory', the King recorded.

(vi)

The period between the Axis surrender in North Africa of May 13, 1943, and the launching of the Allied invasion of Sicily on July 9 provided an opportunity not only for military and political planning but for a general stocktaking of the situation as a whole.   Mr. Churchill had indeed already left on May 5 for a further conference in Washington, bearing with him a letter from the King to President Roosevelt, a message of warm friendship and congratulation on the part played by the American 2nd Corps.[41]   When, therefore, the news reached London of the final surrender at Cap Bon, King George telegraphed his felicitation to the Prime Minister at the White House :

Now that the campaign in Africa has reached a glorious conclusion, I wish to tell you how profoundly I appreciate the fact that its initial conception and successful prosecution are largely due to your vision and to your unflinching determination in the face of early difficulties.   The African campaign has immeasurably increased the debt that this country, and indeed all the United Nations, owe to you.

GEORGE R.I.[42]

To this message the Prime Minister replied :

I am deeply grateful for the most gracious message with which your Majesty has honoured me.   No Minister of the Crown has ever received more kindness and confidence from his Sovereign than I have done during the three fateful years which have passed since I received your Majesty's commission to form a national administration.   This has been a precious aid and comfort to me, especially

1954.   He held office in Sir Anthony Eden's Government as Secretary of State for Foreign Affairs, April–December 1955, and Chancellor of the Exchequer, 1955–1957.   He became Prime Minister, in succession to Sir Anthony Eden, in January 1957.

in the dark time through which we have passed. My father and
my grandfather both served in Cabinets of Queen Victoria's reign,
and I myself have been a Minister under your Majesty's grandfather,
your father, and your self for many years. The signal compliment
which your Majesty has paid me on this occasion goes far beyond
my deserts but will remain as a source of lively pleasure to me as
long as I live.[43]

This exchange between the Sovereign and his Minister,
symbolizing the cordial feeling, the mutual admiration and
co-operation, which existed between them, was very appropriately seized upon by the editor of *The Times* to pay a fitting
tribute to the part played by the King himself in the harrowing
days of war and to draw public attention to the arduous nature
of his responsibilities. Under the title of 'King and Minister',
the editor wrote, on May 18 :

The telegram sent by the King to his Prime Minister of the
United Kingdom on the glorious occasion of the expulsion of the
enemy from Africa and the Prime Minister's reply are sure to
remain in the memory of thoughtful people. There is a historic
element in them appropriate enough to the events which they
commemorate. Their publication lifts for one moment a corner
of the curtain that ordinarily conceals the working of a unique
relationship. Nothing in British institutions does more to preserve
the balance and temperate humanity of politics than the constitutional practice that makes the heads of the Government His
Majesty's 'Ministers'. The Ministers, and especially the 'Prime
Minister' as first among them, enjoy the unreserved confidence of
the Sovereign and bear absolute responsibility. But, while the
responsibility is theirs, it is the Sovereign's part to be fully informed
upon all their activities, and they will not look in vain to him for
counsel and suggestion.

It is easy to read between the lines of the King's message, and
especially of the Prime Minister's reply — even if there were no
other grounds for the presumption — how this ideal is being
realized in daily practice. In his wholehearted attribution of credit
for supreme leadership His Majesty speaks with special knowledge
the sentiments of all his people ; in his moving references to the
aid and comfort he has received in dark times, Mr. Churchill pays
public tribute to the discharge of a duty that only the Sovereign
can perform, and that only the few can see him performing.
Ministers come and go, but the King remains, always at the centre
of public affairs, always participating vigilantly in the work of
government from a standpoint detached from any consideration
but the welfare of his peoples as a whole. He is the continuous

element in the constitution, one of the main safe-guards of its democratic character, and the repository of a knowledge of affairs that before long comes to transcend that of any individual statesman.

The present King's reign is still young; but already he has been served by three Prime Ministers, and has sat on the throne for a longer time than any member of the War Cabinet has been continuously in office. Moreover he now maintains relations with his cabinets in the Dominions, which have been explicitly removed from the cognizance of his Ministers in Whitehall. He thus acquires a wide and rich personal experience. How this personal experience has been used in the past for the informal assistance of statesmanship in many aspects comes ultimately to be read in the memoirs of courtiers and politicians, and especially in the unpublished correspondence of the Sovereigns themselves. But because these documents are published late, it is always a temptation to forget that the unremitting labour which, for instance, Queen Victoria devoted to the daily business of state has been carried on, with at least equal diligence, though in the changing form appropriate to ever-changing times, by her descendants. Mr. Churchill's telegram in grateful acknowledgment of a signal honour, revealing the help that one of the strongest of Prime Ministers has received from his Sovereign, is a powerful reminder that King George VI is doing a work as indispensable for English governance as any of his predecessors, just as he has set his peoples from the first day of the war an unfailing public example of courage, confidence, and devoted energy; and it conveys a hint of how much His Majesty's advisers continue to owe to His Majesty's advice.

(vii)

The lull between the conquest of North Africa and the subsequent assault upon Sicily was seized upon by King George to fulfil a long-cherished wish, namely to visit his victorious armies in the field and to express personally to them his pride in their achievements. As early as March, when the ultimate destruction of the Axis forces in Tunisia was clearly only a matter of time, he had broached the subject to the Prime Minister, who was favourably disposed to the idea.[44] Though conscious of the risks involved, Mr. Churchill also appreciated the immense service which King George would perform in visiting North Africa when the appropriate moment arrived. The presence of His Majesty, it was thought, would not only act as a tonic on British and Imperial troops of the 1st and 8th Armies, but would also have a beneficial effect upon Anglo-American

co-operation in the field, and also upon the relations of the
British and Americans with their somewhat difficult French
Allies. The approval of the War Cabinet was obtained when
the King dined with them at No. 10 Downing Street on
March 31,[45] and plans were immediately set in train with the
greatest secrecy.

The King was pleased at the prospect of again being with
his armies abroad.   His last visit, in December 1939 to the
B.E.F. in France, had greatly interested him, and much had
happened in the interval.   The long journey, however, had
now to be made by air and this prospect, for he really disliked
flying, did not attract him. It was characteristic of his methodical mind that, on the day before his departure, he summoned
his solicitor and placed his affairs in order, recording in his
diary : 'I think it better on this occasion to leave nothing to
chance'.[46]

At the last moment also he was assailed by qualms of
conscience as to whether he should leave the country at this
juncture. 'As the time draws nearer for my departure on
my journey, I wonder if I should go ', he wrote to Queen Mary,
'but I know I shall be doing good in visiting those men who
have done such wonderful deeds for this Country, & who will
shortly be going into action again.' [47]

On June 11 came the encouraging news of the surrender
by the Italians of the strongly fortified island of Pantellaria,
which Mussolini had described as 'the Gibraltar of the Central
Mediterranean', and that night the King, attended by Sir
Alexander Hardinge, Sir Piers Legh and Wing Commander
Fielden,[a] left Northolt airport in the 'York' Transport Air-
craft, which had been specially fitted for the comfort of the
Prime Minister on his travels.[b]

The original programme for the King's journey had called
for a refuelling stop at Gibraltar, but dense fog shrouded the
Rock as the York circled above it and they were compelled
to fly on without landing. This involuntary change of plan

---

[a] The King was also accompanied on his journey, though in a separate aircraft, by two Ministers in Attendance, the Secretary of State for War, Sir James
Grigg, and the Secretary of State for Air, Sir Archibald Sinclair.
[b] Before leaving England the King appointed five Counsellors of State: The
Queen, the Duke of Gloucester, the Princess Royal, Princess Arthur of Connaught
and the Countess of Southesk.

occasioned alarm at home. 'I have had an anxious few hours', the Queen wrote to Queen Mary, 'because at 8.15 I heard that the plane had been heard near Gibraltar, and that it would soon be landing. Then after an hour & a half I heard that there was a thick fog at Gib. & that they were going on to Africa. Then complete silence till a few minutes ago, when a message came that they had landed in Africa, & taken off again. Of course I imagined every sort of horror, & walked up & down my room staring at the telephone.' [48]

Though the plans for the King's journey had been kept a close secret and he had even travelled incognito as 'General Lyon',[49] his arrival in Algiers, shortly after noon on June 12, was soon known all over the city, and some of the more discerning citizens recognized him in his car as he drove to the Villa Germain, a house commandeered from a rich French wine merchant, but in which, as the King noted in his diary, 'like all French houses, the plumbing was defective & erratic'.[50]

There followed a particularly heavy two weeks' programme. The long journeys by air, coupled with unfamiliar climatic conditions, were a severe physical strain. Yet, weary though he often was and sometimes weak from lack of food — for he and his party all fell victims to the prevalent complaint of 'Desert tummy' — the King stood up to the ordeal far better than had been expected, and he spared himself nothing. In all he travelled some 6700 miles.

He conferred at length, not only with the British Commanders, General Alexander, General Montgomery [a] and General Wilson,[b] and their divisional and corps commanders,

[a] Field-Marshal Bernard Law, first Viscount Montgomery of Alamein, K.G., G.C.B., D.S.O. (b. 1887), was at beginning of the Second World War commanding the 3rd Division; thereafter between 1940 and 1942 he commanded the 5th Corps, the 12th Corps and the South-Eastern Command. In July 1942 he assumed command of the 8th Army and conducted its victorious course in the North African, Sicily and Italian campaigns. During the invasion of Europe he commanded the 21st Army Group, and thereafter was successively G.O.C.-in-C. British Army of the Rhine, 1945–1946; Chief of the Imperial General Staff, 1946–1948; Chairman of the Western European Commanders'-in-Chief Committee, 1948–1951; and Deputy Supreme Allied Commander in Europe, 1951–1958.

[b] Field-Marshal Henry Maitland, first Baron Wilson, G.C.B., G.B.E., D.S.O. (b. 1881), was G.O.C.-in-C. Egypt in 1939, G.O.C.-in-C. and Military Governor in Cyrenaica in 1941, and G.O.C.-in-C. British Troops in Greece, 1941. He subsequently served as G.O.C.-in-C. British Forces in Palestine and Transjordan, 1941, and was Allied Commander-in-Chief in Syria in the same year, and also G.O.C.-in-C. 9th Army. He was Commander-in-Chief Persia-Iraq Command, 1942–

but also with General Eisenhower and his military and political advisers. There was also a famous luncheon with the French when the King sat between General Giraud and General de Gaulle, as a result of which, it is said, both withdrew the resignation which they had tendered that same morning. In a blazing sun he inspected the troops of the 1st Army at Bone [a] — 'The men looked very fit & well & the smiles on their faces showed that they were pleased with what they have done' [51] — and later drove slowly through the ranks of some 85,000 men of the 8th Army, whose bearing and appearance suggested a ceremonial appearance on the Horse Guards Parade. He inspected the British and American naval units in the port area of Algiers and he visited General Mark Clark's U.S. 5th Army at Oran. 'They have at last realized that their troops are not fit & hard', was his comment here, 'so they are copying our battle schools & P.T.' [52] And every evening he dined with military and civilian notables.

Wherever he went he impressed all who met him with his knowledge of local problems, his insatiable interest and the dignified simplicity of his bearing.

Of the many incidents which occurred during this momentous visit two may be singled out as having given the King particular pleasure. On one occasion he appeared unheralded on a beach where some five hundred troops, young veterans of the desert, were bathing. In their surprise and delight they crowded about him, singing 'For he's a jolly good fellow', giving him a tremendous ovation, which in its exuberant spontaneity reminded him, as he afterwards said, of his Camps at Southwold and particularly, perhaps, of that August day in the unhappy summer of 1938, when he had been borne ashore from an open boat on the bare shoulders of cheering schoolboys.

The second incident was in Libya, at Castel Benito, where the King saw the troops of the 4th Indian Division,

1943; Commander-in-Chief Middle East Command, 1943, and Supreme Allied Commander, Mediterranean Theatre, 1944. From 1945 until his retirement in 1947 he was Head of the British Joint Staff Mission in Washington. He was appointed Constable of the Tower of London in 1955.

[a] The King, who had been wearing the regulation shorts and a short-sleeved tunic, was badly sunburned on this occasion. Thereafter he wore slacks, and an obliging coloured American sergeant sewed 'extensions' on to the sleeves of his tunics.

which had fought magnificently in every action since El Alamein. At one point His Majesty stopped his car in order to pin the ribbon of the Victoria Cross on the tunic of a Subadar of the 2nd Gurkha Rifles. He later recorded: 'The King-Emperor has never before had the opportunity of doing this in an occupied enemy country'.[53]

Very early on the morning of June 25 the York aircraft touched down at Northolt on the completion of her return journey. She had arrived an hour ahead of schedule, much to the consternation of the Prime Minister and those others who were meeting the King on his arrival. Later in the day the War Cabinet called at Buckingham Palace to congratulate him on his safe return. 'Thus ended a Royal Tour unique in history', wrote one who had accompanied His Majesty, 'and one which will, without doubt, be remembered long after this generation, and the next, have passed away.' [a]

It was most strenuous & I did feel very tired at times [the King wrote to Queen Mary]. I am very relieved that the journey is over as it was a cause for worry & anxiety beforehand on account of its secrecy. However it all went off very well & I am very glad that I carried it out. I do hope & trust that you did not worry too much while I was away.[54]

The success of the King's visit and the deep impression which he had made on all whom he had seen and met could not be in doubt. The effect on the troops was very marked and those in the higher command were equally emphatic in their praise. In addition, messages of congratulation and relief at the King's safe return arrived from all parts of the United Kingdom and the Commonwealth, including one from the Salvation Army. The evident sincerity of their tributes to what he had hoped and tried to do touched his Majesty greatly.

I have had such nice letters from people in every walk of life about my journey [b] [the King wrote again to his mother], it was certainly well worth doing, & did me a great deal of good. I feel I have done some good to the troops who have fought so well.[55]

---

[a] For that part of the story of His Majesty's tour which concerns his visit to Malta, see below, pp. 575-8.

[b] 'Down the road came a big open Ford V.8, flying the Royal Standard', one young soldier wrote to his mother, who forwarded the letter to the King. 'It passed us quite slowly & there nodding to the crowds was the King himself in the uniform of a Field Marshal. *We felt then that we were not quite so far from home.*'

NORTH AFRICA, JUNE 1943

ENTERING THE GRAND HARBOUR OF VALETTA, JUNE 20, 1943

(viii)

The itinerary of King George's visit to the Mediterranean Front had included a visit to Malta and for a very special reason. His Majesty had taken a deep interest in every phase of the island's ordeal; his imagination had been fired by the epic gallantry of the defence, his sympathy aroused by the sufferings and courage of the inhabitants. It was his established purpose to pay personal tribute to this battered outpost of his Empire.

The strategic importance of Malta in Mediterranean strategy is obvious. The line of communications by sea between Italy and Tripoli was brief but exposed and Malta constituted a permanent menace to it. Indeed, after the fall of France it was only from Malta that British naval and air forces could threaten the enemy's vital sea-route to North Africa. The maintenance of the island fortress became as indispensable, therefore, to Allied victory as its elimination was of cardinal importance to the Axis.

With the opening of the Libyan Front in December 1940 the Italian Air Force had made its first attacks upon Malta and these had been repulsed with energy and success, but six months later, when Hitler decided to come to the support of his Italian ally, imperative orders were issued by Goering to Kesselring for the reduction of the strong-point, and the full fury of the combined German and Italian air-fleets was loosed upon the island. For the second time in her history Malta stood siege, and for over a year (June 1941–September 1942) the island was under continual attack by night or day, and sometimes both.

The weight of the assault was very heavy. In the first six months of 1942 over eleven thousand tons of bombs were dropped by the enemy, and in the month of April alone the equivalent of thirty-six times the bomb-tonnage dropped upon Coventry fell upon the island.[56] Food and supplies were running short, yet, in the face of this constant bombardment, the defenders not only fought off their antagonists but carried out their two other essential functions, of themselves inflicting telling damage on the Axis sea-lines of communication and of sending on reinforcement aircraft to the Middle East. The

gallantry of the garrison of the besieged island was matched
by the calmness and endurance of the civilian population,
and both derived inspiration from the indomitable and devout
leadership of the Governor, General William Dobbie.[a]

In London the intrepid resistance of Malta was watched
with admiration but with mounting anxiety. 'Malta is in
my thoughts sleeping and waking', Nelson had written nearly
a century and a half earlier, and in the spring of 1942 it was
no less constantly in the minds of British leaders. Could the
island hold out? Could it be reinforced and reprovisioned?
These were the vital problems, and in the meantime could
any fillip be provided to sustain the morale of the defenders
in their ordeal?

It was at this critical moment that King George's inspiration provided the solution. As one who had shared the
dangers of air assault and had witnessed the heroic endurance
of his people in Britain, he had marked with pride and understanding the valour of this other beleaguered island among
his heritage. His sympathetic imagination conceived the idea
of special recognition, and on his own initiative he proposed
to confer his own decoration, the George Cross, upon the
people and garrison of the island. On April 15 he sent the
following message to the Governor:

To honour her brave people I award the George Cross to the
Island Fortress of Malta to bear witness to a heroism and devotion
that will long be famous in history.[b] [57]

The award could not have been made at a more grim
nor a more propitious moment, and the hard-pressed defenders
accepted with acclaim this symbol of the King's trust in their
continued will and ability to resist and endure.

But the ordeal continued and even the indomitable Dobbie
broke down under the strain. On May 7 he was succeeded
by Lord Gort, and on his return to London was received
in audience at Buckingham Palace. The King greeted him

[a] Lieutenant-General Sir William George Shedden Dobbie, G.C.M.G.,
K.C.B., D.S.O. (b. 1879), Governor and Commander-in-Chief of Malta, 1940–
1942.
[b] The text of the King's message is now inscribed on a tablet of marble on
the wall of the Palace of the Grand Masters of the Order of St. John of Malta in
the Great Square at Valletta.

with honour. 'I knighted him and invested him with the K.C.B., and for his outstanding services in Malta during the last months I invested him with the G.C.M.G. . . . He is a God-fearing man, and lives with a bible in one hand and a sword in the other. He looks very old and tired after his ordeal.' [58]

The situation which confronted Lord Gort on his arrival in Malta might well have daunted the courage of any man. The island had officially sufficient food for only six weeks. It was not bombing but starvation which had nearly brought the defenders to the limit of their resistance. The position was approaching desperation, for, as the King recorded grimly in his diary: 'It has been decided not to try to reinforce Malta in May, and if we cannot do so in June we shall have to try and evacuate it'.[59]

In June, therefore, the attempt was made. Two convoys set out for the relief of Malta on the 13th, one of eleven merchantmen, from Alexandria, the other of six, from Gibraltar. Both were escorted by carriers and destroyers and aircraft but both were heavily attacked by enemy air and surface craft. Losses were heavy and the Alexandria convoy was compelled to return to port. Of the six ships of the Gibraltar group only two made their eventual arrival in the Grand Harbour of Valletta.

The psychological effect of the arrival of these two vessels was immense, their material aid but scanty. It almost seemed as if the sacrifices and heroism of the past months must terminate in eventual defeat, for available food for the garrison and population was now below starvation diet. Lord Gort made all preparations for the surrender of the island. He himself with a party of volunteers planned to set sail for Sicily and sell their lives as dearly as possible.

The gravity of the situation was appreciated in London, and at the close of July Lord Cranborne and the Chief of the Imperial General Staff, Sir Alan Brooke,[a] flew to Malta to

[a] Field-Marshal Alan Francis Brooke, first Viscount Alanbrooke, K.G., G.C.B., O.M., G.C.V.O., D.S.O. (b. 1883), commanded the Second Corps of the British Expeditionary Force in France, 1939–1940, and was Commander-in-Chief Home Forces from 1940 to 1941, when he became Chief of the Imperial General Staff, which position he held until 1946. From 1946 to 1956 he held the appointment of Master Gunner of St. James's Park, and from 1950 to 1955 that of Constable of the Tower of London.

confer with the Governor. With them they bore a letter from King George, a message of encouragement and confidence, in which His Majesty wrote not only for himself but for his Ministers and his people.

31st July 1942

MY DEAR GORT,

I am taking the opportunity of Cranborne's visit to send you this short line of good wishes.

I would like you to know that you are constantly in my thoughts, and that your difficulties and anxieties are fully appreciated at home. I and my Government have, however, entire confidence in your ability to discharge your heavy responsibilities, and it goes without saying that we shall do everything that is humanly possible to help you through.

I wish you the best of luck, and hope that you are keeping fit.

GEORGE R.I.[60]

Once again the expression of the King's trust in the capacity of the defenders of Malta to endure was justified and once again it brought fresh courage to a hard-pressed garrison. Under increasing privation they continued their resistance for a further three weeks, until at dawn on August 20 a considerable convoy, under effective air and sea escort, successfully entered the Grand Harbour and the beginning of relief had come. Two months later came the victory of Alamein, and, with the defeat of Rommel, Malta's ordeal was at an end.

The Battle of Malta stands out as one of the most valiant and glorious episodes of the war. It has all the elements of an adventure of romance; courage and virtue and endurance, and, in the end, victory against heavy odds. For the garrison of Malta not only covered itself with honour in defence, it carried the war into the very vitals of the enemy.[a] It strangled the Axis life-line of communication, held open the door into Europe and materially contributed to the final surrender of the enemy forces at Cap Bon on May 13, 1943. And behind and around the garrison were the Maltese themselves, men,

[a] During the period of June 1, 1941–July 13, 1942, it is estimated that the defenders of Malta shot down six hundred and ninety-three German and Italian aircraft, and British aircraft based on Malta destroyed one hundred and ninety of the enemy on the ground in enemy territory, with thirty-five probably destroyed and two hundred and forty-nine damaged.[61]

women and children, who never lost faith even in the darkest hour of blitz and starvation.

It was to this battered but undaunted island that King George paid a surprise visit on June 20, 1943, less than a year after those gloomy conferences in the Governor's palace at Valletta when the besieged defenders had counted the weeks and days to the moment of their inevitable surrender unless relief arrived in time. The inclusion of Malta in his programme had been in the King's mind from the earliest stages of the planning of his journey. His imagination had been caught and his admiration aroused by the romantic record of the Island Fortress and he was proud of having conceived the idea of awarding it the George Cross, but, with his deep understanding of the mystique of monarchy, he was also conscious of the effect which a personal visit from himself would have upon the population, who now proudly spoke of Malta as 'The King's Island'.

His idea was welcomed in principle by the Prime Minister and his colleagues, but, on the grounds of safety and security, the final decision was left until after the King's arrival in North Africa. For, though the Allied supremacy in the air gave a sufficient guarantee against all but the outside chance of risk, it had to be remembered that the Italian Fleet had not yet surrendered and that only sixty miles to the north of Malta lay Sicily, still in Axis hands. Nor was the danger of air attack from the mainland of Italy a possibility to be ignored, indeed the last raid to be made upon Malta from this quarter was not until October 1944, more than a year later.

The King, however, was determined. He would not run unnecessary risks, but he had every intention of going to Malta if at all possible, and at dinner on the first evening in Algiers he tackled the naval Commander-in-Chief, who was at once impressed with the cogency of his arguments. 'His Majesty was most anxious to visit Malta', Lord Cunningham [a]

[a] Admiral of the Fleet Andrew Browne, first Viscount Cunningham of Hyndhope, K.T., G.C.B., O.M., D.S.O. (b. 1883), was Commander-in-Chief Mediterranean from 1939 to 1942; Head of the British Admiralty Delegation in Washington, 1942; Naval Commander-in-Chief North African Expeditionary Force, 1942, and again Commander-in-Chief Mediterranean, 1943. He served as First Sea Lord and Chief of Naval Staff, 1943–1946, when he retired. He was appointed Lord High Commissioner to the General Assembly of the Church of Scotland in 1950 and again in 1952.

wrote later, 'and pressed the suggestion on me during dinner.
I was most favourably inclined to the idea and needed little
persuasion. The effect on the Maltese would be immense,
and not only upon the Maltese, but throughout the whole
Empire. Nor did I think that if the proper precautions were
taken the risks were prohibitive.' [62] Thus, after consultation
with the responsible authorities at home and locally, the visit
was arranged, and on the night of June 19 the King and his
suite embarked in the cruiser *Aurora* (Capt. W. G. Agnew) for
passage to Malta. The crossing was rough and the King and
his suite, most of whom were suffering from 'Desert tummy'
in more or less severe forms, passed an uncomfortable night.
But as dawn broke the dim outline of Malta was discernible
and the first rays of the sun lit up the battle-scarred ruins of the
undefeated island.

For reasons of security the King's visit had naturally been
kept a close secret. Those high officials who were to welcome
him were warned only the night before, and to the mass of
the civilian population of the island — some 250,000 of them
— and to the armed forces of the Crown, the momentous fact
was not made public until five-thirty on the morning of the
20th of June, when it was announced by means of loud-
speakers. At once excitement mounted. In the shattered
streets of the towns and the bomb-pocked villages decorations
began to appear, flags and such poor bunting as there was,
and, where these were lacking, rugs and carpets and curtains
hung out of the windows — anything to make a show. All
who could reach the harbour thronged the approaches and
stood in a dense black mass upon the rising tiers of buildings.

For he was coming, that King whom in those past agonizing months they had so often prayed God to save — along
with themselves; that King who had chosen Malta from
all other islands of his dominions for the signal award of the
George Cross. His coming would bring to them that manifestation of the Crown to which, after their own fashion, they
were deeply loyal; and perhaps even more — although the
enemy was as yet far from vanquished — it marked the
restored freedom and security of passage of British ships in
the Mediterranean; and his Maltese subjects waited upon the
slopes of their victorious fortress to do him honour.

And then at last he came. In the bright morning sunlight *Aurora* entered the Grand Harbour of Valletta and sailed up its magnificent length. On the bridge, for all to see, stood a slim figure in white naval uniform, his hand at the salute.

'I have witnessed many memorable spectacles, but this was the most impressive of them all', wrote one who accompanied His Majesty. 'The dense throngs of loyal Maltese, men, women and children, were wild with enthusiasm. I have never heard such cheering, and all the bells in the many churches started ringing when he landed.' [63]

The record of the moving events of the next twelve hours, with their triumph and their pathos and their exultation, is best given in the King's own words:

On Sunday at 8.15 a.m. I was on the bridge as we came in to the Grand Harbour. A lovely sunny morning. A wonderful sight. Every bastion & every view point lined with people who cheered as we entered. It was a very moving moment for me. I had made up my mind that I would take a risk to get to Malta & I had got there & by sea. Mussolini called the Mediterranean Sea his Italian Lake a short time ago. Ld Gort the Governor came on board as we secured, & I landed at 9.30 a.m. I drove through cheering crowds to the Palace in Valletta & met the Council. I presented Gort with his F.M.'s baton in their presence. I saw the George Cross I gave to Malta on April 15th, 1942. Then I went on to the Balcony overlooking the Square & received a great ovation from the people below. I then went to the Naval Dockyard & was shown round it by Rear Ad. Mackenzie (the Ad. Supt.) who has been there for $4\frac{1}{2}$ years. There is nothing left above ground but all the workshops, electric light plant etc are now in tunnels underground hewn out mostly by manual labour, under Mackenzie's direction. The parish of Senglea just above the dockyard is a mere shell & I met the R.C. priest who did all he could for his parishioners.[a] Most of his flock are now evacuated, as they cannot live there. Only 80 killed. Gort then took me for a drive round part of the Island to show me some of the devastation of the 6 months 'blitz' which the Island endured. November 1941 to April 1942. We arrived at the Verdala Palace where Gort is now living & had lunch there. I met the R.C. Archbishop of Malta & the R.C. Bishop of Gozo, besides the Lt. Govr. Mr. Campbell. I rested after lunch & then after tea where I met the military staff officers about 20, Gort took me to see the other side of the Island.

[a] This priest, the Rt. Rev. Monsignor Canon Emmanuel Brincat, was later awarded the M.B.E. for his services.

I saw the runways of the R.A.F. airfields made by Maltese labour & the aircraft dispersal points. Air Ml. Sir K. Park, whom I knighted, is in command & has done a great deal in extending the aerodromes in the last year. In each village the population gave me a great reception & I found the profusion of flowers which they threw into the car was quite detrimental to my white uniform.[a] I dined with Gort & later when it was dark I reembarked in the 'Aurora' & left Malta by night. A very strenuous day but a very interesting one to have spent.[64]

The King had been deeply moved by the events of the day, which, it is not too much to say, constituted one of the most important incidents of his reign. All that he had hoped of his visit had been accomplished and surpassed. It had all been wonderfully worth while and this consoled him for his excessive weariness.

'You have made the people of Malta very happy today, Sir,' said the Lieutenant-Governor, Mr. David Campbell, in bidding him farewell, and the King answered: 'But I have been the happiest man in Malta today'.

. . . The real gem of my tour was my visit to Malta [the King wrote to Queen Mary on his return to London]. I had set my heart on that & it was not difficult to persuade the Naval & Air C in C's of its importance or of its effect on the Island itself. The question was which was the safest route, by sea or by air. I knew there was a risk in any case but it was worth taking. So I went by sea & by night. I shall never forget the sight of entering the Grand Harbour at 8.30 a.m. on a lovely sunny day, & seeing the people cheering from every vantage view point, while we were still some way off. Then later, when we anchored inside, hearing the cheers of the people which brought a lump into my throat, knowing what they had suffered from 6 months constant bombing. . . .[65]

(ix)

On his return to Britain from North Africa and Malta King George was confronted with a domestic problem within his own Household; his Private Secretary, Sir Alexander Hardinge, was compelled on grounds of ill-health to resign. For

[a] The only flowers available were scarlet geraniums and of these the Maltese picked off the heads, tied them into posies and threw them at the King. By the time he reached Verdala Palace for luncheon his white drill tunic was stained red from these 'flower bombs'. It was noted that he appeared to be delighted.

nearly a quarter of a century Sir Alexander had served three sovereigns with great devotion and efficiency, and his period as chief Private Secretary, first to King Edward VIII and subsequently to his successor, had been one of unrelieved strain and tension. The events of the Abdication crisis were followed by an inevitably increased load of responsibility for the Private Secretary owing to the fact that the new Sovereign had acceded suddenly and without preparation. The burden thus imposed, together with the gravity of the Munich Crisis, the gradual but inevitable drift towards hostilities and, finally, the years of heavy responsibility under war-time conditions, had taken their toll of one who spared himself nothing either in, or over and above, the call of duty.

Sir Alexander had modelled his conduct of his highly important office [a] on the lines laid down by his predecessor, Lord Stamfordham, under whom he had received his early training, and whose relations with the Sovereign have been so clearly portrayed by Sir Harold Nicolson. It had been the practice of King George V to send for his Private Secretary immediately after a Minister had been received in audience and to tell him the gist of their conversation so that a record of it could be made at once. This practice had not been followed by King George VI, partly because he had a natural difficulty in expression and partly because, disliking any idea of being 'run' by any member of his Household, he preferred to keep his transactions with his Ministers to himself. This had worried Sir Alexander, who felt that his resultant ignorance militated against the efficient discharge of his task in accordance with the high standard of duty which he had set for himself.

The King had been keenly appreciative of Sir Alexander's devoted service and when, in February 1939, Mr. Chamberlain had submitted his name for appointment as Governor of Madras, His Majesty had replied that he could not consider the possibility of losing him, though he hoped that one day he might go to India in this or some other similar capacity.[66] By midsummer of 1943, however, it became evident that the strain of overwhelming anxiety and responsibility made it

---

[a] For a study of the office of Private Secretary to the Sovereign, see Appendix B, p. 817.

impossible for Sir Alexander to continue and, on the medical advice of Lord Dawson of Penn, he submitted his resignation, which was accepted.

'I know I shall miss him in many ways', the King wrote in his diary,[67] and on July 19 he sent Lord Hardinge of Penshurst the following encomium of his son:

MY DEAR LORD HARDINGE,

I would like to write & tell you how very sorry I am that Alec has had to leave my service, due to ill-health. He has exhausted himself during these last very strenuous years in helping me with my work, which has indeed been heavy. You know how Alec will never spare himself when there is a job to be done, & I can never tell you how well he has done the work.

I do hope & trust that he will now be able to take a long & well earned rest to restore his health & energy, & prepare himself for the time when he can again take a further part in public service.

I shall miss him very much & I shall always look back with gratitude to him for his work on my behalf. . . .[68]

Sir Alexander Hardinge was succeeded as Private Secretary by Sir Alan Lascelles, whose wise counsel and sound judgment continued at His Majesty's disposal for the remainder of his reign.

(x)

The golden summer of 1943 continued to bring fresh news of victory. On July 9/10 the Allied combined operation against Sicily began, and less than six weeks later King George, as he began a new volume of his diary, recorded jubilantly: 'I start this volume on a note of victory. A message from Gen. Alexander to the Prime Minister states this fact: "By 10.0 a.m. this morning, 17th August, 1943, the last German soldier was flung out of Sicily & the whole island is now in our hands."'[69] On September 3 — only 16 days after the termination of the Sicilian campaign — British troops landed on the mainland of Italy north of Reggio, virtually without opposition. On September 9 the American 5th Army, under General Mark Clark, consisting of one American and one British Army Corps, effected a landing in the Gulf of Salerno south of Naples. The forces of freedom were once again established on the continent of Europe; the laborious and hard-fought process of liberation had begun.

Shortly thereafter the King was enabled to make a further record of his satisfaction. On September 26 he attended with the Queen a great service of National Thanksgiving at St. Paul's to commemorate the Battle of Britain, and in the afternoon of the same day he took the salute at a march past outside Buckingham Palace of units of the Civil Defence, Royal Air Force and Ministry of Aircraft Production as representing the three factors which had contributed most valiantly to the winning of that battle. 'It was a vivid reminder', he wrote in his diary that night, 'of those days when the enemy "let loose hell" upon London, & how our people "took it".'

In the meantime great events of historical importance had occurred in Rome. Under the impact of the Allied invasion of Sicily and the bombing of Rome (July 19) the Fascist Grand Council had on July 25/26 deposed Mussolini, who was arrested and imprisoned on the Gran Sasso, whence he was kidnapped to freedom by a German task-force on September 12, in one of the most dramatic commando operations of the war. King Victor Emmanuel, meanwhile, had entrusted the premiership to Marshal Badoglio,[a] who had succeeded in forming a government with the object of seeking peace. Secret negotiations for an armistice were opened, through Lisbon, with the Supreme Allied Commander in Sicily, and on September 3 — the day on which British troops landed on 'the toe of Italy' — the instrument of Italian unconditional surrender was signed in Syracuse.

It had been hoped to effect the capture of Rome by means of an airborne operation simultaneously with the announcement of the Italian capitulation, but this proved impracticable and the Germans, who had got wind of the armistice negotiations, lost no time in closing in upon the Eternal City, whence the King and Marshal Badoglio had difficulty in escaping to

[a] Pietro Badoglio, Marshal of Italy, Duke of Addis Ababa and Marquis of Sabotino (1871–1956), distinguished himself as a Corps Commander in the First World War and was Chief of the General Staff from 1919 to 1921. After the establishment of the Fascist régime he served as Ambassador to Brazil from 1924 to 1925 when he was again appointed Chief of the General Staff. He was Governor of Libya 1928–1933 and played the chief rôle in the conquest of Abyssinia in 1935–1936, where he became the first Viceroy and Governor-General until his reappointment as Chief of the General Staff in 1936, a post which he resigned in 1940. He was Prime Minister of Italy from July 1943 until the occupation of Rome by the Allies in June 1944, when he resigned. His memoirs of the Second World War were published in England in 1948.

Brindisi. The Italian Fleet, however, succeeded in evading capture by the Germans and sailed to Malta to surrender to the British on September 11.

The conduct of the war in Italy was complicated by the fact that there existed four forms of government. In the north were Marshal Kesselring and the German High Command, who were virtually masters of that part of the country and paid scant courtesy to Mussolini's tragi-comic opera neo-Fascist 'Republic of Salò', while in the south were the Allied military government and the fugitive régime of King Victor Emmanuel and Marshal Badoglio.

It became a principle of Allied policy that, at any rate for the time being, support must be given to the House of Savoy as the legitimate government of Italy, despite its proved record of collaboration with Fascism. King Victor Emmanuel sought to improve his standing and that of his government in letters addressed through General Eisenhower to King George and President Roosevelt at the end of September, in which he appealed for greater speed in the conduct of the Italian campaign and for the occupation of Rome at the earliest possible juncture. The King also requested the extension of the authority of his government, beyond the province of Apulia and the island of Sardinia, to include the remainder of occupied territory, including Sicily. In addition, he asked for an improvement in the rate of exchange, giving more favourable treatment to the Italians than had been accorded by that set by the Allied Military Government in Sicily.[70]

Such an appeal required the widest form of consideration and consultation before a response was made and, after having taken counsel with the War Cabinet in London, with President Roosevelt and the Soviet Government, and with the Supreme Allied Commander, King George replied on October 9 by telegram in the following terms:

I thank Your Majesty for your personal letter conveyed to me through General Eisenhower.

I and my Government agree that it is most important, in our common interest, that the greatest possible area of Italian territory should be freed from the Germans and, in particular, that Allied troops should reach Rome at the earliest moment with the best assistance that the Italian armed forces can afford them.

My Government are prepared to agree, on a provisional basis, to Your Majesty's suggestion, that your Government's jurisdiction should be extended to Sicily and subsequently to other areas on the mainland of Italy as they are cleared of the Germans, the authority of the Italian Government being exercised under the supervision of the Allied Government. At the same time I must make it clear that, while my Government are prepared to deal with Your Majesty's Government on a *de facto* basis in regard to questions arising out of the execution of the Armistice and the expulsion of the German invader from Italian soil, there is no question of recognizing Your Majesty's Government as an ally. Nor will this provisional arrangement be allowed by my Government to restrict in any way the free choice by the Italian people of the form of democratic Government which they prefer.

I and my Government welcome Your Majesty's reference to the political reconstruction of Italy and the prospect of a return to a parliamentary régime. My Government earnestly hope that all anti-Fascist elements throughout Italy will range themselves round Your Majesty and your Government and that a Coalition Government including all patriotic groups will be formed, with the object of carrying on the struggle against the German invader with the maximum force of the Italian people.

Finally, my Government are prepared to consider the possibility of altering the rate of exchange between the pound and the lira, though I must warn Your Majesty that there may be serious difficulties in the way of any such change.[71]

The reference made by the King in the third paragraph of his telegram to the position of the Royal Italian Government was somewhat clarified a few days later when the status of Italy *vis-à-vis* the Allies was changed from one of a conquered enemy, who had surrendered unconditionally, to that of a 'co-belligerent', and the Badoglio Government declared war on Germany (October 13). It was not, however, until eight months later, not until June 4, 1944 — two days before the landings in Normandy — that British and American forces entered Rome.

(xi)

In the changes and permutations of Anglo-Soviet relations during the past twelve years — from the fierce acerbity of the 'cold war' to the odour of bitter-sweetness which surrounded the visit of Marshal Bulganin and Mr. Kruschev to these islands, and the horror and disgust evoked by Soviet suppression of liberty in Hungary — it is difficult to recapture that atmosphere of heartfelt admiration for Russia which enveloped Britain in the nineteen-forties. The sense of horror and repulsion with which the British people greeted the Nazi-Soviet Pact of August 1939 as deliberate mayhem upon the peace of Europe had been sustained during the two following years by the cold-blooded policy of the U.S.S.R. in Poland, in the Baltic States and in the Balkans. These feelings, how-ever, changed almost overnight when, on June 22, 1941, Hitler invaded Russia, and it was discovered that, contrary to all expectation, the Russians did not collapse before the might of the Wehrmacht but fought back with fierce defiance and eventual success. Here at last was proof that the military machine of the Nazis was not invincible, and with gratitude and relief the people of Britain hailed the fact that they no longer 'stood alone', a condition which, while it had afforded them much cause for pride, they were in no way reluctant to abandon. Henceforth, till the conclusion of the war, the Russians were hailed as valiant brothers-in-arms and, though there was no ideological connotation attached to it, there were few factories in Britain in which the portrait of Marshal Stalin did not hang in company with those of President Roosevelt and Mr. Churchill.

This enthusiasm for Russian military success reached a new point of fervour when on February 1, 1943, the fortress of Stalingrad was surrendered by Field-Marshal von Paulus and ninety thousand German troops became prisoners.[a] Great was the jubilation at this victory and preparations were made to celebrate Red Army Day (February 21), which this year marked the 25th anniversary of the founding of the Army, in a series of public meetings throughout Britain.

The suggestion was made to King George at this moment that he should confer some award on the people of Stalingrad in recognition of their gallant and prolonged resistance against the initial German assault and in their part in the ultimate Russian victory. His Majesty was well disposed to the idea, but there were difficulties in deciding what form such an

---

[a] It is estimated that the German casualties during the siege of Stalingrad were not less than one hundred thousand.

award should take. Precedents existed in that the Military
Cross had been conferred by King George V during the First
World War on the cities of Verdun and Ypres, and King
George VI had himself decorated the island of Malta with
the George Cross. Therein, in fact, lay one of the major
complications. There could be no question of giving the George
Cross to Stalingrad, and yet it was felt that the Russians might
well feel aggrieved if that city received the Military Cross, a
lesser decoration.

The somewhat Ruritanian suggestion that a special Military Cross in brilliants should be prepared for the purpose
was rejected by the King, nor did the proposal for a casket,
similar to those in which the freedom of a city borough is
presented, find favour. An impasse seemed to have been
reached when an official of the Foreign Office suggested an
altogether different and far more appropriate form of recognition in a Sword of Honour to be specially prepared at the
King's command and suitably embellished and inscribed as a
gift from His Majesty to the city of Stalingrad in token of the
admiration of the British people.

This idea the King thought 'quite excellent' and he suggested that on Red Army Day he should send a message to
President Kalinin in which the announcement of the forthcoming gift should be included.[72] This was accordingly done
in the following terms :

To the Chairman of the Praesidium of the Supreme Council of
the Union of Soviet Socialist Republics, Moscow.

Today I and my peoples join with the peoples of the Soviet
Union in whole-hearted tribute to the heroic qualities and magnificent leadership whereby the Red Army, in its struggle against our
common enemies, has, by its resounding triumphs, written new
pages of history.

It was the unyielding resistance of Stalingrad that turned the
tide and heralded the crushing blows which have struck dismay
into the foes of civilization and freedom. To mark the profound
admiration felt by myself and the peoples of the British Empire, I
have given commands for the preparation of a Sword of Honour,
which it would give me pleasure to present to the city of Stalingrad.
My hope would be that this gift might commemorate in the happier
times to come the inflexible courage with which the warrior city
steeled herself against the powerful and persistent onslaughts of her

assailants, and that it might be a token of the admiration not only of the British peoples but of the whole civilized world.

GEORGE R.I.

The announcement of the Stalingrad Sword was received with appreciation in Moscow and with enthusiasm in Britain. The King himself took a keen interest and considered and rejected several draft drawings before approving, just before his departure for North Africa in June, the design of Mr. R. M. Y. Gleadowe, a former Art Master at Winchester and Slade Professor of Fine Art at Oxford. The design of the King's choice was for a two-handed fighting weapon with a broad and convex two-edged blade of the hardest steel, inscribed in severe capitals :

To the steel-hearted citizens of Stalingrad, the gift of King George VI, in token of the homage of the British People.

On its completion in September the Sword was sent on tour throughout Britain in the custody of Corporal Durbin of the Royal Air Force, a young metal-smith who had been temporarily released from active service to join the team of craftsmen who had made the Sword. It was estimated that nearly half a million people saw it in various cities, and many stood in queues for hours to pass before it; in London alone there were 83,000, and a similar number in Edinburgh and Glasgow; in Birmingham 50,000; in Coventry, where the Sword rested in the ruined nave of the Cathedral, 20,000.

The circumstances of the presentation of the King's gift were in themselves felicitous. The three leaders of the Grand Alliance against Nazi Germany had never met. Marshal Stalin had been invited to the Casablanca Conference in January 1943, but 'was unable to attend on account of the offensive he was directing' — that offensive, in fact, of which the capitulation of the Germans at Stalingrad had been an important part. Now, however, at the close of the year they were to meet at last at Teheran,[a] a meeting which was to mark the apogee of the alliance, for, when they met again at Yalta,

[a] President Roosevelt and Mr. Churchill, with their advisers, met with Marshal Chiang Kai-shek at Cairo from November 23 to 26, 1943. They then proceeded to Teheran for the conference with Marshal Stalin from November 28 to December 1. The President and the Prime Minister then returned to Cairo for conversations with President Inönü of Turkey from December 4 to 7.

just over a year later, suspicion and doubt of Soviet designs upon Europe had certainly arisen in Mr. Churchill's mind. At Teheran, however, there was a large measure of mutual confidence and, though there were differences of opinion as to how it was to be achieved, the defeat and conquest of Germany were agreed upon as of the utmost importance in the minds of all three statesmen. The consideration of the next step, after this end had been accomplished, was sufficiently distant as to be described as 'very preliminary'.

By the King's command, Mr. Churchill had taken the Stalingrad Sword with him to Teheran and, before the second plenary session of the conference opened at four o'clock in the afternoon of November 29, he presented it to Marshal Stalin in the presence of President Roosevelt, the British and American Chiefs of Staff and many others. 'The large outer hall was filled with Russian officers and soldiers', Mr. Churchill writes. 'When after a few sentences of explanation, I handed the splendid weapon to Marshal Stalin, he raised it in a most impressive gesture to his lips and kissed the scabbard. He then passed it to Voroshilov who dropped it.' [73]

Other eye-witnesses aver that the Marshal, on being handed the sword, half-drew the blade and kissed it just below the hilt. All agree, however, that he was deeply affected. He had difficulty in replying and when he did speak his voice was so low that he could scarcely be heard. His interpreter's voice, unfortunately, was also so choked with emotion that he was almost equally inaudible, but he was understood to say that the Marshal expressed the deep appreciation of the Russian people for this gesture of their British comrades.

The gratitude of Marshal Stalin to King George was later expressed in suitable terms by the Soviet Ambassador, who was received in audience. 'I received M. Gousev, the Soviet Ambr., who brought me a message of thanks from Stalin, for the gift of the Stalingrad Sword', the King wrote in his diary. 'The Prime Minister handed it to Stalin on my behalf at Teheran.' [a][74]

[a] The Sword was placed by Stalin's order in the War Museum of the rebuilt city of Stalingrad, where it is kept in a small special strong-room together with other tributes to the defenders of Stalingrad. This room is not normally open to the public and its contents are only on show on certain occasions, such as the anniversary of the surrender of von Paulus's army.

(xii)

The year 1943, which had seen so great a change in the military
fortunes of himself and his allies, ended on a note of victory
which, to the King as a sailor, brought particular gratification.

The maintenance of the convoys to Russia around the
North Cape and through the Arctic Ocean to the port of
Archangel had been one of the most onerous and costly naval
operations of the war. German U-boats and surface vessels
had destroyed many merchantmen, together with their escorts,
in the desperate battle to keep open the supply route to the
Soviet Union, and there had been prolonged periods of the
gravest anxiety. In the latter half of 1943, however, two
devastating blows were struck at German naval strength
sheltering in Norwegian waters. On September 22 the
35,000-ton battleship *Tirpitz* was crippled in the northerly
Alter Fjord by British midget submarines, a fact which King
George had noted with satisfaction in his diary,[75] and on
Sunday, December 26, the 26,000-ton battle-cruiser, *Scharnhorst*, whose dramatic escape from Brest, together with *Gneisenau*
and *Prinz Eugen* in February 1942, had caused such mortified
heart-burning in Britain, was sunk not far off the North Cape
after a brilliant naval action which the King followed with avid
interest.

On Sunday morning [he wrote in his diary] I was told that the
'Scharnhorst' was in contact with our Convoy going to Russia in
the vicinity of the North Cape. Rear Ad. Burnett in the 'Belfast',
with 'Norfolk' & 'Sheffield', frustrated two attempted attacks on
the Convoy by the 'Scharnhorst'. The 'Norfolk' was hit aft in
'X' turret but not badly. The C in C. H. Fleet, in the 'Duke of
York', with 'Jamaica' & 4 destroyers, were in position to intercept
from the S.W. Owing to 'S''s superior speed, the 4 destroyers
were despatched to try a torpedo attack. In this they succeeded &
the 'S''s speed was reduced, which enabled the 'Duke of York' to
engage her, & the 'Scharnhorst' sank at 7.45 p.m. This is great
news & I am delighted the 'D of Y' did it. The whole of the
action or most of it took place in the dark owing to its whereabouts
in the Arctic Circle. The Convoy is safe & our casualties few.
The Admiralty have not yet announced the names of the ships
which took part as they have not yet reached port. The destroyers
were 'Savage', 'Saumarez', 'Scorpion' & the Norwegian 'Stord'.
As usual I spent the day wondering what was going on. I was very
hopeful. . . .[76]

A few days later he added a further note of pride in the part which the 'D of Y', his own namesake, had played in the action :

An interesting item has come to light re the 'Scharnhorst' battle. The gunfire of the 'Duke of York' was so accurate & an underwater hit on the 'S' enabled the destroyers to attack as the hit reduced her speed.[77]

But despite the successes of the year, of which the Battle of the North Cape was but the latest, King George was under no illusion about the heavy tasks which lay ahead. Germany was far from conquered and her decisive defeat could only be accomplished by means of invasion across the Channel. Plans for such an operation were already in train, of which the King had been kept fully informed, and he was also aware that the stubborn and able resistance which the German army was still offering in Italy and in Russia betokened an equally bitter opposition whenever the Allied armies might land in Western Europe ; and on the Pacific Front, the forces of Japan, though discomfited, were by no means vanquished. While, therefore, there was cause for satisfaction, gratitude and thanksgiving for what had already been achieved, this was no moment for diminution of effort nor for indulgence in dreams of early victory ; fierce fighting and grim sacrifices were still to be encountered, and it was in a spirit of mingled gratification and warning that His Majesty spoke to his peoples in his Christmas broadcast :

Since I last spoke to you many things have changed. But the spirit of our people has not changed. As we were not downcast by defeat, we are not unduly exalted by victory. While we have bright visions of the future we have no easy dreams of the days that lie close at hand. We know that much hard working and hard fighting, and perhaps harder working and harder fighting than ever before, are necessary for victory. We shall not rest from our task until it is nobly ended. Meanwhile within these islands, we have tried to be worthy of our fathers ; we have tried to carry into the dawn the steadfastness and courage vouchsafed to us when we stood alone in the darkness.

Even the King himself was not entirely free from all wishful thinking, however, for on this Christmas night he wrote in his diary : 'Let us hope next Christmas will see the end of the War'.

CHAPTER IX

VICTORY ACHIEVED
1944–1945

(i)

ESIDES the many vital problems which confronted King
George at the opening of the New Year, there was also
the domestic question of the future status of his elder
daughter, who would attain her eighteenth birthday on
April 21, 1944.

This event, though it did not constitute Princess Elizabeth's
majority, did raise certain live issues of importance. The two
Princesses had spent most of the war at Windsor and in Scotland, but the King had realized for some while that the time
was approaching when Princess Elizabeth would have to enter
public life and that the preparation for this should be put in
hand. To this end he requested Parliament in the previous
autumn so to amend the Regency Act of 1937 as to admit
Princess Elizabeth to be included among the Counsellors of
State whenever the need for their appointment arose, 'in
order that she should have every opportunity of gaining experience in the duties which would fall upon her in the event
of her acceding to the Throne'. Under the existing law the
Princess would not have become eligible as a Counsellor until
the age of twenty-one when she would attain her legal majority.
In September 1943, therefore, a new Regency Bill was introduced,
which provided that 'The Heir Apparent or Heir Presumptive
to the Throne, if not under 18 years, should not be disqualified from being a Counsellor of State by reason only of his
not being of full age'. The Bill met with no opposition in
either House, and received the Royal Assent on November 11,
1943.[a]

The constitutional status of Princess Elizabeth was therefore established, but there remained the somewhat vexed

[a] See Appendix A.   A Regent and Counsellors of State.

question of a potential change in her style and title. From various sources there came indications that appeals would be made to His Majesty to create his elder daughter 'Princess of Wales', and it was held more than likely that the House of Commons would exercise their immemorial privilege of peti-tioning the Sovereign to this effect.[a] The motives for such proposals were for the most part romantic, nationalistic or sentimental; though one eminent politician advocated it on the grounds that it would be a bait to catch Welsh votes in the next General Election!

The expectations of public agitation were fully justified and the King, who was firmly averse to any such action, was anxious to make it clear well in advance of Princess Elizabeth's birthday that he had no intention of changing her title on this occasion. He consulted Mr. Churchill on the subject, with the result that a conflict of thought ensued as to who should make the announcement. The King wrote in his diary:

Tuesday, February 8th
I talked to W. about the question of my putting out a statement to say that I did not intend to give Lilibet any title on her 18th birthday. The Press & other people, especially in Wales, are agitating for her to become 'Princess of Wales'. W. thought he shld. put it out, but I argued that it is a family matter & that the Domn. P.M.s could suggest she shld. have a Domn. title. He agreed to put it before the War Cabinet, & let me know.

The War Cabinet eventually concurred with the King's point of view and on February 12 the following announcement appeared in the Press:

It is officially announced from Buckingham Palace that the King does not contemplate making any change in the style and title of the Princess Elizabeth on the occasion of her approaching eighteenth birthday.[b]

The King's reasons for his decision were, as usual, emi-nently practical. 'How could I create Lilibet the Princess of

[a] The House of Commons had exercised this privilege on more than one occasion, as, for example, when in 1376 they formally petitioned Edward III to make Richard of Bordeaux Prince of Wales.
[b] Princess Elizabeth's eighteenth birthday was widely but erroneously de-scribed as her coming-of-age. Even *The Times* had fallen into this error in com-menting on the announcement of February 12, and had corrected itself two days later.

Wales', he wrote to Queen Mary, 'when it is the recognised title of the wife of the Prince of Wales? Her own name is so nice and what name would she be called by when she marries, I want to know.'[1]

Lilibet's 18th Birthday [he wrote in his diary at Windsor]. The Changing of the Guard took place in the quadrangle and we made it an occasion for her birthday. The Lt. Colonel, Col. J. Prescott, handed her the Colonel's Standard, which will be used on her future inspections. Officers and gdsmen. of Trg. Bn. Grenadier Guards were present.[a] We gave a family lunch to which Mama came. It was a lovely hot day. L. can now act as a Counsellor of State.[2]

(ii)

That which was engaging the King's interest to a major degree at this time was the secret preparation for the major assault upon Europe, now being mounted in the United Kingdom.

It had been at the Casablanca Conference in January 1943 that President Roosevelt and Mr. Churchill had taken the momentous decision to effect a full-scale invasion of the Nazi-dominated continent of Europe, in addition to their projected operations in Italy and their intensified bombing of Axis targets.

We shall concentrate in the United Kingdom a strong American land and air force [they telegraphed to Marshal Stalin on January 26]. These, combined with the British forces in the United Kingdom, will prepare themselves to re-enter the continent of Europe as soon as practicable.[3]

At that precise moment the exact point of attack had not been determined but the military concentration in Britain, since it could not hope to escape the attention of the Germans, would, for that very reason, have the additional advantage of

[a] King George had, in fact, appointed Princess Elizabeth Colonel of the Grenadier Guards in February 1942. Two months later, on her sixteenth birthday, she made her first inspection in impressive circumstances. Under their commanding officers, every battalion of the regiment was represented by small detachments, including units serving with the Guards Armoured Division, the Training and Holding Battalions, the Depôt Companies, and members of the Old Comrades Association. The Princess took the salute at a march past in the Great Quadrangle at Windsor Castle and later gave a party for the six hundred officers and men who had been on parade.

causing them considerable speculation and consequent dissi-
pation of strength throughout the *Festung Europa*. 'They will
not know where or when, or on what scale, we propose striking', the President and the Prime Minister informed the
Marshal. 'They will therefore be compelled to divert both
land and air forces to all the shores of France, the Low Countries,
Corsica, Sardinia, Sicily, the heel of Italy, Yugoslavia, Greece,
Crete and the Dodecanese.'

While the commander of this projected Anglo-American
Army of Liberation was as yet undesignated, a further decision
at Casablanca constituted the nucleus of his general staff under
the short title of 'Cossac' (Chief of Staff, Supreme Allied
Commander), and to this post Lieutenant-General F. E.
Morgan [a] was appointed in April, with headquarters at Norfolk House, St. James's Square.

The first idea for the liberation of Europe which had
commended itself to Mr. Churchill had been to extend the
Mediterranean theatre of operations by the invasion of the
Balkans, with the intention of linking up with the armies of
the Soviet Union and the possibility of bringing Turkey into
the war on the side of the Allies. The strategists of the United
States, however, had expressed a preference for an invasion
of Western Europe, and this was confirmed at the Quebec
Conference of August 1943. By the winter the selection of a
striking-point for 'Operation Overlord' had been narrowed
down to a choice between the Pas-de-Calais and Normandy.

There were those, however, who regretted the abandonment of Mr. Churchill's plan and who feared that the division
of Allied strength between Western Europe and the Mediterranean theatre would result in victory being achieved on
neither front. Amongst these was General Smuts who, in a
series of telegrams to Mr. Churchill after the Quebec Conference, criticized somewhat trenchantly the strategic decisions

---

[a] Lieutenant-General Sir Frederick Edgworth Morgan, K.C.B. (b. 1894),
had commanded the First Corps in North Africa from 1942 to 1943, prior to his
appointment to 'Cossac'. On the formation of the Supreme Headquarters,
Allied Expeditionary Force (SHAEF) in 1944 he became Deputy Chief of Staff
to the Supreme Commander and so continued until the end of the war. He was
chief of UNRRA operations in Germany from 1945 to 1946, when he retired.
In 1951 he was appointed Controller of Atomic Energy and in 1954 Controller
of Atomic Weapons. His book, *Overture to Overlord*, provides an authoritative and
entertaining account of the planning of the invasion of North-Western Europe.

reached there,[4] and, on his arrival in London in October for the meeting of Commonwealth Prime Ministers,[a] essayed to bring about a change of plan.

To General Smuts at this moment it appeared that the course of the war was going deplorably slowly, and it prompted him to remark privately : 'I doubt if we shall ever finish this war, America is more concerned about money matters than beating Germany'.[5]   In Italy it seemed to him that the Allies were bogged down on a line south of Rome, owing to a shortage of men. By the end of the year General Alexander would have fifteen divisions, whereas the Germans already had twenty-four to twenty-eight at their disposal in this theatre, with the possibility of quickly reinforcing this number to sixty if they so wished. General Smuts, therefore, considered that the Allied strength should be concentrated on the Mediterranean Front, and he communicated his misgivings to King George.

Smuts is not happy about 'Overlord' & is doing his best to convince Winston that we must go on with W's own strategy of attacking the 'under belly of the Axis' [the King wrote in his diary after a long audience on October 13]. We are now in Italy, Italy has surrendered to us, & has declared war on Germany today as a co-belligerent, not as an Ally, which means the Italian people will help us in Italy. We are masters of the Mediterranean & the Italian Fleet is ours. S. feels we must capture the Dodecanese & Aegean Islands & from there land in Greece & in Yugoslavia across the Adriatic, thus liberating those 2 countries, which in turn may make Roumania & even Hungary give in. Turkey may come in on our side as well. As arrangements are we are committed to 'Overlord' next May which may mean a stalemate in France. I agree with S. about all this. If you have a good thing stick to it. Why start another front across the Channel. F. D. R. wants to give Marshall [b] a good job here as C in C. The Russians do not want us in the Balkans. They would like to see us fighting in France, so as to have a free hand in the east of Europe.[6]

    [a] It was in the course of this visit to England that General Smuts delivered on October 25, 1943, before the Empire Parliamentary Association, his famous 'Explosive Speech' on the theme 'Thoughts on a New World', in which, 'thinking aloud', he depicted a courageous vision of the rôle which a revitalized British Empire and Commonwealth might play in partnership with the United States and the Soviet Union.
    [b] General of the Army George Catlett Marshall (b. 1880) served with the United States Army in the Philippines, in France in the First World War and later in China. He became deputy Chief of the General Staff of the Army in

So impressed was King George with the arguments of General Smuts that he determined to exercise his constitutional prerogative of warning his Prime Minister. Mr. Churchill was about to set out upon his series of consultations with President Roosevelt and Marshal Stalin at Cairo and Teheran.[a] If any change was to be effected, therefore, in accordance with General Smuts's ideas, in the over-all plan of allied strategy, this was the time — perhaps the last opportunity — to do it. If his United Kingdom and South African Prime Ministers could be brought together with himself to thrash out the matter, much good might come of it. The King thereupon wrote the following letter to Mr. Churchill.

MY DEAR WINSTON,

I had a long talk with Smuts yesterday about the Mediterranean theatre of war. He has discussed this with you, & wants us to go on fighting there, & not to switch over to a new front like 'Overlord'.

I have thought about this matter a lot since then & am wondering whether we three could not discuss it together, I have always thought that your original idea of last year of attacking the 'under belly of the Axis' was the right one & you convinced President Roosevelt & Gen. Marshall to carry out 'Torch'. The present situation as we know has turned out even better than we could have ever hoped for last year & would it not be possible to carry on there. Look at the present position in the Mediterranean. The whole of North Africa is ours, we command the Mediterranean Sea itself, Sicily, Sardinia & Corsica, half the mainland of Italy is ours. Italy is now at war with our enemy Germany; Roumania & Hungary are trying to get into touch with us. What we want to see is Greece & Yugoslavia liberated; then Turkey may come in with us & may be we shall see the 3 Great Powers, Great Britain, U.S.A. & U.S.S.R. fighting together on the same front!!

Let this country be the base from which all bombing operations will take place in an ever increasing intensity on Germany. I was so impressed by what Smuts said that I felt I must pass it on to you. I know there are many difficulties for a change of plan at this late hour, but you, F. D. R. & Stalin are to meet in the near future. I am alone here for dinner tonight, & if there is any

1938 and Chief of the General Staff in 1939, in which capacity he served throughout the Second World War. He was appointed President Truman's Special Ambassador to China, 1945–1947, Secretary of State, 1947–1949, and Secretary of Defence, 1950–1951. In the initial planning of 'Overlord' there was at one moment some uncertainty as to whether General Marshall or General Eisenhower would be appointed Supreme Commander.

[a] See above, p. 586, fn.

possibility of Smuts & you joining me, it would give us all a very good opportunity of talking these things over undisturbed.

Would 8.30 pm or 8.45 pm suit you best?

I am

Yours very sincerely

GEORGE R.I.[7]

The invitation was at once accepted and the King and his two Prime Ministers dined together alone that night. Mr. Churchill maintained the point of view which had been agreed with President Roosevelt at Quebec and succeeded, at least apparently, in convincing General Smuts not only of the impossibility of changing the basis of 'Overlord' at this juncture, but also of the good chances of success for that operation. The discussion was frank and full and the King was well satisfied with his initiative, which had enabled the three of them to deliberate upon the issue in the relaxed atmosphere around a dinner-table.

Both of them came to dinner with me alone [he recorded]. We discussed the whole strategy of the war at length, & W. thinks it possible to arrange for Overlord & the Balkans too. The U.S.S.R. know that we & the U.S.A. are definitely going to do the former but if the situation in the Medn. warrants it we shall go on there, & the divisions will not be withdrawn until later. Both P.M.s had talked seriously to Wavell about India. It was a pleasant evening & I collected a great deal of information from both of them. It is so seldom in this busy life, that people can find time to think & talk about matters which are not current problems.[8]

The King was also gratified to learn that Mr. Churchill had sent His Majesty's letter to the Chiefs of Staff for their consideration. 'They agree that Italy has got to be secured at all costs, before Overlord', he wrote in his diary.[9]

The appointment of General Eisenhower as Supreme Commander of the Allied Expeditionary Force (SCAEF), and of his subordinate commanders, was announced on Christmas Eve,[a] and in the New Year the King entered upon a period of intense activity. As in the days after Dunkirk, he travelled

[a] General Eisenhower's subordinate commanders as announced on December 24, 1943, were as follows: Deputy Supreme Commander, Air Chief Marshal Sir Arthur Tedder; Chief of Staff, General Wallis Bedell Smith; Deputy Chief of Staff, Lieut.-General Sir Frederick Morgan; Commander-in-Chief British Army Group, General Sir Bernard Montgomery; Allied Air Commander-in-Chief, Air Chief Marshal Sir Trafford Leigh-Mallory.

up and down the country inspecting troops and encouraging officers and men in the ordeal which lay before them. In 1940 he had bidden them to be of good heart and to stand firm in the defence of their island fortress; in 1944 he exhorted them to go forward with equal courage in the assault from that island upon the Fortress of Europe.

He kept close contact also with those who were to lead this great operation. When General Eisenhower arrived in London in January he was received at Buckingham Palace, and the King was on more than one occasion the guest of the Supreme Commander at his headquarters at Bushy Park. General Montgomery came to see him and 'drew me a sketch of his plan of attack for "Overlord"', which the King kept among his collection of war souvenirs.[10]

A few days later he received Admiral Sir Bertram Ramsay,[a] who gave him to his intense interest an idea of the problems arising from the naval side of the project:

He told me on what a prodigious scale the operation wld have to be. He wants 15000 officers & men to put one infantry divn ashore, as his men must be accommodated afloat until shore buildings are built. About 2000 ships are needed. The more one goes into it, the more alarming it becomes in its vastness. His actual deputy is R.Ad. Sir Philip Vian,[b] whom I talked to later, who is in charge of 5 Assault Divisions from the Landing Craft side. Three of ours & two American. He is training them now on different parts of the coast.[11]

Much was thought and said at this time about the religious dedication of the troops training in England for D-Day, whose spiritual preparation became a greater cause of concern than on the eve of almost any other great operation of our military history since Henry V's prayer before Agincourt. Archbishop

[a] Admiral Sir Bertram Home Ramsay, K.C.B., K.B.E., M.V.O. (1883–1945), Flag Officer Commanding, Dover, 1939–1942; Naval Commander, Eastern Task Force, Mediterranean, 1943; Allied Naval Commander-in-Chief, Expeditionary Force, 1944 until his death in an air accident on January 2, 1945.

[b] Admiral of the Fleet Sir Philip Vian, G.C.B., K.B.E., D.S.O. (b. 1894), served as Captain (D) in H.M.S. *Cossack*, 1940–1941; commanded Force 'K' (Arctic), 1941; 15th Cruiser Squadron, 1941–1942; Force 'U' at Sicilian and Salerno landings, 1943; British Naval Forces at Normandy landings, 1944; and Carrier Force, Pacific, 1945. He became Second-in-Command of the British Pacific Fleet in 1945, 5th Sea Lord (Air) in 1946 and Deputy-Chief of Naval Staff, 1947. He was Commander-in-Chief Home Fleet from 1950 to 1952.

Temple [a] was desirous that the King should mark D-Day by
calling upon his people for a national observance of prayer
and intercession, and with this suggestion His Majesty was
deeply sympathetic. When, however, there came from an
exalted military quarter a proposal for an elaborate service
for the hallowing of the fighting men who would be engaged
in 'Overlord', to be held in St. Paul's on May 12, the anniversary of the Coronation, and at which the Coronation
regalia were to be paraded, the King rejected it with distaste
and with the very just comment that the Coronation regalia
were already consecrated to a unique purpose. The proposal
was eventually disposed of by Sir Alan Lascelles with a wholly
felicitous quotation from the Younger Pitt, who in 1782 had
said : 'This is neither a fit time nor a proper subject for the
exhibition of a gaudy fancy or the wanton blandishments of
theatrical enchantment'.[12]

The hallowing of the troops was more properly observed
in the many and crowded voluntary services held in country
churches in the areas in which the army of invasion was
concentrated.[b]

The King spent the days of May 10–13 with his fleet at
Scapa, where he visited many ships, great and small, and put
to sea in the aircraft carrier *Victorious*, flying the Royal Standard
at the fore, being greatly impressed by the landing on her deck
of some 40 to 50 'Barracudas' and 'Corsairs' — a truly remarkable sight.

On his return to London he attended, on May 15, the
historic conference at St. Paul's School, at which General
Montgomery had been educated and which was now the
headquarters of his 21st Army Group.[c] At this meeting the
general plan of 'Operation Overlord' was explained by its

---

[a] Most Rev. and Rt. Hon. William Temple (1881–1944), a son of a previous
Archbishop of Canterbury, was ordained in 1908 and, having been Headmaster
of Repton School from 1910 to 1914, was consecrated Bishop of Manchester in
1921. He was Archbishop of York from 1929 to 1942, and of Canterbury from
1942 to 1944.

[b] As a result of these services, and of their own spiritual contemplation, many
young Servicemen decided to offer themselves for the Ministry of the Church of
England after the war, and provision was made by the Archbishop of Canterbury
for their preliminary selection under the charge of the Rev. Kenneth Riches,
now Bishop of Lincoln, as Director of Service Ordinands.

[c] Shortly before D-Day the operational headquarters of the 21st Army Group
were transferred to Portsmouth.

executive commanders to a uniquely distinguished audience. In addition to His Majesty and General Eisenhower, there were present Mr. Churchill and the members of the War Cabinet, the British Chiefs of Staff, the Prime Minister of South Africa, and Admirals, Generals and Air Marshals by the score. Though the meeting had been kept a dead secret, the thought of potential danger and its results was in the minds of more than one of those present. 'Never in all my long experience have I seen a conference chamber more crowded with officers of high rank', wrote one who participated. 'I found myself wondering what might happen if the Germans made a daylight raid in force and landed a bomb on the building'; [13] and Sir Alan Lascelles later recorded: 'I could not help reflecting as I looked round the room, that there had probably been no single assembly in the last four years the annihilation of which by a single well-directed bomb would affect more profoundly the issue of the war'.[a]

The conference was of dramatic significance since it marked the virtual completion of all preliminary planning and preparation for the invasion, and the drama was enhanced by the very simplicity of the surroundings. The room was an ordinary form-room, partly panelled in pitch-pine, and an incongruous element was provided by a notice on the wall to the effect that sons of clergymen who were candidates for scholarships should apply to the High Master. The King and Mr. Churchill were accorded the privilege of armchairs, but the rest of the company sat on school forms facing a large map of the invasion area which hung above a low dais. After a brief introduction by General Eisenhower each commander demonstrated his own particular rôle and task in the invasion. General Montgomery spoke with quiet and deliberate emphasis and remarkable exactness of prophecy; Admiral Ramsay with cheerful pessimism; Air Chief Marshal Leigh-Mallory with radiant confidence; General Spaatz was nervous and stumbling.

When the last commander had concluded his statement on this portentous blue-print of the shape of things to come, the

[a] The same thought had occurred to General Eisenhower, for in closing the afternoon proceedings, at which the King was not present, he prefaced his remarks by saying that in a few moments Hitler would have missed his last chance to wipe out all the leaders of the invasion by a well-placed bomb.

King rose and, to the surprise of all, stepped on to the platform. He had not been expected to speak and he did so
without notes, with impressive brevity and very aptly. The
content of his remarks was as follows : [a]

> I have known of the existence of this Operation ever since it
> was first mooted and I have followed all its preparations very
> carefully. I have heard and seen reports from my P.M. as Minr. of
> Defence, & from the Supreme Comdr. Today I have attended
> this lecture given by the Comdrs. of all 3 Services who are taking
> part in it.
> This is the biggest Combined Operation ever thought out in
> the world. But it is much more than this. It is a Combined Opn.
> of 2 Countries, the United States & the British Empire. As I look
> around this audience of British & Americans I can see that you
> have equally taken a part in its preparation. I wish you all success
> & with God's help you will succeed.[b] [15]

Between the Conference at St. Paul's School and D-Day
itself the King visited each of the assault forces in their ports
of assembly. 'I have now seen all our troops who are taking
part in Overlord', he wrote in his diary.[16]

(iii)

The plans for 'Operation Overlord' were now complete, the
last preparations made. The great host for the liberation of
Europe from Nazi tyranny was gathered in its areas of embarkation; all southern England, lovely in its wild flowers
and early summer green, was a vast military concentration;
the appointed hour of the invasion was dawn on June 5.[c]

[a] Since for security reasons no record was kept of the conference of May 15,
the exact text of the King's remarks is unknown, but the following draft was
found among his papers at Buckingham Palace after his death and is included
here as an indication rather than a record. In his diary for the day His Majesty
refers to a 'short impromptu speech', and adds: 'I stressed the fact that this was
a "combined operation" of the forces of 2 Nations, working together in friendly
rivalry though in perfect harmony. No 2 Nations (U.S.A. & Br. Emp.) had
ever worked so closely before.' [14]

[b] 'The King made a very good short speech . . .', Sir John Kennedy, the
Director of Military Operations, wrote in his diary, 'it was perfect for the occasion
and created an excellent impression on the Americans, as well as on us' (*The
Business of War*, p. 328).

[c] To many young Servicemen who waited at this time in southern Eng-

To the King's intense satisfaction the promise of the Chiefs of Staff in response to his letter concerning the Italian campaign[a] had been fulfilled. On May 11/12 the armies of General Alexander had opened their offensive against the Gustav Line, to be followed on May 23 by the formidable assault launched from the Anzio beach-head. The result of these operations was to be the occupation of Rome on June 4.

King George supported the interval of waiting for D-Day with impatience and with a growing desire to be a witness of this great event. He encountered a similar desire in the mind of Mr. Churchill who, as a soldier, journalist and historian, was irked at the prospect of sniffing the battle from afar. There resulted that conflict of wills between the Sovereign and his Prime Minister, of which the latter has given his own account in his memoirs.[17]

On Tuesday, May 30, Mr. Churchill came to the palace for his usual luncheon-audience. The King made the following note of their conversation :

I asked W. where he would be on D day or rather the night before & he told me glibly he hoped to see the initial attack from one of the bombarding ships. He had asked Ad. Ramsay to work out a plan for him a month ago. I was not surprised & when I suggested that I should go as well (the idea has been in my mind for some time) he reacted well, & he & I are going to talk it over with Ramsay on Thursday. It is a big decision to take on one's own responsibility. W. cannot say no if he goes himself, & I don't want to have to tell him he cannot. So? I told Elizabeth about the idea & she was wonderful as always & encouraged me to do it.[18]

The effect, however, upon Sir Alan Lascelles, when the King broached the project to him, was far from enthusiastic. That wise adviser of the Monarchy was appalled at such a

land for the beginning of this huge hazard the land had never seemed so beautiful. One of them wrote:

And lo, on Hampshire hill and Devon combe
The beacons spoke to friend and enemy.
The call to arms was lit on gorse and broom
That time when all hills ran towards the sea.

I never saw the lanes look lovelier.
The English earth was prodigal as we,
Sparing no umbelled flower nor crucifer
That time when all lanes led towards the sea.
(John Moore, 'England 1944', *Come Rain, Come Shine.*)

[a] See above, p. 596.

hazardous enterprise being undertaken by either the Sovereign
or his Prime Minister and, though he preserved a certain
deliberate impassivity which he was far from feeling, he did
not hesitate to deprecate the idea to the King. By way of
argument, he posed the question whether His Majesty was
prepared to advise Princess Elizabeth on the choice of her
first Prime Minister in the event of her father and Mr. Churchill
being killed simultaneously. He also depicted the intolerable
predicament in which the commander of any vessel would be
placed in having to fight his ship with so august a complement
aboard. These arguments impressed the King and he agreed
to sleep on them.

In the night watches Sir Alan became the more certain that
the idea must be abandoned and he reposed great confidence
in the King's habitual common sense to see the matter likewise
on reflection. When he returned to the attack next morning
he was not disappointed. The King wrote in his diary:

> Lascelles came to me in the morning & told me he had come
> to the conclusion that it was not right for either the P.M. or me to
> go on this expedition & suggested I should write to Winston & tell
> him so. I had also given the whole matter very careful thought &
> my thoughts had come to the same end. I wrote a letter to the
> P.M. saying that I hoped he would reconsider his plan. His going
> would add more to my anxieties at this moment, & that should
> anything happen to him the whole Allied cause would suffer, &
> was it worth it.[19]

The King wrote to his Prime Minister:

MY DEAR WINSTON,

I have been thinking a great deal of our conversation yesterday,
and I have come to the conclusion that it would not be right for
either you or me to be where we planned on D Day. I don't
think I need emphasise what it would mean to me personally, and
to the whole Allied cause, if at this juncture a chance bomb,
torpedo, or even a mine, should remove you from the scene;
equally a change of Sovereign at this moment would be a serious
matter for the country and Empire. We should both, I know, love
to be there, but in all seriousness I would ask you to reconsider
your plan. Our presence, I feel, would be an embarrassment to
those responsible for fighting the ship or ships in which we were,
despite anything we might say to them.

So, as I said, I have very reluctantly come to the conclusion that the right thing to do is what normally falls to those at the top on such occasions, namely, to remain at home and wait. I hope very much that you will see it in this light too. The anxiety of these coming days would be very greatly increased for me if I thought that, in addition to everything else, there was a risk, however remote, of my losing your help and guidance.

          Believe me,
                    Yours very sincerely,
                              GEORGE R.I.[20]

The King added that no reply should be sent to his letter as he would be seeing the Prime Minister on the following day and would discuss his reactions with him and with Admiral Sir Bertram Ramsay.

Accordingly the next afternoon the King, attended by his Private Secretary, went to the Downing Street Annexe in Storey's Gate. There, in the map-room, Admiral Ramsay, who knew only of Mr. Churchill's project and nothing of the King's, expounded to them exactly what would be involved in the Prime Minister's scheme of sailing on D-Day in the cruiser *Belfast*, which would be flying the flag of Admiral Sir Frederick Dalrymple-Hamilton, commanding the ships executing the bombardment. It needed but a few moments to make obvious that any passenger in *Belfast* would run considerable risks from mines and torpedoes; from air attack and shells from the shore batteries. In addition, it was demonstrated that, since the ship would at no time be nearer the coast than 14,000 yards, those on board would see little of the battle to compensate for these dangers, and would indeed have less information about its general progress than those following it in London.

Having made his exposition Admiral Ramsay was asked to withdraw, to be recalled after a few minutes and informed that the operation which he had just described might under certain circumstances include his Sovereign as well as the Prime Minister. To this the unfortunate Admiral, not unnaturally, reacted violently. Mr. Churchill declared that he would feel bound to seek the Cabinet's approval of the King's participation in the expedition but that he would not be able to recommend them to give it. This His Majesty accepted with good grace, but it became clear that Mr. Churchill had no intention of applying this wise decision to himself. Quite regardless of the King's letter, he was still determined to go, and nothing that the King could say at that moment could deter him.

Sir Alan Lascelles was in despair and his feelings were, for once, apparent. 'Your face is getting longer and longer', said the King, and his Private Secretary replied : 'I was thinking, Sir, that it is not going to make things easier for you if you have to find a new Prime Minister in the middle of "Overlord" '. To which Mr. Churchill responded : 'Oh, that's all arranged for [a] and, anyhow, I don't think the risk is 100/1'.

The constitutional issue was then raised and Sir Alan said that he had always understood that no Minister of the Crown could leave the country without the Sovereign's consent. To this Mr. Churchill made riposte that his proposed action did not count as going abroad because he would be in a British man-of-war and therefore on British territory. But, Sir Alan pointed out, he would, even so, be a long way outside British territorial waters. No argument, however, could prevail against the Prime Minister's irrefragable determination, and the King returned to Buckingham Palace.

King George's own account of this interview, together with its sequel, is given in his diary and shows clearly his anxiety and concern at Mr. Churchill's obduracy :

I said I very much deprecated the idea of his [the Prime Minister's] going as a passenger for a 'joy ride'. He said he had flown to U.S.A., Middle East, Moscow & Teheran & had crossed the Atlantic by sea already & that this was nothing. I said he had had to pay those visits on duty for the future strategy of the war, & that this idea was taking unnecessary risks for one holding his important position. He had already received my letter yesterday so knew what I felt about it. I suggested to Ramsay he could get another cruiser for both of us but it was too late to do that. When I left I could see Ramsay was a bit shaken & wished to stop the P.M. going. I saw Gen. Ismay later who was very upset at the P.M.'s attitude. Ramsay also said that there would be little to see at that time, but that if all went well in 5 or 6 days a visit to the beaches would be well worth while. He did promise me that much as soon as it was reasonably safe to do so. I am very worried

See above, pp. 544-6.

over the P.M.'s seemingly selfish way of looking at the matter. He doesn't seem to care about the future, or how much depends on him.[21]

That evening the King went to Windsor to dine and sleep, and with him went Sir Alan Lascelles. Both were troubled and depressed at the negative outcome of the afternoon's meeting, and on the following morning, June 2, the King took further action :

Friday, June 2nd

Ismay sent me a message early to say that the P.M. was wavering & hoped that I would send him another message imploring him not to go on the expedition. I did so & this is what I wrote.

'I want to make one more appeal to you not to go to sea on D Day. Please consider my own position. I am a younger man than you, I am a sailor, & as King I am the head of all three Services. There is nothing I would like better than to go to sea but I have agreed to stop at home ; is it fair that you should then do exactly what I should have liked to do myself? You said yesterday afternoon that it would be a fine thing for the King to lead his troops into battle, as in old days ; if the King cannot do this, it does not seem to me right that his Prime Minister should take his place. Then there is your own position ; you will see very little, you will run a considerable risk, you will be inaccessible at a critical time when vital decisions might have to be taken ; and however unobtrusive you may be, your mere presence on board is bound to be a very heavy additional responsibility to the Admiral & Captain.

'As I said in my previous letter, your being there would add immeasurably to my own anxieties, & your going without consulting your colleagues in the Cabinet would put them in a very difficult position which they would justifiably resent.

'I ask you most earnestly to consider the whole question again & not let your personal wishes, which I very well understand, lead you to depart from your own high standard of duty to the State.'

I have been very worried & anxious over the whole of this business & it is my duty to warn the P.M. on such occasions. No one else can & should anything dreadful happen I should be asked if I had tried to deter him.[22]

The King's letter reached 10 Downing Street just before the Prime Minister's departure in his special train for General Eisenhower's headquarters near Portsmouth. He was reported to have been impressed by the cogent arguments which it contained, but by eleven o'clock that evening he had sent no

reply, nor had he given any definitive indications of his intended
action. The King was now thoroughly disturbed and, in a
telephone conversation with Sir Alan Lascelles, he threatened
to start off from Windsor by car at dawn next morning to
ensure personally that the Prime Minister should not embark
in *Belfast*. Sir Alan rang up the train and received from
Mr. Churchill an assurance that, in deference to the King's
wishes, he would abandon his plan of going to sea. This
assurance he subsequently put in writing to His Majesty, to
the King's intense relief.

I received a letter from the Prime Minister in answer to mine
[the King wrote in his diary on June 3]. He has decided not to
go on the expedition, only because I have asked him not to go.
He thanks me for my letter & goes on 'Sir, I cannot really feel
that the first paragraph of your letter takes sufficient account of
the fact that there is absolutely no comparison in the British Constitution between a Sovereign & a subject. If Your Majesty had
gone, as you desired, on board one of your ships in this bombarding
action, it would have required the Cabinet approval beforehand &
I am very much inclined to think, as I told you, that the Cabinet
would have advised most strongly against Your Majesty going.
On the other hand, as Prime Minister & Minister of Defence, I
ought to be allowed to go where I consider it necessary to the
discharge of my duty, & I do not admit that the Cabinet have
any right to put restrictions on my freedom of movement. I rely
on my own judgment, invoked in many serious matters, as to what
are the proper limits of risk which a person who discharges my
duties is entitled to run. I must most earnestly ask Your Majesty
that no principle shall be laid down which inhibits my freedom of
movement when I judge it necessary to acquaint myself with conditions in the various theatres of war. Since Your Majesty does
me the honour to be so much concerned about my personal safety
on this occasion, I must defer to Your Majesty's wishes & indeed
commands. It is a great comfort to me to know that they arise
from Your Majesty's desire to continue me in your service. Though
I regret that I cannot go, I am deeply grateful to Your Majesty for
the motives which have guided Your Majesty in respect of
    Your Majesty's humble & devoted Servant & Subject
                    (signed) WINSTON S. CHURCHILL.

I am glad this matter is settled [was the King's comment], and
that the P.M. sees the sense of it. I was not raising any constitutional
point. I asked him as a friend not to endanger his life & so put
me & everybody else in a difficult position.[23]

The days of waiting until the moment of the invasion of Europe were now but few. D-Day was scheduled for dawn on June 5, but the weather was execrable, cold and wet, with a gale blowing from the west. Early on the morning of Sunday, June 4, General Eisenhower took his momentous decision to postpone Operation Overlord for twenty-four hours and this news was telephoned to the King at Windsor. His first thought was for the troops. 'This added to my anxieties', he wrote, 'as I knew that the men were going on board the ships at the time, & that their quarters were very cramped'.[24] Forty-eight hours later, however, he was able to record the successful opening of the invasion. 'The assault Divs. had reached their right beaches, had landed & had met little opposition.' [25]

That night at 9 p.m. the King broadcast to his peoples, calling them to prayer and dedication for this great enterprise, the liberation of Europe.

Four years ago, our Nation and Empire stood alone against an overwhelming enemy, with our backs to the wall. Tested as never before in history, in God's providence we survived the test; the spirit of the people, resolute, dedicated, burned like a bright flame, lit surely from those Unseen Fires which nothing can quench.

Now once more a supreme test has to be faced. . . .

At this historic moment surely not one of us is too busy, too young or too old to play a part in a nation-wide, a world-wide, vigil of prayer as the great crusade sets forth. If from every place of worship, from home and factory, from men and women of all ages and many races and occupations, our intercessions rise, then, please God, both now and in a future not remote the predictions of an ancient Psalm may be fulfilled : 'The Lord will give strength unto this people : The Lord will give this people the blessing of peace '.

The importance and influence of this appeal for national dedication and intercession had been much in the King's mind. He had given great care to its composition and had sought the advice of others, in addition to rehearsing it meticulously with Mr. Logue. Its reception and the letters of gratitude which he subsequently received touched him greatly, but perhaps none was more deeply appreciated than that from his mother.

. . . Thank you so much for your note & for your message to me at this time [he wrote to Queen Mary]. They are very anxious days & I do trust that we shall be able to win this fierce struggle which is now going on. It was feared that we would suffer severe casualties on the beaches, but the date was kept a good secret.

I am glad you liked my broadcast. The Bishop of Lichfield [a] helped me with it. It was a great opportunity to call everybody to prayer. I have wanted to do it for a long time.[26]

The first critical days of the invasion were watched by the King and Queen with tense anxiety. The fate of Europe was being decided on the beaches of Normandy and they could only wait and pray for victory. 'We spent a quiet week-end, though not in our thoughts' is a poignant entry in the King's diary at this moment.[27]

Success, however, went with the liberating armies, and the moment was approaching when the King could attain his high ambition of visiting his troops upon the beaches. On June 13, at their Tuesday luncheon, the Prime Minister gave his approval for such a visit, and later in the day the Cabinet also concurred, with the proviso that all possible precautions should be taken for His Majesty's safety. The date was set for June 16. This was to be no sightseeing trip; the King was going on military duty. He was anxious to see for himself the conditions under which his troops were fighting and to give by his presence among them an added proof of the wholehearted support which the army was receiving from the nation at home.

The Cabinet, Mr. Churchill had written, felt no doubt that 'a visit of the King to the Armies in France would be an encouragement to the Allied forces engaged and also make an impression upon our Allies throughout the British Empire and Commonwealth which would be favourable to our cause'.[28]

Attended by Sir Alan Lascelles and Sir Harold Campbell, he left London by train on the night of June 15 and next morning crossed the Channel in a choppy sea and cold and gusty weather, which resulted in a four and a half hours' passage.

I left Portsmouth at 8.0 a.m. in the cruiser 'Arethusa' (Capt. Dalrymple-Smith) to visit the beaches in Normandy [he wrote in

---

[a] Rt. Rev. Edward Sydney Woods, D.D. (1877–1953), Bishop of Croydon 1930–1937, and of Lichfield 1937–1953, was appointed High Almoner to King George VI in 1946.

his diary]. On the way over we passed outgoing & incoming convoys the whole time in the swept channel & saw the mine-sweepers at work. I had the Royal Standard flying at the main. When we reached the other side I got a very good view of the mass of shipping which is there stretching for miles in both directions. To the eastward the 'Nelson' & 'Ramillies' were lying as the bombardment ships. The cruiser 'Hawkins' was actually firing in support of an attack as we came in. I went ashore in a M.L. & changed into a 'Duck' the amphibious craft & drove ashore over the beach where the Canadians landed & was met by Genl. Montgomery at Courcelles beach. We drove to his tactical H.Q. & had lunch. After which I decorated some officers & men. In his caravan he explained to me how the battle was going on. He was very enthusiastic re. the position as it stands now & Rommel is using up his strategic reserves by filling up weak spots where we have dented them. The position at Caen is the most delicate. The enemy has made determined counter attacks & attacks on our positions in this sector which have withstood them with great loss to him. The 3rd Div & the 6th Airborne have fought magnificently here & now the 51st Div is going in to help them to the east of the Orne river. The 6th Armd. Div on the west have inflicted heavy casualties on the 2 Panzer Div which was diverted from Caen to fill up the hole. What Monty wants to do & Genl. Dempsey the 2nd Army Comdr. agrees, is to try a pincer movement with the 7th Armd. Div, 50th & 49th Divs coming round to the east & to attack N of Caen thus giving the 3rd & 51st & 6th Air Divs a chance to attack S of Caen & take it. Monty wants to defeat the enemy here. Meanwhile the U.S. troops will be able to get Cherbourg. This plan is being laid on now, to start next week.[a]

I drove back to the same beach & returned to the 'Arethusa'. It was now 4.0 p.m. & I was not able to see the Mulberries, the artificial harbours, as they were full of mines, I left Normandy & reached Portsmouth at 9.0 p.m. I went to Windsor. A long & very interesting day. It was most encouraging to know that it was possible for me to land on the beaches only 10 days after D Day.[29]

The King's satisfaction was somewhat mitigated by his discovery on his return to England that a new burden had been laid upon his people in the shape of Hitler's first 'secret weapon', the V.1. These pilotless planes filled with ex-plosives made their first descent on the night of June 15, and were to remain a menace for the next nine months or so.

[a] United States forces isolated Cherbourg on June 17 and finally captured the fortress on June 26.

The effect upon public morale was considerable, partly because there had been no aerial attack from Germany for some
considerable time and, as a result, its renewal caused a certain
disappointment and despondency in a people whose power of
endurance had been gravely taxed during five years of war;
partly because they continued, at any rate in the early use
of the weapon, by day and by night,[a] causing lack of sleep
and of relaxation from nervous strain; and partly because of
their uncanny and robot-like nature. As the Queen wrote to
Queen Mary: 'There is something very inhuman about death-
dealing missiles being launched in such an indiscriminate
manner'.[30]

The King's comments on this new and unpleasant phenomenon were characteristically practical: 'A change in our
daily routine will be needed',[31] was his first reaction, and 'the
nuisance value of this bombing may get worse especially at
night'.[32] This was an understatement. The windows of
Buckingham Palace at this period, in company with many
others in London, were almost daily either blown in or sucked
out by blast, and one by one the glass panes were replaced by
small squares of talc set in wooden casements. The King was
deeply shocked at the destruction of the Guards Chapel at
Wellington Barracks, where many of the worshippers were
friends and acquaintances of the Royal Family, and immediately cancelled his investitures for the time being, 'until we
learn more about the technique'. For the same reason he and
the Prime Minister held their Tuesday luncheon for the next
few weeks in the air-raid shelter of Buckingham Palace. The
Palace itself was not struck at this time but a seventy-five-yard
length of its boundary wall was demolished when a bomb fell
in Constitution Hill.

King George took a keen interest in the methods applied
by the Army and Royal Air Force to combat the V.1 and
on several occasions he was a witness of their efficacy.

We motored from here to Maresfield in Sussex to visit an L.A.A.
Battery sited to deal with the Flying Bombs [he wrote on July 12].

[a] It was estimated by the Home Office that, in the first fortnight after the
'Flying Bomb' was launched, over 600 such missiles fell in the London area, as
a result of which 1600 people were killed and 10,000 wounded, and over 200,000
houses were damaged.

WITH FIELD-MARSHAL MONTGOMERY ON THE
NORMANDY BEACHES, JUNE 16, 1944

GREETED BY PRESIDENT TRUMAN IN U.S.S. *Augusta*
AUGUST 2, 1945

Gen Sir F. Pile,[a] C in C Anti Aircraft Comd. met us. We then went to East Grinstead where a F.B. had just fallen & we talked to the people & on to a H.A.A. Battery site. From here we lunched at Lingfield in the mess of a Mixed Battery of H.A.A. The A.T.S. girls work all instruments. After lunch the alarm went & we watched the 3.7″ guns go into action against the F.Bs. Six of them came over at very short intervals at a rate of not less than 400 m.p.h. at 3000 ft. The shooting was very level but a bit 'behind'. This is due to a 'time lag' in the Radar automatic instruments but it will be got over by practice. This battery shot two down out of five fired at yesterday. I hoped it was not because we were there which had made them nervous. They think they hit one later, but a fighter was on its tail as well. We saw 2 fighters left 'standing' by a F.B. at one time. It was most interesting & we got back at 6.30 pm.[33]

A few days later he visited R.A.F. stations near Chichester, whence fighter squadrons flew in support of the Army in Normandy, and held investitures. Once again he was impressed by the inarticulate modesty of these young men: 'Several of our fighter pilots in both places have shot down Flying Bombs, one having had to bale out having been blasted. I find it so difficult to talk to them as they will never say what they have done, and they have all got stories to tell.' [34]

(iv)

Though King George recognized and respected the constitutional inhibitions which prevented his taking an active part as a combatant, he was constantly irked by his inability to see more of his troops in the field. 'He feels so much not being more in the fighting-line', the Queen wrote to Queen Mary.[35] In another age there is no doubt that he would have delighted in the rôle of a warrior-king leading his forces into battle; in the twentieth century he could but encourage them by his presence.

It was with this thought in mind that the King welcomed the opportunity of visiting his armies in Italy. From July 23

---

[a] General Sir Frederick Alfred Pile, second Bt., G.C.B., D.S.O., M.C. (b. 1884), having commanded the 1st Anti-Aircraft Division of the Territorial Army from 1937 to 1939, was appointed G.O.C.-in-C. of Anti-Aircraft Command, a position which he held throughout the war.

to August 3,[a] under the guidance of General Alexander, he saw all that was possible for him to see, inspecting the sites of old battlefields, watching actual fighting and artillery bombardments.[36] In a strenuous programme of eleven days the King travelled 8000 miles by air and 1000 miles by road, visiting and talking not only to British and Imperial troops, but also to units of the American, French, Polish and Brazilian forces which made up General Alexander's composite army. The timing of his visit had been particularly fortunate, for the Army in Italy were beginning to feel a little neglected. 'Alex told me', the King recorded, 'he was particularly glad I had come out just at this moment as the troops rather feared that their campaign had been put in the shade by the Press ever since the landing in Normandy'.[37]

One incident during the King's visit to Naples was not without its medley of humour and pathos. His Majesty was quartered in the Villa Emma, that lovely villa on the Bay of Naples where Lady Hamilton had first met Lord Nelson. During the King's sojourn there a motor-launch patrolled the harbour for his protection, with orders that no craft of any kind should be allowed within a certain limited area. To the consternation of the Lieutenant R.N.V.R. in charge, a small boat suddenly appeared early one morning within the forbidden zone with a lady fishing from the stern. Challenged by the patrol-boat the intruder took no notice whatsoever and the Lieutenant trained his Lewis gun on her. Thereupon the lady composedly produced from among her fishing tackle an immense visiting card, on which the embarrassed Lieutenant read the words, 'The Queen of Italy'. He saluted smartly and withdrew, leaving Queen Elena to the uninterrupted pursuit of her piscatorial activities.

The King's return to England coincided with that forward sweep which carried the Armies of Liberation from Normandy to the Line of the Maas. On July 27 Allied armour had broken through the German lines west of St.-Lô and advanced towards Paris. On August 15 Allied forces landed on the south coast of France and drove northwards to the

---

[a] During His Majesty's absence from the United Kingdom the following were appointed to act as Counsellors of State: the Queen, the Princess Elizabeth, the Duke of Gloucester, the Princess Royal and Princess Arthur of Connaught.

Belfort Gap. Paris was liberated from within by the forces of French resistance on August 23 and two days later General Leclerc's armoured division, which had begun its great trek northwards from Lake Chad, entered the city. Brussels was liberated by British troops on September 3. By October German forces had been virtually driven from France and Belgium and from the southern portion of the Netherlands, and from October 11 to 16 King George experienced the ineffable satisfaction of visiting his victorious 21st Army Group as the guest of General Montgomery.

These visits to his armies in Italy and the Low Countries prompted King George to advance a more ambitious plan which had been germinating in his mind for some time. Why should he not go to India in February and March of the following year and carry a similar message of encouragement to his troops on the South-East Asia Front? The King had long wished to visit his Indian Empire and had genuinely regretted the necessity which had prompted the cancellation of his projected Durbar visit in 1937.[a] The present moment seemed to be propitious. The offensive which the Supreme Allied Commander in South-East Asia, Lord Mountbatten, had planned against the Japanese in Burma had been recently postponed in deference to considerations of grand strategy in other theatres of war. Both the Supreme Commander and the troops were naturally disappointed and, as the King said to Mr. Churchill: 'A visit from me would buck them up.'[38] Moreover, an opportunity would be provided for the King to gain an insight into the workings of the Government of India.

But the Prime Minister feared that the political situation obtaining in India at the time presented too many difficulties. If the King were to go there he would be expected to make some declaration on the constitutional future of the country, and for this His Majesty's Government were not yet ready. The King's view, however, was that a visit from the Sovereign to his armies in the field would have no political significance at all, and for this opinion he gained the approval of other of his Ministers. He was, however, unable to prevail against Mr. Churchill, and the idea was temporarily abandoned. But it did not leave the King's mind, and he was warmly supported

[a] See above, pp. 303-4.

by Lord Mountbatten. Some five months later, when the Burmese front was again active, the Supreme Commander wrote to King George urging him to raise anew the question of a visit to the South-East Asian theatre of war. 'Once we have got Rangoon do *please* come out', he besought the King. 'You can easily do a flying visit via Delhi without any previous announcement and go on after a day or two straight to Rangoon. It's the one chance you will have of visiting your Indian capital without endless political complications and you have NEVER been there, whereas David, your father and grandfather all visited Delhi (1922, 1911 & 1876).'[39]

King George would have readily acquiesced, but when Rangoon ultimately fell on May 3, 1945, events in Europe, both at home and abroad, rendered even a flying visit so far afield impracticable and the last King-Emperor was fated never to set foot within his Indian dominions.

(v)

Though victory in Europe was still far from achieved — as the desperate resistance of the German armies and the brilliant counter-offensive of Field-Marshal von Rundstedt in the Ardennes in December bore witness — the premonitory symptoms were apparent on all sides. Despite the death and destruction wrought by Hitler's second 'vengeance weapon', the V.2,[a] it was generally considered that this would be the last winter of the war. Some relaxation of the stringent precautions for Britain's safety during the last four years was therefore possible.

For example, with the Germans driven to the banks of the Rhine, the danger of invasion was considered to have become so remote that it was judged safe to disband the Home Guard. Their 'stand-down' on December 3 was marked by a review of representative units in Hyde Park at which King

---

[a] The first V.2, the first of some 1250, fell in Chiswick on September 8, 1944. These were ballistic missiles launched from installations in the Netherlands and in the Pas-de-Calais, which rose into the stratosphere and fell with great velocity and no warning in the London area and in south-eastern England. At the same time the Germans continued to keep up the dispatch of their V.1 weapon by launching them from aircraft flying over the North Sea. The casualties caused by these two types of aerial attack during the period of September–December 1944 were 1425 killed and 3134 injured.

George took the salute, and in the evening he broadcast the nation's thanks to them for their 'steadfast devotion' which had 'helped much to ward off the danger of invasion'. But, as was his habit, the King was never content with retrospection; he was ever conscious of the tasks ahead, ever aware of the grim problems of reconstruction. He lost no opportunity of driving home the necessity of carrying into the future the lessons and experience of the past. 'You have gained something for yourselves', he told the veterans of the Home Guard. 'You have discovered in yourselves new capabilities. You have found how men from all kinds of homes and many different occupations can work together in a great cause, and how happy they can be with each other. That is a memory and a knowledge which may help us all in the many peace-time problems that we shall have to tackle before long.'

The same regard for the problems of the future was apparent in the speech which the King made in response to the toast of his health at a private official dinner given on December 19 by the Home Secretary, Mr. Herbert Morrison, to the Regional Commissioners and their Deputies on the occasion of their return to those varied walks of private life from which they had come at a moment of national emergency.

These men and women had, for the better part of four years, administered the power of the Crown in relation to Civil Defence over and above the Local Authorities. Their work had been difficult and arduous, and the King thanked them in his own name and in that of the nation. They had often been brought into contact with him during his frequent tours in the country, and this fact His Majesty recalled in very happy vein, saying that, though he had met nearly all of them before and some on numerous occasions, he had never seen them look so happy and so free from care : 'Usually I have seen you standing anxiously at the exit of some factory — in a north-easterly gale — looking feverishly at your watches and wondering how on earth we could make up a time-lag of 40 minutes; or, at the end of a long day, on the platform of some draughty railway station, with your faces wearing that quite unmistakable expression which can only mean "Well, thank God that's over!"'

It was at the conclusion of his remarks that the King

made reference to the future in the light of their past experience :

> I know my Government has had to ask a great deal of the Local Authorities — not least in the sphere of Civil Defence. You have seen — at close quarters — the good that comes when the feeling between the centre and circumference is that of partners, working together in a common cause. You have seen what progress can be made, however difficult the task, when that is the spirit in which it is undertaken.
>
> It is my hope that our system of Local Government, to which you have contributed so much in these war years, will play the same great part in the years of reconstruction. It will, I know, so long as it attracts men and women of ability and high character.[40]

The King's mind was also active for the future during the latter months of the war in matters which concerned himself even more closely. Conscious as always of the dignity of his high office and of its importance in the life of the nation, the King was anxious to see the pageantry of royalty restored as soon as possible to the nearest approximation to its pre-war standards compatible with national economy. He conferred accordingly with the Prime Minister and with the Earl Marshal, the Duke of Norfolk, on the revival of the State Opening of Parliament after the first post-war general election and as to how the battle-scarred Palace of Westminster could be re-arranged for this ceremony.[a] His own ideas were clear and practical, and, after personally reconnoitring the position, he put them forward to the officials concerned at a meeting in the House of Lords. His suggestion was that, for the purpose of the opening ceremony, the Peers could return to their own Chamber and the Commons could meet in the interval in St. Stephen's Hall, their pristine home under which Guy Fawkes had planned their destruction. He was not, however, certain of the constitutional aspects of this arrangement and

---

[a] Parliament remained in London throughout the war, discarding the plan which had been formulated in 1938 for its possible evacuation to Stratford-on-Avon. Church House in Dean's Yard, Westminster, was, however, selected as an alternative meeting-place and the King opened the new session of Parliament there on November 21, 1940. After the destruction of the House of Commons on May 10, 1941, Parliament met at Church House from May 19 to June 19, but it then returned to Westminster where the Commons sat in the House of Lords and the Peers were temporarily accommodated in the Robing Room. There was a further migration to Church House from June 20 to August 3, 1944, when the flying-bomb danger was at its height.

asked that an inquiry should be instituted and a report made
to him.[41]   As a result, when, a year later, the King again opened
Parliament (August 15, 1945), his suggestions in regard to
venue were adopted and, apart from a certain modification as
to dress, the ancient ceremonial was restored in so far as was
compatible with post-war austerity.

The post-war future of the Army also engaged His Majesty's
attention at this time.   The size and formations of the units
would have to be worked out later, but, as early as October
1944, the King expressed the hope to the Secretary of State for
War that compulsory military service would be retained and that
the age of 18 or 18½ would be chosen.   He was also emphatic
that 'all questions relating to uniform must come before me
before any alterations to it are discussed, let alone settled'.[42]

In this matter of Army uniform he had very emphatic ideas
which he made clear to the Adjutant-General, Sir Ronald
Adam.[a]

I told him I want it to be in Dark Blue & to cut out any idea
of having a shade of khaki as had been suggested in 1939 [the
King wrote in his diary on December 15].   Battle Dress has been
proved in this war to be the most suitable dress for all fighting &
training purposes, so I told him to keep it for those only.   The
Blue Uniform should be worn on all other occasions from Sentry
duty to Ceremonial.   I want the Army to be popular & for soldiers
to have a uniform which they will be proud of.   The Household
Cavalry & the Brigade of Guards to revert to the Full Dress they
had previous to the war.   Adam agreed with all these points.

(vi)

In the wider field of world affairs planning for peace as well
as for victory was also the order of the day.   The second
Quebec Conference (September 1944) and the subsequent
meetings of Mr. Churchill with Marshal Stalin in Moscow
(October 1944) and with President Roosevelt in Malta (February 1945) reached their culmination in the now highly
controversial decisions of the Conference of Yalta where, from

[a] General Sir Ronald Adam, second Bt., G.C.B., D.S.O., O.B.E. (b. 1885),
commanded the 3rd Army Corps, 1939–1940, and was G.O.C.-in-C. Northern
Command, 1940–1941.   He served as Adjutant-General to the Forces from 1941
to 1946, when he retired.   He was President of the M.C.C., 1946–1947, and
Director-General of the British Council, 1947–1954.

February 4 to 11, the Big Three met 'to discuss plans for completing the defeat of the common enemy and building, with their Allies, firm foundations for a lasting peace'.[a] The concrete achievement of the Yalta Conference was the decision to call a conference of the United Nations at San Francisco on April 25 to prepare a Charter for a permanent international organization to replace the League of Nations.

As to the decisions of the Yalta Conference for the solution of the problems of Eastern Europe there was grave dubiety and some bewilderment. These the King shared. He wrote in his diary :

> I find in my daily reading of Cabinet papers & F.O. telegrams, besides the daily papers (Press), that it is almost impossible to keep a clear mind on all that is going on nowadays. . . . The Polish question is by no means settled & Gen. Anders who commands the Polish Army in Italy is here now for talks as neither he nor his troops will take the statement about Poland as it is now written. They took an oath to the Polish Govt. in London not to the Lublin Committee. They are fearful of Russia as they have always been. In Rumania the Rumanian Govt. started off well, & Michael was praised after their liberation. Now orders from Moscow have come to work up agitation against them & to form a minority Communist govt.[b] Stalin, no doubt, after having met Winston, F. D. R. & other people from the Western part of the world appreciates the need for having 2 very useful Allies & is doing his best to be friendly with them, but he has not got enough time in which to teach some of his people on Allied Commissions the same thing. Stalin realises it himself that he must come back into the world, so probably does Molotov, & that making contact with us & the Americans is not such an antipathy to all his ideas. But can he stop his anti-democratic policy in the Balkans in time? Stalin has put his name to some very important negotiations together with those of 2 very modern & enlightened countries & can he play fair? These negotiations are the foundations of the future peace of the World & will they ever be ratified? [44]

[a] The Yalta documents have been published by the United States Department of State in the series of 'Foreign Relations of the United States', *The Conferences at Malta and Yalta, 1945* (Washington, 1955).

[b] King George felt great sympathy with the young King Michael in his exceedingly difficult situation. 'Poor Michael and his mother Zitta [Queen Helen] in Rumania have been having a very worrying time from the Russians and again we can do nothing to help them for the moment', he wrote to Queen Mary. 'I feel so differently towards them, than the attitude taken up by the Government. The latter say Rumania was an enemy and is now in the Russian sphere.' [43]

The King's suspicion of Russia had been of long standing and of considerable prescience. His pragmatic common sense had warned him of the dangers inherent in this quarter when others had been more optimistic. As long ago as the fateful summer of 1940 he had had a conversation with Mr. Churchill and President Beneš as to the relative qualities of Germany and Russia as the greater long-term menace, and had recorded his own opinion : 'I thought Russia would eventually be but they both thought not, as she could be organised'.[45] Now his doubts and suspicions were reawakened.

The most cheering news which reached King George from Yalta was that of the possibility of a visit to Britain of President Roosevelt in the spring or summer. He wrote warmly on March 12:

MY DEAR PRESIDENT ROOSEVELT,

I am very glad to hear that it may be possible for you to make your long promised visit to my Country after the conclusion of the Conference at San Francisco.

You may be sure that you will get a very warm welcome from the people of Great Britain, & I send you and Mrs. Roosevelt a very cordial invitation to be our guests at Buckingham Palace.

We are still under daily bombardment at the moment but we hope & trust the situation will be better in a few months' time.

We shall do our best to make you comfortable here & it would be a real pleasure to the Queen & myself to have you with us & to continue that friendship which started so happily in Washington & at Hyde Park in 1939. So much has happened to us all since those days.

I hope you had a good voyage home from the Crimea, but I was very sorry to hear of the death of your aide Gen. Watson. He will be a great loss to you I fear.

Hoping to meet you here in the not too distant future.

    With all good wishes to you & Mrs. Roosevelt
        Believe me
            Yours very sincerely,
                GEORGE R.I.[46]

It was not to be. A month later came the staggering news of the President's sudden death at Warm Springs, Georgia, on April 12, 1945. The King was greatly saddened.

We were very shocked to hear the sad news of the sudden death of President Roosevelt. [He wrote in his diary.] He was a very great man & his loss will be felt the World over. He was a staunch friend of this country, & Winston will feel his loss most of all in his dealings with Stalin. I had hoped that the Roosevelts would have paid us a visit here this summer, but it cannot be. F. D. R. had not been well & had got frailer in the past year, entirely through overwork due to the war.[47]

The King mourned deeply the loss of one whom he had regarded with genuine admiration, affection and gratitude. He wrote letters in his own hand, expressing his simple and sincere grief, to Mrs. Roosevelt, to Mr. Winant and to the Prime Minister. Mr. Churchill replied : 'The sudden loss of this great friend and comrade in all our affairs is very hard for me. Ties have been torn asunder which years had woven. We have to begin again in many ways.' [48] The Prime Minister would have flown to Washington to attend the funeral, but the King dissuaded him, and Mr. Eden went in his stead. King George ordered a week's Court mourning, and himself attended the Memorial Service in St. Paul's on April 17.[a]

The death of President Roosevelt removed from world affairs a figure of great statesmanship. Great he was — if only for the superb courage and vision with which, in the early days of the war, he risked everything to give all the help he could to Britain in her lone and seemingly hopeless struggle. With the skill of a psychologist, with a sure knowledge of his own countrymen and their national characteristics, he led, cajoled and ordered them into giving that help, almost against their will, until the evil folly of Japan made America Britain's ally. Yet all the time he held his grip on all but a small section, steadily educating them to the realization that this was no war in the old-fashioned sense but a fundamental struggle to the death between the forces of good and evil.

Of Mr. Roosevelt's successor, Vice-President Truman,[b] the

[a] King George VI was represented at the funeral service in Washington by his uncle, the Earl of Athlone, Governor-General of Canada, and by his Ambassador, Lord Halifax. Mr. Roosevelt was eventually buried in the rose-garden of his home at Hyde Park.
[b] Hon. Harry S. Truman (b. 1884) served with the United States Army in France in the First World War as a Captain of Artillery. After serving as Judge of Jackson County, Mo., from 1922 to 1934, he was elected to the United States Senate from Missouri, and during the Second World War became Chairman of the Special Committee to investigate the National Defence Programme. He was chosen by President Roosevelt as Vice-Presidential candidate in the former's campaign for a fourth term in 1944, and was duly elected. He succeeded Mr.

world knew little as yet. It knows considerably more today.
President Truman may well be numbered among the great
leaders of the United States. He differed from his predecessor
in background, character and approach. President Roosevelt's
ancestry was that of the aristocratic patroon families; President
Truman came of virile pioneer stock. Without the subtlety
and agility of mind and the blinding charm of Mr. Roosevelt,
Mr. Truman matched him in courage, in vision and in
bulldog determination, and, when necessary, excelled him in
ruthlessness. Their principles and precepts were identical but,
whereas Mr. Roosevelt arrived at his uncanny understanding
of American public opinion by means of an almost feminine
intuition, Mr. Truman derived his own keen perception of
the views of his countrymen from within himself, through an
upwelling of his own inner consciousness. Truly the comment
of a New York weekly magazine that 'President Roosevelt
was *for* the people; President Truman *is* the people' was
not far off the mark.

The thirty-second President of the United States personi-
fied that combination of fundamental toughness, common
sense and goodness of heart which comprises the average
American. He was more forthright than Mr. Roosevelt, and
by his very forthrightness he prevented the American people
from slipping back into that myopic self-righteous isolationism
which had afflicted them after the First World War. The
fearless and resolute decisions which he took in relation to the
Atom Bomb, to the Berlin Air-lift, to the Communist aggression in Korea and the formation of the North Atlantic Treaty
Organization caused the United States to assert and maintain
that leadership of the free world which had been bequeathed
to them by Mr. Roosevelt. As Winston Churchill, as Franklin
Roosevelt, so Harry S. Truman was the 'lord of his event'.

The world mourned the death of Mr. Roosevelt, but the
pace of the world's events could not be slowed to the tempo
of its mourning. The velocity of victory in the summer of
1945 outpaced even the fleetness of defeat five years' earlier

Roosevelt in 1945 and, to the surprise of all except himself and a few faithful
friends, was elected as President of the United States in 1948. He retired in
1953. Mr. Truman's memoirs, published in 1955–1956, provide a remarkable
first-hand account of his administration written within two years of its termination.

when, with unbelievable rapidity, the German Wehrmacht had made itself master of Western Europe. Now British, American and Canadian forces in the north of Germany and American armies in the south swept eastwards to meet the victorious hosts of the Soviet Union. The junction was made at Torgau on the Elbe on April 25, and simultaneously there reached King George at Sandringham the news of the attempts at peace-making by Count Bernadotte and Heinrich Himmler.[a]

We had to return to London [from Appleton] on Friday afternoon on account of a telegram from Stockholm which said that Count Bernadotte, head of the Swedish Red Cross, had seen Himmler in Germany. Himmler told Bernadotte that Hitler was very ill & was likely to die at any moment & that before this happened he [Himmler] would take over now & surrender the German armies on the Western Front & the troops in Norway & Denmark to Gen. Eisenhower. But he (Himmler) would go on fighting on the Eastern Front. Bernadotte told H. that he must surrender to all Three Powers at once, as he knew U.K. & U.S.A. would not accept it. On receiving this news the Prime Minister at once rang up President Truman & they both sent telegrams to Stalin telling him that they would accept nothing but unconditional surrender to all Three Powers.
Stalin's answer was polite & friendly.[b] [49]

The negotiations proved abortive, for Himmler was unable to make good his authority and could not, in any case, stomach an unconditional surrender to the Russians. But the end could not be very long delayed. As the King wrote in his diary: 'Events are moving very fast now'.[50] The breath of Nemesis was hot on the necks of the Dictators. Mussolini met his fate at the hands of Italian partisans at Mezzegra on April 28, and on May 2 the German armies in Italy surrendered unconditionally at Caserta in the presence of British,

[a] Count Folke Bernadotte (1895-1948), son of Prince Oscar Bernadotte of Sweden, was the head of a Swedish Red Cross Mission to Germany in March-May 1945 for the evacuation of Scandinavian concentration camp prisoners. In 1948 he was appointed United Nations Mediator in Palestine, where he was assassinated in Jerusalem on September 17. The story of the Bernadotte-Himmler negotiations is brilliantly told in Mr. Hugh Trevor-Roper's *The Last Days of Hitler* (3rd ed., 1956, pp. 97, 128-129, 139, 146-149), less effectively by Count Bernadotte himself in *The Curtain Falls* (pp. 105-129, 136-155), and in *The Schellenberg Memoirs* (pp. 428-454).
[b] Mr. Churchill's account of these negotiations and conversations is given in the sixth volume of his memoirs, pp. 465-468.

United States and Soviet military representatives. Meanwhile, in Berlin Hitler had committed suicide on April 30, in the chaotic squalor of the Chancellery bunker, and, two days later (May 2), the capital of the Thousand Year Reich capitulated to the Russians. The transitory German Government of Admiral Doenitz opened negotiations from Flensburg for a final termination of hostilities, and on May 4 Field-Marshal Montgomery reported to General Eisenhower that all enemy forces in Holland, North-West Germany and Denmark had surrendered with effect from eight o'clock on the following morning. This information was at once telephoned by Mr. Churchill to the King who received it with rejoicing. 'This is wonderful news', he wrote,[51] and on the following day recorded the subsequent course of the surrender negotiations :

So the hostilities on our front have now ceased. This surrender involves over one million fighting men. All the Germans prefer to surrender to us than to the Russian Red Army, & this applies to civilians as well. During the day Eisenhower has been receiving German emissaries from Doenitz at his H.Q. about the surrender of Norway, the Channel Islands & the coast 'pockets' such as Dunkirk etc. But the emissary has had to return to Doenitz to fetch the bona fide surrender of all the German Armies everywhere. We hope he will return with his full powers tomorrow. Kesselring has surrendered to Devers [a] the southern group of German armies.[52]

The instrument of unconditional surrender of the German armies to the Western Allies and to Russia was signed in the schoolhouse of Rheims by a weeping Jodl on behalf of the German High Command at 2.41 on the morning of Monday, May 7. The actual moment for the cessation of operations was agreed at 23.01 hours, Central European Time, on May 8.[b]

Thus the moment had arrived for which the world had waited and suffered since the dawn of September 1, 1939. The might of German militarism and of Nazi tyranny had

[a] General Jacob Loucks Devers (b. 1887) was the first Commander of United States troops in the European Theatre of Operations in 1941, and in 1944 became deputy Supreme Commander of the Allied forces in the Mediterranean Area. In 1951 he served as chief military adviser to the United Nations Mission to India and Pakistan.

[b] The formal ratification of the surrender of May 7 was made in Berlin on May 9, when the final act of capitulation was signed by Field-Marshal Keitel in the presence of military representatives from Britain, the United States the Soviet Union and France.

been conclusively defeated. For the first time in six years the guns were stilled in Europe.

But the circumstances of the announcement of this great event were disappointing. Preparations for the celebration of V-E Day had long ago been set in train, and throughout London there were indications of public expectation. The King and the Prime Minister had both made arrangements to broadcast, and it had been hoped that the public announcement of victory could be synchronized in London, Washington and Moscow. But no such agreement had been reached by May 7 and the result was confusion, to the frustration of all, and not least of King George. He had spent the week-end at Windsor anxiously awaiting final news.

We returned to London on Sunday evening [May 6]. Monday morning came the news that the Unconditional Surrender document had been signed in the early hours of this morning. Preparations for the announcement of VE Day today were going on apace, outside Buckingham Palace & other places. Placing of loud speakers & flood lighting lamps etc. The Press had worked everybody up that VE Day would be today as the news was already known. The P.M. wanted to announce it but Prest. Truman & Ml. Stalin want it to be announced tomorrow at 3.0 p.m. as arranged. The time fixed for Unconditional Surrender is Midnight May 8th. This came to me as a terrible anti-climax, having made my broadcast speech for record purposes with cinema photography & with no broadcast at 9.0 p.m. today ! ! [53]

The anti-climax was even greater than His Majesty thought, for, as a result of the wrangling between London, Washington and Moscow, the first official intimation of victory which the avidly awaiting world received was the broadcast by Count Schwerin von Krosigk from Hamburg on May 7, announcing to the German people the tidings of their defeat.

When victory was formally announced on the following day, however, nothing could dim the glory and the thanksgivings of the rejoicings. It was appropriate that it should be a Tuesday and that the King and his Prime Minister should celebrate together and alone the great event for which both had striven so resolutely. They had passed through moments of great strain together, and, at their informal audiences, Mr. Churchill had often been the harbinger of grave news, and more than once of disaster. Now part of that, at least, was

behind them, though neither underestimated the tasks which
lay before.

The Prime Minister came to lunch [the King wrote in his diary].
We congratulated each other on the end of the European War.
The day we have been longing for has arrived at last & we can
look back with thankfulness to God that our tribulation is over.
No more fear of being bombed at home & no more living in air-raid
shelters.   But there is still Japan to be defeated & the restoration
of our country to be dealt with, which will give us many headaches
& hard work in the coming years.[54]

Mr. Churchill made the formal announcement of victory
at 3 o'clock in the afternoon and thereafter London made
holiday.   There were not the scenes of wild excess which had
marked Armistice Day.   The element of surprise, so great in
November 1918, was lacking in May 1945, for the news of
victory had leaked out piecemeal.   Just as the whole nature
of the Second World War had been different from that of the
First, so were the celebrations of its termination in Europe.
There was a greater restraint.   Amid the natural exuberance
and excitement there was also apparent a weary gratitude for
deliverance from privation, death and danger and a knowledge that the struggle was not yet entirely over, that sacrifices
in lives still lay ahead.   It was confidently believed that the
war in the Pacific would continue for at least another eighteen
months.

In one respect, however, the celebrations of May 8, 1945,
bore a marked similarity to those of November 11, 1918.
The people of London demonstrated in jubilant affection their
loyalty and devotion to the Crown.   Great crowds gathered
before Buckingham Palace and clamoured for their King and
Queen, who had shared their sorrows and dangers and with
whom they now desired to share their joy in victory.   The
ovation accorded to Their Majesties on their first appearance
on the Palace balcony with the Princesses was tremendous,
and they were called back again and again.   The King
recorded, 'we went out 8 times altogether during the afternoon
and evening.   We were given a great reception.'

In the course of the afternoon the King received the War
Cabinet and the Chiefs of Staff and exchanged congratulations.   'You have brought this country — I may say you have

brought the whole world — out of deadly peril into complete victory', he told them. 'You have won the gratitude of millions and, I may add, of your Sovereign.'

Later that evening King George — 'speaking from our Empire's oldest capital city, war-battered but never for one moment daunted or discouraged' — called upon his peoples to join with him in an act of thanksgiving. He spoke of the fallen: 'Those who will not come back, their constancy and courage in battle, their sacrifice and endurance in the face of a merciless enemy'; and of those who would return — 'the great host of the living who have brought us victory'; and bade his listeners 'on this day of just triumph and proud sorrow' to take up their work again, 'resolved as a people to do nothing unworthy of those who died for us and to make the world such a world as they would have desired, for their children and for ours'.

Characteristically, on this memorable evening the King thought of the enjoyment of his daughters, and, in order that Princess Elizabeth and Princess Margaret should share in the excitement and festive mood, he confided them to the care of a party of young officers with whom they joined the crowds in Whitehall and the Mall in the almost forgotten luxury of street lights and floodlit buildings. 'Poor darlings, they have never had any fun yet', was his final entry.

The days following were filled with a prolonged series of victory celebrations. On May 9 and 10 the King and Queen made State Drives through East and South London, constantly halted by cheering crowds, who recalled other visits in grimmer days, and each evening they were summoned forth upon the balcony of the Palace to acknowledge great ovations.

It was remarked by the King and Queen that on these drives the horses drawing the Royal Carriage behaved with their usual exemplary restraint and were undeterred by the cheering, jostling crowds. Considering that they had spent the greater part of the war carting hay and other farm crops, this both surprised and pleased the King, and he made enquiry of the Crown Equerry. Sir Dermot Kavanagh [a] explained

---

[a] Colonel Sir Dermot McMorrough Kavanagh, G.C.V.O. (1890–1958), Crown Equerry to King George VI, 1941–1952, and to Queen Elizabeth II, 1952–1955.

that he had been preparing for this eventuality for some weeks past and had conditioned his charges to strange noises by installing a wireless in the Royal Stables and making them listen regularly to the Forces Programme of the B.B.C. !

On May 13 the King and Queen went in state to the City to attend a National Service of Thanksgiving at St. Paul's, and on the 16th, in a brief visit to Edinburgh, were present at a similar ceremony in St. Giles' Cathedral.[a] On the following day, in the Great Hall of Westminster, the King received addresses from both Houses of Parliament. He had a great triumph on this occasion and his reply to the addresses was adjudged by many present to surpass in dignity and eloquence anything which they had previously heard from him. Apart from a prolonged hesitation on the word 'imperishable', his delivery was perfect, and a wholly spontaneous touch gave the speech a dramatic and moving quality, when, in alluding to the Duke of Kent's death, his voice faltered and broke.

Wearied with celebration and deeply touched by the love and loyalty of which they had been witness, the King and Queen sought with relief a short rest at Windsor.

We have spent a very busy fortnight since VE Day & feel rather jaded from it all [the King recorded]. We have been overwhelmed by the kind things people have said over our part in the War. We have only tried to do our duty during these 5½ years.[b] I have found it difficult to rejoice or relax as there is still so much hard work ahead to deal with.[56]

(vii)

There was indeed but little time for relaxation, and the period of untrammelled rejoicing was definitely curtailed. Not only the Japanese war but the political situation at home presented problems which had given King George cause for considerable deliberation for some months past.

It was evident from many signs and portents that the party truce which had been so dominant a feature of the

[a] On June 7 the King and Queen visited the recently liberated Channel Islands and on July 17 they flew to Northern Ireland for a three-day tour.
[b] 'The Queen and I have been overcome in the last fortnight with everybody's great kindness, which has been overwhelming', the King wrote to Archbishop Lang. 'We have tried to do our duty in these 5 long exacting years.'[55]

British national life for the past five years could not be much longer maintained. The political situation was a peculiar one. Though King George VI had been on the Throne for over eight years there had been no General Election in Britain during that period and, of his three Prime Ministers, only one, Mr. Baldwin, had been returned by the electorate as the leader of a victorious party. The parliament of the day was that which had been elected in October 1935 — the same which had rejected the Hoare-Laval Plan, had enthusiastically welcomed Mr. Chamberlain back from Munich and had as decisively overthrown him not three years later.

Throughout the war there had been an electoral moratorium. By agreement between the parties the life of Parliament had been annually prolonged, and when by-elections became necessary a representative of the party to which the last occupant of the seat had belonged was by common consent allowed to retain it without contest. The state of the parties in the House of Commons had therefore remained virtually static since September 1939.[a]

The all-Party National Government which Mr. Churchill had formed in May 1940 had worked together loyally and effectively in defeat and in victory, but the increasing prospects of an early end to the war in Europe brought about a growing strain upon this temporary partnership. Within the Cabinet party differences became more apparent when attention began to be focused on problems of post-war reconstruction. So long as the Cabinet were concerned solely with the direction of the war they were united by the common aim of victory, and Coalition Government was easy. When, however, they turned their minds to post-war problems they found it possible to agree on some things — notably the Beveridge Plan and the scheme for a National Health Service — but on matters of post-war industrial organization, for example, doctrinal differences soon began to emerge. It was

[a] D. C. Somervell, in his excellent study of British politics, points out that 'Those who wished to register dissatisfaction had sometimes, toward the end of the war, an opportunity of voting for a candidate put forward by the Common Wealth Party, an ephemeral organization created by an idealistic landowner, Sir Richard Acland. Common Wealth candidates presented themselves only to Conservative constituencies. The Party was in fact a sort of Labour alias, and shortly after the war it was merged in the Labour Party.' [57]

remarkable that they were able to agree on the principles of a post-war Employment Policy; but the production of the White Paper on that question showed that there were limits beyond which it would be unprofitable to discuss post-war problems. The differences were too great — and these were matters on which compromise might well have given the worst of both worlds.

Both the Prime Minister and Mr. Attlee, therefore, were made increasingly aware of the constitutional need for an appeal to the people of Britain by an election. Mr. Churchill had indeed made this point clearly in the House of Commons on October 31, 1944, when moving the prolongation of Parliament. 'It seems to me', he had said on that occasion, 'that, unless all political parties resolve to maintain the present Coalition until the Japanese are defeated, we must look to the termination of the war against Nazism as a pointer which will fix the date of the General Election. . . . Indeed I have myself a clear view that it would be wrong to continue this Parliament beyond the period of the German war.' [58]

With this view the leaders of the Labour Party had concurred. Following the precedent it had set for itself in 1918, the party were quite decided to leave the Government as soon as the German war was over. But, when the moment of victory in Europe arrived, Mr. Churchill had changed his mind. He now hoped and urged that the Coalition should continue in being until Japan was defeated, the peace settlement made and the troops brought home. In this indefinite prolongation of the life of the Government, however, he was opposed by the Labour Party who would envisage no longer postponement of the break-up of the Coalition than October.

It must be remembered that the general belief at this time was that the Japanese war would continue at least eighteen months after the defeat of Germany. Though the existence of the atom-bomb project was known, its progress and imminent fruition were a closely guarded secret, kept within a very narrow circle, of whom the King was one. Mr. Attlee was himself unaware of it,[59] and Mr. Churchill could manifestly make no use of his own intimate knowledge in his dealings with his Labour and Conservative colleagues.

Mr. Churchill was not enamoured of the idea of an election

in either June or October. He was himself very weary —
'physically so feeble that I had to be carried upstairs in a
chair by the Marines from the Cabinet meetings under the
Annexe' [60] — but he still cherished the hope of preserving the
National Coalition until the end of the Japanese war and of
leading a united government to ultimate and final victory.
It was in this spirit that he made his final offer.

The situation was complicated by the fact that both Mr.
Eden and Mr. Attlee were absent from London attending the
San Francisco Conference. The Prime Minister had therefore
to consult his principal lieutenant by telegram and to conduct
his preliminary conversations with the Labour Party through
Mr. Bevin and Mr. Morrison. The former was disinclined to
see the Coalition break up for reasons perhaps not dissimilar
to those of Mr. Churchill. Mr. Morrison, however, would
not budge beyond the date of October. When Mr. Attlee
returned from America in mid-May he conferred at length
with the Prime Minister at No. 10 Downing Street before
leaving for the annual conference of the Labour Party at
Blackpool. The impression left upon Mr. Churchill's mind
by the interview was that the leader of the Labour Party, like
Mr. Bevin, favoured an indefinite prolongation of the Coalition
Government until the end of the Japanese war and would seek
to obtain the consent of his followers to this course.

Whatever Mr. Attlee's personal feelings may have been,
he found the Blackpool Conference obstinately opposed to
maintaining the Coalition beyond the autumn. The old
Labour Party suspicions of the Conservatives and of Mr.
Churchill had been stilled but not eradicated by their five
years' association. Moreover, the whole of their political
philosophy was opposed to coalitions except under the exigencies of extreme emergency. In addition, they were increasingly
anxious to see legislation passed for the implementation of the
Beveridge Report and the other comprehensive schemes of
social reform which had been formulated and agreed upon
by members of the Conservative, Labour and Liberal parties,
and they were by no means certain that their own anxiety
was matched by an accompanying enthusiasm among the
Conservatives.[61]

There followed an exchange of letters between the Prime

Minister and the Leader of the Labour Party (May 18-22, 1945) in which the arguments on both sides were stated forcefully and well and of which the outcome was the decision for an immediate termination of the Government.[a]

King George had been kept in close touch with each development by the Prime Minister who had also sent him copies of his correspondence with Mr. Attlee. The record of their Tuesday luncheons at this time provides a clear picture of what was in Mr. Churchill's mind from week to week and of the King's reactions to it. On the whole, His Majesty was sympathetic to the idea of a coalition indefinitely prolonged until the end of the Japanese war, which both he and the Prime Minister had reason to believe, because of their knowledge of the progress of the atom-bomb project, might not be as long as was generally expected. This, however, could not be said, and, as between the choice of June or October for a General Election, there could be no doubt that, leaving aside altogether the question of relative party advantages, the interests of the country and of the King's Government would be best served by an early consultation of the electorate. By waiting until October, as Mr. Churchill told the King, 'We should be condemned to between four and five months of uncertainty and electioneering hanging over the whole business of government and administration, both at home and abroad. . . . It would be no service to the nation to go forward with a pretence of union which had in fact lapsed with the attainment of complete victory.'[62]

Having informed the King fully by letter of the reasons which prompted his action, Mr. Churchill sought audience on May 23 to tender the resignation of himself and his Government. King George recorded:

The Prime Minister sent me a letter last night in which he explained the reasons for his writing to the leaders of the other Parties suggesting that the present Govt. should go on till the end of the war with Japan. Unfortunately neither Labour nor Liberal Parties will agree to this course, & the only course suggested by Mr. Attlee is that the present Administration should continue together until October. This course is not acceptable to the P.M.

[a] The text of Mr. Churchill's letters to Mr. Attlee is given in the sixth volume of his memoirs, pp. 515-517; that of Mr. Attlee's reply in his own book, *As it Happened*, pp. 135-138.

as he feels that the government of this country would not be on a
sound basis, & that the work of 'The whole vast process of trans-
formation of industry from war to peace, & of demobilizing the
Armies while at the same time forming the largest possible forces
to be sent to the Far East, as well as that of getting our trade &
industry on the move again, constitutes a task which, though not
so deadly as some which we have surmounted, is in some respects
more complicated.   Mr. Churchill feels that this task can only be
undertaken by a united Government possessing the undisputed
confidence of the people, & actuated by true Ministerial harmony
& agreement such as Your Majesty has the right to expect in any
Administration which may be formed in Your Reign.'   The P.M.
does not feel he can assure me that 'conditions of amity & single-
mindedness would prevail in the present Administration' with a
General Election in the offing.   It would only be a pretence & the
P.M. himself 'is convinced that he could not himself conscientiously
continue to head such an Administration in the circumstances
which he has outlined '.

'He therefore asks Your Majesty to accord him an audience at
some time convenient to Your Majesty tomorrow morning in order
that he may tender his resignation of the various Offices which he
now holds, & thus bring the present not inglorious Administration
to a dignified end in accordance with the highest constitutional
traditions & practice.'

Actual quotations from the letter in inverted commas.

The P.M. came to see me at 12.0 noon & explained fully what
had been going on during the last week with his colleagues, that
he felt he could not continue as the leader of a divided Cabinet &
placed his resignation in my hands.   I did not accept it then.   I
told him I would see him again at 4.0 p.m. when I would give
him my reply.   I had to have a Prime Minister in being during
those intervening 4 hours in case of emergency especially in war
time.   When he came at 4.0 pm I told him at once that I accepted
his resignation & asked him to form a new Government.   So he
became my Prime Minister for the 2nd time.[63]

The King's conduct of this occasion was, as in all things,
most constitutional.   Both he and Mr. Churchill were agreed
that the Sovereign should have a period for reflection and
that for this reason the Prime Minister's resignation could not
be accepted until the second audience, since otherwise any
important decision taken by him between noon and four
o'clock would have been *ultra vires*.   The King's choice in
asking Mr. Churchill to form a government was in itself an
obvious one, for he was the leader of a party which still had

a majority of a hundred over all others in the House of Commons and could therefore with ease have carried on the business of the King's Government indefinitely.　Mr. Churchill, in fact, asked for a dissolution of Parliament immediately after his reappointment as Prime Minister, and this the King granted, special legislation having been passed for an interval of three weeks to elapse before the order became operative, 'in view of the special circumstances prevailing'.

The date of Dissolution was therefore set for June 15, with polling day on July 5, and having made these arrangements the King was free to enjoy with his family a few weeks' well-earned vacation at Balmoral.　Before he left, however, he received his retiring Labour and Liberal Ministers and thanked them for their services over the past five years.　'They were all sorry to leave the War Administration but felt that the time had come to break away', he wrote.　'Parliament is 10 years old, and no one under the age of 30 has ever voted, the House of Commons needs rejuvenating. . . . Thus has ended the Coalition Government which during the War has done admirable work.　Country before Party has been its watchword.　But now what?'[64]

His Majesty had in fact taken the whole affair very philosophically.

We shall be in the throes of a General Election next month [he wrote to his brother the Duke of Gloucester, at that time Governor-General of Australia].　It is just as well to get it over.　The outcome of it is uncertain as no Party may secure a clear working majority, which will make things difficult for any Govt. to try & deal with U.S.A., Russia & France, let alone setting up a Govt. in Germany, & with all the problems of demobilization & housing at home. Then there is the war with Japan to deal with as well.　The outlook as far as I am concerned does not look very peaceful or restful. But I am not pessimistic about the future.　We have all been through so much in the war together that the people will realize things cannot be replaced and rebuilt at once.[65]

The King's remark that the outcome of the General Election was 'uncertain' was indeed a masterpiece of understatement.　Rarely had there been less tangible data for forecasting the result of an electoral contest.　In the 'coupon' election of December 1918, after the conclusion of the First

World War, an overwhelming victory for Mr. Lloyd George's Government had been virtually inevitable. In July 1945, however, with a parliament ten years old, with the German war ended but with the Japanese war then predictably far from finished, there were few political circumstances on which party statisticians could base their calculations. The field was left open to the psephological prophets.

Mr. Churchill toured the country and was received everywhere with enthusiasm and affectionate acclamation — a personal tribute to a great war leader. Mr. Churchill's qualities as a leader in peace-time, however, were not adequately disclosed during the campaign. His election addresses seemed to many to be ill-judged and maladroit, more especially his warning that the Labour Party, if it established Socialism, would also have to establish a Gestapo to maintain it.

In effect, only a brilliant *tour de force* on the part of their leader could have saved the Conservatives from defeat. They had been in power for the whole of the period between the wars save during two brief intervals in 1924 and 1929–1931 in which Labour had held office. All the evils of this unhappy period were thus laid at their door, their rule being popularly identified with that sense of insecurity, due mainly to fear of war and unemployment, which had dogged so many during these years. There was thus a tremendous presumption in favour of change; but the change would deprive the nation of Mr. Churchill's leadership and it was felt by many in all parties that his statesmanship could be ill spared at this juncture. This, then, was the fundamental issue at the polls on July 5. If a voter believed that Mr. Churchill's services were indispensable he would cast his suffrage for the Conservatives. If, however, his distrust of the Tory Party overbore all other considerations in his mind, he would vote Labour.[a]

When the votes were counted on July 26[b] it was perceived that suspicion had triumphed. For the first time in the twentieth century — with the exception of the election of 1906 — the Conservatives had failed to be returned with more

[a] An admirable study of the issues involved may be found in *The British General Election of 1945*, by R. B. McCallum and Alison Readman, pp. 44-68.

[b] Because of the delay in getting in the votes of the troops overseas, an interval of three weeks separated polling day from the declaration of the polls.

votes than any other single party. They lost 160 seats, while Labour gained 230, and the combined number of the Liberals and Independents fell by 55. The Labour Party and its associates had a majority of 180. The final state of the parties was as follows :

Labour	392
Conservatives	189
Liberal Nationals	13
Liberals	12
Ulster Unionists	9
Independent Labour Party	3
Communists	2
Irish Nationalists	2
Common Wealth Party	1 [a]

Thus the British electorate rejected Mr. Churchill — the man who, 'lion-hearted — held half the world at bay, until the other half was shocked into comprehension of the truths which he had long preached in vain' [b] — and summoned Labour in his stead.

Mr. Churchill was both saddened and surprised at being thus 'immediately dismissed by the British electorate from all further conduct of their affairs'.[66] On July 25 he had told King George that he had 'hopes of being returned with a majority of between 30 & 80',[67] but at 2 o'clock on the following afternoon it was clear that the Conservatives had been defeated and that the Labour Party would have a large majority in the new House of Commons. At 4 o'clock the Prime Minister asked Sir Alan Lascelles to call upon him at the Storey's Gate Annexe. His first inclination had been to postpone his resignation until after a Cabinet meeting on Monday, July 30, but he later changed his mind and decided to resign that same evening, saying that, *if the King should ask his advice*, he would recommend His Majesty to send for Mr. Attlee.[68] At 7 o'clock Mr. Churchill drove to the Palace.

The parting between the Sovereign and his great Prime Minister was inevitably a melancholy occasion. All the reluctance which King George had felt in 1940 to Mr. Churchill's

[a] Figures taken from the *Annual Register* for 1945, p. 55.

[b] This tribute to Sir Winston Churchill was offered by former President Truman when the guest of the Pilgrims at a banquet in London on June 21, 1956.

appointment had disappeared. In the crucible of war, in the trials of defeat and the flush of victory, the two men had acquired a mutual admiration, and a unique degree of intimacy had developed between them. The King was deeply appreciative of the leadership which Mr. Churchill had given to the country in its great ordeal and of the extent to which he had always kept his Sovereign informed of all developments — good or bad. For his part, Mr. Churchill had been honoured by the confidence which the King had reposed in him and had valued deeply the unwavering support of the Crown at every turn. Moreover, both he and his colleagues had found that on more than one occasion the questing mind of King George, with its pragmatic common sense, had opened up vistas of thought which had hitherto evaded them.

Now this great partnership was ended and the King felt towards his defeated Prime Minister all that sympathy which five years before had characterized his parting with Mr. Chamberlain. He wrote in his diary :

I saw Winston at 7.0 pm & it was a very sad meeting. I told him I thought the people were very ungrateful after the way they had been led in the War. He was very calm & said that with the majority the Socialists had got over the other parties (153) & with careful management they could remain in power for years. He would be Leader of the Opposition. I asked him if I should send for Mr. Attlee to form a government & he agreed. We said good bye & I thanked him for all his help to me during the 5 War Years.[69]

King George was desirous of rewarding Mr. Churchill's services to the country by appointing him a Knight of the Garter, but this honour he begged leave to decline, feeling that it would not be proper for him to accept while leading the Conservative Party in opposition in the House of Commons. But 'he hoped he would be able to accept it later'. With characteristic generosity, however, he asked the King to give the Garter to Mr. Eden and to this course His Majesty was not averse. But Mr. Eden, when sounded, also begged leave to decline, saying that he could not accept any honour if his Chief would not.[a] [70]

[a] The Garter, which had subsequently become a 'non-political' honour (see below, pp. 755-8), was conferred by Queen Elizabeth II on Mr. Churchill on the occasion of her Coronation in 1953, and on Mr. Eden in the following year.

The King expressed his personal gratitude to Mr. Churchill in the following letter :

MY DEAR WINSTON,

I am writing to tell you how very sad I am that you are no longer my Prime Minister. During the last 5 years of war we have met on dozens, I may say on hundreds, of occasions, when we have discussed the most vital questions concerning the security & welfare of this country & the British Empire in their hours of trial. I shall always remember our talks with the greatest pleasure & only wish they could have continued longer.

You often told me what you thought of people & matters of real interest which I could never have learnt from anyone else. Your breadth of vision & your grasp of the essential things were a great comfort to me in the darkest days of the War, & I like to think that we have never disagreed on any really important matter. For all those things I thank you most sincerely. I feel that your conduct as Prime Minister & Minister of Defence has never been surpassed. You have had many difficulties to deal with both as a politician & as a strategist of war but you have always surmounted them with supreme courage.

Your relations with the Chiefs of Staff have always been most cordial & they have served you with a real devotion.

They I know will regret your leaving the helm at this moment.

For myself personally, I regret what has happened more than perhaps anyone else. I shall miss your counsel to me more than I can say. But please remember that as a friend I hope we shall be able to meet at intervals.

　　　Believe me
　　　　　　I am,
　　　　　　　　　　Yours very sincerely & gratefully
　　　　　　　　　　　　　　　　　　G.R.I.[71]

But the King's Government had to be carried on, and at half-past seven on the evening of July 26 Mr. Clement Attlee followed Mr. Churchill to Buckingham Palace. The extent of Labour's victory at the elections had been as great a surprise to Mr. Attlee as to anyone, and he was in the additional difficulty of having many of his colleagues dispersed throughout the country in their constituencies. Yet certain key positions must be filled at once, since President Truman and Marshal Stalin were waiting at Potsdam to resume the work of the Conference, which had opened on July 17. It is a tribute to Mr. Attlee's powers of organization and to the state of preparedness of his Party that he was enabled to form the beginnings of his Cabinet and depart for Potsdam within twenty-four hours of being summoned to the Palace. In this he was greatly assisted by having a nucleus of men who had been recently in office.

I then saw Mr. Attlee [the King recorded] & asked him to form a government. He accepted & became my new Prime Minister. I told him he would have to appoint a Foreign Secy. & take him to Berlin. I found he was very surprised his Party had won [a] & had had no time to meet or discuss with his colleagues any of the Offices of State. I asked him whom he would make Foreign Secy. & he suggested Dr. Hugh Dalton. I disagreed with him & said that Foreign Affairs was the most important subject at the moment & I hoped he would make Mr. Bevin take it. He said he would but he could not return to Berlin till Saturday at the earliest. I told him I could hold a Council on Saturday to swear in the new Secy. of State. I hoped our relations would be cordial & said that I would always be ready to do my best to help him.[73]

It is appropriate at this point to deal with the rumour that subsequently became current both in Britain and in the United States that, at this first audience with his new Prime Minister, King George 'insisted' on the appointment of Mr. Ernest Bevin as Foreign Secretary and that Mr. Attlee, against his own judgment, complied. This rumour Mr. Attlee has most properly and emphatically denied, saying that Mr. Bevin was his own choice.[74]

What is abundantly clear from the King's own record, and from the memorandum made by Sir Alan Lascelles immediately after the audience,[b] is that His Majesty was exercising one of what Walter Bagehot has defined as the constitutional prerogatives of the Sovereign — the right to advise, and that Mr. Attlee, having taken this advice into consideration, doubtless in conjunction with other factors, made his decision of his own wisdom and free will. There is no conceivable evidence of 'insistence' or 'pressure'. It is true, however, that Mr. Attlee did not apparently inform his colleagues of his conversation with the King, for when the

[a] Mr. Attlee wrote subsequently: 'He [the King] always used to say that I looked very surprised, as indeed I certainly was at the extent of our success'.[72]

[b] 'Mr. Attlee mentioned to the King that he was thinking of appointing Mr. Dalton to be his Foreign Secretary', wrote Sir Alan Lascelles. 'His Majesty begged him to think carefully about this, and suggested that Mr. Bevin would be a better choice.'[75]

new Secretary of State for Foreign Affairs was received in audience somewhat later and the King told him that he had suggested that he should go to the Foreign Office, Mr. Bevin replied that this 'was news to him'.[76]

It was under these somewhat unusual circumstances that the King's new Government came into being. At a Privy Council at Buckingham Palace on the morning of Saturday, July 28, the Prime Minister and six of his principal colleagues received their seals of office,[a] and that same evening Mr. Attlee and Mr. Bevin flew back to Berlin. The remainder of the Ministerial appointments were not completed until August 4.

(viii)

We have it on the authority of Pericles that men rarely adhere to the same views during the course of war which they held upon entering it, and are likely to change their beliefs as to its causes when they look back from the consequence of their actions.[b]

In September 1939 the active belligerent Powers were but four, Germany, Great Britain, France and Poland, and this number rapidly decreased to three. Of the four principal neutral States, Russia, Japan and Italy were considered potential enemies of the West, and the United States a potential friend. Six years later all these Powers had become belligerents, three along the lines anticipated. The great imponderable of the Soviet Union, however, had been added to the forces of the United Nations.

The original attitude of the Western Powers towards Germany had been defined by Mr. Neville Chamberlain in his broadcast on September 4, 1939. 'In this war', he had said, 'we are not fighting against you, the German people, for whom we have no bitter feelings, but against a tyrannous and forsworn régime which has destroyed not only its own people but the whole of Western civilization and all that you

---

[a] The Ministers appointed on July 28 were as follows; Mr. Attlee, First Lord of the Treasury; Mr. Ernest Bevin, Foreign Secretary; Sir William Jowitt, Lord Chancellor; Dr. Hugh Dalton, Chancellor of the Exchequer; Mr. Arthur Greenwood, Lord Privy Seal; and Sir Stafford Cripps, President of the Board of Trade.

[b] Thucydides, Book I, chapter cxl.

and we hold dear.' [a] In the course of the next six years it was clearly apparent that, whatever their inner reservations may have been, the German people were unable or unwilling to free themselves from the Nazi régime, with the inevitable result that they became identified in the minds of those arrayed against them with an upsurging of bitterness — a bitterness which found its ultra-logical apogee in the Morgenthau Plan, formally considered at the Second Quebec Conference of September 1944, by which a defeated Germany would have been forcibly transformed from an industrial into an agricultural country. Though this idea of 'pastoralizing' Germany did not survive, the very fact that it was officially advanced marks a notable change from the sentiments expressed by Mr. Chamberlain. The policy of Unconditional Surrender promulgated at Casablanca in 1943 set the pattern for the ultimate conclusion of the war, a pattern which was finally completed in the school-house of Rheims on May 7, 1945.

Furthermore, the fact that Britain's *casus belli* in September 1939 had been in defence of the independence and integrity of Poland had been somewhat obscured by subsequent events. The emergence of the Soviet Union as a leading partner in the Grand Alliance had had a further — and again, perhaps, an inevitable — sequel in the virtual abandonment of Poland by the Western Powers at Yalta.

When, therefore, the chief representatives of the Grand Alliance met on July 17, 1945, at Potsdam, amid the shattered glories of the Hohenzollerns, it was to consider a Germany in a state of total subjection, her territory occupied by conquering armies and her very sovereignty thrown into commission ; [b] and a Europe of which the whole eastern portion was dominated by the victorious hosts of the Soviet Union. It was at Potsdam, moreover, that that which had been apparent to some for a considerable time now became clear beyond per-

---

[a] Broadcast to the German People, *British Blue Book*, No. 144.

[b] The members of Grand Admiral Doenitz's Government at Flensburg were arrested on May 23, 1945, and thenceforward, until the establishment in 1949 of the Federal Republic in Bonn and the Democratic Republic in Berlin, the government of Germany was in the hands of the Allied Commission of Control. As a result of subsequent events Germany, after 1948, became completely divided, with the British, American and French High Commissioners administering Western and the Soviet High Commissioner Eastern Germany. Full sovereignty was accorded to the Federal Republic under the Bonn Agreement of 1954.

adventure to all : namely, that included among the fruits and favours which flowed from the cornucopia of victory was the bitter apple of Soviet aggression and duplicity. It was yet two years, however, before tepid friendship was transmuted into 'cold war'.

A not unimportant facet of the Potsdam Conference was the lesson in the art of government — for it remains an art and not a science — provided by the British delegation, which afforded an impressive example of the fundamental principle of British politics — the King's Government must go on.

The Conference began during the unusually long interval in the British General Election between polling day and the declaration of the polls. Mr. Churchill, Mr. Eden and Mr. Attlee all attended the opening sessions. They returned to London on July 25, having given their assurance to President Truman and Marshal Stalin that a representative delegation would return by the end of the week. The result of the election replaced Mr. Churchill by Mr. Attlee as Prime Minister and on the evening of July 28 he was back in Potsdam with Mr. Bevin. In a matter of hours the Conference was resumed with the continuity of British representation quite unruffled.

The effect of this embodiment of British phlegm upon the Americans and the Russians was varied but not without interest. To President Truman 'it was a dramatic demonstration of the slow and peaceful way in which a democracy changes its government',[77] but in the bosom of M. Molotov the whole affair evoked a deep distrust. He had asked Mr. Attlee before his departure for London what he thought the result of the election would be and the leader of the Labour Party had replied, with perfect sincerity, that he thought it would be a very close thing. M. Molotov interpreted this remark as a cryptic indication that the result of the election had already been 'fixed' and the change-over by democratic process was a great shock to him, more especially as the new Prime Minister and Foreign Secretary were accompanied on their return to Potsdam by the same official advisers as had served their predecessors, and Mr. Attlee had even taken over as his Principal Private Secretary the same person who had been serving Mr. Churchill in the same capacity. 'But you said the Election would be a close thing and now you have a

big majority', M. Molotov kept repeating in reproachful bewilderment, and thenceforth regarded the British representatives with the darkest suspicion.[78]

(ix)

Ever since the termination of hostilities in Europe King George
had been desirous of a meeting with President Truman and
of establishing with him something of the close personal relations which he had enjoyed with President Roosevelt.   The
difficulty was one of timing, since all were anxious to avoid
reawakening the suspicion which Marshal Stalin had evinced
as a result of the preliminary meetings between Mr. Churchill
and President Roosevelt at Cairo and Malta before the
Teheran and Yalta Conferences.   'By rights Truman should
come here first before seeing Stalin, as F. D. R. had given me
a promise he would', the King wrote in his diary.   'Truman
is frightened of "ganging-up" with Winston in Stalin's eyes.
Then again Truman can't meet Stalin before he meets Winston.
So the meeting must take place first and Truman's visit here
later.'[79]
    King George then made the suggestion that he should
inspect his troops in the British zone; this was approved in
principle and General Eisenhower invited him to come to
SHAEF headquarters at Frankfurt.   Since this visit would
coincide with the Potsdam Conference it was agreed between
the King and Mr. Churchill that His Majesty might come to
Berlin for a day, lunch with Marshal Stalin and in the evening
give a dinner in the British sector at which President Truman
and the Marshal would be his guests.   This proposal was
warmly endorsed by the President and was accepted by
Marshal Stalin,[80] but to the great disappointment of King
George, his hopes of a visit to Germany were dashed by the
strong disinclination of Field-Marshal Montgomery to assume
the responsibility for His Majesty's safety in view of the hostile
state of the country, and the idea was abandoned.[81]
    The King then wrote to President Truman inviting him
to stay at Buckingham Palace on his way back from the Conference to the United States.[82]   The invitation was gladly
accepted on July 12, but only in principle, since Mr. Truman

feared that 'conditions in the United States may require my immediate return when the Conference is over'.[83] What the President had in mind was not the domestic political situation in the United States but the circumstances attendant upon the first use of the atomic weapon. The final decision to drop the atom bomb on a Japanese target was his and his alone, and he was almost daily expecting word from America which might make the taking of this decision immediate.

This is exactly what occurred. On July 16, the day before the Potsdam Conference opened, news came of the successful test carried out in New Mexico, and on July 22 President Truman wrote to King George deeply regretting that it was essential for him to return home immediately after the Conference closed and he must therefore forgo the pleasure of a visit to London.[84] On the following day orders were wired to General Spaatz, the commander of the U.S. Strategic Air Forces, instructing him that the first bomb would be dropped 'as soon after August 3 as weather would permit'.[85]

King George, however, was not to be defeated. He was fully convinced that a meeting between himself and the President, if even for an hour or so, before he left Europe was both desirable and expedient, and he therefore proposed that, as Mr. Truman would be returning in the U.S.S. *Augusta*, it might be possible for her to put in to British territorial waters so that the King might go out from Portsmouth in a barge, board her and have a talk with the President going down the Solent. He would then leave her somewhere off the Needles. With this plan Mr. Truman was delighted, but his travelling arrangements made it necessary to join *Augusta* at Plymouth, whither he flew from Berlin, and thus it came about that the long deferred meeting took place in Plymouth Sound on August 2, 1945.

I arrived at Milbay Station, Plymouth & went on board the 'Renown' which was lying at anchor in the Sound [the King wrote in his diary]. The U.S.S. 'Augusta' was at anchor nearby. President Truman, Secy of State Mr. Byrnes & Fleet Adl. Leahy came on board to call on me at 12.30 pm. I welcomed him to this country & we had ½ hrs. talk before lunch. He told me he was glad he had taken part in the Berlin Conference in that he had made personal contact with Churchill, Stalin & Attlee. He admitted he had learnt a great deal & understood European difficulties from a new standpoint. He could see Stalin wanted to keep what he already had, but he had too much for U.S. & U.K. liking, & concessions from Russia were arranged for under the new Foreign Secys. Council which is to meet at intervals in London to discuss these matters & also to arrange the preliminaries of the Peace Conference. He was horrified at the devastation of Berlin by our combined bombing. He could see that the Big Powers would have to combine for all time to prevent another war. At lunch I talked to Mr. Byrnes. I liked him. Attractive of Irish origin & a great talker. He had many arguments with Molotov, who could take no decision on any matter. Reference to Stalin at all times. He thought Bevin a bit crude in behaviour though a good negotiator. Byrnes wld. discuss the T.A. bomb [a] at length on its potentialities, as he was in charge of its research organisation. After lunch I went on board the 'Augusta' to return the President's visit & later she & the U.S.S. 'Philadelphia' sailed. I returned to my train & reached London at 10.0 pm.[86]

The character of King George at once registered with Mr. Truman. 'I was impressed with the King as a good man', he has written,[87] and there was an immediate affinity between them. The King's modesty, his earnestness and simple kindliness, coupled with his remarkably detailed knowledge of the pattern of the world and his avid eagerness to learn more, all appealed to the President. Before leaving *Augusta* King George asked Mr. Truman if he would give him his autograph 'for my wife and daughters', and the President, delighted to make the discovery which many Americans had made, that the King of England was also a 'human being', thereupon signed several White House cards.

The President's advisers, Mr. Byrnes [b] and Admiral Leahy,[c]

[a] Within the narrow circle of those in Britain who were initiated in the matter of the atomic weapon, the term 'Tube Alloy' (or T.A.) was used in conversation as a security measure. The King scrupulously maintained this precaution in any references which he made to the project in his diary.

[b] Hon. James Francis Byrnes (b. 1879) served as Congressman and Senator from South Carolina, 1911–1941; as Associate Justice of the U.S. Supreme Court, 1941–1942; Director of Economic Stabilization, 1942–1943; Director of the Office of War Mobilization, 1943–1945; and Secretary of State, 1945–1947. He was elected Governor of South Carolina in 1950.

[c] Fleet Admiral William D. Leahy (b. 1875), after a distinguished naval career, was appointed Governor of Puerto Rico by President Roosevelt in 1939 and Ambassador to the Vichy Government of France in 1940. He served as Chief of Staff to President Roosevelt from 1942 to 1945 and to President Truman from 1945 to 1949.

were also astonished at the King's informality and wide knowledge. At luncheon, which was a very gay affair, much of the
conversation turned on the use of the atom bomb, and the King
displayed a considerable intimacy with the project and of the
possible uses of atomic energy after the war. The only member
of the group to be sceptical of its success was Admiral Leahy,
who bluntly stated : 'It sounds like a professor's dream to
me'. 'Would you like to lay a little bet on that, Admiral?'
King George asked, and Admiral Leahy records with honesty :
'Events shortly were to prove that in this respect I was very
much in error'.[88]

On the departure of President Truman, the King and
Queen went to Windsor to attend the Ascot races where, as
the King recorded, 'my horse "Rising Light" beat "Stirling
Castle" in a mile and a half race by a short head. It was
thrilling for me as I had never seen one of my own horses win
before.' [a] [89] But meantime great events were in process.

On August 6 the first atomic bomb was dropped on
Hiroshima. Russia declared war on Japan two days later,
and on the 9th the second bomb was dropped on Nagasaki.
Thereafter the Japanese Government accepted unconditional
surrender, and on August 15 the King opened his first peace-
time Parliament since 1938, amid the jubilation of V-J Day.[b]
In the course of the afternoon and evening the King and
Queen appeared half a dozen times on the balcony of Buckingham Palace in response to the cheering crowd, and the King
received the congratulations of his Ministers. He also received
Mr. Winston Churchill. 'I wish he could have been given a
proper reception by the people', was his thought that night.[90]

Ten days later the King and Queen arrived at Balmoral

[a] The governing words in this quotation from the King's diary are 'my *own*
horses'. He had on June 12, 1942, seen the filly 'Sun Chariot', which he had
leased from the National Stud, carry his racing colours to victory at the Oaks
which, owing to war-time exigencies, was run at Newmarket. 'She got left at
the start & lost 50 yds but made it up in grand style, & beat "Afterthought" by
half a length. I led her in', he had written in his diary on that day.

[b] On this occasion, for the first time in history, *two* Speeches from the Throne
were prepared and signed by the Sovereign for the opening of Parliament. The
cause was that, until a very few hours before the King left for the Palace of
Westminster, it was not known whether Japan had surrendered or not. One
version of the speech, therefore, alluded to the surrender, the other omitted any
reference to it. The former was, of course, the speech which the King actually
delivered.

for a well-earned rest. The weather was lovely though the shooting was poor, as many young grouse had been killed by the frost and snow of the early summer. But the King was thankful for the peace of Deeside — and in the world at large.

The final surrender of Japan was signed in Tokyo Bay on board the U.S.S. 'Missouri', the U.S. Flagship, yesterday [a] [he wrote on September 3]. Thus has ended the World War which started 6 years ago to-day.[91]

[a] Among those present in *Missouri* on this historic occasion was Prince Philip of Greece, later Duke of Edinburgh.

CHAPTER X

THE POST-WAR WORLD
1945–1950

(i)

THE problems with which King George VI was confronted on his return to London from Balmoral in October 1945 were both similar and dissimilar to those which had faced his father after the First World War. In 1918 Germany had also been a prostrate enemy, but in 1945 her defeat was of infinitely greater proportions. At the close of the First World War the United States of America represented a vast new potential in world affairs but one whose co-operation was destined to be withdrawn under the influence of the forces of isolationism ; in 1945 the position of America was the same but with the historic difference that she remained a positive, as opposed to a negative, factor in the comity of nations, throwing, with an almost prodigal generosity, the full weight of her manifold resources into the post-war battle of rehabilitation, reconstruction and mutual defence. France, who at the close of the First World War had been a senior partner in victory and the dominant force in Europe, emerged from the Second as a nation groping painfully forward in the search for the rediscovery of her own soul.

The greatest difference, however, lay in the position of Russia. In 1918 she had reached the depths of political and military disintegration and perhaps the apogee of pure revolutionary fervour. The impact upon the world of Bolshevism as a new ideology was greater even than that of Wilsonism, and even more dangerous to the survival of the Old Order. Dependent almost entirely for its success on the external effect of its propaganda — for it was not until considerably later that the Red Army was reorganized as an effective fighting force — Bolshevism constituted a threat to the countries of Eastern and Central Europe, but a threat which the authority of established governments was, in the main, sufficiently strong to combat successfully. A quarter of a century later, however, the position had greatly changed. By 1945 the inspirational genius of Lenin and the revolutionary fanaticism of Trotsky had both disappeared and in their place was the crude materialism, the stark *Realpolitik*, of Stalin. At the close of the Second World War the Soviet Union was second only to the United States as a military world power, exercising a rigid and ruthless control over all Eastern, Central and South-eastern Europe, with the exception of Austria, Czechoslovakia and Greece, and exhibiting a very patent intention of extending permanently her ideological and political hegemony over all those territories.

In Britain itself the basic problems of post-war reconstruction — demobilization, the reconversion of industry from war-time to peace-time production, housing (a far more pressing question in 1945 by reason of the effects of enemy bombing) and the search for means to pay for the stupendous cost of war — were much the same in nature in 1945 as they had been in 1918, though far greater in magnitude. But there was a clearly defined difference in the methods and motives of tackling them. After the First World War there had been a perceptible desire to get back, as far as the exigencies of the situation permitted, to the 'good old days'. This was no longer the case in 1945. The British people had learned by harsh experience that peace did not necessarily mean prosperity. Their memories of the years between the wars were bitter, especially in regard to unemployment. By contrast, their memories of the war-time period were happier in at least one respect : the diminution of class differences, the great increase in the equality of opportunity, the growth of the idea of share-and-share-alike. Full employment had banished the spectre of want and, as a result of the efficiency of the rationing system, it is certain that the children of the poor were better fed during the war years than they had ever been before.

From these factors was bred a conscious desire for greater social justice; a desire which played an important rôle in bringing about the second great difference in the political situation in Britain from that obtaining at the close of the

First World War.   For, whereas King George V had faced his post-war problems with the advice of a Coalition Government, of which the predominating element was the Conservative Party, King George VI entered upon the difficult path of peace-time reconstruction with a Labour Government, which enjoyed a substantial majority in the House of Commons.

King George had not been prepared for the results of the 1945 elections which, as he wrote to the Duke of Gloucester, 'came as a great surprise to one and all'.[1]   General Smuts had warned him as early as April that in his view there would undoubtedly be a swing to the Left and that the Crown would have to be the stabilizer,[2] but the General had been equally confident that Mr. Churchill would win the Election simply on his record as the leader of a successful War Government.[3] This, indeed, had been the King's own expectation and its complete negation at the polls came as a considerable surprise to him.

It was not that His Majesty was out of sympathy with the prevailing spirit of the times.   From the days of his Camp and of his work with the Industrial Welfare Society no man in Britain had done more than he to gain recognition for the necessity for wider social understanding and greater equality of opportunity.   In every message which he had broadcast to his peoples during the past six years he had not failed to emphasize the vital need of applying to the problems of peace those supreme qualities of common sacrifice and endeavour which had been so nobly demonstrated in time of war, and he was perhaps more aware of its deeper meaning than the leaders of either of the two major political parties.

The King's reaction to the results of the General Election was occasioned partly by his own great and understandable reluctance to disrupt the effective working partnership which he had established with Mr. Churchill, and partly by a genuine sorrow that Britain should be deprived at this most difficult juncture of Mr. Churchill's outstanding power of leadership and wide experience of government.   His Majesty was not pro-Conservative or anti-Socialist.   He would undoubtedly have preferred the continuation of the National Coalition which had brought the war to a successful and victorious conclusion.   What did arouse his apprehension was

the prospect of a new and untried Labour Government — with
its policy of nationalization well to the fore of its programme
— being faced with the responsibility of solving the manifold
and complex problems of post-war reconstruction. He himself
was a progressive in political thought and a reformer in social
conscience but he was distrustful of undue haste and of political
extremism in any form. It was this anxiety which prompted
him to write to General Smuts of the result of the General
Election : 'It was a great shock to me to have to lose Churchill
as my chief adviser, and I am sure the People did not want to
lose him as their leader, after all the years of stupendous work
he did on their behalf in the War.' [4]

But whatever King George's personal misgivings may have
been, he did not permit them to affect his relations with his
new Ministers, with whom he worked in a remarkable degree
of friendship, help and co-operation. Their relative lack of
governmental experience, however, materially increased his own
burden of responsibility. 'You will find that your position will
be greatly strengthened', Lord Mountbatten had written to him
soon after the Election results had been announced, 'since you
are now the old experienced campaigner on whom a new and
partly inexperienced Government will lean for advice and
guidance',[5] and this was indeed true. The audiences which
followed in the latter months of 1945 and the beginning of
1946 provided both Sovereign and Ministers with an opportunity for increased mutual respect and enlightenment. His
advisers learned to appreciate the King's innate probity, his
selflessness of character and his remarkable capacity of knowing in detail exactly what he was talking about, while he grew
to appreciate their very considerable qualities.

With his new Prime Minister the King was well acquainted.
Mr. Attlee is an example of those who have come into public
life by the way of 'good works'. Haileybury and University
College, Oxford, had prepared him for a legal career but,
following the strong family tradition of social service, he combined his practice of the law with work in the East End of
London, first at the Haileybury College Club and later at
Toynbee Hall, of which he became secretary in 1910. His
experience of social conditions and his desire to reform them
caused him to enter local politics in Stepney and to become

BUCKINGHAM PALACE, V-J DAY, AUGUST 15, 1945

a member of the Independent Labour Party. On his return from the First World War he was elected Stepney's first mayor in 1919 and in 1922 entered the House of Commons as Member for Limehouse, a seat which he retained for the next eighteen years.

Owing, in part, to the general respect for his integrity and ability and, in part, to the warring personalities of his colleagues, Mr. Attlee became leader of the Labour Party in 1935, and in this capacity he had entered the Coalition Government in 1940 as deputy to the Prime Minister, proving himself a wise and loyal colleague to Mr. Churchill throughout the war. In the difficult years of his own premiership, though a curiously elusive figure to the public, he exercised great gifts of judgment and leadership within his Cabinet, holding together what was perhaps a difficult team, of which the chief figures were men of such diverse individualism as Mr. Herbert Morrison, Mr. Ernest Bevin, Sir Stafford Cripps, Dr. Hugh Dalton and Mr. Aneurin Bevan.

Mr. Attlee's personal relationship with King George was at first not easy. Both were essentially shy men and the initiation of conversation did not come easily to either of them. At the outset the Prime Minister's audiences were not infrequently marked by long silences. This, however, quickly wore off. Both persevered — and with success. The King writes in his diary later of 'long talks' with Mr. Attlee, in the course of which he was able, apart from conducting the business of the day, to put to the Prime Minister some of the aspects of thought which were current at the time, not infrequently surprising him by the extent, detail and accuracy of his information. 'I told Attlee', he wrote on one occasion, 'that he must give the people here some confidence that the Government was not going to stifle all private enterprise. Everyone wanted to help in rehabilitating the country but they were not allowed to',[6] and again :

We discussed Housing & Clothing. I told him I had heard that Local Authorities had had their plans turned down & were unable to build any houses because they could not get a permit from Health. Papers he had read showed a good improvement in approved permits to build now. But where are the houses, I asked ? The delay is very worrying. Private building contractors had done well. As to Clothing the P.M. told me all available suits etc. go to the Demobilised Men, & the Women's clothes stocks are much exaggerated. I said we must all have new clothes & my family are down to the lowest ebb.[7]

On the subject of strikes also the King was emphatic with his Prime Minister. A stoppage of work by gas employees, which had not been accorded official Trade Union recognition, caused considerable inconvenience during the winter of 1945 and Mr. Attlee expressed the hope that it would be settled quickly. King George commented that 'the liberty of the subject was at stake if a strike interfered with home life. Essential services such as gas, electricity and water should never be used for those purposes in an unofficial strike. He & I could easily go on strike. He would send me no papers and if he did I would not sign them. But we don't!'[8]

With his other new Ministers the King soon established a good working relationship. The fundamental common sense and good judgment of Ernest Bevin made an immediate appeal. 'I was much struck by his knowledge of the Foreign Affairs subject', the King wrote to Queen Mary,[9] and throughout Mr. Bevin's tenure of the Foreign Office their relations were of the best, though the Foreign Secretary did not go often to the Palace.

The King was impressed also with the effervescent personality of Mr. Aneurin Bevan,[a] the Minister of Health. Mr. Bevan also has a Celtic charm and romanticism, both of which were in evidence at his first audience. With becoming diffidence he asked permission to express his long-felt admiration for the amazing way in which King George had overcome his speech defect, adding that, as one who had himself stammered very badly as a boy, he appreciated this achievement in full measure. 'I asked him how he liked the responsibility of a Government Dept. instead of criticising it', the King recorded. 'He laughed at that. I found him easy to talk to. . . . He

---

[a] Rt. Hon. Aneurin Bevan (b. 1897) entered Parliament as member for Ebbw Vale in 1929. His somewhat contumacious nature caused him to be expelled from the Labour Party for a brief period in 1939, and during the war he was a frequent and trenchant critic of Mr. Churchill's leadership. He was Minister of Health from 1945 to 1951, when he became Minister of Labour. He resigned, however, in the same year in protest against Mr. Hugh Gaitskell's budget and remained a critic of Mr. Attlee's leadership of the Party. He was elected Treasurer of the Labour Party in 1956.

thought modern houses should be built as homes not just boxes of brick & designs must suit environment.'[10]

Like many another Party pledged by electoral promises to a sweeping programme of social reforms, the Labour Government was anxious to achieve as much as possible within the life of one Parliament, and the King did not hesitate to warn his Ministers that, in his view, they were overcrowding the parliamentary time-table. He put this point forcefully to Mr. Herbert Morrison when the Lord President was acting Prime Minister during Mr. Attlee's absence in America in November 1945.

We discussed the whole of the Labour programme [he wrote in his diary]. I thought he was going too fast in the new nationalising legislation. Bill drafting takes time, especially with a reduced staff. He did not dissent at this but said the Party would have to carry out its agreed proposals as soon as possible, though he saw the difficulties of getting the people accustomed to the changes. During the Coalition the Labour members had learnt a great deal from the Conservatives in how to govern.[11]

This mantle of elder statesman, upon whose wide experience of government his Ministers relied perhaps more than they realized, lay heavily upon the King's shoulders. He felt a constant burden of responsibility, an ever-increasing anxiety regarding policies from which he did not dissent in principle but which he often regarded as being implemented too precipitately. He was aware that in his talks with Ministers he was not infrequently successful in presenting arguments which caused them to reconsider decisions at which they had already arrived, but the tension and exertion thus entailed fatigued him mightily and now there also came upon him the delayed reaction from the six long years of war. He was exhausted physically and mentally. Ever since he had come to the Throne there had scarcely been a month in which he had been free from care. The sudden circumstances of his accession and their consequent problems had been followed by the Czechoslovak crisis and this by the prolonged perils and grave problems of the war. The strain had been unremitting and, when he went to Sandringham for Christmas — the first to be spent in the Big House since 1940, since, for reasons of security and economy, the Royal Family had used Appleton, Queen

Maud's home, during the war years — the full tide of exhaustion swept over him. 'I feel burned out', was his frequent remark, and he wrote gloomily to the Duke of Gloucester :

. . . I have been suffering from an awful reaction from the strain of the war I suppose & have felt very tired especially down here but I hope I shall soon start to feel well again. Medicine, not even Weir's,[a] is of any use as I really want a rest, away from people & papers but that of course is impossible. I am perfectly well really but feel that I cannot cope competently with all the varied & many questions which come up. My new Government is not too easy & the people are rather difficult to talk to. Bevin is very good & tells me everything that is going on. The others are still learning how to run their departments, & their efforts have not made life any easier so far. Food, clothes & fuel are the main topics of conversation with us all.[12]

The years to come were to bring little to lighten the Sovereign's burdens.

(ii)

That which occurred in Britain between the years 1945 and 1950 was neither more nor less than a Social Revolution; a projection in essence, perhaps, of those great social reforms which Mr. Lloyd George had introduced before the First World War, but far more extensive in character and carrying the very distinctive brand of Socialist ideology. The Labour Party had come into power with a well-defined policy worked out over many years but well calculated to meet the prevailing spirit of the times in this post-war period. It had been set forth very clearly in their Electoral Manifesto and the result of the polls entitled them to consider that they had received a mandate to carry it out.

Basically their object was to create a society founded on social justice, towards which end plans had been made under the Coalition Government with the assent of all three political parties. That Government, in which Conservative support had been a dominant element, had appointed a Liberal, Sir William Beveridge, to prepare a report on Social Insurance and Allied

---

[a] Under the influence of his physician, Sir John Weir, the King became a convinced believer in homoeopathy.

Services. His recommendations, with some changes, had been accepted and these were to be the basis of the Labour Party's social welfare legislation. As a result of the campaigning activities of the Independent Member, Miss Eleanor Rathbone, the Coalition Government had also passed the Family Allowances Act, which the Labour Party put into force in 1946. In addition, a Conservative, Mr. R. A. Butler, was the Minister responsible for the great Education Act of 1944, which again was implemented by the Labour Party.

The Labour Party in 1945, therefore, fell heir to a considerable quantity of social legislation, the value and necessity of which was already agreed. The issue between them and the Conservatives was the cardinal Socialist doctrine that social justice can only be achieved by bringing under public ownership and control the main factors in the national economic system.

Nationalization [Mr. Attlee has written] was not an end in itself but an essential element in achieving the ends we sought. Controls were desirable not for their own sake but because they were necessary in order to gain freedom from the economic power of the owners of capital. A juster distribution of wealth was not a policy to soak the rich or to take revenge, but because a society with gross inequalities of wealth and opportunity is fundamentally unhealthy.

It had always been our practice, in accord with the natural genius of the British people, to work empirically. We were not afraid of compromises and partial solutions. We knew that mistakes would be made and that advances would be often by trial and error. We realized that the application of socialist principles in a country such as Britain with a peculiar economic structure based on international trade required great flexibility.

We were also well aware of the especially difficult situation of the country resulting from the great life-and-death struggle from which we had emerged victorious. But, in our view, this did not make change in the socialist direction less necessary. On the contrary, it was clear that there could be no return to past conditions. The old pattern was worn out and it was for us to weave the new. Thus, the kind of reproach levelled at us by Churchill, that instead of uniting the country by a programme of social reform on the lines of the Beveridge Report, we were following a course dictated by social prejudice or theory, left us completely unmoved. We had not been elected to try to patch up an old system but to make something new. Our policy was not a reformed capitalism, but progress toward a democratic socialism.[13]

This, then, was the course which His Majesty's Government had charted for itself and to which it adhered unwaveringly throughout the duration of its term of office. Beginning with the Bank of England — which, to the surprise of many, was revealed to be already in an advanced stage of nationalization — the ownership of coal mines, railways, road transport, gas and electricity, together with the health services of the country, were all brought in due course under public control, and at length, in the autumn session of 1948, the Government produced its Bill for the nationalization of the iron and steel industry.

The Conservative Party, who had fought the Government's legislation energetically but in vain, were determined to oppose this latest measure by every means at their command, not excluding the use of the House of Lords. They regarded the transfer to state ownership of the steel industry, which was as thriving as the coal industry was the reverse, as a direct threat to a mainstay of the nation's export trade without which the people of Britain would starve. The Government had foreseen this all-out onslaught. They had also realized that the introduction of the Steel Bill had been so long delayed that the next general election would fall due before the Bill could be enacted under the procedure of the Parliament Act of 1911. This Act provided that any measure rejected by the Lords would become law if it had been passed by the Commons in three successive sessions, and also if two years had elapsed between its first appearance for a second reading and its passage through the Commons for a second time. It was on this delay that the Conservatives were counting, for they hoped to win the next election, and it was this delay that the Government were determined to forestall.

Hitherto the Upper House had been very active though far from obstructive. Under the wise and conciliatory guidance of Lord Addison and Lord Salisbury they had provided a necessary corrective to the legislative enthusiasm of the Commons which, as King George had pointed out to Mr. Morrison, was overloading the parliamentary programme and overworking the departmental officials and the parliamentary draughtsmen. The Lords had not considered it their duty to reject — but rather to accept in principle — measures designed by the Government to carry out policies to which the electorate had given approval, but they had not hesitated to send back to the Commons the Bills designed to implement these policies '"blue-pencilled" all over, like the compositions of over-hasty schoolboys after they have passed through the hands of the conscientious schoolmaster'.[14] Ministers had been constrained to accept multitudes of such amendments, some with ill-grace, some with appreciation. The net effect upon the Prime Minister, however, was to convince him that 'the period of delay imposed by this measure [the Parliament Act of 1911] before the will of the elected Chamber could prevail was too long'.[15]

Accordingly, in the parliamentary session prior to the introduction of the Steel Bill, the Government brought forward a measure providing that the period by which legislation could be held up by the House of Lords should be cut from three to two successive sessions of the House of Commons and that only one year, instead of two, need elapse between the first appearance of a Bill for its second reading and its passage through the House of Commons for a second time.

As this new Parliament Bill was clearly designed to clear the way for the passage of the Steel Bill, it was assailed by many Conservatives on the grounds of questionable ethics and the Opposition made a stiff fight against it. They were somewhat disconcerted, however, to find that some of the best oratorial ammunition of the Government was provided by extracts from the speeches of Mr. Churchill, when a Liberal Minister in Mr. Asquith's Government, during the debates on the passage of the Parliament Act of 1911. The Bill became law in December 1949.[a]

When the Steel Bill — which had been denounced by Mr. Churchill as 'a wanton act of party malice' [b] — came in due course before the House of Lords, it was not rejected outright, but so amended that the earliest possible date for its

---

[a] The Parliament Bill was rejected by the House of Lords in June and September 1948; it was passed a third time by the House of Commons on November 14, 1949, and was again rejected by the Lords on November 29. This being the third time of asking, the Bill automatically became law under the procedure of the Act of 1911 and received the Royal Assent on December 16. So far, the provisions of the Act of 1949 have not been called into operation (1958).

[b] Speech at Wolverhampton on July 24, 1949.

coming into operation was one in the autumn of 1950, well beyond the latest possible date of the next General Election. The Conservative Opposition were prepared to accept a proposal which would postpone the final operation of the Act until after it had been pronounced upon by the electorate, but gave notice that, should they be returned to power at the next General Election or thereafter, they would at once expunge the Act from the Statute Book. The Iron and Steel Act, in this state of suspended animation, was finally passed by the Lords on November 24, 1949.

The controversy over the Parliament Act resulted in the resuscitation of that hardy parliamentary perennial, the reform of the House of Lords. Both the major parties favoured some measure of reform; the Labour Party, though formerly in favour of unicameral government, had lately come to realize the advantages of a revising Chamber, while the Conservatives had also realized the weakness of a House of Lords the composition of which included five or six hundred peers, who never attended its sittings but whose voting power was a potential threat to any Government.

All-party discussions on the subject of the reform of the Upper Chamber were held between February and May 1948.[a] They reached a considerable degree of accord as to the composition of a reformed House but failed to find agreement on the issue of its powers and competence. The representatives of the Labour Party 'were prepared to recommend acceptance of the scheme, provided we could be satisfied as to the powers to be entrusted to the reformed House [Mr. Attlee has written]. It was on this that the conference broke down. The Conservatives now regarded the Parliament Act of 1911 as the Ark of the Covenant and were not prepared to relinquish the power of the unrepresentative House to thwart the Commons.'[16] The attempt at reform was therefore abandoned.

Thus ended the last major operation of the Labour Party in the field of nationalization, and the history of its fortunes, together with those of the Parliament Bill, which was so bound

[a] Those who participated in the Conference of Party Leaders were: *Labour*, Mr. Attlee, Mr. Herbert Morrison, Lord Addison, Lord Jowitt and Mr. William Whiteley; *Conservatives*, Mr. Anthony Eden, Lord Salisbury, Lord Swinton and Sir David Maxwell Fyfe; *Liberals*, Lord Samuel and Mr. Clement Davies.

up with it, is indicative of the important and significant changes effected during the first post-war years of King George's reign. In addition to these changes the Labour Government addressed itself with vigour and dispatch to the other major problems of reconstruction. The repatriation and return to civilian life of millions of Servicemen was accomplished more smoothly than after the First World War, and the conversion of industry from war-time to peace-time production was achieved with a very remarkable degree of success.

President Truman has told in his memoirs how, on the recommendation of his economic advisers, he signed on May 8, 1945, without reading it, the order which brought Lend-Lease supplies to Britain to an abrupt termination in August.[17]   The shock of this unexpected decision to British financial and economic computations was substantial, and remedial measures were at once set in train. An agreement was negotiated in Washington by Lord Keynes and Sir Edward Bridges [a] for a credit of $3750 million at 2 per cent, an important feature of which was an undertaking by Britain to make her currency convertible. This was supplemented in March 1946 by the granting of a credit of $1250 million, at the same rate of interest, by the Canadian Government.   Both obligations were to be repaid in fifty annual instalments beginning on January 1, 1951.

The purpose of these two agreements was to enable Britain to sustain herself until 1949 or 1950; but ill-fortune dogged the steps of recovery. The Anglo-American Agreement, which was accorded a stormy passage through the House of Commons,[b] was not approved by the United States Congress until July 1946, and in the meantime Britain had to pay for all

[a] Rt. Hon. Edward, first Baron Bridges, G.C.B., G.C.V.O., M.C. (b. 1892), son of Robert Bridges, the Poet Laureate, served in H.M. Treasury from 1919 till 1938, when he became Secretary of the Cabinet. He was appointed Permanent Secretary of the Treasury in 1945 and so continued until his retirement in 1956.

[b] The Bill to ratify the Anglo-American Financial Agreement, when submitted to the House of Commons on December 12 and 13, 1945, was subjected to bitter criticism by both Conservative and Labour members. The strength of the feeling was evidenced by the fact that a considerable number of members on both sides of the House went into the lobby against it. Despite Mr. Churchill's appeal to his followers to abstain from voting, 71 Conservatives voted against the Bill and with them 23 Labour members. In a very full House the figures in the division were 345 for the motion and 98 against; 8 Conservatives voted with the Government.

supplies received from America. There followed in Britain the disastrous winter of 1946–1947 : the worst on record for sixty-six years. Snow, ice and floods held the life of the country in a paralysing grip. An acute shortage of coal and other fuel brought grave discomfort to many and caused a drop of £200 millions in exports. Meanwhile a 50 per cent rise in American wholesale prices had materially reduced the value of the new credit.

By reason of the exigency of world economic affairs, the lot of the British people in those early post-war years was not an entirely happy one. They had survived the ordeal of war in great measure by dint of hopes of better things to come, but this advent seemed indefinitely deferred. In the life-and-death struggle to increase exports and curtail imports to the minimum the Government were compelled to take drastic measures, and the average Englishman found himself condemned to a seemingly unending drabness of existence, of which the key-words were 'austerity' and 'utility'. War-time rationing and controls were maintained and in certain cases their severity increased. Bread was rationed in 1946 for the first time in our national history. Taxation, direct and indirect, mounted precipitately. Income tax, especially in the higher brackets, reached unprecedented heights, until, as one American observer wrote : 'Where, before the War, Britain could count some seven thousand people who kept incomes of £6000 (then worth approximately $24,000) or over after taxes, the Britain of today counts only sixty people who still retain £6000 (now worth $16,800)'.[18]

And there was worse to come. As the summer of 1947 drew on, it was apparent that Britain was confronted with as serious an economic crisis as that of the dire days of 1931. By the end of June, of those transatlantic credits which, it had been fondly hoped, would see the country through until 1949 and even until 1950, there remained only £250 million of the American credit and £125 million of the Canadian, and beyond this lay only the ultimate bullion reserve of £600 million. The necessary means employed by the Government to counter this situation inevitably entailed further sacrifices by the long-suffering British public. The Chancellor of the Exchequer imposed drastic cuts in the import of tobacco, petrol and newsprint and, though on July 1 the Food Minister denied that there was any food crisis, the weekly meat ration was cut to 1s. 2d. worth two weeks later.

Hitherto the British public had borne the hardships of peace, like Shylock, 'ever with a patient shrug', but now there developed a feeling, voiced in certain organs of the Press as well as in Parliament, that the Government had been caught off their guard by the tempo of events and that the experiment of creating a democratic socialism by means of nationalization was perhaps too costly a luxury.   Mr. Attlee's declaration in the House of Commons on August 6 that 'We are engaged in another Battle of Britain; it cannot be won by the few; it demands a united effort by the whole nation', while it was abundantly true, did not evoke the unhesitating response of 1940.   The magnitude of the problems involved, and the sincere nature of the Government's efforts to solve them, were not fully appreciated by the public at large.

To meet the crisis the Government introduced the Supplies and Services Bill to supplement the Transitional Powers Act of 1945.   This enabled further substantial cuts to be made in food purchases from the hard-currency areas and in imports of timber and luxury consumer goods and other commodities. It also made it possible to impose further restrictions at home on the basic petrol ration, on meals taken in restaurants and on the foreign travel allowance.   To facilitate the movement of coal there would be a diminution in other freight and passenger traffic, and a tighter control was imposed on public and private capital investment.   In addition to the provisions of the Bill, a reduction in the size of the armed services was introduced to increase man-power in industry at home, and the war-time Control of Employment Order was reimposed for those becoming unemployed in order to direct them into essential industries.   For those engaged in certain of these industries, such as the transport workers and coal-miners, longer hours of work and higher targets of production were proposed.

The Bill was subjected to fierce criticism by the Opposition. Mr. Churchill described it as 'a blank cheque for totalitarian government', and Mr. Clement Davies, for the Liberals, voiced abhorrence of an unjustifiable interference with the spiritual liberty of the individual. There was a widespread anxiety that, with these new powers in their hands, the Government would endeavour to conduct a social revolution by Ministerial order, and, though the Lord President of the Council, Mr. Herbert Morrison, denied this in the House, he did not allay apprehension by adding that the Government had no preconceived notion as to how they would use the powers and that they would not be cross-examined as to their intentions. The Bill passed its third reading, nevertheless, on August 12, and eight days later the Chancellor of the Exchequer announced the suspension of the full convertibility of sterling, thus freezing the last $400 million of the American loan.

King George had watched with growing concern and foreboding the course which events had taken during the two years following the end of the war. Anxious himself for progress, yet deeply convinced of the perils of undue precipitancy, he had exercised with constant vigilance throughout this grave period the three great prerogatives of the Sovereign : to advise, to encourage and to warn, but the outcome of the years was not one calculated to bring him peace of mind. 'I have asked Mr. Attlee 3 times now if he is not worried over the domestic situation in this country', he wrote in his diary at the end of January 1947. 'But he won't tell me he is when I feel he is. I know I am worried', and on the following day he told a friend that 'I was doing my best to warn them that they were going too fast in their legislation and were offending every class of people who were ready to help them if they were asked to, but were swept aside by regulations, etc.' [a] [19]

From the beginning of February 1947 till the beginning of May the King, with the Queen and the two Princesses, was absent from Britain on his historic tour of the Union of South Africa,[b] and his return had coincided with the beginning of the more acute phase of the economic crisis. He had followed it carefully in all its stages, discussing with Mr. Attlee the various methods which might be employed to meet the exigencies of the situation. The Prime Minister, however, had apparently had no opportunity to explain the full purport of the Supplies

[a] These are among the last entries in King George's diary which closes on January 30, 1947, on the eve of his departure for South Africa.
[b] See below, pp. 685-92.

and Services Bill to His Majesty before his departure for Balmoral in August, and had, indeed, left with him the impression that it was not a major piece of legislation. When, therefore, the King, who even when on holiday conscientiously kept abreast of national affairs, learned of the repercussions of the Bill through reading the Press and the Parliamentary Debates, it seemed to him that the Prime Minister had gravely underestimated the popular reaction. He was disturbed at the fierce battle or words which the Bill had provoked and, like many of his subjects, he sought reassurance that these sweeping powers which the Government were taking to themselves would not be used to circumvent by Ministerial Order the established rights of Parliament. 'The Government have got themselves into a nasty mess over that Bill, which I was told was not a serious one when it was first thought of', the King wrote to Queen Mary. 'But of course, now that the Opposition have placed a different conception on its clauses, they have tried their best to pooh-pooh it. I have written to Attlee for an explanation.'[20]

He therefore wrote to Mr. Attlee on August 26:

I have carefully read the debates, in both Houses of Parliament, on the Supplies and Services Bill, and am rather perplexed by the different interpretations given it by various speakers of all parties.

The Lord Chancellor,[a] for instance, described the Bill as a purely legal necessity, covering possible loopholes in the application of existing powers to the present emergency ; others, in all parties in the House of Commons, appear to have attributed to it a much wider and more far-reaching significance, suggesting that it might be used to curtail seriously those liberties which the ordinary British citizen has long regarded as his right.

It would be a great help to me if you, as my Prime Minister, would tell me what you yourself intended the purpose, and the scope, of the Bill to be.

You did, I remember, tell me something of this during one of our talks before I left London, but I am bound to say that, at the time, I did not foresee that the passage of this Bill through

[a] Rt. Hon. William Allen, first Earl Jowitt (1885–1957), entered Parliament as a Liberal Member 1922–1924. He later joined the Labour Party and sat in the House of Commons for Preston, and later for Ashton-under-Lyne, from 1929 to 1945, during which time he served as Attorney-General, 1929–1932; Solicitor-General, 1940–1942; Minister without portfolio, 1942–1944; and Minister of National Insurance, 1944–1945. He was appointed Lord Chancellor in Mr. Attlee's first administration in 1945 and so continued until 1951.

Parliament would cause as much controversy as it eventually did, or that it could be open to these widely different interpretations.

I need not say that I know very well that, so long as you are at the head of my Government, due regard will be given to the rights of Parliament itself, and that Parliament will be afforded the opportunity of exercising its proper functions of supervising legislation in respect of any orders made under the Bill. I know that your attitude towards this supremely important matter is the same as my own. But, in view of the fact that the Bill has been the subject of so many different interpretations and that it is now on the Statute Book, a personal account by you of its purpose and scope would be of the greatest value to me.

Finally, I hope that you will not hesitate to let me know at once if you think that my presence in London during the critical weeks ahead of us would be of assistance to you and to the country generally.[21]

To this letter the Prime Minister replied two days later:

I am very glad to have this opportunity of explaining to Your Majesty, as I should have done in person had the occasion offered, what I conceive to be the object and the scope of the Supplies and Services (Extended Purposes) Act. My main intention in introducing the Bill to Parliament, and that of Your Majesty's Government as a whole, was to put it beyond doubt that the powers given by the 1945 Act could be used for the immediate purposes of the present economic crisis. Your Majesty will recall that the purpose of the 1945 Act, as set out in Section I (I), was to maintain supplies and services so as to secure a sufficiency of those essential to the well-being of the community. As both the Lord President and the Lord Chancellor stated in Parliament, it is quite possible to raise a legal argument of some weight in the sense that the purposes of the 1945 Act are broad enough to enable its powers to be applied to any of the needs which might arise out of the present crisis. This was, indeed, the Lord Chancellor's own view. But since it was also possible for a lawyer honestly to hold the contrary view, we felt that it must be the constitutionally correct course to place the matter beyond dispute by a full and open statement of the purposes to which the powers might be put in the new circumstances and to seek the proper authority of Parliament. It was this consideration, rather than any other, which moved Your Majesty's Government to bring in the Bill.

That there should be some criticism of such a Bill could be expected, but I would say frankly that I saw no reason, nor do I now see any, why this measure should upon its own merits excite the bitter attack which was in fact launched upon it. I should perhaps mention, for Your Majesty's own information, that the intentions of Your Government, as I have expressed them above, were privately explained to the Opposition by the Lord President and myself, before introduction of the Bill.   We had reason to think that any grave apprehensions which they held had been removed, and I was afterwards both surprised and sorry that the Leader of the Opposition should choose to take the opportunity to attack the Government fiercely on the grounds that the Bill was designed for ends very different from those which we had in mind.

Your Majesty is kind enough to express confidence in my care that Parliament should have the opportunity of exercising its proper function of supervising legislation.   I can, of course, assure Your Majesty that no question of evading Parliamentary control could arise out of this Act.   The 1945 Supplies and Services Act extended the rights of Parliament by providing that Orders and other Statutory Instruments (as defined in Section 4 of the Act) made under the Defence Regulations should be subject to Parliamentary challenge, whereas this had not previously been the case. This provision is repeated in the new Act, and both Houses therefore have full rights to challenge and annul Orders to which they take exception.

I should perhaps refer also to the argument, which has been raised in certain quarters, that Your Majesty's Government are taking new powers to direct and recruit labour, and so make fresh inroads upon the cherished rights of British citizens.   I am happy to assure Your Majesty that there is no substance in this.   There is, of course, no reference to direction of labour in the Act itself, and in fact these powers already existed and have been used, though with restraint and caution.   The view has indeed been advanced that we have exercised too much restraint and caution, but that is not, of course, a reason for seeking new powers at the present stage.

I shall not hesitate to inform you, Sir, immediately if there should be any occasion for Your presence in London; but I do not feel that a need for this has as yet arisen.   May I add my sincere hope that Your Majesty and the Royal Family are enjoying a restful time in Scotland ? [22]

This lengthy and prosaic explanation from the Prime Minister in justification of the Government's intended use of the Services and Supplies Act, though it allayed the King's anxiety on this specific issue did little to mitigate his depression as to the situation in general.   'I do wish one could see a glimmer of a bright spot anywhere in world affairs', he wrote a few weeks later to Queen Mary from Balmoral.   'Never in the whole history of mankind have things looked gloomier than they do now, and one feels so powerless to do anything to help.'[23]

Nor were the King's forebodings ill-founded. The crisis of 1947 was indeed weathered, but the necessary improvement of the economic state of the country was not forthcoming, and Britain was only saved from what looked like financial ruin by the application of increased American aid under the Marshall Plan. The hideous spiral of rising costs and prices continued to ascend and with it the inevitable claims for increased wages. The year 1948 was one of illusory amelioration and, at its close, the *Economist* wrote of 'the almost magical change in what has occurred in that sensitive barometer of national standing, the prestige and standing of the pound sterling ';[24] the New Year, however, brought a sharp increase in the dollar deficit and on the evening of September 18, 1949, Sir Stafford Cripps, returning from Washington, announced the drastic devaluation of the pound. From its old rate of $4.03 the exchange value of sterling was reduced to $2.80. The response of the Government to this new emergency was to call for more severe sacrifices and greater austerity. In this year the meat ration was reduced to one shilling's worth per person per week and the sugar ration was cut to eight ounces. Nor had the situation materially improved when in January 1950 the Prime Minister decided in favour of a February election.

(iii)

In the field of international affairs the years of the Social Revolution in Britain were remarkable for the rapidity with which the nations of the world regrouped themselves, discarding the political alignments which had wrought the defeat of Germany and Japan in favour of those made necessary by the establishment of the Iron Curtain. The amity of Teheran, which had been replaced by the smouldering suspicion of Yalta, had given way to the fundamental distrust of Potsdam, and these, in all too short a space of time, resulted in the division of Europe, and ultimately of the whole world, into the Eastern and the Western *blocs*, the first dominated by Russia, the second by the United States of America in close alliance with Britain.

The fact that in Britain His Majesty's Government of the day was entrusted to the Labour Party had an important effect upon the formulation of policy both in Moscow and in Washington. 'Heaven', we are assured, 'has no rage like love to hatred turned ; nor hell a fury like a woman scorned',[a] but these passions, it may be believed, are as nothing beside the malignity cherished by the Bolshevik for the Menshevik. Between the Second and the Third Internationals there is a great gulf fixed, as wide and as deep and as unbridgeable as that which separated Dives and Lazarus. For the Bolsheviks regard the moderates of the Left, whether they be labelled Socialist, Labour or Social-Democrat, as sinners against the light in rejecting the 'pure doctrine' of Marx, as interpreted by Lenin, and as wolves in sheep's clothing, deliberately misleading the masses. It was infinitely more congenial to those in the Kremlin to deal with the Tories, whom they regarded as irredeemably benighted, than with the Labour Party, whom they considered as renegade revolutionaries, and no better epitome of this attitude could be provided than the reputed remark of Mr. Kruschev to the Labour leaders at their famous dinner-party in April 1956 : 'If you are Socialists then I'm a Conservative'.

Similarly, in America, where the political standards of all parties are well to the Right of those in Britain and where the supporters of the Socialist and Labour movements are held by Moscow to be rank reactionaries, the Labour Government in Britain was regarded in many quarters with suspicion. The rejection of Mr. Churchill at the polls in July 1945 had been received with dismay in the United States, and it had required all Mr. Attlee's tact and diplomacy, during his brief visit to Washington in November 1945, to restore something of the spirit of confidence and close co-operation which had been so salient a feature of Anglo-American relations during the war years.

For the Labour Party — and not they alone in Britain — were somewhat fearful of the use which the Government of the United States might make of the atomic weapon as an instrument of national policy and indeed that it might become 'trigger-happy' in its dealings with the Soviet Union or any

[a] William Congreve, *The Mourning Bride*, Act III, Scene viii, concluding lines.

other potential aggressor. The desire for reassurance on this point was one of the main objects of Mr. Attlee's visit to President Truman, as he explained to King George on the eve of his departure for Washington. 'He wants Truman to understand that the United Nations Organization has got to work and countries must work together for the common good', the King wrote in his diary. 'The threat of the atomic bomb should help this fact to be kept in the foreground.'[25]

Mr. Attlee's conversations with President Truman and Mr. Mackenzie King, of which both he and the President have given some account in their respective memoirs,[26] resulted in what Mr. Truman described as 'a sound plan of international control of atomic energy', accompanied by a joint reaffirmation of their faith in and their approval for the United Nations, and this became the basis of Britain's foreign policy.

The slender hopes which may have been entertained for the achievement of a peaceful settlement in Europe and of the establishment of a workable system of 'co-existence' with the Soviet Union soon began to wane. The new Russian imperialism began to reveal itself in all its stark ruthlessness. On Eastern Germany, on Poland, on Italy, on Yugoslavia, on Czechoslovakia and on the former enemy states of Bulgaria, Hungary and Rumania, the hand of Moscow lay heavy, and Communist parties sought to establish themselves in the seats of government in response to the behests of the Kremlin.

The situation was revealed with force and clarity by Mr. Churchill on March 5, 1946, in his famous speech at Fulton, Missouri, in the presence of President Truman. Here he outlined the measure of Russian activities in Europe and declared that, though 'we aim at nothing but collaboration and mutual assistance with Russia' and though 'I do not believe that Russia desires war', the real design of the Kremlin was 'the fruits of war and the indefinite expansion of their power and doctrine'. There was nothing that Russia admired so much as strength. 'We cannot afford to work on a narrow margin offering temptation to a trial of strength. If the Western democracies stand together in strict adherence to the principles of the United Nations Charter their influence for furthering those principles will be immense and no one is likely to molest them.' And he added the warning: 'Beware, I say, time may be short'.

The immediate effect of Mr. Churchill's speech was to set the cat among the pigeons. It was greeted with enthusiasm in America, the more so when Marshal Stalin, on March 13, declared it to be 'a dangerous act, calculated to sow seeds of dissent among the Allied nations', and denounced Mr. Churchill as a warmonger. Mr. Churchill himself, in a second speech in New York on March 8, while withdrawing nothing of his charges, repeated his belief that Russia was not contemplating immediate war. 'I do not believe war is inevitable or imminent', he said. 'I do not believe the rulers of Russia wish for war at the present time.' Meanwhile Mr. Bevin emphasized that the Government were not in any way party to Mr. Churchill's speech, and reiterated his willingness to extend the war-time alliance with Russia.[a]

The free world as a whole, however, welcomed Mr. Churchill's ventilation of a state of affairs which was all too obvious, and on his return to London King George took the opportunity of expressing this general satisfaction. 'We talked about his American visit and his Fulton speech', the King recorded. 'I was able to tell him how much good it had done in the world and that Stalin's tirade against him (W) personally showed he had a guilty conscience, and that his (W's) second speech had cleared up many misunderstandings.'[27]

The truth of Mr. Churchill's appraisal of the situation and the seasonableness of his warning that 'Time may be short' were amply revealed in the months that followed. Russia's tactics during the Peace Conference of Paris which, beginning in July 1946, dragged out a frustrating existence till the following February;[b] her hamstringing of the United Nations by her irresponsible use of the veto; her rejection of the Marshall Plan; and her persistent obstruction at conference after conference of any agreement on the future of Austria and Germany, convinced even the most intransigent of optimists that her rulers, while they might not desire war

[a] Speech at Port Talbot, March 16, 1946.
[b] As a result of the Paris Peace Conference treaties of peace were signed on February 10, 1947, with Italy, Rumania, Bulgaria, Hungary and Finland. These were published in a Blue Book (Cmd. 7022).

at the present time, were determined, in Mr. Churchill's phrase, to obtain 'the fruits of war and the indefinite expansion of their power and doctrine'. There came a moment during the Conference of Foreign Ministers in London, in November and December 1947, when the patience of Mr. Bevin reached breaking point. 'Now 'e's gone too bloody far', he remarked to his advisers, after a particularly vitriolic tirade by Mr. Molotov, and from that moment may be traced the re-direction of British foreign policy.

The appointment of Ernest Bevin to the Foreign Office was among the happiest of Mr. Attlee's inspirations. Stolid and trustworthy, kindly but shrewd, well endowed with political vision and common sense, and, though receptive of advice, strongly independent in thought and opinion, Mr. Bevin was no novice in the field of international relations. His experience at meetings of the international Trade Union movement had familiarized him both with the technique of conferences and with the eccentricities of foreigners. He proved a formidable watch-dog of Britain's foreign interests; and, which was also of great importance, the reciprocal affection, loyalty and esteem which existed between him and Mr. Attlee was a vital source of strength to both men, who worked together in perfect trust and harmony. Mr. Bevin's resignation in March 1951, and his death a few weeks later, not only deprived the Prime Minister of a valued friend and an invaluable colleague but marked also the passing of one who may well be numbered among the foremost of British Foreign Secretaries.[a]

Mr. Bevin had not always been antagonistic to Bolshevik Russia. One of his earliest appearances at No. 10 Downing Street had been soon after the First World War when he led a deputation of dockers to protest against Mr. Churchill's policy of intervention against the Bolshevik régime. Since then much had happened. The relentless warfare waged by

[a] Rt. Hon. Ernest Bevin (1881–1951) had been National Organizer of the Dockers' Union, 1910–1921, and General Secretary of the Transport and General Workers' Union, 1921–1940. He entered Parliament in 1940 on his appointment as Minister of Labour in Mr. Churchill's Government, and so continued until the break-up of the Coalition. He was Secretary of State for Foreign Affairs from 1945 to 1951, and died, whilst holding office as Lord Privy Seal, later in that year. A warmly affectionate portrait of Mr. Bevin is given by Lord Strang, who served under him as Permanent Under-Secretary of State for Foreign Affairs, in his memoirs, *Home and Abroad*, pp. 287-300.

the Bolsheviks on the more moderate Marxists had withered
for ever the early blossom of their friendly gestures, and Mr.
Bevin's own first official contacts with the Russians at the
Potsdam Conference in 1945 had left with him an impression
of distrust and hostility.

In the early years after the war, however, the Foreign
Secretary strove to reach an accommodation with Moscow.
Over and over again he proclaimed the desire of the British
Government for co-operation in all spheres of post-war reconstruction, and he had been sincere in his offer to extend the
Anglo-Soviet Alliance for a period of fifty years. The motives
of his policy were twofold; first, it was clearly to Britain's
advantage to have a peaceful Europe working constructively
towards political and economic reconstruction and, secondly,
there was the inherent uncertainty of American policy; the
underlying fear that the United States would once again
retreat behind the barrier of isolation.

As Russian obstruction developed into Russian aggression
and there was still no clear indication of policy from Washington, Mr. Bevin's anxiety deepened. Without the backing of
America there seemed no possibility of halting the economic
depression in Western Europe and the consequent drift towards
Communism. There was imminent danger that Russia might
succeed in extending her power and doctrine by reason of the
very inability of Western Europe to pull itself up by its own
boot-straps.

The answer came on June 5, 1947. On that day General
Marshall, the United States Secretary of State, speaking at
Harvard University, used these words: 'Any Government
that is willing to assist in the task of recovery will find full
co-operation, I am sure, from the United States Government.
Any Government which manœuvres to block the recovery of
other countries cannot expect help from us. Furthermore,
Governments, political parties or groups which seek to perpetuate human misery in order to profit therefrom, politically
or otherwise, will encounter the opposition of the United
States.'

Mr. Bevin was an early riser. He heard a report of that
speech before breakfast at Carlton House Gardens. He was
able to give the Foreign Office the news. 'As he listened',

Sir Oliver Franks [a] has written, 'the first thought that came into his mind was not that this gave a prospect of American economic help for Europe. He saw that, and grasped the chance with both hands; but first came the realization that his chief fear had been banished for good. The Americans were not going to do as they had done after the First World War and retreat into their hemisphere. They had enlarged their horizon and their understanding of the intention of the United States to take in the Atlantic and the several hundred millions of Europeans who lived beyond it. The keystone of Bevin's foreign policy had swung into place.' [28]

Forthwith he took energetic diplomatic initiative and to such effect that on July 12, six weeks after General Marshall's speech, an international conference had assembled in Paris to give practical shape to the proposals which it had contained. From this conference emerged the Marshall Plan. Its application proved the economic and political salvation of Western Europe; its rejection by Russia made clear for all to see her fundamental hostility. [b]

It was not, however, until after the breakdown of the Conference of Foreign Ministers in December 1947 that the British Government took its own diplomatic initiative. In a major speech on foreign affairs in the House of Commons on January 22, 1948, Mr. Bevin called upon the states of Western Europe to unite for their own protection and advantage: 'The free nations of Western Europe must now draw closely

---

[a] Rt. Hon. Sir Oliver Shewell Franks, G.C.M.G., K.C.B., C.B.E. (b. 1905), was, at the outbreak of war, a Fellow of Queen's College, Oxford. He joined the staff of the Ministry of Supply and was its Permanent Secretary from 1945 to 1946, when he returned to Oxford as Provost of Queen's College. Summoned back to Government service by Mr. Bevin in 1947, he played an important rôle in shaping the Marshall Plan at the Paris Conference. In 1948 he was appointed Ambassador in Washington, where he remained until 1952, exerting a dominant and beneficial influence on Anglo-American relations. In 1954 he became Chairman of Lloyds Bank.

[b] Mr. Bevin flew to Paris on June 17 for a preliminary discussion of the Marshall proposals with M. Bidault, the French Foreign Minister. As a result of their joint invitation, Mr. Molotov joined them on June 27. These discussions broke up on July 1 when the Russian delegation rejected the fundamental basis of the American offer. Mr. Bevin and M. Bidault then issued on July 4 a joint invitation to twenty-two countries to a conference in Paris on July 12 which, on September 22, presented an over-all plan to the United States Government. Immediately after the passage of the first European Recovery Act in April 1948 the Organization for European Economic Co-operation (OEEC) was established to implement the Marshall Plan.

together. I believe the time is ripe for a consolidation of
Western Europe.' The response was immediate. On March 17
the Pact of Brussels was signed by representatives of Britain,
France, Belgium, the Netherlands and Luxembourg for the
purpose of closer collaboration in economic, social and cultural
matters and for collective self-defence.[a] Free Europe, sure
now of American economic support, was beginning to take
heed of Mr. Churchill's warning at Fulton, uttered a full
two years before.

The aggressive nature of Russian policy was intensified as
the year progressed. At the close of February a *coup d'état* in
Prague placed Czechoslovakia finally behind the Iron Curtain,
and in March Moscow threatened to demand from Norway
the conclusion of a mutual defence agreement. In June, as a
result of a dispute over currency reform, the Soviet authorities
blockaded the western sector of Berlin, cutting off Germans
and Allies alike from the supplies of food, light and fuel.
There followed that remarkable demonstration of Anglo-
American co-operation and efficiency — the air-lift. For 323
days vital supplies were flown night and day into the western
sectors by the R.A.F. and the United States Air Force until
on May 12, 1949, the Soviet Government reluctantly lifted
its blockade. It was a major victory for the West and it
had far-reaching repercussions, not the least of which were
the establishment of the North Atlantic Treaty Organization
and the decision to integrate a rearmed Western Germany
with Western Europe.

For, against this background of tension, vitally important
decisions had been reached by the United States Government,
who had for some time been in receipt of warnings from
Britain and France of the necessity for a wider system of
defence. The attitude of Washington, however, had been
that, until some evidence had been shown that Western Europe
was prepared to do something for itself, further American
assistance would not be forthcoming. The signature of the
Pact of Brussels provided that evidence, and the subsequent
display of Soviet aggression and defiance was an added proof

[a] After the rejection of the European Defence Community by France, the
organization of the Pact of Brussels became the basis of the Western European
Union established by the London and Paris Conferences of October 1954.

that America must still further justify the rôle of world leadership which had become her heritage from the Second World
War.

On April 28, 1948, the idea of a single mutual defence
system, including and superseding the Brussels Treaty system,
was publicly advocated in the Canadian House of Commons
by the Prime Minister, Mr. St. Laurent.[a] It was welcomed
by Mr. Bevin in the British Parliament a week later, but the
major result occurred on May 12, when the Republican
Senator Arthur H. Vandenberg,[b] chairman of the Senate
Foreign Relations Committee, offered a resolution recommending 'the association of the United States by constitutional
process, with such regional and other collective arrangements
as are based on continuous and effective self-help and mutual
aid, and as affect its national security'. The resolution was
adopted by the United States Senate on June 11, by 64 votes
to 4.

This truly remarkable evolution in American foreign and
defence policies in time of peace — a development of which
President Roosevelt may have dreamed in his more sanguine
moments but which he could never have hoped to accomplish
— made it possible for the United States to enter an Atlantic
Alliance. As a result, the North Atlantic Treaty was signed
in Washington on April 4, 1949, by the Foreign Ministers of
twelve states.[c] The purposes of the Treaty — which, it was
emphasized, was not directed against any nation or group of
nations, but only against the forces of aggression — were defined as the outcome of the decision of its signatories 'to safeguard the freedom, common heritage and civilization of these
peoples, founded on the principle of democracy, individual
liberty and the rule of law; to promote stability and well-

[a] Rt. Hon. Louis Stephen St. Laurent (b. 1882) served as Canadian Ministei
of Justice, 1941-1946 and in 1948, and as Minister of External Affairs, 1946-1948.
He succeeded Mr. Mackenzie King as Leader of the Liberal Party and Prime
Minister of Canada in 1948 and continued in office till the Conservative victory
of 1957. He resigned the leadership of the Liberal Party in 1958.

[b] Hon. Arthur Hendrick Vandenberg (1884-1951), Republican Senator from
the State of Michigan, 1928-1951, was a proponent of the system of bipartisan
foreign policy in the United States Senate.

[c] The original signatories to the North Atlantic Treaty were Belgium, Canada,
Denmark, France, Iceland, Italy, Luxembourg, the Netherlands, Norway, Portugal,
the United Kingdom and the United States. Greece and Turkey acceded to the
Treaty in 1952.

THE KING WITH MEMBERS OF THE LABOUR CABINET AND CHIEFS OF STAFF, 1945

being in the North Atlantic area; and to unite their efforts for collective defence and for the preservation of peace and security'.[a]

There remained the problem of Germany. The Four-Power policy agreed upon at the Potsdam Conference in 1945 had been founded upon two basic principles: first, that though, for occupational purposes, Germany was to be divided into four zones, this segmentation was in no way to prejudice the fundamental unity of the German State nor the subsequent formation of a central German Government; and secondly, that in order to achieve the underlying purpose for which two World Wars had been fought and won, Germany should remain disarmed and no effort should be spared to eradicate the militaristic spirit from the German mind.

Quadripartite solidarity remained in being until the conclusion of the trial of the Major War Criminals at Nuremberg in October 1946, and thenceforth markedly deteriorated. By 1948 it was fully apparent that the Potsdam propositions had reached a condition of *reductio ad absurdum* by reason of the fact that the Iron Curtain separated East Germany impenetrably from the West, and from behind it were perceptible all the premonitory symptoms of the revival of militarism under direct Russian supervision.

In face of this progressive change on the part of the Soviet Union from the status of respected ally, which she had enjoyed at the end of the war, to that of suspect aggressor and *saboteur* of peace, the Western Powers were compelled to take their own measures of defence. It was certainly not to the interests of Britain, the United States and France to allow all Germany to drift into the Communist camp through inertia on the part of the three Occupying Powers inspired by an over-nice respect for the principle of German unity. Under the impulse of a joint Anglo-American initiative, therefore, agreement was reached to restore a limited degree of sovereignty to a West German Federal Republic, composed of the three Western zones of occupation, with its capital at Bonn, it being still

[a] In order to give practical form to this last provision, the NATO Powers established in 1951 a Supreme Headquarters for the Allied Powers in Europe (SHAPE) at Versailles, to which General Eisenhower was appointed as the first Supreme Commander.

emphasized that, despite this temporary dichotomy, the ultimate desire of the three Powers was for a united Germany.

The Federal German Government came into existence in May 1949 and the temporary jettisoning of one of the main Potsdam principles which it represented was shortly followed by another. By reason of the growth of their fear of Russian aggression, and their realization of Mr. Churchill's dictum that 'there is nothing that Russia admires so much as strength', the statesmen in London and Washington were impelled to urge upon the continental states of Western Europe the necessity of even more extraordinary precautions for the protection of their security and independence. These measures involved the creation of a unified Western European defence community with the revolutionary provision for the inclusion of Western Germany, to whom the right of rearmament was to be conceded, albeit hedged about with restrictions and limitations — a shift of policy which would have been as unthinkable in 1945 as was the creation of a North Atlantic Alliance.[a]

(iv)

Thus, within the short space of the first post-war years of King George's reign, there had come about a complete transmogrification of the political and international scene. Within Britain herself there had occurred a Social Revolution of a permanent nature. Mr. Attlee's first Government had attained a notable record of achievement in difficult circumstances. The

[a] The decisions to permit Western Germany to rearm within the framework of a European defence organization were taken at meetings of the Conference of the Three Foreign Ministers and of the North Atlantic Council at New York in September 1950 and of the Council of the Brussels Treaty Organization at Brussels in December 1950. They were confirmed at the Lisbon meeting of the North Atlantic Council in February 1952. The agreement establishing the European Defence Community was signed in Paris on May 27, 1952. Thereafter there were vicissitudes of fortune. France had never been reconciled to the idea of German rearmament, and successive French Governments would not risk bringing the Agreement before the National Assembly. When this was ultimately done by M. Mendès-France in August 1954, the Assembly refused to ratify it. As a result, therefore, of conferences in London and Paris in October, a new formula was devised. By agreements signed on October 23, 1954 — and this time ultimately ratified — the Allied Powers brought to an end their occupation of Germany and restored full sovereignty to the Bonn Government. Western Germany was invited to become a member of NATO and of the Western European Union.

establishment of the Welfare State had carried the country far along the road to Socialism, and the degree of nationalization effected had set a new pattern upon some of the basic industries of the country : a pattern which, though it might be modified, could never be reversed. In addition, the Welfare State had conferred considerable benefits upon the country, and the Labour Party had to its credit other major accomplishments, among them the smooth demobilization of millions of service personnel, and had had no small measure of success in the reconversion of the industry of the country from a war-time basis to peace-time production.

In the world at large the early hopes of a quiescent period of 'peace, retrenchment and reform' had perished before the cold blast of the Soviet menace. Europe, despite her longing for peace, stood again divided into two camps, bond and free, and the Western Powers, resuscitated by Marshall Aid and emboldened by American military support, had placed themselves four-square against the threat of aggression. Germany, having touched the nadir of collapse, had, by the force of circumstances, arisen phoenix-like from the ashes of defeat and was in the process of 'working her passage home' to full partnership in Western Europe integration.

His Majesty's Government, which had shown an undaunted pertinacity in pressing forward with their domestic policies, had displayed equal courage and initiative in the field of world economic reconstruction and in shouldering their share of the burdens of the 'Cold War' which had been forced upon them.

Such was the position, at home and abroad, when in January 1950 Mr. Attlee advised King George to dissolve Parliament.

CHAPTER XI

THE NEW COMMONWEALTH

1945-1949

(i)

IF King George's allegory of the reaction of the man who, on first seeing a giraffe, exclaimed : 'There ain't no such animal',[a] was applicable to the structure of the British Commonwealth of Nations before the war, it was even more apposite in reference to the fourth British association of nations [b] which emerged from that conflict and from the political convulsions which succeeded it. The compromise solution achieved in 1949, while typical of the genius of the British peoples, rendered still more incomprehensible to the foreigner the new relationship of the Crown to the Commonwealth and of the component parts of the Commonwealth to one another. 'A new Athanasianism of many crowns in one monarchy'[1] comes near to an accurate description of the formula which, while acknowledging the divisibility of the Crown, enabled the Commonwealth of sovereign and equal States to discover a new creed of unity. Less academically but more succinctly, it may be summed up in the motto of the Free Foresters : 'United though Untied'.[c]

The circumstances under which King George's governments in the Dominions went to war in 1939 have already been described,[d] and the years which followed provided a

---

[a] See above, p. 379.

[b] It is suggested that the *first* British Empire ended with the American Declaration of Independence in 1776, the *second* with the Balfour Formula of 1926 and the *third*, based upon the Statute of Westminster, with the solution of April 1949.

[c] For the constitutional development of the Commonwealth during this period, see K. C. Wheare, *The Statute of Westminster and Dominion Status* ; Nicholas Mansergh, *The Commonwealth and the Nations* ; Eric Walker, *The British Empire, its Structure and its Spirit* ; and *Documents and Speeches on British Commonwealth Affai,s, 1931-1953*, edited by Nicholas Mansergh.

[d] See above, pp. 408-14.

striking example of the solidarity of the British Commonwealth. The armed forces of Australia and New Zealand fought gallantly in the Mediterranean area, in Burma and in the Pacific and South-East Asia theatres of war; South African and Indian troops shared with their British and American comrades the honours of victory in North Africa; Canadian armies contributed to the liberation of Europe. The air forces and navies of the Commonwealth and Empire fought to keep free the skies and oceans of the world. In his visits to the various battle-fronts King George had seen warriors of all his Dominions united in arms for the common defence of freedom.

Yet this comradeship of arms had not been without its concomitant tensions, and of these one instance may suffice. The entry of Japan into the war, accompanied by the disaster of Pearl Harbour and the equally calamitous campaigns in Malaya, the Philippines and South-East Asia, had their inevitably unfavourable repercussions in the Antipodes. The fact that Australian and New Zealand troops had been employed in Libya, Greece and Crete, and the Australian Navy and Air Force dispersed in the guarding of the lines of communication was held — especially in Labour circles in Canberra — to have reduced defences nearer home to danger point and to have contributed to bringing about the existing situation. It was strongly felt by the Australian Cabinet that they were inadequately represented in the direction of the war at Ministerial level and, at the close of the year, the Prime Minister, Mr. Curtin,[a] issued a public message to the country in this vein. What Australia was demanding in effect was a permanent representative in the War Cabinet.

The view of Mr. Churchill on this matter, based upon his experiences of the First World War, was that it was impracticable to have Dominion Cabinet Ministers in London for too long at a time, but this was hailed in Australia as 'an indication of his disinclination to surrender a jot of his too exorbitant power until surrender is forced upon him'.[2] Moreover, the increasingly bad news from Malaya, where Australian troops

[a] Rt. Hon. John Curtin (1885–1945) entered the Australian House of Representatives in 1928 as a member of the Labour Party, of which he became Leader in 1935. He served as Prime Minister and Minister of Defence from 1941 until his death in 1945.

were engaged, seemed to give point to Mr. Curtin's opinions, which in fine amounted to the view that if Australia did not obtain satisfaction from London she would turn for aid and guidance to Washington. What was being contemplated in Canberra was an independent military alliance with the United States.[a]

Though other leaders of Australian political opinion hastened to dissociate themselves from the Prime Minister's proposed policy, which the veteran ex-Premier 'Billy' Hughes [b] denounced as 'suicidal', Mr. Curtin's pronouncement had the worst effect possible in London and Washington and in other Dominion capitals. Mr. Churchill met the situation with firmness and vigour — 'I hope there will be no pandering to this', he cabled to Mr. Attlee from Washington — and there ensued between himself and Mr. Curtin throughout the month of January 1942 that remarkable exchange of pungent cables reproduced textually in his memoirs.[4]

King George had watched with deep concern a development which might seriously affect the relations of the British Commonwealth as a whole. He feared that a disorientation which started in Australia might spread to other Dominions and recognized the evidence of this in the attitude of the Nationalist Party in South Africa, whose leader Dr. Malan [c] on January 14 had put forward a parliamentary motion

[a] What Mr. Curtin had told the Australian press and people was this: 'I make it clear that Australia looks to America free from any pangs about our traditional links of kinship with Britain. We know Britain's problems. We know her constant threat of invasion. We know the danger of dispersing strength. But we know that Australia can go and Britain still hold on. We are determined that Australia shall not go. We shall exert our energy towards shaping a plan, with the United States as its keystone, giving our country . . . ability to hold out until the tide of the battle swings against the enemy.'[3]

[b] Rt. Hon. William Morris Hughes, C.H. (1864–1952), having emigrated to Australia in 1884, was elected to the New South Wales Parliament ten years later on a Labour programme. He was elected to the Commonwealth Parliament in 1901 and later formed the United Australia Party which he led successfully for many years. Prime Minister from 1915 to 1923, he represented Australia at the Peace Conference of Paris and subsequently served in a number of Cabinet positions. At the outbreak of the Second World War he was Minister of External Affairs, and served as Minister for Industry, 1939–1940, Attorney-General, 1939–1941, and Minister for the Navy, 1940–1941.

[c] Hon. Dr. Daniel François Malan, D.D. (b. 1874), in 1939 succeeded as leader of the Nationalist Party which he led in opposition until 1948 when, as the result of the defeat of General Smuts's Government in a general election, he became Prime Minister and Minister of External Affairs. He resigned in 1954.

calling for the secession of the Union from the British Commonwealth and the establishment of a South African Republic. The proposal was rejected by a vote of 90 votes to 48, but its very appearance was not without its significance. The King was not unsympathetic with the very understandable apprehension of the Australian Government in the face of the threat of invasion, but he felt that they were perhaps somewhat hyperbolic in their arguments and that too much was said in public.

'The Australians are very voluble about invasion, both in the Australian Government and in the Press', he wrote in his diary. 'They blame everyone here for not having foreseen this contingency, when it is obvious that the U.S. Fleet would have prevented this from happening had her fleet been on the high seas instead of at the bottom of Pearl Harbour where it is.'[5]

Because of his strong belief that the Crown had a very special responsibility where Imperial matters were concerned, King George sent to the Prime Minister, on his return from Washington, an expression of his foreboding.

His Majesty is genuinely alarmed at the feeling which appears to be growing in Australia and may well be aggravated by further reverses in the Far East [Sir Alexander Hardinge wrote to Mr. Churchill on January 22]. He very much hopes, therefore, that it may be possible to adopt as soon as possible some procedure which will succeed in arresting these dangerous developments without impairing the efficiency of the existing machinery, though at the same time His Majesty entirely appreciates the additional complication which he fears it may cause for you.[6]

Mr. Churchill's reply was one of bland and lofty reassurance. He enclosed for the King's perusal the exchange of telegrams which had passed between himself and Mr. Curtin, and commented thereon as follows:

Your Majesty will see that in spite of all the arguments we have used, the Commonwealth Government, which has a majority of two, is determined to have recourse to the United States. They have the idea that they can get better service and more support from the United States than they can from us. It would be foolish and vain to obstruct their wishes. From what I know, I fear they will have a very awkward reception in Washington. Access to the supreme power is extremely difficult. It is only granted to few and then in abundant measure. The lengthy telegrams they send will be addressed to subordinate officials and officers. It may be that, having knocked at this door, they will come back again to ours. If so, they will be very welcome. . . . It is always good to let people do what they like and then see whether they like what they do. I do not think they will succeed in displacing the effective centre of gravity from London.[7]

The measures proposed by the British Government to meet the Australian demands were that Sir Earle Page,[a] an Australian Cabinet Minister, should attend meetings of the War Cabinet for purposes of information and that a Far-Eastern War Council should be established in London, on which the Australian, New Zealand, Chinese and Netherlands Governments should be represented by persons of Ministerial status and which would meet under the chairmanship of the Prime Minister of the United Kingdom. This was far from satisfying Mr. Curtin. What he wanted, and what he publicly demanded in a speech[b] on January 24, was that an accredited representative of the Australian Government should have the right to be heard in the War Cabinet in the formulation and direction of war policy. Moreover, it was feared in Canberra that the proposed Far-Eastern War Council in London would be purely advisory and incommensurate with the essential interests of Australia in the Pacific. In addition, it lacked provision for American representation. Mr. Curtin urged that a Pacific War Council be established in Washington : a body functioning as a council of action for the higher direction of the war in the Pacific in association with the Combined Staffs Organization already in existence in Washington, on which the Pacific Council would have service representatives if desired.

In the final result both bodies were set up, though it is doubtful whether their deliberations in either London or

[a] Rt. Hon. Sir Earle Christmas Grafton Page, G.C.M.G., C.H. (b. 1880), forsook a medical career for politics in 1919 and from 1920 to 1939 was the leader of the Australian Country Party. He served in a number of Cabinet positions and was briefly Prime Minister of Australia in 1939. He was Minister of Commerce, 1940–1941, special Envoy to the British War Cabinet, 1941–1942, and a member of the Australian War Cabinet, 1942–1943. He became Minister of Health in Mr. Menzies's Coalition Government in 1949.
[b] At Perth, Western Australia.

Washington materially affected the concepts of grand strategy. 'The war', writes Mr. Churchill, 'continued to be run by the old machinery, but meetings of the Pacific War Councils enabled those countries which were not represented in this permanent machinery to be consulted about what was going on.[a] [8]

(ii)

It had long been foreseen that, in the New World which emerged from the life-and-death struggle of the Second World War, a certain reshaping of the form and basis of the British Commonwealth of Nations would be necessary from that established by the Declaration of 1926 and the Statute of Westminster. The constitutional position at the outbreak of the war in September 1939 had been that of a group of nations, in which the United Kingdom occupied a position of *primus inter pares*; each with a parliament possessing full powers to legislate on all matters affecting its own country; each recognizing the King as Sovereign of that country and taking all formal action in the King's name.[b] The extent of the degree of independence which each unit of the Commonwealth could exercise had been amply proved in 1939, when Eire declared her neutrality and the South African Parliament narrowly defeated a motion by General Hertzog to follow a similar course.

The pressure of the war years had tried the bonds of Commonwealth to the uttermost, but in the main they had proved sound and strong, and the substance of the Commonwealth,

[a] It is a matter of interest that a decade later, in the face of the menace of increasing Communist aggression in the Pacific area, a security agreement between Australia, New Zealand and the United States became an accomplished fact. This was the ANZUS Pact signed in San Francisco on September 1, 1951. Three years later this agreement was expanded, both in scope and composition, with the establishment of the South-East Asia Treaty Organization (SEATO) by the signature at Manila on September 8, 1954, of a Collective Defence Agreement by the Governments of the United Kingdom, the United States, Australia, New Zealand, France, Pakistan, the Philippine Republic and Thailand.

[b] After 1931 the only inequality of status which remained was the residing power left to the United Kingdom Parliament to legislate for a Dominion at the request and with the consent of that Dominion. The retention of this authority was necessary since Canada, and, to a limited extent, New Zealand, had no power to alter their existing constitutions without the participation of the Parliament at Westminster.

which had been defined by the Imperial Conference of 1926 in the following terms, still remained basically true :

The British Empire is not founded on negations. It depends essentially, if not formally, on positive ideals. Free institutions are its lifeblood. Free co-operation is its instrument. Peace, security and progress are among its objects. . . . Though every Dominion is now, and must always remain, the sole judge of the nature and extent of its co-operation, no common course will, in our opinion, be thereby imperilled.

Nevertheless it was apparent to all that some overhauling of the machinery of the Commonwealth was both inevitable and desirable. The spirit of nationalism had increased in all its component parts. Certain of the forms and nomenclature of the past, for example, were held to be outmoded and some of the older Dominions, notably South Africa and Canada, disliked the term 'Dominion Status', while other portions of the Empire, such as Rhodesia, sought to achieve it. The solution of the problem of the future of India was one which could no longer be delayed. And, furthermore, there was the new and not inconsiderable factor of American public opinion.

Our allies the American people [Mr. Attlee has written] had very strong views, shared by the Administration, of the evils of imperialism. Much of their criticism of British rule was very ill informed but its strength could not be denied. Americans drew a sharp distinction between their own expansion from the Atlantic to the Pacific, in voting the Mexican War and the relegation to reserves of the original inhabitants, and British overseas expansion. The absorption of a continent seemed to be a natural process to them, but an empire containing numerous detached portions of land inhabited by various races at different stages of civilization appeared an example of colonialism and rank imperialism.[9]

It was, therefore, to this task of finding some form of association other than the existing Dominion status and in which independent states might continue their association under the Crown, while still retaining the basic substance of the 1926 Report, that His Majesty's Ministers addressed themselves in 1947 — in the first instance through a Cabinet Committee on Commonwealth Relations presided over by the Prime Minister. The first step towards a new relationship was taken in July of that year, when the designation of the Secretary of State for Dominion Affairs was changed to that of 'Commonwealth Relations' and the Dominions Office became the 'Commonwealth Relations Office'.

The year 1947 marked one of the great watersheds in the history of the British Commonwealth. Within its calendar are to be numbered the last days of British rule in India; the secession of Burma — the first country to leave the Empire since the American War of Independence; the entry of the Dominion of Ceylon; and, by no means least in importance, the great imperial mission which King George himself undertook in his tour of the South African Union.

(iii)

The proposal that His Majesty should visit South Africa and should formally open the Union Parliament in Cape Town had been more than once discussed between King George and General Smuts during the latter's war-time visits to London. The King was greatly attracted by this prospect of seeing the youngest of his Dominions. His visits to Australia, New Zealand and Canada had stimulated his mind and had imbued him with an admiration for those countries which can only be derived from first-hand experience.

When, therefore, the suggestion was revived informally in February 1946, the King welcomed it warmly. He spoke of it to Mr. Attlee, who agreed; [10] the Cabinet, the Prime Minister felt, would be in complete accord with the idea of the strengthening of the bonds of Empire through a personal visit by His Majesty. A few days later there arrived the formal invitation from the Governor-General of the Union, Mr. Van Zyl,[a] on behalf of his Ministers, that the King, with the Queen and the two Princesses, should visit the Union during the spring of 1947 and that King George should open Parliament on February 21.[11] It was immediately accepted.[b]

[a] Rt. Hon. Gideon Brand Van Zyl (1873–1956) was Governor-General of the Union of South Africa from 1945 to 1950, being the first holder of this office to be South African born.

[b] The official invitation was communicated to the Prime Minister of the United Kingdom by Sir Alan Lascelles on February 27 and the formal approval of the British Government was given on March 3. The King's acceptance was dispatched on March 6.

Thus, a year later, the Royal Party [a] sailed from Portsmouth on February 1, 1947, on their three weeks' voyage to Cape Town.[b]   They were conveyed in Britain's newest battleship, *Vanguard*, which had been launched on Clydeside by Princess Elizabeth on December 1, 1944, and was commanded by Rear-Admiral William G. Agnew who, as commanding officer of *Aurora*, had conveyed His Majesty to Malta on the occasion of his historic visit in June 1943.

By an unfortunate concatenation of circumstances the Royal journey coincided with the most severe period of cold weather which Britain experienced in that never-to-be-forgotten winter of 1946/47 and which, coupled with the Government's general policy of inevitable post-war austerity, combined to produce considerable hardship and despondency in the United Kingdom.   As *Vanguard* approached her destination in clear weather and bright sunshine, ploughing forward through the blue Atlantic with the majestic rise and fall of a great vessel, the Royal Family were saddened to hear of the conditions at home.   As the news came in of unabated frosts and blizzards, of curtailed coal output and dwindling stocks of fuel, of coal-ships storm-bound in port or sailing gallantly in the teeth of the gales, they shared in spirit the sufferings of their people in Great Britain.

The severity of the crisis was fully reported to the King in a series of telegrams from the Prime Minister, who said that it had merited the same speed and urgency as a major military operation during the war and that he had treated it as such.   On the eve of his arrival at Cape Town the King telegraphed to Mr. Attlee expressing his sympathy and that of the Queen with the people of Britain and their earnest hope for an early alleviation of their present hardships ; this message was made public in London on February 17.

I am very worried over the extra privations which all of you at

[a] Their Majesties were attended on this occasion by Sir Alan Lascelles (Private Secretary to the King); Major Michael Adeane (Assistant Private Secretary) ; Major T. Harvey (Private Secretary to the Queen); Wing-Commander Peter Townsend and Lieut.-Commander Peter Ashmore (Equerries); the Lady Harlech and the Lady Delia Peel (Ladies-in-Waiting to the Queen); Lady Margaret Egerton (Lady-in-Waiting to the Princesses); Surgeon Rear-Admiral H. E. Y. White (Medical Officer); and Captain (S) Lewis Ritchie (Press Secretary).
[b] Before leaving the United Kingdom His Majesty appointed as Counsellors of State the Duke of Gloucester, the Princess Royal and Lord Lascelles.

home are having to put up with in that ghastly cold weather with no light or fuel [King George wrote to Queen Mary shortly after his arrival]. In many ways I wish I was with you having borne so many trials with them. [12]

Their Majesties were also deeply concerned and not a little grieved by the rumours reaching them of ill-informed criticism of their absence from Britain at this juncture. To a man of King George's conscientiousness of spirit this divided loyalty to duty was a mental torment. He genuinely desired to share with his people in Great Britain their trials and privations as he had suffered with them the war-time dangers of blitz and bombardment, yet he knew that he owed an obligation of devoir to his peoples of South Africa where an opportunity to perform an important service to the Commonwealth awaited him. Anxiously he reviewed various means by which this conflict of duties might be resolved. He considered the possibility of interrupting the Royal Tour, or even of cutting it short, and consulted Mr. Attlee on this premise.

This tour is being very strenuous as I feared it would be & doubly hard for Bertie who feels he should be at home [the Queen wrote to Queen Mary]. But there is very little he could do now, and even if he interrupted the tour & flew home, it would be very exhausting, & possibly make it difficult to return here. We think of home all the time, & Bertie has offered to return but Mr. Attlee thought that it would only make people feel that things were getting worse, & was not anxious for him to come back. [13]

The Prime Minister had, indeed, been emphatic in his reassurance. He fully appreciated the desire of King George to take his part in the crisis at home, but he was equally aware of the importance of the mission on which he was engaged.

I hope that the King will not add to his burden by anxiety about his absence from this country at this time [he telegraphed to Sir Alan Lascelles on March 4]. There has not been any serious criticism on this score and I feel confident that there will not be. It is realized that the King's duties must carry him on occasions to the Dominions and that he is kept in touch with affairs of State while he is abroad. Apart from other effects, the curtailment of the tour would magnify unduly the extent of the difficulties we are facing and surmounting at home, especially in the eyes of foreign observers. I hope, therefore, you will reassure the King on this account.

Acting, therefore, on the advice of his Prime Minister in the United Kingdom, King George, though he could not banish from his mind the sufferings of Britain, abandoned all thought of curtailing his South African visit and devoted himself to the vitally important matter in hand.[a]

The visit of King George to the Union of South Africa had in certain respects an even deeper significance than those which he had paid to other states of the Commonwealth. Canada, Australia and New Zealand had long been members of the British family of nations, and their traditions (with the exception of French Canada) were basically British in their origin.   This was not true of South Africa where at every turn it is brought home to the traveller that this is a land in which two distinct white races — British and Dutch — maintain their separate ideals and have still to find the final terms on which they may share the country and on which they may both live with the vast native population.

It was not yet half a century since the Peace of Vereeniging had brought to a close a war in which the full resources of the Empire, including troops from Canada, Australia, New Zealand and India, had been required to defeat the armies of the Boer Republics.   It was not yet forty years since certain Boer generals — De Wet, De la Rey and Beyers — had raised the standard of rebellion against the Union Government at a moment of grave peril to the British Commonwealth.   In 1939 the Union had entered the war by a narrow majority and, as late as 1942, the Nationalist Party had put forward a motion for secession from the British Crown.

Though the great act of Liberal statesmanship in 1910 had brought into being the youngest of the British Dominions, the division between the two white races had left its mark deeply imprinted upon the constitution of the new nation.   In South Africa alone there are two capitals — the seat of Parliament at Cape Town and that of the executive government in Pretoria ;   two national anthems, in one of which, the Dutch,

[a] Speaking at the Lord Mayor's luncheon at Guildhall on May 15, 1947, shortly after his return to Britain, King George used these words ; 'The ordeals through which my peoples here have passed during my absence have never been far from my thoughts.   I was often torn between my duty towards the wonderful country that I have just left and my anxiety to share at first hand, as I have always tried to do, the troubles which faced you here.'

the name of the Sovereign is not mentioned ; and two national flags. Moreover, though the King's official host in South Africa, the Prime Minister of the Union, Field-Marshal Smuts, a Boer signatory at Vereeniging, was now established as the elder statesman of the British Commonwealth, it was noticeable when, on the day of arrival in Cape Town, King George decorated him with the Order of Merit before the members of the South African Parliament, that the Senators and Representatives of the Nationalist Party were largely conspicuous by their absence from the ceremony.

The hidden shoals and reefs which beset the course of the King and his advisers during these momentous weeks of the Royal Tour are therefore manifest.[a] He was the constitutional Sovereign of South Africa and must therefore limit himself, as in the United Kingdom, to those three great constitutional prerogatives — to advise, to encourage and to warn ; yet he never allowed an opportunity to escape him for furthering the great task of reconciliation. It was not for nothing that at Bloemfontein he welcomed as his Minister in attendance Dr. Colin Steyn, the son of the last President of the Orange Free State Republic,[b] nor that he paid an unexpected and informal visit to the 82-year-old widow of the President.—'She sent you many messages', the Queen wrote to Queen Mary, 'and said that she always remembered a luncheon in London when you were Princess of Wales, & how much she admired you. A wonderful old lady.' [14] It was not for nothing that in Cecil Rhodes's house, Groote Schuur, the King handed to General Smuts President Kruger's bible, which had been captured among his effects during the South African War and which the King had brought with him from London ; nor that, in the message to the South African people which he broadcast from Pretoria on a day when he had been greeted by over a thousand

---

[a] A brilliant account of the tour, *The Royal Family in Africa* (London, 1947), has been written by Mr. Dermot Morrah, the editor of the *Round Table*, who accompanied the Royal Party.

[b] Martinus Theunis Steyn (1857–1916) was President of the Orange Free State Republic from 1896 to 1900. He endeavoured to mediate between President Kruger of the Transvaal and Sir Alfred Milner, but when war broke out supported Kruger. Rejecting the Peace of Vereeniging, he continued to support the separatist movement which led to the rebellion of 1914. His son, Colin Fraser Steyn (b. 1887), mediated between General Botha and General De Wet after the suppression of this rising, and served in General Smuts's Government as Minister of Justice (1939–1945) and of Labour (1945–1948).

Oudstryders (the Boer veterans of the South African War), he gave as their watchword to the youth of the country Kruger's own words : 'Take from the past all that is good and beautiful ; shape your ideal therewith and build your future on this ideal'.

It was to see South Africa that the Royal Family had come, and see it they did in so far as that was possible in ten crowded weeks. They travelled many thousands of miles by car and train and air, going from Cape Town as far north as the Rhodesias, where they spent ten days. The King performed the State opening of the Southern Rhodesian Parliament in the House of Assembly at Salisbury, on April 7, and, some days later, the Royal Party made pilgrimage from Bulawayo to that bald hill-top in the Matopos Range which is the last resting-place of Cecil Rhodes. In Northern Rhodesia they visited Livingstone, and gazed spellbound upon the mighty 'smoking water' of the Victoria Falls, standing where, less than a century before, David Livingstone, the first white man to see it, had looked upon this majestic phenomenon.

Though, as the King was forced to admit, their tour was at times both arduous and fatiguing, their interest never flagged, and the great pageant of the African scene which unrolled before them held them fascinated and spellbound. Nor was their effort unrequited. The warmth and sincerity of the enthusiasm with which they met at every turn, from Boer and Briton, Basuto and Zulu, was eloquent of the fact that they were accepted, not as the Sovereign and Consort of some alien power, but as the King and Queen of South Africa, an intimate part of the body politic of the Union, who came to greet and be greeted by the members of the great heterogeneous African family of which they were the heads.

Not the least important aspect of the South African tour was the King's decision that, for the first time in history, the Royal Family should make the journey together and that it should coincide with the coming-of-age of Princess Elizabeth, the heir to this great royal heritage. This event took place at Cape Town, four days before the departure for England. Throughout the tour the demeanour of Princess Elizabeth had been remarkable for its youthful dignity, commingled with her spontaneous gaiety and enthusiasm. Now, on the evening of April 21, at the threshold of her own tremendous destiny,

WITH FIELD-MARSHAL SMUTS AT PRETORIA

sitting alone in a quiet room in Government House, she broadcast her birthday message to her father's subjects. Her words,
though they were addressed to all the five hundred millions
of the British Commonwealth and Empire, contained a special
message for the people of South Africa. 'When', wrote one
who heard her, 'she said that, even though six thousand miles
from the country where she was born, she still felt herself at
home, she might have been summing up not only for herself
but for all the Royal Family the meaning and the achievement
of the tour. The King, the Queen and their children had
been taken to the heart of the people, and would henceforth
be regarded as true South Africans.' [15]

The Princess's clear young voice, vibrant with emotion,
carried across the spheres her solemn act of self-dedication.
'I should like', she said, 'to make that dedication now. It is
very simple. I declare before you all that my whole life,
whether it be long or short, shall be devoted to your service
and the service of our great Imperial Commonwealth to which
we all belong. But I shall not have strength to carry out this
resolution unless you join in it with me, as I now invite you
to do; I know that your support will be unfailingly given.
God bless all of you who are willing to share it.'

To the many millions of those who heard the broadcast
there came an impression of an instant summons, a summons
of unalloyed sincerity, to share with Princess Elizabeth the
task and the mission which were to be hers. She was taking
up at that moment the duties, sufficiently onerous in themselves, of an heir to the throne, duties which all too soon she
was to exchange for the infinitely greater burden of the Crown
itself. No event could have marked more vividly or more
appropriately the ending of a great Imperial journey, and the
fact that this moving act of self-dedication took place in one
of the member states of the Commonwealth served to emphasize that journey as a new milestone in that Commonwealth's history.

Three days later, on April 24, the journey came to an end,
and the King, with the happy choice of the phrase ' Tot
Siens',[a] said farewell to the Union of South Africa. In the
glorious autumn sunshine, *Vanguard* drew away from the

---

[a] ' Tot Siens' is the Afrikaans equivalent of 'Au revoir' or 'Auf Wiedersehen'.

harbour; gradually the outline of Table Mountain faded on the horizon, and the Royal Family, very weary, sincerely regretful yet deeply content, turned their faces towards home.

Despite the fatigue and tension of the tour, which had been very considerable, King George had enjoyed his South African visit. He had done what he always enjoyed doing, namely getting to know people and problems at first hand. Moreover, he was justly confident that the impression created in the minds of many South Africans by meeting personally their Sovereign, his consort and their daughters, might well — as had been the case in Canada — have placed the whole idea of the Crown, and of their own relation to it, in a new and more favourable perspective. The King of South Africa had come among his South African subjects.

As *Vanguard* neared the shores of Britain the King wrote something of all this to General Smuts:

It has given me a new outlook on life after those terrible war years in Britain, which to me were a period of great strain, & followed by the life of austerity which we are compelled to undergo as a result of our exertion in the war. I have been able to relax for a bit, & I feel that I shall now be able to return to my work in London with renewed energy. Now that our visit is over I don't mind confessing to you alone that I was rather fearful about it, after reading various books & reports on South Africa, but my mind was completely set at rest the day we landed in Cape Town & ever after. The wonderfully friendly welcome given to us by all in South Africa made such a deep impression on us, & by it made our part all the easier. If, & I firmly believe it has, our visit has altered the conception of monarchy to some South Africans & has given them a new viewpoint from our personal contacts with them, then our tour has been well worth while & I for one will have gained immeasurably by my contacts with them.[16]

(iv)

The position of the Indian Empire within the British Commonwealth was a problem which had caused constant concern to successive governments during the latter part of the reign of King George V. An anomalous position had been created by the fact that India, in company with the Dominions, had been a signatory of the Treaties of Peace in 1919 and had thus automatically become a charter member of the League of Nations, though her legal status fell short of the requirement stated in the preamble to the Covenant : namely, that membership could only be enjoyed by 'completely self-governing States, Dominions or Colonies'.

The Montagu-Chelmsford Reforms, as embodied in the Government of India Act of 1919, had carried the Indian Empire a considerable distance along the road to self-government, albeit by means of the tortuous and troubled method of 'dyarchy'. Thereafter attempts to attain further progress toward the conscious goal of dominion status within the Commonwealth were essayed through the Simon Commission, the First and Second Round Table Conferences (1930 and 1933) and the labours of the Joint Select Parliamentary Committee on Indian Constitutional Reforms (1933–1934). From these discussions, and after passionate debate within the House of Commons, there emerged the new Government of India Act of 1935.

The purpose of this piece of legislation was twofold. It aimed at the establishment of an all-Indian Federation, to which the Princes could adhere if they so desired, with a central Government, whose ministers, responsible to a Legislature composed of two Chambers, would be in full charge of all matters, except Defence and External Affairs. These two reserved subjects were to be administered by the Viceroy, aided by Counsellors nominated by himself. Within the provincial governments complete self-government was accorded, with certain provisions in case of deadlock or breakdown.

The new Act became operative in respect of the provincial governments on April 1, 1937, and was therefore the constitutional basis of relations between India and the Commonwealth at the outset of the reign of King George VI.

Grave and, as it subsequently appeared, insuperable obstacles were encountered in the establishment of the Central Government and the All-India Federation. The Congress Party of Mr. Gandhi, though they had won control in eight out of the eleven provincial governments, were reluctant to assume greater responsibilities in a national cabinet. The Muslim League of Mr. Jinnah were inclined to bargain for a promise of ultimate partition. The rulers of the Indian States were apprehensive of infringements of their sovereignty. However, the Viceroy, Lord Linlithgow, was tireless in his efforts to bring these conflicting elements together, and, at the outset, was not unoptimistic of success.

    . . . I have been much occupied since my return to duty [he wrote to the King-Emperor at the beginning of December 1938] by the final preparations of the terms upon which, in accordance with Part II of the Act of 1935, the Princes are to be invited to accede to the all-India Federation. I hope to send these terms to the Rulers very early in the present month, and I am asking them to give me their answers—for or against Federation — within a period of 6 months from their receiving my communication. So far as I am at present able to judge, this should make possible the laying of the Instruments of Accession on the tables of both Houses of Parliament by the autumn of 1939. This would be followed, all being well, by the voting of an address to Your Majesty before Xmas, 1939, and, if it pleases Your Majesty, to the issue of your Royal Proclamation in the spring of 1940. The way will then be clear for the preparation of the new electoral rolls in the Provinces upon which the Upper Chamber of the new Federal Legislature will be elected. I contemplate the first elections to the Federal Legislature in the autumn of 1940, and the summoning of the first Federal Legislature and swearing in of the first Federal Ministry in the early months of 1941. I think, Sir, that you may like to have my tentative programme.[17]

This sanguine forecast was, however, never destined to be fulfilled. By September 1939 the Princes were still in process of replying to the Viceroy's offer and the requisite number of states had failed to accede. Moreover, the Muslim League had definitely rejected any scheme of Federation and the Congress Party had refused to consider the possibility of partition. Being, therefore, without a responsible central government the Viceroy declared India to be at war by virtue of the powers still vested in him under the Indian Act of 1919, without preliminary discussion with the Indian leaders. This caused the Congress Party to make an open demonstration of protest. They absented themselves from the discussion on the Defence of India Bill, which was introduced into the Central Assembly two days after the declaration of war, thus shirking the responsibility of either agreeing or refusing to support the Allies, and they withdrew their Ministers from the provincial governments, which were taken over by the governors.

Apart from this demonstration, as Lord Linlithgow wrote to King George, 'the declaration of war was the signal for widespread and enthusiastic manifestation of loyalty and of eagerness to support Your Majesty's cause in the conflict'.[18] The Princes came forward in large numbers with offers of personal service and material aid, and the other political parties promised full co-operation in the war effort.   Indian troops served with conspicuous gallantry in East Africa and in the expulsion of the enemy from Libya and Tunisia.

Lord Linlithgow did not abate his efforts to reach a constitutional solution, and these were followed by King George with interest and sympathy.   'It seems to His Majesty that your conciliatory attitude puts both Hindus and Moslems in the wrong', Sir Alexander Hardinge wrote to the Viceroy, 'and that they ought to blame each other rather than you for any lack of progress in India's constitutional development.'[19]

But the deadlock persisted.   The Muslim League at the Lahore Conference (March 25, 1940) adopted as its constitutional goal the political division of India into two parts in one of which the Muslims should be in a permanent majority. This appeared to them the sole means of escape from the dilemma in which they found themselves as a result of the introduction of democratic institutions.   Lord Linlithgow thereupon made his 'August Offer', repeating the pledge of dominion status for India immediately after the war provided that communal agreement was reached, but reiterating that His Majesty's Government could not transfer power to any body whose authority was denied by powerful minorities.   In the meantime, he announced, the Viceroy's Council would consist of eight Indians and four Europeans, the portfolios of Defence and Foreign Affairs remaining in his own hands. The Congress Party, however, would accept nothing short of complete independence, and the Muslim League demanded recognition of the principle of partition.

The deadlock was unresolved when, on December 7, 1941, the whole situation in the Orient underwent a cataclysmic change by the entry of Japan into the war and the consequent decline in British prestige.   Hong Kong surrendered on December 25, Singapore on February 15, and with each disaster the attitude of the Congress Party worsened.   The

Party leaders utilized a visit by Marshal Chiang Kai-shek to Delhi to bring pressure upon the British Government to yield to their demands and, though these were refused, it was found impossible to resist the pressure brought by President Roosevelt upon Mr. Churchill, both personally at Washington and subsequently by cable, to make a further declaration of the terms of self-government for India after the war.[20] The Viceroy also urged that some new *démarche* be made.

It was not easy for Mr. Churchill, who had so vehemently opposed in all its stages the passing of the India Act of 1935, to bear responsibility in 1942 for constitutional concessions which were far more sweeping. But he had never shirked a political duty, however distasteful, nor had he ever failed to look facts squarely in the face, and he now took up the burden with his usual vigour. India's continued participation in the Commonwealth war effort must be assured and at this moment above all others it was necessary to maintain a unanimity of outlook with Washington. Forthwith he set in train the drafting of a declaration of policy and, as usual, he kept the King fully informed.

The Prime Minister came to lunch [the King wrote in his diary on March 3]. He looked rather tired. He told me about the India Declaration for Dominion status after the war, about which a Cabinet meeting had been held this morning. F. D. R. had urged Winston to give India a promise of Dominion status now, as he thought it would unite all Indians to work for the war effort, especially in face of Japanese aggression, when Indian troops were being exposed to the Japanese troops. W. explained to F. D. R. that India was a continent the size of Europe, with many sects, languages, etc & that it was very difficult to reconcile the differences between Hindus & Mahommedans. The latter are a minority of 100,000,000, & most of the Indian troops are Mahommedans. The draft declaration states to create a new Indian Union which shall constitute a Dominion associated with the U.K. & other Domns. by a common allegiance to the Crown, but equal to them in every respect, & free to remain in or to separate itself from the equal partnership of the British Commonwealth of Nations. Why mention secession as it is what Congress has always wanted to do. Many Provinces won't want to join it, or the Indian Princes either. Many Indians still want to owe allegiance to me as King-Emperor. W. is not satisfied with it, & told me he is not going to ask my approval for anything that will not help now & work later. It is a very important though difficult matter, & whatever is said now, cannot please everybody & will have bad repercussions on the Indian Army, in Afghanistan, the N.W. Frontier, & Nepal. Anything to upset the loyalty of the Gurkhas would be tragic.[21]

It was considered, however, that, if the Declaration were to be made without preliminary sounding of public opinion in India, it would have little chance of success, and Sir Stafford Cripps volunteered to go out and conduct preliminary discussions with the party leaders on behalf of the British Government, leaving the Viceroy and the Commander-in-Chief uncommitted to responsibility. He arrived in Karachi on March 22, bearing with him a long-term and a short-term plan, the details of which were made public on March 30.[a]

The draft declaration was indeed a full-blooded offer of complete self-government at the end of the war. The British Government undertook to create immediately after the cessation of hostilities an Indian Union, equal in every respect to the other dominions of the British Commonwealth and having a constitution framed by a constituent body elected by Indians. There were, however, two conditions : any province not satisfied with the new constitution might refuse to accede to the Union and, secondly, a treaty negotiated between the British Government and the Constituent Assembly would safeguard the rights of minorities.

Despite the King's expressed distrust of the wisdom of including a 'secession clause', it was made clear in the statement, and still more so in press conferences, that the Indian Union would have the right to leave the Commonwealth if it so wished.[b]

The short-term plan proposed that each of the main political parties should have representatives in the Central Cabinet which, except for the Viceroy and the Commander-in-Chief, would be entirely Indian. Even the responsibilities of the

[a] White Paper, Cmd. 6350. The story of this Mission is told at length in Sir Reginald Coupland's *The Cripps Mission* and in Mr. Churchill's memoirs, vol. iv, chapter 12. See also *The Life of Sir Stafford Cripps*, by Dr. Colin Cooke (pp. 283-94).

[b] Section (c) ii of the draft declaration, which provided for the treaty between the British Government and the Constituent Assembly, stated that 'it [the Treaty] will not impose any restriction on the power of the Indian Union to decide in the future its relationship to the other Member States of the British Commonwealth'.

Commander-in-Chief were to be shared with an Indian Defence Minister, though certain safeguards were to be retained in British hands until after the war.

For nearly two weeks Sir Stafford Cripps laboured in the jungle of oriental negotiation. His sincerity was undoubted, his assiduity beyond question, but his enthusiastic desire to find a solution caused him to take certain actions which some regarded as being of questionable tact and wisdom. He communicated his formula to the Congress Party leaders without having first informed the Viceroy and the Commander-in-Chief of its details, and he felt constrained to take counsel with the head of the United States supply mission, Colonel Louis Johnson.[a] There was anxiety at home that Sir Stafford's zeal might have outpaced his discretion and this was shared by the King. 'There is no excuse for this [the keeping of the Viceroy and the Commander-in-Chief in ignorance] or for bringing Col. Johnson, an American, into the negotiations', the King wrote in his diary. 'The latter knows nothing about India, & is F. D. R.'s expert sent to deal with supply and munition matters. In fact the whole matter is in a most unsatisfactory state.'[22]

On April 10 the Congress Party rejected the British proposals and on the following day the Muslim League did likewise. On April 13 Sir Stafford Cripps, having broadcast to the people of India the reason for the failure of the negotiations, returned to England.

The King never had much confidence that the declaration would commend itself to the party leaders in India [Sir Alexander Hardinge later wrote to the Viceroy]. Nevertheless, the fact that we made such an offer has done much to put us right in the eyes of the world; and the Indian political leaders have done their cause little good by their rejection of it.[23]

The King's own reflection had indeed been in these terms. 'The Cripps Mission may have failed', he wrote in his diary on April 12, 'but it has cleared up many ambiguities for the rest of the world, especially America, as to our rule in India

---

[a] Louis Johnson (b. 1891) served as U.S. Assistant Secretary for War, 1937–1940, and as President Roosevelt's personal representative in India from March to December 1942. He was Secretary for Defence in President Truman's Cabinet from 1949 to 1950.

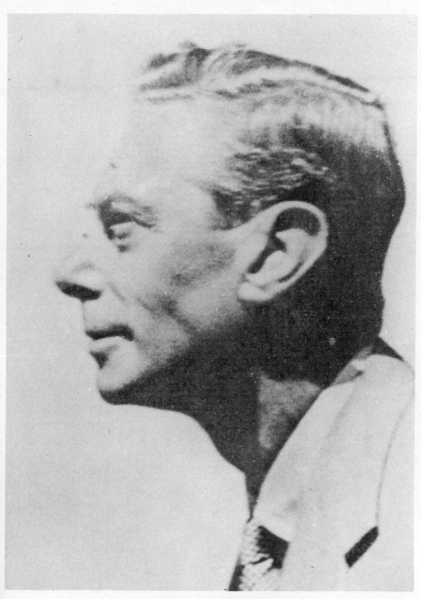

IN SOUTH AFRICA

(Photograph taken by a South African student)

& what it has done for the Indian peoples. The Hindus will now have to make up their minds whether to hinder our war effort or not.'[24]

The position could not have been put more succinctly. The terms of the offer brought by Sir Stafford Cripps and their rejection by the principal parties in India created a profound impression upon public opinion both at home and in the United States, where the critics of British policy, who had been accustomed to attribute every difficulty to the alleged failure of any British Government to commit themselves, had been completely discomfited. A new attitude was immediately manifest, and not least apparently among the United States troops then serving in India. Within a few weeks the Congress leaders, who had for years conducted virulent anti-British propaganda in the United States, had lost a large part of their hold over American public opinion. Nor was their subsequent action calculated to re-establish that hold.

'The Hindus will now have to make up their minds whether to hinder our war effort or not' had been the King's thought, and the question was soon answered. The Japanese, having overrun Burma, were now upon the frontiers of India itself and the Congress leaders became obsessed with the idea that Britain was on the verge of defeat. On July 14 the Working Committee of the Congress Party demanded the immediate withdrawal of British rule from India and this demand was endorsed by the All-India Committee on August 8. The Viceroy had no alternative but to declare the Party an illegal body and to intern the members of the Working Committee, including Mr. Gandhi and Mr. Nehru, for the duration of the war. Violent disorders broke out in certain of the provinces, which appeared to be planned to synchronize with a Japanese invasion of India, but these were suppressed. India, rallying in the face of danger, made a supreme effort in the raising of new armed forces and in becoming the centre of the Eastern supply group and the base from which the ultimate defeat of the Japanese armies was planned and accomplished.

In the spring of the following year the question of the choice of a new Viceroy greatly exercised the minds of the King and of Mr. Churchill. Lord Linlithgow was due to retire in the late summer at the close of a term of office which

had been distinguished for the patient and courageous statesmanship of a man who had a soul above frustration and who
had refused to be soured by the failure which had dogged
his every effort to find a constitutional solution to the Indian
problem. He would be a difficult man to succeed and the
best was not too good. The Prime Minister, backed by the
Secretary of State for India, Mr. Leopold Amery, at first
favoured the appointment of Mr. Eden who, when sounded
on the subject, expressed the view, as Mr. Churchill wrote to
King George, 'that he was not only willing to go if he were
strongly pressed, but was powerfully attracted to the idea of
rendering this great service to the British Empire'.[25]

The King weighed the matter in his own mind. He
realized the importance of the appointment of someone of the
calibre and abilities of the Foreign Secretary, but he doubted
whether it would be possible to do without these same great
qualities in the councils of the Empire at home. 'India is in
a bad state, & Eden, with his knowledge of foreign affairs,
his visit to U.S.A. & high reputation would be able to cope
with the position', he wrote in his diary. 'We must not lose
India by keeping our best people here, but I do not feel that
Eden can be spared at present.'[26] He considered the matter
fully at Windsor during his brief Easter holiday, and in the
meantime, on his instructions, Sir Alexander Hardinge had
discussed the matter with Mr. Eden himself and with Lord
Cranborne.[27] On April 28, having now reached a conclusion,
the King wrote to the Prime Minister :

I am grateful to you for letting me know the way your mind
has been working since we discussed the matter at our last Tuesday
luncheon. I fully recognize the force of your arguments in favour
of sending Anthony Eden, and I have little doubt that he would
do the job better than anyone else who is available. I am equally
sure that he would subordinate himself to the national interest
whatever his real personal feelings might be.

At the same time there are, in my opinion, several strong
arguments against his appointment at the present time. From the
point of view of the general conduct of the war he is, I know, very
much in your confidence. He is, so to speak, your Second-in-
Command in many respects, and, while I appreciate your readiness
to let him go, I cannot help feeling that you might well find the
loss of his assistance and support too great an addition to the

heavy burden which you already have to bear. As regards Foreign
Affairs, he has won for himself a unique position among the United
Nations. He enjoys, in an exceptional degree, the confidence both
of the United States and of our Soviet Allies. If he were to go
away to India now, the benefit which the country derives from his
very special position would be, to a large extent, lost to it, just at
a time when the delicate international problems of the post-war
settlement are coming more and more to the front. I think, too,
that it might be rather disturbing to the country to feel that his
part in the general conduct of the war against Germany was thus
being brought to a close, and while I agree that we ought in
principle to send overseas the best men that we can spare, the
conduct of the war from the United Kingdom must, I feel, take
precedence over everything else.

Admittedly the gesture would be a significant one ; but I
cannot help wondering if the political situation in India, unsatisfactory as it undoubtedly is, will yield to treatment at the hands of
any individual Statesman for some time to come.

These are some of the reasons for my serious misgivings about
the appointment of Eden. I feel that the matter is one of great
importance and, as Linlithgow's term of office has still some months
to run, I very much hope that no decision will be reached for the
next week or two, during which we can all give this new suggestion
the amount of thought which it deserves.[28]

As a result of the King's letter Mr. Eden was temporarily
dropped from consideration and he himself had by now
reached the conclusion that his place was at home. The
King discussed the matter very frankly with him, telling him
that later on he could certainly be reconsidered, but at the
moment he was indispensable : 'I told him that when the
P.M. goes off to U.S.A. I must have him with whom I can
discuss matters'.[29]   In June, however, Mr. Churchill, having
considered and rejected various other candidates for the Viceroyalty, returned again to the King with the somewhat extraordinary proposal that Mr. Eden should, in effect, both be
Viceroy and remain in the counsels of the Government,[a] but
this suggestion King George, with his usual practical common
sense, scouted at once. 'He is thinking of Eden with a 3 year
term of office & frequent visits home [he wrote in his diary].
I asked him how he could be in 2 places at once, as being

[a] A precedent for this lay in Lord Halifax's retention of his membership of
the War Cabinet on his appointment as Ambassador in Washington. (See above,
p. 520.)

Viceroy is a whole-time job.'[30]   This cogent argument appeared finally to convince the Prime Minister.   There was no
more talk about Mr. Eden and on June 19, 1943, the appointment of Field-Marshal Lord Wavell was announced.   He was
installed as Viceroy and Governor-General on October 20.

As a soldier Lord Wavell had shown himself the epitome
of Mr. Churchill's maxim : 'In defeat — defiance ;   in victory
— magnanimity', and as an imperial pro-consul he was to
demonstrate the two other elements of the Churchillian
precept : 'In war — resolution ;   in peace — goodwill'.   No
Viceroy viewed more dispassionately nor more clearly the
problems which beset the India he served ; no Viceroy assumed
office at a moment more fraught with difficulty ;   nor strove
more diligently to overcome the obstacles to a peaceful settlement.

Politically the Cripps Mission had marked a stage in the
retrocession of the British from power in India which it was
never possible to retrace.   The repression of the 1942 Rebellion
had showed that the prestige and power of the British were
still high, when they chose to exercise them ;   but they were
definitely in danger, since events had shown how easy it was
for agitators to inflame the mobs and to make ordered government impossible over large parts of the country.

To Lord Wavell, therefore, it seemed that the essential
principle of his task, as he later wrote to the King-Emperor,
was :

The vital necessity, not only to the British Commonwealth but
to the whole world, of a united, stable and friendly India ;   and
that therefore all our efforts in the next few years must be directed
to promoting this stability and, as far as possible, friendliness.   The
first obvious difficulty was that real stability seemed only possible
if we retained our own control ;   but that if we did so it was unlikely
that we should secure the friendliness at any rate of the educated
part of the population.   I was also convinced in my own mind,
from what I had seen of the psychology of our people at the end
of the First World War and during this last one, that it was most
unlikely that the British could be induced to make the necessary
effort to retain control of India against the wishes of a large part
of its population.   Nor did I think it was right that we should do so.[31]

In pursuance of this general principle Lord Wavell conceived the original idea of beginning his Viceroyalty with a

great act of clemency.   He proposed to release Mr. Gandhi and Mr. Nehru from prison and to invite them to become members of his Executive Council.   This suggestion, however, received no support at all from London and made King George very angry.   'Gandhi is now discredited in U.S.A. & in India', he wrote in his diary, '& to let him out of confinement now is a suicidal policy.   I was very annoyed when I heard of it some days ago.'[32]

The King indeed had been genuinely alarmed at the degree to which the idea of the transfer of power in India had become an admitted inevitability in the minds of British political party leaders, a fact which had been gloomily disclosed to him by Mr. Churchill at one of their Tuesday luncheons in July 1942.

He [the P.M.] amazed me by saying that his colleagues & both, or all 3, parties in Parliament were quite prepared to give up India to the Indians after the war.   He felt they had already been talked into giving up India.   Cripps, the Press & U.S. public opinion have all contributed to make their minds up that our rule in India is wrong & has always been wrong for India.   I disagree & have always said India has got to be governed, & this will have to be our policy.[33]

The King regretted more and more acutely that he had never set foot in his Indian Empire, had never been brought into contact with its political leaders nor seen the teeming millions of its population.   It was in character with his whole concept of kingship that he should wish to acquaint himself at first hand with the setting and problems of the Indian constitutional issue, and it was in pursuit of this desire that he proposed to the Prime Minister in the winter of 1944 that he should go to the South-East Asia front, visiting India on the way.   Mr. Churchill, however, was discouraging and in deference to his Prime Minister's objections the King reluctantly abandoned the idea.[a][34]

The year 1945 saw the decisive defeat of the Japanese armies in Burma and the liberation of that country.   In a masterly campaign the Fourteenth Army turned the retreat of the enemy into a disastrous rout, and, in a successful race

[a] See above, p. 613.

against the monsoon, Sir William Slim [a] occupied Rangoon on May 3. In a message of congratulation on the occasion of the Victory Parade on June 15, the King wrote to the Supreme Allied Commander, Lord Mountbatten: 'Your victory is a victory not only over the Japanese enemy but over climate, distance and disease. It will go down to history as a magnificent feat of arms.'

It had seemed to Lord Wavell for some time that the moment had arrived for a further effort to secure the co-operation of the Indian political leaders in the formation of something in the nature of a provisional government, but it took him six months to obtain the approval of the British Government. He returned to London for consultation in the summer and was received on May 2 by King George, whom he told that he hoped to begin his conversations in India before the end of the Japanese war.[35] On June 15 the Viceroy announced at Delhi that, without prejudice to the final constitutional settlement, — in which connection, it was stated, that the Cripps offer 1942 'stands in its entirety without change or qualification' — he was prepared to reconstitute his Executive Council with members chosen from among the leaders of Indian political life, and as a gesture of clemency he released the members of the Working Committee of the Congress Party who had been in confinement for nearly three years.

There followed the Simla Conference of June 25, at which the Viceroy hoped to arrive at the selection of the new members of his Council. Once again, however, failure resulted from the intransigence of the leaders of the Congress Party and Muslim League. The conference dispersed on July 21 having reached no agreement and, with characteristic magnanimity, Lord Wavell took upon himself the blame for its breakdown.

The advent of the Labour Government to power in Britain gave a new complexion to the Indian issue. Mr. Attlee, as a member of the Simon Commission of 1928, and of the Joint Select Committee in 1933, had had some first-hand experience

---

[a] Field-Marshal Sir William Joseph Slim, G.C.B., G.C.M.G., G.C.V.O., G.B.E., D.S.O., M.C. (b. 1891), commanded the Fourteenth Army in the Burma Campaign and was Commander-in-Chief Land Forces, South-East Asia, 1945–1946. On his return to England he became Commandant of the Imperial Defence College, 1946–1947, and Chief of the Imperial General Staff, 1948–1952. In 1953 he was appointed Governor-General of the Commonwealth of Australia.

of Indian problems. Sir Stafford Cripps had tried and failed
to find a solution in 1942. But the Government was determined
to try again and, this time, to succeed at all costs. Indian
elections were decreed at which the Congress Party won
sweeping victories in eight provinces and the Muslim League
captured nearly all the seats reserved for Muslims; when the
new Central Legislative Assembly met on January 25, 1946,
Lord Wavell spoke of the 'determination' of the British
Government to establish an Executive Council made up of
political leaders, and to call into existence an all-India Constituent Assembly.

To further this end a Cabinet Mission was dispatched to
India, arriving there in May 1946.[a] Of their labours Lord
Wavell wrote to the King:

I do not think any men could have worked more wholeheartedly
and with greater patience and good temper than did the Mission.
. . . Their achievements were also very considerable. They certainly convinced Indian opinion, except perhaps the most extreme,
that we really do intend to give India her freedom as soon as
possible; they persuaded the Congress and Muslim League leaders
to meet at Simla; they produced an admirable compromise plan
in the statement of May 16; and they succeeded, after almost
interminable haggling on the part of Congress, in getting it accepted
by the two main Parties — though both had, I am afraid, more
than mental reservations in their acceptance.[36]

The Mission, however, failed in its efforts to bring about
an Interim Government, but in September the Viceroy succeeded in persuading Mr. Nehru to form one composed of
twelve members, with five places held available for the Muslim
League, which were eventually filled by nominees of Mr.
Jinnah. But, in the months which followed, it became all too
apparent that Lord Wavell's suspicion of 'mental reservations' was amply justified. Dissension between the leaders of
the Congress Party and the Muslim League became more and
more acute and the League threatened to boycott the sessions
of the Constituent Assembly which was due to open on December 9. In a further effort to seek a solution the British

[a] The Mission consisted of Lord Pethick-Lawrence, Secretary of State for
India; Sir Stafford Cripps, President of the Board of Trade; and Mr. A. V.
Alexander, First Lord of the Admiralty.

Government, on the initiative of Lord Wavell, invited the Viceroy to come to London, together with two Congress Party and two League leaders. After the usual period of haggling the invitation was accepted, and on December 3 Lord Wavell arrived, accompanied by Mr. Jinnah and Mr. Liaquat Ali Khan, for the Muslim League, and Mr. Nehru and Sardar Baldau Singh, the Sikh Minister of Defence.

Now for the first time King George was presented with an opportunity of meeting the leading protagonists in the Indian problem. He had followed the various stages of the negotiations with close attention and mounting anxiety, reading with deep interest the dispatches of the Viceroy and discussing the current issues with his Prime Minister. With his innate dislike of undue precipitancy he was anxious that no decision should be taken from reasons of pure expediency, though he fully realized that no turning-back of the clock was now possible.

He received both Mr. Attlee and Lord Wavell on December 3, and recorded the following impression of his conversations with them :

The Hindu & Moslem attitude towards India's future govt. is very different & the question is whether they can come to some agreement while they are here. The only alternative is Civil War between Hindu & Moslem, which we will be powerless to prevent, as the Indian Army, mixed as it is, may put religion before all else & our troops are not in sufficient numbers without the I. Army to cope with an open rebellion. I saw Ld. Wavell with the P.M. & after he had left. The Viceroy has done very well in trying to keep the 2 sides together & to have brought them here for conversations.[37]

Two days later the four Indian leaders were entertained at a luncheon party at Buckingham Palace. The occasion only served to depress the King still further. He sat between Mr. Nehru and Mr. Jinnah. 'The former was very uncommunicative on any subject', he recorded. 'The latter told me a great deal. I talked with the other 2 afterwards. I had prepared a few words to say but, as the moment, I felt, was most unpropitious, I said nothing. The leaders of the 2 parties I feel will never agree. We have gone too fast for them."[38]

The King's forebodings were soon translated into hard

facts. The conference ran foul of the obstinate determination of Mr. Nehru to achieve the domination by the Congress Party of any central government in India and the equally adamant refusal of Mr. Jinnah to accept such a situation. It was becoming increasingly clear that the principle of partition must be conceded to the Muslims, whose fear of the Hindus could only be assuaged by the establishment of Pakistan.

On December 8 the conference dispersed without any agreement having been reached, and two days later King George had a very serious discussion of the situation with Mr. Attlee.

I saw the Prime Minister [he wrote]. I told him I was very worried over the breakdown of the Indian Leaders talks, & that I could see no alternative to Civil War between Hindus & Moslems for which we should be held responsible as we have not enough troops or authority with which to keep order. The P.M. agreed & said that he had discussed the Constitutional Position with the Cabinet that morning. Nehru's present policy seemed to be to secure complete domination by Congress throughout the Govt. of India. The Muslims would never stand for it & would probably fight for Pakistan which the Hindus dislike so much. The 2 main political parties in India had no real will to reach agreement among themselves; the situation might so develop as to result in Civil War in India, & there seemed to be little realisation among Indian leaders of the risk that ordered govt. might collapse. We have plans to evacuate India, but we cannot do so without leaving India with a workable Constitution. The Indian leaders have got to learn that the responsibility is theirs & that they must learn how to govern.[39]

It was now a matter beyond peradventure that the transfer of power in India could not long be delayed. The vital necessity was to assure that this operation should take place as peacefully as possible, from the point of view of the shedding of both British and Indian blood. The protection of minorities was an essential provision of any such transfer and this appeared to be impossible without recognizing the partition of Pakistan from India.

The Constituent Assembly duly met on December 9 without the representation of the Muslim League, but displayed little hope of progress. Believing a breakdown to be inevitable and that British authority would not be sufficient to prevent the resultant widespread disorders, Lord Wavell urged the

British Government to decide upon a definite programme in the event of such a breakdown and the announcement of a date, not later than March 1948, by which, in the absence of agreement, British power would be transferred to successor authorities.   He recommended a withdrawal by stages beginning with the Congress-controlled provinces of peninsular India and allowing for a concentration in Northern India of British administrative and military forces.   Lord Wavell gave a clear exposition of this policy in the last letter which, as Viceroy, he wrote to the King-Emperor :

I put before the Prime Minister and Committee the absolute necessity for a definite policy of some kind, and said that I could see four courses open to us if the Mission Plan broke down :

(a) To make up our minds to re-establish our power and prestige in India, and to rule the country for a further period, which must be for at least fifteen years if we were to obtain any effective support whatever within the country.   The Prime Minister made it quite clear that this policy was totally inacceptable, it was the one point on which I got a definite decision.

(b) To try and deal the cards afresh, i.e. to make one further attempt to bring the two Parties together.   This seemed to me to involve a recognition of Pakistan in one form or another, and I did not think that we should do this.

(c) To support the majority party, i.e. the Congress, in establishing their control over India.   I did not think that this policy was a just or honourable one, in view of our pledges to the Minorities and to the Indian States ; we might not be able to protect them any longer, but it would be wrong to help the Congress to suppress them, which was what this policy might amount to.

(d) To recognise that we had failed to reconcile the two main parties, and that it would be better for the interests both of ourselves and of India to remove our control as soon as possible, and leave Indians to determine their own future.   This was the policy which I advocated, and I recommended the withdrawal of British control by stages, beginning with the south of India, as the safest method of proceeding.   (I had put this proposal to a civil and military committee in India in the previous autumn, and they had been unable to recommend to me any better plan.)   The date I recommended for final transfer of power was March 31st, 1948.

I failed, after many hours of conference, to get any definite policy from Your Majesty's Government.   Their chief difficulty was reluctance to face Parliament with any proposal which would make it clear that we were withdrawing our control very shortly.

My own view was that our own interests would probably best

be served now by a definite decision to withdraw our control from India by a given date, thus enabling our nationals, of whom there are about 100,000 excluding military, to take a decision whether or not to leave India, while we still have the power to protect them.   We should also thus avoid being responsible for, and probably involved in, any widespread breakdown of law and order which may result from the communal situation or from labour troubles induced by revolutionary preaching or economic conditions.   The worst danger for us is an anti-European movement which might result in the killing of some of our nationals, and of our having to carry out an ignominious forced withdrawal ; instead of leaving in our own time and voluntarily.

On the other hand it is probably in India's best interests that we should remain as long as we possibly can and still try and influence events in the direction of political sanity. We still have a great deal of prestige and may still be able to do great service to India.   But the longer we stay the more risk we run of becoming involved in a civil war, or in anti-European troubles and being eventually forced to scuttle out ignominiously ; or of being compelled to make an effort to re-establish law and order and protect our nationals, or prevent civil war, which might throw a great strain on our resources and gravely retard our economic recovery.

My efforts since I returned from England have been directed to the following objects, so far as internal security is concerned :

(a) That we should have as good and detailed a plan as possible for the protection and withdrawal of our nationals in an emergency ;

(b) that we should try to prevent British troops being used for the suppression of one party in the interests of another, and that we should not become involved in communal or labour disturbances if we can avoid it ; and

(c) that we should for as long as possible maintain the stability and integrity of the Indian Army, which is at the present time perhaps the brightest part of the Indian outlook.[40]

His Majesty's Government, however, refused to accept the Viceroy's plan, which they regarded as altogether too precipitate a retreat, but authorized him to prepare secret plans for withdrawal, varying in accordance with the several contingencies in which a breakdown might occur.   Moreover, their confidence in Lord Wavell's ability to handle the possible contingencies was undermined.

Attlee told me [the King wrote in mid-December] that Ld. Wavell's plan for our leaving India savours too much of a military retreat & does not realise it is a political problem & not a military one. Wavell has done very good work up to now but Attlee doubts whether he has the finesse to negotiate the next steps when we must keep the 2 Indian parties friendly to us all the time.[41]

Mr. Attlee had now reached the conclusion that the hope of achieving an agreement between the Indian leaders by the way of discussion was pure delusion. As long as Britain held power she would inevitably be held responsible for failure. He had also become convinced that, though Muslims and Hindus might establish a state of 'co-existence' in terms of independence, they would never live as subjects of the same dominion. The Government were preparing a statement on these lines. They were not very hopeful of success but they were prepared to stake a great deal on the personality of a new Viceroy.

The choice of Lord Mountbatten as successor to Lord Wavell came as a surprise in some quarters, but in selecting him Mr. Attlee had taken many essential factors into consideration. Lord Mountbatten's war record had been brilliant, both as a dashing Captain of Destroyers and as a successful Supreme Allied Commander in South-East Asia. In this latter capacity he had had to work with the Americans and with the Chinese and to command troops of many nationalities; he had done so with notable felicity. He was possessed of tremendous energy, of imagination, tact and charm, together with a certain romanticism and considerable ruthlessness. This combination of qualities convinced the Prime Minister that he was 'the one man who might pull it off'.[42]

There was, however, a further major factor to be considered. Lord Mountbatten was a member of the Royal Family. Not only was he King George's cousin [a] but probably his closest personal friend, and as such it might have been considered hazardous to send him out on a mission whose object was nothing less than the liquidation of the Indian Empire. Mr. Attlee was at first hesitant in putting his name before the King but when he did so, on December 17, he found that His Majesty very warmly approved his choice. One stipulation, however, the King did make. 'Lord Mountbatten', he

---

[a] King George and Lord Mountbatten were cousins by virtue of their both being great-grandchildren of Queen Victoria. The Queen's daughter, Princess Alice, married Louis IV, Prince of Hesse and the Rhine ; their daughter, Princess Victoria, married Prince Louis of Battenberg, Lord Mountbatten's father.

said, 'must have concrete orders as to what he is to do. Is he to lead the retreat out of India or is he to work for the reconciliation of Hindus and Muslims?'[43]

Lord Mountbatten, when approached two days later, was found to 'welcome the fact that his task was to end one régime and to inaugurate a new one'.[44] He was convinced, however, that there could be no hope of his success, if the manner of his appointment suggested to the Indians that Britain wished to perpetuate the Viceregal system, and he impressed upon the Government the absolute necessity of stating some definite date for the withdrawal of the British *Raj* from India. Both these points were accepted by the Cabinet. Lord Mountbatten was indeed somewhat surprised at the degree to which he was to be given a free hand in executing the new policy and insisted upon receiving a written directive.

They offered me 'carte blanche' [he wrote to King George] & said I could take anyone out on my staff I liked.[a] Sir Stafford 'bouleversed' me by offering to come out himself on my staff if I'd accept & the P.M. agreed! That was a swift one because if I do have to go I don't want to be hamstrung by bringing out a third version of the Cripps offer!!!

After over an hour we broke up & the next day Stafford came round to see me & again assured me of his desire to place his services at my disposal — so I had a brain-wave & said 'I'll accept your offer on one condition & that is that you take the appointment which I consider would help me most' — He fell for that & agreed & then I said 'I'd like him to go to the India Office & thus be my rear-link with H.M.G.' He was a bit staggered but finally agreed, subject to the P.M.

I then sat down & wrote the P.M. a letter (a copy of which I enclose) & when I next saw him & Stafford I asked the P.M. to put him at the India Office & he said he'd give this request favourable consideration. . . .

I only await the directive & announcement before giving a final answer.[45]

The announcement of the new policy and of Lord Mountbatten's appointment as Viceroy was duly made on February 20, 1947. It was declared that the definite intention of His Majesty's Government was to effect the transfer of power to

[a] Lord Mountbatten took with him Lord Ismay as Chief of Staff and Sir Eric Miéville as Principal Secretary.

Indian hands by a date not later than June 1, 1948, and, if an Indian Constitution had not been worked out by a fully representative Assembly by that date, 'His Majesty's Government will have to consider to whom the powers of the Central Government in British India should be handed over, on the due date, whether as a whole to some form of Central Government for British India, or in some areas to the existing Provincial Governments, or in such other way as may seem most reasonable and in the best interests of the Indian people'.

The issue was thereby placed for the first time squarely before the Indian leaders. The object for which the Government was at first striving was to achieve a single government for the whole of India, but, if this proved impossible, it was indicated that other methods must be found. The Government's policy received a handsome majority in the House of Commons but met with considerable criticism in the House of Lords, where for a time it appeared that an adverse vote was possible. A speech of great statesmanship by Lord Halifax, however, averted a division.

Thus when King George sailed for South Africa the die nad been cast for a final solution of the Indian problem. The ultimate outcome was still in doubt but a definite time limit had been set.

To Lord Wavell, on whom an earldom was conferred, the King's appreciation and gratitude were conveyed by his Private Secretary:

For me to say how highly His Majesty values your services to the Crown in India, both as Commander-in-Chief and as Viceroy, seems to me, even though I write under orders, almost an impertinence [wrote Sir Alan Lascelles]; it would also be unnecessary, for I am sure you know it already. What you may not know, perhaps, is how fully the King has understood, all through these recent years, the immense difficulties with which you have had to cope. Nobody, not even the King, who is not actually in India can ever grasp to their full extent the problems with which a Viceroy is faced all day and every day, and the peculiar complexity of the instruments with which he has to work; but no man who is so comprehensively well informed as His Majesty could fail to realize that, in all the history of British rule in India, there has never been a Viceroy with a harder task — made all the harder by the trend of circumstances — than fell to your lot.

One thing especially The King charged me to say to you; on the purely personal side, he is very grateful indeed to you for the extremely generous references which you have made, in private and in public, to the appointment of Dickie Mountbatten as your successor. . . . The King feels that you have done a great deal towards giving him a good start, and is very grateful to you.[46]

Lord Mountbatten assumed office in March and at the beginning of May, when King George returned to Britain from South Africa, the first stage of his negotiations had been concluded. This had resulted in a purely negative outcome. Hindus and Muslims had found it impossible to agree on the basis of a single government for India and the issue of partition had become one which could no longer be ignored. Moreover, the tense situation in India had convinced both the Viceroy and the Government in London that the transfer of power must take place considerably before the stated date of June 1948.

During conferences in London with the Viceroy in the month of May it was decided to establish two self-governing Dominions of India and Pakistan, equal in all respects with the other Member States of the Commonwealth and both having the right, in accordance with the Statute of Westminster, to decide whether or not they remained within the Commonwealth. The final decision in respect of partition was left to the votes of the Provincial Governments of the Punjab and Bengal and it was agreed that, in the event of a favourable vote, a Boundary Commission would be appointed.

These decisions were made public on June 3. Their acceptance by Mr. Nehru and Mr. Jinnah was due in very large measure to the dynamic energy and forceful personality of Lord Mountbatten, who was determined to succeed. Thenceforward events moved with remarkable celerity. The Punjab and Bengal Legislatures voted in favour of partition,[a] and on July 10 the Indian Independence Bill was introduced into the House of Commons by Mr. Attlee; it was passed through both Houses of Parliament without a division and became law on July 18. The transfer of power to the Governments of the

[a] The Bengal Legislature voted in favour of partition on June 20, the Punjab Legislature on June 23.

two new Dominions was accomplished on August 15, Lord Mountbatten becoming Governor-General of the Dominion of India and Mr. Jinnah of the Dominion of Pakistan.[a]

It was unfortunate that the realization of statehood on the Indian sub-continent should have been marred by massacre and rapine. The complicated and arduous task of the Punjab and Bengal Boundary Commissions, headed by Sir Cyril Radcliffe,[b] had been carried on under the most difficult conditions. The Hindu and Muslim members of the Commissions were unwilling to arrive at any independent decisions and the final awards were therefore made by Sir Cyril alone. In the Punjab, unlike Bengal, partition was accompanied by widespread murder and atrocities committed by both sides, preceding and following the announcement of the awards, and the ensuing movement of population from one Dominion to another was accompanied by the death of hundreds of thousands.

Thus passed, on August 15, 1947, the glory that was the Indian Empire — that 'bright jewel' which Disraeli had presented to Queen Victoria not quite seventy years before. On that date ended also the much longer rule of the British in India; that long and honourable record of men who, before and since the Mutiny, gave of their unselfish best in generations of dedicated service to the Indian peoples. Of these men Lord Radcliffe has written: 'It may be some service to think of them at those times when one falls to wondering whether those who are given power must always use it for selfish ends or forget its purpose in the pride of its possession. When one asks whether there must always be a "governing clan" to whom power is to be entrusted, it may help to recall the origins and training of these men. What was their secret? Pride of Race? Sense of duty? Sound Schooling? All these things

[a] It had originally been hoped by Lord Mountbatten and his staff that he might be asked to serve as Governor-General of both the new Dominions. It was not until he had accepted this office in respect of India that Mr. Jinnah, at the last moment, decided that he wished himself to be Governor-General of Pakistan.

[b] Rt. Hon. Cyril John, Baron Radcliffe, G.B.E. (b. 1899), a distinguished Chancery Counsel, was Director-General of the Ministry of Information, 1941–1945. After serving as Chairman of the Punjab and Bengal Boundary Commissions in 1947, he was appointed a Lord of Appeal in Ordinary in 1949 and Chairman of the Royal Commission on Taxation of Profits and Means in 1952. More recently (1956–1957) he has been occupied with the constitutional problems of the island of Cyprus.

were present, and yet the quality that strikes one most is a certain unaffected readiness to be themselves.'[47]

Amongst the many problems involved in the dissolution of the Indian Empire there was that of the necessary change in the King's title. As from August 15, 1947, he was no longer Emperor of India and was therefore no longer entitled to sign 'G. R. I.'. This first became an issue with the passage of the Indian Independence Act which provided (Section 7 [2]) for the omission of the styles 'Indiae Imperator' and 'Emperor of India', and the change had to be regularized by a Royal Proclamation.

However, the preamble to the Statute of Westminster declared that any change in the Royal Style and Titles was a matter of concern to all the members of the Commonwealth, and though, with the exception of Eire, all the Dominion Governments had agreed to pass the necessary legislation, it was not possible that all these parliamentary processes could be completed by August 15, the date on which India and Pakistan became self-governing Dominions.

This difficulty was presented to the King in a letter from the Prime Minister in which it was proposed that the issue of the Royal Proclamation should be deferred until after the Dominion Parliaments had enacted their legislation, but that the change in the King's title should be made at once in view of the necessity of issuing the Commissions and Letters Patent for the appointment of the two Governors-General which would come into effect on August 15 and must therefore be issued some time before that date. But how should the King sign these documents? It was suggested that the use of the letter 'I' should be discontinued forthwith.[48]

King George agreed to the postponement of the Proclamation but in the matter of the signature he did not feel that the suggested procedure was entirely correct, since the immediate discontinuance of the letter 'I' in his signature would anticipate the Dominion legislation. He therefore proposed to Mr. Attlee, at an audience on July 29, that he should use the signature 'George R.' for all papers relating to India and Pakistan, but would continue to sign all other documents 'George R. I.' until all the Dominions had enacted the necessary legislation and the Royal Proclamation could be made, and to this the Prime Minister agreed.[49]

On further reflection, however, Mr. Attlee felt unhappy about this dichotomy of signature, both on the grounds that it was undesirable that the King should have different titles in different parts of the Commonwealth and also because all cases might not be absolutely clear and difficulty might arise in deciding which title to use. He therefore suggested [50] that the change in the style and title, and also in the King's signature, should become effective for all documents on August 15, and *before* that date for the Commission of Appointment of the Governors-General and other documents relating to India and Pakistan. The exception would be in the issue of the final India Honours List which, though it was to be issued on January 1, 1948, would still be signed 'G. R. I.' as the King's final act as Emperor of India. To this proposal the King assented.[a] [51]

For himself the King had but one personal request and one which reflected his strong sense of historical tradition. On receiving Lord Listowel,[b] his last Secretary of State for India, at Balmoral on August 15, he asked that the last of the Union Jacks which had flown day and night above the Residency at Lucknow since the memorable siege of 1857, might be presented to him so that it might hang at Windsor with other historical flags already there, and this wish was fulfilled some six weeks later.[c] [52]

---

[a] The change in the King's signature was at once commented upon by Queen Mary, who wrote on the back of the envelope of a letter received from him on August 18, 1947: 'The first time Bertie wrote me a letter with the *I* for Emperor of India left out, very sad'.

[b] Rt. Hon. William Francis Hare, fifth Earl of Listowel (b. 1906), served as Postmaster-General, 1945-1947; Secretary of State for India, April-August 1947, and for Burma, 1947-1948; Minister of State for Colonial Affairs, 1948-1950; and Joint Parliamentary Secretary for the Ministry of Agriculture and Fisheries, 1950-1951. In 1957 he was appointed the first Governor-General of Ghana.

[c] The question of the disposal of the Crown of India, especially fashioned for the Coronation Durbar at Delhi in 1911, also came under discussion. The Crown had been purchased out of Indian Revenues at the cost of £60,000 by the Secretary of State in Council on behalf of the Government of India and was vested in His Majesty. It was agreed between the King and the Prime Minister that, as long as the two new Dominions remained within the Commonwealth, it would seem appropriate that the Crown should be retained among the Crown jewels; but that, if at a later date one, or both, of the Dominions of India and Pakistan were to secede, it might be contended that, in view of the fact that it had been purchased out of Indian funds, the Crown should be vested in some Indian authority.[53]

(v)

In the early post-war years of King George's reign other events, besides those in the sub-continent of India, had a vital effect upon the structure of the British Commonwealth which, in the course of the years 1947–1949, experienced one adhesion and two secessions. By an Act of Parliament, which received the Royal Assent on December 10, 1947, the Colony of Ceylon was established as a fully self-governing dominion within the British Commonwealth, with effect from February 4, 1948. On the other hand, Burma, which had been separated from the Indian Empire in 1937 with a limited degree of self-government, elected, on the morrow of her liberation from Japanese occupation by British forces, to secede from the British Crown. In June 1947 the Constituent Assembly adopted a resolution declaring that Burma's future status should be that of an independent sovereign republic outside the British Commonwealth, but bound to the United Kingdom by a treaty of alliance. This attitude was accepted by the British Government on the basis of Mr. Attlee's dictum that: 'We want no unwilling partners in the British Commonwealth'. The treaty was signed in London on October 17, 1947, and implemented by the passage of the Burma Independence Act on November 14.[a]

The post-war reactions of Eire were characteristically both unexpected and contradictory. Throughout the period of hostilities Mr. De Valera had persistently refused to be wooed from his declared position of neutrality, though, under pressure of events during the disastrous days of 1940, he had sufficiently receded from this position to agree to the holding of staff talks with Britain for the mutual defence of Eire against a German invasion.[b] Both during and after the war, however, he had consistently adhered to the tenuous relationship with the Crown established by the External

[a] The Treaty of Alliance with Burma was supplemented by the signature on January 4, 1948, of a Defence Agreement with the United Kingdom.

[b] How seriously the German Government considered the possibility of an invasion of Eire at this time may be seen from the material published in *Documents on German Foreign Policy, 1918–1945*. Series D, vol. ix, March 18–June 22, 1940.

Relations Act of 1936 [a] and its shadowy nexus with the Commonwealth.[b]

But as a result of the General Election of February 4, 1948, Mr. De Valera's sixteen years of office were brought to a close and his administration gave place to a coalition government, of which the leaders of the dominant party, Fine Gael, had pledged themselves during the election campaign to maintain the *status quo* in relation to the Commonwealth.[c] However, in the course of a visit to Canada and the United States in the autumn of 1948, the new Taoiseach, Mr. John Costello, himself a leader of Fine Gael, announced somewhat unexpectedly on September 7 [d] the intention of his government to repeal the External Relations Act of 1936, thereby severing the last link with the Crown. 'Friendship with Britain', he declared, 'did not depend on archaic forms, but on principles of association unrelated to outworn formulae.'

The Bill to give legal form to this intention — The Republic of Ireland Act, 1948 — was introduced into the Dail on November 17 and passed its third reading ten days later. The Republic of Ireland was formally proclaimed on Easter Monday (April 18) 1949 at the General Post Office in Dublin where, thirty-three years before, it had enjoyed a brief and informal existence. King George sent a message of good-will to President O'Kelly in which, mindful 'of the neighbourly links which hold the people of the Republic of Ireland in close association with my subjects of the United Kingdom', he expressed his sincere good wishes, adding that he held 'in most grateful

[a] See above, p. 324.

[b] Mr. De Valera said in the Dail on June 24, 1947: 'I did not say that we are in the Commonwealth. I carefully pointed out that if being in the Commonwealth implied in any way allegiance, or acceptance of the British King as King here, we are not in the Commonwealth, because the position here is that we do not accept either of those things. Our position in relation to the Commonwealth is accepted and understood by the people immediately concerned in Britain, and it is understood by everybody who wants to understand it abroad.'

[c] General Richard Mulcahy (Fine Gael), who subsequently became Minister of Education in Mr. Costello's Cabinet, had declared that his party, if elected, would not alter the Constitution in relation to external affairs, adding: 'The present position has been accepted by all members of the British Commonwealth as being in consonance with membership'. On the other hand, Mr. Sean MacBride, the leader of the Republican Party, who became Mr. Costello's Minister for External Affairs, declared during the campaign that he favoured the repeal of the External Relations Act in view of the anomalous position which it created.

[d] Before the Canadian Bar Association at Ottawa.

memory the services and sacrifices of the men and women of your country who rendered gallant assistance to our cause in the recent war'.

Eire had formally seceded from the Commonwealth, but, by virtue of that splendidly illogical genius which has guided Anglo-Irish affairs since 1936, it was mutually agreed that the citizens of Eire and of the Commonwealth countries were not to be regarded as foreigners, and Anglo-Irish affairs still continued to be dealt with in London by the Commonwealth Relations Office.

King George's comment on the new relationship was given a few weeks later when, on the occasion of the signing of the Statute of the Council of Europe,[a] he received the Eire Minister of External Affairs as one of the signatories. 'Tell me, Mr. MacBride,' he asked, 'what does this new legislation of yours make *me* in Ireland, an undesirable alien?' Mr. MacBride's reply is unrecorded.

(vi)

For republics such as Burma and Ireland to *withdraw* from the aegis of the British Crown was one thing — and a fairly normal thing at that — but for a state with a republican form of government to wish to *remain* within the British Commonwealth was an entirely different matter and one which affected the very essence and basis of the Commonwealth structure. It was with this remarkable contingency that King George and his Ministers were confronted in the winter of 1948.

The Government of India, having achieved dominion status on August 15, 1947, proceeded to establish its Constituent Assembly. From this body, after a year's discussion, there emerged on November 26, 1948, the new Indian Constitution, in the preamble to which it was declared that the people of India had solemnly resolved to constitute their country a sovereign democratic republic, and this measure was destined to become law on January 26, 1950.

Lord Mountbatten had laid down his commission as

---

[a] The Statute was signed in London on May 5, 1949, by the Foreign Ministers of Denmark, France, the Irish Republic, Italy, Luxembourg, the Netherlands, Norway, Sweden and the United Kingdom, and the Belgian Ambassador. The King received the signatories at a party at Buckingham Palace on May 3.

Governor-General of the Dominion of India in June 1948, having, in the words of Mr. Nehru, 'acted in India's interests as zealously as any Indian could have done'.[a] He was now to leave his mark still more deeply upon the future of both the Dominion and the Commonwealth. For it was very largely due to his persuasive powers that Mr. Nehru, when he arrived in London in the autumn of 1948, displayed an unexpectedly helpful attitude concerning the future relations of his country with the Commonwealth.

In attaining this view Mr. Nehru had been influenced not only by the arguments and friendship of Lord Mountbatten but also by the practical and sympathetic attitude of King George. The King had watched the career and activities of his cousin in India with admiration. He admired Lord Mountbatten's energetic drive and executive ability and was proud of the fact that these qualities should be so vividly displayed by a member of his own family. He also shared his cousin's opinion that no legitimate means should be neglected of keeping India within the Commonwealth. With his strong sense of tradition he had been saddened that the proud style of 'Emperor of India' had been shorn from the Royal title, but he was no Bourbon, he knew both how to learn and how to forget, and he never confused the substance with the shadow.

When, therefore, Mr. Nehru came to London King George received him with interest, and this time, in contrast to a former occasion,[b] the Indian Premier was expansive in his conversation. 'I had a long talk with Nehru last night', the King wrote to Lord Mountbatten on October 12. 'I expect he told you about it as he dined with you. I liked him very much.' The effect of this talk upon Mr. Nehru, together with that of his other conversations during his London visit, was such that he left behind him an impression of his real desire to keep India within the Commonwealth, provided always that the imperial compass could be boxed and a constitutional formula found which would be acceptable to the Indian Constituent Assembly and conformable with the expressed intention that India should be a Republic.

[a] Accounts of Lord Mountbatten's period of office as Viceroy and/or Governor-General have been written by Alan Campbell Johnson in *Mission with Mountbatten* and by Roy Murphy in *Last Viceroy*.

[b] See above, p. 706.

The problem thus posed had not taken the British Government unawares. Since May 1947 Mr. Attlee and his colleagues had given the gravest consideration to the future structure of the Commonwealth, through the medium of the Cabinet Committee on Commonwealth Relations, of which the Prime Minister himself was chairman. Their task had been the search for a formula to 'enable the greatest number of independent units to adhere to the Commonwealth without excessive uniformity in their internal constitutions', but until March 1948 their efforts were concentrated on attempts to devise some form of relationship through the Crown. Various other possibilities were examined, including the setting up of a 'Commonwealth' of 'British and Associated States' and the 'redefining' of the Commonwealth so as to avoid terminology and procedure that might cause difficulty to India or Pakistan, but the conclusion was always reached that some link with the Crown was essential.

In the late summer of 1948 the Secretary to the Cabinet, Sir Norman Brook,[a] had visited Canada, Australia and New Zealand for the purpose of discussing the problem with the political leaders of those countries, and his letters to Sir Alan Lascelles during his journey had afforded King George an admirable picture of the reactions which he had received. These amounted, in sum, to the view that, if some Commonwealth countries were unable to accept the jurisdiction of the Crown for internal purposes, they might qualify for continuing membership of the Commonwealth if they were content to accept the King's jurisdiction in their external relations; and a plan was made to discuss this proposal at a meeting of Commonwealth Prime Ministers in October. Before this could happen, however, there were two developments which vitally changed the situation — the repeal of the External Relations Act by Eire and the news that India proposed to proclaim herself a 'Sovereign Independent Republic'.

[a] Rt. Hon. Sir Norman Craven Brook, G.C.B. (b. 1902), had entered the Home Office in 1925, of which in 1940 he was Principal Assistant Secretary. He became successively Deputy Secretary to the War Cabinet, 1942; Permanent Secretary, Office of Minister of Reconstruction, 1943–1945; and Additional Secretary to the Cabinet in 1945. In 1947 he was appointed Secretary of the Cabinet, and in 1956 he assumed the additional duties of Joint Permanent Secretary of the Treasury and Head of the Civil Service.

This new situation resulted in the production of a paper by the Committee on Commonwealth Relations in January 1949, which the King read with deep interest. Shortly thereafter Sir Norman Brook visited His Majesty's Private Secretary at Windsor, and, as a result of their conversation, Sir Alan Lascelles prepared a memorandum. It was not optimistic in tone :

The outstanding facts are that India, though anxious to stay in (on her own terms) is determined either to stay in or go right out — she will not be satisfied with any compromise such as that accepted for Ireland in 1921 ; that there is no hope of inducing India to stay in on condition that she pays allegiance to the Crown as do the older Dominions ; and that none of the artificial 'links with the Crown' which have been suggested in the discussions is really worth anything at all ; they are all so obviously artificial and 'machine-made' as to be worthless. The idea of keeping the 'Fountain of Honour' as a link seemed to have possibilities at one time, but it would never do as the sole permanent acknowledgment of the Crown, and it becomes futile when we know (as we do) that the Indians are already determined that any new Indian decorations shall be entirely devoid of any outward association with the Crown, or with any 'British' symbol.

The last proposal — that the King should act as President of a Commonwealth Conference — is equally unrealistic ; as Brook told the Committee, what makes 'The King' a vital and permanent link for most of us is that it is an ideal for which men are prepared to work, to fight, and to die ; but nobody is going to die for a Conference. So the plain fact is that all attempts to find a substitute-link have failed.

Thus we are at a fork in the road. If we follow one arm, we tell India that, unless she agrees to pay allegiance to the Crown, she must go. She will then go — with the consequence which anybody can foresee.

If we follow the other arm, we agree to the principle of 'inner and outer' membership of the Commonwealth : we admit that the Balfour declaration must be revised ; that the 'common allegiance to the Crown' is no longer the *sine qua non* of membership ; that it is possible for membership, with all its political & economic privileges, to be enjoyed by states that do not recognize the Crown — in other words, by republics. . . .

. . . I told Brook that in no circumstances might any definite recommendation on this matter be made to Your Majesty without the concurrence of, not only your Ministers in this country, but also the leaders of the Opposition, *and* Ministers in the older

Dominions. I said too that The King ought also to be perfectly free to consult, if he wished, individuals not actually in office — such as Smuts or Mackenzie King. . . .ᵃ

On the question of finding a 'link', Brook reminded me of Mackenzie King's point — that any such search would inevitably tend to make the position and functions of the Sovereign the subject of violent political discussion not only in India itself but all over the world. This might do much harm and provides another argument against trying to make some artificial and makeshift 'link'. I mentioned the point that, if 'outer' membership is permitted, it might encourage S. Africa to abandon her present 'inner' membership, and go 'outer'. He said he had discussed this at length with Evelyn Baring ᵇ not long ago. Evelyn had said that already the precedent of Eire had made the idea of 'outer' membership a familiar one in S. Africa and that it was even now becoming increasingly popular. Consequently, if India were allowed to have 'outer' membership, it would, in his opinion, start nothing new in S. Africa, though it would no doubt accelerate the present tendency.

On the other hand, the recognition of 'outer' membership might quite possibly bring Burma, and Eire, back into the Commonwealth, which is something to put on the credit side. . . .⁵⁴

In the weeks which followed, the Committee on Commonwealth Relations gave prolonged study to the problem of India's relationship to the Commonwealth. Mr. Nehru was co-operative within the limits of his very curious position. In an attempt to find a compromise he put forward a 'Ten Points' memorandum which, however, was found unsatisfactory on legal grounds. He then prepared an 'Eight Points' memorandum which provided, if anything, even less in the way of a connection with the Crown; and by February 1949, talks with Canada, Australia and New Zealand had shown that neither of these memoranda provided a sufficient basis for India's continued membership. Despite all efforts, therefore, a suitable formula defied discovery.

It was, however, imperative in Mr. Attlee's mind that every possible step should be taken to prevent this vital matter

ᵃ General Smuts had been defeated in the South African General Election of 1948 and Mr. King had resigned the Canadian Premiership in the same year.

ᵇ Hon. Sir Evelyn Baring, G.C.M.G., K.C.V.O. (b. 1903), was Governor of Southern Rhodesia, 1942–1944, and High Commissioner of the United Kingdom in the Union of South Africa, 1944–1951. In 1952 he was appointed Governor of Kenya.

affecting the Crown from becoming a subject of political controversy. He therefore informed the King, on February 17, that he considered it essential to convene a Conference of Commonwealth Prime Ministers in London not later than May in order to reach a collective decision.

In his letter containing this advice, the Prime Minister set out once again the difficulties and dangers inherent in the problems involved.

Mr. Attlee has always found it difficult to discover any satisfactory nexus for the Commonwealth other than allegiance to the Crown, and it is therefore difficult to see how a Republic can be included. He is, at the same time, impressed by the fact that India is anxious to remain within the Commonwealth, and that other Dominions, especially Australia and New Zealand, have stressed strongly the desirability of retaining her. If India, against her will, is obliged to leave the Commonwealth, it would encourage Russia in her efforts to disrupt South-East Asia, while India, as the most important national state in that area, would tend to become the leader of an anti-European Asiatic movement. On the other hand, if she remains in the Commonwealth, there is a great possibility of building up in South-East Asia something analogous to Western Union. The arguments are therefore well balanced. It is an open question whether the inclusion of a Republic in the Commonwealth would lead to the spread of Republicanism, or whether the insistence on allegiance to the Crown as an essential nexus might not lead to other Commonwealth states going out. In Mr. Attlee's view it is clear that this question can only be settled at a Commonwealth Conference, and it is impossible to forecast what conclusion will be reached by the Conference members.[55]

The interval between Mr. Attlee's letter to King George and the opening of the Commonwealth Premiers' Conference some two months later was utilized for a further diligent consideration of the problem in all its aspects and the ultimately successful outcome was due, in great measure to the initiative and determination of the Prime Minister. Convinced that a new approach to the problem was essential, Mr. Attlee urged in Cabinet, on March 3, that the political advantages of retaining India within the Commonwealth were so great as to justify adapting the Commonwealth to include a republican country owing no allegiance to the Crown. He carried his colleagues with him and the Cabinet decision of March 3

marks a definite milestone in the history of the British Commonwealth.

It had an added immediate importance. It broke the
deadlock which had seemed insoluble and put new life into
the discussions. Time was now short, since the new Indian
Constitution was to be enacted in July, and on the Prime
Minister's suggestion personal emissaries [a] were dispatched on
March 12, to discuss this new approach with the other Commonwealth Prime Ministers. On April 1, towards the end of
Mr. Gordon Walker's [b] discussions in Delhi, the idea was first
mooted that India might recognize the King's position in the
Commonwealth as distinct from his position in India, and
therefrom a formula of compromise was gradually evolved; a
compromise which did full justice to the peculiar genius which
the British have always displayed in this respect.

The essence of the formula was a new interpretation of the
relation of the Sovereign to the Commonwealth. Hitherto
allegiance to the Crown had been a prerequisite of Commonwealth membership, but this — as both Mr. Attlee and Sir
Alan Lascelles had pointed out to the King — was clearly
incompatible with India's declared intention to become a
Republic. On the other hand, though India was not prepared
to recognize King George as her King she was ready to acknowledge him as Head of the Commonwealth, and the other
member states indicated a willingness to acquiesce in India's
continued association in the Commonwealth on these terms.
Thus allegiance to the Crown would cease to be regarded as
the intrinsic requirement of Commonwealth membership as
declared in the Balfour statement of 1926 and in the Statute of
Westminster, and the essential position of the Crown would
become that of a symbol of association.

It was obvious that, if this formula became the accepted
basis of the new Commonwealth, a vitally important conse-

[a] Lord Listowel, Mr. Gordon Walker, Sir Percival Liesching and Sir Norman
Brook.
[b] Rt. Hon. Patrick Gordon Walker (b. 1907) was, before the Second World
War, a Student and Tutor at Christ Church, Oxford, and was occupied during
the war in the European Services of the British Broadcasting Corporation,
specializing in broadcasts to German workers. Elected to Parliament in 1945 as
Labour member for Smethwick, he served successively as Parliamentary Under-
Secretary of State at the Commonwealth Relations Office, 1947–1950, and
Secretary of State for Commonwealth Affairs, 1950–1951.

quence would be the appropriate form of the King's style and title arising from the new constitutional position thus created. In this matter King George took the greatest personal interest. Certain proposals were put before him by his Ministers and on these he made his own comments. From His Majesty's notes his Assistant Private Secretary, Major Adeane,[a] prepared the following memorandum :

THE KING'S TITLE

1. Assuming for the time being that there are to be seven major and entirely self-governing parts of the Commonwealth as well as the dependent territories, and that all seven recognise The King, the following possible alterations and amplifications are suggested :

(1) The title : 'United Kingdom of Great Britain and Ireland (or N. Ireland)' is cumbrous. Could it be improved by including Northern Ireland in Great Britain (as Scotland and Wales are already included) and making this part of the title read simply : 'Great Britain'?

(2) The longer the title becomes the more misleading it is to place the all-important word King towards the end of it. It would be better perhaps to put it immediately before : 'of Great Britain'.

(3) Those parts of the Commonwealth which recognize The King could with advantage be called Kingdoms, which in fact they are. The thesis for the divisibility of the Crown is in any case to be strengthened by the Committee's proposals, and this would add nothing further. The word 'countries' could be reserved for the dependent territories.

(4) 'By the Grace of God' and 'Defender of the Faith' to be optional as suggested.

2. On these lines The King's title for Great Britain would become 'George the Sixth by the Grace of God King of Great Britain and of the other Kingdoms and countries of the Commonwealth, Defender of the Faith'. While for Canada, for example, it would be : 'George the Sixth (by the Grace of God) King of Canada and of the other Kingdoms and countries of the Commonwealth (Defender of the Faith)'.

3. Should the Commonwealth in future include one or more

[a] Rt. Hon. Sir Michael Edward Adeane, K.C.B., K.C.V.O. (b. 1910), a grandson of Lord Stamfordham, was appointed Assistant Private Secretary to King George VI in 1937, and continued to serve Queen Elizabeth II in the same capacity until, in 1953, he succeeded Sir Alan Lascelles as Private Secretary to the Sovereign.

republican states it would be possible to adapt the title for use in a non-Republican unit of the Commonwealth (as suggested in paragraph 8) as follows: 'George the Sixth by the Grace of God King of Great Britain and of the other Kingdoms and countries of the Commonwealth which owe him allegiance, Defender of the Faith'.[56]

The King's Ministers, while giving careful consideration to His Majesty's views, felt that some objection might attach to the words 'and of the other countries in the Commonwealth which owe him allegiance'. An alternative formula was suggested:

George the Sixth (by the Grace of God) King of Great Britain and Northern Ireland and of his other Kingdoms and countries in the Commonwealth, (Defender of the Faith).

In each of the other self-governing states of the Commonwealth, save India, the name of the country would be substituted for 'Great Britain and Northern Ireland'.

In this formula, which went far towards meeting the King's ideas, the whole importance lay in the word 'his'. If India did not owe allegiance to the King, she would not be one of 'his Kingdoms'. His Majesty, however, still foresaw certain difficulties and possible future confusion which he outlined in a note to Sir Alan Lascelles:

I suggested Great Britain and Northern Ireland as a substitute for the United Kingdom of G.B. & N.I. so that the word 'British' could be left out of the term The British Commonwealth as some of the members did not quite like it.

If I am to be recognised as King of Australia, Australia will have to drop the term 'Commonwealth of Australia'. Commonwealth is, I understand, another word for Union.

Is Canada willing to drop the 'Dominion of'?

Is South Africa willing to drop the 'Union of'? This I very much doubt.

If the title Head of the Commonwealth as opposed to head of the British Commonwealth is going to be used then Australia I feel must alter her name.

All the members of the Commonwealth must use the same designation.[57]

The King's points were met by the insertion of the term 'Head of the Commonwealth' in his title, this being accepted by all parties concerned. The several states agreed that, for this purpose of the Royal Title, their individual designations of 'Dominion', 'Union' or 'Commonwealth' should be omitted. A further amendment substituted the word 'Realms' for 'Kingdoms and countries'.

The necessary processes of legislation for the changes in the Sovereign's Title were not completed before the death of King George in 1952. Nevertheless, on the accession of Queen Elizabeth II, some departures were made from the form in which King George VI had been proclaimed, in the light of the changes which had been proposed. Thus the description 'Head of the Commonwealth' was introduced for the first time and the accession proclamation referred to the Queen as :

'Queen Elizabeth the Second, by the Grace of God Queen of this Realm and of all Her other Realms and Territories, Head of the Commonwealth, Defender of the Faith.'

The Commonwealth Prime Ministers at their Conference in December 1952 considered the form of the Royal Title and agreed that the existing title of the Sovereign was not in accord with current constitutional relations within the Commonwealth. They recognized the need for a new form of title which would, in particular, reflect the special position of the Sovereign as Head of the Commonwealth and, further, the desirability of each member country using for its own purposes a form of title suitable to its own particular circumstances but retaining a substantial element which was common to all. The decision was reached that each country should pass the necessary legislation as soon as possible.

The United Kingdom Government accordingly introduced the Royal Titles Act which received Royal Assent on March 26, 1953, giving the Queen power, in accordance with precedent, to proclaim her title. By a Proclamation made on May 28 Her Majesty declared that her title for use in the United Kingdom should be :

'Elizabeth the Second, by the Grace of God of the United Kingdom of Great Britain and Northern Ireland and of Her other Realms and Territories, Queen, Defender of the Faith.'

In Canada, Australia and New Zealand the Sovereign's title is the same, with the substitution of the name of the respective country for that of the United Kingdom; in Ceylon, Pakistan and South Africa the title 'Defender of the Faith' was omitted.[a]

The Conference of Commonwealth Prime Ministers which opened in London on April 21, 1949, was the first to meet without a representative of Eire and also the first to be attended by the Premiers of India, Pakistan and Ceylon.[b] Within a week they had reached a satisfactory conclusion and at an audience with the King on the afternoon of Tuesday, April 26, Mr. Attlee suggested that the seven Prime Ministers and Mr. Pearson[c] should wait upon His Majesty on the following day and together advise him of the result of their discussions on the impending constitutional changes in India. The King agreed and appointed the hour of 12.30 p.m., at which time he received his Ministers in the White Drawing Room at Buckingham Palace. No member of the Household was present at this meeting, at which Mr. Attlee as chairman of the Conference read aloud the approved text of their final conclusions. The King asked if all present were in agreement and, when they had signified their assent,[38] he then addressed them:

GENTLEMEN,

I am glad to be able to congratulate you on the promptitude with which you have finished the task on which you started only a few days ago.

[a] The years 1956 and 1957 were momentous in the history of the British Commonwealth and provided additional evidence of the adaptability of its structure. On March 23, 1956, Pakistan declared itself a republic, ceasing thereby to acknowledge the Queen as Sovereign but continuing to recognize Her Majesty as Head of the Commonwealth. On the other hand, on March 7, 1957, the West African State of Ghana achieved autonomous status within the Commonwealth with the Queen as Sovereign. 'Defender of the Faith' was omitted from the title. On August 31, 1957, the Federation of Malaya entered the Commonwealth as an elective monarchy, recognizing the Queen as the Head of the Commonwealth.

[b] Those attending the Conference were Mr. Attlee (United Kingdom); Mr. Chifley (Australia); Mr. Fraser (New Zealand); Dr. Malan (South Africa); Mr. Nehru (India); Mr. Liaquat Ali Khan (Pakistan); Mr. Senanayake (Ceylon); and Mr. Lester Pearson, Canadian Minister for External Affairs, representing Mr. St. Laurent.

[c] Hon. Lester Bowles Pearson, O.B.E. (b. 1897), having served as a lecturer and Assistant Professor in Modern History at the University of Toronto, entered the Canadian Department of External Affairs in 1928. He served as Minister-Counsellor and as Ambassador in Washington from 1942 to 1946, when he was appointed Under-Secretary of State in Ottawa. Elected to Parliament in 1948 he became Minister of External Affairs and held that office till 1957. In this same year he was awarded the Nobel Peace Prize.

I wish that certain other countries, who are not privileged to belong to our British Commonwealth, could show an equal degree of commonsense and good temper when they meet us round the Conference table.

The problem of which you have just offered me your solution is one that has given us all very grave concern. That solution is a striking example of the elasticity of our system.

So far, it has stood tests such as no other association of nations in history has ever survived. Believing as I do that it has in it immense powers of good for humanity generally, I sincerely trust that it may not in the future be subjected to any greater strain.

Meanwhile, I thank you, gentlemen, for the wisdom and toleration which you have all shown in your handling of this present problem. I hope with all my heart that the arrangement which you now propose may redound to the greater happiness of all those millions whose well-being is the responsibility of all of us in this room today.

The conclusions reached by Commonwealth Premiers which Mr. Attlee read to King George represent as important a document as any in the history of the development of the British Empire; it is to be numbered in importance with the Balfour Formula of 1926 and with the Statute of Westminster itself. The Declaration of April 27, 1949, is as follows:

'The Governments of the United Kingdom, Canada, Australia, New Zealand, South Africa, India, Pakistan and Ceylon, whose countries are united as Members of the British Commonwealth of Nations and owe a common allegiance to the Crown, which is also the symbol of their free association, have considered the impending constitutional changes in India.

'The Government of India have informed the other Governments of the Commonwealth of the intention of the Indian people that under the new constitution which is about to be adopted India shall become a sovereign independent Republic. The Government of India have, however, declared and affirmed India's desire to continue her full membership of the Commonwealth of Nations and her acceptance of The King as the symbol of the free association of its independent member nations and as such the Head of the Commonwealth.

'The Governments of the other countries of the Commonwealth, the basis of whose membership of the Commonwealth is not hereby changed, accept and recognise India's continuing membership in accordance with the terms of the declaration.

'Accordingly the United Kingdom, Canada, Australia, New Zealand, South Africa, India, Pakistan and Ceylon hereby declare that they remain united as free and equal members of the Commonwealth of Nations, freely co-operating in the pursuit of peace, liberty and progress.'

By this Declaration the whole structure of the British Commonwealth was remodelled, adapting it to the exigencies of the time, giving to the Crown a new significance, and proving once again the infinite and invaluable capacity of British institutions to adjust themselves to changing situations. The result was hailed with virtually universal approval throughout the world and with great relief that the new status of India· had been thus embodied in the fabric of the Commonwealth instead of an impassable gulf being opened between the two.[a] Concessions had been made by all, but the outcome was one by which, in Mr. Churchill's words, 'neither the majesty of the Crown nor the personal dignity of the King had been impaired by the conditions under which India was continuing her membership of the Commonwealth'.

One aspect of the new structure of the Commonwealth is not without irony. The Declaration of April 27, 1949, virtually accepts as the new basis of Commonwealth relations that formula of 'External Association' which Mr. De Valera expounded to Mr. Lloyd George in July 1921 and from which he never receded. It was the essence of his opposition to the ratification of the Anglo-Irish Treaty in the Dail in 1922 and of his own legislation of 1936 and 1937. It is therefore ironical that the inauguration on April 18, 1949, of the Republic of Ireland, *outside* the Commonwealth, preceded by only a few days the enunciation of the Declaration of April 27, of which, by inference, Mr. De Valera may be said to be the original progenitor.

[a] The Declaration of April 27, 1949, was submitted by Mr. Nehru to the Indian Constituent Assembly on May 16-17, and ratified by an overwhelming majority.

CHAPTER XII

THE KING AND THE MAN

(i)

KING GEORGE VI was in every sense *un Roi de métier*, and one of the most remarkable personal aspects of his reign was the manner in which he developed in the fulfilment of his high office. When he ascended the Throne, at the age of forty, his unexpected elevation found him unprepared and untrained for the heavy responsibilities which he was suddenly called upon to bear. Though dedicated to the faithful discharge of these new and onerous duties, he was untried and unskilled in the ways of statecraft. At his death, fifteen years later, he had achieved, by diligent application and pragmatic common sense, a wisdom and an understanding which were unreservedly respected by the statesmen and leaders in all the countries of his Commonwealth and Empire.

This growth of stature was apparent not only in retrospect. It was notable at the time and frequently remarked upon by those in contact with His Majesty. One distinguished imperial proconsul, returning to Britain in the latter part of the war after an absence of five years, was asked what most impressed him in the changed conditions which he found. He replied unhesitatingly that it was the degree to which the King had matured in the formation and expression of his judgments and in his singularly wide and detailed knowledge of affairs.

Perhaps more than any monarch of modern times, King George maintained an even balance between the aloof position of a Sovereign and the 'homespun dignity of man'. None was more fully conscious than he of his position as the hierophant of the *mystique* of monarchy, nor of the vital importance of the Crown in the structure of the Commonwealth and Empire. None guarded more jealously, nor exercised with greater rectitude, the constitutional prerogatives of his office, and the duties and privileges of his status as the Fount of Honour.

Yet, from first to last, he was 'The People's King'. His concept of monarchy was two fold; the mystical aloofness of the monarch combined with the close identification of the Sovereign with the interests and problems and welfare of his peoples. This principle of royalty he had evolved and established for himself, as Duke of York, in his work for Industrial Welfare and it had been one of the basic ideas behind his annual Camp. He carried it with him into his kinghood and thereby ensured for himself an unchallengeable position in the hearts of his subjects.

Like his father and grandfather before him, King George was keenly aware of his loyalties and obligations as a member of the Guild of Sovereigns, which he regarded in the sense of a 'Royal Trade Union'. Being himself so conscious of his own responsibilities he was ever sympathetic with the burdens and difficulties of his fellow monarchs. It was in a great measure this guild-loyalty — over and above the ties of kinship and the bonds of common humanity — which prompted the warmth and hospitality with which he received King Haakon of Norway, Queen Wilhelmina of the Netherlands and King George of Greece during their temporary war-time exile; which induced the sympathy he displayed with King Peter of Yugoslavia [a] and King Michael of Rumania [b] in the circumstances which rendered their exile more permanent; and which evoked his broad-minded understanding of the terrible dilemmas which beset King Leopold of the Belgians, Prince Paul of Yugoslavia and King Boris of Bulgaria. '*Mon*

[a] As King Peter's 'Koom' King George offered his godson much wise advice in the conduct of his political affairs and was of no small assistance to him in the somewhat complicated arrangements of his marriage. To this both King Peter and Queen Alexandra have paid tribute in their respective memoirs.

[b] King George had been deeply concerned regarding King Michael and his mother, Queen Helen (see above, p. 618 fn.) and had thought highly of the manner in which the young monarch had comported himself in very difficult circumstances, in opposition to both the Nazis and the Russians. When King Michael came to attend the wedding of Princess Elizabeth in November 1947 he recounted, at King George's request, the story of his *coup* against Marshal Antonescu, to His Majesty's great interest. A few weeks later, on King Michael's arrival in Lausanne after his abdication, the British Minister at Berne called upon him, at King George's instruction, to express His Majesty's personal sympathy and to obtain for him a first-hand account of the events which had preceded King Michael's departure from Bucharest. The story of these events and of the overthrow of Antonescu is to be found in Air Vice-Marshal Gould Lee's book, *Crown against Sickle, the Story of King Michael of Rumania.*

métier à moi est d'être Roi', King Edward VII had said on a memorable occasion,[a] and this was also the attitude of his grandson, who could not be indifferent to the fortunes and misfortunes of his fellow guildsmen.

It was in response to this same guild-spirit, coupled with his own strong feeling for historical tradition and the proper order of things, that King George in 1939 caused the three Stuart Pretenders — Prince James Edward, Prince Charles Edward and Henry, Cardinal of York — whose graves in the crypt of St. Peter's at Rome had fallen into neglect and dis-repair, to be reburied in a tomb of suitable dignity, the cost being borne by the King himself.[1]

With Chaucer's Knight

> He loved chyvalrye,
> Trouthe and honour, freedom and curtesie.

(ii)

King George VI was a zealous Freemason, maintaining that contact of the Royal Family with the Craft which, with the exception of a brief period in the middle years of the nineteenth century, had remained unbroken since George III's youngest son, Ernest Augustus, Duke of Cumberland, had been installed as Grand Master in 1782.[b] With this family tradition and his own personal inclination, it is not surprising that the King, as a young man, found himself drawn towards the Order. He was initiated in 1919 in the Navy Lodge No. 2612 to which many of his service comrades belonged.[c] Happy and deeply interested in the new world into which he was now introduced, he at once applied himself with characteristic diligence to the mastering of the ceremonial and its import with the intention of qualifying for the highest office in his lodge; this he duly attained, being installed Master in 1921. His promotion in the higher degrees of the Order came rapidly, not only because of his rank but also of his personal ability. In 1924 he accepted

---

[a] See above, p. 145.

[b] The Duke of Connaught held the office of Grand Master for a period of thirty-eight years, retiring in 1939 for reasons of health and advanced age. (He was then 89.)

[c] Both the Duke of Kent and the Duke of Edinburgh were initiated into Freemasonry in the same Lodge : the former in 1928, the latter in 1952.

the charge, as Grand Master, of the Masonic Province of Middlesex and retained this position until his accession.

Nor was the King's connection confined to English Masonry alone. As Duke of York, he became affiliated to Scottish Masonry in June 1936, being received into the Lodge Glamis No. 99 at the hands of Brother Beattie, the village postman, and on St. Andrew's Day of the same year he was installed Grand Master Mason of the Grand Lodge of Scotland. His accession to the Throne a few days later terminated the holding of all active Masonic offices, but his interest did not languish. Indeed, he made Masonic history by creating the precedent of a British Sovereign publicly participating in the observances of the Order. He was ceremonially inducted as Past Grand Master before a great audience of Masons in the Albert Hall in 1937 and as such he personally installed three Grand Masters — the Duke of Kent in 1939, Lord Harewood in 1943 and the Duke of Devonshire in 1948 — and only illness prevented his performing a similar office for Lord Scarbrough in November 1951.

There was much in Masonry which appealed consciously and deeply to King George : its hierarchic discipline ; the dignity and simplicity of its ceremonial, of which he was a knowledgeable student ; the simplicity and vitality of its three great tenets — brotherly love, relief and truth. His belief in the Order became the more apparent to those with whom he conversed about it as the years passed ; he was influenced by its symbolism, and the record of his daily life bore witness to his strict adherence to its moral and spiritual precepts.

(iii)

King George was possessed not only of an inquiring intellect, which penetrated into unexpected recesses of a subject and retained every detail of what it discovered, but also of a most agile mind which, with the hovering volatility of a humming-bird, would dart from subject to subject, often with bewildering rapidity. In conversation he was not infrequently (to change the metaphor !) several jumps ahead of the rest of the field, of whom some managed to catch up with him but many were left toiling behind.

But it was the King's eagle eye which caused awe and

sometimes fear to those about him. No sartorial irregularity, no unusual detail of dress escaped him, and he never failed to comment. On the occasion of a Gillies' Ball at Balmoral the King had scarcely entered when he sent for the pipe-major and asked him if he saw anything amiss with the kilt of one of the pipers. The answer was in the negative. 'Why, the pleats are pressed the wrong way round; I noticed it as soon as I came into the ballroom', said the King.

Nor was this an isolated instance. At the stand-down parade of the Windsor Home Guard towards the end of the war, the King, as he passed down the line, noticed that Lord Gowrie, V.C., was wearing, embedded in his five rows of decorations, both the China Medal for the Relief of the Peking Legations and Queen Victoria's medal for the first part of the South African War. Turning to the Officer Commanding, Sir Owen Morshead,[a] the King asked : 'Have *you* ever known another case of a man's holding both these medals ? *I* never have. How on earth did he get from China to South Africa in time ?'

The King's eye for detail was not dimmed by sentiment. His first act on returning to Buckingham Palace after the wedding of Princess Elizabeth was to cause inquiries to be made as to why a certain distinguished Admiral had omitted to wear his sword.

Matters of dress had always been of importance to the King. He himself, whether in uniform or civilian clothes, achieved a standard of *soigné* impeccability which it would be difficult to surpass. He also possessed great physical elegance, his every movement, whether dancing or riding or taking a cigarette from his case and lighting it, being beautifully co-ordinated. Neither fop nor dandy, he nevertheless recognized the importance of correct attire and the part which it played in the dignity of human life. His essential practicality of mind was displayed in this, as in other facets of his character,

---

[a] Sir Owen Frederick Morshead, K.C.B., K.C.V.O., D.S.O., M.C. (b. 1893), having served with gallantry and distinction in the First World War, became a Fellow of Magdalene College, Cambridge, and Pepys Librarian. He was appointed Librarian of Windsor Castle and Assistant Keeper of the Royal Archives in 1926, in which capacity he served King George V, King Edward VIII, King George VI and Queen Elizabeth II, retiring in 1958. During the Second World War Sir Owen commanded the 9th Berkshire Battalion of the Home Guard.

for he himself designed the war-time livery, based on battle-dress, which is still worn, except on State occasions, by the pages and footmen of the Royal Household in the interests of national economy.

His Majesty would not, however, tolerate any irregularity in the wearing of uniform, and on one occasion during the war this severity transcended his sense of 'guildsmanship' between Sovereigns. King Peter of Yugoslavia came to call upon him wearing the uniform of the Royal Yugoslav Air Force, with a thin gold watch-chain threaded through the two upper pockets of the tunic. 'Is that part of the uniform?' inquired King George coldly. 'No', replied King Peter. 'Then', said his 'Koom', 'take it off. It looks damned silly and damned sloppy.'²

An example of the King's interest in modern developments and of his scrupulous attention to detail is to be found in an incident during the planning for the State Visit of the President of the French Republic in March 1950. M. Vincent Auriol's arrival at Victoria Station, where he was to be received by the King, was to be shown on television — then a compara-tively new medium — and His Majesty took the keenest interest in the preparations. 'Please arrange', he wrote to Com-mander Richard Colville, the Royal press relations officer, 'for the television camera to be placed on a platform above the train so that it can "see" the arrival from the front. When I introduce the President to the dignitaries it will "see" what is going on from the side and not from the back', and he accompanied this instruction with a sketch of how it was to be implemented. His orders were carried out to the letter and have since become regular procedure.

Not the least remarkable metamorphosis in the King's tastes was in his attitude towards works of art. The change was gradual, though steady and clearly apparent. At the time of his Accession his reaction was one of normal interest, but, as the years passed, his appreciation quickened and he developed the best kind of taste of an English country gentleman. King George's awakened interests were largely confined to the pictures at Windsor, but he took an active concern in the post-war rehabilitation of the Royal Collection as a whole. Here, again, there was a further connection with the King's strong sense of historical tradition and of the mystique of monarchy.

In addition to the pleasure which he derived from their beauty, he felt great pride of ownership in this splendid aggregate of pictures which his Tudor, Stuart and Hanoverian ancestors had made and handed down, yet regarded himself not merely as owner but also as trustee for posterity.

Nor did the King's interest in the care and maintenance of the Collection proceed along entirely conservative lines. He followed, with increasingly keen attention, the cleaning and restoration of his favourite pictures, among them Holbein's portrait of Derich Born; Gainsborough's group of the three eldest daughters of George III, which the King hung in his Audience Room at Buckingham Palace; and the set of portraits by the same artist of the family of George III, which were rearranged by the King in accordance with Gainsborough's original scheme for them.

Humour and an innate sense of fun were dominant among the King's personal traits. He had that sense of flippancy which is always endearing in human relationships, and, in the bosom of his family, would be prostrated by gales of irrepressible laughter. Nor was he above leading a 'Conga' through the halls and corridors of Buckingham Palace at the private dances given for his daughters. The jocularity of Tommy Handley's 'ITMA' programme on the wireless delighted him and, while recuperating from his illness in 1951, he had a special wireless installed in his room at Buckingham Palace in order that he might listen in to the Royal Variety Performance.

The King's wit — quick, pungent and salty — was a part of that great humanity which placed him in uncommon relationship with his people of every class. Those who served him in his household, those who ministered to him in his illness, those whose contact with him was but fleeting and transient, were at one in their impression of a man essentially human and, as such, subject to the frailties of humanity, but with an acute sensitiveness for the welfare of others and a genuine and generous gratitude to those upon whose services he counted.[a]

[a] Of this, a by no means isolated example is that of the King's visit to the sick-bed of his physician, Sir Maurice Cassidy, shortly before his death in October 1949, in order to invest him personally with the insignia of a G.C.V.O.

It was this capacity for interest and sympathy which captured the imagination and the affection of the peoples of Canada and South Africa and, indeed, of the United States, and which, in the United Kingdom, assured for King George a nation's love,

> No little thing :
> A vast dumb tenderness beyond all price.

(iv)

An admirable and delightful account of the King as a sportsman has been written by Mr. Aubrey Buxton in *The King in his Country*; indeed his sporting life at Sandringham and Balmoral provided almost His Majesty's only relaxation. He was not a man of hobbies. His father, in addition to a love for shooting, had other pastimes in his yachting and his stamp collecting. King George VI had neither of these distractions. Yachting he enjoyed, but he was not happy in the atmosphere of Cowes ; and, while he gave careful attention to the upkeep of the Royal stamp collection, he lacked the avid philatelic pleasure of King George V. Nor, though he took a keen interest in the fortunes of the Royal racing stables and was delighted with their successes, did he share that fondness for the Turf which is enjoyed by Her Majesty Queen Elizabeth II.

Moreover, his affection for Sandringham and Balmoral was deeper and more comprehensive than the facilities for sport that they afforded. King George, who, under other circumstances, might have been a capable senior naval officer or, in the view of one of his medical advisers, an efficient doctor, was essentially a country gentleman, taking a meticulous concern in the day-to-day details of his estates, the welfare of his tenants and the upkeep of his properties. In his State residences of Buckingham Palace and Windsor, as well as at Royal Lodge, Sandringham and Balmoral, which were his own property, he gave eager attention to every detail.

Indeed he wore himself out with his care for detail. No addition could be made to a cottage at either Sandringham or Balmoral, no new tenant taken on, no employee discharged, no tree cut down, without the King's approval, the decision being submitted to him personally, even if he was in London. In this correspondence he replied invariably in his own hand.

It had been as Squire of Sandringham that he had found a common basis of personal interest with President Roosevelt at Hyde Park. It was in Sandringham, where he had been born and where he was to die, that his heart delighted. 'Dear old Sandringham', King George V had called it, 'the place I love better than anywhere else in the world', and his son had inherited the sentiment. He liked, too, to think of this affection being transmitted to future generations. 'I want Lilibet & Philip to get to know it too as I have always been so happy here & I love the place', he wrote to Queen Mary;[3] and to Princess Elizabeth he wrote, when she was in Malta with her husband and Prince Charles was spending Christmas with his grandparents: 'He is too sweet stumping around the room & we shall love having him at Sandringham. He is the fifth generation to live there & I hope he will get to love the place.'

It was fitting that King George should die peacefully where he had loved so well.

(v)

It was as head of his family that King George was more profoundly happy than in any other capacity. From the first days of his marriage his home life was his refuge and safeguard against the world, and on the love and companionship of the Queen was based his lifelong contentment. As the family circle widened with the advent of his daughters so did the ambit of his happiness increase in an all-embracing affection.

The war had caused a partial separation, for the Princesses had lived at Windsor Castle, whereas the King and Queen had spent most of their time in London, though at certain periods of grave peril they slept at Windsor after their day's work at Buckingham Palace. It was frequently and regretfully in the King's mind that his daughters were being deprived of much of the entertainment and companionship which should legitimately have been theirs and he did all in his power to mitigate this in so far as war-time conditions permitted. There was, for example, an occasion in December 1940 when they took part with the children of the King's tenants at the Park School in a Nativity Play. 'Margaret as the "child" played her part remarkably well and was not shy. I wept through most of it. It is such a wonderful story', was the King's comment.[4] The Princesses were also encouraged to produce an annual pantomime, which delighted their father.

Later, as they grew older, small and informal dances were arranged for them and, whenever possible, the King himself rode with them in Windsor Great Park.

It was in the post-war years, however, that the Princesses came into full companionship with their parents. The happiness thus engendered was immense. The King watched with pride the development of their two characters along quite different lines. In Princess Elizabeth he saw emerge certain of his own traits: a love of sport, a skilled proficiency with rod and rifle and an admirable seat on horseback; and also his own combination of humour and dignity, his penetrating mind, his pragmatic common sense, his eagle eye for detail and his deep devotion to public service. All these things pleased him and, as the Princess continued to mature in her married life and earned for herself a place in the affections of his people, his pleasure increased many-fold and his pride, as father and grandfather, waxed abundantly.

In his younger daughter King George found some tastes in common with himself and others with her elder sister. Princess Margaret had the same quick mind and with it a vivacious charm, a sparkling sense of wit, an appreciation of the ludicrous, and a brilliant gift of mimicry. She also possessed an amazing ability to play the piano by ear, passing from classical items to songs and music-hall tunes of the First World War, to modern dance music, with equal facility. She it was who could always make her father laugh — even when he was angry with her — and who, perhaps more than any other of her family, could reduce him to giggles. She it was who could entertain him by the hour with songs and tunes and drolleries. Yet both she and Princess Elizabeth could talk with him on serious subjects.

So closely knit were the personalities of the King and Queen that the Princesses were apt to think of them collectively rather than as individuals. There was nothing which the daughters felt they could not discuss with their parents and there was nothing from which they were excluded. Yet they were not spoiled. In their early girlhood the King was a strict but sympathetic father, never failing to chide when necessary — and his daughters were no youthful paragons — yet always with a loving kindness which emphasized rather than diminished the effectiveness of the rebuke. He never nagged ; once the reproach had been administered it was over and done with, and an affectionate reception awaited repentance.

As the years passed and they grew to womanhood, the King desired for his daughters the utmost enjoyment of liberty compatible with their station, and himself entered into all their pleasures in so far as his busy days allowed. But he insisted on their taking their ever-increasing responsibilities with the full seriousness which these demanded. Himself a devotee to duty, he demanded equal devotion in others.

Home and family were to King George the epitome of his personal felicity. Together, he and the Queen and their daughters were united in deep happiness and mutual understanding.

(vi)

Like his father, King George VI was sincerely religious. Religion was a part of his ordered life, both as a Sovereign and as a man. He was mindful of his title of Defender of the Faith and of the unique position which he occupied in the established churches of both England and Scotland, yet at the same time no private worshipper came more humbly in prayer before his Maker.

Not only was the King a regular attendant at Divine Service but, in true Victorian tradition, he expected similar regularity in others. At Sandringham and at Balmoral he liked to see all the heads of departments on his estate present in church, together with their wives, and, if he noticed an absentee (and he always noticed), he made immediate and emphatic enquiries after his health. He himself worshipped as the Squire attending the parish church with his family and not as a Sovereign in his private chapel. By his express desire no greater notice was taken of them than of any other leading family in similar circumstances, save that they left the church before the rest of the congregation. This was true also of the children's Carol Service on Christmas Eve at Sandringham. The King and Queen, with their daughters, never missed this happiest service of the whole year, regarding it as a part of their family Christmas.

As a man of simple faith the King preferred simplicity in matters of worship. Ceremonial he loved but not ritual. The magnificent prose of the English Liturgy evoked his admiration but his practical mind boggled at certain of its anomalies. He took exception, for example, to the word 'indifferently' in the prayer for those in authority — 'that they may truly and *indifferently* minister justice' — and authorized at Sandringham the substitution of 'impartially',[a] adding characteristically: 'the other doesn't make sense'.

His position as Head of the Established Church did not render the King unmindful of the welfare of the other Christian Churches within his realms. His interest in the work of Nonconformity was great and, although a strong Protestant by conviction and vocation, he held the Roman Catholic Church in respect. He particularly esteemed the part played during the war by Cardinal Hinsley,[b] whose lifelong loyalty to the Crown, clear-sightedness and desire for Christian co-operation had aroused his admiration. When the Cardinal died in 1943 it was the King's immediate thought that he should be represented at the Requiem Mass at Westminster Cathedral, both as a mark of his respect for an eminent patriot and Churchman and as a gesture to his many Roman Catholic subjects. The advice tendered to His Majesty was, however, to the contrary, partly on the basis of precedent[c] and partly

---

[a] It is to be noted that in the 'Alternative Order of the Communion' provided by the 1928 Prayer Book the word 'impartially' is substituted for 'indifferently' in the prayer for the whole state of Christ's Church.

[b] His Eminence Arthur Cardinal Hinsley (1865–1943) was Headmaster of St. Bede's Grammar School, Bradford, from 1899 to 1904 and a parish priest from 1904 to 1917, when he became Rector of the English College at Rome. In 1927 he was appointed Visitor Apostolic to the Catholic Missions in Africa and Apostolic Delegate in Africa in 1930. He was consecrated Archbishop of Westminster in 1935 and created Cardinal two years later.

[c] King George V had not been represented at the funeral of Cardinal Bourne in 1935, nor was Her Majesty Queen Elizabeth II at that of Cardinal Griffin in 1956.

because of the danger that the Defender of the Faith might be criticized for giving such formal and public recognition to the Roman Catholic Church,[5] but it was agreed that a laudatory telegram should be dispatched in the King's name to the Bishop Auxiliary. King George, therefore, relinquished the idea of sending a representative, but only with considerable vexation.

No one was more annoyed than I when I was 'advised' not to be represented at Cardinal Hinsley's funeral [he wrote to Queen Mary]. I know how much he had done to bring his church into line with our churches here & I was going to see him & thank him personally. . . . I feel it was a great chance missed when relations are definitely better.[6]

The King's faith was sincere and profound, with a simplicity consistent with his normal and uncomplicated character. He enjoyed the discussion of religious subjects which he carried on freely and without embarrassment. A regular listener to the 'Lift up your hearts' programme on the wireless, he would not infrequently introduce the topic of the morning into his conversation at luncheon or dinner — sometimes with disconcerting directness. 'What do you think of the Ten Commandments?' he once unexpectedly asked a lady sitting next to him who, thus suddenly taxed, was somewhat inhibited in her reply.

King George's spiritual life, as distinct from his interest in matters religious, grew with advancing years. The spiritual guidance which he and the Queen had sought in preparation for their Coronation was a dominant factor throughout their lives. Always a regular communicant at the great festivals of the Church, he and his family asked for a special early celebration on the morning of their departure from Sandringham before sailing for South Africa, and a similar request was made for a special service in the house at Royal Lodge when, after his first operation, the King was unable to walk far or to kneel. This latter inability caused him great distress and, with his proper sense of conduct in all things, he repeatedly apologized for having to receive the Sacrament seated.

He made a practice of reading certain spiritual works, notably Patterson Smythe's *Life of Christ* and Bishop Carey's

Prayer, and was deeply impressed by what appeared to him to be the incontrovertibility of the arguments on the Resurrection contained in Frank Morrison's *Who moved the Stone?* But, in contrast to his lack of inhibition in conversing on religious subjects, he was shy and diffident in embarking on any discussion of the deeper spiritual issues. His references to them were oblique but eloquent of his own profound Christian faith. 'Your prayers on my behalf have been answered in no uncertain way & I am truly grateful', he wrote to a friend after his second illness.

It was in his own code of conduct that the King's spiritual life was most clearly observed. 'A king shall reign in righteousness and princes shall rule in judgment', wrote the prophet Isaiah,[7] and this was essentially true of King George. To this truth were added the salient traits of a great Christian gentleman : quiet and resolute courage ; loyalty to friends ; love of home and family ; simplicity, sincerity and frankness ; steadfastness in the path of duty ; and mindfulness of God.

CHAPTER XIII

THE LATTER YEARS

1947–1952

(i)

WITHIN two months of the return to London of the Royal Family from South Africa King George announced the engagement of his elder daughter, Princess Elizabeth, to Lieutenant Philip Mountbatten, R.N., son of Prince and Princess Andrew of Greece.[a]

Born on the island of Corfu on June 10, 1921, Prince Philip of Greece became an infant exile from his homeland a year later, when the Greek monarchy, as a result of the military débâcle in Asia Minor, suffered one of those periods of eclipse with which it has been intermittently afflicted. The torrent of Turkish nationalism, newly released by Mustapha Kemal Pasha, not only swept the Greek army out of Asia but also the Greek monarch from his throne. King Constantine abdicated (for the second time) in favour of his eldest son, the Diadoch George, who himself ended his first tenure of the throne, a short and unhappy one, in December 1923.

Before this date, however, King Constantine's youngest brother, Prince Andrew, who had had the misfortune to command one of the defeated Greek army corps, had narrowly escaped the blood-bath with which the Revolutionary Committee of General Plastiras vented the vengeance of the new régime upon the leaders of the old, and which had resulted in the judicial murder of three ex-Premiers, two former Ministers

---

[a] Prince Andrew of Greece married, in 1903, Princess Alice, eldest daughter of Admiral of the Fleet Prince Louis of Battenberg, first Marquess of Milford Haven. Their family consisted, in addition to Prince Philip who was the youngest child, of four daughters: Princess Margarita (b. 1905) married Gottfried, Hereditary Prince of Hohenlohe-Langenburg; Princess Theodora (b. 1906) married Prince Bertold Frederik, Margrave of Baden; Princess Cecilia (b. 1911) married the Grand Duke George of Hesse-and-the-Rhine and, with him and their two sons, was killed in an air crash in 1937; and Princess Sophie (b. 1914) who married, firstly, Prince Christopher of Hesse and, after his death on active service in 1943, secondly, Prince George of Hanover. Prince Andrew died in Paris in 1944.

WITH PRINCE CHARLES OF EDINBURGH
OCTOBER 2, 1950

SANDRINGHAM, CHRISTMAS 1951

and the Commander-in-Chief of the Army.ᵃ   Only the personal intervention of King George V and other sovereigns
had saved Prince Andrew from a like fate.   Instead, he was
sentenced to deprivation of rank and banishment for life, and
with his wife and family found refuge in Paris.

The tragedy which had overwhelmed the Royal House of
Greece, and the bitter experiences through which they themselves had passed, determined Prince Philip's parents that
their son should be brought up as far removed as possible from
the dangers and intrigues of Greek politics.   The only country
where those of royal birth seemed safe was Britain, and at the
age of eight Prince Philip's upbringing was confided to the
British branch of his mother's family.   To all intents and purposes he became a second son to Lord Milford Haven,ᵇ and,
on his death in 1938, the guardianship was assumed by his
younger brother, Lord Louis Mountbatten.

After four years at 'Old Tabor School' at Cheam in Surrey,ᶜ
Prince Philip came under the influence of that educational
genius Dr. Kurt Hahn, who had been Prince Max of Baden's
personal adviser during that unhappy statesman's period of
office in 1918 as the Kaiser's last Chancellor.   In 1920 Prince
Max had set aside a wing of the Schloss Salem as a modern
public school which, under the guidance of Dr. Hahn, was to
combine the best of both the British and German methods of
character-building and the instilling of knowledge.   In ten
years Salem School had grown from a brave adventure of four
pupils to an established college with five hundred boarders, and
the system on which it was based had come to be recognized
throughout Europe as one of the most daringly successful
educational experiments of our time.

To Salem, therefore, Prince Philip went in 1934, but his
stay there was not of long duration.   There was no room in

ᵃ On November 18, 1922, MM. Gounaris, Stratos, Baltatzes, Theotokes, and
Protopapadakes and General Hadjianestes were condemned to death by an
extraordinary court-martial and shot.   The executions shocked Europe, and
Great Britain withdrew her Minister from Athens.

ᵇ George Louis Victor Henry Sergius Mountbatten, second Marquess of
Milford Haven, G.C.V.O. (1892–1938), was the elder son of Prince Louis of
Battenberg.   He married Nadejda, daughter of the Grand Duke Michael of Russia
and Countess Torby, and was succeeded by his only son, David.

ᶜ Shortly after the departure of Prince Philip, the school was removed from
Cheam to Headley, near Newbury in Berkshire, where it is known as Cheam
School.   It was here that Prince Charles became a boarder in 1957.

Hitler's Germany for men of Kurt Hahn's liberal outlook and, moreover, his earlier association with Prince Max of Baden, 'the Man of November 1918', marked him from the start as a target for Nazi abuse and persecution. He was arrested as an 'enemy of the state' and his release was with difficulty obtained by the personal intervention of Prince Bertold of Baden with President von Hindenburg, backed by the protests of friends in Britain and elsewhere in Europe. Undeterred by fate, Dr. Hahn re-established his school at Gordonstoun in Morayshire and thither Prince Philip followed him.

With the sea-going traditions of the British branch of the Mountbattens in his blood it was not unnatural that Prince Philip should select the Royal Navy as his career. He entered Dartmouth in 1939 and it was during the Royal visit to the College in the summer of that year that he first met Princess Elizabeth.[a] He was eighteen years old at the time and she thirteen.

Prince Philip had within him, in addition to other great gifts of grace and character, the attributes of a born naval officer, a fact which had been early descried by Dr. Hahn.

He is universally trusted, liked and respected [his headmaster had written prophetically in December 1938]. He has the greatest sense of service of all the boys in the school. Prince Philip is a born leader, but will need the exacting demands of a great service to do justice to himself. His best is outstanding — his second best is not good enough. Prince Philip will make his mark in any profession where he will have to prove himself in a full trial of strength. His gifts would run to waste if he was soon condemned to lead a life where neither superior officers nor the routine of the day forced him to tap his hidden resources.[1]

This forecast and analysis of character were fulfilled in every respect. Prince Philip's career as a naval officer was indeed outstanding. He won the King's Dirk at Dartmouth. His first captain's opinion of him was succinct: 'My best midshipman'; and his first admiral wrote of him that he was the best junior commanding officer in the Fleet. His conduct in the battleship *Valiant* at the Battle of Cape Matapan[b]

---

[a] See above, pp. 396-7.
[b] On March 28, 1941, the British Fleet, in co-operation with the R.A.F. operating from Greece, caught an Italian squadron off Cape Matapan, sinking four cruisers and three destroyers and severely damaging several other warships.

earned him his Captain's commendation in the following terms: 'Thanks to his alertness and appreciation of the situation, we were able to sink in five minutes two eight-inch-gun Italian cruisers'.

This was the man with whom Princess Elizabeth had been in love from their first meeting. A cousinly correspondence was maintained throughout the war and Prince Philip spent several of his rare leaves at Windsor, where on at least one occasion he entertained King George with an account of his adventures in the Mediterranean.[2] Though the situation between him and Princess Elizabeth was clear, both the King and Queen agreed to ignore it for the present, and when King George of Greece spoke to them on behalf of his young kinsman he received no encouragement.

We both think she is too young for that now, as she has never met any young men of her own age [the King wrote to Queen Mary]. . . . I like Philip. He is intelligent, has a good sense of humour & thinks about things in the right way. . . . We are going to tell George that P. had better not think any more about it for the present.[3]

Prince Philip meanwhile was anxious to regularize his future status as a British naval officer, a matter not without its complications. Though he had been domiciled in Britain since the age of eight and had served in the Navy throughout the war, his position had only been covered by the temporary Defence (Armed Services) Regulations of 1939. According to Admiralty Regulations he could only receive a permanent commission if he became a British subject, and this he was most anxious to do. King George, however, with his strict sense of correct conduct between Sovereigns, felt that the King of Greece must first approve such action. He advised Lord Louis Mountbatten, who was urging his nephew's desires, to consult the Greek King in Cairo, and that monarch's consent was obtained in the autumn of 1944.

The matter hung fire until the following spring when, on the King's initiative, it was raised with the Home Office and became a matter of earnest discussion between the Home Secretary, the Prime Minister and the Secretary of State for Foreign Affairs. For, though Prince Philip was entirely willing to renounce his membership of the Greek and Danish Royal

Families, and the King of Greece had given his assent to this, there were other aspects of foreign policy to be considered.

The dramatic visit of Mr. Churchill and Mr. Eden to Athens on Christmas Day 1944, which had resulted in the appointment of Archbishop Damaskinos as Regent of Greece and General Plastiras as Prime Minister, had been followed by a period of uneasy political activity, with lapses into armed conflict between Right and Left. It was far from clear in the spring of 1945 that King George of Greece would return to his throne.

In these circumstances it was felt that the naturalization of a member of the Greek Royal House as a British subject would be open to misrepresentation from two aspects. On the one hand, it might be said that this was an indication of British support for the Greek Royalists; on the other, it might be held to be a sign that the future prospects of the Greek monarchy were so dark that members of the Greek Royal House were seeking refuge in other countries. His Majesty was therefore advised by his Ministers that it would be better to postpone the question of Prince Philip's naturalization until after March 1946 when the Greek General Election and the plebiscite on the monarchy would have taken place, and this advice was adopted.

The plebiscite resulted in a declaration calling upon the King of Greece to return to Athens, which he did on September 28, 1946. This, however, provided a further source of delay in the matter of Prince Philip's affairs, since it was now held that it would be unhelpful to the Greek King's cause if a member of his House, in the direct succession, were to renounce his Greek nationality immediately after the King had returned to his throne.

By the close of 1946, however, the matter of Prince Philip's naturalization was once more in train, but there remained the vexed question of the name by which he would be known. On the precedent of the two daughters of Prince Christian of Schleswig-Holstein and Princess Helena,[a] who, at the time of

---

[a] On July 5, 1866, Queen Victoria's third daughter, Princess Helena Augusta Victoria, was married to Prince Christian of Schleswig-Holstein. They had five children: three sons, of whom the eldest died at Pretoria during the South African War, the second succeeded as Duke of Schleswig-Holstein in 1921 and died ten years later, and the third died in infancy, and two daughters, Princess Helena Victoria (1870-1948) and Princess Marie-Louise (1872-1956).

the great shedding of German titles in 1917, merely dropped 'Schleswig-Holstein' from their names and retained the style of 'Highness', the King was prepared to grant the right and privilege of the title 'His Royal Highness Prince Philip', and this was agreed to by the Prime Minister and Lord Mountbatten. The matter, however, was unexpectedly disposed of by Prince Philip himself, who announced, with some determination, that, while he greatly appreciated His Majesty's offer, he preferred not to take advantage of it but to be known, after his naturalization as a British subject, simply as 'Lieutenant Philip . . . R.N.'. This decision both pleased and impressed King George, who at once assented to it.

The question of title being thus settled, there remained only the problem of finding a suitable surname. The Royal House of Greece and Denmark has no family name and the suggestion of 'Oldcastle' — an anglicized form of Oldenburg, whence the House of Schleswig-Holstein-Sonderburg-Glucksburg had originally sprung — was not well thought of. It remained for the Home Secretary, Mr. Chuter Ede,[a] to suggest that the new British subject take his mother's name of Mountbatten. This was at once agreed to by all parties [4] and the announcement was accordingly made in the *London Gazette* of March 18, 1947.

At this time the Royal Family were in South Africa and, though it was popularly believed that Prince Philip's naturalization was but a preliminary to the announcement of his engagement to Princess Elizabeth, of which rumours had been in circulation for some time past and officially denied, King George still withheld his consent. He had always liked Prince Philip and had grown to esteem him highly, being most favourably impressed by his conduct in the matter of his name and title, but he still found it difficult to believe that his elder daughter had really fallen in love with the first young man she had ever met, and perhaps he also dreaded losing her from that compact and happy family circle which had been his delight and solace since his early married days in Royal Lodge. In

---

[a] Rt. Hon. James Chuter Ede, C.H. (b. 1882), sat as a Labour Member of Parliament for Mitcham, Surrey, in 1923, for South Shields, 1929–1931, and since 1935. He was Chairman of the Surrey County Council from 1933 to 1937 and served as Home Secretary in Mr. Attlee's Government from 1945 to 1951.

any case, he was anxious that no final decision should be reached until after the conclusion of the South African tour, by which time Princess Elizabeth would have come of age.

On the return of the Royal Family to England, however, there could no longer be any question as to the wishes and affections of both parties, and their pertinacity and patience were rewarded when, on July 10, the following announcement was made from Buckingham Palace :

It is with the greatest pleasure that The King and Queen announce the betrothal of their dearly beloved daughter The Princess Elizabeth to Lieutenant Philip Mountbatten, R.N., son of the late Prince Andrew of Greece and Princess Andrew (Princess Alice of Battenberg), to which union The King has gladly given his consent.

The announcement of the betrothal evoked a new upsurging of loyalty and devotion to the Monarchy and to the Royal Family. Princess Elizabeth had already won a place in the hearts of her father's peoples, the more so by reason of that moving act of dedication to their service and welfare which she had so recently performed and which had been so warmly and gratefully received. There was also the added thought that she, who was by birth the leader and representative of the youth of the Commonwealth, would make her representation the clearer by being withdrawn a little from the King, the universal representative, and would multiply its power by sharing it with another who was also young.

But the pleasure of the public was all the greater because it was apparent that the engagement could have had no motive but the impulse of their own hearts to bring this young couple together. The people were delighted with Princess Elizabeth's choice of a husband. Lieutenant Mountbatten's manifest charm and handsome appearance, his gallant war record and his obvious devotion, made a special appeal to all that love of romance and affection for the Monarchy which lies so close beneath the surface of the so-called 'undemonstrative' British public. 'By a happy accident', wrote one, 'the Princess has bestowed her hand in such a way that two apparently divergent opinions about the qualifications of a consort are simultaneously satisfied — the opinions of those on the one hand who would wish him to be a British subject and of those on the other who consider Royal blood essential'.*[a] [5]

Four months later they were married, on November 20 ; but before this event King George took occasion to mark his pleasure and approval by bestowing honours upon both of them.

I am giving the Garter to Lilibet next Tuesday, November 11th [he wrote to Queen Mary], so that she will be senior to Philip, to whom I am giving it on November 19th. I have arranged that he shall be created a Royal Highness & that the titles of his peerage will be

Baron Greenwich, Earl of Merioneth
& Duke of Edinburgh.

These will be announced in the morning papers of November 20th, including the Garter.

It is a great deal to give a man all at once, but I know Philip understands his new responsibilities on his marriage to Lilibet.[b] [6]

The wedding of Princess Elizabeth and Lieutenant Philip Mountbatten was solemnized in Westminster Abbey with the pomp and dignity imperatively required by a King's daughter who would be Queen hereafter, yet with all the beauty and simplicity of the marriage rite of the Church of England, which, as the Archbishop of Canterbury emphasized in his address, was 'in all essentials exactly the same as it would be for any cottager who might be married this afternoon in some small country church in a remote village in the dales'.[c] Kings,

[a] Queen Elizabeth II and Prince Philip are third cousins through the lineage of Queen Victoria, second cousins once removed through King Christian IX of Denmark, and fourth cousins once removed through collateral descendants of King George III.

[b] The announcement of the conferring of these honours upon Prince Philip was duly made in the press of November 20, 1947, and he wore the insignia of the Garter at the wedding, but, because the King's intentions had been kept strictly secret and the order of the service had to be printed well in advance, the name of the bridegroom appeared in it as 'Lieutenant Philip Mountbatten, R.N.'. He signed the register simply as 'Philip'. The matter of the Duke of Edinburgh's title remained to some degree an anomaly. He had been created a 'Royal Highness' but not a Prince, though he became popularly known as 'Prince Philip'. This situation was ended on February 22, 1957, when, on the advice of her Prime Minister, Mr. Macmillan, the Queen granted to the Duke of Edinburgh the style and title of a Prince of the United Kingdom in recognition of the services which he had rendered to the country and to the life of the Commonwealth.

[c] Shortly after the announcement of the Royal betrothal the Archbishop of Canterbury drew the attention of the King to the fact that, though Prince Philip had worshipped regularly as an Anglican throughout his service in the Royal Navy, he did in fact remain a member of the Greek Orthodox Church into which

Queens and Princes were met together in one of the largest gatherings of royalty, regnant and exiled, of the century,[a] and there were also present in the great assemblage of distinguished guests those veteran leaders of the Commonwealth, Mr. Churchill, Mr. Mackenzie King and General Smuts.   The British public greeted the occasion with manifest rejoicing, welcoming the opportunity to reaffirm their loyalty to the Crown and their good-will towards the bridal couple, while, by means of broadcasting and television, people in all countries were able to follow the ceremonies with enthusiastic interest.

Nor was the Royal wedding merely an event in the history of the British Commonwealth.   To every foreigner present it was an object lesson, doubly expressive in the existing distressed state of Europe, of the stability of Britain's political institutions, and of the unity of the nation in its respect for tradition and its loyalty to the throne.   It was a lesson which was well marked and not without its value.   As a distinguished foreign guest at the party at Buckingham Palace expressed it : 'A country which can throw such a party as that will never go under'.

For King George it was a day of mixed emotions.   His love for his daughter, his pleasure in her happiness and his confidence in her future were mingled with a deep sorrow at losing her from his own home.   Something of all this he wrote to Princess Elizabeth in a heart-warming letter during her honeymoon.

. . . I was so proud of you & thrilled at having you so close to me on our long walk in Westminster Abbey, but when I handed your hand to the Archbishop I felt that I had lost something very precious.   You were so calm & composed during the Service &

---

he had been baptized.   The Archbishop suggested that all concerned 'might feel it to be more fitting and happy that he should have his position regularized as a member of the Church of England' by being formally received into that body.[7]   This proposal received unanimous approval and at the King's suggestion the ceremony was performed privately by the Archbishop in the Chapel of Lambeth Palace.   (*The Times*, October 4, 1947.)

[a] There were present at the Royal wedding the King and Queen of Denmark, the Kings of Norway, Rumania and Iraq, the King and Queen of Yugoslavia, the Queen of the Hellenes, the Princess Regent and Prince Bernhard of the Netherlands, the Prince Regent of Belgium, the Crown Prince and Crown Princess of Sweden, the Count and Countess of Barcelona, Queen Helen of Rumania, Queen Victoria Eugénie of Spain, Prince Jean and Princess Elizabeth of Luxembourg, and the Duchess of Aosta.

PRINCESS ELIZABETH'S WEDDING, November 20, 1947

1. Prince George of Denmark
2. Princess George of Greece
3. King Peter of Yugoslavia
4. Queen Alexandra of Yugoslavia
5. Lord Mountbatten of Burma
6. Count of Barcelona
7. Prince Bernhard of the Netherlands
8. King of Norway
9. Prince Charles of Belgium
10. Prince George of Greece
11. Prince René of Bourbon-Parma
12. King of Denmark
13. King of Rumania
14. Prince Michael of Bourbon-Parma
15. Duchess of Aosta
16. Hereditary Prince of Luxemburg
17. Princess Eugénie of Greece
18. Lady Milford Haven
19. Princess Andrew of Greece
20. Lady Mountbatten of Burma
21. Duchess of Kent
22. Princess Juliana of the Netherlands
23. Queen of Greece
24. Queen Mary
25. Queen Victoria Eugénie
26. Queen of Denmark
27. Crown Princess of Sweden
28. Princess Margaret
29. Lord Milford Haven
30. Princess Elizabeth
31. Duke of Edinburgh
32. Princess Alexandra of Kent
33. The King

34. The Queen
35. Duke of Gloucester
36. Duchess of Gloucester
37. Princess René of Bourbon-Parma
38. Princess Marie Louise
39. Crown Prince of Sweden
40. Prince William of Gloucester
41. Prince Michael of Kent
42. Prince Richard of Gloucester
43. Princess Helena Victoria

said your words with such conviction, that I knew everything was all right.

I am so glad you wrote & told Mummy that you think the long wait before your engagement & the long time before the wedding was for the best. I was rather afraid that you had thought I was being hard hearted about it. I was so anxious for you to come to South Africa as you knew. Our family, us four, the 'Royal Family' must remain together with additions of course at suitable moments!! I have watched you grow up all these years with pride under the skilful direction of Mummy, who as you know is the most marvellous person in the World in my eyes, & I can, I know, always count on you, & now Philip, to help us in our work. Your leaving us has left a great blank in our lives but do remember that your old home is still yours & do come back to it as much & as often as possible. I can see that you are sublimely happy with Philip which is right but don't forget us is the wish of

Your ever loving & devoted

PAPA.

(ii)

The bestowal of the Order of the Garter upon Princess Elizabeth and her husband at the time of their wedding and their installation at Windsor on April 23, 1948, on the occasion of the six-hundredth anniversary of the founding of the Order, were a part of the deep and dedicated interest which King George evinced in the status and conduct of this oldest order of chivalry, of which the Sovereign is head.

Since the foundation of the Order by Edward III in 1348 the right of bestowal had always been a prerogative of the Sovereign — a prerogative which, however, had been exercised under varying circumstances. Until the eighteenth century a system obtained of election by the existing Knights for the purpose of affording the King assistance and advice in making new appointments. On the death of a Knight the members of the Order were summoned to meet their Sovereign and, a quorum of six being required, each presented to him the names of nine candidates 'without reproach'. These nominations were laid by the Prelate of the Order before the King, who chose 'of them that be named he that shall have the most voices and also he that the Sovereign shall esteem to be the most profitable to his Crown and Realm'.[a]

---

[a] The Twentieth Statute of the Order of the Garter.

At what exact date this practice was discontinued is uncertain, but Charles II certainly conferred the Garter freely upon his illegitimate sons and it is probable also that George I took his principal Minister's advice on appointments to the Order because of his lack of knowledge of English persons and politics — and indeed of the English language. By gradual process, therefore, an established but unwritten custom had developed, accepted by both Sovereign and Premier, whereby the one would make no appointments to the Order except on the recommendation of the other.

Thus, though the Prime Minister of the day exercised the greatest care in offering his counsel to the Sovereign in order that the high purpose and irreproachable standard of the membership of the Order should be maintained, it was undeniable that the Garter had become a 'political' honour bestowed in accordance with party recommendation.[a] It had also lost something of its Christian character since, in deference to the demands of foreign policy, it had been conferred at one time or another upon the Shah of Persia and the Emperor of Japan.

King George VI's interest in the future of the Garter and his desire to see it redeemed from the influence of politics dated from the earliest days of his reign. He believed sincerely that this great and oldest of the orders of chivalry, which he had felt so honoured to receive from the hands of his father[b] and of which he was most proud to be the head, should be non-political in character. This was a part of his strong belief in the *mystique* of monarchy, of which the Fount of Honour was so vital an attribute, and, while he fully recognized the necessity of 'political' honours, he was equally convinced that the bestowal of membership in the major Orders, the Garter, the Thistle and the Patrick, should, like the Order of Merit, be in the unfettered gift of the Sovereign.

He had had it in mind to raise the issue with Mr. Chamberlain but the war had intervened. At its close, however, there were seven vacancies in the membership of the Garter and the existing political situation was confederate to the fulfilment of

---

[a] For an illuminating if fictional discussion of this point see chapter xliv of Anthony Trollope's *The Prime Minister.*

[b] See above, p. 100.

the King's desires in filling them. Apart from the great commanders on sea and land and in the air, many of the possible
recipients in the political field were active members of the
Conservative Party whom a Labour Government could scarcely
be expected to recommend. Moreover, the Labour Party were
essentially chary of honours as a whole.

In seeking, therefore, for likely candidates, King George
rejected the romantic suggestion of Mr. Churchill, who shared
his views and had himself twice refused the Garter, that he
return to the principles of the Founder of the Order, Edward III,
and appoint 'Young paladins',[8] and posed the question directly
to his new Prime Minister in May 1946.

> I spoke to Attlee about the future K.G.s [he wrote in his diary].
> His people are against accepting honours & most recipients would
> have to be of the other party. I want it non-political & in my
> gift. Naturally I would tell him my ideas.[9]

From this conversation there ensued consultations between
the Prime Minister and Mr. Churchill and others of the King's
advisers, with the result that on July 23 Mr. Attlee was enabled
to tender advice to the King that not only the Garter but also
the Thistle and the Patrick should be conferred by His Majesty
on the same basis as that of the Order of Merit, namely without
any formal submission by the Prime Minister.[10] This principle
had been clearly established in 1902 when the Order of Merit
was founded and the new procedure for the great orders of
chivalry became similar to that which the Sovereign had
always retained in respect of his near relations and members
of foreign Royal Families, namely the right to confer after
consultation with, but not on advice from, his Ministers.[11]

King George was highly satisfied with the outcome of his
negotiations, which had resulted in so favourable a solution
in accordance with his wishes and with what he believed to
be right and proper. In a letter to Queen Mary he informed
her of the new status of the Order, at the same time acquainting her with his intended appointments, the choice of which
was particularly happy.

> . . . At the moment there are 7 vacancies in the Order of the
> Garter & after a talk with the P.M. & Winston I have arranged
> for the Garter & Thistle appts. to be in my hands like those of the

Order of Merit. In December the following new Knights will be announced.

> Ld. Addison, Ld. Cranborne, Ld. Mountbatten, Ld. Alanbrooke, Ld. Alexander, Ld. Portal (airman), and Ld. Montgomery.

Addison accepts as Leader of the House of Lords & Bobbety [Lord Cranborne [a]] as Opposition Leader. The others for their great work in the War.

As there are 6 out of 7 in this country I feel it would be nice were I to have a special Investiture for them in the Bow Room, having the other Knights present as well.

I do hope you will be able to come to it & the date I suggest is Tuesday Dec. 17th at 3.15 pm. I propose that the Knights should wear Mantles & collars over plain clothes, so would you wear yours & the special hat. If you & Elizabeth would like to wear the riband & star please do on a day dress.

I am working out the details of the ceremony with Garter King of Arms. I want to give you as much notice as possible.[12]

The announcement of the reversion to the King of the appointment of Knights of the Garter and of those persons whom he had thus chosen to honour was made on December 7, 1946, and ten days later, as he had planned, His Majesty held his special investiture at Buckingham Palace. It was only the second such ceremony to be held in the twentieth century and the King applied himself diligently to the ordering of the procedure, from which, with the passage of time, various essential parts had come to be omitted. He was greatly concerned that emphasis should be laid upon the fundamental principles of the Order and particularly upon its Christian character. To this end he decided to depart from precedent and himself address the assembled Knights. He did so in words of moving simplicity:

This is the first Investiture held since before the Great War (1914–18) and the first in which any of the present Knights have taken part. Our Order, besides being one of Chivalry, is above all a Christian one. During the actual Investiture you will find that the Ancient Admonitions will be said as the separate emblems of

---

[a] Lord Cranborne's father, Lord Salisbury, was also a Knight of the Garter at this time, and it is believed that this is the first occasion for five hundred years that father and son were both members of the Order simultaneously. The previous occasion was that of the father and brother of Elizabeth Woodville, King Edward IV's Queen.

the Order are presented, signifying their Christian purport. These Admonitions have been revived after many years of disuse.

His own account of the proceedings is given in his diary for the day (December 17) :

In the afternoon I held a Chapter of the Order of the Garter, the first one since 1911. All the Knights except Ld. Derby were present, & I invested six out of seven of the Knights-elect. Lds. Addison, Cranborne, Mountbatten, Alanbrooke, Portal & Montgomery. Ld. Alexander was in Canada. The ceremony I had to adapt from ancient usage modernising it to suit the time we live in. The old Admonitions were said as each emblem of the Order was presented & the new Knights took the Oath. I held it in the Bow Room. We all wore our Garter Mantles & Collars over plain clothes or service uniform. I thought it went very well.[13]

The King's deep interest and concern in the great Order of which he was the Sovereign were not confined to the ceremonies of the Garter itself. Once, on the occasion of a production of *Henry VIII* at Stratford, he visited Mr. Anthony Quayle in his dressing-room, congratulated him on his performance and explained to him, illustrating the point on his own leg, how the Garter should be correctly worn.

The six-hundredth anniversary of the founding of the Most Noble Order of the Garter was celebrated by a special Chapter meeting of the Knights held on April 23, 1948 (St. George's Day). On this occasion the full pageantry of the Order was revived and in the Throne Room of Windsor Castle King George invested Princess Elizabeth with the insignia of a Lady of the Most Noble Order, and the Duke of Edinburgh and five others [a] as Knights Companion, repeating the address which he had composed two years before.

After this ceremony, the King and Queen, attended by twenty-two Knights together with the Officers of the Order and the gorgeous habiliments of Heralds, Pursuivants and Kings of Arms, went in procession from the Castle to a special service in St. George's Chapel. The day was one of perfect spring weather. Sunlight glinted on the helmets and armour and the drawn sabres of the Household Cavalry and upon the jewelled insignia of the Knights. The crowds of spectators

---

[a] The other Knights to be invested on this occasion were Lord Alexander, the Duke of Portland, Lord Harlech, the Earl of Scarbrough and Lord Cranworth.

who thronged the processional way cheered their Sovereign and his Consort as they passed amid the stately pomp in which Britain excels and in which the British people delight. They had been starved of it during the gloom of the war years and the brief glimpses of colour and splendour afforded them amid the grim distress of post-war austerity were especially welcomed. The crowds acclaimed the King and Queen enthusiastically and they cheered again as the new Royal Knight and his Lady of Grace went on their way.

Until the reign of King George it would appear that the gatherings of the Order had been fortuitous for at least a hundred and fifty years, and it was His Majesty's intention that after the six-hundredth anniversary they should be held annually. In 1949 his illness made this impossible, but in 1950 there was a full procession and Service at St. George's and a year later, on May 9, 1951, the King invested King Frederik IX of Denmark, together with the Duke of Wellington, Lord Fortescue and Lord Allendale.

(iii)

Three days after the majestic ceremonies of the sexcentenary of the Order of the Garter, King George and Queen Elizabeth celebrated a more intimate anniversary; April 26, 1948, was their Silver Wedding Day. Though the event was essentially and primarily a personal one, it was made the occasion of yet another great and spontaneous demonstration of love and loyalty. In brilliant sunshine the King and Queen drove in a state landau to St. Paul's through cheering crowds, to attend, in the midst of their family and before a congregation of some four hundred people, a service of thanksgiving and celebration. In the afternoon they motored in an open car through twenty miles of London streets and were again given a great ovation. On their return to the Palace they were called several times to the balcony to acknowledge further enthusiastic manifestations, and that evening both of them made broadcasts.

It was a day both of thanksgiving and re-dedication: thanksgiving by King George and Queen Elizabeth for this long period of happiness together and by their people for their

Sovereign and his Consort, who for twenty-five years had spared themselves no effort and shrunk from no danger to make themselves the most richly representative family in all their dominions; re-dedication of both the King and Queen to the welfare and service of their peoples and of their peoples' loyalty and devotion to them.

'A princely marriage is the brilliant edition of a universal fact, and as such it rivets mankind', Walter Bagehot had written eighty years before. 'We have come to believe that it is natural to have a virtuous sovereign, and that domestic virtues are as likely to be found on thrones as they are eminent when there.' For the twenty-five years of their married life and the eleven years of the King's reign, King George and Queen Elizabeth had given to the world an epitome of these principles. The high promise which they had shown as Duke and Duchess of York had been amply fulfilled in the years which had followed when, together, they had shared the perils and trials of the nation. With their daughters they had come to be the conjoined and united symbol of the whole national life of their peoples, their work and play, their arts and sciences, and especially of the kindly relations of family life. Of King George, with his Queen at his side and inseparable from him in the thoughts of all, it could be said, in the simple words of the Scriptures: 'All the people took notice of it and it pleased them; as whatsoever the King did pleased all the people'.[a]

It was this general and popular approbation of Their Majesties which gave to the demonstrations at the time of their Silver Wedding a special significance. It was widely (if vainly) hoped that Britain was on the threshold of a period of economic improvement and that the years to come would bring a greater sense of well-earned peace and enjoyment for all and especially to the King and Queen. All shared the prayer of the Poet Laureate:

> To These, to-day (to them a sacred day)
> Our hopes become a praying that the stress
> Of these, their cruel years, may pass away
> And happy years succeed, and Wisdom bless.[b]

[a] 2 Samuel iii. 36.
[b] John Masefield, 'Lines Written on the Silver Wedding of the King and Queen' (*The Times*, April 26, 1948).

To the King and Queen themselves these widespread up-
surgings of loyalty and devotion, evidence of which poured in
upon them from every corner of the Commonwealth, came as
a genuine though gratifying surprise. 'We were both dumb-
founded over our reception', King George wrote to his mother.
'We have received so many nice letters from all and sundry
thanking us for what we have tried to do during these years.
It does spur us on to further efforts.'[14]

And, indeed, it seemed at the outset of 1948 that a new
chapter of service and activity was opening before the King.
For on March 6 it had been announced that, with the Queen
and Princess Margaret, he proposed in the following spring
to make a visit to Australia and New Zealand, similar to those
which he had made as Sovereign to Canada and South Africa.
Apart from the cares of state, which always weighed heavily
upon him, he appeared to be in excellent health, and in the
month of April, a crowded month, during which there occurred,
among other exacting engagements, the unveiling of the
memorial to President Roosevelt in Grosvenor Square, the
Garter ceremonies and the Silver Wedding celebrations, it had
been openly remarked how well he looked.

These appearances were, however, misleading. The King
had not fully recovered from the war years which had exhausted him alike in mind and body. The South African tour,
though he had greatly enjoyed it, had fatigued him greatly —
he had lost 17 lb. in the course of it — and his temperament
was not one which facilitated a rapid replenishing of nervous
and physical reserves. For some time he had been suffering
from cramp in both legs — he had first noticed it in January
— and, though he at first made no mention of it, it became
progressively worse, so that by August he was in 'discomfort
most of the time'.[a] At the beginning of his holiday at Balmoral
he experienced an improvement. Exercise, he found, did him
good and he was not physically tired at the end of a day's
shooting, but by October there was a perceptible deterioration;
his left foot was numb all day and the pain kept him awake
at night. Later the main centre of trouble shifted to the right
foot.

[a] King George kept a rough record of the development of his symptoms which
he handed to his doctors at their first consultation.

SANDRINGHAM, NOVEMBER 1949

The King returned to London on October 8 and a fortnight later (October 20) summoned Sir Morton Smart [a] who
had treated him for many years for strains and similar ail-
ments. Sir Morton was gravely alarmed at the condition in
which he found the King's right foot and insisted upon having
the further opinion of His Majesty's general medical adviser,
Sir Maurice Cassidy. In the meantime he gave the patient
treatment which to some extent relieved him.

The Royal Calendar was very full at the time. The King
and Queen of Denmark arrived on a visit on October 24 and
two days later the King opened Parliament in full state for
the first time since the war. It was not until October 30 that
he was examined by Sir Maurice Cassidy, Sir Morton Smart
and Sir Thomas Dunhill.[b] All were agreed on the King's
serious condition. They at once decided to call in Professor
James Learmonth,[c] of Edinburgh, one of the greatest authorities on vascular complaints in the country, and at the same
time they warned Sir Alan Lascelles that, in their opinion,
the proposed visit to Australia and New Zealand should not,
in the King's interests, be undertaken. Such a decision was
a serious matter, for the planning of the Royal Tour had
already reached an advanced stage of preparation, and
Brigadier Norman Gwatkin [d] was about to leave for Australia
for the co-ordination of arrangements in Canberra and the
State capitals. So strong were the representations of the
doctors that Brigadier Gwatkin was advised to postpone his
departure until after X-ray photographs and blood tests could
be taken, and until Professor Learmonth had made his examination on November 12.

[a] Commander Sir Morton Smart, G.C.V.O., D.S.O., M.D., Ch.B. (1878–1956),
had had, as an R.N.V.R. officer, an adventurous career in the First World
War. He became Manipulative Surgeon to King George VI in 1937 and Extra
Manipulative Surgeon in 1949.
[b] Sir Thomas Peel Dunhill, G.C.V.O., C.M.G., M.D., F.R.C.S. (1876–1957),
served as Surgeon to King George V, as Serjeant-Surgeon to King George VI,
and as Extra-Surgeon to Queen Elizabeth II.
[c] Sir James Learmonth, K.C.V.O., C.B.E., M.B., Ch.M., F.R.C.S. (b. 1895),
having been Regius Professor of Surgery at Aberdeen University from 1932, was
appointed Professor of Surgery at the University of Edinburgh in 1939 and Regius
Professor of Clinical Surgery in 1946.
[d] Brigadier Sir Norman Gwatkin, K.C.V.O., D.S.O. (b. 1899), Assistant
Comptroller of the Lord Chamberlain's Office since 1936 and an Extra Equerry
to King George VI and Queen Elizabeth II.

In the meantime the King had insisted upon fulfilling a number of fatiguing engagements, including a review of the Territorial Army in Hyde Park on October 31 and the Remembrance Day Service at the Cenotaph on Sunday, November 7. He persisted in attending the latter ceremony against medical advice, and, anxious as ever to spare others the burden of additional worry, he would allow no word of his serious condition to be told to Princess Elizabeth, who was then expecting the birth of her first child.

Professor Learmonth's examination on November 12 disclosed — and those also present concurred in his diagnosis *ᵃ* — that the King's condition was one of early arteriosclerosis; there was a danger of gangrene developing and at first there was grave fear that his right leg might have to be amputated.

The question of the Royal Tour was also debated. The doctors were unanimously agreed that it should not be undertaken, but the King was determined to go if he could, partly because he very much wanted to do so, partly because of the great disappointment and inconvenience which he knew a postponement or cancellation would occasion to the peoples of Australia and New Zealand, and partly because of his inherent disinclination to give up anything under any circumstances. He asked that consideration should be given to the alternative of a shorter programme with much less work, but on this point also his medical advisers were adamant. They could not agree even to a curtailed tour when at that moment they all believed that amputation was unavoidable. The King's objections were finally overcome on November 16 and, after the cancellation of the tour had been communicated to his Prime Ministers in the United Kingdom, Australia and New Zealand, the following bulletin was made public on November 23.*ᵇ*

ᵃ Those present at the consultation on November 12 in addition to Professor Learmonth were Sir Maurice Cassidy, Sir Morton Smart and Sir Thomas Dunhill.

ᵇ With characteristic consideration the King wrote in his own hand to his doctor at Balmoral, Dr. George Middleton, on November 22, so that the letter should arrive on the morning of the announcement. 'You having helped me so much this year at Balmoral', he wrote, 'I thought it only fair to you that I should tell you in my layman's language what is really the matter with me', and he proceeded to give Dr. Middleton a detailed précis of the doctors' report and of the treatment prescribed. 'It is a great nuisance having to lie up', he added, 'but I am very glad the doctors have found the cause of the trouble. Of course, it will take me some time to recover from it but with rest and care I am sure I shall.'

The King is suffering from an obstruction to the circulation through the arteries of the legs, which has only recently become acute ; the defective blood supply to the right foot causes anxiety. Complete rest has been advised and treatment to improve the circulation in the legs has been initiated and must be maintained for an immediate and prolonged period. Though His Majesty's general health, including the condition of his heart, gives no reason for concern, there is no doubt that the strain of the last twelve years has appreciably affected his resistance to physical fatigue.

We have come to the conclusion that it would be hazardous for His Majesty to embark upon a long journey, which might delay his recovery, and which might well involve serious risk to the limb. With deep regret, therefore, we have advised that the King's visit to Australia and New Zealand should not be undertaken next year.

Having taken this decision with great reluctance, King George became an extremely good patient. He was very tired, and, once the surrender had been made, he settled down well under conservative treatment, welcoming the period of enforced inactivity. His health improved rapidly and all danger of amputation had disappeared by the beginning of December. 'I think even Learmonth is surprised & pleased with the fortnight's treatment, so I am feeling happier to-day', he wrote to Queen Mary. 'But I am getting tired & bored with bed as I am feeling so much more rested which is a good thing.'[15]

A great joy had come to him on November 14 in the birth of his first grandchild, and he was particularly glad to be sufficiently well to attend the little Prince's christening a month later.[a]

Both the King and the Queen had been filled with gratitude for the great upwelling of good-will and affection which had been elicited during the past year ; a year that had seen those vivid personal experiences in their lives, their Silver Wedding, the birth of their grandchild and the King's illness. From all over the world had come countless messages of love and loyalty and, latterly, of sympathy, and for this the King expressed his thanks in his Christmas broadcast, given on this occasion from Buckingham Palace.

Of his illness he said :

By an unkind stroke of fate, it fell to me a month ago to make a decision that caused me much distress — to postpone, on the advice

---

[a] The Prince was christened on December 15, 1948, at Buckingham Palace by the names of Charles Philip Arthur George.

of my doctors, the journey for which my peoples in Australia and
New Zealand had been making such kindly preparations. But
here, against the disappointment that I knew I was causing others,
I can set the wave of sympathy and concern which flowed back to
me not only from the Australians and New Zealanders themselves
but from friends known and unknown in this old country and in
every one of the great brotherhood of nations to which we all
belong — and, indeed, from many hundreds of people in foreign
lands who wish us well. The Queen and I have been deeply
touched and much comforted by these expressions of love and
loyalty from our people.

Under the treatment prescribed by his doctors the King's
local condition and also his general health had sufficiently
improved for him to go to Sandringham in the New Year.
He had become keenly interested in his own case, and, greatly
to the pleasure of Professor Learmonth, who was in constant
attendance, had himself devised and constructed certain appliances for his own use. He was able to take short walks and
by January 18 was well enough to shoot, but he dutifully
rested in bed in the afternoons. On his return to London at
the end of February he resumed a limited programme of
audiences and held an investiture. He believed himself to be
well set on the road to complete recovery.

Great was the King's disappointment, therefore, at the
outcome of a full consultation of his doctors on March 3.[a]
Their considered opinion was that, though their patient had
reacted so well to the treatment prescribed, his improved
state of health would only be maintained on the present basis
if he continued to lead the life of an invalid, and this, by reason
of his temperament alone, was impossible. It was necessary
for his future happiness that he should live out the rest of his
life as normally as possible, and to this end they recommended
that he undergo a right lumbar sympathectomy operation.

The King's initial reaction to this suggestion, when it
was put to him by Professor Learmonth and Professor Paterson
Ross,[b] was one of extreme annoyance. 'So all our treatment
has been a waste of time', he said. He was quickly mollified,

[a] Those present at the consultation of March 3 were Sir Maurice Cassidy,
Sir Thomas Dunhill, Sir John Weir, Sir Horace Evans, Professor Learmonth and
Professor Paterson Ross.
[b] Sir James Paterson Ross, K.C.V.O., M.B., F.R.C.S. (b. 1895), was appointed Professor of Surgery at the University of London in 1935.

however, when it was pointed out to him that by his patient co-operation during the past weeks he would be able to stand the operation much better than he could have done without the treatment. 'And it might have been a very different operation too', he replied at once, for he had all the time been aware of the risk of losing his right leg.

It was first thought that, in view of the complicated nature of modern surgery, the operation should be performed in a hospital, and the Royal Masonic was suggested. The King was not averse in principle. 'I suppose I have a good right to go to a Masonic Hospital', was his comment, 'but I've never heard of a King going to a hospital before.' In the end, however, it was deemed more expedient to carry out the operation in Buckingham Palace, where a complete surgical theatre was established in rooms overlooking the Mall.

The operation was successfully performed on the morning of Saturday, March 12, 1949, by Professor Learmonth, assisted by Professor Paterson Ross. The King was very calm. 'I am not in the least worried', he said as the anaesthetic was administered.

Great was the concern of the public at the King's illness and great their relief at the success of the operation. The news spread from the crowds outside the Palace and was relayed to other thousands in the terse but affectionate notice on the placards of newsvendors : 'He's all right'.

His Majesty was sufficiently recovered to hold a Privy Council on March 29, and a month later to receive his seven Prime Ministers and Mr. Lester Pearson on the memorable occasion of their presenting to him, on April 27, the findings of the Commonwealth Conference.[a] By May he was able to undertake a good many official duties, to receive in audience and to attend to numerous papers without too great fatigue, and on June 9 he drove in an open carriage to watch his Brigade of Guards troop the Colour, at which ceremony Princess Elizabeth rode at the head of the parade. Ascot Week did not unduly try him, but it was thought wise that he should have a week's rest at Balmoral which, as he wrote to Professor Learmonth, 'did me a world of good and now I feel a different person'.

[a] See above, p. 729.

Despite this new buoyancy the King was not deceived into believing that his recovery would restore him to complete activity. He requested guidance from Professor Learmonth, who replied with a letter of wise counsel. The problem was both psychological and physical, and the change in the tempo of the King's life must be permanent. The future was in his own hands, thenceforward, and he was warned that a second attack of thrombosis would be difficult to weather. He was urged to consider changing some of his major interests and to live a quieter life generally.[a]

This practical approach, demanding his own co-operation in his own case, appealed to the King, whose interest in medical matters was considerable, and he at once set about devising means for putting the recommended régime into force at Balmoral when he returned there in August. He had promised not to over-tire himself but he did not want to interfere with his normal shooting programme more than was absolutely necessary. His inventive mind soon hit upon the solution. He knew that he was all right on level ground but that pain recurred in his legs on greater exertion. He arranged, therefore, to go as far as possible in a Land-Rover and then, not being able to ride, to have a long trace fastened around his waist and attached to a pony, which pulled him uphill. As he explained : 'I've only got to *move* my legs without having to exert myself at all'. Somebody asked : 'What if the pony bolted, Sir?' But the King had provided for that contingency also. At his end of the trace he had had fitted a quick-release mechanism similar to that of a Royal Air Force parachute !

But the cares of state still continued to disturb him. The economic condition of Britain had again deteriorated, and both Mr. Bevin and Sir Stafford Cripps were in Washington and Ottawa seeking a solution. The King's enjoyment of his new

[a] Professor Learmonth was in almost constant attendance upon King George from November 12, 1948, till January 11, 1949, and again from March 1 till March 25, 1949, and thenceforward was in frequent consultation until the end of the year. There is no doubt that his unremitting care and the wise advice which he gave the King about the necessary change in the tempo of his life and activities were a major factor in saving his right leg from amputation. This the King appreciated. On the occasion of Professor Learmonth's final examination His Majesty asked him, at its conclusion, to give him his bath-robe and slippers; then, pushing forward a stool and picking up a sword which he had hitherto concealed, he said : 'You used a knife on me, now I'm going to use one on you', and bidding him kneel, bestowed upon him the accolade of knighthood.

sense of well-being was tempered by his concern for his country. 'I feel ever so well in this good fresh air & am trying to worry less about matters political', he wrote to Queen Mary towards the end of August. 'If the talks [in Washington] do not go well we may have a General Election this year. What I fear is another 1931 crisis.' [16] A month later the King's fears were all but realized. Though the North American mission of the Chancellor of the Exchequer had not been without its favourable results,[a] Sir Stafford Cripps's return from Washington was followed by a major diminution in the value of the pound sterling,[b] for which official action was required by His Majesty.

It is curious [he wrote to Queen Mary] how Balmoral is always the place where one worries most, but on the whole it is worth it, as one can get out & away from it all for a few hours. I held a Privy Council here to sign the Proclamation for the Bank Holiday, but it was so secret that I could not tell anybody about the £ devaluation. I fear it is only a palliative & not a cure for our financial position.[17]

By the end of November the King's doctors were sufficiently satisfied with his progress to recommend that, with certain safeguards, it would be possible for him to resume his plans for the Royal Tour of Australia and New Zealand. It was then too late to arrange for the visit in 1950, and the celebrations for the Festival of Britain rendered it unfeasible in 1951 : it was therefore proposed that he should go, if all went well, in 1952.

(iv)

The New Year opened darkly. It was generally realized that the country had only avoided a major economic crisis by the

---

[a] The results of Sir Stafford Cripps's conversations with the United States and Canadian Governments were announced on September 12, 1949. America's investments abroad, especially in British colonies, were to be increased; there were to be larger stock-piling and facilities for the sale of natural rubber in America and Canada ; a simpler form of United States Customs procedure and lower tariffs by agreement with other countries were promised, as were more liberal intra-European trade and payments arrangements. The most substantial result was the widening of the terms of Britain's eligibility for Marshall Aid, permitting the purchase of Canadian wheat with American dollars.

[b] See above, p. 666.

skin of its teeth and that it was still far from complete recovery. Moreover, while the fact was gratefully appreciated that, as one American put it, 'the United States appears to have recognized that we simply cannot permit the collapse of Great Britain', there was a general recognition of the fact that this status of a privileged pensionary was both unhealthy and undignified.

We are deeply grateful to our good friends in the United States for the imagination and sympathy with which they first realised our problems and then set to work to help us over them [the King had said in his Christmas broadcast]. Without this understanding help we could not have made the progress towards recovery that has already been achieved. But none of us can be satisfied till we are again standing upright and supporting our own weight, and we have a long way to go before we do that. It is bound to be a tough business and if we are to see it through, as we shall, we must put the good of our country first every time.

The political situation at the close of 1949 had also convinced Mr. Attlee that he must take cognizance of the marked swing of public opinion towards an early consulting of the electorate and that the continuance of the existing suspense and uncertainty could not be in the nation's interest. He therefore wrote in this vein to King George at Sandringham on January 5, 1950, requesting a dissolution of Parliament on February 3 and the holding of a General Election on February 23.[18]

There had been very few instances of a Prime Minister asking the Sovereign for a Dissolution by letter since the time of Queen Victoria, to whom both Mr. Disraeli and Mr. Gladstone made such a request,[a] the Queen replying in her own hand. The last recorded instance was in October 1935, when Mr. Baldwin wrote to King George V at Sandringham and His Majesty replied by the hand of Lord Wigram, granting approval. King George VI, however, preferred to follow the example of his great-grandmother, and he replied to Mr. Attlee in his own hand, giving his letter of assent personally to the Prime Minister when he motored over from Chequers to luncheon on January 7.[19] The Dissolution was publicly announced three days later.

[a] Mr. Disraeli in 1868; Mr. Gladstone in 1874 and in 1886.

Both the major political parties entered the General Election of 1950 with guarded optimism. 'We had now been in power for more than four years', Mr. Attlee has written, 'and had carried out the programme which we had put forward at the last General Election. We had no reason to think that we had lost the confidence of the country, for we had created a record in having never lost a by-election.'[20] The Conservatives, on the other hand, seemed confident that the country as a whole was satiated with nationalization, wearied of austerity, and had lost confidence in the ability of the Labour Party to achieve national economic recovery.

In the result both sides were disappointed. The Conservatives were defeated but so was nationalization, though both by the barest of margins. The electoral battle of February 23 was in fact, as the Duke of Wellington said to Mr. Creevey of the battle of Waterloo: 'A damned near run thing'. There was a spell in the returns — it lasted for about ten minutes — when the combined totals of the Conservatives and Liberals drew level with Labour. Four times Labour's lead was wiped out, but each time their total edged forward by one seat. It was not until 6.20 p.m. that they knew for certain that they would be the largest single party in the new House of Commons. The final results were:

Labour	315
Conservatives and National Liberals	298
Liberals	9
Irish Nationalists	2
Speaker	1 [a]

'A British General Election is generally expected to do three things:' wrote one commentator, 'return a government, provide a "mandate", and educate the electorate by the processes of public debate. The General Election of 1950, though it had many admirable features, failed to perform any of these functions satisfactorily.'[21] It had indeed returned the Labour Government of Mr. Attlee, but with a majority so narrow that it would not enable them to proceed, nor justify them in trying to proceed, with their distinctively socialist policies.

[a] Of the hundred Communist candidates nominated none was returned and ninety forfeited their deposits, and of the 476 Liberal candidates over three hundred suffered a similar fate.

The situation was certainly precarious. The Labour Party could only command an over-all majority of 8; a majority which gave little margin for safety. Either Mr. Attlee would be defeated or he might decide once again to ask for a Dissolution. This latter possibility aroused great interest among the public generally and among constitutional lawyers in particular. The debated question was whether the King had a right to refuse such a request, such action being considered tantamount to demanding the Prime Minister's resignation. The case of Lord Byng's action in Canada in 1926, when he refused a Dissolution to Mr. Mackenzie King but later granted it to Mr. Meighen, was widely discussed.[a] There was some talk of an all-party conference to consider the question of carrying on the King's Government, but this idea was rejected by both the Prime Minister, who was determined to meet the new House of Commons, and by Mr. Churchill, who, in a letter to Sir Alan Lascelles, expressed the view that 'the principle that a new House of Commons has a right to live if it can and should not be destroyed until some fresh issue or situation has arisen to place before the electors, is, I believe, sound'.[22] Mr. Attlee was, therefore, received by the King at 5.30 on February 27 and agreed to continue in office and to form a Government.

In the new Parliament, which was formally opened by the

[a] In 1926 Mr. Mackenzie King, having been returned to power in a General Election with a small majority, asked for a second Dissolution when the new Parliament was only eight months old. The Governor-General, Field-Marshal Lord Byng, refused this request, having received from the Conservative leader, Mr. Meighen, an assurance that he could form a Government and carry on in the existing House of Commons if Mr. Mackenzie King resigned — as he immediately did. Mr. Meighen gave this assurance in good faith, having reached an agreement for co-operation and support with the leader of the Agricultural Party. This guarantee, however, proved to be illusory. Within a few days of taking office, Mr. Meighen was deserted by his allies and was defeated in the House. He thereupon advised the Governor-General to send for Mr. King, but added that his Party strongly desired a Dissolution. Lord Byng after consideration refused to send for Mr. King a second time and granted the Dissolution. In the ensuing election Mr. King was returned with an immense majority.

The view was widely held, and, amongst others, by Mr. Mackenzie King himself, that, while Lord Byng had been entirely within his rights in refusing a Dissolution to Mr. King in the first place, he was not acting in consonance with constitutional principle in granting it subsequently to Mr. Meighen, and that he should have sent for the Liberal leader immediately after the defeat of the Conservatives in the House of Commons. The incident left a legacy of bitterness against Crown Government in many Canadian hearts.

King on March 6, the strategy of the Conservative Party was to move two amendments to the Address, one on the Iron and Steel Bill and the other on Housing, and to let it be known that both would be pressed to a division. In the event of defeat, Mr. Attlee could either request a Dissolution or, if asked, tender advice to the King to send for Mr. Churchill. The Conservatives would then be compelled to take responsibility for the situation which they had created. They would be a minority Government at the mercy of the Opposition. But the Labour Party, by thus putting the Conservatives in office, would themselves be faced with the choice of either putting them out again and precipitating a new General Election, or of condoning — or, at any rate, refraining from challenging — legislation and policies at variance with their principles and distasteful to their electoral supporters.

What, then, was the constitutional duty of the Sovereign in this complicated situation, which, though admittedly hypothetical, might well become actual at any moment? For the King's guidance and information, Sir Alan Lascelles took careful soundings among the leaders of the Government and the Opposition and also in official circles. As a result of these he reached the conclusion that, despite appearances, the real imminence of a parliamentary crisis was not as great as it seemed. The majority of the Conservative front bench were not anxious to bring down the Government at the moment and the political manœuvres then in progress were being conducted, as it were, with blank rounds rather than with live ammunition.

This tactical forecast he placed before the King on April 21, saying that, if it were true, His Majesty would not be called upon to make any difficult decision at the moment.

But it may be false [Sir Alan continued] and then account would have to be taken of what may be called general strategical considerations.

If Mr. Attlee is beaten, two courses are open to him :

(1) He can ask The King to accept his resignation and (if asked) advise His Majesty to send for Mr. Churchill. There could not be much doubt about what to do then, and The King's problem is simple. (I am told, however, on good authority that Mr. Attlee would *not* adopt this course, though the temptation to try and put

the other side in on a very sticky wicket would obviously be strong.)

(2) He can ask The King to dissolve Parliament. The King would be perfectly entitled to refuse this request if he were convinced that the present Parliament had not exhausted its present usefulness and that the country's interests demanded that the holding of another general election should be postponed as long as possible. It is doubtful whether the argument is valid in present circumstances ; could anybody else form a Government capable of doing anything but exist precariously on a tiny majority — or even a minority ? And would withholding a dissolution now do more than postpone the inevitable general election for more than a few weeks ? So there does not seem to be sufficient reason here for the Sovereign to break the precedent followed by his predecessors for more than a century by refusing his Prime Minister a dissolution. In Canada, of course, Lord Byng did, on a famous occasion, refuse a dissolution ; but, though he acted from the very best motives, it is questionable if this refusal did anybody any good in the long run, and it undoubtedly left in certain quarters in Canada a considerable legacy of bitterness against the Crown. (I am aware that Mr. Churchill might argue in a directly contrary sense, but I do not believe that more than a small minority of his party would do so.)

But even if The King decided to grant a dissolution, he should certainly not do so save on the condition that it should not become operative until Parliament has done its duty of making at' least a minimum provision for the national finance ; no Prime Minister should ever be allowed to close the national legislative premises — particularly at this time of year — unless he can leave them in good financial order. Consequently The King would be bound to insist that the dissolution asked for by Mr. Attlee should not take effect until Parliament had dealt with a Minimal Finance Act, and an Appropriation Act, as explained in the attached copy of a Treasury paper given me this evening by Sir E. Bridges. As the Prime Minister himself called for this paper, it may fairly be presumed that, if he should ask The King for a dissolution, he would himself stipulate that Parliament should be made to sit until this minimal business were completed — a period, I understand, of at least ten days or even a fortnight. So, in the event of Mr. Attlee asking His Majesty for a dissolution on Thursday, April 27th, it could not take place until about May 10th.

To sum up, then : it does not seem probable that the Government will be faced with resignation during the next few weeks, but even if this should happen the only difficult problem which The King might be called on to solve is the decision to grant or to withhold a dissolution ; in present circumstances the arguments in favour of granting it seem to outweigh those against it.[23]

Sir Alan Lascelles' forecast was justified to the full. Mr. Attlee's second administration continued to maintain its tenuous hold upon life for a further eighteen months, but the ever-present threat of defeat in the division lobbies laid upon Ministers and Members alike the heaviest parliamentary burden in a century.

Nevertheless the question of the Sovereign's rights and powers in the granting of a Dissolution continued to be the subject of a somewhat desultory correspondence in the columns of *The Times*, until it received a quietus on May 2 with the publication of a letter over a pseudonym which masked the identity of Sir Alan Lascelles himself :

Sir,

It is surely indisputable (and common sense) that a Prime Minister may ask — not demand — that his Sovereign will grant him a dissolution of Parliament ; and that the Sovereign, if he so chooses, may refuse to grant this request. The problem of such a choice is entirely personal to the Sovereign, though he is, of course, free to seek informal advice from anybody whom he thinks fit to consult.

Insofar as this matter can be publicly discussed, it can be properly assumed that no wise Sovereign — that is, one who has at heart the true interest of the country, the constitution, and the Monarchy — would deny a dissolution to his Prime Minister unless he were satisfied that : (1) the existing Parliament was still vital, viable, and capable of doing its job ; (2) a General Election would be detrimental to the national economy ; (3) he could rely on finding another Prime Minister who could carry on his Government, for a reasonable period, with a working majority in the House of Commons. When Sir Patrick Duncan refused a dissolution to his Prime Minister in South Africa in 1939, all these conditions were satisfied : when Lord Byng did the same in Canada in 1926, they appeared to be, but in the event the third proved illusory.

I am, &c.,

Senex.

(v)

The uneasy state of peace — shading into 'cold war' — which had prevailed in the world since September 1945, received its first major shock on June 25, 1950, when Northern Korean forces crossed the 38th parallel in their first invasion of the

South Korean Republic.[a] Here was a direct and deliberate challenge by a Russian-controlled to an American-controlled Government. It was met by President Truman with courage and initiative. On the day of the invasion itself the United States representative submitted to an emergency meeting of the Security Council of the United Nations a resolution calling on the North Korean authorities to withdraw their troops, and two days later Mr. Truman made his momentous announcement that United States air and sea forces would give cover and support to the South Korean forces.

'Naked aggression and it must be checked', was Mr. Attlee's comment in the House of Commons on the same evening (June 27) and he at once pledged the United Kingdom's support for the American proposal to the Security Council that members of the United Nations should furnish such support as might be necessary to check the North Korean invasion. This amounted, in the first instance, to the British naval strength in the Far East, but, in response to an appeal by the Security Council for ground troops, a brigade was dispatched which, together with other Commonwealth contingents, later formed part of the extremely efficient Commonwealth Division.

There followed bitter fighting, of which the brunt was initially borne by the United States forces. Within a few weeks, however, the troops of 14 United Nations' member states were in the field and with these the Supreme Commander, General MacArthur,[b] first stabilized his line north

[a] The ancient Empire of Korea, which, since the Russo-Japanese War of 1904–1905, had become virtually a Japanese protectorate, was formally annexed by Japan in 1910. The restoration of Korean independence had been promised at the Cairo Conference of 1943, and at the close of the Japanese War the country was occupied by Russian and American troops to enforce the surrender of Japanese forces. The country had been divided for mutual military convenience into two portions, separated by the 38th parallel, and abortive negotiations between Washington and Moscow as to the future of Korea continued until 1946. Thereafter the Soviet military authorities proclaimed the Korean People's Republic in their zone in 1948, and in the same year President Rhee was inaugurated President of the Republic of Korea at Seoul in the south. This was the position at the outbreak of the Korean war.

[b] General of the Army Douglas MacArthur (b. 1880), having served in the First World War and in the Philippine Islands, became Chief of Staff of the United States Army in 1930. In 1935 he was appointed Director of the Organization of National Defence by the Philippine Commonwealth Government who also created for him the rank of Field-Marshal. He served as Supreme Commander of Allied Forces in the South-West Pacific from 1942 to 1945, when he assumed control on behalf of the Allies of the occupation of Japan.

of Taegu and along the Naktong River, and then, on September 14, in a brilliant amphibious operation, began a victorious advance.

In Britain the Korean war had serious political repercussions. Mr. Attlee's Government, faced with the problem of squaring the indisputable necessity of rearmament in the face of Russian aggression with the delicate state of the nation's economic situation, had introduced a Defence White Paper in March which, though providing for expenditure amounting to 7·6 per cent of the national income, or £15 per head of the population, was now recognized as being too meagre. On July 26 Mr. Shinwell, the Minister of Defence,[a] announced that a further £100 million would be allocated to armaments in the national budget, but these new proposals were denounced by Mr. Churchill as 'few and far between'. However, the Government were not at the moment prepared for a further increase. The House of Commons rose, however, at a moment when the United States were inquiring what additional measures the Western Powers were prepared to take in the field of rearmament, to which the British Government at length replied, on August 8, that they agreed in principle to the expenditure of £3400 million in three years for defence, an increase which involved a rise of from 8 to 10 per cent of the national revenue.

The House rose on August 5, but such was the gravity of the Korean situation, where at that moment it appeared as if the United Nations forces might not be able to preserve even their toe-hold at Pusan, that a week later the Speaker issued notices of recall for September 12. This appeared to the leaders of the Conservative and Liberal Opposition as altogether too far distant a date. In their view Parliament should be informed immediately of the decisions which the Government proposed to take. They protested in this sense to Mr. Attlee on August 17, but the Prime Minister remained firm, for reasons which he explained to King George :

[a] Rt. Hon. Emanuel Shinwell (b. 1884) has sat in the House of Commons intermittently since 1922. He was Financial Secretary to the War Office, 1929–1930; Parliamentary Secretary to the Department of Mines in 1924 and 1930–1931; Minister of Fuel and Power, 1945–1947; Secretary of State for War, 1947–1950; and Minister of Defence, 1950–1951.

Sir,

Mr. Churchill, Mr. Eden and Mr. Clement Davies came to see me yesterday to ask that Parliament should be recalled next week. Mr. Bevin was with me.

I explained that we had decided on the date of September 12th in order that we might put to the House our full proposals and indicated the reasons which weighed with us in not suggesting an earlier date.

Mr. Churchill talked at considerable length on the dangers of the present situation mostly on the lines of his last speech in the Defence debate in the House.

I was unable to find any substantial reason for an earlier recall as it did not seem to me that another debate without definite action to be taken by the House would be useful.

Mr. Churchill showed considerable annoyance and suggested that in not accepting his date the Government were acting dictatorially. I was unable to accept this view as it would seem that Mr. Churchill's demand might be considered as an attempt to dictate to the Government.

Mr. Clement Davies has issued a statement in which he sets out his reasons and I understand that Mr. Churchill proposes to broadcast.

I am proposing to broadcast to the Services probably on August 30th.

I have the honour to be, Sir,
Your Majesty's obedient humble servant
C. R. ATTLEE.[24]

There was no doubt that public feeling was deeply stirred by the situation in Korea and in its possible repercussions for the rest of the world, especially in Europe. Had the Third World War in fact already begun, men asked themselves, and were the more disturbed since it was known that Russia was now in possession of precious atomic secrets.

The King's reply to Mr. Attlee reflected his own deep interest and concern, both for the situation as a whole and for the health of his Prime Minister.

It seems certain [he wrote from Balmoral] that when Parliament does meet on September 12th, you will have a difficult, and even critical debate, the course of which the general public will, I believe, follow with deeper interest than it has felt about any debate in recent years. So I hope very much that it will be possible for you to get some rest between now and then as, so far, you cannot have had a real holiday.[25]

An exchange of broadcasts between the Prime Minister and Mr. Churchill on the wireless was but a preliminary to the spirited three-day debate which opened on September 12, in which the Government gave details of the further steps which they proposed to take to place the nation's defence in order. The period of National Service was to be extended from eighteen months to two years, and within the next three years it was proposed to establish from six to ten divisions in the Regular Army, and from 1951 there would be 12 Territorial divisions available for a call-up. On the wider front of European defence, notice was given of the agreement reached for the integration of the Brussels Pact machinery and NATO for the purpose of establishing a unified command.

Public anxiety was somewhat assuaged by the turn for the better in the military situation in Korea. General MacArthur's brilliant landing at Inchon on September 15 was followed by the recapture of the South Korean capital of Seoul on the 26th, and by the end of the month the North Korean invaders had been thrust back beyond the 38th parallel. A memorable decision was now taken by the Supreme Commander, the wisdom of which was to be hotly debated in the weeks and months which followed. The Government of President Rhee, now reinstated in Seoul, claimed sovereignty over the whole of Korea and called for a general advance beyond the 38th parallel. This operation was begun by General MacArthur on October 9, on the implicit, though not entirely clear, authority of a resolution of the United Nations General Assembly which had established a Commission for the Unification and Rehabilitation of Korea. This advance swept northwards, meeting a steadily weakening resistance, and by the last week of November General MacArthur was well beyond the North Korean capital of Pyongyang. Now, however, a new factor appeared. The victorious advance of the United Nations army was first checked and then repulsed by a powerful and well-equipped force of Chinese 'volunteers'. There was heavy fighting, several of the United Nations divisions being severely mauled. A general retirement was ordered and the Commonwealth forces covered the retreat of the main United Nations forces to the 38th parallel where, at the close of the year, they stood awaiting a further attack from the North.

This reverse of arms had its inevitable repercussions upon the Anglo-American Alliance. In Britain there had been considerable criticism of the decision to carry the military operation into North Korea, and, although Mr. Bevin assured the House of Commons on November 29 that the Supreme Commander's objectives were those of the United Nations, his colleague, Mr. Shinwell, expressed the opinion [a] that 'it would appear that General MacArthur went beyond the objectives which we understood to be the objectives at the beginning of the affair'. In the United States, on the other hand, the smarting of defeat demanded a whipping boy, and strictures were levelled at what was alleged to be the paucity of Britain's contribution to the Korean war. Moreover, the fact that Britain was on terms of diplomatic relations with Communist China while the United States still recognized the Nationalist régime of Marshal Chiang Kai-shek in Formosa as the legitimate Chinese Government, proved an additional source of friction.[b] Passions were stirred and apprehensions aroused on both sides of the Atlantic. In Britain it was feared that the Americans had lost sight of the fact that, despite the immediate hostilities in Korea, the real threat to world peace lay in the danger of Russian and not Chinese aggression, and that President Truman's Administration was contemplating an all-out offensive against China. This, it was believed, would almost certainly result in full-scale support for China by the Soviet Union and the precipitation of a Third World War. In America there were those who whispered that Britain, in an effort to appease the Peking Government, wished to liquidate the Korean War by the negotiating of an armistice agreement not unfavourable to North Korea, and that, if unsuccessful in this purpose, she would withdraw from the battle.

So acute did the tension in Anglo-American relations become that Mr. Attlee decided that only personal contact could restore the position. The idea, welcomed in Washington and in Westminster, received the warm approval of King George.

[a] In a speech at Durham on December 3.
[b] The United Kingdom Government recognized the Communist Government of China on January 6, 1950.

Throughout these difficult months King George had shared
to the full the general anxiety of his people. He had been
heartened by successes of United Nations arms in Korea, but
the situation created by the intervention of China and its
effect upon Anglo-American relations filled him with gloom.
In their meetings together the Prime Minister had more than
once referred to his desire to talk matters out face to face with
President Truman, and the King had assented whole-heartedly.
It was a question of choosing the most appropriate moment
and this was afforded by the formidable statement of the
President at his press conference on November 30 that he did
not exclude the use of the atom-bomb in meeting the situation
in Korea. 'Does that mean that there is active consideration
of the use of the atomic bomb?' a journalist asked, and Mr.
Truman replied : 'There has always been active consideration
of its use. I don't want to see it used. It is a terrible weapon,
and it should not be used on innocent men, women and
children who have nothing whatever to do with this military
aggression. That happens when it is used.' [26]

These words determined in Mr. Attlee's mind the necessity
for immediate action. He sought and obtained the approval
of the King, who was at Sandringham, and after a fortuitous
but fortunate visit from the French Premier and Foreign
Minister, he set out on December 3.

Before his departure the Prime Minister received the following letter from King George :

My dear Prime Minister,
    I am writing, on the eve of your departure to America for your
talks with President Truman, to wish you all success.
    I know that you have contemplated this visit for some time, &
I feel that this is the right moment when, as head of my Government
in the United Kingdom you can explain to the President the true
picture as we see it, of the present world situation. I wish I could
have told you this personally, but events nowadays happen so
quickly. I have been very worried lately over affairs in general,
so I am very glad that you will be able to put our case fairly &
squarely before the President.
    I am most interested to see that M. Pleven & M. Schumann
are having talks with you today which I hope shows that the
French do at last realise the urgent necessity of getting their Defence
programme started.

I am quite confident that you will be able to deal with all the important outstanding problems & I trust that your visit will not be too exacting. I shall look forward to our next meeting in London with much anticipation.

I am
Yours very sincerely
GEORGE R.[27]

In thanking the King for his good wishes, Mr. Attlee replied in relation to the subject of his forthcoming talks with Mr. Truman :

I should have wished to have discussed these matters with Your Majesty, but although the idea of this meeting has been under consideration for some time, the actual timing was dictated by events. The unfortunate statements of the President required immediate action.

The visit of the French Ministers was unexpected but in the result useful, though they have still some way to go towards meeting the views of the other members of the Atlantic Treaty. I have the impression that French public opinion is in advance of that of the French Parliament and that the Ministers dare not go as far as they would wish.

I agree respectfully with Your Majesty that I should put the whole position very fully and frankly to the President, pointing out that it is not possible for this country to do what it wishes to do in the field of defence, unless the United States Government makes its economic policy conform to the needs of the situation.

I think that the Americans realise that to get heavily involved in the Far East would be to play the Russian game, and that we must have regard to the broad world strategy.

Your Majesty's gracious letter gave me much encouragement to deal with the tasks confronting me.[28]

Mr. Attlee's conversations in Washington (December 4–8), of which Mr. Truman has given an account in his memoirs,[29] were only partially successful. The Prime Minister was able to disabuse the minds of the President and his advisers of the idea that the United Kingdom contemplated any withdrawal from its commitments in Korea, but he did not succeed in effecting any material change in the attitude of the United States toward China. The suggestion that the Communist régime in Peking should be admitted to the United Nations (of which Nationalist China was a charter member) was scouted at the outset as a betrayal of the United States recognition of the Formosa Government, and the only assurance gained was the somewhat ambiguous statement of the Secretary of State, Mr. Dean Acheson,[a] that there were 'not many of the President's advisers' who would urge him to follow the course of an all-out war on China. There was agreement, however, between both parties as to their determination to rearm as speedily and intelligently as possible against attacks on freedom in both Europe and Asia, and Mr. Attlee gained some satisfaction from the President in the matter of the use of the atomic weapon.

Nevertheless it was not a very cheering report which Mr. Attlee made to the King on December 12. His Majesty's fifty-fifth year and the first half of the twentieth century were closing in an atmosphere of suspicion, menace and aggression which deeply depressed him. The outlook was sombre in the extreme.

(vi)

The year 1951 was dominated by the depression occasioned by the continuous ebb and flow of the fighting in Korea,[b] by the hysterically fanatical politics of Dr. Mussadiq in Teheran, culminating in the nationalization of the Anglo-Iranian Oil Company,[c] by the persistence of the *malaise* which afflicted

[a] Hon. Dean Acheson (b. 1893), having served as private secretary to Associate Justice Brandeis, of the U.S. Supreme Court, from 1919 to 1921, practised law in New York until 1941, when he entered the Department of State as Assistant Secretary of State, becoming Under-Secretary in 1945. He retired in 1947, but was recalled to public service as Secretary of State in 1949 by President Truman, in whose cabinet he continued to serve until 1953.

[b] In January 1951 the expected Communist offensive was launched and the U.N. forces were driven nearly to the 37th parallel. In March, however, they counter-attacked, recapturing Seoul and recrossing the 38th parallel in April. On April 11 President Truman dismissed General MacArthur on account of certain statements not in conformity with U.N. policy, among them a warning that China's failure to accept a negotiated peace settlement might widen the scope of the war. Bitter fighting, with varying success, continued until the end of June when a series of desultory truce negotiations opened and continued into the New Year.

[c] A crisis in Anglo-Persian relations was precipitated in March 1951 when, after the assassination of the Persian Premier, General Rasmara, the government passed into the hands of the fanatical Dr. Mussadiq, who shortly thereafter passed a bill nationalizing the holdings of the Anglo-Iranian Oil Company, of which he was an inveterate opponent. After a period of abortive negotiation, in which both British and American politicians participated, the whole of the Anglo-Iranian staff were expelled from Abadan in October.

the country's economic condition, and by the uncertainty of life of a Government which depended upon an exiguous majority of 8. Some relief from these fears and dejections was afforded by the Festival of Britain, with which His Majesty's Government, under the impetus and enthusiasm of the Lord President of the Council, Mr. Herbert Morrison (who delighted in the sobriquet of 'Lord Festival' bestowed upon him by the press), had decided to celebrate the centenary of the Great Exhibition of 1851.

This vast enterprise, for which preparations had been in process for four years, was intended not only to mark the hundredth anniversary of Prince Albert's Exhibition of 1851, when the Crystal Palace was built in Hyde Park, but to show to the world the degree to which Britain had achieved recuperation after the ordeal of war and the task of recon-struction. In announcing the project in Parliament, Mr. Morrison invited the House to recall that Exposition in Paris to which the world had been invited in 1878 to demonstrate the recovery of France from the débâcle of the Franco-Prussian War. The spirit of this great occasion had been epitomized by George Augustus Sala in the phrase : 'Paris herself again', but there were many who wondered whether this phrase could be legitimately applied to the situation of Britain in 1951 when austerity was still the keyword of national life and the country seemed still to be teetering on the brink of economic crisis.

The Festival, nevertheless, played an important part in the year's events, not only by reason of the Exhibition on the South Bank and the Fun Fair in Battersea Park, but also because it was nation-wide. All over the British Isles that summer the spirit of the Festival found expression in events and celebrations which, if they were criticized by some, gave abundant pleasure to many, and which, taken together, afforded a united act of national reassessment and a corporate reaffirmation of faith in the nation's future.

It was, however, the condition of King George's health which was the main concern and preoccupation of the peoples of the United Kingdom and of the Commonwealth during 1951.

In accordance with the advice of Sir James Learmonth,

the King's programme of public engagements had been curtailed and restricted to those of the most outstanding importance. He had learned the importance of rest and relaxation
whenever opportunity was afforded, and he was aware of the
dangers inherent in further attacks of thrombosis. Even with
these precautions, however, the King became very tired, and
his general appearance began to give rise to public comment.
Nor could he, by virtue of his temperament, divorce his mind
from anxiety over the affairs of state. 'The incessant worries
& crises through which we have to live got me down properly',
he wrote to a friend.

The King paid visits to the Midlands and to Cambridge
University in April, opened the Festival of Britain from the
steps of St. Paul's on May 3 and a week later received the
King and Queen of Denmark on a State visit, installing King
Frederik as a Knight of the Garter at Windsor on May 9.
He enjoyed a week's holiday in the third week of the month
and looked forward to a visit with the Queen to Northern
Ireland in June, and to their departure in December on their
postponed tour of Australia and New Zealand.

On his return to London the King went in state, on May 24,
to instal his brother, the Duke of Gloucester, as Great Master
of the Order of the Bath at a special service in King Henry VII's
Chapel, Westminster Abbey. This gathering of the Knights
of the Bath was unique in a number of aspects. It was the
first to be held during His Majesty's reign, the first in almost
a quarter of a century at which the Sovereign of the Order had
been present,[a] and also the first in which the King himself
had participated, since prior to his accession he had not been
appointed a member of the Order. Mindful of these facts, it
was the King's desire to signalize the event by some personal
act of self-dedication. The thought came to him that the most
appropriate oblation would be the symbolic knightly gesture
of offering his own sword : the sword which had been given
to him by his father when he received his commission as a
naval officer in 1915. He had worn it on all subsequent
occasions when naval uniform was the order of the day and
had frequently used it to bestow the accolade of knighthood.

[a] King George V attended the Service of the Order of the Bath in 1928, but
was unable to be present at that held in 1935.

The King's desire was communicated to the Officers of the Order and a suitable interpolation was made in the programme of the Service. When the Sovereign had completed the traditional offering of gold and silver at the Altar, he drew his sword and handed it to the Dean of Westminster, who placed it on the Altar, whence, after a short interval, he returned it to the King.[a]

King George was already unwell when he went to the Abbey, and it was remarked by many present on that occasion how ill he looked. He had a temperature but insisted upon going through with the ceremony, and in the afternoon visited the Imperial Institute in South Kensington. That evening he retired to bed with influenza.

His Majesty did not make the quick recovery that had been hoped for and anticipated. His doctors [b] took the opportunity of making an exhaustive examination of his physical condition, and as a result advised him not to attend the Derby and to cancel his proposed visit to Northern Ireland. They had discovered a small area of catarrhal inflammation in the left lung.

The King took his usual keen interest in his own case. As one of his medical advisers once remarked, under other circumstances he might have made a very good doctor. He was attracted by the general subject of medicine, insisting upon having every point of detail explained to him in terms which he could understand, and asking innumerable questions.

. . . At last the doctors have found the cause of the temperature [he wrote to Queen Mary at the end of May]. I have a condition on the left lung known as pneumonitis. It is not pneumonia though if left it might become it. I was X-rayed & the photographs showed a shadow. So I am having daily injections of penicillin for about a week. This condition has only been on the lung for a few days at the most so it should resolve itself with treatment.

The doctors think the cause of the cough was below the larynx & has now moved into the lung. Whether I can do anything next

---

[a] After the death of King George VI this sword was presented to the Order by Her Majesty Queen Elizabeth II and Queen Elizabeth the Queen Mother. It now stands in a glass case in the Henry VII Chapel.

[b] The doctors in attendance on His Majesty at this period were Sir Horace Evans, Sir Daniel Davies, Sir John Weir and Dr. Geoffrey Marshall.

week remains to be seen but I must get well first & the sooner the better.

Everyone is very relieved at this revelation & the doctors are happier about me tonight than they have been for a week.[30]

Despite all efforts, the King's complete recovery was still elusive and he was becoming wearied, both physically and mentally, at 'not being able to chuck out the bug', as he expressed it. A prolonged period of convalescence was prescribed, and, during June and July, he rested first at Royal Lodge and then at Sandringham. The only semi-public engagement which he undertook in these weeks was at Windsor where, on July 7, he opened the York Club, a community centre designed for the welfare and enjoyment of his tenants in the Great Park.

On August 3 the King moved to Balmoral. The two months' rest had had some of the desired effect and had confirmed his own confidence. 'I am getting stronger every day', he had written to a friend from Sandringham. The hills of Deeside — so cherished, so beloved — would, he hoped, exercise their soothing influence upon his mind and body. He looked forward to a full enjoyment of his curtailed activities with gun and rifle.

And at first all went well. It was found that the King could enjoy a whole day's shooting without undue fatigue, but the weather was very wet and cold, and he developed a chill and sore throat. His doctors were summoned to Balmoral for a conference on September 1, and, at their earnest request, he agreed to return briefly to London for further examination and X-rays. This he did on September 8 after attending the Braemar Gathering two days earlier.[a]

Sir Horace Evans [b] and his medical colleagues already had their suspicions as to the cause of the King's illness. They called into consultation Mr. Clement Price Thomas,[c] a

[a] The King travelled to London by train on the night of September 7 and flew back to Scotland on the 8th after his medical examination.

[b] Horace, first Baron Evans, G.C.V.O., M.D., F.R.C.P. (b. 1903), was Physician to King George VI from 1949 to 1952 and subsequently to Queen Elizabeth II, and also Physician to the London Hospital and the Royal Masonic Hospital.

[c] Sir Clement Price Thomas, K.C.V.O., F.R.C.S., L.R.C.P. (b. 1893), Surgeon to the Westminster Hospital and to the Brompton Hospital for Diseases of the Chest.

leading surgical authority on malignant diseases of the chest, and the result of their conference was tendered to His Majesty at Balmoral on September 11. Their unanimous advice was that the King should undergo a bronchoscopy for the purpose of removing a portion of tissue from the lung for histological examination.

The King at once assented to this proposal. He cut short his holiday and returned to Buckingham Palace on September 15, where, on the following day, he was bronchoscoped by Mr. Price Thomas. The result of the examination confirmed previous suspicions. The King was suffering from a malignant growth. At a further medical conference it was agreed, again unanimously, that, despite the risk of cardiac complications, there was no alternative to an operation for the removal of the whole left lung.

This decision was communicated to King George by Mr. Price Thomas on September 18. He was not told that he was suffering from cancer — nor, in so far as is known, did he ever know it. The reason given for the operation was that his complaint was caused by a blockage of one of the bronchial tubes which necessitated the removal of his lung.

The King accepted the situation with courage. He was, in a sense, consoled by the thought that the ill-health which had irked him all summer might now be relieved permanently. He received the Prime Minister on September 18 and informed him of the forthcoming operation and then composed himself to await what lay ahead.

He displayed great fortitude, for he dreaded the prospect of a second operation. 'If it's going to help to get me well again I don't mind but the very idea of the surgeon's knife again is hell', he wrote to a friend.

But the King's great sense of humanity — which deeply impressed all who were brought into contact with him at this time — never deserted him. His consideration was for the suspense which the Queen and his daughters would be undergoing at this time, for the burden of responsibility placed upon his doctors and for the anxiety of his people at large. Both he and the Queen paid minute attention to the wording of the bulletins issued to the public, so that no false impression should be given of the gravity of the King's illness.[a]   Their constant thought was for others, and one of His Majesty's last acts before undergoing the operation was an instruction to the Master of the Household, written in his own hand, to send three brace of grouse to the house where the Duke of Windsor was then staying in London, adding : 'I understand he is fond of grouse'.

The operation was performed by Mr. Price Thomas on the morning of Sunday, September 23. It was completely successful, but the circumstances were grave. It was recognized by all concerned that the coronary thrombosis, which subsequently caused the King's death, might occur at any moment while the operation was in process or a few days later. This was a risk which had to be taken. But there was a further hazard. After preliminary exploration, Mr. Price Thomas found that certain nerves of the larynx would have to be sacrificed ; this might conceivably mean that His Majesty would not be able to speak again above a whisper. After a conference with the doctors in attendance, it was decided that this risk too must be taken. For those about the King it was a day of gloom and anguished suspense.

All, however, went smoothly and the King's response was satisfactory. The anxiety regarding both his heart and his vocal chords was gradually allayed, and three days later, though still very weak, he was able to sign in a firm hand the warrant authorizing the issue of Letters Patent appointing Counsellors of State.[b]

Once again the King's illness was the occasion of widespread concern throughout the world and his recovery one of

[a] The first announcement to the public was made on September 18, in the following bulletin:

> During the King's recent illness a series of examinations have been carried out, including radiology and bronchoscopy. These investigations now show structural changes to have developed in the lung. His Majesty has been advised to stay in London for further treatment.

A bulletin warning of an imminent operation was issued on September 21, and, two days later, it was announced at 4.30 p.m.:

> The King underwent an operation for lung resection this morning. Whilst anxiety must remain for some days, His Majesty's immediate post-operative condition is satisfactory.

[b] The Counsellors of State appointed on this occasion were the Queen, Princess Elizabeth, Princess Margaret, the Duke of Gloucester and the Princess Royal.

universal rejoicing.   Day after day, often in gloom and drizzle, the silent crowds waited outside the Palace for word of their ailing Sovereign.   Their mute patience was in itself an eloquent witness to their solicitude.

The sentiments of the Commonwealth were unanimous in their concern and solicitude. The King's health was the primary anxiety of all his peoples, and from every corner of his possessions there came deep and sincere testimony of loyalty and affection.   From Canada came an earnest request that the departure of Princess Elizabeth and the Duke of Edinburgh on October 1 on their projected visit might be postponed until the King's recovery should be better assured,[a] and there was little surprise, though deep disappointment, when it was decided on October 9 that the King would not be able to undertake his own tour of Australia and New Zealand in the coming year.   The profound regret of the peoples of the two countries was mitigated by the announcement that the Princess and her husband would come to them in the place of their Sovereign.

Gradually the King's strength returned, and, by mid-October, he could write with renewed confidence to Queen Mary :

. . . At last I am feeling a bit better after all I have been through in the last 3 weeks. I do seem to go through the most serious operations anybody can do, but thank goodness there were no complications & everything has gone according to plan.   I have been most beautifully looked after from the surgeon to the nurses & the doctors. They have all done their best to make me as comfortable as possible. I have been sitting up in a chair for the last week & have had my meals up as well.   So I am getting stronger & can walk to the bathroom. It will take some time for me to recover from the ordeal I have been through. I have seen many of the wonderful messages from all & sundry for my recovery which have been a great comfort.

I must now start to get up & do more to get stronger. Always an ordeal to begin with as one does not know how much one can do on one's own.[31]

(vii)

But world events and the affairs of state did not wait upon the King's health.   For nearly eighteen months the United

---

[a] Princess Elizabeth and Prince Philip left by air for Canada on October 7.

Kingdom had been governed by an administration which, because of its attenuated majority, had maintained a mere hand-to-mouth existence, balanced precariously upon the razor-edge of uncertainty. The Opposition, failing to bring down the Government by a series of adverse motions, adopted a policy of 'guerrilla warfare', designed to wear down the resistance of their opponents by making the House sit late every night. These tactics imposed a not inconsiderable strain upon Ministers, whose duties did not end with their attendance at the House of Commons, and upon their supporters who lived in the outer districts of London and spent much of their free time shuttling back and forth to Westminster. It needed but the breakdown in health of a few to put the Government in a minority. The strain upon the members of the Opposition was also heavy, but in a lesser degree since their leaders had no Ministerial duties. Nevertheless the health of all was sorely taxed. Members on both sides of the House rose from their sick-beds to attend divisions until, as one remarked, the appearance of the Lobbies resembled that of the Pool of Siloam, lacking only the presence of an angel. 'It was not pleasant', wrote Mr. Attlee, 'to have Members coming from hospital at the risk of their lives to prevent a defeat in the House.'[32]

To King George, his Government's uncertainty of tenure had long been a cause of worry. The gravity of conditions both at home and abroad, he considered, merited a government, from whichever political party it might be drawn, more representative of a majority of the electorate. Moreover, he had hesitated to go forward with the plans for his tour of Australia and New Zealand in the New Year with the over-shadowing possibility that some political crisis might bring down the Government and necessitate a General Election during his absence from the United Kingdom.

The King raised the question of the unstable situation in the House of Commons with the Prime Minister at an audience on June 24 and Mr. Attlee then said that he would ask for a Dissolution in the autumn, but did not mention any specific date.[33] The situation remained in the same state of uncertainty when some six weeks later His Majesty left for Balmoral. There he gave further consideration to the plans for his tour, in which two factors gave him much concern.

On September 1 he consulted Mr. Attlee upon both of them. The first was the question of the advisability of his passage through the Suez Canal in view of 'our present unhappy relations with Egypt' and the possibility of adopting an alternative route. He then continued :

The other matter which troubles me is the political situation in this country. As I said at one of our talks in the summer (and you agreed with me) it would be very difficult indeed for me to go away for five or six months unless it was reasonably certain that political stability would prevail during my absence.

On the other hand, it would be disastrous if my visits to three [a] of the self-governing countries of the British Commonwealth (not to mention some of our Colonies) had to be postponed, or even interrupted, on account of political upheavals at home. You, as a former Secretary of State for the Dominions and as one who has an exceptionally wide experience of Commonwealth affairs, will need no reminder from me that the people of those countries which I have promised to visit would never understand the reason for such a postponement or interruption — and would never forgive it.

It would be a very great relief to me if you could now — or even in the next few weeks — give me some assurance that would set my mind at rest on this score.[34]

The Prime Minister had himself reached a similar conclusion. He had in fact made up his mind before the House rose for the Autumn Recess. The continuation of the factors in international and domestic issues presented difficulties to meet which the Government required more adequate support from the country and in the House of Commons, and Mr. Attlee fully appreciated the additional burden of anxiety which a prolongation of the existing situation would lay upon the Sovereign's shoulders during his projected absence from Britain.[35] By the time the King's letter reached him he had returned from his holiday in Norway, and on September 5 he replied :

I have been giving much anxious thought to the question of a General Election. Among the factors to which I have given particular attention was the need for avoiding any political crises while Your Majesty was out of the country. I have come to the conclusion that the right course would be to have a dissolution of

[a] The King and Queen were to have visited Ceylon *en route* for Australia and New Zealand.

Parliament in the first week of October. A later date would, I think, be undesirable as November is seldom a good month from the point of view of the weather.

I should, therefore, like to make a submission to Your Majesty in about a fortnight's time for the prorogation and dissolution of Parliament in the first week in October. This would, I think, give reasonable notice without unduly lengthening the election period.[36]

King George replied on the following day, expressing his relief at Mr. Attlee's decision to seek a Dissolution and appointing September 21 as the date on which he would welcome the Prime Minister at Balmoral and receive his submission.[37]

But by that date Fate had decreed otherwise. The King had written his original letter of September 5 in the complete faith that he would leave the United Kingdom according to programme early in the New Year. He had no idea how ill he was, and it was not until his doctors reported their findings to him on September 11 that he had any inkling of the gravity of his condition. He flew back to London on the 15th and the bronchoscopy was performed next day; it was therefore at Buckingham Palace and not at Balmoral that the Prime Minister made his submission for the Prorogation and Dissolution of Parliament.

In view of these facts it seemed right to Sir Alan Lascelles that the course of events should be recorded, lest any wrong construction should be placed upon them in the future. He therefore wrote a 'Personal and Secret' letter to Mr. Attlee on September 21 :

So that there may be no misinterpretation of recent events by historians in the future, I want to put the following record in our secret archives here : when The King wrote to you from Balmoral on September 1st urging that a decision should be taken to ensure political stability in this country before he left on his projected Commonwealth tour next January, he had no conception that his physical condition might make it necessary for him to abandon this tour ; indeed, he still believes today, on the eve of his serious operation, that he will be able to carry out the tour more or less as planned.

I should be very grateful if you could send me a brief acknowledgment of this letter.[a] [38]

[a] Mr. Attlee wrote on September 23 confirming the facts as quoted in Sir Alan's letter.[39]

The wisdom of the King's Private Secretary in thus placing upon record a change of circumstances dictated by forces beyond the King's knowledge or control is fully justified. Misunderstandings can occur all too easily in the search for truth.

On October 4 a Privy Council was held at Buckingham Palace, presided over by the Queen and Princess Elizabeth as Counsellors of State, at which an Order for the Prorogation of Parliament was approved. The final act of Dissolution, however, was performed by the Sovereign himself.[a] A second Council was summoned on the following day for this purpose. The King was still very weak. The Counsellors [b] stood in the doorway which separated the Audience Chamber from his bedroom and listened while the order of business was read by the Lord President. The King, with difficulty, uttered the word 'Approved'; then Sir Alan Lascelles carried to the bedside the three documents requiring signature and held them while the King affixed his name.[c]

The General Election of 1951, for which polling was held on October 25, was fought largely on general issues. The Labour Party claimed that they were the party of peace and coined the slogan: 'You can't trust the Tories'. The Con-

[a] Under Section 6 of the Regency Act of 1937 Counsellors of State are explicitly debarred from the power of dissolving Parliament 'otherwise than on the express instruction of the Sovereign', and so grave was the King's state of health immediately after his operation that, on September 28, a meeting of officials was held to consider the forms the Proclamation for the Dissolution of Parliament should take in the event of His Majesty's being compelled to issue these 'express instructions'. The drafts were prepared against the emergency but were not used because the King was able to hold the Council himself.

At a further meeting of officials on October 3 the point was raised as to what would happen to Parliament in the event of the demise of the Crown after the date of Dissolution. The answer was provided by the representative of the Home Office who cited the Meeting of Parliament Act of 1797. Under Section 3 of this measure it is provided that, if the Sovereign died after the Dissolution but before the assembly of a new Parliament, the dissolved Parliament should immediately convene and sit at Westminster for no longer than six months, unless sooner prorogued or dissolved. Similarly, Section 5 of the same Act further states that if the Sovereign died on the day appointed for calling a new Parliament and before that Parliament should have met and sat, it should immediately convene after the demise and sit for six months as above.

[b] The Privy Counsellors present on this occasion were the Lord Chancellor, Lord Jowitt; the Lord President, Lord Addison; the Home Secretary, Mr. Chuter Ede, and Sir Alan Lascelles.

[c] The three signatures required of the King were on the two Proclamations, one of which was in duplicate.

servatives responded by emphasizing the high cost of living and urged the electorate to 'Look what a mess Labour has made'. Full employment and housing came in the rank of secondary importance in the campaign; nationalization played little part at all.[40]

As the electoral campaign progressed there were few, if any, portents that the virtual stalemate of 1950 might not be repeated, with one or other of the major parties being returned by a bare majority. In view of this possibility Sir Alan Lascelles sought advice as to how King George might best proceed in such a contingency. On the eve of the declaration of the poll he sent His Majesty the following memorandum:

With my humble duty:

I saw John Anderson this afternoon, & asked his opinion on the best way Your Majesty could deal with the situation if neither side has a working majority after the election.

If Attlee is returned with the same sort of majority that he has now, then he thought that Your Majesty should warn him that a continuance of the present state of affairs would be very bad for the country, & suggest to him that he should try to form a National Govt.

If Attlee rejected this advice & said he would prefer to face the House of Commons, then the only course would be to let him do so — even if he only had a majority of one, or two.

Anderson thought this was the line Attlee would take, & that Winston would, if he got in with a tiny majority, take the same line; he knew Winston didn't like the idea of a Coalition, except in time of war.

But Winston *might* say to you that, though he didn't want to form a National Govt. himself, he was ready to make way for some other Conservative leader (e.g. Eden) & let him try.

If, in such circumstances, the Conservatives were to make a genuine attempt to form a National Govt. & the Labour Party were to refuse to join one, whether Winston, or A. Eden or anybody else were the head of it, then the only thing to be done would be to hold another General Election on that issue.

All this is very much the same as what Bobbety [Lord Salisbury] said to me at Hatfield a week ago.

Anderson's forecast seemed to be that the Conservatives would come back with a 30/40 majority, & that seems to be the most general opinion.[41]

In the event, Sir John Anderson's forecast proved to be over-optimistic. The contest resulted in no overwhelming majority for either of the major parties. When the last results became known they were as follows :

Conservatives	321
Labour	295
Liberals	6
Others	3

The Conservatives had thus achieved a majority of 17 (16 when one of their number had been elected Speaker) or twice that of Labour in 1950; but, despite this majority in seats, they had received 231,000 votes fewer than Labour in a poll which had accorded both parties a greater total of votes than any party had ever secured before.[a] [42] The Liberal Party, contesting 109 seats, pertinaciously refused to die.

King George, though barely convalescent, had followed the campaign with keen interest : 'I must be ready for the result of the General Election on the 25th', he had written to Queen Mary ten days earlier [43] — and he now awaited developments. Mr. Attlee conceded defeat on the afternoon of October 26 and intimated his intention to resign. He came to the Palace at 5 p.m. and received the thanks of his Sovereign for his great and important services during the arduous course of the past six and a half years. During this period Mr. Attlee had come to know the King well and to respect greatly his nobility of character, his humanity of outlook, his constitutional rectitude and his sense of duty. 'Few people realize how much time and care he gave to public affairs', he said later,[b] ' but visitors from overseas were often astonished at his close familiarity with all kinds of questions. With this close study went a good judgment and a sure instinct for what was really vital. During his reign there were developments in the Commonwealth, some of which entailed the abandonment of outward forms which a lesser man might have felt it difficult to surrender, but he was essentially broad-minded and was ready to accept changes that seemed necessary.'

For his part the King had grown to appreciate to the full the integrity and ability of one who had served him for eleven years as one of his Ministers and for six of them as Prime

[a] The Conservatives in 1951 received 13,717,538 votes as against 13,948,605 cast for Labour.
[b] In the House of Commons on February 11, 1952.

Minister.   On November 5 he received Mr. Attlee in audience
and conferred upon him the Order of Merit.[a]

At 5.45 on the afternoon of October 26 Mr. Churchill
drove to Buckingham Palace to receive from the King for
the third time, at the age of seventy-six, the mandate to
form a Government.   He accepted and at once embarked
upon the task of Cabinet-making.   This process was somewhat
complicated by the tendency on the part of the Prime Minister
to appoint Ministers to constitutionally non-existent offices.
His first list of submissions, for example, contained the name
of Mr. Eden as Secretary of State for Foreign Affairs and
'Deputy Prime Minister' — an office which does not exist in
the British constitutional hierarchy.   The King at once noticed
this irregularity and on his instructions the latter title was
deleted from Mr. Eden's appointment.[44]

The term 'Deputy Prime Minister' had, in fact, had an
unofficial existence for some time previous to this date.   Mr.
Churchill had initiated the custom in the Coalition Government
during the war when he wished to mark the special position of
Mr. Attlee as Leader of the Labour Party.   Mr. Herbert
Morrison had also had this additional title, as a matter of
usage, from the first appointment of the Labour Government
in 1945, and, when the Government was reconstituted in 1947,
the official announcement from 10 Downing Street said that
he would continue to act as 'Deputy Prime Minister'.   In these
circumstances Mr. Churchill's constitutional solecism of recommending Mr. Eden to the King as 'Foreign Secretary and
Deputy Prime Minister' is perhaps not surprising, since the
practice had become established by unofficial usage over the
preceding eleven years.

Nevertheless, it would seem highly undesirable that the
office of 'Deputy Prime Minister' should be officially recognized,
since such recognition would certainly imply the establishment
of a line of succession and would thereby impose a certain
restriction upon one of the unquestioned prerogatives of the
Sovereign — namely, the unfettered choice of a successor in
the event of the death or resignation of the Prime Minister.

The fact that the King was still in no very advanced a

---

[a] The King had written to Mr. Attlee on November 1 thanking him for his
services and notifying him of his desire to confer the Order of Merit upon him.

state of convalescence made the whole process of filling the
Ministerial posts somewhat abnormal, in that it was rendered
impossible for the Prime Minister to adhere to the traditional
custom of discussing these appointments with the Sovereign
privatim et seriatim.   Moreover, owing to the urgency of national
affairs at the moment, Mr. Churchill was naturally anxious
to get his Administration functioning, in all its departments,
with the least possible delay.   The King held the necessary
Privy Councils on October 27 and 30, for the reception of his
senior Ministers, and contented himself with Mr. Churchill's
informally acquainting him with the other appointments.

The King's state of health also precluded him from receiving individually each of his outgoing Administration,
amounting to 17 members of the Cabinet and 16 other
Ministers, as was normally his custom.   They therefore took
leave of him collectively, and each received a personal letter
of thanks.[45]

The process of Cabinet-making and leave-taking was completed by the end of the first week of November and the new
Parliament met on November 6, the King's Speech being read
by the Lord Chancellor.

(viii)

With the tension and excitement of the General Election
behind him, King George's recuperation progressed apace.
On November 30 he went out for the first time, motoring to
Royal Lodge, where he spent the week-end and walked in the
grounds of Windsor Castle.   He was delighted to be home
again.   'As we drove through the gates we felt at once the
calm of this place', he wrote to a friend.   Sunday, December 2,
was appointed as a day of National Thanksgiving for the
King's recovery, and on December 10 he signed the warrant
revoking the mandate of the Counsellors of State.

A great happiness came to him at this time in the success
of the first imperial mission to be undertaken personally by
Princess Elizabeth.   With the Duke of Edinburgh she had left
Britain on October 7 on a tour of Canada and a visit to the
United States.   In 35 days they crossed the North American
continent twice and travelled nearly 10,000 miles in Canada

alone, visiting every province of the Dominion, including that of newly incorporated Newfoundland.ᵃ Everywhere they encountered the still glowing memories of the visit of the King and Queen in the summer of 1939, and they left behind them felicitous impressions of themselves.

The press of the continent bore witness to the success of this mission. Though it was remarked that the anxiety caused by her father's illness, and the precarious state of health in which she had left him, had placed their mark upon the Princess,ᵇ she returned to London, in the happy phrase of the editor of *The Times*, 'adorned with the laurels of a glittering victory over the hearts of the Canadian people'.[46] In addition to her own personality and charm, Princess Elizabeth had renewed in the Canadian people their sense of possession. 'Here at least', wrote one of them, 'is something that the Americans have not got. Almost universally Canadians feel that Americans are always one gadget ahead of them. Here the Canadians had royalty, and it was their own, and the Americans had not got it.'

But the Americans, from the President to the man in the street, also claimed and acclaimed Princess Elizabeth and Prince Philip. None responded more cordially than President Truman. Warm-hearted and generous, he owed much of his political influence to the fact that the American people saw in him a reflection of themselves. He was deeply moved by the youth and charm of his guests and spoke repeatedly in terms of the highest admiration of the responsible and attentive manner in which they carried out their engagements.

We've just had a visit from a lovely young lady and her personable husband [he later wrote to King George].

They went to the hearts of all the citizens of the United States. We tried to make their visit a happy one.

As one father to another, we can be very proud of our daughters. You have the better of me — because you have two ! [47]

ᵃ Newfoundland, which had been a Crown Colony since 1855 and a Dominion since 1917, was, as a result of financial difficulties, placed under a form of Government by Commission in 1934 and so continued for the next fifteen years, when, as the result of a referendum, it was incorporated as a province into the Dominion of Canada in 1949.

ᵇ Princess Elizabeth was only too well aware of the dangerous condition of the King at the time of her departure. She took with her a sealed envelope containing, *inter alia*, the draft Accession Declaration and a Message to both Houses of Parliament, to be opened only in the event of the King's death.

The success of the visit of Princess Elizabeth and her husband was not one of mere emotional fervour. It established once again in the American mind a respect for both the humanity and the *mystique* of royalty,[a] and it played an important part in cementing still more firmly the structure of the Anglo-American Alliance. These facts were reported at length to King George by Sir Oliver Franks.

It is my good fortune to have been Your Majesty's Ambassador in Washington at the time of this visit [he wrote] and to share with others the very stimulating effect the visit has had on our good relations with the people of the United States. I am sure that the presence of Their Royal Highnesses here for this short visit of two days, enabled a large number of Americans, who have a very sincere affection for all things British and believe Your Majesty and the members of Your Family are the embodiment of all they so much admire in Britain, to be given an opportunity to demonstrate that affection and admiration. This is an aspect of American life which often seems to disappear under the pressures of politics, the stress of international affairs and the rapid tempo of the American way of life. But such occasions as last week's visit prove that, given the opportunity, the American people delight to show that there is a real and abiding bond between themselves and the British people.[48]

No circumstances, no congeries of events, could have delighted the heart of King George more supremely than these encomiums. His love for his daughter, a part of that great affection of family which was so vital a factor of his life, mingled with a new pride in her success in this her first mission overseas, and a new confidence in her evident and eminent ability to discharge her duty as his heir to a mighty heritage. He was keenly appreciative also of the considerable part played by Prince Philip, both in support of Princess Elizabeth and in his own right.

The King was determined, perhaps with memories of the lack of appreciation displayed by King George V of his own early missions abroad, to signify his pleasure at the triumph of Princess Elizabeth and the Duke of Edinburgh in a special

---

[a] 'I cannot believe that such a little girl can possess such quiet strength and serenity', a citizen of Washington wrote to a friend in England. 'This cannot be all trained into her; there is something deeper, God-given, I believe. She will be great in the days to come, because of this sweetness and humility which accompanies keen intelligence and perception' (*The Times*, November 17, 1951).

manner, by an act which would express at one and the same time both his pleasure as a father and his approbation as a Sovereign. He therefore wrote to Princess Elizabeth on November 28 :

To mark the return to this Country from your & Philip's most successful visit to Canada I propose to have you both introduced into the Privy Council. In other words to make you Privy Counsellors. I am holding a Council next Tuesday Dec. 4th, at 12.15 p.m. which I wish you to attend. Will you please come at 12.0 so that I can show you what you will have to do.

> From
>
> Your very loving & devoted
>
> PAPA.

King George's recovery was now well advanced; but a troublesome cough developed early in December which necessitated a second bronchoscopy by Sir Clement Price Thomas on the 13th. This was entirely successful and resulted in the disappearance of the cough; though a certain hoarseness remained, which was apparent in the King's Christmas broadcast, it was practically unnoticeable in his normal speech.

A great sense of peace and happiness now descended upon him. His sense of well-being returned and he looked forward to a period of years during which he could devote himself to the training of Princess Elizabeth in the art of statecraft. His immediate anxieties as to the political uncertainty in the country had been allayed by the result of the General Election, which had at least ensured a Government with a more secure lease of life than its predecessor. Serene in the affection of his family, the love of the Queen and of his daughters, and his own growing interest in his two grandchildren,[a] he was more contented in mind and confident in health than he had been at any time since the war. He looked forward with pleasure to the prospect of a private visit, as the guest of the Union Government, to South Africa, where Dr. Malan had placed a house at the disposal of the King and Queen, so that they might enjoy the warmth and sunshine so often denied to Britain in the spring. Plans were made for their departure on March 10.

[a] Princess Elizabeth's second child, the Princess Anne, was born on August 15, 1950.

In the meantime the King continued to live a quiet life in accordance with the normal precautions necessitated by his past illness. He celebrated his fifty-sixth birthday at Buckingham Palace and on December 21 went down to Sandringham. The family Christmas was a particularly happy one and it was remarked that the King himself was especially gay and carefree. He had been relieved of the burden of delivering his broadcast on Christmas Day, as the strain of so continuous a period of utterance had been considered too great. The broadcast had been recorded piece by piece as his strength allowed, and in it he expressed his deep thankfulness for his recovery and his gratitude for the sympathy that had been so lavishly bestowed upon him.

For not only by the grace of God and through the faithful skill of my doctors, surgeons and nurses have I come through my illness, but I have learned once again that it is in bad times that we value most highly the support and sympathy of our friends. From my peoples in these islands and in the British Commonwealth and Empire — as well as from many other countries — this support and sympathy has reached me, and I thank you now from my heart. I trust that you yourselves realize how greatly your prayers and good wishes have helped and are helping me in my recovery.

This note of hope and confidence was sustained in the New Year. The King continued to take his habitual avid interest in the course of events at home and abroad and also devoted much of his time to the affairs of his estate. With the approval of his doctors he had begun shooting soon after his arrival at Sandringham and was delighted to find that he achieved his normally high standard.

His confidence in his ultimate complete recovery of health was undimmed. 'I am seeing all my doctors next Tuesday morning, & I hope they will be pleased with my progress', he wrote to Queen Mary.[49] His expectations were fulfilled; after their examination at Buckingham Palace on January 29 the King's doctors were very well satisfied with their patient.

Next evening the Royal Family went to the theatre for the first time since the King's illness. They saw *South Pacific* at Drury Lane. It was in the nature of a celebration, partly in honour of the King's recovery, partly because it was to be the last occasion on which they were to be together for some

NOVEMBER 1951

time, since, on the morrow, Princess Elizabeth and the Duke of Edinburgh were to depart on the first stage of the journey which was to take them to East Africa, Australia and New Zealand. On the morning of January 31, hatless and wind-blown, the King waved good-bye to them at London Airport. The following day he returned, with the Queen and Princess Margaret, to Sandringham where a small party of friends assembled.

February 5 was a day of perfect weather, dry and cold and sunny. King George had never been in better form. It was a 'Keepers' Day', a day of rural sport, and the King shot hares with his usual accuracy. He was as carefree and happy as those about him had ever known him to be. At the end of the day he sent a word of congratulation to each of the keepers, and that evening, with his customary precision, he planned the next day's sport.

At dinner he was relaxed and contented. He retired to his room at 10.30 and was occupied with his personal affairs until about midnight, when a watchman in the garden observed him affixing the latch of his bedroom window, to which a new fastening had lately been attached. Then he went to bed and peacefully to sleep.

Very early on the morning of February 6 his heart stopped beating.

CHAPTER XIV

EPILOGUE

No more fitting epilogue to the life of King George VI, no better epitome of his character, can be found than in the words of Her Majesty Queen Elizabeth II on the occasion of the unveiling of King George's Memorial in the Mall on October 21, 1955. On that day Her Majesty said :

. . . Like his father, he expected to support the Throne rather than to fill it, but the unsparing devotion which he gave to his duties as Duke of York enabled him to assume with resolution the burden of Sovereignty. The pledge which he then gave to uphold the honour of the Realm and to promote the happiness of his peoples was the guiding principle of his life. To this he gave unremitting service and all his strength.

Within three years of his Accession to the Throne his peoples were faced with the challenge of war. His fortitude, determination and confidence throughout the perilous summer of 1940 and the anxious years that followed were an inspiration to all who loved freedom. He was the living symbol of our steadfastness. He never wavered in his faith that, with God's help, the cause of freedom would prevail. When London became the target he, like so many other gallant Londoners, stayed in his Capital and saw bombs fall on his home. There are many who remember to this day the comfort which he and my mother, during their visits to areas which had been bombed, gave to those who had suffered and had lost relatives, friends, and worldly possessions.

The friendliness and simplicity which so endeared him to his peoples during the trials of war were the fruit of a lifelong interest in his fellow men and of a human sympathy which was one of my father's most lovable qualities. . . .

It was this unassuming humanity, this respect for the 'homespun dignity of man', which enabled my father to preserve in a changing world that affection and respect for the Crown by which our free Commonwealth of Nations is united. In his broadcasts and his visits to the Empire and to Commonwealth countries he made himself the friend of peoples all over the World, and as the first British Sovereign to enter the United States of America he made a signal contribution to Anglo-American understanding. I know how deep was his regret that, after his tour of South Africa, he was prevented by illness from continuing the series of visits to the Commonwealth to which he had looked forward so keenly. . . .

Much was asked of my father in personal sacrifice and endeavour, often in the face of illness; his courage in overcoming it endeared him to everybody. He shirked no task, however difficult, and to the end he never faltered in his duty to his peoples. Throughout all the strains of his public life he remained a man of warm and friendly sympathies — a man who by the simple qualities of loyalty, resolution and service won for himself such a place in the affection of all of us that when he died millions mourned for him as for a true and trusted friend. . . .

APPENDICES

A REGENT AND COUNSELLORS OF STATE

I T is an essential and inevitable part of the structure of monarchy that provision be made for the maintenance of the Royal authority and of the machinery of government in the event of the minority or the incapacity, permanent or temporary, of the Sovereign, or of his absence from the country. The post-Conquest history of Britain is rich in varied examples of these precautions.

Thus, when in 1216 King John succumbed, as it is alleged, to a surfeit of ripe peaches and new cider, his heir Henry III was but nine years old, and a committee of prelates and barons entrusted the guardianship of the King to the Earl Marshal of England, William, Earl of Pembroke, with the title of *Rector Regis et Regni*. When Henry III died in 1272 his son and successor, Edward I, was abroad but, by arrangements made before his departure, the government of the realm was carried on under the Great Seal in the custody of the Archbishop of York (the see of Canterbury being vacant) until the King's return to England two years later. Edward III and Richard II both succeeded to the Throne as minors, but in neither case was a Regent appointed. In the first instance a Council of Bishops, Earls and Barons was constituted by Parliament to advise the King; in the second, the Lords themselves nominated a Council, without whose concurrence no measure might be put into effect.

For the infant Henry VI his uncle John, Duke of Bedford, was appointed by Parliament in 1422 as Regent for the Crowns of England and France, and during the King's two periods of insanity the Lords 'elected and nominated Richard Duke of York to be protector and defender of England during the King's pleasure'. There was also the debatable regency of Richard, Duke of Gloucester, for the youthful Edward V in 1483.

The first Regency Act proper in our history was that of 1536, whereby Henry VIII sought to secure the government of the realm should his children succeed to the Throne under the age of eighteen in the case of sons and sixteen in that of daughters. By his will the King appointed his sixteen executors to constitute the Privy Council which was to exercise collective authority until his son came of age. However, on his death in 1547, the Council set aside the King's wishes and appointed the Earl of Hertford, later Duke of Somerset, as Protector of the Realm and guardian of the new

King's person. This act was confirmed by the Lords temporal and spiritual, and by Letters Patent secured by the Protector from his young charge, Edward VI.

For the next two hundred years no provision was made for a Regency, though the disturbed state of the country on various occasions might well have warranted it.[a] But in 1751, George II being then sixty-eight years of age and his grandson and successor but thirteen, an Act was passed providing that, in the event of a minority succession, the Dowager Princess of Wales, the masterful Princess Augusta, should be Regent and Guardian of the Sovereign assisted by a Council of Regency, of whom the Duke of Cumberland was to be the head. The provisions of this Act were never exercised since George III was twenty-two on his accession, but his several illnesses and his eventual incurable insanity were the occasion of Regency Acts in 1765, 1788 and 1811.

Within the last hundred and forty-six years six Regency Acts have been passed in Britain, in 1830, 1840, 1910, 1937, 1943 and 1953, each providing in varying terms for the necessary contingencies. It has happily been the case that the provision of a Regent has been unnecessary, but there have been numerous occasions on which the Sovereign's illness or absence from the country has necessitated the appointment of Counsellors of State to whom the Royal functions have been delegated.

Before 1937 Counsellors of State were appointed under the Royal Prerogative. A Privy Council was held at which a draft Commission for the conduct of the business of the Realm was read and approved by the King, who then nominated the Counsellors of State. The Order in Council directed the Home Secretary to prepare a Commission in accordance with the draft approved by the King in Council.

This was the procedure followed in 1911, when King George V went to India for his Coronation Durbar; in March 1925, when the King went abroad; in December 1928, after he had declared in Council that 'having been stricken by illness, he was unable for the time being to give attention to the affairs of the Realm'; and again immediately before His Majesty's death in January 1936.

The circumstances attending this delegation of the Royal functions were undeniably complicated and cumbersome, and, after his illness in 1928, King George V gave much thought to the means

---

[a] On the death of Queen Anne in 1714 the Government was, in fact, carried on by the Lords Justices from August 1 to September 14, when George I arrived from Hanover. This was in pursuance of an Act (6 Anne, Cap. 7) which provided that if, at the death of the Queen, the heir-presumptive should be out of the Kingdom, the holders of certain great offices should be Lords Justices to exercise Royal Authority until the King arrived or determined their authority, there being no person qualified to be Regent.

by which the procedure might be simplified and improved. Both
he and King Edward VIII had intended to draw the attention of
Parliament to the matter, but this was not actually done until after
the accession of King George VI, one of whose first acts was to
send to both Houses of Parliament on January 26, 1937, a message
which recalled the difficulties which had arisen at the time of his
father's illnesses and added :

> The uncertainty of human life, and a deep sense of My duty
> to My People, render it incumbent upon Me to recommend to
> you to consider contingencies which may hereafter arise, and to
> make such provision as will, in any event, secure the exercise of
> the Royal Authority.

In response to this request a Bill was mmediately laid before
Parliament providing that, in the event of a Sovereign's being under
eighteen years of age, a Regent, who should be the person next in
line of succession to the Throne, should be appointed to perform
all the Royal functions until the Sovereign should have attained
that age. A Regent might also be appointed if the Sovereign were
certified by three of five personages, of whom one was the next of
kin (*i.e.* wife or husband), to be incapacitated by infirmity of body
or mind to give due attention to the affairs of the Realm.[a]

The Bill, which received the Royal Assent on March 19, 1937,
also changed and greatly simplified the procedure for the appointing of Counsellors of State, to whom a limited delegation of Royal
authority was to be made. Those prescribed by the Act to serve
in this capacity were the wife (or husband) of the Sovereign and
the four persons next in line of succession.

The change in the category of persons from whom Counsellors
of State may be appointed is of its own significance. When such
an appointment was made in 1928 the six Counsellors nominated
included, in addition to Members of the Royal Family, certain of
the great dignitaries of the Realm : the Archbishop of Canterbury,
the Lord Chancellor and the Prime Minister. Since that time,
however, the structure of the British Commonwealth had changed.
As a result of the developments to which legal effect was given by
the Statute of Westminster of 1931, the former supremacy of the
United Kingdom over the countries then known as Dominions had
been abrogated. For this reason it was held to be inconsonant with
the spirit of the new British Commonwealth that the Sovereign
should delegate his authority and functions to officials, however
distinguished they might be, of *one* of his kingdoms and, when the

---

[a] The four personages, other than the next of kin, were stated to be the Lord
Chancellor, the Speaker of the House of Commons, the Lord Chief Justice and
the Master of the Rolls. The Act required the certification of the Sovereign's
incapacity to be made by at least 'any three or more' of these persons.

next occasion arose in 1936 for the appointment of Counsellors of State, it was noticeable that they were confined to members of the Royal Family. This principle is now legally enshrined in the Regency Act of 1937.

The provisions of the Act of 1937 still remain the basic authority on the question of a delegation of Royal power and functions, but they have been subject to certain amendments. In 1943 a new Regency Act was passed containing two important changes. These were, first, that any one of the persons eligible as Counsellors of State who intended to be absent from the United Kingdom might be exempted from the duties of the delegation of powers; and second, that the heir-apparent, or heir-presumptive, to the Throne was declared to be eligible to serve as a Counsellor if not under eighteen years of age.

When King George VI went to visit his armies in Italy in 1944,[a] Letters Patent were issued appointing as Counsellors of State the Queen, Princess Elizabeth, the Duke of Gloucester, the Princess Royal and Princess Arthur of Connaught. The question was later raised as to whether Lord Lascelles, fourth in line of succession and then a prisoner of war in Germany, should have been nominated in place of Princess Arthur of Connaught. Absence from the United Kingdom *simpliciter* and unaccompanied by a change of domicile, did not, it was urged, constitute 'disqualification' within the meaning of the Regency Acts and, in any case, a prisoner of war does not cease to be domiciled in the country of his birth or origin. The matter was referred to the Lord Chancellor of the day, Lord Jowitt; after consideration he admitted that the Letters Patent were irregular in this respect and that Lord Lascelles should have been included in place of Princess Arthur who, in point of fact, never signed any documents as Counsellor of State.[b]

A further complication in the appointment of Counsellors of State arose in 1946 in the preparation for the Royal visit to South Africa in the following year. Of those eligible, the Queen and Princess Elizabeth would be accompanying the King, the Duke of Gloucester was in Australia as Governor-General and Lord Lascelles was serving as A.D.C. to the Governor-General of Canada. The Princess Royal alone was available.

Now the Regency Act of 1937 provides, subject to the amendment of 1943, that the Counsellors shall be the wife or husband of the Sovereign (if the Sovereign is married) and the four persons who, excluding any persons disqualified under this Act from

[a] See above, pp. 611-12.
[b] This point was originally raised by Mr. Edward F. Iwi, whose indefatigable researches have not infrequently led to the discovery of most interesting lacunae and imperfections in the legal sphere. Some account of these has been given in his book *Laws and Flaws*.

becoming Regent, are next in the line of succession to the Crown, or if the number of such persons next in the line of succession is less than four, then all such persons; and, moreover, that 'any functions delegated under this section shall be exercised jointly by the Counsellors of State, or by such number of them as may be specified in the Letters Patent, and subject to such conditions, if any, as may be therein prescribed'.

The custom had grown up that the delegated functions should be exercised jointly by two Counsellors of State acting together.[a] The question therefore arose as to who should be appointed in addition to the Princess Royal and, mindful of the irregularity of 1944, it was held that the fifth in succession to the Throne, Princess Arthur of Connaught, was again ineligible, since neither the Duke of Gloucester nor Lord Lascelles had changed his domicile, both being absent from the United Kingdom in the service of the Crown. It was therefore found necessary to terminate the Duke's term of office as Governor-General somewhat prematurely, in order that he might be in England by the time the Royal party left for South Africa in February 1947, and both he and Lord Lascelles were appointed to assist the Princess Royal as Counsellors of State.

Under the Regency Act of 1937 the actual method of procedure in the appointment of Counsellors of State is very simple. It might well have been designed to cause the least possible effort to a sick man, though it is, of course, called into effect for other causes than that of sickness. The Sovereign simply signs one document, and the signature does not even require a witness. It must, however, be countersigned by the Home Secretary, but not necessarily in the Sovereign's presence. This document is a Warrant addressed to the Lord Chancellor, directing him to cause the Great Seal of the Realm to be affixed to Letters Patent in the terms stated in the Warrant.

These Letters Patent constitute at once both the authority of and the charge to the Counsellors, and they remain in force until revoked by another Warrant under the King's hand. They read as follows: [b]

George the Sixth, by the Grace of God, of Great Britain, Northern Ireland and the British Dominions beyond the Seas, King, Defender of the Faith: To All Archbishops, Dukes, Marquesses, Earls, Viscounts, Bishops, Barons, Baronets, Knights,

---

[a] It is a matter of importance that, though the powers delegated to Counsellors of State are exercised by them jointly, or by such number as may be specified, they do not at any time constitute a Council of State.

[b] The following excerpt is taken from the Letters Patent issued on September 27, 1951, after King George VI's second operation, when the Queen, Princess Elizabeth, Princess Margaret, the Duke of Gloucester and the Princess Royal were appointed Counsellors of State.

Citizens and Burgesses and all Our other faithful Subjects what-soever to whom these Presents shall come, Greeting.

Whereas by section six of an Act passed in the first year of Our Reign intituled 'The Regency Act of 1937' it is amongst other things enacted that in the event of Our illness We may in order to prevent delay or difficulty in the despatch of public business by Letters Patent under the Great Seal delegate for the period of that illness to Counsellors of State such of Our Royal Functions as may, subject to the exception provided in the said Act, be specified in the Letters Patent, and Whereas by reason of Our illness We deem it expedient to delegate pursuant to the said section the Royal Functions hereinafter specified and Whereas the persons to whom the Royal Functions may by virtue of the said section as amended by an Act passed in the seventh year of Our Reign intituled 'The Regency Act of 1943', now be delegated by Us as Counsellors of State are . . .

The purpose of the delegation of the Royal functions is, in the words of the Act of 1937, 'to prevent delay or difficulty in the dispatch of public business'. The Letters Patent exclude from the authority of Counsellors of State not only the power to dissolve Parliament otherwise than on the express instructions of the Sovereign, to grant any rank, title or dignity of the peerage (as required by the Act) and to receive any homage required to be done to the Sovereign, but, in addition, the giving of the Royal Assent to any Act touching any of the matters for which provision is made in the Act of Settlement or touching the Royal Style and Titles, and also the approval or signature of warrants, fiats, sub-missions or other documents in connection with :

1. Awards of honours, decorations and medals.
2. Precedence to rank among nobility.
3. The use by British subjects of foreign titles and the wearing of foreign Orders in the United Kingdom.
4. Issue of writs in Peerage claims for the determination of abeyances.
5. Disbandment of Regiments and other Army Units and changes in Army and Air Force dress.
6. Matters arising in connection with the General Assembly of the Church of Scotland.
7. Amendment of Statutes of Orders.

The Counsellors are enjoined by the Letters Patent that if

        (a) the Sovereign has signified, or
        (b) it appears to them

that they should not act in any matter or for any purpose without previous special approval of the Sovereign, they should not act without that approval.

It is a matter of some importance that, generally speaking, the provisions of the Regency Acts do not bind the Governments of the Commonwealth, other than the United Kingdom Government, and are operative only in the United Kingdom and the Colonial Empire. Accordingly a Regent appointed under the Acts could not legally perform Royal Functions in other parts of the Commonwealth without his position being formally recognized by them, and, should those countries desire the Royal Functions to be performed by the Regent, appropriate legislation would be required.

Similarly, with regard to Counsellors of State; the temporary delegation of the Royal Functions and powers made to them by the Sovereign under the United Kingdom Acts would require special Commonwealth legislation to make it operative in the other component parts. In point of fact, however, it is always possible for the Sovereign, in the event of absence from the United Kingdom, to exercise these functions in respect of Commonwealth countries wherever he or she may be, and an instance of this is to be found in the fact that the Commission appointing Mr. William McKell to be Governor-General of the Commonwealth of Australia in 1947 was forwarded to King George VI in South Africa for signature.

The last occasion in the life of King George VI when the provisions of the Regency Act of 1937, as amended in 1943, were called into operation was the appointment of Counsellors of State in September 1951. His death and the accession of Queen Elizabeth II in the following year created certain anomalies in the terms of the Acts which required legislative correction.

On Wednesday, November 3, 1953, a Message from The Queen to Parliament invited the consideration of certain amendments to the Regency Act of 1937, in respect of its provisions for the appointment of a Regent. Under the then existing provisions the person who would become Regent, if the Duke of Cornwall or any other child of The Queen and the Duke of Edinburgh were to succeed to the Throne while under the age of eighteen, or if The Queen became totally incapacitated and there were no child or grandchild of sufficient years, would be the Princess Margaret, the Duke of Edinburgh being thus debarred from becoming Regent or guardian of his own children. Both The Queen and Princess Margaret were now desirous that the statutory provisions should be so amended that, should the necessity arise, His Royal Highness should become Regent though, in the event of his death, such amendment would cease to have effect and the Regency would revert to Princess Margaret.

The argument in favour of such a provision was clear and was placed before the House of Commons by the Home Secretary, Sir David Maxwell Fyfe:

> I cannot imagine anyone thinking that it could be right that, in the event of his child succeeding to the Throne under age, His Royal Highness the Duke of Edinburgh should not be the guardian of the Sovereign. As soon as it is thought right that he should be the guardian, we are faced with the position of the Sovereign during the important and formative years immediately before he assumes the Royal Power. Only from the Regent would he receive the practical instruction in the relative problems which he will have to face. I do not need to look into the past, or speculate whether opposing households are still a possibility of the present. The interests of the prospective Sovereign surely make a combination of Regency, guardianship and paternal influence, in the same hand, the most desirable course. . . .
>
> I hope that no one will think it out of place on my part if I say — indeed, I am sure that everyone will agree — that the Duke of Edinburgh has already won such a high place in the affection of the country, and has already proved himself such a great help to The Queen, as undoubtedly to merit a place in the line of potential Regents.[a]

These proposals, which had already received the approval of the Prime Ministers of the Commonwealth in the course of their discussions in London at the occasion of the Coronation, now commended themselves to the House of Commons, as did also The Queen's wish that the Act of 1937 be further amended to provide for the continued eligibility of Queen Elizabeth The Queen Mother to serve as a Counsellor of State, since this had lapsed on her ceasing to be the wife of the Sovereign.

The result was the Regency Act of 1953, wherein it is provided that, in the event of the succession to the Throne while under eighteen years of age of one of the children of The Queen and the Duke of Edinburgh, the Duke shall be Regent, and, further, that, if a Regency should become necessary during The Queen's lifetime, the Duke shall also be Regent 'unless, or (as the case may be) until, there is a child or grandchild of Her Majesty and His Royal Highness who can under the provision of the said Act [of 1937] be the Regent'.

It is further provided that Queen Elizabeth The Queen Mother should continue to be eligible as a Counsellor of State, in addition to the five persons qualified to serve under the Act of 1937.

[a] *Parliamentary Debates*, House of Commons, November 11, 1953, col. 952.

THE SOVEREIGN'S PRIVATE SECRETARY

IT is perhaps characteristic of what foreigners are apt to regard as the inveterate tendency to 'amateurism' in the British Way of Life — a tendency which has, more than once, proved to be our salvation — that the British Constitution, which remained steadfastly silent as to the position of a Prince Consort and for forty years refused recognition of the office of Prime Minister,[a] should be equally incognizant of so important a factor in its functioning as the Private Secretary to the Sovereign. The ponderous tomes of Anson and Dicey, the sparkling pages of Bagehot, the weighty treatises of Professor Berriedale Keith and Sir Ivor Jennings, though they have collectively illuminated to a very great degree our knowledge of what has been called 'the complicated metaphysics of limited monarchy', have shed but little light upon this vital link between the Crown and the Cabinet, between the Monarch and the machinery of government, and between the Sovereign and the Commonwealth.

The origin and growth of the office of Private Secretary to the Sovereign are in themselves amply illustrative of the advantages of an unwritten Constitution which, being a living organism, retains the power to adapt itself to necessities and the ability to accept the *de facto* with the same equanimity as the *de jure*: that genius for assimilation which has proved so vital in preserving the Monarchy, the Realm and the Commonwealth.

The Sovereign has always had his advisers. Originally these were the Lords of the Council assisted by clerks and secretaries. Secretaries of State emerged during the reign of Queen Elizabeth I, and, as the effective power of government passed from the Privy Council to Parliament, the Secretaries of State, as the executive committee of the Privy Council, became the Cabinet, bearing collective responsibility for the advice tendered to the Sovereign through their presiding officer and chief, the First Lord of the

---

[a] The traditional title of the head of the Sovereign's Government is the First Lord of the Treasury. The first mention of the office of Prime Minister is said to occur in a document signed by Mr. Disraeli during his second administration (1874–1880) (Paul H. Emden, *Behind the Throne*, p. 16); it was not accorded official recognition in the table of precedence until the reign of King Edward VII, and it was not until 1937 that the office was first established (Section 4 (1) of the Ministers of the Crown Act, 1937) when it was provided that a payment of an annual salary of £10,000 be paid to 'the person who is Prime Minister and First Lord of the Treasury'.

Treasury. It was customary for the King to attend the meetings of his Council, and though, for various reasons, George I
and George II frequently absented themselves and left much of
the transaction of the business of State to their First Ministers,
George III gave assiduous attention to the affairs of the realm, not
only conducting his own correspondence but keeping copies of his
letters in his own hand.

The constitutional theory obtaining at this time was that the
Secretary of State for Home Affairs was the King's Private Secretary,
and that it was both undesirable and irregular for anyone not a
Privy Counsellor to have access to Cabinet secrets.[a]   In 1805,
however, George III, having become almost totally blind, appointed,
in defiance of tradition, Lieut.-General Sir Herbert Taylor to be
his Private Secretary. This step, revolutionary in itself, was of the
greater importance because, in addition to his blindness, the King's
mental condition was rapidly deteriorating. General Taylor continued to give him valuable assistance until the final attack of
insanity in 1810 resulted in the establishment of the Regency.

Parliament, which had been highly suspicious of the appointment of Sir Herbert Taylor, proved definitely hostile when the
Prince Regent sought in 1812 to nominate Colonel McMahon as
his Private Secretary at a salary of £2000 a year. The House of
Commons raised a great clamour, one member declaring that the
office of Private Secretary was 'dangerous and unconstitutional,
rendering the person holding it the secret adviser of the Sovereign
with a degree of influence over his mind totally at variance with
the forms of Government in England. . . . The office [he continued]
would be destructive of a fundamental principle of the constitution,
which was that no one ought to use the name of the Sovereign,
give him advice, or be the bearer of his commands, unless he be one
of the responsible ministers of the Crown, and answerable to
Parliament.' In a division in a House of nearly three hundred
members the appointment of the Prince Regent's Secretary was
carried by seventy votes.[b]

The Prince Regent retained Colonel McMahon's services for
a while, creating him a Privy Counsellor, and subsequently a
baronet. Later, however, the Regent circumvented the objections
of the House of Commons by employing Sir William Knighton,
an eminent physician, as Keeper of the Privy Purse, in which
capacity he also served as Private Secretary. Sir William gave the
Regent remarkably good advice not only on political matters but
also in the highly complicated state of His Royal Highness's finances.

William IV recalled Sir Herbert Taylor from retirement and

    [a] Lord Ponsonby of Shulbrede, *Henry Ponsonby, Queen Victoria's Private Secretary*,
p. 34.
    [b] Randolph Churchill, *They serve the Queen*, pp. 51-52.

that tried veteran, who had been admitted to the Privy Council after serving as Ambassador in Berlin, gave patient and diplomatic counsel to his Sovereign during the period of agitation for Reform, in the course of which the King caused his Cabinet no little anxiety. This same experienced counsellor was summoned by Queen Victoria shortly after her accession to the Throne and consulted on the question of the appointment of a Private Secretary. 'Is Your Majesty afraid of the work?' Sir Herbert inquired, and on receiving the Queen's 'No', he continued: 'Then don't have a Private Secretary'.[a] This advice the Queen followed, at least in form. Lord Melbourne combined the office of Prime Minister with that of private mentor and there followed the beneficent influence of Prince Albert as the Queen's chief adviser. Baron Stockmar acted in the capacity of Her Majesty's Private Secretary but was never so called, and it was not until after the death of the Prince Consort that the Queen appointed his former Private Secretary as her own — General Charles Grey, son of the Prime Minister of the Reform Bill.

General Grey served the Queen from 1861 to 1870 when he was succeeded by Colonel Henry Ponsonby. By this time the office of Private Secretary had become officially recognized, though Colonel Ponsonby was not sworn of the Privy Council until ten years after his appointment. On his death in 1895 he was in turn succeeded by Sir Arthur Bigge, later Lord Stamfordham.

King Edward VII on his accession appointed Sir Francis (later Viscount) Knollys, who had been his Private Secretary when Prince of Wales, in succession to Sir Arthur Bigge, who joined the Household of the Duke of Cornwall and York. When the latter came to the Throne as King George V he recalled Sir Arthur, while still retaining Lord Knollys, and the office of Private Secretary was held in diarchy until the retirement of Lord Knollys in 1913.   Lord Stamfordham continued to serve until his death in 1931.

Thereafter the Private Secretaries to the Sovereign have been as follows:

George V   Sir Clive Wigram, 1931–1935.
Edward VIII   Major Alexander Hardinge, January–December 1936.
George VI   Sir Alexander Hardinge, 1936–1943.
              Sir Alan Lascelles, 1943–1951.
Elizabeth II Sir Alan Lascelles, 1951–1953.
              Sir Michael Adeane, 1953–.

Though the office of Private Secretary to the Sovereign was officially accepted during the incumbency of General Grey, it is to Sir Henry Ponsonby and Lord Stamfordham, who between them

[a] Emden, p. 14.

occupied the office for over fifty years, that it owed the establishment of its prestige and importance. Theirs was the wisdom, the patience and the discretion which established the office, both in the mind of the Sovereign and in the mind of successive governments, as what Lord Rosebery did not hesitate to describe as being 'the most important in the public service',[a] — a far cry from the criticisms raised in the House of Commons a hundred years before. Moreover — a development of equal importance — they set the pattern and example which their successors in office have followed so ably.

What, then, was this pattern of conduct for the Sovereign's Private Secretary which has been handed down? It may be epitomized in the triple formula of the Sovereign's own prerogatives defined by Walter Bagehot — 'the right to be consulted, the right to encourage and the right to warn'. These guiding principles may equally well apply to the Private Secretary, though, under the pressure of this modern period, too strict an interpretation of the 'right to be consulted' would be impossible.

The Private Secretary is the eyes and ears of his Sovereign. For, in order that the machinery of government may function smoothly, it is essential that the Sovereign must be fully informed on all current topics and on all basic issues. The Private Secretary plays a leading rôle, perhaps *the* leading rôle, in the maintenance of friendly relations between the Sovereign and the Ministers of the Crown; indeed, it is he more than anyone else who creates for the Sovereign the background of the régime, and from him, through his constant intercourse with all national leaders, that the general impression of the reign is largely drawn. He must owe loyalty to none but the Sovereign, whose complete confidence he must enjoy. Never must he be a Civil Servant in forced allegiance to the Government of the day. His complete independence of view must inspire confidence in the Opposition Party, which will show a good return when this party comes into power. He must know all that is going on and must be ready to advise upon all. Yet he must never so advise that he appears to influence the decision of the Sovereign in terms of the premise of his own thought.

Those who have read Lord Ponsonby's biography of his father and Sir Harold Nicolson's penetrating study of Lord Stamfordham in his biography of King George V will realize the degree to which these two men adhered in practice to the principles of their conception. Under their influence the office of Private Secretary attained the heights which it today maintains and to which so striking a tribute was paid by the late Professor Harold Laski in a review of Lord Ponsonby's book: [b]

[a] Emden, p. 224.
[b] Harold J. Laski, 'The King's Secretary', *Fortnightly Review*, vol. 158, July–December 1942.

. . . He [the Private Secretary] is the confidant of all Ministers, but he must never leave the impression that he is anybody's man. He must intrude without ever seeming to intrude. He must learn how to deflect the lightning from others. He must be able to carry the burden of the Sovereign's mistakes. He must not know the meaning of fatigue. He must take correction without being provoked to the humanity of remonstrance. He must accept condescension as a favour, and he must know when to be deaf and blind. He must have the art of translating attitudes into the gestures which make the royal relations possible. Receiving a thousand secrets, he must discriminate between what may emerge and what shall remain obscure. And he has to steer his way through the complicated labyrinth of anxious politicians, jealous courtiers, the mass of continental royalties, each of whom is on the watch lest a right be withheld or a claim denied.

It is a life passed amid circumstances in which the most trifling incident may lead to major disaster. It is a life, too, which affords the maximum opportunity for the mischief-maker. The royal secretary walks on a tight-rope below which he is never unaware that an abyss is yawning. If the Monarch is lazy, like Edward VII, his very presence may almost become an error of judgment. If the Monarch is hard-working, like Queen Victoria, all his tact and discretion are required to keep firmly drawn the possible lines of working relations in a constitutional system. He has to be himself, since his sincerity is the crux of his position; but he must never be so insistently himself that Ministers are disturbed by his influence. It is vital that he be a judge of character; he has to thread his way through a host of influences the effective measurement of which is essential to the Monarch's position. He has to translate the obvious decisions of common sense into the elaborate formulae which the etiquette of the system requires. He must accept its pomps and ceremonies without fatigue; and he must be able to make the elegant minuet he is constantly performing capable of adaptation to a world which is constantly changing. Half of him must be in a real sense a statesman, and the other half must be prepared, if the occasion arise, to be something it is not very easy to distinguish from a lacquey. . . .

For he has to put aside his personal views; a private secretary to the Monarch who pushed his ideas might easily precipitate a crisis. He must be pretty nearly selfless; once private ambition begins to colour his horizons, his usefulness is over. He must move serenely amid all the events which move other men to passionate statement; he must seem, therefore, never to feel while he never appears to be without the power of sympathetic

response. The secretary to the Monarch, in short, occupies to
the Crown much the same position that the Crown itself in our
system occupies to the Government ; he must advise and encourage
and warn. But whereas the Monarch can speak his mind — as
we know from the royal letters of the last hundred years — the
private secretary has no such luxury. He interprets as best
he can a tradition which is never quite the same from one
Monarch to another with the same Monarch. . . .

. . . I do not think it is beyond the mark to say that a bad
private secretary, one who was rash, or indiscreet, or untrust-
worthy, might easily make the system of constitutional monarchy
unworkable unless the Monarch himself was a person of extraordinary wisdom. This is so because the system is built on
compromises, accommodations, a process of half-measures, in which
an attempt, on either side, to dominate might rapidly produce
an explosive atmosphere. The Monarch, with us, has grown in
influence as he has surrendered power and the very fact of that
growth means that those who are playing for power will seek to
capture his influence. To keep the Monarch nicely balanced in
the delicate position he occupies is likely to call for a diplomatic
talent of the first order.

This tribute of Professor Laski's, though directed primarily
toward the conduct of Sir Henry Ponsonby, is entirely applicable
to the office of Private Secretary in the present day. Within the
last half-century there have been certain occasions in which, without his wise and tactful counsel, a situation might have developed
in which the Crown might have become the arbiter of national
destiny — a situation which it must ever be his object to prevent.
Bad advice by Lord Stamfordham in 1923, when Mr. Bonar Law
resigned and the choice of a successor as Prime Minister lay
between Mr. Baldwin and Lord Curzon, or a year later, when the
Labour Party first took office, might have induced a major political
crisis. Similarly, an indiscretion by Sir Clive Wigram in the
delicate and dangerous conditions which underlay the crisis of
1931, when King George V invited Mr. MacDonald to form a
National Government, might have provoked a political conflict of
the first magnitude. There was the melancholy duty of Sir Alexander Hardinge in writing his famous letter to King Edward VIII
in November 1936, in which he warned the Sovereign of impending
crisis, and there were not infrequent occasions during the post-war
years of King George VI's reign when a faulty judgment by Sir
Alan Lascelles might have led to grave difficulties.

Complex and sensitive though the task of the Sovereign's
Private Secretary has always been, it is increasingly so today and
its importance is even more greatly enhanced. For upon his

shoulders lies the major responsibility for maintaining the Crown as 'a dignified emollient', an essential and vital element in the metaphysics of constitutional monarchy. Nor is this all. With the emergence of the New Commonwealth the Private Secretary has become the sole link between the Sovereign and her Governors-General overseas, and between Her Majesty and her Prime Ministers, not only in Westminster but also in Ottawa, Canberra, Wellington, Cape Town, Colombo and Accra. He must 'shape the whisper to the Throne' as it is spoken in not one but seven countries, for all have equal right of access to their Sovereign, and the channel of that access is the office of the Private Secretary.

Such is the task and the trust of one of the least known but most responsible officers of the Crown, for in his hands, more perhaps than in those of any other individual in the Commonwealth, lies the continued well-being of the Monarchy. As Sir Alan Lascelles informed the Select Committee on the Civil List in December 1947 :

> Any Member of the Committee who may have read Sir Henry Ponsonby's letters, or an excellent article by Professor Harold Laski in the *Fortnightly* a year or two ago, will know what I mean when I say that life in that office is not by any means beer and skittles. His [the Private Secretary's] work, both in volume and in responsibility, is continually increasing. . . .
>
> In my office at present we compare unfavourably with our relative opposite numbers in the Civil Service, as regards man-hours per day, as regards pay, and as regards leave. We serve, I may remind you, one of the very few men in this world who never gets a holiday at all and who, unlike the rest of us, can look forward to no period of retirement at the end of his Service, for his Service never ends.

APPENDIX C

MINISTERS OF KING GEORGE VI

1936-1952

MINISTERS OF KING GEORGE VI
1936-1952

	December 1936	May 28, 1937
Prime Minister	Stanley Baldwin	Neville Chamberlain
Lord Chancellor	Lord Hailsham	Lord Hailsham Lord Maugham
Lord President	Ramsay MacDonald	Lord Halifax Lord Hailsham Lord Runciman
Lord Privy Seal	Lord Halifax	Lord De La Warr Sir John Anderson
Home Office	Sir John Simon	Sir Samuel Hoare
Foreign Office	Anthony Eden	Anthony Eden Lord Halifax
Exchequer	Neville Chamberlain	Sir John Simon
Dominions Office	Malcolm MacDonald	Malcolm MacDonald Lord Stanley Sir Thomas Inskip
Colonial Office	William Ormsby-Gore	William Ormsby-Gore Malcolm MacDonald
Scotland	Walter Elliot	Walter Elliot D. J. Colville
Defence*	Sir Thomas Inskip	Sir Thomas Inskip Lord Chatfield
Admiralty	Sir Samuel Hoare	Alfred Duff Cooper Lord Stanhope
War	Alfred Duff Cooper	Leslie Hore-Belisha
Air	Lord Swinton	Lord Swinton Sir Kingsley Wood
Labour	Ernest Brown	Ernest Brown
Board of Trade	Walter Runciman	Oliver Stanley
Health	Sir Kingsley Wood	Sir Kingsley Wood Walter Elliot
Agriculture	W. S. Morrison	W. S. Morrison Sir Reginald Dorman-Smith
Education	Oliver Stanley	Lord Stanhope Lord De La Warr
India	Lord Zetland	Lord Zetland

* Minister for the Co-ordination of Defence, 1936-1940. Mr. Winston Churchill assumed the office of Minister of Defence together with that of Prime Minister in May 1940 and Mr. Attlee continued to hold both offices until the Ministry of Defence was formally established as a Government department by an Act of 1946.

	September 3, 1939	*May 11, 1940*
Prime Minister	Neville Chamberlain	Winston S. Churchill
Lord Chancellor	Lord Caldecote	Lord Simon
Lord President	Lord Stanhope	Neville Chamberlain Sir John Anderson Clement Attlee
Lord Privy Seal	Sir Kingsley Wood	Clement Attlee Sir Stafford Cripps Lord Beaverbrook
Home Office	Sir John Anderson	Sir John Anderson Herbert Morrison
Foreign Office	Lord Halifax	Lord Halifax Anthony Eden
Exchequer	Sir John Simon	Sir Kingsley Wood Sir John Anderson
Dominions Office	Anthony Eden	Lord Caldecote Lord Cranborne Clement Attlee Lord Cranborne
Colonial Office	Malcolm MacDonald	Lord Lloyd Lord Moyne Lord Cranborne Oliver Stanley
Scotland	D. J. Colville	Ernest Brown Thomas Johnston
Defence*	Lord Chatfield	Winston S. Churchill
Admiralty	Winston S. Churchill	A. V. Alexander
War	Leslie Hore-Belisha Oliver Stanley	Anthony Eden David Margesson Sir James Grigg
Air	Sir Kingsley Wood Sir Samuel Hoare	Sir Archibald Sinclair
Labour	Ernest Brown	Ernest Bevin
Board of Trade	Oliver Stanley Sir Andrew Duncan	Sir Andrew Duncan Oliver Lyttelton Sir Andrew Duncan J. J. Llewellin Hugh Dalton
Health	Walter Elliot	Malcolm MacDonald Ernest Brown H. U. Willink
Agriculture	Sir Reginald Dorman-Smith	R. S. Hudson
Education	Lord De La Warr H. Ramsbotham	H. Ramsbotham R. A. Butler
India	Lord Zetland	L. S. Amery

	May 23, 1945	*July 26, 1945*
Prime Minister	Winston S. Churchill	Clement Attlee
Lord Chancellor	Lord Simon	Lord Jowitt
Lord President	Lord Woolton	Herbert Morrison
Lord Privy Seal	Lord Beaverbrook	Arthur Greenwood Lord Inman Lord Addison
Home Office	Sir Donald Somervell	J. Chuter Ede
Foreign Office	Anthony Eden	Ernest Bevin
Exchequer	Sir John Anderson	Hugh Dalton Sir Stafford Cripps
Dominions Office (until 1947)	Lord Cranborne	Lord Addison
Commonwealth Relations (from 1947)		Philip Noel-Baker
Colonial Office	Oliver Stanley	G. H. Hall A. Creech Jones
Scotland	Lord Rosebery	Joseph Westwood Arthur Woodburn
Defence*	Winston S. Churchill	Clement Attlee A. V. Alexander
Admiralty	Brendan Bracken	A. V. Alexander Lord Hall
War	Sir James Grigg	J. J. Lawson F. J. Bellenger Emanuel Shinwell
Air	Harold Macmillan	Lord Stansgate Philip Noel-Baker Arthur Henderson
Labour	R. A. Butler	George Isaacs
Board of Trade	Oliver Lyttelton	Sir Stafford Cripps Harold Wilson
Health	H. U. Willink	Aneurin Bevan
Agriculture	R. S. Hudson	Tom Williams
Education	Richard Law	Ellen Wilkinson George Tomlinson
India (until 1947)	L. S. Amery	Lord Pethick-Lawrence Lord Listowel

	March 1, 1950	*October 26, 1951*
Prime Minister	Clement Attlee	Winston S. Churchill
Lord Chancellor	Lord Jowitt	Lord Simonds
Lord President	Herbert Morrison Lord Addison	Lord Woolton
Lord Privy Seal	Lord Addison Richard Stokes	Lord Salisbury
Home Office	J. Chuter Ede	Sir David Maxwell Fyfe
Foreign Office	Ernest Bevin Herbert Morrison	Anthony Eden
Exchequer	Sir Stafford Cripps Hugh Gaitskell	R. A. Butler
Commonwealth Relations	Patrick Gordon Walker	Lord Ismay
Colonial Office	James Griffiths	Oliver Lyttelton
Scotland	Hector McNeill	James Stuart
Defence	Emanuel Shinwell	Winston S. Churchill
Admiralty	Lord Hall Lord Pakenham	J. P. L. Thomas
War	John Strachey	Antony Head
Air	Arthur Henderson	Lord De L'Isle and Dudley
Labour	George Isaacs Aneurin Bevan Alfred Robens	Sir Walter Monckton
Board of Trade	Harold Wilson Sir Hartley Shawcross	Peter Thorneycroft
Health	Aneurin Bevan H. A. Marquand	Harry Crookshank
Agriculture	Tom Williams	Sir Thomas Dugdale
Education	George Tomlinson	Florence Horsbrugh
Local Government	Hugh Dalton	Harold Macmillan

BIBLIOGRAPHY

THE books listed below are all, except where stated, published in Great Britain.

For purposes of general reference I have used *Hansard Debates*, the latest available edition of the *Encyclopaedia Britannica*, the 1950 edition of *Chambers's Encyclopaedia*, *The Annual Register*, *The Statesman's Year-Book*, *Whitaker's Almanack*, and that admirable publication once issued — but, alas, no longer — by the Royal Institute of International Affairs, at first under the title of the *Bulletin of International News* and latterly as *The World To-day*, *Chronology and Documents*. I have also used the files of *The Times* and the *Scotsman* and other newspapers. I wish to acknowledge my indebtedness to all these publications and also to the staff of *The Times* Reference Room for their unfailing help and courtesy.

J. W. W.-B.

(i) BIOGRAPHY AND AUTOBIOGRAPHY

AMERY, L. S. *My Political Life*, 3 vols. (1953–1955).
ARTHUR, Sir George. *King George V, a Sketch of a Great Ruler* (1929).
ASPINALL-OGLANDER, G. *Roger Keyes* (1951).
ASQUITH, Lady Cynthia. *The Family Life of Her Majesty Queen Elizabeth* (1937).
ATTLEE, C. R. *As it Happened* (1954).
BALDWIN, A. W. *My Father, the True Story* (1955).
BOLITHO, Hector. *King George VI* (1937).
BROAD, Lewis. *Sir Anthony Eden* (1955).
   Winston Churchill (1956).
BROMAGE, Mary C. *De Valera and the March of a Nation* (1956).
BROME, Vincent. *Aneurin Bevan, a Biography* (1953).
BRYANT, Sir Arthur. *The Turn of the Tide* (1957).
BUCHAN, John. *The King's Grace* (1935).
BUXTON, Aubrey. *The King in his Country* (1955).
BYRNES, James F. *Speaking Frankly* (New York, 1947).
CECIL, Lady Gwendoline. *Life of Robert, Marquess of Salisbury* (1931).
CHURCHILL, Sir Winston S. *The Second World War*, 6 vols. (1948–1954).
   The World Crisis (1931).
Ciano's Diplomatic Papers (1948).
CLARK, General Mark. *Calculated Risk* (1951).
COOKE, Dr. Colin. *The Life of Richard Stafford Cripps* (1957).
CRAWFORD, Marion. *The Little Princesses* (1950).
CUNNINGHAM, Admiral of the Fleet Lord. *A Sailor's Odyssey* (1951).
CURZON, Marchioness of. *Reminiscences* (1955).

DALTON, Dr. Hugh. *The Fateful Years, 1931–45* (1957).
DARBYSHIRE, Taylor. *In the Words of the King* (1938).
King George VI, an Intimate and Authentic Biography (1937).
DUGDALE, Mrs. Edgar. *Arthur James Balfour* (1936).
EASTWOOD, G. G. *George Isaacs* (1952).
EISENHOWER, General Dwight D. *Crusade in Europe* (1948).
ELLIS, Jennifer. *The Royal Mother* (1954).
FEILING, Keith. *The Life of Neville Chamberlain* (1946).
FULFORD, Roger. *The Prince Consort* (1949).
GAULLE, General Charles de. *The Call to Honour* (1955).
GORE, John. *King George V, a Personal Memoir* (1941).
GRIGG, Sir James. *Prejudice and Judgment* (1948).
HALIFAX, Earl of. *Fulness of Days* (1957).
Hitler's Table Talk (1953).
ICKES, Harold L. *Secret Diary*, 3 vols. (1955).
JOHNSON, Alan Campbell. *Anthony Eden* (1938).
Viscount Halifax (1941).
JONES, Thomas. *A Diary with Letters* (1954).
KENNEDY, Major-General Sir John. *The Business of War* (1957).
King George VI to his Peoples, 1936–1951 (1952).
KING PETER II of Yugoslavia. *A King's Heritage* (1955).
LEAHY, Admiral William D. *I was There* (1950).
LEE, Sir Sidney. *King Edward VII. A Biography*, 2 vols. (1925–1927).
LEGGE, Edward. *King Edward VII in his True Colours* (1913).
LLOYD, Air Marshal Sir Hugh. *Briefed to Attack* (1949).
LLOYD GEORGE, David. *War Memoirs* (1933–1936).
LOCKHART, J. G. *Cosmo Gordon Lang* (1949).
McINTIRE, Vice-Admiral Ross T. *Twelve Years with Roosevelt* (1948).
McNAIR, John. *James Maxton, the Beloved Rebel* (1955).
MARTIN, Sir Theodore. *The Life of the Prince Consort*, 5 vols. (1874–1876).
MAUGHAM, Viscount. *At the End of the Day* (1954).
Memoirs of Cordell Hull (New York, 1955).
MORRAH, Dermot. *The Royal Family in Africa* (1947).
MURPHY, Ray. *The Last Viceroy* (1948).
NICOLSON, Sir Harold. *King George V: His Life and Reign* (1952).
NORWICH, Viscount. *Old Men Forget* (1953).
OWEN, Frank. *Tempestuous Journey* (1954).
PONSONBY, Sir Frederick. *Recollections of Three Reigns* (1951).
PONSONBY, Lord. *Henry Ponsonby* (1943).
PRINCESS MARIE LOUISE. *My Memories of Six Reigns* (1956).
PUDNEY, John. *His Majesty King George VI, a Study* (1952).
QUEEN ALEXANDRA of Yugoslavia. *For Love of a King* (1956).
QUEEN VICTORIA. *Letters, 1837–1901*, 3 series.
Leaves from the Journal of our Life in the Highlands (1868).
More Leaves (1884).
REITH, Rev. George M. *Reminiscences of the United Free Church General Assembly, 1900–1929* (1933).
REITH, Lord. *Into the Wind* (1949).
ROOSEVELT, Eleanor. *This I Remember* (New York, 1949).
SAMUEL, Viscount. *Memories* (1945).

832 BIBLIOGRAPHY

SHAKESPEARE, Sir Geoffrey. *Let Candles be brought in* (1949).
SHERWOOD, Robert E. *Roosevelt and Hopkins* (New York, 1948).
SHEW, Betty Spencer. *Queen Elizabeth, the Queen Mother* (1955).
SIMON, Viscount. *Retrospect* (1952).
SMUTS, J. C. *Jan Christian Smuts* (1952).
SOMERVELL, D. C. *Stanley Baldwin* (1953).
SPEARS, Sir Edward. *Assignment to Catastrophe,* 2 vols. (1954).
SPENDER, J. A., and ASQUITH, Cyril. *Life of Lord Oxford and Asquith* (1932).
STIMSON, Henry L., and BUNDY, McGeorge. *On Active Service* (New York, 1948).
SWINTON, Viscount. *I Remember* (1948).
TEMPLEWOOD, Viscount. *Nine Troubled Years* (1954).
THOMPSON, George Malcolm. *The Life and Times of King George VI* (1953).
TRUMAN, Harry S. *Year of Decisions* (New York, 1955).
Years of Trial and Hope (New York, 1956).
WATSON, Francis. *Dawson of Penn* (1951).
WELLES, Sumner. *The Time for Decision* (New York, 1944).
WHIBLEY, Charles. *William Pitt* (1906).
WILLIAMS, Francis. *Ernest Bevin* (1952).
WINANT, John G. *A Letter from Grosvenor Square* (1947).
WINDSOR, Duchess of. *The Heart has its Reasons* (1956).
WINDSOR, H.R.H. the Duke of. *A King's Story* (1951).
WINTERTON, Earl. *Orders of the Day* (1953).
WRENCH, Sir Evelyn. *Geoffrey Dawson and our Times* (1955).
WRIGHT, Rev. G. N. *The Life and Reign of King William the Fourth* (1837).
YOUNG, G. M. *Stanley Baldwin* (1952).

(ii) HISTORY AND POLITICS

AMERY, L. S. *Thoughts on the Constitution* (1953).
ATTLEE, C. R. *The Labour Party in Perspective* (1937).
BAGEHOT, Walter. *The English Constitution* (1949).
BEVERIDGE, Lady. *Beveridge and his Plan* (1954).
BEVERIDGE, Lord. *Full Employment in a Free Society* (1944).
BROOKS, Graham. *Dukes of York* (1927).
BUCHAN, John, and SMITH, George Adam. *The Kirk in Scotland* (1930).
BUTLER, D. E. *The British General Election of 1951* (1952).
BUTLER, R. A., and others. *Conservatism, 1945–1950* (1950).
CARTER, Byrnes E. *The Office of Prime Minister* (1956).
COLLIER, Basil. *The Defence of the United Kingdom* (1957).
CORBETT, Sir Julian. *History of the Great War, Naval Operations,* Vol. III (1923).
COUPLAND, Sir Reginald. *The Cripps Mission* (1942).
Documents on German Foreign Policy, 1918–1945 (1949).
DRUMMOND, Donald F. *The Passing of American Neutrality* (1955).
ELLIS, Major L. F. *The War in France and Flanders, 1939–1940* (1953).
FALLS, Cyril. *The Second World War* (1948).
FLEMING, Peter. *Invasion 1940* (1957).

Foreign Relations of the United States; The Conferences at Malta and Yalta, 1945 (Washington, 1955).

FULLER, Major-General J. F. G. *The Second World War, 1939–1945* (1948).

GARBETT, Most Rev. Cyril, Archbishop of York. *The Claims of the Church of England* (1947).

GRIFFITHS, Sir Percival. *The British Impact on India* (1952).

HENDERSON, Dr. G. D. *The Church of Scotland* (1939).

History of 'The Times', The, Part II (1952).

IWI, Edward F. *Laws and Flaws* (1956).

JACKSON, J. Hampden. *The Post-War Decade* (1955).

JENNINGS, Sir Ivor. *Cabinet Government* (1936).

KEITH, A. B. *The British Cabinet System* (1939).
   The Constitution of England from Victoria to George VI (1940).
   The King, the Constitution, the Empire and Foreign Affairs, 1936–1937 (1938).

KENNEDY, Senator John F. *Profiles in Courage* (1956).

McCALLUM, R. B., and READMAN, Alison. *The British General Election of 1945* (1947).

McKENZIE, R. T. *British Political Parties* (1955).

McMILLAN, Rev. W. *The Office of the Lord High Commissioner to the General Assembly of the Church of Scotland* (1924).

MANSERGH, Nicholas. *Documents and Speeches on British Commonwealth Affairs, 1931–1952*, 2 vols. (1953).
   Survey of British Commonwealth Affairs, 1931–1939 (1952).
   The Commonwealth and the Nations (1948).

MOOREHEAD, Alan. *African Trilogy* (1944).

MORRISON, Herbert. *Government and Parliament* (1954).

MOWAT, Charles Loch. *Britain between the Wars. 1918–1940* (1955).

NICHOLAS, H. G. *The British General Election of 1950* (1951).

O'BRIEN, Terence H. *Civil Defence* (1955).

PETRIE, Sir Charles. *Monarchy in the Twentieth Century* (1952).

PLAYFAIR, Major-General I. S. O. *The Mediterranean and the Middle East*, 2 vols. (1954–1956).

RALEIGH, Sir Walter, and JONES, H. A. *The War in the Air* (1922–1937).

SCHUSTER, Sir George, and WINT, Guy. *India and Democracy* (1941).

SIMON, Viscount. *The Crown and the Commonwealth* (1953).

SOMERVELL, D. C. *British Politics since 1900* (1953).

Stalin's Correspondence with Churchill, Attlee, Roosevelt and Truman, 1941–1945 (1958).

TOYNBEE, Arnold. *Survey of International Affairs*, 6 vols. (1938–1950).

WATT, Hugh. *Thomas Chalmers and the Disruption* (1943).

WHEARE, Kenneth C. *The Statute of Westminster and Dominion Status* (1953).

WILMOT, Chester. *The Struggle for Europe* (1952).

WINT, Guy. *The British in India* (1947).

(iii) GENERAL

'BARTIMEUS.' *The Navy Eternal* (1918).

BERTON, Pierre. *The Royal Family* (New York, 1954).

BLACK, Percy. *The Mystique of Modern Monarchy* (1953).

BROWN, Ivor. *Balmoral* (1955).

CHURCHILL, Randolph. *They Serve the Queen* (1953).

EELES, Francis C. *The Coronation Service* (1953).

EMDEN, Paul H. *Behind the Throne* (1934).

FLETCHER, I. H. *The British Court : its Traditions and Ceremonial* (1953).

HARDINGE OF PENSHURST, Lady. *The Path of Kings* (1952).

HOGART, A. M. *Kingship* (1927).

HUGHES, E. A. *The Royal Naval College, Dartmouth* (1950).

HYDE, Sir Robert. *The Camp Book* (1930).

LYSONS, Rev. Daniel. *The Environs of London* (1792).

MACKENZIE, Sir Compton. *The Queen's House* (1953).

MICHIE, Allan A. *The Crown and the People* (1952).

NARES, Gordon. *Royal Homes* (1953).

PERKINS, Jocelyn. *The Crowning of the Sovereign* (1953).

RADCLIFFE, Lord. *The Problem of Power* (1952).

ROPER, Lanning. *Royal Gardens* (1953).

SHEWELL-COOPER, W. E. *The Royal Gardeners* (1952).

WINDSOR, H.R.H. the Duke of. *The Crown and the People, 1902-1953* (1953).

REFERENCES

PART I

PRINCE ALBERT, 1895–1920

CHAPTER I

THE NURSERY AND THE SCHOOLROOM, 1895–1908

1. R.A. G.V. AA. 7/7-14.
2. *The London Gazette*, December 13, 1895, Special Supplement dated December 14.
3. H.R.H. The Duke of Windsor, *A King's Story*, p. 1.
4. R.A. G.V. AA. 31/42.
5. R.A. G.V. AA. 44/31.
6. R.A. King George V's Diary, December 14, 1895.
7. R.A. Vic. Z. 477/222.
8. R.A. Vic. Z. 58/60.
9. R.A. G.V. AA. 20/64.
10. R.A. G.V. AA. 20/65.
11. R.A. Vic. Z. 477/235.
12. R.A. Queen Victoria's Diary, December 14, 1895.
13. R.A. { Vic. Z. 477/236.
        { G.V. AA. 11/11.
14. R.A. (Queen Mary's Papers) undated.
15. *The Times*, February 18, 1896.
16. R.A. Queen Mary's Diary, December 14, 1895.
17. R.A. King George V's and Queen Mary's Diaries, February 17, 1896.
18. R.A. G.V. AA. 12/43.
19. John Gore, *King George V, A Personal Memoir*, pp. 128-129.
20. Sir Harold Nicolson, *King George V, His Life and Reign*, p. 51.
21. Gore, pp. 367-370.
22. Duke of Windsor, *A King's Story*, p. 7.
23. R.A. Queen Victoria's Diary, May 10, 1898.
24. R.A. G.V. AA. 58/1.
25. Duke of Windsor, *A King's Story*, p. 13.
26. R.A. (Queen Mary's Papers) Prince Albert to the Duke and Duchess of Cornwall and York, March 12, 1901.
27. Duke of Windsor, *A King's Story*, p. 17.
28. Sir Sidney Lee, *King Edward VII: a Biography*, Vol. I, p. 27.
29. *Ibid.* p. 28.
30. Nicolson, p. 7.
31. *Ibid.* p. 105.
32. Duke of Windsor, *A King's Story*, p. 39.
33. R.A. (Queen Mary's Papers) Prince Albert to the Princess of Wales, February 26, 1904.
34. Duke of Windsor, *The Crown and the People*, p. 14.
35. R.A. G.V. AA. 58/58.
36. R.A. G.V. AA. 63/I/21.
37. R.A. G.V. AA. 58/59.

38. R.A. G.V. AA. 63/I/43.
39. R.A. G.V. O. 2573/15.
40. R.A. G.V. O. 2573/31.
41. Duke of Windsor, *A King's Story*, p. 44.

CHAPTER II

OSBORNE, DARTMOUTH AND 'CUMBERLAND', 1908–1912

1. Sir Theodore Martin, *Life of the Prince Consort*, Vol. I, p. 247.
2. R.A. Vic. Y. 92/16.
3. Martin, Vol. I, pp. 247, 249.
4. Duke of Windsor, *A King's Story*, p. 13.
5. R.A. (Queen Mary's Papers). Prince of Wales to the Princess of Wales, August 4, 1903.
6. Letter from Messrs. Gieves to the author, March 18, 1953.
7. E. A. Hughes, *The Royal Naval College, Dartmouth*, p. 50.
8. R.A. (Queen Mary's Papers) Prince Albert to the Princess of Wales, January 19, 1909.
9. R.A. (Queen Mary's Papers) Prince Edward to the Princess of Wales, January 24, 31, and February 14, 1909.
10. R.A. G.V. AA. 63/I/56.
11. 'Bartimeus', *The Navy Eternal*, p. 41.
12. R.A. G.V. O. 2575/134.
13. R.A. G.V. AA. 63/I/53.
14. Lee, Vol. II, p. 692.
15. R.A. G.V. O. 2575/172.
16. R.A. G.V. O. 2575/181.
17. Duke of Windsor, *A King's Story*, p. 68.
18. Nicolson, p. 125.
19. R.A. G.V. O. 2575/184.
20. R.A. G.V. O. 2575/166 and 203.
21. R.A. G.V. AA. 58/155.
22. R.A. G.V. O. 2575/199.
23. R.A. G.V. O. 2573/37.
24. Hughes, p. 20.
25. *The Lancet*, February 18, 1911.
26. Duke of Windsor, *A King's Story*, p. 77.
27. R.A. G.V. O. 2573/38.
28. R.A. G.V. O. 2575/372.
29. R.A. G.V. AA. 58/319.
30. *Daily Graphic*, February 28, 1912.
31. R.A. (Queen Mary's Papers) Prince Albert to Queen Mary, February 28, 1912.
32. R.A. G.V. AA. 59/14.
33. R.A. G.V. AA. 59/15.
34. Nicolson, p. 159.
35. R.A. G.V. AA. 59/50 and 51.
36. R.A. Queen Mary's Diary, and Prince Albert's Diary, April 18, 1912.
37. St. Luke xxii. 19.
38. Prince Albert to Bishop Boyd-Carpenter, April 17, 1914. (British Museum Dept. of Manuscripts, Boyd-Carpenter Papers, Vol. VI, Additional Manuscript, 46722.)
39. R.A. (Queen Mary's Papers) Prince Albert to Queen Mary, October 2, 1912, and Prince Albert's Diary, October 1, 1912.

40. R.A. G.V. O. 2575/403.
41. R.A. G.V. O. 2575/203.
42. Duke of Windsor, *A King's Story*, p. 75.
43. R.A. G.V. AA. 63/III/73.
44. R.A. (Queen Mary's Papers) Prince Albert to Queen Mary, January 26, 1913.
45. Hector Bolitho, *George VI*, p. 40.
46. R.A. Prince Albert's Diary, March 8, 1913.
47. R.A. G.V. AA. 59/133.
48. R.A. G.V. AA. 59/19.
49. Prince Albert's Diary, June 6, 1913.
50. R.A. G.V. O. 2573/41.

CHAPTER III

NAVAL CAREER, 1913-1917

1. R.A. Prince Albert's Diary, November 24, 1913.
2. R.A. G.V. AA. 47/211.
3. R.A. G.V. AA. 59/208.
4. R.A. Prince Albert's Diary, December 1, 1913.
5. *Ibid.* December 14, 1913.
6. R.A. (Queen Mary's Papers) Prince Albert to Queen Mary, December 14, 1913.
7. R.A. G.V. AA. 59/226.
8. R.A. G.V. AA. 59/228.
9. Nicolson, pp. 237-239.
10. R.A. G.V. AA. 59/245.
11. R.A. G.V. AA. 59/240.
12. R.A. G.V. AA. 59/242.
13. R.A. Prince Albert's Diary, July 1, 1914.
14. Winston S. Churchill, *The World Crisis*, pp. 108-109.
15. R.A. Prince Albert's Diary, July 20, 1914.
16. R.A. G.V. AA. 59/285.
17. R.A. G.V. AA. 59/287.
18. Churchill, *The World Crisis*, p. 124.
19. R.A. Prince Albert's Diary, August 5, 1914.
20. R.A. King George V's Diary, August 5, 1914.
21. R.A. G.V. AA. 59/290.
22. R.A. G.V. AA. 59/291.
23. R.A. G.V. AA. 65/19
24. R.A. G.V. AA. 59/304.
25. R.A. G.V. AA. 59/296.
26. R.A. Prince Albert's Diary, September 19, 1914.
27. R.A. G.V. AA. 59/314.
28. R.A. G.V. AA. 59/324.
29. R.A. G.V. AA. 59/325.
30. R.A. G.V. AA. 59/328.
31. R.A. G.V. AA. 60/8.
32. R.A. G.V. AA. 60/9.
33. R.A. G.V. AA. 60/18.
34. R.A. G.V. AA. 60/43.
35. R.A. G.V. AA. 60/24.
36. R.A. G.V. AA. 60/34.

37. R.A. G.V. AA. 60/37.
38. R.A. G.V. AA. 65/58.
39. R.A. G.V. AA. 65/59.
40. R.A. G.V. AA. 65/71.
41. R.A. G.V. AA. 65/66.
42. Sir Julian Corbett, *History of the Great War, Naval Operations,* Vol. III, pp. 320-321.
43. R.A. (George VI Collection).
44. R.A. G.V. Q. 832/435.
45. R.A. (George VI Collection).
46. R.A. G.V. Q. 832/366.
47. R.A. Vic. Addl. MSS. A/15/6596.
48. R.A. (George VI Collection).
49. R.A. (George VI Collection).
50. R.A. G.V. AA. 60/126.
51. R.A. G.V. AA. 60/135.
52. Queen Mary's Diary, September 2, 1916.
53. R.A. G.V. AA. 60/175.
54. R.A. G.V. AA. 60/178.
55. R.A. (Queen Mary's Papers) Prince Albert to Queen Mary, December 20, 1916.
56. R.A. G.V. AA. 60/179.
57. R.A. (Queen Mary's Papers) Prince Albert to Queen Mary, June 13, 1917.
58. R.A. G.V. AA. 60/240.
59. R.A. G.V. AA. 60/244.
60. R.A. G.V. AA. 60/249.
61. R.A. G.V. AA. 60/251.
62. R.A. G.V. AA. 60/257.
63. R.A. G.V. AA. 63/III/118.

CHAPTER IV

CRANWELL AND CAMBRIDGE, 1918–1920

1. Sir Walter Raleigh, *The War in the Air,* Vol. I, pp. 198-213.
2. R.A. G.V. AA. 60/280.
3. R.A. (Queen Mary's Papers) Prince Albert to Queen Mary, February 6, 1918.
4. R.A. (Queen Mary's Papers) Prince Albert to Queen Mary, March 5, 1918.
5. R.A. (Queen Mary's Papers) Prince Albert to Queen Mary, April 24, 1918.
6. H. A. Jones, *The War in the Air,* Vol. VI, pp. 26-27.
7. R.A. G.V. AA. 60/301.
8. R.A. G.V. AA. 60/302.
9. Jones, *The War in the Air,* Vol. VI, pp. 101-117.
10. R.A. G.V. AA. 60/304.
11. R.A. G.V. AA. 60/309.
12. R.A. G.V. AA. 60/345.
13. R.A. (Queen Mary's Papers) Prince Albert to Queen Mary, November 6, 1918.
14. R.A. G.V. AA. 60/365.
15. R.A. G.V. AA. 60/371.
16. R.A. G.V. AA. 60/375.
17. R.A. (Queen Mary's Papers) Prince of Wales to Queen Mary, December 6, 1918.

18. R.A. (Queen Mary's Papers) Prince Albert to Queen Mary, January 1, 1919, and G.V. AA. 60/381.

19. R.A. G.V. AA. 60/383.

20. R.A. G.V. AA. 60/388.

21. Roger Fulford, *The Prince Consort*, pp. 258-259.

22. Rudyard Kipling, 'The Scholars', *Rudyard Kipling's Verse*, Definitive Edition.

23. Bolitho, pp. 111-112.

24. R.A. G.V. O. 1595/1.

25. Walter Bagehot, *The English Constitution*, World's Classics Edition, p. 35.

26. *Ibid.* p. 53.

27. *Ibid.* pp. 34-35.

28. *Ibid.* p. 37.

29. Professor J. R. M. Butler, 'H.M. King George VI as a Trinity Man', *The Trinity Magazine*, May Term 1952.

30. The Marchioness Curzon of Kedleston, *Reminiscences*, p. 133.

31. Privy Purse File, No. 10792.

32. R.A. G.V. AA. 61/14.

33. R.A. (Queen Mary's Papers) Prince Albert to Queen Mary, April 30, 1920.

34. *The London Gazette*, June 4, 1920, Second Supplement, June 5, 1920.

PART II

DUKE OF YORK, 1920–1936

CHAPTER I

ENGAGEMENT AND MARRIAGE, 1920–1923

1. Nicolson, p. 47.
2. R.A. G.V. AA. 10/39.
3. R.A. G.V. AA. 61/27.
4. R.A. (G. VI Collection) King George V to Duke of York, June 7, 1920.
5. R.A. G.V. P. 1675/8.
6. Lee, Vol. II, pp. 272-273.
7. Edward Legge, *King Edward in his True Colours*, pp. 81-82.
8. R.A. G.V. AA. 43. Addenda.
9. R.A. G.V. P. 1788/2.
10. R.A. (Queen Mary's Papers) Lord Stamfordham to Queen Mary, October 24, 1922.
11. R.A. (Queen Mary's Papers) Duke of York to Queen Mary, January 16, 1923.
12. R.A. G.V. AA. 61/179.
13. Lord Reith, *Into the Wind*, p. 94.
14. Bagehot, p. 34.
15. Graham Brooks, *The Dukes of York*.
16. *The Times*, Special Supplement, April 25, 1923.
17. R.A. (Queen Mary's Papers) Duke of York to Queen Mary, May 25, 1923.
18. R.A. (Queen Mary's Papers) Duke of York to Queen Mary, April 27, 1923.
19. R.A. G.V. AA. 61/156.

CHAPTER II

INDUSTRIAL RELATIONS

1. Duke of Windsor, *A King's Story*, p. 120.
2. David Lloyd George, *War Memoirs*, Vol. IV, p. 1963.
3. R.A. Conf. G.V. O./1341.
4. R.A. G.V. Q. 724.110.
5. Frank Owen, *Tempestuous Journey*, pp. 498-499.
6. Duke of Windsor, *A King's Story*, pp. 131-132.
7. Lloyd George, Vol. I, pp. 347-353.
8. Owen, p. 302.
9. Mr. Hyde to Dr. Bell, January 22, 1919.
10. Wing Cdr. Louis Greig to Mr. Hyde, March 19, 1919.
11. Mr. Hyde to the Archbishop of Canterbury, April 16, 1919.
12. Prince Albert to the Industrial Welfare Society, May 1919.
13. *The Times*, February 2, 1952.

14. *Yorkshire Post*, April 27, 1928.
15. Duke of York to Mr. Hyde, September 4, 1934.

CHAPTER III

'MY CAMP'

1. R.A. (King George VI's Papers) Duke of York to Sir Alexander Grant, December 14, 1933.
2. Robert R. Hyde, *The Camp Book*, p. 11.
3. Article signed CALO, *Bedfordshire Times and Independent*, August 26, 1921.
4. Hyde, p. 81.
5. *Ibid.* p. 38.
6. R.A. (King George VI's Papers) Duke of York to Sir Alexander Grant, April 10, 1930.
7. R.A. Duke of York to Captain J. G. Paterson, January 24, 1933.

CHAPTER IV

WIDENING EXPERIENCE, 1923–1926

1. Rev. Daniel Lysons, *The Environs of London* (1792), Vol. I.
2. Sir Walter Scott, *The Heart of Midlothian*, chapter 37.
3. C. Pellew, *Life and Correspondence of Henry Addington, 1st Lord Sidmouth*, Vol. II, p. 37; Rear-Admiral Alfred Thayer Mahan, *Life of Nelson*, pp. 703-704; Carola Oman, *Nelson*, p. 600.
4. Lee, Vol. I, pp. 48-49.
5. R.A. (Queen Mary's Papers) Duke of York to Queen Mary, June 21, 1923.
6. R.A. Diaries of King George V and Queen Mary, June 28, 1923.
7. R.A. G.V. AA. 61/189.
8. *Ibid.*
9. King Peter II of Yugoslavia, *A King's Heritage*, p. 1.
10. R.A. G.V. AA. 61/189.
11. Nicolson, pp. 379-384.
12. R.A. G.V. AA. 61/196.
13. R.A. (Queen Mary's Papers) Duke of York to Queen Mary, April 4, 1924.
14. Nicolson, pp. 351-352.
15. R.A. G.V. AA. 61/213.
16. R.A. G.V. AA. 61/227.
17. R.A. G.V. AA. 61/232.
18. *Ibid.*
19. *Ibid.*
20. R.A. Duke of York's Diary, December 28, 1924.
21. *Ibid.* December 28, 1924.
22. R.A. G.V. AA. 61/235.
23. R.A. (Queen Mary's Papers) Duke of York to Queen Mary, January 3, 1925.
24. R.A. G.V. AA. 61/234.
25. R.A. Duke of York's Diary, February 11, 1925.
26. R.A. G.V. AA. 61/244.
27. *Ibid.*

28. R.A. G.V. AA. 61/249.
29. Reith, p. 96.
30. R.A. King George V's Diary, April 23, 1924.
31. R.A. G.V. AA. 61/250.
32. R.A. G.V. AA. 61/252.
33. Duke of Windsor, *A King's Story*, p. 211.
34. R.A. (Queen Mary's Papers) Duke of York to Queen Mary, April 22, 1926.
35. R.A. G.V. AA. 61/310.
36. R.A. G.V. AA. 61/311.
37. R.A. (Queen Mary's Papers) King George V to Queen Mary, April 25, 1926.

CHAPTER V

THE WORLD TOUR AND AFTER, 1927–1929

1. Nicolson, pp. 66-68.
2. Duke of Windsor, *A King's Story*, pp. 152-161.
3. R.A. G.V. AA. 61/337.
4. *Logue Papers*, Duke of York to Mr. Logue, January 5, 1927.
5. *Ibid.* Duke of York to Mr. Logue, September 11, 1927.
6. R.A. (Queen Mary's Papers) King George V to Queen Mary, August 29, 1927.
7. Nicolson, pp. 427-428.
8. R.A. G.V. AA. 62/17.
9. R.A. G.V. AA. 62/20.
10. R.A. G.V. AA. 62/2.
11. R.A. G.V. P. 476/71.
12. R.A. G.V. NC. 44029.
13. R.A. (Queen Mary's Papers) Duke of York to Queen Mary, February 27, 1927.
14. R.A. G.V. P. 476/77.
15. R.A. G.V. AA. 62/6.
16. R.A. G.V. AA. 62/15.
17. R.A. G.V. P. 476/78.
18. R.A. G.V. NC. 44029.
19. R.A. (Queen Mary's Papers) Mr. P. K. Hodgson to Queen Mary, April 11, 1927.
20. R.A. G.V. AA. 62/20.
21. R.A. (Queen Mary's Papers) Duke of York to Queen Mary, March 26, 1927.
22. R.A. Mr. P. K. Hodgson to Queen Mary, May 10, 1927.
23. R.A. G.V. NC. 44029.
24. R.A. G.V. AA. 62/30. May 12–June 12/1927.
25. R.A. G.V. P. 1867/14.
26. R.A. G.V. AA. 62/30. May 12–June 12/1927.
27. R.A. G.V. AA. 62/31.
28. Duke of Windsor, *A King's Story*, pp. 211-212.
29. Nicolson, pp. 430-432.
30. Duke of Windsor, *A King's Story*, p. 224.
31. *Ibid.* p. 230.
32. John Buchan, *The King's Grace*, p. 305.
33. *Logue Papers*, Letter from the Duke of York, December 15, 1928.

CHAPTER VI

LORD HIGH COMMISSIONER TO THE GENERAL
ASSEMBLY OF THE CHURCH OF SCOTLAND, 1929

1. R.A. Vic. Y. 93/48.
2. R.A. Vic. Y. 96/36.
3. R.A. Queen Victoria's Diary.
4. Fulford, p. 82.
5. R.A. G.V. 4866/A.
6. R.A. G.V. 4866/A.
7. R.A. G.V. 4866/A.
8. R.A. G.V. 4866/A.
9. Rev. George M. Reith, *Reminiscences of the United Free Church General Assembly, 1900-1929*, pp. 336-337.
10. R.A. G.V. 4866/A.
11. R.A. G.V. 4866/A.
12. *The Scotsman* (Editorial), May 20, 1929.
13. R.A. (Queen Mary's Papers) Duchess of York to Queen Mary, May 25, 1929.
14. R.A. G.V. 4866/B.
15. R.A. G.V. AA. 62/100.
16. *The Glasgow Herald*, October 3, 1929.
17. John Buchan and George Adam Smith, *The Kirk in Scotland, 1560-1929*, p. 212.
18. R.A. G.V. AA. 62/101.

CHAPTER VII

SIX QUIET YEARS, 1930-1935

1. R.A. G.V. P. 780/64.
2. R.A. (Queen Mary's Papers) Duke of York to Queen Mary, August 10, 1930.
3. R.A. G.V. AA. 62/113.
4. R.A. King George V's Diary, August 22, 1930.
5. R.A. Queen Mary's Diary, August 30, 1930.
6. R.A. (Queen Mary's Papers) Duchess of York to Queen Mary, August 27, 1930.
7. R.A. (Queen Mary's Papers) Duchess of York to Queen Mary, September 6, 1930.
8. R.A. G.V. L. 2314/21.
9. R.A. G.V. L. 2314/27.
10. R.A. G.V. L. 2314/28.
11. R.A. G.V. AA. 62/144.
12. R.A. G.V. AA. 62/145.
13. *Ibid.*
14. Duke of York to Mr. Ronald Tree, September 18, 1931.
15. Duke of York to Commander Colin Buist, September 17, 1931.
16. W. E. Shewell-Cooper, *The Royal Gardeners*, p. 49.
17. Duke of York to the Countess of Stair, May 27, 1935.
18. R.A. (King George VI's Papers) Countess of Stair to the Duke of York, June 2, 1935.

19. Nicolson, p. 525.
20. Duke of Windsor, *A King's Story*, p. 254.
21. R.A. Queen Mary's Diary, January 16, 1936.
22. R.A. Queen Mary's Diary, January 17, 1936.
23. Duke of Windsor, *A King's Story*, p. 262.
24. R.A. Queen Mary's Diary, January 20, 1936.

CHAPTER VIII

THE REIGN OF KING EDWARD VIII:
JANUARY–DECEMBER 1936

1. *The Times*, January 22, 1936.
2. Duke of Windsor, *A King's Story*, p. 278.
3. *Ibid.* pp. 283-384.
4. *Ibid.* p. 278.
5. Duchess of Windsor, *The Heart has its Reasons*, p. 224.
6. Duke of Windsor, *A King's Story*, p. 265.
7. *Ibid.* pp. 292-293.
8. *Ibid.* p. 258.
9. R.A. (Queen Mary's Papers) Duke of York to Queen Mary, October 13, 1936.
10. Duke of Windsor, *A King's Story*, p. 306.
11. *The History of 'The Times'*, Part II, p. 1027.
12. Duke of Windsor, *A King's Story*, p. 315.
13. Viscount Templewood, *Nine Troubled Years*, p. 219.
14. R.A. (Queen Mary's Papers) Duke of York to Queen Mary, November 6, 1936.
15. R.A. Queen Mary's Diary, December 9, 1936.
16. Ecclesiasticus, ii. 5.
17. Reith, p. 270.

PART III

KING GEORGE VI, 1936-1952

CHAPTER I

THE FIRST YEAR, 1936-1937

1. R.A. (George VI, Private Papers, Box No. 2) Duke of Connaught to King George VI, December 15, 1936.
2. J. G. Lockhart, *Cosmo Gordon Lang*, p. 407.
3. R.A. (Queen Mary's Collection) Queen Elizabeth to Queen Mary, December 14, 1936.
4. King George VI to Mr. Baldwin, December 31, 1936 (*Baldwin Papers*, Cambridge University Library).
5. R.A. G.VI Conf./342, Mr. Baldwin to King George VI, January 2, 1937.
6. Sir Charles Petrie, *Monarchy in the Twentieth Century*, p. 111.
7. *House of Commons Debates*, December 11, 1936, col. 2218.
8. Sir Evelyn Wrench, *Geoffrey Dawson and Our Times*, p. 358.
9. *The Times*, 'Review of the Year 1936', January 1, 1937.
10. R.A. G.VI. Conf./62A, Lord Wigram to Sir A. Hardinge, January 27, 1937.
11. R.A. G.VI. Conf./62A, Lord Zetland to Lord Wigram, January 27, 1937.
12. R.A. G.VI. Conf./62A, King George VI to Lord Zetland, February 3, 1937.
13. Dr. Cyril Garbett, Archbishop of York, *The Claims of the Church of England*, p. 189.
14. Lockhart, p. 409.
15. Reith, p. 280.
16. Nicholas Mansergh, *Survey of British Commonwealth Affairs, External Policy, 1931-1939*, p. 48, fn.
17. Lockhart, pp. 412-413.
18. Lee, Vol. II, pp. 22-25; Nicolson, pp. 162-163.
19. See *News Chronicle*, February 11, 1937; *Sunday Referee*, February 28, 1937; *Daily Express*, May 13, 1937; and *Daily Sketch*, December 11, 1937.
20. *Co-Partnership*, June 1937, Vol. XLV, No. 46.
21. *The Times*, December 14, 1936.
22. *Logue Papers*.
23. Lockhart, p. 417.
24. R.A. (George VI, Private Papers, Box No. 5) Bishop of St. Albans to Queen Elizabeth, May 21, 1937.
25. *Logue Papers*.
26. R.A. G.VI. Conf./342, Archbishop of Canterbury to King George VI, December 10, 1937.

CHAPTER II

THE KING'S HERITAGE

1. R.A. G.VI. Conf./34.
2. King George VI to Mr. Baldwin, May 29, 1937 (*Baldwin Papers*, Cambridge University Library).

3. Keith Feiling, *The Life of Neville Chamberlain*, p. 303.
4. *House of Commons Debates*, March 26, 1936, cols. 1435-1449.
5. Feiling, pp. 321, 324.
6. *Ibid.* p. 300.
7. *Summary of the Proceedings of the Imperial Conference of 1937.* (Cmd. 5482), p. 16.
8. *Ibid.* p. 21.
9. Mansergh, *Survey of British Commonwealth Affairs*, p. 89.
10. Cmd. 5482.
11. *The Times*, December 30, 1937.
12. Winston Churchill, *The Second World War*, Vol. I, p. 248.
13. Feiling, p. 310.
14. R.A. G.VI. Conf./18c, Sir A. Hardinge to Mr. MacDonald, March 12, 1938.
15. *Ibid.* Mr. Chamberlain to King George VI, April 25, 1938.
16. *Ibid.* King George VI to Mr. Chamberlain, April 26, 1938.

CHAPTER III

THE TWILIGHT OF PEACE,
NOVEMBER 1937–MARCH 1939

1. Templewood, p. 282.
2. Feiling, pp. 332-333.
3. *Documents on German Foreign Policy, 1918–1945*, Series D, Vol. I, p. 29.
4. Sumner Welles, *The Time for Decision*, pp. 64-68.
5. Feiling, p. 336.
6. Templewood, p. 262.
7. Feiling, p. 337.
8. *Ciano's Diplomatic Papers.* Report from Count Grandi, February 19, 1938, pp. 164-184.
9. *Ibid.* p. 183.
10. Feiling, p. 338.
11. R.A. G.VI. Conf./63, Note by Sir A. Hardinge, February 20, 1938.
12. R.A. G.VI. Conf./67, Sir A. Hardinge to Sir M. Hankey, February 21, 1938.
13. Churchill, *The Second World War*, Vol. I, p. 231.
14. Earl Winterton, *Orders of the Day*, p. 232.
15. Chester Wilmot, *The Struggle for Europe*, p. 35.
16. Winterton, p. 235.
17. Viscount Swinton, *I Remember*, p. 147.
18. R.A. King George VI to Mr. Chamberlain, May 16, 1938.
19. R.A. King George VI to Mr. Chamberlain, August 14, 1938.
20. R.A. Mr. Chamberlain to King George VI, September 6, 1938.
21. R.A. G.VI. Conf./235, Mr. Chamberlain to King George VI, September 13, 1938.
22. *Ibid.*
23. R.A. G.VI. Conf./235, King George VI to Mr. Chamberlain, September 16, 1938.
24. R.A. King George VI to Queen Mary, September 16, 1938.
25. R.A. King George VI to Mr. Chamberlain, September 30, 1938.
26. R.A. (Queen Mary's Collection) King George VI to Queen Mary, October 1, 1938.
27. *Ibid.*
28. Feiling, p. 375.

29. Viscount Norwich, *Old Men Forget*, p. 243.

30. R.A. (Queen Mary's Collection) Queen Mary to King George VI, October, 4, 1938.

31. Feiling, p. 382.

32. R.A. G.VI. Conf./239, Memorandum by Sir A. Hardinge, October 19, 1938.

33. R.A. G.VI. Conf./90, Memorandum by Sir A. Hardinge, and G.VI. Conf./239, Mr. Chamberlain to King George VI, October 26, 1938.

34. R.A. G.VI. Conf./156.

35. R.A. G.VI. Conf. /84.

36. R.A. Mr. Chamberlain to King George VI, January 17, 1939.

37. R.A. King George VI to Mr. Chamberlain, January 19, 1939.

38. R.A. King George VI to Mr. Chamberlain, March 18, 1939.

CHAPTER IV

THE APPROACH OF WAR, MARCH–SEPTEMBER 1939

1. *House of Commons Debates*, March 24, 1938, cols. 1403-1407.

2. Feiling, p. 407.

3. *House of Commons Debates*, October 3, 1939, cols. 1876-1877.

4. *Ibid.* March 31, 1939, col. 2415.

5. Letters exchanged between Hon. James Gerard and President Roosevelt, June 30 and July 6, 1939. *Papers of President Franklin D. Roosevelt*, Hyde Park, New York, hereinafter referred to as *Roosevelt Archives*. (President's Secretary's File, Box 44.)

6. *Ibid.* President Roosevelt to Mr. Gerard, July 6, 1939.

7. R.A. (George VI, Private Papers, Box No. 3) President Roosevelt to King George VI, September 17, 1938.

8. *Roosevelt Archives*, King George VI to President Roosevelt, October 8, 1938.

9. R.A. G.VI. Non.Conf.3400/3, Memorandum by Sir A. Hardinge, March 16, 1939.

10. R.A. G.VI. Non.Conf.3400/3, King George VI to Mr. King, March 28, 1939.

11. R.A. (Queen Mary's Collection) King George VI to Queen Mary, May 1, 1939.

12. R.A. G.VI. Non.Conf.3400/5, Sir A. Hardinge to Lord Stanhope, April 12 and 19, 1939.

13. R.A. (Queen Mary's Collection) Queen Elizabeth to Queen Mary, May 15, 1939.

14. R.A. (Queen Mary's Collection) King George VI to Queen Mary, May 17, 1939.

15. Lee, Vol. I, p. 95.

16. Rev. G. N. Wright, *The Life and Reign of King William the Fourth*, Vol. I, p. 67.

17. Eleanor Roosevelt, *This I Remember*, pp. 183-184.

18. *Roosevelt Archives*, Mrs. Roosevelt's Diary, June 9, 1939 (President's Secretary's File, Box 44).

19. *The Secret Diary of Harold L. Ickes*, Vol. II, p. 650.

20. *Ibid.* Vol. II, pp. 645, 646.

21. Eleanor Roosevelt, p. 196.

22. Vice-Admiral Ross T. McIntire, *Twelve Years with Roosevelt*, p. 118.

23. *Roosevelt Archives*, Hon. Daniel C. Roper, U.S. Minister in Ottawa, to President Roosevelt, July 5, 1939 (Papers of Harry L. Hopkins, Box 4).

24. *Roosevelt Archives*, Mr. Mackenzie King to President Roosevelt, July 1, 1939 (President's Secretary's File, Box 44) ; and Eleanor Roosevelt, p. 197.

25. R.A. (Queen Mary's Collection) Queen Elizabeth to Queen Mary, June 11, 1939.

26. *Roosevelt Archives*, Mrs. Roosevelt's Diary, June 12, 1939 (President's Secretary's File, Box 44).

27. *Roosevelt Archives*, Mr. Roper to President Roosevelt, July 5, 1939 (*op. cit.*).

28. *Logue Papers.*

29. King George VI to Sir Louis Greig, July 4, 1939.

30. R.A. King George VI to Mr. Chamberlain, July 3, 1939.

31. R.A. (Queen Mary's Collection) King George VI to Queen Mary, August 13, 1939.

32. *Ibid.*

33. R.A. Queen Mary to Queen Elizabeth, August 23, 1939.

34. R.A. G.VI. Conf./120, Sir A. Hardinge to Sir A. Cadogan, August 26, 1939.

35. R.A. G.VI. Conf./111, Memorandum by Sir A. Hardinge, August 29, 1939.

36. Leopold Amery, *My Political Life*; Vol. III, *The Unforgiving Years, 1929–1940*, p. 324.

CHAPTER V

THE WAR OF NERVES, SEPTEMBER 1939–MAY 1940

1. Mansergh, *Survey of British Commonwealth Affairs*, p. 365.

2. *Ibid.* p. 368.

3. Nicolson, pp. 255-256.

4. J. A. Spender and Cyril Asquith, *Life of Lord Oxford and Asquith*, Vol. II, p. 109.

5. King's Diary, September 4, 1939.

6. *Ibid.* September 11, 1939.

7. R.A. King George VI to Mr. Chamberlain, September 14, 1939.

8. Duchess of Windsor, p. 324.

9. R.A. G.VI. Conf./42H.

10. Lady Gwendoline Cecil, *Life of Robert, Marquess of Salisbury*, Vol. III, p. 191 ; also Mrs. Edgar Dugdale, *Arthur James Balfour*, Vol. I, p. 297.

11. *Hitler's Table Talk*, p. 389.

12. R.A. G.VI. Conf./114, King George VI to King Boris, September 19, 1939.

13. King's Diary, October 11, 1939.

14. R.A. G.VI. Conf./116, General Ismay to Sir A. Hardinge, October 17, 1939.

15. King's Diary, November 7, 1939.

16. *The Times*, November 13, 1939.

17. King's Diary, November 11, 1939.

18. *Ibid.* October 7, 1939.

19. *Ibid.* September 6, 1939.

20. R.A. (George VI, Private Papers, Box No. 5), Sir P. Legh to Queen Elizabeth, December 11, 1939.

21. King's Diary, December 25, 1939.

22. Feiling, p. 419.

23. *Ibid.* p. 420.

24. Amery, *My Political Life*, Vol. III, p. 330.

25. C. R. Attlee, *As It Happened*, p. 105.
26. King's Diary, October 17, 1939.
27. *Ibid*. October 24, 1939.
28. Feiling, p. 434.
29. Churchill, *The Second World War*, Vol. I, p. 318.
30. *Ibid*. Vol. II, p. 33.
31. King's Diary, December 20, 1939.
32. King George VI to the Duke of Gloucester, January 5, 1940.
33. R.A. Mr. Chamberlain to King George VI, January 8, 1940.
34. King's Diary, January 9, 1940.
35. *Annual Register*, 1940, pp. 2-3, 5.
36. King's Diary, February 17, 1940.
37. *Ibid*. March 11, 1940.
38. *Ibid*. March 16/17, 1940.
39. *Ibid*. April 2, 1940.
40. *Ibid*. April 9, 1940.
41. *Ibid*. May 7, 1940.
42. Norwich, p. 279.
43. Amery, *My Political Life*, Vol. III, pp. 368-369.
44. Feiling, p. 422.
45. Churchill, *The Second World War*, Vol. I, pp. 597-598; also Lord Halifax, *Fulness of Days*, pp. 219-220.
46. Amery, *My Political Life*, Vol. III, pp. 371-372; Attlee, *As It Happened*, pp. 112-113.
47. King's Diary, May 9, 1940.
48. Nicolson, pp. 287-288.
49. Churchill, *The Second World War*, Vol. I, p. 599.
50. Senator John F. Kennedy, *Profiles in Courage*, p. 69.
51. Churchill, *The Second World War*, Vol. I, pp. 197-198.
52. King's Diary, May 11, 1940.
53. Churchill, *The Second World War*, Vol. II, p. 335.
54. King's Diary, February 8 and 9, 1941.

CHAPTER VI

THE DECISIVE STRUGGLE, MAY 1940–JUNE 1941

1. King's Diary, May 13, 1940.
2. *Ibid*.
3. *Ibid*. May 28, 1940.
4. R.A. G.VI. Conf./166.
5. Robert E. Sherwood, *Roosevelt and Hopkins*, p. 252.
6. R.A. G.VI. Conf./130.
7. R.A. G.VI. Non.Conf. 4188/5.
8. R.A. G.VI. Non.Conf. 4188/6.
9. Churchill, *The Second World War*, Vol. II, p. 210.
10. King's Diary, June 22, 1940.
11. R.A. (Queen Mary's Collection) King George VI to Queen Mary, June 27, 1940.
12. Churchill, *The Second World War*, Vol. II, pp. 334-335.
13. Templewood, pp. 392-393.
14. King's Diary, August 5, 1940.
15. R.A. G.VI. Conf./204, King George VI to the King of Sweden, August 12, 1940.

16. King's Diary, November 27, 1940.
17. R.A. Mr. Churchill to King George VI, January 5, 1941.
18. King's Diary, September 9 and 10, 1940.
19. *Ibid.* September 13, 1940.
20. *Ibid.* September 19, 1940.
21. R.A. Lord Mountbatten to King George VI, September 17, 1940.
22. King's Diary, October 14, 1940.
23. Betty Spencer Shew, *Queen Elizabeth, the Queen Mother*, p. 76.
24. R.A. (Queen Mary's Collection) Queen Elizabeth to Queen Mary, October 19, 1940.
25. R.A. (Queen Mary's Collection) King George VI to Queen Mary, September 26, 1940.
26. R.A. King George VI to Mr. Chamberlain, October 8, 1940.
27. Feiling, p. 453.
28. R.A. (Queen Mary's Collection) King George VI to Queen Mary, October 14, 1940.
29. R.A. (Queen Mary's Collection) King George VI to Queen Mary, November 18, 1940.
30. King's Diary, November 18, 1940.
31. R.A. G.VI. Non.Conf./4932.
32. R.A. (Queen Mary's Collection) King George VI to Queen Mary, November 18, 1940.
33. King's Diary, November 17 and 18, 1940.
34. Charles de Gaulle, *War Memoirs*, Vol. I, *The Call to Honour*, p. 106.
35. Churchill, *The Second World War*, Vol. II, p. 450.
36. *Ibid.* Vol. II, pp. 451-453.
37. R.A. G.VI. Conf./204.
38. King's Diary, November 6 and 7, 1940.
39. Alan Moorehead, *African Trilogy*, p. 22.
40. R.A. G.VI. Conf./97.
41. King's Diary, June 22/23, 1940.
42. R.A. G.VI. Conf./203.
43. R.A. G.VI. Conf./114.
44. R.A. G.VI. Conf. 148.
45. R.A. G.VI. Conf./140.
46. Churchill, *The Second World War*, Vol. III, pp. 141-142.
47. King's Diary, March 22, 1941.
48. R.A. G.VI. Conf./148.
49. King's Diary, September 24, 1941.
50. *Ibid.* June 22, 1941.
51. R.A. G.VI. Conf./140.

CHAPTER VII

ANGLO-AMERICAN RELATIONS, 1939-1942

1. Donald F. Drummond, *The Passing of American Neutrality, 1937-1941*, pp. 372-373.
2. King's Diary, March 5, 1940.
3. *Ibid.* March 12, 1940.
4. *Roosevelt Archives*, President's Secretary's File, Box 69.
5. R.A. (George VI, Private Papers, Box No. 3), President Roosevelt to King George VI, May 1, 1940.
6. *Roosevelt Archives*, President's Secretary's File, Box, 69.

7. R.A. G.VI. Conf./244, Sir A. Hardinge to Lord Halifax, August 5, 1940.

8. *Ibid.* Sir A. Hardinge to Lord Halifax, August 16, 1940.

9. R.A. (George VI, Private Papers, Box No. 3), President Roosevelt to King George VI, May 1, 1940.

10. Churchill, *The Second World War*, Vol. II, pp. 125-126.

11. *Roosevelt Archives*, President's Secretary's File, Box 69.

12. *Ibid.*

13. King's Diary, December 30, 1940.

14. R.A. G.VI. Conf./139.

15. *Ibid.* Sir A. Hardinge to Lord Lloyd, December 31, 1940.

16. *Roosevelt Archives*, President's Secretary's File, Box 69.

17. R.A. (George VI, Private Papers, Box No. 3) President Roosevelt to King George VI, November 22, 1940.

18. King's Diary, December 12, 1940.

19. *Roosevelt Archives*, President's Secretary's File, Box 76.

20. King's Diary, March 1, 1941.

21. John G. Winant, *A Letter from Grosvenor Square*, p. 19.

22. King's Diary, December 31, 1940.

23. Churchill, *The Second World War*, Vol. II, pp. 494-501.

24. King's Diary, March 11, 1941.

25. *Ibid.* January 30, 1941.

26. Sherwood, pp. 250-253.

27. Henry L. Stimson and McGeorge Bundy, *On Active Service*, pp. 369-370.

28. R.A. (George VI, Private Papers, Box No. 3) Telegram from King George VI to President Roosevelt, May 30, 1941.

29. *Roosevelt Archives*, President's Secretary's File, Box 82.

30. Winant, p. 26.

31. *Roosevelt Archives*, President's Secretary's File, Box 82.

32. King's Diary, August 18, 1941.

33. *Ibid.* August 25, 1941.

34. R.A. (Queen Mary's Collection) King George VI to Queen Mary, August 17, 1941.

35. R.A. (George VI, Private Papers, Box No. 3) President Roosevelt to King George VI, August 11, 1941.

36. King's Diary, February 20/21, 1941.

37. *Roosevelt Archives*, President's Secretary's File, Box 76.

38. King's Diary, November 15/17, 1941.

39. *Memoirs of Cordell Hull*, Vol. II, p. 1018.

40. *Ibid.* pp. 1093-1094.

41. R.A. G.VI. Non.Conf./4188(14).

CHAPTER VIII

THE TIDE OF VICTORY, 1942–1943

1. King's Diary, January 19, 1942.

2. Churchill, *The Second World War*, Vol. IV, p. 88.

3. R.A. (Queen Mary's Collection) King George VI to Queen Mary, February 16, 1942.

4. King's Diary, February 17, 1942.

5. *Ibid.* February 19, 1942.

6. *Ibid.* February 24, 1942.

7. Churchill, *The Second World War*, Vol. IV, pp. 167-173.

8. *Roosevelt Archives*, President's Secretary's File, Box 96.

9. R.A. (Queen Mary's Collection) King George VI to Queen Mary. May 31, 1942.

10. King's Diary, April 30, 1942.

11. *Ibid.* July 7, 1942.

12. R.A. (George VI, Private Papers, Box No. 3) President Roosevelt to King George VI, October 17, 1942.

13. Churchill, *The Second World War*, Vol. III, p. 383.

14. *Ibid.* Vol. IV, p. 337.

15. Sir Ivor Jennings, *Cabinet Government*, p. 40.

16. R.A. (George VI, Private Papers, Box No. 3) President Roosevelt to King George VI, October 17, 1942.

17. King's Diary, August 24/26, 1942.

18. *Ibid.* August 9, 1942.

19. *Ibid.* September 7/14, 1942.

20. R.A. (George VI, Private Papers, Box No. 3) President Roosevelt to King George VI, October 17, 1942.

21. R.A. (Queen Mary's Collection) Queen Elizabeth to Queen Mary, October 19, 1942.

22. *Roosevelt Archives*, Papers of Mrs. Franklin D. Roosevelt. Diary of Trip to Great Britain October–November 1942.

23. Eleanor Roosevelt, p. 265.

24. *Roosevelt Archives*, President's Secretary's File, Box 96.

25. Eleanor Roosevelt, p. 264.

26. *Logue Papers.*

27. King's Diary, November 4, 1942.

28. *Ibid.* November 28/30, 1942.

29. *Ibid.* December 29, 1942.

30. *Ibid.* January 13, 1943.

31. R.A. (Queen Mary's Collection) King George VI to Queen Mary, February 2, 1943.

32. King's Diary, January 14/17, 1942.

33. *Roosevelt Archives*, President's Secretary's File, Box 117.

34. R.A. (George VI, Private Papers, Box No. 3) President Roosevelt to King George VI, January 24, 1943.

35. King's Diary, February 4, 1943.

36. *Ibid.* February 6/8, 1943.

37. *Ibid.* February 16, 1943.

38. *Ibid.* February 20/22, 1943.

39. Churchill, *The Second World War*, Vol. IV, pp. 657-659.

40. King's Diary, May 8/10, 1943.

41. *Roosevelt Archives*, President's Secretary's File, Box 117.

42. Churchill, *The Second World War*, Vol. IV, p. 698.

43. R.A. Mr. Churchill to King George VI, May 15, 1943.

44. King's Diary, March 23, 1943.

45. *Ibid.* March 31, 1943.

46. *Ibid.* June 11, 1943.

47. R.A. (Queen Mary's Collection) King George VI to Queen Mary, June 10, 1943.

48. R.A. (Queen Mary's Collection) Queen Elizabeth to Queen Mary, June 12, 1943.

49. Admiral of the Fleet Lord Cunningham, *A Sailor's Odyssey*, p. 543.

50. King's Diary, June 12, 1943.

51. *Ibid.* June 17, 1943.

52. *Ibid.* June 14, 1943.

53. *Ibid.* June 19, 1943.

54. R.A. (Queen Mary's Collection) King George VI to Queen Mary, June 28, 1943.
55. R.A. (Queen Mary's Collection) King George VI to Queen Mary, July 3, 1943.
56. Air Marshal Sir Hugh Lloyd, *Briefed to Attack*, p. 161.
57. King's Diary, April 16, 1942.
58. *Ibid.* May 11, 1942.
59. *Ibid.* April 22, 1942.
60. R.A. G.VI. Conf./173.
61. Lloyd, p. 229.
62. Cunningham, pp. 543-544.
63. *Ibid.* pp. 544-545.
64. King's Diary, June 20, 1943.
65. R.A. (Queen Mary's Collection) King George VI to Queen Mary, June 28, 1943.
66. R.A. King George VI to Mr. Chamberlain, February 3, 1939.
67. King's Diary, July 6, 1943.
68. R.A. (George VI, Private Papers, Box 1) King George VI to Lord Hardinge of Penshurst, July 19, 1943.
69. King's Diary, August 17/22, 1943.
70. R.A. G.VI. Conf./156.
71. *Ibid.*
72. R.A. G.VI. Non.Conf./6484, Sir A. Hardinge to Sir A. Cadogan, February 14, 1943.
73. Churchill, *The Second World War*, Vol. V, p. 321.
74. King's Diary, December 15, 1943.
75. *Ibid.* October 1/3, 1943.
76. *Ibid.* December 27/28, 1943.
77. *Ibid.* December 30/31, 1943.

CHAPTER IX

VICTORY ACHIEVED, 1944–1945

1. R.A. (Queen Mary's Collection) King George VI to Queen Mary, February 20, 1944.
2. King's Diary, April 21, 1944.
3. Churchill, *The Second World War*, Vol. IV, p. 664.
4. *Ibid.* Vol. V, pp. 112-116.
5. Major J. C. Smuts, *Jan Christiaan Smuts*, p. 437.
6. King's Diary, October 13, 1943.
7. King George VI to Mr. Churchill, October 14, 1943.
8. King's Diary, October 14, 1943.
9. *Ibid.* October 26, 1943.
10. *Ibid.* February 1, 1944.
11. *Ibid.* February 3, 1944.
12. Charles Whibley, *William Pitt*, p. 47.
13. Cunningham, p. 602.
14. King's Diary, May 15, 1922.
15. R.A. G.VI. Non.Conf./9105.
16. King's Diary, May 22, 1944.
17. Churchill, *The Second World War*, Vol. V, pp. 546-551.
18. King's Diary, May 30, 1944.
19. *Ibid.* May 31, 1944.

20. King George VI to Mr. Churchill, May 31, 1944.
21. King's Diary, June 1, 1944.
22. *Ibid.* June 2, 1944.
23. *Ibid.* June 3, 1944.
24. *Ibid.* June 4/5, 1944.
25. *Ibid.* June 6, 1944.
26. R.A. (Queen Mary's Collection) King George VI to Queen Mary, June 10, 1944.
27. King's Diary, June 10/12, 1944.
28. R.A. Mr. Churchill to King George VI, June 13, 1944.
29. King's Diary, June 16, 1944.
30. R.A. (Queen Mary's Collection) Queen Elizabeth to Queen Mary, July 8, 1944.
31. King's Diary, June 16, 1944.
32. *Ibid.* June 20, 1944.
33. *Ibid.* July 12, 1944.
34. *Ibid.* July 14, 1944.
35. R.A. (Queen Mary's Collection) Queen Elizabeth to Queen Mary, July 26, 1944.
36. King's Diary, July 25, 1944, *passim.*
37. *Ibid.* August 3, 1944.
38. *Ibid.* November 7, 1944.
39. R.A. Lord Mountbatten to King George VI, April 1, 1945.
40. R.A. G.VI. Non.Conf./7324.
41. King's Diary, July 25, 1944.
42. *Ibid.* October 26, 1944.
43. R.A. (Queen Mary's Collection) King George VI to Queen Mary, March 25, 1945.
44. King's Diary, February 23/26, 1945.
45. *Ibid.* August 13, 1940.
46. *Roosevelt Archives,* President's Secretary's File, Box 150.
47. King's Diary, April 13, 1945.
48. R.A. Mr. Churchill to King George VI, April 13, 1945.
49. King's Diary, April 23/27, 1945.
50. *Ibid.* April 28/30, 1945.
51. *Ibid.* May 4, 1945.
52. *Ibid.* May 5, 1945.
53. *Ibid.* May 6/7, 1945.
54. *Ibid.* May 8, 1945.
55. King George VI to Archbishop Lang, May 19, 1945.
56. King's Diary, May 18/20, 1945.
57. D. C. Somervell, *British Politics since 1900,* p. 237.
58. Churchill, *The Second World War,* Vol. VI, p. 510.
59. Attlee, *As It Happened,* p. 135.
60. Churchill, *The Second World War,* Vol. VI, pp. 512-513.
61. Attlee, *As It Happened,* p. 132.
62. R.A. Mr. Churchill to King George VI, May 22, 1945.
63. King's Diary, May 23, 1945.
64. *Ibid.* May 29, 1945.
65. King George VI to the Duke of Gloucester, May 29, 1945.
66. Churchill, *The Second World War,* Vol. I, p. 601.
67. King's Diary, July 25, 1945.
68. R.A. G.VI. Conf./254.   Memorandum by Sir A. Lascelles, July 26, 1945.
69. King's Diary, July 26, 1945.
70. *Ibid.* July 28, 1945.
71. King George VI to Mr. Churchill, July 31, 1945.

72. Attlee, *As It Happened*, p. 148.
73. King's Diary, July 26, 1945.
74. *Daily Herald*, February 20, 1952.
75. R.A. G.VI. Conf./254.
76. King's Diary, August 23, 1945.
77. Harry S. Truman, *Year of Decisions*, p. 395.
78. Attlee, *As It Happened*, p. 149.
79. King's Diary, May 29, 1945.
80. Truman, *Year of Decisions*, p. 333; *Stalin's Correspondence with Churchill, Attlee, Roosevelt aud Truman, 1941–45*, Vol. I, p. 370.
81. King's Diary, June 29, 1945.
82. R.A. G.VI. Conf./255, June 28, 1945.
83. *Ibid.* July 12, 1945.
84. *Ibid.* July 22, 1945.
85. Truman, *Year of Decisions*, pp. 420-421.
86. King's Diary, August 2, 1945.
87. Truman, *Year of Decisions*, p. 413.
88. Fleet Admiral William D. Leahy, *I was There*, pp. 502-503; James F. Byrnes, *Speaking Frankly*, pp. 263-264.
89. King's Diary, August 4/6, 1945.
90. *Ibid.* August 15, 1945.
91. *Ibid.* September 3, 1945.

CHAPTER X

THE POST-WAR WORLD, 1945–1950

1. King George VI to the Duke of Gloucester, September 13, 1945.
2. King's Diary, April 5, 1945.
3. *Ibid.* July 2, 1945.
4. *Smuts Archives*, King George VI to General Smuts, November 20, 1945.
5. R.A. Lord Mountbatten to King George VI, July 28, 1945.
6. King's Diary, November 20, 1945.
7. *Ibid.* February 26, 1946.
8. *Ibid.* November 27, 1945.
9. R.A. (Queen Mary's Collection) King George VI to Queen Mary, September 2, 1945.
10. King's Diary, October 31, 1945.
11. *Ibid.* November 13, 1945.
12. King George VI to the Duke of Gloucester, January 21, 1946.
13. Attlee, *As It Happened*, p. 163.
14. Somervell, p. 247.
15. Attlee, *As It Happened*, p. 167.
16. *Ibid.* p. 168.
17. Truman, *Year of Decisions*, pp. 227-228.
18. Quoted by J. Hampden Jackson in *The Post-War Decade*, p. 184.
19. King's Diary, January 28 and 29, 1947.
20. R.A. (Queen Mary's Collection) King George VI to Queen Mary, August 18 [28 ?], 1947.
21. R.A. King George VI to Mr. Attlee, August 26, 1947.
22. R.A. Mr. Attlee to King George VI, August 28, 1947.
23. R.A. (Queen Mary's Collection) King George VI to Queen Mary, September 14, 1947.
24. *The Economist*, December 25, 1948.

25. King's Diary, November 6, 1945.
26. Attlee, *As It Happened*, pp. 161-162; Truman, *Year of Decisions*, pp. 538-544.
27. King's Diary, April 22/28, 1946.
28. Sir Oliver Franks, *The Listener*, June 14, 1956.

CHAPTER XI

THE NEW COMMONWEALTH, 1945–1949

1. Nicholas Mansergh, *Documents and Speeches on British Commonwealth Affairs, 1931–1952*, Vol. I, p. xxxviii.
2. *Sydney Bulletin*, January 7, 1942.
3. *Melbourne Herald*, December 27, 1941.
4. Churchill, *The Second World War*, Vol. IV, pp. 7-17.
5. King's Diary, January 23, 1942.
6. R.A. G.VI. Conf./207, Sir A. Hardinge to Mr. Churchill, January 22, 1942.
7. R.A. G.VI. Conf./207, Mr. Churchill to King George VI, January 22, 1942.
8. Churchill, *The Second World War*, Vol. IV, p. 17.
9. Attlee, *As It Happened*, p. 180.
10. King's Diary, February 12, 1946.
11. R.A. G.VI. Conf./8100/1A, Mr. Van Zyl to King George VI, February 14, 1946.
12. R.A. (Queen Mary's Collection) King George VI to Queen Mary, March 3, 1947.
13. R.A. (Queen Mary's Collection) Queen Elizabeth to Queen Mary, March 9, 1947.
14. *Ibid.*
15. Dermot Morrah, *The Royal Family in Africa*, p. 124.
16. *Smuts Archives*, King George VI to General Smuts, May 2, 1947.
17. R.A. G.VI. Conf./52, Lord Linlithgow to King George VI, December 4, 1938.
18. *Ibid.* October 19, 1939.
19. R.A. G.VI. Conf./52, Sir A. Hardinge to Lord Linlithgow, March 7, 1940.
20. Churchill, *The Second World War*, Vol. IV, pp. 185-190.
21. King's Diary, March 3, 1942.
22. *Ibid.* April 9, 1942.
23. R.A. G.VI. Conf./52, Sir A. Hardinge to Lord Linlithgow, May 25, 1942.
24. King's Diary, April 10/12, 1942.
25. R.A. Mr. Churchill to King George VI, April 24, 1943.
26. King's Diary, April 21/25, 1943.
27. *Ibid.* April 26/May 3, 1943.
28. R.A. King George VI to Mr. Churchill, April 28, 1943.
29. King's Diary, May 8, 1943.
30. *Ibid.* June 8, 1943.
31. R.A. Lord Wavell to King George VI, February 24, 1947.
32. King's Diary, October 12, 1943.
33. *Ibid.* July 28, 1942.
34. *Ibid.* December 5, 1944.
35. *Ibid.* May 2, 1945.
36. R.A. Lord Wavell to King George VI, July 8, 1946.
37. King's Diary, December 3, 1946.
38. *Ibid.* December 5, 1946.

39. *Ibid.* December 10, 1946.
40. R.A. Lord Wavell to King George VI, February 24, 1947.
41. King's Diary, December 17, 1946.
42. Attlee, *As It Happened*, pp. 183-184.
43. King's Diary, December 17, 1946.
44. Attlee, *As It Happened*, p. 184.
45. R.A. Lord Mountbatten to King George VI, January 4, 1947.
46. R.A. Sir A. Lascelles to Lord Wavell, March 30, 1947.
47. Lord Radcliffe, *The Problem of Power*, p. 79.
48. R.A. G.VI. Conf./280(4), Mr. Attlee to Sir A. Lascelles, July 25, 1947.
49. *Ibid.* King George VI to Sir A. Lascelles, July 29, 1947 ; Sir A. Lascelles to Mr. Attlee, July 30, 1947.
50. *Ibid.* Mr. Attlee to Sir A. Lascelles, July 31, 1947.
51. *Ibid.* Sir A. Lascelles to Mr. Attlee, August 1, 1947.
52. R.A. G.VI. Conf./280(2), Sir A. Lascelles to Mr. R. M. J. Harris, India Office, August 16, 1947.
53. R.A. G.VI. Conf./280(11).
54. R.A. Sir A. Lascelles to King George VI, January 17, 1949.
55. R.A. Mr. Attlee to King George VI, February 17, 1949.
56. R.A. G.VI. Conf./329, April 6, 1949.
57. *Ibid.*
58. R.A. G.VI. Conf./310, Memorandum by Sir A. Lascelles, April 27, 1949.

CHAPTER XII

THE KING AND THE MAN

1. R.A. G.VI. Non.Conf./2917.
2. Queen Alexandra of Yugoslavia, *For a King's Love*, p. 112.
3. R.A. (Queen Mary's Collection) King George VI to Queen Mary, January 22, 1951.
4. King's Diary, December 21, 1940.
5. R.A. G.VI. Non.Conf./6305, Memorandum by Sir A. Hardinge, March 26, 1943.
6. R.A. (Queen Mary's Collection) King George VI to Queen Mary, March 24, 1943.
7. Isaiah xxxii. 1.

CHAPTER XIII

THE LATTER YEARS, 1947-1952

1. R.A. G.VI. Conf./270.
2. King's Diary, October 18/20, 1941.
3. R.A. (Queen Mary's Collection) King George VI to Queen Mary, March 17, 1944.
4. R.A. G.VI. Conf./270.
5. *The Times*, July 10, 1947.
6. R.A. (Queen Mary's Collection) King George VI to Queen Mary, November 6, 1947.
7. R.A. G.VI. Non.Conf./8644(7), Archbishop of Canterbury to King George VI, July 14, 1947.
8. R.A. G.VI. Conf./273.

9. King's Diary, May 8, 1946.

10. *Ibid.* July 23, 1946.

11. R.A. G.VI. Conf./279.

12. R.A. (Queen Mary's Collection) King George VI to Queen Mary, November 21, 1946.

13. King's Diary, December 17, 1946.

14. R.A. (Queen Mary's Collection) King George VI to Queen Mary, May 3, 1948.

15. R.A. (Queen Mary's Collection) King George VI to Queen Mary, December 1, 1948.

16. R.A. (Queen Mary's Collection) King George VI to Queen Mary, August 24, 1949.

17. R.A. (Queen Mary's Collection) King George VI to Queen Mary, September 25, 1949.

18. R.A. G.VI. Conf./320, Mr. Attlee to King George VI, January 5, 1950.

19. *Ibid.*

20. Attlee, *As It Happened*, p. 193.

21. H. G. Nicholas, *The British General Election of 1950*, p. 303.

22. R.A. G.VI. Conf./320.

23. *Ibid.*

24. R.A. Mr. Attlee to King George VI, August 18, 1950.

25. R.A. King George VI to Mr. Attlee, August 21, 1950.

26. Truman, *Years of Trial and Hope*, p. 395.

27. R.A. King George VI to Mr. Attlee, December 2, 1950.

28. R.A. Mr. Attlee to King George VI, December 3, 1950.

29. Truman, *Years of Trial and Hope*, pp. 396-413.

30. R.A. (Queen Mary's Collection) King George VI to Queen Mary, May 31, 1951.

31. R.A. (Queen Mary's Collection) King George VI to Queen Mary, October 14, 1951.

32. Attlee, *As It Happened*, p. 206.

33. R.A. Memorandum from King George VI to Sir A. Lascelles, June 24, 1951.

34. R.A. G.VI. Conf./340, King George VI to Mr. Attlee, September 1, 1951.

35. Attlee, *As It Happened*, p. 207.

36. R.A. G.VI. Conf./340, Mr. Attlee to King George VI, September 5, 1951.

37. *Ibid.* King George VI to Mr. Attlee, September 6, 1951.

38. *Ibid.* Sir A. Lascelles to Mr. Attlee, September 21, 1951.

39. *Ibid.* Mr. Attlee to Sir A. Lascelles, September 23, 1951.

40. D. E. Butler, *The British General Election of 1951*, p. 105.

41. R.A. G.VI. Conf./340, Sir A. Lascelles to King George VI, October 23, 1951.

42. Butler, D. E., p. 237.

43. R.A. (Queen Mary's Collection) King George VI to Queen Mary, October 14, 1951.

44. R.A. G.VI. Non.Conf./9826.

45. R.A. G.VI. Conf./340, Notes by Sir A. Lascelles, November 26, 1951.

46. *The Times*, November 17, 1951.

47. R.A. G.VI. Non.Conf./10135(3).

48. *Ibid.*

49. R.A. (Queen Mary's Collection) King George VI to Queen Mary, January 23, 1952.

INDEX

and exchange of ambassadors with U.S., early 1941, 519-21; and Atlantic Charter, 526-30; and Pearl Harbour, 532-4; and Far East disasters, 533, 536-7; and criticism of Churchill's conduct of the war, 536-538; and Baedeker Raids, 540; Churchill's advice concerning his successor, 543-6, 604; and death of Duke of Kent, 546-9, 558; and visit of Eleanor Roosevelt, 549-52, 559; and Allied progress in N. Africa, 552-564; and problems in French N. Africa, 556, 559-61, 562, 569; and Casablanca, 558 ff.; and plans for invasion of Italy, 561; visit to troops in N. Africa, 566-70; visit to Malta, 571, 575-8; and change of Private Secretary, 578-80; and victory in Sicily, 580; and Stalingrad Sword of Honour, 584-7; and constitutional status and future title of Princess Elizabeth, 590-2; and 'Second Front', 592, 594; and preparation of forces for D-Day, 596-8, 600; and planning for 'Overlord', 597, 598-600; and plans to accompany invasion, 601-6; and D-Day, 607; and visit to Normandy, 608-9; and Hitler's vengeance weapons, 609-611; visits forces in Italy and Low Countries, 611-13, 812; suggests visit to Far East forces, 613-14, 703; and stand-down of Home Guard, 614-15; and Regional Commissioners, 615; and Parliamentary ceremonial, 616-17; and the postwar Army, 617; and Yalta, 618-19; and relations with Russia, 619; and death of President Roosevelt, 619-20; and German surrender, 623-7; and U.K. political situation after VE-Day, 627-33; and General Election 1945, 633-5, 649; and defeat of Churchill, 635-7; invites Attlee to form government, 637-9; his meeting with President Truman, 642-5; and VJ-Day, 645-46

THE POST-WAR YEARS

and Labour government, 649-50, 653; concern for domestic situation in U.K., 662-6, 686-7, 769, 791, 801; visit to South Africa and the Rhodesias, 662, 685-92, 762; and General Election, 1950, 677, 770-2; and Indian constitutional problems,

692-716, 719 ff.; and Indian leaders, 703, 706, 720; and Royal style and title, 715-16, 720, 725-8; and new status of Ireland, 719; and 1949 Commonwealth Conference and Declaration, 729-31; and Royal Art Collection, 737-8; and marriage of Princess Elizabeth, 749-55; bestows Garter on Princess Elizabeth and Duke of Edinburgh, 753, 755; and Silver Wedding Anniversary, 760-2, 765; and proposed visit to Australia and New Zealand, 762, 763, 764, 765, 766, 769, 790, 791-2, 793; and operation, March 12, 1949, 762-8; and visits of King Frederik IX of Denmark, 763, 785; birth of Prince Charles, 765 and n.; and Korean War, 778; and deterioration in health, 784 ff.; second operation, 788-90; and General Election, 1951, 791-6; invites Churchill to form government, 797; and Princess Elizabeth's visit to Canada and U.S., 798-801; birth of Princess Anne, 801 n.; and departure of Princess Elizabeth for Commonwealth Tour, 803; his death, 803

Characteristics and Attributes

sensitive and retiring nature, 17, 27, 39, 42, 60, 61-2, 64-5, 104, 164, 181, 207, 214, 220, 227, 288, 293, 361, 651; nervousness, 17, 18, 27, 39, 41, 42, 208, 227, 309, 310, 429; affectionate nature, 17, 18, 20-1, 31, 44, 60, 148; kindness and generosity, 58, 288, 451, 549; high-spirited and intelligent, 25, 26 n.; modesty and humility, 296, 311, 428, 644, 732, 745, 804; speech impediment, 27, 33, 39, 42, 61-2, 65, 121-2, 131, 133 n., 134-5, 164, 207, 208, 212-15, 218, 230, 232, 236, 293, 309-10, 314, 394, 429, 627, 652; left-handed, 27, 49; determination and courage, 41, 42, 45, 49, 50, 62, 104, 121, 131, 133 n., 134, 152-3, 179, 186, 208, 296, 297, 309, 575, 745, 764, 804, 805; integrity and sense of honour, 34, 42, 104, 132, 296, 404, 426; friendly and gay personality, 41, 58, 104, 109, 155, 181-3, 384, 804; loyalty, 41, 58, 181, 356, 474, 536, 645, 745, 805; sense of humour, 50, 53, 54, 65, 104, 134, 169, 231, 235, 738, 741; consideration for others, 58, 59, 79, 104, 549,

738 and *n.*, 764, 778, 788-9; poor sailor, 61, 66; linguistic ability, 90; common touch and human understanding, 59, 68, 104, 109, 167, 172, 218-19, 294, 296, 380, 393, 692, 738-739, 796, 804; zeal and sense of duty, 104, 109, 110, 115, 121, 129, 132, 155, 156, 165, 167, 171, 194, 196, 206, 209, 216, 220, 221, 227, 254, 258, 263, 296, 297, 300-1, 311, 312, 315, 342, 376, 415, 438, 449, 479, 565-6, 567, 741, 742, 745, 761, 792, 796, 804, 805; common sense, 104, 166, 181, 271, 294-5, 296, 304, 380, 602, 619, 741; temper, 27, 32, 104, 131, 155; sense of appreciation, 104, 185, 198, 214, 354, 474, 553, 738 and *n.*, 790; dignity and bearing, 146, 152, 212, 219, 230, 246, 288, 569, 627, 732, 736, 741; love of family life, 110, 155-6, 215, 246, 251, 254-5, 259, 263, 297, 740-2, 745, 798, 801; informality, 164, 165, 168, 177, 181-2, 223, 380, 384, 393, 398, 467, 569, 644-5; inspiration and leadership, 180, 300, 355, 448-9, 463, 474, 478, 565-6; good memory, 183; attention to detail, 185, 312, 313, 336, 471-2, 567, 586, 617, 650, 735-738, 739-40, 741, 742, 758, 759, 786, 788-9, 797; idealism, 186, 225, 228-229, 232, 315, 382, 406-7; response to challenge, 33, 214, 220; his faith, 56-7, 240, 249, 296, 297, 304-6, 310-311, 406-7, 429-30, 449-50, 473, 499, 742-5, 802; progressive outlook, 272-3, 649, 737, 796; sympathy, 364, 439-40, 443, 479, 491; statesmanship and diplomatic ability, 419 ff., 431, 490 ff., 503, 511-15, 521, 523-4, 569, 663-4; popularity, 58, 156, 467, 517, 569, 762, 805; growth in stature and confidence, 300, 310, 315, 316, 335, 392-3, 394, 564-6, 597-8, 638, 650, 653, 663-4, 732; love for Balmoral, 30-1, 239-40, 273, 398, 739, 787; love for Sandringham, 15, 31, 271, 297, 739-40

Health and Physique

gastric disorders, 17, 77, 84-9, 98-9, 102-4, 342; knock-knees, 28-9; whooping-cough, 42; measles and mumps, 50; appendicitis, 78-81; stamina, 49, 104, 143; false rumours about, 308-9; strain of war years, 653-4, 692, 762; arteriosclerosis and first operation, March 12, 1949, 762-8; deterioration in health, 784-785, 794, 799 and *n.*, 801; pneumonitis, 786-90; cancer and second operation, September 23, 1951, 788

Pursuits

beagling, 49; dancing, 64-5, 69, 74, 148; driving, 109; fishing, 43, 65, 83, 219, 741; golf, 29, 50, 83, 131, 169-70; hunting, 148, 196, 208, 234, 258; nature, 398; racing, 645, 739; riding, 29, 49, 62, 80, 109, 123, 146, 219, 258, 741; rowing, 49; running, 49; shooting, 52, 80, 89-90, 148, 200-2, 204-5, 240, 646, 741, 766, 768, 787, 802, 803; tennis, 49, 62, 109, 123, 131, 142, 219

Interests

the constitution, 131-2; estate management and gardening, 259-62, 271-272, 389, 739-40, 742-3, 802; freemasonry, 283, 285, 287, 734-5; his Camp, 148, 177 ff., 314, 344, 393, 399, 733; industrial welfare, 148, 153, 164-72, 173 ff., 733; international affairs, 328, 336, 344-55, 357-8, 388-9, 390-2, 402, 423, 480, 505-6, 552, 644, 665-6, 778, 780-3, 796, 802; medals and decorations, 471, 736; medicine, 739, 766, 768, 786; Orders of Chivalry, 755-760, 785-6; sport and fitness, 116, 181, 739-740, 741; theory of monarchy, 186, 226, 393, 466-7, 479, 703, 732, 733, 756

Personal Relationships

with father, 27, 42, 65, 77, 83, 154-5, 212, 215, 220, 232, 233, 272, 293 (*see also* Letters); with mother, 235 (*see also* Letters); support from consort, 198, 212, 214, 219-20, 263, 287, 288, 296-7, 342, 601, 740, 755, 761, 801; with daughters, 740-2, 754, 800-1; with Prince Philip, 749, 751-2, 753; his 'double', 62; early friendships, 41, 43; with Clement Attlee, 431, 650, 651-2, 662-5, 778, 796-7; with Aneurin Bevan, 652-3; with Ernest Bevin, 652, 654; with Colin Buist, 190-1; with Neville Chamberlain, 319, 328, 346 ff., 353, 364, 431, 439, 443-4, 445, 446, 473-4; with Winston Churchill, 416, 445-7, 526, 536-7, 558, 564-5, 601-6, 635-7; with

THE END